fifth edition

Financial Accounting
Information for Decisions

John J. Wild

www.mhhe.com/wildfa5e

2010
for use with
Financial Accounting
Information for Decisions, 5e

by
John J. Wild

Where in the World is IFRS?

Abu Dhabi-United Arab Emirates	Cyprus	Hong Kong	Mauritius	Serbia
Anguilla	Czech Republic	Hungary	Mongolia	Slovenia
Antigua and Barbuda	Denmark	Iceland	Montenegro	Slovak Republic
Armenia	Dominica	Iraq	Morocco	South Africa
Aruba	Dominican Republic	Ireland	Mozambique	Spain
Austria	Dubai-United Arab Emirates	Israel	Myanmar	Sri Lanka
Australia	Ecuador	Italy	Namibia	Suriname
Azerbaijan	Egypt	Jamaica	Netherlands	Sweden
Bahamas	El Salvador	Jordan	Netherlands Antilles	Swaziland
Bahrain	Estonia	Kazakhstan	Nepal	Switzerland
Barbados	Fiji	Kenya	New Zealand	Tajikistan
Belgium	Finland	Kuwait	Nicaragua	Tanzania
Belarus	France	Kyrgyzstan	Norway	Trinidad and Tobago
Bermuda	Germany	Laos	Oman	Turkey
Bolivia	Georgia	Latvia	Panama	Uganda
Bosnia and Herzegovina	Ghana	Lebanon	Papua New Guinea	Ukraine
Botswana	Gibraltar	Liechtenstein	Paraguay	United Kingdom
Brazil	Grenada	Lesotho	Peru	Venezuela
Bulgaria	Greece	Lithuania	Poland	Virgin Islands (British)
Canada	Guatemala	Luxembourg	Portugal	West Bank/Gaza
Cayman Islands	Guyana	Macedonia	Qatar	Zambia
Chile	Haiti	Malawi	Romania	Zimbabwe
Costa Rica	Honduras	Maldives	Russia	
		Malta	St. Kitts and Nevis	

For updates on countries joining the IFRS ranks, see www.IASplus.com/country/useias.htm

ISBN 13: 978-0-07-740532-8
ISBN 10: 0-07-740532-3

What in the World is IFRS?

What is IFRS? IFRS is an abbreviation for International Financial Reporting Standards, which are set by the International Accounting Standards Board (IASB), headquartered in London. The majority of companies throughout the world report financial statements following IFRS. However, companies listing their stock on U.S. stock exchanges report financial statements following U.S. GAAP, which is set by the Financial Accounting Standards Board (FASB), headquartered in Connecticut. There is increasing pressure on many fronts for the U.S. to adopt IFRS for financial reporting. Already, many international subsidiaries of U.S. companies prepare financial statements following IFRS, not U.S. GAAP.

The illustration to the side shows the general structure and the responsible parties for the setting of IFRS. The key parties are identified in this graphic and are defined below. This illustration shows that IFRS is established by the IASB. The IASB reports to (overseen by) the International Accounting Standards Committee Foundation (IASCF). That Foundation is appointed by a Monitoring Board. The Foundation appoints the Standards Advisory Council (SAC) and the International Financial Reporting Interpretations Committee (IFRIC). More detail on each of these groups is provided below.

The IASB and FASB have mutually agreed to a *Memorandum of Understanding*, which is a commitment to cooperate on making existing and future standards compatible. The U.S. Securities and Exchange Commission (SEC) has also stepped in with a *Roadmap to Convergence*. These developments have set in motion what most believe is inevitable; that is, the convergence of U.S. GAAP to IFRS, and the conversion of financial statements under U.S. GAAP to IFRS. No one knows the exact timetable, but we do know that IFRS is already the business language for much of the world.

Monitoring Board — Approve and oversee trustees

IASC Foundation — 22 trustees; appoint, oversee, raise funds

Standards Advisory Council — Approximately 40 members

International Financial Reporting Interpretations Committee — 14 members

IASB — 15 members (maximum 3 part-time). Set technical agenda; approve standards, exposure drafts and interpretations

IFRS (International Financial Reporting Standards)

Key: Appoints → Reports to → Advises

Monitoring Board
The Monitoring Board serves as a source of communication between key market participants and the IASCF. One of its goals is to aid regulators in requiring IFRS in their jurisdictions. This board also aids in appointing trustees and in providing advice to those trustees. Members include leaders from the European Commission, the Financial Services Agency of Japan, the U.S. Securities and Exchange Commission, the Emerging Markets Committee of IOSCO, and the Technical Committee of IOSCO.

International Accounting Standards Committee Foundation (IASCF)
The IASCF is a nonprofit, private sector group who represents the public interest when appointing and overseeing the Board. Members include six from North America, six from Europe, six from the Asia/Oceania region, and four from any area. Members also include a balance of professional backgrounds, including auditors, preparers, users, academics, and others.

International Accounting Standards Board (IASB)
The IASB approves standards, exposure drafts, and interpretations. Members normally include four from the Asia/Oceania region, four from Europe, four from North America, one each from Africa and South America, and the remainder appointed from any area. Members are professionally competent with a diversity of international business experience.

Standards Advisory Council (SAC)
SAC serves the IASB as a means to consult a wide range of representatives from user groups, preparers, financial analysts, academics, auditors, regulators, professional accounting bodies, and investor groups that are affected by and interested in the IASB's work.

International Financial Reporting Interpretations Committee (IFRIC)
The IFRIC is the interpretative body of the IASC Foundation. Its mandate is to review on a timely basis widespread accounting issues that have arisen within the context of current IFRS. The work of the IFRIC is aimed at reaching consensus on the proper accounting treatment (IFRIC Interpretations) and providing authoritative guidance on those issues.

International Financial Reporting Standards (IFRS)
A single set of high quality, understandable international financial reporting standards (IFRS) for general-purpose financial statements.

Photo Credits: IMS Communications Ltd./Capstone Design. All Rights Reserved; Geoff Manasse/Getty Images; Annie Reynolds/PhotoLink/Getty Images; T.O'Keffe/PhotoLink/Getty Images; Punchstock; Alamy; RF/Corbis; RF/Corbis; Brand X Pictures; Pixtal/age footstock; RF/Corbis; ©The McGraw-Hill Companies, Inc./Barry Barker, photographer; ©The McGraw-Hill Companies, Inc./Barry Barker, photographer; ©The McGraw-Hill Companies, Inc./Barry Barker, photographer; Stockbyte/Getty Images

Where in Time is IFRS?

Where are we with IFRS?

Accounting impacts companies across the world, which requires us to adopt a global view. Consider the following:
- IFRS now adopted or accepted in over 115 countries, including over 30 member-states of the EU
- FASB and IASB are attempting to converge IFRS and U.S. GAAP
- Regulators consider a transition entirely from U.S. GAAP to IFRS for U.S. companies
- U.S. Securities and Exchange Commission (SEC) proposes a "roadmap" for use of IFRS by U.S. companies (see following roadmap)

IFRS Roadmap

2001	IASB established
2002	IASB and FASB agree on efforts to converge IFRS and U.S. GAAP
2005	SEC proposes a "Roadmap" for foreign companies to use IFRS without reconciliation to U.S. GAAP
2007	Foreign companies can use IFRS in lieu of U.S. GAAP for U.S. SEC filings
2008	SEC proposes a "Roadmap for Potential Use of Financial Statements Prepared in Accordance with IFRS by U.S. Issuers"
2010	SEC seeks company volunteers to convert to IFRS
2011	Potential for early adoption of IFRS
2012	SEC targeted decision point on mandating IFRS
2014	Potential phase-in of IFRS for large, accelerated companies
2015	Potential phase-in of IFRS for medium-sized, accelerated companies
2016	Potential phase-in of IFRS for smaller, nonaccelerated companies

What hurdles exist with IFRS?

- Cost estimates are $30 to $40 million per large company to transition to IFRS
- Convergence between IFRS and U.S. GAAP is slower than anticipated
- Skeptics assert convergence is unlikely and that IFRS and U.S. GAAP will never be identical
- Critics assert that U.S. GAAP is the "gold standard" and that IFRS will yield reports of less quality
- Both U.S. executives and accountants are not yet prepared for IFRS (see following survey results)

Survey of U.S. CPAs on IFRS readiness

- Currently preparing for adoption of IFRS: 55%
- Not yet preparing for adoption of IFRS: 45%

Survey of U.S. executives on adopting IFRS

- Would not consider adopting IFRS immediately: 42%
- Would consider adopting IFRS immediately: 30%
- Undecided: 28%

Global survey of business leaders on importance of IFRS for economic growth

- "Very Important" 55%
- "Important" 35%
- "Somewhat Important" 9%
- "Not Important" 1%

Source: International Financial Reporting Standards (IFRS): An AICPA Backgrounder "International Federation of Accountants survey", p. 2 © 2008, American Institute of Certified Public Accountants, New York, NY 10036-8775

What benefits exist to IFRS?

- IFRS is becoming the global norm for accounting standards, and nonadopters run the risk of being marginalized
- Global IFRS usage enhances analysis and capital allocations
- Global standards aid users in comparative analysis and help companies raise financing throughout the world
- High quality global standards promote financial disclosure and transparency
- IFRS emphasizes "principles-based" standards that encourage disclosure of economically relevant and transparent business activities
- One set of global standards can reduce long-run costs of the accounting for, analysis of, and translations with business activities
- Uniform, global standards allow companies to centralize financial reporting and simplify its processes
- Enhanced global standards and transparency reduce the cost of capital
- U.S. adoption of IFRS would align the U.S. with the rest of the world and encourage economic growth (see chart to the side)

Topic	Similarities	Differences
Analyzing and recording transactions (Chapters 1 & 2)	• U.S. GAAP and IFRS apply the identical double-entry accounting system • Debits and credits are applied in an identical manner • Accounting (4-step) processes of identifying, analyzing, recording, and posting are identical • Use of general ledgers, account ledgers, balance column accounts, and the trial balance is identical • Accounting equation applies for both systems at all times	• IFRS is more "principles-based" versus "rules-based," which emphasizes the spirit of the accounting standard rather than strict adherence to a written rule • IFRS derives from a conceptual framework that is similar to that for U.S. GAAP but emphasizes stewardship to a greater extent and includes more measurement options beyond historical cost and U.S.-based fair value options • IFRS has similar revenue recognition criteria, but offer much less detailed (industry-specific) guidance vis-à-vis U.S. GAAP
Accounting adjustments (Chapter 3)	• Adjusting (3-step) processes of determining current balance, determining what it should be, and recording adjustments are identical • Adjustments are similarly categorized as prepaid expenses, unearned revenues, accrued expenses, and accrued revenues • Use of adjusted and post-closing trial balances is identical • Accounts similarly classified as temporary or permanent • Identical steps in the accounting cycle, including the 4-step closing process	• IFRS and U.S. GAAP apply similar revenue and expense recognition criteria, but some differences can result in accounting adjustments being recorded in different periods under IFRS versus U.S. GAAP • IFRS employs classified balance sheets, but the ordering of assets and liabilities is normally from least liquid to most liquid (reverse of U.S. GAAP)

Survey of AICPA members on company preparedness for IFRS

Category	Percentage
Actively preparing	4.5%
Ready to adopt; adopted	4.7%
Preliminary discussions	12.8%
Planning to adopt; not yet begun	15.7%
Still evaluating whether to adopt	29.5%
Does not apply; no plans to adopt in next 5 years	32.6%

Source: AICPA IFRS Preparedness Survey Results Conducted 3/3 through 3/17, 2009 © 2009 AICPA

Topic	Similarities	Differences
Financial statements (Chapters 1, 2, 3)	• IFRS and U.S. GAAP require four basic statements: income statement, balance sheet (also called statement of financial position), statement of changes in equity, and statement of cash flows • Financial statements apply similar account titles with some notable differences such as *finance costs* for interest expense, and *finance revenues* for interest revenue	• IFRS income statement reports expenses by function or nature; U.S. GAAP is usually by function and applies a single-step or multiple-step format • IFRS balance sheets commonly report assets and liabilities in reverse order of liquidity; unique subtotals commonly arise such as net current assets and net assets
Merchandising operations and inventory (Chapters 4 & 5)	• IFRS and U.S. GAAP define inventories similarly; and both measure inventories at cost using generally similar criteria • Merchandising entries are similar under IFRS and U.S. GAAP for purchases, sales, adjustments, and closing	• IFRS and U.S. GAAP apply similar cost flow assumptions such as specific identification, FIFO, and average costs; however, IFRS prohibits LIFO • IFRS and U.S. GAAP apply lower of cost or market, but both define market a bit differently and IFRS permits a reversal of write downs
Cash and Internal Controls (Chapter 6)	• Principles, procedures, and motivations for internal controls are similar for companies worldwide • IFRS and U.S. GAAP define cash and cash equivalents similarly • Controls involving cash receipts and disbursements, bank reconciliations, and vouchers are similar for companies worldwide	• Sarbanes-Oxley (SOX) internal control requirements (Section 404) are only applicable to companies that list their securities on U.S. exchanges; some argue that this creates a competitive disadvantage for U.S. exchanges (and U.S. companies) relative to non-U.S. exchanges (and non-U.S. companies)

Topic	Similarities	Differences
Equity (Chapter 11)	• IFRS and U.S. GAAP apply similar accounting for equity, including its definition, issuance, classification, and reporting • Accounting for basic and diluted earnings per share is similar under IFRS and U.S. GAAP; slight differences exist in detailed calculations	• IFRS and U.S. GAAP have some terminology differences that commonly include the following: U.S. GAAP / IFRS Common stock / Share capital Paid-In capital in excess of par / Share premium Accumulated other comp income / General reserve & other
Statement of Cash Flows (Chapter 12)	• IFRS and U.S. GAAP similarly require a statement of cash flows that classifies cash flows as either operating, investing, or financing activities • This statement is prepared using either the indirect or direct method; indirect is more popular for companies reporting under IFRS and for those under U.S. GAAP • IFRS and U.S. GAAP require disclosure of noncash investing and financing activities; however, U.S. GAAP (not IFRS) permits disclosure in the body of the statement	• IFRS and U.S. GAAP differ on the classification of the following cash flows as operating, investing, or financing: Transaction / U.S. GAAP / IFRS Interest paid / Operating / Financing or Operating Dividends paid / Financing / Financing or Operating Interest received / Operating / Operating or Investing Dividends received / Operating / Operating or Investing Income taxes / Operating / Operating unless linked with financing or investing items
Financial Analysis (Chapter 13)	• IFRS and U.S. GAAP are similar in not requiring any substantial analysis of the financial statements; ratios are limited to items such as earnings per share • IFRS and U.S. GAAP have converged their reporting for discontinued operations, error corrections, accounting policy changes, and accounting estimate changes	• U.S. GAAP presents a transaction that is both unusual and infrequent as Extraordinary on the income statement or notes; IFRS prohibits any classification as Extraordinary and, instead, encourages descriptive titles for such items
Investments (Appendix C)	• IFRS and U.S. GAAP apply similar accounting for available-for-sale, held-to-maturity, and trading securities • IFRS and U.S. GAAP determine the accounting for equity securities based on the level of control the investor has; the presumption is an investor lacks significant influence if holding less than 20% of the voting rights, but has significant influence if holding between 20% and 50% • Both IFRS and U.S. GAAP presume an investor controls an entity if it holds more than 50% of the voting rights	• IFRS and U.S. GAAP use similar titles for available-for-sale and held-to-maturity securities; they differ on the following categories: U.S. GAAP / IFRS Trading securities / Financial assets at fair value through profit or loss (Nothing similar) / Loans & receivables • IFRS permits recoveries of impairment losses on investments under certain conditions; U.S. GAAP does not • IFRS uses "associate investment" in lieu of U.S. GAAP's "equity investment" terminology

Survey of AICPA members on IFRS knowledge

- Expert Knowledge—Very Familiar with Specifics, Could Train Others 0.5%
- Advanced Knowledge—Very Familiar with Most Specifics 5.7%
- Some Knowledge—Familiar with Some Specifics 24%
- Basic Knowledge—Familiar with High Level Concepts 42.7%
- No Knowledge 22.1%
- Does Not Apply—No Plans to Learn 5%

Source: AICPA IFRS Preparedness Survey Results Conducted 3/3 through 3/17, 2009 © 2009 AICPA

Survey of U.S. executives on whether IFRS adoption makes the U.S. more globally competitive

- Yes 34%
- No 38%
- Not Sure 28%

Source: "IFRS Survey Results 2009: Current Issues" © 2009 Deloitte Development LLC.

Topic	Similarities	Differences
Receivables (Chapter 7)	• Recognizing and valuing receivables are similar under IFRS and U.S. GAAP, including estimating bad debts and allowances • The "fair value option" applies to receivables under both IFRS and U.S. GAAP	• Allowance for Doubtful Accounts under U.S. GAAP is commonly titled Provision for Doubtful Accounts under IFRS • Both IFRS and U.S. GAAP require recognition of any impairment losses from receivables; however, IFRS, unlike U.S. GAAP, permits reversals of impairment losses • IFRS and U.S. GAAP apply similar accounting when disposing of receivables; however, IFRS focuses on tests of risk and reward for disposition, while U.S. GAAP focuses on tests of control
Plant Assets (Chapter 8)	• IFRS and U.S. GAAP apply similar accounting for cost determination, depreciation, additional expenditures, and disposition ("cost model") • Similar depreciation methods are applied under IFRS and U.S. GAAP • Impairment tests are similar, but not identical, under IFRS and U.S. GAAP; impairment entries are identical	• IFRS permits (does not require) a "revaluation model" for plant assets, which uses the assets' fair value at the balance sheet date of revaluation • IFRS requires "component depreciation" if asset components have different useful lives; U.S. GAAP permits it, but does not require it • IFRS permits recoveries of impairments, U.S. GAAP does not
Intangible Assets (Chapter 8)	• IFRS and U.S. GAAP apply similar accounting for intangible assets having indefinite lives and for those having limited lives ("cost model") • IFRS and U.S. GAAP apply impairment testing, but tests are different under IFRS and U.S. GAAP • U.S. GAAP treats research and development expenditures as expenses in the period incurred; IFRS treatment is similar for research expenditures	• IFRS permits (does not require) a "revaluation model" for intangible assets *having limited lives*, which uses the assets' fair value at the balance sheet date of revaluation • IFRS permits recoveries of impairments (except for goodwill), whereas U.S. GAAP does not • IFRS treats development expenditures meeting certain criteria as intangible assets (capitalized)
Current Liabilities (Chapter 9)	• IFRS and U.S. GAAP apply similar accounting for current liabilities, including definitions, classifications, and reporting • IFRS and U.S. GAAP recognize contingent liabilities applying generally similar criteria • Accounting for income taxes is similar under IFRS and U.S. GAAP, with obvious differences in computations linked to different tax rates across countries	• IFRS has different requirements for current liabilities that are refinanced, are in violation of covenants, and reflect bank overdrafts • IFRS estimates of contingent liabilities tend to be at the mid-point of possible values, whereas U.S. GAAP estimates are at the lower end of values • IFRS commonly titles contingent liabilities as a "provision" for those liabilities • Liabilities are commonly presented in order of liquidity; U.S. GAAP from most liquid to least, whereas IFRS from least liquid to most
Long-Term Liabilities (Chapter 10)	• IFRS and U.S. GAAP apply similar accounting for bonds and notes, including their definitions, classifications, and reporting • Accounting for pensions and leases is similar under IFRS and U.S. GAAP; the respective boards are attempting to converge any minor differences	• Accounting for bonds and notes that carry characteristics of equity such as mandatorily redeemable notes or convertible bonds is different under IFRS and U.S. GAAP; IFRS attempts to identify them (or a component) as either a liability or equity • A capital lease under U.S. GAAP is referred to as a finance lease under IFRS

Survey of U.S. executives on SEC's IFRS roadmap

- Not Sure 18%
- Reject it Entirely 12%
- Approve as is 19%
- Approve but Consider Extending Deadline by 1 Year 51%

Survey of AICPA members on SEC's IFRS roadmap

- Not Sure 25.2%
- Accelerate IFRS Implementation 6.1%
- Approve as is 21.8%
- Delay IFRS Implementation 46.8%

Source: AICPA IFRS Preparedness Survey Results Conducted 3/3 through 3/17, 2009 © 2009 AICPA

Topic	Similarities	Differences
Analyzing and Recording Transactions (Chapters 1 & 2)	<ul><li>U.S. GAAP and IFRS apply the identical double-entry accounting system</li><li>Debits and credits are applied in an identical manner</li><li>Accounting (4-step) processes of identifying, analyzing, recording, and posting are identical</li><li>Use of general ledgers, account ledgers, balance column accounts, and the trial balance is identical</li><li>Accounting equation applies for both systems at all times</li></ul>	<ul><li>IFRS is more "principles-based" versus "rules-based," which emphasizes the spirit of the accounting standard rather than strict adherence to a written rule</li><li>IFRS derives from a conceptual framework that is similar to that for U.S. GAAP but emphasizes stewardship to a greater extent and includes more measurement options beyond historical cost and U.S.-based fair value options</li><li>IFRS has similar revenue recognition criteria, but offer much less detailed (industry-specific) guidance vis-à-vis U.S. GAAP</li></ul>
Accounting Adjustments (Chapter 3)	<ul><li>Adjusting (3-step) processes of determining current balance, determining what it should be, and recording adjustments are identical</li><li>Adjustments are similarly categorized as prepaid expenses, unearned revenues, accrued expenses, and accrued revenues</li><li>Use of adjusted and post-closing trial balances is identical</li><li>Accounts similarly classified as temporary or permanent</li><li>Identical steps in the accounting cycle, including the 4-step closing process</li></ul>	<ul><li>IFRS and U.S. GAAP apply similar revenue and expense recognition criteria, but some differences can result in accounting adjustments being recorded in different periods under IFRS versus U.S. GAAP</li><li>IFRS employs classified balance sheets, but the ordering of assets and liabilities is normally from least liquid to most liquid (reverse of U.S. GAAP)</li></ul>

Survey of AICPA members on company preparedness for IFRS

Category	Percentage
Actively preparing	4.5%
Ready to adopt; adopted	4.7%
Preliminary discussions	12.8%
Planning to adopt; not yet begun	15.7%
Still evaluating whether to adopt	29.5%
Does not apply; no plans to adopt in next 5 years	32.6%

Source: AICPA IFRS Preparedness Survey Results Conducted 3/3 through 3/17, 2009 © 2009 AICPA

Topic	Similarities	Differences
Financial Statements (Chapters 1, 2, 3)	<ul><li>IFRS and U.S. GAAP require four basic statements: income statement, balance sheet (also called statement of financial position), statement of changes in equity, and statement of cash flows</li><li>Financial statements apply similar account titles with some notable differences such as *finance costs* for interest expense, and *finance revenues* for interest revenue</li></ul>	<ul><li>IFRS income statement reports expenses by function or nature; U.S. GAAP is usually by function and applies a single-step or multiple-step format</li><li>IFRS balance sheets commonly report assets and liabilities in reverse order of liquidity; unique subtotals commonly arise such as net current assets and net assets</li></ul>
Merchandising Operations and Inventory (Chapters 4 & 5)	<ul><li>IFRS and U.S. GAAP define inventories similarly; and both measure inventories at cost using generally similar criteria</li><li>Merchandising entries are similar under IFRS and U.S. GAAP for purchases, sales, adjustments, and closing</li></ul>	<ul><li>IFRS and U.S. GAAP apply similar cost flow assumptions such as specific identification, FIFO, and average costs; however, IFRS prohibits LIFO</li><li>IFRS and U.S. GAAP apply lower of cost or market, but both define market a bit differently and IFRS permits a reversal of write downs</li></ul>
Cash and Internal Controls (Chapter 6)	<ul><li>Principles, procedures, and motivations for internal controls are similar for companies worldwide</li><li>IFRS and U.S. GAAP define cash and cash equivalents similarly</li><li>Controls involving cash receipts and disbursements, bank reconciliations, and vouchers are similar for companies worldwide</li></ul>	<ul><li>Sarbanes-Oxley (SOX) internal control requirements (Section 404) are only applicable to companies that list their securities on U.S. exchanges; some argue that this creates a competitive disadvantage for U.S. exchanges (and U.S. companies) relative to non-U.S. exchanges (and non-U.S. companies)</li></ul>

Selected Material from

Financial Accounting
Sixth Edition
Information for Decisions

John J. Wild
University of Wisconsin–Madison

Eastern Connecticut State University

Professor Candice Deal
Dr. Mohd RuJoub
Dr. Richard Silkoff

McGraw Hill Learning Solutions

Boston Burr Ridge, IL Dubuque, IA New York San Francisco St. Louis
Bangkok Bogotá Caracas Lisbon London Madrid
Mexico City Milan New Delhi Seoul Singapore Sydney Taipei Toronto

Selected Material from
FINANCIAL ACCOUNTING: INFORMATION FOR DECISIONS, Sixth Edition
Professor Candice Deal | Dr. Mohd RuJoub | Dr. Richard Silkoff

Copyright © 2013 by The McGraw-Hill Companies, Inc. All rights reserved. Printed in the United States of America. Except as permitted under the United States Copyright Act of 1976, no part of this publication may be reproduced or distributed in any form or by any means, or stored in a data base retrieval system, without prior written permission of the publisher.

This book is a McGraw-Hill Learning Solutions textbook and contains select material from *Financial Accounting*, Sixth Edition by John J. Wild. Copyright © 2013, 2011, 2008, 2005, 2003, 2000 by The McGraw-Hill Companies, Inc. Reprinted with permission of the publisher. Many custom published texts are modified versions or adaptations of our best-selling textbooks. Some adaptations are printed in black and white to keep prices at a minimum, while others are in color.

1 2 3 4 5 6 7 8 9 0   BRP BRP   14 13 12

ISBN-13: 978-0-07-777644-2
ISBN-10: 0-07-777644-5

Learning Solutions Consultant: Stephanie Corby
Learning Solutions Representative: Cindy Hedley
Production Editor: Larry Jackson
Printer/Binder: BR Printers

Dear Colleagues/Friends,

As we roll out the new edition of *Financial Accounting*, I wish to thank each of you who provided suggestions to improve our textbook. As teachers, we know how important it is to select the right book for our course. This new edition reflects the advice and wisdom of many dedicated reviewers, students, instructors, and symposium and workshop participants. Together, we have created the most readable, concise, current, accurate, and innovative accounting book available today.

Throughout the writing process, I steered this book in the manner you directed. Reviewers, instructors, and students say this book's enhanced presentation, graphics, and technology cater to different learning styles and help students better understand accounting. McGraw-Hill *Connect Accounting*® offers new features to improve student learning and to assist instructor teaching and grading. LearnSmart, Self-Quiz and Study, Guided Examples, and Interactive Presentations provide additional tools and resources needed to achieve success through faster learning, more efficient studying, and higher retention of knowledge. You and your students will find all these tools easy to apply.

I owe the success of this book to you and our colleagues who graciously took time to help us focus on the changing needs of today's instructors and students. I feel fortunate to have witnessed our profession's extraordinary devotion to teaching. Your feedback and suggestions are reflected in everything I write. Please accept my heartfelt thanks for your dedication in helping today's students learn, understand, and appreciate accounting.

With kindest regards,

John J. Wild

About the Author

JOHN J. WILD is a distinguished professor of accounting at the University of Wisconsin at Madison. He previously held appointments at Michigan State University and the University of Manchester in England. He received his BBA, MS, and PhD from the University of Wisconsin.

Professor Wild teaches accounting courses at both the undergraduate and graduate levels. He has received numerous teaching honors, including the Mabel W. Chipman Excellence-in-Teaching Award, the departmental Excellence-in-Teaching Award, and the Teaching Excellence Award from the 2003 and 2005 business graduates at the University of Wisconsin. He also received the Beta Alpha Psi and Roland F. Salmonson Excellence-in-Teaching Award from Michigan State University. Professor Wild has received several research honors and is a past KPMG Peat Marwick National Fellow and is a recipient of fellowships from the American Accounting Association and the Ernst and Young Foundation.

Professor Wild is an active member of the American Accounting Association and its sections. He has served on several committees of these organizations, including the Outstanding Accounting Educator Award, Wildman Award, National Program Advisory, Publications, and Research Committees. Professor Wild is author of *Fundamental Accounting Principles, Financial Accounting Fundamentals, Managerial Accounting,* and *College Accounting*, each published by McGraw-Hill/Irwin. His research articles on accounting and analysis appear in *The Accounting Review; Journal of Accounting Research; Journal of Accounting and Economics; Contemporary Accounting Research; Journal of Accounting, Auditing and Finance; Journal of Accounting and Public Policy;* and other journals. He is past associate editor of *Contemporary Accounting Research* and has served on several editorial boards including *The Accounting Review.*

In his leisure time, Professor Wild enjoys hiking, sports, travel, people, and spending time with family and friends.

© Getty Images

Helping Students Achieve New Heights

Financial Accounting, 6e

Assist your students in achieving new heights by giving them what they need to succeed in today's financial accounting course.

Whether the goal is to become an accountant or a businessperson, or simply to be an informed consumer of accounting information, *Financial Accounting (FA)* has helped thousands of students succeed by giving them support in the form of leading-edge accounting content that engages students, paired with state-of-the-art technology that elevates their understanding of key accounting principles.

With *FA* on your side, you'll be provided with **engaging content** in a **motivating style** to help students see the relevance of accounting. Students are motivated when reading materials that are clear and pertinent. *FA* excels at engaging students. Its chapter-opening vignettes showcase dynamic, successful entrepreneurial individuals and companies guaranteed to **interest and excite students**. This edition's featured companies—**Research In Motion** (maker of BlackBerry), **Apple**, **Nokia**, and **Palm**—captivate students with their products and annual reports, which are a pathway for learning financial statements. Further, this book's coverage of the accounting cycle fundamentals is widely praised for its clarity and effectiveness.

FA also delivers innovative technology to help student performance. **Connect Accounting**® provides students with instant grading and feedback for assignments that are completed online. **Connect Accounting Plus**® integrates an online version of the textbook with *Connect Accounting*. Our algorithmic test bank offers infinite variations of numerical test bank questions. The Self-Quiz and Study, Guided Examples, Interactive Presentations, and LearnSmart all provide additional support to help reinforce concepts and keep students motivated.

We're confident you'll agree that *FA* **will help your students achieve new heights**.

McGraw-Hill connect | ACCOUNTING

Students' Connection to

McGraw-Hill *Connect Accounting*® is an online assignment and assessment solution that connects your students with the tools and resources needed to achieve success through faster learning, more efficient studying, and higher retention of knowledge.

Online Assignments: *Connect Accounting* helps students learn more efficiently by providing feedback and practice material when they need it, where they need it. *Connect* grades homework automatically and gives immediate feedback on any questions students may have missed.

Interactive Presentations: The interactive presentations provide engaging narratives of all chapter learning objectives in an interactive online format. The presentations are tied specifically to *Financial Accounting*, 6e. They follow the structure of the text and are organized to match the learning objectives within each chapter. While the interactive presentations are not meant to replace the textbook in this course, they provide additional explanation and enhancement of material from the text chapter, allowing students to learn, study, and practice with instant feedback at their own pace.

Student Resource Library: The *Connect Accounting* Student Study Center gives access to additional resources such as recorded lectures, online practice materials, an eBook, and more.

Achieve New Heights!

Guided Examples: The Guided Examples in *Connect Accounting* provide a narrated, animated, step-by-step walk-through of select exercise similar to those assigned. These short presentations provide reinforcement when students need it most.

LearnSmart: LearnSmart adaptive self-study technology within *Connect Accounting* helps students make the best use of their study time. LearnSmart provides a seamless combination of practice, assessment, and remediation for every concept in the textbook. LearnSmart's intelligent software adapts to students by supplying questions on a new concept when they are ready to learn it. With LearnSmart, students will spend less time on topics they understand and practice more on those they have yet to master.

Self-Quiz and Study: The Self-Quiz and Study (SQS) connects students to the learning resources students need to succeed in the course. For each chapter, students can take a practice quiz and immediately see how well they performed. A study plan then recommends specific readings from the text, supplemental study material, and practice exercises that will improve students' understanding and mastery of each learning objective.

Connect Accounting

Connect Accounting® offers a number of powerful tools and features to make managing assignments easier, so faculty can spend more time teaching. With *Connect Accounting*, students can engage with their coursework anytime and anywhere, making the learning process more accessible and efficient. (Please see previous page for a description of the student tools available within *Connect Accounting*.)

Simple Assignment Management and Smart Grading

With *Connect Accounting*, creating assignments is easier than ever, so you can spend more time teaching and less time managing. *Connect Accounting* enables you to:

- Create and deliver assignments easily with select end-of-chapter questions and test bank items.
- Go paperless with the eBook and online submission and grading of student assignments.
- Have assignments scored automatically, giving students immediate feedback on their work and side-by-side comparisons with correct answers.
- Reinforce classroom concepts with practice tests and instant quizzes.

Student Reporting

Connect Accounting keeps instructors informed about how each student, section, and class is performing, allowing for more productive use of lecture and office hours. The reporting function enables you to:

- View scored work immediately and track individual or group performance with assignment and grade reports.
- Access an instant view of student or class performance relative to learning objectives.
- Collect data and generate reports required by many accreditation organizations, such as AACSB and AICPA.

©iStock Images

Instructor Library

The *Connect Accounting* Instructor Library is your repository for additional resources to improve student engagement in and out of class. You can select and use any asset that enhances your lecture. The *Connect Accounting* Instructor Library includes: access to the eBook version of the text, PowerPoint files, Solutions Manual, Instructor Resource Manual, and Test Bank.

> "I have nothing but praise for *Connect*. It saves me a significant amount of time by grading homework for me. The majority of students like that (1) it's always available/conforms to their schedule, (2) provides immediate feedback, . . . (3) the way they can access the eBook from *Connect Plus* for targeted help."
>
> —Eric Carstensen, MiraCosta College

Tools for Instructors

McGraw-Hill *Connect Plus Accounting*®

McGraw-Hill reinvents the textbook learning experience for the modern student with *Connect Plus Accounting*. A seamless integration of an eBook and *Connect Accounting*, *Connect Plus Accounting* provides all of the *Connect Accounting* features plus:

- An integrated eBook, allowing for anytime, anywhere access to the textbook.
- Dynamic links between the problems or questions you assign to your students and the location in the eBook where that problem or question is covered.
- A powerful search function to pinpoint and connect key concepts in a snap.

For more information about *Connect*, go to www.mcgrawhillconnect.com, or contact your local McGraw-Hill sales representative.

Tegrity Campus: Lectures 24/7

Tegrity Campus is a service that makes class time available 24/7 by automatically capturing every lecture. With a simple one-click start-and-stop process, you capture all computer screens and corresponding audio in a format that is easily searchable, frame by frame. Students can replay any part of any class with easy-to-use browser-based viewing on a PC or Mac, an iPod, or other mobile device.

Educators know that the more students can see, hear, and experience class resources, the better they learn. In fact, studies prove it. Tegrity Campus's unique search feature helps students efficiently find what they need, when they need it, across an entire semester of class recordings. Help turn your students' study time into learning moments immediately supported by your lecture. With Tegrity Campus, you also increase intent listening and class participation by easing students' concerns about note-taking. Lecture Capture will make it more likely you will see students' faces, not the tops of their heads.

To learn more about Tegrity watch a two-minute Flash demo at http://tegritycampus.mhhe.com.

McGraw-Hill Customer Experience Contact Information

At McGraw-Hill, we understand that getting the most from new technology can be challenging. That's why our services don't stop after you purchase our products. You can e-mail our Product Specialists 24 hours a day to get product training online. Or you can search our knowledge bank of Frequently Asked Questions on our support Website. For Customer Support, call 800-331-5094 or visit www.mhhe.com/support. One of our Technical Support Analysts will be able to assist you in a timely fashion.

©Getty Images

How Can Text-Related Web Resources Enrich My Course?

Online Learning Center (OLC)

We offer an Online Learning Center (OLC) that follows *Financial Accounting* chapter by chapter. It doesn't require any building or maintenance on your part. It's ready to go the moment you and your students type in the URL:
www.mhhe.com/wildFA6e

As students study and learn from *Financial Accounting*, they can visit the Student Edition of the OLC Website to work with a multitude of helpful tools:

- Generic Template Working Papers
- Chapter Learning Objectives
- Interactive Chapter Quizzes
- PowerPoint® Presentations
- Narrated PowerPoint® Presentations*
- Video Library
- Excel Template Assignments
- iPod Content*

* indicates Premium Content

A secured Instructor Edition stores essential course materials to save you prep time before class. Everything you need to run a lively classroom and an efficient course is included. All resources available to students, plus:

- Instructor's Resource Manual
- Solutions Manual
- Solutions to Excel Template Assignments
- Test Bank

The OLC Website also serves as a doorway to other technology solutions, like course management systems.

©iStock Images

McGraw-Hill Higher Education and Blackboard have teamed up. What does this mean for you?

1. **Your life, simplified.** Now you and your students can access McGraw-Hill's Connect® and Create™ right from within your Blackboard course—all with one single sign-on. Say goodbye to the days of logging in to multiple applications.

2. **Deep integration of content and tools.** Not only do you get single sign-on with Connect® and Create™, you also get deep integration of McGraw-Hill content and content engines right in Blackboard. Whether you're choosing a book for your course or building Connect® assignments, all the tools you need are right where you want them—inside Blackboard.

3. **Seamless Gradebooks.** Are you tired of keeping multiple gradebooks and manually synchronizing grades into Blackboard? We thought so. When a student completes an integrated Connect® assignment, the grade for that assignment automatically (and instantly) feeds your Blackboard grade center.

4. **A solution for everyone.** Whether your institution is already using Blackboard or you just want to try Blackboard on your own, we have a solution for you. McGraw-Hill and Blackboard can now offer you easy access to industry-leading technology and content, whether your campus hosts it, or we do. Be sure to ask your local McGraw-Hill representative for details.

CourseSmart

CourseSmart is a new way to find and buy eTextbooks. CourseSmart has the largest selection of eTextbooks available anywhere, offering thousands of the most commonly adopted textbooks from a wide variety of higher education publishers. CourseSmart eTextbooks are available in one standard online reader with full text search, notes, and highlighting, and email tools for sharing between classmates. Visit www.CourseSmart.com for more information on ordering.

How Students Can Study On the Go Using Their iPods

iPod Content

Harness the power of one of the most popular technology tools students use today—the Apple iPod. Our innovative approach allows students to download audio and video presentations right into their iPod and take learning materials with them wherever they go. Students just need to visit the Online Learning Center at www.mhhe.com/wildFA6e to download our iPod content. For each chapter of the book they will be able to download audio narrated lecture presentations for use on various versions of iPods. iPod Touch users can even access self-quizzes.

It makes review and study time as easy as putting on headphones.

How Can McGraw-Hill Help Teach My Course Online?

Improve Student Learning Outcomes and Save Instructor Time with ALEKS®

ALEKS is an assessment and learning program that provides individualized instruction in accounting. Available online in partnership with McGraw-Hill/Irwin, ALEKS interacts with students much like a skilled human tutor, with the ability to assess precisely a student's knowledge and provide instruction on the exact topics the student is most ready to learn. By providing topics to meet individual students' needs, allowing students to move between explanation and practice, correcting and analyzing errors, and defining terms, ALEKS helps students to master course content quickly and easily.

ALEKS also includes an Instructor Module with powerful, assignment-driven features and extensive content flexibility. The complimentary Instructor Module provides a course calendar, a customizable gradebook with automatically graded homework, textbook integration, and dynamic reports to monitor student and class progress. ALEKS simplifies course management and allows instructors to spend less time with administrative tasks and more time directing student learning.

To learn more about ALEKS, visit www.aleks.com/highered/business.

ALEKS is a registered trademark of ALEKS Corporation.

Innovative Textbook Features

Using Accounting for Decisions

Whether we prepare, analyze, or apply accounting information, one skill remains essential: decision-making. To help develop good decision-making habits and to illustrate the relevance of accounting, our book uses a unique pedagogical framework we call the Decision Center. This framework is comprised of a variety of approaches and subject areas, giving students insight into every aspect of business decision-making; see three examples to the right and one below. Answers to Decision Maker and Ethics boxes are at the end of each chapter.

Decision Insight

Revenue Spread The New Orleans Saints have Unearned Revenues of about $60 million in advance ticket sales. When the team plays its home games, it settles this liability to its ticket holders and then transfers the amount earned to Ticket Revenues.

Decision Ethics — Answer — p. 184

Credit Manager As a new credit manager, you are being trained by the outgoing manager. She explains that the system prepares checks for amounts net of favorable cash discounts, and the checks are dated the last day of the discount period. She also tells you that checks are not mailed until five days later, adding that "the company gets free use of cash for an extra five days, and our department looks better. When a supplier complains, we blame the computer system and the mailroom." Do you continue this payment policy?

Decision Maker — Answer — p. 185

Supplier A retailer requests to purchase supplies on credit from your company. You have no prior experience with this retailer. The retailer's current ratio is 2.1, its acid-test ratio is 0.5, and inventory makes up most of its current assets. Do you extend credit?

CAP Model

The Conceptual/Analytical/Procedural (CAP) Model allows courses to be specially designed to meet your teaching needs or those of a diverse faculty. This model identifies learning objectives, textual materials, assignments, and test items by C, A, or P, allowing different instructors to teach from the same materials, yet easily customize their courses toward a conceptual, analytical, or procedural approach (or a combination thereof) based on personal preferences.

Global View

This section explains international accounting practices relating to the material covered in that chapter. This section is purposefully located at the end of each chapter so that each instructor can decide what emphasis, if at all, is to be assigned to it. The aim of this Global View section is to describe accounting practices and to identify the similarities and differences in international accounting practices versus that in the U.S. As we move toward global convergence in accounting practices, and as we witness the likely conversion of U.S. GAAP to IFRS, the importance of student familiarity with international accounting grows. This innovative section helps us begin down that path of learning and teaching global accounting practices.

New Fraud Boxes

Stewardship is a crucial part of modern business and accounting. Fraud is a gross violation of stewardship. Each chapter introduces one or more new features devoted to accounting's role in fraud detection and prevention. These features describe, or relate to, provocative real-life scenarios of people who pursued fraudulent accounting activities for personal gain.

Bring Accounting To Life

Chapter Preview With Flowchart

This flowchart feature provides a handy textual/visual guide at the start of every chapter. Students can now begin their reading with a clear understanding of what they will learn and when, allowing them to stay more focused and organized along the way.

Quick Check

These short question/answer features reinforce the material immediately preceding them. They allow the reader to pause and reflect on the topics described, then receive immediate feedback before going on to new topics. Answers are provided at the end of each chapter.

Quick Check — Answers — p. 130

17. Classify the following assets as (1) current assets, (2) plant assets, or (3) intangible assets: (a) land used in operations, (b) office supplies, (c) receivables from customers due in 10 months, (d) insurance protection for the next 9 months, (e) trucks used to provide services to customers, (f) trademarks.
18. Cite at least two examples of assets classified as investments on the balance sheet.
19. Explain the operating cycle for a service company.

"Once again, I think this is an exceptional book. During the review, I found myself enjoying just reading the book and looking at all the wonderful examples.... It has relevant stories that most students would enjoy reading about.... These stories about entrepreneurs show why accounting is relevant to a student's business understanding."

—Norman Colter, University of New Mexico

Marginal Student Annotations

These annotations provide students with additional hints, tips, and examples to help them more fully understand the concepts and retain what they have learned. The annotations also include notes on global implications of accounting and further examples.

Point: The Association of Certified Fraud Examiners (cfenet.com) estimates that employee fraud costs small companies more than $100,000 per incident.

"This text captures students' interest with a lively writing style and contemporary examples/cases. Technically accurate and lends itself to use by instructors who use a variety of teaching styles."

—Gerald Smith, University of Northern Iowa

Outstanding Assignment Material

Once a student has finished reading the chapter, how well he or she retains the material can depend greatly on the questions, exercises, and problems that reinforce it. This book leads the way in comprehensive, accurate assignments.

Demonstration Problems present both a problem and a complete solution, allowing students to review the entire problem-solving process and achieve success.

Chapter Summaries provide students with a review organized by learning objectives. Chapter Summaries are a component of the CAP model (see page xii), which recaps each conceptual, analytical, and procedural objective.

Key Terms are bolded in the text and repeated at the end of the chapter with page numbers indicating their location. The book also includes a complete Glossary of Key Terms.

Multiple Choice Quiz Questions quickly test chapter knowledge before a student moves on to complete Quick Studies, Exercises, and Problems.

Quick Study assignments are short exercises that often focus on one learning objective. Most are included in *Connect Accounting*. There are usually 8-10 Quick Study assignments per chapter.

Exercises are one of this book's many strengths and a competitive advantage. There are about 10-15 per chapter and most are included in *Connect Accounting*.

Problem Sets A & B are proven problems that can be assigned as homework or for in-class projects. All problems are coded according to the CAP model (see page xii), and Set A is included in *Connect Accounting*.

PUT AWAY YOUR RED PEN!

We pride ourselves on the accuracy of this book's assignment materials. Independent research reports that instructors and reviewers point to the accuracy of this book's assignment materials as one of its key competitive advantages.

Helps Students Master Key Concepts

Beyond the Numbers exercises ask students to use accounting figures and understand their meaning. Students also learn how accounting applies to a variety of business situations. These creative and fun exercises are all new or updated and are divided into sections:

- Reporting in Action
- Comparative Analysis
- Ethics Challenge
- Communicating in Practice
- Taking It To The Net
- Teamwork in Action
- Hitting the Road
- Entrepreneurial Decision
- Global Decision

Serial Problem uses a continuous running case study to illustrate chapter concepts in a familiar context. The Serial Problem can be followed continuously from the first chapter or picked up at any later point in the book; enough information is provided to ensure students can get right to work.

> "Wild's *Financial Accounting* is a masterful teaching textbook. Every accounting topic is eloquently taught. End-of-chapter materials are fabulous. Layout is enjoyable and info-graphics are creative."
>
> —Sherry Gordon, Palomar College

The End of the Chapter Is Only the Beginning Our valuable and proven assignments aren't just confined to the book. From problems that require technological solutions to materials found exclusively online, this book's end-of-chapter material is fully integrated with its technology package.

- Quick Studies, Exercises, and Problems available in *Connect* are marked with an icon.
- Online Learning Center (OLC) includes Interactive Quizzes, Excel template assignments, and more.
- Problems supported with Microsoft Excel template assignments are marked with an icon.
- Material that receives additional coverage (slide shows, videos, audio, etc.) available in iPod ready format are marked with an icon.
- Assignments that focus on global accounting practices and companies are often identified with an icon.

mhhe.com/wildFA6e

The authors extend a special thanks to accuracy checkers Barbara Schnathorst, The Write Solution, Inc.; Helen Roybark, Radford University; Donna Grace, Sheridan College; Yvonne Phang, Borough of Manhattan Community College; Mitchell Franklin, Syracuse University; Beth Woods; Judith Zander, Grossmont College; Wanda Wong, Chabot College; and David Krug, Johnson County Community College.

Enhancements in This Edition

This edition's revisions are driven by instructors and students. General revisions to the entire book are in the following bulleted list; specific chapter-by-chapter revisions follow.

- New coverage in each chapter on fraud and accounting controls, with explanation on the role of accounting
- Revised and updated assignments throughout
- Updated ratio (tool) analyses for each chapter
- New material on International Financial Reporting Standards (IFRS) in most chapters, including new global examples
- New and revised entrepreneurial examples and elements
- Revised serial problem through nearly all chapters
- New art program, visual info-graphics, and text layout
- New Research In Motion (maker of BlackBerry) annual report with comparisons to Apple, Palm, and Nokia (IFRS) with new assignments for each
- Updated graphics added to each chapter's analysis section
- New technology content integrated and referenced in the book
- Revised Global View section in each chapter referencing international accounting with examples using global companies
- Updated assignments covering international accounting

Chapter 1

Twitter NEW opener with new entrepreneurial assignment

New section on fraud, including explanation of the *fraud triangle*

Streamlined and consolidated learning objectives

New section on International Standards and convergence

Updated section on accounting principles, assumptions, and constraints

New section on accounting effects of the Dodd-Frank *Wall Street Reform and Consumer Protection Act*

New graphic discussing fraud control in accounting

Updated compensation data in exhibit

Chapter 2

CitySlips NEW opener with new entrepreneurial assignment

Reorganized and streamlined learning objectives

Enhanced introduction of double-entry accounting

New box on the fraud risks with religious organizations

New coverage on reading and using an annual report

Enhanced layout for transaction analysis

New discussion on accounting quality

Chapter 3

Cheezburger Network NEW opener with new entrepreneurial assignment

Revised and streamlined presentation of accounting adjustments

Enhanced info-graphics for adjusting entries

Revised exhibit on steps in preparing financial statements

Expanded discussion of global accounting

New box on fraud and lack of controls on assets within government agencies

Revised graphics for closing process

Enhanced details for general ledger after the closing process

Chapter 4

Heritage Link Brands REVISED opener with new entrepreneurial assignment

Streamlined learning objectives

Revised 2-step presentation for recording merchandise sales and its costs

New box on the accounting quality implications of accounting for sales returns

New discussion on fraud and invoices

Revised discussion of gross margin

Chapter 5

Fitness Anywhere NEW opener with new entrepreneurial assignment

Color-coded graphic for introducing cost flow assumptions

Revised discussion on inventory controls

Revised discussion of inventory accounting under IFRS

For Better Learning

Chapter 6

New Belgium Brewing Company NEW opener with new entrepreneurial assignment

Revised SOX discussion of controls, including the role of COSO

Streamlined learning objectives

New material on drivers of human fraud

New graphic introducing a bank reconciliation with links to bank and book balances

Revised graphic on frequent cyber frauds

New graphic on drivers of financial misconduct

Chapter 7

Johnny Cupcakes NEW opener with new entrepreneurial assignment

Streamlined learning objectives

Reorganized recording of credit sales

Further clarification of interest formula

New boxes covering fraud risks with accounts receivable and some potential controls

Chapter 8

Games2U NEW opener with new entrepreneurial assignment

Reorganized learning objectives

Added entry to record impairment

Enhanced discussion of asset sales

Updated all real world examples and graphics

New box highlighting fraud risks with long-term assets

Chapter 9

SnorgTees NEW opener with new entrepreneurial assignment

New box highlighting fraud risks with payables

Updated tax illustrations and assignments using most recent government rates

New data on frauds involving employee payroll

New entry to reclassify long- to short-term debt

Updated all real world examples and graphics

Chapter 10

CakeLove NEW opener with new entrepreneurial assignment

Enhanced graphics for bonds and notes

Revised discussion of debt-to-equity

Enhanced explanation of how U.S. GAAP and IFRS determine fair value

New fraud discussion on hidden liabilities

Chapter 11

Clean Air Lawn Care NEW opener with new entrepreneurial assignment

Streamlined learning objectives

Inserted numerous key margin computations for entries involving equity

New box highlighting fraud risks with stock valuation

Updated all real world examples and graphics

Chapter 12

Animoto NEW opener with new entrepreneurial assignment

Streamlined learning objectives

New box highlighting fraud risks and cash controls

Updated discussion of different classifications for certain cash flows under IFRS

Increased number and range of assignments

Chapter 13

Motley Fool REVISED opener with new entrepreneurial assignment

Streamlined learning objectives

New discussion on analysis tools to help identify fraud

New companies—**Research In Motion**, **Apple**, **Palm** and **Nokia**—and new data throughout the chapter, exhibits, and illustrations

Enhanced horizontal and vertical analysis using new company and industry data

Enhanced discussion of common-size graphics

Revised ratio analysis using new company and industry data

Supplements

Instructor's Resource CD-ROM
ISBN13: 9780077429959
ISBN10: 0077429958

This is your all-in-one resource. It allows you to create custom presentations from your own materials or from the following text-specific materials provided in the CD's asset library:

- **Instructor's Resource Manual**
  Written by April Mohr, Jefferson Community and Technical College SW.

  This manual contains (for each chapter) a Lecture Outline, a chart linking all assignment materials to Learning Objectives, a list of relevant active learning activities, and additional visuals with transparency masters.

- **Solutions Manual**
  Prepared by John J. Wild.
  Includes detailed solutions and explanations for all assignments.

- **Test Bank, Computerized Test Bank**
  Prepared by Stacie Mayes, Rose State College, and Margaret Tanner, University of Arkansas-Fort Smith.

- **PowerPoint® Presentations**
  Prepared by Debra Schmidt, Cerritos College.

  Presentations allow for revision of lecture slides, and includes a viewer, allowing screens to be shown with or without the software.

- **Link to PageOut**

Working Papers
ISBN13: 9780077429980
ISBN10: 0077429982

Written by John J. Wild.

Blank solution and financial statement templates for students to complete that are specifically customized to each assignment throughout the book.

Assurance of Learning Ready

Many educational institutions today are focused on the notion of assurance of learning, an important element of some accreditation standards. *Financial Accounting* is designed specifically to support your assurance of learning initiatives with a simple, yet powerful solution. Each test bank question for *Financial Accounting* maps to a specific chapter learning objective listed in the text. You can use our test bank software, EZ Test and EZ Test Online, or *Connect Accounting* to easily query for learning objectives that directly relate to the learning objectives for your course. You can then use the reporting features of EZ Test to aggregate student results in similar fashion, making the collection and presentation of assurance of learning data simple and easy.

AACSB Statement

The McGraw-Hill Companies is a proud corporate member of AACSB International. Understanding the importance and value of AACSB accreditation, *Financial Accounting* recognizes the curricula guidelines detailed in the AACSB standards for business accreditation by connecting selected questions in the test bank to the six general knowledge and skill guidelines in the AACSB standards. The statements contained in *Financial Accounting* are provided only as a guide for the users of this textbook. The AACSB leaves content coverage and assessment within the purview of individual schools, the mission of the school, and the faculty. While *Financial Accounting* and the teaching package make no claim of any specific AACSB qualification or evaluation, we have within *Financial Accounting* labeled select questions according to the six general knowledge and skills areas.

The authors extend a special thanks to our contributing and technology supplement authors:
Contributing Author: Anita Kroll, University of Wisconsin–Madison
LearnSmart Authors: April Mohr, Jefferson Community and Technical College, SW; Anna Boulware, St. Charles Community College; Brenda Mattison, Tri County Technical College; and Dominique Svarc, William Rainey Harper College
Online Quizzes: Constance Hylton, George Mason University
Connect Self-Quiz and Study: Jeannine Metzler, Northampton Community College
Interactive Presentations: Jeannie Folk, College of DuPage
Guided Examples: Kathleen O'Donnell, Onondaga Community College

©Getty Images

Acknowledgments

John J. Wild and McGraw-Hill/Irwin would like to recognize the following instructors for their valuable feedback and involvement in the development of *Financial Accounting,* 6e. We are thankful for their suggestions, counsel, and encouragement.

Dawn P. Addington, Central New Mexico Community College

Dave Alldredge, Salt Lake Community College

Sylvia Allen, Los Angeles Valley College

Sheryl Alley, Ball State University

Sheila Ammons, Austin Community College

Jack Aschkenazi, American Intercontinental University

Progyan Basu, University of Maryland

Joe Beams, University of New Orleans

Gerard L. Berardino, Community College of Allegheny County-Boyce Campus

Swati Bhandarkar, University of Georgia

Jaswinder Bhangal, Chabot College

David Borjarsky, California State University-Long Beach

Anna Marie Boulware, St. Charles Community College

Charles Boxell, Owens Community College

Mia Breen, DeAnza College

Philip Brown, Harding University

Eric Carstensen, MiraCosta College

Donna Chadwick, Sinclair Community College

Barbara Chaney, University of Montana

Betty Chavis, California State University Fullerton

Robert Churchman, Harding University

Marilyn Ciolino, Delgado Community College

Norman H. Colter, University of New Mexico

Laurie Dahlin, Worcester State College

Rosemond Desir, Colorado State University

Jap Efendi, University of Texas-Arlington

Terry Elliott, Morehead State University-Ashland

Stephanie Farewell, University of Arkansas-Little Rock

Carol Flowers, Orange Coast College

Mike Foland, Southwestern Illinois College

Jeannie Folk, College of DuPage

Amy Ford, Western Illinois University

Mitch Franklin, Syracuse University

Virginia Fullwood, Texas A&M University

Hubert Gill, University of North Florida

Saturnino Gonzalez Jr., El Paso Community College

Sherry L. Gordon, Palomar College

Marina Grau, Houston Community College

Jeannie Harrington, Middle Tennessee State University

Tracey Hawkins, University of Cincinnati, Clermont College

Roger G. Hehman, Raymond Walters College

Cecil Hill, Jackson State University

Tom Hrubec, Franklin University

Constance Hylton, George Mason University

Catherine Jeppson, California State University-Northridge

Christie W. Johnson, Montana State University

Vern Jorgensen, Southwestern Community College

Irene Kim, George Mason University

Phillip Korb, University of Baltimore

Anita Kroll, University of Wisconsin-Madison

David Krug, Johnson County Community College

Don Lucy, Indian River State College

Stacie Mayes, Rose State College

Allison McLeod, University of North Texas

Kathleen Michele, Sun Prairie College

Jeanne Miller, Cypress College

Tim Mills, Eastern Illinois University

Susan Minke, Indiana University/Purdue University at Ft. Wayne

April Mohr, Jefferson Community and Technical College, SW

Audrey S. Morrison, Pensacola Junior College

Matt Muller, Adirondack Community College

Kathleen Munter, Pima Community College

Karen Nunez, Elon University

Ash Patel, Normandale Community College

Reed Peoples, Austin Community College

Karin Petruska, Youngstown State University

Yvonne Phang, Borough of Manhattan Community College

Eric Primuth, Cuyahoga Community College Western-Parma

Allan M. Rabinowitz, Pace University

Ruthie Reynolds, Howard University

Lawrence A. Roman, Cuyahoga Community College

Lou Rosamilia, Hudson Valley Community College

Pamela Rouse, Butler University

Helen Roybark, Radford University

Joan Ryan, Clackamas Community College

Judith Sage, Texas A&M International University

Marilyn Sagrillo, University of Wisconsin-Green Bay

Christine Schalow, University of Wisconsin-Stevens Point

Albert Schepanski, University of Iowa

Debra Schmidt, Cerritos College

Randall Serrett, University of Houston-Downtown

Vicki Shipley, Ball State University

Gerald Smith, University of Northern Iowa

Nancy Snow, University of Toledo

Dale Spencer, New Mexico State University

Gloria Stuart, Georgia Southern University

Gracelyn V. Stuart-Tuggle, Palm Beach Community College-South

Diane Sturek, Indiana University-Indianapolis

Dominique Svarc, William Rainey Harper College

Diane Tanner, University of North Florida

Margaret Tanner, University of Arkansas-Fort Smith

Janet Tarase, Lorain County Community College

Karen Varnell, Tarleton State University

Donna J. Viens, Johnson & Wales University

Stephen J. Walsh, Clark College

Terri Walsh, Seminole State College of Florida

William J. Walsh, Syracuse University

James Weglin, North Seattle Community College

Dave Welch, Franklin University

Jean Wells, Howard Univeristy

Jane Wiese, Valencia Community College

Kenneth L. Wild, University of London

Gayle Williams, Sacramento City College

Scott Williams, County College of Morris

Karen Wisniewski, County College of Morris

Darryl Woolley, University of Idaho

Judith Zander, Grossmont College

In addition to the helpful and generous colleagues listed above, I thank the entire McGraw-Hill/Irwin *Financial Accounting*, 6e, team, including Tim Vertovec, Dana Woo, Christina Sanders, Aaron Downey of Matrix Productions, Lori Koetters, Matthew Baldwin, Carol Bielski, Patricia Plumb, Ron Nelms, and Brian Nacik. I also thank the great marketing and sales support staff, including Kathleen Klehr and Brad Parkins. Many talented educators and professionals worked hard to create the supplements for this book, and for their efforts we're grateful. Finally, many more people I either did not meet or whose efforts we did not personally witness nevertheless helped to make this book everything that it is, and we thank them all.

John J. Wild

Brief Contents

1 Introducing Accounting in Business 2
2 Analyzing and Recording Transactions 50
3 Adjusting Accounts and Preparing Financial Statements 94
4 Reporting and Analyzing Merchandising Operations 156
5 Reporting and Analyzing Inventories 204
6 Reporting and Analyzing Cash and Internal Controls 248
7 Reporting and Analyzing Receivables 292
8 Reporting and Analyzing Long-Term Assets 326
9 Reporting and Analyzing Current Liabilities 368
10 Reporting and Analyzing Long-Term Liabilities 412
11 Reporting and Analyzing Equity 456
Appendix A Financial Statement Information A-1

Contents

1 Introducing Accounting in Business 2

Importance of Accounting 4
- *Users of Accounting Information 5*
- *Opportunities in Accounting 6*

Fundamentals of Accounting 8
- *Ethics—A Key Concept 8*
- *Fraud Triangle 8*
- *Generally Accepted Accounting Principles 9*
- *International Standards 9*
- *Conceptual Framework and Convergence 10*
- *Sarbanes–Oxley (SOX) 13*
- *Dodd-Frank 14*

Transaction Analysis and the Accounting Equation 15
- *Accounting Equation 15*
- *Transaction Analysis 16*
- *Summary of Transactions 19*

Financial Statements 20
- *Income Statement 20*
- *Statement of Retained Earnings 20*
- *Balance Sheet 22*
- *Statement of Cash Flows 22*

Global View 22
Decision Analysis—Return on Assets 24
Appendix 1A Return and Risk Analysis 28
Appendix 1B Business Activities and the Accounting Equation 28

2 Analyzing and Recording Transactions 50

Analyzing and Recording Process 52
- *Source Documents 52*
- *The Account and Its Analysis 53*

Analyzing and Processing Transactions 56
- *Ledger and Chart of Accounts 56*
- *Debits and Credits 57*
- *Double-Entry Accounting 57*
- *Journalizing and Posting Transactions 58*
- *Analyzing Transactions—An Illustration 61*
- *Accounting Equation Analysis 65*

Trial Balance 67
- *Preparing a Trial Balance 67*
- *Using a Trial Balance to Prepare Financial Statements 68*

Global View 71
Decision Analysis—Debt Ratio 72

3 Adjusting Accounts and Preparing Financial Statements 94

Timing and Reporting 96
- *The Accounting Period 96*
- *Accrual Basis versus Cash Basis 97*
- *Recognizing Revenues and Expenses 98*

xxiii

Adjusting Accounts 98
Framework for Adjustments 98
Prepaid (Deferred) Expenses 99
Unearned (Deferred) Revenues 102
Accrued Expenses 103
Accrued Revenues 105
Links to Financial Statements 107
Adjusted Trial Balance 108

Preparing Financial Statements 108

Closing Process 110
Temporary and Permanent Accounts 110
Recording Closing Entries 110
Post-Closing Trial Balance 112
Accounting Cycle 114

Classified Balance Sheet 115
Classification Structure 115
Classification Categories 116

Global View 118
Decision Analysis—Profit Margin and Current Ratio 119
Appendix 3A Alternative Accounting for Prepayments 123
Appendix 3B Work Sheet as a Tool 125
Appendix 3C Reversing Entries 127

4 Reporting and Analyzing Merchandising Operations 156

Merchandising Activities 158
Reporting Income for a Merchandiser 158
Reporting Inventory for a Merchandiser 159
Operating Cycle for a Merchandiser 159
Inventory Systems 159

Accounting for Merchandise Purchases 160
Purchase Discounts 161
Purchase Returns and Allowances 162
Transportation Costs and Ownership Transfer 163

Accounting for Merchandise Sales 165
Sales of Merchandise 165
Sales Discounts 166
Sales Returns and Allowances 166

Completing the Accounting Cycle 168
Adjusting Entries for Merchandisers 168
Preparing Financial Statements 169
Closing Entries for Merchandisers 169
Summary of Merchandising Entries 169

Financial Statement Formats 170
Multiple-Step Income Statement 171
Single-Step Income Statement 172
Classified Balance Sheet 172

Global View 173
Decision Analysis—Acid-Test and Gross Margin Ratios 174
Appendix 4A Periodic Inventory System 179
Appendix 4B Work Sheet—Perpetual System 183

Contents   xxv

5 Reporting and Analyzing Inventories 204

Inventory Basics 206
Determining Inventory Items 206
Determining Inventory Costs 207
Internal Controls and Taking a Physical Count 207

Inventory Costing under a Perpetual System 208
Inventory Cost Flow Assumptions 208
Inventory Costing Illustration 209
Specific Identification 209
First-In, First-Out 211
Last-In, First-Out 211
Weighted Average 212
Financial Statement Effects of Costing Methods 214
Consistency in Using Costing Methods 215

Valuing Inventory at LCM and the Effects of Inventory Errors 215
Lower of Cost or Market 215
Financial Statement Effects of Inventory Errors 216

Global View 218
Decision Analysis—Inventory Turnover and Days' Sales in Inventory 219
Appendix 5A Inventory Costing under a Periodic System 224
Appendix 5B Inventory Estimation Methods 229

6 Reporting and Analyzing Cash and Internal Controls 248

Internal Control 250
Purpose of Internal Control 250
Principles of Internal Control 251
Technology and Internal Control 253
Limitations of Internal Control 254

Control of Cash 255
Cash, Cash Equivalents, and Liquidity 255
Cash Management 255
Control of Cash Receipts 256
Control of Cash Disbursements 258

Banking Activities as Controls 262
Basic Bank Services 262
Bank Statement 264
Bank Reconciliation 265

Global View 268
Decision Analysis—Days' Sales Uncollected 269
Appendix 6A Documentation and Verification 272
Appendix 6B Control of Purchase Discounts 275

7 Reporting and Analyzing Receivables 292

Accounts Receivable 294
Recognizing Accounts Receivable 294
Valuing Accounts Receivable—Direct Write-Off Method 297
Valuing Accounts Receivable—Allowance Method 298
Estimating Bad Debts—Percent of Sales Method 300
Estimating Bad Debts—Percent of Receivables Method 301
Estimating Bad Debts—Aging of Receivables Method 302

Notes Receivable 304
Computing Maturity and Interest 304
Recognizing Notes Receivable 305
Valuing and Settling Notes 306

Disposal of Receivables 307
Selling Receivables 307
Pledging Receivables 308

Global View 308
Decision Analysis—Accounts Receivable Turnover 309

8 Reporting and Analyzing Long-Term Assets 326

SECTION 1—Plant Assets 328
Cost Determination 329
Land 329
Land Improvements 330
Buildings 330
Machinery and Equipment 330
Lump-Sum Purchase 330

Depreciation 331
Factors in Computing Depreciation 331
Depreciation Methods 332
Partial-Year Depreciation 336
Change in Estimates for Depreciation 337
Reporting Depreciation 337

Additional Expenditures 338
Ordinary Repairs 338
Betterments and Extraordinary Repairs 339

Disposals of Plant Assets 339
Discarding Plant Assets 340
Selling Plant Assets 340

SECTION 2—Natural Resources 342
Cost Determination and Depletion 342
Plant Assets Used in Extracting 343

SECTION 3—Intangible Assets 343
Cost Determination and Amortization 343
Types of Intangibles 344

Global View 346
Decision Analysis—Total Asset Turnover 347
Appendix 8A Exchanging Plant Assets 350

9 Reporting and Analyzing Current Liabilities 368

Characteristics of Liabilities 370
Defining Liabilities 370
Classifying Liabilities 370
Uncertainty in Liabilities 371

Known Liabilities 372
Accounts Payable 372
Sales Taxes Payable 372
Unearned Revenues 373
Short-Term Notes Payable 373
Payroll Liabilities 375
Multi-Period Known Liabilities 378

Estimated Liabilities 379
Health and Pension Benefits 379
Vacation Benefits 380
Bonus Plans 380
Warranty Liabilities 380
Multi-Period Estimated Liabilities 381

Contingent Liabilities 382
Accounting for Contingent Liabilities 382
Reasonably Possible Contingent Liabilities 382
Uncertainties That Are Not Contingencies 383

Global View 383
Decision Analysis—Times Interest Earned Ratio 384
Appendix 9A Payroll Reports, Records, and Procedures 387
Appendix 9B Corporate Income Taxes 393

10 Reporting and Analyzing Long-Term Liabilities 412

Basics of Bonds 414
Bond Financing 414
Bond Trading 415
Bond-Issuing Procedures 416

Bond Issuances 416
Issuing Bonds at Par 416
Bond Discount or Premium 417
Issuing Bonds at a Discount 417
Issuing Bonds at a Premium 420
Bond Pricing 422

Bond Retirement 423
Bond Retirement at Maturity 423
Bond Retirement before Maturity 423
Bond Retirement by Conversion 424

Long-Term Notes Payable 424
Installment Notes 425
Mortgage Notes and Bonds 426

Global View 427
Decision Analysis—Debt Features and the Debt-to-Equity Ratio 428
Appendix 10A Present Values of Bonds and Notes 432
Appendix 10B Effective Interest Amortization 434
Appendix 10C Issuing Bonds between Interest Dates 436
Appendix 10D Leases and Pensions 438

11 Reporting and Analyzing Equity 456

Corporate Form of Organization 458
Characteristics of Corporations 458
Corporate Organization and Management 459
Stockholders of Corporations 460
Basics of Capital Stock 461

Common Stock 462
Issuing Par Value Stock 462
Issuing No-Par Value Stock 463
Issuing Stated Value Stock 464
Issuing Stock for Noncash Assets 464

Dividends 465
Cash Dividends 465
Stock Dividends 466
Stock Splits 468

Preferred Stock 468
Issuance of Preferred Stock 469
Dividend Preference of Preferred Stock 469
Convertible Preferred Stock 470
Callable Preferred Stock 471
Reasons for Issuing Preferred Stock 471

Treasury Stock 472
Purchasing Treasury Stock 472
Reissuing Treasury Stock 473
Retiring Stock 474

Reporting of Equity 474
Statement of Retained Earnings 474
Statement of Stockholders' Equity 475
Reporting Stock Options 476

Global View 476
Decision Analysis—Earnings per Share, Price-Earnings Ratio, Dividend Yield, and Book Value per Share 477

Appendix A Financial Statement Information A-1
Research In Motion A-2
Apple A-19
Palm A-24
Nokia A-29

Glossary G-1
Index IND

Financial Accounting

INFORMATION FOR DECISIONS

A Look at This Chapter

Accounting is crucial in our information age. In this chapter, we discuss the importance of accounting to different types of organizations and describe its many users and uses. We explain that ethics are essential to accounting. We also explain business transactions and how they are reflected in financial statements.

A Look Ahead

Chapter 2 describes and analyzes business transactions. We explain the analysis and recording of transactions, the ledger and trial balance, and the double-entry system. More generally, Chapters 2 and 3 show (via the accounting cycle) how financial statements reflect business activities.

1 Introducing Accounting in Business

Learning Objectives

Learning Objectives are classified as conceptual, analytical, or procedural.

CAP

CONCEPTUAL

C1 Explain the purpose and importance of accounting. (p. 4)

C2 Identify users and uses of, and opportunities in, accounting. (p. 5)

C3 Explain why ethics are crucial to accounting. (p. 8)

C4 Explain generally accepted accounting principles and define and apply several accounting principles. (p. 9)

C5 *Appendix 1B*—Identify and describe the three major activities of organizations. (p. 28)

ANALYTICAL

A1 Define and interpret the accounting equation and each of its components. (p. 15)

A2 Compute and interpret return on assets. (p. 24)

A3 *Appendix 1A*—Explain the relation between return and risk. (p. 28)

LP1

PROCEDURAL

P1 Analyze business transactions using the accounting equation. (p. 16)

P2 Identify and prepare basic financial statements and explain how they interrelate. (p. 20)

Decision Insight

*A **Decision Feature** launches each chapter showing the relevance of accounting for a real entrepreneur. An **Entrepreneurial Decision** problem at the end of the assignments returns to this feature with a mini-case.*

Accounting for Twitter

"There is so much going on here..."
—**BIZ STONE** (RIGHT)

SAN FRANCISCO—"We came across the word 'twitter,' and it was just perfect," recalls Jack Dorsey (center of photo). "The definition was 'a short burst of inconsequential information,' and 'chirps from birds,' and that's exactly what the product was." Today, Twitter boasts over 200 million users. Founded by Jack, along with Biz Stone (right) and Evan Williams (left), **Twitter** (**Twitter.com**) is "facilitating connections between businesses and individuals in meaningful and relevant ways," says Jack. Along the way, the young entrepreneurs had to learn accounting and the details of preparing and interpreting financial statements.

"There is so much going on here," explains Biz when describing Twitter's business model. However, admits Evan, "We did a poor job of communicating." Important questions involving business formation, transaction analysis, and financial reporting arose. The entrepreneurs eventually met those challenges and, in the process, set Twitter apart. "If you stand pat," says Evan, "you risk being stagnant."

Information is the focus within Twitter's accounting records and systems. Jack recalls that when they launched Twitter, there were all these reasons why they would not succeed. He applied their similar "can-do" approach to accounting information. "My whole philosophy is making tech [and accounting] more accessible and human," says Jack. This includes using accounting information to make key business decisions.

Twitter is the language of micro-blogging, and accounting is the language of business. "Twitter is so many things: a messaging service, a customer-service tool, a real-time search," explains Biz, and the accounting system had to capture those things. Biz adds that Twitter is exploring additional "interesting ways to generate revenue." That revenue-stream is reflected in its financial statements, which are based on transaction analysis and accounting concepts.

Twitter's revenues exhibit growth and reflect what experts call the *monetizing* of its business. A recent study by the marketing firm SocialTwist found that the click-through rate was 19 for Twitter, which is the number of clicks on an embedded link. This compares with 3 clicks for Facebook links. Twitter's revenues in the recent year were estimated at $45 million, which are projected to exceed $100 million next year. Twitter also tracks its expenses and asset purchases. Twitter owners have an estimated valuation of between $5 and $10 billion!

The three entrepreneurs emphasize that accounting records must be in order for Twitter to realize its full potential. Many experts predict a public offering of its stock within the next two years, which could generate untold wealth. Still, Evan recognizes that "so many people here [at Twitter] contribute to that success." He also emphasizes that learning is a key to their business success. "I realized," insists Evan, "I could buy books and learn something that people spent years learning."

[Sources: Twitter Website, January 2012; *Entrepreneur,* December 2010; *USA Today,* May 2009; Smedio.com, June 2011; *San Francisco Chronicle,* March 2011; SocialTwist.com, October 2010; *The Wall Street Journal,* February 2011]

Chapter Preview

*A **Preview** opens each chapter with a summary of topics covered.*

Today's world is one of information—its preparation, communication, analysis, and use. Accounting is at the core of this information age. Knowledge of accounting gives us career opportunities and the insight to take advantage of them. This book introduces concepts, procedures, and analyses that help us make better decisions, including career choices. In this chapter we describe accounting, the users and uses of accounting information, the forms and activities of organizations, and several accounting principles. We also introduce transaction analysis and financial statements.

Introducing Accounting in Business

Importance of Accounting
- Accounting information users
- Opportunities in accounting

Fundamentals of Accounting
- Ethics—key concept
- Generally accepted accounting principles
- International standards

Transaction Analysis
- Accounting equation
- Transaction analysis—illustrated

Financial Statements
- Income statement
- Statement of retained earnings
- Balance sheet
- Statement of cash flows

IMPORTANCE OF ACCOUNTING

C1 Explain the purpose and importance of accounting.

Why is accounting so popular on campuses? Why are there so many accounting jobs for graduates? Why is accounting so important to companies? Why do politicians and business leaders focus on accounting regulations? The answer is that we live in an information age, where that information, and its reliability, impacts the financial well-being of us all.

Accounting is an information and measurement system that identifies, records, and communicates relevant, reliable, and comparable information about an organization's business activities. *Identifying* business activities requires selecting transactions and events relevant to an organization. Examples are the sale of iPhones by **Apple** and the receipt of ticket money by **TicketMaster**. *Recording* business activities requires keeping a chronological log of transactions and events measured in dollars and classified and summarized in a useful format. *Communicating* business activities requires preparing accounting reports such as financial statements. It also requires analyzing and interpreting such reports. (The financial statements and notes of **Research In Motion**, the maker of BlackBerry, are shown in Appendix A near the end of this book. This appendix also shows the financial statements of **Apple**, **Palm**, and **Nokia**.) Exhibit 1.1 summarizes accounting activities.

Real company names are printed in bold magenta.

We must guard against a narrow view of accounting. Our most common contact with accounting is through credit approvals, checking accounts, tax forms, and payroll. These experiences are limited and tend to focus on the recordkeeping parts of accounting. **Recordkeeping,** or **bookkeeping,** is the recording of transactions and events, either manually or electronically. This is just one part of accounting. Accounting also identifies and communicates information on transactions and events, and it includes the crucial processes of analysis and interpretation.

EXHIBIT 1.1
Accounting Activities

Identifying — Select transactions and events

Recording — Input, measure, and classify

Communicating — Prepare, analyze, and interpret

Technology is a key part of modern business and plays a major role in accounting. Technology reduces the time, effort, and cost of recordkeeping while improving clerical accuracy. Some small organizations continue to perform various accounting tasks manually, but even they are impacted by technology. As technology has changed the way we store, process, and summarize masses of data, accounting has been freed to expand. Consulting, planning, and other financial services are now closely linked to accounting. These services require sorting through data, interpreting their meaning, identifying key factors, and analyzing their implications.

Point: Technology is only as useful as the accounting data available, and users' decisions are only as good as their understanding of accounting. The best software and recordkeeping cannot make up for lack of accounting knowledge.

Margin notes further enhance the textual material.

Users of Accounting Information

Accounting is often called the *language of business* because all organizations set up an accounting information system to communicate data to help people make better decisions. Exhibit 1.2 shows that the accounting information system serves many kinds of users (this is a partial listing) who can be divided into two groups: external users and internal users.

External users

- Lenders
- Shareholders
- Governments
- Consumer groups
- External auditors
- Customers

Internal users

- Officers
- Managers
- Internal auditors
- Sales staff
- Budget officers
- Controllers

EXHIBIT 1.2
Users of Accounting Information

Infographics reinforce key concepts through visual learning.

External Information Users *External users* of accounting information are *not* directly involved in running the organization. They include shareholders (investors), lenders, directors, customers, suppliers, regulators, lawyers, brokers, and the press. External users have limited access to an organization's information. Yet their business decisions depend on information that is reliable, relevant, and comparable.

Financial accounting is the area of accounting aimed at serving external users by providing them with *general-purpose financial statements*. The term *general-purpose* refers to the broad range of purposes for which external users rely on these statements.

Each external user has special information needs depending on the types of decisions to be made. *Lenders* (creditors) loan money or other resources to an organization. Banks, savings and loans, co-ops, and mortgage and finance companies are lenders. Lenders look for information to help them assess whether an organization is likely to repay its loans with interest. *Shareholders* (investors) are the owners of a corporation. They use accounting reports in deciding whether to buy, hold, or sell stock. Shareholders typically elect a *board of directors* to oversee their interests in an organization. Since directors are responsible to shareholders, their information needs are similar. *External* (independent) *auditors* examine financial statements to verify that they are prepared according to generally accepted accounting principles. *Nonexecutive employees* and *labor unions* use financial statements to judge the fairness of wages, assess job prospects, and bargain for better wages. *Regulators* often have legal authority over certain activities of organizations. For example, the Internal Revenue Service (IRS) and other tax authorities require organizations to file accounting reports in computing taxes. Other regulators include utility boards that use accounting information to set utility rates and securities regulators that require reports for companies that sell their stock to the public.

C2 Identify users and uses of, and opportunities in, accounting.

Accounting serves the needs of many other external users. *Voters, legislators,* and *government officials* use accounting information to monitor and evaluate government receipts and expenses. *Contributors* to nonprofit organizations use accounting information to evaluate the use and impact of their donations. *Suppliers* use accounting information to judge the soundness of a customer before making sales on credit, and *customers* use financial reports to assess the staying power of potential suppliers.

Internal Information Users **Internal users** of accounting information are those directly involved in managing and operating an organization. They use the information to help improve the efficiency and effectiveness of an organization. **Managerial accounting** is the area of accounting that serves the decision-making needs of internal users. Internal reports are not subject to the same rules as external reports and instead are designed with the special needs of internal users in mind.

There are several types of internal users, and many are managers of key operating activities. *Research and development managers* need information about projected costs and revenues of any proposed changes in products and services. *Purchasing managers* need to know what, when, and how much to purchase. *Human resource managers* need information about employees' payroll, benefits, performance, and compensation. *Production managers* depend on information to monitor costs and ensure quality. *Distribution managers* need reports for timely, accurate, and efficient delivery of products and services. *Marketing managers* use reports about sales and costs to target consumers, set prices, and monitor consumer needs, tastes, and price concerns. *Service managers* require information on the costs and benefits of looking after products and services. Decisions of these and other internal users depend on accounting reports.

Both internal and external users rely on internal controls to monitor and control company activities. *Internal controls* are procedures set up to protect company property and equipment, ensure reliable accounting reports, promote efficiency, and encourage adherence to company policies. Examples are good records, physical controls (locks, passwords, guards), and independent reviews.

Decision Insight

Virtuous Returns Virtue is not always its own reward. Compare the S&P 500 with the Domini Social Index (DSI), which covers 400 companies that have especially good records of social responsibility. We see that returns for companies with socially responsible behavior are at least as high as those of the S&P 500. ■

Copyright © 2010 by KLD Research & Analytics, Inc. The "FTSE KLD 400 Social Index" is a service mark of KLD Research & Analytics.

Opportunities in Accounting

Accounting information affects many aspects of our lives. When we earn money, pay taxes, invest savings, budget earnings, and plan for the future, we are influenced by accounting. Accounting has four broad areas of opportunities: financial, managerial, taxation, and accounting-related. Exhibit 1.3 lists selected opportunities in each area.

EXHIBIT 1.3

Accounting Opportunities

Opportunities in Accounting

Financial	Managerial	Taxation	Accounting-related	
• Preparation	• General accounting	• Preparation	• Lenders	• FBI investigators
• Analysis	• Cost accounting	• Planning	• Consultants	• Market researchers
• Auditing	• Budgeting	• Regulatory	• Analysts	• Systems designers
• Regulatory	• Internal auditing	• Investigations	• Traders	• Merger services
• Consulting	• Consulting	• Consulting	• Directors	• Business valuation
• Planning	• Controller	• Enforcement	• Underwriters	• Forensic accounting
• Criminal investigation	• Treasurer	• Legal services	• Planners	• Litigation support
	• Strategy	• Estate plans	• Appraisers	• Entrepreneurs

The majority of accounting opportunities are in *private accounting,* which are employees working for businesses, as shown in Exhibit 1.4. *Public accounting* offers the next largest number of opportunities, which involve services such as auditing and tax advice to a vast range of businesses. Still other opportunities exist in government and not-for-profit agencies, including business regulation and investigation of law violations.

EXHIBIT 1.4

Accounting Jobs by Area

- Private accounting 60%
- Government, not-for-profit and education 16%
- Public accounting 24%

Accounting specialists are highly regarded and their professional standing is often denoted by a certificate. Certified public accountants (CPAs) must meet education and experience requirements, pass an examination, and exhibit ethical character. Many accounting specialists hold certificates in addition to or instead of the CPA. Two of the most common are the certificate in management accounting (CMA) and the certified internal auditor (CIA). Employers also look for specialists with designations such as certified bookkeeper (CB), certified payroll professional (CPP), personal financial specialist (PFS), certified fraud examiner (CFE), and certified forensic accountant (CrFA).

Point: The largest accounting firms are Deloitte, Ernst & Young, KPMG, and PricewaterhouseCoopers.

Individuals with accounting knowledge are always in demand as they can help with financial analysis, strategic planning, e-commerce, product feasibility analysis, information technology, and financial management. Benefit packages can include flexible work schedules, telecommuting options, career path alternatives, casual work environments, extended vacation time, and child and elder care.

Demand for accounting specialists is strong. Exhibit 1.5 reports average annual salaries for several accounting positions. Salary variation depends on location, company size, professional designation, experience, and other factors. For example, salaries for chief financial officers (CFO) range from under $75,000 to more than $1 million per year. Likewise, salaries for bookkeepers range from under $30,000 to more than $80,000.

Point: Census Bureau (2009) reports that for workers 18 and over, higher education yields higher average pay:
Advanced degree.......... $80,977
Bachelor's degree.......... 57,181
High school degree 31,286
No high school degree...... 21,484

Field	Title (experience)	2010 Salary	2015 Estimate*
Public Accounting	Partner..........................	$191,000	$211,000
	Manager (6–8 years)	94,500	104,000
	Senior (3–5 years)..................	72,000	79,500
	Junior (0–2 years)	51,500	57,000
Private Accounting	CFO............................	232,000	256,000
	Controller/Treasurer	147,500	163,000
	Manager (6–8 years)	87,500	96,500
	Senior (3–5 years)..................	72,500	80,000
	Junior (0–2 years)	49,000	54,000
Recordkeeping	Full-charge bookkeeper	57,500	63,500
	Accounts manager..................	51,000	56,500
	Payroll manager	54,500	60,000
	Accounting clerk (0–2 years)	37,500	41,500

EXHIBIT 1.5

Accounting Salaries for Selected Fields

* Estimates assume a 2% compounded annual increase over current levels (rounded to nearest $500).

Point: For updated salary information:
Abbott-Langer.com
www.AICPA.org
Kforce.com

Quick Check

Answers — p. 30

Quick Check is a chance to stop and reflect on key points.

1. What is the purpose of accounting?
2. What is the relation between accounting and recordkeeping?
3. Identify some advantages of technology for accounting.
4. Who are the internal and external users of accounting information?
5. Identify at least five types of managers who are internal users of accounting information.
6. What are internal controls and why are they important?

Point: U.S. Bureau of Labor (June 2011) reports higher education results in less unemployment:
Bachelor's degree or more 4.4%
High school degree 10.0%
No high school degree........ 14.3%

FUNDAMENTALS OF ACCOUNTING

Accounting is guided by principles, standards, concepts, and assumptions. This section describes several of these key fundamentals of accounting.

Ethics—A Key Concept

C3 Explain why ethics are crucial to accounting.

The goal of accounting is to provide useful information for decisions. For information to be useful, it must be trusted. This demands ethics in accounting. **Ethics** are beliefs that distinguish right from wrong. They are accepted standards of good and bad behavior.

Identifying the ethical path is sometimes difficult. The preferred path is a course of action that avoids casting doubt on one's decisions. For example, accounting users are less likely to trust an auditor's report if the auditor's pay depends on the success of the client's business. To avoid such concerns, ethics rules are often set. For example, auditors are banned from direct investment in their client and cannot accept pay that depends on figures in the client's reports. Exhibit 1.6 gives guidelines for making ethical decisions.

Point: Sarbanes-Oxley Act requires each issuer of securities to disclose whether it has adopted a code of ethics for its senior financial officers and the contents of that code.

EXHIBIT 1.6
Guidelines for Ethical Decision Making

Identify ethical concerns → **Analyze options** → **Make ethical decision**

Use personal ethics to recognize an ethical concern.

Consider all good and bad consequences.

Choose best option after weighing all consequences.

Providers of accounting information often face ethical choices as they prepare financial reports. These choices can affect the price a buyer pays and the wages paid to workers. They can even affect the success of products and services. Misleading information can lead to a wrongful closing of a division that harms workers, customers, and suppliers. There is an old saying: *Good ethics are good business.*

Some people extend ethics to *social responsibility,* which refers to a concern for the impact of actions on society. An organization's social responsibility can include donations to hospitals, colleges, community programs, and law enforcement. It also can include programs to reduce pollution, increase product safety, improve worker conditions, and support continuing education. These programs are not limited to large companies. For example, many small businesses offer discounts to students and senior citizens. Still others help sponsor events such as the Special Olympics and summer reading programs.

Point: The American Institute of Certified Public Accountants' *Code of Professional Conduct* is available at www.AICPA.org.

Fraud Triangle

The fraud triangle is a model created by a criminologist, which asserts the following *three* factors must exist for a person to commit fraud: opportunity, pressure, and rationalization.

Opportunity is one side of the fraud triangle. A person must envision a way to commit fraud with a low perceived risk of getting caught. Employers can directly reduce this risk. An example of some control on opportunity is a pre-employment background check. *Pressure,* or incentive, is another side of the fraud triangle. A person must be motivated to commit fraud. Examples are unpaid bills and addictions. *Rationalization,* or attitude, is the third side of the fraud triangle. A person who rationalizes fails to see the criminal nature of the fraud or justifies the action.

The key to dealing with fraud is to focus on prevention. It is cheaper and more effective to prevent fraud from happening than it is to try to detect the crime. By the time the fraud is discovered, the money is gone and chances are slim to none that it will be recovered. Additionally, it is costly and time consuming to investigate a fraud.

It is important to recognize that all three factors of the fraud triangle must usually exist for fraud to occur. The absence of one or more factors suggests fraud is unlikely. When we focus on fraud prevention, it almost always involves reducing opportunity. It is generally less costly to prevent fraud than to cover losses from fraud.

Fraud

They Fought the Law Our economic and social welfare depends on reliable accounting. Some individuals forgot that and are now paying their dues. They include Bernard Madoff (in photo) of **Madoff Investment Securities**, convicted of falsifying securities records; Bernard Ebbers of **WorldCom**, convicted of an $11 billion accounting scandal; Andrew Fastow of **Enron**, guilty of hiding debt and inflating income; and Ramalinga Raju of **Satyam Computers**, accused of overstating assets by $1.5 billion.

Generally Accepted Accounting Principles

Financial accounting practice is governed by concepts and rules known as **generally accepted accounting principles (GAAP).** To use and interpret financial statements effectively, we need to understand these principles, which can change over time in response to the demands of users. GAAP aims to make information in financial statements *relevant, reliable,* and *comparable.* Relevant information affects the decisions of its users. Reliable information is trusted by users. Comparable information is helpful in contrasting organizations.

In the United States, the **Securities and Exchange Commission (SEC),** a government agency, has the legal authority to set GAAP. The SEC also oversees proper use of GAAP by companies that raise money from the public through issuances of their stock and debt. Those companies that issue their stock on U.S. exchanges include both *U.S. SEC registrants* (companies incorporated in the United States) and *non-U.S. SEC registrants* (companies incorporated under non-U.S. laws). The SEC has largely delegated the task of setting U.S. GAAP to the **Financial Accounting Standards Board (FASB),** which is a private-sector group that sets both broad and specific principles.

C4 Explain generally accepted accounting principles and define and apply several accounting principles.

Point: State ethics codes require CPAs who audit financial statements to disclose areas where those statements fail to comply with GAAP. If CPAs fail to report noncompliance, they can lose their licenses and be subject to criminal and civil actions and fines.

International Standards

In today's global economy, there is increased demand by external users for comparability in accounting reports. This demand often arises when companies wish to raise money from lenders and investors in different countries. To that end, the **International Accounting Standards Board (IASB),** an independent group (consisting of individuals from many countries), issues **International Financial Reporting Standards (IFRS)** that identify preferred accounting practices.

If standards are harmonized, one company can potentially use a single set of financial statements in all financial markets. Differences between U.S. GAAP and IFRS are slowly fading as the FASB and IASB pursue a *convergence* process aimed to achieve a single set of accounting standards for global use. More than 115 countries now require or permit companies to prepare financial reports following IFRS. Further, non-U.S. SEC registrants can use IFRS in financial reports filed with the SEC (with no reconciliation to U.S. GAAP). This means there are *two* sets of accepted accounting principles in the United States: (1) U.S. GAAP for U.S. SEC registrants and (2) either IFRS or U.S. GAAP for non-U.S. SEC registrants.

The convergence process continues and the SEC has set a roadmap for use of IFRS by publicly traded U.S. companies. This roadmap tentatively proposes that large U.S. companies adopt IFRS by 2014, with midsize and small companies following in 2015 and 2016, respectively. Early adoption is permitted for large multinationals that meet certain criteria. For updates on this roadmap, we can check with the AICPA (**IFRS.com**), FASB (**FASB.org**), and IASB (**IASB.org.uk**).

IFRS

Like the FASB, the IASB uses a conceptual framework to aid in revising or drafting new standards. However, unlike the FASB, the IASB's conceptual framework is used as a reference when specific guidance is lacking. The IASB also requires that transactions be accounted for according to their substance (not only their legal form), and that financial statements give a fair presentation, whereas the FASB narrows that scope to fair presentation *in accordance with U.S. GAAP.*

Conceptual Framework and Convergence

The FASB and IASB are attempting to converge and enhance the **conceptual framework** that guides standard setting. The framework consists broadly of the following:

- **Objectives**—to provide information useful to investors, creditors, and others.
- **Qualitative characteristics**—to require information that is relevant, reliable, and comparable.
- **Elements**—to define items that financial statements can contain.
- **Recognition and measurement**—to set criteria that an item must meet for it to be recognized as an element; and how to measure that element.

For updates on this joint FASB and IASB conceptual framework convergence we can check with FASB.org or IASB.org.uk Websites. We must remember that U.S. GAAP and IFRS are two similar, but not identical, systems. However, their similarities greatly outweigh any differences. The remainder of this section describes key principles and assumptions of accounting.

Decision Insight

Principles and Scruples Auditors, directors, and lawyers are using principles to improve accounting reports. Examples include accounting restatements at **Navistar**, financial restatements at **Nortel**, accounting reviews at **Echostar**, and expense adjustments at **Electronic Data Systems**. Principles-based accounting has led accounting firms to drop clients deemed too risky. Examples include **Grant Thornton**'s resignation as auditor of **Fremont General** due to alleged failures in providing information when promised, and **Ernst and Young**'s resignation as auditor of **Catalina Marketing** due to alleged accounting errors. ■

Principles and Assumptions of Accounting Accounting principles (and assumptions) are of two types. *General principles* are the basic assumptions, concepts, and guidelines for preparing financial statements. *Specific principles* are detailed rules used in reporting business transactions and events. General principles stem from long-used accounting practices. Specific principles arise more often from the rulings of authoritative groups.

We need to understand both general and specific principles to effectively use accounting information. Several general principles are described in this section that are relied on in later chapters. General principles (in purple font with white shading) and assumptions (in red font with yellow shading) are portrayed as building blocks of GAAP in Exhibit 1.7. The specific principles are described as we encounter them in the book.

EXHIBIT 1.7
Building Blocks for GAAP

Accounting Principles

General principles consist of at least four basic principles, four assumptions, and two constraints.

The **measurement principle,** also called the **cost principle,** usually means that accounting information is based on actual cost (with a potential for subsequent adjustments to market). Cost is measured on a cash or equal-to-cash basis. This means if cash is given for a service, its cost is measured as the amount of cash paid. If something besides cash is exchanged (such as a car traded for a truck), cost is measured as the cash value of what is given up or received. The cost principle emphasizes reliability and verifiability, and information based on cost is considered objective. *Objectivity* means that information is supported by independent, unbiased evidence; it demands more than a person's opinion. To illustrate, suppose a company pays $5,000 for equipment. The cost principle requires that this purchase be recorded at a cost of $5,000. It makes no difference if the owner thinks this equipment is worth $7,000. Later in the book we introduce *fair value* measures.

Point: The cost principle is also called the *historical cost principle*.

Revenue (sales) is the amount received from selling products and services. The **revenue recognition principle** provides guidance on when a company must recognize revenue. To *recognize* means to record it. If revenue is recognized too early, a company would look more profitable than it is. If revenue is recognized too late, a company would look less profitable than it is.

Three concepts are important to revenue recognition. (1) *Revenue is recognized when earned.* The earnings process is normally complete when services are performed or a seller transfers ownership of products to the buyer. (2) *Proceeds from selling products and services need not be in cash.* A common noncash proceed received by a seller is a customer's promise to pay at a future date, called *credit sales*. (3) *Revenue is measured by the cash received plus the cash value of any other items received.*

Example: When a bookstore sells a textbook on credit is its earnings process complete? *Answer:* A bookstore can record sales for these books minus an amount expected for returns.

The **expense recognition principle,** also called the **matching principle,** prescribes that a company record the expenses it incurred to generate the revenue reported. The principles of matching and revenue recognition are key to modern accounting.

The **full disclosure principle** prescribes that a company report the details behind financial statements that would impact users' decisions. Those disclosures are often in footnotes to the statements.

Decision Insight

Revenues for the **Green Bay Packers** and **Dallas Cowboys** football teams include ticket sales, television and cable broadcasts, radio rights, concessions, and advertising. Revenues from ticket sales are earned when the NFL team plays each game. Advance ticket sales are not revenues; instead, they represent a liability until the NFL team plays the game for which the ticket was sold. At that point, the liability is removed and revenues are reported.

Accounting Assumptions There are four accounting assumptions: the going concern assumption, the monetary unit assumption, the time period assumption, and the business entity assumption.

The **going-concern assumption** means that accounting information reflects a presumption that the business will continue operating instead of being closed or sold. This implies, for example, that property is reported at cost instead of, say, liquidation values that assume closure.

The **monetary unit assumption** means that we can express transactions and events in monetary, or money, units. Money is the common denominator in business. Examples of monetary units are the dollar in the United States, Canada, Australia, and Singapore; and the peso in Mexico, the Philippines, and Chile. The monetary unit a company uses in its accounting reports usually depends on the country where it operates, but many companies today are expressing reports in more than one monetary unit.

Point: For currency conversion: xe.com

The **time period assumption** presumes that the life of a company can be divided into time periods, such as months and years, and that useful reports can be prepared for those periods.

The **business entity assumption** means that a business is accounted for separately from other business entities, including its owner. The reason for this assumption is that separate information about each business is necessary for good decisions. A business entity can take one of three legal forms: *proprietorship, partnership,* or *corporation.*

Point: Abuse of the entity assumption was a main culprit in **Enron**'s collapse.

1. A **sole proprietorship,** or simply **proprietorship,** is a business owned by one person in which that person and the company are viewed as one entity for tax and liability purposes.

EXHIBIT 1.8
Attributes of Businesses

Attribute Present	Proprietorship	Partnership	Corporation
One owner allowed............	yes	no	yes
Business taxed.................	no	no	yes
Limited liability.................	no*	no*	yes
Business entity.................	yes	yes	yes
Legal entity....................	no	no	yes
Unlimited life..................	no	no	yes

* Proprietorships and partnerships that are set up as LLCs provide limited liability.

No special legal requirements must be met to start a proprietorship. It is a separate entity for accounting purposes, but it is *not* a separate legal entity from its owner. This means, for example, that a court can order an owner to sell personal belongings to pay a proprietorship's debt. This *unlimited liability* of a proprietorship is a disadvantage. However, an advantage is that a proprietorship's income is not subject to a business income tax but is instead reported and taxed on the owner's personal income tax return. Proprietorship attributes are summarized in Exhibit 1.8, including those for partnerships and corporations.

2. A **partnership** is a business owned by two or more people, called *partners,* which are jointly liable for tax and other obligations. Like a proprietorship, no special legal requirements must be met in starting a partnership. The only requirement is an agreement between partners to run a business together. The agreement can be either oral or written and usually indicates how income and losses are to be shared. A partnership, like a proprietorship, is *not* legally separate from its owners. This means that each partner's share of profits is reported and taxed on that partner's tax return. It also means *unlimited liability* for its partners. However, at least three types of partnerships limit liability. A *limited partnership* (*LP*) includes a general partner(s) with unlimited liability and a limited partner(s) with liability restricted to the amount invested. A *limited liability partnership* (*LLP*) restricts partners' liabilities to their own acts and the acts of individuals under their control. This protects an innocent partner from the negligence of another partner, yet all partners remain responsible for partnership debts. A *limited liability company* (*LLC*) offers the limited liability of a corporation and the tax treatment of a partnership (and proprietorship). Most proprietorships and partnerships are now organized as LLCs.

Point: Proprietorships and partnerships are usually managed by their owners. In a corporation, the owners (shareholders) elect a board of directors who appoint managers to run the business.

3. A **corporation,** also called *C corporation,* is a business legally separate from its owner or owners, meaning it is responsible for its own acts and its own debts. Separate legal status means that a corporation can conduct business with the rights, duties, and responsibilities of a person. A corporation acts through its managers, who are its legal agents. Separate legal status also means that its owners, who are called **shareholders** (or **stockholders**), are not personally liable for corporate acts and debts. This limited liability is its main advantage. A main disadvantage is what's called *double taxation*—meaning that (1) the corporation income is taxed and (2) any distribution of income to its owners through dividends is taxed as part of the owners' personal income, usually at the 15% rate. (For lower income taxpayers, the dividend tax is less than 15%, and in some cases zero.) An *S corporation,* a corporation with special attributes, does not owe corporate income tax. Owners of S corporations report their share of corporate income with their personal income. Ownership of all corporations is divided into units called **shares** or **stock.** When a corporation issues only one class of stock, we call it **common stock** (or *capital stock*).

Decision Ethics boxes are role-playing exercises that stress ethics in accounting and business.

Decision Ethics Answer — p. 29

Entrepreneur You and a friend develop a new design for in-line skates that improves speed by 25% to 30%. You plan to form a business to manufacture and market those skates. You and your friend want to minimize taxes, but your prime concern is potential lawsuits from individuals who might be injured on these skates. What form of organization do you set up? ■

Accounting Constraints There are two basic constraints on financial reporting. The **materiality constraint** prescribes that only information that would influence the decisions of a reasonable person need be disclosed. This constraint looks at both the importance and relative size of an amount. The **cost-benefit constraint** prescribes that only information with benefits of disclosure greater than the costs of providing it need be disclosed.

Sarbanes–Oxley (SOX)

Congress passed the **Sarbanes–Oxley Act,** also called *SOX,* to help curb financial abuses at companies that issue their stock to the public. SOX requires that these public companies apply both accounting oversight and stringent internal controls. The desired results include more transparency, accountability, and truthfulness in reporting transactions.

Compliance with SOX requires documentation and verification of internal controls and increased emphasis on internal control effectiveness. Failure to comply can yield financial penalties, stock market delisting, and criminal prosecution of executives. Management must issue a report stating that internal controls are effective. CEOs and CFOs who knowingly sign off on bogus accounting reports risk millions of dollars in fines and years in prison. **Auditors** also must verify the effectiveness of internal controls.

A listing of some of the more publicized accounting scandals in recent years follows.

Point: An audit examines whether financial statements are prepared using GAAP. It does *not* attest to absolute accuracy of the statements.

Point: *BusinessWeek* reports that external audit costs run about $35,000 for start-ups, up from $15,000 pre-SOX.

Company	Alleged Accounting Abuses
Enron	Inflated income, hid debt, and bribed officials
WorldCom	Understated expenses to inflate income and hid debt
Fannie Mae	Inflated income
Adelphia Communications	Understated expenses to inflate income and hid debt
AOL Time Warner	Inflated revenues and income
Xerox	Inflated income
Bristol-Myers Squibb	Inflated revenues and income
Nortel Networks	Understated expenses to inflate income
Global Crossing	Inflated revenues and income
Tyco	Hid debt, and CEO evaded taxes
Halliburton	Inflated revenues and income
Qwest Communications	Inflated revenues and income

To reduce the risk of accounting fraud, companies set up *governance systems.* A company's governance system includes its owners, managers, employees, board of directors, and other important stakeholders, who work together to reduce the risk of accounting fraud and increase confidence in accounting reports.

The impact of SOX regulations for accounting and business is discussed throughout this book. Ethics and investor confidence are key to company success. Lack of confidence in accounting numbers impacts company value as evidenced by huge stock price declines for **Enron**, **WorldCom**, **Tyco**, and **ImClone** after accounting misconduct was uncovered.

Fraud

Economic Downturn, Fraud Upturn? Executives polled show that 80% believe that the economic downturn has or will have a significant impact on fraud control in their companies (Deloitte 2009). The top three responses to the question "What activity would best counter this increased fraud risk?" are tallied in the graphic to the right.

- Increased fraud awareness training: 38.7%
- Greater fraud assessment: 21.5%
- Expanded internal auditing: 20.3%

Dodd-Frank

Congress recently passed the **Dodd-Frank Wall Street Reform and Consumer Protection Act**, or *Dodd-Frank,* in a desire to (1) promote U.S. financial stability by improving accountability and transparency in the financial system, (2) put an end to the notion of "too big to fail," (3) protect the taxpayer by ending bailouts, and (4) protect consumers from abusive financial services practices. It includes provisions whose impacts are unknown until regulators set detailed rules. This section provides a preview of its key financial reporting implications.

Exemption from Section 404(b) of SOX For smaller public entities, there is an exemption for nonaccelerated filers (whose public value is less than $75 million) from the requirement to obtain an external audit on the effectiveness of internal control over financial reporting per SOX.

Enhancements to Asset-Backed Securitization Dodd-Frank requires that securitizers of financial assets retain an economic interest in a portion of the credit risk of those assets. It requires securitizers to have "skin in the game" when securitizing financial assets. It also requires additional disclosures of the securitization.

Additional Rules on Compensation Dodd-Frank requires independence for all members of the compensation committee. That committee is also responsible for appointment, compensation, and oversight of independent compensation consultants and other advisers. The act requires public companies to allow shareholders a nonbinding vote on the compensation of officers at least once every three years. The SEC must set rules requiring that, in the event of an accounting restatement, an entity set policies mandating recovery ("clawback") of excess incentive compensation. Also, regulators must set rules that (a) require certain financial institutions to disclose all incentive-based compensation arrangements and (b) prohibit incentive-based arrangements that encourage inappropriate risk taking that could result in material losses. The SEC must require disclosures on whether employees and directors are allowed to hedge the value of the entity's securities. The Federal Reserve must require certain financial institutions to set up risk committees.

Revisions to SEC Authority and Operations Dodd-Frank alters and expands SEC power. It requires the SEC, when sanctions exceed $1 million, to pay whistleblowers between 10 percent and 30 percent of the sanction. It requires the SEC to set up a permanent Investor Advisory Committee made up of outside members to consult the SEC on investor interests. The SEC must set up an Office of Investor Advocate to (a) assist investors, (b) consult with the SEC, and (3) annually report to Congress.

Volcker Rule The *Volcker Rule* aims to limit speculative investments by large financial firms and to prohibit most banking entities from engaging in proprietary trading or sponsoring, or investing in, a hedge or private equity fund.

Regulation of OTC Derivatives The act requires entities to trade most derivatives on regulated exchanges to increase transparency. For those derivatives not regulated ("cleared"), there are new reporting and disclosure requirements.

It will take several years for us to assess the costs versus the benefits of the Dodd-Frank Act.

Quick Check

Answers — p. 30

7. What three-step guidelines can help people make ethical decisions?
8. Why are ethics and social responsibility valuable to organizations?
9. Why are ethics crucial in accounting?
10. Who sets U.S. accounting rules?
11. How are U.S. companies affected by international accounting standards?
12. How are the objectivity concept and cost principle related?
13. Why is the business entity assumption important?
14. Why is the revenue recognition principle important?
15. What are the three basic forms of business organization?
16. Identify the owners of corporations and the terminology for ownership units.

TRANSACTION ANALYSIS AND THE ACCOUNTING EQUATION

To understand accounting information, we need to know how an accounting system captures relevant data about transactions, and then classifies, records, and reports data.

Accounting Equation

The accounting system reflects two basic aspects of a company: what it owns and what it owes. *Assets* are resources a company owns or controls. Examples are cash, supplies, equipment, and land, where each carries expected benefits. The claims on a company's assets—what it owes—are separated into owner and nonowner claims. *Liabilities* are what a company owes its nonowners (creditors) in future payments, products, or services. *Equity* (also called owner's equity or capital) refers to the claims of its owner(s). Together, liabilities and equity are the source of funds to acquire assets. The relationship of assets, liabilities, and equity is reflected in the following **accounting equation:**

$$\text{Assets} = \text{Liabilities} + \text{Equity}$$

A1 Define and interpret the accounting equation and each of its components.

Liabilities are usually shown before equity in this equation because creditors' claims must be paid before the claims of owners. (The terms in this equation can be rearranged; for example, Assets − Liabilities = Equity.) The accounting equation applies to all transactions and events, to all companies and forms of organization, and to all points in time. For example, **Research In Motion**'s assets equal $10,204,409, its liabilities equal $2,601,746, and its equity equals $7,602,663 ($ in thousands). Let's now look at the accounting equation in more detail.

Assets Assets are resources a company owns or controls. These resources are expected to yield future benefits. Examples are Web servers for an online services company, musical instruments for a rock band, and land for a vegetable grower. The term *receivable* is used to refer to an asset that promises a future inflow of resources. A company that provides a service or product on credit is said to have an account receivable from that customer.

Point: The phrases "on credit" and "on account" imply that cash payment will occur at a future date.

Liabilities Liabilities are creditors' claims on assets. These claims reflect company obligations to provide assets, products, or services to others. The term *payable* refers to a liability that promises a future outflow of resources. Examples are wages payable to workers, accounts payable to suppliers, notes payable to banks, and taxes payable to the government.

Equity Equity is the owner's claim on assets. Equity is equal to assets minus liabilities. This is the reason equity is also called *net assets* or *residual equity*.

A corporation's equity—often called stockholders' or shareholders' equity—has two parts: contributed capital and retained earnings. **Contributed capital** refers to the amount that stockholders invest in the company—included under the title **common stock. Retained earnings** refer to **income** (revenues less expenses) that has *not* been distributed to its stockholders. The distribution of assets to stockholders is called **dividends,** which reduce retained earnings. **Revenues** increase retained earnings (via net income) and are resources generated from a company's earnings activities. Examples are consulting services provided, sales of products, facilities rented to others, and commissions from services. **Expenses** decrease retained earnings and are the cost of assets or services used to earn revenues. Examples are costs of employee time, use of supplies, and advertising, utilities, and insurance services from others. In sum, retained earnings is the accumulated revenues less the accumulated expenses and dividends since the company began. This breakdown of equity yields the following **expanded accounting equation:**

Key **terms** are printed in bold and defined again in the end-of-book **glossary.**

$$\text{Assets} = \text{Liabilities} + \overbrace{\text{Contributed Capital} + \text{Retained Earnings}}^{\text{Equity}}$$
$$= \text{Liabilities} + \overbrace{\text{Common Stock} - \text{Dividends} + \text{Revenues} - \text{Expenses}}$$

Net income occurs when revenues exceed expenses. Net income increases equity. A **net loss** occurs when expenses exceed revenues, which decreases equity.

Decision Insight

Web Info Most organizations maintain Websites that include accounting data—see **Research In Motion (RIM.com)** as an example. The SEC keeps an online database called **EDGAR (www.sec.gov/edgar.shtml)**, which has accounting information for thousands of companies that issue stock to the public (EDGAR is being upgraded and renamed **IDEA**). Information services such as **Finance.Google.com** and **Finance.Yahoo.com** offer additional online data and analysis.

Transaction Analysis

P1 Analyze business transactions using the accounting equation.

Business activities can be described in terms of transactions and events. **External transactions** are exchanges of value between two entities, which yield changes in the accounting equation. An example is the sale of ad space by **Twitter**. **Internal transactions** are exchanges within an entity, which may or may not affect the accounting equation. An example is Twitter's use of its supplies, which are reported as expenses when used. **Events** refer to happenings that affect the accounting equation *and* are reliably measured. They include business events such as changes in the market value of certain assets and liabilities and natural events such as floods and fires that destroy assets and create losses. They do not include, for example, the signing of service or product contracts, which by themselves do not impact the accounting equation.

This section uses the accounting equation to analyze 11 selected transactions and events of FastForward, a start-up consulting (service) business, in its first month of operations. Remember that each transaction and event leaves the equation in balance and that assets *always* equal the sum of liabilities and equity.

Point: There are 3 basic types of company operations: (1) **Services**—providing customer services for profit, (2) **Merchandisers**—buying products and re-selling them for profit, and (3) **Manufacturers**—creating products and selling them for profit.

Transaction 1: Investment by Owner On December 1, Chas Taylor forms a consulting business, named FastForward and set up as a corporation, that focuses on assessing the performance of footwear and accessories. Taylor owns and manages the business. The marketing plan for the business is to focus primarily on publishing online reviews and consulting with clubs, athletes, and others who place orders for footwear and accessories with manufacturers. Taylor personally invests $30,000 cash in the new company and deposits the cash in a bank account opened under the name of FastForward. After this transaction, the cash (an asset) and the stockholders' equity each equal $30,000. The source of increase in equity is the owner's investment (stock issuance), which is included in the column titled Common Stock. The effect of this transaction on FastForward is reflected in the accounting equation as follows:

	Assets	=	Liabilities	+	Equity
	Cash	=			Common Stock
(1)	+$30,000	=			+$30,000

Transaction 2: Purchase Supplies for Cash FastForward uses $2,500 of its cash to buy supplies of brand name footwear for performance testing over the next few months. This transaction is an exchange of cash, an asset, for another kind of asset, supplies. It merely changes the form of assets from cash to supplies. The decrease in cash is exactly equal to the increase in supplies. The supplies of footwear are assets because of the expected future benefits from the test results of their performance. This transaction is reflected in the accounting equation as follows:

	Assets			=	Liabilities	+	Equity
	Cash	+	Supplies	=			Common Stock
Old Bal.	$30,000			=			$30,000
(2)	−2,500	+	$2,500				
New Bal.	$27,500	+	$ 2,500	=			$30,000
	$30,000				$30,000		

Transaction 3: Purchase Equipment for Cash FastForward spends $26,000 to acquire equipment for testing footwear. Like transaction 2, transaction 3 is an exchange of one asset, cash, for another asset, equipment. The equipment is an asset because of its expected future benefits from testing footwear. This purchase changes the makeup of assets but does not change the asset total. The accounting equation remains in balance.

	Assets					=	Liabilities	+	Equity
	Cash	+	Supplies	+	Equipment	=			Common Stock
Old Bal.	$27,500	+	$2,500			=			$30,000
(3)	−26,000			+	$26,000				
New Bal.	$ 1,500	+	$2,500	+	$ 26,000	=			$30,000
			$30,000						$30,000

Transaction 4: Purchase Supplies on Credit Taylor decides more supplies of footwear and accessories are needed. These additional supplies total $7,100, but as we see from the accounting equation in transaction 3, FastForward has only $1,500 in cash. Taylor arranges to purchase them on credit from CalTech Supply Company. Thus, FastForward acquires supplies in exchange for a promise to pay for them later. This purchase increases assets by $7,100 in supplies, and liabilities (called *accounts payable* to CalTech Supply) increase by the same amount. The effects of this purchase follow:

Example: If FastForward pays $500 cash in transaction 4, how does this partial payment affect the liability to CalTech? What would be FastForward's cash balance? *Answers:* The liability to CalTech would be reduced to $6,600 and the cash balance would be reduced to $1,000.

	Assets					=	Liabilities	+	Equity
	Cash	+	Supplies	+	Equipment	=	Accounts Payable	+	Common Stock
Old Bal.	$1,500	+	$2,500	+	$26,000	=			$30,000
(4)		+	7,100				+$7,100		
New Bal.	$1,500	+	$9,600	+	$26,000	=	$ 7,100	+	$30,000
			$37,100						$37,100

Transaction 5: Provide Services for Cash FastForward earns revenues by selling online ad space to manufacturers and by consulting with clients about test results on footwear and accessories. It earns net income only if its revenues are greater than its expenses incurred in earning them. In one of its first jobs, FastForward provides consulting services to a power-walking club and immediately collects $4,200 cash. The accounting equation reflects this increase in cash of $4,200 and in equity of $4,200. This increase in equity is identified in the far right column under Revenues because the cash received is earned by providing consulting services.

	Assets					=	Liabilities	+	Equity		
	Cash	+	Supplies	+	Equipment	=	Accounts Payable	+	Common Stock	+	Revenues
Old Bal.	$1,500	+	$9,600	+	$26,000	=	$7,100	+	$30,000		
(5)	+4,200									+	$4,200
New Bal.	$5,700	+	$9,600	+	$26,000	=	$7,100	+	$30,000	+	$ 4,200
			$41,300						$41,300		

Transactions 6 and 7: Payment of Expenses in Cash FastForward pays $1,000 rent to the landlord of the building where its facilities are located. Paying this amount allows FastForward to occupy the space for the month of December. The rental payment is reflected in the following accounting equation as transaction 6. FastForward also pays the biweekly $700 salary of the company's only employee. This is reflected in the accounting equation as transaction 7. Both transactions 6 and 7 are December expenses for FastForward. The costs of both rent and salary are expenses, as opposed to assets, because their benefits are used in December (they

18   Chapter 1   Introducing Accounting in Business

By definition, increases in expenses yield decreases in equity.

have no future benefits after December). These transactions also use up an asset (cash) in carrying out FastForward's operations. The accounting equation shows that both transactions reduce cash and equity. The far right column identifies these decreases as Expenses.

	Assets					=	Liabilities	+	Equity				
	Cash	+	Supplies	+	Equipment	=	Accounts Payable	+	Common Stock	+	Revenues	−	Expenses
Old Bal.	$5,700	+	$9,600	+	$26,000	=	$7,100	+	$30,000	+	$4,200		
(6)	−1,000											−	$1,000
Bal.	4,700	+	9,600	+	26,000	=	7,100	+	30,000	+	4,200	−	1,000
(7)	− 700											−	700
New Bal.	$4,000	+	$9,600	+	$26,000	=	$7,100	+	$30,000	+	$4,200	−	$1,700
			$39,600						$39,600				

Transaction 8: Provide Services and Facilities for Credit   FastForward provides consulting services of $1,600 and rents its test facilities for $300 to a podiatric services center. The rental involves allowing members to try recommended footwear and accessories at FastForward's testing area. The center is billed for the $1,900 total. This transaction results in a new asset, called *accounts receivable,* from this client. It also yields an increase in equity from the two revenue components reflected in the Revenues column of the accounting equation:

	Assets							=	Liabilities	+	Equity				
	Cash	+	Accounts Receivable	+	Supplies	+	Equipment	=	Accounts Payable	+	Common Stock	+	Revenues	−	Expenses
Old Bal.	$4,000	+		+	$9,600	+	$26,000	=	$7,100	+	$30,000	+	$4,200	−	$1,700
(8)		+	$1,900									+	1,600		
												+	300		
New Bal.	$4,000	+	$1,900	+	$9,600	+	$26,000	=	$7,100	+	$30,000	+	$6,100	−	$1,700
				$41,500							$41,500				

Transaction 9: Receipt of Cash from Accounts Receivable   The client in transaction 8 (the podiatric center) pays $1,900 to FastForward 10 days after it is billed for consulting services. This transaction 9 does not change the total amount of assets and does not affect liabilities or equity. It converts the receivable (an asset) to cash (another asset). It does not create new revenue. Revenue was recognized when FastForward rendered the services in transaction 8, not when the cash is now collected. This emphasis on the earnings process instead of cash flows is a goal of the revenue recognition principle and yields useful information to users. The new balances follow:

Point: Receipt of cash is not always a revenue.

	Assets							=	Liabilities	+	Equity				
	Cash	+	Accounts Receivable	+	Supplies	+	Equipment	=	Accounts Payable	+	Common Stock	+	Revenues	−	Expenses
Old Bal.	$4,000	+	$1,900	+	$9,600	+	$26,000	=	$7,100	+	$30,000	+	$6,100	−	$1,700
(9)	+1,900	−	1,900												
New Bal.	$5,900	+	$ 0	+	$9,600	+	$26,000	=	$7,100	+	$30,000	+	$6,100	−	$1,700
				$41,500							$41,500				

Transaction 10: Payment of Accounts Payable   FastForward pays CalTech Supply $900 cash as partial payment for its earlier $7,100 purchase of supplies (transaction 4), leaving $6,200 unpaid. The accounting equation shows that this transaction decreases FastForward's cash by $900 and decreases its liability to CalTech Supply by $900. Equity does not change. This event does not create an expense even though cash flows out of FastForward (instead the expense is recorded when FastForward derives the benefits from these supplies).

	Assets	=	Liabilities	+	Equity	
	Cash + Accounts Receivable + Supplies + Equipment	=	Accounts Payable	+	Common Stock + Revenues − Expenses	
Old Bal.	$5,900 + $ 0 + $9,600 + $26,000	=	$7,100	+	$30,000 + $6,100 − $1,700	
(10)	− 900		− 900			
New Bal.	$5,000 + $ 0 + $9,600 + $26,000	=	$6,200	+	$30,000 + $6,100 − $1,700	
	$40,600				$40,600	

Transaction 11: Payment of Cash Dividend FastForward declares and pays a $200 cash dividend to its owner. Dividends (decreases in equity) are not reported as expenses because they are not part of the company's earnings process. Since dividends are not company expenses, they are not used in computing net income.

By definition, increases in dividends yield decreases in equity.

	Assets	=	Liabilities	+	Equity
	Cash + Accounts Receivable + Supplies + Equipment	=	Accounts Payable	+	Common Stock − Dividends + Revenues − Expenses
Old Bal.	$5,000 + $ 0 + $9,600 + $26,000	=	$6,200	+	$30,000 + $6,100 − $1,700
(11)	− 200				− $200
New Bal.	$4,800 + $ 0 + $9,600 + $26,000	=	$6,200	+	$30,000 − $200 + $6,100 − $1,700
	$40,400				$40,400

Summary of Transactions

We summarize in Exhibit 1.9 the effects of these 11 transactions of FastForward using the accounting equation. First, we see that the accounting equation remains in balance after each transaction. Second, transactions can be analyzed by their effects on components of the

EXHIBIT 1.9

Summary of Transactions Using the Accounting Equation

	Assets	=	Liabilities	+	Equity
	Cash + Accounts Receivable + Supplies + Equipment	=	Accounts Payable + Common Stock	−	Dividends + Revenues − Expenses
(1)	$30,000	=		+	$30,000
(2)	− 2,500 + $2,500				
Bal.	27,500 + 2,500	=		+	30,000
(3)	−26,000 + $26,000				
Bal.	1,500 + 2,500 + 26,000	=		+	30,000
(4)	+ 7,100	=	+$7,100		
Bal.	1,500 + 9,600 + 26,000	=	7,100	+	30,000
(5)	+ 4,200				+ $4,200
Bal.	5,700 + 9,600 + 26,000	=	7,100	+	30,000 + 4,200
(6)	− 1,000				− $1,000
Bal.	4,700 + 9,600 + 26,000	=	7,100	+	30,000 + 4,200 − 1,000
(7)	− 700				− 700
Bal.	4,000 + 9,600 + 26,000	=	7,100	+	30,000 + 4,200 − 1,700
(8)	+ $1,900				+ 1,600
					+ 300
Bal.	4,000 + 1,900 + 9,600 + 26,000	=	7,100	+	30,000 + 6,100 − 1,700
(9)	+ 1,900 − 1,900				
Bal.	5,900 + 0 + 9,600 + 26,000	=	7,100	+	30,000 + 6,100 − 1,700
(10)	− 900		− 900		
Bal.	5,000 + 0 + 9,600 + 26,000	=	6,200	+	30,000 + 6,100 − 1,700
(11)	− 200				− $200
Bal.	$ 4,800 + $ 0 + $ 9,600 + $ 26,000	=	$ 6,200	+	$ 30,000 − $ 200 + $6,100 − $1,700

Point: Knowing how financial statements are prepared improves our analysis of them. We develop the skills for analysis of financial statements throughout the book. Chapter 13 focuses on financial statement analysis.

accounting equation. For example, in transactions 2, 3, and 9, one asset increased while another asset decreased by equal amounts.

Quick Check
Answers — p. 30

17. When is the accounting equation in balance, and what does that mean?
18. How can a transaction not affect any liability and equity accounts?
19. Describe a transaction increasing equity and one decreasing it.
20. Identify a transaction that decreases both assets and liabilities.

FINANCIAL STATEMENTS

P2 Identify and prepare basic financial statements and explain how they interrelate.

This section introduces us to how financial statements are prepared from the analysis of business transactions. The four financial statements and their purposes are:

1. **Income statement**—describes a company's revenues and expenses along with the resulting net income or loss over a period of time due to earnings activities.
2. **Statement of retained earnings**—explains changes in retained earnings from net income (or loss) and from any dividends over a period of time.
3. **Balance sheet**—describes a company's financial position (types and amounts of assets, liabilities, and equity) at a point in time.
4. **Statement of cash flows**—identifies cash inflows (receipts) and cash outflows (payments) over a period of time.

We prepare these financial statements, in this order, using the 11 selected transactions of FastForward. (These statements are technically called *unadjusted*—we explain this in Chapters 2 and 3.)

Income Statement

FastForward's income statement for December is shown at the top of Exhibit 1.10. Information about revenues and expenses is conveniently taken from the Equity columns of Exhibit 1.9. Revenues are reported first on the income statement. They include consulting revenues of $5,800 from transactions 5 and 8 and rental revenue of $300 from transaction 8. Expenses are reported after revenues. (For convenience in this chapter, we list larger amounts first, but we can sort expenses in different ways.) Rent and salary expenses are from transactions 6 and 7. Expenses reflect the costs to generate the revenues reported. Net income (or loss) is reported at the bottom of the statement and is the amount earned in December. Stockholders' investments and dividends are *not* part of income.

Point: Net income is sometimes called *earnings* or *profit*.

Statement of Retained Earnings

The statement of retained earnings reports information about how retained earnings changes over the reporting period. This statement shows beginning retained earnings, events that increase it (net income), and events that decrease it (dividends and net loss). Ending retained earnings is computed in this statement and is carried over and reported on the balance sheet. FastForward's statement of retained earnings is the second report in Exhibit 1.10. The beginning balance is measured as of the start of business on December 1. It is zero because FastForward did not exist before then. An existing business reports the beginning balance equal to that as of the end of the prior reporting period (such as from November 30). FastForward's statement shows the $4,400 of net income earned during the period. This links the income statement to the statement of retained earnings (see line ①). The statement also reports the $200 cash dividend and FastForward's end-of-period retained earnings balance.

Point: The statement of retained earnings is also called the *statement of changes in retained earnings*. Note: Beg. Retained Earnings + Net Income − Dividends = End. Retained Earnings

EXHIBIT 1.10

Financial Statements and Their Links

FASTFORWARD
Income Statement
For Month Ended December 31, 2011

Revenues		
Consulting revenue ($4,200 + $1,600)	$ 5,800	
Rental revenue	300	
Total revenues		$ 6,100
Expenses		
Rent expense	1,000	
Salaries expense	700	
Total expenses		1,700
Net income		**$ 4,400**

Point: A statement's heading identifies the company, the statement title, and the date or time period.

FASTFORWARD
Statement of Retained Earnings
For Month Ended December 31, 2011

Retained earnings, December 1, 2011	$ 0
Plus: Net income	4,400
	4,400
Less: Dividends	200
Retained earnings, December 31, 2011	**$ 4,200**

Point: Arrow lines show how the statements are linked. ① Net income is used to compute equity. ② Retained earnings is used to prepare the balance sheet. ③ Cash from the balance sheet is used to reconcile the statement of cash flows.

FASTFORWARD
Balance Sheet
December 31, 2011

Assets		Liabilities	
Cash	**$ 4,800**	Accounts payable	$ 6,200
Supplies	9,600	Total liabilities	6,200
Equipment	26,000	**Equity**	
		Common stock	30,000
		Retained earnings	4,200
		Total equity	34,200
Total assets	$40,400	Total liabilities and equity	$40,400

Point: The income statement, the statement of retained earnings, and the statement of cash flows are prepared for a *period* of time. The balance sheet is prepared as of a *point* in time.

FASTFORWARD
Statement of Cash Flows
For Month Ended December 31, 2011

Cash flows from operating activities		
Cash received from clients ($4,200 + $1,900)	$ 6,100	
Cash paid for supplies ($2,500 + $900)	(3,400)	
Cash paid for rent	(1,000)	
Cash paid to employee	(700)	
Net cash provided by operating activities		$ 1,000
Cash flows from investing activities		
Purchase of equipment	(26,000)	
Net cash used by investing activities		(26,000)
Cash flows from financing activities		
Investments by stockholder	30,000	
Dividends to stockholder	(200)	
Net cash provided by financing activities		29,800
Net increase in cash		$ 4,800
Cash balance, December 1, 2011		0
Cash balance, December 31, 2011		$ 4,800

Point: A single ruled line denotes an addition or subtraction. Final totals are double underlined. Negative amounts are often in parentheses.

Balance Sheet

FastForward's balance sheet is the third report in Exhibit 1.10. This statement refers to FastForward's financial condition at the close of business on December 31. The left side of the balance sheet lists FastForward's assets: cash, supplies, and equipment. The upper right side of the balance sheet shows that FastForward owes $6,200 to creditors. Any other liabilities (such as a bank loan) would be listed here. The equity balance is $34,200. Line ② shows the link between the ending balance of the statement of retained earnings and the retained earnings balance on the balance sheet. (This presentation of the balance sheet is called the *account form:* assets on the left and liabilities and equity on the right. Another presentation is the *report form:* assets on top, followed by liabilities and then equity at the bottom. Either presentation is acceptable.) As always, we see the accounting equation applies: Assets of $40,400 = Liabilities of $6,200 + Equity of $34,200.

Decision Maker boxes are role-playing exercises that stress the relevance of accounting.

Decision Maker   Answer — p. 29

Retailer You open a wholesale business selling entertainment equipment to retail outlets. You find that most of your customers demand to buy on credit. How can you use the balance sheets of these customers to help you decide which ones to extend credit to?

Statement of Cash Flows

FastForward's statement of cash flows is the final report in Exhibit 1.10. The first section reports cash flows from *operating activities*. It shows the $6,100 cash received from clients and the $5,100 cash paid for supplies, rent, and employee salaries. Outflows are in parentheses to denote subtraction. Net cash provided by operating activities for December is $1,000. If cash paid exceeded the $5,100 cash received, we would call it "cash used by operating activities." The second section reports *investing activities,* which involve buying and selling assets such as land and equipment that are held for *long-term use* (typically more than one year). The only investing activity is the $26,000 purchase of equipment. The third section shows cash flows from *financing activities,* which include the *long-term* borrowing and repaying of cash from lenders and the cash investments from, and dividends to, stockholders. FastForward reports $30,000 from the owner's initial investment and the $200 cash dividend. The net cash effect of all financing transactions is a $29,800 cash inflow. The final part of the statement shows FastForward increased its cash balance by $4,800 in December. Since it started with no cash, the ending balance is also $4,800—see line ③. We see that cash flow numbers are different from income statement (*accrual*) numbers, which is common.

Point: Statement of cash flows has three main sections: operating, investing, and financing.

Point: Payment for supplies is an operating activity because supplies are expected to be used up in short-term operations (typically less than one year).

Point: Investing activities refer to long-term asset investments by the company, *not* to owner investments.

Quick Check   Answers — p. 30

21. Explain the link between the income statement and the statement of retained earnings.
22. Describe the link between the balance sheet and the statement of retained earnings.
23. Discuss the three major sections of the statement of cash flows.

GLOBAL VIEW

Accounting according to U.S. GAAP is similar, but not identical, to IFRS. Throughout the book we use this last section to identify major similarities and differences between IFRS and U.S. GAAP for the materials in each chapter.

Basic Principles Both U.S. GAAP and IFRS include broad and similar guidance for accounting. However, neither system specifies particular account names nor the detail required. (A typical *chart of accounts* is shown near the end of this book.) IFRS does require certain minimum line items be reported in the balance sheet along with other minimum disclosures that U.S. GAAP does not. On the other hand, U.S. GAAP requires disclosures for the current and prior two years for the income statement, statement of cash flows, and statement of retained earnings (equity), while IFRS requires disclosures for the current and prior year. Still, the basic principles behind these two systems are similar.

Transaction Analysis Both U.S. GAAP and IFRS apply transaction analysis identically as shown in this chapter. Although some variations exist in revenue and expense recognition and other principles, all of the transactions in this chapter are accounted for identically under these two systems. It is often said that U.S. GAAP is more *rules-based* whereas IFRS is more *principles-based*. The main difference on the rules versus principles focus is with the approach in deciding how to account for certain transactions. Under U.S. GAAP, the approach is more focused on strictly following the accounting rules; under IFRS, the approach is more focused on a review of the situation and how accounting can best reflect it. This difference typically impacts advanced topics beyond the introductory course.

Financial Statements Both U.S. GAAP and IFRS prepare the same four basic financial statements. To illustrate, a condensed version of Nokia's income statement follows (numbers are in euros millions). Nokia is a leader in mobile technology, from smartphones to mobile computers. Similar condensed versions can be prepared for the other three statements.

NOKIA
Income Statement (in € millions)
For Year Ended December 31, 2009

Net sales	40,984
Cost of sales	27,720
Research, selling, administrative, and other expenses	12,302
Taxes	702
Net income (profit)	260

Status of IFRS Accounting impacts companies across the world, which requires us to take a global view. IFRS is now adopted or accepted in over 115 countries, including over 30 member-states of the EU. The map below gives us some sense of its prevalence. The FASB and IASB continue to work on the convergence of IFRS and U.S. GAAP. Further, the SEC has a "roadmap" for ultimate use of IFRS by U.S. companies. Currently, the roadmap extends out over the next three to five years.

Yellow marks jurisdictions that permit or require IFRS for some or all domestic companies; a lighter yellow indicates jurisdictions that either modify or delay full implementation of IFRS.

Decision Analysis

Return on Assets

A2 Compute and interpret return on assets.

A *Decision Analysis* section at the end of each chapter is devoted to financial statement analysis. We organize financial statement analysis into four areas: (1) liquidity and efficiency, (2) solvency, (3) profitability, and (4) market prospects—Chapter 13 has a ratio listing with definitions and groupings by area. When analyzing ratios, we need benchmarks to identify good, bad, or average levels. Common benchmarks include the company's prior levels and those of its competitors.

This chapter presents a profitability measure: return on assets. Return on assets is useful in evaluating management, analyzing and forecasting profits, and planning activities. **Dell** has its marketing department compute return on assets for *every* order. **Return on assets (ROA),** also called *return on investment (ROI)*, is defined in Exhibit 1.11.

EXHIBIT 1.11
Return on Assets

$$\text{Return on assets} = \frac{\text{Net income}}{\text{Average total assets}}$$

Net income is from the annual income statement, and average total assets is computed by adding the beginning and ending amounts for that same period and dividing by 2. To illustrate, **Best Buy** reports net income of $1,317 million for fiscal year 2010. At the beginning of fiscal 2010, its total assets are $15,826 million and at the end of fiscal 2010, they total $18,302 million. Best Buy's return on assets for fiscal 2010 is:

$$\text{Return on assets} = \frac{\$1{,}317 \text{ million}}{(\$15{,}826 \text{ million} + \$18{,}302 \text{ million})/2} = 7.7\%$$

Is a 7.7% return on assets good or bad for Best Buy? To help answer this question, we compare (benchmark) Best Buy's return with its prior performance, the returns of competitors (such as **RadioShack**, **Conn's**, and **Rex Stores**), and the returns from alternative investments. Best Buy's return for each of the prior five years is in the second column of Exhibit 1.12, which ranges from 7.0% to 10.8%.

EXHIBIT 1.12
Best Buy and Industry Returns

Fiscal Year	Return on Assets — Best Buy	Return on Assets — Industry
2010	7.7%	2.9%
2009	7.0	2.5
2008	10.7	3.4
2007	10.8	3.5
2006	10.3	3.3

Best Buy shows a fairly stable pattern of good returns that reflect its productive use of assets. There is a decline in its 2009 return reflecting the recessionary period. We compare Best Buy's return to the normal return for similar merchandisers of electronic products (third column). Industry averages are available from services such as **Dun & Bradstreet**'s *Industry Norms and Key Ratios* and **The Risk Management Association**'s *Annual Statement Studies*. When compared to the industry, Best Buy performs well.

Decision Maker

Answer — p. 29

Business Owner You own a small winter ski resort that earns a 21% return on its assets. An opportunity to purchase a winter ski equipment manufacturer is offered to you. This manufacturer earns a 19% return on its assets. The industry return for this manufacturer is 14%. Do you purchase this manufacturer?

Each Decision Analysis section ends with a role-playing scenario to show the usefulness of ratios.

The Demonstration Problem is a review of key chapter content. The Planning the Solution offers strategies in solving the problem.

DEMONSTRATION PROBLEM

After several months of planning, Jasmine Worthy started a haircutting business called Expressions. The following events occurred during its first month of business.

a. On August 1, Worthy invested $3,000 cash and $15,000 of equipment in Expressions in exchange for its common stock.
b. On August 2, Expressions paid $600 cash for furniture for the shop.
c. On August 3, Expressions paid $500 cash to rent space in a strip mall for August.
d. On August 4, it purchased $1,200 of equipment on credit for the shop (using a long-term note payable).
e. On August 5, Expressions opened for business. Cash received from haircutting services in the first week and a half of business (ended August 15) was $825.
f. On August 15, it provided $100 of haircutting services on account.
g. On August 17, it received a $100 check for services previously rendered on account.
h. On August 17, it paid $125 cash to an assistant for hours worked during the grand opening.
i. Cash received from services provided during the second half of August was $930.
j. On August 31, it paid a $400 installment toward principal on the note payable entered into on August 4.
k. On August 31, it paid $900 in cash dividends to Worthy.

Required

1. Arrange the following asset, liability, and equity titles in a table similar to the one in Exhibit 1.9: Cash; Accounts Receivable; Furniture; Store Equipment; Note Payable; Common Stock; Dividends; Revenues; and Expenses. Show the effects of each transaction using the accounting equation.
2. Prepare an income statement for August.
3. Prepare a statement of retained earnings for August.
4. Prepare a balance sheet as of August 31.
5. Prepare a statement of cash flows for August.
6. Determine the return on assets ratio for August.

PLANNING THE SOLUTION

- Set up a table like Exhibit 1.9 with the appropriate columns for accounts.
- Analyze each transaction and show its effects as increases or decreases in the appropriate columns. Be sure the accounting equation remains in balance after each transaction.
- Prepare the income statement, and identify revenues and expenses. List those items on the statement, compute the difference, and label the result as *net income* or *net loss*.
- Use information in the Equity columns to prepare the statement of retained earnings.
- Use information in the last row of the transactions table to prepare the balance sheet.
- Prepare the statement of cash flows; include all events listed in the Cash column of the transactions table. Classify each cash flow as operating, investing, or financing.
- Calculate return on assets by dividing net income by average assets.

SOLUTION TO DEMONSTRATION PROBLEM

1.

	Assets							=	Liabilities	+			Equity			
	Cash	+	Accounts Receivable	+	Furniture	+	Store Equipment	=	Note Payable	+	Common Stock	−	Dividends	+	Revenues	−	Expenses
a.	$3,000						$15,000				$18,000						
b.	− 600			+	$600												
Bal.	2,400	+		+	600	+	15,000	=			18,000						
c.	− 500																− $500
Bal.	1,900	+		+	600	+	15,000	=			18,000						− 500
d.						+	1,200		+$1,200								
Bal.	1,900	+		+	600	+	16,200	=	1,200	+	18,000						− 500
e.	+ 825													+	$ 825		
Bal.	2,725	+		+	600	+	16,200	=	1,200	+	18,000			+	825	−	500
f.		+	$100											+	100		
Bal.	2,725	+	100	+	600	+	16,200	=	1,200	+	18,000			+	925	−	500
g.	+ 100	−	100														
Bal.	2,825	+	0	+	600	+	16,200	=	1,200	+	18,000			+	925	−	500
h.	− 125															−	125
Bal.	2,700	+	0	+	600	+	16,200	=	1,200	+	18,000			+	925	−	625
i.	+ 930													+	930		
Bal.	3,630	+	0	+	600	+	16,200	=	1,200	+	18,000			+	1,855	−	625
j.	− 400								− 400								
Bal.	3,230	+	0	+	600	+	16,200	=	800	+	18,000			+	1,855	−	625
k.	− 900											−	$900				
Bal.	$ 2,330	+	0	+	$600	+	$ 16,200	=	$ 800	+	$ 18,000	−	$900	+	$1,855	−	$625

2.

EXPRESSIONS
Income Statement
For Month Ended August 31

Revenues		
Haircutting services revenue		$1,855
Expenses		
Rent expense	$500	
Wages expense	125	
Total expenses		625
Net Income		$1,230

3.

EXPRESSIONS
Statement of Retained Earnings
For Month Ended August 31

Retained earnings, August 1*.........		$ 0
Plus: Net income		1,230
		1,230
Less: Dividend to owner		900
Retained earnings, August 31		$ 330

* If Expressions had been an existing business from a prior period, the beginning retained earnings balance would equal the retained earnings balance from the end of the prior period.

4.

EXPRESSIONS				
Balance Sheet				
August 31				
Assets		**Liabilities**		
Cash	$ 2,330	Note payable	$ 800	
Furniture	600	**Equity**		
Store equipment	16,200	Common stock	18,000	
		Retained earnings	330	
		Total equity	18,330	
Total assets	$19,130	Total liabilities and equity	$19,130	

5.

EXPRESSIONS	
Statement of Cash Flows	
For Month Ended August 31	
Cash flows from operating activities	
Cash received from customers	$1,855
Cash paid for rent	(500)
Cash paid for wages	(125)
Net cash provided by operating activities	$1,230
Cash flows from investing activities	
Cash paid for furniture	(600)
Cash flows from financing activities	
Investments from stockholders	3,000
Cash dividends to stockholders	(900)
Partial repayment of (long-term) note payable	(400)
Net cash provided by financing activities	1,700
Net increase in cash	$2,330
Cash balance, August 1	0
Cash balance, August 31	$2,330

6. $\text{Return on assets} = \dfrac{\text{Net income}}{\text{Average assets}} = \dfrac{\$1{,}230}{(\$18{,}000^* + \$19{,}130)/2} = \dfrac{\$1{,}230}{\$18{,}565} = \underline{\underline{6.63\%}}$

** Uses the initial $18,000 investment as the beginning balance for the *start-up period only*.*

APPENDIX 1A

Return and Risk Analysis

This appendix explains return and risk analysis and its role in business and accounting.

Net income is often linked to **return.** Return on assets (ROA) is stated in ratio form as income divided by assets invested. For example, banks report return from a savings account in the form of an interest return such as 4%. If we invest in a savings account or in U.S. Treasury bills, we expect a return of around 2% to 7%. We could also invest in a company's stock, or even start our own business. How do we decide among these investment options? The answer depends on our trade-off between return and risk.

A3 Explain the relation between return and risk.

Risk is the uncertainty about the return we will earn. All business investments involve risk, but some investments involve more risk than others. The lower the risk of an investment, the lower is our expected return. The reason that savings accounts pay such a low return is the low risk of not being repaid with interest (the government guarantees most savings accounts from default). If we buy a share of eBay or any other company, we might obtain a large return. However, we have no guarantee of any return; there is even the risk of loss.

EXHIBIT 1A.1
Average Returns for Bonds with Different Risks

Bond Type	Annual Return
U.S. Treasury	3.6%
Low-risk corporate	4.8%
Medium-risk corporate	6.3%
High-risk corporate	8.0%

The bar graph in Exhibit 1A.1 shows recent returns for 10-year bonds with different risks. *Bonds* are written promises by organizations to repay amounts loaned with interest. U.S. Treasury bonds provide a low expected return, but they also offer low risk since they are backed by the U.S. government. High-risk corporate bonds offer a much larger potential return but with much higher risk.

The trade-off between return and risk is a normal part of business. Higher risk implies higher, but riskier, expected returns. To help us make better decisions, we use accounting information to assess both return and risk.

APPENDIX 1B — Business Activities and the Accounting Equation

C5 Identify and describe the three major activities of organizations.

This appendix explains how the accounting equation is derived from business activities.

There are three major types of business activities: financing, investing, and operating. Each of these requires planning. *Planning* involves defining an organization's ideas, goals, and actions. Most public corporations use the *Management Discussion and Analysis* section in their annual reports to communicate plans. However, planning is not cast in stone. This adds *risk* to both setting plans and analyzing them.

Financing *Financing activities* provide the means organizations use to pay for resources such as land, buildings, and equipment to carry out plans. Organizations are careful in acquiring and managing financing activities because they can determine success or failure. The two sources of financing are owner and nonowner. *Owner financing* refers to resources contributed by the owner along with any income the owner leaves in the organization. *Nonowner* (or *creditor*) *financing* refers to resources contributed by creditors (lenders). *Financial management* is the task of planning how to obtain these resources and to set the right mix between owner and creditor financing.

Point: Management must understand accounting data to set financial goals, make financing and investing decisions, and evaluate operating performance.

Investing *Investing activities* are the acquiring and disposing of resources (assets) that an organization uses to acquire and sell its products or services. Assets are funded by an organization's financing. Organizations differ on the amount and makeup of assets. Some require land and factories to operate. Others need only an office. Determining the amount and type of assets for operations is called *asset management*. Invested amounts are referred to as *assets*. Financing is made up of creditor and owner financing, which hold claims on assets. Creditors' claims are called *liabilities*, and the owner's claim is called *equity*. This basic equality is called the *accounting equation* and can be written as: Assets = Liabilities + Equity.

Point: Investing (assets) and financing (liabilities plus equity) totals are *always* equal.

EXHIBIT 1B.1
Activities of Organizations

Operating *Operating activities* involve using resources to research, develop, purchase, produce, distribute, and market products and services. Sales and revenues are the inflow of assets from selling products and services. Costs and expenses are the outflow of assets to support operating activities. *Strategic management* is the process of determining the right mix of operating activities for the type of organization, its plans, and its market.

Exhibit 1B.1 summarizes business activities. Planning is part of each activity and gives them meaning and focus. Investing

Summary

*← A **Summary** organized by learning objectives concludes each chapter.*

C1 **Explain the purpose and importance of accounting.** Accounting is an information and measurement system that aims to identify, record, and communicate relevant, reliable, and comparable information about business activities. It helps assess opportunities, products, investments, and social and community responsibilities.

C2 **Identify users and uses of, and opportunities in, accounting.** Users of accounting are both internal and external. Some users and uses of accounting include (a) managers in controlling, monitoring, and planning; (b) lenders for measuring the risk and return of loans; (c) shareholders for assessing the return and risk of stock; (d) directors for overseeing management; and (e) employees for judging employment opportunities. Opportunities in accounting include financial, managerial, and tax accounting. They also include accounting-related fields such as lending, consulting, managing, and planning.

C3 **Explain why ethics are crucial to accounting.** The goal of accounting is to provide useful information for decision making. For information to be useful, it must be trusted. This demands ethical behavior in accounting.

C4 **Explain generally accepted accounting principles and define and apply several accounting principles.** Generally accepted accounting principles are a common set of standards applied by accountants. Accounting principles aid in producing relevant, reliable, and comparable information. Four principles underlying financial statements were introduced: cost, revenue recognition, matching, and full disclosure. Financial statements also reflect four assumptions: going-concern, monetary unit, time period, and business entity.

C5[B] **Identify and describe the three major activities of organizations.** Organizations carry out three major activities: financing, investing, and operating. Financing is the means used to pay for resources such as land, buildings, and machines. Investing refers to the buying and selling of resources used in acquiring and selling products and services. Operating activities are those necessary for carrying out the organization's plans.

A1 **Define and interpret the accounting equation and each of its components.** The accounting equation is: Assets = Liabilities + Equity. Assets are resources owned by a company. Liabilities are creditors' claims on assets. Equity is the owner's claim on assets (*the residual*). The expanded accounting equation is: Assets = Liabilities + [Common Stock − Dividends + Revenues − Expenses].

A2 **Compute and interpret return on assets.** Return on assets is computed as net income divided by average assets. For example, if we have an average balance of $100 in a savings account and it earns $5 interest for the year, the return on assets is $5/$100, or 5%.

A3[A] **Explain the relation between return and risk.** *Return* refers to income, and *risk* is the uncertainty about the return we hope to make. All investments involve risk. The lower the risk of an investment, the lower is its expected return. Higher risk implies higher, but riskier, expected return.

P1 **Analyze business transactions using the accounting equation.** A *transaction* is an exchange of economic consideration between two parties. Examples include exchanges of products, services, money, and rights to collect money. Transactions always have at least two effects on one or more components of the accounting equation. This equation is always in balance.

P2 **Identify and prepare basic financial statements and explain how they interrelate.** Four financial statements report on an organization's activities: balance sheet, income statement, statement of retained earnings, and statement of cash flows.

Guidance Answers to Decision Maker and Decision Ethics

Entrepreneur You should probably form the business as a corporation if potential lawsuits are of prime concern. The corporate form of organization protects your personal property from lawsuits directed at the business and places only the corporation's resources at risk. A downside of the corporate form is double taxation: The corporation must pay taxes on its income, and you normally must pay taxes on any money distributed to you from the business (even though the corporation already paid taxes on this money). You should also examine the ethical and socially responsible aspects of starting a business in which you anticipate injuries to others. Formation as an LLC or S corp. should also be explored.

Retailer You can use the accounting equation (Assets = Liabilities + Equity) to help identify risky customers to whom you would likely not want to extend credit. A balance sheet provides amounts for each of these key components. The lower a customer's equity is relative to liabilities, the less likely you would be to extend credit. A low equity means the business has little value that does not already have creditor claims to it.

Business Owner The 19% return on assets for the manufacturer exceeds the 14% industry return (and many others). This is a positive factor for a potential purchase. Also, the purchase of this manufacturer is an opportunity to spread your risk over two businesses as opposed to one. Still, you should hesitate to purchase a business whose return of 19% is lower than your current resort's return of 21%. You are probably better off directing efforts to increase investment in your resort, assuming you can continue to earn a 21% return.

Guidance Answers to Quick Checks

1. Accounting is an information and measurement system that identifies, records, and communicates relevant information to help people make better decisions.

2. Recordkeeping, also called *bookkeeping,* is the recording of financial transactions and events, either manually or electronically. Recordkeeping is essential to data reliability; but accounting is this and much more. Accounting includes identifying, measuring, recording, reporting, and analyzing business events and transactions.

3. Technology offers increased accuracy, speed, efficiency, and convenience in accounting.

4. External users of accounting include lenders, shareholders, directors, customers, suppliers, regulators, lawyers, brokers, and the press. Internal users of accounting include managers, officers, and other internal decision makers involved with strategic and operating decisions.

5. Internal users (managers) include those from research and development, purchasing, human resources, production, distribution, marketing, and servicing.

6. Internal controls are procedures set up to protect assets, ensure reliable accounting reports, promote efficiency, and encourage adherence to company policies. Internal controls are crucial for relevant and reliable information.

7. Ethical guidelines are threefold: (1) identify ethical concerns using personal ethics, (2) analyze options considering all good and bad consequences, and (3) make ethical decisions after weighing all consequences.

8. Ethics and social responsibility yield good behavior, and they often result in higher income and a better working environment.

9. For accounting to provide useful information for decisions, it must be trusted. Trust requires ethics in accounting.

10. Two major participants in setting rules include the SEC and the FASB. (*Note:* Accounting rules reflect society's needs, not those of accountants or any other single constituency.)

11. Most U.S. companies are not directly affected by international accounting standards. International standards are put forth as preferred accounting practices. However, stock exchanges and other parties are increasing the pressure to narrow differences in worldwide accounting practices. International accounting standards are playing an important role in that process.

12. The objectivity concept and cost principle are related in that most users consider information based on cost as objective. Information prepared using both is considered highly reliable and often relevant.

13. Users desire information about the performance of a specific entity. If information is mixed between two or more entities, its usefulness decreases.

14. The revenue recognition principle gives preparers guidelines on when to recognize (record) revenue. This is important; for example, if revenue is recognized too early, the statements report revenue sooner than it should and the business looks more profitable than it is. The reverse is also true.

15. The three basic forms of business organization are sole proprietorships, partnerships, and corporations.

16. Owners of corporations are called *shareholders* (or *stockholders*). Corporate ownership is divided into units called *shares* (or *stock*). The most basic of corporate shares is common stock (or capital stock).

17. The accounting equation is: Assets = Liabilities + Equity. This equation is always in balance, both before and after each transaction.

18. A transaction that changes the makeup of assets would not affect liability and equity accounts. FastForward's transactions 2 and 3 are examples. Each exchanges one asset for another.

19. Earning revenue by performing services, as in FastForward's transaction 5, increases equity (and assets). Incurring expenses while servicing clients, such as in transactions 6 and 7, decreases equity (and assets). Other examples include owner investments (stock issuances) that increase equity and dividends that decrease equity.

20. Paying a liability with an asset reduces both asset and liability totals. One example is FastForward's transaction 10 that reduces a payable by paying cash.

21. An income statement reports a company's revenues and expenses along with the resulting net income or loss. A statement of retained earnings shows changes in retained earnings, including that from net income or loss. Both statements report transactions occurring over a period of time.

22. The balance sheet describes a company's financial position (assets, liabilities, and equity) at a point in time. The retained earnings amount in the balance sheet is obtained from the statement of retained earnings.

23. Cash flows from operating activities report cash receipts and payments from the primary business the company engages in. Cash flows from investing activities involve cash transactions from buying and selling long-term assets. Cash flows from financing activities include long-term cash borrowings and repayments to lenders and the cash investments from, and dividends to, the stockholders.

Key Terms

Accounting (p. 4)
Accounting equation (p. 15)
Assets (p. 15)
Audit (p. 13)
Auditors (p. 13)
Balance sheet (p. 20)
Bookkeeping (p. 4)
Business entity assumption (p. 11)
Common stock (p. 12)
Conceptual framework (p. 10)
Contributed capital (p. 15)
Corporation (p. 12)
Cost-benefit constraint (p. 13)
Cost principle (p. 11)
Dividends (p. 15)
Equity (p. 15)
Ethics (p. 8)
Events (p. 16)
Expanded accounting equation (p. 15)
Expense recognition principle (p. 11)
Expenses (p. 15)
External transactions (p. 16)

External users (p. 5)
Financial accounting (p. 5)
Financial Accounting Standards Board (FASB) (p. 9)
Full disclosure principle (p. 11)
Generally accepted accounting principles (GAAP) (p. 9)
Going-concern assumption (p. 11)
Income (p. 15)
Income statement (p. 20)
Internal transactions (p. 16)
Internal users (p. 6)
International Accounting Standards Board (IASB) (p. 9)
International Financial Reporting Standards (IFRS) (p. 9)
Liabilities (p. 15)
Managerial accounting (p. 6)
Matching principle (p. 11)
Materiality constraint (p. 13)
Measurement principle (p. 11)
Monetary unit assumption (p. 11)
Net income (p. 15)

Net loss (p. 15)
Partnership (p. 12)
Proprietorship (p. 11)
Recordkeeping (p. 4)
Retained earnings (p. 15)
Return (p. 28)
Return on assets (p. 24)
Revenue recognition principle (p. 11)
Revenues (p. 15)
Risk (p. 28)
Sarbanes–Oxley Act (p. 13)
Securities and Exchange Commission (SEC) (p. 9)
Shareholders (p. 12)
Shares (p. 12)
Sole proprietorship (p. 11)
Statement of cash flows (p. 20)
Statement of retained earnings (p. 20)
Stock (p. 12)
Stockholders (p. 12)
Time period assumption (p. 11)

Multiple Choice Quiz

Answers on p. 49 mhhe.com/wildFA6e

Additional quiz questions are available at the book's Website.

1. A building is offered for sale at $500,000 but is currently assessed at $400,000. The purchaser of the building believes the building is worth $475,000, but ultimately purchases the building for $450,000. The purchaser records the building at:
   a. $50,000
   b. $400,000
   c. $450,000
   d. $475,000
   e. $500,000

2. On December 30, 2010, **KPMG** signs a $150,000 contract to provide accounting services to one of its clients in 2011. KPMG has a December 31 year-end. Which accounting principle or assumption requires KPMG to record the accounting services revenue from this client in 2011 and not 2010?
   a. Business entity assumption
   b. Revenue recognition principle
   c. Monetary unit assumption
   d. Cost principle
   e. Going-concern assumption

3. If the assets of a company increase by $100,000 during the year and its liabilities increase by $35,000 during the same year, then the change in equity of the company during the year must have been:
   a. An increase of $135,000.
   b. A decrease of $135,000.
   c. A decrease of $65,000.
   d. An increase of $65,000.
   e. An increase of $100,000.

4. **Brunswick** borrows $50,000 cash from Third National Bank. How does this transaction affect the accounting equation for Brunswick?
   a. Assets increase by $50,000; liabilities increase by $50,000; no effect on equity.
   b. Assets increase by $50,000; no effect on liabilities; equity increases by $50,000.
   c. Assets increase by $50,000; liabilities decrease by $50,000; no effect on equity.
   d. No effect on assets; liabilities increase by $50,000; equity increases by $50,000.
   e. No effect on assets; liabilities increase by $50,000; equity decreases by $50,000.

5. **Geek Squad** performs services for a customer and bills the customer for $500. How would Geek Squad record this transaction?
  a. Accounts receivable increase by $500; revenues increase by $500.
  b. Cash increases by $500; revenues increase by $500.
  c. Accounts receivable increase by $500; revenues decrease by $500.
  d. Accounts receivable increase by $500; accounts payable increase by $500.
  e. Accounts payable increase by $500; revenues increase by $500.

A(B) *Superscript letter A (B) denotes assignments based on Appendix 1A (1B).*
 Icon denotes assignments that involve decision making.

Discussion Questions

1. What is the purpose of accounting in society?
2. Technology is increasingly used to process accounting data. Why then must we study and understand accounting?
3. Identify four kinds of external users and describe how they use accounting information.
4. What are at least three questions business owners and managers might be able to answer by looking at accounting information?
5. Identify three actual businesses that offer services and three actual businesses that offer products.
6. Describe the internal role of accounting for organizations.
7. Identify three types of services typically offered by accounting professionals.
8. What type of accounting information might be useful to the marketing managers of a business?
9. Why is accounting described as a service activity?
10. What are some accounting-related professions?
11. How do ethics rules affect auditors' choice of clients?
12. What work do tax accounting professionals perform in addition to preparing tax returns?
13. What does the concept of *objectivity* imply for information reported in financial statements? Why?
14. A business reports its own office stationery on the balance sheet at its $400 cost, although it cannot be sold for more than $10 as scrap paper. Which accounting principle and/or assumption justifies this treatment?
15. Why is the revenue recognition principle needed? What does it demand?
16. Describe the three basic forms of business organization and their key attributes.
17. Define (*a*) assets, (*b*) liabilities, (*c*) equity, and (*d*) net assets.
18. What events or transactions change equity?
19. Identify the two main categories of accounting principles.
20. What do accountants mean by the term *revenue*?
21. Define *net income* and explain its computation.
22. Identify the four basic financial statements of a business.
23. What information is reported in an income statement?
24. Give two examples of expenses a business might incur.
25. What is the purpose of the statement of retained earnings?
26. What information is reported in a balance sheet?
27. The statement of cash flows reports on what major activities?
28. Define and explain return on assets.
29.A Define return and risk. Discuss the trade-off between them.
30.B Describe the three major business activities in organizations.
31.B Explain why investing (assets) and financing (liabilities and equity) totals are always equal.
32. Refer to the financial statements of **Research In Motion** in Appendix A near the end of the book. To what level of significance are dollar amounts rounded? What time period does its income statement cover?
33. Identify the dollar amounts of **Apple**'s 2009 assets, liabilities, and equity as reported in its statements in Appendix A near the end of the book.
34. Refer to **Nokia**'s balance sheet in Appendix A near the end of the book. Confirm that its total assets equal its total liabilities plus total equity.
35. Access the SEC EDGAR database (www.sec.gov) and retrieve **Palm**'s 2009 10-K (filed July 24, 2009; ticker PALM). Identify its auditor. What responsibility does its independent auditor claim regarding Palm's financial statements?

Connect reproduces assignments online, in static or algorithmic mode, which allows instructors to monitor, promote, and assess student learning. It can be used for practice, homework, or exams.

Quick Study exercises give readers a brief test of key elements.

QUICK STUDY

QS 1-1
Identifying accounting terms   C1

Reading and interpreting accounting reports requires some knowledge of accounting terminology. (*a*) Identify the meaning of these accounting-related acronyms: GAAP, SEC, FASB, IASB and IFRS. (*b*) Briefly explain the importance of the knowledge base or organization that is referred to for each of the accounting-related acronyms.

An important responsibility of many accounting professionals is to design and implement internal control procedures for organizations. Explain the purpose of internal control procedures. Provide two examples of internal controls applied by companies.	**QS 1-2** Explaining internal control C1	

Identify the following users as either external users (E) or internal users (I).
QS 1-3 Identifying accounting users C2

a. Lenders d. Sales staff g. Brokers j. Managers
b. Controllers e. FBI and IRS h. Suppliers k. Business press
c. Shareholders f. Consumer group i. Customers l. District attorney

---

There are many job opportunities for those with accounting knowledge. Identify at least three main areas of opportunities for accounting professionals. For each area, identify at least three job possibilities linked to accounting.

QS 1-4 Accounting opportunities C2

Accounting professionals must sometimes choose between two or more acceptable methods of accounting for business transactions and events. Explain why these situations can involve difficult matters of ethical concern.

QS 1-5 Identifying ethical concerns C3

This icon highlights assignments that enhance decision-making skills.

Identify which accounting principle or assumption best describes each of the following practices:

QS 1-6 Identifying accounting principles C4

a. If $51,000 cash is paid to buy land, the land is reported on the buyer's balance sheet at $51,000.
b. Alissa Kees owns both Sailing Passions and Dockside Supplies. In preparing financial statements for Dockside Supplies, Kees makes sure that the expense transactions of Sailing Passions are kept separate from Dockside's transactions and financial statements.
c. In December 2010, Ace Landscaping received a customer's order and cash prepayment to install sod at a new house that would not be ready for installation until March 2011. Ace should record the revenue from the customer order in March 2011, not in December 2010.

---

a. Total assets of Caldwell Company equal $40,000 and its equity is $10,000. What is the amount of its liabilities?
b. Total assets of Waterworld equal $55,000 and its liabilities and equity amounts are equal to each other. What is the amount of its liabilities? What is the amount of its equity?

QS 1-7 Applying the accounting equation A1

Use the accounting equation to compute the missing financial statement amounts (a), (b), and (c).

QS 1-8 Applying the accounting equation A1

Company	Assets	=	Liabilities	+	Equity
1	$ 30,000		$ (a)		$ 20,000
2	(b)		50,000		30,000
3	90,000		10,000		(c)

Accounting provides information about an organization's business transactions and events that both affect the accounting equation and can be reliably measured. Identify at least two examples of both (a) business transactions and (b) business events that meet these requirements.

QS 1-9 Identifying transactions and events P1

Use **Apple**'s September 26, 2009, financial statements, in Appendix A near the end of the book, to answer the following:

QS 1-10 Identifying and computing assets, liabilities, and equity P1

a. Identify the dollar amounts of Apple's 2009 (1) assets, (2) liabilities, and (3) equity.
b. Using Apple's amounts from part a, verify that Assets = Liabilities + Equity.

QS 1-11
Computing and interpreting return on assets

A2

In a recent year's financial statements, **Home Depot** reported the following results. Compute and interpret Home Depot's return on assets (assume competitors average a 5% return on assets).

Sales	$71,288 million
Net income	2,260 million
Average total assets	42,744 million

QS 1-12
Identifying items with financial statements

P2

Indicate in which financial statement each item would most likely appear: income statement (I), balance sheet (B), statement of retained earnings (RE), or statement of cash flows (CF).

a. Assets
b. Revenues
c. Liabilities
d. Equipment
e. Dividends
f. Expenses
g. Total liabilities and equity
h. Cash from operating activities
i. Net decrease (or increase) in cash

QS 1-13
International accounting standards C4

This icon highlights assignments that focus on IFRS-related content.

Answer each of the following questions related to international accounting standards.

a. The International Accounting Standards Board (IASB) issues preferred accounting practices that are referred to as what?
b. The FASB and IASB are working on a convergence process for what purpose?
c. The SEC has proposed a roadmap for use of IFRS by U.S. companies. What is the proposed adoption date for large U.S. companies to adopt IFRS?

EXERCISES

Exercise 1-1
Classifying activities reflected in the accounting system

C1

Accounting is an information and measurement system that identifies, records, and communicates relevant, reliable, and comparable information about an organization's business activities. Classify the following activities as part of the identifying (I), recording (R), or communicating (C) aspects of accounting.

_____ 1. Determining employee tasks behind a service.
_____ 2. Establishing revenues generated from a product.
_____ 3. Maintaining a log of service costs.
_____ 4. Measuring the costs of a product.
_____ 5. Preparing financial statements.
_____ 6. Analyzing and interpreting reports.
_____ 7. Presenting financial information.

Exercise 1-2
Identifying accounting users and uses

C2

Part A. Identify the following users of accounting information as either an internal (I) or an external (E) user.

_____ 1. Shareholders
_____ 2. Creditors
_____ 3. Nonexecutive employee
_____ 4. Research and development director
_____ 5. Purchasing manager
_____ 6. Human resources director
_____ 7. Production supervisors
_____ 8. Distribution managers

Part B. Identify the following questions as most likely to be asked by an internal (I) or an external (E) user of accounting information.

_____ 1. What are the costs of our service to customers?
_____ 2. Should we make a five-year loan to that business?
_____ 3. Should we spend further research on our product?
_____ 4. Do income levels justify the current stock price?
_____ 5. What are reasonable payroll benefits and wages?
_____ 6. Which firm reports the highest sales and income?
_____ 7. What are the costs of our product's ingredients?

Exercise 1-3
Describing accounting responsibilities

C2

Many accounting professionals work in one of the following three areas:

A. Managerial accounting
B. Financial accounting
C. Tax accounting

Identify the area of accounting that is most involved in each of the following responsibilities:

_____ 1. Reviewing reports for SEC compliance.
_____ 2. Planning transactions to minimize taxes.
_____ 3. Investigating violations of tax laws.
_____ 4. Preparing external financial statements.
_____ 5. Budgeting.
_____ 6. Cost accounting.
_____ 7. External auditing.
_____ 8. Internal auditing.

Exercise 1-4
Identifying ethical concerns
C3

Assume the following role and describe a situation in which ethical considerations play an important part in guiding your decisions and actions:
a. You are a student in an introductory accounting course.
b. You are an accounting professional with audit clients that are competitors in business.
c. You are an accounting professional preparing tax returns for clients.
d. You are a manager with responsibility for several employees.

Exercise 1-5
Learning the language of business
C1–C3

Match each of the numbered descriptions with the term or phrase it best reflects. Indicate your answer by writing the letter for the term or phrase in the blank provided.
A. Audit   C. Ethics   E. SEC   G. Net income
B. GAAP   D. Tax accounting   F. Public accountants   H. IASB
____ 1. Amount a business earns after paying all expenses and costs associated with its sales and revenues.
____ 2. An examination of an organization's accounting system and records that adds credibility to financial statements.
____ 3. Principles that determine whether an action is right or wrong.
____ 4. Accounting professionals who provide services to many clients.
____ 5. An accounting area that includes planning future transactions to minimize taxes paid.

Exercise 1-6
Identifying accounting principles and assumptions
C4

Match each of the numbered descriptions with the principle or assumption it best reflects. Enter the letter for the appropriate principle or assumption in the blank space next to each description.
A. Cost principle   E. General accounting principle
B. Matching principle   F. Business entity assumption
C. Specific accounting principle   G. Revenue recognition principle
D. Full disclosure principle   H. Going-concern assumption
____ 1. Revenue is recorded only when the earnings process is complete.
____ 2. Information is based on actual costs incurred in transactions.
____ 3. Usually created by a pronouncement from an authoritative body.
____ 4. Financial statements reflect the assumption that the business continues operating.
____ 5. A company reports details behind financial statements that would impact users' decisions.
____ 6. A company records the expenses incurred to generate the revenues reported.
____ 7. Derived from long-used and generally accepted accounting practices.
____ 8. Every business is accounted for separately from its owner or owners.

Exercise 1-7
Distinguishing business organizations
C4

The following describe several different business organizations. Determine whether the description refers to a sole proprietorship, partnership, or corporation.
a. A-1 pays its own income taxes and has two owners.
b. Ownership of Zeller Company is divided into 1,000 shares of stock.
c. Waldron is owned by Mary Malone, who is personally liable for the company's debts.
d. Micah Douglas and Nathan Logan own Financial Services, a financial services provider. Neither Douglas nor Logan has personal responsibility for the debts of Financial Services.
e. Bailey and Kay own Squeaky Clean, a cleaning service. Both are personally liable for the debts of the business.
f. Plasto Products does not pay income taxes and has one owner.
g. Ian LLC does not have separate legal existence apart from the one person who owns it.

Exercise 1-8
Using the accounting equation
A1 P1

Answer the following questions. (*Hint:* Use the accounting equation.)
a. Office Mart has assets equal to $123,000 and liabilities equal to $53,000 at year-end. What is the total equity for Office Mart at year-end?
b. At the beginning of the year, Logan Company's assets are $200,000 and its equity is $150,000. During the year, assets increase $70,000 and liabilities increase $30,000. What is the equity at the end of the year?
c. At the beginning of the year, Keller Company's liabilities equal $60,000. During the year, assets increase by $80,000, and at year-end assets equal $180,000. Liabilities decrease $10,000 during the year. What are the beginning and ending amounts of equity?

Check (c) Beg. equity, $40,000

Exercise 1-9
Using the accounting equation
A1

Determine the missing amount from each of the separate situations *a*, *b*, and *c* below.

	Assets	=	Liabilities	+	Equity
(a)	$?		$ 30,000		$ 65,000
(b)	89,000		22,000		?
(c)	132,000		?		20,000

Exercise 1-10
Identifying effects of transactions on the accounting equation
P1

Provide an example of a transaction that creates the described effects for the separate cases *a* through *g*.

a. Increases an asset and decreases an asset.
b. Decreases an asset and decreases a liability.
c. Decreases a liability and increases a liability.
d. Increases an asset and increases a liability.
e. Decreases an asset and decreases equity.
f. Increases a liability and decreases equity.
g. Increases an asset and increases equity.

Exercise 1-11
Identifying effects of transactions using the accounting equation
P1

Lena Gold began a professional practice on June 1 and plans to prepare financial statements at the end of each month. During June, Gold (the owner) completed these transactions:

a. Owner invested $50,000 cash in the company along with equipment that had a $10,000 market value in exchange for common stock.
b. The company paid $1,600 cash for rent of office space for the month.
c. The company purchased $12,000 of additional equipment on credit (payment due within 30 days).
d. The company completed work for a client and immediately collected the $2,000 cash earned.
e. The company completed work for a client and sent a bill for $7,000 to be received within 30 days.
f. The company purchased additional equipment for $8,000 cash.
g. The company paid an assistant $2,400 cash as wages for the month.
h. The company collected $5,000 cash as a partial payment for the amount owed by the client in transaction *e*.
i. The company paid $12,000 cash to settle the liability created in transaction *c*.
j. The company paid $500 cash for dividends.

Required

Check Net income, $5,000

Create a table like the one in Exhibit 1.9, using the following headings for columns: Cash; Accounts Receivable; Equipment; Accounts Payable; Common Stock; Dividends; Revenues; and Expenses. Then use additions and subtractions to show the effects of the transactions on individual items of the accounting equation. Show new balances after each transaction.

Exercise 1-12
Analysis using the accounting equation
P1

Zelda began a new consulting firm on January 5. The accounting equation showed the following balances after each of the company's first five transactions. Analyze the accounting equation for each transaction and describe each of the five transactions with their amounts.

			Assets							=	Liabilities	+		Equity	
Trans-action	Cash	+	Accounts Receivable	+	Office Supplies	+	Office Furniture	=	Accounts Payable	+	Common Stock	+	Revenues
a.	$20,000	+	$ 0	+	$ 0	+	$ 0	=	$ 0	+	$20,000	+	$ 0
b.	19,000	+	0	+	1,500	+	0	=	500	+	20,000	+	0
c.	11,000	+	0	+	1,500	+	8,000	=	500	+	20,000	+	0
d.	11,000	+	3,000	+	1,500	+	8,000	=	500	+	20,000	+	3,000
e.	11,500	+	3,000	+	1,500	+	8,000	=	500	+	20,000	+	3,500

Exercise 1-13
Identifying effects of transactions on accounting equation
P1

The following table shows the effects of five transactions (*a* through *e*) on the assets, liabilities, and equity of Vera's Boutique. Write short descriptions of the probable nature of each transaction.

	Assets							=	Liabilities	+	Equity		
	Cash	+	Accounts Receivable	+	Office Supplies	+	Land	=	Accounts Payable	+	Common Stock	+	Revenues
	$ 10,500	+	$ 0	+	$1,500	+	$ 9,500	=	$ 0	+	$21,500	+	$ 0
a.	− 2,000						2,000						
b.					500				+500				
c.		+	950									+	950
d.	− 500								−500				
e.	+ 950	−	950										
	$ 8,950	+	$ 0	+	$2,000	+	$11,500	=	$ 0	+	$21,500	+	$950

Exercise 1-14
Preparing an income statement
P2

On October 1, Natalie King organized Real Solutions, a new consulting firm. On October 31, the company's records show the following items and amounts. Use this information to prepare an October income statement for the business.

Cash	$ 2,000	Cash dividends	$ 3,360
Accounts receivable	13,000	Consulting fees earned	15,000
Office supplies	4,250	Rent expense	2,550
Land	36,000	Salaries expense	6,000
Office equipment	28,000	Telephone expense	660
Accounts payable	7,500	Miscellaneous expenses	680
Common stock	74,000		

Check Net income, $5,110

Exercise 1-15
Preparing a statement of retained earnings P2

Use the information in Exercise 1-14 to prepare an October statement of retained earnings for Real Solutions.

Exercise 1-16
Preparing a balance sheet P2

Use the information in Exercise 1-14 (if completed, you can also use your solution to Exercise 1-15) to prepare an October 31 balance sheet for Real Solutions.

Exercise 1-17
Preparing a statement of cash flows
P2

Use the information in Exercise 1-14 to prepare an October 31 statement of cash flows for Real Solutions. Also assume the following:
a. The owner's initial investment consists of $38,000 cash and $36,000 in land in exchange for common stock.
b. The company's $28,000 equipment purchase is paid in cash.
c. The accounts payable balance of $7,500 consists of the $4,250 office supplies purchase and $3,250 in employee salaries yet to be paid.
d. The company's rent, telephone, and miscellaneous expenses are paid in cash.
e. $2,000 has been collected on the $15,000 consulting fees earned.

Check Net increase in cash, $2,000

Exercise 1-18
Analysis of return on assets
A2

Geneva Group reports net income of $20,000 for 2011. At the beginning of 2011, Geneva Group had $100,000 in assets. By the end of 2011, assets had grown to $150,000. What is Geneva Group's 2011 return on assets? How would you assess its performance if competitors average a 10% return on assets?

Exercise 1-19
Identifying sections of the statement of cash flows
P2

Indicate the section where each of the following would appear on the statement of cash flows.
A. Cash flows from operating activity
B. Cash flows from investing activity
C. Cash flows from financing activity

_____ 1. Cash paid for wages
_____ 2. Cash paid for dividends
_____ 3. Cash purchase of equipment
_____ 4. Cash paid for advertising
_____ 5. Cash paid on an account payable
_____ 6. Cash received from stock issued
_____ 7. Cash received from clients
_____ 8. Cash paid for rent

Exercise 1-20[B]
Identifying business activities
C5

Match each transaction or event to one of the following activities of an organization: financing activities (F), investing activities (I), or operating activities (O).

1. _____ An owner contributes resources to the business in exchange for stock.
2. _____ An organization purchases equipment.
3. _____ An organization advertises a new product.
4. _____ The organization borrows money from a bank.
5. _____ An organization sells some of its land.

Exercise 1-21
Preparing an income statement for a global company
P2

Nintendo Company reports the following income statement accounts for the year ended March 31, 2009. (Japanese yen in millions.)

Net sales	¥1,838,622
Cost of sales	1,044,981
Selling, general and administrative expenses	238,378
Other expenses	276,174

Use this information to prepare Nintendo's income statement for the year ended March 31, 2009.

Problem Set B located at the end of Problem Set A is provided for each problem to reinforce the learning process.

PROBLEM SET A

Problem 1-1A
Identifying effects of transactions on financial statements
A1 P1

Identify how each of the following separate transactions affects financial statements. For the balance sheet, identify how each transaction affects total assets, total liabilities, and total equity. For the income statement, identify how each transaction affects net income. For the statement of cash flows, identify how each transaction affects cash flows from operating activities, cash flows from financing activities, and cash flows from investing activities. For increases, place a "+" in the column or columns. For decreases, place a "−" in the column or columns. If both an increase and a decrease occur, place a "+/−" in the column or columns. The first transaction is completed as an example.

	Transaction	Balance Sheet — Total Assets	Total Liab.	Total Equity	Income Statement — Net Income	Operating Activities	Financing Activities	Investing Activities
1	Owner invests cash for stock	+		+			+	
2	Incurs legal costs on credit							
3	Pays cash for employee wages							
4	Borrows cash by signing long-term note payable							
5	Receives cash for services provided							
6	Buys land by signing note payable							
7	Buys office equipment for cash							
8	Provides services on credit							
9	Collects cash on receivable from (8)							
10	Pays cash dividend							

The following financial statement information is from five separate companies:

	Company A	Company B	Company C	Company D	Company E
December 31, 2010					
Assets..................	$45,000	$35,000	$29,000	$80,000	$123,000
Liabilities	23,500	22,500	14,000	38,000	?
December 31, 2011					
Assets..................	48,000	41,000	?	125,000	112,500
Liabilities	?	27,500	19,000	64,000	75,000
During year 2011					
Stock issuances	5,000	1,500	7,750	?	4,500
Net income (loss) ..	7,500	?	9,000	12,000	18,000
Cash dividends	2,500	3,000	3,875	0	9,000

Problem 1-2A
Computing missing information using accounting knowledge

A1 P1

Required

1. Answer the following questions about Company A:
   a. What is the amount of equity on December 31, 2010?
   b. What is the amount of equity on December 31, 2011?
   c. What is the amount of liabilities on December 31, 2011?
2. Answer the following questions about Company B:
   a. What is the amount of equity on December 31, 2010?
   b. What is the amount of equity on December 31, 2011?
   c. What is net income for year 2011?
3. Calculate the amount of assets for Company C on December 31, 2011.
4. Calculate the amount of stock issuances for Company D during year 2011.
5. Calculate the amount of liabilities for Company E on December 31, 2010.

Check (1b) $31,500

(2c) $2,500
(3) $46,875

The following is selected financial information for Affiliated Company as of December 31, 2011: liabilities, $34,000; equity, $56,000; assets, $90,000.

Problem 1-3A
Preparing a balance sheet
P2

Required
Prepare the balance sheet for Affiliated Company as of December 31, 2011.

The following is selected financial information for Sun Energy Company for the year ended December 31, 2011: revenues, $65,000; expenses, $50,000; net income, $15,000.

Problem 1-4A
Preparing an income statement
P2

Required
Prepare the 2011 calendar-year income statement for Sun Energy Company.

Following is selected financial information for Boardwalk for the year ended December 31, 2011.

Retained earnings, Dec. 31, 2011.........	$15,000	Cash dividends	$2,000
Net income	9,000	Retained earnings, Dec. 31, 2010	8,000

Problem 1-5A
Preparing a statement of retained earnings
P2

Required
Prepare the 2011 statement of retained earnings for Boardwalk.

Problem 1-6A
Preparing a statement of cash flows
P2

Following is selected financial information of Trimark for the year ended December 31, 2011.

Cash used by investing activities	$(3,000)
Net increase in cash	200
Cash used by financing activities	(3,800)
Cash from operating activities	7,000
Cash, December 31, 2010	3,300

Check Cash balance, Dec. 31, 2011, $3,500

Required

Prepare the 2011 statement of cash flows for Trimark Company.

Problem 1-7A
Analyzing effects of transactions
C4 P1 P2 A1

Miranda Right started Right Consulting, a new business, and completed the following transactions during its first year of operations.

a. M. Right invests $60,000 cash and office equipment valued at $30,000 in the company in exchange for common stock.
b. The company purchased a $300,000 building to use as an office. Right paid $50,000 in cash and signed a note payable promising to pay the $250,000 balance over the next 10 years.
c. The company purchased office equipment for $6,000 cash.
d. The company purchased $4,000 of office supplies and $1,000 of office equipment on credit.
e. The company paid a local newspaper $1,000 cash for printing an announcement of the office's opening.
f. The company completed a financial plan for a client and billed that client $4,000 for the service.
g. The company designed a financial plan for another client and immediately collected an $8,000 cash fee.
h. The company paid $1,800 cash for dividends.
i. The company received $3,000 cash as partial payment from the client described in transaction *f*.
j. The company made a partial payment of $500 cash on the equipment purchased in transaction *d*.
k. The company paid $2,500 cash for the office secretary's wages for this period.

Required

1. Create a table like the one in Exhibit 1.9, using the following headings for the columns: Cash; Accounts Receivable; Office Supplies; Office Equipment; Building; Accounts Payable; Notes Payable; Common Stock; Dividends; Revenues; and Expenses.
2. Use additions and subtractions within the table created in part 1 to show the dollar effects of each transaction on individual items of the accounting equation. Show new balances after each transaction.
3. Once you have completed the table, determine the company's net income.

Check (2) Ending balances: Cash, $9,200; Expenses, $3,500; Notes Payable, $250,000

(3) Net income, $8,500

Problem 1-8A
Analyzing transactions and preparing financial statements
C4 P1 P2

mhhe.com/wildFA6e

J. D. Simpson started The Simpson Co., a new business that began operations on May 1. The Simpson Co. completed the following transactions during its first month of operations.

May 1 J. D. Simpson invested $60,000 cash in the company in exchange for common stock.
  1 The company rented a furnished office and paid $3,200 cash for May's rent.
  3 The company purchased $1,680 of office equipment on credit.
  5 The company paid $800 cash for this month's cleaning services.
  8 The company provided consulting services for a client and immediately collected $4,600 cash.
 12 The company provided $3,000 of consulting services for a client on credit.
 15 The company paid $850 cash for an assistant's salary for the first half of this month.
 20 The company received $3,000 cash payment for the services provided on May 12.
 22 The company provided $2,800 of consulting services on credit.
 25 The company received $2,800 cash payment for the services provided on May 22.
 26 The company paid $1,680 cash for the office equipment purchased on May 3.
 27 The company purchased $60 of advertising in this month's (May) local paper on credit; cash payment is due June 1.
 28 The company paid $850 cash for an assistant's salary for the second half of this month.
 30 The company paid $200 cash for this month's telephone bill.
 30 The company paid $480 cash for this month's utilities.
 31 The company paid $1,200 cash for dividends.

Required

1. Arrange the following asset, liability, and equity titles in a table like Exhibit 1.9: Cash; Accounts Receivable; Office Equipment; Accounts Payable; Common Stock; Dividends; Revenues; and Expenses.

2. Show effects of the transactions on the accounts of the accounting equation by recording increases and decreases in the appropriate columns. Do not determine new account balances after each transaction. Determine the final total for each account and verify that the equation is in balance.

3. Prepare an income statement for May, a statement of retained earnings for May, a May 31 balance sheet, and a statement of cash flows for May.

Check (2) Ending balances: Cash, $61,140; Expenses, $6,440

(3) Net income, $3,960; Total assets, $62,820

Curtis Hamilton started a new business and completed these transactions during December.

Dec. 1 Curtis Hamilton transferred $56,000 cash from a personal savings account to a checking account in the name of Hamilton Electric in exchange for common stock.
2 The company rented office space and paid $800 cash for the December rent.
3 The company purchased $14,000 of electrical equipment by paying $3,200 cash and agreeing to pay the $10,800 balance in 30 days.
5 The company purchased office supplies by paying $900 cash.
6 The company completed electrical work and immediately collected $1,000 cash for these services.
8 The company purchased $3,800 of office equipment on credit.
15 The company completed electrical work on credit in the amount of $4,000.
18 The company purchased $500 of office supplies on credit.
20 The company paid $3,800 cash for the office equipment purchased on December 8.
24 The company billed a client $600 for electrical work completed; the balance is due in 30 days.
28 The company received $4,000 cash for the work completed on December 15.
29 The company paid the assistant's salary of $1,200 cash for this month.
30 The company paid $440 cash for this month's utility bill.
31 The company paid $700 cash for dividends.

Problem 1-9A
Analyzing transactions and preparing financial statements
C4 P1 P2

mhhe.com/wildFA6e

Required

1. Arrange the following asset, liability, and equity titles in a table like Exhibit 1.9: Cash; Accounts Receivable; Office Supplies; Office Equipment; Electrical Equipment; Accounts Payable; Common Stock; Dividends; Revenues; and Expenses.
2. Use additions and subtractions to show the effects of each transaction on the accounts in the accounting equation. Show new balances after each transaction.
3. Use the increases and decreases in the columns of the table from part 2 to prepare an income statement, a statement of retained earnings, and a statement of cash flows—each of these for the current month. Also prepare a balance sheet as of the end of the month.

Check (2) Ending balances: Cash, $49,960, Accounts Payable, $11,300

(3) Net income, $3,160; Total assets, $69,760

Analysis Component

4. Assume that the owner investment transaction on December 1 was $40,000 cash instead of $56,000 and that Hamilton Electric obtained another $16,000 in cash by borrowing it from a bank. Explain the effect of this change on total assets, total liabilities, and total equity.

Nolan manufactures, markets, and sells cellular telephones. The average total assets for Nolan is $250,000. In its most recent year, Nolan reported net income of $55,000 on revenues of $455,000.

Problem 1-10A
Determining expenses, liabilities, equity, and return on assets
A1 A2

Required

1. What is Nolan's return on assets?
2. Does return on assets seem satisfactory for Nolan given that its competitors average a 12% return on assets?
3. What are total expenses for Nolan in its most recent year?
4. What is the average total amount of liabilities plus equity for Nolan?

Check (3) $400,000
(4) $250,000

Coca-Cola and PepsiCo both produce and market beverages that are direct competitors. Key financial figures (in $ millions) for these businesses over the past year follow.

Problem 1-11A
Computing and interpreting return on assets
A2

Key Figures ($ millions)	Coca-Cola	PepsiCo
Sales	$30,990	$43,232
Net income	6,906	5,979
Average assets	44,595	37,921

Chapter 1 Introducing Accounting in Business

Check (1a) 15.5%; (1b) 15.8%

Required

1. Compute return on assets for (a) Coca-Cola and (b) PepsiCo.
2. Which company is more successful in its total amount of sales to consumers?
3. Which company is more successful in returning net income from its assets invested?

Analysis Component

4. Write a one-paragraph memorandum explaining which company you would invest your money in and why. (Limit your explanation to the information provided.)

Problem 1-12A^A
Identifying risk and return
A3

All business decisions involve aspects of risk and return.

Required

Identify both the risk and the return in each of the following activities:
1. Investing $1,000 in a 4% savings account.
2. Placing a $1,000 bet on your favorite sports team.
3. Investing $10,000 in Yahoo! stock.
4. Taking out a $10,000 college loan to earn an accounting degree.

Problem 1-13A^B
Describing organizational activities C5

An organization undertakes various activities in pursuit of business success. Identify an organization's three major business activities, and describe each activity.

Problem 1-14A^B
Describing organizational activities
C5

A start-up company often engages in the following transactions in its first year of operations. Classify those transactions in one of the three major categories of an organization's business activities.

F. Financing   I. Investing   O. Operating

_____ 1. Owner investing land in business.
_____ 2. Purchasing a building.
_____ 3. Purchasing land.
_____ 4. Borrowing cash from a bank.
_____ 5. Purchasing equipment.
_____ 6. Selling and distributing products.
_____ 7. Paying for advertising.
_____ 8. Paying employee wages.

PROBLEM SET B

Problem 1-1B
Identifying effects of transactions on financial statements A1 P1

Identify how each of the following separate transactions affects financial statements. For the balance sheet, identify how each transaction affects total assets, total liabilities, and total equity. For the income statement, identify how each transaction affects net income. For the statement of cash flows, identify how each transaction affects cash flows from operating activities, cash flows from financing activities, and cash flows from investing activities. For increases, place a "+" in the column or columns. For decreases, place a "−" in the column or columns. If both an increase and a decrease occur, place "+/−" in the column or columns. The first transaction is completed as an example.

		Balance Sheet			Income Statement	Statement of Cash Flows		
	Transaction	Total Assets	Total Liab.	Total Equity	Net Income	Operating Activities	Financing Activities	Investing Activities
1	Owner invests cash for stock	+		+			+	
2	Buys building by signing note payable							
3	Pays cash for salaries incurred							
4	Provides services for cash							
5	Pays cash for rent incurred							
6	Incurs utilities costs on credit							
7	Buys store equipment for cash							
8	Pays cash dividend							
9	Provides services on credit							
10	Collects cash on receivable from (9)							

Problem 1-2B
Computing missing information using accounting knowledge
A1 P1

The following financial statement information is from five separate companies.

	Company V	Company W	Company X	Company Y	Company Z
December 31, 2010					
Assets	$45,000	$70,000	$121,500	$82,500	$124,000
Liabilities	30,000	50,000	58,500	61,500	?
December 31, 2011					
Assets	49,000	90,000	136,500	?	160,000
Liabilities	26,000	?	55,500	72,000	52,000
During year 2011					
Stock issuances	6,000	10,000	?	38,100	40,000
Net income or (loss)	?	30,000	16,500	24,000	32,000
Cash dividends	4,500	2,000	0	18,000	6,000

Required

1. Answer the following questions about Company V:
   a. What is the amount of equity on December 31, 2010?
   b. What is the amount of equity on December 31, 2011?
   c. What is the net income or loss for the year 2011?
2. Answer the following questions about Company W:
   a. What is the amount of equity on December 31, 2010?
   b. What is the amount of equity on December 31, 2011?
   c. What is the amount of liabilities on December 31, 2011?
3. Calculate the amount of stock issuances for Company X during 2011.
4. Calculate the amount of assets for Company Y on December 31, 2011.
5. Calculate the amount of liabilities for Company Z on December 31, 2010.

Check (1b) $23,000

(2c) $32,000

(4) $137,100

The following is selected financial information for RWB Company as of December 31, 2011.

Liabilities	$74,000	Equity	$40,000	Assets	$114,000

Problem 1-3B
Preparing a balance sheet
P2

Required
Prepare the balance sheet for RWB Company as of December 31, 2011.

Selected financial information for Online Company for the year ended December 31, 2011, follows.

Revenues	$58,000	Expenses	$30,000	Net income	$28,000

Problem 1-4B
Preparing an income statement
P2

Required
Prepare the 2011 income statement for Online Company.

Following is selected financial information of ComEx for the year ended December 31, 2011.

Retained earnings, Dec. 31, 2011	$47,000	Cash dividends	$ 8,000
Net income	6,000	Retained earnings, Dec. 31, 2010	49,000

Problem 1-5B
Preparing a statement of retained earnings
P2

Required
Prepare the 2011 statement of retained earnings for ComEx.

Problem 1-6B
Preparing a statement of cash flows
P2

Selected financial information of BuyRight Company for the year ended December 31, 2011, follows.

Cash from investing activities	$2,600
Net increase in cash	1,400
Cash from financing activities	2,800
Cash used by operating activities	(4,000)
Cash, December 31, 2010	1,300

Required

Prepare the 2011 statement of cash flows for BuyRight Company.

Problem 1-7B
Analyzing effects of transactions
C4 P1 P2 A1

Tiana Moore started a new business, Tiana's Solutions, and completed the following transactions during its first year of operations.

a. T. Moore invests $95,000 cash and office equipment valued at $20,000 in the company in exchange for common stock.
b. The company purchased a $120,000 building to use as an office. It paid $20,000 in cash and signed a note payable promising to pay the $100,000 balance over the next 10 years.
c. The company purchased office equipment for $20,000 cash.
d. The company purchased $1,400 of office supplies and $3,000 of office equipment on credit.
e. The company paid a local newspaper $400 cash for printing an announcement of the office's opening.
f. The company completed a financial plan for a client and billed that client $1,800 for the service.
g. The company designed a financial plan for another client and immediately collected a $2,000 cash fee.
h. The company paid $5,000 cash for dividends.
i. The company received $1,800 cash from the client described in transaction *f*.
j. The company made a payment of $2,000 cash on the equipment purchased in transaction *d*.
k. The company paid $2,000 cash for the office secretary's wages.

Required

1. Create a table like the one in Exhibit 1.9, using the following headings for the columns: Cash; Accounts Receivable; Office Supplies; Office Equipment; Building; Accounts Payable; Notes Payable; Common Stock; Dividends; Revenues; and Expenses.
2. Use additions and subtractions within the table created in part 1 to show the dollar effects of each transaction on individual items of the accounting equation. Show new balances after each transaction.
3. Once you have completed the table, determine the company's net income.

Check (2) Ending balances: Cash, $49,400; Expenses, $2,400; Notes Payable, $100,000
(3) Net income, $1,400

Problem 1-8B
Analyzing transactions and preparing financial statements
C4 P1 P2

Ken Stone launched a new business, Ken's Maintenance Co., that began operations on June 1. The following transactions were completed by the company during that first month.

June 1 K. Stone invested $120,000 cash in the company in exchange for common stock.
 2 The company rented a furnished office and paid $4,500 cash for June's rent.
 4 The company purchased $2,400 of equipment on credit.
 6 The company paid $1,125 cash for this month's advertising of the opening of the business.
 8 The company completed maintenance services for a customer and immediately collected $750 cash.
 14 The company completed $6,300 of maintenance services for City Center on credit.
 16 The company paid $900 cash for an assistant's salary for the first half of the month.
 20 The company received $6,300 cash payment for services completed for City Center on June 14.
 21 The company completed $3,500 of maintenance services for Skyway Co. on credit.
 24 The company completed $825 of maintenance services for Comfort Motel on credit.
 25 The company received $3,500 cash payment from Skyway Co. for the work completed on June 21.
 26 The company made payment of $2,400 cash for equipment purchased on June 4.
 28 The company paid $900 cash for an assistant's salary for the second half of this month.
 29 The company paid $2,000 cash for dividends.
 30 The company paid $120 cash for this month's telephone bill.
 30 The company paid $525 cash for this month's utilities.

Required

1. Arrange the following asset, liability, and equity titles in a table like Exhibit 1.9: Cash; Accounts Receivable; Equipment; Accounts Payable; Common Stock; Dividends; Revenues; and Expenses.

2. Show the effects of the transactions on the accounts of the accounting equation by recording increases and decreases in the appropriate columns. Do not determine new account balances after each transaction. Determine the final total for each account and verify that the equation is in balance.

3. Prepare a June income statement, a June statement of retained earnings, a June 30 balance sheet, and a June statement of cash flows.

Check (2) Ending balances: Cash, $118,080; Expenses, $8,070

(3) Net income, $3,305; Total assets, $121,305

Problem 1-9B
Analyzing transactions and preparing financial statements

C4 P1 P2

Swender Excavating Co., owned by Patrick Swender, began operations in July and completed these transactions during that first month of operations.

July 1 P. Swender invested $60,000 cash in the company in exchange for common stock.
2 The company rented office space and paid $500 cash for the July rent.
3 The company purchased excavating equipment for $4,000 by paying $800 cash and agreeing to pay the $3,200 balance in 30 days.
6 The company purchased office supplies for $500 cash.
8 The company completed work for a customer and immediately collected $2,200 cash for the work.
10 The company purchased $3,800 of office equipment on credit.
15 The company completed work for a customer on credit in the amount of $2,400.
17 The company purchased $1,920 of office supplies on credit.
23 The company paid $3,800 cash for the office equipment purchased on July 10.
25 The company billed a customer $5,000 for work completed; the balance is due in 30 days.
28 The company received $2,400 cash for the work completed on July 15.
30 The company paid an assistant's salary of $1,260 cash for this month.
31 The company paid $260 cash for this month's utility bill.
31 The company paid $1,200 cash for dividends.

Required

1. Arrange the following asset, liability, and equity titles in a table like Exhibit 1.9: Cash; Accounts Receivable; Office Supplies; Office Equipment; Excavating Equipment; Accounts Payable; Common Stock; Dividends; Revenues; and Expenses.
2. Use additions and subtractions to show the effects of each transaction on the accounts in the accounting equation. Show new balances after each transaction.
3. Use the increases and decreases in the columns of the table from part 2 to prepare an income statement, a statement of retained earnings, and a statement of cash flows—each of these for the current month. Also prepare a balance sheet as of the end of the month.

Check (2) Ending balances: Cash, $56,280; Accounts Payable, $5,120

(3) Net income, $7,580; Total assets, $71,500

Analysis Component

4. Assume that the $4,000 purchase of excavating equipment on July 3 was financed from an owner investment of another $4,000 cash in the business in exchange for more common stock (instead of the purchase conditions described in the transaction). Explain the effect of this change on total assets, total liabilities, and total equity.

Aspen Company manufactures, markets, and sells ATV and snowmobile equipment and accessories. The average total assets for Aspen is $2,000,000. In its most recent year, Aspen reported net income of $100,000 on revenues of $1,200,000.

Problem 1-10B
Determining expenses, liabilities, equity, and return on assets

A1 A2

Required

1. What is Aspen Company's return on assets?
2. Does return on assets seem satisfactory for Aspen given that its competitors average a 9.5% return on assets?
3. What are the total expenses for Aspen Company in its most recent year?
4. What is the average total amount of liabilities plus equity for Aspen Company?

Check (3) $1,100,000
(4) $2,000,000

AT&T and **Verizon** produce and market telecommunications products and are competitors. Key financial figures (in $ millions) for these businesses over the past year follow.

Problem 1-11B
Computing and interpreting return on assets

A2

Key Figures ($ millions)	AT&T	Verizon
Sales	$123,018	$107,808
Net income	12,535	10,358
Average assets	266,999	214,937

Required

Check (1a) 4.7%; (1b) 4.8%

1. Compute return on assets for (a) AT&T and (b) Verizon.
2. Which company is more successful in the total amount of sales to consumers?
3. Which company is more successful in returning net income from its assets invested?

Analysis Component

4. Write a one-paragraph memorandum explaining which company you would invest your money in and why. (Limit your explanation to the information provided.)

Problem 1-12B^A
Identifying risk and return
A3

All business decisions involve aspects of risk and return.

Required

Identify both the risk and the return in each of the following activities:

1. Stashing $1,000 cash under your mattress.
2. Placing a $500 bet on a horse running in the Kentucky Derby.
3. Investing $10,000 in Nike stock.
4. Investing $10,000 in U.S. Savings Bonds.

Problem 1-13B^B
Describing organizational activities C5

Identify in outline format the three major business activities of an organization. For each of these activities, identify at least two specific transactions or events normally undertaken by the business's owners or its managers.

Problem 1-14B^B
Describing organizational activities
C5

A start-up company often engages in the following activities during its first year of operations. Classify each of the following activities into one of the three major activities of an organization.

A. Financing **B.** Investing **C.** Operating

_____ 1. Providing client services. _____ 5. Supervising workers.
_____ 2. Obtaining a bank loan. _____ 6. Owner investing money in business.
_____ 3. Purchasing machinery. _____ 7. Renting office space.
_____ 4. Research for its products. _____ 8. Paying utilities expenses.

This serial problem starts in this chapter and continues throughout most chapters of the book. It is most readily solved if you use the Working Papers that accompany this book (but working papers are not required).

SERIAL PROBLEM
Business Solutions
C4   P1

SP 1 On October 1, 2011, Santana Rey launched a computer services company, **Business Solutions,** that is organized as a corporation and provides consulting services, computer system installations, and custom program development. Rey adopts the calendar year for reporting purposes and expects to prepare the company's first set of financial statements on December 31, 2011.

Required

Create a table like the one in Exhibit 1.9 using the following headings for columns: Cash; Accounts Receivable; Computer Supplies; Computer System; Office Equipment; Accounts Payable; Common Stock; Dividends; Revenues; and Expenses. Then use additions and subtractions within the table created to show the dollar effects for each of the following October transactions for Business Solutions on the individual items of the accounting equation. Show new balances after each transaction.

Oct. 1   S. Rey invested $45,000 cash, a $20,000 computer system, and $8,000 of office equipment in the company in exchange for common stock.
    3   The company purchased $1,420 of computer supplies on credit from Harris Office Products.
    6   The company billed Easy Leasing $4,800 for services performed in installing a new Web server.
    8   The company paid $1,420 cash for the computer supplies purchased from Harris Office Products on October 3.
    10 The company hired Lyn Addie as a part-time assistant for $125 per day, as needed.
    12 The company billed Easy Leasing another $1,400 for services performed.
    15 The company received $4,800 cash from Easy Leasing as partial payment toward its account.
    17 The company paid $805 cash to repair computer equipment damaged when moving it.
    20 The company paid $1,728 cash for advertisements published in the local newspaper.
    22 The company received $1,400 cash from Easy Leasing toward its account.
    28 The company billed IFM Company $5,208 for services performed.
    31 The company paid $875 cash for Lyn Addie's wages for seven days of work this month.
    31 The company paid $3,600 cash for dividends.

Check Ending balances: Cash, $42,772; Revenues, $11,408; Expenses, $3,408

Chapter 1 Introducing Accounting in Business   47

Beyond the Numbers (BTN) is a special problem section aimed to refine communication, conceptual, analysis, and research skills. It includes many activities helpful in developing an active learning environment.

Beyond the Numbers

BTN 1-1 Key financial figures for **Research In Motion**'s fiscal year ended February 27, 2010, follow.

Key Figure	In Millions
Liabilities + Equity.........	$10,204
Net income	2,457
Revenues	14,953

REPORTING IN ACTION
A1 A2 A3

RIM

Required
1. What is the total amount of assets invested in Research In Motion?
2. What is Research In Motion's return on assets? Its assets at February 28, 2009, equal $8,101 (in millions).
3. How much are total expenses for Research In Motion for the year ended February 27, 2010?
4. Does Research In Motion's return on assets seem satisfactory if competitors average an 18% return?

Check (2) 26.8%

Fast Forward
5. Access Research In Motion's financial statements (Form 10-K) for fiscal years ending after February 27, 2010, from its Website (**RIM.com**) or from the SEC Website (**www.SEC.gov**) and compute its return on assets for those fiscal years. Compare the February 27, 2010, fiscal year-end return on assets to any subsequent years' returns you are able to compute, and interpret the results.

BTN 1-2 Key comparative figures ($ millions) for both **Research In Motion** and **Apple** follow.

Key Figure	Research In Motion	Apple
Liabilities + Equity.........	$10,204	$47,501
Net income	2,457	8,235
Revenues and sales	14,953	42,905

COMPARATIVE ANALYSIS
A1 A2 A3

RIM
Apple

Required
1. What is the total amount of assets invested in (*a*) Research In Motion and (*b*) Apple?
2. What is the return on assets for (*a*) Research In Motion and (*b*) Apple? Research In Motion's beginning-year assets equal $8,101 (in millions) and Apple's beginning-year assets equal $36,171 (in millions).
3. How much are expenses for (*a*) Research In Motion and (*b*) Apple?
4. Is return on assets satisfactory for (*a*) Research In Motion and (*b*) Apple? (Assume competitors average an 18% return.)
5. What can you conclude about Research In Motion and Apple from these computations?

Check (2b) 19.7%

BTN 1-3 Madison Thorne works in a public accounting firm and hopes to eventually be a partner. The management of Allnet Company invites Thorne to prepare a bid to audit Allnet's financial statements. In discussing the audit fee, Allnet's management suggests a fee range in which the amount depends on the reported profit of Allnet. The higher its profit, the higher will be the audit fee paid to Thorne's firm.

ETHICS CHALLENGE
C3 C4

Required
1. Identify the parties potentially affected by this audit and the fee plan proposed.
2. What are the ethical factors in this situation? Explain.
3. Would you recommend that Thorne accept this audit fee arrangement? Why or why not?
4. Describe some ethical considerations guiding your recommendation.

COMMUNICATING IN PRACTICE
A1 C2

BTN 1-4 Refer to this chapter's opening feature about **Twitter**. Assume that the owners desire to expand their online services to meet people's demands regarding online services. They eventually decide to meet with their banker to discuss a loan to allow Twitter to expand.

Required

1. Prepare a half-page report outlining the information you would request from the owners if you were the loan officer.
2. Indicate whether the information you request and your loan decision are affected by the form of business organization for Twitter.

TAKING IT TO THE NET
A2

BTN 1-5 Visit the EDGAR database at (www.sec.gov). Access the Form 10-K report of **Rocky Mountain Chocolate Factory** (ticker RMCF) filed on May 26, 2009, covering its 2009 fiscal year.

Required

1. Item 6 of the 10-K report provides comparative financial highlights of RMCF for the years 2005–2009. How would you describe the revenue trend for RMCF over this five-year period?
2. Has RMCF been profitable (see net income) over this five-year period? Support your answer.

TEAMWORK IN ACTION
C1

BTN 1-6 Teamwork is important in today's business world. Successful teams schedule convenient meetings, maintain regular communications, and cooperate with and support their members. This assignment aims to establish support/learning teams, initiate discussions, and set meeting times.

Required

1. Form teams and open a team discussion to determine a regular time and place for your team to meet between each scheduled class meeting. Notify your instructor via a memorandum or e-mail message as to when and where your team will hold regularly scheduled meetings.
2. Develop a list of telephone numbers and/or e-mail addresses of your teammates.

ENTREPRENEURIAL DECISION
A1 P1

BTN 1-7 Refer to this chapter's opening feature about **Twitter**. Assume that the owners decide to open a new Website devoted to micro-blogging for accountants and those studying accounting. This new company will be called **AccounTwit**.

Required

1. AccounTwit obtains a $500,000 loan and the three owners contribute $250,000 in total from their own savings in exchange for common stock in the new company.
   a. What is the new company's total amount of liabilities plus equity?
   b. What is the new company's total amount of assets?
2. If the new company earns $80,000 in net income in the first year of operation, compute its return on assets (assume average assets equal $750,000). Assess its performance if competitors average a 10% return.

Check (2) 10.7%

HITTING THE ROAD
C2

BTN 1-8 You are to interview a local business owner. (This can be a friend or relative.) Opening lines of communication with members of the business community can provide personal benefits of business networking. If you do not know the owner, you should call ahead to introduce yourself and explain your position as a student and your assignment requirements. You should request a 30-minute appointment for a face-to-face or phone interview to discuss the form of organization and operations of the business. Be prepared to make a good impression.

Required

1. Identify and describe the main operating activities and the form of organization for this business.
2. Determine and explain why the owner(s) chose this particular form of organization.
3. Identify any special advantages and/or disadvantages the owner(s) experiences in operating with this form of business organization.

BTN 1-9 Nokia (www.Nokia.com) is a leading manufacturer of mobile devices and services, and it competes to some extent with both **Research In Motion** and **Apple**. Key financial figures for Nokia follow.

GLOBAL DECISION

A1 A2 A3

NOKIA

RIM

Apple

Key Figure*	Euro (EUR) in Millions
Average assets	37,660
Net income	260
Revenue	40,984
Return on assets	0.7%

* Figures prepared in accordance with International Financial Reporting Standards.

Required

1. Identify any concerns you have in comparing Nokia's income and revenue figures to those of Research In Motion and Apple (in BTN 1-2) for purposes of making business decisions.
2. Identify any concerns you have in comparing Nokia's return on assets ratio to those of Research In Motion and Apple (computed for BTN 1-2) for purposes of making business decisions.

ANSWERS TO MULTIPLE CHOICE QUIZ

1. c; $450,000 is the actual cost incurred.
2. b; revenue is recorded when earned.
3. d;

Assets	=	Liabilities	+	Equity
+$100,000	=	+35,000	+	?

Change in equity = $100,000 − $35,000 = $65,000

4. a
5. a

A Look Back

Chapter 1 defined accounting and introduced financial statements. We described forms of organizations and identified users and uses of accounting. We defined the accounting equation and applied it to transaction analysis.

A Look at This Chapter

This chapter focuses on the accounting process. We describe transactions and source documents, and we explain the analysis and recording of transactions. The accounting equation, T-account, general ledger, trial balance, and debits and credits are key tools in the accounting process.

A Look Ahead

Chapter 3 extends our focus on processing information. We explain the importance of adjusting accounts and the procedures in preparing financial statements.

2 Analyzing and Recording Transactions

Learning Objectives

CAP

CONCEPTUAL

- **C1** Explain the steps in processing transactions and the role of source documents. (p. 52)
- **C2** Describe an account and its use in recording transactions. (p. 53)
- **C3** Describe a ledger and a chart of accounts. (p. 56)
- **C4** Define *debits* and *credits* and explain double-entry accounting. (p. 57)

ANALYTICAL

- **A1** Analyze the impact of transactions on accounts and financial statements. (p. 61)
- **A2** Compute the debt ratio and describe its use in analyzing financial condition. (p. 72)

LP2

PROCEDURAL

- **P1** Record transactions in a journal and post entries to a ledger. (p. 58)
- **P2** Prepare and explain the use of a trial balance. (p. 67)
- **P3** Prepare financial statements from business transactions. (p. 68)

Decision Insight

Sole Sisters

"Every way we can cut costs, we do!"
—SUSIE LEVITT (on right)

NEW YORK—"High heels were killing our feet, but we didn't want to give them up because we aren't the tallest people out there," insists Susie Levitt, who stands no taller than 5'2". "So we came up with the idea of emergency footwear." Susie, along with Katie Shea, designed a stylish, foldable slip-on ballet flat with a pouch that is readily tucked into a handbag and pulled out when their feet cry for mercy. The empty pouch then expands into a tote bag to hold their "killer" heels for carrying home. Launched from their college apartment, Susie and Katie invested "less than $10,000" for the cost of their first order of 1,000 pairs, including Website design, to launch **CitySlips** (**www.cityslips.com**).

To pursue their business ambitions, Susie and Katie took business courses, including accounting. They learned and applied recordkeeping processes, transaction analysis, inventory accounting, and financial statement reporting. "We were careful to get a handle on our financial situation," says Katie. Today, the two are running a profitable business and have a reliable accounting system to help them make good business decisions.

"We had to account for product costs, design expenses, supplier payments, patent fees, and other expenses," says Susie. At the same time, the two have grown sales and expanded their product line. "It was all done online," says Susie. "We became nocturnal!"

The two insist that it is crucial to track and account for all revenues and expenses, and what is invested in the business. They maintain that success requires proper accounting for and analysis of the financial side. Susie also suggests that young entrepreneurs "network with your professors and other staff members. They have years of experience and can often help you, or introduce you to people who can help you, with your business."

"The bigger message of our company," says Susie, "is promoting comfort and confidence for women." Adds Katie, "Regardless of what your business is, the story of starting while in college differentiates you from the beginning!"

[Sources: *CitySlips Website,* January 2012; *Entrepreneur,* December 2009; *Examiner.com,* December 2009; *CNN.com,* August 2009; *Daily News,* May 2009; *Teen Business Forum,* March 11, 2011, Video]

Chapter Preview

Financial statements report on the financial performance and condition of an organization. Knowledge of their preparation, organization, and analysis is important. A main goal of this chapter is to illustrate how transactions are recorded, how they are reflected in financial statements, and how they impact analysis of financial statements. Debits and credits are introduced and identified as a tool in helping analyze and process transactions.

Analyzing and Recording Transactions

Analyzing and Recording Process
- Source documents
- The account and its analysis
- Types of accounts

Analyzing and Processing Transactions
- General ledger
- Double-entry accounting
- Journalizing and posting
- An illustration

Trial Balance
- Trial balance preparation
- Search for and correction of errors
- Trial balance use

ANALYZING AND RECORDING PROCESS

The accounting process identifies business transactions and events, analyzes and records their effects, and summarizes and presents information in reports and financial statements. These reports and statements are used for making investing, lending, and other business decisions. The steps in the accounting process that focus on *analyzing and recording* transactions and events are shown in Exhibit 2.1.

EXHIBIT 2.1

The Analyzing and Recording Process

Analyze each transaction and event from source documents → Record relevant transactions and events in a journal → Post journal information to ledger accounts → Prepare and analyze the trial balance

C1 Explain the steps in processing transactions and the role of source documents.

Business transactions and events are the starting points. Relying on source documents, the transactions and events are analyzed using the accounting equation to understand how they affect company performance and financial position. These effects are recorded in accounting records, informally referred to as the *accounting books,* or simply the *books*. Additional steps such as posting and then preparing a trial balance help summarize and classify the effects of transactions and events. Ultimately, the accounting process provides information in useful reports or financial statements to decision makers.

Source Documents

Source documents identify and describe transactions and events entering the accounting process. They are the sources of accounting information and can be in either hard copy or electronic form. Examples are sales tickets, checks, purchase orders, bills from suppliers, employee earnings records, and bank statements. To illustrate, when an item is purchased on credit, the seller usually prepares at least two copies of a sales invoice. One copy is given to the buyer. Another copy, often sent electronically, results in an entry in the seller's information system to record the sale. Sellers use invoices for recording sales and for control; buyers use them for recording purchases and for monitoring purchasing activity. Many cash registers record information for each sale on a tape or electronic file locked inside the register. This record can be used as a source document for recording sales in the accounting records. Source documents, especially if obtained from outside the organization, provide objective and reliable evidence about transactions and events and their amounts.

Point: To ensure that all sales are rung up on the register, most sellers require customers to have their receipts to exchange or return purchased items.

Decision Ethics
Answer — p. 76

Cashier Your manager requires that you, as cashier, immediately enter each sale. Recently, lunch hour traffic has increased and the assistant manager asks you to avoid delays by taking customers' cash and making change without entering sales. The assistant manager says she will add up cash and enter sales after lunch. She says that, in this way, the register will always match the cash amount when the manager arrives at three o'clock. What do you do?

The Account and Its Analysis

An **account** is a record of increases and decreases in a specific asset, liability, equity, revenue, or expense item. Information from an account is analyzed, summarized, and presented in reports and financial statements. The **general ledger,** or simply **ledger,** is a record containing all accounts used by a company. The ledger is often in electronic form. While most companies' ledgers contain similar accounts, a company often uses one or more unique accounts because of its type of operations. As shown in Exhibit 2.2, accounts are classified into three general categories based on the accounting equation: asset, liability, or equity.

C2 Describe an account and its use in recording transactions.

Asset Accounts = Liability Accounts + Equity Accounts

EXHIBIT 2.2

Accounts Organized by the Accounting Equation

Asset Accounts Assets are resources owned or controlled by a company, and those resources have expected future benefits. Most accounting systems include (at a minimum) separate accounts for the assets described here.

A *Cash* account reflects a company's cash balance. All increases and decreases in cash are recorded in the Cash account. It includes money and any medium of exchange that a bank accepts for deposit (coins, checks, money orders, and checking account balances).

Accounts receivable are held by a seller and refer to promises of payment from customers to sellers. These transactions are often called *credit sales* or *sales on account* (or *on credit*). Accounts receivable are increased by credit sales and are decreased by customer payments. A company needs a separate record for each customer, but for now, we use the simpler practice of recording all increases and decreases in receivables in a single account called Accounts Receivable.

Point: Customers and others who owe a company are called its **debtors.**

A *note receivable,* or promissory note, is a written promise of another entity to pay a definite sum of money on a specified future date to the holder of the note. A company holding a promissory note signed by another entity has an asset that is recorded in a Note (or Notes) Receivable account.

Prepaid accounts (also called *prepaid expenses*) are assets that represent prepayments of future expenses (*not* current expenses). When the expenses are later incurred, the amounts in prepaid accounts are transferred to expense accounts. Common examples of prepaid accounts include prepaid insurance, prepaid rent, and prepaid services (such as club memberships). Prepaid accounts expire with the passage of time (such as with rent) or through use (such as with prepaid meal tickets). When financial statements are prepared, prepaid accounts are adjusted so that (1) all expired and used prepaid accounts are recorded as regular expenses and (2) all unexpired and unused prepaid accounts are recorded as assets (reflecting future use in

Point: A college parking fee is a prepaid account from the student's standpoint. At the beginning of the term, it represents an asset that entitles a student to park on or near campus. The benefits of the parking fee expire as the term progresses. At term-end, prepaid parking (asset) equals zero as it has been entirely recorded as parking expense.

Point: Prepaid accounts that apply to current and future periods are assets. These assets are adjusted at the end of each period to reflect only those amounts that have not yet expired, and to record as expenses those amounts that have expired.

future periods). To illustrate, when an insurance fee, called a *premium,* is paid in advance, the cost is typically recorded in the asset account Prepaid Insurance. Over time, the expiring portion of the insurance cost is removed from this asset account and reported in expenses on the income statement. Any unexpired portion remains in Prepaid Insurance and is reported on the balance sheet as an asset. (An exception exists for prepaid accounts that will expire or be used before the end of the current accounting period when financial statements are prepared. In this case, the prepayments *can* be recorded immediately as expenses.)

Supplies are assets until they are used. When they are used up, their costs are reported as expenses. The costs of unused supplies are recorded in a Supplies asset account. Supplies are often grouped by purpose—for example, office supplies and store supplies. *Office supplies* include stationery, paper, toner, and pens. *Store supplies* include packaging materials, plastic and paper bags, gift boxes and cartons, and cleaning materials. The costs of these unused supplies can be recorded in an Office Supplies or a Store Supplies asset account. When supplies are used, their costs are transferred from the asset accounts to expense accounts.

Equipment is an asset. When equipment is used and gets worn down, its cost is gradually reported as an expense (called depreciation). Equipment is often grouped by its purpose—for example, office equipment and store equipment. *Office equipment* includes computers, printers, desks, chairs, and shelves. Costs incurred for these items are recorded in an Office Equipment asset account. The Store Equipment account includes the costs of assets used in a store, such as counters, showcases, ladders, hoists, and cash registers.

Point: Some assets are described as *intangible* because they do not have physical existence or their benefits are highly uncertain. A recent balance sheet for **Coca-Cola Company** shows nearly $1 billion in intangible assets.

Buildings such as stores, offices, warehouses, and factories are assets because they provide expected future benefits to those who control or own them. Their costs are recorded in a Buildings asset account. When several buildings are owned, separate accounts are sometimes kept for each of them.

The cost of *land* owned by a business is recorded in a Land account. The cost of buildings located on the land is separately recorded in one or more building accounts.

Decision Insight

Women Entrepreneurs The Center for Women's Business Research reports that women-owned businesses, such as **CitySlips**, are growing and that they:

- Total approximately 11 million and employ nearly 20 million workers.
- Generate $2.5 trillion in annual sales and tend to embrace technology.
- Are philanthropic—70% of owners volunteer at least once per month.
- Are more likely funded by individual investors (73%) than venture firms (15%).

Liability Accounts Liabilities are claims (by creditors) against assets, which means they are obligations to transfer assets or provide products or services to others. **Creditors** are individuals and organizations that have rights to receive payments from a company. If a company fails to pay its obligations, the law gives creditors a right to force the sale of that company's assets to obtain the money to meet creditors' claims. When assets are sold under these conditions, creditors are paid first, but only up to the amount of their claims. Any remaining money, the residual, goes to the owners of the company. Creditors often use a balance sheet to help decide whether to loan money to a company. A loan is less risky if the borrower's liabilities are small in comparison to assets because this means there are more resources than claims on resources. Common liability accounts are described here.

Point: Accounts payable are also called *trade payables.*

Accounts payable refer to oral or implied promises to pay later, which usually arise from purchases of merchandise. Payables can also arise from purchases of supplies, equipment, and services. Accounting systems keep separate records about each creditor. We describe these individual records in Chapter 4.

A *note payable* refers to a formal promise, usually denoted by the signing of a promissory note, to pay a future amount. It is recorded in either a short-term Note Payable account or a long-term Note Payable account, depending on when it must be repaid. We explain details of short- and long-term classification in Chapter 3.

Unearned revenue refers to a liability that is settled in the future when a company delivers its products or services. When customers pay in advance for products or services (before revenue is earned), the revenue recognition principle requires that the seller consider this payment as unearned revenue. Examples of unearned revenue include magazine subscriptions collected in advance by a publisher, sales of gift certificates by stores, and season ticket sales by sports teams. The seller would record these in liability accounts such as Unearned Subscriptions, Unearned Store Sales, and Unearned Ticket Revenue. When products and services are later delivered, the earned portion of the unearned revenue is transferred to revenue accounts such as Subscription Fees, Store Sales, and Ticket Sales.[1]

Accrued liabilities are amounts owed that are not yet paid. Examples are wages payable, taxes payable, and interest payable. These are often recorded in separate liability accounts by the same title. If they are not large in amount, one or more ledger accounts can be added and reported as a single amount on the balance sheet. (Financial statements often have amounts reported that are a summation of several ledger accounts.)

Point: If a subscription is canceled, the publisher is expected to refund the unused portion to the subscriber.

Decision Insight

Revenue Spread The **New Orleans Saints** have *Unearned Revenues* of about $60 million in advance ticket sales. When the team plays its home games, it settles this liability to its ticket holders and then transfers the amount earned to *Ticket Revenues*.

Equity Accounts The owner's claim on a company's assets is called *equity,* or *stockholders' equity,* or *shareholders' equity*. Equity is the owners' *residual interest* in the assets of a business after deducting liabilities. Equity is impacted by four types of accounts: common stock, dividends, revenues, and expenses. We show this visually in Exhibit 2.3 by expanding the accounting equation. (As Chapter 1 explains, the accounts for dividends, revenues, and expenses are reflected in the retained earnings account, and that account is reported in the balance sheet.)

Point: Equity is also called *net assets*.

EXHIBIT 2.3

Expanded Accounting Equation

When an owner invests in a company in exchange for common stock, the invested amount is recorded in an account titled **Common Stock.** Any further owner investments are recorded in this account. When the company pays any cash dividends, it decreases both the company's assets and its total equity. Dividends are not expenses of the business. They are simply the opposite of owner investments. A **Dividends** account is used in recording asset distributions to stockholders (owners).

Revenues and expenses also impact equity. Examples of revenue accounts are Sales, Commissions Earned, Professional Fees Earned, Rent Revenue, and Interest Revenue. *Revenues increase equity* and result from products and services provided to customers. Examples of expense accounts are Advertising Expense, Store Supplies Expense, Office Salaries Expense, Office Supplies Expense, Rent Expense, Utilities Expense, and Insurance Expense. *Expenses decrease equity* and result from assets and services used in a company's operations. The variety of revenues and expenses can be seen by looking at the *chart of accounts* that follows the index at the

Point: The Dividends account is sometimes referred to as a *contra equity* account because it reduces the normal balance of equity.

Point: The withdrawal of assets by the owners of a corporation is called a *dividend*.

---

[1] In practice, account titles vary. As one example, Subscription Fees is sometimes called Subscription Fees Revenue, Subscription Fees Earned, or Earned Subscription Fees. As another example, Rent Earned is sometimes called Rent Revenue, Rental Revenue, or Earned Rent Revenue. We must use good judgment when reading financial statements because titles can differ even within the same industry. For example, product sales are called *revenue* at **Research In Motion**, but *net sales* at **Apple**. Generally, the term *revenues* or *fees* is more commonly used with service businesses, and *net sales* or *sales* with product businesses.

back of this book. (Different companies sometimes use different account titles than those in this book's chart of accounts. For example, some might use Interest Revenue instead of Interest Earned, or Rental Expense instead of Rent Expense. It is important only that an account title describe the item it represents.)

> **Decision Insight**
>
> **Sporting Accounts** The Los Angeles Lakers and the other NBA teams have the following major revenue and expense accounts:
>
> | Revenues | Expenses |
> |---|---|
> | Basketball ticket sales | Team salaries |
> | TV & radio broadcast fees | Game costs |
> | Advertising revenues | NBA franchise costs |
> | Basketball playoff receipts | Promotional costs |

ANALYZING AND PROCESSING TRANSACTIONS

This section explains several tools and processes that comprise an accounting system. These include a ledger, T-account, debits and credits, double-entry accounting, journalizing, and posting.

Ledger and Chart of Accounts

C3 Describe a ledger and a chart of accounts.

The collection of all accounts and their balances for an information system is called a *ledger* (or *general ledger*). If accounts are in files on a hard drive, the sum of those files is the ledger. If the accounts are pages in a file, that file is the ledger. A company's size and diversity of operations affect the number of accounts needed. A small company can get by with as few as 20 or 30 accounts; a large company can require several thousand. The **chart of accounts** is a list of all ledger accounts and includes an identification number assigned to each account. A small business might use the following numbering system for its accounts:

101–199	Asset accounts
201–299	Liability accounts
301–399	Equity accounts
401–499	Revenue accounts
501–699	Expense accounts

These numbers provide a three-digit code that is useful in recordkeeping. In this case, the first digit assigned to asset accounts is a 1, the first digit assigned to liability accounts is a 2, and so on. The second and third digits relate to the accounts' subcategories. Exhibit 2.4 shows a partial chart of accounts for FastForward, the focus company of Chapter 1. (Please review the more complete chart of accounts that follows the index at the back of this book.)

EXHIBIT 2.4
Partial Chart of Accounts for FastForward

Acct. No.	Account Name	Acct. No.	Account Name	Acct. No.	Account Name
101	Cash	236	Unearned consulting revenue	406	Rental revenue
106	Accounts receivable			622	Salaries expense
126	Supplies	307	Common stock	637	Insurance expense
128	Prepaid insurance	318	Retained earnings	640	Rent expense
167	Equipment	319	Dividends	652	Supplies expense
201	Accounts payable	403	Consulting revenue	690	Utilities expense

Debits and Credits

A **T-account** represents a ledger account and is a tool used to understand the effects of one or more transactions. Its name comes from its shape like the letter **T**. The layout of a T-account, shown in Exhibit 2.5, is (1) the account title on top, (2) a left, or debit side, and (3) a right, or credit, side.

The left side of an account is called the **debit** side, often abbreviated *Dr*. The right side is called the **credit** side, abbreviated *Cr*.[2] To enter amounts on the left side of an account is to *debit* the account. To enter amounts on the right side is to *credit* the account. Do not make the error of thinking that the terms *debit* and *credit* mean increase or decrease. Whether a debit or a credit is an increase or decrease depends on the account. For an account where a debit is an increase, the credit is a decrease; for an account where a debit is a decrease, the credit is an increase. The difference between total debits and total credits for an account, including any beginning balance, is the **account balance.** When the sum of debits exceeds the sum of credits, the account has a *debit balance*. It has a *credit balance* when the sum of credits exceeds the sum of debits. When the sum of debits equals the sum of credits, the account has a *zero balance*.

Account Title	
(Left side)	(Right side)
Debit	**Credit**

EXHIBIT 2.5
The T-Account

Point: Think of *debit* and *credit* as accounting directions for left and right.

C4 Define *debits* and *credits* and explain double-entry accounting.

Double-Entry Accounting

Double-entry accounting requires that for each transaction:

- At least two accounts are involved, with at least one debit and one credit.
- The total amount debited must equal the total amount credited.
- The accounting equation must not be violated.

This means the sum of the debits for all entries must equal the sum of the credits for all entries, and the sum of debit account balances in the ledger must equal the sum of credit account balances.

The system for recording debits and credits follows from the usual accounting equation—see Exhibit 2.6. Two points are important here. First, like any simple mathematical relation, net increases or decreases on one side have equal net effects on the other side. For example, a net increase in assets must be accompanied by an identical net increase on the liabilities and equity

"Total debits equal total credits for each entry."

Assets	=	Liabilities	+	Equity
Debit for increases | Credit for decreases		Debit for decreases | Credit for increases		Debit for decreases | Credit for increases
+ | −		− | +		− | +
Normal		Normal		Normal

EXHIBIT 2.6
Debits and Credits in the Accounting Equation

side. Recall that some transactions affect only one side of the equation, meaning that two or more accounts on one side are affected, but their net effect on this one side is zero. Second, the left side is the *normal balance* side for assets, and the right side is the *normal balance* side for liabilities and equity. This matches their layout in the accounting equation where assets are on the left side of this equation, and liabilities and equity are on the right.

Recall that equity increases from revenues and stock issuances, and it decreases from expenses and dividends. These important equity relations are conveyed by expanding the accounting equation to include debits and credits in double-entry form as shown in Exhibit 2.7.

Increases (credits) to common stock and revenues *increase* equity; increases (debits) to dividends and expenses *decrease* equity. The normal balance of each account (asset, liability, common stock, dividends, revenue, or expense) refers to the left or right (debit or credit) side where

Point: Debits and credits do not mean favorable or unfavorable. A debit to an asset increases it, as does a debit to an expense. A credit to a liability increases it, as does a credit to a revenue.

---

[2] These abbreviations are remnants of 18th-century English recordkeeping practices where the terms *debitor* and *creditor* were used instead of *debit* and *credit*. The abbreviations use the first and last letters of these terms, just as we still do for Saint (St.) and Doctor (Dr.).

EXHIBIT 2.7

Debit and Credit Effects for Component Accounts

Assets	=	Liabilities	+	Common Stock	−	Dividends	+	Revenues	−	Expenses
Dr. for increases / Cr. for decreases		Dr. for decreases / Cr. for increases		Dr. for decreases / Cr. for increases		Dr. for increases / Cr. for decreases		Dr. for decreases / Cr. for increases		Dr. for increases / Cr. for decreases
+ / −		− / +		− / +		+ / −		− / +		+ / −
Normal		Normal		Normal		Normal		Normal		Normal

(Equity bracket spans Common Stock through Expenses.)

increases are recorded. Understanding these diagrams and rules is required to prepare, analyze, and interpret financial statements.

The T-account for FastForward's Cash account, reflecting its first 11 transactions (from Exhibit 1.9), is shown in Exhibit 2.8. The total increases in its Cash account are $36,100, the total decreases are $31,300, and the account's debit balance is $4,800. (We illustrate use of T-accounts later in this chapter.)

EXHIBIT 2.8

Computing the Balance for a T-Account

Cash			
Receive investment by owner for stock	30,000	Purchase of supplies	2,500
Consulting services revenue earned	4,200	Purchase of equipment	26,000
Collection of account receivable	1,900	Payment of rent	1,000
		Payment of salary	700
		Payment of account payable	900
		Payment of cash dividend	200
Balance	4,800		

Point: The ending balance is on the side with the larger dollar amount. Also, a plus (+) and minus (−) are not used in a T-account.

Quick Check
Answers — p. 77

1. Identify examples of accounting source documents.
2. Explain the importance of source documents.
3. Identify each of the following as either an asset, a liability, or equity: (*a*) Prepaid Rent, (*b*) Unearned Fees, (*c*) Building, (*d*) Wages Payable, and (*e*) Office Supplies.
4. What is an account? What is a ledger?
5. What determines the number and types of accounts a company uses?
6. Does *debit* always mean increase and *credit* always mean decrease?
7. Describe a chart of accounts.

Journalizing and Posting Transactions

P1 Record transactions in a journal and post entries to a ledger.

Processing transactions is a crucial part of accounting. The four usual steps of this process are depicted in Exhibit 2.9. Steps 1 and 2—involving transaction analysis and the accounting equation—were introduced in prior sections. This section extends that discussion and focuses on steps 3 and 4 of the accounting process. Step 3 is to record each transaction chronologically in a journal. A **journal** gives a complete record of each transaction in one place. It also shows debits and credits for each transaction. The process of recording transactions in a journal is called **journalizing**. Step 4 is to transfer (or *post*) entries from the journal to the ledger. The process of transferring journal entry information to the ledger is called **posting.**

Journalizing Transactions The process of journalizing transactions requires an understanding of a journal. While companies can use various journals, every company uses a **general journal**. It can be used to record any transaction and includes the following information about each transaction: (*a*) date of transaction, (*b*) titles of affected accounts, (*c*) dollar amount of each

EXHIBIT 2.9

Steps in Processing Transactions

debit and credit, and ⓓ explanation of the transaction. Exhibit 2.10 shows how the first two transactions of FastForward are recorded in a general journal. This process is similar for manual and computerized systems. Computerized journals are often designed to look like a manual journal page, and also include error-checking routines that ensure debits equal credits for each entry. Shortcuts allow recordkeepers to select account names and numbers from pull-down menus.

EXHIBIT 2.10

Partial General Journal for FastForward

To record entries in a general journal, apply these steps; refer to the entries in Exhibit 2.10 when reviewing these steps. (1) Date the transaction: Enter the year at the top of the first column and the month and day on the first line of each journal entry. (2) Enter titles of accounts debited and then enter amounts in the Debit column on the same line. Account titles are taken from the chart of accounts and are aligned with the left margin of the Account Titles and Explanation column. (3) Enter titles of accounts credited and then enter amounts in the Credit column on the same line. Account titles are from the chart of accounts and are indented from the left margin of the Account Titles and Explanation column to distinguish them from debited accounts. (4) Enter a brief explanation of the transaction on the line below the entry (it often references a source document). This explanation is indented about half as far as the credited account titles to avoid confusing it with accounts, and it is italicized.

Point: There are no exact rules for writing journal entry explanations. An explanation should be short yet describe why an entry is made.

🌐 IFRS

IFRS requires that companies report the following four basic financial statements with explanatory notes:

- Balance sheet
- Statement of changes in equity (or statement of recognized revenue and expense)
- Income statement
- Statement of cash flows

IFRS does not prescribe specific formats, and comparative information is required for the preceding period only.

A blank line is left between each journal entry for clarity. When a transaction is first recorded, the **posting reference (PR) column** is left blank (in a manual system). Later, when posting entries to the ledger, the identification numbers of the individual ledger accounts are entered in the PR column.

Balance Column Account T-accounts are simple and direct means to show how the accounting process works. However, actual accounting systems need more structure and therefore use **balance column accounts,** such as that in Exhibit 2.11.

EXHIBIT 2.11

Cash Account in Balance Column Format

Cash					Account No. 101
Date	Explanation	PR	Debit	Credit	Balance
2011					
Dec. 1		G1	30,000		30,000
Dec. 2		G1		2,500	27,500
Dec. 3		G1		26,000	1,500
Dec. 10		G1	4,200		5,700

The balance column account format is similar to a T-account in having columns for debits and credits. It is different in including transaction date and explanation columns. It also has a column with the balance of the account after each entry is recorded. To illustrate, FastForward's Cash account in Exhibit 2.11 is debited on December 1 for the $30,000 owner investment, yielding a $30,000 debit balance. The account is credited on December 2 for $2,500, yielding a $27,500 debit balance. On December 3, it is credited again, this time for $26,000, and its debit balance is reduced to $1,500. The Cash account is debited for $4,200 on December 10, and its debit balance increases to $5,700; and so on.

The heading of the Balance column does not show whether it is a debit or credit balance. Instead, an account is assumed to have a *normal balance.* Unusual events can sometimes temporarily

Point: Explanations are typically included in ledger accounts only for unusual transactions or events.

EXHIBIT 2.12

Posting an Entry to the Ledger

Point: The fundamental concepts of a manual (pencil-and-paper) system are identical to those of a computerized information system.

Key:
1. Identify debit account in Ledger: enter date, journal page, amount, and balance.
2. Enter the debit account number from the Ledger in the PR column of the journal.
3. Identify credit account in Ledger: enter date, journal page, amount, and balance.
4. Enter the credit account number from the Ledger in the PR column of the journal.

give an account an abnormal balance. An *abnormal balance* refers to a balance on the side where decreases are recorded. For example, a customer might mistakenly overpay a bill. This gives that customer's account receivable an abnormal (credit) balance. An abnormal balance is often identified by circling it or by entering it in red or some other unusual color. A zero balance for an account is usually shown by writing zeros or a dash in the Balance column to avoid confusion between a zero balance and one omitted in error.

Posting Journal Entries Step 4 of processing transactions is to post journal entries to ledger accounts (see Exhibit 2.9). To ensure that the ledger is up-to-date, entries are posted as soon as possible. This might be daily, weekly, or when time permits. All entries must be posted to the ledger before financial statements are prepared to ensure that account balances are up-to-date. When entries are posted to the ledger, the debits in journal entries are transferred into ledger accounts as debits, and credits are transferred into ledger accounts as credits. Exhibit 2.12 shows the *four steps to post a journal entry*. First, identify the ledger account that is debited in the entry; then, in the ledger, enter the entry date, the journal and page in its PR column, the debit amount, and the new balance of the ledger account. (The letter *G* shows it came from the General Journal.) Second, enter the ledger account number in the PR column of the journal. Steps 3 and 4 repeat the first two steps for credit entries and amounts. The posting process creates a link between the ledger and the journal entry. This link is a useful cross-reference for tracing an amount from one record to another.

Point: Computerized systems often provide a code beside a balance such as *dr.* or *cr.* to identify its balance. Posting is automatic and immediate with accounting software.

Point: A journal is often referred to as the *book of original entry*. The ledger is referred to as the *book of final entry* because financial statements are prepared from it.

Analyzing Transactions—An Illustration

We return to the activities of FastForward to show how double-entry accounting is useful in analyzing and processing transactions. Analysis of each transaction follows the four steps of Exhibit 2.9.

A1 Analyze the impact of transactions on accounts and financial statements.

Step 1 Identify the transaction and any source documents.
Step 2 Analyze the transaction using the accounting equation.
Step 3 Record the transaction in journal entry form applying double-entry accounting.
Step 4 Post the entry (for simplicity, we use T-accounts to represent ledger accounts).

Study each transaction thoroughly before proceeding to the next. The first 11 transactions are from Chapter 1, and we analyze five additional December transactions of FastForward (numbered 12 through 16) that were omitted earlier.

1. Receive Investment by Owner

1 IDENTIFY FastForward receives $30,000 cash from Chas Taylor in exchange for common stock.

2 ANALYZE

Assets	=	Liabilities	+	Equity
Cash				Common Stock
+30,000	=	0	+	30,000

3 RECORD

| (1) | Cash | 101 | 30,000 | |
| | Common Stock | 307 | | 30,000 |

4 POST

Cash	101
(1) 30,000	

Common Stock	307
	(1) 30,000

2. Purchase Supplies for Cash

1 IDENTIFY FastForward pays $2,500 cash for supplies.

2 ANALYZE

Assets		=	Liabilities	+	Equity
Cash	Supplies				
−2,500	+2,500	=	0	+	0

Changes the composition of assets but not the total.

3 RECORD

| (2) | Supplies | 126 | 2,500 | |
| | Cash | 101 | | 2,500 |

4 POST

Supplies	126
(2) 2,500	

Cash	101
(1) 30,000	(2) 2,500

3. Purchase Equipment for Cash

1 IDENTIFY FastForward pays $26,000 cash for equipment.

2 ANALYZE

Assets	=	Liabilities	+	Equity
Cash Equipment				
−26,000 +26,000	=	0	+	0

Changes the composition of assets but not the total.

3 RECORD

| (3) | Equipment | 167 | 26,000 | |
| | Cash | 101 | | 26,000 |

4 POST

Equipment		167
(3) 26,000		

Cash		101
(1) 30,000	(2) 2,500
	(3) 26,000

4. Purchase Supplies on Credit

1 IDENTIFY FastForward purchases $7,100 of supplies on credit from a supplier.

2 ANALYZE

Assets	=	Liabilities	+	Equity
Supplies		Accounts Payable		
+7,100	=	+7,100	+	0

3 RECORD

| (4) | Supplies | 126 | 7,100 | |
| | Accounts Payable | 201 | | 7,100 |

4 POST

Supplies		126
(2) 2,500		
(4) 7,100		

Accounts Payable		201
	(4) 7,100

5. Provide Services for Cash

1 IDENTIFY FastForward provides consulting services and immediately collects $4,200 cash.

2 ANALYZE

Assets	=	Liabilities	+	Equity
Cash				Consulting Revenue
+4,200	=	0	+	+4,200

3 RECORD

| (5) | Cash | 101 | 4,200 | |
| | Consulting Revenue | 403 | | 4,200 |

4 POST

Cash		101
(1) 30,000	(2) 2,500
(5) 4,200	(3) 26,000

Consulting Revenue		403
	(5) 4,200

6. Payment of Expense in Cash

1 IDENTIFY FastForward pays $1,000 cash for December rent.

2 ANALYZE

Assets	=	Liabilities	+	Equity
Cash				Rent Expense
−1,000	=	0	+	−1,000

3 RECORD

| (6) | Rent Expense | 640 | 1,000 | |
| | Cash | 101 | | 1,000 |

4 POST

Rent Expense		640
(6) 1,000		

Cash		101
(1) 30,000	(2) 2,500
(5) 4,200	(3) 26,000
	(6) 1,000

7. Payment of Expense in Cash

1 IDENTIFY FastForward pays $700 cash for employee salary.

2 ANALYZE

Assets	=	Liabilities	+	Equity
Cash				Salaries Expense
−700	=	0	+	−700

3 RECORD

| (7) | Salaries Expense | 622 | 700 | |
| | Cash | 101 | | 700 |

4 POST

Salaries Expense		622
(7) 700		

Cash		101
(1) 30,000	(2) 2,500
(5) 4,200	(3) 26,000
	(6) 1,000
	(7) 700

Point: *Salary* usually refers to compensation for an employee who receives a fixed amount for a given time period, whereas *wages* usually refers to compensation based on time worked.

8. Provide Consulting and Rental Services on Credit

1 IDENTIFY FastForward provides consulting services of $1,600 and rents its test facilities for $300. The customer is billed $1,900 for these services.

2 ANALYZE

Assets	=	Liabilities	+	Equity	
Accounts Receivable				Consulting Revenue	Rental Revenue
+1,900	=	0		+1,600	+300

3 RECORD

(8)	Accounts Receivable	106	1,900	
	Consulting Revenue	403		1,600
	Rental Revenue	406		300

4 POST

Accounts Receivable		106
(8) 1,900		

Consulting Revenue		403
	(5)	4,200
	(8)	1,600

Rental Revenue		406
	(8)	300

Point: Transaction 8 is a **compound journal entry,** which affects three or more accounts.

9. Receipt of Cash on Account

1 IDENTIFY FastForward receives $1,900 cash from the client billed in transaction 8.

2 ANALYZE

Assets		=	Liabilities	+	Equity
Cash	Accounts Receivable				
+1,900	−1,900	=	0	+	0

3 RECORD

(9)	Cash	101	1,900	
	Accounts Receivable	106		1,900

4 POST

Cash				101
(1)	30,000	(2)	2,500	
(5)	4,200	(3)	26,000	
(9)	1,900	(6)	1,000	
		(7)	700	

Accounts Receivable				106
(8)	1,900	(9)	1,900	

Point: The *revenue recognition principle* requires revenue to be recognized when earned, which is when the company provides products and services to a customer. This is not necessarily the same time that the customer pays. A customer can pay before or after products or services are provided.

10. Partial Payment of Accounts Payable

1 IDENTIFY FastForward pays CalTech Supply $900 cash toward the payable of transaction 4.

2 ANALYZE

Assets	=	Liabilities	+	Equity
Cash		Accounts Payable		
−900	=	−900	+	0

3 RECORD

(10)	Accounts Payable	201	900	
	Cash	101		900

4 POST

Accounts Payable				201
(10)	900	(4)	7,100	

Cash				101
(1)	30,000	(2)	2,500	
(5)	4,200	(3)	26,000	
(9)	1,900	(6)	1,000	
		(7)	700	
		(10)	900	

11. Payment of Cash Dividend

1 IDENTIFY FastForward pays $200 cash for dividends

2 ANALYZE

Assets	=	Liabilities	+	Equity
Cash				Dividends
−200	=	0		−200

3 RECORD

(11)	Dividends	319	200	
	Cash	101		200

4 POST

Dividends		319
(11) 200		

Cash				101
(1)	30,000	(2)	2,500	
(5)	4,200	(3)	26,000	
(9)	1,900	(6)	1,000	
		(7)	700	
		(10)	900	
		(11)	200	

12. Receipt of Cash for Future Services

1 IDENTIFY FastForward receives $3,000 cash in advance of providing consulting services to a customer.

2 ANALYZE

Assets	=	Liabilities	+	Equity
Cash		Unearned Consulting Revenue		
+3,000	=	+3,000	+	0

Accepting $3,000 cash obligates FastForward to perform future services and is a liability. No revenue is earned until services are provided.

3 RECORD

(12)	Cash	101	3,000	
	Unearned Consulting Revenue	236		3,000

4 POST

Cash			101
(1)	30,000	(2)	2,500
(5)	4,200	(3)	26,000
(9)	1,900	(6)	1,000
(12)	**3,000**	(7)	700
		(10)	900
		(11)	200

Unearned Consulting Revenue			236
		(12)	**3,000**

Point: Luca Pacioli, a 15th-century monk, is considered a pioneer in accounting and the first to devise double-entry accounting.

13. Pay Cash for Future Insurance Coverage

1 IDENTIFY FastForward pays $2,400 cash (insurance premium) for a 24-month insurance policy. Coverage begins on December 1.

2 ANALYZE

Assets		=	Liabilities	+	Equity
Cash	Prepaid Insurance				
−2,400	+2,400	=	0	+	0

Changes the composition of assets from cash to prepaid insurance. Expense is incurred as insurance coverage expires.

3 RECORD

(13)	Prepaid Insurance	128	2,400	
	Cash	101		2,400

4 POST

Prepaid Insurance			128
(13)	**2,400**		

Cash			101
(1)	30,000	(2)	2,500
(5)	4,200	(3)	26,000
(9)	1,900	(6)	1,000
(12)	3,000	(7)	700
		(10)	900
		(11)	200
		(13)	**2,400**

14. Purchase Supplies for Cash

1 IDENTIFY FastForward pays $120 cash for supplies.

2 ANALYZE

Assets		=	Liabilities	+	Equity
Cash	Supplies				
−120	+120	=	0	+	0

3 RECORD

(14)	Supplies	126	120	
	Cash	101		120

4 POST

Supplies			126
(2)	2,500		
(4)	7,100		
(14)	**120**		

Cash			101
(1)	30,000	(2)	2,500
(5)	4,200	(3)	26,000
(9)	1,900	(6)	1,000
(12)	3,000	(7)	700
		(10)	900
		(11)	200
		(13)	2,400
		(14)	**120**

15. Payment of Expense in Cash

1 IDENTIFY FastForward pays $230 cash for December utilities expense.

2 ANALYZE

Assets	=	Liabilities	+	Equity
Cash				Utilities Expense
−230	=	0		−230

3 RECORD

(15)	Utilities Expense	690	230
	Cash	101	230

4 POST

Utilities Expense		690
(15)	230	

Cash			101
(1)	30,000	(2)	2,500
(5)	4,200	(3)	26,000
(9)	1,900	(6)	1,000
(12)	3,000	(7)	700
		(10)	900
		(11)	200
		(13)	2,400
		(14)	120
		(15)	230

16. Payment of Expense in Cash

1 IDENTIFY FastForward pays $700 cash in employee salary for work performed in the latter part of December.

2 ANALYZE

Assets	=	Liabilities	+	Equity
Cash				Salaries Expense
−700	=	0		−700

3 RECORD

(16)	Salaries Expense	622	700
	Cash	101	700

4 POST

Salaries Expense		622
(7)	700	
(16)	700	

Cash			101
(1)	30,000	(2)	2,500
(5)	4,200	(3)	26,000
(9)	1,900	(6)	1,000
(12)	3,000	(7)	700
		(10)	900
		(11)	200
		(13)	2,400
		(14)	120
		(15)	230
		(16)	700

Point: We could merge transactions 15 and 16 into one *compound entry*.

Accounting Equation Analysis

Exhibit 2.13 shows the ledger accounts (in T-account form) of FastForward after all 16 transactions are recorded and posted and the balances computed. The accounts are grouped into three major columns corresponding to the accounting equation: assets, liabilities, and equity. Note several important points. First, as with each transaction, the totals for the three columns must obey the accounting equation. Specifically, assets equal $42,470 ($4,350 + $0 + $9,720 + $2,400 + $26,000); liabilities equal $9,200 ($6,200 + $3,000); and equity equals $33,270 ($30,000 − $200 + $5,800 + $300 − $1,400 − $1,000 − $230). These numbers prove the accounting equation: Assets of $42,470 = Liabilities of $9,200 + Equity of $33,270. Second, the common stock, dividends, revenue, and expense accounts reflect the transactions that change equity. The latter three account categories underlie the statement of retained earnings. Third, the revenue and expense account balances will be summarized and reported in the income statement. Fourth, increases and decreases in the cash account make up the elements reported in the statement of cash flows.

Debit and Credit Rules

Accounts	Increase (normal bal.)	Decrease
Asset	Debit	Credit
Liability	Credit	Debit
Common stock	Credit	Debit
Dividends	Debit	Credit
Revenue	Credit	Debit
Expense	Debit	Credit

Point: Technology does not provide the judgment required to analyze most business transactions. Analysis requires the expertise of skilled and ethical professionals.

EXHIBIT 2.13

Ledger for FastForward (in T-Account Form)

Assets			=	Liabilities		+	Equity	

Cash 101

(1)	30,000	(2)	2,500
(5)	4,200	(3)	26,000
(9)	1,900	(6)	1,000
(12)	3,000	(7)	700
		(10)	900
		(11)	200
		(13)	2,400
		(14)	120
		(15)	230
		(16)	700
Balance	4,350		

Accounts Receivable 106

(8)	1,900	(9)	1,900
Balance	0		

Supplies 126

(2)	2,500		
(4)	7,100		
(14)	120		
Balance	9,720		

Prepaid Insurance 128

(13)	2,400

Equipment 167

(3)	26,000

$42,470

Accounts Payable 201

(10)	900	(4)	7,100
		Balance	6,200

Unearned Consulting Revenue 236

(12)	3,000

$9,200

Common Stock 307

(1)	30,000

Dividends 319

(11)	200

Consulting Revenue 403

		(5)	4,200
		(8)	1,600
		Balance	5,800

Rental Revenue 406

(8)	300

Salaries Expense 622

(7)	700		
(16)	700		
Balance	1,400		

Rent Expense 640

(6)	1,000

Utilities Expense 690

(15)	230

Accounts in this white area reflect those reported on the income statement.

$33,270

Quick Check
Answers — p. 77

8. What types of transactions increase equity? What types decrease equity?
9. Why are accounting systems called *double-entry*?
10. For each transaction, double-entry accounting requires which of the following? (a) Debits to asset accounts must create credits to liability or equity accounts, (b) a debit to a liability account must create a credit to an asset account, or (c) total debits must equal total credits.
11. An owner invests $15,000 cash along with equipment having a market value of $23,000 in a company in exchange for common stock. Prepare the necessary journal entry.
12. Explain what a compound journal entry is.
13. Why are posting reference numbers entered in the journal when entries are posted to ledger accounts?

TRIAL BALANCE

Double-entry accounting requires the sum of debit account balances to equal the sum of credit account balances. A trial balance is used to confirm this. A **trial balance** is a list of accounts and their balances at a point in time. Account balances are reported in their appropriate debit or credit columns of a trial balance. A trial balance can be used to confirm this and to follow up on any abnormal or unusual balances. Exhibit 2.14 shows the trial balance for FastForward after its 16 entries have been posted to the ledger. (This is an *unadjusted* trial balance—Chapter 3 explains the necessary adjustments.)

FASTFORWARD
Trial Balance
December 31, 2011

	Debit	Credit
Cash	$ 4,350	
Accounts receivable	0	
Supplies	9,720	
Prepaid insurance	2,400	
Equipment	26,000	
Accounts payable		$ 6,200
Unearned consulting revenue		3,000
Common stock		30,000
Dividends	200	
Consulting revenue		5,800
Rental revenue		300
Salaries expense	1,400	
Rent expense	1,000	
Utilities expense	230	
Totals	$ 45,300	$ 45,300

EXHIBIT 2.14
Trial Balance (Unadjusted)

Point: The ordering of accounts in a trial balance typically follows their identification number from the chart of accounts.

Preparing a Trial Balance

Preparing a trial balance involves three steps:

1. List each account title and its amount (from ledger) in the trial balance. If an account has a zero balance, list it with a zero in its normal balance column (or omit it entirely).
2. Compute the total of debit balances and the total of credit balances.
3. Verify (*prove*) total debit balances equal total credit balances.

P2 Prepare and explain the use of a trial balance.

Fraud

Heavenly accounting. Religious organizations are especially vulnerable to fraud. Due to "trust" among religious cohorts, the opportunity factor in the fraud triangle looms large for such entities. In many cases, the recording of transactions has few or no controls. For example, in 2011, a mother and son team from Morristown, Tennessee, pleaded guilty to defrauding a local church. They had recorded nearly 2,000 checks to "cash," amounting to more than $1.5 million, which they cashed and pocketed. An independent review of transactions or a requirement for documentation would have reduced the opportunity factor.

Point: A trial balance is *not* a financial statement but a mechanism for checking equality of debits and credits in the ledger. Financial statements do not have debit and credit columns.

Example: If a credit to Unearned Revenue was incorrectly posted from the journal as a credit to the Revenue ledger account, would the ledger still balance? Would the financial statements be correct? *Answers:* The ledger would balance, but liabilities would be understated, equity would be overstated, and income would be overstated (all because of overstated revenues).

Point: The IRS requires companies to keep records that can be audited.

The total of debit balances equals the total of credit balances for the trial balance in Exhibit 2.14. Equality of these two totals does not guarantee that no errors were made. For example, the column totals still will be equal when a debit or credit of a correct amount is made to a wrong account. Another error that does not cause unequal column totals occurs when equal debits and credits of an incorrect amount are entered.

Searching for and Correcting Errors If the trial balance does not balance (when its columns are not equal), the error (or errors) must be found and corrected. An efficient way to search for an error is to check the journalizing, posting, and trial balance preparation in *reverse order*. Step 1 is to verify that the trial balance columns are correctly added. If step 1 fails to find the error, step 2 is to verify that account balances are accurately entered from the ledger. Step 3 is to see whether a debit (or credit) balance is mistakenly listed in the trial balance as a credit (or debit). A clue to this error is when the difference between total debits and total credits equals twice the amount of the incorrect account balance. If the error is still undiscovered, Step 4 is to recompute each account balance in the ledger. Step 5 is to verify that each journal entry is properly posted. Step 6 is to verify that the original journal entry has equal debits and credits. At this point, the errors should be uncovered.[3]

If an error in a journal entry is discovered before the error is posted, it can be corrected in a manual system by drawing a line through the incorrect information. The correct information is written above it to create a record of change for the auditor. Many computerized systems allow the operator to replace the incorrect information directly.

If an error in a journal entry is not discovered until after it is posted, we do not strike through both erroneous entries in the journal and ledger. Instead, we correct this error by creating a *correcting entry* that removes the amount from the wrong account and records it to the correct account. As an example, suppose a $100 purchase of supplies is journalized with an incorrect debit to Equipment, and then this incorrect entry is posted to the ledger. The Supplies ledger account balance is understated by $100, and the Equipment ledger account balance is overstated by $100. The correcting entry is: debit Supplies and credit Equipment (both for $100).

Using a Trial Balance to Prepare Financial Statements

This section shows how to prepare *financial statements* from the trial balance in Exhibit 2.14 and from information on the December transactions of FastForward. These statements differ from those in Chapter 1 because of several additional transactions. These statements are also more precisely called *unadjusted statements* because we need to make some further accounting adjustments (described in Chapter 3).

How financial statements are linked in time is illustrated in Exhibit 2.15. A balance sheet reports on an organization's financial position at a *point in time*. The income statement, statement of retained earnings, and statement of cash flows report on financial performance over a *period of time*. The three statements in the middle column of Exhibit 2.15 link balance sheets from the

P3 Prepare financial statements from business transactions.

EXHIBIT 2.15

Links between Financial Statements across Time

---

[3] *Transposition* occurs when two digits are switched, or transposed, within a number. If transposition is the only error, it yields a difference between the two trial balance totals that is evenly divisible by 9. For example, assume that a $691 debit in an entry is incorrectly posted to the ledger as $619. Total credits in the trial balance are then larger than total debits by $72 ($691 − $619). The $72 error is *evenly* divisible by 9 (72/9 = 8). The first digit of the quotient (in our example it is 8) equals the difference between the digits of the two transposed numbers (the 9 and the 1). The number of digits in the quotient also tells the location of the transposition, starting from the right. The quotient in our example had only one digit (8), so it tells us the transposition is in the first digit. Consider another example where a transposition error involves posting $961 instead of the correct $691. The difference in these numbers is $270, and its quotient is 30 (270/9). The quotient has two digits, so it tells us to check the second digit from the right for a transposition of two numbers that have a difference of 3.

beginning to the end of a reporting period. They explain how financial position changes from one point to another.

Preparers and users (including regulatory agencies) determine the length of the reporting period. A one-year, or annual, reporting period is common, as are semiannual, quarterly, and monthly periods. The one-year reporting period is known as the *accounting,* or *fiscal, year.* Businesses whose accounting year begins on January 1 and ends on December 31 are known as *calendar-year* companies. Many companies choose a fiscal year ending on a date other than December 31. **Research In Motion** is a *noncalendar-year* company as reflected in the headings of its February 27 year-end financial statements in Appendix A near the end of the book.

Point: A statement's heading lists the 3 W's: **W**ho—name of organization, **W**hat—name of statement, **W**hen—statement's point in time or period of time.

Income Statement An income statement reports the revenues earned less the expenses incurred by a business over a period of time. FastForward's income statement for December is shown at the top of Exhibit 2.16. Information about revenues and expenses is conveniently taken from the trial balance in Exhibit 2.14. Net income of $3,470 is reported at the bottom of the statement. Owner investments and dividends are *not* part of income.

EXHIBIT 2.16

Financial Statements and Their Links

FASTFORWARD
Income Statement
For Month Ended December 31, 2011

Revenues		
Consulting revenue ($4,200 + $1,600)	$ 5,800	
Rental revenue	300	
Total revenues		$ 6,100
Expenses		
Rent expense	1,000	
Salaries expense	1,400	
Utilities expense	230	
Total expenses		2,630
Net income		$ 3,470

FASTFORWARD
Statement of Retained Earnings
For Month Ended December 31, 2011

Retained earnings, December 1, 2011		$ 0
Plus: Net income		3,470
		3,470
Less: Cash dividends		200
Retained earnings, December 31, 2011		$ 3,270

Point: Arrow lines show how the statements are linked.

FASTFORWARD
Balance Sheet
December 31, 2011

Assets		Liabilities	
Cash	$ 4,350	Accounts payable	$ 6,200
Supplies	9,720	Unearned revenue	3,000
Prepaid insurance	2,400	Total liabilities	9,200
Equipment	26,000	**Equity**	
		Common stock	30,000
		Retained earnings	3,270
		Total equity	33,270
Total assets	$42,470	Total liabilities and equity	$42,470

Point: To *foot* a column of numbers is to add them.

Statement of Retained Earnings The statement of retained earnings reports information about how retained earnings changes over the reporting period. FastForward's statement of retained earnings is the second report in Exhibit 2.16. It shows the $3,470 of net income, the $200 dividend, and the $3,270 end-of-period balance. (The beginning balance in the statement of retained earnings is rarely zero; an exception is for the first period of operations. The beginning retained earnings balance in January 2012 is $3,270, which is December's ending balance.)

Balance Sheet The balance sheet reports the financial position of a company at a point in time, usually at the end of a month, quarter, or year. FastForward's balance sheet is the third report in Exhibit 2.16. This statement refers to financial condition at the close of business on December 31. The left side of the balance sheet lists its assets: cash, supplies, prepaid insurance, and equipment. The upper right side of the balance sheet shows that it owes $6,200 to creditors and $3,000 in services to customers who paid in advance. The equity section shows an ending balance of $33,270. Note the link between the ending balance of the statement of retained earnings and the retained earnings balance. (Recall that this presentation of the balance sheet is called the *account form:* assets on the left and liabilities and equity on the right. Another presentation is the *report form:* assets on top, followed by liabilities and then equity. Either presentation is acceptable.)

Presentation Issues Dollar signs are not used in journals and ledgers. They do appear in financial statements and other reports such as trial balances. The usual practice is to put dollar signs beside only the first and last numbers in a column. **Research In Motion**'s financial statements in Appendix A show this. When amounts are entered in a journal, ledger, or trial balance, commas are optional to indicate thousands, millions, and so forth. However, commas are always used in financial statements. Companies also commonly round amounts in reports to the nearest dollar, or even to a higher level. Research In Motion is typical of many companies in that it rounds its financial statement amounts to the nearest thousand or million. This decision is based on the perceived impact of rounding for users' business decisions.

Reading and Using an Annual Report An *annual report* is required of more than 10,000 corporations in the United States that trade their stock *publicly*. This requirement is imposed by the SEC. Another nearly 5 million corporations in the United States do not trade their shares publicly, and are called *private* or *closely held* corporations, which are not subject to SEC oversight.

Appendix A, near the end of this book, shows key excerpts from the annual report of **Research In Motion (RIM)**. This appendix also reproduces financial statements from the annual reports of **Apple**, **Palm**, and **Nokia**. The key excerpts are identified and explained on page A-1. Page A-3 includes a report on the audit of RIM's financial statements, and page A-4 has the report on internal controls over its financial reporting. Pages A-5 through A-8 report the four financial statements. Pages A-9 to A-18 contain footnotes that expand on details underlying those statements. We review and use the annual report for many business decisions, especially for valuing corporate stock.

Point: An income statement is also called an *earnings statement, a statement of operations,* or a *P&L* (profit and loss) *statement.* A balance sheet is also called a *statement of financial position.*

Point: While revenues increase equity, and expenses decrease equity, the amounts are not reported in detail in the statement of retained earnings. Instead, their effects are reflected through net income.

Point: Knowing how financial statements are prepared improves our analysis of them.

Quick Check
Answers — p. 77

14. Where are dollar signs typically entered in financial statements?
15. If a $4,000 debit to Equipment in a journal entry is incorrectly posted to the ledger as a $4,000 credit, and the ledger account has a resulting debit balance of $20,000, what is the effect of this error on the Trial Balance column totals?
16. Describe the link between the income statement and the statement of retained earnings.
17. Explain the link between the balance sheet and the statement of retained earnings.
18. Define and describe revenues and expenses.
19. Define and describe assets, liabilities, and equity.

GLOBAL VIEW

Financial accounting according to U.S. GAAP is similar, but not identical, to IFRS. This section discusses differences in analyzing and recording transactions, and with the preparation of financial statements.

Analyzing and Recording Transactions Both U.S. GAAP and IFRS include broad and similar guidance for financial accounting. As the FASB and IASB work toward a common conceptual framework over the next few years, even those differences will fade. Further, both U.S. GAAP and IFRS apply transaction analysis and recording as shown in this chapter—using the same debit and credit system and accrual accounting. Although some variations exist in revenue and expense recognition and other accounting principles, all of the transactions in this chapter are accounted for identically under these two systems.

Financial Statements Both U.S. GAAP and IFRS prepare the same four basic financial statements. A few differences within each statement do exist and we will discuss those throughout the book. For example, both U.S. GAAP and IFRS require balance sheets to separate current items from noncurrent items. However, while U.S. GAAP balance sheets report current items first, IFRS balance sheets normally (but are not required to) present noncurrent items first, and equity before liabilities. To illustrate, a condensed version of **Nokia**'s balance sheet follows (numbers using euros in millions).

NOKIA
Balance Sheet (in EUR millions)
December 31, 2009

Assets		Equity and Liabilities	
Noncurrent assets	12,125	Total equity	14,749
Current assets	23,613	Noncurrent liabilities	5,801
		Current liabilities	15,188
Total assets	35,738	Total equity and liabilities	35,738

Accounting Controls and Assurance Accounting systems depend on control procedures that assure the proper principles were applied in processing accounting information. The passage of SOX legislation strengthened U.S. control procedures in recent years. However, global standards for control are diverse and so are enforcement activities. Consequently, while global accounting standards are converging, their application in different countries can yield different outcomes depending on the quality of their auditing standards and enforcement.

Fraud

Accounting control. Recording valid transactions, and not recording fraudulent transactions, enhances the quality of financial statements. The graph here shows the percentage of employees in information technology that report observing specific types of misconduct within the past year.

[Source: KPMG 2009]

Type of Misconduct	Percent
Breaching database controls	23%
Mishandling private information	22%
Breaching customer privacy	16%
Falsifying accounting data	9%

Percent Citing Misconduct

Decision Analysis

Debt Ratio

A2 Compute the debt ratio and describe its use in analyzing financial condition.

An important business objective is gathering information to help assess a company's risk of failing to pay its debts. Companies finance their assets with either liabilities or equity. A company that finances a relatively large portion of its assets with liabilities is said to have a high degree of *financial leverage*. Higher financial leverage involves greater risk because liabilities must be repaid and often require regular interest payments (equity financing does not). The risk that a company might not be able to meet such required payments is higher if it has more liabilities (is more highly leveraged). One way to assess the risk associated with a company's use of liabilities is to compute the **debt ratio** as in Exhibit 2.17.

EXHIBIT 2.17
Debt Ratio

$$\text{Debt ratio} = \frac{\text{Total liabilities}}{\text{Total assets}}$$

Point: Compare the equity amount to the liability amount to assess the extent of owner versus nonowner financing.

To see how to apply the debt ratio, let's look at **Skechers**'s liabilities and assets. The company designs, markets, and sells footwear for men, women, and children under the Skechers brand. Exhibit 2.18 computes and reports its debt ratio at the end of each year from 2005 to 2009.

EXHIBIT 2.18
Computation and Analysis of Debt Ratio

$ in millions	2009	2008	2007	2006	2005
Total liabilities	$246	$204	$201	$288	$238
Total assets	$996	$876	$828	$737	$582
Debt ratio	**0.25**	**0.23**	**0.24**	**0.39**	**0.41**
Industry debt ratio	0.51	0.50	0.46	0.48	0.47

Skechers's debt ratio ranges from a low of 0.23 to a high of 0.41—also, see graph in margin. Its ratio is lower, and has been generally declining, compared with the industry ratio. This analysis implies a low risk from its financial leverage. Is financial leverage good or bad for Skechers? To answer that question we need to compare the company's return on the borrowed money to the rate it is paying creditors. If the company's return is higher, it is successfully borrowing money to make more money. A company's success with making money from borrowed money can quickly turn unprofitable if its own return drops below the rate it is paying creditors.

Decision Maker
Answer — p. 76

Investor You consider buying stock in **Converse**. As part of your analysis, you compute its debt ratio for 2009, 2010, and 2011 as: 0.35, 0.74, and 0.94, respectively. Based on the debt ratio, is Converse a low-risk investment? Has the risk of buying Converse stock changed over this period? (The industry debt ratio averages 0.40.)

DEMONSTRATION PROBLEM

(This problem extends the demonstration problem of Chapter 1.) After several months of planning, Jasmine Worthy started a haircutting business called Expressions. The following events occurred during its first month.

a. On August 1, Worthy invested $3,000 cash and $15,000 of equipment in Expressions in exchange for common stock.
b. On August 2, Expressions paid $600 cash for furniture for the shop.
c. On August 3, Expressions paid $500 cash to rent space in a strip mall for August.
d. On August 4, it purchased $1,200 of equipment on credit for the shop (using a long-term note payable).
e. On August 5, Expressions opened for business. Cash received from haircutting services in the first week and a half of business (ended August 15) was $825.
f. On August 15, it provided $100 of haircutting services on account.
g. On August 17, it received a $100 check for services previously rendered on account.
h. On August 17, it paid $125 to an assistant for hours worked during the grand opening.
i. Cash received from services provided during the second half of August was $930.

j. On August 31, it paid a $400 installment toward principal on the note payable entered into on August 4.

k. On August 31, it paid $900 cash for dividends.

Required

1. Open the following ledger accounts in balance column format (account numbers are in parentheses): Cash (101); Accounts Receivable (102); Furniture (161); Store Equipment (165); Note Payable (240); Common Stock (307); Dividends (319); Haircutting Services Revenue (403); Wages Expense (623); and Rent Expense (640). Prepare general journal entries for the transactions.

2. Post the journal entries from (1) to the ledger accounts.

3. Prepare a trial balance as of August 31.

4. Prepare an income statement for August.

5. Prepare a statement of retained earnings for August.

6. Prepare a balance sheet as of August 31.

7. Determine the debt ratio as of August 31.

Extended Analysis

8. In the coming months, Expressions will experience a greater variety of business transactions. Identify which accounts are debited and which are credited for the following transactions. (*Hint:* We must use some accounts not opened in part 1.)

   a. Purchase supplies with cash.

   b. Pay cash for future insurance coverage.

   c. Receive cash for services to be provided in the future.

   d. Purchase supplies on account.

PLANNING THE SOLUTION

- Analyze each transaction and use the debit and credit rules to prepare a journal entry for each.
- Post each debit and each credit from journal entries to their ledger accounts and cross-reference each amount in the posting reference (PR) columns of the journal and ledger.
- Calculate each account balance and list the accounts with their balances on a trial balance.
- Verify that total debits in the trial balance equal total credits.
- To prepare the income statement, identify revenues and expenses. List those items on the statement, compute the difference, and label the result as *net income* or *net loss*.
- Use information in the ledger to prepare the statement of retained earnings.
- Use information in the ledger to prepare the balance sheet.
- Calculate the debt ratio by dividing total liabilities by total assets.
- Analyze the future transactions to identify the accounts affected and apply debit and credit rules.

SOLUTION TO DEMONSTRATION PROBLEM

1. General journal entries:

General Journal Entry

Page 1

Date		Account Titles and Explanation	PR	Debit	Credit
Aug. 1		Cash	101	3,000	
		Store Equipment	165	15,000	
		Common Stock	307		18,000
		Owner's investment for stock.			
	2	Furniture	161	600	
		Cash	101		600
		Purchased furniture for cash.			
	3	Rent Expense	640	500	
		Cash	101		500
		Paid rent for August.			
	4	Store Equipment	165	1,200	
		Note Payable	240		1,200
		Purchased additional equipment on credit.			

[continued on next page]

[continued from previous page]

	15	Cash	101	825	
		Haircutting Services Revenue	403		825
		Cash receipts from first half of August.			
	15	Accounts Receivable	102	100	
		Haircutting Services Revenue	403		100
		To record revenue for services provided on account.			
	17	Cash	101	100	
		Accounts Receivable	102		100
		To record cash received as payment on account.			
	17	Wages Expense	623	125	
		Cash	101		125
		Paid wages to assistant.			
	31	Cash	101	930	
		Haircutting Services Revenue	403		930
		Cash receipts from second half of August.			
	31	Note Payable	240	400	
		Cash	101		400
		Paid an installment on the note payable.			
	31	Dividends	319	900	
		Cash	101		900
		Paid cash dividend.			

2. Post journal entries from part 1 to the ledger accounts:

General Ledger

Cash — Account No. 101

Date	PR	Debit	Credit	Balance
Aug. 1	G1	3,000		3,000
2	G1		600	2,400
3	G1		500	1,900
15	G1	825		2,725
17	G1	100		2,825
17	G1		125	2,700
31	G1	930		3,630
31	G1		400	3,230
31	G1		900	2,330

Accounts Receivable — Account No. 102

Date	PR	Debit	Credit	Balance
Aug. 15	G1	100		100
17	G1		100	0

Furniture — Account No. 161

Date	PR	Debit	Credit	Balance
Aug. 2	G1	600		600

Store Equipment — Account No. 165

Date	PR	Debit	Credit	Balance
Aug. 1	G1	15,000		15,000
4	G1	1,200		16,200

Note Payable — Account No. 240

Date	PR	Debit	Credit	Balance
Aug. 4	G1		1,200	1,200
31	G1	400		800

Common Stock — Account No. 307

Date	PR	Debit	Credit	Balance
Aug. 1	G1		18,000	18,000

Dividends — Account No. 319

Date	PR	Debit	Credit	Balance
Aug. 31	G1	900		900

Haircutting Services Revenue — Account No. 403

Date	PR	Debit	Credit	Balance
Aug. 15	G1		825	825
15	G1		100	925
31	G1		930	1,855

Wages Expense — Account No. 623

Date	PR	Debit	Credit	Balance
Aug. 17	G1	125		125

Rent Expense — Account No. 640

Date	PR	Debit	Credit	Balance
Aug. 3	G1	500		500

3. Prepare a trial balance from the ledger:

EXPRESSIONS
Trial Balance
August 31

	Debit	Credit
Cash	$ 2,330	
Accounts receivable	0	
Furniture	600	
Store equipment	16,200	
Note payable		$ 800
Common stock		18,000
Dividends	900	
Haircutting services revenue		1,855
Wages expense	125	
Rent expense	500	
Totals	$20,655	$20,655

4.

EXPRESSIONS
Income Statement
For Month Ended August 31

Revenues		
Haircutting services revenue		$1,855
Operating expenses		
Rent expense	$500	
Wages expense	125	
Total operating expenses		625
Net income		$1,230

5.

EXPRESSIONS
Statement of Retained Earnings
For Month Ended August 31

Retained earnings, August 1	$ 0
Plus: Net income	1,230
	1,230
Less: Cash dividends	900
Retained earnings, August 31	$ 330

6.

EXPRESSIONS
Balance Sheet
August 31

Assets		Liabilities	
Cash	$ 2,330	Note payable	$ 800
Furniture	600	**Equity**	
Store equipment	16,200	Common stock	18,000
		Retained earnings	330
		Total equity	18,330
Total assets	$19,130	Total liabilities and equity	$19,130

7. Debt ratio = $\dfrac{\text{Total liabilities}}{\text{Total assets}} = \dfrac{\$800}{\$19{,}130} = \underline{\underline{4.18\%}}$

8a. Supplies *debited*
Cash *credited*

8b. Prepaid Insurance *debited*
Cash *credited*

8c. Cash *debited*
Unearned Services Revenue *credited*

8d. Supplies *debited*
Accounts Payable *credited*

Summary

C1 Explain the steps in processing transactions and the role of source documents. The accounting process identifies business transactions and events, analyzes and records their effects, and summarizes and prepares information useful in making decisions. Transactions and events are the starting points in the accounting process. Source documents identify and describe transactions and events. Examples are sales tickets, checks, purchase orders, bills, and bank statements. Source documents provide objective and reliable evidence, making information more useful. The effects of transactions and events are recorded in journals. Posting along with a trial balance helps summarize and classify these effects.

C2 Describe an account and its use in recording transactions. An account is a detailed record of increases and decreases in a specific asset, liability, equity, revenue, or expense. Information from accounts is analyzed, summarized, and presented in reports and financial statements for decision makers.

C3 Describe a ledger and a chart of accounts. The ledger (or general ledger) is a record containing all accounts used by a company and their balances. It is referred to as the *books*. The chart of accounts is a list of all accounts and usually includes an identification number assigned to each account.

C4 Define *debits* and *credits* and explain double-entry accounting. *Debit* refers to left, and *credit* refers to right. Debits increase assets, expenses, and dividends while credits decrease them. Credits increase liabilities, common stock, and revenues; debits decrease them. Double-entry accounting means each transaction affects at least two accounts and has at least one debit and one credit. The system for recording debits and credits follows from the accounting equation. The left side of an account is the normal balance for assets, dividends, and expenses, and the right side is the normal balance for liabilities, common stock, and revenues.

A1 Analyze the impact of transactions on accounts and financial statements. We analyze transactions using concepts of double-entry accounting. This analysis is performed by determining a transaction's effects on accounts. These effects are recorded in journals and posted to ledgers.

A2 Compute the debt ratio and describe its use in analyzing financial condition. A company's debt ratio is computed as total liabilities divided by total assets. It reveals how much of the assets are financed by creditor (nonowner) financing. The higher this ratio, the more risk a company faces because liabilities must be repaid at specific dates.

P1 Record transactions in a journal and post entries to a ledger. Transactions are recorded in a journal. Each entry in a journal is posted to the accounts in the ledger. This provides information that is used to produce financial statements. Balance column accounts are widely used and include columns for debits, credits, and the account balance.

P2 Prepare and explain the use of a trial balance. A trial balance is a list of accounts from the ledger showing their debit or credit balances in separate columns. The trial balance is a summary of the ledger's contents and is useful in preparing financial statements and in revealing recordkeeping errors.

P3 Prepare financial statements from business transactions. The balance sheet, the statement of retained earnings, the income statement, and the statement of cash flows use data from the trial balance (and other financial statements) for their preparation.

Guidance Answers to Decision Maker and Decision Ethics

Cashier The advantages to the process proposed by the assistant manager include improved customer service, fewer delays, and less work for you. However, you should have serious concerns about internal control and the potential for fraud. In particular, the assistant manager could steal cash and simply enter fewer sales to match the remaining cash. You should reject her suggestion without the manager's approval. Moreover, you should have an ethical concern about the assistant manager's suggestion to ignore store policy.

Investor The debt ratio suggests the stock of Converse is of higher risk than normal and that this risk is rising. The average industry ratio of 0.40 further supports this conclusion. The 2011 debt ratio for Converse is twice the industry norm. Also, a debt ratio approaching 1.0 indicates little to no equity.

Guidance Answers to Quick Checks

1. Examples of source documents are sales tickets, checks, purchase orders, charges to customers, bills from suppliers, employee earnings records, and bank statements.
2. Source documents serve many purposes, including record-keeping and internal control. Source documents, especially if obtained from outside the organization, provide objective and reliable evidence about transactions and their amounts.
3.

Assets	Liabilities	Equity
a,c,e	b,d	—

4. An account is a record in an accounting system that records and stores the increases and decreases in a specific asset, liability, equity, revenue, or expense. The ledger is a collection of all the accounts of a company.
5. A company's size and diversity affect the number of accounts in its accounting system. The types of accounts depend on information the company needs to both effectively operate and report its activities in financial statements.
6. No. Debit and credit both can mean increase or decrease. The particular meaning in a circumstance depends on the *type of account*. For example, a debit increases the balance of asset, dividends, and expense accounts, but it decreases the balance of liability, common stock, and revenue accounts.
7. A chart of accounts is a list of all of a company's accounts and their identification numbers.
8. Equity is increased by revenues and by owner investments. Equity is decreased by expenses and dividends.
9. The name *double-entry* is used because all transactions affect at least two accounts. There must be at least one debit in one account and at least one credit in another account.
10. The answer is (*c*).
11.

Cash	15,000	
Equipment	23,000	
Common Stock		38,000
Investment by owner of cash and equipment.		

12. A compound journal entry affects three or more accounts.
13. Posting reference numbers are entered in the journal when posting to the ledger as a cross-reference that allows the recordkeeper or auditor to trace debits and credits from one record to another.
14. At a minimum, dollar signs are placed beside the first and last numbers in a column. It is also common to place dollar signs beside any amount that appears after a ruled line to indicate that an addition or subtraction has occurred.
15. The Equipment account balance is incorrectly reported at $20,000—it should be $28,000. The effect of this error understates the trial balance's Debit column total by $8,000. This results in an $8,000 difference between the column totals.
16. An income statement reports a company's revenues and expenses along with the resulting net income or loss. A statement of retained earnings reports changes in retained earnings, including that from net income or loss. Both statements report transactions occurring over a period of time.
17. The balance sheet describes a company's financial position (assets, liabilities, and equity) at a point in time. The retained earnings amount in the balance sheet is obtained from the statement of retained earnings.
18. Revenues are inflows of assets in exchange for products or services provided to customers as part of the main operations of a business. Expenses are outflows or the using up of assets that result from providing products or services to customers.
19. Assets are the resources a business owns or controls that carry expected future benefits. Liabilities are the obligations of a business, representing the claims of others against the assets of a business. Equity reflects the owner's claims on the assets of the business after deducting liabilities.

Key Terms

Account (p. 53)
Account balance (p. 57)
Balance column account (p. 60)
Chart of accounts (p. 56)
Common stock (p. 55)
Compound journal entry (p. 63)
Credit (p. 57)
Creditors (p. 54)
Debit (p. 57)

Debtors (p. 53)
Debt ratio (p. 72)
Dividends (p. 55)
Double-entry accounting (p. 57)
General journal (p. 58)
General ledger (p. 53)
Journal (p. 58)
Journalizing (p. 58)
Ledger (p. 53)

Posting (p. 58)
Posting reference (PR) column (p. 60)
Source documents (p. 52)
T-account (p. 57)
Trial balance (p. 67)
Unearned revenue (p. 54)

Multiple Choice Quiz

Answers on p. 93   mhhe.com/wildFA6e

Additional quiz questions are available at the book's Website.

1. Amalia Company received its utility bill for the current period of $700 and immediately paid it. Its journal entry to record this transaction includes a
   a. Credit to Utility Expense for $700.
   b. Debit to Utility Expense for $700.
   c. Debit to Accounts Payable for $700.
   d. Debit to Cash for $700.
   e. Credit to Common Stock for $700.

2. On May 1, Mattingly Lawn Service collected $2,500 cash from a customer in advance of five months of lawn service. Mattingly's journal entry to record this transaction includes a
   a. Credit to Unearned Lawn Service Fees for $2,500.
   b. Debit to Lawn Service Fees Earned for $2,500.
   c. Credit to Cash for $2,500.
   d. Debit to Unearned Lawn Service Fees for $2,500.
   e. Credit to Common Stock for $2,500.

3. Liang Shue contributed $250,000 cash and land worth $500,000 to open his new business, Shue Consulting Corporation. Which of the following journal entries does Shue Consulting make to record this transaction?
   a. Cash Assets 750,000
      Common Stock   750,000
   b. Common Stock 750,000
      Assets   750,000
   c. Cash 250,000
      Land 500,000
      Common Stock   750,000
   d. Common Stock 750,000
      Cash   250,000
      Land   500,000

4. A trial balance prepared at year-end shows total credits exceed total debits by $765. This discrepancy could have been caused by
   a. An error in the general journal where a $765 increase in Accounts Payable was recorded as a $765 decrease in Accounts Payable.
   b. The ledger balance for Accounts Payable of $7,650 being entered in the trial balance as $765.
   c. A general journal error where a $765 increase in Accounts Receivable was recorded as a $765 increase in Cash.
   d. The ledger balance of $850 in Accounts Receivable was entered in the trial balance as $85.
   e. An error in recording a $765 increase in Cash as a credit.

5. Bonaventure Company has total assets of $1,000,000, liabilities of $400,000, and equity of $600,000. What is its debt ratio (rounded to a whole percent)?
   a. 250%
   b. 167%
   c. 67%
   d. 150%
   e. 40%

Icon denotes assignments that involve decision making.

Discussion Questions

1. Provide the names of two (a) asset accounts, (b) liability accounts, and (c) equity accounts.
2. What is the difference between a note payable and an account payable?
3. Discuss the steps in processing business transactions.
4. What kinds of transactions can be recorded in a general journal?
5. Are debits or credits typically listed first in general journal entries? Are the debits or the credits indented?
6. If assets are valuable resources and asset accounts have debit balances, why do expense accounts also have debit balances?
7. Should a transaction be recorded first in a journal or the ledger? Why?
8. Why does the recordkeeper prepare a trial balance?
9. If an incorrect amount is journalized and posted to the accounts, how should the error be corrected?
10. Identify the four financial statements of a business.
11. What information is reported in an income statement?
12. Why does the user of an income statement need to know the time period that it covers?
13. What information is reported in a balance sheet?
14. Define (a) assets, (b) liabilities, (c) equity, and (d) net assets.
15. Which financial statement is sometimes called the statement of financial position?
16. Review the **Research In Motion** balance sheet in Appendix A. Identify three accounts on its balance sheet that carry debit balances and three accounts on its balance sheet that carry credit balances.
17. Review the **Apple** balance sheet in Appendix A. Identify an asset with the word receivable in its account title and a liability with the word payable in its account title.
18. Locate **Palm**'s income statement in Appendix A. What is the title of its revenue account?
19. Refer to **Nokia**'s balance sheet in Appendix A. What does Nokia title its current asset referring to merchandise available for sale?

QUICK STUDY

QS 2-1
Identifying financial statement items
C2 P3

Identify the financial statement(s) where each of the following items appears. Use I for income statement, E for statement of retained earnings, and B for balance sheet.
- a. Accounts payable
- b. Cash
- c. Rent expense
- d. Office supplies
- e. Prepaid insurance
- f. Revenue
- g. Office equipment
- h. Cash dividends
- i. Unearned rent revenue

QS 2-2
Identifying source documents
C1

Identify the items from the following list that are likely to serve as source documents.
- a. Bank statement
- b. Sales ticket
- c. Income statement
- d. Trial balance
- e. Telephone bill
- f. Invoice from supplier
- g. Company revenue account
- h. Balance sheet
- i. Prepaid rent

QS 2-3
Analyzing debit or credit by account
A1

Identify whether a debit or credit yields the indicated change for each of the following accounts.
- a. To increase Store Equipment
- b. To increase Land
- c. To decrease Cash
- d. To increase Utilities Expense
- e. To increase Fees Earned
- f. To decrease Unearned Revenue
- g. To decrease Prepaid Insurance
- h. To increase Notes Payable
- i. To decrease Accounts Receivable
- j. To increase Common Stock

QS 2-4
Identifying normal balance
C4

Identify the normal balance (debit or credit) for each of the following accounts.
- a. Equipment
- b. Wages Expense
- c. Repair Services Revenue
- d. Office Supplies
- e. Dividends
- f. Accounts Receivable
- g. Prepaid Insurance
- h. Wages Payable
- i. Common Stock

QS 2-5
Linking debit or credit with normal balance
C4

Indicate whether a debit or credit *decreases* the normal balance of each of the following accounts.
- a. Land
- b. Service Revenue
- c. Interest Payable
- d. Accounts Receivable
- e. Salaries Expense
- f. Common Stock
- g. Prepaid Insurance
- h. Buildings
- i. Interest Revenue
- j. Dividends
- k. Unearned Revenue
- l. Accounts Payable

QS 2-6
Preparing journal entries
P1

Prepare journal entries for each of the following selected transactions.
- a. On January 15, Kolby Anderson opens a remodeling company called Fancy Kitchens by investing $75,000 cash along with equipment having a $30,000 value in exchange for common stock.
- b. On January 21, Fancy Kitchens purchases office supplies on credit for $650.
- c. On January 25, Fancy Kitchens receives $8,700 cash for performing remodeling services.
- d. On January 30, Fancy Kitchens receives $4,000 cash in advance of providing remodeling services to a customer.

QS 2-7
Identifying a posting error
P2

A trial balance has total debits of $20,000 and total credits of $24,500. Which one of the following errors would create this imbalance? Explain.
- a. A $2,250 debit posting to Accounts Receivable was posted mistakenly to Cash.
- b. A $4,500 debit posting to Equipment was posted mistakenly to Supplies.
- c. An entry debiting Cash and crediting Accounts Payable for $4,500 was mistakenly not posted.
- d. A $2,250 credit to Revenue in a journal entry is incorrectly posted to the ledger as a $2,250 debit, leaving the Revenue account with a $6,300 credit balance.
- e. A $4,500 debit to Rent Expense in a journal entry is incorrectly posted to the ledger as a $4,500 credit, leaving the Rent Expense account with a $750 debit balance.
- f. A $2,250 debit to Utilities Expense in a journal entry is incorrectly posted to the ledger as a $2,250 credit, leaving the Utilities Expense account with a $3,000 debit balance.

QS 2-8
Classifying accounts in financial statements
P3

Indicate the financial statement on which each of the following items appears. Use I for income statement, E for statement of retained earnings, and B for balance sheet.

a. Buildings
b. Interest Expense
c. Dividends
d. Office Supplies
e. Rental Revenue
f. Insurance Expense
g. Services Revenue
h. Interest Payable
i. Accounts Receivable
j. Salaries Expense
k. Equipment
l. Prepaid Insurance

QS 2-9
International accounting standards
C4

Answer each of the following questions related to international accounting standards.

a. What type of entry system is applied when accounting follows IFRS?
b. Identify the number and usual titles of the financial statements prepared under IFRS.
c. How do differences in accounting controls and enforcement impact accounting reports prepared across different countries?

EXERCISES

Exercise 2-1
Steps in analyzing and recording transactions C1

Order the following steps in the accounting process that focus on analyzing and recording transactions.

____ a. Record relevant transactions in a journal.
____ b. Prepare and analyze the trial balance.
____ c. Analyze each transaction from source documents.
____ d. Post journal information to ledger accounts.

Exercise 2-2
Identifying and classifying accounts
C2

Enter the number for the item that best completes each of the descriptions below.

1. Account
2. Three
3. Asset
4. Liability
5. Equity

a. Common stock and dividends are examples of ____ accounts.
b. Accounts payable, unearned revenue, and note payable are examples of ____ accounts.
c. Accounts receivable, prepaid accounts, supplies, and land are examples of ____ accounts.
d. Accounts are arranged into ____ general categories.
e. An ____ is a record of increases and decreases in a specific asset, liability, equity, revenue, or expense item.

Exercise 2-3
Identifying a ledger and chart of accounts
C3

Enter the number for the item that best completes each of the descriptions below.

1. General ledger
2. Chart

a. The ____ is a record containing all accounts used by a company.
b. A ____ of accounts is a list of all accounts a company uses.

Exercise 2-4
Identifying type and normal balances of accounts
C4

For each of the following (1) identify the type of account as an asset, liability, equity, revenue, or expense, (2) identify the normal balance of the account, and (3) enter *debit* (*Dr.*) or *credit* (*Cr.*) to identify the kind of entry that would increase the account balance.

a. Fees Earned
b. Equipment
c. Notes Payable
d. Common Stock
e. Cash
f. Legal Expense
g. Prepaid Insurance
h. Land
i. Accounts Receivable
j. Dividends
k. License Fee Revenue
l. Unearned Revenue

Exercise 2-5
Analyzing effects of transactions on accounts
A1

Taylor Co. bills a client $48,000 for services provided and agrees to accept the following three items in full payment: (1) $7,500 cash, (2) computer equipment worth $75,000, and (3) to assume responsibility for a $34,500 note payable related to the computer equipment. The entry Taylor makes to record this transaction includes which one or more of the following?

a. $34,500 increase in a liability account
b. $7,500 increase in the Cash account
c. $7,500 increase in a revenue account
d. $48,000 increase in an asset account
e. $48,000 increase in a revenue account
f. $34,500 increase in an equity account

Exercise 2-6
Analyzing account entries and balances
A1

Use the information in each of the following separate cases to calculate the unknown amount.

a. During October, Shandra Company had $97,500 of cash receipts and $101,250 of cash disbursements. The October 31 Cash balance was $16,800. Determine how much cash the company had at the close of business on September 30.

b. On September 30, Mordish Co. had a $97,500 balance in Accounts Receivable. During October, the company collected $88,950 from its credit customers. The October 31 balance in Accounts Receivable was $100,500. Determine the amount of sales on account that occurred in October.

c. Nasser Co. had $147,000 of accounts payable on September 30 and $136,500 on October 31. Total purchases on account during October were $270,000. Determine how much cash was paid on accounts payable during October.

Exercise 2-7
Preparing general journal entries
P1

Prepare general journal entries for the following transactions of a new company called Pose for Pics.

Aug. 1 Kasey Madison, the owner, invested $7,500 cash and $32,500 of photography equipment in the company in exchange for common stock.
2 The company paid $3,000 cash for an insurance policy covering the next 24 months.
5 The company purchased office supplies for $1,400 cash.
20 The company received $2,650 cash in photography fees earned.
31 The company paid $875 cash for August utilities.

Exercise 2-8
Preparing T-accounts (ledger) and a trial balance P2

Use the information in Exercise 2-7 to prepare an August 31 trial balance for Pose for Pics. Begin by opening these T-accounts: Cash; Office Supplies; Prepaid Insurance; Photography Equipment; Common Stock; Photography Fees Earned; and Utilities Expense. Then, post the general journal entries to these T-accounts (which will serve as the ledger), and prepare the trial balance.

Exercise 2-9
Recording effects of transactions in T-accounts
A1

Prepare general journal entries to record the transactions below for Dexter Company by using the following accounts: Cash; Accounts Receivable; Office Supplies; Office Equipment; Accounts Payable; Common Stock; Dividends; Fees Earned; and Rent Expense. Use the letters beside each transaction to identify entries. After recording the transactions, post them to T-accounts, which serves as the general ledger for this assignment. Determine the ending balance of each T-account.

a. Macy Dexter, owner, invested $12,750 cash in the company in exchange for common stock.
b. The company purchased office supplies for $375 cash.
c. The company purchased $7,050 of office equipment on credit.
d. The company received $1,500 cash as fees for services provided to a customer.
e. The company paid $7,050 cash to settle the payable for the office equipment purchased in transaction c.
f. The company billed a customer $2,700 as fees for services provided.
g. The company paid $525 cash for the monthly rent.
h. The company collected $1,125 cash as partial payment for the account receivable created in transaction f.
i. The company paid $1,000 cash for dividends.

Check Cash ending balance, $6,425

Exercise 2-10
Preparing a trial balance P2

After recording the transactions of Exercise 2-9 in T-accounts and calculating the balance of each account, prepare a trial balance. Use May 31, 2011, as its report date.

Exercise 2-11
Analyzing and journalizing revenue transactions
A1 P1

Examine the following transactions and identify those that create revenues for Jade Services, a company owned by Mia Jade. Prepare general journal entries to record those revenue transactions and explain why the other transactions did not create revenues.

a. Mia Jade invests $38,250 cash in the company in exchange for common stock.
b. The company provided $1,350 of services on credit.
c. The company provided services to a client and immediately received $1,575 cash.
d. The company received $9,150 cash from a client in payment for services to be provided next year.
e. The company received $4,500 cash from a client in partial payment of an account receivable.
f. The company borrowed $150,000 cash from the bank by signing a promissory note.

Exercise 2-12
Analyzing and journalizing expense transactions
A1 P1

Examine the following transactions and identify those that create expenses for Jade Services. Prepare general journal entries to record those expense transactions and explain why the other transactions did not create expenses.

a. The company paid $14,100 cash for payment on a 14-month old liability for office supplies.
b. The company paid $1,125 cash for the just completed two-week salary of the receptionist.
c. The company paid $45,000 cash for equipment purchased.
d. The company paid $930 cash for this month's utilities.
e. The company paid $5,000 cash for dividends.

Exercise 2-13
Preparing an income statement
C3 P3

Dominick Lopez operates a consulting firm called Tech Today, which began operations on August 1. On August 31, the company's records show the following accounts and amounts for the month of August. Use this information to prepare an August income statement for the business.

Cash	$ 8,360	Dividends	$ 3,000
Accounts receivable	17,000	Consulting fees earned	17,000
Office supplies	3,250	Rent expense	4,550
Land	46,000	Salaries expense	8,000
Office equipment	18,000	Telephone expense	560
Accounts payable	8,000	Miscellaneous expenses	280
Common Stock	84,000		

Check Net income, $3,610

Exercise 2-14
Preparing a statement of retained earnings P3

Use the information in Exercise 2-13 to prepare an August statement of retained earnings for Tech Today. (The owner invested $84,000 cash in the company in exchange for common stock on August 1.)

Check End. Ret. Earn., $610

Exercise 2-15
Preparing a balance sheet P3

Use the information in Exercise 2-13 (if completed, you can also use your solution to Exercise 2-14) to prepare an August 31 balance sheet for Tech Today.

Exercise 2-16
Computing net income
A1

A corporation had the following assets and liabilities at the beginning and end of this year.

	Assets	Liabilities
Beginning of the year	$ 70,000	$30,000
End of the year	115,000	46,000

Determine the net income earned or net loss incurred by the business during the year for each of the following *separate* cases:

a. Owner made no investments in the business and no dividends were paid during the year.
b. Owner made no investments in the business, but dividends were $1,250 cash per month.
c. No dividends were paid during the year, but the owner did invest an additional $45,000 cash in exchange for common stock.
d. Dividends were $1,250 cash per month and the owner invested an additional $25,000 cash in exchange for common stock.

Exercise 2-17
Analyzing changes in a company's equity
P3

Compute the missing amount for each of the following separate companies *a* through *d*.

	(a)	(b)	(c)	(d)
Equity, December 31, 2010	$ 0	$ 0	$ 0	$ 0
Owner investments during the year	120,000	?	87,000	210,000
Dividends during the year	?	54,000	10,000	55,000
Net income (loss) for the year	31,500	81,000	(4,000)	?
Equity, December 31, 2011	102,000	99,000	?	110,000

Exercise 2-18
Interpreting and describing transactions from T-accounts
A1

Assume the following T-accounts reflect Joy Co.'s general ledger and that seven transactions *a* through *g* are posted to them. Provide a short description of each transaction. Include the amounts in your descriptions.

Cash			
(a)	7,000	(b)	3,600
(e)	2,500	(c)	600
		(f)	2,400
		(g)	700

Office Supplies			
(c)	600		
(d)	200		

Prepaid Insurance			
(b)	3,600		

Equipment			
(a)	5,600		
(d)	9,400		

Automobiles			
(a)	11,000		

Accounts Payable			
(f)	2,400	(d)	9,600

Common Stock			
		(a)	23,600

Delivery Services Revenue			
		(e)	2,500

Gas and Oil Expense			
(g)	700		

Exercise 2-19
Preparing general journal entries
P1

Use information from the T-accounts in Exercise 2-18 to prepare general journal entries for each of the seven transactions *a* through *g*.

Exercise 2-20
Identifying effects of posting errors on the trial balance
A1 P2

Posting errors are identified in the following table. In column (1), enter the amount of the difference between the two trial balance columns (debit and credit) due to the error. In column (2), identify the trial balance column (debit or credit) with the larger amount if they are not equal. In column (3), identify the account(s) affected by the error. In column (4), indicate the amount by which the account(s) in column (3) is under- or overstated. Item (a) is completed as an example.

	Description of Posting Error	(1) Difference between Debit and Credit Columns	(2) Column with the Larger Total	(3) Identify Account(s) Incorrectly Stated	(4) Amount that Account(s) Is Over- or Understated
a.	$2,400 debit to Rent Expense is posted as a $1,590 debit.	$810	Credit	Rent Expense	Rent Expense understated $810
b.	$4,050 credit to Cash is posted twice as two credits to Cash.				
c.	$9,900 debit to the Dividends account is debited to Common Stock.				
d.	$2,250 debit to Prepaid Insurance is posted as a debit to Insurance Expense.				
e.	$42,000 debit to Machinery is posted as a debit to Accounts Payable.				
f.	$4,950 credit to Services Revenue is posted as a $495 credit.				
g.	$1,440 debit to Store Supplies is not posted.				

Exercise 2-21
Analyzing a trial balance error
A1 P2

You are told the column totals in a trial balance are not equal. After careful analysis, you discover only one error. Specifically, a correctly journalized credit purchase of a computer for $16,950 is posted from the journal to the ledger with a $16,950 debit to Office Equipment and another $16,950 debit to Accounts Payable. The Office Equipment account has a debit balance of $40,100 on the trial balance. Answer each of the following questions and compute the dollar amount of any misstatement.

a. Is the debit column total of the trial balance overstated, understated, or correctly stated?
b. Is the credit column total of the trial balance overstated, understated, or correctly stated?
c. Is the Office Equipment account balance overstated, understated, or correctly stated in the trial balance?
d. Is the Accounts Payable account balance overstated, understated, or correctly stated in the trial balance?
e. If the debit column total of the trial balance is $360,000 before correcting the error, what is the total of the credit column before correction?

Exercise 2-22
Interpreting the debt ratio and return on assets

A2

a. Calculate the debt ratio and the return on assets using the year-end information for each of the following six separate companies ($ thousands).

Case	Assets	Liabilities	Average Assets	Net Income
Company 1	$147,000	$56,000	$200,000	$21,000
Company 2	104,500	51,500	70,000	12,000
Company 3	90,500	12,000	100,000	20,000
Company 4	92,000	31,000	40,000	7,500
Company 5	64,000	47,000	40,000	3,800
Company 6	32,500	26,500	50,000	660

b. Of the six companies, which business relies most heavily on creditor financing?
c. Of the six companies, which business relies most heavily on equity financing?
d. Which two companies indicate the greatest risk?
e. Which two companies earn the highest return on assets?
f. Which one company would investors likely prefer based on the risk–return relation?

Exercise 2-23
Preparing a balance sheet following IFRS

P3

BMW reports the following balance sheet accounts for the year ended December 31, 2009 (euro in millions). Prepare the balance sheet for this company as of December 31, 2009, following the usual IFRS formats.

Current liabilities	€ 8,350	Noncurrent liabilities	€10,943
Current assets	17,663	Noncurrent assets	6,984
Total equity	5,354		

PROBLEM SET A

Problem 2-1A
Preparing and posting journal entries; preparing a trial balance

C3 C4 A1 P1 P2

mhhe.com/wildFA6e

Gary Bauer opens a computer consulting business called Technology Consultants and completes the following transactions in April.

April 1 Bauer invested $100,000 cash along with $24,000 in office equipment in the company in exchange for common stock.
2 The company prepaid $7,200 cash for twelve months' rent for an office. (*Hint:* Debit Prepaid Rent for $7,200.)
3 The company made credit purchases of office equipment for $12,000 and office supplies for $2,400. Payment is due within 10 days.
6 The company completed services for a client and immediately received $2,000 cash.
9 The company completed an $8,000 project for a client, who must pay within 30 days.
13 The company paid $14,400 cash to settle the account payable created on April 3.
19 The company paid $6,000 cash for the premium on a 12-month insurance policy. (*Hint:* Debit Prepaid Insurance for $6,000.)
22 The company received $6,400 cash as partial payment for the work completed on April 9.
25 The company completed work for another client for $2,640 on credit.
28 The company paid $6,200 cash for dividends.
29 The company purchased $800 of additional office supplies on credit.
30 The company paid $700 cash for this month's utility bill.

Required

1. Prepare general journal entries to record these transactions (use the account titles listed in part 2).
2. Open the following ledger accounts—their account numbers are in parentheses (use the balance column format): Cash (101); Accounts Receivable (106); Office Supplies (124); Prepaid Insurance (128);

Prepaid Rent (131); Office Equipment (163); Accounts Payable (201); Common Stock (307); Dividends (319); Services Revenue (403); and Utilities Expense (690). Post the journal entries from part 1 to the ledger accounts and enter the balance after each posting.

3. Prepare a trial balance as of the end of April.

Check (2) Ending balances: Cash, $73,900; Accounts Receivable, $4,240; Accounts Payable, $800
(3) Total debits, $137,440

Shelton Engineering completed the following transactions in the month of June.

a. Shana Shelton, the owner, invested $105,000 cash, office equipment with a value of $6,000, and $45,000 of drafting equipment to launch the company in exchange for common stock.
b. The company purchased land worth $54,000 for an office by paying $5,400 cash and signing a long-term note payable for $48,600.
c. The company purchased a portable building with $75,000 cash and moved it onto the land acquired in b.
d. The company paid $6,000 cash for the premium on an 18-month insurance policy.
e. The company completed and delivered a set of plans for a client and collected $5,700 cash.
f. The company purchased $22,500 of additional drafting equipment by paying $10,500 cash and signing a long-term note payable for $12,000.
g. The company completed $12,000 of engineering services for a client. This amount is to be received in 30 days.
h. The company purchased $2,250 of additional office equipment on credit.
i. The company completed engineering services for $18,000 on credit.
j. The company received a bill for rent of equipment that was used on a recently completed job. The $1,200 rent cost must be paid within 30 days.
k. The company collected $7,200 cash in partial payment from the client described in transaction g.
l. The company paid $1,500 cash for wages to a drafting assistant.
m. The company paid $2,250 cash to settle the account payable created in transaction h.
n. The company paid $675 cash for minor maintenance of its drafting equipment.
o. The company paid $9,360 cash for dividends.
p. The company paid $1,500 cash for wages to a drafting assistant.
q. The company paid $3,000 cash for advertisements in the local newspaper during June.

Problem 2-2A
Preparing and posting journal entries; preparing a trial balance
C3 C4 A1 P1 P2

Required

1. Prepare general journal entries to record these transactions (use the account titles listed in part 2).
2. Open the following ledger accounts—their account numbers are in parentheses (use the balance column format): Cash (101); Accounts Receivable (106); Prepaid Insurance (108); Office Equipment (163); Drafting Equipment (164); Building (170); Land (172); Accounts Payable (201); Notes Payable (250); Common Stock (307); Dividends (319); Engineering Fees Earned (402); Wages Expense (601); Equipment Rental Expense (602); Advertising Expense (603); and Repairs Expense (604). Post the journal entries from part 1 to the accounts and enter the balance after each posting.
3. Prepare a trial balance as of the end of June.

Check (2) Ending balances: Cash, $2,715; Accounts Receivable, $22,800; Accounts Payable, $1,200

(3) Trial balance totals, $253,500

The accounting records of Fabiano Distribution show the following assets and liabilities as of December 31, 2010 and 2011.

December 31	2010	2011
Cash	$ 52,500	$ 18,750
Accounts receivable	28,500	22,350
Office supplies	4,500	3,300
Office equipment	138,000	147,000
Trucks	54,000	54,000
Building	0	180,000
Land	0	45,000
Accounts payable	7,500	37,500
Note payable	0	105,000

Problem 2-3A
Computing net income from equity analysis, preparing a balance sheet, and computing the debt ratio
C2 A1 A2 P3

mhhe.com/wildFA6e

Late in December 2011, the business purchased a small office building and land for $225,000. It paid $120,000 cash toward the purchase and a $105,000 note payable was signed for the balance. Mr. Fabiano had to invest $35,000 cash in the business (in exchange for stock) to enable it to pay the $120,000 cash. The business also pays $3,000 cash per month for dividends.

Required

1. Prepare balance sheets for the business as of December 31, 2010 and 2011. (*Hint:* Report only total equity on the balance sheet and remember that total equity equals the difference between assets and liabilities.)
2. By comparing equity amounts from the balance sheets and using the additional information presented in this problem, prepare a calculation to show how much net income was earned by the business during 2011.
3. Compute the 2011 year-end debt ratio for the business.

Check (2) Net income, $58,900

(3) Debt ratio, 30.29%

Problem 2-4A
Preparing and posting journal entries; preparing a trial balance
C3 C4 A1 P1 P2

Santo Birch opens a Web consulting business called Show-Me-the-Money and completes the following transactions in its first month of operations.

March 1 Birch invests $150,000 cash along with office equipment valued at $22,000 in the company in exchange for common stock.
2 The company prepaid $6,000 cash for twelve months' rent for office space. (*Hint:* Debit Prepaid Rent for $6,000.)
3 The company made credit purchases for $3,000 in office equipment and $1,200 in office supplies. Payment is due within 10 days.
6 The company completed services for a client and immediately received $4,000 cash.
9 The company completed a $7,500 project for a client, who must pay within 30 days.
13 The company paid $4,200 cash to settle the account payable created on March 3.
19 The company paid $5,000 cash for the premium on a 12-month insurance policy. (*Hint:* Debit Prepaid Insurance for $5,000.)
22 The company received $3,500 cash as partial payment for the work completed on March 9.
25 The company completed work for another client for $3,820 on credit.
29 The company paid $5,100 cash for dividends.
30 The company purchased $600 of additional office supplies on credit.
31 The company paid $200 cash for this month's utility bill.

Required

1. Prepare general journal entries to record these transactions (use account titles listed in part 2).
2. Open the following ledger accounts—their account numbers are in parentheses (use the balance column format): Cash (101); Accounts Receivable (106); Office Supplies (124); Prepaid Insurance (128); Prepaid Rent (131); Office Equipment (163); Accounts Payable (201); Common Stock (307); Dividends (319); Services Revenue (403); and Utilities Expense (690). Post journal entries from part 1 to the ledger accounts and enter the balance after each posting.
3. Prepare a trial balance as of March 31.

Check (2) Ending balances: Cash, $137,000; Accounts Receivable, $7,820; Accounts Payable, $600

(3) Total debits, $187,920

Problem 2-5A
Recording transactions; posting to ledger; preparing a trial balance
C3 A1 P1 P2

Business transactions completed by Eric Pense during the month of September are as follows.

a. Pense invested $23,000 cash along with office equipment valued at $12,000 in exchange for common stock of a new company named EP Consulting.
b. The company purchased land valued at $8,000 and a building valued at $33,000. The purchase is paid with $15,000 cash and a long-term note payable for $26,000.
c. The company purchased $600 of office supplies on credit.
d. Pense invested his personal automobile in the company in exchange for more common stock. The automobile has a value of $7,000 and is to be used exclusively in the business.
e. The company purchased $1,100 of additional office equipment on credit.
f. The company paid $800 cash salary to an assistant.
g. The company provided services to a client and collected $2,700 cash.
h. The company paid $430 cash for this month's utilities.
i. The company paid $600 cash to settle the account payable created in transaction *c*.
j. The company purchased $4,000 of new office equipment by paying $4,000 cash.
k. The company completed $2,400 of services for a client, who must pay within 30 days.
l. The company paid $800 cash salary to an assistant.
m. The company received $1,000 cash in partial payment on the receivable created in transaction *k*.
n. The company paid $1,050 cash for dividends.

Required

1. Prepare general journal entries to record these transactions (use account titles listed in part 2).
2. Open the following ledger accounts—their account numbers are in parentheses (use the balance column format): Cash (101); Accounts Receivable (106); Office Supplies (108); Office Equipment (163); Automobiles (164); Building (170); Land (172); Accounts Payable (201); Notes Payable (250); Common Stock (307); Dividends (319); Fees Earned (402); Salaries Expense (601); and Utilities Expense (602). Post the journal entries from part 1 to the ledger accounts and enter the balance after each posting.
3. Prepare a trial balance as of the end of September.

Check (2) Ending balances: Cash, $4,020; Office Equipment, $17,100

(3) Trial balance totals, $74,200

Carlos Beltran started an engineering firm called Beltran Engineering. He began operations and completed seven transactions in May, which included his initial investment of $17,000 cash. After those seven transactions, the ledger included the following accounts with normal balances.

Problem 2-6A
Analyzing account balances and reconstructing transactions

C1　C3　A1　P2

Cash	$26,660
Office supplies	660
Prepaid insurance	3,200
Office equipment	16,500
Accounts payable	16,500
Common Stock	17,000
Dividends	3,740
Engineering fees earned	24,000
Rent expense	6,740

Required

1. Prepare a trial balance for this business as of the end of May.

Analysis Components

2. Analyze the accounts and their balances and prepare a list that describes each of the seven most likely transactions and their amounts.
3. Prepare a report of cash received and cash paid showing how the seven transactions in part 2 yield the $26,660 ending Cash balance.

Check (1) Trial balance totals, $57,500

(3) Cash paid, $14,340

Shaw Management Services opens for business and completes these transactions in November.

Nov. 1　Kita Shaw, the owner, invested $30,000 cash along with $15,000 of office equipment in the company in exchange for common stock.
　　2　The company prepaid $4,500 cash for six months' rent for an office. (*Hint:* Debit Prepaid Rent for $4,500.)
　　4　The company made credit purchases of office equipment for $2,500 and of office supplies for $600. Payment is due within 10 days.
　　8　The company completed work for a client and immediately received $3,400 cash.
　12　The company completed a $10,200 project for a client, who must pay within 30 days.
　13　The company paid $3,100 cash to settle the payable created on November 4.
　19　The company paid $1,800 cash for the premium on a 24-month insurance policy.
　22　The company received $5,200 cash as partial payment for the work completed on November 12.
　24　The company completed work for another client for $1,750 on credit.
　28　The company paid $5,300 cash for dividends.
　29　The company purchased $249 of additional office supplies on credit.
　30　The company paid $531 cash for this month's utility bill.

PROBLEM SET B

Problem 2-1B
Preparing and posting journal entries; preparing a trial balance

C3　C4　A1　P1　P2

Required

1. Prepare general journal entries to record these transactions (use account titles listed in part 2).
2. Open the following ledger accounts—their account numbers are in parentheses (use the balance column format): Cash (101); Accounts Receivable (106); Office Supplies (124); Prepaid Insurance (128); Prepaid Rent (131); Office Equipment (163); Accounts Payable (201); Common Stock (307); Dividends (319); Services Revenue (403); and Utilities Expense (690). Post the journal entries from part 1 to the ledger accounts and enter the balance after each posting.
3. Prepare a trial balance as of the end of November.

Check (2) Ending balances: Cash, $23,369; Accounts Receivable, $6,750; Accounts Payable, $249

(3) Total debits, $60,599

Problem 2-2B
Preparing and posting journal entries; preparing a trial balance
C3 C4 A1 P1 P2

At the beginning of April, Brooke Gable launched a custom computer solutions company called Softways. The company had the following transactions during April.

a. Brooke Gable invested $45,000 cash, office equipment with a value of $4,500, and $28,000 of computer equipment in the company in exchange for common stock.
b. The company purchased land worth $24,000 for an office by paying $4,800 cash and signing a long-term note payable for $19,200.
c. The company purchased a portable building with $21,000 cash and moved it onto the land acquired in b.
d. The company paid $6,600 cash for the premium on a two-year insurance policy.
e. The company provided services to a client and immediately collected $3,200 cash.
f. The company purchased $3,500 of additional computer equipment by paying $700 cash and signing a long-term note payable for $2,800.
g. The company completed $3,750 of services for a client. This amount is to be received within 30 days.
h. The company purchased $750 of additional office equipment on credit.
i. The company completed client services for $9,200 on credit.
j. The company received a bill for rent of a computer testing device that was used on a recently completed job. The $320 rent cost must be paid within 30 days.
k. The company collected $4,600 cash in partial payment from the client described in transaction i.
l. The company paid $1,600 cash for wages to an assistant.
m. The company paid $750 cash to settle the payable created in transaction h.
n. The company paid $425 cash for minor maintenance of the company's computer equipment.
o. The company paid $3,875 cash for dividends.
p. The company paid $1,600 cash for wages to an assistant.
q. The company paid $800 cash for advertisements in the local newspaper during April.

Required

1. Prepare general journal entries to record these transactions (use account titles listed in part 2).

Check (2) Ending balances: Cash, $10,650; Accounts Receivable, $8,350; Accounts Payable, $320

2. Open the following ledger accounts—their account numbers are in parentheses (use the balance column format): Cash (101); Accounts Receivable (106); Prepaid Insurance (108); Office Equipment (163); Computer Equipment (164); Building (170); Land (172); Accounts Payable (201); Notes Payable (250); Common Stock (307); Dividends (319); Fees Earned (402); Wages Expense (601); Computer Rental Expense (602); Advertising Expense (603); and Repairs Expense (604). Post the journal entries from part 1 to the accounts and enter the balance after each posting.

(3) Trial balance totals, $115,970

3. Prepare a trial balance as of the end of April.

Problem 2-3B
Computing net income from equity analysis, preparing a balance sheet, and computing the debt ratio
C2 A1 A2 P3

The accounting records of Schmit Co. show the following assets and liabilities as of December 31, 2010 and 2011.

December 31	2010	2011
Cash	$14,000	$10,000
Accounts receivable	25,000	30,000
Office supplies	10,000	12,500
Office equipment	60,000	60,000
Machinery	30,500	30,500
Building	0	260,000
Land	0	65,000
Accounts payable	5,000	15,000
Note payable	0	260,000

Late in December 2011, the business purchased a small office building and land for $325,000. It paid $65,000 cash toward the purchase and a $260,000 note payable was signed for the balance. Janet Schmit, the owner, had to invest an additional $25,000 cash (in exchange for common stock) to enable it to pay the $65,000 cash toward the purchase. The company also pays $1,000 cash per month for dividends.

Required

1. Prepare balance sheets for the business as of December 31, 2010 and 2011. (*Hint:* Report only total equity on the balance sheet and remember that total equity equals the difference between assets and liabilities.)

2. By comparing equity amounts from the balance sheets and using the additional information presented in the problem, prepare a calculation to show how much net income was earned by the business during 2011.
3. Calculate the December 31, 2011, debt ratio for the business.

Check (2) Net income, $45,500

(3) Debt ratio, 58.76%

Lummus Management Services opens for business and completes these transactions in September.

Sept. 1 Rhonda Lummus, the owner, invests $28,000 cash along with office equipment valued at $25,000 in the company in exchange for common stock.
 2 The company prepaid $10,500 cash for 12 months' rent for office space. (*Hint:* Debit Prepaid Rent for $10,500.)
 4 The company made credit purchases for $9,000 in office equipment and $1,200 in office supplies. Payment is due within 10 days.
 8 The company completed work for a client and immediately received $2,600 cash.
 12 The company completed a $13,400 project for a client, who must pay within 30 days.
 13 The company paid $10,200 cash to settle the payable created on September 4.
 19 The company paid $5,200 cash for the premium on an 18-month insurance policy. (*Hint:* Debit Prepaid Insurance for $5,200.)
 22 The company received $7,800 cash as partial payment for the work completed on September 12.
 24 The company completed work for another client for $1,900 on credit.
 28 The company paid $5,300 cash for dividends.
 29 The company purchased $1,700 of additional office supplies on credit.
 30 The company paid $460 cash for this month's utility bill.

Problem 2-4B
Preparing and posting journal entries; preparing a trial balance
C3 C4 A1 P1 P2

Required

1. Prepare general journal entries to record these transactions (use account titles listed in part 2).
2. Open the following ledger accounts—their account numbers are in parentheses (use the balance column format): Cash (101); Accounts Receivable (106); Office Supplies (124); Prepaid Insurance (128); Prepaid Rent (131); Office Equipment (163); Accounts Payable (201); Common Stock (307); Dividends (319); Service Fees Earned (401); and Utilities Expense (690). Post journal entries from part 1 to the ledger accounts and enter the balance after each posting.
3. Prepare a trial balance as of the end of September.

Check (2) Ending balances: Cash, $6,740; Accounts Receivable, $7,500; Accounts Payable, $1,700

(3) Total debits, $72,600

Cooke Consulting completed the following transactions during June.

a. Chris Cooke, the owner, invested $80,000 cash along with office equipment valued at $30,000 in the new company in exchange for common stock.
b. The company purchased land valued at $30,000 and a building valued at $170,000. The purchase is paid with $40,000 cash and a long-term note payable for $160,000.
c. The company purchased $2,400 of office supplies on credit.
d. C. Cooke invested his personal automobile in the company in exchange for more common stock. The automobile has a value of $18,000 and is to be used exclusively in the business.
e. The company purchased $6,000 of additional office equipment on credit.
f. The company paid $1,500 cash salary to an assistant.
g. The company provided services to a client and collected $6,000 cash.
h. The company paid $800 cash for this month's utilities.
i. The company paid $2,400 cash to settle the payable created in transaction *c*.
j. The company purchased $20,000 of new office equipment by paying $20,000 cash.
k. The company completed $5,200 of services for a client, who must pay within 30 days.
l. The company paid $1,500 cash salary to an assistant.
m. The company received $3,800 cash in partial payment on the receivable created in transaction *k*.
n. The company paid $6,400 cash for dividends.

Problem 2-5B
Recording transactions; posting to ledger; preparing a trial balance
C3 A1 P1 P2

Required

1. Prepare general journal entries to record these transactions (use account titles listed in part 2).
2. Open the following ledger accounts—their account numbers are in parentheses (use the balance column format): Cash (101); Accounts Receivable (106); Office Supplies (108); Office Equipment (163); Automobiles (164); Building (170); Land (172); Accounts Payable (201); Notes Payable (250); Common Stock (307); Dividends (319); Fees Earned (402); Salaries Expense (601); and Utilities Expense (602). Post the journal entries from part 1 to the ledger accounts and enter the balance after each posting.
3. Prepare a trial balance as of the end of June.

Check (2) Ending balances: Cash, $17,200; Office Equipment, $56,000

(3) Trial balance totals, $305,200

Problem 2-6B
Analyzing account balances and reconstructing transactions
C1 C3 A1 P2

Michael Gould started a Web consulting firm called Gould Solutions. He began operations and completed seven transactions in April that resulted in the following accounts, which all have normal balances.

Cash	$12,485
Office supplies	560
Prepaid rent	1,500
Office equipment	11,450
Accounts payable	11,450
Common Stock	10,000
Dividends	6,200
Consulting fees earned	16,400
Operating expenses	5,655

Required

Check (1) Trial balance total, $37,850

1. Prepare a trial balance for this business as of the end of April.

Analysis Component

2. Analyze the accounts and their balances and prepare a list that describes each of the seven most likely transactions and their amounts.

(3) Cash paid, $13,915

3. Prepare a report of cash received and cash paid showing how the seven transactions in part 2 yield the $12,485 ending Cash balance.

SERIAL PROBLEM
Business Solutions
A1 P1 P2

(This serial problem started in Chapter 1 and continues through most of the chapters. If the Chapter 1 segment was not completed, the problem can begin at this point. It is helpful, but not necessary, to use the Working Papers that accompany this book.)

SP 2 On October 1, 2011, Santana Rey launched a computer services company called **Business Solutions,** which provides consulting services, computer system installations, and custom program development. Rey adopts the calendar year for reporting purposes and expects to prepare the company's first set of financial statements on December 31, 2011. The company's initial chart of accounts follows.

Account	No.	Account	No.
Cash	101	Common Stock	307
Accounts Receivable	106	Dividends	319
Computer Supplies	126	Computer Services Revenue	403
Prepaid Insurance	128	Wages Expense	623
Prepaid Rent	131	Advertising Expense	655
Office Equipment	163	Mileage Expense	676
Computer Equipment	167	Miscellaneous Expenses	677
Accounts Payable	201	Repairs Expense—Computer	684

Required

1. Prepare journal entries to record each of the following transactions for Business Solutions.

Oct. 1 S. Rey invested $45,000 cash, a $20,000 computer system, and $8,000 of office equipment in the company in exchange for its common stock.
 2 The company paid $3,300 cash for four months' rent. (*Hint:* Debit Prepaid Rent for $3,300.)
 3 The company purchased $1,420 of computer supplies on credit from Harris Office Products.
 5 The company paid $2,220 cash for one year's premium on a property and liability insurance policy. (*Hint:* Debit Prepaid Insurance for $2,220.)
 6 The company billed Easy Leasing $4,800 for services performed in installing a new Web server.
 8 The company paid $1,420 cash for the computer supplies purchased from Harris Office Products on October 3.
 10 The company hired Lyn Addie as a part-time assistant for $125 per day, as needed.
 12 The company billed Easy Leasing another $1,400 for services performed.

15	The company received $4,800 cash from Easy Leasing as partial payment on its account.	
17	The company paid $805 cash to repair computer equipment that was damaged when moving it.	
20	The company paid $1,728 cash for advertisements published in the local newspaper.	
22	The company received $1,400 cash from Easy Leasing on its account.	
28	The company billed IFM Company $5,208 for services performed.	
31	The company paid $875 cash for Lyn Addie's wages for seven days' work.	
31	The company paid $3,600 cash for dividends.	
Nov. 1	The company reimbursed S. Rey in cash for business automobile mileage allowance (Rey logged 1,000 miles at $0.32 per mile).	
2	The company received $4,633 cash from Liu Corporation for computer services performed.	
5	The company purchased computer supplies for $1,125 cash from Harris Office Products.	
8	The company billed Gomez Co. $5,668 for services performed.	
13	The company received notification from Alex's Engineering Co. that Business Solutions' bid of $3,950 for an upcoming project is accepted.	
18	The company received $2,208 cash from IFM Company as partial payment of the October 28 bill.	
22	The company donated $250 cash to the United Way in the company's name.	
24	The company completed work for Alex's Engineering Co. and sent it a bill for $3,950.	
25	The company sent another bill to IFM Company for the past-due amount of $3,000.	
28	The company reimbursed S. Rey in cash for business automobile mileage (1,200 miles at $0.32 per mile).	
30	The company paid $1,750 cash for Lyn Addie's wages for 14 days' work.	
30	The company paid $2,000 cash for dividends.	

2. Open ledger accounts (in balance column format) and post the journal entries from part 1 to them.

3. Prepare a trial balance as of the end of November.

Check (2) Cash, Nov. 30 bal., $38,264
(3) Trial bal. totals, $98,659

Beyond the Numbers

BTN 2-1 Refer to **Research In Motion**'s financial statements in Appendix A for the following questions.

Required

1. What amount of total liabilities does it report for each of the fiscal years ended February 28, 2009, and February 27, 2010?
2. What amount of total assets does it report for each of the fiscal years ended February 28, 2009, and February 27, 2010?
3. Compute its debt ratio for each of the fiscal years ended February 28, 2009, and February 27, 2010.
4. In which fiscal year did it employ more financial leverage (February 28, 2009, or February 27, 2010)? Explain.

Fast Forward

5. Access its financial statements (10-K report) for a fiscal year ending after February 27, 2010, from its Website (**RIM.com**) or the SEC's EDGAR database (**www.sec.gov**). Recompute its debt ratio for any subsequent year's data and compare it with the debt ratio for 2009 and 2010.

REPORTING IN ACTION
A1 A2
RIM

BTN 2-2 Key comparative figures for **Research In Motion** and **Apple** follow.

	Research In Motion		Apple	
($ millions)	Current Year	Prior Year	Current Year	Prior Year
Total liabilities	$ 2,602	$ 2,227	$15,861	$13,874
Total assets	10,204	8,101	47,501	36,171

COMPARATIVE ANALYSIS
A1 A2
RIM
Apple

1. What is the debt ratio for Research In Motion in the current year and for the prior year?
2. What is the debt ratio for Apple in the current year and for the prior year?
3. Which of the two companies has the higher degree of financial leverage? What does this imply?

ETHICS CHALLENGE
C1

BTN 2-3 Review the *Decision Ethics* case from the first part of this chapter involving the cashier. The guidance answer suggests that you should not comply with the assistant manager's request.

Required

Propose and evaluate two other courses of action you might consider, and explain why.

COMMUNICATING IN PRACTICE
C1 C2 A1 P3

BTN 2-4 Mora Stanley is an aspiring entrepreneur and your friend. She is having difficulty understanding the purposes of financial statements and how they fit together across time.

Required

Write a one-page memorandum to Stanley explaining the purposes of the four financial statements and how they are linked across time.

TAKING IT TO THE NET
A1

BTN 2-5 Access EDGAR online (www.sec.gov) and locate the 2009 year 10-K report of **Amazon.com** (ticker AMZN) filed on January 29, 2010. Review its financial statements reported for years ended 2009, 2008, and 2007 to answer the following questions.

Required

1. What are the amounts of its net income or net loss reported for each of these three years?
2. Do Amazon's operating activities provide cash or use cash for each of these three years?
3. If Amazon has a 2009 net income of more than $900 million and 2009 operating cash flows of more than $3,000 million, how is it possible that its cash balance at December 31, 2009, increases by less than $700 million relative to its balance at December 31, 2008?

TEAMWORK IN ACTION
C1 C2 C4 A1

BTN 2-6 The expanded accounting equation consists of assets, liabilities, common stock, dividends, revenues, and expenses. It can be used to reveal insights into changes in a company's financial position.

Required

1. Form *learning teams* of six (or more) members. Each team member must select one of the six components and each team must have at least one expert on each component: (*a*) assets, (*b*) liabilities, (*c*) common stock, (*d*) dividends, (*e*) revenues, and (*f*) expenses.
2. Form *expert teams* of individuals who selected the same component in part 1. Expert teams are to draft a report that each expert will present to his or her learning team addressing the following:
   a. Identify for its component the (i) increase and decrease side of the account and (ii) normal balance side of the account.
   b. Describe a transaction, with amounts, that increases its component.
   c. Using the transaction and amounts in (*b*), verify the equality of the accounting equation and then explain any effects on the income statement and statement of cash flows.
   d. Describe a transaction, with amounts, that decreases its component.
   e. Using the transaction and amounts in (*d*), verify the equality of the accounting equation and then explain any effects on the income statement and statement of cash flows.
3. Each expert should return to his/her learning team. In rotation, each member presents his/her expert team's report to the learning team. Team discussion is encouraged.

ENTREPRENEURIAL DECISION
A1 A2 P3

BTN 2-7 Assume Susie Levitt and Katie Shea of **CitySlips** plan on expanding their business to accommodate more product lines. They are considering financing their expansion in one of two ways: (1) contributing more of their own funds to the business or (2) borrowing the funds from a bank.

Required

Identify at least two issues that Susie and Katie should consider when trying to decide on the method for financing their expansion.

BTN 2-8 Lisa Langely is a young entrepreneur who operates Langely Music Services, offering singing lessons and instruction on musical instruments. Langely wishes to expand but needs a $15,000 loan. The bank requests Langely to prepare a balance sheet and key financial ratios. Langely has not kept formal records but is able to provide the following accounts and their amounts as of December 31, 2011.

ENTREPRENEURIAL DECISION
A1 A2 P3

Cash	$ 1,800	Accounts Receivable	$4,800	Prepaid Insurance	$ 750
Prepaid Rent	4,700	Store Supplies	3,300	Equipment	25,000
Accounts Payable	1,100	Unearned Lesson Fees	7,800	Total Equity*	31,450
Annual net income	20,000				

* The total equity amount reflects all owner investments, dividends, revenues, and expenses as of December 31, 2011.

Required
1. Prepare a balance sheet as of December 31, 2011, for Langely Music Services. (Report only the total equity amount on the balance sheet.)
2. Compute Langely's debt ratio and its return on assets (the latter ratio is defined in Chapter 1). Assume average assets equal its ending balance.
3. Do you believe the prospects of a $15,000 bank loan are good? Why or why not?

BTN 2-9 Obtain a recent copy of the most prominent newspaper distributed in your area. Research the classified section and prepare a report answering the following questions (attach relevant classified clippings to your report). Alternatively, you may want to search the Web for the required information. One suitable Website is CareerOneStop (www.CareerOneStop.org). For documentation, you should print copies of Websites accessed.

HITTING THE ROAD
C1

1. Identify the number of listings for accounting positions and the various accounting job titles.
2. Identify the number of listings for other job titles, with examples, that require or prefer accounting knowledge/experience but are not specifically accounting positions.
3. Specify the salary range for the accounting and accounting-related positions if provided.
4. Indicate the job that appeals to you, the reason for its appeal, and its requirements.

BTN 2-10 Nokia (www.Nokia.com) is a leading global manufacturer of mobile devices and services, and it competes to some extent with both Research In Motion and Apple. Key financial ratios for the current fiscal year follow.

GLOBAL DECISION
A2

NOKIA
RIM
Apple

Key Figure	Nokia	Research In Motion	Apple
Return on assets	0.7%	26.8%	19.7%
Debt ratio	58.7%	25.5%	33.4%

Required
1. Which company is most profitable according to its return on assets?
2. Which company is most risky according to the debt ratio?
3. Which company deserves increased investment based on a joint analysis of return on assets and the debt ratio? Explain.

ANSWERS TO MULTIPLE CHOICE QUIZ

1. b; debit Utility Expense for $700, and credit Cash for $700.
2. a; debit Cash for $2,500, and credit Unearned Lawn Service Fees for $2,500.
3. c; debit Cash for $250,000, debit Land for $500,000, and credit Common Stock for $750,000.
4. d
5. e; Debt ratio = $400,000/$1,000,000 = 40%

A Look Back

Chapter 2 explained the analysis and recording of transactions. We showed how to apply and interpret company accounts, T-accounts, double-entry accounting, ledgers, postings, and trial balances.

A Look at This Chapter

This chapter explains the timing of reports and the need to adjust accounts. Adjusting accounts is important for recognizing revenues and expenses in the proper period. We describe how to prepare financial statements from an adjusted trial balance, and how the closing process works.

A Look Ahead

Chapter 4 looks at accounting for merchandising activities. We describe the sale and purchase of merchandise and their implications for preparing and analyzing financial statements.

3 Adjusting Accounts and Preparing Financial Statements

Learning Objectives

CAP

CONCEPTUAL

- **C1** Explain the importance of periodic reporting and the time period assumption. (p. 96)
- **C2** Explain accrual accounting and how it improves financial statements. (p. 97)
- **C3** Identify steps in the accounting cycle. (p. 114)
- **C4** Explain and prepare a classified balance sheet. (p. 115)

ANALYTICAL

- **A1** Explain how accounting adjustments link to financial statements. (p. 107)
- **A2** Compute profit margin and describe its use in analyzing company performance. (p. 119)
- **A3** Compute the current ratio and describe what it reveals about a company's financial condition. (p. 119)

PROCEDURAL

- **P1** Prepare and explain adjusting entries. (p. 98)
- **P2** Explain and prepare an adjusted trial balance. (p. 108)
- **P3** Prepare financial statements from an adjusted trial balance. (p. 108)
- **P4** Describe and prepare closing entries. (p. 110)
- **P5** Explain and prepare a post-closing trial balance. (p. 112)
- **P6** *Appendix 3A*—Explain the alternatives in accounting for prepaids. (p. 123)
- **P7** *Appendix 3B*—Prepare a work sheet and explain its usefulness. (p. 125)
- **P8** *Appendix 3C*—Prepare reversing entries and explain their purpose. (p. 128)

LP3

Decision Insight

Huh? Yes!

"Make sure that whatever commitment you make . . . you keep."
—BEN HUH

SEATTLE—"When we were starting this thing, people asked who was going to run it, and I said, 'I will, and my wife.' And they said, 'You're crazy.' And I said, 'Yes!'" Meet Ben Huh. His thing? **Cheezburger Network (Cheezburger.com/sites),** which controls over 30 Websites devoted to Internet memes. (Memes are running gags, usually in JPEG or video format, which spawn and spread on the Web.) His sites include ICanHasCheezburger?, FailBlog, IHasAHotdog!, ROFLrazzi, and TotallyLooksLike. Since launching his company just a few years ago, his network has nearly 200 million page views per month and annual revenue in the millions. Revenue comes from display ads, along with some merchandise sales.

Ben explains that he set up an accounting system early on to account for all business activities, including cash, revenues, receivables, and payables. He also had to learn about the deferral and accrual of revenues and expenses. Setting up a good accounting system is an important part of success, explains Ben. "I learned how to keep costs low."

In spite of his quirky business, Ben insists "it is very serious business." He also seriously monitors the adjusting of accounts so that revenues and expenses are properly reported so that good decisions are made. Adds Ben, "No matter how strange or ridiculous a business looks, those fundamentals still need to be there."

Financial statement preparation and analysis is a process that Ben emphasizes. Although he insists on timely and accurate accounting reports, Ben says "we're just having fun . . . we've always been very much counterculture." To achieve the fun part, Ben first took time to understand accounting adjustments and their effects. It is part of the larger picture. We "make people happy for five minutes every day." But, for Ben to do that, he insists that a reliable accounting system is necessary . . . otherwise his business would fail.

"We'd like to continue to do what we do . . . build bigger communities and just kind of evangelize the idea that the user is great at creating excellent content," says Ben. "The market is far more efficient than any one company . . . but we haven't applied that theory to [Web] content."

[Sources: *Cheezburger Website* and *BenHuh Website,* January 2012; *Entrepreneur,* August 2009; *Wired,* February 2010; *The New York Times,* April 2009; *Time,* August 2009; *Silicon Prairie News,* June 2011]

Chapter Preview

Chapters 1 and 2 described how transactions and events are analyzed, journalized, and posted. This chapter describes important adjustments that are often necessary to properly reflect revenues when earned and expenses when incurred. This chapter also describes financial statement preparation. It explains the closing process that readies revenue, expense, and dividend accounts for the next reporting period and updates retained earnings. It also explains how accounts are classified on a balance sheet to increase their usefulness to decision makers.

Adjusting Accounts and Preparing Financial Statements

Timing and Reporting
- Accounting period
- Accrual versus cash
- Recognition of revenues and expenses

Adjusting Accounts
- Prepaid expenses
- Unearned revenues
- Accrued expenses
- Accrued revenues
- Adjusted trial balance

Preparing Financial Statements
- Income statement
- Statement of retained earnings
- Balance sheet

Closing Process
- Temporary and permanent accounts
- Closing entries
- Post-closing trial balance
- Accounting cycle summary

Classified Balance Sheet
- Classification structure
- Classification categories

TIMING AND REPORTING

This section describes the importance of reporting accounting information at regular intervals and its impact for recording revenues and expenses.

The Accounting Period

C1 Explain the importance of periodic reporting and the time period assumption.

The value of information is often linked to its timeliness. Useful information must reach decision makers frequently and promptly. To provide timely information, accounting systems prepare reports at regular intervals. This results in an accounting process impacted by the time period (or periodicity) assumption. The **time period assumption** presumes that an organization's activities can be divided into specific time periods such as a month, a three-month quarter, a six-month interval, or a year. Exhibit 3.1 shows various **accounting,** or *reporting,* **periods.** Most organizations use a year as their primary accounting period. Reports covering a one-year period are known as **annual financial statements.** Many organizations also prepare **interim financial statements** covering one, three, or six months of activity.

"RIM announces annual income of . . ."

EXHIBIT 3.1
Accounting Periods

The annual reporting period is not always a calendar year ending on December 31. An organization can adopt a **fiscal year** consisting of any 12 consecutive months. It is also acceptable to adopt an annual reporting period of 52 weeks. For example, Gap's fiscal year consistently ends the final week of January or the first week of February each year.

Companies with little seasonal variation in sales often choose the calendar year as their fiscal year. The financial statements of The Kellogg Company (the company that controls characters such as Tony the Tiger, Snap! Crackle! Pop!, and Keebler Elf) reflect a fiscal year that ends on the Saturday nearest December 31. Companies experiencing seasonal variations in sales often choose a **natural business year** end, which is when sales activities are at their lowest level for the year. The natural business year for retailers such as Walmart, Target, and Macy's usually ends around January 31, after the holiday season.

Accrual Basis versus Cash Basis

After external transactions and events are recorded, several accounts still need adjustments before their balances appear in financial statements. This need arises because internal transactions and events remain unrecorded. **Accrual basis accounting** uses the adjusting process to recognize revenues when earned and expenses when incurred (matched with revenues).

Cash basis accounting recognizes revenues when cash is received and records expenses when cash is paid. This means that cash basis net income for a period is the difference between cash receipts and cash payments. Cash basis accounting is not consistent with generally accepted accounting principles (neither U.S. GAAP nor IFRS).

It is commonly held that accrual accounting better reflects business performance than information about cash receipts and payments. Accrual accounting also increases the *comparability* of financial statements from one period to another. Yet cash basis accounting is useful for several business decisions—which is the reason companies must report a statement of cash flows.

To see the difference between these two accounting systems, let's consider FastForward's Prepaid Insurance account. FastForward paid $2,400 for 24 months of insurance coverage that began on December 1, 2011. Accrual accounting requires that $100 of insurance expense be reported on December 2011's income statement. Another $1,200 of expense is reported in year 2012, and the remaining $1,100 is reported as expense in the first 11 months of 2013. Exhibit 3.2 illustrates this allocation of insurance cost across these three years. Any unexpired premium is reported as a Prepaid Insurance asset on the accrual basis balance sheet.

C2 Explain accrual accounting and how it improves financial statements.

EXHIBIT 3.2

Accrual Accounting for Allocating Prepaid Insurance to Expense

Alternatively, a cash basis income statement for December 2011 reports insurance expense of $2,400, as shown in Exhibit 3.3. The cash basis income statements for years 2012 and 2013 report no insurance expense. The cash basis balance sheet never reports an insurance asset because it is immediately expensed. This shows that cash basis income for 2011–2013 fails to match the cost of insurance with the insurance benefits received for those years and months.

EXHIBIT 3.3

Cash Accounting for Allocating Prepaid Insurance to Expense

Point: Recording revenue early overstates current-period revenue and income; recording it late understates current-period revenue and income.

Point: Recording expense early overstates current-period expense and understates current-period income; recording it late understates current-period expense and overstates current-period income.

Recognizing Revenues and Expenses

We use the time period assumption to divide a company's activities into specific time periods, but not all activities are complete when financial statements are prepared. Thus, adjustments often are required to get correct account balances.

We rely on two principles in the adjusting process: revenue recognition and expense recognition (the latter is often referred to as matching). Chapter 1 explained that the *revenue recognition principle* requires that revenue be recorded when earned, not before and not after. Most companies earn revenue when they provide services and products to customers. A major goal of the adjusting process is to have revenue recognized (reported) in the time period when it is earned. The **expense recognition** (or **matching**) **principle** aims to record expenses in the same accounting period as the revenues that are earned as a result of those expenses. This matching of expenses with the revenue benefits is a major part of the adjusting process.

Matching expenses with revenues often requires us to predict certain events. When we use financial statements, we must understand that they require estimates and therefore include measures that are not precise. **Walt Disney**'s annual report explains that its production costs from movies, such as its *Pirates of the Caribbean* series, are matched to revenues based on a ratio of current revenues from the movie divided by its predicted total revenues.

Quick Check
Answers — p. 130

1. Describe a company's annual reporting period.
2. Why do companies prepare interim financial statements?
3. What two accounting principles most directly drive the adjusting process?
4. Is cash basis accounting consistent with the matching principle? Why or why not?
5. If your company pays a $4,800 premium on April 1, 2011, for two years' insurance coverage, how much insurance expense is reported in 2012 using cash basis accounting?

ADJUSTING ACCOUNTS

Adjusting accounts is a three-step process:

Step 1: Determine what the current account balance *equals*.

Step 2: Determine what the current account balance *should equal*.

Step 3: Record an adjusting entry to get from step *1* to step *2*.

Framework for Adjustments

P1 Prepare and explain adjusting entries.

Adjustments are necessary for transactions and events that extend over more than one period. It is helpful to group adjustments by the timing of cash receipt or cash payment in relation to the recognition of the related revenues or expenses. Exhibit 3.4 identifies four types of adjustments.

The upper half of this exhibit shows prepaid expenses (including depreciation) and unearned revenues, which reflect transactions when cash is paid or received *before* a related expense or revenue is recognized. They are also called *deferrals* because the recognition of an expense (or revenue) is *deferred* until after the related cash is paid (or received). The lower half of this exhibit shows accrued expenses and accrued revenues, which reflect transactions when cash is paid or received *after* a related expense or revenue is recognized. Adjusting entries are necessary for each of these so that revenues, expenses, assets, and liabilities are correctly reported. Specifically, an **adjusting entry** is made at the end of an accounting period to reflect a transaction or event that is not yet recorded. Each adjusting entry affects one or more income statement accounts *and* one or more balance sheet accounts (but never the Cash account).

Point: Source documents provide information for most daily transactions, and in many businesses the recordkeepers record them. Adjustments require more knowledge and are usually handled by senior accounting professionals.

EXHIBIT 3.4
Types of Adjustments

Prepaid (Deferred) Expenses

Prepaid expenses refer to items *paid for* in advance of receiving their benefits. Prepaid expenses are assets. When these assets are used, their costs become expenses. Adjusting entries for prepaids increase expenses and decrease assets as shown in the T-accounts of Exhibit 3.5. Such adjustments reflect transactions and events that use up prepaid expenses (including passage of time). To illustrate the accounting for prepaid expenses, we look at prepaid insurance, supplies, and depreciation.

EXHIBIT 3.5
Adjusting for Prepaid Expenses

Prepaid Insurance We use our three-step process for this and all accounting adjustments.

Step 1: We determine that the current balance of FastForward's prepaid insurance is equal to its $2,400 payment for 24 months of insurance benefits that began on December 1, 2011.

Step 2: With the passage of time, the benefits of the insurance gradually expire and a portion of the Prepaid Insurance asset becomes expense. For instance, one month's insurance coverage expires by December 31, 2011. This expense is $100, or 1/24 of $2,400, which leaves $2,300.

Step 3: The adjusting entry to record this expense and reduce the asset, along with T-account postings, follows:

	Adjustment (a)		
Dec. 31	Insurance Expense	100	
	Prepaid Insurance		100
	To record first month's expired insurance.		

Insurance Expense	637
Dec. 31 100	

Prepaid Insurance			128
Dec. 6	2,400	Dec. 31	100
Balance	2,300		

Assets = Liabilities + Equity
−100   −100

Explanation After adjusting and posting, the $100 balance in Insurance Expense and the $2,300 balance in Prepaid Insurance are ready for reporting in financial statements. *Not* making the adjustment on or before December 31 would (1) understate expenses by $100 and overstate net income by $100 for the December income statement and (2) overstate both prepaid insurance (assets) and equity (because of net income) by $100 in the December 31 balance sheet. (Exhibit 3.2 showed that 2012's adjustments must transfer a total of $1,200 from Prepaid Insurance to Insurance Expense, and 2013's adjustments must transfer the remaining $1,100 to Insurance Expense.) The following table highlights the December 31, 2011, adjustment for prepaid insurance.

Point: Many companies record adjusting entries only at the end of each year because of the time and cost necessary.

100   Chapter 3   Adjusting Accounts and Preparing Financial Statements

Before Adjustment	Adjustment	After Adjustment
Prepaid Insurance = $2,400	Deduct $100 from Prepaid Insurance Add $100 to Insurance Expense	Prepaid Insurance = $2,300
Reports $2,400 policy for 24-months' coverage.	Record current month's $100 insurance expense and $100 reduction in prepaid amount.	Reports $2,300 in coverage for remaining 23 months.

Supplies   Supplies are a prepaid expense requiring adjustment.

Step 1: FastForward purchased $9,720 of supplies in December and some of them were used during this month. When financial statements are prepared at December 31, the cost of supplies used during December must be recognized.

Step 2: When FastForward computes (takes physical count of) its remaining unused supplies at December 31, it finds $8,670 of supplies remaining of the $9,720 total supplies. The $1,050 difference between these two amounts is December's supplies expense.

Step 3: The adjusting entry to record this expense and reduce the Supplies asset account, along with T-account postings, follows:

Supplies
Dec. 2, 6, 26   Purchase supplies and record asset

Dec. 31   Supplies used and record expense

Assets = Liabilities + Equity
−1,050   −1,050

Adjustment (b)

Dec. 31	Supplies Expense	1,050	
	Supplies		1,050
	To record supplies used.		

Supplies Expense		652
Dec. 31 1,050		

Supplies			126
Dec. 2	2,500	Dec. 31	1,050
6	7,100		
26	120		
Balance	8,670		

Explanation   The balance of the Supplies account is $8,670 after posting—equaling the cost of the remaining supplies. *Not* making the adjustment on or before December 31 would (1) understate expenses by $1,050 and overstate net income by $1,050 for the December income statement and (2) overstate both supplies and equity (because of net income) by $1,050 in the December 31 balance sheet. The following table highlights the adjustment for supplies.

Before Adjustment	Adjustment	After Adjustment
Supplies = $9,720	Deduct $1,050 from Supplies Add $1,050 to Supplies Expense	Supplies = $8,670
Reports $9,720 in supplies.	Record $1,050 in supplies used and $1,050 as supplies expense.	Reports $8,670 in supplies.

Other Prepaid Expenses   Other prepaid expenses, such as Prepaid Rent, are accounted for exactly as Insurance and Supplies are. We should note that some prepaid expenses are both paid for and fully used up within a single accounting period. One example is when a company pays monthly rent on the first day of each month. This payment creates a prepaid expense on the first day of each month that fully expires by the end of the month. In these special cases, we can record the cash paid with a debit to an expense account instead of an asset account. This practice is described more completely later in the chapter.

Point: We assume that prepaid and unearned items are recorded in balance sheet accounts. An alternative is to record them in income statement accounts; Appendix 3A discusses this alternative. The adjusted financial statements are identical.

🟩 Decision Maker   Answer — p. 130

Investor   A small publishing company signs a well-known athlete to write a book. The company pays the athlete $500,000 to sign plus future book royalties. A note to the company's financial statements says that "prepaid expenses include $500,000 in author signing fees to be matched against future expected sales." Is this accounting for the signing bonus acceptable? How does it affect your analysis? ∎

Depreciation A special category of prepaid expenses is **plant assets,** which refers to long-term tangible assets used to produce and sell products and services. Plant assets are expected to provide benefits for more than one period. Examples of plant assets are buildings, machines, vehicles, and fixtures. All plant assets, with a general exception for land, eventually wear out or decline in usefulness. The costs of these assets are deferred but are gradually reported as expenses in the income statement over the assets' useful lives (benefit periods). **Depreciation** is the process of allocating the costs of these assets over their expected useful lives. Depreciation expense is recorded with an adjusting entry similar to that for other prepaid expenses.

Point: Plant assets are also called *Plant & Equipment,* or *Property, Plant & Equipment.*

Point: Depreciation does not necessarily measure decline in market value.

Point: An asset's expected value at the end of its useful life is called *salvage value.*

Step 1: Recall that FastForward purchased equipment for $26,000 in early December to use in earning revenue. This equipment's cost must be depreciated.

Step 2: The equipment is expected to have a useful life (benefit period) of four years and to be worth about $8,000 at the end of four years. This means the *net* cost of this equipment over its useful life is $18,000 ($26,000 − $8,000). We can use any of several methods to allocate this $18,000 net cost to expense. FastForward uses a method called **straight-line depreciation,** which allocates equal amounts of the asset's net cost to depreciation during its useful life. Dividing the $18,000 net cost by the 48 months in the asset's useful life gives a monthly cost of $375 ($18,000/48).

Step 3: The adjusting entry to record monthly depreciation expense, along with T-account postings, follows:

	Adjustment (c)		
Dec. 31	Depreciation Expense	375	
	Accumulated Depreciation—Equipment		375
	To record monthly equipment depreciation.		

Assets = Liabilities + Equity
−375   −375

Depreciation Expense—Equipment	612		Equipment	167		Accumulated Depreciation—Equipment	168
Dec. 31	375		Dec. 3	26,000			Dec. 31	375

Explanation After posting the adjustment, the Equipment account ($26,000) less its Accumulated Depreciation ($375) account equals the $25,625 net cost (made up of $17,625 for the 47 remaining months in the benefit period plus the $8,000 value at the end of that time). The $375 balance in the Depreciation Expense account is reported in the December income statement. *Not* making the adjustment at December 31 would (1) understate expenses by $375 and overstate net income by $375 for the December income statement and (2) overstate both assets and equity (because of income) by $375 in the December 31 balance sheet. The following table highlights the adjustment for depreciation.

Before Adjustment	Adjustment	After Adjustment
Equipment, net = $26,000	Deduct $375 from Equipment, net Add $375 to Depreciation Expense	Equipment, net = $25,625
Reports $26,000 in equipment.	Record $375 in depreciation and $375 as accumulated depreciation, which is deducted from equipment.	Reports $25,625 in equipment, net of accumulated depreciation.

Accumulated depreciation is kept in a separate contra account. A **contra account** is an account linked with another account, where the contra account has a normal balance opposite of the account it is linked with. It is reported as a subtraction from that other account's balance. For instance, FastForward's contra account of Accumulated Depreciation—Equipment is subtracted from the Equipment account in the balance sheet (see Exhibit 3.7). This contra account allows balance sheet readers to know both the full costs of assets and the total depreciation.

The title of the contra account, *Accumulated Depreciation,* reveals that this account includes total depreciation expense for all prior periods for which the asset was used. To illustrate, the Equipment and the Accumulated Depreciation accounts appear as in Exhibit 3.6 on February 28, 2012, after three months of adjusting entries. The $1,125 balance in the accumulated depreciation account can be subtracted from its related $26,000 asset cost. The difference ($24,875) between these two balances is the cost of the asset that has not yet been depreciated. This difference is

Point: The cost principle requires an asset to be initially recorded at acquisition cost. Depreciation causes the asset's book value (cost less accumulated depreciation) to decline over time.

102   Chapter 3   Adjusting Accounts and Preparing Financial Statements

EXHIBIT 3.6

Accounts after Three Months of Depreciation Adjustments

Equipment	167
Dec. 3 26,000	

Accumulated Depreciation—Equipment	168
	Dec. 31 375
	Jan. 31 375
	Feb. 28 375
	Balance 1,125

Point: The net cost of equipment is also called the *depreciable basis*.

called the **book value,** or the *net amount,* which equals the asset's costs less its accumulated depreciation.

These account balances are reported in the assets section of the February 28 balance sheet in Exhibit 3.7.

EXHIBIT 3.7

Equipment and Accumulated Depreciation on February 28 Balance Sheet

Assets (at February 28, 2012)

Cash		$ ____
⋮		
Equipment	$26,000	
Less accumulated depreciation	1,125	24,875
Total Assets		$ ____

← Commonly titled *Equipment, net*

Fraud

Where Are the Assets? The U.S. government seems to lose assets. The **Center for Disease Control and Prevention** (CDC) seems especially vulnerable. In a recent year, the CDC lost track of over $8 million in computer and video equipment. In another year it was unable to account for nearly $6 million in computers, microscopes, and vehicles. The president of *Citizens Against Government Waste* said "It's just a good thing they haven't lost any diseases!"

Unearned (Deferred) Revenues

The term **unearned revenues** refers to cash received in advance of providing products and services. Unearned revenues, also called *deferred revenues,* are liabilities. When cash is accepted, an obligation to provide products or services is accepted. As products or services are provided, the unearned revenues become *earned* revenues. Adjusting entries for unearned revenues involve increasing revenues and decreasing unearned revenues, as shown in Exhibit 3.8.

EXHIBIT 3.8

Adjusting for Unearned Revenues

Liability (Decreased) — Debit adjustment | Unadjusted balance
Revenue (Increased) — Credit adjustment
Dr. Liability..... #
Cr. Revenue... #

Point: To *defer* is to postpone. We postpone reporting amounts received as revenues until they are earned.

An example of unearned revenues is from **The New York Times Company**, which reports unexpired (unearned) subscriptions of $81 million: "Proceeds from ... subscriptions are deferred at the time of sale and are recognized in earnings on a pro rata basis over the terms of the subscriptions." Unearned revenues are nearly 10% of the current liabilities for the Times. Another example comes from the **Boston Celtics**. When the Celtics receive cash from advance ticket sales and broadcast fees, they record it in an unearned revenue account called *Deferred Game Revenues*. The Celtics recognize this unearned revenue with adjusting entries on a game-by-game basis. Since the NBA regular season begins in October and ends in April, revenue recognition is mainly limited to this period. For a recent season, the Celtics' quarterly revenues were $0 million for July–September; $34 million for October–December; $48 million for January–March; and $17 million for April–June.

Unearned Revenues

Dec. 26   Cash received in advance and record liability

"Thanks for cash in advance. I'll work now through Feb. 24."

Dec. 31   Provided services and record revenue

Returning to FastForward, it also has unearned revenues. It agreed on December 26 to provide consulting services to a client for a fixed fee of $3,000 for 60 days.

Step 1: On December 26, the client paid the 60-day fee in advance, covering the period December 27 to February 24. The entry to record the cash received in advance is

Dec. 26	Cash	3,000	
	Unearned Consulting Revenue		3,000
	Received advance payment for services over the next 60 days.		

Assets = Liabilities + Equity
+3,000   +3,000

This advance payment increases cash and creates an obligation to do consulting work over the next 60 days.

Step 2: As time passes, FastForward earns this payment through consulting. By December 31, it has provided five days' service and earned 5/60 of the $3,000 unearned revenue. This amounts to $250 ($3,000 × 5/60). The *revenue recognition principle* implies that $250 of unearned revenue must be reported as revenue on the December income statement.

Step 3: The adjusting entry to reduce the liability account and recognize earned revenue, along with T-account postings, follows:

Adjustment (d)

Dec. 31	Unearned Consulting Revenue	250	
	Consulting Revenue		250
	To record earned revenue that was received in advance ($3,000 × 5/60).		

Assets = Liabilities + Equity
            −250   +250

Unearned Consulting Revenue			236
Dec. 31	250	Dec. 26	3,000
		Balance	2,750

Consulting Revenue		403
	Dec. 5	4,200
	12	1,600
	31	250
	Balance	6,050

Explanation The adjusting entry transfers $250 from unearned revenue (a liability account) to a revenue account. *Not* making the adjustment (1) understates revenue and net income by $250 in the December income statement and (2) overstates unearned revenue and understates equity by $250 on the December 31 balance sheet. The following highlights the adjustment for unearned revenue.

Before Adjustment	Adjustment	After Adjustment
Unearned Consulting Revenue = $3,000	Deduct $250 from Unearned Consulting Revenue Add $250 to Consulting Revenue	Unearned Consulting Revenue = $2,750
Reports $3,000 in unearned revenue for consulting services promised for 60 days.	Record 5 days of earned consulting revenue, which is 5/60 of unearned amount.	Reports $2,750 in unearned revenue for consulting services owed over next 55 days.

Accounting for unearned revenues is crucial to many companies. For example, the **National Retail Federation** reports that gift card sales, which are unearned revenues for sellers, exceed $20 billion annually. Gift cards are now the top selling holiday gift.

Accrued Expenses

Accrued expenses refer to costs that are incurred in a period but are both unpaid and unrecorded. Accrued expenses must be reported on the income statement of the period when incurred. Adjusting entries for recording accrued expenses involve increasing expenses and increasing liabilities as shown in Exhibit 3.9. This adjustment recognizes expenses incurred in a period but not yet paid. Common examples of accrued expenses are salaries, interest, rent, and taxes. We use salaries and interest to show how to adjust accounts for accrued expenses.

Point: Accrued expenses are also called accrued liabilities.

EXHIBIT 3.9

Adjusting for Accrued Expenses

Expense (Increased) — Debit adjustment
Liability (Increased) — Credit adjustment

Dr. Expense..... #
    Cr. Liability... #

Chapter 3 Adjusting Accounts and Preparing Financial Statements

Accrued Salaries Expense FastForward's employee earns $70 per day, or $350 for a five-day workweek beginning on Monday and ending on Friday.

Step 1: Its employee is paid every two weeks on Friday. On December 12 and 26, the wages are paid, recorded in the journal, and posted to the ledger.

Step 2: The calendar in Exhibit 3.10 shows three working days after the December 26 payday (29, 30, and 31). This means the employee has earned three days' salary by the close of business

EXHIBIT 3.10

Salary Accrual and Paydays

Point: An employer records salaries expense and a vacation pay liability when employees earn vacation pay.

on Wednesday, December 31, yet this salary cost has not been paid or recorded. The financial statements would be incomplete if FastForward fails to report the added expense and liability to the employee for unpaid salary from December 29, 30, and 31.

Step 3: The adjusting entry to account for accrued salaries, along with T-account postings, follows:

Assets = Liabilities + Equity
         +210   −210

Adjustment (e)

Dec. 31	Salaries Expense	210	
	Salaries Payable		210
	To record three days' accrued salary (3 × $70).		

Salaries Expense	622		Salaries Payable	209
Dec. 12	700		Dec. 31	210
26	700			
31	210			
Balance	1,610			

Explanation Salaries expense of $1,610 is reported on the December income statement and $210 of salaries payable (liability) is reported in the balance sheet. *Not* making the adjustment (1) understates salaries expense and overstates net income by $210 in the December income statement and (2) understates salaries payable (liabilities) and overstates equity by $210 on the December 31 balance sheet. The following highlights the adjustment for salaries incurred.

Before Adjustment	Adjustment	After Adjustment
Salaries Payable = $0	Add $210 to Salaries Payable Add $210 to Salaries Expense	Salaries Payable = $210
Reports $0 from employee salaries incurred but not yet paid in cash.	Record 3 days' salaries owed to employee, but not yet paid, at $70 per day.	Reports $210 salaries payable to employee but not yet paid.

Accrued Interest Expense Companies commonly have accrued interest expense on notes payable and other long-term liabilities at the end of a period. Interest expense is incurred with the passage of time. Unless interest is paid on the last day of an accounting period, we need to adjust for interest expense incurred but not yet paid. This means we must accrue interest cost from the most recent payment date up to the end of the period. The formula for computing accrued interest is:

Principal amount owed × Annual interest rate × Fraction of year since last payment date.

To illustrate, if a company has a $6,000 loan from a bank at 6% annual interest, then 30 days' accrued interest expense is $30—computed as $6,000 × 0.06 × 30/360. The adjusting entry would be to debit Interest Expense for $30 and credit Interest Payable for $30.

Point: Interest computations assume a 360-day year; known as the *bankers' rule*.

Future Payment of Accrued Expenses Adjusting entries for accrued expenses foretell cash transactions in future periods. Specifically, accrued expenses at the end of one accounting period result in *cash payment* in a *future period*(s). To illustrate, recall that FastForward recorded accrued salaries of $210. On January 9, the first payday of the next period, the following entry settles the accrued liability (salaries payable) and records salaries expense for seven days of work in January:

Jan. 9	Salaries Payable (3 days at $70 per day)	210	
	Salaries Expense (7 days at $70 per day)	490	
	Cash		700
	Paid two weeks' salary including three days accrued in December.		

Assets = Liabilities + Equity
−700   −210   −490

The $210 debit reflects the payment of the liability for the three days' salary accrued on December 31. The $490 debit records the salary for January's first seven working days (including the New Year's Day holiday) as an expense of the new accounting period. The $700 credit records the total amount of cash paid to the employee.

Accrued Revenues

The term **accrued revenues** refers to revenues earned in a period that are both unrecorded and not yet received in cash (or other assets). An example is a technician who bills customers only when the job is done. If one-third of a job is complete by the end of a period, then the technician must record one-third of the expected billing as revenue in that period—even though there is no billing or collection. The adjusting entries for accrued revenues increase assets and increase revenues as shown in Exhibit 3.11. Accrued revenues commonly arise from services, products, interest, and rent. We use service fees and interest to show how to adjust for accrued revenues.

Point: Accrued revenues are also called *accrued assets*.

EXHIBIT 3.11
Adjusting for Accrued Revenues

Increased → Asset — Debit adjustment
Increased → Revenue — Credit adjustment
Dr. Asset......... #
Cr. Revenue... #

Accrued Services Revenue Accrued revenues are not recorded until adjusting entries are made at the end of the accounting period. These accrued revenues are earned but unrecorded because either the buyer has not yet paid for them or the seller has not yet billed the buyer. FastForward provides an example.

Step 1: In the second week of December, it agreed to provide 30 days of consulting services to a local fitness club for a fixed fee of $2,700. The terms of the initial agreement call for FastForward to provide services from December 12, 2011, through January 10, 2012, or 30 days of service. The club agrees to pay FastForward $2,700 on January 10, 2012, when the service period is complete.

Step 2: At December 31, 2011, 20 days of services have already been provided. Since the contracted services have not yet been entirely provided, FastForward has neither billed the club nor recorded the services already provided. Still, FastForward has earned two-thirds of the 30-day fee, or $1,800 ($2,700 × 20/30). The *revenue recognition principle* implies that it must report the $1,800 on the December income statement. The balance sheet also must report that the club owes FastForward $1,800.

Accrued Revenues
Dec. 31 Record revenue and receivable for services provided but unbilled

Pay me next month

Jan. 10 Receive cash and reduce receivable

Step 3: The year-end adjusting entry to account for accrued services revenue is

Assets = Liabilities + Equity
+1,800   +1,800

Adjustment (f)		
Dec. 31	Accounts Receivable 1,800	
	Consulting Revenue	1,800
	To record 20 days' accrued revenue.	

Accounts Receivable			106
Dec. 12	1,900	Dec. 22	1,900
31	**1,800**		
Balance	1,800		

Consulting Revenue			403
		Dec. 5	4,200
		12	1,600
		31	250
		31	**1,800**
		Balance	7,850

Example: What is the adjusting entry if the 30-day consulting period began on December 22? *Answer:* One-third of the fee is earned:
Accounts Receivable 900
    Consulting Revenue 900

Explanation Accounts receivable are reported on the balance sheet at $1,800, and the $7,850 total of consulting revenue is reported on the income statement. *Not* making the adjustment would understate (1) both consulting revenue and net income by $1,800 in the December income statement and (2) both accounts receivable (assets) and equity by $1,800 on the December 31 balance sheet. The following table highlights the adjustment for accrued revenue.

Before Adjustment	Adjustment	After Adjustment
Accounts Receivable = $0	Add $1,800 to Accounts Receivable Add $1,800 to Consulting Revenue	**Accounts Receivable = $1,800**
Reports $0 from revenue earned but not yet received in cash.	Record 20 days of earned consulting revenue, which is 20/30 of total contract amount.	Reports $1,800 in accounts receivable from consulting services provided.

Accrued Interest Revenue In addition to the accrued interest expense we described earlier, interest can yield an accrued revenue when a debtor owes money (or other assets) to a company. If a company is holding notes or accounts receivable that produce interest revenue, we must adjust the accounts to record any earned and yet uncollected interest revenue. The adjusting entry is similar to the one for accruing services revenue. Specifically, we debit Interest Receivable (asset) and credit Interest Revenue.

Future Receipt of Accrued Revenues Accrued revenues at the end of one accounting period result in *cash receipts* in a *future period*(s). To illustrate, recall that FastForward made an adjusting entry for $1,800 to record 20 days' accrued revenue earned from its consulting contract. When FastForward receives $2,700 cash on January 10 for the entire contract amount, it makes the following entry to remove the accrued asset (accounts receivable) and recognize the revenue earned in January. The $2,700 debit reflects the cash received. The $1,800 credit reflects the removal of the receivable, and the $900 credit records the revenue earned in January.

Assets = Liabilities + Equity
+2,700   +900
−1,800

Jan. 10	Cash 2,700	
	Accounts Receivable (20 days at $90 per day)	1,800
	Consulting Revenue (10 days at $90 per day)	900
	Received cash for the accrued asset and recorded earned consulting revenue for January.	

Decision Maker Answer — p. 130

Loan Officer The owner of an electronics store applies for a business loan. The store's financial statements reveal large increases in current-year revenues and income. Analysis shows that these increases are due to a promotion that let consumers buy now and pay nothing until January 1 of next year. The store recorded these sales as accrued revenue. Does your analysis raise any concerns? ■

Links to Financial Statements

The process of adjusting accounts is intended to bring an asset or liability account balance to its correct amount. It also updates a related expense or revenue account. These adjustments are necessary for transactions and events that extend over more than one period. (Adjusting entries are posted like any other entry.)

Exhibit 3.12 summarizes the four types of transactions requiring adjustment. Understanding this exhibit is important to understanding the adjusting process and its importance to financial statements. Remember that each adjusting entry affects one or more income statement accounts *and* one or more balance sheet accounts (but never cash).

A1 Explain how accounting adjustments link to financial statements.

Category	BEFORE Adjusting — Balance Sheet	BEFORE Adjusting — Income Statement	Adjusting Entry
Prepaid expenses†	Asset overstated / Equity overstated	Expense understated	Dr. Expense / Cr. Asset*
Unearned revenues†	Liability overstated / Equity understated	Revenue understated	Dr. Liability / Cr. Revenue
Accrued expenses	Liability understated / Equity overstated	Expense understated	Dr. Expense / Cr. Liability
Accrued revenues	Asset understated / Equity understated	Revenue understated	Dr. Asset / Cr. Revenue

EXHIBIT 3.12
Summary of Adjustments and Financial Statement Links

* For depreciation, the credit is to Accumulated Depreciation (contra asset).
† Exhibit assumes that prepaid expenses are initially recorded as assets and that unearned revenues are initially recorded as liabilities.

Information about some adjustments is not always available until several days or even weeks after the period-end. This means that some adjusting and closing entries are recorded later than, but dated as of, the last day of the period. One example is a company that receives a utility bill on January 10 for costs incurred for the month of December. When it receives the bill, the company records the expense and the payable as of December 31. Other examples include long-distance phone usage and costs of many Web billings. The December income statement reflects these additional expenses incurred, and the December 31 balance sheet includes these payables, although the amounts were not actually known on December 31.

Decision Ethics — Answer — p. 130

Financial Officer At year-end, the president instructs you, the financial officer, not to record accrued expenses until next year because they will not be paid until then. The president also directs you to record in current-year sales a recent purchase order from a customer that requires merchandise to be delivered two weeks after the year-end. Your company would report a net income instead of a net loss if you carry out these instructions. What do you do? ■

Quick Check — Answers — p. 130

6. If an adjusting entry for accrued revenues of $200 at year-end is omitted, what is this error's effect on the year-end income statement and balance sheet?
7. What is a contra account? Explain its purpose.
8. What is an accrued expense? Give an example.
9. Describe how an unearned revenue arises. Give an example.

Adjusted Trial Balance

An **unadjusted trial balance** is a list of accounts and balances prepared *before* adjustments are recorded. An **adjusted trial balance** is a list of accounts and balances prepared *after* adjusting entries have been recorded and posted to the ledger.

Exhibit 3.13 shows both the unadjusted and the adjusted trial balances for FastForward at December 31, 2011. The order of accounts in the trial balance is usually set up to match the order in the chart of accounts. Several new accounts arise from the adjusting entries.

P2 Explain and prepare an adjusted trial balance.

EXHIBIT 3.13
Unadjusted and Adjusted Trial Balances

FASTFORWARD
Trial Balances
December 31, 2011

Acct. No.	Account Title	Unadjusted Trial Balance Dr.	Unadjusted Trial Balance Cr.	Adjustments Dr.	Adjustments Cr.	Adjusted Trial Balance Dr.	Adjusted Trial Balance Cr.
101	Cash	$ 4,350				$ 4,350	
106	Accounts receivable	0		(f) $1,800		1,800	
126	Supplies	9,720			(b) $1,050	8,670	
128	Prepaid insurance	2,400			(a) 100	2,300	
167	Equipment	26,000				26,000	
168	Accumulated depreciation—Equip.		$ 0		(c) 375		$ 375
201	Accounts payable		6,200				6,200
209	Salaries payable		0		(e) 210		210
236	Unearned consulting revenue		3,000	(d) 250			2,750
307	Common stock		30,000				30,000
318	Retained earnings		0				0
319	Dividends	200				200	
403	Consulting revenue		5,800		(d) 250		7,850
					(f) 1,800		
406	Rental revenue		300				300
612	Depreciation expense—Equip.	0		(c) 375		375	
622	Salaries expense	1,400		(e) 210		1,610	
637	Insurance expense	0		(a) 100		100	
640	Rent expense	1,000				1,000	
652	Supplies expense	0		(b) 1,050		1,050	
690	Utilities expense	230				230	
	Totals	$45,300	$45,300	$3,785	$3,785	$47,685	$47,685

Each adjustment (see middle columns) is identified by a letter in parentheses that links it to an adjusting entry explained earlier. Each amount in the Adjusted Trial Balance columns is computed by taking that account's amount from the Unadjusted Trial Balance columns and adding or subtracting any adjustment(s). To illustrate, Supplies has a $9,720 Dr. balance in the unadjusted columns. Subtracting the $1,050 Cr. amount shown in the adjustments columns yields an adjusted $8,670 Dr. balance for Supplies. An account can have more than one adjustment, such as for Consulting Revenue. Also, some accounts might not require adjustment for this period, such as Accounts Payable.

PREPARING FINANCIAL STATEMENTS

P3 Prepare financial statements from an adjusted trial balance.

We can prepare financial statements directly from information in the *adjusted* trial balance. An adjusted trial balance (see the right-most columns in Exhibit 3.13) includes all accounts and balances appearing in financial statements, and is easier to work from than the entire ledger when preparing financial statements.

Chapter 3 Adjusting Accounts and Preparing Financial Statements 109

EXHIBIT 3.14

Preparing Financial Statements (Adjusted Trial Balance from Exhibit 3.13)

FASTFORWARD
Adjusted Trial Balance
December 31, 2011

Acct. No.	Account Title	Debit	Credit
101	Cash	$ 4,350	
106	Accounts receivable	1,800	
126	Supplies	8,670	
128	Prepaid insurance	2,300	
167	Equipment	26,000	
168	Accumulated depreciation—Equip.		$ 375
201	Accounts payable		6,200
209	Salaries payable		210
236	Unearned consulting revenue		2,750
307	Common stock		30,000
318	Retained earnings		0
319	Dividends	200	
403	Consulting revenue		7,850
406	Rental revenue		300
612	Depreciation expense—Equip.	375	
622	Salaries expense	1,610	
637	Insurance expense	100	
640	Rent expense	1,000	
652	Supplies expense	1,050	
690	Utilities expense	230	
	Totals	$47,685	$47,685

Steps to Prepare Financial Statements

Step 1 Prepare income statement using revenue and expense accounts from trial balance.

Step 2 Prepare statement of retained earnings using retained earnings and dividends from trial balance; and pull net income from step 1.

Step 3 Prepare balance sheet using asset and liability accounts, and common stock, from trial balance; and pull updated retained earnings from step 2.

Step 4 Prepare statement of cash flows from changes in cash flows for the period (not shown).

Step 3 Prepare balance sheet

FASTFORWARD
Balance Sheet
December 31, 2011

Assets
Cash		$ 4,350
Accounts receivable		1,800
Supplies		8,670
Prepaid insurance		2,300
Equipment	$26,000	
Less accumulated depreciation	375	25,625
Total assets		$42,745

Liabilities
Accounts payable	$ 6,200
Salaries payable	210
Unearned consulting revenue	2,750
Total liabilities	9,160

Equity
Common stock	30,000
Retained earnings	3,585
Total equity	33,585
Total liabilities and equity	$42,745

Step 2 Prepare statement of retained earnings

FASTFORWARD
Statement of Retained Earnings
For Month Ended December 31, 2011

Retained earnings, December 1	$ 0
Plus: Net income	3,785
	3,785
Less: Cash dividends	200
Retained earnings, December 31	$3,585

Step 1 Prepare income statement

FASTFORWARD
Income Statement
For Month Ended December 31, 2011

Revenues		
Consulting revenue	$7,850	
Rental revenue	300	
Total revenues		$8,150
Expenses		
Depreciation expense—Equip.	375	
Salaries expense	1,610	
Insurance expense	100	
Rent expense	1,000	
Supplies expense	1,050	
Utilities expense	230	
Total expenses		4,365
Net income		$3,785

Exhibit 3.14 shows how revenue and expense balances are transferred from the adjusted trial balance to the income statement (red lines). The net income and the dividends amount are then used to prepare the statement of retained earnings (black lines). Asset and liability balances on the adjusted trial balance are then transferred to the balance sheet (blue lines). The ending retained earnings is determined on the statement of retained earnings and transferred to the balance sheet (green lines).

Point: Sarbanes-Oxley Act requires that financial statements filed with the SEC be certified by the CEO and CFO, including a declaration that the statements fairly present the issuer's operations and financial condition. Violators can receive fines and/or prison terms.

110   Chapter 3   Adjusting Accounts and Preparing Financial Statements

Point: Each trial balance amount is used in only *one* financial statement and, when financial statements are completed, each account will have been used once.

We prepare financial statements in the following order: income statement, statement of retained earnings, and balance sheet. This order makes sense because the balance sheet uses information from the statement of retained earnings, which in turn uses information from the income statement. The statement of cash flows is usually the final statement prepared.

Quick Check   Answers — p. 130

10. Music-Mart records $1,000 of accrued salaries on December 31. Five days later, on January 5 (the next payday), salaries of $7,000 are paid. What is the January 5 entry?

11. Jordan Air has the following information in its unadjusted and adjusted trial balances. What are the adjusting entries that Jordan Air likely recorded?

	Unadjusted		Adjusted	
	Debit	Credit	Debit	Credit
Prepaid insurance	$6,200		$5,900	
Salaries payable		$ 0		$1,400

12. What accounts are taken from the adjusted trial balance to prepare an income statement?

13. In preparing financial statements from an adjusted trial balance, what statement is usually prepared second?

CLOSING PROCESS

P4 Describe and prepare closing entries.

Temporary Accounts
(closed at period-end)
Revenues
Expenses
Dividends
Income Summary

Permanent Accounts
(not closed at period-end)
Assets
Liabilities
Common Stock
Retained Earnings

The **closing process** is an important step at the end of an accounting period *after* financial statements have been completed. It prepares accounts for recording the transactions and the events of the *next* period. In the closing process we must (1) identify accounts for closing, (2) record and post the closing entries, and (3) prepare a post-closing trial balance. The purpose of the closing process is twofold. First, it resets revenue, expense, and dividends account balances to zero at the end of each period. This is done so that these accounts can properly measure income and dividends for the next period. Second, it helps in summarizing a period's revenues and expenses. This section explains the closing process.

Temporary and Permanent Accounts

Temporary (or *nominal*) **accounts** accumulate data related to one accounting period. They include all income statement accounts, the dividends account, and the Income Summary account. They are temporary because the accounts are opened at the beginning of a period, used to record transactions and events for that period, and then closed at the end of the period. *The closing process applies only to temporary accounts.* **Permanent** (or *real*) **accounts** report on activities related to one or more future accounting periods. They carry their ending balances into the next period and generally consist of all balance sheet accounts. These asset, liability, and equity accounts are not closed.

Recording Closing Entries

To record and post **closing entries** is to transfer the end-of-period balances in revenue, expense, and dividends accounts to the permanent retained earnings account. Closing entries are necessary at the end of each period after financial statements are prepared because

- Revenue, expense, and dividends accounts must begin each period with zero balances.
- Retained earnings must reflect prior periods' revenues, expenses, and dividends.

An income statement aims to report revenues and expenses for a *specific accounting period*. The statement of retained earnings reports similar information, including dividends. Since revenue, expense, and dividends accounts must accumulate information separately for each period, they must start each period with zero balances. To close these accounts, we transfer their balances first to an account called *Income Summary*. **Income Summary** is a temporary account (only used for the closing process) that contains a credit for the sum of all revenues (and gains) and a debit for the sum of all expenses (and losses). Its balance equals net income or net loss and it is transferred to retained earnings. Next the dividends account balance is transferred to retained earnings. After these closing entries are posted, the revenue, expense, dividends, and Income Summary accounts have zero balances. These accounts are then said to be *closed* or *cleared*.

Exhibit 3.15 uses the adjusted account balances of FastForward (from the left side of Exhibit 3.14) to show the four steps necessary to close its temporary accounts. We explain each step.

Point: To understand the closing process, focus on its *outcomes*—updating the retained earnings account balance to its proper ending balance, and getting *temporary accounts* to show *zero balances* for purposes of accumulating data for the next period.

EXHIBIT 3.15
Four-Step Closing Process

Expense Accounts

Depreciation Expense—Equip.	
Balance 375	375

Salaries Expense	
Balance 1,610	1,610

Insurance Expense	
Balance 100	100

Rent Expense	
Balance 1,000	1,000

Supplies Expense	
Balance 1,050	1,050

Utilities Expense	
Balance 230	230

Four-Step Closing Process
1. Close income statement credit balances
2. Close income statement debit balances
3. Close income summary account
4. Close dividends account

Revenue Accounts

Consulting Revenue	
7,850	Balance 7,850

Rental Revenue	
300	Balance 300

Income Summary

4,365	8,150
3,785	Balance 3,785

Retained Earnings

	Balance 0
200	3,785
	Balance 3,585

Dividends

| Balance 200 | 200 |

Point: Retained Earnings is the only *permanent account* in Exhibit 3.15.

Step 1: Close Credit Balances in Revenue Accounts to Income Summary
The first closing entry transfers credit balances in revenue (and gain) accounts to the Income Summary account. We bring accounts with credit balances to zero by debiting them. For FastForward, this journal entry is step 1 in Exhibit 3.16. This entry closes revenue accounts and leaves them with zero balances. The accounts are now ready to record revenues when they occur in the next period. The $8,150 credit entry to Income Summary equals total revenues for the period.

Step 2: Close Debit Balances in Expense Accounts to Income Summary
The second closing entry transfers debit balances in expense (and loss) accounts to the Income Summary account. We bring expense accounts' debit balances to zero by crediting them. With a balance of zero, these accounts are ready to accumulate a record of expenses for the next period. This second closing entry for FastForward is step 2 in Exhibit 3.16. Exhibit 3.15 shows that posting this entry gives each expense account a zero balance.

Point: It is possible to close revenue and expense accounts directly to retained earnings. Computerized accounting systems do this.

Chapter 3 Adjusting Accounts and Preparing Financial Statements

FASTFORWARD
Adjusted Trial Balance
December 31, 2011

	Debit	Credit
Cash	$ 4,350	
Accounts receivable	1,800	
Supplies	8,670	
Prepaid insurance	2,300	
Equipment	26,000	
Accumulated depreciation—Equip.		$ 375
Accounts payable		6,200
Salaries payable		210
Unearned consulting revenue		2,750
Common stock		30,000
Retained earnings		0
Dividends	200	
Consulting revenue		7,850
Rental revenue		300
Depreciation expense—Equip.	375	
Salaries expense	1,610	
Insurance expense	100	
Rent expense	1,000	
Supplies expense	1,050	
Utilities expense	230	
Totals	$47,685	$47,685

Step 1: General Journal

Dec. 31	Consulting Revenue	7,850	
	Rental Revenue	300	
	Income Summary		8,150
	To close revenue accounts.		

Step 2:

Dec. 31	Income Summary	4,365	
	Depreciation Expense—Equipment		375
	Salaries Expense		1,610
	Insurance Expense		100
	Rent Expense		1,000
	Supplies Expense		1,050
	Utilities Expense		230
	To close expense accounts.		

Step 3:

Dec. 31	Income Summary	3,785	
	Retained Earnings		3,785
	To close Income Summary account.		

Step 4:

Dec. 31	Retained Earnings	200	
	Dividends		200
	To close the dividends account.		

EXHIBIT 3.16
Preparing Closing Entries

Step 3: Close Income Summary to Retained Earnings After steps 1 and 2, the balance of Income Summary is equal to December's net income of $3,785 ($8,150 credit less $4,365 debit). The third closing entry transfers the balance of the Income Summary account to retained earnings. This entry closes the Income Summary account–see step 3 in Exhibit 3.16. The Income Summary account has a zero balance after posting this entry. It continues to have a zero balance until the closing process again occurs at the end of the next period. (If a net loss occurred because expenses exceeded revenues, the third entry is reversed: debit Retained Earnings and credit Income Summary.)

Step 4: Close Dividends Account to Retained Earnings The fourth closing entry transfers any debit balance in the dividends account to retained earnings—see step 4 in Exhibit 3.16. This entry gives the dividends account a zero balance, and the account is now ready to accumulate next period's dividends. This entry also reduces the retained earnings balance to the $3,585 amount reported on the balance sheet.

We could also have selected the accounts and amounts needing to be closed by identifying individual revenue, expense, and dividends accounts in the ledger. This is illustrated in Exhibit 3.16 where we prepare closing entries using the adjusted trial balance. (Information for closing entries is also in the financial statement columns of a work sheet—see Appendix 3B.)

Post-Closing Trial Balance

P5 Explain and prepare a post-closing trial balance.

Exhibit 3.17 shows the entire ledger of FastForward as of December 31 after adjusting and closing entries are posted. (The transaction entries are in Chapter 2.) The temporary accounts (revenues, expenses, and dividends) have ending balances equal to zero.

A **post-closing trial balance** is a list of permanent accounts and their balances from the ledger after all closing entries have been journalized and posted. It lists the balances for all accounts not closed. These accounts comprise a company's assets, liabilities, and equity, which are identical to those in the balance sheet. The aim of a post-closing trial balance is to verify that

EXHIBIT 3.17

General Ledger after the Closing Process for FastForward

Asset Accounts

Cash — Acct. No. 101

Date	Explan.	PR	Debit	Credit	Balance
2011					
Dec. 1	(1)	G1	30,000		30,000
2	(2)	G1		2,500	27,500
3	(3)	G1		26,000	1,500
5	(5)	G1	4,200		5,700
6	(13)	G1		2,400	3,300
12	(6)	G1		1,000	2,300
12	(7)	G1		700	1,600
22	(9)	G1	1,900		3,500
24	(10)	G1		900	2,600
24	(11)	G1		200	2,400
26	(12)	G1	3,000		5,400
26	(14)	G1		120	5,280
26	(15)	G1		230	5,050
26	(16)	G1		700	**4,350**

Accounts Receivable — Acct. No. 106

Date	Explan.	PR	Debit	Credit	Balance
2011					
Dec. 12	(8)	G1	1,900		1,900
22	(9)	G1		1,900	0
31	Adj.(f)	G1	1,800		**1,800**

Supplies — Acct. No. 126

Date	Explan.	PR	Debit	Credit	Balance
2011					
Dec. 2	(2)	G1	2,500		2,500
6	(4)	G1	7,100		9,600
26	(14)	G1	120		9,720
31	Adj.(b)	G1		1,050	**8,670**

Prepaid Insurance — Acct. No. 128

Date	Explan.	PR	Debit	Credit	Balance
2011					
Dec. 6	(13)	G1	2,400		2,400
31	Adj.(a)	G1		100	**2,300**

Equipment — Acct. No. 167

Date	Explan.	PR	Debit	Credit	Balance
2011					
Dec. 3	(3)	G1	26,000		**26,000**

Accumulated Depreciation— Equipment — Acct. No. 168

Date	Explan.	PR	Debit	Credit	Balance
2011					
Dec. 31	Adj.(c)	G1		375	**375**

Liability and Equity Accounts

Accounts Payable — Acct. No. 201

Date	Explan.	PR	Debit	Credit	Balance
2011					
Dec. 6	(4)	G1		7,100	7,100
24	(10)	G1	900		**6,200**

Salaries Payable — Acct. No. 209

Date	Explan.	PR	Debit	Credit	Balance
2011					
Dec. 31	Adj.(e)	G1		210	**210**

Unearned Consulting Revenue — Acct. No. 236

Date	Explan.	PR	Debit	Credit	Balance
2011					
Dec. 26	(12)	G1		3,000	3,000
31	Adj.(d)	G1	250		**2,750**

Common Stock — Acct. No. 307

Date	Explan.	PR	Debit	Credit	Balance
2011					
Dec. 1	(1)	G1		30,000	30,000

Retained Earnings — Acct. No. 318

Date	Explan.	PR	Debit	Credit	Balance
2011					
Dec. 31	Clos.(3)	G1		3,785	3,785
31	Clos.(4)	G1	200		**3,585**

Dividends — Acct. No. 319

Date	Explan.	PR	Debit	Credit	Balance
2011					
Dec. 24	(11)	G1	200		200
31	Clos.(4)	G1		200	**0**

Revenue and Expense Accounts (Including Income Summary)

Consulting Revenue — Acct. No. 403

Date	Explan.	PR	Debit	Credit	Balance
2011					
Dec. 5	(5)	G1		4,200	4,200
12	(8)	G1		1,600	5,800
31	Adj.(d)	G1		250	6,050
31	Adj.(f)	G1		1,800	7,850
31	Clos.(1)	G1	7,850		**0**

Rental Revenue — Acct. No. 406

Date	Explan.	PR	Debit	Credit	Balance
2011					
Dec. 12	(8)	G1		300	300
31	Clos.(1)	G1	300		**0**

Depreciation Expense— Equipment — Acct. No. 612

Date	Explan.	PR	Debit	Credit	Balance
2011					
Dec. 31	Adj.(c)	G1	375		375
31	Clos.(2)	G1		375	**0**

Salaries Expense — Acct. No. 622

Date	Explan.	PR	Debit	Credit	Balance
2011					
Dec. 12	(7)	G1	700		700
26	(16)	G1	700		1,400
31	Adj.(e)	G1	210		1,610
31	Clos.(2)	G1		1,610	**0**

Insurance Expense — Acct. No. 637

Date	Explan.	PR	Debit	Credit	Balance
2011					
Dec. 31	Adj.(a)	G1	100		100
31	Clos.(2)	G1		100	**0**

Rent Expense — Acct. No. 640

Date	Explan.	PR	Debit	Credit	Balance
2011					
Dec. 12	(6)	G1	1,000		1,000
31	Clos.(2)	G1		1,000	**0**

Supplies Expense — Acct. No. 652

Date	Explan.	PR	Debit	Credit	Balance
2011					
Dec. 31	Adj.(b)	G1	1,050		1,050
31	Clos.(2)	G1		1,050	**0**

Utilities Expense — Acct. No. 690

Date	Explan.	PR	Debit	Credit	Balance
2011					
Dec. 26	(15)	G1	230		230
31	Clos.(2)	G1		230	**0**

Income Summary — Acct. No. 901

Date	Explan.	PR	Debit	Credit	Balance
2011					
Dec. 31	Clos.(1)	G1		8,150	8,150
31	Clos.(2)	G1	4,365		3,785
31	Clos.(3)	G1	3,785		**0**

114   Chapter 3 Adjusting Accounts and Preparing Financial Statements

(1) total debits equal total credits for permanent accounts and (2) all temporary accounts have zero balances. FastForward's post-closing trial balance is shown in Exhibit 3.18. The post-closing trial balance usually is the last step in the accounting process.

EXHIBIT 3.18

Post-Closing Trial Balance

FASTFORWARD
Post-Closing Trial Balance
December 31, 2011

	Debit	Credit
Cash	$ 4,350	
Accounts receivable	1,800	
Supplies	8,670	
Prepaid insurance	2,300	
Equipment	26,000	
Accumulated depreciation—Equipment		$ 375
Accounts payable		6,200
Salaries payable		210
Unearned consulting revenue		2,750
Common stock		30,000
Retained earnings		3,585
Totals	$43,120	$43,120

Accounting Cycle

C3 Identify steps in the accounting cycle.

The term **accounting cycle** refers to the steps in preparing financial statements. It is called a *cycle* because the steps are repeated each reporting period. Exhibit 3.19 shows the 10 steps in the cycle, beginning with analyzing transactions and ending with a post-closing trial balance or

EXHIBIT 3.19

Steps in the Accounting Cycle*

1. Analyze transactions → 2. Journalize → 3. Post → 4. Prepare unadjusted trial balance → 5. Adjust → 6. Prepare adjusted trial balance → 7. Prepare statements → 8. Close → 9. Prepare post-closing trial balance → 10. Reverse (Optional) → (back to 1)

Explanations

1. Analyze transactions	Analyze transactions to prepare for journalizing.
2. Journalize	Record accounts, including debits and credits, in a journal.
3. Post	Transfer debits and credits from the journal to the ledger.
4. Prepare unadjusted trial balance	Summarize unadjusted ledger accounts and amounts.
5. Adjust	Record adjustments to bring account balances up to date; journalize and post adjustments.
6. Prepare adjusted trial balance	Summarize adjusted ledger accounts and amounts.
7. Prepare statements	Use adjusted trial balance to prepare financial statements.
8. Close	Journalize and post entries to close temporary accounts.
9. Prepare post-closing trial balance	Test clerical accuracy of the closing procedures.
10. Reverse (optional)	Reverse certain adjustments in the next period—optional step; see Appendix 3C.

* Steps 4, 6, and 9 can be done on a work sheet. A work sheet is useful in planning adjustments, but adjustments (step 5) must always be journalized and posted. Steps 3, 4, 6, and 9 are automatic with a computerized system.

reversing entries. Steps 1 through 3 usually occur regularly as a company enters into transactions. Steps 4 through 9 are done at the end of a period. *Reversing entries* in step 10 are optional and are explained in Appendix 3C.

Quick Check

Answers — p. 130

14. What are the major steps in preparing closing entries?
15. Why are revenue and expense accounts called *temporary?* Identify and list the types of temporary accounts.
16. What accounts are listed on the post-closing trial balance?

CLASSIFIED BALANCE SHEET

Our discussion to this point has been limited to unclassified financial statements. This section describes a classified balance sheet. The next chapter describes a classified income statement. An **unclassified balance sheet** is one whose items are broadly grouped into assets, liabilities, and equity. One example is FastForward's balance sheet in Exhibit 3.14. A **classified balance sheet** organizes assets and liabilities into important subgroups that provide more information to decision makers.

C4 Explain and prepare a classified balance sheet.

Classification Structure

A classified balance sheet has no required layout, but it usually contains the categories in Exhibit 3.20. One of the more important classifications is the separation between current and noncurrent items for both assets and liabilities. Current items are those expected to come due (either collected or owed) within one year or the company's operating cycle, whichever is longer. The **operating cycle** is the time span from when *cash is used* to acquire goods and services until *cash is received* from the sale of goods and services. "Operating" refers to company operations and "cycle" refers to the circular flow of cash used for company inputs and then cash received from its outputs. The length of a company's operating cycle depends on its activities. For a service company, the operating cycle is the time span between (1) paying employees who perform the services and (2) receiving cash from customers. For a merchandiser selling products, the operating cycle is the time span between (1) paying suppliers for merchandise and (2) receiving cash from customers.

Point: Current and Noncurrent are also referred to as Short-Term and Long-Term, respectively.

Assets	Liabilities and Equity
Current assets	Current liabilities
Noncurrent assets	Noncurrent liabilities
Long-term investments	Equity
Plant assets	
Intangible assets	

EXHIBIT 3.20

Typical Categories in a Classified Balance Sheet

Most operating cycles are less than one year. This means most companies use a one-year period in deciding which assets and liabilities are current. A few companies have an operating cycle longer than one year. For instance, producers of certain beverages (wine) and products (ginseng) that require aging for several years have operating cycles longer than one year. A balance sheet lists current assets before noncurrent assets and current liabilities before noncurrent liabilities. This consistency in presentation allows users to quickly identify current assets that are most easily converted to cash and current liabilities that are shortly coming due. Items in current assets and current liabilities are listed in the order of how quickly they will be converted to, or paid in, cash.

EXHIBIT 3.21

Example of a Classified Balance Sheet

SNOWBOARDING COMPONENTS
Balance Sheet
January 31, 2011

Assets

Current assets
Cash	$ 6,500	
Short-term investments	2,100	
Accounts receivable, net	4,400	
Merchandise inventory	27,500	
Prepaid expenses	2,400	
Total current assets		$ 42,900

Long-term investments
Notes receivable	1,500	
Investments in stocks and bonds	18,000	
Land held for future expansion	48,000	
Total long-term investments		67,500

Plant assets
Equipment and buildings	203,200	
Less accumulated depreciation	53,000	
Equipment and buildings, net		150,200
Land		73,200
Total plant assets		223,400
Intangible assets		10,000
Total assets		$343,800

Liabilities

Current liabilities
Accounts payable	$ 15,300	
Wages payable	3,200	
Notes payable	3,000	
Current portion of long-term liabilities	7,500	
Total current liabilities		$ 29,000
Long-term liabilities (net of current portion)		150,000
Total liabilities		179,000

Equity

Common stock	50,000
Retained earnings	114,800
Total equity	164,800
Total liabilities and equity	$343,800

Classification Categories

This section describes the most common categories in a classified balance sheet. The balance sheet for Snowboarding Components in Exhibit 3.21 shows the typical categories. Its assets are classified as either current or noncurrent. Its noncurrent assets include three main categories: long-term investments, plant assets, and intangible assets. Its liabilities are classified as either current or long-term. Not all companies use the same categories of assets and liabilities for their balance sheets. **K2 Inc.**, a manufacturer of snowboards, reported a balance sheet with only three asset classes: current assets; property, plant and equipment; and other assets.

Current Assets Current assets are cash and other resources that are expected to be sold, collected, or used within one year or the company's operating cycle, whichever is longer. Examples are cash, short-term investments, accounts receivable, short-term notes receivable, goods for sale (called *merchandise* or *inventory*), and prepaid expenses. The individual prepaid expenses of a company are usually small in amount compared to many other assets and are often combined and shown as a single item. The prepaid expenses likely include items such as prepaid insurance, prepaid rent, office supplies, and store supplies. Prepaid expenses are usually listed last because they will not be converted to cash (instead, they are used).

Long-Term Investments A second major balance sheet classification is **long-term** (or *noncurrent*) **investments.** Notes receivable and investments in stocks and bonds are long-term assets when they are expected to be held for more than the longer of one year or the operating cycle. Land held for future expansion is a long-term investment because it is *not* used in operations.

Plant Assets Plant assets are tangible assets that are both *long-lived* and *used to produce* or *sell products and services*. Examples are equipment, machinery, buildings, and land that are used to produce or sell products and services. The order listing for plant assets is usually from most liquid to least liquid such as equipment and machinery to buildings and land.

Intangible Assets Intangible assets are long-term resources that benefit business operations, usually lack physical form, and have uncertain benefits. Examples are patents, trademarks, copyrights, franchises, and goodwill. Their value comes from the privileges or rights granted to or held by the owner. **K2, Inc.**, reported intangible assets of $228 million, which is nearly 20 percent of its total assets. Its intangibles included trademarks, patents, and licensing agreements.

Current Liabilities Current liabilities are obligations due to be paid or settled within one year or the operating cycle, whichever is longer. They are usually settled by paying out current assets such as cash. Current liabilities often include accounts payable, notes payable, wages payable, taxes payable, interest payable, and unearned revenues. Also, any portion of a long-term liability due to be paid within one year or the operating cycle, whichever is longer, is a current liability. Unearned revenues are current liabilities when they will be settled by delivering products or services within one year or the operating cycle, whichever is longer. Current liabilities are reported in the order of those to be settled first.

Long-Term Liabilities Long-term liabilities are obligations *not* due within one year or the operating cycle, whichever is longer. Notes payable, mortgages payable, bonds payable, and lease obligations are common long-term liabilities. If a company has both short- and long-term items in each of these categories, they are commonly separated into two accounts in the ledger.

Equity Equity is the owner's claim on assets. The equity section for a corporation is divided into two main subsections, common stock and retained earnings.

Point: Current is also called *short-term*, and noncurrent is also called *long-term*.

Point: Plant assets are also called *fixed assets; property, plant and equipment;* or *long-lived assets.*

Point: Many financial ratios are distorted if accounts are not classified correctly.

Point: Only assets and liabilities are classified as current or noncurrent.

Quick Check
Answers — p. 130

17. Classify the following assets as (1) current assets, (2) plant assets, or (3) intangible assets: (*a*) land used in operations, (*b*) office supplies, (*c*) receivables from customers due in 10 months, (*d*) insurance protection for the next 9 months, (*e*) trucks used to provide services to customers, (*f*) trademarks.
18. Cite at least two examples of assets classified as investments on the balance sheet.
19. Explain the operating cycle for a service company.

GLOBAL VIEW

We explained that accounting under U.S. GAAP is similar, but not identical, to that under IFRS. This section discusses differences in adjusting accounts, preparing financial statements, and reporting assets and liabilities on a balance sheet.

Adjusting Accounts Both U.S. GAAP and IFRS include broad and similar guidance for adjusting accounts. Although some variations exist in revenue and expense recognition and other principles, all of the adjustments in this chapter are accounted for identically under the two systems. In later chapters we describe how certain assets and liabilities can result in different adjusted amounts using fair value measurements.

Preparing Financial Statements Both U.S. GAAP and IFRS prepare the same four basic financial statements following the same process discussed in this chapter. Chapter 2 explained how both U.S. GAAP and IFRS require current items to be separated from noncurrent items on the balance sheet (yielding a classified balance sheet). U.S. GAAP balance sheets report current items first. Assets are listed from most liquid to least liquid, where liquid refers to the ease of converting an asset to cash. Liabilities are listed from nearest to maturity to furthest from maturity, maturity refers to the nearness of paying off the liability. IFRS balance sheets normally present noncurrent items first (and equity before liabilities), but this is not a requirement. Other differences with financial statements exist, which we identify in later chapters. **Nokia** provides the following example of IFRS reporting for its assets, liabilities, and equity within the balance sheet:

NOKIA
Balance Sheet (in EUR millions)
December 31, 2009

Assets		Equity and Liabilities	
Noncurrent assets		Total equity	14,749
Goodwill and other intangibles	8,076	Noncurrent liabilities	
Property, plant and equipment	1,867	Long-term interest-bearing liabilities	4,432
Other noncurrent assets	2,182	Other long-term liabilities	1,369
Total noncurrent assets	12,125	Total noncurrent liabilities	5,801
Current assets		Current liabilities	
Inventories	1,865	Current portion of long-term loans	44
Accounts receivable, net	7,981	Short-term borrowings and other liabilities	972
Prepaid expenses and accrued income	4,551	Accounts payable	4,950
Other current assets	8,074	Accrued expenses	6,504
Cash	1,142	Provisions	2,718
Total current assets	23,613	Total current liabilities	15,188
Total assets	35,738	Total equity and liabilities	35,738

Closing Process The closing process is identical under U.S. GAAP and IFRS. Although unique accounts can arise under either system, the closing process remains the same.

IFRS

Revenue and expense recognition are key to recording accounting adjustments. IFRS tends to be more *principles-based* relative to U.S. GAAP, which is viewed as more *rules-based*. A principles-based system depends heavily on control procedures to reduce the potential for fraud or misconduct. Failure in judgment led to improper accounting adjustments at **Fannie Mae**, **Xerox**, **WorldCom**, and others. A KPMG 2009 survey of accounting and finance employees found that 13% of them had witnessed falsification or manipulation of accounting data within the past year. Internal controls and governance processes are directed at curtailing such behavior.

Decision Analysis

Profit Margin and Current Ratio

A useful measure of a company's operating results is the ratio of its net income to net sales. This ratio is called **profit margin,** or *return on sales,* and is computed as in Exhibit 3.22.

$$\text{Profit margin} = \frac{\text{Net income}}{\text{Net sales}}$$

A2 Compute profit margin and describe its use in analyzing company performance.

EXHIBIT 3.22
Profit Margin

This ratio is interpreted as reflecting the percent of profit in each dollar of sales. To illustrate how we compute and use profit margin, let's look at the results of **Limited Brands, Inc.**, in Exhibit 3.23 for its fiscal years 2006 through 2010.

$ in millions	2010	2009	2008	2007	2006
Net income	$ 448	$ 220	$ 718	$ 676	$ 683
Net sales	$8,632	$9,043	$10,134	$10,671	$9,699
Profit margin	5.2%	2.4%	7.1%	6.3%	7.0%
Industry profit margin	0.9%	0.3%	1.1%	1.6%	1.5%

EXHIBIT 3.23
Limited Brands' Profit Margin

The Limited's average profit margin is 5.6% during this 5-year period. This favorably compares to the average industry profit margin of 1.1%. However, Limited's profit margin has declined in the most recent two years—from 7.1% in 2008 to 2.4% and 5.2% for the recent recessionary periods (see margin graph). Future success depends on Limited maintaining its market share and increasing its profit margin.

Current Ratio

An important use of financial statements is to help assess a company's ability to pay its debts in the near future. Such analysis affects decisions by suppliers when allowing a company to buy on credit. It also affects decisions by creditors when lending money to a company, including loan terms such as interest rate, due date, and collateral requirements. It can also affect a manager's decisions about using cash to pay debts when they come due. The **current ratio** is one measure of a company's ability to pay its short-term obligations. It is defined in Exhibit 3.24 as current assets divided by current liabilities.

$$\text{Current ratio} = \frac{\text{Current assets}}{\text{Current liabilities}}$$

A3 Compute the current ratio and describe what it reveals about a company's financial condition.

EXHIBIT 3.24
Current Ratio

Using financial information from **Limited Brands, Inc.**, we compute its current ratio for the recent four-year period. The results are in Exhibit 3.25.

$ in millions	2010	2009	2008	2007	2006
Current assets	$3,250	$2,867	$2,919	$2,771	$2,784
Current liabilities	$1,322	$1,255	$1,374	$1,709	$1,575
Current ratio	2.5	2.3	2.1	1.6	1.8
Industry current ratio	1.9	2.0	2.1	2.3	2.4

EXHIBIT 3.25
Limited Brands' Current Ratio

Limited Brands' current ratio averaged 2.1 for its fiscal years 2006 through 2010. The current ratio for each of these years suggests that the company's short-term obligations can be covered with its short-term assets. However, if its ratio would approach 1.0, Limited would expect to face challenges in covering liabilities. If the ratio were *less* than 1.0, current liabilities would exceed current assets, and the company's ability to pay short-term obligations could be in doubt.

Decision Maker

Answer — p. 130

Analyst You are analyzing the financial condition of a company to assess its ability to meet upcoming loan payments. You compute its current ratio as 1.2. You also find that a major portion of accounts receivable is due from one client who has not made any payments in the past 12 months. Removing this receivable from current assets lowers the current ratio to 0.7. What do you conclude? ■

DEMONSTRATION PROBLEM 1

The following information relates to Fanning's Electronics on December 31, 2011. The company, which uses the calendar year as its annual reporting period, initially records prepaid and unearned items in balance sheet accounts (assets and liabilities, respectively).

a. The company's weekly payroll is $8,750, paid each Friday for a five-day workweek. Assume December 31, 2011, falls on a Monday, but the employees will not be paid their wages until Friday, January 4, 2012.

b. Eighteen months earlier, on July 1, 2010, the company purchased equipment that cost $20,000. Its useful life is predicted to be five years, at which time the equipment is expected to be worthless (zero salvage value).

c. On October 1, 2011, the company agreed to work on a new housing development. The company is paid $120,000 on October 1 in advance of future installation of similar alarm systems in 24 new homes. That amount was credited to the Unearned Services Revenue account. Between October 1 and December 31, work on 20 homes was completed.

d. On September 1, 2011, the company purchased a 12-month insurance policy for $1,800. The transaction was recorded with an $1,800 debit to Prepaid Insurance.

e. On December 29, 2011, the company completed a $7,000 service that has not been billed and not recorded as of December 31, 2011.

Required

1. Prepare any necessary adjusting entries on December 31, 2011, in relation to transactions and events *a* through *e*.

2. Prepare T-accounts for the accounts affected by adjusting entries, and post the adjusting entries. Determine the adjusted balances for the Unearned Revenue and the Prepaid Insurance accounts.

3. Complete the following table and determine the amounts and effects of your adjusting entries on the year 2011 income statement and the December 31, 2011, balance sheet. Use up (down) arrows to indicate an increase (decrease) in the Effect columns.

Entry	Amount in the Entry	Effect on Net Income	Effect on Total Assets	Effect on Total Liabilities	Effect on Total Equity

PLANNING THE SOLUTION

- Analyze each situation to determine which accounts need to be updated with an adjustment.
- Calculate the amount of each adjustment and prepare the necessary journal entries.
- Show the amount of each adjustment in the designated accounts, determine the adjusted balance, and identify the balance sheet classification of the account.
- Determine each entry's effect on net income for the year and on total assets, total liabilities, and total equity at the end of the year.

SOLUTION TO DEMONSTRATION PROBLEM 1

1. Adjusting journal entries.

(a) Dec. 31	Wages Expense		1,750	
	Wages Payable			1,750
	To accrue wages for the last day of the year ($8,750 × 1/5).			
(b) Dec. 31	Depreciation Expense—Equipment		4,000	
	Accumulated Depreciation—Equipment			4,000
	To record depreciation expense for the year ($20,000/5 years = $4,000 per year).			
(c) Dec. 31	Unearned Services Revenue		100,000	
	Services Revenue			100,000
	To recognize services revenue earned ($120,000 × 20/24).			
(d) Dec. 31	Insurance Expense		600	
	Prepaid Insurance			600
	To adjust for expired portion of insurance ($1,800 × 4/12).			
(e) Dec. 31	Accounts Receivable		7,000	
	Services Revenue			7,000
	To record services revenue earned.			

2. T-accounts for adjusting journal entries *a* through *e*.

Wages Expense				Wages Payable	
(a)	1,750			(a)	1,750

Depreciation Expense—Equipment				Accumulated Depreciation—Equipment	
(b)	4,000			(b)	4,000

Unearned Revenue				Services Revenue	
		Unadj. Bal.	120,000	(c)	100,000
(c)	100,000			(e)	7,000
		Adj. Bal.	20,000	Adj. Bal.	107,000

Insurance Expense				Prepaid Insurance	
(d)	600		Unadj. Bal.	1,800	
					(d) 600
Accounts Receivable			Adj. Bal.	1,200	
(e)	7,000				

3. Financial statement effects of adjusting journal entries.

Entry	Amount in the Entry	Effect on Net Income	Effect on Total Assets	Effect on Total Liabilities	Effect on Total Equity
a	$ 1,750	$ 1,750 ↓	No effect	$ 1,750 ↑	$ 1,750 ↓
b	4,000	4,000 ↓	$4,000 ↓	No effect	4,000 ↓
c	100,000	100,000 ↑	No effect	$100,000 ↓	100,000 ↑
d	600	600 ↓	$ 600 ↓	No effect	600 ↓
e	7,000	7,000 ↑	$7,000 ↑	No effect	7,000 ↑

DEMONSTRATION PROBLEM 2

Use the following adjusted trial balance to answer questions 1–3.

CHOI COMPANY
Adjusted Trial Balance
December 31

	Debit	Credit
Cash	$ 3,050	
Accounts receivable	400	
Prepaid insurance	830	
Supplies	80	
Equipment	217,200	
Accumulated depreciation—Equipment		$ 29,100
Wages payable		880
Interest payable		3,600
Unearned rent		460
Long-term notes payable		150,000
Common stock		10,000
Retained earnings		30,340
Dividends	21,000	
Rent earned		57,500
Wages expense	25,000	
Utilities expense	1,900	
Insurance expense	3,200	
Supplies expense	250	
Depreciation expense—Equipment	5,970	
Interest expense	3,000	
Totals	$281,880	$281,880

1. Prepare the annual income statement from the adjusted trial balance of Choi Company.

Answer:

CHOI COMPANY
Income Statement
For Year Ended December 31

Revenues		
Rent earned		$57,500
Expenses		
Wages expense	$25,000	
Utilities expense	1,900	
Insurance expense	3,200	
Supplies expense	250	
Depreciation expense—Equipment	5,970	
Interest expense	3,000	
Total expenses		39,320
Net income		$18,180

2. Prepare a statement of retained earnings from the adjusted trial balance of Choi Company.

Answer:

CHOI COMPANY
Statement of Retained Earnings
For Year Ended December 31

Retained earnings, December 31 prior year-end	$30,340
Plus: Net income	18,180
	48,520
Less: Dividends	21,000
Retained earnings, December 31 current year-end	$27,520

3. Prepare a balance sheet from the adjusted trial balance of Choi Company.

Answer:

CHOI COMPANY
Balance Sheet
December 31

Assets

Cash		$ 3,050
Accounts receivable		400
Prepaid insurance		830
Supplies		80
Equipment	$217,200	
Less accumulated depreciation	29,100	188,100
Total assets		$192,460

Liabilities

Wages payable	$ 880
Interest payable	3,600
Unearned rent	460
Long-term notes payable	150,000
Total liabilities	154,940

Equity

Common stock	10,000
Retained earnings	27,520
Total equity	37,520
Total liabilities and equity	$192,460

APPENDIX 3A

Alternative Accounting for Prepayments

This appendix explains an alternative in accounting for prepaid expenses and unearned revenues.

Recording Prepayment of Expenses in Expense Accounts An alternative method is to record *all* prepaid expenses with debits to expense accounts. If any prepaids remain unused or unexpired at the end of an accounting period, then adjusting entries must transfer the cost of the unused portions from expense accounts to prepaid expense (asset) accounts. This alternative method is acceptable. The financial statements are identical under either method, but the adjusting entries are different. To illustrate the differences between these two methods, let's look at FastForward's cash payment of December 6 for 24 months of insurance coverage beginning on December 1. FastForward recorded that payment with a debit to an asset account, but it could have recorded a debit to an expense account. These alternatives are shown in Exhibit 3A.1.

P6 Explain the alternatives in accounting for prepaids.

EXHIBIT 3A.1
Alternative Initial Entries for Prepaid Expenses

			Payment Recorded as Asset		Payment Recorded as Expense	
Dec. 6	Prepaid Insurance		2,400			
	Cash			2,400		
Dec. 6	Insurance Expense				2,400	
	Cash					2,400

At the end of its accounting period on December 31, insurance protection for one month has expired. This means $100 ($2,400/24) of insurance coverage expired and is an expense for December. The adjusting entry depends on how the original payment was recorded. This is shown in Exhibit 3A.2.

EXHIBIT 3A.2

Adjusting Entry for Prepaid Expenses for the Two Alternatives

			Payment Recorded as Asset	Payment Recorded as Expense
Dec. 31	Insurance Expense		100	
	Prepaid Insurance		100	
Dec. 31	Prepaid Insurance			2,300
	Insurance Expense			2,300

When these entries are posted to the accounts in the ledger, we can see that these two methods give identical results. The December 31 adjusted account balances in Exhibit 3A.3 show Prepaid Insurance of $2,300 and Insurance Expense of $100 for both methods.

EXHIBIT 3A.3

Account Balances under Two Alternatives for Recording Prepaid Expenses

Payment Recorded as Asset	Payment Recorded as Expense

Prepaid Insurance		128
Dec. 6 2,400	Dec. 31 100	
Balance 2,300		

Prepaid Insurance		128
Dec. 31 2,300		

Insurance Expense		637
Dec. 31 100		

Insurance Expense		637
Dec. 6 2,400	Dec. 31 2,300	
Balance 100		

Recording Prepayment of Revenues in Revenue Accounts As with prepaid expenses, an alternative method is to record *all* unearned revenues with credits to revenue accounts. If any revenues are unearned at the end of an accounting period, then adjusting entries must transfer the unearned portions from revenue accounts to unearned revenue (liability) accounts. This alternative method is acceptable. The adjusting entries are different for these two alternatives, but the financial statements are identical. To illustrate the accounting differences between these two methods, let's look at FastForward's December 26 receipt of $3,000 for consulting services covering the period December 27 to February 24. FastForward recorded this transaction with a credit to a liability account. The alternative is to record it with a credit to a revenue account, as shown in Exhibit 3A.4.

EXHIBIT 3A.4

Alternative Initial Entries for Unearned Revenues

			Receipt Recorded as Liability	Receipt Recorded as Revenue
Dec. 26	Cash		3,000	
	Unearned Consulting Revenue		3,000	
Dec. 26	Cash			3,000
	Consulting Revenue			3,000

By the end of its accounting period on December 31, FastForward has earned $250 of this revenue. This means $250 of the liability has been satisfied. Depending on how the initial receipt is recorded, the adjusting entry is as shown in Exhibit 3A.5.

Chapter 3 Adjusting Accounts and Preparing Financial Statements

		Receipt Recorded as Liability	Receipt Recorded as Revenue
Dec. 31	Unearned Consulting Revenue	250	
	Consulting Revenue		250
Dec. 31	Consulting Revenue		2,750
	Unearned Consulting Revenue		2,750

EXHIBIT 3A.5

Adjusting Entry for Unearned Revenues for the Two Alternatives

After adjusting entries are posted, the two alternatives give identical results. The December 31 adjusted account balances in Exhibit 3A.6 show unearned consulting revenue of $2,750 and consulting revenue of $250 for both methods.

Receipt Recorded as Liability

Unearned Consulting Revenue			236
Dec. 31	250	Dec. 26	3,000
		Balance	2,750

Consulting Revenue		403
	Dec. 31	250

Receipt Recorded as Revenue

Unearned Consulting Revenue		236
	Dec. 31	2,750

Consulting Revenue			403
Dec. 31	2,750	Dec. 26	3,000
		Balance	250

EXHIBIT 3A.6

Account Balances under Two Alternatives for Recording Unearned Revenues

APPENDIX 3B

Work Sheet as a Tool

Information preparers use various analyses and internal documents when organizing information for internal and external decision makers. Internal documents are often called **working papers.** One widely used working paper is the **work sheet,** which is a useful tool for preparers in working with accounting information. It is usually not available to external decision makers.

Benefits of a Work Sheet (Spreadsheet) A work sheet is *not* a required report, yet using a manual or electronic work sheet has several potential benefits. Specifically, a work sheet:

- Aids the preparation of financial statements.
- Reduces the possibility of errors when working with many accounts and adjustments.
- Links accounts and adjustments to their impacts in financial statements.
- Assists in planning and organizing an audit of financial statements—as it can be used to reflect any adjustments necessary.
- Helps in preparing interim (monthly and quarterly) financial statements when the journalizing and posting of adjusting entries are postponed until the year-end.
- Shows the effects of proposed or "what if" transactions.

P7 Prepare a work sheet and explain its usefulness.

Use of a Work Sheet (Spreadsheet) When a work sheet is used to prepare financial statements, it is constructed at the end of a period before the adjusting process. The complete work sheet includes a list of the accounts, their balances and adjustments, and their sorting into financial statement columns. It provides two columns each for the unadjusted trial balance, the adjustments, the adjusted trial balance, the income statement, and the balance sheet. To describe and interpret the work sheet, we

Point: Since a work sheet is *not* a required report or an accounting record, its format is flexible and can be modified by its user to fit his/her preferences.

use the information from FastForward. Preparing the work sheet has five important steps. Each step, 1 through 5, is color-coded and explained with reference to Exhibit 3B.1.

① Step 1. Enter Unadjusted Trial Balance

The first step in preparing a work sheet is to list the title of every account and its account number that is expected to appear on its financial statements. This includes all accounts in the ledger plus any new ones from adjusting entries. Most adjusting entries—including expenses from salaries, supplies, depreciation, and insurance—are predictable and recurring. The unadjusted balance for each account is then entered in the appropriate Debit or Credit column of the unadjusted trial balance columns. The totals of these two columns must be equal. Exhibit 3B.1 shows FastForward's work sheet after completing this first step. Sometimes blank lines are left on the work sheet based on past experience to indicate where lines will be needed for adjustments to certain accounts. Exhibit 3B.1 shows Consulting Revenue as one example. An alternative is to squeeze adjustments on one line or to combine the effects of two or more adjustments in one amount. In the unusual case when an account is not predicted, we can add a new line for such an account following the *Totals* line.

② Step 2. Enter Adjustments

The second step in preparing a work sheet is to enter adjustments in the Adjustments columns. The adjustments shown are the same ones shown in Exhibit 3.13. An identifying letter links the debit and credit of each adjusting entry. This is called *keying* the adjustments. After preparing a work sheet, adjusting entries must still be entered in the journal and posted to the ledger. The Adjustments columns provide the information for those entries.

③ Step 3. Prepare Adjusted Trial Balance

Point: To avoid omitting the transfer of an account balance, start with the first line (cash) and continue in account order.

The adjusted trial balance is prepared by combining the adjustments with the unadjusted balances for each account. As an example, the Prepaid Insurance account has a $2,400 debit balance in the Unadjusted Trial Balance columns. This $2,400 debit is combined with the $100 credit in the Adjustments columns to give Prepaid Insurance a $2,300 debit in the Adjusted Trial Balance columns. The totals of the Adjusted Trial Balance columns confirm the equality of debits and credits.

④ Step 4. Sort Adjusted Trial Balance Amounts to Financial Statements

This step involves sorting account balances from the adjusted trial balance to their proper financial statement columns. Expenses go to the Income Statement Debit column and revenues to the Income Statement Credit column. Assets and Dividends go to the Balance Sheet Debit column. Liabilities, Retained Earnings, and Common Stock go to the Balance Sheet Credit column.

⑤ Step 5. Total Statement Columns, Compute Income or Loss, and Balance Columns

Each financial statement column (from Step 4) is totaled. The difference between the totals of the Income Statement columns is net income or net loss. This occurs because revenues are entered in the Credit column and expenses in the Debit column. If the Credit total exceeds the Debit total, there is net income. If the Debit total exceeds the Credit total, there is a net loss. For FastForward, the Credit total exceeds the Debit total, giving a $3,785 net income.

The net income from the Income Statement columns is then entered in the Balance Sheet Credit column. Adding net income to the last Credit column implies that it is to be added to retained earnings. If a loss occurs, it is added to the Debit column. This implies that it is to be subtracted from retained earnings. The ending balance of retained earnings does not appear in the last two columns as a single amount, but it is computed in the statement of retained earnings using these account balances. When net income or net loss is added to the proper Balance Sheet column, the totals of the last two columns must balance. If they do not, one or more errors have been made. The error can either be mathematical or involve sorting one or more amounts to incorrect columns.

Work Sheet Applications and Analysis A work sheet does not substitute for financial statements. It is a tool we can use at the end of an accounting period to help organize data and prepare financial statements. FastForward's financial statements are shown in Exhibit 3.14. Its income statement amounts are taken from the Income Statement columns of the work sheet. Similarly, amounts for its balance sheet and its statement of retained earnings are taken from the Balance Sheet columns of the work sheet.

Work sheets are also useful in analyzing the effects of proposed, or what-if, transactions. This is done by entering financial statement amounts in the Unadjusted (what-if) columns. Proposed transactions are then entered in the Adjustments columns. We then compute "adjusted" amounts from these proposed transactions. The extended amounts in the financial statement columns show the effects of these proposed transactions. These financial statement columns yield **pro forma financial statements** because they show the statements *as if* the proposed transactions occurred.

Chapter 3 Adjusting Accounts and Preparing Financial Statements 127

EXHIBIT 3B.1

Work Sheet

FASTFORWARD
Work Sheet
For Month Ended December 31, 2011

No.	Account	Unadjusted Trial Balance Dr.	Unadjusted Trial Balance Cr.	Adjustments Dr.	Adjustments Cr.	Adjusted Trial Balance Dr.	Adjusted Trial Balance Cr.	Income Statement Dr.	Income Statement Cr.	Balance Sheet Dr.	Balance Sheet Cr.
101	Cash	4,350				4,350				4,350	
106	Accounts receivable	0		(f)1,800		1,800				1,800	
126	Supplies	9,720			(b)1,050	8,670				8,670	
128	Prepaid insurance	2,400			(a) 100	2,300				2,300	
167	Equipment	26,000				26,000				26,000	
168	Accumulated depreciation—Equip.		0		(c) 375		375				375
201	Accounts payable		6,200				6,200				6,200
209	Salaries payable		0		(e) 210		210				210
236	Unearned consulting revenue		3,000	(d) 250			2,750				2,750
307	Common stock		30,000				30,000				30,000
318	Retained earnings		0				0				0
319	Dividends	200				200				200	
403	Consulting revenue		5,800		(d) 250 (f)1,800		7,850		7,850		
406	Rental revenue		300				300		300		
612	Depreciation expense—Equip.	0		(c) 375		375		375			
622	Salaries expense	1,400		(e) 210		1,610		1,610			
637	Insurance expense	0		(a) 100		100		100			
640	Rent expense	1,000				1,000		1,000			
652	Supplies expense	0		(b)1,050		1,050		1,050			
690	Utilities expense	230				230		230			
	Totals	45,300	45,300	3,785	3,785	47,685	47,685	4,365	8,150	43,320	39,535
	Net income							3,785			3,785
	Totals							8,150	8,150	43,320	43,320

(1) List all accounts from the ledger and those expected to arise from adjusting entries.

(2) Enter all amounts available from ledger accounts. Column totals must be equal.

(3)(4) A work sheet collects and summarizes information used to prepare adjusting entries, financial statements, and closing entries.

APPENDIX

Reversing Entries

3C

Reversing entries are optional. They are recorded in response to accrued assets and accrued liabilities that were created by adjusting entries at the end of a reporting period. The purpose of reversing entries is to simplify a company's recordkeeping. Exhibit 3C.1 shows an example of FastForward's reversing entries. The top of the exhibit shows the adjusting entry FastForward recorded on December 31 for its employee's earned but unpaid salary. The entry recorded three days' salary of $210, which increased December's total salary expense to $1,610. The entry also recognized a liability of $210. The expense is reported on December's income statement. The expense account is then closed. The ledger on January 1, 2012, shows a $210 liability and a zero balance in the Salaries Expense account. At this point, the choice is made between using or not using reversing entries.

Point: As a general rule, adjusting entries that create new asset or liability accounts are likely candidates for reversing.

EXHIBIT 3C.1
Reversing Entries for an Accrued Expense

Accrue salaries expense on December 31, 2011

Salaries Expense	210	
Salaries Payable		210

Salaries Expense

Date	Expl.	Debit	Credit	Balance
2011				
Dec. 12	(7)	700		700
26	(16)	700		1,400
31	(e)	210		1,610

Salaries Payable

Date	Expl.	Debit	Credit	Balance
2011				
Dec. 31	(e)		210	210

WITHOUT Reversing Entries — OR — **WITH Reversing Entries**

No reversing entry recorded on January 1, 2012 — *Reversing entry recorded on January 1, 2012*

WITHOUT Reversing Entries

NO ENTRY

Salaries Expense

Date	Expl.	Debit	Credit	Balance
2012				

Salaries Payable

Date	Expl.	Debit	Credit	Balance
2011				
Dec. 31	(e)		210	210
2012				

WITH Reversing Entries

Salaries Payable	210	
Salaries Expense		210

Salaries Expense*

Date	Expl.	Debit	Credit	Balance
2012				
Jan. 1			210	(210)

Salaries Payable

Date	Expl.	Debit	Credit	Balance
2011				
Dec. 31	(e)		210	210
2012				
Jan. 1		210		0

Pay the accrued and current salaries on January 9, the first payday in 2012

WITHOUT Reversing Entries

Salaries Expense	490	
Salaries Payable	210	
Cash		700

Salaries Expense

Date	Expl.	Debit	Credit	Balance
2012				
Jan. 9		490		**490**

Salaries Payable

Date	Expl.	Debit	Credit	Balance
2011				
Dec. 31	(e)		210	210
2012				
Jan. 9		210		0

WITH Reversing Entries

Salaries Expense	700	
Cash		700

Salaries Expense*

Date	Expl.	Debit	Credit	Balance
2012				
Jan. 1			210	(210)
Jan. 9		700		**490**

Salaries Payable

Date	Expl.	Debit	Credit	Balance
2011				
Dec. 31	(e)		210	210
2012				
Jan. 1		210		0

Under both approaches, the expense and liability accounts have identical balances after the cash payment on January 9.

Salaries Expense	$490
Salaries Payable	$ 0

*Circled numbers in the Balance column indicate abnormal balances.

Accounting *without* Reversing Entries The path down the left side of Exhibit 3C.1 is described in the chapter. To summarize here, when the next payday occurs on January 9, we record payment with a compound entry that debits both the expense and liability accounts and credits Cash. Posting that entry creates a $490 balance in the expense account and reduces the liability account balance to zero because the debt has been settled. The disadvantage of this approach is the slightly more complex entry required on January 9. Paying the accrued liability means that this entry differs from the routine entries made on all other paydays. To construct the proper entry on January 9, we must recall the effect of the December 31 adjusting entry. Reversing entries overcome this disadvantage.

P8 Prepare reversing entries and explain their purpose.

Accounting *with* Reversing Entries The right side of Exhibit 3C.1 shows how a reversing entry on January 1 overcomes the disadvantage of the January 9 entry when not using reversing entries.

A reversing entry is the exact opposite of an adjusting entry. For FastForward, the Salaries Payable liability account is debited for $210, meaning that this account now has a zero balance after the entry is posted. The Salaries Payable account temporarily understates the liability, but this is not a problem since financial statements are not prepared before the liability is settled on January 9. The credit to the Salaries Expense account is unusual because it gives the account an *abnormal credit balance*. We highlight an abnormal balance by circling it. Because of the reversing entry, the January 9 entry to record payment is straightforward. This entry debits the Salaries Expense account and credits Cash for the full $700 paid. It is the same as all other entries made to record 10 days' salary for the employee. Notice that after the payment entry is posted, the Salaries Expense account has a $490 balance that reflects seven days' salary of $70 per day (see the lower right side of Exhibit 3C.1). The zero balance in the Salaries Payable account is now correct. The lower section of Exhibit 3C.1 shows that the expense and liability accounts have exactly the same balances whether reversing entries are used or not. This means that both approaches yield identical results.

Summary

C1 **Explain the importance of periodic reporting and the time period assumption.** The value of information is often linked to its timeliness. To provide timely information, accounting systems prepare periodic reports at regular intervals. The time period assumption presumes that an organization's activities can be divided into specific time periods for periodic reporting.

C2 **Explain accrual accounting and how it improves financial statements.** Accrual accounting recognizes revenue when earned and expenses when incurred—not necessarily when cash inflows and outflows occur. This information is valuable in assessing a company's financial position and performance.

C3 **Identify steps in the accounting cycle.** The accounting cycle consists of 10 steps: (1) analyze transactions, (2) journalize, (3) post, (4) prepare an unadjusted trial balance, (5) adjust accounts, (6) prepare an adjusted trial balance, (7) prepare statements, (8) close, (9) prepare a post-closing trial balance, and (10) prepare (optional) reversing entries.

C4 **Explain and prepare a classified balance sheet.** Classified balance sheets report assets and liabilities in two categories: current and noncurrent. Noncurrent assets often include long-term investments, plant assets, and intangible assets. A corporation separates equity into common stock and retained earnings.

A1 **Explain how accounting adjustments link to financial statements.** Accounting adjustments bring an asset or liability account balance to its correct amount. They also update related expense or revenue accounts. Every adjusting entry affects one or more income statement accounts *and* one or more balance sheet accounts. An adjusting entry never affects cash.

A2 **Compute profit margin and describe its use in analyzing company performance.** *Profit margin* is defined as the reporting period's net income divided by its net sales. Profit margin reflects on a company's earnings activities by showing how much income is in each dollar of sales.

A3 **Compute the current ratio and describe what it reveals about a company's financial condition.** A company's current ratio is defined as current assets divided by current liabilities. We use it to evaluate a company's ability to pay its current liabilities out of current assets.

P1 **Prepare and explain adjusting entries.** *Prepaid expenses* refer to items paid for in advance of receiving their benefits. Prepaid expenses are assets. Adjusting entries for prepaids involve increasing (debiting) expenses and decreasing (crediting) assets. *Unearned* (or *prepaid*) *revenues* refer to cash received in advance of providing products and services. Unearned revenues are liabilities. Adjusting entries for unearned revenues involve increasing (crediting) revenues and decreasing (debiting) unearned revenues. *Accrued expenses* refer to costs incurred in a period that are both unpaid and unrecorded. Adjusting entries for recording accrued expenses involve increasing (debiting) expenses and increasing (crediting) liabilities. *Accrued revenues* refer to revenues earned in a period that are both unrecorded and not yet received in cash. Adjusting entries for recording accrued revenues involve increasing (debiting) assets and increasing (crediting) revenues.

P2 **Explain and prepare an adjusted trial balance.** An adjusted trial balance is a list of accounts and balances prepared after recording and posting adjusting entries. Financial statements are often prepared from the adjusted trial balance.

P3 **Prepare financial statements from an adjusted trial balance.** Revenue and expense balances are reported on the income statement. Asset, liability, and equity balances are reported on the balance sheet. We usually prepare statements in the following order: income statement, statement of retained earnings, balance sheet, and statement of cash flows.

P4 **Describe and prepare closing entries.** Closing entries involve four steps: (1) close credit balances in revenue (and gain) accounts to Income Summary, (2) close debit balances in expense (and loss) accounts to Income Summary, (3) close Income Summary to retained earnings, and (4) close dividends account to retained earnings.

P5 **Explain and prepare a post-closing trial balance.** A post-closing trial balance is a list of permanent accounts and their balances after all closing entries have been journalized and posted. Its purpose is to verify that (1) total debits equal total credits for permanent accounts and (2) all temporary accounts have zero balances.

P6[A] **Explain the alternatives in accounting for prepaids.** Charging all prepaid expenses to expense accounts when they are purchased is acceptable. When this is done, adjusting entries must transfer any unexpired amounts from expense accounts to asset accounts. Crediting all unearned revenues to revenue accounts when cash is received is also acceptable. In this case, the adjusting entries must transfer any unearned amounts from revenue accounts to unearned revenue accounts.

P7B Prepare a work sheet and explain its usefulness. A work sheet can be a useful tool in preparing and analyzing financial statements. It is helpful at the end of a period in preparing adjusting entries, an adjusted trial balance, and financial statements. A work sheet usually contains five pairs of columns: Unadjusted Trial Balance, Adjustments, Adjusted Trial Balance, Income Statement, and Balance Sheet & Statement of Equity.

P8C Prepare reversing entries and explain their purpose. Reversing entries are an optional step. They are applied to accrued expenses and revenues. The purpose of reversing entries is to simplify subsequent journal entries. Financial statements are unaffected by the choice to use or not use reversing entries.

Guidance Answers to Decision Maker and Decision Ethics

Investor Prepaid expenses are items paid for in advance of receiving their benefits. They are assets and are expensed as they are used up. The publishing company's treatment of the signing bonus is acceptable provided future book sales can at least match the $500,000 expense. As an investor, you are concerned about the risk of future book sales. The riskier the likelihood of future book sales is, the more likely your analysis is to treat the $500,000, or a portion of it, as an expense, not a prepaid expense (asset).

Loan Officer Your concern in lending to this store arises from analysis of current-year sales. While increased revenues and income are fine, your concern is with collectibility of these promotional sales. If the owner sold products to customers with poor records of paying bills, then collectibility of these sales is low. Your analysis must assess this possibility and recognize any expected losses.

Financial Officer Omitting accrued expenses and recognizing revenue early can mislead financial statement users. One action is to request a second meeting with the president so you can explain that accruing expenses when incurred and recognizing revenue when earned are required practices. If the president persists, you might discuss the situation with legal counsel and any auditors involved. Your ethical action might cost you this job, but the potential pitfalls for falsification of statements, reputation and personal integrity loss, and other costs are too great.

Analyst A current ratio of 1.2 suggests that current assets are sufficient to cover current liabilities, but it implies a minimal buffer in case of errors in measuring current assets or current liabilities. Removing the past due receivable reduces the current ratio to 0.7. Your assessment is that the company will have some difficulty meeting its loan payments.

Guidance Answers to Quick Checks

1. An annual reporting (or accounting) period covers one year and refers to the preparation of annual financial statements. The annual reporting period is not always a calendar year that ends on December 31. An organization can adopt a fiscal year consisting of any consecutive 12 months or 52 weeks.
2. Interim financial statements (covering less than one year) are prepared to provide timely information to decision makers.
3. The revenue recognition principle and the expense recognition (matching) principle lead most directly to the adjusting process.
4. No. Cash basis accounting is not consistent with the matching principle because it reports revenue when received, not necessarily when earned, and expenses when paid, not necessarily in the period when the expenses were incurred as a result of the revenues earned.
5. No expense is reported in 2012. Under cash basis accounting, the entire $4,800 is reported as an expense in April 2011 when the premium is paid.
6. If the accrued revenues adjustment of $200 is not made, then both revenues and net income are understated by $200 on the current year's income statement, and both assets and equity are understated by $200 on the balance sheet.
7. A contra account is an account that is subtracted from the balance of a related account. Use of a contra account provides more information than simply reporting a net amount.
8. An accrued expense is a cost incurred in a period that is both unpaid and unrecorded prior to adjusting entries. One example is salaries earned but not yet paid at period-end.
9. An unearned revenue arises when a firm receives cash (or other assets) from a customer before providing the services or products to the customer. A magazine subscription paid in advance is one example; season ticket sales is another.
10. Salaries Payable 1,000
    Salaries Expense 6,000
        Cash 7,000
    Paid salary including accrual from December.
11. The probable adjusting entries of Jordan Air are:
    Insurance Expense 300
        Prepaid Insurance 300
    To record insurance expired.
    Salaries Expense 1,400
        Salaries Payable 1,400
    To record accrued salaries.
12. Revenue accounts and expense accounts.
13. Statement of retained earnings.
14. The major steps in preparing closing entries are to close (1) credit balances in revenue accounts to Income Summary, (2) debit balances in expense accounts to Income Summary,

(3) Income Summary to retained earnings, and (4) any dividends account to retained earnings.

15. Revenue (and gain) and expense (and loss) accounts are called *temporary* because they are opened and closed each period. The Income Summary and Dividends accounts are also temporary.

16. Permanent accounts make up the post-closing trial balance, which consist of asset, liability, and equity accounts.

17. Current assets: (b), (c), (d). Plant assets: (a), (e). Item (f) is an intangible asset.

18. Investment in common stock, investment in bonds, and land held for future expansion.

19. For a service company, the operating cycle is the usual time between (1) paying employees who do the services and (2) receiving cash from customers for services provided.

Key Terms

Accounting cycle (p. 114)
Accounting period (p. 96)
Accrual basis accounting (p. 97)
Accrued expenses (p. 103)
Accrued revenues (p. 105)
Adjusted trial balance (p. 108)
Adjusting entry (p. 98)
Annual financial statements (p. 96)
Book value (p. 102)
Cash basis accounting (p. 97)
Classified balance sheet (p. 115)
Closing entries (p. 110)
Closing process (p. 110)
Contra account (p. 101)
Current assets (p. 116)

Current liabilities (p. 117)
Current ratio (p. 119)
Depreciation (p. 101)
Expense recognition (or matching) principle (p. 98)
Fiscal year (p. 97)
Income summary (p. 111)
Intangible assets (p. 117)
Interim financial statements (p. 96)
Long-term investments (p. 117)
Long-term liabilities (p. 117)
Natural business year (p. 97)
Operating cycle (p. 115)
Permanent accounts (p. 110)
Plant assets (p. 101)

Post-closing trial balance (p. 112)
Prepaid expenses (p. 99)
Pro forma financial statements (p. 126)
Profit margin (p. 119)
Reversing entries (p. 127)
Straight-line depreciation method (p. 101)
Temporary accounts (p. 110)
Time period assumption (p. 96)
Unadjusted trial balance (p. 108)
Unclassified balance sheet (p. 115)
Unearned revenues (p. 102)
Working papers (p. 125)
Work sheet (p. 125)

Multiple Choice Quiz

Answers on p. 155

mhhe.com/wildFA6e

Additional quiz questions are available at the book's Website.

1. A company forgot to record accrued and unpaid employee wages of $350,000 at period-end. This oversight would
   a. Understate net income by $350,000.
   b. Overstate net income by $350,000.
   c. Have no effect on net income.
   d. Overstate assets by $350,000.
   e. Understate assets by $350,000.

2. Prior to recording adjusting entries, the Supplies account has a $450 debit balance. A physical count of supplies shows $125 of unused supplies still available. The required adjusting entry is:
   a. Debit Supplies $125; Credit Supplies Expense $125.
   b. Debit Supplies $325; Credit Supplies Expense $325.
   c. Debit Supplies Expense $325; Credit Supplies $325.
   d. Debit Supplies Expense $325; Credit Supplies $125.
   e. Debit Supplies Expense $125; Credit Supplies $125.

3. On May 1, 2011, a two-year insurance policy was purchased for $24,000 with coverage to begin immediately. What is the amount of insurance expense that appears on the company's income statement for the year ended December 31, 2011?
   a. $4,000
   b. $8,000
   c. $12,000
   d. $20,000
   e. $24,000

4. On November 1, 2011, Stockton Co. receives $3,600 cash from Hans Co. for consulting services to be provided evenly over the period November 1, 2011, to April 30, 2012—at which time Stockton credited $3,600 to Unearned Consulting Fees. The adjusting entry on December 31, 2011 (Stockton's year-end), would include a
   a. Debit to Unearned Consulting Fees for $1,200.
   b. Debit to Unearned Consulting Fees for $2,400.
   c. Credit to Consulting Fees Earned for $2,400.
   d. Debit to Consulting Fees Earned for $1,200.
   e. Credit to Cash for $3,600.

5. If a company had $15,000 in net income for the year, and its sales were $300,000 for the same year, what is its profit margin?
   a. 20%
   b. 2,000%
   c. $285,000
   d. $315,000
   e. 5%

6. Based on the following information from Repicor Company's balance sheet, what is Repicor Company's current ratio?

a. 2.10
b. 1.50
c. 1.00
d. 0.95
e. 0.67

Current assets	$ 75,000	Current liabilities	$ 50,000
Investments	30,000	Long-term liabilities	60,000
Plant assets	300,000	Common stock	295,000

A(B,C) Superscript letter A(B,C) denotes assignments based on Appendix 3A(3B,3C).

Icon denotes assignments that involve decision making.

Discussion Questions

1. What is the difference between the cash basis and the accrual basis of accounting?
2. Why is the accrual basis of accounting generally preferred over the cash basis?
3. What type of business is most likely to select a fiscal year that corresponds to its natural business year instead of the calendar year?
4. What is a prepaid expense and where is it reported in the financial statements?
5. What type of assets require adjusting entries to record depreciation?
6. What contra account is used when recording and reporting the effects of depreciation? Why is it used?
7. **Apple** has unearned revenue. What is unearned revenue and where is it reported in financial statements? **Apple**
8. What is an accrued revenue? Give an example.
9.[A] If a company initially records prepaid expenses with debits to expense accounts, what type of account is debited in the adjusting entries for those prepaid expenses?
10. Review the balance sheet of **Research In Motion** in Appendix A. Identify one asset account that requires adjustment before annual financial statements can be prepared. What would be the effect on the income statement if this asset account were not adjusted? **RIM**
11. Review the balance sheet of **Nokia** in Appendix A. Identify the amount for property, plant, and equipment. What adjusting entry is necessary (no numbers required) for this account when preparing financial statements? **NOKIA**
12. Refer to **Palm**'s balance sheet in Appendix A. If it made an adjustment for unpaid wages at year-end, where would the accrued wages be reported on its balance sheet? **Palm**
13. What accounts are affected by closing entries? What accounts are not affected?
14. What two purposes are accomplished by recording closing entries?
15. What are the steps in recording closing entries?
16. What is the purpose of the Income Summary account?
17. Explain whether an error has occurred if a post-closing trial balance includes a Depreciation Expense account.
18.[B] What tasks are aided by a work sheet?
19.[B] Why are the debit and credit entries in the Adjustments columns of the work sheet identified with letters?
20. What is a company's operating cycle?
21. What classes of assets and liabilities are shown on a typical classified balance sheet?
22. How is unearned revenue classified on the balance sheet?
23. What are the characteristics of plant assets?
24.[C] How do reversing entries simplify recordkeeping?
25.[C] If a company recorded accrued salaries expense of $500 at the end of its fiscal year, what reversing entry could be made? When would it be made?
26. Refer to the balance sheet for **Research In Motion** in Appendix A. What five main noncurrent asset categories are used on its classified balance sheet? **RIM**
27. Refer to **Nokia**'s balance sheet in Appendix A. Identify and list its 9 current assets. **NOKIA**
28. Refer to **Apple**'s balance sheet in Appendix A. Identify the three accounts listed as current liabilities. **Apple**
29. Refer to **Palm**'s financial statements in Appendix A. What journal entry was likely recorded as of May 31, 2009, to close its Income Summary account? **Palm**

QUICK STUDY

QS 3-1
Identifying accounting adjustments
P1

Classify the following adjusting entries as involving prepaid expenses (PE), unearned revenues (UR), accrued expenses (AE), or accrued revenues (AR).

a. _____ To record revenue earned that was previously received as cash in advance.
b. _____ To record annual depreciation expense.
c. _____ To record wages expense incurred but not yet paid (nor recorded).
d. _____ To record revenue earned but not yet billed (nor recorded).
e. _____ To record expiration of prepaid insurance.

QS 3-2
Adjusting prepaid expenses
P1

a. On July 1, 2011, Baxter Company paid $1,800 for six months of insurance coverage. No adjustments have been made to the Prepaid Insurance account, and it is now December 31, 2011. Prepare the journal entry to reflect expiration of the insurance as of December 31, 2011.

b. Tyrell Company has a Supplies account balance of $1,000 on January 1, 2011. During 2011, it purchased $3,000 of supplies. As of December 31, 2011, a supplies inventory shows $1,300 of supplies available. Prepare the adjusting journal entry to correctly report the balance of the Supplies account and the Supplies Expense account as of December 31, 2011.

QS 3-3
Adjusting for depreciation
P1

a. Carlos Company purchases $30,000 of equipment on January 1, 2011. The equipment is expected to last five years and be worth $5,000 at the end of that time. Prepare the entry to record one year's depreciation expense of $5,000 for the equipment as of December 31, 2011.

b. Chaves Company purchases $40,000 of land on January 1, 2011. The land is expected to last indefinitely. What depreciation adjustment, if any, should be made with respect to the Land account as of December 31, 2011?

QS 3-4
Adjusting for unearned revenues
A1 P1

a. Eager Co. receives $20,000 cash in advance for 4 months of legal services on October 1, 2011, and records it by debiting Cash and crediting Unearned Revenue both for $20,000. It is now December 31, 2011, and Eager has provided legal services as planned. What adjusting entry should Eager make to account for the work performed from October 1 through December 31, 2011?

b. Rutherford Co. started a new publication called *Contest News*. Its subscribers pay $48 to receive 12 issues. With every new subscriber, Rutherford debits Cash and credits Unearned Subscription Revenue for the amounts received. The company has 100 new subscribers as of July 1, 2011. It sends *Contest News* to each of these subscribers every month from July through December. Assuming no changes in subscribers, prepare the journal entry that Rutherford must make as of December 31, 2011, to adjust the Subscription Revenue account and the Unearned Subscription Revenue account.

QS 3-5
Accruing salaries
A1 P1

Marsha Moder employs one college student every summer in her coffee shop. The student works the five weekdays and is paid on the following Monday. (For example, a student who works Monday through Friday, June 1 through June 5, is paid for that work on Monday, June 8.) Moder adjusts her books monthly, if needed, to show salaries earned but unpaid at month-end. The student works the last week of July—Friday is August 1. If the student earns $100 per day, what adjusting entry must Moder make on July 31 to correctly record accrued salaries expense for July?

QS 3-6
Recording and analyzing adjusting entries
A1

Adjusting entries affect at least one balance sheet account and at least one income statement account. For the following entries, identify the account to be debited and the account to be credited. Indicate which of the accounts is the income statement account and which is the balance sheet account.

a. Entry to record revenue earned that was previously received as cash in advance.
b. Entry to record annual depreciation expense.
c. Entry to record wage expenses incurred but not yet paid (nor recorded).
d. Entry to record revenue earned but not yet billed (nor recorded).
e. Entry to record expiration of prepaid insurance.

QS 3-7
Computing accrual and cash income
C2 A1

In its first year of operations, Harden Co. earned $39,000 in revenues and received $33,000 cash from these customers. The company incurred expenses of $22,500 but had not paid $2,250 of them at year-end. The company also prepaid $3,750 cash for expenses that would be incurred the next year. Calculate the first year's net income under both the cash basis and the accrual basis of accounting.

QS 3-8
Interpreting adjusting entries
C2 P2

The following information is taken from Cruz Company's unadjusted and adjusted trial balances.

	Unadjusted Debit	Unadjusted Credit	Adjusted Debit	Adjusted Credit
Prepaid insurance..........	$4,100		$3,700	
Interest payable		$ 0		$800

Given this information, which of the following is likely included among its adjusting entries?
a. A $400 credit to Prepaid Insurance and an $800 debit to Interest Payable.
b. A $400 debit to Insurance Expense and an $800 debit to Interest Payable.
c. A $400 debit to Insurance Expense and an $800 debit to Interest Expense.

QS 3-9
Determining effects of adjusting entries
A1

In making adjusting entries at the end of its accounting period, Gomez Consulting failed to record $1,600 of insurance coverage that had expired. This $1,600 cost had been initially debited to the Prepaid Insurance account. The company also failed to record accrued salaries expense of $1,000. As a result of these two oversights, the financial statements for the reporting period will [choose one] (1) understate assets by $1,600; (2) understate expenses by $2,600; (3) understate net income by $1,000; or (4) overstate liabilities by $1,000.

QS 3-10
Preparing adjusting entries
P1

During the year, Lyle Co. recorded prepayments of expenses in asset accounts, and cash receipts of unearned revenues in liability accounts. At the end of its annual accounting period, the company must make three adjusting entries: (1) accrue salaries expense, (2) adjust the Unearned Services Revenue account to recognize earned revenue, and (3) record services revenue earned for which cash will be received the following period. For each of these adjusting entries (1), (2), and (3), indicate the account from *a* through *i* to be debited and the account to be credited.

a. Prepaid Salaries
b. Salaries Expense
c. Services Revenue
d. Salaries Payable
e. Equipment
f. Cash
g. Unearned Services Revenue
h. Accounts Receivable
i. Accounts Payable

QS 3-11
Analyzing profit margin A2

Yang Company reported net income of $37,925 and net sales of $390,000 for the current year. Calculate the company's profit margin and interpret the result. Assume that its competitors earn an average profit margin of 15%.

QS 3-12^A
Preparing adjusting entries
P6

Diego Consulting initially records prepaid and unearned items in income statement accounts. Given this company's accounting practices, which of the following applies to the preparation of adjusting entries at the end of its first accounting period?

a. Earned but unbilled (and unrecorded) consulting fees are recorded with a debit to Unearned Consulting Fees and a credit to Consulting Fees Earned.
b. Unpaid salaries are recorded with a debit to Prepaid Salaries and a credit to Salaries Expense.
c. The cost of unused office supplies is recorded with a debit to Supplies Expense and a credit to Office Supplies.
d. Unearned fees (on which cash was received in advance earlier in the period) are recorded with a debit to Consulting Fees Earned and a credit to Unearned Consulting Fees.

QS 3-13
International accounting standards P3

Answer each of the following questions related to international accounting standards.
a. Do financial statements prepared under IFRS normally present assets from least liquid to most liquid or vice-versa?
b. Do financial statements prepared under IFRS normally present liabilities from furthest from maturity to nearest to maturity or vice-versa?

QS 3-14
Identifying the accounting cycle
C3

List the following steps of the accounting cycle in their proper order.
a. Preparing the post-closing trial balance.
b. Posting the journal entries.
c. Journalizing and posting adjusting entries.
d. Preparing the adjusted trial balance.
e. Journalizing and posting closing entries.
f. Analyzing transactions and events.
g. Preparing the financial statements.
h. Preparing the unadjusted trial balance.
i. Journalizing transactions and events.

QS 3-15
Identifying current accounts and computing the current ratio
A3

Compute Jamar Company's current ratio using the following information.

Accounts receivable	$15,000	Long-term notes payable	$20,000
Accounts payable	10,000	Office supplies	1,800
Buildings	42,000	Prepaid insurance	2,500
Cash	6,000	Unearned services revenue	4,000

QS 3-16
Classifying balance sheet items
C4

The following are common categories on a classified balance sheet.
- A. Current assets
- B. Long-term investments
- C. Plant assets
- D. Intangible assets
- E. Current liabilities
- F. Long-term liabilities

For each of the following items, select the letter that identifies the balance sheet category where the item typically would appear.

_____ 1. Trademarks
_____ 2. Accounts receivable
_____ 3. Land not currently used in operations
_____ 4. Notes payable (due in three years)
_____ 5. Cash
_____ 6. Wages payable
_____ 7. Store equipment
_____ 8. Accounts payable

QS 3-17
Prepare closing entries from the ledger P4

The ledger of Avril Company includes the following accounts with normal balances: Common Stock $6,000; Dividends $400; Services Revenue $10,000; Wages Expense $5,200; and Rent Expense $800. Prepare the necessary closing entries from the available information at December 31.

QS 3-18
Identify post-closing accounts P5

Identify the accounts listed in QS 3-17 that would be included in a post-closing trial balance.

QS 3-19^B
Preparing a partial work sheet P7

The ledger of Terrel Company includes the following unadjusted normal balances: Prepaid Rent $800, Services Revenue $11,600, and Wages Expense $5,000. Adjusting entries are required for (a) accrued rent expense $240; (b) accrued services revenue $180; and (c) accrued wages expense $160. Enter these unadjusted balances and the necessary adjustments on a work sheet and complete the work sheet for these accounts. *Note:* Also include the following accounts: Accounts Receivable, Wages Payable, and Rent Expense.

QS 3-20^C
Reversing entries P8

On December 31, 2010, Lester Co. prepared an adjusting entry for $6,700 of earned but unrecorded management fees. On January 16, 2011, Lester received $15,500 cash in management fees, which included the accrued fees earned in 2010. Assuming the company uses reversing entries, prepare the January 1, 2011, reversing entry and the January 16, 2011, cash receipt entry.

EXERCISES

Exercise 3-1
Preparing adjusting entries P1

For each of the following separate cases, prepare adjusting entries required of financial statements for the year ended (date of) December 31, 2011. (Assume that prepaid expenses are initially recorded in asset accounts and that fees collected in advance of work are initially recorded as liabilities.)

a. One-third of the work related to $30,000 cash received in advance is performed this period.
b. Wages of $9,000 are earned by workers but not paid as of December 31, 2011.
c. Depreciation on the company's equipment for 2011 is $19,127.
d. The Office Supplies account had a $480 debit balance on December 31, 2010. During 2011, $5,349 of office supplies are purchased. A physical count of supplies at December 31, 2011, shows $587 of supplies available.
e. The Prepaid Insurance account had a $5,000 balance on December 31, 2010. An analysis of insurance policies shows that $2,200 of unexpired insurance benefits remain at December 31, 2011.
f. The company has earned (but not recorded) $750 of interest from investments in CDs for the year ended December 31, 2011. The interest revenue will be received on January 10, 2012.
g. The company has a bank loan and has incurred (but not recorded) interest expense of $3,500 for the year ended December 31, 2011. The company must pay the interest on January 2, 2012.

Check (e) Dr. Insurance Expense, $2,800; (f) Cr. Interest Revenue, $750

Exercise 3-2
Preparing adjusting entries P1

Prepare adjusting journal entries for the year ended (date of) December 31, 2011, for each of these separate situations. Assume that prepaid expenses are initially recorded in asset accounts. Also assume that fees collected in advance of work are initially recorded as liabilities.

a. Depreciation on the company's equipment for 2011 is computed to be $16,000.
b. The Prepaid Insurance account had a $7,000 debit balance at December 31, 2011, before adjusting for the costs of any expired coverage. An analysis of the company's insurance policies showed that $1,040 of unexpired insurance coverage remains.
c. The Office Supplies account had a $300 debit balance on December 31, 2010; and $2,680 of office supplies were purchased during the year. The December 31, 2011, physical count showed $354 of supplies available.

Check (c) Dr. Office Supplies Expense, $2,626; (e) Dr. Insurance Expense, $4,600

d. One-half of the work related to $10,000 of cash received in advance was performed this period.

e. The Prepaid Insurance account had a $5,600 debit balance at December 31, 2011, before adjusting for the costs of any expired coverage. An analysis of insurance policies showed that $4,600 of coverage had expired.

f. Wage expenses of $4,000 have been incurred but are not paid as of December 31, 2011.

Exercise 3-3
Adjusting and paying accrued expenses
A1

Check (b) May 20 Dr. Interest Expense, $4,160

The following three separate situations require adjusting journal entries to prepare financial statements as of April 30. For each situation, present both the April 30 adjusting entry and the subsequent entry during May to record the payment of the accrued expenses.

a. On April 1, the company retained an attorney for a flat monthly fee of $2,500. This amount is paid to the attorney on the 12th day of the following month in which it was earned.

b. A $780,000 note payable requires 9.6% annual interest, or $6,240 to be paid at the 20th day of each month. The interest was last paid on April 20 and the next payment is due on May 20. As of April 30, $2,080 of interest expense has accrued.

c. Total weekly salaries expense for all employees is $9,000. This amount is paid at the end of the day on Friday of each five-day workweek. April 30 falls on Tuesday of this year, which means that the employees had worked two days since the last payday. The next payday is May 3.

Exercise 3-4
Determining cost flows through accounts
C1 A1

Determine the missing amounts in each of these four separate situations a through d.

	a	b	c	d
Supplies available—prior year-end	$ 300	$1,600	$1,360	?
Supplies purchased during the current year	2,100	5,400	?	$6,000
Supplies available—current year-end	750	?	1,840	800
Supplies expense for the current year	?	1,300	9,600	6,575

Exercise 3-5
Adjusting and paying accrued wages
C1 P1

Pablo Management has five part-time employees, each of whom earns $100 per day. They are normally paid on Fridays for work completed Monday through Friday of the same week. They were paid in full on Friday, December 28, 2011. The next week, the five employees worked only four days because New Year's Day was an unpaid holiday. Show (a) the adjusting entry that would be recorded on Monday, December 31, 2011, and (b) the journal entry that would be made to record payment of the employees' wages on Friday, January 4, 2012.

Exercise 3-6
Analyzing and preparing adjusting entries
A1 P3

Following are two income statements for Kendall Co. for the year ended December 31. The left column is prepared before any adjusting entries are recorded, and the right column includes the effects of adjusting entries. The company records cash receipts and payments related to unearned and prepaid items in balance sheet accounts. Analyze the statements and prepare the eight adjusting entries that likely were recorded. (Note: 30% of the $6,000 adjustment for Fees Earned has been earned but not billed, and the other 70% has been earned by performing services that were paid for in advance.)

KENDALL CO.
Income Statements
For Year Ended December 31

	Unadjusted	Adjusted
Revenues		
Fees earned	$24,000	$30,000
Commissions earned	42,500	42,500
Total revenues	66,500	72,500
Expenses		
Depreciation expense—Computers	0	1,500
Depreciation expense—Office furniture	0	1,750
Salaries expense	12,500	14,950
Insurance expense	0	1,300
Rent expense	4,500	4,500
Office supplies expense	0	480
Advertising expense	3,000	3,000
Utilities expense	1,250	1,320
Total expenses	21,250	28,800
Net income	$45,250	$43,700

Exercise 3-7
Computing and interpreting profit margin
A2

Use the following information to compute profit margin for each separate company *a* through *e*.

	Net Income	Net Sales		Net Income	Net Sales
a.	$ 5,390	$ 44,830	d.	$55,234	$1,458,999
b.	87,644	398,954	e.	70,158	435,925
c.	93,385	257,082			

Which of the five companies is the most profitable according to the profit margin ratio? Interpret that company's profit margin ratio.

Exercise 3-8[A]
Recording and reporting revenues received in advance
P6

Corbel Company experienced the following events and transactions during July.

July 1 Received $2,000 cash in advance of performing work for Beth Oker.
    6 Received $8,400 cash in advance of performing work for Lisa Poe.
    12 Completed the job for Oker.
    18 Received $7,500 cash in advance of performing work for Henry Coe.
    27 Completed the job for Poe.
    31 None of the work for Coe has been performed.

a. Prepare journal entries (including any adjusting entries as of the end of the month) to record these events using the procedure of initially crediting the Unearned Fees account when payment is received from a customer in advance of performing services.

b. Prepare journal entries (including any adjusting entries as of the end of the month) to record these events using the procedure of initially crediting the Fees Earned account when payment is received from a customer in advance of performing services.

c. Under each method, determine the amount of earned fees reported on the income statement for July and the amount of unearned fees reported on the balance sheet as of July 31.

Check (c) Fees Earned—using entries from part b, $10,400

Exercise 3-9[A]
Adjusting for prepaids recorded as expenses and unearned revenues recorded as revenues
P6

On-The-Mark Construction began operations on December 1. In setting up its accounting procedures, the company decided to debit expense accounts when it prepays its expenses and to credit revenue accounts when customers pay for services in advance. Prepare journal entries for items *a* through *d* and the adjusting entries as of its December 31 period-end for items *e* through *g*.

a. Supplies are purchased on December 1 for $3,000 cash.
b. The company prepaid its insurance premiums for $1,440 cash on December 2.
c. On December 15, the company receives an advance payment of $12,000 cash from a customer for remodeling work.
d. On December 28, the company receives $3,600 cash from another customer for remodeling work to be performed in January.
e. A physical count on December 31 indicates that On-The-Mark has $1,920 of supplies available.
f. An analysis of the insurance policies in effect on December 31 shows that $240 of insurance coverage had expired.
g. As of December 31, only one remodeling project has been worked on and completed. The $6,300 fee for this project had been received in advance and recorded as unearned remodeling fees.

Check (f) Cr. Insurance Expense, $1,200; (g) Dr. Remodeling Fees Earned, $9,300

Exercise 3-10
Preparing a balance sheet following IFRS
P3

adidas AG reports the following balance sheet accounts for the year ended December 31, 2009 (euros in millions). Prepare the balance sheet for this company as of December 31, 2009, following usual IFRS practices.

Tangible and other assets	€1,410	Intangible assets	€2,980
Total equity	3,776	Total current liabilities	2,836
Receivables and financial assets	1,753	Inventories	1,471
Total noncurrent liabilities	2,263	Total liabilities	5,099
Cash and cash equivalents	775	Other current assets	486
Total current assets	4,485	Total noncurrent assets	4,390

Exercise 3-11
Preparing financial statements
C3 P3

Use the following adjusted trial balance of Webb Trucking Company to prepare the (1) income statement and (2) statement of retained earnings, for the year ended December 31, 2011. The retained earnings account balance is $151,000 at December 31, 2010.

Account Title	Debit	Credit
Cash	$ 7,000	
Accounts receivable	16,500	
Office supplies	2,000	
Trucks	170,000	
Accumulated depreciation—Trucks		$ 35,000
Land	75,000	
Accounts payable		11,000
Interest payable		3,000
Long-term notes payable		52,000
Common stock		10,000
Retained earnings		151,000
Dividends	19,000	
Trucking fees earned		128,000
Depreciation expense—Trucks	22,500	
Salaries expense	60,000	
Office supplies expense	7,000	
Repairs expense—Trucks	11,000	
Totals	$390,000	$390,000

Exercise 3-12
Preparing a classified balance sheet C4

Use the information in the adjusted trial balance reported in Exercise 3-11 to prepare Webb Trucking Company's classified balance sheet as of December 31, 2011.

Check Total assets, $235,500

Exercise 3-13
Computing the current ratio A3

Use the information in the adjusted trial balance reported in Exercise 3-11 to compute the current ratio as of the balance sheet date (round the ratio to two decimals). Interpret the current ratio for the Webb Trucking Company. (Assume that the industry average for the current ratio is 1.5.)

Exercise 3-14
Computing and analyzing the current ratio A3

Calculate the current ratio in each of the following separate cases (round the ratio to two decimals). Identify the company case with the strongest liquidity position. (These cases represent competing companies in the same industry.)

	Current Assets	Current Liabilities
Case 1	$ 78,000	$31,000
Case 2	104,000	75,000
Case 3	44,000	48,000
Case 4	84,500	80,600
Case 5	60,000	99,000

Exercise 3-15[A]
Preparing reversing entries P8

The following two events occurred for Tanger Co. on October 31, 2011, the end of its fiscal year.

a. Tanger rents a building from its owner for $3,200 per month. By a prearrangement, the company delayed paying October's rent until November 5. On this date, the company paid the rent for both October and November.

b. Tanger rents space in a building it owns to a tenant for $750 per month. By prearrangement, the tenant delayed paying the October rent until November 8. On this date, the tenant paid the rent for both October and November.

Required

1. Prepare adjusting entries that the company must record for these events as of October 31.
2. Assuming Tanger does *not* use reversing entries, prepare journal entries to record Tanger's payment of rent on November 5 and the collection of rent on November 8 from Tanger's tenant.
3. Assuming that the company uses reversing entries, prepare reversing entries on November 1 and the journal entries to record Tanger's payment of rent on November 5 and the collection of rent on November 8 from Tanger's tenant.

Exercise 3-16
Preparing closing entries
P4

Following are **Nintendo**'s revenue and expense accounts for a recent calendar year (yen in millions). Prepare the company's closing entries for its revenues and its expenses.

Sales	¥1,838,622
Cost of sales (expense)	1,044,981
Advertising expense	117,308
Other expense, net	397,244

Exercise 3-17
Completing a worksheet
P7

The following data are taken from the unadjusted trial balance of the Madison Company at December 31, 2011. Each account carries a normal balance and the accounts are shown here in alphabetical order.

Accounts Payable	$ 2	Prepaid Insurance	$ 6	Retained earnings	$11
Accounts Receivable	4	Revenue	25	Dividends	2
Accumulated Depreciation—Equip.	5	Salaries Expense	6	Unearned Revenue	4
Cash	7	Supplies	8	Utilities Expense	4
Equipment	13	Common stock	3		

1. Use the data above to prepare a worksheet. Enter the accounts in proper order and enter their balances in the correct debit or credit column.
2. Use the following adjustment information to complete the worksheet.
   a. Depreciation on equipment, $1
   b. Accrued salaries, $2
   c. The $4 of unearned revenue has been earned
   d. Supplies available at December 31, 2011, $5
   e. Expired insurance, $5

PROBLEM SET A

Problem 3-1A
Preparing adjusting and subsequent journal entries
C1 A1 P1

Meyer Co. follows the practice of recording prepaid expenses and unearned revenues in balance sheet accounts. The company's annual accounting period ends on December 31, 2011. The following information concerns the adjusting entries to be recorded as of that date.

a. The Office Supplies account started the year with a $3,000 balance. During 2011, the company purchased supplies for $12,400, which was added to the Office Supplies account. The inventory of supplies available at December 31, 2011, totaled $2,640.

b. An analysis of the company's insurance policies provided the following facts.

Policy	Date of Purchase	Months of Coverage	Cost
A	April 1, 2010	24	$15,840
B	April 1, 2011	36	13,068
C	August 1, 2011	12	2,700

The total premium for each policy was paid in full (for all months) at the purchase date, and the Prepaid Insurance account was debited for the full cost. (Year-end adjusting entries for Prepaid Insurance were properly recorded in all prior years.)

c. The company has 15 employees, who earn a total of $2,100 in salaries each working day. They are paid each Monday for their work in the five-day workweek ending on the previous Friday. Assume that December 31, 2011, is a Tuesday, and all 15 employees worked the first two days of that week. Because New Year's Day is a paid holiday, they will be paid salaries for five full days on Monday, January 6, 2012.

d. The company purchased a building on January 1, 2011. It cost $855,000 and is expected to have a $45,000 salvage value at the end of its predicted 30-year life. Annual depreciation is $27,000.

e. Since the company is not large enough to occupy the entire building it owns, it rented space to a tenant at $2,400 per month, starting on November 1, 2011. The rent was paid on time on November 1, and the amount received was credited to the Rent Earned account. However, the tenant has not paid the December rent. The company has worked out an agreement with the tenant, who has promised to pay both December and January rent in full on January 15. The tenant has agreed not to fall behind again.

f. On November 1, the company rented space to another tenant for $2,175 per month. The tenant paid five months' rent in advance on that date. The payment was recorded with a credit to the Unearned Rent account.

Check (1b) Dr. Insurance Expense, $12,312 (1d) Dr. Depreciation Expense, $27,000

Required

1. Use the information to prepare adjusting entries as of December 31, 2011.
2. Prepare journal entries to record the first subsequent cash transaction in 2012 for parts *c* and *e*.

Problem 3-2A
Identifying adjusting entries with explanations
P1

For each of the following entries, enter the letter of the explanation that most closely describes it in the space beside each entry. (You can use letters more than once.)

A. To record receipt of unearned revenue.
B. To record this period's earning of prior unearned revenue.
C. To record payment of an accrued expense.
D. To record receipt of an accrued revenue.
E. To record an accrued expense.
F. To record an accrued revenue.
G. To record this period's use of a prepaid expense.
H. To record payment of a prepaid expense.
I. To record this period's depreciation expense.

___	1.	Rent Expense	2,000
		Prepaid Rent	2,000
___	2.	Interest Expense	1,000
		Interest Payable	1,000
___	3.	Depreciation Expense	4,000
		Accumulated Depreciation	4,000
___	4.	Unearned Professional Fees	3,000
		Professional Fees Earned	3,000
___	5.	Insurance Expense	4,200
		Prepaid Insurance	4,200
___	6.	Salaries Payable	1,400
		Cash	1,400
___	7.	Prepaid Rent	4,500
		Cash	4,500
___	8.	Salaries Expense	6,000
		Salaries Payable	6,000
___	9.	Interest Receivable	5,000
		Interest Revenue	5,000
___	10.	Cash	9,000
		Accounts Receivable (from consulting)	9,000
___	11.	Cash	7,500
		Unearned Professional Fees	7,500
___	12.	Cash	2,000
		Interest Receivable	2,000

Problem 3-3A
Preparing adjusting entries, adjusted trial balance, and financial statements
A1 P1 P2 P3

mhhe.com/wildFA6e

Watson Technical Institute (WTI), a school owned by Tom Watson, provides training to individuals who pay tuition directly to the school. WTI also offers training to groups in off-site locations. Its unadjusted trial balance as of December 31, 2011, follows. WTI initially records prepaid expenses and unearned revenues in balance sheet accounts. Descriptions of items *a* through *h* that require adjusting entries on December 31, 2011, follow.

Additional Information Items

a. An analysis of WTI's insurance policies shows that $3,000 of coverage has expired.
b. An inventory count shows that teaching supplies costing $2,600 are available at year-end 2011.
c. Annual depreciation on the equipment is $12,000.
d. Annual depreciation on the professional library is $6,000.
e. On November 1, WTI agreed to do a special six-month course (starting immediately) for a client. The contract calls for a monthly fee of $2,200, and the client paid the first five months' fees in advance. When the cash was received, the Unearned Training Fees account was credited. The fee for the sixth month will be recorded when it is collected in 2012.

Chapter 3 Adjusting Accounts and Preparing Financial Statements

f. On October 15, WTI agreed to teach a four-month class (beginning immediately) for an individual for $3,000 tuition per month payable at the end of the class. The class started on October 15, but no payment has yet been received. (WTI's accruals are applied to the nearest half-month; for example, October recognizes one-half month accrual.)

g. WTI's two employees are paid weekly. As of the end of the year, two days' salaries have accrued at the rate of $100 per day for each employee.

h. The balance in the Prepaid Rent account represents rent for December.

WATSON TECHNICAL INSTITUTE
Unadjusted Trial Balance
December 31, 2011

	Debit	Credit
Cash	$ 26,000	
Accounts receivable	0	
Teaching supplies	10,000	
Prepaid insurance	15,000	
Prepaid rent	2,000	
Professional library	30,000	
Accumulated depreciation — Professional library		$ 9,000
Equipment	70,000	
Accumulated depreciation — Equipment		16,000
Accounts payable		36,000
Salaries payable		0
Unearned training fees		11,000
Common stock		10,000
Retained earnings		53,600
Dividends	40,000	
Tuition fees earned		102,000
Training fees earned		38,000
Depreciation expense — Professional library	0	
Depreciation expense — Equipment	0	
Salaries expense	48,000	
Insurance expense	0	
Rent expense	22,000	
Teaching supplies expense	0	
Advertising expense	7,000	
Utilities expense	5,600	
Totals	$ 275,600	$ 275,600

Required

1. Prepare T-accounts (representing the ledger) with balances from the unadjusted trial balance.
2. Prepare the necessary adjusting journal entries for items *a* through *h* and post them to the T-accounts. Assume that adjusting entries are made only at year-end.
3. Update balances in the T-accounts for the adjusting entries and prepare an adjusted trial balance.
4. Prepare Watson Technical Institute's income statement and statement of retained earnings for the year 2011 and prepare its balance sheet as of December 31, 2011.

Check (2*e*) Cr. Training Fees Earned, $4,400; (2*f*) Cr. Tuition Fees Earned, $7,500; (3) Adj. Trial balance totals, $301,500; (4) Net income, $38,500

A six-column table for JJW Company follows. The first two columns contain the unadjusted trial balance for the company as of July 31, 2011. The last two columns contain the adjusted trial balance as of the same date.

Problem 3-4A
Interpreting unadjusted and adjusted trial balances, and preparing financial statements

A1 P1 P2 P3

Required

Analysis Component

1. Analyze the differences between the unadjusted and adjusted trial balances to determine the eight adjustments that likely were made. Show the results of your analysis by inserting these adjustment amounts in the table's two middle columns. Label each adjustment with a letter *a* through *h* and provide a short description of it at the bottom of the table.

mhhe.com/wildFA6e

142 Chapter 3 Adjusting Accounts and Preparing Financial Statements

Preparation Component

Check (2) Net income, $37,020; Total assets, $131,340

2. Use the information in the adjusted trial balance to prepare the company's (*a*) income statement and its statement of retained earnings for the year ended July 31, 2011 (*note:* retained earnings at July 31, 2010, was $23,420, and the current-year dividends were $10,000), and (*b*) the balance sheet as of July 31, 2011.

	Unadjusted Trial Balance		Adjustments		Adjusted Trial Balance	
Cash	$ 27,000				$ 27,000	
Accounts receivable	12,000				22,460	
Office supplies	18,000				3,000	
Prepaid insurance	7,320				4,880	
Office equipment	92,000				92,000	
Accum. depreciation—Office equip.		$ 12,000				$ 18,000
Accounts payable		9,300				10,200
Interest payable		0				800
Salaries payable		0				6,600
Unearned consulting fees		16,000				14,300
Long-term notes payable		44,000				44,000
Common stock		5,000				5,000
Retained earnings		23,420				23,420
Dividends	10,000				10,000	
Consulting fees earned		156,000				168,160
Depreciation expense—Office equip.	0				6,000	
Salaries expense	71,000				77,600	
Interest expense	1,400				2,200	
Insurance expense	0				2,440	
Rent expense	13,200				13,200	
Office supplies expense	0				15,000	
Advertising expense	13,800				14,700	
Totals	$265,720	$265,720			$290,480	$290,480

Problem 3-5A
Preparing financial statements from the adjusted trial balance and calculating profit margin
P3 A1 A2

The adjusted trial balance for Callahay Company as of December 31, 2011, follows.

	Debit	Credit
Cash	$ 22,000	
Accounts receivable	44,000	
Interest receivable	10,000	
Notes receivable (due in 90 days)	160,000	
Office supplies	8,000	
Automobiles	160,000	
Accumulated depreciation—Automobiles		$ 42,000
Equipment	130,000	
Accumulated depreciation—Equipment		10,000
Land	70,000	
Accounts payable		88,000
Interest payable		12,000
Salaries payable		11,000
Unearned fees		22,000
Long-term notes payable		130,000
Common stock		20,000

[continued on next page]

[continued from previous page]

Retained earnings		227,800
Dividends	38,000	
Fees earned		420,000
Interest earned		16,000
Depreciation expense—Automobiles	18,000	
Depreciation expense—Equipment	10,000	
Salaries expense	180,000	
Wages expense	32,000	
Interest expense	24,000	
Office supplies expense	26,000	
Advertising expense	50,000	
Repairs expense—Automobiles	16,800	
Totals	$998,800	$998,800

Required

1. Use the information in the adjusted trial balance to prepare (*a*) the income statement for the year ended December 31, 2011; (*b*) the statement of retained earnings for the year ended December 31, 2011; and (*c*) the balance sheet as of December 31, 2011.
2. Calculate the profit margin for year 2011.

Check (1) Total assets, $552,000

Problem 3-6A
Determining balance sheet classifications
C4

In the blank space beside each numbered balance sheet item, enter the letter of its balance sheet classification. If the item should not appear on the balance sheet, enter a Z in the blank.

A. Current assets **D.** Intangible assets **F.** Long-term liabilities
B. Long-term investments **E.** Current liabilities **G.** Equity
C. Plant assets

____ 1. Office equipment
____ 2. Office supplies
____ 3. Buildings
____ 4. Store supplies
____ 5. Accumulated depreciation—Trucks
____ 6. Land (used in operations)
____ 7. Repairs expense
____ 8. Cash
____ 9. Current portion of long-term note payable
____ 10. Long-term investment in stock
____ 11. Depreciation expense—Building
____ 12. Prepaid rent
____ 13. Interest receivable
____ 14. Taxes payable
____ 15. Automobiles
____ 16. Notes payable (due in 3 years)
____ 17. Accounts payable
____ 18. Prepaid insurance
____ 19. Common stock
____ 20. Unearned services revenue

Problem 3-7A
Applying the accounting cycle
P1 P2 P3 P4 P5

mhhe.com/wildFA6e

On April 1, 2011, Jennifer Stafford created a new travel agency, See-It-Now Travel. The following transactions occurred during the company's first month.

April 1 Stafford invested $20,000 cash and computer equipment worth $40,000 in the company in exchange for common stock.
  2 The company rented furnished office space by paying $1,700 cash for the first month's (April) rent.
  3 The company purchased $1,100 of office supplies for cash.
  10 The company paid $3,600 cash for the premium on a 12-month insurance policy. Coverage begins on April 11.
  14 The company paid $1,800 cash for two weeks' salaries earned by employees.
  24 The company collected $7,900 cash on commissions from airlines on tickets obtained for customers.
  28 The company paid $1,800 cash for two weeks' salaries earned by employees.
  29 The company paid $250 cash for minor repairs to the company's computer.
  30 The company paid $650 cash for this month's telephone bill.
  30 The company paid $1,500 cash for dividends.

The company's chart of accounts follows:

101	Cash	405	Commissions Earned
106	Accounts Receivable	612	Depreciation Expense—Computer Equip.
124	Office Supplies	622	Salaries Expense
128	Prepaid Insurance	637	Insurance Expense
167	Computer Equipment	640	Rent Expense
168	Accumulated Depreciation—Computer Equip.	650	Office Supplies Expense
209	Salaries Payable	684	Repairs Expense
307	Common Stock	688	Telephone Expense
318	Retained Earnings	901	Income Summary
319	Dividends		

Required

1. Use the balance column format to set up each ledger account listed in its chart of accounts.
2. Prepare journal entries to record the transactions for April and post them to the ledger accounts. The company records prepaid and unearned items in balance sheet accounts.
3. Prepare an unadjusted trial balance as of April 30.
4. Use the following information to journalize and post adjusting entries for the month:
   a. Two-thirds of one month's insurance coverage has expired.
   b. At the end of the month, $700 of office supplies are still available.
   c. This month's depreciation on the computer equipment is $600.
   d. Employees earned $320 of unpaid and unrecorded salaries as of month-end.
   e. The company earned $1,650 of commissions that are not yet billed at month-end.
5. Prepare the income statement and the statement of retained earnings for the month of April and the balance sheet at April 30, 2011.
6. Prepare journal entries to close the temporary accounts and post these entries to the ledger.
7. Prepare a post-closing trial balance.

Check (3) Unadj. trial balance totals, $67,900

(4a) Dr. Insurance Expense, $200

(5) Net income, $1,830; Total assets, $60,650

(7) P-C trial balance totals, $61,250

Problem 3-8A
Preparing closing entries, financial statements, and ratios
C4 A2 A3 P3 P4

The adjusted trial balance for Sharp Construction as of December 31, 2011, follows.

SHARP CONSTRUCTION
Adjusted Trial Balance
December 31, 2011

No.	Account Title	Debit	Credit
101	Cash	$ 4,000	
104	Short-term investments	22,000	
126	Supplies	7,100	
128	Prepaid insurance	6,000	
167	Equipment	39,000	
168	Accumulated depreciation—Equipment		$ 20,000
173	Building	130,000	
174	Accumulated depreciation—Building		55,000
183	Land	45,000	
201	Accounts payable		15,500
203	Interest payable		1,500
208	Rent payable		2,500
210	Wages payable		1,500
213	Property taxes payable		800
233	Unearned professional fees		6,500

[continued on next page]

[continued from previous page]

251	Long-term notes payable		66,000
307	Common stock		20,000
318	Retained earnings		62,700
319	Dividends	12,000	
401	Professional fees earned		96,000
406	Rent earned		13,000
407	Dividends earned		1,900
409	Interest earned		1,000
606	Depreciation expense—Building	10,000	
612	Depreciation expense—Equipment	5,000	
623	Wages expense	31,000	
633	Interest expense	4,100	
637	Insurance expense	9,000	
640	Rent expense	12,400	
652	Supplies expense	6,400	
682	Postage expense	3,200	
683	Property taxes expense	4,000	
684	Repairs expense	7,900	
688	Telephone expense	2,200	
690	Utilities expense	3,600	
	Totals	$363,900	$363,900

J. Sharp invested $50,000 cash in the business in exchange for more common stock during year 2011 (the December 31, 2010, credit balance of retained earnings was $62,700). Sharp Construction is required to make a $6,600 payment on its long-term notes payable during 2012.

Required

1. Prepare the income statement and the statement of retained earnings for the calendar year 2011 and the classified balance sheet at December 31, 2011.
2. Prepare the necessary closing entries at December 31, 2011.
3. Use the information in the financial statements to compute these ratios: (*a*) return on assets (total assets at December 31, 2010, was $200,000), (*b*) debt ratio, (*c*) profit margin ratio (use total revenues as the denominator), and (*d*) current ratio.

Check (1) Total assets (12/31/2011), $178,100; Net income, $13,100

Nomo Co. follows the practice of recording prepaid expenses and unearned revenues in balance sheet accounts. The company's annual accounting period ends on October 31, 2011. The following information concerns the adjusting entries that need to be recorded as of that date.

a. The Office Supplies account started the fiscal year with a $500 balance. During the fiscal year, the company purchased supplies for $3,650, which was added to the Office Supplies account. The supplies available at October 31, 2011, totaled $700.

b. An analysis of the company's insurance policies provided the following facts.

PROBLEM SET B

Problem 3-1B
Preparing adjusting and subsequent journal entries
C1 A1 P1

Policy	Date of Purchase	Months of Coverage	Cost
A	April 1, 2010	24	$3,000
B	April 1, 2011	36	3,600
C	August 1, 2011	12	660

The total premium for each policy was paid in full (for all months) at the purchase date, and the Prepaid Insurance account was debited for the full cost. (Year-end adjusting entries for Prepaid Insurance were properly recorded in all prior fiscal years.)

c. The company has four employees, who earn a total of $800 for each workday. They are paid each Monday for their work in the five-day workweek ending on the previous Friday. Assume that October 31, 2011, is a Monday, and all four employees worked the first day of that week. They will be paid salaries for five full days on Monday, November 7, 2011.

d. The company purchased a building on November 1, 2010, that cost $155,000 and is expected to have a $20,000 salvage value at the end of its predicted 25-year life. Annual depreciation is $5,400.

e. Since the company does not occupy the entire building it owns, it rented space to a tenant at $600 per month, starting on September 1, 2011. The rent was paid on time on September 1, and the amount received was credited to the Rent Earned account. However, the October rent has not been paid. The company has worked out an agreement with the tenant, who has promised to pay both October and November rent in full on November 15. The tenant has agreed not to fall behind again.

f. On September 1, the company rented space to another tenant for $525 per month. The tenant paid five months' rent in advance on that date. The payment was recorded with a credit to the Unearned Rent account.

Required

Check (1*b*) Dr. Insurance Expense, $2,675; (1*d*) Dr. Depreciation Expense, $5,400

1. Use the information to prepare adjusting entries as of October 31, 2011.
2. Prepare journal entries to record the first subsequent cash transaction in November 2011 for parts *c* and *e*.

Problem 3-2B
Identifying adjusting entries with explanations

P1

For each of the following entries, enter the letter of the explanation that most closely describes it in the space beside each entry. (You can use letters more than once.)

A. To record payment of a prepaid expense.
B. To record this period's use of a prepaid expense.
C. To record this period's depreciation expense.
D. To record receipt of unearned revenue.
E. To record this period's earning of prior unearned revenue.
F. To record an accrued expense.
G. To record payment of an accrued expense.
H. To record an accrued revenue.
I. To record receipt of accrued revenue.

___	1.	Unearned Professional Fees	6,000	
		Professional Fees Earned		6,000
___	2.	Interest Receivable	3,500	
		Interest Revenue		3,500
___	3.	Salaries Payable	9,000	
		Cash		9,000
___	4.	Depreciation Expense	8,000	
		Accumulated Depreciation		8,000
___	5.	Cash	9,000	
		Unearned Professional Fees		9,000
___	6.	Insurance Expense	4,000	
		Prepaid Insurance		4,000
___	7.	Interest Expense	5,000	
		Interest Payable		5,000
___	8.	Cash	1,500	
		Accounts Receivable (from services)		1,500
___	9.	Salaries Expense	7,000	
		Salaries Payable		7,000
___	10.	Cash	1,000	
		Interest Receivable		1,000
___	11.	Prepaid Rent	3,000	
		Cash		3,000
___	12.	Rent Expense	7,500	
		Prepaid Rent		7,500

Following is the unadjusted trial balance for Alcorn Institute as of December 31, 2011, which initially records prepaid expenses and unearned revenues in balance sheet accounts. The Institute provides one-on-one training to individuals who pay tuition directly to the business and offers extension training to groups in off-site locations. Shown after the trial balance are items *a* through *h* that require adjusting entries as of December 31, 2011.

Problem 3-3B
Preparing adjusting entries, adjusted trial balance, and financial statements
A1 P1 P2 P3

ALCORN INSTITUTE
Unadjusted Trial Balance
December 31, 2011

	Debit	Credit
Cash	$ 50,000	
Accounts receivable	0	
Teaching supplies	60,000	
Prepaid insurance	18,000	
Prepaid rent	2,600	
Professional library	10,000	
Accumulated depreciation—Professional library		$ 1,500
Equipment	30,000	
Accumulated depreciation—Equipment		16,000
Accounts payable		12,200
Salaries payable		0
Unearned training fees		27,600
Common stock		12,000
Retained earnings		56,500
Dividends	20,000	
Tuition fees earned		105,000
Training fees earned		62,000
Depreciation expense—Professional library	0	
Depreciation expense—Equipment	0	
Salaries expense	43,200	
Insurance expense	0	
Rent expense	28,600	
Teaching supplies expense	0	
Advertising expense	18,000	
Utilities expense	12,400	
Totals	$ 292,800	$292,800

Additional Information Items

a. An analysis of the Institute's insurance policies shows that $6,400 of coverage has expired.

b. An inventory count shows that teaching supplies costing $2,500 are available at year-end 2011.

c. Annual depreciation on the equipment is $4,000.

d. Annual depreciation on the professional library is $2,000.

e. On November 1, the Institute agreed to do a special four-month course (starting immediately) for a client. The contract calls for a $4,600 monthly fee, and the client paid the first two months' fees in advance. When the cash was received, the Unearned Training Fees account was credited. The last two months' fees will be recorded when collected in 2012.

f. On October 15, the Institute agreed to teach a four-month class (beginning immediately) to an individual for $2,200 tuition per month payable at the end of the class. The class started on October 15, but no payment has yet been received. (Alcorn's accruals are applied to the nearest half-month; for example, October recognizes one-half month accrual.)

g. The Institute's only employee is paid weekly. As of the end of the year, three days' salaries have accrued at the rate of $180 per day.

h. The balance in the Prepaid Rent account represents rent for December.

Required

1. Prepare T-accounts (representing the ledger) with balances from the unadjusted trial balance.
2. Prepare the necessary adjusting journal entries for items *a* through *h*, and post them to the T-accounts. Assume that adjusting entries are made only at year-end.
3. Update balances in the T-accounts for the adjusting entries and prepare an adjusted trial balance.
4. Prepare the company's income statement and statement of retained earnings for the year 2011, and prepare its balance sheet as of December 31, 2011.

Check (2e) Cr. Training Fees Earned, $9,200; (2f) Cr. Tuition Fees Earned, $5,500; (3) Adj. trial balance totals, $304,840; (4) Net income, $6,460

Problem 3-4B
Interpreting unadjusted and adjusted trial balances, and preparing financial statements
A1 P1 P2 P3

A six-column table for Daxu Consulting Company follows. The first two columns contain the unadjusted trial balance for the company as of December 31, 2011, and the last two columns contain the adjusted trial balance as of the same date.

	Unadjusted Trial Balance		Adjustments		Adjusted Trial Balance	
Cash	$ 48,000				$ 48,000	
Accounts receivable	70,000				76,660	
Office supplies	30,000				7,000	
Prepaid insurance	13,200				8,600	
Office equipment	150,000				150,000	
Accumulated depreciation—Office equip.		$ 30,000				$ 40,000
Accounts payable		36,000				42,000
Interest payable		0				1,600
Salaries payable		0				11,200
Unearned consulting fees		30,000				17,800
Long-term notes payable		80,000				80,000
Common stock		4,000				4,000
Retained earnings		66,200				66,200
Dividends	10,000				10,000	
Consulting fees earned		264,000				282,860
Depreciation expense—Office equip.	0				10,000	
Salaries expense	115,600				126,800	
Interest expense	6,400				8,000	
Insurance expense	0				4,600	
Rent expense	24,000				24,000	
Office supplies expense	0				23,000	
Advertising expense	43,000				49,000	
Totals	$510,200	$510,200			$545,660	$545,660

Required

Analysis Component

1. Analyze the differences between the unadjusted and adjusted trial balances to determine the eight adjustments that likely were made. Show the results of your analysis by inserting these adjustment amounts in the table's two middle columns. Label each adjustment with a letter *a* through *h* and provide a short description of it at the bottom of the table.

Preparation Component

2. Use the information in the adjusted trial balance to prepare this company's (*a*) income statement and its statement of retained earnings for the year ended December 31, 2011 (*note:* retained earnings at December 31, 2010, was $66,200, and the current-year dividends were $10,000), and (*b*) the balance sheet as of December 31, 2011.

Check (2) Net income, $37,460; Total assets, $250,260

The adjusted trial balance for Lightning Courier as of December 31, 2011, follows.

Problem 3-5B
Preparing financial statements from the adjusted trial balance and calculating profit margin

P3 A1 A2

	Debit	Credit
Cash	$ 48,000	
Accounts receivable	110,000	
Interest receivable	6,000	
Notes receivable (due in 90 days)	200,000	
Office supplies	12,000	
Trucks	124,000	
Accumulated depreciation—Trucks		$ 48,000
Equipment	260,000	
Accumulated depreciation—Equipment		190,000
Land	90,000	
Accounts payable		124,000
Interest payable		22,000
Salaries payable		30,000
Unearned delivery fees		110,000
Long-term notes payable		190,000
Common stock		15,000
Retained earnings		100,000
Dividends	40,000	
Delivery fees earned		580,000
Interest earned		24,000
Depreciation expense—Trucks	24,000	
Depreciation expense—Equipment	46,000	
Salaries expense	64,000	
Wages expense	290,000	
Interest expense	25,000	
Office supplies expense	33,000	
Advertising expense	26,400	
Repairs expense—Trucks	34,600	
Totals	$1,433,000	$1,433,000

Required

1. Use the information in the adjusted trial balance to prepare (*a*) the income statement for the year ended December 31, 2011, (*b*) the statement of retained earnings for the year ended December 31, 2011, and (*c*) the balance sheet as of December 31, 2011.
2. Calculate the profit margin for year 2011.

Check (1) Total assets, $612,000

In the blank space beside each numbered balance sheet item, enter the letter of its balance sheet classification. If the item should not appear on the balance sheet, enter a Z in the blank.

A. Current assets
B. Long-term investments
C. Plant assets
D. Intangible assets
E. Current liabilities
F. Long-term liabilities
G. Equity

Problem 3-6B
Determining balance sheet classifications

C4

_____ 1. Machinery
_____ 2. Prepaid insurance
_____ 3. Current portion of long-term note payable
_____ 4. Interest receivable
_____ 5. Rent receivable
_____ 6. Land (used in operations)
_____ 7. Copyrights
_____ 8. Rent revenue
_____ 9. Depreciation expense—Trucks

_____ 10. Long-term investment in stock
_____ 11. Office supplies
_____ 12. Interest payable
_____ 13. Common stock
_____ 14. Notes receivable (due in 120 days)
_____ 15. Accumulated depreciation—Trucks
_____ 16. Salaries payable
_____ 17. Commissions earned
_____ 18. Income taxes payable
_____ 19. Office equipment
_____ 20. Notes payable (due in 15 years)

Problem 3-7B
Applying the accounting cycle
P1 P2 P3 P4 P5

On July 1, 2011, Lucinda Fogle created a new self-storage business, KeepSafe Co. The following transactions occurred during the company's first month.

July 1 Fogle invested $20,000 cash and buildings worth $120,000 in the company in exchange for common stock.
2 The company rented equipment by paying $1,800 cash for the first month's (July) rent.
5 The company purchased $2,300 of office supplies for cash.
10 The company paid $5,400 cash for the premium on a 12-month insurance policy. Coverage begins on July 11.
14 The company paid an employee $900 cash for two weeks' salary earned.
24 The company collected $8,800 cash for storage fees from customers.
28 The company paid $900 cash for two weeks' salary earned by an employee.
29 The company paid $850 cash for minor repairs to a leaking roof.
30 The company paid $300 cash for this month's telephone bill.
31 The company paid $1,600 cash for dividends.

The company's chart of accounts follows:

101	Cash	401	Storage Fees Earned
106	Accounts Receivable	606	Depreciation Expense—Buildings
124	Office Supplies	622	Salaries Expense
128	Prepaid Insurance	637	Insurance Expense
173	Buildings	640	Rent Expense
174	Accumulated Depreciation—Buildings	650	Office Supplies Expense
209	Salaries Payable	684	Repairs Expense
307	Common Stock	688	Telephone Expense
318	Retained Earnings	901	Income Summary
319	Dividends		

Required

1. Use the balance column format to set up each ledger account listed in its chart of accounts.
2. Prepare journal entries to record the transactions for July and post them to the ledger accounts. Record prepaid and unearned items in balance sheet accounts.
3. Prepare an unadjusted trial balance as of July 31.
4. Use the following information to journalize and post adjusting entries for the month:
   a. Two-thirds of one month's insurance coverage has expired.
   b. At the end of the month, $1,550 of office supplies are still available.
   c. This month's depreciation on the buildings is $1,200.
   d. An employee earned $180 of unpaid and unrecorded salary as of month-end.
   e. The company earned $950 of storage fees that are not yet billed at month-end.
5. Prepare the income statement and the statement of retained earnings for the month of July and the balance sheet at July 31, 2011.
6. Prepare journal entries to close the temporary accounts and post these entries to the ledger.
7. Prepare a post-closing trial balance.

Check (3) Unadj. trial balance totals, $148,800

(4a) Dr. Insurance Expense, $300

(5) Net income, $2,570; Total assets, $141,150

(7) P-C trial balance totals, $142,350

Chapter 3 Adjusting Accounts and Preparing Financial Statements

The adjusted trial balance for Giovanni Co. as of December 31, 2011, follows.

Problem 3-8B
Preparing closing entries, financial statements, and ratios

C4 A2 A3 P3 P4

GIOVANNI COMPANY
Adjusted Trial Balance
December 31, 2011

No.	Account Title	Debit	Credit
101	Cash	$ 6,400	
104	Short-term investments	10,200	
126	Supplies	3,600	
128	Prepaid insurance	800	
167	Equipment	18,000	
168	Accumulated depreciation—Equipment		$ 3,000
173	Building	90,000	
174	Accumulated depreciation—Building		9,000
183	Land	28,500	
201	Accounts payable		2,500
203	Interest payable		1,400
208	Rent payable		200
210	Wages payable		1,180
213	Property taxes payable		2,330
233	Unearned professional fees		650
251	Long-term notes payable		32,000
307	Common stock		30,000
318	Retained earnings		61,800
319	Dividends	6,000	
401	Professional fees earned		47,000
406	Rent earned		3,600
407	Dividends earned		500
409	Interest earned		1,120
606	Depreciation expense—Building	2,000	
612	Depreciation expense—Equipment	1,000	
623	Wages expense	17,500	
633	Interest expense	1,200	
637	Insurance expense	1,425	
640	Rent expense	1,800	
652	Supplies expense	900	
682	Postage expense	310	
683	Property taxes expense	3,825	
684	Repairs expense	579	
688	Telephone expense	421	
690	Utilities expense	1,820	
	Totals	$196,280	$196,280

J. Giovanni invested $30,000 cash in the business in exchange for more common stock during year 2011 (the December 31, 2010, credit balance of retained earnings was $61,800). Giovanni Company is required to make a $6,400 payment on its long-term notes payable during 2012.

Required

1. Prepare the income statement and the statement of retained earnings for the calendar year 2011 and the classified balance sheet at December 31, 2011.
2. Prepare the necessary closing entries at December 31, 2011.
3. Use the information in the financial statements to calculate these ratios: (*a*) return on assets (total assets at December 31, 2010, were $150,000), (*b*) debt ratio, (*c*) profit margin ratio (use total revenues as the denominator), and (*d*) current ratio.

Check (1) Total assets (12/31/2011), $145,500; Net income, $19,440

SERIAL PROBLEM
Business Solutions
P1 P2 P3 P4 P5

(This serial problem began in Chapter 1 and continues through most of the book. If previous chapter segments were not completed, the serial problem can still begin at this point. It is helpful, but not necessary, to use the Working Papers that accompany the book.)

SP 3 After the success of the company's first two months, Santana Rey continues to operate Business Solutions. (Transactions for the first two months are described in the serial problem of Chapter 2.) The November 30, 2011, unadjusted trial balance of Business Solutions (reflecting its transactions for October and November of 2011) follows.

No.	Account Title	Debit	Credit
101	Cash	$38,264	
106	Accounts receivable	12,618	
126	Computer supplies	2,545	
128	Prepaid insurance	2,220	
131	Prepaid rent	3,300	
163	Office equipment	8,000	
164	Accumulated depreciation—Office equipment		$ 0
167	Computer equipment	20,000	
168	Accumulated depreciation—Computer equipment		0
201	Accounts payable		0
210	Wages payable		0
236	Unearned computer services revenue		0
307	Common stock		73,000
318	Retained earnings		0
319	Dividends	5,600	
403	Computer services revenue		25,659
612	Depreciation expense—Office equipment	0	
613	Depreciation expense—Computer equipment	0	
623	Wages expense	2,625	
637	Insurance expense	0	
640	Rent expense	0	
652	Computer supplies expense	0	
655	Advertising expense	1,728	
676	Mileage expense	704	
677	Miscellaneous expenses	250	
684	Repairs expense—Computer	805	
	Totals	$98,659	$98,659

Business Solutions had the following transactions and events in December 2011.

Dec. 2 Paid $1,025 cash to Hillside Mall for Business Solutions' share of mall advertising costs.
     3 Paid $500 cash for minor repairs to the company's computer.
     4 Received $3,950 cash from Alex's Engineering Co. for the receivable from November.
    10 Paid cash to Lyn Addie for six days of work at the rate of $125 per day.
    14 Notified by Alex's Engineering Co. that Business Solutions' bid of $7,000 on a proposed project has been accepted. Alex's paid a $1,500 cash advance to Business Solutions.
    15 Purchased $1,100 of computer supplies on credit from Harris Office Products.
    16 Sent a reminder to Gomez Co. to pay the fee for services recorded on November 8.
    20 Completed a project for Liu Corporation and received $5,625 cash.
22–26 Took the week off for the holidays.
    28 Received $3,000 cash from Gomez Co. on its receivable.
    29 Reimbursed S. Rey for business automobile mileage (600 miles at $0.32 per mile).
    31 The business paid $1,500 cash for dividends.

The following additional facts are collected for use in making adjusting entries prior to preparing financial statements for the company's first three months:

a. The December 31 inventory count of computer supplies shows $580 still available.
b. Three months have expired since the 12-month insurance premium was paid in advance.
c. As of December 31, Lyn Addie has not been paid for four days of work at $125 per day.
d. The computer system, acquired on October 1, is expected to have a four-year life with no salvage value.
e. The office equipment, acquired on October 1, is expected to have a five-year life with no salvage value.
f. Three of the four months' prepaid rent has expired.

Required

1. Prepare journal entries to record each of the December transactions and events for Business Solutions. Post those entries to the accounts in the ledger.
2. Prepare adjusting entries to reflect *a* through *f*. Post those entries to the accounts in the ledger.
3. Prepare an adjusted trial balance as of December 31, 2011.
4. Prepare an income statement for the three months ended December 31, 2011.
5. Prepare a statement of retained earnings for the three months ended December 31, 2011.
6. Prepare a balance sheet as of December 31, 2011.
7. Record and post the necessary closing entries for Business Solutions.
8. Prepare a post-closing trial balance as of December 31, 2011.

Check (3) Adjusted trial balance totals, $109,034

(6) Total assets, $83,460
Check Post-closing trial balance totals, $85,110

Beyond the Numbers

BTN 3-1 Refer to **Research In Motion**'s financial statements in Appendix A to answer the following.
1. Identify and write down the revenue recognition principle as explained in the chapter.
2. Review Research In Motion's footnotes to discover how it applies the revenue recognition principle and when it recognizes revenue. Report what you discover.
3. What is Research In Motion's profit margin for fiscal years ended February 28, 2009, and February 27, 2010?
4. For the fiscal year ended February 27, 2010, what amount is credited to Income Summary to summarize its revenues earned?
5. For the fiscal year ended February 27, 2010, what amount is debited to Income Summary to summarize its expenses incurred?
6. For the fiscal year ended February 27, 2010, what is the balance of its Income Summary account before it is closed?

REPORTING IN ACTION
C1 C2 A1 A2 P4

RIM

Fast Forward

7. Access RIM's annual report (10-K) for fiscal years ending after February 27, 2010, at its Website (**RIM.com**) or the SEC's EDGAR database (**www.sec.gov**). Assess and compare the February 27, 2010, fiscal year profit margin to any subsequent year's profit margin that you compute.

BTN 3-2 Key figures for the recent two years of both **Research In Motion** and **Apple** follow.

COMPARATIVE ANALYSIS
A2 A3

RIM
Apple

($ millions)	Research In Motion Current Year	Research In Motion Prior Year	Apple Current Year	Apple Prior Year
Net income	$ 2,457	$ 1,893	$ 8,235	$ 6,119
Net sales	14,953	11,065	42,905	37,491
Current assets	5,813	4,842	31,555	30,006
Current liabilities	2,432	2,115	11,506	11,361

Required

1. Compute profit margins for (*a*) Research In Motion and (*b*) Apple for the two years of data shown.
2. Which company is more successful on the basis of profit margin? Explain.
3. Compute the current ratio for both years for both companies.
4. Which company has the better ability to pay short-term obligations according to the current ratio?
5. Analyze and comment on each company's current ratios for the past two years.
6. How do RIM's and Apple's current ratios compare to their industry (assumed) average ratio of 2.4?

ETHICS CHALLENGE
C1 C2 A1

BTN 3-3 Jackie Bergez works for Sea Biscuit Co. She and Bob Welch, her manager, are preparing adjusting entries for annual financial statements. Bergez computes depreciation and records it as

Depreciation Expense—Equipment	123,000	
Accumulated Depreciation—Equipment		123,000

Welch agrees with her computation but says the credit entry should be directly to the Equipment account. Welch argues that while accumulated depreciation is technically correct, "it is less hassle not to use a contra account and just credit the Equipment account directly. And besides, the balance sheet shows the same amount for total assets under either method."

Required

1. How should depreciation be recorded? Do you support Bergez or Welch?
2. Evaluate the strengths and weaknesses of Welch's reasons for preferring his method.
3. Indicate whether the situation Bergez faces is an ethical problem. Explain.

COMMUNICATING IN PRACTICE
P4

BTN 3-4 Assume that one of your classmates states that a company's books should be ongoing and therefore not closed until that business is terminated. Write a half-page memo to this classmate explaining the concept of the closing process by drawing analogies between (1) a scoreboard for an athletic event and the revenue and expense accounts of a business or (2) a sports team's record book and retained earnings. (*Hint:* Think about what would happen if the scoreboard is not cleared before the start of a new game.)

TAKING IT TO THE NET
C1 A2

BTN 3-5 Access EDGAR online (www.sec.gov) and locate the 10-K report of **The Gap, Inc.,** (ticker GPS) filed on March 26, 2010. Review its financial statements reported for the year ended January 30, 2010, to answer the following questions.

Required

1. What are Gap's main brands?
2. What is Gap's fiscal year-end?
3. What is Gap's net sales for the period ended January 30, 2010?
4. What is Gap's net income for the period ended January 30, 2010?
5. Compute Gap's profit margin for the year ended January 30, 2010.
6. Do you believe Gap's decision to use a year-end of late January or early February relates to its natural business year? Explain.

TEAMWORK IN ACTION
A1 P1

BTN 3-6 Four types of adjustments are described in the chapter: (1) prepaid expenses, (2) unearned revenues, (3) accrued expenses, and (4) accrued revenues.

Required

1. Form *learning teams* of four (or more) members. Each team member must select one of the four adjustments as an area of expertise (each team must have at least one expert in each area).

Chapter 3 Adjusting Accounts and Preparing Financial Statements

2. Form *expert teams* from the individuals who have selected the same area of expertise. Expert teams are to discuss and write a report that each expert will present to his or her learning team addressing the following:
   a. Description of the adjustment and why it's necessary.
   b. Example of a transaction or event, with dates and amounts, that requires adjustment.
   c. Adjusting entry(ies) for the example in requirement *b*.
   d. Status of the affected account(s) before and after the adjustment in requirement *c*.
   e. Effects on financial statements of not making the adjustment.
3. Each expert should return to his or her learning team. In rotation, each member should present his or her expert team's report to the learning team. Team discussion is encouraged.

BTN 3-7 Review the opening feature of this chapter dealing with **Cheezburger Network**.

ENTREPRENEURIAL DECISION

A2

Required
1. Assume that Cheezburger Network sells a $300 gift certificate to a customer, collecting the $300 cash in advance. Prepare the journal entry for the (*a*) collection of the cash for delivery of the gift certificate to the customer and (*b*) revenue from the subsequent delivery of merchandise when the gift certificate is used.
2. How can keeping less inventory help to improve Cheezburger Network's profit margin?
3. Ben Huh understands that many companies carry considerable inventory, and Ben is thinking of carrying additional inventory of merchandise for sale. Ben desires your advice on the pros and cons of carrying such inventory. Provide at least one reason for and one reason against carrying additional inventory.

BTN 3-8 Select a company that you can visit in person or interview on the telephone. Call ahead to the company to arrange a time when you can interview an employee (preferably an accountant) who helps prepare the annual financial statements. Inquire about the following aspects of its *accounting cycle:*

HITTING THE ROAD

C1

1. Does the company prepare interim financial statements? What time period(s) is used for interim statements?
2. Does the company use the cash or accrual basis of accounting?
3. Does the company use a work sheet in preparing financial statements? Why or why not?
4. Does the company use a spreadsheet program? If so, which software program is used?
5. How long does it take after the end of its reporting period to complete annual statements?

BTN 3-9 **Nokia** (www.Nokia.com) is a leading global manufacturer of mobile devices and services.

GLOBAL DECISION

A2 A3 C1 C2

NOKIA

Required
1. Locate the notes to its December 31, 2009, financial statements at the company's Website, and read note *1 Accounting Principles—Revenue Recognition,* first paragraph only. When is revenue recognized by Nokia?
2. Refer to Nokia's financials in Appendix A. What is Nokia's profit margin for the year ended December 31, 2009?
3. Compute Nokia's current ratio for both the current year and the prior year.
4. Comment on any change from the prior year to the current year for the current ratio.

ANSWERS TO MULTIPLE CHOICE QUIZ

1. b; the forgotten adjusting entry is: *dr.* Wages Expense, *cr.* Wages Payable.
2. c; Supplies used = $450 − $125 = $325
3. b; Insurance expense = $24,000 × (8/24) = $8,000; adjusting entry is: *dr.* Insurance Expense for $8,000, *cr.* Prepaid Insurance for $8,000.
4. a; Consulting fees earned = $3,600 × (2/6) = $1,200; adjusting entry is: *dr.* Unearned Consulting Fee for $1,200, *cr.* Consulting Fees Earned for $1,200.
5. e; Profit margin = $15,000/$300,000 = 5%
6. b

A Look Back
Chapter 3 focused on the final steps of the accounting process. We explained the importance of proper revenue and expense recognition and described the adjusting and closing processes. We also prepared financial statements.

A Look at This Chapter
This chapter emphasizes merchandising activities. We explain how reporting merchandising activities differs from reporting service activities. We also analyze and record merchandise purchases and sales transactions, and explain the adjustments and closing process for merchandisers.

A Look Ahead
Chapter 5 extends our analysis of merchandising activities and focuses on the valuation of inventory. Topics include the items in inventory, costs assigned, costing methods used, and inventory estimation techniques.

4 Reporting and Analyzing Merchandising Operations

Learning Objectives

CAP

CONCEPTUAL

- **C1** Describe merchandising activities and identify income components for a merchandising company. (p. 158)
- **C2** Identify and explain the inventory asset and cost flows of a merchandising company. (p. 159)

ANALYTICAL

- **A1** Compute the acid-test ratio and explain its use to assess liquidity. (p. 174)
- **A2** Compute the gross margin ratio and explain its use to assess profitability. (p. 174)

LP4

PROCEDURAL

- **P1** Analyze and record transactions for merchandise purchases using a perpetual system. (p. 160)
- **P2** Analyze and record transactions for merchandise sales using a perpetual system. (p. 165)
- **P3** Prepare adjustments and close accounts for a merchandising company. (p. 168)
- **P4** Define and prepare multiple-step and single-step income statements. (p. 170)
- **P5** *Appendix 4A*—Record and compare merchandising transactions using both periodic and perpetual inventory systems. (p. 179)

Decision Insight

Out of Africa

"We are changing history and . . . we are all going to make a whole lot of money."
—SELENA CUFFE

LOS ANGELES—Selena Cuffe was in Johannesburg as part of a student exchange program when she discovered wine at the Soweto Wine Festival. "They have wine here?" asked a puzzled Selena. That festival unleashed Selena's passion to pursue the merchandising of wine. But not just any wine—she would import and distribute wine produced by indigenous African vintners. She and her husband, Khary, launched **Heritage Link Brands** (**HeritageLinkBrands.com**). Our mission, says Selena, is "to showcase the very best wines from Africa and the African Diaspora."

But the start-up was a struggle. "Our business is a family business so whatever decisions we make have to be made with the best interest of my family and those we work with," explains Selena. She describes how the business required a merchandising accounting system to account for purchases and sales transactions and to effectively track the levels of the various wines. Inventory was especially important to account for and monitor. Khary explains, "It is very easy to underestimate expenses."

To succeed, Selena and Khary needed to make smart business decisions. They set up an accounting system to capture and communicate costs and sales information. Tracking merchandising activities was necessary to set prices and to manage discounts, allowances, and returns of both sales and purchases. A perpetual inventory system enabled them to stock the right kind and amount of merchandise and to avoid the costs of out-of-stock and excess inventory. Khary stressed that they monitored current assets and current liabilities (working capital). "Understand working capital," insists Khary. "If you don't understand working capital, stop right here and open an accounting book."

Mastering accounting for merchandising is a means to an end for Selena and Khary. "My training is really about how to run a successful business," says Selena. "How to get the most profit you can out of something." Still, Selena recognizes that her merchandising business is more than profits and losses. "What we're able to do and how we're able to make an impact with this business only matters in as much as the people here and on the continent are able to be successful and thrive."

[Sources: *Heritage Link Brands Website,* January 2012; *TIME,* September 2007; *Black Enterprise,* May 2009; *Inc,* March 2009; *SpreadLuv,* May 2011]

Chapter Preview

Buyers of merchandise expect many products, discount prices, inventory on demand, and high quality. This chapter introduces the accounting practices used by companies engaged in merchandising. We show how financial statements reflect merchandising activities and explain the new financial statement items created by merchandising activities. We also analyze and record merchandise purchases and sales, and explain the adjustments and the closing process for these companies.

Reporting and Analyzing Merchandising Operations

Merchandising Activities	Merchandising Purchases	Merchandising Sales	Accounting Cycle	Financial Statement Formats
• Reporting income • Reporting inventory • Operating cycles • Inventory systems	• Purchase discounts • Purchase returns and allowances • Transportation costs	• Sales of merchandise • Sales discounts • Sales returns and allowances	• Adjusting entries • Preparing financial statements • Closing entries	• Multiple-step income statement • Single-step income statement • Classified balance sheet

MERCHANDISING ACTIVITIES

C1 Describe merchandising activities and identify income components for a merchandising company.

Previous chapters emphasized the accounting and reporting activities of service companies. A merchandising company's activities differ from those of a service company. **Merchandise** consists of products, also called *goods,* that a company acquires to resell to customers. A **merchandiser** earns net income by buying and selling merchandise. Merchandisers are often identified as either wholesalers or retailers. A **wholesaler** is an *intermediary* that buys products from manufacturers or other wholesalers and sells them to retailers or other wholesalers. A **retailer** is an intermediary that buys products from manufacturers or wholesalers and sells them to consumers. Many retailers sell both products and services.

Reporting Income for a Merchandiser

Net income for a merchandiser equals revenues from selling merchandise minus both the cost of merchandise sold to customers and the cost of other expenses for the period, see Exhibit 4.1. The

EXHIBIT 4.1

Computing Income for a Merchandising Company versus a Service Company

Service Company

Revenues → Minus → Expenses → Equals → Net income

Merchandiser

Net sales → Minus → Cost of goods sold → Equals → Gross profit → Minus → Expenses → Equals → Net income

usual accounting term for revenues from selling merchandise is *sales,* and the term used for the expense of buying and preparing the merchandise is **cost of goods sold.** (Some service companies use the term *sales* instead of revenues; and cost of goods sold is also called *cost of sales.*)

The income statement for Z-Mart in Exhibit 4.2 illustrates these key components of a merchandiser's net income. The first two lines show that products are acquired at a cost of $230,400 and sold for $314,700. The third line shows an $84,300 **gross profit,** also called

Point: Fleming, SuperValu, and SYSCO are wholesalers. Gap, Oakley, Target, and Walmart are retailers.

158

EXHIBIT 4.2

Merchandiser's Income Statement

Z-MART
Income Statement
For Year Ended December 31, 2011

Net sales	$314,700
Cost of goods sold	230,400
Gross profit	84,300
Expenses	71,400
Net income	$ 12,900

gross margin, which equals net sales less cost of goods sold. Additional expenses of $71,400 are reported, which leaves $12,900 in net income.

Point: Analysis of gross profit is important to effective business decisions, and is described later in the chapter.

Reporting Inventory for a Merchandiser

A merchandiser's balance sheet includes a current asset called *merchandise inventory,* an item not on a service company's balance sheet. **Merchandise inventory,** or simply *inventory,* refers to products that a company owns and intends to sell. The cost of this asset includes the cost incurred to buy the goods, ship them to the store, and make them ready for sale.

C2 Identify and explain the inventory asset and cost flows of a merchandising company.

Operating Cycle for a Merchandiser

A merchandising company's operating cycle begins by purchasing merchandise and ends by collecting cash from selling the merchandise. The length of an operating cycle differs across the types of businesses. Department stores often have operating cycles of two to five months. Operating cycles for grocery merchants usually range from two to eight weeks.

Exhibit 4.3 illustrates an operating cycle for a merchandiser with credit sales. The cycle moves from (*a*) cash purchases of merchandise to (*b*) inventory for sale to (*c*) credit sales to (*d*) accounts receivable to (*e*) cash. Companies try to keep their operating cycles short because assets tied up in inventory and receivables are not productive. Cash sales shorten operating cycles.

EXHIBIT 4.3

Merchandiser's Operating Cycle

Inventory Systems

Cost of goods sold is the cost of merchandise sold to customers during a period. It is often the largest single expense on a merchandiser's income statement. **Inventory** refers to products a company owns and expects to sell in its normal operations. Exhibit 4.4 shows that a company's merchandise available for sale consists of what it begins with (beginning inventory) and what it

EXHIBIT 4.4

Merchandiser's Cost Flow for a Single Time Period

Point: Mathematically, Exhibit 4.4 says

BI + NP = MAS,

where BI is beginning inventory, NP is net purchases, and MAS is merchandise available for sale. Exhibit 4.4 also says

MAS = EI + COGS,

which can be rewritten as MAS − EI = COGS or MAS − COGS = EI, where EI is ending inventory and COGS is cost of goods sold.

Point: Growth of superstores such as **Costco** and **Sam's** is fueled by efficient use of perpetual inventory.

purchases (net purchases). The merchandise available is either sold (cost of goods sold) or kept for future sales (ending inventory).

Two alternative inventory accounting systems can be used to collect information about cost of goods sold and cost of inventory: *perpetual system* or *periodic system*. The **perpetual inventory system** continually updates accounting records for merchandising transactions—specifically, for those records of inventory available for sale and inventory sold. The **periodic inventory system** updates the accounting records for merchandise transactions only at the *end of a period*. Technological advances and competitive pressures have dramatically increased the use of the perpetual system. It gives managers immediate access to detailed information on sales and inventory levels, where they can strategically react to sales trends, cost changes, consumer tastes, and so forth, to increase gross profit. Selena and Khary Cuffe (see chapter opening feature) use perpetual records to track their wine inventories. (Some companies use a *hybrid* system where the perpetual system is used for tracking units available and the periodic system is used to compute cost of sales.)

Quick Check

Answers — p. 185

1. Describe a merchandiser's cost of goods sold.
2. What is gross profit for a merchandising company?
3. Explain why use of the perpetual inventory system has dramatically increased.

The following sections, consisting of the next 10 pages on purchasing, selling, and adjusting merchandise, use the perpetual system. Appendix 4A uses the periodic system (with the perpetual results on the side). An instructor can choose to cover either one or both inventory systems.

ACCOUNTING FOR MERCHANDISE PURCHASES

P1 Analyze and record transactions for merchandise purchases using a perpetual system.

Assets = Liabilities + Equity
+1,200
−1,200

The cost of merchandise purchased for resale is recorded in the Merchandise Inventory asset account. To illustrate, Z-Mart records a $1,200 cash purchase of merchandise on November 2 as follows:

Nov. 2	Merchandise Inventory	1,200	
	Cash		1,200
	Purchased merchandise for cash.		

The invoice for this merchandise is shown in Exhibit 4.5. The buyer usually receives the original invoice, and the seller keeps a copy. This *source document* serves as the purchase invoice of Z-Mart (buyer) and the sales invoice for Trex (seller). The amount recorded for merchandise inventory includes its purchase cost, shipping fees, taxes, and any other costs necessary to make it ready for sale. This section explains how we compute the recorded cost of merchandise purchases.

Point: The Merchandise Inventory account reflects the cost of goods available for resale.

Decision Insight

Trade Discounts When a manufacturer or wholesaler prepares a catalog of items it has for sale, it usually gives each item a **list price**, also called a *catalog price*. However, an item's intended *selling price* equals list price minus a given percent called a **trade discount**. The amount of trade discount usually depends on whether a buyer is a wholesaler, retailer, or final consumer. A wholesaler buying in large quantities is often granted a larger discount than a retailer buying in smaller quantities. A buyer records the net amount of list price minus trade discount. For example, in the November 2 purchase of merchandise by Z-Mart, the merchandise was listed in the seller's catalog at $2,000 and Z-Mart received a 40% trade discount. This meant that Z-Mart's purchase price was $1,200, computed as $2,000 − (40% × $2,000). ■

EXHIBIT 4.5

Invoice

INVOICE	① **TREX**
	W9797 Cherry Rd.
	Antigo, WI 54409

SOLD TO ③

Firm Name	Z-Mart
Attention of	Tom Novak, Purchasing Agent
Address	10 Michigan Street
City	Chicago
State	Illinois Zip 60521

② Invoice Date: 11/2/11 Number: 4657-2

④ P.O. Date	⑤ Salesperson	Terms	⑥ Freight	Ship
10/30/11	#141	2/10, n/30	FOB Destination	Via FedEx

Model No.	Description	Quantity	Price	Amount
⑦ CH015	Challenger X7	1	490	490
SD099	Speed Demon	1	710	710

See reverse for terms of sale and returns.

SubTotal	1,200
Shipping	—
Tax	—
⑧ Total	1,200

Key: ① Seller ② Invoice date ③ Purchaser ④ Order date ⑤ Credit terms
⑥ Freight terms ⑦ Goods ⑧ Total invoice amount

Purchase Discounts

The purchase of goods on credit requires a clear statement of expected future payments and dates to avoid misunderstandings. **Credit terms** for a purchase include the amounts and timing of payments from a buyer to a seller. Credit terms usually reflect an industry's practices. To illustrate, when sellers require payment within 10 days after the end of the month of the invoice date, the invoice will show credit terms as "n/10 EOM," which stands for net 10 days after end of month (**EOM**). When sellers require payment within 30 days after the invoice date, the invoice shows credit terms of "n/30," which stands for *net 30 days*.

Exhibit 4.6 portrays credit terms. The amount of time allowed before full payment is due is called the **credit period**. Sellers can grant a **cash discount** to encourage buyers to pay earlier. A buyer views a cash discount as a **purchase discount**. A seller views a cash discount as a **sales discount**. Any cash discounts are described in the credit terms on the invoice. For example, credit terms of "2/10, n/60" mean that full payment is due within a 60-day credit period, but the buyer can deduct 2% of the invoice amount if payment is made within 10 days of the invoice date. This reduced payment applies only for the **discount period**.

Point: Since both the buyer and seller know the invoice date, this date is used in setting the discount and credit periods.

EXHIBIT 4.6

Credit Terms

*Discount refers to a purchase discount for a buyer and a sales discount for a seller.

Point: Appendix 4A repeats journal entries *a* through *f* using a periodic inventory system.

To illustrate how a buyer accounts for a purchase discount, assume that Z-Mart's $1,200 purchase of merchandise is on credit with terms of 2/10, n/30. Its entry is

Assets = Liabilities + Equity
+1,200   +1,200

(a) Nov. 2	Merchandise Inventory	1,200	
	Accounts Payable		1,200
	Purchased merchandise on credit, invoice dated Nov. 2, terms 2/10, n/30.		

If Z-Mart pays the amount due on (or before) November 12, the entry is

Assets = Liabilities + Equity
−24   −1,200
−1,176

(b) Nov. 12	Accounts Payable	1,200	
	Merchandise Inventory		24
	Cash		1,176
	Paid for the $1,200 purchase of Nov. 2 less the discount of $24 (2% × $1,200).		

Point: These entries illustrate what is called the *gross method* of accounting for purchases with discount terms.

The Merchandise Inventory account after these entries reflects the net cost of merchandise purchased, and the Accounts Payable account shows a zero balance. Both ledger accounts, in T-account form, follow:

Merchandise Inventory				Accounts Payable			
Nov. 2	1,200	Nov. 12	24	Nov. 12	1,200	Nov. 2	1,200
Balance	1,176					Balance	0

A buyer's failure to pay within a discount period can be expensive. To illustrate, if Z-Mart does not pay within the 10-day 2% discount period, it can delay payment by 20 more days. This delay costs Z-Mart $24, computed as 2% × $1,200. Most buyers take advantage of a purchase discount because of the usually high interest rate implied from not taking it.[1] Also, good cash management means that no invoice is paid until the last day of the discount or credit period.

Decision Maker *Answer — p. 184*

Entrepreneur You purchase a batch of products on terms of 3/10, n/90, but your company has limited cash and you must borrow funds at an 11% annual rate if you are to pay within the discount period. Do you take advantage of the purchase discount? ■

Purchase Returns and Allowances

Purchase returns refer to merchandise a buyer acquires but then returns to the seller. A *purchase allowance* is a reduction in the cost of defective or unacceptable merchandise that a buyer acquires. Buyers often keep defective but still marketable merchandise if the seller grants an acceptable allowance. When a buyer returns or takes an allowance on merchandise, the buyer issues a **debit memorandum** to inform the seller of a debit made to the seller's account in the buyer's records.

Point: The sender (maker) of a *debit memorandum* will debit the account of the memo's receiver. The memo's receiver will credit the sender's account.

---

[1] The *implied annual interest rate* formula is:

(365 days ÷ [Credit period − Discount period]) × Cash discount rate.

For terms of 2/10, n/30, missing the 2% discount for an additional 20 days is equal to an annual interest rate of 36.5%, computed as [365 days/(30 days − 10 days)] × 2% discount rate. *Favorable purchase discounts* are those with implied annual interest rates that exceed the purchaser's annual rate for borrowing money.

Purchase Allowances To illustrate purchase allowances, assume that on November 15, Z-Mart (buyer) issues a $300 debit memorandum for an allowance from Trex for defective merchandise. Z-Mart's November 15 entry to update its Merchandise Inventory account to reflect the purchase allowance is

(c) Nov. 15	Accounts Payable	300	
	Merchandise Inventory		300
	Allowance for defective merchandise.		

Assets = Liabilities + Equity
−300   −300

The buyer's allowance for defective merchandise is usually offset against the buyer's current account payable balance to the seller. When cash is refunded, the Cash account is debited instead of Accounts Payable.

Purchase Returns Returns are recorded at the net costs charged to buyers. To illustrate the accounting for returns, suppose Z-Mart purchases $1,000 of merchandise on June 1 with terms 2/10, n/60. Two days later, Z-Mart returns $100 of goods before paying the invoice. When Z-Mart later pays on June 11, it takes the 2% discount only on the $900 remaining balance. When goods are returned, a buyer can take a purchase discount on only the remaining balance of the invoice. The resulting discount is $18 (2% × $900) and the cash payment is $882 ($900 − $18). The following entries reflect this illustration.

June 1	Merchandise Inventory	1,000	
	Accounts Payable		1,000
	Purchased merchandise, invoice dated June 1, terms 2/10, n/60.		
June 3	Accounts Payable	100	
	Merchandise Inventory		100
	Returned merchandise to seller.		
June 11	Accounts Payable	900	
	Merchandise Inventory		18
	Cash		882
	Paid for $900 merchandise ($1,000 − $100) less $18 discount (2% × $900).		

Example: Assume Z-Mart pays $980 cash for $1,000 of merchandise purchased within its 2% discount period. Later, it returns $100 of the original $1,000 merchandise. The return entry is
Cash 98
   Merchandise Inventory 98

■ Decision Ethics   Answer — p. 184

Credit Manager As a new credit manager, you are being trained by the outgoing manager. She explains that the system prepares checks for amounts net of favorable cash discounts, and the checks are dated the last day of the discount period. She also tells you that checks are not mailed until five days later, adding that "the company gets free use of cash for an extra five days, and our department looks better. When a supplier complains, we blame the computer system and the mailroom." Do you continue this payment policy? ■

Transportation Costs and Ownership Transfer

The buyer and seller must agree on who is responsible for paying any freight costs and who bears the risk of loss during transit for merchandising transactions. This is essentially the same as asking at what point ownership transfers from the seller to the buyer. The point of transfer is called the **FOB** (*free on board*) point, which determines who pays transportation costs (and often other incidental costs of transit such as insurance).

Exhibit 4.7 identifies two alternative points of transfer. (1) *FOB shipping point,* also called *FOB factory,* means the buyer accepts ownership when the goods depart the seller's place of business. The buyer is then responsible for paying shipping costs and bearing the risk of damage or loss when goods are in transit. The goods are part of the buyer's inventory when they are in transit since ownership has transferred to the buyer. **1-800-FLOWERS.COM**, a floral and gift

EXHIBIT 4.7

Ownership Transfer and Transportation Costs

Shipping point → Carrier → Destination

	Ownership Transfers When Goods Passed to	Transportation Costs Paid by
FOB shipping point	Carrier	Buyer
FOB destination	Buyer	Seller

Point: The party not responsible for shipping costs sometimes pays the carrier. In these cases, the party paying these costs either bills the party responsible or, more commonly, adjusts its account payable or account receivable with the other party. For example, a buyer paying a carrier when terms are FOB destination can decrease its account payable to the seller by the amount of shipping cost.

merchandiser, and **Bare Escentuals**, a cosmetic manufacturer, both use FOB shipping point. (2) *FOB destination* means ownership of goods transfers to the buyer when the goods arrive at the buyer's place of business. The seller is responsible for paying shipping charges and bears the risk of damage or loss in transit. The seller does not record revenue from this sale until the goods arrive at the destination because this transaction is not complete before that point. **Kyocera**, a manufacturer, uses FOB destination.

Z-Mart's $1,200 purchase on November 2 is on terms of FOB destination. This means Z-Mart is not responsible for paying transportation costs. When a buyer is responsible for paying transportation costs, the payment is made to a carrier or directly to the seller depending on the agreement. The cost principle requires that any necessary transportation costs of a buyer (often called *transportation-in* or *freight-in*) be included as part of the cost of purchased merchandise. To illustrate, Z-Mart's entry to record a $75 freight charge from an independent carrier for merchandise purchased FOB shipping point is

Assets = Liabilities + Equity
+75
−75

(d) Nov. 24	Merchandise Inventory	75	
	Cash		75
	Paid freight costs on purchased merchandise.		

A seller records the costs of shipping goods to customers in a Delivery Expense account when the seller is responsible for these costs. Delivery Expense, also called *transportation-out* or *freight-out,* is reported as a selling expense in the seller's income statement.

In summary, purchases are recorded as debits to Merchandise Inventory. Any later purchase discounts, returns, and allowances are credited (decreases) to Merchandise Inventory. Transportation-in is debited (added) to Merchandise Inventory. Z-Mart's itemized costs of merchandise purchases for year 2011 are in Exhibit 4.8.

EXHIBIT 4.8

Itemized Costs of Merchandise Purchases

Z-MART
Itemized Costs of Merchandise Purchases
For Year Ended December 31, 2011

Invoice cost of merchandise purchases	$235,800
Less: Purchase discounts received	(4,200)
Purchase returns and allowances	(1,500)
Add: Costs of transportation-in	2,300
Total cost of merchandise purchases	**$232,400**

Point: Some companies have separate accounts for purchase discounts, returns and allowances, and transportation-in. These accounts are then transferred to Merchandise Inventory at period-end. This is a *hybrid system* of perpetual and periodic. That is, Merchandise Inventory is updated on a perpetual basis but only for purchases and cost of goods sold.

The accounting system described here does not provide separate records (accounts) for total purchases, total purchase discounts, total purchase returns and allowances, and total transportation-in. Yet nearly all companies collect this information in supplementary records because managers need this information to evaluate and control each of these cost elements. **Supplementary records,** also called *supplemental records,* refer to information outside the usual general ledger accounts.

Chapter 4 Reporting and Analyzing Merchandising Operations

> **Quick Check** Answers — p. 185
>
> 4. How long are the credit and discount periods when credit terms are 2/10, n/60?
> 5. Identify which items are subtracted from the *list* amount and not recorded when computing purchase price: (a) freight-in; (b) trade discount; (c) purchase discount; (d) purchase return.
> 6. What does FOB mean? What does FOB destination mean?

ACCOUNTING FOR MERCHANDISE SALES

Merchandising companies also must account for sales, sales discounts, sales returns and allowances, and cost of goods sold. A merchandising company such as Z-Mart reflects these items in its gross profit computation, as shown in Exhibit 4.9. This section explains how this information is derived from transactions.

P2 Analyze and record transactions for merchandise sales using a perpetual system.

EXHIBIT 4.9
Gross Profit Computation

Z-MART
Computation of Gross Profit
For Year Ended December 31, 2011

Sales..................................		$321,000
Less: Sales discounts...................	$4,300	
Sales returns and allowances.........	2,000	6,300
Net sales.............................		314,700
Cost of goods sold...................		230,400
Gross profit.........................		**$ 84,300**

Sales of Merchandise

Each sales transaction for a seller of merchandise involves two parts.

> 1. **Revenue received in the form of an asset from the customer.**
> 2. **Cost recognition of the merchandise sold to the customer.**

Accounting for a sales transaction under the perpetual system requires recording information about both parts. This means that each sales transaction for merchandisers, whether for cash or on credit, requires *two entries:* one for revenue and one for cost. To illustrate, Z-Mart sold $2,400 of merchandise on credit on November 3. The revenue part of this transaction is recorded as

(e) Nov. 3	Accounts Receivable.............................	2,400	
	Sales...		2,400
	Sold merchandise on credit.		

Assets = Liabilities + Equity
+2,400   +2,400

This entry reflects an increase in Z-Mart's assets in the form of accounts receivable. It also shows the increase in revenue (Sales). If the sale is for cash, the debit is to Cash instead of Accounts Receivable.

The cost part of each sales transaction ensures that the Merchandise Inventory account under a perpetual inventory system reflects the updated cost of the merchandise available for sale. For example, the cost of the merchandise Z-Mart sold on November 3 is $1,600, and the entry to record the cost part of this sales transaction is

(e) Nov. 3	Cost of Goods Sold.............................	1,600	
	Merchandise Inventory........................		1,600
	To record the cost of Nov. 3 sale.		

Assets = Liabilities + Equity
−1,600   −1,600

Decision Insight

Suppliers and Demands Large merchandising companies often bombard suppliers with demands. These include discounts for bar coding and technology support systems, and fines for shipping errors. Merchandisers' goals are to reduce inventories, shorten lead times, and eliminate errors.

Sales Discounts

Sales discounts on credit sales can benefit a seller by decreasing the delay in receiving cash and reducing future collection efforts. At the time of a credit sale, a seller does not know whether a customer will pay within the discount period and take advantage of a discount. This means the seller usually does not record a sales discount until a customer actually pays within the discount period. To illustrate, Z-Mart completes a credit sale for $1,000 on November 12 with terms of 2/10, n/60. The entry to record the revenue part of this sale is

Assets = Liabilities + Equity
+1,000   +1,000

Nov. 12	Accounts Receivable	1,000	
	Sales		1,000
	Sold merchandise under terms of 2/10, n/60.		

This entry records the receivable and the revenue as if the customer will pay the full amount. The customer has two options, however. One option is to wait 60 days until January 11 and pay the full $1,000. In this case, Z-Mart records that payment as

Assets = Liabilities + Equity
+1,000
−1,000

Jan. 11	Cash	1,000	
	Accounts Receivable		1,000
	Received payment for Nov. 12 sale.		

The customer's second option is to pay $980 within a 10-day period ending November 22. If the customer pays on (or before) November 22, Z-Mart records the payment as

Assets = Liabilities + Equity
+980   −20
−1,000

Nov. 22	Cash	980	
	Sales Discounts	20	
	Accounts Receivable		1,000
	Received payment for Nov. 12 sale less discount.		

Sales Discounts is a contra revenue account, meaning the Sales Discounts account is deducted from the Sales account when computing a company's net sales (see Exhibit 4.9). Management monitors Sales Discounts to assess the effectiveness and cost of its discount policy.

Sales Returns and Allowances

Point: Published income statements rarely disclose sales discounts, returns and allowances.

Sales returns refer to merchandise that customers return to the seller after a sale. Many companies allow customers to return merchandise for a full refund. *Sales allowances* refer to reductions in the selling price of merchandise sold to customers. This can occur with damaged or defective merchandise that a customer is willing to purchase with a decrease in selling price. Sales returns and allowances usually involve dissatisfied customers and the possibility of lost future sales, and managers monitor information about returns and allowances.

Sales Returns To illustrate, recall Z-Mart's sale of merchandise on November 3 for $2,400 that had cost $1,600. Assume that the customer returns part of the merchandise on

November 6, and the returned items sell for $800 and cost $600. The revenue part of this transaction must reflect the decrease in sales from the customer's return of merchandise as follows:

(f) Nov. 6	Sales Returns and Allowances	800	
	Accounts Receivable		800
	Customer returns merchandise of Nov. 3 sale.		

Assets = Liabilities + Equity
−800   −800

If the merchandise returned to Z-Mart is not defective and can be resold to another customer, Z-Mart returns these goods to its inventory. The entry to restore the cost of such goods to the Merchandise Inventory account is

Nov. 6	Merchandise Inventory	600	
	Cost of Goods Sold		600
	Returned goods added to inventory.		

Assets = Liabilities + Equity
+600   +600

This entry changes if the goods returned are defective. In this case the returned inventory is recorded at its estimated value, not its cost. To illustrate, if the goods (costing $600) returned to Z-Mart are defective and estimated to be worth $150, the following entry is made: Dr. Merchandise Inventory for $150, Dr. Loss from Defective Merchandise for $450, and Cr. Cost of Goods Sold for $600.

Fraud

Reversing Returns. On May 3, 2011, Green Mountain Coffee Roasters beat analysts' earnings estimates by $0.10 per share for the 13-week period ended March 26, 2011. The next day the stock price rose $11.91 per share to close at $75.98 per share, an 18.5% increase over the prior day's closing price. In the weeks that followed, some analysts raised questions about the quality of Green Mountain's earnings because of its accounting for sales returns. They allege that a large part of that earnings increase was due to an accounting adjustment that reversed much of a reserve that was set up for sales returns in prior periods.

Sales Allowances To illustrate sales allowances, assume that $800 of the merchandise Z-Mart sold on November 3 is defective but the buyer decides to keep it because Z-Mart offers a $100 price reduction. Z-Mart records this allowance as follows:

Nov. 6	Sales Returns and Allowances	100	
	Accounts Receivable		100
	To record sales allowance on Nov. 3 sale.		

Assets = Liabilities + Equity
−100   −100

The seller usually prepares a credit memorandum to confirm a buyer's return or allowance. A seller's **credit memorandum** informs a buyer of the seller's credit to the buyer's Account Receivable (on the seller's books).

Point: The sender (maker) of a credit memorandum will *credit* the account of the receiver. The receiver of a credit memorandum will *debit* the sender's account.

Quick Check
Answers — p. 185

7. Why are sales discounts and sales returns and allowances recorded in contra revenue accounts instead of directly in the Sales account?
8. Under what conditions are two entries necessary to record a sales return?
9. When merchandise is sold on credit and the seller notifies the buyer of a price allowance, does the seller create and send a credit memorandum or a debit memorandum?

COMPLETING THE ACCOUNTING CYCLE

Exhibit 4.10 shows the flow of merchandising costs during a period and where these costs are reported at period-end. Specifically, beginning inventory plus the net cost of purchases is the merchandise available for sale. As inventory is sold, its cost is recorded in cost of goods sold on the income statement; what remains is ending inventory on the balance sheet. A period's ending inventory is the next period's beginning inventory.

EXHIBIT 4.10

Merchandising Cost Flow in the Accounting Cycle

Adjusting Entries for Merchandisers

P3 Prepare adjustments and close accounts for a merchandising company.

Each of the steps in the accounting cycle described in the prior chapter for a service company applies to a merchandiser. This section and the next two further explain three steps of the accounting cycle for a merchandiser—adjustments, statement preparation, and closing.

Adjusting entries are generally the same for merchandising companies and service companies, including those for prepaid expenses (including depreciation), accrued expenses, unearned revenues, and accrued revenues. However, a merchandiser using a perpetual inventory system is usually required to make another adjustment to update the Merchandise Inventory account to reflect any loss of merchandise, including theft and deterioration. **Shrinkage** is the term used to refer to the loss of inventory and it is computed by comparing a physical count of inventory with recorded amounts. A physical count is usually performed at least once annually.

To illustrate, Z-Mart's Merchandise Inventory account at the end of year 2011 has a balance of $21,250, but a physical count reveals that only $21,000 of inventory exists. The adjusting entry to record this $250 shrinkage is

Point: About two-thirds of shoplifting losses are thefts by employees.

Assets = Liabilities + Equity
−250   −250

Dec. 31	Cost of Goods Sold	250	
	Merchandise Inventory		250
	To adjust for $250 shrinkage revealed by a physical count of inventory.		

Preparing Financial Statements

The financial statements of a merchandiser, and their preparation, are similar to those for a service company described in Chapters 2 and 3. The income statement mainly differs by the inclusion of *cost of goods sold* and *gross profit*. Also, net sales is affected by discounts, returns, and allowances, and some additional expenses are possible such as delivery expense and loss from defective merchandise. The balance sheet mainly differs by the inclusion of *merchandise inventory* as part of current assets. The statement of retained earnings is unchanged. A work sheet can be used to help prepare these statements, and one is illustrated in Appendix 4B for Z-Mart.

Point: Staples's costs of shipping merchandise to its stores is included in its costs of inventories as required by the cost principle.

Closing Entries for Merchandisers

Closing entries are similar for service companies and merchandising companies using a perpetual system. The difference is that we must close some new temporary accounts that arise from merchandising activities. Z-Mart has several temporary accounts unique to merchandisers: Sales (of goods), Sales Discounts, Sales Returns and Allowances, and Cost of Goods Sold. Their existence in the ledger means that the first two closing entries for a merchandiser are slightly different from the ones described in the prior chapter for a service company. These differences are set in **red boldface** in the closing entries of Exhibit 4.11.

Point: The Inventory account is not affected by the closing process under a perpetual system.

EXHIBIT 4.11
Closing Entries for a Merchandiser

Step 1: Close Credit Balances in Temporary Accounts to Income Summary.

Dec. 31	Sales	321,000	
	Income Summary		321,000
	To close credit balances in temporary accounts.		

Step 2: Close Debit Balances in Temporary Accounts to Income Summary.

Dec. 31	Income Summary	308,100	
	Sales Discounts		**4,300**
	Sales Returns and Allowances		**2,000**
	Cost of Goods Sold		**230,400**
	Depreciation Expense		3,700
	Salaries Expense		43,800
	Insurance Expense		600
	Rent Expense		9,000
	Supplies Expense		3,000
	Advertising Expense		11,300
	To close debit balances in temporary accounts.		

Step 3: Close Income Summary to Retained Earnings.

The third closing entry is identical for a merchandising company and a service company. The $12,900 amount is net income reported on the income statement.

Dec. 31	Income Summary	12,900	
	Retained Earnings		12,900
	To close the Income Summary account.		

Step 4: Close Dividends Account to Retained Earnings.

The fourth closing entry is identical for a merchandising company and a service company. It closes the Dividends account and adjusts the Retained Earnings account to the amount shown on the balance sheet.

Dec. 31	Retained Earnings	4,000	
	Dividends		4,000
	To close the Dividends account.		

Summary of Merchandising Entries

Exhibit 4.12 summarizes the key adjusting and closing entries of a merchandiser (using a perpetual inventory system) that are different from those of a service company described in prior chapters (the Demonstration Problem 2 illustrates these merchandising entries).

EXHIBIT 4.12
Summary of Merchandising Entries

	Merchandising Transactions	Merchandising Entries	Dr.	Cr.
Purchases	Purchasing merchandise for resale.	Merchandise Inventory Cash or Accounts Payable	#	#
	Paying freight costs on purchases; FOB shipping point.	Merchandise Inventory Cash	#	#

	Paying within discount period.	Accounts Payable
		    Merchandise Inventory
		    Cash
			#	#
				#

	Recording purchase returns or allowances.	Cash or Accounts Payable Merchandise Inventory	#	#

Sales	Selling merchandise.	Cash or Accounts Receivable
		    Sales
		Cost of Goods Sold
		    Merchandise Inventory
			#
			
			#
			
				#
				
				#

	Receiving payment within discount period.	Cash Sales Discounts Accounts Receivable	# #	 #

	Granting sales returns or allowances.	Sales Returns and Allowances
		    Cash or Accounts Receivable
		Merchandise Inventory
		    Cost of Goods Sold
			#
			
			#
				
				#
				
				#

	Paying freight costs on sales; FOB destination.	Delivery Expense Cash	#	#

	Merchandising Events	Adjusting and Closing Entries	Dr.	Cr.
Adjusting	Adjusting due to shrinkage (occurs when recorded amount larger than physical inventory).	Cost of Goods Sold Merchandise Inventory	#	#
Closing	Closing temporary accounts with credit balances.	Sales Income Summary	#	#

	Closing temporary accounts with debit balances.	Income Summary
		    Sales Returns and Allowances
		    Sales Discounts
		    Cost of Goods Sold
		    Delivery Expense
		    "Other Expenses"
			#	#
				#
				#
				#
				#

Quick Check
Answers — p. 185

10. When a merchandiser uses a perpetual inventory system, why is it sometimes necessary to adjust the Merchandise Inventory balance with an adjusting entry?
11. What temporary accounts do you expect to find in a merchandising business but not in a service business?
12. Describe the closing entries normally made by a merchandising company.

FINANCIAL STATEMENT FORMATS

P4 Define and prepare multiple-step and single-step income statements.

Generally accepted accounting principles do not require companies to use any one presentation format for financial statements so we see many different formats in practice. This section describes two common income statement formats: multiple-step and single-step. The classified balance sheet of a merchandiser is also explained.

Multiple-Step Income Statement

A **multiple-step income statement** format shows detailed computations of net sales and other costs and expenses, and reports subtotals for various classes of items. Exhibit 4.13 shows a multiple-step income statement for Z-Mart. The statement has three main parts: (1) *gross profit,* determined by net sales less cost of goods sold, (2) *income from operations,* determined by gross profit less operating expenses, and (3) *net income,* determined by income from operations adjusted for nonoperating items.

EXHIBIT 4.13

Multiple-Step Income Statement

Z-MART
Income Statement
For Year Ended December 31, 2011

Sales		$321,000
Less: Sales discounts	$ 4,300	
Sales returns and allowances	2,000	6,300
Net sales		314,700
Cost of goods sold*		230,400
Gross profit		84,300
Operating Expenses		
Selling expenses		
Depreciation expense—Store equipment	3,000	
Sales salaries expense	18,500	
Rent expense—Selling space	8,100	
Store supplies expense	1,200	
Advertising expense	11,300	
Total selling expenses	42,100	
General and administrative expenses		
Depreciation expense—Office equipment	700	
Office salaries expense	25,300	
Insurance expense	600	
Rent expense—Office space	900	
Office supplies expense	1,800	
Total general and administrative expenses	29,300	
Total operating expenses		71,400
Income from operations		12,900
Other revenues and gains (expenses and losses)		
Interest revenue	1,000	
Gain on sale of building	2,500	
Interest expense	(1,500)	
Total other revenue and gains (expenses and losses)		2,000
Net income		$ 14,900

- Gross profit computation
- Income from operations computation
- Nonoperating activities computation

*Cost of goods sold consists of the following:

Beginning inventory	$ 19,000
Cost of goods purchased	232,400
Cost of goods available for sale	251,400
Less ending inventory	21,000
Cost of goods sold	$230,400

Operating expenses are classified into two sections. **Selling expenses** include the expenses of promoting sales by displaying and advertising merchandise, making sales, and delivering goods to customers. **General and administrative expenses** support a company's overall operations and include expenses related to accounting, human resource management, and financial management. Expenses are allocated between sections when they contribute to more than one. Z-Mart allocates rent expense of $9,000 from its store building between two sections: $8,100 to selling expense and $900 to general and administrative expense.

Nonoperating activities consist of other expenses, revenues, losses, and gains that are unrelated to a company's operations. *Other revenues and gains* commonly include interest revenue,

Point: Z-Mart did not have any nonoperating activities; however, Exhibit 4.13 includes some for illustrative purposes.

dividend revenue, rent revenue, and gains from asset disposals. *Other expenses and losses* commonly include interest expense, losses from asset disposals, and casualty losses. When a company has no reportable nonoperating activities, its income from operations is simply labeled net income.

Single-Step Income Statement

Point: Many companies report interest expense and interest revenue in separate categories after operating income and before subtracting income tax expense. As one example, see **Palm**'s income statement in Appendix A.

A **single-step income statement** is another widely used format and is shown in Exhibit 4.14 for Z-Mart. It lists cost of goods sold as another expense and shows only one subtotal for total expenses. Expenses are grouped into very few, if any, categories. Many companies use formats that combine features of both the single- and multiple-step statements. Provided that income statement items are shown sensibly, management can choose the format. (In later chapters, we describe some items, such as extraordinary gains and losses, that must be reported in certain locations on the income statement.) Similar presentation options are available for the statement of retained earnings and statement of cash flows.

EXHIBIT 4.14

Single-Step Income Statement

Z-MART
Income Statement
For Year Ended December 31, 2011

Revenues		
Net sales		$314,700
Interest revenue		1,000
Gain on sale of building		2,500
Total revenues		318,200
Expenses		
Cost of goods sold	$230,400	
Selling expenses	42,100	
General and administrative expenses	29,300	
Interest expense	1,500	
Total expenses		303,300
Net income		$ 14,900

Classified Balance Sheet

The merchandiser's classified balance sheet reports merchandise inventory as a current asset, usually after accounts receivable according to an asset's nearness to liquidity. Inventory is usually less liquid than accounts receivable because inventory must first be sold before cash can be received; but it is more liquid than supplies and prepaid expenses. Exhibit 4.15 shows the current asset section of Z-Mart's classified balance sheet (other sections are as shown in Chapter 3).

EXHIBIT 4.15

Classified Balance Sheet (partial) of a Merchandiser

Z-MART
Balance Sheet (partial)
December 31, 2011

Current assets	
Cash	$ 8,200
Accounts receivable	11,200
Merchandise inventory	**21,000**
Office supplies	550
Store supplies	250
Prepaid insurance	300
Total current assets	$41,500

Fraud

Merchandising Shenanigans. Accurate invoices are important to both sellers and buyers. Merchandisers rely on invoices to make certain they receive all monies for products provided—no more, no less. To achieve this, controls are set up. Still, failures arise. A survey reports that 9% of employees in sales and marketing witnessed false or misleading invoices sent to customers. Another 14% observed employees violating contract terms with customers (KPMG 2009).

GLOBAL VIEW

This section discusses similarities and differences between U.S. GAAP and IFRS in accounting and reporting for merchandise purchases and sales, and for the income statement.

Accounting for Merchandise Purchases and Sales Both U.S. GAAP and IFRS include broad and similar guidance for the accounting of merchandise purchases and sales. Specifically, all of the transactions presented and illustrated in this chapter are accounted for identically under the two systems. The closing process for merchandisers also is identical for U.S. GAAP and IFRS. In the next chapter we describe how inventory valuation can, in some cases, be different for the two systems.

Income Statement Presentation We explained that net income, profit, and earnings refer to the same (*bottom line*) item. However, IFRS tends to use the term *profit* more than any other term, whereas U.S. statements tend to use *net income* more than any other term. Both U.S. GAAP and IFRS income statements begin with the net sales or net revenues (*top line*) item. For merchandisers and manufacturers, this is followed by cost of goods sold. The presentation is similar for the remaining items with the following differences.

- U.S. GAAP offers little guidance about the presentation or order of expenses. IFRS requires separate disclosures for financing costs (interest expense), income tax expense, and some other special items.
- Both systems require separate disclosure of items when their size, nature, or frequency are important for proper interpretation.
- IFRS permits expenses to be presented by their function or their nature. U.S. GAAP provides no direction but the SEC requires presentation by function.
- Neither U.S. GAAP nor IFRS define *operating* income; this means classification of expenses into operating or nonoperating reflects considerable management discretion.
- IFRS permits alternative measures of income on the income statement; U.S. GAAP prohibits disclosure of alternative income measures in financial statements.

Nokia provides the following example of income statement reporting.

NOKIA
Income Statement (in Euros million)
For Year Ended December 31, 2009

Net sales	40,984
Cost of sales	27,720
Gross profit	13,264
Research and development expenses	5,909
Selling and marketing expenses	3,933
Administrative and general expenses	1,145
Other income and expenses	1,080
Operating profit	1,197
Financial income and expenses (and other)	235
Profit before tax	962
Tax	702
Profit	260

Balance Sheet Presentation Chapters 2 and 3 explained how both U.S. GAAP and IFRS require current items to be separated from noncurrent items on the balance sheet (yielding a *classified balance sheet*). As discussed, U.S. GAAP balance sheets report current items first. Assets are listed from most liquid to least liquid, whereas liabilities are listed from nearest to maturity to furthest from maturity. IFRS balance sheets normally present noncurrent items first (and equity before liabilities), but this is *not* a requirement. **Nokia** provides an example of IFRS reporting for the balance sheet in Appendix A.

Decision Analysis

Acid-Test and Gross Margin Ratios

Acid-Test Ratio

A1 Compute the acid-test ratio and explain its use to assess liquidity.

For many merchandisers, inventory makes up a large portion of current assets. Inventory must be sold and any resulting accounts receivable must be collected before cash is available. Chapter 3 explained that the current ratio, defined as current assets divided by current liabilities, is useful in assessing a company's ability to pay current liabilities. Because it is sometimes unreasonable to assume that inventories are a source of payment for current liabilities, we look to other measures.

One measure of a merchandiser's ability to pay its current liabilities (referred to as its *liquidity*) is the acid-test ratio. It differs from the current ratio by excluding less liquid current assets such as inventory and prepaid expenses that take longer to be converted to cash. The **acid-test ratio,** also called *quick ratio,* is defined as *quick assets* (cash, short-term investments, and current receivables) divided by current liabilities—see Exhibit 4.16.

EXHIBIT 4.16
Acid-Test (Quick) Ratio

$$\text{Acid-test ratio} = \frac{\text{Cash and cash equivalents} + \text{Short-term investments} + \text{Current receivables}}{\text{Current liabilities}}$$

Exhibit 4.17 shows both the acid-test and current ratios of retailer **JCPenney** for fiscal years 2007 through 2010—also see margin graph. JCPenney's acid-test ratio reveals a general increase from 2007 through 2010 that exceeds the industry average. Further, JCPenney's current ratio (never less than 1.90) suggests that its short-term obligations can be confidently covered with short-term assets.

EXHIBIT 4.17
JCPenney's Acid-Test and Current Ratios

($ millions)	2010	2009	2008	2007
Total quick assets	$3,406	$2,704	$2,845	$2,901
Total current assets	$6,652	$6,220	$6,751	$6,648
Total current liabilities	$3,249	$2,794	$3,338	$3,492
Acid-test ratio	**1.05**	**0.97**	**0.85**	**0.83**
Current ratio	**2.05**	**2.23**	**2.02**	**1.90**
Industry acid-test ratio	0.59	0.63	0.62	0.58
Industry current ratio	2.15	2.31	2.39	2.43

An acid-test ratio less than 1.0 means that current liabilities exceed quick assets. A rule of thumb is that the acid-test ratio should have a value near, or higher than, 1.0 to conclude that a company is unlikely to face near-term liquidity problems. A value much less than 1.0 raises liquidity concerns unless a company can generate enough cash from inventory sales or if much of its liabilities are not due until late in the next period. Similarly, a value slightly larger than 1.0 can hide a liquidity problem if payables are due shortly and receivables are not collected until late in the next period. Analysis of JCPenney shows no need for concern regarding its liquidity even though its acid-test ratio is less than one. This is because retailers such as JCPenney pay many current liabilities from inventory sales. Further, in all years, JCPenney's acid-test ratios exceed the industry norm (and its inventory is fairly liquid).

Point: Successful use of a just-in-time inventory system can narrow the gap between the acid-test ratio and the current ratio.

Decision Maker
Answer — p. 185

Supplier A retailer requests to purchase supplies on credit from your company. You have no prior experience with this retailer. The retailer's current ratio is 2.1, its acid-test ratio is 0.5, and inventory makes up most of its current assets. Do you extend credit? ■

Gross Margin Ratio

A2 Compute the gross margin ratio and explain its use to assess profitability.

The cost of goods sold makes up much of a merchandiser's expenses. Without sufficient gross profit, a merchandiser will likely fail. Users often compute the gross margin ratio to help understand this relationship. It differs from the profit margin ratio in that it excludes all costs except cost of goods sold. The **gross margin ratio** (also called *gross profit ratio*) is defined as *gross margin* (net sales minus cost of goods sold) divided by net sales—see Exhibit 4.18.

EXHIBIT 4.18
Gross Margin Ratio

$$\text{Gross margin ratio} = \frac{\text{Net sales} - \text{Cost of goods sold}}{\text{Net sales}}$$

Exhibit 4.19 shows the gross margin ratio of **JCPenney** for fiscal years 2007 through 2010. For JCPenney, each $1 of sales in 2010 yielded about 39.4¢ in gross margin to cover all other expenses and still produce a net income. This 39.4¢ margin is up from 39.3¢ in 2007. This slight increase is a favorable development. Success for merchandisers such as JCPenney depends on adequate gross margin. For example, the 0.1¢ increase in the gross margin ratio, computed as 39.4¢ − 39.3¢, means that JCPenney has $17.6 million more in gross margin! (This is computed as net sales of $17,556 million multiplied by the 0.1% increase in gross margin.) Management's discussion in its annual report attributes this improvement to its "strategy to sell a greater portion of merchandise at regular promotional prices and less at clearance prices."

Point: The power of a ratio is often its ability to identify areas for more detailed analysis.

EXHIBIT 4.19
JCPenney's Gross Margin Ratio

($ millions)	2010	2009	2008	2007
Gross margin	$ 6,910	$ 6,915	$ 7,671	$ 7,825
Net sales	$17,556	$18,486	$19,860	$19,903
Gross margin ratio	39.4%	37.4%	38.6%	39.3%

Decision Maker
Answer — p. 184

Financial Officer Your company has a 36% gross margin ratio and a 17% net profit margin ratio. Industry averages are 44% for gross margin and 16% for net profit margin. Do these comparative results concern you? ■

DEMONSTRATION PROBLEM 1

Use the following adjusted trial balance and additional information to complete the requirements.

KC ANTIQUES
Adjusted Trial Balance
December 31, 2011

	Debit	Credit
Cash	$ 7,000	
Accounts receivable	13,000	
Merchandise inventory	60,000	
Store supplies	1,500	
Equipment	45,600	
Accumulated depreciation—Equipment		$ 16,600
Accounts payable		9,000
Salaries payable		2,000
Common stock		20,000
Retained earnings		59,000
Dividends	10,000	
Sales		343,250
Sales discounts	5,000	
Sales returns and allowances	6,000	
Cost of goods sold	159,900	
Depreciation expense—Store equipment	4,100	
Depreciation expense—Office equipment	1,600	
Sales salaries expense	30,000	
Office salaries expense	34,000	
Insurance expense	11,000	
Rent expense (70% is store, 30% is office)	24,000	
Store supplies expense	5,750	
Advertising expense	31,400	
Totals	$449,850	$449,850

KC Antiques' *supplementary records* for 2011 reveal the following itemized costs for merchandising activities:

Invoice cost of merchandise purchases	$150,000
Purchase discounts received	2,500
Purchase returns and allowances	2,700
Cost of transportation-in	5,000

Required

1. Use the supplementary records to compute the total cost of merchandise purchases for 2011.
2. Prepare a 2011 multiple-step income statement. (Inventory at December 31, 2010, is $70,100.)
3. Prepare a single-step income statement for 2011.
4. Prepare closing entries for KC Antiques at December 31, 2011.
5. Compute the acid-test ratio and the gross margin ratio. Explain the meaning of each ratio and interpret them for KC Antiques.

PLANNING THE SOLUTION

- Compute the total cost of merchandise purchases for 2011.
- To prepare the multiple-step statement, first compute net sales. Then, to compute cost of goods sold, add the net cost of merchandise purchases for the year to beginning inventory and subtract the cost of ending inventory. Subtract cost of goods sold from net sales to get gross profit. Then classify expenses as selling expenses or general and administrative expenses.
- To prepare the single-step income statement, begin with net sales. Then list and subtract the expenses.
- The first closing entry debits all temporary accounts with credit balances and opens the Income Summary account. The second closing entry credits all temporary accounts with debit balances. The third entry closes the Income Summary account to the retained earnings account, and the fourth entry closes the dividends account to the retained earnings account.
- Identify the quick assets on the adjusted trial balance. Compute the acid-test ratio by dividing quick assets by current liabilities. Compute the gross margin ratio by dividing gross profit by net sales.

SOLUTION TO DEMONSTRATION PROBLEM 1

1.

Invoice cost of merchandise purchases	$150,000
Less: Purchases discounts received	2,500
Purchase returns and allowances	2,700
Add: Cost of transportation-in	5,000
Total cost of merchandise purchases	$149,800

2. Multiple-step income statement

KC ANTIQUES
Income Statement
For Year Ended December 31, 2011

Sales		$343,250
Less: Sales discounts	$ 5,000	
Sales returns and allowances	6,000	11,000
Net sales		332,250
Cost of goods sold*		159,900
Gross profit		172,350
Expenses		
Selling expenses		
Depreciation expense—Store equipment	4,100	
Sales salaries expense	30,000	
Rent expense—Selling space	16,800	
Store supplies expense	5,750	
Advertising expense	31,400	
Total selling expenses	88,050	

[continued on next page]

[continued from previous page]

General and administrative expenses		
Depreciation expense—Office equipment	1,600	
Office salaries expense	34,000	
Insurance expense	11,000	
Rent expense—Office space	7,200	
Total general and administrative expenses	53,800	
Total operating expenses		141,850
Net income		$ 30,500

* Cost of goods sold can also be directly computed (applying concepts from Exhibit 4.4):

Merchandise inventory, December 31, 2010	$ 70,100
Total cost of merchandise purchases (from part 1)	149,800
Goods available for sale	219,900
Merchandise inventory, December 31, 2011	60,000
Cost of goods sold	$159,900

3. Single-step income statement

KC ANTIQUES
Income Statement
For Year Ended December 31, 2011

Net sales		$332,250
Expenses		
Cost of goods sold	$159,900	
Selling expenses	88,050	
General and administrative expenses	53,800	
Total expenses		301,750
Net income		$ 30,500

4.

Dec. 31	Sales	343,250	
	Income Summary		343,250
	To close credit balances in temporary accounts.		
Dec. 31	Income Summary	312,750	
	Sales Discounts		5,000
	Sales Returns and Allowances		6,000
	Cost of Goods Sold		159,900
	Depreciation Expense—Store Equipment		4,100
	Depreciation Expense—Office Equipment		1,600
	Sales Salaries Expense		30,000
	Office Salaries Expense		34,000
	Insurance Expense		11,000
	Rent Expense		24,000
	Store Supplies Expense		5,750
	Advertising Expense		31,400
	To close debit balances in temporary accounts.		
Dec. 31	Income Summary	30,500	
	Retained Earnings		30,500
	To close the Income Summary account.		
Dec. 31	Retained Earnings	10,000	
	Dividends		10,000
	To close the Dividends account.		

5. Acid-test ratio = (Cash and equivalents + Short-term investments + Current receivables)/ Current liabilities

= (Cash + Accounts receivable/(Accounts payable + Salaries payable)
= ($7,000 + $13,000)/($9,000 + $2,000) = $20,000/$11,000 = <u>1.82</u>

Gross margin ratio = Gross profit/Net sales = $172,350/$332,250 = <u>0.52</u> (or 52%)

KC Antiques has a healthy acid-test ratio of 1.82. This means it has more than $1.80 in liquid assets to satisfy each $1.00 in current liabilities. The gross margin of 0.52 shows that KC Antiques spends 48¢ ($1.00 − $0.52) of every dollar of net sales on the costs of acquiring the merchandise it sells. This leaves 52¢ of every dollar of net sales to cover other expenses incurred in the business and to provide a net profit.

DEMONSTRATION PROBLEM 2

Prepare journal entries to record the following merchandising transactions for both the seller (BMX) and buyer (Sanuk).

May 4   BMX sold $1,500 of merchandise on account to Sanuk, terms FOB shipping point, n/45, invoice dated May 4. The cost of the merchandise was $900.
May 6   Sanuk paid transportation charges of $30 on the May 4 purchase from BMX.
May 8   BMX sold $1,000 of merchandise on account to Sanuk, terms FOB destination, n/30, invoice dated May 8. The cost of the merchandise was $700.
May 10 BMX paid transportation costs of $50 for delivery of merchandise sold to Sanuk on May 8.
May 16 BMX issued Sanuk a $200 credit memorandum for merchandise returned. The merchandise was purchased by Sanuk on account on May 8. The cost of the merchandise returned was $140.
May 18 BMX received payment from Sanuk for purchase of May 8.
May 21 BMX sold $2,400 of merchandise on account to Sanuk, terms FOB shipping point, 2/10, n/EOM. BMX prepaid transportation costs of $100, which were added to the invoice. The cost of the merchandise was $1,440.
May 31 BMX received payment from Sanuk for purchase of May 21, less discount (2% × $2,400).

SOLUTION TO DEMONSTRATION PROBLEM 2

BMX (Seller)

Date	Account	Debit	Credit
May 4	Accounts Receivable—Sanuk	1,500	
	Sales		1,500
	Cost of Goods Sold	900	
	Merchandise Inventory		900
6	No entry.		
8	Accounts Receivable—Sanuk	1,000	
	Sales		1,000
	Cost of Goods Sold	700	
	Merchandise Inventory		700
10	Delivery Expense	50	
	Cash		50
16	Sales Returns & Allowances	200	
	Accounts Receivable—Sanuk		200
	Merchandise Inventory	140	
	Cost of Goods Sold		140
18	Cash	800	
	Accounts Receivable—Sanuk		800
21	Accounts Receivable—Sanuk	2,400	
	Sales		2,400
	Accounts Receivable—Sanuk	100	
	Cash		100
	Cost of Goods Sold	1,440	
	Merchandise Inventory		1,440
31	Cash	2,452	
	Sales Discounts	48	
	Accounts Receivable—Sanuk		2,500

Sanuk (Buyer)

Date	Account	Debit	Credit
May 4	Merchandise Inventory	1,500	
	Accounts Payable—BMX		1,500
6	Merchandise Inventory	30	
	Cash		30
8	Merchandise Inventory	1,000	
	Accounts Payable—BMX		1,000
10	No entry.		
16	Accounts Payable—BMX	200	
	Merchandise Inventory		200
18	Accounts Payable—BMX	800	
	Cash		800
21	Merchandise Inventory	2,500	
	Accounts Payable—BMX		2,500
31	Accounts Payable—BMX	2,500	
	Merchandise Inventory		48
	Cash		2,452

Chapter 4 Reporting and Analyzing Merchandising Operations

APPENDIX

Periodic Inventory System

4A

A periodic inventory system requires updating the inventory account only at the *end of a period* to reflect the quantity and cost of both the goods available and the goods sold. Thus, during the period, the Merchandise Inventory balance remains unchanged. It reflects the beginning inventory balance until it is updated at the end of the period. During the period the cost of merchandise is recorded in a temporary *Purchases* account. When a company sells merchandise, it records revenue **but not the cost of the goods sold.** At the end of the period when a company prepares financial statements, it takes a *physical count of inventory* by counting the quantities and costs of merchandise available. The cost of goods sold is then computed by subtracting the ending inventory amount from the cost of merchandise available for sale.

Recording Merchandise Transactions Under a periodic system, purchases, purchase returns and allowances, purchase discounts, and transportation-in transactions are recorded in separate temporary accounts. At period-end, each of these temporary accounts is closed and the Merchandise Inventory account is updated. To illustrate, journal entries under the periodic inventory system are shown for the most common transactions (codes *a* through *f* link these transactions to those in the chapter, and we drop explanations for simplicity). For comparison, perpetual system journal entries are shown to the right of each periodic entry, where differences are in green font.

> **P5** Record and compare merchandising transactions using both periodic and perpetual inventory systems.

Purchases The periodic system uses a temporary *Purchases* account that accumulates the cost of all purchase transactions during each period. Z-Mart's November 2 entry to record the purchase of merchandise for $1,200 on credit with terms of 2/10, n/30 is

(a)

Periodic			Perpetual		
Purchases	1,200		Merchandise Inventory	1,200	
Accounts Payable		1,200	Accounts Payable		1,200

Purchase Discounts The periodic system uses a temporary *Purchase Discounts* account that accumulates discounts taken on purchase transactions during the period. If payment in (*a*) is delayed until after the discount period expires, the entry is to debit Accounts Payable and credit Cash for $1,200 each. However, if Z-Mart pays the supplier for the previous purchase in (*a*) within the discount period, the required payment is $1,176 ($1,200 × 98%) and is recorded as

(b)

Periodic			Perpetual		
Accounts Payable	1,200		Accounts Payable	1,200	
Purchase Discounts		24	Merchandise Inventory		24
Cash		1,176	Cash		1,176

Purchase Returns and Allowances Z-Mart returned merchandise purchased on November 2 because of defects. In the periodic system, the temporary *Purchase Returns and Allowances* account accumulates the cost of all returns and allowances during a period. The recorded cost (including discounts) of the defective merchandise is $300, and Z-Mart records the November 15 return with this entry:

(c)

Periodic			Perpetual		
Accounts Payable	300		Accounts Payable	300	
Purchase Returns and Allowances		300	Merchandise Inventory		300

Transportation-In Z-Mart paid a $75 freight charge to transport merchandise to its store. In the periodic system, this cost is charged to a temporary *Transportation-In* account.

(d)

Periodic			Perpetual		
Transportation-In	75		Merchandise Inventory	75	
Cash		75	Cash		75

Sales Under the periodic system, the cost of goods sold is *not* recorded at the time of each sale. (We later show how to compute total cost of goods sold at the end of a period.) Z-Mart's November 3 entry to record sales of $2,400 in merchandise on credit (when its cost is $1,600) is:

(e)

Periodic			Perpetual		
Accounts Receivable	2,400		Accounts Receivable	2,400	
Sales		2,400	Sales		2,400
			Cost of Goods Sold	1,600	
			Merchandise Inventory		1,600

Sales Returns A customer returned part of the merchandise from the transaction in (*e*), where the returned items sell for $800 and cost $600. (*Recall:* The periodic system records only the revenue effect, not the cost effect, for sales transactions.) Z-Mart restores the merchandise to inventory and records the November 6 return as

(f)

Periodic			Perpetual		
Sales Returns and Allowances	800		Sales Returns and Allowances	800	
Accounts Receivable ...		800	Accounts Receivable		800
			Merchandise Inventory	600	
			Cost of Goods Sold		600

Sales Discounts To illustrate sales discounts, assume that the remaining $1,600 of receivables (computed as $2,400 from *e* less $800 for *f*) has credit terms of 3/10, n/90 and that customers all pay within the discount period. Z-Mart records this payment as

Periodic			Perpetual		
Cash	1,552		Cash	1,552	
Sales Discounts ($1,600 × .03)	48		Sales Discounts ($1,600 × .03) ...	48	
Accounts Receivable ...		1,600	Accounts Receivable		1,600

Adjusting and Closing Entries The periodic and perpetual inventory systems have slight differences in adjusting and closing entries. The period-end Merchandise Inventory balance (unadjusted) is $19,000 under the periodic system and $21,250 under the perpetual system. Since the periodic system does not update the Merchandise Inventory balance during the period, the $19,000 amount is the beginning inventory. However, the $21,250 balance under the perpetual system is the recorded ending inventory before adjusting for any inventory shrinkage.

A physical count of inventory taken at the end of the period reveals $21,000 of merchandise available. The adjusting and closing entries for the two systems are shown in Exhibit 4A.1. The periodic system records the ending inventory of $21,000 in the Merchandise Inventory account (which includes

EXHIBIT 4A.1

Comparison of Adjusting and Closing Entries—Periodic and Perpetual

PERIODIC			PERPETUAL		
Adjusting Entry—Shrinkage			**Adjusting Entry—Shrinkage**		
None			Cost of Goods Sold	250	
			Merchandise Inventory		250

[continued on next page]

[continued from previous page]

PERIODIC		
Closing Entries		
(1) Sales	321,000	
Merchandise Inventory	21,000	
Purchase Discounts	4,200	
Purchase Returns and Allowances	1,500	
Income Summary		347,700
(2) Income Summary	334,800	
Sales Discounts		4,300
Sales Returns and Allowances		2,000
Merchandise Inventory		19,000
Purchases		235,800
Transportation-In		2,300
Depreciation Expense		3,700
Salaries Expense		43,800
Insurance Expense		600
Rent Expense		9,000
Supplies Expense		3,000
Advertising Expense		11,300
(3) Income Summary	12,900	
Retained Earnings		12,900
(4) Retained Earnings	4,000	
Dividends		4,000

PERPETUAL		
Closing Entries		
(1) Sales	321,000	
Income Summary		321,000
(2) Income Summary	308,100	
Sales Discounts		4,300
Sales Returns and Allowances		2,000
Cost of Goods Sold		230,400
Depreciation Expense		3,700
Salaries Expense		43,800
Insurance Expense		600
Rent Expense		9,000
Supplies Expense		3,000
Advertising Expense		11,300
(3) Income Summary	12,900	
Retained Earnings		12,900
(4) Retained Earnings	4,000	
Dividends		4,000

shrinkage) in the first closing entry and removes the $19,000 beginning inventory balance from the account in the second closing entry.[2]

By updating Merchandise Inventory and closing Purchases, Purchase Discounts, Purchase Returns and Allowances, and Transportation-In, the periodic system transfers the cost of goods sold amount to Income Summary. Review the periodic side of Exhibit 4A.1 and notice that the **boldface** items affect Income Summary as follows.

Credit to Income Summary in the first closing entry includes amounts from:	
Merchandise inventory (ending)	$ 21,000
Purchase discounts	4,200
Purchase returns and allowances	1,500
Debit to Income Summary in the second closing entry includes amounts from:	
Merchandise inventory (beginning)	(19,000)
Purchases	(235,800)
Transportation-in	(2,300)
Net effect on Income Summary	**$(230,400)**

This $230,400 effect on Income Summary is the cost of goods sold amount. The periodic system transfers cost of goods sold to the Income Summary account but without using a Cost of Goods Sold account. Also, the periodic system does not separately measure shrinkage. Instead, it computes cost of goods available

---

[2] This approach is called the *closing entry method*. An alternative approach, referred to as the *adjusting entry method*, would not make any entries to Merchandise Inventory in the closing entries of Exhibit 4A.1, but instead would make two adjusting entries. Using Z-Mart data, the two adjusting entries would be: (1) Dr. Income Summary and Cr. Merchandise Inventory for $19,000 each, and (2) Dr. Merchandise Inventory and Cr. Income Summary for $21,000 each. The first entry removes the beginning balance of Merchandise Inventory, and the second entry records the actual ending balance.

for sale, subtracts the cost of ending inventory, and defines the difference as cost of goods sold, which includes shrinkage.

Preparing Financial Statements The financial statements of a merchandiser using the periodic system are similar to those for a service company described in prior chapters. The income statement mainly differs by the inclusion of *cost of goods sold* and *gross profit*—of course, net sales is affected by discounts, returns, and allowances. The cost of goods sold section under the periodic system follows

Calculation of Cost of Goods Sold
For Year Ended December 31, 2011

Beginning inventory	$ 19,000
Cost of goods purchased	232,400
Cost of goods available for sale	251,400
Less ending inventory	21,000
Cost of goods sold	$230,400

The balance sheet mainly differs by the inclusion of *merchandise inventory* in current assets—see Exhibit 4.15. The statement of retained earnings is unchanged. A work sheet can be used to help prepare these statements. The only differences under the periodic system from the work sheet illustrated in Appendix 4B using the perpetual system are highlighted as follows in **blue boldface** font.

	No.	Account	Unadjusted Trial Balance Dr.	Cr.	Adjustments Dr.	Cr.	Adjusted Trial Balance Dr.	Cr.	Income Statement Dr.	Cr.	Balance Sheet Dr.	Cr.
3	101	Cash	8,200				8,200				8,200	
4	106	Accounts receivable	11,200				11,200				11,200	
5	119	**Merchandise Inventory**	19,000				19,000		19,000	21,000	21,000	
6	126	Supplies	3,800			(b) 3,000	800				800	
7	128	Prepaid insurance	900			(a) 600	300				300	
8	167	Equipment	34,200				34,200				34,200	
9	168	Accumulated depr.—Equip.		3,700		(c) 3,700		7,400				7,400
10	201	Accounts payable		16,000				16,000				16,000
11	209	Salaries payable				(d) 800		800				800
12	307	Common stock		10,000				10,000				10,000
13	318	Retained earnings		32,600				32,600				32,600
14	319	Dividends	4,000				4,000				4,000	
15	413	Sales		321,000				321,000		321,000		
16a	414	Sales returns and allowances	2,000				2,000		2,000			
16b	415	Sales discounts	4,300				4,300		4,300			
16c	505	**Purchases**	235,800				235,800		235,800			
16d	506	**Purchases returns & allowance**		1,500				1,500		1,500		
17	507	**Purchases discounts**		4,200				4,200		4,200		
18	508	**Transportation-in**	2,300				2,300		2,300			
19	612	Depreciation expense—Equip.			(c) 3,700		3,700		3,700			
20	622	Salaries expense	43,000		(d) 800		43,800		43,800			
21	637	Insurance expense			(a) 600		600		600			
22	640	Rent expense	9,000				9,000		9,000			
23	652	Supplies expense			(b) 3,000		3,000		3,000			
24	655	Advertising expense	11,300				11,300		11,300			
25		Totals	389,000	389,000	8,100	8,100	393,500	393,500	334,800	347,700	79,700	66,800
26		Net income							12,900			12,900
27		Totals							347,700	347,700	79,700	79,700

Quick Check

Answers — p. 185

13. What account is used (for journalizing entries) in a perpetual inventory system but not in a periodic system?
14. Which of the following accounts are temporary accounts under a periodic system? (*a*) Merchandise Inventory; (*b*) Purchases; (*c*) Transportation-In.
15. How is cost of goods sold computed under a periodic inventory system?
16. Do reported amounts of ending inventory and net income differ if the adjusting entry method of recording the change in inventory is used instead of the closing entry method?

APPENDIX 4B

Work Sheet—Perpetual System

Exhibit 4B.1 shows the work sheet for preparing financial statements of a merchandiser. It differs slightly from the work sheet layout in Chapter 3—the differences are in **red boldface**. Also, the adjustments in the work sheet reflect the following: (*a*) Expiration of $600 of prepaid insurance. (*b*) Use of $3,000 of supplies. (*c*) Depreciation of $3,700 for equipment. (*d*) Accrual of $800 of unpaid salaries. (*e*) Inventory shrinkage of $250. Once the adjusted amounts are extended into the financial statement columns, the information is used to develop financial statements.

EXHIBIT 4B.1

Work Sheet for Merchandiser (using a perpetual system)

No.	Account	Unadjusted Trial Balance Dr.	Cr.	Adjustments Dr.	Cr.	Adjusted Trial Balance Dr.	Cr.	Income Statement Dr.	Cr.	Balance Sheet Dr.	Cr.
101	Cash	8,200				8,200				8,200	
106	Accounts receivable	11,200				11,200				11,200	
119	**Merchandise Inventory**	21,250			(e) 250	21,000				21,000	
126	Supplies	3,800			(b) 3,000	800				800	
128	Prepaid insurance	900			(a) 600	300				300	
167	Equipment	34,200				34,200				34,200	
168	Accumulated depr.—Equip.		3,700		(c) 3,700		7,400				7,400
201	Accounts payable		16,000				16,000				16,000
209	Salaries payable				(d) 800		800				800
307	Common stock		10,000				10,000				10,000
318	Retained earnings		32,600				32,600				32,600
319	Dividends	4,000				4,000				4,000	
413	**Sales**		321,000				321,000		321,000		
414	**Sales returns and allowances**	2,000				2,000		2,000			
415	**Sales discounts**	4,300				4,300		4,300			
502	**Cost of goods sold**	230,150		(e) 250		230,400		230,400			
612	Depreciation expense—Equip.			(c) 3,700		3,700		3,700			
622	Salaries expense	43,000		(d) 800		43,800		43,800			
637	Insurance expense			(a) 600		600		600			
640	Rent expense	9,000				9,000		9,000			
652	Supplies expense			(b) 3,000		3,000		3,000			
655	Advertising expense	11,300				11,300		11,300			
	Totals	383,300	383,300	8,350	8,350	387,800	387,800	308,100	321,000	79,700	66,800
	Net income							12,900			12,900
	Totals							321,000	321,000	79,700	79,700

Summary

C1 **Describe merchandising activities and identify income components for a merchandising company.** Merchandisers buy products and resell them. Examples of merchandisers include Walmart, Home Depot, The Limited, and Barnes & Noble. A merchandiser's costs on the income statement include an amount for cost of goods sold. Gross profit, or gross margin, equals sales minus cost of goods sold.

C2 **Identify and explain the inventory asset and cost flows of a merchandising company.** The current asset section of a merchandising company's balance sheet includes *merchandise inventory,* which refers to the products a merchandiser sells and are available for sale at the balance sheet date. Cost of merchandise purchases flows into Merchandise Inventory and from there to Cost of Goods Sold on the income statement. Any remaining inventory is reported as a current asset on the balance sheet.

A1 **Compute the acid-test ratio and explain its use to assess liquidity.** The acid-test ratio is computed as quick assets (cash, short-term investments, and current receivables) divided by current liabilities. It indicates a company's ability to pay its current liabilities with its existing quick assets. An acid-test ratio equal to or greater than 1.0 is often adequate.

A2 **Compute the gross margin ratio and explain its use to assess profitability.** The gross margin ratio is computed as gross margin (net sales minus cost of goods sold) divided by net sales. It indicates a company's profitability before considering other expenses.

P1 **Analyze and record transactions for merchandise purchases using a perpetual system.** For a perpetual inventory system, purchases of inventory (net of trade discounts) are added to the Merchandise Inventory account. Purchase discounts and purchase returns and allowances are subtracted from Merchandise Inventory, and transportation-in costs are added to Merchandise Inventory.

P2 **Analyze and record transactions for merchandise sales using a perpetual system.** A merchandiser records sales at list price less any trade discounts. The cost of items sold is transferred from Merchandise Inventory to Cost of Goods Sold. Refunds or credits given to customers for unsatisfactory merchandise are recorded in Sales Returns and Allowances, a contra account to Sales. If merchandise is returned and restored to inventory, the cost of this merchandise is removed from Cost of Goods Sold and transferred back to Merchandise Inventory. When cash discounts from the sales price are offered and customers pay within the discount period, the seller records Sales Discounts, a contra account to Sales.

P3 **Prepare adjustments and close accounts for a merchandising company.** With a perpetual system, it is often necessary to make an adjustment for inventory shrinkage. This is computed by comparing a physical count of inventory with the Merchandise Inventory balance. Shrinkage is normally charged to Cost of Goods Sold. Temporary accounts closed to Income Summary for a merchandiser include Sales, Sales Discounts, Sales Returns and Allowances, and Cost of Goods Sold.

P4 **Define and prepare multiple-step and single-step income statements.** Multiple-step income statements include greater detail for sales and expenses than do single-step income statements. They also show details of net sales and report expenses in categories reflecting different activities.

P5[A] **Record and compare merchandising transactions using both periodic and perpetual inventory systems.** A perpetual inventory system continuously tracks the cost of goods available for sale and the cost of goods sold. A periodic system accumulates the cost of goods purchased during the period and does not compute the amount of inventory or the cost of goods sold until the end of a period. Transactions involving the sale and purchase of merchandise are recorded and analyzed under both the periodic and perpetual inventory systems. Adjusting and closing entries for both inventory systems are illustrated and explained.

Guidance Answers to Decision Maker and Decision Ethics

Entrepreneur For terms of 3/10, n/90, missing the 3% discount for an additional 80 days equals an implied annual interest rate of 13.69%, computed as (365 days ÷ 80 days) × 3%. Since you can borrow funds at 11% (assuming no other processing costs), it is better to borrow and pay within the discount period. You save 2.69% (13.69% − 11%) in interest costs by paying early.

Credit Manager Your decision is whether to comply with prior policy or to create a new policy and not abuse discounts offered by suppliers. Your first step should be to meet with your superior to find out if the late payment policy is the actual policy and, if so, its rationale. If it is the policy to pay late, you must apply your own sense of ethics. One point of view is that the late payment policy is unethical. A deliberate plan to make late payments means the company lies when it pretends to make payment within the discount period. Another view is that the late payment policy is acceptable. In some markets, attempts to take discounts through late payments are accepted as a continued phase of "price negotiation." Also, your company's suppliers can respond by billing your company for the discounts not accepted because of late payments. However, this is a dubious viewpoint, especially since the prior manager proposes that you dishonestly explain late payments as computer or mail problems and since some suppliers have complained.

Supplier A current ratio of 2.1 suggests sufficient current assets to cover current liabilities. An acid-test ratio of 0.5 suggests, however, that quick assets can cover only about one-half of current liabilities. This implies that the retailer depends on money from sales of inventory to pay current liabilities. If sales of inventory decline or profit margins decrease, the likelihood that this retailer will default on its payments increases. Your decision is probably not to extend credit. If you do extend credit, you are likely to closely monitor the retailer's financial condition. (It is better to hold unsold inventory than uncollectible receivables.)

Financial Officer Your company's net profit margin is about equal to the industry average and suggests typical industry performance. However, gross margin reveals that your company is paying far more in cost of goods sold or receiving far less in sales price than competitors. Your attention must be directed to finding the problem with cost of goods sold, sales, or both. One positive note is that your company's expenses make up 19% of sales (36% − 17%). This favorably compares with competitors' expenses that make up 28% of sales (44% − 16%).

Guidance Answers to Quick Checks

1. Cost of goods sold is the cost of merchandise purchased from a supplier that is sold to customers during a specific period.
2. Gross profit (or gross margin) is the difference between net sales and cost of goods sold.
3. Widespread use of computing and related technology has dramatically increased the use of the perpetual inventory system.
4. Under credit terms of 2/10, n/60, the credit period is 60 days and the discount period is 10 days.
5. (b) trade discount.
6. *FOB* means "free on board." It is used in identifying the point when ownership transfers from seller to buyer. *FOB destination* means that the seller transfers ownership of goods to the buyer when they arrive at the buyer's place of business. It also means that the seller is responsible for paying shipping charges and bears the risk of damage or loss during shipment.
7. Recording sales discounts and sales returns and allowances separately from sales gives useful information to managers for internal monitoring and decision making.
8. When a customer returns merchandise *and* the seller restores the merchandise to inventory, two entries are necessary. One entry records the decrease in revenue and credits the customer's account. The second entry debits inventory and reduces cost of goods sold.
9. Credit memorandum—seller credits accounts receivable from buyer.
10. Merchandise Inventory may need adjusting to reflect shrinkage.
11. Sales (of goods), Sales Discounts, Sales Returns and Allowances, and Cost of Goods Sold (and maybe Delivery Expense).
12. Four closing entries: (1) close credit balances in temporary accounts to Income Summary, (2) close debit balances in temporary accounts to Income Summary, (3) close Income Summary to retained earnings, and (4) close dividends account to retained earnings.
13. Cost of Goods Sold.
14. (b) Purchases and (c) Transportation-In.
15. Under a periodic inventory system, the cost of goods sold is determined at the end of an accounting period by adding the net cost of goods purchased to the beginning inventory and subtracting the ending inventory.
16. Both methods report the same ending inventory and income.

Key Terms

Acid-test ratio (p. 174)
Cash discount (p. 161)
Cost of goods sold (p. 158)
Credit memorandum (p. 167)
Credit period (p. 161)
Credit terms (p. 161)
Debit memorandum (p. 162)
Discount period (p. 161)
EOM (p. 161)
FOB (p. 163)
General and administrative expenses (p. 171)

Gross margin (p. 159)
Gross margin ratio (p. 174)
Gross profit (p. 158)
Inventory (p. 159)
List price (p. 160)
Merchandise (p. 158)
Merchandise inventory (p. 159)
Merchandiser (p. 158)
Multiple-step income statement (p. 171)
Periodic inventory system (p. 160)
Perpetual inventory system (p. 160)

Purchase discount (p. 161)
Retailer (p. 158)
Sales discount (p. 161)
Selling expenses (p. 171)
Shrinkage (p. 168)
Single-step income statement (p. 172)
Supplementary records (p. 164)
Trade discount (p. 160)
Wholesaler (p. 158)

Multiple Choice Quiz

Answers on p. 203   mhhe.com/wildFA6e

Additional quiz questions are available at the book's Website.

1. A company has $550,000 in net sales and $193,000 in gross profit. This means its cost of goods sold equals
   a. $743,000
   b. $550,000
   c. $357,000
   d. $193,000
   e. $(193,000)

2. A company purchased $4,500 of merchandise on May 1 with terms of 2/10, n/30. On May 6, it returned $250 of that merchandise. On May 8, it paid the balance owed for merchandise, taking any discount it is entitled to. The cash paid on May 8 is
   a. $4,500
   b. $4,250
   c. $4,160
   d. $4,165
   e. $4,410

3. A company has cash sales of $75,000, credit sales of $320,000, sales returns and allowances of $13,700, and sales discounts of $6,000. Its net sales equal
   a. $395,000
   b. $375,300
   c. $300,300
   d. $339,700
   e. $414,700

4. A company's quick assets are $37,500, its current assets are $80,000, and its current liabilities are $50,000. Its acid-test ratio equals
   a. 1.600
   b. 0.750
   c. 0.625
   d. 1.333
   e. 0.469

5. A company's net sales are $675,000, its costs of goods sold are $459,000, and its net income is $74,250. Its gross margin ratio equals
   a. 32%
   b. 68%
   c. 47%
   d. 11%
   e. 34%

A(B) *Superscript letter A (B) denotes assignments based on Appendix 4A (4B).*

I Icon denotes assignments that involve decision making.

Discussion Questions

1. In comparing the accounts of a merchandising company with those of a service company, what additional accounts would the merchandising company likely use, assuming it employs a perpetual inventory system?
2. What items appear in financial statements of merchandising companies but not in the statements of service companies?
3. **I** Explain how a business can earn a positive gross profit on its sales and still have a net loss.
4. **I** Why do companies offer a cash discount?
5. How does a company that uses a perpetual inventory system determine the amount of inventory shrinkage?
6. Distinguish between cash discounts and trade discounts. Is the amount of a trade discount on purchased merchandise recorded in the accounts?
7. What is the difference between a sales discount and a purchase discount?
8. **I** Why would a company's manager be concerned about the quantity of its purchase returns if its suppliers allow unlimited returns?
9. Does the sender (maker) of a debit memorandum record a debit or a credit in the recipient's account? What entry (debit or credit) does the recipient record?
10. What is the difference between the single-step and multiple-step income statement formats?
11. **I** Refer to the balance sheet and income statement for **Research In Motion** in Appendix A. What does the company title its inventory account? Does the company present a detailed calculation of its cost of sales? **RIM**
12. Refer to **Nokia**'s income statement in Appendix A. What title does it use for cost of goods sold? **NOKIA**
13. Refer to the income statement for **Apple** in Appendix A. What does Apple title its cost of goods sold account? **Apple**
14. Refer to the income statement of **Palm** in Appendix A. Does its income statement report a gross profit figure? If yes, what is the amount? **Palm**
15. **I** Buyers negotiate purchase contracts with suppliers. What type of shipping terms should a buyer attempt to negotiate to minimize freight-in costs?

QUICK STUDY

QS 4-1
Applying merchandising terms
C1

Enter the letter for each term in the blank space beside the definition that it most closely matches.
A. Cash discount
B. Credit period
C. Discount period
D. FOB destination
E. FOB shipping point
F. Gross profit
G. Merchandise inventory
H. Purchase discount
I. Sales discount
J. Trade discount

_____ 1. Ownership of goods is transferred when delivered to the buyer's place of business.
_____ 2. Time period in which a cash discount is available.
_____ 3. Difference between net sales and the cost of goods sold.
_____ 4. Reduction in a receivable or payable if it is paid within the discount period.
_____ 5. Purchaser's description of a cash discount received from a supplier of goods.
_____ 6. Ownership of goods is transferred when the seller delivers goods to the carrier.
_____ 7. Reduction below list or catalog price that is negotiated in setting the price of goods.
_____ 8. Seller's description of a cash discount granted to buyers in return for early payment.
_____ 9. Time period that can pass before a customer's payment is due.
_____ 10. Goods a company owns and expects to sell to its customers.

The cost of merchandise inventory includes which of the following:

a. Costs incurred to buy the goods.
b. Costs incurred to ship the goods to the store(s).
c. Costs incurred to make the goods ready for sale.
d. Both a and b.
e. a, b, and c.

QS 4-2
Identifying inventory costs
C2

Prepare journal entries to record each of the following purchases transactions of a merchandising company. Show supporting calculations and assume a perpetual inventory system.

Mar. 5   Purchased 500 units of product at a cost of $5 per unit. Terms of the sale are 2/10, n/60; the invoice is dated March 5.
Mar. 7   Returned 50 defective units from the March 5 purchase and received full credit.
Mar. 15 Paid the amount due from the March 5 purchase, less the return on March 7.

QS 4-3
Recording purchases—perpetual system
P1

Prepare journal entries to record each of the following sales transactions of a merchandising company. Show supporting calculations and assume a perpetual inventory system.

Apr. 1   Sold merchandise for $2,000, granting the customer terms of 2/10, EOM; invoice dated April 1. The cost of the merchandise is $1,400.
Apr. 4   The customer in the April 1 sale returned merchandise and received credit for $500. The merchandise, which had cost $350, is returned to inventory.
Apr. 11 Received payment for the amount due from the April 1 sale less the return on April 4.

QS 4-4
Recording sales—perpetual system
P2

Compute net sales, gross profit, and the gross margin ratio for each separate case *a* through *d*. Interpret the gross margin ratio for case *a*.

	a	b	c	d
Sales	$130,000	$512,000	$35,700	$245,700
Sales discounts	4,200	16,500	400	3,500
Sales returns and allowances	17,000	5,000	5,000	700
Cost of goods sold	76,600	326,700	21,300	125,900

QS 4-5
Computing and analyzing gross margin
A2

Nix'It Company's ledger on July 31, its fiscal year-end, includes the following selected accounts that have normal balances (Nix'It uses the perpetual inventory system).

Merchandise inventory	$ 34,800	Sales returns and allowances	$ 3,500
Retained earnings	115,300	Cost of goods sold	102,000
Dividends	7,000	Depreciation expense	7,300
Sales	157,200	Salaries expense	29,500
Sales discounts	1,700	Miscellaneous expenses	2,000

QS 4-6
Accounting for shrinkage—perpetual system
P3

A physical count of its July 31 year-end inventory discloses that the cost of the merchandise inventory still available is $32,900. Prepare the entry to record any inventory shrinkage.

QS 4-7
Closing entries P3

Refer to QS 4-6 and prepare journal entries to close the balances in temporary revenue and expense accounts. Remember to consider the entry for shrinkage that is made to solve QS 4-6.

QS 4-8
Computing and interpreting acid-test ratio
A1

Use the following information on current assets and current liabilities to compute and interpret the acid-test ratio. Explain what the acid-test ratio of a company measures.

Cash	$1,200	Prepaid expenses	$ 600
Accounts receivable	2,700	Accounts payable	4,750
Inventory	5,000	Other current liabilities	950

QS 4-9
Contrasting liquidity ratios A1

Identify similarities and differences between the acid-test ratio and the current ratio. Compare and describe how the two ratios reflect a company's ability to meet its current obligations.

QS 4-10
Multiple-step income statement
P4

The multiple-step income statement normally includes which of the following:
a. Detailed computations of net sales.
b. Detailed computations of expenses, including subtotals for various expense categories.
c. Operating expenses are usually classified into (1) selling expenses and (2) general and administrative expenses.
d. Both a and c.
e. a, b, and c.

QS 4-11[A]
Contrasting periodic and perpetual systems
P5

Identify whether each description best applies to a periodic or a perpetual inventory system.
a. Provides more timely information to managers.
b. Requires an adjusting entry to record inventory shrinkage.
c. Markedly increased in frequency and popularity in business within the past decade.
d. Records cost of goods sold each time a sales transaction occurs.
e. Updates the inventory account only at period-end.

QS 4-12[A]
Recording purchases—periodic system P5

Refer to QS 4-3 and prepare journal entries to record each of the merchandising transactions assuming that the periodic inventory system is used.

QS 4-13[A]
Recording purchases—periodic system P5

Refer to QS 4-4 and prepare journal entries to record each of the merchandising transactions assuming that the periodic inventory system is used.

QS 4-14
IFRS income statement presentation
P4

Income statement information for **adidas**, a German footwear, apparel, and accessories manufacturer, for the year ended December 31, 2009, follows. The company applies IFRS, as adopted by the European Union, and reports its results in millions of euros. Prepare its calendar year 2009 (1) multiple-step income statement and (2) single-step income statement.

Net income	€ 245
Financial income	19
Financial expenses	169
Operating profit	508
Cost of sales	5,669
Income taxes	113
Income before taxes	358
Gross profit	4,712
Royalty and commission income	86
Other operating income	100
Other operating expenses	4,390
Net sales	10,381

Answer each of the following questions related to international accounting standards.

a. Explain how the accounting for merchandise purchases and sales is different between accounting under IFRS versus U.S. GAAP.

b. Income statements prepared under IFRS usually report an item titled *finance costs*. What do finance costs refer to?

c. U.S. GAAP prohibits alternative measures of income reported on the income statement. Does IFRS permit such alternative measures on the income statement?

QS 4-15
International accounting standards
C1

EXERCISES

Prepare journal entries to record the following transactions for a retail store. Assume a perpetual inventory system.

Apr.	2	Purchased merchandise from Blue Company under the following terms: $3,600 price, invoice dated April 2, credit terms of 2/15, n/60, and FOB shipping point.
	3	Paid $200 for shipping charges on the April 2 purchase.
	4	Returned to Blue Company unacceptable merchandise that had an invoice price of $600.
	17	Sent a check to Blue Company for the April 2 purchase, net of the discount and the returned merchandise.
	18	Purchased merchandise from Fox Corp. under the following terms: $7,500 price, invoice dated April 18, credit terms of 2/10, n/30, and FOB destination.
	21	After negotiations, received from Fox a $2,100 allowance on the April 18 purchase.
	28	Sent check to Fox paying for the April 18 purchase, net of the discount and allowance.

Exercise 4-1
Recording entries for merchandise purchases
P1

Check April 28, Cr. Cash $5,292

Taos Company purchased merchandise for resale from Tuscon Company with an invoice price of $22,000 and credit terms of 3/10, n/60. The merchandise had cost Tuscon $15,000. Taos paid within the discount period. Assume that both buyer and seller use a perpetual inventory system.

1. Prepare entries that the buyer should record for (*a*) the purchase and (*b*) the cash payment.

2. Prepare entries that the seller should record for (*a*) the sale and (*b*) the cash collection.

3. Assume that the buyer borrowed enough cash to pay the balance on the last day of the discount period at an annual interest rate of 11% and paid it back on the last day of the credit period. Compute how much the buyer saved by following this strategy. (Assume a 365-day year and round dollar amounts to the nearest cent, including computation of interest per day.)

Exercise 4-2
Analyzing and recording merchandise transactions—both buyer and seller
P1 P2

Check (3) $338.50 savings (rounded)

The operating cycle of a merchandiser with credit sales includes the following five activities. Starting with merchandise acquisition, identify the chronological order of these five activities.

a. _____ purchases of merchandise.
b. _____ credit sales to customers.
c. _____ inventory made available for sale.
d. _____ cash collections from customers.
e. _____ accounts receivable accounted for.

Exercise 4-3
Operating cycle for merchandiser
C2

Spare Parts was organized on May 1, 2011, and made its first purchase of merchandise on May 3. The purchase was for 1,000 units at a price of $10 per unit. On May 5, Spare Parts sold 600 of the units for $14 per unit to DeSoto Co. Terms of the sale were 2/10, n/60. Prepare entries for Spare Parts to record the May 5 sale and each of the following separate transactions *a* through *c* using a perpetual inventory system.

a. On May 7, DeSoto returns 200 units because they did not fit the customer's needs. Spare Parts restores the units to its inventory.

b. On May 8, DeSoto discovers that 50 units are damaged but are still of some use and, therefore, keeps the units. Spare Parts sends DeSoto a credit memorandum for $300 to compensate for the damage.

c. On May 15, DeSoto discovers that 72 units are the wrong color. DeSoto keeps 43 of these units because Spare Parts sends a $92 credit memorandum to compensate. DeSoto returns the remaining 29 units to Spare Parts. Spare Parts restores the 29 returned units to its inventory.

Exercise 4-4
Recording sales returns and allowances
P2

Check (c) Dr. Merchandise Inventory $290

Refer to Exercise 4-4 and prepare the appropriate journal entries for DeSoto Co. to record the May 5 purchase and each of the three separate transactions *a* through *c*. DeSoto is a retailer that uses a perpetual inventory system and purchases these units for resale.

Exercise 4-5
Recording purchase returns and allowances
P1

Exercise 4-6
Analyzing and recording merchandise transactions—both buyer and seller
P1 P2

Check (1) May 20, Cr. Cash $27,936

On May 11, Smythe Co. accepts delivery of $30,000 of merchandise it purchases for resale from Hope Corporation. With the merchandise is an invoice dated May 11, with terms of 3/10, n/90, FOB shipping point. The goods cost Hope $20,000. When the goods are delivered, Smythe pays $335 to Express Shipping for delivery charges on the merchandise. On May 12, Smythe returns $1,200 of goods to Hope, who receives them one day later and restores them to inventory. The returned goods had cost Hope $800. On May 20, Smythe mails a check to Hope Corporation for the amount owed. Hope receives it the following day. (Both Smythe and Hope use a perpetual inventory system.)

1. Prepare journal entries that Smythe Co. records for these transactions.
2. Prepare journal entries that Hope Corporation records for these transactions.

Exercise 4-7
Sales returns and allowances
C1

Business decision makers desire information on sales returns and allowances. (1) Explain why a company's manager wants the accounting system to record customers' returns of unsatisfactory goods in the Sales Returns and Allowances account instead of the Sales account. (2) Explain whether this information would be useful for external decision makers.

Exercise 4-8
Recording effects of merchandising activities
P1 P2

The following supplementary records summarize Titus Company's merchandising activities for year 2011. Set up T-accounts for Merchandise Inventory and Cost of Goods Sold. Then record the summarized activities in those T-accounts and compute account balances.

Cost of merchandise sold to customers in sales transactions	$186,000
Merchandise inventory, December 31, 2010	27,000
Invoice cost of merchandise purchases	190,500
Shrinkage determined on December 31, 2011	700
Cost of transportation-in	1,900
Cost of merchandise returned by customers and restored to inventory	2,200
Purchase discounts received	1,600
Purchase returns and allowances	4,100

Check Year-End Merchandise Inventory Dec. 31, $29,200

Exercise 4-9
Computing revenues, expenses, and income
C1 C2

Using your accounting knowledge, fill in the blanks in the following separate income statements *a* through *e*. Identify any negative amount by putting it in parentheses.

	a	b	c	d	e
Sales	$60,000	$42,500	$36,000	$?	$23,600
Cost of goods sold					
Merchandise inventory (beginning)	6,000	17,050	7,500	7,000	2,560
Total cost of merchandise purchases	36,000	?	?	32,000	5,600
Merchandise inventory (ending)	?	(2,700)	(9,000)	(6,600)	?
Cost of goods sold	34,050	15,900	?	?	5,600
Gross profit	?	?	3,750	45,600	?
Expenses	9,000	10,650	12,150	2,600	6,000
Net income (loss)	$?	$15,950	$ (8,400)	$43,000	$?

Exercise 4-10
Preparing adjusting and closing entries for a merchandiser
P3

The following list includes selected permanent accounts and all of the temporary accounts from the December 31, 2011, unadjusted trial balance of Deacon Co., a business owned by Julie Deacon. Use these account balances along with the additional information to journalize (*a*) adjusting entries and (*b*) closing entries. Deacon Co. uses a perpetual inventory system.

	Debit	Credit
Merchandise inventory	$ 28,000	
Prepaid selling expenses	5,000	
Dividends	2,200	
Sales		$429,000
Sales returns and allowances	16,500	
Sales discounts	4,000	
Cost of goods sold	211,000	
Sales salaries expense	47,000	
Utilities expense	14,000	
Selling expenses	35,000	
Administrative expenses	95,000	

[continued on next page]

Additional Information

Accrued sales salaries amount to $1,600. Prepaid selling expenses of $2,000 have expired. A physical count of year-end merchandise inventory shows $27,450 of goods still available.

Check Entry to close Income Summary: Cr. Retained Earnings $2,350

A retail company recently completed a physical count of ending merchandise inventory to use in preparing adjusting entries. In determining the cost of the counted inventory, company employees failed to consider that $2,000 of incoming goods had been shipped by a supplier on December 31 under an FOB shipping point agreement. These goods had been recorded in Merchandise Inventory as a purchase, but they were not included in the physical count because they were in transit. Explain how this overlooked fact affects the company's financial statements and the following ratios: return on assets, debt ratio, current ratio, and acid-test ratio.

Exercise 4-11
Interpreting a physical count error as inventory shrinkage
A1

Refer to the information in Exercise 4-11 and explain how the error in the physical count affects the company's gross margin ratio and its profit margin ratio.

Exercise 4-12
Physical count error and profits
A2

Compute the current ratio and acid-test ratio for each of the following separate cases. (Round ratios to two decimals.) Which company case is in the best position to meet short-term obligations? Explain.

Exercise 4-13
Computing and analyzing acid-test and current ratios
A1

	Case A	Case B	Case C
Cash	$ 800	$ 510	$3,200
Short-term investments	0	0	1,100
Current receivables	0	790	800
Inventory	2,000	1,600	1,900
Prepaid expenses	1,200	600	300
Total current assets	$4,000	$3,500	$7,300
Current liabilities	$2,200	$1,100	$3,650

Journalize the following merchandising transactions for CSI Systems assuming it uses a perpetual inventory system.

1. On November 1, CSI Systems purchases merchandise for $1,400 on credit with terms of 2/5, n/30, FOB shipping point; invoice dated November 1.
2. On November 5, CSI Systems pays cash for the November 1 purchase.
3. On November 7, CSI Systems discovers and returns $100 of defective merchandise purchased on November 1 for a cash refund.
4. On November 10, CSI Systems pays $80 cash for transportation costs with the November 1 purchase.
5. On November 13, CSI Systems sells merchandise for $1,500 on credit. The cost of the merchandise is $750.
6. On November 16, the customer returns merchandise from the November 13 transaction. The returned items would sell for $200 and cost $100; the items were not damaged and were returned to inventory.

Exercise 4-14
Preparing journal entries—perpetual system
P1 P2

A company reports the following sales-related information: Sales (gross) of $100,000; Sales discounts of $2,000; Sales returns and allowances of $8,000; Sales salaries expense of $5,000. Prepare the net sales portion only of this company's multiple-step income statement.

Exercise 4-15
Multiple-step income statement
P4

Refer to Exercise 4-1 and prepare journal entries to record each of the merchandising transactions assuming that the periodic inventory system is used.

Exercise 4-16ᴬ
Recording purchases—periodic system P5

Refer to Exercise 4-2 and prepare journal entries to record each of the merchandising transactions assuming that the periodic inventory system is used by both the buyer and the seller. (Skip the part 3 requirement.)

Exercise 4-17ᴬ
Recording purchases and sales—periodic system P5

Exercise 4-18[A]
Buyer and seller transactions—periodic system P5

Refer to Exercise 4-6 and prepare journal entries to record each of the merchandising transactions assuming that the periodic inventory system is used by both the buyer and the seller.

Exercise 4-19[A]
Recording purchases—periodic system P5

Refer to Exercise 4-14 and prepare journal entries to record each of the merchandising transactions assuming that the periodic inventory system is used.

Exercise 4-20
Preparing an income statement following IFRS
P4

L'Oréal reports the following income statement accounts for the year ended December 31, 2009 (euros in millions). Prepare the income statement for this company for the year ended December 31, 2009, following usual IFRS practices.

Net profit	€ 1,794.9	Income tax expense	€ 676.1
Finance costs	76.0	Profit before tax expense	2,471.0
Net sales	17,472.6	Research and development expense	609.2
Gross profit	12,311.0	Selling, general and administrative expense	3,735.5
Other expense	30.6	Advertising and promotion expense	5,388.7
Cost of sales	5,161.6		

PROBLEM SET A

Problem 4-1A
Preparing journal entries for merchandising activities—perpetual system
P1 P2

Check Aug. 9, Dr. Delivery Expense, $120

Aug. 18, Cr. Cash $4,695

Aug. 29, Dr. Cash $2,970

Prepare journal entries to record the following merchandising transactions of Stone Company, which applies the perpetual inventory system. (*Hint:* It will help to identify each receivable and payable; for example, record the purchase on August 1 in Accounts Payable—Abilene.)

Aug. 1 Purchased merchandise from Abilene Company for $6,000 under credit terms of 1/10, n/30, FOB destination, invoice dated August 1.
 4 At Abilene's request, Stone paid $100 cash for freight charges on the August 1 purchase, reducing the amount owed to Abilene.
 5 Sold merchandise to Lux Corp. for $4,200 under credit terms of 2/10, n/60, FOB destination, invoice dated August 5. The merchandise had cost $3,000.
 8 Purchased merchandise from Welch Corporation for $5,300 under credit terms of 1/10, n/45, FOB shipping point, invoice dated August 8. The invoice showed that at Stone's request, Welch paid the $240 shipping charges and added that amount to the bill. (*Hint:* Discounts are not applied to freight and shipping charges.)
 9 Paid $120 cash for shipping charges related to the August 5 sale to Lux Corp.
 10 Lux returned merchandise from the August 5 sale that had cost Stone $500 and been sold for $700. The merchandise was restored to inventory.
 12 After negotiations with Welch Corporation concerning problems with the merchandise purchased on August 8, Stone received a credit memorandum from Welch granting a price reduction of $800.
 15 Received balance due from Lux Corp. for the August 5 sale less the return on August 10.
 18 Paid the amount due Welch Corporation for the August 8 purchase less the price reduction granted.
 19 Sold merchandise to Trax Co. for $3,600 under credit terms of 1/10, n/30, FOB shipping point, invoice dated August 19. The merchandise had cost $2,500.
 22 Trax requested a price reduction on the August 19 sale because the merchandise did not meet specifications. Stone sent Trax a $600 credit memorandum to resolve the issue.
 29 Received Trax's cash payment for the amount due from the August 19 sale.
 30 Paid Abilene Company the amount due from the August 1 purchase.

Problem 4-2A
Preparing journal entries for merchandising activities—perpetual system
P1 P2

Prepare journal entries to record the following merchandising transactions of Bask Company, which applies the perpetual inventory system. (*Hint:* It will help to identify each receivable and payable; for example, record the purchase on July 1 in Accounts Payable—Black.)

July 1 Purchased merchandise from Black Company for $6,000 under credit terms of 1/15, n/30, FOB shipping point, invoice dated July 1.
 2 Sold merchandise to Coke Co. for $800 under credit terms of 2/10, n/60, FOB shipping point, invoice dated July 2. The merchandise had cost $500.
 3 Paid $100 cash for freight charges on the purchase of July 1.

Chapter 4 Reporting and Analyzing Merchandising Operations

8 Sold merchandise that had cost $1,200 for $1,600 cash.
9 Purchased merchandise from Lane Co. for $2,300 under credit terms of 2/15, n/60, FOB destination, invoice dated July 9.
11 Received a $200 credit memorandum from Lane Co. for the return of part of the merchandise purchased on July 9.
12 Received the balance due from Coke Co. for the invoice dated July 2, net of the discount.
16 Paid the balance due to Black Company within the discount period.
19 Sold merchandise that cost $900 to AKP Co. for $1,250 under credit terms of 2/15, n/60, FOB shipping point, invoice dated July 19.
21 Issued a $150 credit memorandum to AKP Co. for an allowance on goods sold on July 19.
24 Paid Lane Co. the balance due after deducting the discount.
30 Received the balance due from AKP Co. for the invoice dated July 19, net of discount.
31 Sold merchandise that cost $3,200 to Coke Co. for $5,000 under credit terms of 2/10, n/60, FOB shipping point, invoice dated July 31.

Check July 12, Dr. Cash $784
July 16, Cr. Cash $5,940

July 24, Cr. Cash $2,058
July 30, Dr. Cash $1,078

The following unadjusted trial balance is prepared at fiscal year-end for Rex Company.

Problem 4-3A
Preparing adjusting entries and income statements; and computing gross margin, acid-test, and current ratios

A1 A2 P3 P4

mhhe.com/wildFA6e

REX COMPANY
Unadjusted Trial Balance
January 31, 2011

		Debit	Credit
2	Cash	$ 2,200	
3	Merchandise inventory	11,500	
4	Store supplies	4,800	
5	Prepaid insurance	2,300	
6	Store equipment	41,900	
7	Accumulated depreciation—Store equipment		$ 15,000
8	Accounts payable		9,000
9	Common stock		5,000
10	Retained earnings		27,000
11	Dividends	2,000	
12	Sales		104,000
13	Sales discounts	1,000	
14	Sales returns and allowances	2,000	
15	Cost of goods sold	37,400	
16	Depreciation expense—Store equipment	0	
17	Salaries expense	31,000	
18	Insurance expense	0	
19	Rent expense	14,000	
20	Store supplies expense	0	
21	Advertising expense	9,900	
22	Totals	$160,000	$160,000

Rent expense and salaries expense are equally divided between selling activities and the general and administrative activities. Rex Company uses a perpetual inventory system.

Required

1. Prepare adjusting journal entries to reflect each of the following:
   a. Store supplies still available at fiscal year-end amount to $1,650.
   b. Expired insurance, an administrative expense, for the fiscal year is $1,500.
   c. Depreciation expense on store equipment, a selling expense, is $1,400 for the fiscal year.
   d. To estimate shrinkage, a physical count of ending merchandise inventory is taken. It shows $11,100 of inventory is still available at fiscal year-end.

Check (2) Gross profit, $63,200; (3) Total expenses, $98,750; Net income, $2,250

2. Prepare a multiple-step income statement for fiscal year 2011.
3. Prepare a single-step income statement for fiscal year 2011.
4. Compute the current ratio, acid-test ratio, and gross margin ratio as of January 31, 2011.

Problem 4-4A
Computing merchandising amounts and formatting income statements
C2 P4

BizKid Company's adjusted trial balance on August 31, 2011, its fiscal year-end, follows.

	Debit	Credit
Merchandise inventory	$ 31,000	
Other (noninventory) assets	120,400	
Total liabilities		$ 35,000
Common stock		10,000
Retained earnings		91,650
Dividends	8,000	
Sales		212,000
Sales discounts	3,250	
Sales returns and allowances	14,000	
Cost of goods sold	82,600	
Sales salaries expense	29,000	
Rent expense—Selling space	10,000	
Store supplies expense	2,500	
Advertising expense	18,000	
Office salaries expense	26,500	
Rent expense—Office space	2,600	
Office supplies expense	800	
Totals	$348,650	$348,650

On August 31, 2010, merchandise inventory was $25,000. Supplementary records of merchandising activities for the year ended August 31, 2011, reveal the following itemized costs.

Invoice cost of merchandise purchases	$91,000
Purchase discounts received	1,900
Purchase returns and allowances	4,400
Costs of transportation-in	3,900

Required

1. Compute the company's net sales for the year.
2. Compute the company's total cost of merchandise purchased for the year.
3. Prepare a multiple-step income statement that includes separate categories for selling expenses and for general and administrative expenses.
4. Prepare a single-step income statement that includes these expense categories: cost of goods sold, selling expenses, and general and administrative expenses.

Check (2) $88,600;
(3) Gross profit, $112,150; Net income, $22,750;
(4) Total expenses, $172,000

Problem 4-5A
Preparing closing entries and interpreting information about discounts and returns
C2 P3

Use the data for BizKid Company in Problem 4-4A to complete the following requirements.

Required

1. Prepare closing entries as of August 31, 2011 (the perpetual inventory system is used).

Analysis Component

2. The company makes all purchases on credit, and its suppliers uniformly offer a 3% sales discount. Does it appear that the company's cash management system is accomplishing the goal of taking all available discounts? Explain.
3. In prior years, the company experienced a 5% returns and allowance rate on its sales, which means approximately 5% of its gross sales were eventually returned outright or caused the company to grant allowances to customers. How do this year's results compare to prior years' results?

Check (1) $22,750 Dr. to close Income Summary
(3) Current-year rate, 6.6%

Refer to the data and information in Problem 4-3A.

Required

Prepare and complete the entire 10-column work sheet for Rex Company. Follow the structure of Exhibit 4B.1 in Appendix 4B.

Problem 4-6A[B]
Preparing a work sheet for a merchandiser
P3

Prepare journal entries to record the following merchandising transactions of Wave Company, which applies the perpetual inventory system. (*Hint:* It will help to identify each receivable and payable; for example, record the purchase on July 3 in Accounts Payable—CAP.)

July 3 Purchased merchandise from CAP Corp. for $15,000 under credit terms of 1/10, n/30, FOB destination, invoice dated July 3.
4 At CAP's request, Wave paid $250 cash for freight charges on the July 3 purchase, reducing the amount owed to CAP.
7 Sold merchandise to Morris Co. for $10,500 under credit terms of 2/10, n/60, FOB destination, invoice dated July 7. The merchandise had cost $7,500.
10 Purchased merchandise from Murdock Corporation for $14,200 under credit terms of 1/10, n/45, FOB shipping point, invoice dated July 10. The invoice showed that at Wave's request, Murdock paid the $600 shipping charges and added that amount to the bill. (*Hint:* Discounts are not applied to freight and shipping charges.)
11 Paid $300 cash for shipping charges related to the July 7 sale to Morris Co.
12 Morris returned merchandise from the July 7 sale that had cost Wave $1,250 and been sold for $1,750. The merchandise was restored to inventory.
14 After negotiations with Murdock Corporation concerning problems with the merchandise purchased on July 10, Wave received a credit memorandum from Murdock granting a price reduction of $2,000.
17 Received balance due from Morris Co. for the July 7 sale less the return on July 12.
20 Paid the amount due Murdock Corporation for the July 10 purchase less the price reduction granted.
21 Sold merchandise to Ulsh for $9,000 under credit terms of 1/10, n/30, FOB shipping point, invoice dated July 21. The merchandise had cost $6,250.
24 Ulsh requested a price reduction on the July 21 sale because the merchandise did not meet specifications. Wave sent Ulsh a credit memorandum for $1,500 to resolve the issue.
30 Received Ulsh's cash payment for the amount due from the July 21 sale.
31 Paid CAP Corp. the amount due from the July 3 purchase.

PROBLEM SET B

Problem 4-1B
Preparing journal entries for merchandising activities—perpetual system
P1 P2

Check July 17, Dr. Cash $8,575
July 20, Cr. Cash $12,678

July 30, Dr. Cash $7,425

Prepare journal entries to record the following merchandising transactions of Yang Company, which applies the perpetual inventory system. (*Hint:* It will help to identify each receivable and payable; for example, record the purchase on May 2 in Accounts Payable—Bots.)

May 2 Purchased merchandise from Bots Co. for $9,000 under credit terms of 1/15, n/30, FOB shipping point, invoice dated May 2.
4 Sold merchandise to Chase Co. for $1,200 under credit terms of 2/10, n/60, FOB shipping point, invoice dated May 4. The merchandise had cost $750.
5 Paid $150 cash for freight charges on the purchase of May 2.
9 Sold merchandise that had cost $1,800 for $2,400 cash.
10 Purchased merchandise from Snyder Co. for $3,450 under credit terms of 2/15, n/60, FOB destination, invoice dated May 10.
12 Received a $300 credit memorandum from Snyder Co. for the return of part of the merchandise purchased on May 10.
14 Received the balance due from Chase Co. for the invoice dated May 4, net of the discount.
17 Paid the balance due to Bots Co. within the discount period.
20 Sold merchandise that cost $1,450 to Tex Co. for $2,800 under credit terms of 2/15, n/60, FOB shipping point, invoice dated May 20.
22 Issued a $400 credit memorandum to Tex Co. for an allowance on goods sold from May 20.
25 Paid Snyder Co. the balance due after deducting the discount.
30 Received the balance due from Tex Co. for the invoice dated May 20, net of discount and allowance.
31 Sold merchandise that cost $4,800 to Chase Co. for $7,500 under credit terms of 2/10, n/60, FOB shipping point, invoice dated May 31.

Problem 4-2B
Preparing journal entries for merchandising activities—perpetual system
P1 P2

Check May 14, Dr. Cash $1,176
May 17, Cr. Cash $8,910

May 30, Dr. Cash $2,352

Problem 4-3B
Preparing adjusting entries and income statements; and computing gross margin, acid-test, and current ratios

A1 A2 P3 P4

The following unadjusted trial balance is prepared at fiscal year-end for FAB Products Company.

FAB PRODUCTS COMPANY
Unadjusted Trial Balance
October 31, 2011

	Debit	Credit
Cash	$ 4,400	
Merchandise inventory	23,000	
Store supplies	9,600	
Prepaid insurance	4,600	
Store equipment	83,800	
Accumulated depreciation—Store equipment		$ 30,000
Accounts payable		16,000
Common stock		4,000
Retained earnings		60,000
Dividends	2,000	
Sales		208,000
Sales discounts	2,000	
Sales returns and allowances	4,000	
Cost of goods sold	74,800	
Depreciation expense—Store equipment	0	
Salaries expense	62,000	
Insurance expense	0	
Rent expense	28,000	
Store supplies expense	0	
Advertising expense	19,800	
Totals	$318,000	$318,000

Rent expense and salaries expense are equally divided between selling activities and the general and administrative activities. FAB Products Company uses a perpetual inventory system.

Required

1. Prepare adjusting journal entries to reflect each of the following.
   a. Store supplies still available at fiscal year-end amount to $3,300.
   b. Expired insurance, an administrative expense, for the fiscal year is $3,000.
   c. Depreciation expense on store equipment, a selling expense, is $2,800 for the fiscal year.
   d. To estimate shrinkage, a physical count of ending merchandise inventory is taken. It shows $22,200 of inventory is still available at fiscal year-end.
2. Prepare a multiple-step income statement for fiscal year 2011.
3. Prepare a single-step income statement for fiscal year 2011.
4. Compute the current ratio, acid-test ratio, and gross margin ratio as of October 31, 2011.

Check (2) Gross profit, $126,400; (3) Total expenses, $197,500; Net income, $4,500

Problem 4-4B
Computing merchandising amounts and formatting income statements

C1 C2 P4

Albin Company's adjusted trial balance on March 31, 2011, its fiscal year-end, follows.

	Debit	Credit
Merchandise inventory	$ 46,500	
Other (noninventory) assets	190,600	
Total liabilities		$ 52,500
Common stock		12,000
Retained earnings		140,475
Dividends	2,000	

[continued on next page]

[continued from previous page]

Sales		318,000
Sales discounts	4,875	
Sales returns and allowances	21,000	
Cost of goods sold	123,900	
Sales salaries expense	43,500	
Rent expense—Selling space	15,000	
Store supplies expense	3,750	
Advertising expense	27,000	
Office salaries expense	39,750	
Rent expense—Office space	3,900	
Office supplies expense	1,200	
Totals	$522,975	$522,975

On March 31, 2010, merchandise inventory was $37,500. Supplementary records of merchandising activities for the year ended March 31, 2011, reveal the following itemized costs.

Invoice cost of merchandise purchases	$136,500
Purchase discounts received	2,850
Purchase returns and allowances	6,600
Costs of transportation-in	5,850

Required

1. Calculate the company's net sales for the year.
2. Calculate the company's total cost of merchandise purchased for the year.
3. Prepare a multiple-step income statement that includes separate categories for selling expenses and for general and administrative expenses.
4. Prepare a single-step income statement that includes these expense categories: cost of goods sold, selling expenses, and general and administrative expenses.

Check (2) $132,900;
(3) Gross profit, $168,225; Net income, $34,125;
(4) Total expenses, $258,000

Use the data for Albin Company in Problem 4-4B to complete the following requirements.

Required

1. Prepare closing entries as of March 31, 2011 (the perpetual inventory system is used).

Analysis Component

2. The company makes all purchases on credit, and its suppliers uniformly offer a 3% sales discount. Does it appear that the company's cash management system is accomplishing the goal of taking all available discounts? Explain.
3. In prior years, the company experienced a 5% returns and allowance rate on its sales, which means approximately 5% of its gross sales were eventually returned outright or caused the company to grant allowances to customers. How do this year's results compare to prior years' results?

Problem 4-5B
Preparing closing entries and interpreting information about discounts and returns

C2 P3

Check (1) $34,125 Dr. to close Income Summary

(3) Current-year rate, 6.6%

Refer to the data and information in Problem 4-3B.

Required

Prepare and complete the entire 10-column work sheet for FAB Products Company. Follow the structure of Exhibit 4B.1 in Appendix 4B.

Problem 4-6B^B
Preparing a work sheet for a merchandiser

P3

SERIAL PROBLEM
Business Solutions
P1 P2 P3 P4

(This serial problem began in Chapter 1 and continues through most of the book. If previous chapter segments were not completed, the serial problem can begin at this point. It is helpful, but not necessary, to use the Working Papers that accompany the book.)

SP 4 Santana Rey created Business Solutions on October 1, 2011. The company has been successful, and its list of customers has grown. To accommodate the growth, the accounting system is modified to set up separate accounts for each customer. The following chart of accounts includes the account number used for each account and any balance as of December 31, 2011. Santana Rey decided to add a fourth digit with a decimal point to the 106 account number that had been used for the single Accounts Receivable account. This change allows the company to continue using the existing chart of accounts.

No.	Account Title	Dr.	Cr.
101	Cash	$48,372	
106.1	Alex's Engineering Co.	0	
106.2	Wildcat Services	0	
106.3	Easy Leasing	0	
106.4	IFM Co.	3,000	
106.5	Liu Corp.	0	
106.6	Gomez Co.	2,668	
106.7	Delta Co.	0	
106.8	KC, Inc.	0	
106.9	Dream, Inc.	0	
119	Merchandise inventory	0	
126	Computer supplies	580	
128	Prepaid insurance	1,665	
131	Prepaid rent	825	
163	Office equipment	8,000	
164	Accumulated depreciation—Office equipment		$ 400
167	Computer equipment	20,000	
168	Accumulated depreciation—Computer equipment		1,250
201	Accounts payable		1,100

No.	Account Title	Dr.	Cr.
210	Wages payable		$ 500
236	Unearned computer services revenue		1,500
307	Common stock		73,000
318	Retained earnings		7,360
319	Dividends	$0	
403	Computer services revenue		0
413	Sales		0
414	Sales returns and allowances	0	
415	Sales discounts	0	
502	Cost of goods sold	0	
612	Depreciation expense—Office equipment	0	
613	Depreciation expense—Computer equipment	0	
623	Wages expense	0	
637	Insurance expense	0	
640	Rent expense	0	
652	Computer supplies expense	0	
655	Advertising expense	0	
676	Mileage expense	0	
677	Miscellaneous expenses	0	
684	Repairs expense—Computer	0	

In response to requests from customers, S. Rey will begin selling computer software. The company will extend credit terms of 1/10, n/30, FOB shipping point, to all customers who purchase this merchandise. However, no cash discount is available on consulting fees. Additional accounts (Nos. 119, 413, 414, 415, and 502) are added to its general ledger to accommodate the company's new merchandising activities. Also, Business Solutions does not use reversing entries and, therefore, all revenue and expense accounts have zero beginning balances as of January 1, 2012. Its transactions for January through March follow:

Jan. 4 The company paid cash to Lyn Addie for five days' work at the rate of $125 per day. Four of the five days relate to wages payable that were accrued in the prior year.
    5 Santana Rey invested an additional $25,000 cash in the company in exchange for more common stock.
    7 The company purchased $5,800 of merchandise from Kansas Corp. with terms of 1/10, n/30, FOB shipping point, invoice dated January 7.
    9 The company received $2,668 cash from Gomez Co. as full payment on its account.

Chapter 4 Reporting and Analyzing Merchandising Operations   199

11 The company completed a five-day project for Alex's Engineering Co. and billed it $5,500, which is the total price of $7,000 less the advance payment of $1,500.

Check Jan. 11, Dr. Unearned Computer Services Revenue $1,500

13 The company sold merchandise with a retail value of $5,200 and a cost of $3,560 to Liu Corp., invoice dated January 13.
15 The company paid $600 cash for freight charges on the merchandise purchased on January 7.
16 The company received $4,000 cash from Delta Co. for computer services provided.
17 The company paid Kansas Corp. for the invoice dated January 7, net of the discount.
20 Liu Corp. returned $500 of defective merchandise from its invoice dated January 13. The returned merchandise, which had a $320 cost, is discarded. (The policy of Business Solutions is to leave the cost of defective products in cost of goods sold.)

Check Jan. 20, No entry to Cost of Goods Sold

22 The company received the balance due from Liu Corp., net of both the discount and the credit for the returned merchandise.
24 The company returned defective merchandise to Kansas Corp. and accepted a credit against future purchases. The defective merchandise invoice cost, net of the discount, was $496.
26 The company purchased $9,000 of merchandise from Kansas Corp. with terms of 1/10, n/30, FOB destination, invoice dated January 26.
26 The company sold merchandise with a $4,640 cost for $5,800 on credit to KC, Inc., invoice dated January 26.
31 The company paid cash to Lyn Addie for 10 days' work at $125 per day.

Feb. 1 The company paid $2,475 cash to Hillside Mall for another three months' rent in advance.
3 The company paid Kansas Corp. for the balance due, net of the cash discount, less the $496 amount in the credit memorandum.
5 The company paid $600 cash to the local newspaper for an advertising insert in today's paper.
11 The company received the balance due from Alex's Engineering Co. for fees billed on January 11.
15 The company paid $4,800 cash for dividends.
23 The company sold merchandise with a $2,660 cost for $3,220 on credit to Delta Co., invoice dated February 23.
26 The company paid cash to Lyn Addie for eight days' work at $125 per day.
27 The company reimbursed Santana Rey for business automobile mileage (600 miles at $0.32 per mile).

Mar. 8 The company purchased $2,730 of computer supplies from Harris Office Products on credit, invoice dated March 8.
9 The company received the balance due from Delta Co. for merchandise sold on February 23.
11 The company paid $960 cash for minor repairs to the company's computer.
16 The company received $5,260 cash from Dream, Inc., for computing services provided.
19 The company paid the full amount due to Harris Office Products, consisting of amounts created on December 15 (of $1,100) and March 8.
24 The company billed Easy Leasing for $9,047 of computing services provided.
25 The company sold merchandise with a $2,002 cost for $2,800 on credit to Wildcat Services, invoice dated March 25.
30 The company sold merchandise with a $1,048 cost for $2,220 on credit to IFM Company, invoice dated March 30.
31 The company reimbursed Santana Rey for business automobile mileage (400 miles at $0.32 per mile).

The following additional facts are available for preparing adjustments on March 31 prior to financial statement preparation:

a. The March 31 amount of computer supplies still available totals $2,005.
b. Three more months have expired since the company purchased its annual insurance policy at a $2,220 cost for 12 months of coverage.
c. Lyn Addie has not been paid for seven days of work at the rate of $125 per day.
d. Three months have passed since any prepaid rent has been transferred to expense. The monthly rent expense is $825.
e. Depreciation on the computer equipment for January 1 through March 31 is $1,250.
f. Depreciation on the office equipment for January 1 through March 31 is $400.
g. The March 31 amount of merchandise inventory still available totals $704.

Chapter 4 Reporting and Analyzing Merchandising Operations

Check (2) Ending balances at March 31: Cash, $68,057; Sales, $19,240;

(3) Unadj. totals, $151,557; Adj. totals, $154,082;

(4) Net income, $18,833;

(6) Total assets, $120,268

Required

1. Prepare journal entries to record each of the January through March transactions.
2. Post the journal entries in part 1 to the accounts in the company's general ledger. (*Note:* Begin with the ledger's post-closing adjusted balances as of December 31, 2011.)
3. Prepare a partial work sheet consisting of the first six columns (similar to the one shown in Exhibit 4B.1) that includes the unadjusted trial balance, the March 31 adjustments (*a*) through (*g*), and the adjusted trial balance. Do not prepare closing entries and do not journalize the adjustments or post them to the ledger.
4. Prepare an income statement (from the adjusted trial balance in part 3) for the three months ended March 31, 2012. Use a single-step format. List all expenses without differentiating between selling expenses and general and administrative expenses.
5. Prepare a statement of retained earnings (from the adjusted trial balance in part 3) for the three months ended March 31, 2012.
6. Prepare a classified balance sheet (from the adjusted trial balance) as of March 31, 2012.

Beyond the Numbers

REPORTING IN ACTION
A1
RIM

BTN 4-1 Refer to **Research In Motion**'s financial statements in Appendix A to answer the following.

Required

1. Assume that the amounts reported for inventories and cost of sales reflect items purchased in a form ready for resale. Compute the net cost of goods purchased for the fiscal year ended February 27, 2010.
2. Compute the current ratio and acid-test ratio as of February 27, 2010, and February 28, 2009. Interpret and comment on the ratio results. How does Research In Motion compare to the industry average of 2.4 for the current ratio and 1.5 for the acid-test ratio?

Fast Forward

3. Access Research In Motion's financial statements (form 10-K) for fiscal years ending after February 27, 2010, from its Website (**RIM.com**) or the SEC's EDGAR database (**www.sec.gov**). Recompute and interpret the current ratio and acid-test ratio for these current fiscal years.

COMPARATIVE ANALYSIS
A2
RIM
Apple

BTN 4-2 Key comparative figures for both **Research In Motion** and **Apple** follow.

($ millions)	Research In Motion Current Year	Research In Motion Prior Year	Apple Current Year	Apple Prior Year
Revenues (net sales)	$14,953	$11,065	$42,905	$37,491
Cost of sales	8,369	5,968	25,683	24,294

Required

1. Compute the dollar amount of gross margin and the gross margin ratio for the two years shown for each of these companies.
2. Which company earns more in gross margin for each dollar of net sales? How do they compare to the industry average of 40.0%?
3. Did the gross margin ratio improve or decline for these companies?

ETHICS CHALLENGE
C1 P2

BTN 4-3 Ashton Martin is a student who plans to attend approximately four professional events a year at her college. Each event necessitates a financial outlay of $100 to $200 for a new suit and accessories. After incurring a major hit to her savings for the first event, Ashton developed a different approach. She buys the suit on credit the week before the event, wears it to the event, and returns it the next week to the store for a full refund on her charge card.

Required
1. Comment on the ethics exhibited by Ashton and possible consequences of her actions.
2. How does the merchandising company account for the suits that Ashton returns?

COMMUNICATING IN PRACTICE
C2 P3 P5

BTN 4-4 You are the financial officer for Music Plus, a retailer that sells goods for home entertainment needs. The business owner, Jamie Madsen, recently reviewed the annual financial statements you prepared and sent you an e-mail stating that he thinks you overstated net income. He explains that although he has invested a great deal in security, he is sure shoplifting and other forms of inventory shrinkage have occurred, but he does not see any deduction for shrinkage on the income statement. The store uses a perpetual inventory system.

Required
Prepare a brief memorandum that responds to the owner's concerns.

TAKING IT TO THE NET
A2 C1

BTN 4-5 Access the SEC's EDGAR database (www.sec.gov) and obtain the March 19, 2010, filing of its fiscal 2010 10-K report (for year ended January 30, 2010) for **J. Crew Group, Inc** (ticker: JCG).

Required
Prepare a table that reports the gross margin ratios for J. Crew using the revenues and cost of goods sold data from J. Crew's income statement for each of its most recent three years. Analyze and comment on the trend in its gross margin ratio.

TEAMWORK IN ACTION
C1 C2

BTN 4-6 Best Brands' general ledger and supplementary records at the end of its current period reveal the following.

Sales	$430,000	Merchandise inventory (beginning of period)	$ 49,000
Sales returns and allowances	18,000	Invoice cost of merchandise purchases	180,000
Sales discounts	6,600	Purchase discounts received	4,500
Cost of transportation-in	11,000	Purchase returns and allowances	5,500
Operating expenses	20,000	Merchandise inventory (end of period)	42,000

Required
1. *Each* member of the team is to assume responsibility for computing *one* of the following items. You are not to duplicate your teammates' work. Get any necessary amounts to compute your item from the appropriate teammate. Each member is to explain his or her computation to the team in preparation for reporting to the class.
   - a. Net sales
   - b. Total cost of merchandise purchases
   - c. Cost of goods sold
   - d. Gross profit
   - e. Net income
2. Check your net income with the instructor. If correct, proceed to step 3.
3. Assume that a physical inventory count finds that actual ending inventory is $38,000. Discuss how this affects previously computed amounts in step 1.

Point: In teams of four, assign the same student *a* and *e*. Rotate teams for reporting on a different computation and the analysis in step 3.

ENTREPRENEURIAL DECISION
C1 C2 P4

BTN 4-7 Refer to the opening feature about **Heritage Link Brands**. Assume that Selena and Khary Cuffe report current annual sales at approximately $10 million and disclose the following income statement.

Heritage Link Brands
Income Statement
For Year Ended January 31, 2010

Net sales	$10,000,000
Cost of sales	6,100,000
Expenses (other than cost of sales)	2,000,000
Net income	$ 1,900,000

Selena and Khary Cuffe sell to various individuals and retailers, ranging from small shops to large chains. Assume that they currently offer credit terms of 1/15, n/60, and ship FOB destination. To improve their cash flow, they are considering changing credit terms to 3/10, n/30. In addition, they propose to change shipping terms to FOB shipping point. They expect that the increase in discount rate will increase net sales by 9%, but the gross margin ratio (and ratio of cost of sales divided by net sales) is expected to remain unchanged. They also expect that delivery expenses will be zero under this proposal; thus, expenses other than cost of sales are expected to increase only 6%.

Required

1. Prepare a forecasted income statement for the year ended January 31, 2011, based on the proposal.
2. Based on the forecasted income statement alone (from your part 1 solution), do you recommend that Selena and Khary implement the new sales policies? Explain.
3. What else should Selena and Khary consider before deciding whether or not to implement the new policies? Explain.

HITTING THE ROAD
C1

Point: This activity complements the Ethics Challenge assignment.

BTN 4-8 Arrange an interview (in person or by phone) with the manager of a retail shop in a mall or in the downtown area of your community. Explain to the manager that you are a student studying merchandising activities and the accounting for sales returns and sales allowances. Ask the manager what the store policy is regarding returns. Also find out if sales allowances are ever negotiated with customers. Inquire whether management perceives that customers are abusing return policies and what actions management takes to counter potential abuses. Be prepared to discuss your findings in class.

GLOBAL DECISION
A2 P4

NOKIA
RIM
Apple

BTN 4-9 Nokia (www.Nokia.com), Research In Motion, and Apple are competitors in the global marketplace. Key comparative figures for each company follow.

	Net Sales	Cost of Sales
Nokia*	40,984	27,720
Research In Motion†	$14,953	$ 8,369
Apple†	$42,905	$25,683

* EUR millions for Nokia.
† $ millions for Research In Motion and Apple.

Required

1. Rank the three companies (highest to lowest) based on the gross margin ratio.
2. Which of the companies uses a multiple-step income statement format? (These companies' income statements are in Appendix A.)

ANSWERS TO MULTIPLE CHOICE QUIZ

1. c; Gross profit = $550,000 − $193,000 = $357,000
2. d; ($4,500 − $250) × (100% − 2%) = $4,165
3. b; Net sales = $75,000 + $320,000 − $13,700 − $6,000 = $375,300
4. b; Acid-test ratio = $37,500/$50,000 = 0.750
5. a; Gross margin ratio = ($675,000 − $459,000)/$675,000 = 32%

A Look Back

Chapter 4 focused on merchandising activities and how they are reported. We analyzed and recorded purchases and sales and explained accounting adjustments and closing for merchandisers.

A Look at This Chapter

This chapter emphasizes accounting for inventory. We describe methods for assigning costs to inventory and we explain the items and costs making up merchandise inventory. We also discuss methods of estimating and measuring inventory.

A Look Ahead

Chapter 6 focuses on internal controls and accounting for cash and cash equivalents. We explain good internal control procedures and their importance to accounting.

5 Reporting and Analyzing Inventories

Learning Objectives

CAP

CONCEPTUAL

- **C1** Identify the items making up merchandise inventory. (p. 206)
- **C2** Identify the costs of merchandise inventory. (p. 207)

ANALYTICAL

- **A1** Analyze the effects of inventory methods for both financial and tax reporting. (p. 214)
- **A2** Analyze the effects of inventory errors on current and future financial statements. (p. 216)
- **A3** Assess inventory management using both inventory turnover and days' sales in inventory. (p. 219)

LP5

PROCEDURAL

- **P1** Compute inventory in a perpetual system using the methods of specific identification, FIFO, LIFO, and weighted average. (p. 208)
- **P2** Compute the lower of cost or market amount of inventory. (p. 215)
- **P3** *Appendix 5A*—Compute inventory in a periodic system using the methods of specific identification, FIFO, LIFO, and weighted average. (p. 224)
- **P4** *Appendix 5B*—Apply both the retail inventory and gross profit methods to estimate inventory. (p. 229)

Decision Insight

The Gizmo!

"I wanted to re-create the SEAL team environment."
—RANDY HETRICK

SAN FRANCISCO—The Navy SEALs call it "the gizmo." This gizmo, created by former Navy SEAL Randy Hetrick, CEO of Fitness Anywhere, Inc. and the inventor of Suspension Training®, is a resistance exercise device officially named the TRX Suspension Trainer. It is the hallmark product of Randy's start-up exercise equipment business, **Fitness Anywhere Inc. (FitnessAnywhere.com).**

Randy explains that to keep himself in shape for clandestine missions, he stitched parachute webbing into straps that he could fasten to almost anything and then use as a pulley system where his own body weight served as resistance. After leaving the Navy, Randy headed to business school and devoted himself to producing and marketing his new invention.

However, the entrepreneurial road was rough. Randy struggled with inventory production and sales planning, and had to deal with discounts, returns, and allowances. A major challenge was maintaining appropriate inventories while controlling costs. Randy admits that mistakes are part of entrepreneurial endeavors, but that he just had to throw himself into it and learn.

And, learn he did. Applying inventory management, and old-fashion trial-and-error, Randy learned to fill orders, collect money, and maintain the right inventory. "I wanted to re-create the SEAL team environment," explains Randy. To help, he set up a perpetual inventory system to account for inventory sales and purchases in real time. Randy insists that it is really important to serve customers' needs, which demands sound inventory accounting.

But business success requires more than good products and perpetual inventory management, explains Randy. It requires commitment, patience, energy, faith, and maybe some luck. "I thought this was a commando tool, pure and simple," laughs Randy. "Man, was I wrong!"

While Randy continues to measure, monitor, and manage inventories and costs, his success and growth are pushing him into new products and opportunities. He explains that he now has a line of portable, resistance exercise devices. Still, Randy demands that his business stay true to "the small, flat, high-performance . . . kind of [SEALs] culture." His inventory procedures and office setting contribute to that lean and mean culture. "Working out [in the office] is not only sanctioned," says Randy, "it almost is required."

[Sources: *FitnessAnywhere Website,* January 2012; *Entrepreneur,* February 2010; *Triathlete Magazine,* December 2009; *Wall Street Journal,* September 2009]

Chapter Preview

Merchandisers' activities include the purchasing and reselling of merchandise. We explained accounting for merchandisers in Chapter 4, including that for purchases and sales. In this chapter, we extend the study and analysis of inventory by explaining the methods used to assign costs to merchandise inventory *and* to cost of goods sold. Retailers, wholesalers, and other merchandising companies that purchase products for resale use the principles and methods described here. Understanding inventory accounting helps in the analysis and interpretation of financial statements and helps people run their businesses.

Reporting and Analyzing Inventories

Inventory Basics	Inventory Costing under a Perpetual System	Inventory Valuation and Errors
• Determining inventory items • Determining inventory costs • Internal control of inventory • Taking a physical count	• Cost flow assumptions • Specific identification • First-in, first-out • Last-in, first-out • Weighted average • Financial statement effects	• Inventory valuation at lower of cost or market • Financial statement effects of inventory errors

INVENTORY BASICS

This section identifies the items and costs making up merchandise inventory. It also describes the importance of internal controls in taking a physical count of inventory.

Determining Inventory Items

C1 Identify the items making up merchandise inventory.

Merchandise inventory includes all goods that a company owns and holds for sale. This rule holds regardless of where the goods are located when inventory is counted. Certain inventory items require special attention, including goods in transit, goods on consignment, and goods that are damaged or obsolete.

Goods in Transit Does a purchaser's inventory include goods in transit from a supplier? The answer is that if ownership has passed to the purchaser, the goods are included in the purchaser's inventory. We determine this by reviewing the shipping terms: *FOB destination* or *FOB shipping point*. If the purchaser is responsible for paying freight, ownership passes when goods are loaded on the transport vehicle. If the seller is responsible for paying freight, ownership passes when goods arrive at their destination.

Goods on Consignment Goods on consignment are goods shipped by the owner, called the **consignor,** to another party, the **consignee.** A consignee sells goods for the owner. The consignor continues to own the consigned goods and reports them in its inventory. **Upper Deck**, for instance, pays sports celebrities such as Tony Romo of the Dallas Cowboys to sign memorabilia, which are offered to shopping networks on consignment. Upper Deck, the consignor, must report these items in its inventory until sold.

Goods Damaged or Obsolete Damaged and obsolete (and deteriorated) goods are not counted in inventory if they cannot be sold. If these goods can be sold at a reduced price, they are included in inventory at a conservative estimate of their **net realizable value.** Net realizable value is sales price minus the cost of making the sale. The period when damage or obsolescence (or deterioration) occurs is the period when the loss in value is reported.

> **Decision Insight**
>
> A wireless portable device with a two-way radio allows clerks to quickly record inventory by scanning bar codes and to instantly send and receive inventory data. It gives managers access to up-to-date information on inventory and its location.

Determining Inventory Costs

Merchandise inventory includes costs of expenditures necessary, directly or indirectly, to bring an item to a salable condition and location. This means that the cost of an inventory item includes its invoice cost minus any discount, and plus any incidental costs necessary to put it in a place and condition for sale. Incidental costs can include import duties, freight, storage, insurance, and costs incurred in an aging process (for example, aging wine or cheese).

Accounting principles prescribe that incidental costs be added to inventory. Also, the *matching (expense recognition) principle* states that inventory costs should be recorded against revenue in the period when inventory is sold. However, some companies use the *materiality constraint (cost-to-benefit constraint)* to avoid assigning some incidental costs of acquiring merchandise to inventory. Instead, they expense them when incurred. These companies argue either that those incidental costs are immaterial or that the effort in assigning them outweighs the benefit.

C2 Identify the costs of merchandise inventory.

Internal Controls and Taking a Physical Count

The Inventory account under a perpetual system is updated for each purchase and sale, but events can cause the Inventory account balance to differ from the actual inventory available. Such events include theft, loss, damage, and errors. Thus, nearly all companies take a *physical count of inventory* at least once each year—informally called *taking an inventory*. This often occurs at the end of a fiscal year or when inventory amounts are low. This physical count is used to adjust the Inventory account balance to the actual inventory available.

Point: The Inventory account is a controlling account for the inventory subsidiary ledger. This *subsidiary ledger* contains a separate record (units and costs) for each separate product, and it can be in electronic or paper form. Subsidiary records assist managers in planning and monitoring inventory.

> **Fraud**
>
> A company applies internal controls when taking a physical count of inventory that usually include the following:
>
> - *Prenumbered inventory tickets* are prepared and distributed to the *counters*—each ticket must be accounted for.
> - Counters of inventory are assigned and do not include those responsible for inventory.
> - Counters confirm the validity of inventory, including its existence, amount, and quality.
> - A second count is taken by a different counter.
> - A manager confirms that all inventories are ticketed once, and only once.

Quick Check
Answers — p. 231

1. What accounting principle most guides the allocation of cost of goods available for sale between ending inventory and cost of goods sold?
2. If **Skechers** sells goods to **Target** with terms FOB shipping point, which company reports these goods in its inventory while they are in transit?
3. An art gallery purchases a painting for $11,400 on terms FOB shipping point. Additional costs in obtaining and offering the artwork for sale include $130 for transportation-in, $150 for import duties, $100 for insurance during shipment, $180 for advertising, $400 for framing, and $800 for office salaries. For computing inventory, what cost is assigned to the painting?

INVENTORY COSTING UNDER A PERPETUAL SYSTEM

Accounting for inventory affects both the balance sheet and the income statement. A major goal in accounting for inventory is to properly match costs with sales. We use the *matching principle* to decide how much of the cost of the goods available for sale is deducted from sales and how much is carried forward as inventory and matched against future sales.

Management decisions in accounting for inventory involve the following:

- Items included in inventory and their costs.
- Costing method (specific identification, FIFO, LIFO, or weighted average).
- Inventory system (perpetual or periodic).
- Use of market values or other estimates.

The first point was explained on the prior two pages. The second and third points will be addressed now. The fourth point is the focus at the end of this chapter. Decisions on these points affect the reported amounts for inventory, cost of goods sold, gross profit, income, current assets, and other accounts.

One of the most important issues in accounting for inventory is determining the per unit costs assigned to inventory items. When all units are purchased at the same unit cost, this process is simple. When identical items are purchased at different costs, however, a question arises as to which amounts to record in cost of goods sold and which amounts remain in inventory.

Four methods are commonly used to assign costs to inventory and to cost of goods sold: (1) specific identification; (2) first-in, first-out; (3) last-in, first-out; and (4) weighted average. Exhibit 5.1 shows the frequency in the use of these methods.

EXHIBIT 5.1
Frequency in Use of Inventory Methods

- Other* 3%
- FIFO 50%
- Weighted Average 20%
- LIFO 27%

*Includes specific identification.

Each method assumes a particular pattern for how costs flow through inventory. Each of these four methods is acceptable whether or not the actual physical flow of goods follows the cost flow assumption. Physical flow of goods depends on the type of product and the way it is stored. (Perishable goods such as fresh fruit demand that a business attempt to sell them in a first-in, first-out physical flow. Other products such as crude oil and minerals such as coal, gold, and decorative stone can be sold in a last-in, first-out physical flow.) **Physical flow and cost flow need not be the same.**

Inventory Cost Flow Assumptions

P1 Compute inventory in a perpetual system using the methods of specific identification, FIFO, LIFO, and weighted average.

This section introduces inventory cost flow assumptions. For this purpose, assume that three identical units are purchased separately at the following three dates and costs: May 1 at $45, May 3 at $65, and May 6 at $70. One unit is then sold on May 7 for $100. Exhibit 5.2 gives a visual layout of the flow of costs to either the gross profit section of the income statement or the inventory reported on the balance sheet for FIFO, LIFO, and weighted average.

(1) *FIFO assumes costs flow in the order incurred.* The unit purchased on May 1 for $45 is the earliest cost incurred—it is sent to cost of goods sold on the income statement first. The remaining two units ($65 and $70) are reported in inventory on the balance sheet.

(2) *LIFO assumes costs flow in the reverse order incurred.* The unit purchased on May 6 for $70 is the most recent cost incurred—it is sent to cost of goods sold on the income statement. The remaining two units ($45 and $65) are reported in inventory on the balance sheet.

(3) *Weighted average assumes costs flow at an average of the costs available.* The units available at the May 7 sale average $60 in cost, computed as ($45 + $65 + $70)/3. One unit's $60 average cost is sent to cost of goods sold on the income statement. The remaining two units' average costs are reported in inventory at $120 on the balance sheet.

Cost flow assumptions can markedly impact gross profit and inventory numbers. Exhibit 5.2 shows that gross profit as a percent of net sales ranges from 30% to 55% due to nothing else but the cost flow assumption.

Point: It is helpful to recall the cost flow of inventory from Exhibit 4.4.

Beginning inventory + Net purchases = Merchandise available for sale

Ending inventory + Cost of goods sold

EXHIBIT 5.2

Cost Flow Assumptions

1. First-in, first-out (FIFO)
Costs flow in the order incurred.

$70 May 6
$65 May 3
$45 May 1

Income Statement	
Net sales.............	$100
Cost of goods sold..	45
Gross profit.............	$ 55

Balance Sheet	
Inventory.................	$135

2. Last-in, first-out (LIFO)
Costs flow in the *reverse* order incurred.

$70 May 6
$65 May 3
$45 May 1

Income Statement	
Net sales.............	$100
Cost of goods sold..	70
Gross profit.............	$ 30

Balance Sheet	
Inventory.................	$110

3. Weighted average
Costs flow at an average of costs available.

$70 May 6
$65 May 3
$45 May 1

$\frac{\$180}{3}$ = $60 each

× 1   × 2

Income Statement	
Net sales.............	$100
Cost of goods sold..	60
Gross profit.............	$ 40

Balance Sheet	
Inventory.................	$120

The following sections on inventory costing use the perpetual system. Appendix 5A uses the periodic system. An instructor can choose to cover either one or both systems. If the perpetual system is skipped, then read Appendix 5A and return to the section (six pages ahead) titled "Valuing Inventory at LCM and . . ."

Inventory Costing Illustration

This section provides a comprehensive illustration of inventory costing methods. We use information from Trekking, a sporting goods store. Among its many products, Trekking carries one type of mountain bike whose sales are directed at resorts that provide inexpensive mountain bikes for complimentary guest use. Its customers usually purchase in amounts of 10 or more bikes. We use Trekking's data from August. Its mountain bike (unit) inventory at the beginning of August and its purchases and sales during August are shown in Exhibit 5.3. It ends August with 12 bikes remaining in inventory.

EXHIBIT 5.3

Purchases and Sales of Goods

Date	Activity	Units Acquired at Cost	Units Sold at Retail	Unit Inventory
Aug. 1	Beginning inventory	10 units @ $ 91 = $ 910		10 units
Aug. 3	Purchases	15 units @ $106 = $1,590		25 units
Aug. 14	Sales		20 units @ $130	5 units
Aug. 17	Purchases	20 units @ $115 = $2,300		25 units
Aug. 28	Purchases	10 units @ $119 = $1,190		35 units
Aug. 31	Sales		23 units @ $150	**12 units**
	Totals	**55 units** $5,990	**43 units**	

Trekking uses the perpetual inventory system, which means that its merchandise inventory account is continually updated to reflect purchases and sales. **(Appendix 5A describes the assignment of costs to inventory using a periodic system.)** Regardless of what inventory method or system is used, cost of goods available for sale must be allocated between cost of goods sold and ending inventory.

Point: The perpetual inventory system is now the most dominant system for U.S. businesses.

Point: Cost of goods sold plus ending inventory equals cost of goods available for sale.

Specific Identification

When each item in inventory can be identified with a specific purchase and invoice, we can use **specific identification** (also called *specific invoice inventory pricing*) to assign costs. We also

210   Chapter 5   Reporting and Analyzing Inventories

need sales records that identify exactly which items were sold and when. Trekking's internal documents reveal the following specific unit sales:

| August 14 | Sold 8 bikes costing $91 each and 12 bikes costing $106 each |
| August 31 | Sold 2 bikes costing $91 each, 3 bikes costing $106 each, 15 bikes costing $115 each, and 3 bikes costing $119 each |

Point: Three key variables determine the dollar value of ending inventory: (1) inventory quantity, (2) costs of inventory, and (3) cost flow assumption.

Applying specific identification, and using the information above and from Exhibit 5.3, we prepare Exhibit 5.4. This exhibit starts with 10 bikes at $91 each in beginning inventory. On August 3, 15 more bikes are purchased at $106 each for $1,590. Inventory available now consists of 10 bikes at $91 each and 15 bikes at $106 each, for a total of $2,500. On August 14 (see sales above), 20 bikes costing $2,000 are sold—leaving 5 bikes costing $500 in inventory. On August 17, 20 bikes costing $2,300 are purchased, and on August 28, another 10 bikes costing $1,190 are purchased, for a total of 35 bikes costing $3,990 in inventory. On August 31 (see sales above), 23 bikes costing $2,582 are sold, which leaves 12 bikes costing $1,408 in ending inventory. Carefully study this exhibit and the boxed explanations to see the flow of costs both in and out of inventory. Each unit, whether sold or remaining in inventory, has its own specific cost attached to it.

EXHIBIT 5.4
Specific Identification Computations

"goods in"   "goods out"   "what's left"

Date	Goods Purchased	Cost of Goods Sold	Inventory Balance
Aug. 1	Beginning balance		10 @ $91 = $910
Aug. 3	15 @ $106 = $1,590		10 @ $91 15 @ $106 } = $2,500
Aug. 14		8 @ $91 = $728 12 @ $106 = $1,272 } = $2,000*	2 @ $91 3 @ $106 } = $500
Aug. 17	20 @ $115 = $2,300		2 @ $91 3 @ $106 20 @ $115 } = $2,800
Aug. 28	10 @ $119 = $1,190		2 @ $91 3 @ $106 20 @ $115 10 @ $119 } = $3,990
Aug. 31		2 @ $91 = $182 3 @ $106 = $318 15 @ $115 = $1,725 3 @ $119 = $357 } = $2,582*	5 @ $115 7 @ $119 } = $1,408
		$4,582	

For the 20 units sold on Aug. 14, the company specifically identified that 8 of those had cost $91 and 12 had cost $106.

For the 23 units sold on Aug. 31, the company specifically identified each bike sold and its acquisition cost from prior purchases.

* Identification of items sold (and their costs) is obtained from internal documents that track each unit from its purchase to its sale.

When using specific identification, Trekking's cost of goods sold reported on the income statement totals **$4,582**, the sum of $2,000 and $2,582 from the third column of Exhibit 5.4. Trekking's ending inventory reported on the balance sheet is **$1,408**, which is the final inventory balance from the fourth column of Exhibit 5.4.

The purchases and sales entries for Exhibit 5.4 follow (the colored boldface numbers are those impacted by the cost flow assumption).

Point: Specific identification is usually practical only for companies with expensive, custom-made inventory.

Purchases

Aug. 3	Merchandise Inventory	1,590	
	Accounts Payable		1,590
17	Merchandise Inventory	2,300	
	Accounts Payable		2,300
28	Merchandise Inventory	1,190	
	Accounts Payable		1,190

Sales

Aug. 14	Accounts Receivable	2,600	
	Sales		2,600
14	Cost of Goods Sold	**2,000**	
	Merchandise Inventory		**2,000**
31	Accounts Receivable	3,450	
	Sales		3,450
31	Cost of Goods Sold	**2,582**	
	Merchandise Inventory		**2,582**

First-In, First-Out

The **first-in, first-out (FIFO)** method of assigning costs to both inventory and cost of goods sold assumes that inventory items are sold in the order acquired. When sales occur, the costs of the earliest units acquired are charged to cost of goods sold. This leaves the costs from the most recent purchases in ending inventory. Use of FIFO for computing the cost of inventory and cost of goods sold is shown in Exhibit 5.5.

This exhibit starts with beginning inventory of 10 bikes at $91 each. On August 3, 15 more bikes costing $106 each are bought for $1,590. Inventory now consists of 10 bikes at $91 each and 15 bikes at $106 each, for a total of $2,500. On August 14, 20 bikes are sold—applying FIFO, the first 10 sold cost $91 each and the next 10 sold cost $106 each, for a total cost of $1,970. This leaves 5 bikes costing $106 each, or $530, in inventory. On August 17, 20 bikes costing $2,300 are purchased, and on August 28, another 10 bikes costing $1,190 are purchased, for a total of 35 bikes costing $4,020 in inventory. On August 31, 23 bikes are sold—applying FIFO, the first 5 bikes sold cost $530 and the next 18 sold cost $2,070, which leaves 12 bikes costing $1,420 in ending inventory.

Point: The "Goods Purchased" column is identical for all methods. Data are taken from Exhibit 5.3.

EXHIBIT 5.5
FIFO Computations—Perpetual System

Date	Goods Purchased	Cost of Goods Sold	Inventory Balance
Aug. 1	Beginning balance		10 @ $ 91 = $ 910
Aug. 3	15 @ $106 = $1,590		10 @ $ 91 15 @ $106 } = $2,500
Aug. 14		10 @ $ 91 = $ 910 10 @ $106 = $1,060 } = $1,970	5 @ $106 = $ 530
Aug. 17	20 @ $115 = $2,300		5 @ $106 20 @ $115 } = $2,830
Aug. 28	10 @ $119 = $1,190		5 @ $106 20 @ $115 10 @ $119 } = $4,020
Aug. 31		5 @ $106 = $ 530 18 @ $115 = $2,070 } = $2,600	2 @ $115 10 @ $119 } = $1,420
		$4,570	

For the 20 units sold on Aug. 14, the first 10 sold are assigned the earliest cost of $91 (from beg. bal.). The next 10 sold are assigned the next earliest cost of $106.

For the 23 units sold on Aug. 31, the first 5 sold are assigned the earliest available cost of $106 (from Aug. 3 purchase). The next 18 sold are assigned the next earliest cost of $115 (from Aug. 17 purchase).

Trekking's FIFO cost of goods sold reported on its income statement (reflecting the 43 units sold) is **$4,570** ($1,970 + $2,600), and its ending inventory reported on the balance sheet (reflecting the 12 units unsold) is **$1,420**.

The purchases and sales entries for Exhibit 5.5 follow (the colored boldface numbers are those affected by the cost flow assumption).

Point: Under FIFO, a unit sold is assigned the earliest (oldest) cost from inventory. This leaves the most recent costs in ending inventory.

Purchases			
Aug. 3	Merchandise Inventory	1,590	
	Accounts Payable		1,590
17	Merchandise Inventory	2,300	
	Accounts Payable		2,300
28	Merchandise Inventory	1,190	
	Accounts Payable		1,190

Sales			
Aug. 14	Accounts Receivable	2,600	
	Sales		2,600
14	Cost of Goods Sold	1,970	
	Merchandise Inventory		1,970
31	Accounts Receivable	3,450	
	Sales		3,450
31	Cost of Goods Sold	2,600	
	Merchandise Inventory		2,600

Last-In, First-Out

The **last-in, first-out (LIFO)** method of assigning costs assumes that the most recent purchases are sold first. These more recent costs are charged to the goods sold, and the costs of the earliest purchases are assigned to inventory. As with other methods, LIFO is acceptable even when the physical flow of goods does not follow a last-in, first-out pattern. One appeal of LIFO is that by

Point: Under LIFO, a unit sold is assigned the most recent (latest) cost from inventory. This leaves the oldest costs in inventory.

assigning costs from the most recent purchases to cost of goods sold, LIFO comes closest to matching current costs of goods sold with revenues (compared to FIFO or weighted average).

Exhibit 5.6 shows the LIFO computations. It starts with beginning inventory of 10 bikes at $91 each. On August 3, 15 more bikes costing $106 each are bought for $1,590. Inventory now consists of 10 bikes at $91 each and 15 bikes at $106 each, for a total of $2,500. On August 14, 20 bikes are sold—applying LIFO, the first 15 sold are from the most recent purchase costing $106 each, and the next 5 sold are from the next most recent purchase costing $91 each, for a total cost of $2,045. This leaves 5 bikes costing $91 each, or $455, in inventory. On August 17, 20 bikes costing $2,300 are purchased, and on August 28, another 10 bikes costing $1,190 are purchased, for a total of 35 bikes costing $3,945 in inventory. On August 31, 23 bikes are sold—applying LIFO, the first 10 bikes sold are from the most recent purchase costing $1,190, and the next 13 sold are from the next most recent purchase costing $1,495, which leaves 12 bikes costing $1,260 in ending inventory.

EXHIBIT 5.6

LIFO Computations— Perpetual System

For the 20 units sold on Aug. 14, the first 15 sold are assigned the most recent cost of $106. The next 5 sold are assigned the next most recent cost of $91.

For the 23 units sold on Aug. 31, the first 10 sold are assigned the most recent cost of $119. The next 13 sold are assigned the next most recent cost of $115.

Date	Goods Purchased	Cost of Goods Sold	Inventory Balance
Aug. 1	Beginning balance		10 @ $91 = $910
Aug. 3	15 @ $106 = $1,590		10 @ $91 } = $2,500 15 @ $106
Aug. 14		15 @ $106 = $1,590 } = $2,045 5 @ $91 = $455	5 @ $91 = $455
Aug. 17	20 @ $115 = $2,300		5 @ $91 } = $2,755 20 @ $115
Aug. 28	10 @ $119 = $1,190		5 @ $91 20 @ $115 } = $3,945 10 @ $119
Aug. 31		10 @ $119 = $1,190 } = $2,685 13 @ $115 = $1,495 $4,730	5 @ $91 } = $1,260 7 @ $115

Trekking's LIFO cost of goods sold reported on the income statement is **$4,730** ($2,045 + $2,685), and its ending inventory reported on the balance sheet is **$1,260**.

The purchases and sales entries for Exhibit 5.6 follow (the colored boldface numbers are those affected by the cost flow assumption).

Purchases				Sales			
Aug. 3	Merchandise Inventory	1,590		Aug. 14	Accounts Receivable	2,600	
	Accounts Payable		1,590		Sales		2,600
17	Merchandise Inventory	2,300		14	Cost of Goods Sold	**2,045**	
	Accounts Payable		2,300		Merchandise Inventory		**2,045**
28	Merchandise Inventory	1,190		31	Accounts Receivable	3,450	
	Accounts Payable		1,190		Sales		3,450
				31	Cost of Goods Sold	**2,685**	
					Merchandise Inventory		**2,685**

Weighted Average

The **weighted average** (also called **average cost**) method of assigning cost requires that we use the weighted average cost per unit of inventory at the time of each sale. Weighted average cost per unit at the time of each sale equals the cost of goods available for sale divided by the units available. The results using weighted average (WA) for Trekking are shown in Exhibit 5.7.

This exhibit starts with beginning inventory of 10 bikes at $91 each. On August 3, 15 more bikes costing $106 each are bought for $1,590. Inventory now consists of 10 bikes at $91 each and 15 bikes at $106 each, for a total of $2,500. The average cost per bike for that inventory is $100, computed as $2,500/(10 bikes + 15 bikes). On August 14, 20 bikes are sold—applying WA, the 20 sold are assigned the $100 average cost, for a total cost of $2,000. This leaves

EXHIBIT 5.7
Weighted Average Computations—Perpetual System

Date	Goods Purchased	Cost of Goods Sold	Inventory Balance	
Aug. 1	Beginning balance		10 @ $91	= $910
Aug. 3	15 @ $106 = $1,590		10 @ $91 15 @ $106	= $2,500 (or $100 per unit)[a]
Aug. 14		20 @ $100 = $2,000	5 @ $100	= $500 (or $100 per unit)[b]
Aug. 17	20 @ $115 = $2,300		5 @ $100 20 @ $115	= $2,800 (or $112 per unit)[c]
Aug. 28	10 @ $119 = $1,190		5 @ $100 20 @ $115 10 @ $119	= $3,990 (or $114 per unit)[d]
Aug. 31		23 @ $114 = $2,622	12 @ $114	= **$1,368** (or $114 per unit)[e]
		$4,622		

For the 20 units sold on Aug. 14, the cost assigned is the $100 *average cost* per unit from the inventory balance column at the time of sale.

For the 23 units sold on Aug. 31, the cost assigned is the $114 *average cost* per unit from the inventory balance column at the time of sale.

[a] $100 per unit = ($2,500 inventory balance ÷ 25 units in inventory).
[b] $100 per unit = ($500 inventory balance ÷ 5 units in inventory).
[c] $112 per unit = ($2,800 inventory balance ÷ 25 units in inventory).
[d] $114 per unit = ($3,990 inventory balance ÷ 35 units in inventory).
[e] $114 per unit = ($1,368 inventory balance ÷ 12 units in inventory).

5 bikes with an average cost of $100 each, or $500, in inventory. On August 17, 20 bikes costing $2,300 are purchased, and on August 28, another 10 bikes costing $1,190 are purchased, for a total of 35 bikes costing $3,990 in inventory at August 28. The average cost per bike for the August 28 inventory is $114, computed as $3,990/(5 bikes + 20 bikes + 10 bikes). On August 31, 23 bikes are sold—applying WA, the 23 sold are assigned the $114 average cost, for a total cost of $2,622. This leaves 12 bikes costing $1,368 in ending inventory.

Trekking's cost of goods sold reported on the income statement (reflecting the 43 units sold) is **$4,622** ($2,000 + $2,622), and its ending inventory reported on the balance sheet (reflecting the 12 units unsold) is **$1,368**.

The purchases and sales entries for Exhibit 5.7 follow (the colored boldface numbers are those affected by the cost flow assumption).

Point: Under weighted average, a unit sold is assigned the average cost of all items currently available for sale at the date of each sale.

Purchases

Aug. 3	Merchandise Inventory	1,590		
	Accounts Payable		1,590	
17	Merchandise Inventory	2,300		
	Accounts Payable		2,300	
28	Merchandise Inventory	1,190		
	Accounts Payable		1,190	

Sales

Aug. 14	Accounts Receivable	2,600		
	Sales		2,600	
14	Cost of Goods Sold	**2,000**		
	Merchandise Inventory		**2,000**	
31	Accounts Receivable	3,450		
	Sales		3,450	
31	Cost of Goods Sold	**2,622**		
	Merchandise Inventory		**2,622**	

This completes computations under the four most common perpetual inventory costing methods. Advances in technology have greatly reduced the cost of a perpetual inventory system. Many companies now ask whether they can afford *not* to have a perpetual inventory system because timely access to inventory information is a competitive advantage and it can help reduce the amount of inventory, which reduces costs.

Fraud

Inventory Control. Companies must safeguard inventory and properly report it. Safeguards include restricted access, use of authorized requisitions, security measures, and controlled environments to prevent damage. Proper accounting includes matching inventory received with purchase order terms and quality requirements, preventing misstatements, and controlling access to inventory records. A study reports that 23% of employees in purchasing and procurement observed inappropriate kickbacks or gifts from suppliers (KPMG 2009). Another 23% of employees in production witnessed fabrication of product quality results.

EXHIBIT 5.8

Financial Statement Effects of Inventory Costing Methods

Financial Statement Effects of Costing Methods

When purchase prices do not change, each inventory costing method assigns the same cost amounts to inventory and to cost of goods sold. When purchase prices are different, however, the methods nearly always assign different cost amounts. We show these differences in Exhibit 5.8 using Trekking's data.

A1 Analyze the effects of inventory methods for both financial and tax reporting.

TREKKING COMPANY
For Month Ended August 31

	Specific Identification	FIFO	LIFO	Weighted Average
Income Statement				
Sales	$ 6,050	$ 6,050	$ 6,050	$ 6,050
Cost of goods sold	4,582	4,570	4,730	4,622
Gross profit	1,468	1,480	1,320	1,428
Expenses	450	450	450	450
Income before taxes	1,018	1,030	870	978
Income tax expense (30%)	305	309	261	293
Net income	$ 713	$ 721	$ 609	$ 685
Balance Sheet				
Inventory	$1,408	$1,420	$1,260	$1,368

This exhibit reveals two important results. First, when purchase costs *regularly rise,* as in Trekking's case, the following occurs:

- FIFO assigns the lowest amount to cost of goods sold—yielding the highest gross profit and net income.
- LIFO assigns the highest amount to cost of goods sold—yielding the lowest gross profit and net income, which also yields a temporary tax advantage by postponing payment of some income tax.
- Weighted average yields results between FIFO and LIFO.
- Specific identification always yields results that depend on which units are sold.

Point: Managers prefer FIFO when costs are rising *and* incentives exist to report higher income for reasons such as bonus plans, job security, and reputation.

Second, when costs *regularly decline,* the reverse occurs for FIFO and LIFO. Namely, FIFO gives the highest cost of goods sold—yielding the lowest gross profit and income. However, LIFO then gives the lowest cost of goods sold—yielding the highest gross profit and income.

All four inventory costing methods are acceptable. However, a company must disclose the inventory method it uses in its financial statements or notes. Each method offers certain advantages as follows:

Point: LIFO inventory is often less than the inventory's replacement cost because LIFO inventory is valued using the oldest inventory purchase costs.

- FIFO assigns an amount to inventory on the balance sheet that approximates its current cost; it also mimics the actual flow of goods for most businesses.
- LIFO assigns an amount to cost of goods sold on the income statement that approximates its current cost; it also better matches current costs with revenues in computing gross profit.
- Weighted average tends to smooth out erratic changes in costs.
- Specific identification exactly matches the costs of items with the revenues they generate.

Decision Maker   Answer — p. 231

Financial Planner   One of your clients asks if the inventory account of a company using FIFO needs any "adjustments" for analysis purposes in light of recent inflation. What is your advice? Does your advice depend on changes in the costs of these inventories? ■

Tax Effects of Costing Methods   Trekking's segment income statement in Exhibit 5.8 includes income tax expense (at a rate of 30%) because it was formed as a corporation. Since inventory costs affect net income, they have potential tax effects. Trekking gains a temporary tax advantage by using LIFO. Many companies use LIFO for this reason.

Companies can and often do use different costing methods for financial reporting and tax reporting. *The only exception is when LIFO is used for tax reporting; in this case, the IRS requires that it also be used in financial statements*—called the LIFO conformity rule.

Consistency in Using Costing Methods

The **consistency concept** prescribes that a company use the same accounting methods period after period so that financial statements are comparable across periods—the only exception is when a change from one method to another will improve its financial reporting. The *full-disclosure principle* prescribes that the notes to the statements report this type of change, its justification, and its effect on income.

The consistency concept does *not* require a company to use one method exclusively. For example, it can use different methods to value different categories of inventory.

■ Decision Ethics   Answer — p. 231

Inventory Manager Your compensation as inventory manager includes a bonus plan based on gross profit. Your superior asks your opinion on changing the inventory costing method from FIFO to LIFO. Since costs are expected to continue to rise, your superior predicts that LIFO would match higher current costs against sales, thereby lowering taxable income (and gross profit). What do you recommend? ■

Quick Check   Answers — p. 231

4. Describe one advantage for each of the inventory costing methods: specific identification, FIFO, LIFO, and weighted average.
5. When costs are rising, which method reports higher net income—LIFO or FIFO?
6. When costs are rising, what effect does LIFO have on a balance sheet compared to FIFO?
7. A company takes a physical count of inventory at the end of 2010 and finds that ending inventory is understated by $10,000. Would this error cause cost of goods sold to be overstated or understated in 2010? In year 2011? If so, by how much?

VALUING INVENTORY AT LCM AND THE EFFECTS OF INVENTORY ERRORS

This section examines the role of market costs in determining inventory on the balance sheet and also the financial statement effects of inventory errors.

Lower of Cost or Market

We explained how to assign costs to ending inventory and cost of goods sold using one of four costing methods (FIFO, LIFO, weighted average, or specific identification). However, *accounting principles require that inventory be reported at the market value (cost) of replacing inventory when market value is lower than cost*. Merchandise inventory is then said to be reported on the balance sheet at the **lower of cost or market (LCM).**

P2 Compute the lower of cost or market amount of inventory.

Computing the Lower of Cost or Market *Market* in the term *LCM* is defined as the current replacement cost of purchasing the same inventory items in the usual manner. A decline in replacement cost reflects a loss of value in inventory. When the recorded cost of inventory is higher than the replacement cost, a loss is recognized. When the recorded cost is lower, no adjustment is made.

LCM is applied in one of three ways: (1) to each individual item separately, (2) to major categories of items, or (3) to the whole of inventory. The less similar the items that make up inventory, the more likely companies are to apply LCM to individual items or categories. With the increasing application of technology and inventory tracking, companies increasingly apply

EXHIBIT 5.9

Lower of Cost or Market Computations

$140,000 is the lower of $160,000 or $140,000

Market amount of $265,000 is lower than the $295,000 recorded cost

Inventory Items	Units	Per Unit Cost	Per Unit Market	Total Cost	Total Market	LCM Applied to Items
Cycles						
Roadster	20	$8,000	$7,000	$160,000	$140,000	$140,000
Sprint	10	5,000	6,000	50,000	60,000	50,000
Off-Road						
Trax-4	8	5,000	6,500	40,000	52,000	40,000
Blazer	5	9,000	7,000	45,000	35,000	35,000
Totals				$295,000		$265,000

LCM to each individual item separately. Accordingly, we show that method only; however, advanced courses cover the other two methods. To illustrate LCM, we apply it to the ending inventory of a motorsports retailer in Exhibit 5.9.

LCM Applied to Individual Items When LCM is applied to individual *items* of inventory, the number of comparisons equals the number of items. For Roadster, $140,000 is the lower of the $160,000 cost and the $140,000 market. For Sprint, $50,000 is the lower of the $50,000 cost and the $60,000 market. For Trax-4, $40,000 is the lower of the $40,000 cost and the $52,000 market. For Blazer, $35,000 is the lower of the $45,000 cost and the $35,000 market. This yields a $265,000 reported inventory, computed from $140,000 for Roadster plus $50,000 for Sprint plus $40,000 for Trax-4 plus $35,000 for Blazer.

RIM The manufacturer **Research In Motion** applies LCM and reports that its "inventories are stated at the lower of cost and net realizable value [or replacement cost]."

Point: Advances in technology encourage the individual-item approach for LCM.

Recording the Lower of Cost or Market Inventory must be adjusted downward when market is less than cost. To illustrate, if LCM is applied to the individual items of inventory in Exhibit 5.9, the Merchandise Inventory account must be adjusted from the $295,000 recorded cost down to the $265,000 market amount as follows.

Cost of Goods Sold	30,000	
Merchandise Inventory		30,000
To adjust inventory cost to market.		

Accounting rules require that inventory be adjusted to market when market is less than cost, but inventory normally cannot be written up to market when market exceeds cost. If recording inventory down to market is acceptable, why are companies not allowed to record inventory up to market? One view is that a gain from a market increase should not be realized until a sales transaction verifies the gain. However, this problem also applies when market is less than cost. A second and primary reason is the **conservatism constraint,** which prescribes the use of the less optimistic amount when more than one estimate of the amount to be received or paid exists and these estimates are about equally likely.

Financial Statement Effects of Inventory Errors

A2 Analyze the effects of inventory errors on current and future financial statements.

Companies must be careful both in taking a physical count of inventory and in assigning a cost to it. An inventory error causes misstatements in cost of goods sold, gross profit, net income, current assets, and equity. It also causes misstatements in the next period's statements because ending inventory of one period is the beginning inventory of the next. As we consider the financial statement effects in this section, it is helpful if we recall the following *inventory relation.*

Beginning inventory + Net purchases − Ending inventory = Cost of goods sold

Income Statement Effects Exhibit 5.10 shows the effects of inventory errors on key amounts in the current and next periods' income statements. Let's look at row 1 and year 1. We see that understating ending inventory overstates cost of goods sold. This can be seen from the above inventory relation where we subtract a smaller ending inventory amount in computing cost of goods sold. Then a higher cost of goods sold yields a lower income.

To understand year 2 of row 1, remember that an understated ending inventory for year 1 becomes an understated beginning inventory for year 2. Using the above inventory relation, we see that if beginning inventory is understated, then cost of goods sold is understated (because we are starting with a smaller amount). A lower cost of goods sold yields a higher income.

Turning to overstatements, let's look at row 2 and year 1. If ending inventory is overstated, we use the inventory relation to see that cost of goods sold is understated. A lower cost of goods sold yields a higher income.

For year 2 of row 2, we again recall that an overstated ending inventory for year 1 becomes an overstated beginning inventory for year 2. If beginning inventory is overstated, we use the inventory relation to see that cost of goods sold is overstated. A higher cost of goods sold yields a lower income.

EXHIBIT 5.10

Effects of Inventory Errors on the Income Statement

Ending Inventory	Year 1 Cost of Goods Sold	Year 1 Net Income	Year 2 Cost of Goods Sold	Year 2 Net Income
Understated ↓	Overstated ↑	Understated ↓	Understated ↓	Overstated ↑
Overstated* ↑	Understated ↓	Overstated ↑	Overstated ↑	Understated ↓

* This error is less likely under a perpetual system because it implies more inventory than is recorded (or less shrinkage than expected). Management will normally follow up and discover and correct this error before it impacts any accounts.

To illustrate, consider an inventory error for a company with $100,000 in sales for each of the years 2010, 2011, and 2012. If this company maintains a steady $20,000 inventory level during this period and makes $60,000 in purchases in each of these years, its cost of goods sold is $60,000 and its gross profit is $40,000 each year.

Ending Inventory Understated—Year 1 Assume that this company errs in computing its 2010 ending inventory and reports $16,000 instead of the correct amount of $20,000. The effects of this error are shown in Exhibit 5.11. The $4,000 understatement of 2010 ending inventory causes a $4,000 overstatement in 2010 cost of goods sold and a $4,000 understatement in both gross profit and net income for 2010. We see that these effects match the effects predicted in Exhibit 5.10.

EXHIBIT 5.11

Effects of Inventory Errors on Three Periods' Income Statements

	Income Statements 2010	2011	2012
Sales	$100,000	$100,000	$100,000
Cost of goods sold			
Beginning inventory	$20,000	$16,000*	$20,000
Cost of goods purchased	60,000	60,000	60,000
Goods available for sale	80,000	76,000	80,000
Ending inventory	16,000*	20,000	20,000
Cost of goods sold	64,000†	56,000†	60,000
Gross profit	36,000	44,000	40,000
Expenses	10,000	10,000	10,000
Net income	$ 26,000	$ 34,000	$ 30,000

Correct income is $30,000 for each year

* Correct amount is $20,000.   † Correct amount is $60,000.

Ending Inventory Understated—Year 2 The 2010 understated ending inventory becomes the 2011 understated *beginning* inventory. We see in Exhibit 5.11 that this error causes an understatement in 2011 cost of goods sold and a $4,000 overstatement in both gross profit and net income for 2011.

Ending Inventory Understated—Year 3 Exhibit 5.11 shows that the 2010 ending inventory error affects only that period and the next. It does not affect 2012 results or any period thereafter. An inventory error is said to be *self-correcting* because it always yields an offsetting error in the next period. This does not reduce the severity of inventory errors. Managers, lenders, owners, and others make important decisions from analysis of income and costs.

Example: If 2010 ending inventory in Exhibit 5.11 is overstated by $3,000 (not understated by $4,000), what is the effect on cost of goods sold, gross profit, assets, and equity? *Answer:* Cost of goods sold is understated by $3,000 in 2010 and overstated by $3,000 in 2011. Gross profit and net income are overstated in 2010 and understated in 2011. Assets and equity are overstated in 2010.

218 Chapter 5 Reporting and Analyzing Inventories

Point: A former internal auditor at Coca-Cola alleges that just before midnight at a prior calendar year-end, fully loaded Coke trucks were ordered to drive about 2 feet away from the loading dock so that Coke could record millions of dollars in extra sales.

We can also do an analysis of beginning inventory errors. The income statement effects are the opposite of those for ending inventory.

Balance Sheet Effects Balance sheet effects of an inventory error can be seen by considering the accounting equation: Assets = Liabilities + Equity. For example, understating ending inventory understates both current and total assets. An understatement in ending inventory also yields an understatement in equity because of the understatement in net income. Exhibit 5.12 shows the effects of inventory errors on the current period's balance sheet amounts. Errors in *beginning* inventory do not yield misstatements in the end-of-period balance sheet, but they do affect that current period's income statement.

EXHIBIT 5.12

Effects of Inventory Errors on Current Period's Balance Sheet

Ending Inventory	Assets	Equity
Understated ↓	Understated ↓	Understated ↓
Overstated ↑	Overstated ↑	Overstated ↑

Quick Check
Answers — p. 231

8. Use LCM applied separately to the following individual items to compute ending inventory.

Product	Units	Unit Recorded Cost	Unit Market Cost
A	20	$ 6	$ 5
B	40	9	8
C	10	12	15

GLOBAL VIEW

This section discusses differences between U.S. GAAP and IFRS in the items and costs making up merchandise inventory, in the methods to assign costs to inventory, and in the methods to estimate inventory values.

Items and Costs Making Up Inventory Both U.S. GAAP and IFRS include broad and similar guidance for the items and costs making up merchandise inventory. Specifically, under both accounting systems, merchandise inventory includes all items that a company owns and holds for sale. Further, merchandise inventory includes costs of expenditures necessary, directly or indirectly, to bring those items to a salable condition and location.

Assigning Costs to Inventory Both U.S. GAAP and IFRS allow companies to use specific identification in assigning costs to inventory. Further, both systems allow companies to apply a *cost flow assumption*. The usual cost flow assumptions are: FIFO, Weighted Average, and LIFO. However, IFRS does not (currently) allow use of LIFO. As the convergence project progresses, this prohibition may or may not persist.

Estimating Inventory Costs The value of inventory can change while it awaits sale to customers. That value can decrease or increase.

Decreases in Inventory Value Both U.S. GAAP and IFRS require companies to write down (reduce the cost recorded for) inventory when its value falls below the cost recorded. This is referred to as the *lower of cost or market* method explained in this chapter. U.S. GAAP prohibits any later increase in the recorded value of that inventory even if that decline in value is reversed through value increases in later periods. However, IFRS allows reversals of those write downs up to the original acquisition cost. For example, if Research In Motion wrote down its 2010 inventory from $622 million to $600 million, it could not reverse this in future periods even if its value increased to more than $622 million. However, if RIM applied IFRS, it could reverse that previous loss. (Another difference is that value refers to *replacement cost* under U.S. GAAP, but *net realizable value* under IFRS.)

Increases in Inventory Value Neither U.S. GAAP nor IFRS allow inventory to be adjusted upward beyond the original cost. (One exception is that IFRS requires agricultural assets such as animals, forests, and plants to be measured at fair value less point-of-sale costs.)

Nokia provides the following description of its inventory valuation procedures:

> Inventories are stated at the lower of cost or net realizable value. Cost...approximates actual cost on a FIFO (First-in First-out) basis. Net realizable value is the amount that can be realized from the sale of the inventory in the normal course of business after allowing for the costs of realization.

Inventory Turnover and Days' Sales in Inventory — Decision Analysis

Inventory Turnover

Earlier chapters described two important ratios useful in evaluating a company's short-term liquidity: current ratio and acid-test ratio. A merchandiser's ability to pay its short-term obligations also depends on how quickly it sells its merchandise inventory. **Inventory turnover,** also called *merchandise inventory turnover,* is one ratio used to assess this and is defined in Exhibit 5.13.

$$\text{Inventory turnover} = \frac{\text{Cost of goods sold}}{\text{Average inventory}}$$

This ratio reveals how many *times* a company turns over (sells) its inventory during a period. If a company's inventory greatly varies within a year, average inventory amounts can be computed from interim periods such as quarters or months.

Users apply inventory turnover to help analyze short-term liquidity and to assess whether management is doing a good job controlling the amount of inventory available. A low ratio compared to that of competitors suggests inefficient use of assets. The company may be holding more inventory than it needs to support its sales volume. Similarly, a very high ratio compared to that of competitors suggests inventory might be too low. This can cause lost sales if customers must back-order merchandise. Inventory turnover has no simple rule except to say *a high ratio is preferable provided inventory is adequate to meet demand.*

Days' Sales in Inventory

To better interpret inventory turnover, many users measure the adequacy of inventory to meet sales demand. **Days' sales in inventory,** also called *days' stock on hand,* is a ratio that reveals how much inventory is available in terms of the number of days' sales. It can be interpreted as the number of days one can sell from inventory if no new items are purchased. This ratio is often viewed as a measure of the buffer against out-of-stock inventory and is useful in evaluating liquidity of inventory. It is defined in Exhibit 5.14.

$$\text{Days' sales in inventory} = \frac{\text{Ending inventory}}{\text{Cost of goods sold}} \times 365$$

Days' sales in inventory focuses on ending inventory and it estimates how many days it will take to convert inventory at the end of a period into accounts receivable or cash. Days' sales in inventory focuses on *ending* inventory whereas inventory turnover focuses on *average* inventory.

A3 Assess inventory management using both inventory turnover and days' sales in inventory.

EXHIBIT 5.13
Inventory Turnover

Point: We must take care when comparing turnover ratios across companies that use different costing methods (such as FIFO and LIFO).

Point: Inventory turnover is higher and days' sales in inventory is lower for industries such as foods and other perishable products. The reverse holds for nonperishable product industries.

EXHIBIT 5.14
Days' Sales in Inventory

Point: Days' sales in inventory for many Ford models has risen: Freestyle, 122 days; Montego, 109 days; Five Hundred, 118 days. The industry average is 73 days. (*BusinessWeek*)

Decision Insight

Dell-ocity From its roots in a college dorm room, **Dell** now sells over 50 million dollars' worth of computers each day from its Website. The speed of Web technology has allowed Dell to slash inventories. Dell's inventory turnover is 88 and its days' sales in inventory is 5 days. Michael Dell asserts, "Speed is everything in this business." ∎

Analysis of Inventory Management

Inventory management is a major emphasis for merchandisers. They must both plan and control inventory purchases and sales. **Toys "R" Us** is one of those merchandisers. Its inventory in fiscal year 2009 was $1,781 million. This inventory constituted 59% of its current assets and 21% of its total assets. We apply the analysis tools in this section to Toys "R" Us, as shown in Exhibit 5.15—also see margin graph.

EXHIBIT 5.15

Inventory Turnover and Days' Sales in Inventory for Toys "R" Us

($ millions)	2009	2008	2007	2006
Cost of goods sold	$8,976	$8,987	$8,638	$7,652
Ending inventory	$1,781	$1,998	$1,690	$1,488
Inventory turnover	**4.8** times	**4.9** times	**5.4** times	**4.5** times
Industry inventory turnover	3.2 times	3.4 times	3.0 times	2.8 times
Days' sales in inventory	**72** days	**81** days	**71** days	**71** days
Industry days' sales in inventory	124 days	135 days	129 days	135 days

Its 2009 inventory turnover of 4.8 times means that Toys "R" Us turns over its inventory 4.8 times per year, or once every 76 days (365 days ÷ 4.8). We prefer inventory turnover to be high provided inventory is not out of stock and the company is not losing customers. The second metric, the 2009 days' sales in inventory of 72 days, reveals that it is carrying 72 days of sales in inventory. This inventory buffer seems more than adequate. Toys "R" Us would benefit from further management efforts to increase inventory turnover and reduce inventory levels.

Decision Maker
Answer — p. 231

Entrepreneur Analysis of your retail store yields an inventory turnover of 5.0 and a days' sales in inventory of 73 days. The industry norm for inventory turnover is 4.4 and for days' sales in inventory is 74 days. What is your assessment of inventory management? ■

DEMONSTRATION PROBLEM

Craig Company uses a perpetual inventory system for its one product. Its beginning inventory, purchases, and sales during calendar year 2011 follow.

Date	Activity	Units Acquired at Cost	Units Sold at Retail	Unit Inventory
Jan. 1	Beg. Inventory	400 units @ $14 = $ 5,600		400 units
Jan. 15	Sale		200 units @ $30	200 units
March 10	Purchase	200 units @ $15 = $ 3,000		400 units
April 1	Sale		200 units @ $30	200 units
May 9	Purchase	300 units @ $16 = $ 4,800		500 units
Sept. 22	Purchase	250 units @ $20 = $ 5,000		750 units
Nov. 1	Sale		300 units @ $35	450 units
Nov. 28	Purchase	100 units @ $21 = $ 2,100		550 units
Totals		1,250 units $20,500	700 units	

Additional tracking data for specific identification: (1) January 15 sale—200 units @ $14, (2) April 1 sale—200 units @ $15, and (3) November 1 sale—200 units @ $14 and 100 units @ $20.

Required

1. Calculate the cost of goods available for sale.
2. Apply the four different methods of inventory costing (FIFO, LIFO, weighted average, and specific identification) to calculate ending inventory and cost of goods sold under each method.
3. Compute gross profit earned by the company for each of the four costing methods in part 2. Also, report the inventory amount reported on the balance sheet for each of the four methods.

4. In preparing financial statements for year 2011, the financial officer was instructed to use FIFO but failed to do so and instead computed cost of goods sold according to LIFO. Determine the impact on year 2011's income from the error. Also determine the effect of this error on year 2012's income. Assume no income taxes.
5. Management wants a report that shows how changing from FIFO to another method would change net income. Prepare a table showing (1) the cost of goods sold amount under each of the four methods, (2) the amount by which each cost of goods sold total is different from the FIFO cost of goods sold, and (3) the effect on net income if another method is used instead of FIFO.

PLANNING THE SOLUTION

- Compute cost of goods available for sale by multiplying the units of beginning inventory and each purchase by their unit costs to determine the total cost of goods available for sale.
- Prepare a perpetual FIFO table starting with beginning inventory and showing how inventory changes after each purchase and after each sale (see Exhibit 5.5).
- Prepare a perpetual LIFO table starting with beginning inventory and showing how inventory changes after each purchase and after each sale (see Exhibit 5.6).
- Make a table of purchases and sales recalculating the average cost of inventory prior to each sale to arrive at the weighted average cost of ending inventory. Total the average costs associated with each sale to determine cost of goods sold (see Exhibit 5.7).
- Prepare a table showing the computation of cost of goods sold and ending inventory using the specific identification method (see Exhibit 5.4).
- Compare the year-end 2011 inventory amounts under FIFO and LIFO to determine the misstatement of year 2011 income that results from using LIFO. The errors for year 2011 and 2012 are equal in amount but opposite in effect.
- Create a table showing cost of goods sold under each method and how net income would differ from FIFO net income if an alternate method is adopted.

SOLUTION TO DEMONSTRATION PROBLEM

1. Cost of goods available for sale (this amount is the same for all methods).

Date		Units	Unit Cost	Cost
Jan. 1	Beg. Inventory	400	$14	$ 5,600
March 10	Purchase	200	15	3,000
May 9	Purchase	300	16	4,800
Sept. 22	Purchase	250	20	5,000
Nov. 28	Purchase	100	21	2,100
Total goods available for sale		1,250		$20,500

2a. FIFO perpetual method.

Date	Goods Purchased	Cost of Goods Sold	Inventory Balance
Jan. 1	Beginning balance		400 @ $14 = $ 5,600
Jan. 15		200 @ $14 = $2,800	200 @ $14 = $ 2,800
Mar. 10	200 @ $15 = $3,000		200 @ $14 } = $ 5,800 200 @ $15
April 1		200 @ $14 = $2,800	200 @ $15 = $ 3,000
May 9	300 @ $16 = $4,800		200 @ $15 } = $ 7,800 300 @ $16
Sept. 22	250 @ $20 = $5,000		200 @ $15 300 @ $16 } = $12,800 250 @ $20
Nov. 1		200 @ $15 = $3,000 100 @ $16 = $1,600	200 @ $16 } = $ 8,200 250 @ $20
Nov. 28	100 @ $21 = $2,100		200 @ $16 250 @ $20 } = $10,300 100 @ $21
Total cost of goods sold		$10,200	

Note to students: **In a classroom situation,** once we compute cost of goods available for sale, we can compute the amount for either cost of goods sold or ending inventory—it is a matter of preference. **In practice,** the costs of items sold are identified as sales are made and immediately transferred from the inventory account to the cost of goods sold account. The previous solution showing the line-by-line approach illustrates actual application in practice. The following alternate solutions illustrate that, once the concepts are understood, other solution approaches are available. Although this is only shown for FIFO, it could be shown for all methods.

Alternate Methods to Compute FIFO Perpetual Numbers

[FIFO Alternate No. 1: Computing cost of goods sold first]

Cost of goods available for sale (from part 1)			$ 20,500
Cost of goods sold			
Jan. 15	Sold (200 @ $14)	$2,800	
April 1	Sold (200 @ $14)	2,800	
Nov. 1	Sold (200 @ $15 and 100 @ $16)	4,600	10,200
Ending inventory			$10,300

[FIFO Alternate No. 2: Computing ending inventory first]

Cost of goods available for sale (from part 1)			$ 20,500
Ending inventory*			
Nov. 28	Purchase (100 @ $21)	$2,100	
Sept. 22	Purchase (250 @ $20)	5,000	
May 9	Purchase (200 @ $16)	3,200	
Ending inventory			10,300
Cost of goods sold			$10,200

* Since FIFO assumes that the earlier costs are the first to flow out, we determine ending inventory by assigning the most recent costs to the remaining items.

2b. LIFO perpetual method.

Date	Goods Purchased	Cost of Goods Sold	Inventory Balance
Jan. 1	Beginning balance		400 @ $14 = $ 5,600
Jan. 15		200 @ $14 = $2,800	200 @ $14 = $ 2,800
Mar. 10	200 @ $15 = $3,000		200 @ $14 200 @ $15 } = $ 5,800
April 1		200 @ $15 = $3,000	200 @ $14 = $ 2,800
May 9	300 @ $16 = $4,800		200 @ $14 300 @ $16 } = $ 7,600
Sept. 22	250 @ $20 = $5,000		200 @ $14 300 @ $16 250 @ $20 } = $12,600
Nov. 1		250 @ $20 = $5,000 50 @ $16 = $ 800	200 @ $14 250 @ $16 } = $ 6,800
Nov. 28	100 @ $21 = $2,100		200 @ $14 250 @ $16 100 @ $21 } = $8,900
Total cost of goods sold		**$11,600**	

2c. Weighted average perpetual method.

Date	Goods Purchased	Cost of Goods Sold	Inventory Balance
Jan. 1	Beginning balance		400 @ $14 = $ 5,600
Jan. 15		200 @ $14 = $2,800	200 @ $14 = $ 2,800
Mar. 10	200 @ $15 = $3,000		200 @ $14 200 @ $15 } = $ 5,800 (avg. cost is $14.5)
April 1		200 @ $14.5 = $2,900	200 @ $14.5 = $ 2,900
May 9	300 @ $16 = $4,800		200 @ $14.5 300 @ $16 } = $ 7,700 (avg. cost is $15.4)
Sept. 22	250 @ $20 = $5,000		200 @ $14.5 300 @ $16 250 @ $20 } = $ 12,700 (avg. cost is $16.93)
Nov. 1		300 @ $16.93 = $5,079	450 @ $16.93 = $ 7,618.5
Nov. 28	100 @ $21 = $2,100		450 @ $16.93 100 @ $21 } = **$9,718.5**
Total cost of goods sold*		**$10,779**	

* The cost of goods sold ($10,779) plus ending inventory ($9,718.5) is $2.5 less than the cost of goods available for sale ($20,500) due to rounding.

2d. Specific identification method.

Date	Goods Purchased	Cost of Goods Sold	Inventory Balance
Jan. 1	Beginning balance		400 @ $14 = $ 5,600
Jan. 15		200 @ $14 = $2,800	200 @ $14 = $ 2,800
Mar. 10	200 @ $15 = $3,000		200 @ $14 200 @ $15 } = $ 5,800
April 1		200 @ $15 = $3,000	200 @ $14 = $ 2,800
May 9	300 @ $16 = $4,800		200 @ $14 300 @ $16 } = $ 7,600
Sept. 22	250 @ $20 = $5,000		200 @ $14 300 @ $16 250 @ $20 } = $ 12,600
Nov. 1		200 @ $14 = $2,800 100 @ $20 = $2,000	300 @ $16 150 @ $20 } = $ 7,800
Nov. 28	100 @ $21 = $2,100		300 @ $16 150 @ $20 100 @ $21 } = **$ 9,900**
Total cost of goods sold		**$10,600**	

3.

	FIFO	LIFO	Weighted Average	Specific Identification
Income Statement				
Sales*	$22,500	$22,500	$22,500	$22,500
Cost of goods sold	10,200	11,600	10,779	10,600
Gross profit	$12,300	$10,900	$11,721	$11,900
Balance Sheet				
Inventory	$10,300	$8,900	$9,718.5	$9,900

* Sales = (200 units × $30) + (200 units × $30) + (300 units × $35) = $22,500

4. Mistakenly using LIFO when FIFO should have been used overstates cost of goods sold in year 2011 by $1,400, which is the difference between the FIFO and LIFO amounts of ending inventory. It understates income in 2011 by $1,400. In year 2012, income is overstated by $1,400 because of the understatement in beginning inventory.

5. Analysis of the effects of alternative inventory methods.

	Cost of Goods Sold	Difference from FIFO Cost of Goods Sold	Effect on Net Income If Adopted Instead of FIFO
FIFO	$10,200	—	—
LIFO	11,600	+$1,400	$1,400 lower
Weighted average	10,779	+ 579	579 lower
Specific identification	10,600	+ 400	400 lower

APPENDIX 5A

Inventory Costing under a Periodic System

P3 Compute inventory in a periodic system using the methods of specific identification, FIFO, LIFO, and weighted average.

The basic aim of the periodic system and the perpetual system is the same: to assign costs to inventory and cost of goods sold. The same four methods are used to assign costs under both systems: specific identification; first-in, first-out; last-in, first-out; and weighted average. We use information from Trekking to show how to assign costs using these four methods with a periodic system. Data for sales and purchases are in Exhibit 5A.1. Also, recall that we explained the accounting entries under a periodic system in Appendix 4A.

EXHIBIT 5A.1

Purchases and Sales of Goods

Date	Activity	Units Acquired at Cost	Units Sold at Retail	Unit Inventory
Aug. 1	Beginning inventory	10 units @ $91 = $910		10 units
Aug. 3	Purchases	15 units @ $106 = $1,590		25 units
Aug. 14	Sales		20 units @ $130	5 units
Aug. 17	Purchases	20 units @ $115 = $2,300		25 units
Aug. 28	Purchases	10 units @ $119 = $1,190		35 units
Aug. 31	Sales		23 units @ $150	12 units
	Totals	55 units $5,990	43 units	

Specific Identification We use the above sales and purchases information and the specific identification method to assign costs to ending inventory and units sold. Trekking's internal data reveal the following specific unit sales:

- **August 14** Sold 8 bikes costing $91 each and 12 bikes costing $106 each
- **August 31** Sold 2 bikes costing $91 each, 3 bikes costing $106 each, 15 bikes costing $115 each, and 3 bikes costing $119 each

Applying specific identification and using the information above, we prepare Exhibit 5A.2. This exhibit starts with 10 bikes at $91 each in beginning inventory. On August 3, 15 more bikes are purchased at $106 each for $1,590. Inventory available now consists of 10 bikes at $91 each and 15 bikes at $106 each, for a total of $2,500. On August 14 (see specific sales data above), 20 bikes costing $2,000 are sold—leaving 5 bikes costing $500 in inventory. On August 17, 20 bikes costing $2,300 are purchased, and on August 28, another 10 bikes costing $1,190 are purchased, for a total of 35 bikes costing $3,990 in inventory. On August 31 (see specific sales above), 23 bikes costing $2,582 are sold, which leaves 12 bikes costing $1,408 in ending inventory. Carefully study Exhibit 5A.2 to see the flow of costs both in and out of inventory. Each unit, whether sold or remaining in inventory, has its own specific cost attached to it.

EXHIBIT 5A.2

Specific Identification Computations

Date	Goods Purchased ("goods in")	Cost of Goods Sold ("goods out")	Inventory Balance ("what's left")
Aug. 1	Beginning balance		10 @ $ 91 = $ 910
Aug. 3	15 @ $106 = $1,590		10 @ $ 91 15 @ $106 } = $2,500
Aug. 14		8 @ $ 91 = $ 728 12 @ $106 = $1,272 } = $2,000*	2 @ $ 91 3 @ $106 } = $ 500
Aug. 17	20 @ $115 = $2,300		2 @ $ 91 3 @ $106 20 @ $115 } = $2,800
Aug. 28	10 @ $119 = $1,190		2 @ $ 91 3 @ $106 20 @ $115 10 @ $119 } = $3,990
Aug. 31		2 @ $ 91 = $ 182 3 @ $106 = $ 318 15 @ $115 = $1,725 3 @ $119 = $ 357 } = $2,582*	5 @ $115 7 @ $119 } = $1,408
		$4,582	

For the 20 units sold on Aug. 14, the company specifically identified that 8 of those had cost $91 and 12 had cost $106.

For the 23 units sold on Aug. 31, the company specifically identified each bike sold and its acquisition cost from prior purchases.

* Identification of items sold (and their costs) is obtained from internal documents that track each unit from its purchase to its sale.

When using specific identification, Trekking's cost of goods sold reported on the income statement totals **$4,582**, the sum of $2,000 and $2,582 from the third column of Exhibit 5A.2. Trekking's ending inventory reported on the balance sheet is **$1,408**, which is the final inventory balance from the fourth column. The purchases and sales entries for Exhibit 5A.2 follow (the colored boldface numbers are those affected by the cost flow assumption).

Point: The assignment of costs to the goods sold and to inventory using specific identification is the same for both the perpetual and periodic systems.

Purchases

Aug. 3	Purchases	. . . .	1,590	
	Accounts Payable	. . . .		1,590
17	Purchases	. . . .	2,300	
	Accounts Payable	. . . .		2,300
28	Purchases	. . . .	1,190	
	Accounts Payable	. . . .		1,190

Sales

Aug. 14	Accounts Receivable	. . . .	2,600	
	Sales.			2,600
31	Accounts Receivable	. . . .	3,450	
	Sales.			3,450

Adjusting Entry

31	Merchandise Inventory	. . . .	**1,408**	
	Income Summary.			498
	Merchandise Inventory			910

First-In, First-Out The first-in, first-out (FIFO) method of assigning costs to inventory assumes that inventory items are sold in the order acquired. When sales occur, the costs of the earliest units acquired are charged to cost of goods sold. This leaves the costs from the most recent purchases in ending inventory. Use of FIFO for computing the cost of inventory and cost of goods sold is shown in Exhibit 5A.3.

This exhibit starts with computing $5,990 in total units available for sale—this is given to us at the start of this appendix. Applying FIFO, we know that the 12 units in ending inventory will be reported at the cost of the most recent 12 purchases. Reviewing purchases in reverse order, we assign costs to the 12 bikes in ending inventory as follows: $119 cost to 10 bikes and $115 cost to 2 bikes. This yields 12 bikes costing $1,420 in ending inventory. We then subtract this $1,420 in ending inventory from $5,990 in cost of goods available to get $4,570 in cost of goods sold.

EXHIBIT 5A.3

FIFO Computations—Periodic System

Exhibit 5A.1 shows that the 12 units in ending inventory consist of 10 units from the latest purchase on Aug. 28 and 2 units from the next latest purchase on Aug. 17.

Total cost of 55 units available for sale (from Exhibit 5A.1)		$5,990
Less ending inventory priced using FIFO		
10 units from August 28 purchase at $119 each	$1,190	
2 units from August 17 purchase at $115 each	230	
Ending inventory		1,420
Cost of goods sold		$4,570

Point: The assignment of costs to the goods sold and to inventory using FIFO is the same for both the perpetual and periodic systems.

Trekking's ending inventory reported on the balance sheet is **$1,420**, and its cost of goods sold reported on the income statement is **$4,570**. These amounts are the same as those computed using the perpetual system. This always occurs because the most recent purchases are in ending inventory under both systems. The purchases and sales entries for Exhibit 5A.3 follow (the colored boldface numbers are those affected by the cost flow assumption).

Purchases

Aug. 3	Purchases	1,590	
	Accounts Payable		1,590
17	Purchases	2,300	
	Accounts Payable		2,300
28	Purchases	1,190	
	Accounts Payable		1,190

Sales

Aug. 14	Accounts Receivable	2,600	
	Sales		2,600
31	Accounts Receivable	3,450	
	Sales		3,450

Adjusting Entry

31	Merchandise Inventory	**1,420**	
	Income Summary		510
	Merchandise Inventory		**910**

Last-In, First-Out The last-in, first-out (LIFO) method of assigning costs assumes that the most recent purchases are sold first. These more recent costs are charged to the goods sold, and the costs of the earliest purchases are assigned to inventory. LIFO results in costs of the most recent purchases being assigned to cost of goods sold, which means that LIFO comes close to matching current costs of goods sold with revenues. Use of LIFO for computing cost of inventory and cost of goods sold is shown in Exhibit 5A.4.

This exhibit starts with computing $5,990 in total units available for sale—this is given to us at the start of this appendix. Applying LIFO, we know that the 12 units in ending inventory will be reported at the cost of the earliest 12 purchases. Reviewing the earliest purchases in order, we assign costs to the 12 bikes in ending inventory as follows: $91 cost to 10 bikes and $106 cost to 2 bikes. This yields 12 bikes costing $1,122 in ending inventory. We then subtract this $1,122 in ending inventory from $5,990 in cost of goods available to get $4,868 in cost of goods sold.

EXHIBIT 5A.4

LIFO Computations—Periodic System

Exhibit 5A.1 shows that the 12 units in ending inventory consist of 10 units from the earliest purchase (beg. inv.) and 2 units from the next earliest purchase on Aug. 3.

Total cost of 55 units available for sale (from Exhibit 5A.1)		$5,990
Less ending inventory priced using LIFO		
10 units in beginning inventory at $91 each	$910	
2 units from August 3 purchase at $106 each	212	
Ending inventory		1,122
Cost of goods sold		$4,868

Trekking's ending inventory reported on the balance sheet is **$1,122**, and its cost of goods sold reported on the income statement is **$4,868**. When LIFO is used with the periodic system, cost of goods sold is assigned costs from the most recent purchases for the period. With a perpetual system, cost of goods sold is assigned costs from the most recent purchases at the point of *each sale*. The purchases and sales entries for Exhibit 5A.4 follow (the colored boldface numbers are those affected by the cost flow assumption).

Purchases		Sales	
Aug. 3 Purchases 1,590		Aug. 14 Accounts Receivable 2,600	
Accounts Payable	1,590	Sales	2,600
17 Purchases 2,300		31 Accounts Receivable 3,450	
Accounts Payable	2,300	Sales	3,450
28 Purchases 1,190		**Adjusting Entry**	
Accounts Payable	1,190	31 Merchandise Inventory **1,122**	
		Income Summary	212
		Merchandise Inventory	**910**

Weighted Average The **weighted average** or **WA** (also called **average cost**) method of assigning cost requires that we use the average cost per unit of inventory at the end of the period. Weighted average cost per unit equals the cost of goods available for sale divided by the units available. The weighted average method of assigning cost involves three important steps. The first two steps are shown in Exhibit 5A.5. First, multiply the per unit cost for beginning inventory and each particular purchase by the corresponding number of units (from Exhibit 5A.1). Second, add these amounts and divide by the total number of units available for sale to find the weighted average cost per unit.

Step 1:
- 10 units @ $ 91 = $ 910
- 15 units @ $106 = 1,590
- 20 units @ $115 = 2,300
- 10 units @ $119 = 1,190
- 55 $5,990

Step 2: $5,990/55 units = **$108.91** weighted average cost per unit

EXHIBIT 5A.5
Weighted Average Cost per Unit

Example: In Exhibit 5A.5, if 5 more units had been purchased at $120 each, what would be the weighted average cost per unit?
Answer: $109.83 ($6,590/60)

The third step is to use the weighted average cost per unit to assign costs to inventory and to the units sold as shown in Exhibit 5A.6.

Step 3:	Total cost of 55 units available for sale (from Exhibit 5A.1)	$ 5,990
	Less **ending inventory** priced on a weighted average cost basis: 12 units at $108.91 each (from Exhibit 5A.5)	1,307
	Cost of goods sold	**$4,683**

EXHIBIT 5A.6
Weighted Average Computations—Periodic

Trekking's ending inventory reported on the balance sheet is **$1,307**, and its cost of goods sold reported on the income statement is **$4,683** when using the weighted average (periodic) method. The purchases and sales entries for Exhibit 5A.6 follow (the colored boldface numbers are those affected by the cost flow assumption).

Purchases		Sales	
Aug. 3 Purchases 1,590		Aug. 14 Accounts Receivable 2,600	
Accounts Payable	1,590	Sales	2,600
17 Purchases 2,300		31 Accounts Receivable 3,450	
Accounts Payable	2,300	Sales	3,450
28 Purchases 1,190		**Adjusting Entry**	
Accounts Payable	1,190	31 Merchandise Inventory **1,307**	
		Income Summary	397
		Merchandise Inventory	**910**

Point: Weighted average usually yields different results for the perpetual and the periodic systems because under a perpetual system it recomputes the per unit cost prior to each sale, whereas under a periodic system, the per unit cost is computed only at the end of a period.

Point: LIFO inventory is often less than the inventory's replacement cost because LIFO inventory is valued using the oldest inventory purchase costs.

Financial Statement Effects When purchase prices do not change, each inventory costing method assigns the same cost amounts to inventory and to cost of goods sold. When purchase prices are different, however, the methods nearly always assign different cost amounts. We show these differences in Exhibit 5A.7 using Trekking's data.

EXHIBIT 5A.7

Financial Statement Effects of Inventory Costing Methods

TREKKING COMPANY
For Month Ended August 31

	Specific Identification	FIFO	LIFO	Weighted Average
Income Statement				
Sales	$ 6,050	$ 6,050	$ 6,050	$ 6,050
Cost of goods sold	4,582	4,570	4,868	4,683
Gross profit	1,468	1,480	1,182	1,367
Expenses	450	450	450	450
Income before taxes	1,018	1,030	732	917
Income tax expense (30%)	305	309	220	275
Net income	$ 713	$ 721	$ 512	$ 642
Balance Sheet				
Inventory	$1,408	$1,420	$1,122	$1,307

This exhibit reveals two important results. First, when purchase costs *regularly rise,* as in Trekking's case, observe the following:

- FIFO assigns the lowest amount to cost of goods sold—yielding the highest gross profit and net income.
- LIFO assigns the highest amount to cost of goods sold—yielding the lowest gross profit and net income, which also yields a temporary tax advantage by postponing payment of some income tax.
- Weighted average yields results between FIFO and LIFO.
- Specific identification always yields results that depend on which units are sold.

Second, when costs *regularly decline,* the reverse occurs for FIFO and LIFO. FIFO gives the highest cost of goods sold—yielding the lowest gross profit and income. And LIFO gives the lowest cost of goods sold—yielding the highest gross profit and income.

All four inventory costing methods are acceptable in practice. A company must disclose the inventory method it uses. Each method offers certain advantages as follows:

- FIFO assigns an amount to inventory on the balance sheet that approximates its current cost; it also mimics the actual flow of goods for most businesses.
- LIFO assigns an amount to cost of goods sold on the income statement that approximates its current cost; it also better matches current costs with revenues in computing gross profit.
- Weighted average tends to smooth out erratic changes in costs.
- Specific identification exactly matches the costs of items with the revenues they generate.

Quick Check

Answers — p. 231

9. A company reports the following beginning inventory and purchases, and it ends the period with 30 units in inventory.

Beginning inventory	100 units at $10 cost per unit
Purchase 1	40 units at $12 cost per unit
Purchase 2	20 units at $14 cost per unit

a. Compute ending inventory using the FIFO periodic system.
b. Compute cost of goods sold using the LIFO periodic system.

APPENDIX 5B

Inventory Estimation Methods

Inventory sometimes requires estimation for two reasons. First, companies often require **interim statements** (financial statements prepared for periods of less than one year), but they only annually take a physical count of inventory. Second, companies may require an inventory estimate if some casualty such as fire or flood makes taking a physical count impossible. Estimates are usually only required for companies that use the periodic system. Companies using a perpetual system would presumably have updated inventory data.

This appendix describes two methods to estimate inventory.

P4 Apply both the retail inventory and gross profit methods to estimate inventory.

Retail Inventory Method To avoid the time-consuming and expensive process of taking a physical inventory each month or quarter, some companies use the **retail inventory method** to estimate cost of goods sold and ending inventory. Some companies even use the retail inventory method to prepare the annual statements. **Home Depot**, for instance, says in its annual report: "Inventories are stated at the lower of cost (first-in, first-out) or market, as determined by the retail inventory method." A company may also estimate inventory for audit purposes or when inventory is damaged or destroyed.

The retail inventory method uses a three-step process to estimate ending inventory. We need to know the amount of inventory a company had at the beginning of the period in both *cost* and *retail* amounts. We already explained how to compute the cost of inventory. The *retail amount of inventory* refers to its dollar amount measured using selling prices of inventory items. We also need to know the net amount of goods purchased (minus returns, allowances, and discounts) in the period, both at cost and at retail. The amount of net sales at retail is also needed. The process is shown in Exhibit 5B.1.

Point: When a retailer takes a physical inventory, it can restate the retail value of inventory to a cost basis by applying the cost-to-retail ratio. It can also estimate the amount of shrinkage by comparing the inventory computed with the amount from a physical inventory.

Step 1: Goods available for sale at retail − Net sales at retail = Ending inventory at retail

Step 2: Goods available for sale at cost ÷ Goods available for sale at retail = Cost-to-retail ratio

Step 3: Ending inventory at retail × Cost-to-retail ratio = Estimated ending inventory at cost

EXHIBIT 5B.1
Retail Inventory Method of Inventory Estimation

The reasoning behind the retail inventory method is that if we can get a good estimate of the cost-to-retail ratio, we can multiply ending inventory at retail by this ratio to estimate ending inventory at cost. We show in Exhibit 5B.2 how these steps are applied to estimate ending inventory for a typical company. First, we find that $100,000 of goods (at retail selling prices) were available for sale. We see that $70,000 of these goods were sold, leaving $30,000 (retail value) of merchandise in ending inventory. Second, the cost of these goods is 60% of the $100,000 retail value. Third, since cost for these goods is 60% of retail, the estimated cost of ending inventory is $18,000.

Example: What is the cost of ending inventory in Exhibit 5B.2 if the cost of beginning inventory is $22,500 and its retail value is $34,500? *Answer:* $30,000 × 62% = $18,600

EXHIBIT 5B.2
Estimated Inventory Using the Retail Inventory Method

	At Cost	At Retail
Goods available for sale		
Beginning inventory	$ 20,500	$ 34,500
Cost of goods purchased	39,500	65,500
Goods available for sale	60,000	100,000
Step 1: Deduct net sales at retail		70,000
Ending inventory at retail		$ 30,000
Step 2: Cost-to-retail ratio: ($60,000 ÷ $100,000) = 60%		
Step 3: Estimated ending inventory at cost ($30,000 × 60%)	$18,000	

Gross Profit Method

The **gross profit method** estimates the cost of ending inventory by applying the gross profit ratio to net sales (at retail). This type of estimate often is needed when inventory is destroyed, lost, or stolen. These cases require an inventory estimate so that a company can file a claim with its insurer. Users also apply this method to see whether inventory amounts from a physical count are reasonable. This method uses the historical relation between cost of goods sold and net sales to estimate the proportion of cost of goods sold making up current sales. This cost of goods sold estimate is then subtracted from cost of goods available for sale to estimate the ending inventory at cost. These two steps are shown in Exhibit 5B.3.

EXHIBIT 5B.3
Gross Profit Method of Inventory Estimation

Step 1: Net sales at retail × (1.0 − gross profit ratio) = Estimated cost of goods sold

Step 2: Goods available for sale at cost − Estimated cost of goods sold = Estimated ending inventory at cost

Point: A fire or other catastrophe can result in an insurance claim for lost inventory or income. Backup and off-site storage of data help ensure coverage for such losses.

Point: Reliability of the gross profit method depends on a good estimate of the gross profit ratio.

To illustrate, assume that a company's inventory is destroyed by fire in March 2011. When the fire occurs, the company's accounts show the following balances for January through March: sales, $31,500; sales returns, $1,500; inventory (January 1, 2011), $12,000; and cost of goods purchased, $20,500. If this company's gross profit ratio is 30%, then 30% of each net sales dollar is gross profit and 70% is cost of goods sold. We show in Exhibit 5B.4 how this 70% is used to estimate lost inventory of $11,500. To understand this exhibit, think of subtracting the cost of goods sold from the goods available for sale to get the ending inventory.

EXHIBIT 5B.4
Estimated Inventory Using the Gross Profit Method

Goods available for sale		
Inventory, January 1, 2011		$12,000
Cost of goods purchased		20,500
Goods available for sale (at cost)		32,500
Net sales at retail ($31,500 − $1,500)		$30,000
Step 1: Estimated cost of goods sold ($30,000 × 70%)		(21,000) ← × 0.70
Step 2: Estimated March inventory at cost		$11,500

Quick Check
Answer — p. 231

10. Using the retail method and the following data, estimate the cost of ending inventory.

	Cost	Retail
Beginning inventory	$324,000	$530,000
Cost of goods purchased	195,000	335,000
Net sales		320,000

Summary

C1 Identify the items making up merchandise inventory. Merchandise inventory refers to goods owned by a company and held for resale. Three special cases merit our attention. Goods in transit are reported in inventory of the company that holds ownership rights. Goods on consignment are reported in the consignor's inventory. Goods damaged or obsolete are reported in inventory at their net realizable value.

C2 Identify the costs of merchandise inventory. Costs of merchandise inventory include expenditures necessary to bring an item to a salable condition and location. This includes its invoice cost minus any discount plus any added or incidental costs necessary to put it in a place and condition for sale.

A1 Analyze the effects of inventory methods for both financial and tax reporting. When purchase costs are rising or falling, the inventory costing methods are likely to assign different costs to inventory. Specific identification exactly matches costs and revenues. Weighted average smooths out cost changes. FIFO assigns an amount to inventory closely approximating current replacement cost. LIFO assigns the most recent costs incurred to cost of goods sold and likely better matches current costs with revenues.

A2 **Analyze the effects of inventory errors on current and future financial statements.** An error in the amount of ending inventory affects assets (inventory), net income (cost of goods sold), and equity for that period. Since ending inventory is next period's beginning inventory, an error in ending inventory affects next period's cost of goods sold and net income. Inventory errors in one period are offset in the next period.

A3 **Assess inventory management using both inventory turnover and days' sales in inventory.** We prefer a high inventory turnover, provided that goods are not out of stock and customers are not turned away. We use days' sales in inventory to assess the likelihood of goods being out of stock. We prefer a small number of days' sales in inventory if we can serve customer needs and provide a buffer for uncertainties.

P1 **Compute inventory in a perpetual system using the methods of specific identification, FIFO, LIFO, and weighted average.** Costs are assigned to the cost of goods sold account *each time* a sale occurs in a perpetual system. Specific identification assigns a cost to each item sold by referring to its actual cost (for example, its net invoice cost). Weighted average assigns a cost to items sold by dividing the current balance in the inventory account by the total items available for sale to determine cost per unit. We then multiply the number of units sold by this cost per unit to get the cost of each sale. FIFO assigns cost to items sold assuming that the earliest units purchased are the first units sold. LIFO assigns cost to items sold assuming that the most recent units purchased are the first units sold.

P2 **Compute the lower of cost or market amount of inventory.** Inventory is reported at market cost when market is *lower* than recorded cost, called the *lower of cost or market (LCM) inventory*. Market is typically measured as replacement cost. Lower of cost or market can be applied separately to each item, to major categories of items, or to the entire inventory.

P3^A **Compute inventory in a periodic system using the methods of specific identification, FIFO, LIFO, and weighted average.** Periodic inventory systems allocate the cost of goods available for sale between cost of goods sold and ending inventory *at the end of a period*. Specific identification and FIFO give identical results whether the periodic or perpetual system is used. LIFO assigns costs to cost of goods sold assuming the last units purchased for the period are the first units sold. The weighted average cost per unit is computed by dividing the total cost of beginning inventory and net purchases for the period by the total number of units available. Then, it multiplies cost per unit by the number of units sold to give cost of goods sold.

P4^B **Apply both the retail inventory and gross profit methods to estimate inventory.** The retail inventory method involves three steps: (1) goods available at retail minus net sales at retail equals ending inventory at retail, (2) goods available at cost divided by goods available at retail equals the cost-to-retail ratio, and (3) ending inventory at retail multiplied by the cost-to-retail ratio equals estimated ending inventory at cost. The gross profit method involves two steps: (1) net sales at retail multiplied by 1 minus the gross profit ratio equals estimated cost of goods sold, and (2) goods available at cost minus estimated cost of goods sold equals estimated ending inventory at cost.

Guidance Answers to Decision Maker and Decision Ethics

Financial Planner The FIFO method implies that the oldest costs are the first ones assigned to cost of goods sold. This leaves the most recent costs in ending inventory. You report this to your client and note that in most cases, the ending inventory of a company using FIFO is reported at or near its replacement cost. This means that your client need not in most cases adjust the reported value of inventory. Your answer changes only if there are major increases in replacement cost compared to the cost of recent purchases reported in inventory. When major increases in costs occur, your client might wish to adjust inventory (for internal reports) for the difference between the reported cost of inventory and its replacement cost. (*Note:* Decreases in costs of purchases are recognized under the lower of cost or market adjustment.)

Inventory Manager It seems your company can save (or at least postpone) taxes by switching to LIFO, but the switch is likely to reduce bonus money that you think you have earned and deserve. Since the U.S. tax code requires companies that use LIFO for tax reporting also to use it for financial reporting, your options are further constrained. Your best decision is to tell your superior about the tax savings with LIFO. You also should discuss your bonus plan and how this is likely to hurt you unfairly. You might propose to compute inventory under the LIFO method for reporting purposes but use the FIFO method for your bonus calculations. Another solution is to revise the bonus plan to reflect the company's use of the LIFO method.

Entrepreneur Your inventory turnover is markedly higher than the norm, whereas days' sales in inventory approximates the norm. Since your turnover is already 14% better than average, you are probably best served by directing attention to days' sales in inventory. You should see whether you can reduce the level of inventory while maintaining service to customers. Given your higher turnover, you should be able to hold less inventory.

Guidance Answers to Quick Checks

1. The matching principle.
2. Target reports these goods in its inventory.
3. Total cost assigned to the painting is $12,180, computed as $11,400 + $130 + $150 + $100 + $400.
4. Specific identification exactly matches costs and revenues. Weighted average tends to smooth out cost changes. FIFO assigns an amount to inventory that closely approximates current replacement cost. LIFO assigns the most recent costs incurred to cost of goods sold and likely better matches current costs with revenues.
5. FIFO—it gives a lower cost of goods sold, a higher gross profit, and a higher net income when costs are rising.

6. When costs are rising, LIFO gives a lower inventory figure on the balance sheet as compared to FIFO. FIFO's inventory amount approximates current replacement costs.
7. Cost of goods sold would be overstated by $10,000 in 2010 and understated by $10,000 in year 2011.
8. The reported LCM inventory amount (using items) is $540, computed as [(20 × $5) + (40 × $8) + (10 × $12)].
9.[A] a. FIFO periodic inventory = (20 × $14) + (10 × $12)
= $400
   b. LIFO periodic cost of goods sold
= (20 × $14) + (40 × $12) + (70 × $10)
= $1,460

10.[B] Estimated ending inventory (at cost) is $327,000. It is computed as follows:
Step 1: ($530,000 + $335,000) − $320,000 = $545,000
Step 2: $\frac{\$324,000 + \$195,000}{\$530,000 + \$335,000} = 60\%$
Step 3: $545,000 × 60\% = \underline{\$327,000}$

Key Terms

Average cost (p. 212)
Conservatism constraint (p. 216)
Consignee (p. 206)
Consignor (p. 206)
Consistency concept (p. 215)
Days' sales in inventory (p. 219)

First-in, first-out (FIFO) (p. 211)
Gross profit method (p. 230)
Interim statements (p. 229)
Inventory turnover (p. 219)
Last-in, first-out (LIFO) (p. 211)
Lower of cost or market (LCM) (p. 215)

Net realizable value (p. 206)
Retail inventory method (p. 229)
Specific identification (p. 209)
Weighted average (p. 212)

Multiple Choice Quiz

Answers on p. 247

mhhe.com/wildFA6e

Additional quiz questions are available at the book's Website.

Use the following information from Marvel Company for the month of July to answer questions 1 through 4.

July 1	Beginning inventory	75 units @ $25 each
July 3	Purchase	348 units @ $27 each
July 8	Sale	300 units
July 15	Purchase	257 units @ $28 each
July 23	Sale	275 units

1. Assume that Marvel uses a perpetual FIFO inventory system. What is the dollar value of its ending inventory?
   a. $2,940
   b. $2,685
   c. $2,625
   d. $2,852
   e. $2,705

2. Assume that Marvel uses a perpetual LIFO inventory system. What is the dollar value of its ending inventory?
   a. $2,940
   b. $2,685
   c. $2,625
   d. $2,852
   e. $2,705

3. Assume that Marvel uses a perpetual specific identification inventory system. Its ending inventory consists of 20 units from beginning inventory, 40 units from the July 3 purchase, and 45 units from the July 15 purchase. What is the dollar value of its ending inventory?
   a. $2,940
   b. $2,685
   c. $2,625
   d. $2,852
   e. $2,840

4.[A] Assume that Marvel uses a *periodic* FIFO inventory system. What is the dollar value of its ending inventory?
   a. $2,940
   b. $2,685
   c. $2,625
   d. $2,852
   e. $2,705

5. A company has cost of goods sold of $85,000 and ending inventory of $18,000. Its days' sales in inventory equals:
   a. 49.32 days
   b. 0.21 days
   c. 4.72 days
   d. 77.29 days
   e. 1,723.61 days

[A(B)] *Superscript letter A (B) denotes assignments based on Appendix 5A (5B).*
Icon denotes assignments that involve decision making.

Discussion Questions

1. Describe how costs flow from inventory to cost of goods sold for the following methods: (*a*) FIFO and (*b*) LIFO.
2. Where is the amount of merchandise inventory disclosed in the financial statements?
3. Why are incidental costs sometimes ignored in inventory costing? Under what accounting constraint is this permitted?
4. If costs are declining, will the LIFO or FIFO method of inventory valuation yield the lower cost of goods sold? Why?

5. What does the full-disclosure principle prescribe if a company changes from one acceptable accounting method to another?
6. Can a company change its inventory method each accounting period? Explain.
7. Does the accounting concept of consistency preclude any changes from one accounting method to another?
8. If inventory errors are said to correct themselves, why are accounting users concerned when such errors are made?
9. Explain the following statement: "Inventory errors correct themselves."
10. What is the meaning of *market* as it is used in determining the lower of cost or market for inventory?
11. What guidance does the accounting constraint of conservatism offer?
12. What factors contribute to (or cause) inventory shrinkage?
13.^A What accounts are used in a periodic inventory system but not in a perpetual inventory system?
14. Refer to **Research In Motion**'s financial statements in Appendix A. On February 27, 2010, what percent of current assets are represented by inventory? **RIM**
15. Refer to **Apple**'s financial statements in Appendix A and compute its cost of goods available for sale for the year ended September 26, 2009. **Apple**
16. Refer to **Nokia**'s financial statements in Appendix A. Compute its cost of goods available for sale for the year ended December 31, 2009. **NOKIA**
17. Refer to **Palm**'s financial statements in Appendix A. What percent of its current assets are inventory as of May 31, 2008 and 2009? **Palm**
18.^B When preparing interim financial statements, what two methods can companies utilize to estimate cost of goods sold and ending inventory?

connect

A company reports the following beginning inventory and purchases for the month of January. On January 26, the company sells 360 units. What is the cost of the 155 units that remain in ending inventory at January 31, assuming costs are assigned based on a perpetual inventory system and use of FIFO? (Round per unit costs to three decimals, but inventory balances to the dollar.)

	Units	Unit Cost
Beginning inventory on January 1	320	$6.00
Purchase on January 9	85	6.40
Purchase on January 25	110	6.60

QUICK STUDY

QS 5-1
Inventory costing with FIFO perpetual
P1

Refer to the information in QS 5-1 and assume the perpetual inventory system is used. Determine the costs assigned to ending inventory when costs are assigned based on LIFO. (Round per unit costs to three decimals, but inventory balances to the dollar.)

QS 5-2
Inventory costing with LIFO perpetual P1

Refer to the information in QS 5-1 and assume the perpetual inventory system is used. Determine the costs assigned to ending inventory when costs are assigned based on weighted average. (Round per unit costs to three decimals, but inventory balances to the dollar.)

QS 5-3
Inventory costing with weighted average perpetual P1
Check $960

Segoe Company reports beginning inventory of 10 units at $50 each. Every week for four weeks it purchases an additional 10 units at respective costs of $51, $52, $55 and $60 per unit for weeks 1 through 4. Calculate the cost of goods available for sale and the units available for sale for this four-week period. Assume that no sales occur during those four weeks.

QS 5-4
Computing goods available for sale P1

Mercedes Brown starts a merchandising business on December 1 and enters into three inventory purchases:

December 7	10 units @ $ 9 cost
December 14	20 units @ $10 cost
December 21	15 units @ $12 cost

Brown sells 18 units for $35 each on December 15. Seven of the sold units are from the December 7 purchase and eleven are from the December 14 purchase. Brown uses a perpetual inventory system. Determine the costs assigned to the December 31 ending inventory based on FIFO. (Round per unit costs to three decimals, but inventory balances to the dollar.)

QS 5-5
Assigning costs with FIFO perpetual
P1

QS 5-6
Inventory costing with LIFO perpetual P1

Refer to the information in QS 5-5 and assume the perpetual inventory system is used. Determine the costs assigned to ending inventory when costs are assigned based on LIFO. (Round per unit costs to three decimals, but inventory balances to the dollar.)

QS 5-7
Inventory costing with weighted average perpetual P1

Check End. Inv. = $296

Refer to the information in QS 5-5 and assume the perpetual inventory system is used. Determine the costs assigned to ending inventory when costs are assigned based on weighted average. (Round per unit costs to three decimals, but inventory balances to the dollar.)

QS 5-8
Inventory costing with specific identification perpetual P1

Refer to the information in QS 5-5 and assume the perpetual inventory system is used. Determine the costs assigned to ending inventory when costs are assigned based on specific identification. (Round per unit costs to three decimals, but inventory balances to the dollar.)

QS 5-9
Contrasting inventory costing methods
A1

Identify the inventory costing method best described by each of the following separate statements. Assume a period of increasing costs.
1. The preferred method when each unit of product has unique features that markedly affect cost.
2. Matches recent costs against net sales.
3. Provides a tax advantage (deferral) to a corporation when costs are rising.
4. Yields a balance sheet inventory amount often markedly less than its replacement cost.
5. Results in a balance sheet inventory amount approximating replacement cost.

QS 5-10
Inventory ownership
C1

Crafts Galore, a distributor of handmade gifts, operates out of owner Jenny Finn's house. At the end of the current period, Jenny reports she has 1,500 units (products) in her basement, 30 of which were damaged by water and cannot be sold. She also has another 250 units in her van, ready to deliver per a customer order, terms FOB destination, and another 70 units out on consignment to a friend who owns a retail store. How many units should Jenny include in her company's period-end inventory?

QS 5-11
Inventory costs
C2

A car dealer acquires a used car for $3,000, terms FOB shipping point. Additional costs in obtaining and offering the car for sale include $150 for transportation-in, $200 for import duties, $50 for insurance during shipment, $25 for advertising, and $250 for sales staff salaries. For computing inventory, what cost is assigned to the used car?

QS 5-12
Applying LCM to inventories
P2

Tailspin Trading Co. has the following products in its ending inventory. Compute lower of cost or market for inventory applied separately to each product.

Product	Quantity	Cost per Unit	Market per Unit
Mountain bikes	9	$360	$330
Skateboards	12	210	270
Gliders	25	480	420

QS 5-13
Inventory errors
A2

In taking a physical inventory at the end of year 2011, Nadir Company forgot to count certain units. Explain how this error affects the following: (a) 2011 cost of goods sold, (b) 2011 gross profit, (c) 2011 net income, (d) 2012 net income, (e) the combined two-year income, and (f) income for years after 2012.

QS 5-14
Analyzing inventory A3

Market Company begins the year with $200,000 of goods in inventory. At year-end, the amount in inventory has increased to $230,000. Cost of goods sold for the year is $1,600,000. Compute Market's inventory turnover and days' sales in inventory. Assume that there are 365 days in the year.

QS 5-15ᴬ
Assigning costs with FIFO periodic P3

Refer to the information in QS 5-1 and assume the periodic inventory system is used. Determine the costs assigned to the ending inventory when costs are assigned based on FIFO. (Round per unit costs to three decimals, but inventory balances to the dollar.)

QS 5-16ᴬ Inventory costing with LIFO periodic P3

Refer to the information in QS 5-1 and assume the periodic inventory system is used. Determine the costs assigned to ending inventory when costs are assigned based on LIFO. (Round per unit costs to three decimals, but inventory balances to the dollar.)

QS 5-17ᴬ Inventory costing with weighted average periodic P3

Refer to the information in QS 5-1 and assume the periodic inventory system is used. Determine the costs assigned to ending inventory when costs are assigned based on weighted average. (Round per unit costs to three decimals, but inventory balances to the dollar.)

QS 5-18ᴬ Inventory costing with FIFO periodic P3

Refer to the information in QS 5-5 and assume the periodic inventory system is used. Determine the costs assigned to the December 31 ending inventory when costs are assigned based on FIFO. (Round per unit costs to three decimals, but inventory balances to the dollar.)

QS 5-19ᴬ Inventory costing with LIFO periodic P3

Refer to the information in QS 5-5 and assume the periodic inventory system is used. Determine the costs assigned to ending inventory when costs are assigned based on LIFO. (Round per unit costs to three decimals, but inventory balances to the dollar.)

QS 5-20ᴬ Inventory costing with weighted average periodic P3

Refer to the information in QS 5-5 and assume the periodic inventory system is used. Determine the costs assigned to ending inventory when costs are assigned based on weighted average. (Round per unit costs to three decimals, but inventory balances to the dollar.)

QS 5-21ᴬ Inventory costing with specific identification periodic P3

Refer to the information in QS 5-5 and assume the periodic inventory system is used. Determine the costs assigned to ending inventory when costs are assigned based on specific identification. (Round per unit costs to three decimals, but inventory balances to the dollar.)

QS 5-22ᴮ Estimating inventories—gross profit method P4

Dooling Store's inventory is destroyed by a fire on September 5, 2011. The following data for year 2011 are available from the accounting records. Estimate the cost of the inventory destroyed.

Jan. 1 inventory	$180,000
Jan. 1 through Sept. 5 purchases (net)	$342,000
Jan. 1 through Sept. 5 sales (net)	$675,000
Year 2011 estimated gross profit rate	42%

QS 5-23 International accounting standards C1 C2 P2

Answer each of the following questions related to international accounting standards.
a. Explain how the accounting for items and costs making up merchandise inventory is different between IFRS and U.S. GAAP.
b. Can companies reporting under IFRS apply a cost flow assumption in assigning costs to inventory? If yes, identify at least two acceptable cost flow assumptions.
c. Both IFRS and U.S. GAAP apply the lower of cost or market method for reporting inventory values. If inventory is written down from applying the lower of cost or market method, explain in general terms how IFRS and U.S. GAAP differ in accounting for any subsequent period reversal of that reported decline in inventory value.

EXERCISES

Exercise 5-1 Inventory ownership C1

1. Jolie Company has shipped $500 of goods to China Co., and China Co. has arranged to sell the goods for Jolie. Identify the consignor and the consignee. Which company should include any unsold goods as part of its inventory?
2. At year-end, Jolie Co. had shipped $850 of merchandise FOB destination to China Co. Which company should include the $850 of merchandise in transit as part of its year-end inventory?

Exercise 5-2 Inventory costs C2

Duke Associates, antique dealers, purchased the contents of an estate for $37,500. Terms of the purchase were FOB shipping point, and the cost of transporting the goods to Duke Associates' warehouse was $1,200. Duke Associates insured the shipment at a cost of $150. Prior to putting the goods up for sale, they cleaned and refurbished them at a cost of $490. Determine the cost of the inventory acquired from the estate.

Exercise 5-3
Inventory costing methods—perpetual
P1

Park Company reported the following March purchases and sales data for its only product.

Date	Activities	Units Acquired at Cost	Units Sold at Retail
Mar. 1	Beginning inventory	150 units @ $7.00 = $1,050	
Mar. 10	Sales		90 units @ $15
Mar. 20	Purchase	220 units @ $6.00 = 1,320	
Mar. 25	Sales		145 units @ $15
Mar. 30	Purchase	90 units @ $5.00 = 450	
	Totals	460 units $2,820	235 units

Park uses a perpetual inventory system. Determine the cost assigned to ending inventory and to cost of goods sold using (a) specific identification, (b) weighted average, (c) FIFO, and (d) LIFO. (Round per unit costs to three decimals, but inventory balances to the dollar.) For specific identification, ending inventory consists of 225 units, where 90 are from the March 30 purchase, 80 are from the March 20 purchase, and 55 are from beginning inventory.

Check Ending inventory: LIFO, $1,320; WA, $1,289

Exercise 5-4
Income effects of inventory methods
A1

Use the data in Exercise 5-3 to prepare comparative income statements for the month of January for Park Company similar to those shown in Exhibit 5.8 for the four inventory methods. Assume expenses are $1,600, and that the applicable income tax rate is 30%.

1. Which method yields the highest net income?
2. Does net income using weighted average fall between that using FIFO and LIFO?
3. If costs were rising instead of falling, which method would yield the highest net income?

Exercise 5-5
Inventory costing methods (perpetual)—FIFO and LIFO
P1

Harold Co. reported the following current-year purchases and sales data for its only product.

Date	Activities	Units Acquired at Cost	Units Sold at Retail
Jan. 1	Beginning inventory	100 units @ $10 = $ 1,000	
Jan. 10	Sales		90 units @ $40
Mar. 14	Purchase	250 units @ $15 = 3,750	
Mar. 15	Sales		140 units @ $40
July 30	Purchase	400 units @ $20 = 8,000	
Oct. 5	Sales		300 units @ $40
Oct. 26	Purchase	600 units @ $25 = 15,000	
	Totals	1,350 units $27,750	530 units

Check Ending inventory: LIFO, $18,750

Harold uses a perpetual inventory system. Determine the costs assigned to ending inventory and to cost of goods sold using (a) FIFO and (b) LIFO. Compute the gross margin for each method.

Exercise 5-6
Specific identification P1

Refer to the data in Exercise 5-5. Assume that ending inventory is made up of 100 units from the March 14 purchase, 120 units from the July 30 purchase, and all 600 units from the October 26 purchase. Using the specific identification method, calculate (a) the cost of goods sold and (b) the gross profit.

Exercise 5-7
Lower of cost or market
P2

Ripken Company's ending inventory includes the following items. Compute the lower of cost or market for ending inventory applied separately to each product.

		Per Unit	
Product	Units	Cost	Market
Helmets	22	$50	$54
Bats	15	78	72
Shoes	36	95	91
Uniforms	40	36	36

Check LCM = $6,896

Exercise 5-8
Analysis of inventory errors
A2

Ringo Company had $900,000 of sales in each of three consecutive years 2010–2012, and it purchased merchandise costing $500,000 in each of those years. It also maintained a $200,000 physical inventory from the beginning to the end of that three-year period. In accounting for inventory, it made an error at the end of year 2010 that caused its year-end 2010 inventory to appear on its statements as $180,000 rather than the correct $200,000.

1. Determine the correct amount of the company's gross profit in each of the years 2010–2012.
2. Prepare comparative income statements as in Exhibit 5.11 to show the effect of this error on the company's cost of goods sold and gross profit for each of the years 2010–2012.

Check 2010 reported gross profit, $380,000

Exercise 5-9
Comparing LIFO numbers to FIFO numbers; ratio analysis
A1 A3

Chess Company uses LIFO for inventory costing and reports the following financial data. It also recomputed inventory and cost of goods sold using FIFO for comparison purposes.

	2011	2010
LIFO inventory	$150	$100
LIFO cost of goods sold	730	670
FIFO inventory	220	125
FIFO cost of goods sold	685	—
Current assets (using LIFO)	210	180
Current liabilities	190	170

1. Compute its current ratio, inventory turnover, and days' sales in inventory for 2011 using (a) LIFO numbers and (b) FIFO numbers. (Round answers to one decimal.)
2. Comment on and interpret the results of part 1.

Check (1) FIFO: Current ratio, 1.5; Inventory turnover, 4.0 times

---

Exercise 5-10
Inventory turnover and days' sales in inventory
A3

Use the following information for Ryder Co. to compute inventory turnover for 2011 and 2010, and its days' sales in inventory at December 31, 2011 and 2010. (Round answers to one decimal.) Comment on Ryder's efficiency in using its assets to increase sales from 2010 to 2011.

	2011	2010	2009
Cost of goods sold	$643,825	$426,650	$391,300
Ending inventory	96,400	86,750	91,500

Exercise 5-11^A
Inventory costing—periodic system P3

Refer to Exercise 5-3 and assume the periodic inventory system is used. Determine the costs assigned to ending inventory and to cost of goods sold using (a) specific identification, (b) weighted average, (c) FIFO, and (d) LIFO. (Round per unit costs to three decimals, but inventory balances to the dollar.)

Exercise 5-12^A
Inventory costing—periodic system P3

Refer to Exercise 5-5 and assume the periodic inventory system is used. Determine the costs assigned to ending inventory and to cost of goods sold using (a) FIFO and (b) LIFO. Then (c) compute the gross margin for each method.

Exercise 5-13^A
Alternative cost flow assumptions—periodic
P3

Lopez Co. reported the following current-year data for its only product. The company uses a periodic inventory system, and its ending inventory consists of 300 units—100 from each of the last three purchases. Determine the cost assigned to ending inventory and to cost of goods sold using (a) specific identification, (b) weighted average, (c) FIFO, and (d) LIFO. (Round per unit costs to three decimals, but inventory balances to the dollar.) Which method yields the highest net income?

Jan. 1	Beginning inventory	200 units @ $2.00 =	$ 400
Mar. 7	Purchase	440 units @ $2.25 =	990
July 28	Purchase	1080 units @ $2.50 =	2,700
Oct. 3	Purchase	960 units @ $2.80 =	2,688
Dec. 19	Purchase	320 units @ $2.90 =	928
	Totals	3,000 units	$7,706

Check Inventory; LIFO, $625; FIFO, $870

Exercise 5-14[A]
Alternative cost flow assumptions—periodic
P3

Candis Gifts reported the following current-year data for its only product. The company uses a periodic inventory system, and its ending inventory consists of 300 units—100 from each of the last three purchases. Determine the cost assigned to ending inventory and to cost of goods sold using (*a*) specific identification, (*b*) weighted average, (*c*) FIFO, and (*d*) LIFO. (Round per unit costs to three decimals, but inventory balances to the dollar.) Which method yields the lowest net income?

Jan. 1	Beginning inventory	280 units @ $3.00 =	$ 840
Mar. 7	Purchase	600 units @ $2.80 =	1,680
July 28	Purchase	800 units @ $2.50 =	2,000
Oct. 3	Purchase	1,100 units @ $2.30 =	2,530
Dec. 19	Purchase	250 units @ $2.00 =	500
	Totals	3,030 units	$7,550

Check Inventory: LIFO, $896; FIFO, $615

Exercise 5-15[B]
Estimating ending inventory—retail method
P4

In 2011, Wichita Company had net sales (at retail) of $130,000. The following additional information is available from its records at the end of 2011. Use the retail inventory method to estimate Wichita's 2011 ending inventory at cost.

	At Cost	At Retail
Beginning inventory	$ 31,900	$64,200
Cost of goods purchased	57,810	98,400

Check End. Inventory, $17,930

Exercise 5-16[B]
Estimating ending inventory—gross profit method
P4

On March 1, KB Shop had $450,000 of inventory at cost. In the first quarter of the year, it purchased $1,590,000 of merchandise, returned $23,100, and paid freight charges of $37,600 on purchased merchandise, terms FOB shipping point. The company's gross profit averages 30%, and the store had $2,000,000 of net sales (at retail) in the first quarter of the year. Use the gross profit method to estimate its cost of inventory at the end of the first quarter.

Exercise 5-17
Accounting for inventory following IFRS
P2

Samsung Electronics reports the following regarding its accounting for inventories.

> Inventories are stated at the lower of cost or net realizable value. Cost is determined using the average cost method, except for materials-in-transit which are stated at actual cost as determined using the specific identification method. Losses on valuation of inventories and losses on inventory obsolescence are recorded as part of cost of sales. As of December 31, 2008, losses on valuation of inventories amounted to ₩651,296 million (₩ is Korean won).

1. What cost flow assumption(s) does Samsung apply in assigning costs to its inventories?
2. What has Samsung recorded for 2008 as a write-down on valuation of its inventories?
3. If at year-end 2009 there was an increase in the value of its inventories such that there was a reversal of ₩900 million for the 2008 write-down, how would Samsung account for this under IFRS? Would Samsung's accounting be different for this reversal if it reported under U.S. GAAP? Explain.

PROBLEM SET A

Problem 5-1A
Alternative cost flows—perpetual
P1

Anthony Company uses a perpetual inventory system. It entered into the following purchases and sales transactions for March.

Date	Activities	Units Acquired at Cost	Units Sold at Retail
Mar. 1	Beginning inventory	50 units @ $50/unit	
Mar. 5	Purchase	200 units @ $55/unit	
Mar. 9	Sales		210 units @ $85/unit
Mar. 18	Purchase	60 units @ $60/unit	
Mar. 25	Purchase	100 units @ $62/unit	
Mar. 29	Sales		80 units @ $95/unit
	Totals	410 units	290 units

Required

1. Compute cost of goods available for sale and the number of units available for sale.
2. Compute the number of units in ending inventory.
3. Compute the cost assigned to ending inventory using (*a*) FIFO, (*b*) LIFO, (*c*) weighted average, and (*d*) specific identification. (Round per unit costs to three decimals, but inventory balances to the dollar.) For specific identification, the March 9 sale consisted of 40 units from beginning inventory and 170 units from the March 5 purchase; the March 29 sale consisted of 20 units from the March 18 purchase and 60 units from the March 25 purchase.
4. Compute gross profit earned by the company for each of the four costing methods in part 3.

Check (3) Ending Inventory: FIFO, $7,400; LIFO, $6,840; WA, $7,176

(4) LIFO gross profit, $8,990

Problem 5-2A
Alternative cost flows—perpetual

P1

Marlow Company uses a perpetual inventory system. It entered into the following calendar-year 2011 purchases and sales transactions.

Date	Activities	Units Acquired at Cost	Units Sold at Retail
Jan. 1	Beginning inventory	600 units @ $44/unit	
Feb. 10	Purchase	200 units @ $40/unit	
Mar. 13	Purchase	100 units @ $20/unit	
Mar. 15	Sales		400 units @ $75/unit
Aug. 21	Purchase	160 units @ $60/unit	
Sept. 5	Purchase	280 units @ $48/unit	
Sept. 10	Sales		200 units @ $75/unit
	Totals	1,340 units	600 units

Required

1. Compute cost of goods available for sale and the number of units available for sale.
2. Compute the number of units in ending inventory.
3. Compute the cost assigned to ending inventory using (*a*) FIFO, (*b*) LIFO, (*c*) specific identification—units sold consist of 500 units from beginning inventory and 100 units from the March 13 purchase, and (*d*) weighted average. (Round per unit costs to three decimals, but inventory balances to the dollar.)
4. Compute gross profit earned by the company for each of the four costing methods in part 3.

Check (3) Ending inventory: FIFO, $33,040; LIFO, $35,440; WA, $34,055;

(4) LIFO gross profit, $21,000

Analysis Component

5. If the company's manager earns a bonus based on a percent of gross profit, which method of inventory costing will the manager likely prefer?

A physical inventory of Helmke Company taken at December 31 reveals the following.

Problem 5-3A
Lower of cost or market

P2

			Per Unit	
Item		Units	Cost	Market
Audio equipment				
Receivers		335	$ 90	$ 98
CD players		250	111	100
MP3 players		316	86	95
Speakers		194	52	41
Video equipment				
Handheld LCDs		470	150	125
VCRs		281	93	84
Camcorders		202	310	322
Car audio equipment				
Satellite radios		175	70	84
CD/MP3 radios		160	97	105

Required

1. Calculate the lower of cost or market for the inventory applied separately to each item.
2. If the market amount is less than the recorded cost of the inventory, then record the LCM adjustment to the Merchandise Inventory account.

Check $263,024

Problem 5-4A
Analysis of inventory errors
A2

mhhe.com/wildFA6e

Doubletree Company's financial statements show the following. The company recently discovered that in making physical counts of inventory, it had made the following errors: Inventory on December 31, 2010, is understated by $50,000, and inventory on December 31, 2011, is overstated by $20,000.

For Year Ended December 31	2010	2011	2012
(a) Cost of goods sold	$ 725,000	$ 955,000	$ 790,000
(b) Net income	268,000	275,000	250,000
(c) Total current assets	1,247,000	1,360,000	1,230,000
(d) Total equity	1,387,000	1,580,000	1,245,000

Required

1. For each key financial statement figure—(a), (b), (c), and (d) above—prepare a table similar to the following to show the adjustments necessary to correct the reported amounts.

Figure:	2010	2011	2012
Reported amount			
Adjustments for: 12/31/2010 error			
12/31/2011 error			
Corrected amount			

Check (1) Corrected net income: 2010, $318,000; 2011, $205,000; 2012, $270,000

Analysis Component

2. What is the error in total net income for the combined three-year period resulting from the inventory errors? Explain.

3. Explain why the understatement of inventory by $50,000 at the end of 2010 results in an understatement of equity by the same amount in that year.

Problem 5-5A[A]
Alternative cost flows—periodic
P3

mhhe.com/wildFA6e

Viper Company began year 2011 with 20,000 units of product in its January 1 inventory costing $15 each. It made successive purchases of its product in year 2011 as follows. The company uses a periodic inventory system. On December 31, 2011, a physical count reveals that 35,000 units of its product remain in inventory.

Mar. 7	28,000 units @ $18 each
May 25	30,000 units @ $22 each
Aug. 1	20,000 units @ $24 each
Nov. 10	33,000 units @ $27 each

Required

1. Compute the number and total cost of the units available for sale in year 2011.

2. Compute the amounts assigned to the 2011 ending inventory and the cost of goods sold using (a) FIFO, (b) LIFO, and (c) weighted average. (Round per unit costs to three decimals, but inventory balances to the dollar.)

Check (2) Cost of goods sold: FIFO, $1,896,000; LIFO, $2,265,000; WA, $2,077,557

Problem 5-6A[A]
Income comparisons and cost flows—periodic
A1 P3

Botch Corp. sold 5,500 units of its product at $45 per unit in year 2011 and incurred operating expenses of $6 per unit in selling the units. It began the year with 600 units in inventory and made successive purchases of its product as follows.

Jan. 1	Beginning inventory	600 units @ $18 per unit
Feb. 20	Purchase	1,500 units @ $19 per unit
May 16	Purchase	700 units @ $20 per unit
Oct. 3	Purchase	400 units @ $21 per unit
Dec. 11	Purchase	3,300 units @ $22 per unit
	Total	6,500 units

Required

1. Prepare comparative income statements similar to Exhibit 5.8 for the three inventory costing methods of FIFO, LIFO, and weighted average. (Round per unit costs to three decimals, but inventory balances

Check (1) Net income: FIFO, $71,540; LIFO, $69,020; WA, $70,603

to the dollar.) Include a detailed cost of goods sold section as part of each statement. The company uses a periodic inventory system, and its income tax rate is 30%.

2. How would the financial results from using the three alternative inventory costing methods change if Botch had been experiencing declining costs in its purchases of inventory?

3. What advantages and disadvantages are offered by using (*a*) LIFO and (*b*) FIFO? Assume the continuing trend of increasing costs.

Problem 5-7A[B]
Retail inventory method
P4

The records of Nilson Company provide the following information for the year ended December 31.

	At Cost	At Retail
January 1 beginning inventory	$ 471,350	$ 927,150
Cost of goods purchased	3,276,030	6,279,350
Sales		5,495,700
Sales returns		44,600

Required

1. Use the retail inventory method to estimate the company's year-end inventory at cost.
2. A year-end physical inventory at retail prices yields a total inventory of $1,675,800. Prepare a calculation showing the company's loss from shrinkage at cost and at retail.

Check (1) Inventory, $912,808 cost;
(2) Inventory shortage at cost, $41,392

Wayman Company wants to prepare interim financial statements for the first quarter. The company wishes to avoid making a physical count of inventory. Wayman's gross profit rate averages 35%. The following information for the first quarter is available from its records.

Problem 5-8A[B]
Gross profit method
P4

January 1 beginning inventory	$ 300,260
Cost of goods purchased	939,050
Sales	1,191,150
Sales returns	9,450

Required

Use the gross profit method to estimate the company's first quarter ending inventory.

Check Estimated ending inventory, $471,205

CCO Company uses a perpetual inventory system. It entered into the following purchases and sales transactions for April.

PROBLEM SET B

Problem 5-1B
Alternative cost flows—perpetual
P1

Date	Activities	Units Acquired at Cost	Units Sold at Retail
Apr. 1	Beginning inventory	15 units @ $3,000/unit	
Apr. 6	Purchase	35 units @ $3,500/unit	
Apr. 9	Sales		18 units @ $12,000/unit
Apr. 17	Purchase	8 units @ $4,500/unit	
Apr. 25	Purchase	10 units @ $4,580/unit	
Apr. 30	Sales		30 units @ $14,000/unit
	Total	68 units	48 units

Required

1. Compute cost of goods available for sale and the number of units available for sale.
2. Compute the number of units in ending inventory.
3. Compute the cost assigned to ending inventory using (*a*) FIFO, (*b*) LIFO, (*c*) weighted average, and (*d*) specific identification. (Round per unit costs to three decimals, but inventory balances to the dollar.) For specific identification, the April 9 sale consisted of 8 units from beginning inventory and 10 units from the April 6 purchase; the April 30 sale consisted of 20 units from the April 6 purchase and 10 units from the April 25 purchase.
4. Compute gross profit earned by the company for each of the four costing methods in part 3.

Check (3) Ending inventory: FIFO, $88,800; LIFO, $62,500; WA, $75,600

(4) LIFO gross profit, $449,200

Problem 5-2B
Alternative cost flows—perpetual
P1

Venus Company uses a perpetual inventory system. It entered into the following calendar-year 2011 purchases and sales transactions.

Date	Activities	Units Acquired at Cost	Units Sold at Retail
Jan. 1	Beginning inventory	600 units @ $55/unit	
Jan. 10	Purchase	450 units @ $56/unit	
Feb. 13	Purchase	200 units @ $57/unit	
Feb. 15	Sales		430 units @ $90/unit
July 21	Purchase	230 units @ $58/unit	
Aug. 5	Purchase	345 units @ $59/unit	
Aug. 10	Sales		335 units @ $90/unit
	Total	1,825 units	765 units

Required
1. Compute cost of goods available for sale and the number of units available for sale.
2. Compute the number of units in ending inventory.
3. Compute the cost assigned to ending inventory using (a) FIFO, (b) LIFO, (c) specific identification—units sold consist of 600 units from beginning inventory and 165 units from the February 13 purchase, and (d) weighted average. (Round per unit costs to three decimals, but inventory balances to the dollar.)
4. Compute gross profit earned by the company for each of the four costing methods in part 3.

Check (3) Ending inventory: FIFO, $61,055; LIFO, $59,250; WA, $60,293

(4) LIFO gross profit, $24,805

Analysis Component
5. If the company's manager earns a bonus based on a percent of gross profit, which method of inventory costing will the manager likely prefer?

Problem 5-3B
Lower of cost or market
P2

A physical inventory of Office Deals taken at December 31 reveals the following.

Item	Units	Cost (Per Unit)	Market (Per Unit)
Office furniture			
Desks	436	$261	$305
Credenzas	295	227	256
Chairs	587	49	43
Bookshelves	321	93	82
Filing cabinets			
Two-drawer	214	81	70
Four-drawer	398	135	122
Lateral	175	104	118
Office equipment			
Fax machines	430	168	200
Copiers	545	317	288
Telephones	352	125	117

Required

Check $584,444

1. Compute the lower of cost or market for the inventory applied separately to each item.
2. If the market amount is less than the recorded cost of the inventory, then record the LCM adjustment to the Merchandise Inventory account.

Problem 5-4B
Analysis of inventory errors
A2

Watson Company's financial statements show the following. The company recently discovered that in making physical counts of inventory, it had made the following errors: Inventory on December 31, 2010, is overstated by $70,000, and inventory on December 31, 2011, is understated by $55,000.

For Year Ended December 31	2010	2011	2012
(a) Cost of goods sold	$ 655,000	$ 957,000	$ 799,000
(b) Net income	225,000	277,000	244,000
(c) Total current assets	1,251,000	1,360,000	1,200,000
(d) Total equity	1,387,000	1,520,000	1,250,000

Required

1. For each key financial statement figure—(a), (b), (c), and (d) above—prepare a table similar to the following to show the adjustments necessary to correct the reported amounts.

Figure: _____	2010	2011	2012
Reported amount	____	____	____
Adjustments for: 12/31/2010 error	____	____	____
12/31/2011 error	____	____	____
Corrected amount	____	____	____

Check (1) Corrected net income: 2010, $155,000; 2011, $402,000; 2012, $189,000

Analysis Component

2. What is the error in total net income for the combined three-year period resulting from the inventory errors? Explain.

3. Explain why the overstatement of inventory by $70,000 at the end of 2010 results in an overstatement of equity by the same amount in that year.

Solaris Co. began year 2011 with 6,300 units of product in its January 1 inventory costing $35 each. It made successive purchases of its product in year 2011 as follows. The company uses a periodic inventory system. On December 31, 2011, a physical count reveals that 16,500 units of its product remain in inventory.

Problem 5-5B^A
Alternative cost flows—periodic
P3

Jan. 4	10,500 units @ $33 each
May 18	13,000 units @ $32 each
July 9	12,000 units @ $29 each
Nov. 21	15,500 units @ $26 each

Required

1. Compute the number and total cost of the units available for sale in year 2011.

2. Compute the amounts assigned to the 2011 ending inventory and the cost of goods sold using (a) FIFO, (b) LIFO, and (c) weighted average. (Round per unit costs to three decimals, but inventory balances to the dollar.)

Check (2) Cost of goods sold: FIFO, $1,302,000; LIFO, $1,176,900; WA, $1,234,681

Rikkers Company sold 2,500 units of its product at $98 per unit in year 2011 and incurred operating expenses of $14 per unit in selling the units. It began the year with 740 units in inventory and made successive purchases of its product as follows.

Problem 5-6B^A
Income comparisons and cost flows—periodic
A1 P3

Jan. 1	Beginning inventory	740 units @ $58 per unit
April 2	Purchase	700 units @ $59 per unit
June 14	Purchase	600 units @ $61 per unit
Aug. 29	Purchase	500 units @ $64 per unit
Nov. 18	Purchase	800 units @ $65 per unit
	Total	3,340 units

Required

1. Prepare comparative income statements similar to Exhibit 5.8 for the three inventory costing methods of FIFO, LIFO, and weighted average. (Round per unit costs to three decimals, but inventory balances to the dollar.) Include a detailed cost of goods sold section as part of each statement. The company uses a periodic inventory system, and its income tax rate is 25%.

2. How would the financial results from using the three alternative inventory costing methods change if the company had been experiencing decreasing prices in its purchases of inventory?

3. What advantages and disadvantages are offered by using (a) LIFO and (b) FIFO? Assume the continuing trend of increasing costs.

Check (1) Net income: LIFO, $40,500; FIFO, $44,805; WA, $42,519

The records of Saturn Co. provide the following information for the year ended December 31.

Problem 5-7B^B
Retail inventory method
P4

	At Cost	At Retail
January 1 beginning inventory	$ 81,670	$114,610
Cost of goods purchased	492,250	751,730
Sales		786,120
Sales returns		4,480

Check (1) Inventory, $55,902 cost; (2) Inventory shortage at cost, $4,059

Required

1. Use the retail inventory method to estimate the company's year-end inventory.
2. A year-end physical inventory at retail prices yields a total inventory of $78,550. Prepare a calculation showing the company's loss from shrinkage at cost and at retail.

Problem 5-8B
Gross profit method
P4

Ernst Equipment Co. wants to prepare interim financial statements for the first quarter. The company wishes to avoid making a physical count of inventory. Ernst's gross profit rate averages 30%. The following information for the first quarter is available from its records.

January 1 beginning inventory	$ 752,880
Cost of goods purchased	2,159,630
Sales	3,710,250
Sales returns	74,200

Check Estim. ending inventory, $367,275

Required

Use the gross profit method to estimate the company's first quarter ending inventory.

SERIAL PROBLEM
Business Solutions
P2 A3

(This serial problem began in Chapter 1 and continues through most of the book. If previous chapter segments were not completed, the serial problem can begin at this point.)

SP 5
Part A

Santana Rey of Business Solutions is evaluating her inventory to determine whether it must be adjusted based on lower of cost or market rules. Business Solutions has three different types of software in its inventory and the following information is available for each.

Inventory Items	Units	Per Unit Cost	Per Unit Market
Office productivity	3	$ 76	$ 74
Desktop publishing	2	103	100
Accounting	3	90	96

Required

1. Compute the lower of cost or market for ending inventory assuming Rey applies the lower of cost or market rule to inventory as a whole. Must Rey adjust the reported inventory value? Explain.
2. Assume that Rey had instead applied the lower of cost or market rule to each product in inventory. Under this assumption, must Rey adjust the reported inventory value? Explain.

Part B

Selected accounts and balances for the three months ended March 31, 2012, for Business Solutions follow.

January 1 beginning inventory	$ 0
Cost of goods sold	14,052
March 31 ending inventory	704

Required

1. Compute inventory turnover and days' sales in inventory for the three months ended March 31, 2012.
2. Assess the company's performance if competitors average 15 times for inventory turnover and 25 days for days' sales in inventory.

Beyond the Numbers

REPORTING IN ACTION
C2 A3
RIM

BTN 5-1 Refer to **Research In Motion**'s financial statements in Appendix A to answer the following.

Required

1. What amount of inventories did Research In Motion report as a current asset on February 27, 2010? On February 28, 2009?
2. Inventories represent what percent of total assets on February 27, 2010? On February 28, 2009?

3. Comment on the relative size of Research In Motion's inventories compared to its other types of assets.
4. What accounting method did Research In Motion use to compute inventory amounts on its balance sheet?
5. Compute inventory turnover for fiscal year ended February 27, 2010, and days' sales in inventory as of February 27, 2010.

Fast Forward

6. Access Research In Motion's financial statements for fiscal years ended after February 27, 2010, from its Website (RIM.com) or the SEC's EDGAR database (www.sec.gov). Answer questions 1 through 5 using the current RIM information and compare results to those prior years.

BTN 5-2 Comparative figures for **Research In Motion** and **Apple** follow.

COMPARATIVE ANALYSIS

A3

	Research In Motion			Apple		
($ millions)	Current Year	One Year Prior	Two Years Prior	Current Year	One Year Prior	Two Years Prior
Inventory............	$ 622	$ 682	$ 396	$ 455	$ 509	$ 346
Cost of sales.........	8,369	5,968	2,929	25,683	24,294	16,426

RIM

Apple

Required

1. Compute inventory turnover for each company for the most recent two years shown.
2. Compute days' sales in inventory for each company for the three years shown.
3. Comment on and interpret your findings from parts 1 and 2. Assume an industry average for inventory turnover of 10.

BTN 5-3 Golf Mart is a retail sports store carrying golf apparel and equipment. The store is at the end of its second year of operation and is struggling. A major problem is that its cost of inventory has continually increased in the past two years. In the first year of operations, the store assigned inventory costs using LIFO. A loan agreement the store has with its bank, its prime source of financing, requires the store to maintain a certain profit margin and current ratio. The store's owner is currently looking over Golf Mart's preliminary financial statements for its second year. The numbers are not favorable. The only way the store can meet the required financial ratios agreed on with the bank is to change from LIFO to FIFO. The store originally decided on LIFO because of its tax advantages. The owner recalculates ending inventory using FIFO and submits those numbers and statements to the loan officer at the bank for the required bank review. The owner thankfully reflects on the available latitude in choosing the inventory costing method.

ETHICS CHALLENGE

A1

Required

1. How does Golf Mart's use of FIFO improve its net profit margin and current ratio?
2. Is the action by Golf Mart's owner ethical? Explain.

BTN 5-4 You are a financial adviser with a client in the wholesale produce business that just completed its first year of operations. Due to weather conditions, the cost of acquiring produce to resell has escalated during the later part of this period. Your client, Raphaela Gonzalez, mentions that because her business sells perishable goods, she has striven to maintain a FIFO flow of goods. Although sales are good, the increasing cost of inventory has put the business in a tight cash position. Gonzalez has expressed concern regarding the ability of the business to meet income tax obligations.

COMMUNICATING IN PRACTICE

A1

Required

Prepare a memorandum that identifies, explains, and justifies the inventory method you recommend your client, Ms. Gonzalez, adopt.

BTN 5-5 Access the 2009 annual 10-K report for **Polaris Industries** (Ticker PII), filed on March 1, 2010, from the EDGAR filings at www.sec.gov.

TAKING IT TO THE NET

A3

Required

1. What products are manufactured by Polaris?
2. What inventory method does Polaris use? (*Hint:* See the Note 1 to its financial statements.)

Chapter 5 Reporting and Analyzing Inventories

3. Compute its gross margin and gross margin ratio for the 2009 calendar year. Comment on your computations—assume an industry average of 27% for the gross margin ratio.
4. Compute its inventory turnover and days' sales in inventory for the year ended December 31, 2009. Comment on your computations—assume an industry average of 5.9 for inventory turnover and 55 for days' sales in inventory.

TEAMWORK IN ACTION
A1 P1

BTN 5-6 Each team member has the responsibility to become an expert on an inventory method. This expertise will be used to facilitate teammates' understanding of the concepts relevant to that method.

1. Each learning team member should select an area for expertise by choosing one of the following inventory methods: specific identification, LIFO, FIFO, or weighted average.
2. Form expert teams made up of students who have selected the same area of expertise. The instructor will identify where each expert team will meet.
3. Using the following data, each expert team must collaborate to develop a presentation that illustrates the relevant concepts and procedures for its inventory method. Each team member must write the presentation in a format that can be shown to the learning team.

Point: Step 1 allows four choices or areas for expertise. Larger teams will have some duplication of choice, but the specific identification method should not be duplicated.

Data

The company uses a perpetual inventory system. It had the following beginning inventory and current year purchases of its product.

Jan. 1	Beginning inventory.........	50 units @ $10 = $ 500
Jan. 14	Purchase	150 units @ $12 = 1,800
Apr. 30	Purchase	200 units @ $15 = 3,000
Sept. 26	Purchase	300 units @ $20 = 6,000

The company transacted sales on the following dates at a $35 per unit sales price.

Jan. 10	30 units	(specific cost: 30 @ $10)
Feb. 15	100 units	(specific cost: 100 @ $12)
Oct. 5	350 units	(specific cost: 100 @ $15 and 250 @ $20)

Concepts and Procedures to Illustrate in Expert Presentation

a. Identify and compute the costs to assign to the units sold. (Round per unit costs to three decimals.)
b. Identify and compute the costs to assign to the units in ending inventory. (Round inventory balances to the dollar.)
c. How likely is it that this inventory costing method will reflect the actual physical flow of goods? How relevant is that factor in determining whether this is an acceptable method to use?
d. What is the impact of this method versus others in determining net income and income taxes?
e. How closely does the ending inventory amount reflect replacement cost?

4. Re-form learning teams. In rotation, each expert is to present to the team the presentation developed in part 3. Experts are to encourage and respond to questions.

ENTREPRENEURIAL DECISION
A3

BTN 5-7 Review the chapter's opening feature highlighting Randy Hetrick and his company, **Fitness Anywhere**. Assume that Fitness Anywhere consistently maintains an inventory level of $300,000, meaning that its average and ending inventory levels are the same. Also assume its annual cost of sales is $1,200,000. To cut costs, Randy proposes to slash inventory to a constant level of $150,000 with no impact on cost of sales. He plans to work with suppliers to get quicker deliveries and to order smaller quantities more often.

Required

1. Compute the company's inventory turnover and its days' sales in inventory under (*a*) current conditions and (*b*) proposed conditions.
2. Evaluate and comment on the merits of his proposal given your analysis for part 1. Identify any concerns you might have about the proposal.

HITTING THE ROAD
C1 C2

BTN 5-8 Visit four retail stores with another classmate. In each store, identify whether the store uses a barcoding system to help manage its inventory. Try to find at least one store that does not use bar-coding. If a store does not use bar-coding, ask the store's manager or clerk whether he or she knows which type of inventory method the store employs. Create a table that shows columns for the name of store visited, type of merchandise sold, use or nonuse of bar-coding, and the inventory method used if bar-coding is not employed. You might also inquire as to what the store's inventory turnover is and how often physical inventory is taken.

BTN 5-9 Key figures (EUR millions) for Nokia (www.Nokia.com), which is a leading global manufacturer of mobile devices and services, follow.

EUR millions	Current Year	One Year Prior	Two Years Prior
Inventory	1,865	2,533	2,876
Cost of sales	27,720	33,337	33,781

GLOBAL DECISION
A3

NOKIA
RIM
Apple

Required
1. Use these data and those from BTN 5-2 to compute (a) inventory turnover and (b) days' sales in inventory for the most recent two years shown for Nokia, Research In Motion, and Apple.
2. Comment on and interpret your findings from part 1.

ANSWERS TO MULTIPLE CHOICE QUIZ

1. a; FIFO perpetual

Date	Goods Purchased	Cost of Goods Sold	Inventory Balance
July 1			75 units @ $25 = $ 1,875
July 3	348 units @ $27 = $9,396		75 units @ $25 348 units @ $27 } = $11,271
July 8		75 units @ $25 225 units @ $27 } = $ 7,950	123 units @ $27 = $ 3,321
July 15	257 units @ $28 = $7,196		123 units @ $27 257 units @ $28 } = $10,517
July 23		123 units @ $27 152 units @ $28 } = $ 7,577 $15,527	105 units @ $28 = $ 2,940

2. b; LIFO perpetual

Date	Goods Purchased	Cost of Goods Sold	Inventory Balance
July 1			75 units @ $25 = $ 1,875
July 3	348 units @ $27 = $9,396		75 units @ $25 348 units @ $27 } = $11,271
July 8		300 units @ $27 = $ 8,100	75 units @ $25 48 units @ $27 } = $ 3,171
July 15	257 units @ $28 = $7,196		75 units @ $25 48 units @ $27 257 units @ $28 } = $10,367
July 23		257 units @ $28 18 units @ $27 } = $ 7,682 $15,782	75 units @ $25 30 units @ $27 } = $ 2,685

3. e; Specific identification perpetual—Ending inventory computation.

20 units @ $25	$ 500
40 units @ $27	1,080
45 units @ $28	1,260
105 units	$2,840

4. a; FIFO periodic—Ending inventory computation.
105 units @ $28 each = $2,940; The FIFO periodic inventory computation is identical to the FIFO perpetual inventory computation (see question 1).

5. d; Days' sales in inventory = (Ending inventory/Cost of goods sold × 365)
= ($18,000/$85,000) × 365 = 77.29 days

A Look Back	A Look at This Chapter	A Look Ahead
Chapters 4 and 5 focused on merchandising activities and accounting for inventory. We explained inventory systems, accounting for inventory transactions, and assigning costs to inventory.	This chapter extends our study of accounting to internal control and the analysis of cash. We describe procedures that are good for internal control. We also explain the control of and the accounting for cash, including control features of banking activities.	Chapter 7 focuses on receivables. We explain how to account and report on receivables and their related accounts. This includes estimating uncollectible receivables and computing interest earned.

6 Reporting and Analyzing Cash and Internal Controls

Learning Objectives

CAP

CONCEPTUAL

- **C1** Define internal control and identify its purpose and principles. (p. 250)
- **C2** Define cash and cash equivalents and explain how to report them. (p. 255)

ANALYTICAL

- **A1** Compute the days' sales uncollected ratio and use it to assess liquidity. (p. 269)

PROCEDURAL

- **P1** Apply internal control to cash receipts and disbursements. (p. 256)
- **P2** Explain and record petty cash fund transactions. (p. 260)
- **P3** Prepare a bank reconciliation. (p. 265)
- **P4** *Appendix 6A*—Describe the use of documentation and verification to control cash disbursements. (p. 272)
- **P5** *Appendix 6B*—Apply the net method to control purchase discounts. (p. 275)

LP6

Decision Insight

Successful Brew

"It's just following your instincts, knowing the basics, and sticking with what's important."
—KIM JORDAN

FORT COLLINS, CO—Kim Jordan's entrepreneurial roots were anything but frothy. "For about eight months, we didn't pay ourselves," explains Kim. "We borrowed money from parents and made payroll . . . looking at the bills, we had to decide which to pay." From those meager beginnings, Kim created **New Belgium Brewing Company (NewBelgium.com)**, which is committed to the Belgian brewing tradition of delicious beers.

"We did have a set of values, a purpose, and some outcomes that we wanted to achieve," says Kim. "Four things were important to us: to produce world class Belgium-style beers, to promote beer culture, to be environmental stewards, and to have fun!" To achieve those goals, Kim set up an accounting system to measure, track, summarize, and report on operations. "It is important to have the ability to read financial statements," insists Kim. "And, to understand ratios." Those expectations and priorities fundamentally shaped Kim's accounting system and controls.

"There has to be execution," explains Kim. That focus on execution includes applying internal controls and managing cash. Kim maintains control procedures to monitor New Belgium's business activities and safeguard its assets. Kim explains that such controls raise productivity and cut expenses. Her company's cash management practices are impressive, involving controls over cash receipts, disbursements, and petty cash. The use of bank reconciliations further helps with the control and management of cash. Kim says she takes advantage of available banking services to enhance control of cash.

"Working hard and being dedicated or committed to an outcome are keys," asserts Kim. "Our co-workers [all employees] get to see all of our financials!" Kim explains that this helps shape the control procedures applied in the brewery.

Kim's company is riding high with the right accounting systems and controls for long-run success. "Stasis is not an option," says Kim. "If we're all in the same place today that we were five years ago, that wouldn't be very interesting." Kim smiles and adds, "There's something wrong if making beer can't be fun!"

[Sources: *NewBelgium Website,* January 2012; *Entrepreneur,* November 2009; *50entrepreneurs.com,* March 2010; *CNNMoney.com,* June 2009; *Beverage World,* September 2009; *Mutineer,* April 2011]

Chapter Preview

We all are aware of theft and fraud. They affect us in several ways: We lock doors, chain bikes, review sales receipts, and acquire alarm systems. A company also takes actions to safeguard, control, and manage what it owns. Experience tells us that small companies are most vulnerable, usually due to weak internal controls. It is management's responsibility to set up policies and procedures to safeguard a company's assets, especially cash. To do so, management *and* employees must understand and apply principles of internal control. This chapter describes these principles and how to apply them. It focuses special attention on cash because it is easily transferable and is often at high risk of loss.

Reporting and Analyzing Cash and Internal Controls

- **Internal Control**
  - Purpose of controls
  - Principles of controls
  - Technology and controls
  - Limitations of controls

- **Control of Cash**
  - Cash, cash equivalents, and liquidity
  - Control of receipts
  - Control of disbursements

- **Banking Activities as Controls**
  - Basic bank services
  - Bank statement
  - Bank reconciliation

INTERNAL CONTROL

This section describes internal control and its fundamental principles. We also discuss the impact of technology on internal control and the limitations of control procedures.

Purpose of Internal Control

C1 Define internal control and identify its purpose and principles.

Managers (or owners) of small businesses often control the entire operation. These managers usually purchase all assets, hire and manage employees, negotiate all contracts, and sign all checks. They know from personal contact and observation whether the business is actually receiving the assets and services paid for. Most companies, however, cannot maintain this close personal supervision. They must delegate responsibilities and rely on formal procedures rather than personal contact in controlling business activities.

Internal Control System Managers use an internal control system to monitor and control business activities. An **internal control system** consists of the policies and procedures managers use to

- Protect assets.
- Ensure reliable accounting.
- Promote efficient operations.
- Urge adherence to company policies.

A properly designed internal control system is a key part of systems design, analysis, and performance. Managers place a high priority on internal control systems because they can prevent avoidable losses, help managers plan operations, and monitor company and employee performance. Internal controls do not provide guarantees, but they lower the company's risk of loss.

Sarbanes-Oxley Act (SOX) The **Sarbanes-Oxley Act (SOX)** requires the managers and auditors of companies whose stock is traded on an exchange (called *public companies*) to document and certify the system of internal controls. Following are some of the specific requirements:

- Auditors must evaluate internal controls and issue an internal control report.
- Auditors of a client are restricted as to what consulting services they can provide that client.
- The person leading an audit can serve no more than seven years without a two-year break.
- Auditors' work is overseen by the *Public Company Accounting Oversight Board* (PCAOB).
- Harsh penalties exist for violators—sentences up to 25 years in prison with severe fines.

SOX has markedly impacted companies, and the costs of its implementation are high. Importantly, **Section 404** of SOX requires that managers document and assess the effectiveness of all internal control processes that can impact financial reporting. The benefits include greater confidence in accounting systems and their related reports. However, the public continues to debate the costs versus the benefits of SOX as nearly all business activities of these companies are impacted by SOX. Section 404 of SOX requires that managers document and assess their internal controls *and* that auditors provide an opinion on managers' documentation and assessment. Costs of complying with Section 404 for companies is reported to average $4 million (source: Financial Executives Institute).

Principles of Internal Control

Internal control policies and procedures vary from company to company according to such factors as the nature of the business and its size. Certain fundamental internal control principles apply to all companies. The **principles of internal control** are to

1. Establish responsibilities.
2. Maintain adequate records.
3. Insure assets and bond key employees.
4. Separate recordkeeping from custody of assets.
5. Divide responsibility for related transactions.
6. Apply technological controls.
7. Perform regular and independent reviews.

This section explains these seven principles and describes how internal control procedures minimize the risk of fraud and theft. These procedures also increase the reliability and accuracy of accounting records. A framework for how these seven principles improve the quality of financial reporting is provided by the **Committee of Sponsoring Organizations (COSO)** (www.COSO.org). Specifically, these principles link to five aspects of internal control: control activities, control environment, risk assessment, monitoring, and communication.

Establish Responsibilities Proper internal control means that responsibility for a task is clearly established and assigned to one person. When a problem occurs in a company where responsibility is not identified, determining who is at fault is difficult. For instance, if two salesclerks share the same cash register and there is a cash shortage, neither clerk can be held accountable. To prevent this problem, one clerk might be given responsibility for handling all cash sales. Alternately, a company can use a register with separate cash drawers for each clerk. Most of us have waited at a retail counter during a shift change while employees swap cash drawers.

Maintain Adequate Records Good recordkeeping is part of an internal control system. It helps protect assets and ensures that employees use prescribed procedures. Reliable records are also a source of information that managers use to monitor company activities. When detailed records of equipment are kept, for instance, items are unlikely to be lost or stolen without detection. Similarly, transactions are less likely to be entered in wrong accounts if a chart of accounts is set up and carefully used. Many preprinted forms and internal documents are also designed for use in a good internal control system. When sales slips are properly designed, for instance, sales personnel can record needed information efficiently with less chance of errors or delays to customers. When sales slips are prenumbered and controlled, each one issued is the responsibility of one salesperson, preventing the salesperson from pocketing cash by making a sale and destroying the sales slip. Computerized point-of-sale systems achieve the same control results.

Insure Assets and Bond Key Employees Good internal control means that assets are adequately insured against casualty and that employees handling large amounts of cash and easily transferable assets are bonded. An employee is *bonded* when a company purchases an insurance policy, or a bond, against losses from theft by that employee. Bonding reduces the risk of loss. It also discourages theft because bonded employees know an independent bonding company will be involved when theft is uncovered and is unlikely to be sympathetic with an employee involved in theft.

Point: Sarbanes-Oxley Act (SOX) requires that each annual report contain an *internal control report*, which must: (1) state managers' responsibility for establishing and maintaining adequate internal controls for financial reporting; and (2) assess the effectiveness of those controls.

Point: Many companies have a mandatory vacation policy for employees who handle cash. When another employee must cover for the one on vacation, it is more difficult to hide cash frauds.

Point: The Association of Certified Fraud Examiners (cfenet.com) estimates that employee fraud costs small companies more than $100,000 per incident.

Fraud

Tag Control. A novel technique exists for marking physical assets. It involves embedding a less than one-inch-square tag of fibers that creates a unique optical signature recordable by scanners. Manufacturers hope to embed tags in everything from compact discs and credit cards to designer clothes for purposes of internal control and efficiency.

Separate Recordkeeping from Custody of Assets A person who controls or has access to an asset must not keep that asset's accounting records. This principle reduces the risk of theft or waste of an asset because the person with control over it knows that another person keeps its records. Also, a recordkeeper who does not have access to the asset has no reason to falsify records. This means that to steal an asset and hide the theft from the records, two or more people must *collude*—or agree in secret to commit the fraud.

Divide Responsibility for Related Transactions Good internal control divides responsibility for a transaction or a series of related transactions between two or more individuals or departments. This is to ensure that the work of one individual acts as a check on the other. This principle, often called *separation of duties,* is not a call for duplication of work. Each employee or department should perform unduplicated effort. Examples of transactions with divided responsibility are placing purchase orders, receiving merchandise, and paying vendors. These tasks should not be given to one individual or department. Assigning responsibility for two or more of these tasks to one party increases mistakes and perhaps fraud. Having an independent person, for example, check incoming goods for quality and quantity encourages more care and attention to detail than having the person who placed the order do the checking. Added protection can result from identifying a third person to approve payment of the invoice. A company can even designate a fourth person with authority to write checks as another protective measure.

Point: There's a new security device—a person's ECG (electrocardiogram) reading—that is as unique as a fingerprint and a lot harder to lose or steal than a PIN. ECGs can be read through fingertip touches. An ECG also shows that a living person is actually there, whereas fingerprint and facial recognition software can be fooled.

Apply Technological Controls Cash registers, check protectors, time clocks, and personal identification scanners are examples of devices that can improve internal control. Technology often improves the effectiveness of controls. A cash register with a locked-in tape or electronic file makes a record of each cash sale. A check protector perforates the amount of a check into its face and makes it difficult to alter the amount. A time clock registers the exact time an employee both arrives at and departs from the job. Mechanical change and currency counters quickly and accurately count amounts, and personal scanners limit access to only authorized individuals. Each of these and other technological controls are an effective part of many internal control systems.

Decision Insight

About Face Face-recognition software snaps a digital picture of the face and converts key facial features—say, the distance between the eyes—into a series of numerical values. These can be stored on an ID or ATM card as a simple bar code to prohibit unauthorized access.

Perform Regular and Independent Reviews Changes in personnel, stress of time pressures, and technological advances present opportunities for shortcuts and lapses. To counter these factors, regular reviews of internal control systems are needed to ensure that procedures are followed. These reviews are preferably done by internal auditors not directly involved in the activities. Their impartial perspective encourages an evaluation of the efficiency as well as the effectiveness of the internal control system. Many companies also pay for audits by independent, external auditors. These external auditors test the company's financial records to give an opinion as to whether its financial statements are presented fairly. Before external auditors decide on how much testing is needed, they evaluate the effectiveness of the internal control system. This evaluation is often helpful to a client.

> **Decision Maker** — Answer — p. 277
>
> **Entrepreneur** As owner of a start-up information services company, you hire a systems analyst. One of her first recommendations is to require all employees to take at least one week of vacation per year. Why would she recommend a "forced vacation" policy? ■

Technology and Internal Control

The fundamental principles of internal control are relevant no matter what the technological state of the accounting system, from purely manual to fully automated systems. Technology impacts an internal control system in several important ways. Perhaps the most obvious is that technology allows us quicker access to databases and information. Used effectively, technology greatly improves managers' abilities to monitor and control business activities. This section describes some technological impacts we must be alert to.

Reduced Processing Errors Technologically advanced systems reduce the number of errors in processing information. Provided the software and data entry are correct, the risk of mechanical and mathematical errors is nearly eliminated. However, we must remember that erroneous software or data entry does exist. Also, less human involvement in data processing can cause data entry errors to go undiscovered. Moreover, errors in software can produce consistent but erroneous processing of transactions. Continually checking and monitoring all types of systems are important.

More Extensive Testing of Records A company's review and audit of electronic records can include more extensive testing when information is easily and rapidly accessed. When accounting records are kept manually, auditors and others likely select only small samples of data to test. When data are accessible with computer technology, however, auditors can quickly analyze large samples or even the entire database.

Limited Evidence of Processing Many data processing steps are increasingly done by computer. Accordingly, fewer hard-copy items of documentary evidence are available for review. Yet technologically advanced systems can provide new evidence. They can, for instance, record who made the entries, the date and time, the source of the entry, and so on. Technology can also be designed to require the use of passwords or other identification before access to the system is granted. This means that internal control depends more on the design and operation of the information system and less on the analysis of its resulting documents.

Crucial Separation of Duties Technological advances in accounting information systems often yield some job eliminations or consolidations. While those who remain have the special skills necessary to operate advanced programs and equipment, a company with a reduced workforce risks losing its crucial separation of duties. The company must establish ways to control and monitor employees to minimize risk of error and fraud. For instance, the person who designs and programs the information system must not be the one who operates it. The company must also separate control over programs and files from the activities related to cash receipts and disbursements. For instance, a computer operator should not control check-writing activities. Achieving acceptable separation of duties can be especially difficult and costly in small companies with few employees.

Increased E-Commerce Technology has encouraged the growth of e-commerce. **Amazon** and **eBay** are examples of companies that have successfully exploited e-commerce. Most companies have some e-commerce transactions. All such transactions involve at least three risks. (1) *Credit card number theft* is a risk of using, transmitting, and storing such data online. This increases the cost of e-commerce. (2) *Computer viruses* are malicious programs that attach themselves to innocent files for purposes of infecting and harming other files and programs. (3) *Impersonation* online can result in charges of sales to bogus accounts, purchases of inappropriate materials, and the unknowing giving up of confidential information to hackers. Companies use both firewalls and encryption to

Point: Information on Internet fraud can be found at these Websites:
sec.gov/investor/pubs/cyberfraud.htm
ftc.gov/bcp/consumer.shtm
www.fraud.org

Point: Evidence of any internal control failure for a company reduces user confidence in its financial statements.

Point: We look to several sources when assessing a company's internal controls. Sources include the auditor's report, management report on controls (if available), management discussion and analysis, and financial press.

Point: COSO organizes control components into five types:
- Control environment
- Control activities
- Risk assessment
- Monitoring
- Information and communication

"Worst case of identity theft I've ever seen!"
Copyright 2004 by Randy Glasbergen. www.glasbergen.com

combat some of these risks—firewalls are points of entry to a system that require passwords to continue, and encryption is a mathematical process to rearrange contents that cannot be read without the process code. Nearly 5% of Americans already report being victims of identity theft, and roughly 10 million say their privacy has been compromised.

> **Decision Insight**
>
> **Cheery Fraud Victim** Certified Fraud Examiners Website reports the following: Andrew Cameron stole Jacqueline Boanson's credit card. Cameron headed to the racetrack and promptly charged two bets for $150 on the credit card—winning $400. Unfortunately for Cameron the racetrack refused to pay him cash as its internal control policy is to credit winnings from bets made on a credit card to that same card. Cameron was later nabbed; and the racetrack let Ms. Boanson keep the winnings. ■

Limitations of Internal Control

All internal control policies and procedures have limitations that usually arise from either (1) the human element or (2) the cost–benefit principle.

Internal control policies and procedures are applied by people. This human element creates several potential limitations that we can categorize as either (1) human error or (2) human fraud. *Human error* can occur from negligence, fatigue, misjudgment, or confusion. *Human fraud* involves intent by people to defeat internal controls, such as *management override,* for personal gain. Fraud also includes collusion to thwart the separation of duties. The human element highlights the importance of establishing an *internal control environment* to convey management's commitment to internal control policies and procedures. Human fraud is driven by the *triple-threat* of fraud:

- **Opportunity**—refers to internal control deficiencies in the workplace.
- **Pressure**—refers to financial, family, society, and other stresses to succeed.
- **Rationalization**—refers to employees justifying fraudulent behavior.

The second major limitation on internal control is the *cost–benefit principle,* which dictates that the costs of internal controls must not exceed their benefits. Analysis of costs and benefits must consider all factors, including the impact on morale. Most companies, for instance, have a legal right to read employees' e-mails, yet companies seldom exercise that right unless they are confronted with evidence of potential harm to the company. The same holds for drug testing, phone tapping, and hidden cameras. The bottom line is that managers must establish internal control policies and procedures with a net benefit to the company.

Point: Cybercrime.gov pursues computer and intellectual property crimes, including that of e-commerce.

Address: www.hacker'sguidetocyberspace.com   GO

Hacker's Guide to Cyberspace

Pharming Viruses attached to e-mails and Websites load software onto your PC that monitors keystrokes; when you sign on to financial Websites, it steals your passwords.

Phishing Hackers send e-mails to you posing as banks; you are asked for information using fake Websites where they reel in your passwords and personal data.

WI-Phishing Cybercrooks set up wireless networks hoping you use them to connect to the Web; your passwords and data are stolen as you use their network.

Bot-Networking Hackers send remote-control programs to your PC that take control to send out spam and viruses; they even rent your bot to other cybercrooks.

Typo-Squatting Hackers set up Websites with addresses similar to legit outfits; when you make a typo and hit their sites, they infect your PC with viruses or take them over as bots.

> **Quick Check**   Answers — p. 277
>
> 1. Principles of internal control suggest that (choose one): (*a*) Responsibility for a series of related transactions (such as placing orders, receiving and paying for merchandise) should be assigned to one employee; (*b*) Responsibility for individual tasks should be shared by more than one employee so that one serves as a check on the other; or (*c*) Employees who handle considerable cash and easily transferable assets should be bonded.
> 2. What are some impacts of computing technology on internal control?

CONTROL OF CASH

Cash is a necessary asset of every company. Most companies also own *cash equivalents* (defined below), which are assets similar to cash. Cash and cash equivalents are the most liquid of all assets and are easily hidden and moved. An effective system of internal controls protects these assets and it should meet three basic guidelines:

1. Handling cash is separate from recordkeeping of cash.
2. Cash receipts are promptly deposited in a bank.
3. Cash disbursements are made by check.

The first guideline applies separation of duties to minimize errors and fraud. When duties are separated, two or more people must collude to steal cash and conceal this action in the accounting records. The second guideline uses immediate (say, daily) deposits of all cash receipts to produce a timely independent record of the cash received. It also reduces the likelihood of cash theft (or loss) and the risk that an employee could personally use the money before depositing it. The third guideline uses payments by check to develop an independent bank record of cash disbursements. This guideline also reduces the risk of cash theft (or loss).

This section begins with definitions of cash and cash equivalents. Discussion then focuses on controls and accounting for both cash receipts and disbursements. The exact procedures used to achieve control over cash vary across companies. They depend on factors such as company size, number of employees, volume of cash transactions, and sources of cash.

Cash, Cash Equivalents, and Liquidity

Good accounting systems help in managing the amount of cash and controlling who has access to it. Cash is the usual means of payment when paying for assets, services, or liabilities. **Liquidity** refers to a company's ability to pay for its near-term obligations. Cash and similar assets are called **liquid assets** because they can be readily used to settle such obligations. A company needs liquid assets to effectively operate.

Cash includes currency and coins along with the amounts on deposit in bank accounts, checking accounts (called *demand deposits*), and many savings accounts (called *time deposits*). Cash also includes items that are acceptable for deposit in these accounts such as customer checks, cashier's checks, certified checks, and money orders. **Cash equivalents** are short-term, highly liquid investment assets meeting two criteria: (1) readily convertible to a known cash amount and (2) sufficiently close to their due date so that their market value is not sensitive to interest rate changes. Only investments purchased within three months of their due date usually satisfy these criteria. Examples of cash equivalents are short-term investments in assets such as U.S. Treasury bills and money market funds. To increase their return, many companies invest idle cash in cash equivalents. Most companies combine cash equivalents with cash as a single item on the balance sheet.

C2 Define cash and cash equivalents and explain how to report them.

Point: The most liquid assets are usually reported first on a balance sheet; the least liquid assets are reported last.

Point: Google reports cash and cash equivalents of $10,198 million in its balance sheet. This amount makes up nearly 25% of its total assets.

Cash Management

When companies fail, one of the most common causes is their inability to manage cash. Companies must plan both cash receipts and cash payments. The goals of cash management are twofold:

1. Plan cash receipts to meet cash payments when due.
2. Keep a minimum level of cash necessary to operate.

The *treasurer* of the company is responsible for cash management. Effective cash management involves applying the following cash management principles.

- **Encourage collection of receivables.** The more quickly customers and others pay the company, the more quickly that company can use the money. Some companies have cash-only sales policies. Others might offer discounts for payments received early.
- **Delay payment of liabilities.** The more delayed a company is in paying others, the more time it has to use the money. Some companies regularly wait to pay their bills until the last possible day allowed—although, a company must take care not to hurt its credit standing.
- **Keep only necessary levels of assets.** The less money tied up in idle assets, the more money to invest in productive assets. Some companies maintain *just-in-time* inventory; meaning they plan inventory to be available at the same time orders are filled. Others might lease out excess warehouse space or rent equipment instead of buying it.
- **Plan expenditures.** Money should be spent only when it is available. Companies must look at seasonal and business cycles to plan expenditures.
- **Invest excess cash.** Excess cash earns no return and should be invested. Excess cash from seasonal cycles can be placed in a bank account or other short-term investment for income. Excess cash beyond what's needed for regular business should be invested in productive assets like factories and inventories.

Decision Insight

Days' Cash Expense Coverage The ratio of *cash* (*and cash equivalents*) to *average daily cash expenses* indicates the number of days a company can operate without additional cash inflows. It reflects on company liquidity and on the potential of excess cash. ■

Control of Cash Receipts

P1 Apply internal control to cash receipts and disbursements.

Internal control of cash receipts ensures that cash received is properly recorded and deposited. Cash receipts can arise from transactions such as cash sales, collections of customer accounts, receipts of interest earned, bank loans, sales of assets, and owner investments. This section explains internal control over two important types of cash receipts: over-the-counter and by mail.

Over-the-Counter Cash Receipts For purposes of internal control, over-the-counter cash receipts from sales should be recorded on a cash register at the time of each sale. To help ensure that correct amounts are entered, each register should be located so customers can read the amounts entered. Clerks also should be required to enter each sale before wrapping merchandise and to give the customer a receipt for each sale. The design of each cash register should provide a permanent, locked-in record of each transaction. In many systems, the register is directly linked with computing and accounting services. Less advanced registers simply print a record of each transaction on a paper tape or electronic file locked inside the register.

Proper internal control prescribes that custody over cash should be separate from its recordkeeping. For over-the-counter cash receipts, this separation begins with the cash sale. The clerk who has access to cash in the register should not have access to its locked-in record. At the end of the clerk's work period, the clerk should count the cash in the register, record the amount, and turn over the cash and a record of its amount to the company cashier. The cashier, like the clerk, has access to the cash but should not have access to accounting records (or the register tape or file). A third employee, often a supervisor, compares the record of total register transactions (or the register tape or file) with the cash receipts reported by the cashier. This record is the basis for a journal entry recording over-the-counter cash receipts. The third employee has access to the records for cash but not to the actual cash. The clerk and the cashier have access to cash but not to the accounting records. None of them can make a mistake or divert cash without the difference being revealed—see the following diagram.

Cash over and short. Sometimes errors in making change are discovered from differences between the cash in a cash register and the record of the amount of cash receipts. Although a clerk is careful, one or more customers can be given too much or too little change. This means that at the end of a work period, the cash in a cash register might not equal the record of cash receipts. This difference is reported in the **Cash Over and Short** account, also called *Cash Short and Over,* which is an income statement account recording the income effects of cash overages and cash shortages. To illustrate, if a cash register's record shows $550 but the count of cash in the register is $555, the entry to record cash sales and its overage is

Cash...	555	
Cash Over and Short........................		5
Sales..		550
To record cash sales and a cash overage.		

Assets = Liabilities + Equity
+555   + 5
                                      +550

Point: Retailers often require cashiers to restrictively endorse checks immediately on receipt by stamping them "For deposit only."

On the other hand, if a cash register's record shows $625 but the count of cash in the register is $621, the entry to record cash sales and its shortage is

Cash...	621	
Cash Over and Short........................	4	
Sales..		625
To record cash sales and a cash shortage.		

Assets = Liabilities + Equity
+621   − 4
                                      +625

Since customers are more likely to dispute being shortchanged than being given too much change, the Cash Over and Short account usually has a debit balance at the end of an accounting period. A debit balance reflects an expense. It is reported on the income statement as part of general and administrative expenses. (Since the amount is usually small, it is often combined with other small expenses and reported as part of *miscellaneous expenses*—or as part of *miscellaneous revenues* if it has a credit balance.)

Point: Merchants begin a business day with a *change fund* in their cash register. The accounting for a change fund is similar to that for petty cash, including that for cash shortages or overages.

Cash Receipts by Mail Control of cash receipts that arrive through the mail starts with the person who opens the mail. Preferably, two people are assigned the task of, and are present for, opening the mail. In this case, theft of cash receipts by mail requires collusion between these two employees. Specifically, the person(s) opening the mail enters a list (in triplicate) of money received. This list should contain a record of each sender's name, the amount, and an explanation of why the money is sent. The first copy is sent with the money to the cashier. A second copy is sent to the recordkeeper in the accounting area. A third copy is kept by the

Point: Collusion implies that two or more individuals are knowledgeable or involved with the activities of the other(s).

clerk(s) who opened the mail. The cashier deposits the money in a bank, and the recordkeeper records the amounts received in the accounting records.

This process reflects good internal control. That is, when the bank balance is reconciled by another person (explained later in the chapter), errors or acts of fraud by the mail clerks, the cashier, or the recordkeeper are revealed. They are revealed because the bank's record of cash deposited must agree with the records from each of the three. Moreover, if the mail clerks do not report all receipts correctly, customers will question their account balances. If the cashier does not deposit all receipts, the bank balance does not agree with the recordkeeper's cash balance. The recordkeeper and the person who reconciles the bank balance do not have access to cash and therefore have no opportunity to divert cash to themselves. This system makes errors and fraud highly unlikely. The exception is employee collusion.

Decision Insight

Perpetual Accounting Walmart uses a network of information links with its point-of-sale cash registers to coordinate sales, purchases, and distribution. Its supercenters, for instance, ring up 15,000 separate sales on heavy days. By using cash register information, the company can fix pricing mistakes quickly and capitalize on sales trends.

Control of Cash Disbursements

Control of cash disbursements is especially important as most large thefts occur from payment of fictitious invoices. One key to controlling cash disbursements is to require all expenditures to be made by check. The only exception is small payments made from petty cash. Another key is to deny access to the accounting records to anyone other than the owner who has the authority to sign checks. A small business owner often signs checks and knows from personal contact that the items being paid for are actually received. This arrangement is impossible in large businesses. Instead, internal control procedures must be substituted for personal contact. Such procedures are designed to assure the check signer that the obligations recorded are properly incurred and should be paid. This section describes these and other internal control procedures, including the voucher system and petty cash system. A method for management of cash disbursements for purchases is described in Appendix 6B.

Decision Insight

Cash Budget Projected cash receipts and cash disbursements are often summarized in a *cash budget*. Provided that sufficient cash exists for effective operations, companies wish to minimize the cash they hold because of its risk of theft and its low return versus other investment opportunities.

Voucher System of Control A **voucher system** is a set of procedures and approvals designed to control cash disbursements and the acceptance of obligations. The voucher system of control establishes procedures for

- Verifying, approving, and recording obligations for eventual cash disbursement.
- Issuing checks for payment of verified, approved, and recorded obligations.

A reliable voucher system follows standard procedures for every transaction. This applies even when multiple purchases are made from the same supplier.

A voucher system's control over cash disbursements begins when a company incurs an obligation that will result in payment of cash. A key factor in this system is that only approved departments and individuals are authorized to incur such obligations. The system often limits the type of obligations that a department or individual can incur. In a large retail store, for instance, only a purchasing department should be authorized to incur obligations for merchandise inventory. Another key factor is that procedures for purchasing, receiving, and paying for merchandise are divided among several departments (or individuals). These departments include the one requesting the purchase, the purchasing department, the receiving department, and the accounting department. To coordinate and control responsibilities of these departments, a company uses

Point: MCI, formerly **WorldCom,** paid a whopping $500 million in SEC fines for accounting fraud. Among the charges were that it inflated earnings by as much as $10 billion. Its CEO, Bernard Ebbers, was sentenced to 25 years.

EXHIBIT 6.1

Document Flow in a Voucher System

Sender	Receiver(s)
Cashier	Supplier (vendor)
Accounting	Cashier
Receiving	Accounting; Requesting; and Purchasing
Supplier (vendor)	Accounting
Purchasing	Supplier; Requesting; Receiving; and Accounting
Requesting	Purchasing; and Accounting

several different business documents. Exhibit 6.1 shows how documents are accumulated in a **voucher,** which is an internal document (or file) used to accumulate information to control cash disbursements and to ensure that a transaction is properly recorded. This specific example begins with a *purchase requisition* and concludes with a *check* drawn against cash. Appendix 6A describes the documentation and verification necessary for a voucher system of control. It also describes the internal control objective served by each document.

A voucher system should be applied not only to purchases of inventory but to all expenditures. To illustrate, when a company receives a monthly telephone bill, it should review and verify the charges, prepare a voucher (file), and insert the bill. This transaction is then recorded with a journal entry. If the amount is currently due, a check is issued. If not, the voucher is filed for payment on its due date. If no voucher is prepared, verifying the invoice and its amount after several days or weeks can be difficult. Also, without records, a dishonest employee could collude with a dishonest supplier to get more than one payment for an obligation, payment for excessive amounts, or payment for goods and services not received. An effective voucher system helps prevent such frauds.

Point: A *voucher* is an internal document (or file).

Point: The basic purposes of paper and electronic documents are similar. However, the internal control system must change to reflect different risks, including confidential and competitive-sensitive information that is at greater risk in electronic systems.

Fraud

Cyber Setup. The FTC is on the cutting edge of cybersleuthing. Opportunists in search of easy money are lured to **WeMarket4U.net/SundaeStation** and **WeMarket4U.net/FatFoe**. Take the bait and you get warned. The top 5 fraud complaints as compiled by the Bureau of Consumer Protection are shown to the right.

Percent of all fraud complaints:
- Identity theft: 32%
- Catalog sales: 8%
- Internet services: 5%
- Foreign money offers: 4%
- Lotteries and prizes: 4%

Quick Check
Answers — p. 277

3. Why must a company hold liquid assets?
4. Why does a company hold cash equivalent assets in addition to cash?
5. Identify at least two assets that are classified as cash equivalents.
6. Good internal control procedures for cash include which of the following? (*a*) All cash disbursements, other than those for very small amounts, are made by check; (*b*) One employee counts cash received from sales and promptly deposits cash receipts; or (*c*) Cash receipts by mail are opened by one employee who is then responsible for recording and depositing them.
7. Should all companies require a voucher system? At what point in a company's growth would you recommend a voucher system?

P2 Explain and record petty cash fund transactions.

Petty Cash System of Control A basic principle for controlling cash disbursements is that all payments must be made by check. An exception to this rule is made for *petty cash disbursements,* which are the small payments required for items such as postage, courier fees, minor repairs, and low-cost supplies. To avoid the time and cost of writing checks for small amounts, a company sets up a petty cash fund to make small payments. (**Petty cash** activities are part of an *imprest system,* which designates advance money to establish the fund, to withdraw from the fund, and to reimburse the fund.)

Operating a petty cash fund. Establishing a petty cash fund requires estimating the total amount of small payments likely to be made during a short period such as a week or month. A check is then drawn by the company cashier for an amount slightly in excess of this estimate. This check is recorded with a debit to the Petty Cash account (an asset) and a credit to Cash. The check is cashed, and the currency is given to an employee designated as the *petty cashier* or *petty cash custodian*. The petty cashier is responsible for keeping this cash safe, making payments from the fund, and keeping records of it in a secure place referred to as the *petty cashbox*.

When each cash disbursement is made, the person receiving payment should sign a prenumbered *petty cash receipt,* also called *petty cash ticket*—see Exhibit 6.2. The petty cash receipt is then placed in the petty cashbox with the remaining money. Under this system, the sum of all receipts plus the remaining cash equals the total fund amount. A $100 petty cash fund, for instance, contains any combination of cash and petty cash receipts that totals $100 (examples are $80 cash plus $20 in receipts, or $10 cash plus $90 in receipts). Each disbursement reduces cash and increases the amount of receipts in the petty cashbox.

Point: A petty cash fund is used only for business expenses.

EXHIBIT 6.2
Petty Cash Receipt

Z-Mart No. 9
PETTY CASH RECEIPT
For *Freight charges*
Date *November 5, 2009*   Approved by
Charge to *Merchandise Inventory*
Amount *$6.75*   Received by

Point: Petty cash receipts with either no signature or a forged signature usually indicate misuse of petty cash. Companies respond with surprise petty cash counts for verification.

The petty cash fund should be reimbursed when it is nearing zero and at the end of an accounting period when financial statements are prepared. For this purpose, the petty cashier sorts the paid receipts by the type of expense or account and then totals the receipts. The petty cashier presents all paid receipts to the company cashier, who stamps all receipts *paid* so they cannot be reused, files them for recordkeeping, and gives the petty cashier a check for their sum. When this check is cashed and the money placed in the cashbox, the total money in the cashbox is restored to its original amount. The fund is now ready for a new cycle of petty cash payments.

Illustrating a petty cash fund. To illustrate, assume Z-Mart establishes a petty cash fund on November 1 and designates one of its office employees as the petty cashier. A $75 check is drawn, cashed, and the proceeds given to the petty cashier. The entry to record the setup of this petty cash fund is

Assets = Liabilities + Equity
+75
−75

Nov. 1	Petty Cash	75	
	Cash		75
	To establish a petty cash fund.		

Point: Reducing or eliminating a petty cash fund requires a credit to Petty Cash.

Point: Although *individual* petty cash disbursements are not evidenced by a check, the initial petty cash fund is evidenced by a check, and later petty cash expenditures are evidenced by a check to replenish them *in total*.

After the petty cash fund is established, the Petty Cash account is not debited or credited again unless the amount of the fund is changed. (A fund should be increased if it requires reimbursement too frequently. On the other hand, if the fund is too large, some of its money should be redeposited in the Cash account.)

Next, assume that Z-Mart's petty cashier makes several November payments from petty cash. Each person who received payment is required to sign a receipt. On November 27, after making a $26.50 cash payment for tile cleaning, only $3.70 cash remains in the fund. The petty cashier then summarizes and totals the petty cash receipts as shown in Exhibit 6.3.

EXHIBIT 6.3
Petty Cash Payments Report

Z-MART
Petty Cash Payments Report

Miscellaneous Expenses			
Nov. 2	Cleaning of LCD panels	$20.00	
Nov. 27	Tile cleaning	26.50	$ 46.50
Merchandise Inventory (transportation-in)			
Nov. 5	Transport of merchandise purchased	6.75	
Nov. 20	Transport of merchandise purchased	8.30	15.05
Delivery Expense			
Nov. 18	Customer's package delivered		5.00
Office Supplies Expense			
Nov. 15	Purchase of office supplies immediately used		4.75
Total			**$71.30**

Point: This report can also include receipt number and names of those who approved and received cash payment (see Demo Problem 2).

The petty cash payments report and all receipts are given to the company cashier in exchange for a $71.30 check to reimburse the fund. The petty cashier cashes the check and puts the $71.30 cash in the petty cashbox. The company records this reimbursement as follows.

Nov. 27	Miscellaneous Expenses	46.50	
	Merchandise Inventory	15.05	
	Delivery Expense	5.00	
	Office Supplies Expense	4.75	
	Cash		71.30
	To reimburse petty cash.		

Assets = Liabilities + Equity
−71.30   −46.50
                   −15.05
                   − 5.00
                   − 4.75

A petty cash fund is usually reimbursed at the end of an accounting period so that expenses are recorded in the proper period, even if the fund is not low on money. If the fund is not reimbursed at the end of a period, the financial statements would show both an overstated cash asset and understated expenses (or assets) that were paid out of petty cash. Some companies do not reimburse the petty cash fund at the end of each period under the notion that this amount is immaterial to users of financial statements.

Point: To avoid errors in recording petty cash reimbursement, follow these steps: (1) prepare payments report, (2) compute cash needed by subtracting cash remaining from total fund amount, (3) record entry, and (4) check "Dr. = Cr." in entry. Any difference is Cash Over and Short.

Increasing or decreasing a petty cash fund. A decision to increase or decrease a petty cash fund is often made when reimbursing it. To illustrate, assume Z-Mart decides to *increase* its petty cash fund from $75 to $100 on November 27 when it reimburses the fund. The entries required are to (1) reimburse the fund as usual (see the preceding November 27 entry) and (2) increase the fund amount as follows.

Nov. 27	Petty Cash	25	
	Cash		25
	To increase the petty cash fund amount.		

Alternatively, if Z-Mart *decreases* the petty cash fund from $75 to $55 on November 27, the entry is to (1) credit Petty Cash for $20 (decreasing the fund from $75 to $55) and (2) debit Cash for $20 (reflecting the $20 transfer from Petty Cash to Cash).

Cash over and short. Sometimes a petty cashier fails to get a receipt for payment or overpays for the amount due. When this occurs and the fund is later reimbursed, the petty cash payments report plus the cash remaining will not total to the fund balance. This mistake causes the fund to be *short*. This shortage is recorded as an expense in the reimbursing entry with a debit to the Cash Over and Short account. (An overage in the petty cash fund is recorded with a credit to Cash Over and Short in the reimbursing entry.) To illustrate, prepare the June 1 entry

Summary of Petty Cash Accounting

Event	Petty Cash	Cash	Expenses
Set up fund	Dr.	Cr.	—
Reimburse fund	—	Cr.	Dr.
Increase fund	Dr.	Cr.	—
Decrease fund	Cr.	Dr.	—

$200 Petty Cash Fund

to reimburse a $200 petty cash fund when its payments report shows $178 in miscellaneous expenses and $15 cash remains.

June 1	Miscellaneous Expenses	178	
	Cash Over and Short	7	
	Cash		185
	To reimburse petty cash.		

Decision Insight

Warning Signs There are clues to internal control violations. Warning signs from accounting include (1) an increase in customer refunds—could be fake, (2) missing documents—could be used for fraud, (3) differences between bank deposits and cash receipts—could be cash embezzled, and (4) delayed recording—could reflect fraudulent records. Warning signs from employees include (1) lifestyle change—could be embezzlement, (2) too close with suppliers—could signal fraudulent transactions, and (3) failure to leave job, even for vacations—could conceal fraudulent activities. ■

Quick Check
Answers — p. 277

8. Why are some cash payments made from a petty cash fund and not by check?
9. Why should a petty cash fund be reimbursed at the end of an accounting period?
10. Identify at least two results of reimbursing a petty cash fund.

BANKING ACTIVITIES AS CONTROLS

Banks (and other financial institutions) provide many services, including helping companies control cash. Banks safeguard cash, provide detailed and independent records of cash transactions, and are a source of cash financing. This section describes these services and the documents provided by banking activities that increase managers' control over cash.

Basic Bank Services

This section explains basic bank services—such as the bank account, the bank deposit, and checking—that contribute to the control of cash.

Bank Account, Deposit, and Check A *bank account* is a record set up by a bank for a customer. It permits a customer to deposit money for safekeeping and helps control withdrawals. To limit access to a bank account, all persons authorized to write checks on the account must sign a **signature card,** which bank employees use to verify signatures on checks. Many companies have more than one bank account to serve different needs and to handle special transactions such as payroll.

Each bank deposit is supported by a **deposit ticket,** which lists items such as currency, coins, and checks deposited along with their corresponding dollar amounts. The bank gives the customer a copy of the deposit ticket or a deposit receipt as proof of the deposit. Exhibit 6.4 shows one type of deposit ticket.

To withdraw money from an account, the depositor can use a **check,** which is a document signed by the depositor instructing the bank to pay a specified amount of money to a designated recipient. A check involves three parties: a *maker* who signs the check, a *payee* who is the recipient, and a *bank* (or *payer*) on which the check is drawn. The bank provides a depositor the checks that are serially numbered and imprinted with the name and address of both the depositor and bank. Both checks and deposit tickets are imprinted with identification codes in magnetic ink

Point: Online banking services include the ability to stop payment on a check, move money between accounts, get up-to-date balances, and identify cleared checks and deposits.

EXHIBIT 6.4

Deposit Ticket

for computer processing. Exhibit 6.5 shows one type of check. It is accompanied with an optional *remittance advice* explaining the payment. When a remittance advice is unavailable, the *memo* line is often used for a brief explanation.

Electronic Funds Transfer Electronic funds transfer (EFT) is the electronic transfer of cash from one party to another. No paper documents are necessary. Banks simply transfer cash from one account to another with a journal entry. Companies are increasingly using EFT

EXHIBIT 6.5

Check with Remittance Advice

because of its convenience and low cost. For instance, it can cost up to 50 cents to process a check through the banking system, whereas EFT cost is near zero. We now commonly see items such as payroll, rent, utilities, insurance, and interest payments being handled by EFT. The bank statement lists cash withdrawals by EFT with the checks and other deductions. Cash receipts by EFT are listed with deposits and other additions. A bank statement is sometimes a depositor's only notice of an EFT. *Automated teller machines (ATMs)* are one form of EFT, which allows bank customers to deposit, withdraw, and transfer cash.

Bank Statement

Point: Good internal control is to deposit all cash receipts daily and make all payments for goods and services by check. This controls access to cash and creates an independent record of all cash activities.

Usually once a month, the bank sends each depositor a **bank statement** showing the activity in the account. Although a monthly statement is common, companies often regularly access information on their banking transactions. (Companies can choose to record any accounting adjustments required from the bank statement immediately or later, say, at the end of each day, week, month, or when reconciling a bank statement.) Different banks use different formats for their bank statements, but all of them include the following items of information:

1. Beginning-of-period balance of the depositor's account.
2. Checks and other debits decreasing the account during the period.
3. Deposits and other credits increasing the account during the period.
4. End-of-period balance of the depositor's account.

This information reflects the bank's records. Exhibit 6.6 shows one type of bank statement. Identify each of these four items in that statement. Part Ⓐ of Exhibit 6.6 summarizes changes in the account. Part Ⓑ lists paid checks along with other debits. Part Ⓒ lists deposits and credits to the account, and part Ⓓ shows the daily account balances.

In reading a bank statement note that a depositor's account is a liability on the bank's records. This is so because the money belongs to the depositor, not the bank. When a depositor increases

EXHIBIT 6.6

Bank Statement

FN First National
Hillcrest, New York 11750

Bank Statement

Member FDIC

VideoBuster Company
901 Main Street
Hillcrest, NY 11749

October 31, 2011
Statement Date

494 504 2
Account Number

Ⓐ

Previous Balance	Total Checks and Debits	Total Deposits and Credits	Current Balance
1,609.58	723.00	1,163.42	2,050.00

Ⓑ **Checks and Debits** | Ⓒ **Deposits and Credits** | Ⓓ **Daily Balance**

Date	No.	Amount	Date	Amount	Date	Amount
10/03	119	55.00	10/02	240.00	10/01	1,609.58
10/09	120	200.00	10/09	180.00	10/02	1,849.58
10/10	121	120.00	10/15	100.00 EFT	10/03	1,794.58
10/12		23.00 DM	10/16	150.00	10/09	1,774.58
10/14	122	70.00	10/23	485.00 CM	10/10	1,654.58
10/16	123	25.00	10/31	8.42 IN	10/12	1,631.58
10/23	125	15.00			10/14	1,561.58
10/25		20.00 NSF			10/15	1,661.58
		10.00 DM			10/16	1,786.58
10/26	127	50.00			10/23	2,256.58
10/29	128	135.00			10/25	2,226.58
					10/26	2,176.58
					10/29	2,041.58
					10/31	2,050.00

Symbols: **CM**–Credit Memo **EC**–Error Correction **NSF**–Non-Sufficient Funds **SC**–Service Charge
DM–Debit Memo **IN**–Interest Earned **EFT**–Electronic Funds Transfer **OD**–Overdraft

< Reconcile the account immediately. >

Point: Many banks separately report other debits and credits apart from checks and deposits.

the account balance, the bank records it with a *credit* to that liability account. This means that debit memos from the bank produce *credits* on the depositor's books, and credit memos from the bank produce *debits* on the depositor's books.

Enclosed with a bank statement is a list of the depositor's canceled checks (or the actual canceled checks) along with any debit or credit memoranda affecting the account. Increasingly, banks are showing canceled checks electronically via online access to accounts. **Canceled checks** are checks the bank has paid and deducted from the customer's account during the period. Other deductions that can appear on a bank statement include (1) service charges and fees assessed by the bank, (2) checks deposited that are uncollectible, (3) corrections of previous errors, (4) withdrawals through automated teller machines (ATMs), and (5) periodic payments arranged in advance by a depositor. (Most company checking accounts do not allow ATM withdrawals because of the company's desire to make all disbursements by check.) Except for service charges, the bank notifies the depositor of each deduction with a debit memorandum when the bank reduces the balance. A copy of each debit memorandum is usually sent with the statement (again, this information is often available earlier via online access and notifications).

Transactions that increase the depositor's account include amounts the bank collects on behalf of the depositor and the corrections of previous errors. Credit memoranda notify the depositor of all increases when they are recorded. A copy of each credit memorandum is often sent with the bank statement. Banks that pay interest on checking accounts often compute the amount of interest earned on the average cash balance and credit it to the depositor's account each period. In Exhibit 6.6, the bank credits $8.42 of interest to the account.

Global: If cash is in more than one currency, a company usually translates these amounts into U.S. dollars using the exchange rate as of the balance sheet date. Also, a company must disclose any restrictions on cash accounts located outside the U.S.

Bank Reconciliation

When a company deposits all cash receipts and makes all cash payments (except petty cash) by check, it can use the bank statement for proving the accuracy of its cash records. This is done using a **bank reconciliation,** which is a report explaining any differences between the checking account balance according to the depositor's records and the balance reported on the bank statement. The figure below reflects this process, which we describe in the following sections.

P3 Prepare a bank reconciliation.

Bank Balance

Bank Statement
Checks & debits ...... #
Deposits & credits.... #
Balance.................. #

Bank Reconciliation

Bank balance............. #
Add & deduct:
• Timing differences #
• Any errors #
Adjusted bank bal....... #

Book balance............. #
Add & deduct:
• Timing differences #
• Any errors #
Adjusted book bal....... #

Book Balance

Cash Account
Cash receipts | #
Cash disbursements | #
Balance | #

Purpose of Bank Reconciliation The balance of a checking account reported on the bank statement rarely equals the balance in the depositor's accounting records. This is usually due to information that one party has that the other does not. We must therefore prove the accuracy of both the depositor's records and those of the bank. This means we must *reconcile* the two balances and explain or account for any differences in them. Among the factors causing the bank statement balance to differ from the depositor's book balance are these:

- **Outstanding checks. Outstanding checks** are checks written (or drawn) by the depositor, deducted on the depositor's records, and sent to the payees but not yet received by the bank for payment at the bank statement date.

- **Deposits in transit** (also called **outstanding deposits**). **Deposits in transit** are deposits made and recorded by the depositor but not yet recorded on the bank statement. For example, companies can make deposits (in the night depository) at the end of a business day after the bank is closed. If such a deposit occurred on a bank statement date, it would not appear on this period's statement. The bank would record such a deposit on the next business day, and it would appear on the next period's bank statement. Deposits mailed to the bank near the end of a period also can be in transit and unrecorded when the statement is prepared.

- **Deductions for uncollectible items and for services.** A company sometimes deposits another party's check that is uncollectible (usually meaning the balance in that party's account is not large enough to cover the check). This check is called a *non-sufficient funds (NSF)* check. The bank would have initially credited the depositor's account for the amount of the

Forms of Check Fraud (CkFraud.org)

- Forged signatures—legitimate blank checks with fake payer signature
- Forged endorsements—stolen check that is endorsed and cashed by someone other than the payee
- Counterfeit checks—fraudulent checks with fake payer signature
- Altered checks—legitimate check altered (such as changed payee or amount) to benefit perpetrator
- Check kiting—deposit check from one bank account (without sufficient funds) into a second bank account

check. When the bank learns the check is uncollectible, it debits (reduces) the depositor's account for the amount of that check. The bank may also charge the depositor a fee for processing an uncollectible check and notify the depositor of the deduction by sending a debit memorandum. The depositor should record each deduction when a debit memorandum is received, but an entry is sometimes not made until the bank reconciliation is prepared. Other possible bank charges to a depositor's account that are first reported on a bank statement include printing new checks and service fees.

- **Additions for collections and for interest.** Banks sometimes act as collection agents for their depositors by collecting notes and other items. Banks can also receive electronic funds transfers to the depositor's account. When a bank collects an item, it is added to the depositor's account, less any service fee. The bank also sends a credit memorandum to notify the depositor of the transaction. When the memorandum is received, the depositor should record it; yet it sometimes remains unrecorded until the bank reconciliation is prepared. The bank statement also includes a credit for any interest earned.

- **Errors.** Both banks and depositors can make errors. Bank errors might not be discovered until the depositor prepares the bank reconciliation. Also, depositor errors are sometimes discovered when the bank balance is reconciled. Error testing includes: (a) comparing deposits on the bank statement with deposits in the accounting records and (b) comparing canceled checks on the bank statement with checks recorded in the accounting records.

Illustration of a Bank Reconciliation We follow nine steps in preparing the bank reconciliation. It is helpful to refer to the bank reconciliation in Exhibit 6.7 when studying steps ① through ⑨.

Point: Small businesses with few employees often allow recordkeepers to both write checks and keep the general ledger. If this is done, it is essential that the owner do the bank reconciliation.

Point: The person preparing the bank reconciliation should not be responsible for processing cash receipts, managing checks, or maintaining cash records.

EXHIBIT 6.7

Bank Reconciliation

	VIDEOBUSTER						
	Bank Reconciliation						
	October 31, 2011						
① Bank statement balance			$ 2,050.00	⑤ Book balance			$ 1,404.58
② Add				⑥ Add			
Deposit of Oct. 31 in transit			145.00	Collect $500 note less $15 fee		$485.00	
			2,195.00	Interest earned		8.42	493.42
③ Deduct							1,898.00
Outstanding checks				⑦ Deduct			
No. 124		$150.00		Check printing charge		23.00	
No. 126		200.00	350.00	NSF check plus service fee		30.00	53.00
④ **Adjusted bank balance**			**$1,845.00**	⑧ **Adjusted book balance**			**$1,845.00**
				⑨ Balances are equal (reconciled)			

① Identify the bank statement balance of the cash account (*balance per bank*). VideoBuster's bank balance is $2,050.

② Identify and list any unrecorded deposits and any bank errors understating the bank balance. Add them to the bank balance. VideoBuster's $145 deposit placed in the bank's night depository on October 31 is not recorded on its bank statement.

③ Identify and list any outstanding checks and any bank errors overstating the bank balance. Deduct them from the bank balance. VideoBuster's comparison of canceled checks with its books shows two checks outstanding: No. 124 for $150 and No. 126 for $200.

④ Compute the *adjusted bank balance*, also called the *corrected* or *reconciled balance.*

⑤ Identify the company's book balance of the cash account (*balance per book*). VideoBuster's book balance is $1,404.58.

⑥ Identify and list any unrecorded credit memoranda from the bank, any interest earned, and errors understating the book balance. Add them to the book balance. VideoBuster's bank statement includes a credit memorandum showing the bank collected a note receivable for the

Point: Outstanding checks are identified by comparing canceled checks on the bank statement with checks recorded. This includes identifying any outstanding checks listed on the *previous* period's bank reconciliation that are not included in the canceled checks on this period's bank statement.

company on October 23. The note's proceeds of $500 (minus a $15 collection fee) are credited to the company's account. VideoBuster's bank statement also shows a credit of $8.42 for interest earned on the average cash balance. There was no prior notification of this item, and it is not yet recorded.

7 Identify and list any unrecorded debit memoranda from the bank, any service charges, and errors overstating the book balance. Deduct them from the book balance. Debits on VideoBuster's bank statement that are not yet recorded include (a) a $23 charge for check printing and (b) an NSF check for $20 plus a related $10 processing fee. (The NSF check is dated October 16 and was included in the book balance.)

8 Compute the *adjusted book balance,* also called *corrected* or *reconciled balance.*

9 Verify that the two adjusted balances from steps 4 and 8 are equal. If so, they are reconciled. If not, check for accuracy and missing data to achieve reconciliation.

Point: Adjusting entries can be combined into one compound entry.

Adjusting Entries from a Bank Reconciliation A bank reconciliation often identifies unrecorded items that need recording by the company. In VideoBuster's reconciliation, the adjusted balance of $1,845 is the correct balance as of October 31. But the company's accounting records show a $1,404.58 balance. We must prepare journal entries to adjust the book balance to the correct balance. It is important to remember that only the items reconciling the book balance require adjustment. A review of Exhibit 6.7 indicates that four entries are required for VideoBuster.

Collection of note. The first entry is to record the proceeds of its note receivable collected by the bank less the expense of having the bank perform that service.

Oct. 31	Cash	485	
	Collection Expense	15	
	Notes Receivable...........................		500
	To record the collection fee and proceeds		
	for a note collected by the bank.		

Assets = Liabilities + Equity
+485   −15
−500

Interest earned. The second entry records interest credited to its account by the bank.

Oct. 31	Cash	8.42	
	Interest Revenue		8.42
	To record interest earned on the cash		
	balance in the checking account.		

Assets = Liabilities + Equity
+8.42   +8.42

Check printing. The third entry records expenses for the check printing charge.

Oct. 31	Miscellaneous Expenses.........................	23	
	Cash		23
	Check printing charge.		

Assets = Liabilities + Equity
−23   −23

NSF check. The fourth entry records the NSF check that is returned as uncollectible. The $20 check was originally received from T. Woods in payment of his account and then deposited. The bank charged $10 for handling the NSF check and deducted $30 total from VideoBuster's account. This means the entry must reverse the effects of the original entry made when the check was received and must record (add) the $10 bank fee.

Point: The company will try to collect the entire NSF amount of $30 from customer.

Oct. 31	Accounts Receivable—T. Woods	30	
	Cash		30
	To charge Woods' account for $20 NSF check		
	and $10 bank fee.		

Assets = Liabilities + Equity
+30
−30

Point: The Demo Problem 1 shows an adjusting entry for an error correction.

Cash			
Unadj. bal.	1,404.58		
(6)	485.00	(7)	23.00
(6)	8.42	(7)	30.00
Adj. bal.	1,845.00		

After these four entries are recorded, the book balance of cash is adjusted to the correct amount of $1,845 (computed as $1,404.58 + $485 + $8.42 − $23 − $30). The Cash T-account to the side shows the same computation, where entries are keyed to the numerical codes in Exhibit 6.7.

Fraud

Fraud. A survey reports that 74% of employees had 'personally seen' or had 'firsthand knowledge of' fraud or misconduct in their company within the past year. These employees also identified factors that would drive employees and managers to engage in misconduct. They cited pressures to meet targets, lack of standards, and other root causes—see graphic (KPMG 2009).

Percent Citing These Root Causes
- Pressure to meet targets: 59%
- Results oriented, means irrelevant: 52%
- Lack of standards: 51%
- Code of conduct dismissed: 51%

Quick Check
Answers — p. 277

11. What is a bank statement?
12. What is the meaning of the phrase *to reconcile a bank balance*?
13. Why do we reconcile the bank statement balance of cash and the depositor's book balance of cash?
14. List at least two items affecting the *bank balance* side of a bank reconciliation and indicate whether the items are added or subtracted.
15. List at least three items affecting the *book balance* side of a bank reconciliation and indicate whether the items are added or subtracted.

GLOBAL VIEW

This section discusses similarities and differences between U.S. GAAP and IFRS regarding internal controls and in the accounting and reporting of cash.

Internal Control Purposes, Principles, and Procedures Both U.S. GAAP and IFRS aim for high-quality financial reporting. That aim translates into enhanced internal controls worldwide. Specifically, the purposes and principles of internal control systems are fundamentally the same across the globe. However, culture and other realities suggest different emphases on the mix of control procedures, and some sensitivity to different customs and environments when establishing that mix. Nevertheless, the discussion in this chapter applies internationally. **Nokia** provides the following description of its control activities.

NOKIA

> Nokia has an internal audit function that acts as an independent appraisal function by examining and evaluating the adequacy and effectiveness of the company's system of internal control.

Control of Cash Accounting definitions for cash are similar for U.S. GAAP and IFRS. The need for control of cash is universal and applies globally. This means that companies worldwide desire to apply cash management procedures as explained in this chapter and aim to control both cash receipts and disbursements. Accordingly, systems that employ tools such as cash monitoring mechanisms, verification of documents, and petty cash processes are applied worldwide. The basic techniques explained in this chapter are part of those control procedures.

Banking Activities as Controls There is a global demand for banking services, bank statements, and bank reconciliations. To the extent feasible, companies utilize banking services as part of their effective control procedures. Further, bank statements are similarly used along with bank reconciliations to control and monitor cash.

IFRS

Internal controls are crucial to companies that convert from U.S. GAAP to IFRS. Major risks include misstatement of financial information and fraud. Other risks are ineffective communication of the impact of this change for investors, creditors and others, and management's inability to certify the effectiveness of controls over financial reporting. ●

Decision Analysis

Days' Sales Uncollected

A1 Compute the days' sales uncollected ratio and use it to assess liquidity.

An important part of cash management is monitoring the receipt of cash from receivables. If customers and others who owe money to a company are delayed in payment, then that company can find it difficult to pay its obligations when they are due. A company's customers are crucial partners in its cash management. Many companies attract customers by selling to them on credit. This means that cash receipts from customers are delayed until accounts receivable are collected.

One measure of how quickly a company can convert its accounts receivable into cash is the **days' sales uncollected**, also called *days' sales in receivables*. This measure is computed by dividing the current balance of receivables by net credit sales over the year just completed and then multiplying by 365 (number of days in a year). Since net credit sales usually are not reported to external users, the net sales (or revenues) figure is commonly used in the computation as in Exhibit 6.8.

$$\text{Days' sales uncollected} = \frac{\text{Accounts receivable}}{\text{Net sales}} \times 365$$

EXHIBIT 6.8
Days' Sales Uncollected

We use days' sales uncollected to estimate how much time is likely to pass before the current amount of accounts receivable is received in cash. For evaluation purposes, we need to compare this estimate to that for other companies in the same industry. We also make comparisons between current and prior periods.

To illustrate, we select data from the annual reports of two toy manufacturers, **Hasbro** and **Mattel**. Their days' sales uncollected figures are shown in Exhibit 6.9.

Company	Figure ($ millions)	2009	2008	2007	2006	2005
Hasbro	Accounts receivable	$1,039	$612	$655	$556	$523
	Net sales	$4,068	$4,022	$3,838	$3,151	$3,088
	Days' sales uncollected	93 days	56 days	62 days	64 days	62 days
Mattel	Accounts receivable	$749	$874	$991	$944	$761
	Net sales	$5,431	$5,918	$5,970	$5,650	$5,179
	Days' sales uncollected	50 days	54 days	61 days	61 days	54 days

EXHIBIT 6.9
Analysis Using Days' Sales Uncollected

Days' sales uncollected for Hasbro in 2009 is computed as ($1,039/$4,068) × 365 days = 93 days. This means that it will take about 93 days to collect cash from ending accounts receivable. This number reflects one or more of the following factors: a company's ability to collect receivables, customer financial health, customer payment strategies, and discount terms. To further assess days' sales uncollected for Hasbro, we compare it to four prior years and to those of Mattel. We see that Hasbro's days' sales uncollected has worsened in 2009 as it takes much longer to collect its receivables relative to the prior four years. In comparison, Mattel fluctuated on days' sales uncollected for each of those years—from 54 days, to 61 days for two years, then back down to 54 days, and then down to the current 50 days. For all years, Mattel is superior to Hasbro on this measure of cash management. The less time that money is tied up in receivables often translates into increased profitability.

Decision Maker

Answer — p. 277

Sales Representative The sales staff is told to take action to help reduce days' sales uncollected for cash management purposes. What can you, a salesperson, do to reduce days' sales uncollected? ■

DEMONSTRATION PROBLEM 1

Prepare a bank reconciliation for Jamboree Enterprises for the month ended November 30, 2011. The following information is available to reconcile Jamboree Enterprises' book balance of cash with its bank statement balance as of November 30, 2011:

a. After all posting is complete on November 30, the company's book balance of Cash has a $16,380 debit balance, but its bank statement shows a $38,520 balance.

b. Checks No. 2024 for $4,810 and No. 2026 for $5,000 are outstanding.

c. In comparing the canceled checks on the bank statement with the entries in the accounting records, it is found that Check No. 2025 in payment of rent is correctly drawn for $1,000 but is erroneously entered in the accounting records as $880.

d. The November 30 deposit of $17,150 was placed in the night depository after banking hours on that date, and this amount does not appear on the bank statement.

e. In reviewing the bank statement, a check written by Jumbo Enterprises in the amount of $160 was erroneously drawn against Jamboree's account.

f. A credit memorandum enclosed with the bank statement indicates that the bank collected a $30,000 note and $900 of related interest on Jamboree's behalf. This transaction was not recorded by Jamboree prior to receiving the statement.

g. A debit memorandum for $1,100 lists a $1,100 NSF check received from a customer, Marilyn Welch. Jamboree had not recorded the return of this check before receiving the statement.

h. Bank service charges for November total $40. These charges were not recorded by Jamboree before receiving the statement.

PLANNING THE SOLUTION

- Set up a bank reconciliation with a bank side and a book side (as in Exhibit 6.7). Leave room to both add and deduct items. Each column will result in a reconciled, equal balance.
- Examine each item *a* through *h* to determine whether it affects the book or the bank balance and whether it should be added or deducted from the bank or book balance.
- After all items are analyzed, complete the reconciliation and arrive at a reconciled balance between the bank side and the book side.
- For each reconciling item on the book side, prepare an adjusting entry. Additions to the book side require an adjusting entry that debits Cash. Deductions on the book side require an adjusting entry that credits Cash.

SOLUTION TO DEMONSTRATION PROBLEM 1

JAMBOREE ENTERPRISES
Bank Reconciliation
November 30, 2011

Bank statement balance		$ 38,520	Book balance		$ 16,380
Add			Add		
Deposit of Nov. 30	$17,150		Collection of note	$30,000	
Bank error (Jumbo)	160	17,310	Interest earned	900	30,900
		55,830			47,280
Deduct			Deduct		
Outstanding checks			NSF check (M. Welch)	1,100	
No. 2024	4,810		Recording error (# 2025)	120	
No. 2026	5,000	9,810	Service charge	40	1,260
Adjusted bank balance		**$46,020**	**Adjusted book balance**		**$46,020**

Chapter 6 Reporting and Analyzing Cash and Internal Controls

Required Adjusting Entries for Jamboree

Date	Account	Debit	Credit
Nov. 30	Cash	30,900	
	Notes Receivable		30,000
	Interest Earned		900
	To record collection of note with interest.		
Nov. 30	Accounts Receivable—M. Welch	1,100	
	Cash		1,100
	To reinstate account due from an NSF check.		
Nov. 30	Rent Expense	120	
	Cash		120
	To correct recording error on check no. 2025.		
Nov. 30	Bank Service Charges	40	
	Cash		40
	To record bank service charges.		

Point: Error correction can alternatively involve (1) reversing the error entry, and (2) recording the correct entry.

DEMONSTRATION PROBLEM 2

Bacardi Company established a $150 petty cash fund with Dean Martin as the petty cashier. When the fund balance reached $19 cash, Martin prepared a petty cash payment report, which follows.

Petty Cash Payments Report

Receipt No.	Account Charged		Approved by	Received by
12	Delivery Expense	$ 29	Martin	A. Smirnoff
13	Merchandise Inventory	18	Martin	J. Daniels
15	(Omitted)	32	Martin	C. Carlsberg
16	Miscellaneous Expense	41	(Omitted)	J. Walker
	Total	$120		

Required

1. Identify four internal control weaknesses from the payment report.
2. Prepare general journal entries to record:
   a. Establishment of the petty cash fund.
   b. Reimbursement of the fund. (Assume for this part only that petty cash receipt no. 15 was issued for miscellaneous expenses.)
3. What is the Petty Cash account balance immediately before reimbursement? Immediately after reimbursement?

SOLUTION TO DEMONSTRATION PROBLEM 2

1. Four internal control weaknesses are
   a. Petty cash ticket no. 14 is missing. Its omission raises questions about the petty cashier's management of the fund.
   b. The $19 cash balance means that $131 has been withdrawn ($150 − $19 = $131). However, the total amount of the petty cash receipts is only $120 ($29 + $18 + $32 + $41). The fund is $11 short of cash ($131 − $120 = $11). Was petty cash receipt no. 14 issued for $11? Management should investigate.
   c. The petty cashier (Martin) did not sign petty cash receipt no. 16. This omission could have been an oversight on his part or he might not have authorized the payment. Management should investigate.
   d. Petty cash receipt no. 15 does not indicate which account to charge. This omission could have been an oversight on the petty cashier's part. Management could check with C. Carlsberg and the petty cashier (Martin) about the transaction. Without further information, debit Miscellaneous Expense.

2. Petty cash general journal entries.

   a. Entry to establish the petty cash fund.

Petty Cash	150	
Cash		150

   b. Entry to reimburse the fund.

Delivery Expense	29	
Merchandise Inventory	18	
Miscellaneous Expense ($41 + $32)	73	
Cash Over and Short	11	
Cash		131

3. The Petty Cash account balance *always* equals its fund balance, in this case $150. This account balance does not change unless the fund is increased or decreased.

APPENDIX 6A — Documentation and Verification

This appendix describes the important business documents of a voucher system of control.

P4 Describe the use of documentation and verification to control cash disbursements.

Purchase Requisition Department managers are usually not allowed to place orders directly with suppliers for control purposes. Instead, a department manager must inform the purchasing department of its needs by preparing and signing a **purchase requisition,** which lists the merchandise needed and requests that it be purchased—see Exhibit 6A.1. Two copies of the purchase requisition are sent to the purchasing department, which then sends one copy to the accounting department. When the accounting department receives a purchase requisition, it creates and maintains a voucher for this transaction. The requesting department keeps the third copy.

EXHIBIT 6A.1
Purchase Requisition

Z-Mart

PURCHASE REQUISITION — No. 917

From: Sporting Goods Department
To: Purchasing Department
Date: October 28, 2011
Preferred Vendor: Trex

Request purchase of the following item(s):

MODEL NO.	DESCRIPTION	QUANTITY
CH 015	Challenger X7	1
SD 099	SpeedDemon	1

Reason for Request: Replenish inventory
Approval for Request: T.Z.

For Purchasing Department use only: Order Date 10/30/11 P.O. No. P98

Point: A voucher system is designed to uniquely meet the needs of a specific business. Thus, we should read this appendix as one example of a common voucher system design, but *not* the only design.

Purchase Order A **purchase order** is a document the purchasing department uses to place an order with a **vendor** (seller or supplier). A purchase order authorizes a vendor to ship ordered merchandise at the stated price and terms—see Exhibit 6A.2. When the purchasing department receives a purchase requisition, it prepares at least five copies of a purchase order. The copies are distributed as follows: *copy 1* to the vendor as a purchase request and as authority to ship merchandise; *copy 2,* along with a copy of the purchase requisition, to the accounting department, where it is entered in the voucher and used in approving payment of the invoice; *copy 3* to the requesting department to inform its manager that action is being taken; *copy 4* to the receiving department without order quantity so it can compare with goods received and provide independent count of goods received; and *copy 5* retained on file by the purchasing department.

EXHIBIT 6A.2

Purchase Order

Z-Mart — 10 Michigan Street, Chicago, Illinois 60521

PURCHASE ORDER No. P98

To: Trex, W9797 Cherry Road, Antigo, Wisconsin 54409

Date: 10/30/11
FOB: Destination
Ship by: As soon as possible
Terms: 2/15, n/30

Request shipment of the following item(s):

Model No.	Description	Quantity	Price	Amount
CH 015	Challenger X7	1	490	490
SD 099	SpeedDemon	1	710	710

All shipments and invoices must include purchase order number

J.W.
ORDERED BY

Invoice An **invoice** is an itemized statement of goods prepared by the vendor listing the customer's name, items sold, sales prices, and terms of sale. An invoice is also a bill sent to the buyer from the supplier. From the vendor's point of view, it is a *sales invoice*. The buyer, or **vendee**, treats it as a *purchase invoice*. When receiving a purchase order, the vendor ships the ordered merchandise to the buyer and includes or mails a copy of the invoice covering the shipment to the buyer. The invoice is sent to the buyer's accounting department where it is placed in the voucher. (Refer back to Exhibit 4.5, which shows Z-Mart's purchase invoice.)

Receiving Report Many companies maintain a separate department to receive all merchandise and purchased assets. When each shipment arrives, this receiving department counts the goods and checks them for damage and agreement with the purchase order. It then prepares four or more copies of a **receiving report,** which is used within the company to notify the appropriate persons that ordered goods have been received and to describe the quantities and condition of the goods. One copy is sent to accounting and placed in the voucher. Copies are also sent to the requesting department and the purchasing department to notify them that the goods have arrived. The receiving department retains a copy in its files.

Invoice Approval When a receiving report arrives, the accounting department should have copies of the following documents in the voucher: purchase requisition, purchase order, and invoice. With the information in these documents, the accounting department can record the purchase and approve its payment. In approving an invoice for payment, it checks and compares information across all documents. To facilitate this checking and to ensure that no step is omitted, it often uses an **invoice approval,** also called *check authorization*—see Exhibit 6A.3. An invoice approval is a checklist of steps necessary for approving an invoice for recording and payment. It is a separate document either filed in the voucher or preprinted (or stamped) on the voucher.

EXHIBIT 6A.3

Invoice Approval

INVOICE APPROVAL

DOCUMENT		BY	DATE
Purchase requisition	917	TZ	10/28/11
Purchase order	P98	JW	10/30/11
Receiving report	R85	SK	11/03/11
Invoice:	4657		11/12/11
Price		JK	11/12/11
Calculations		JK	11/12/11
Terms		JK	11/12/11
Approved for payment		BC	

Point: Recording a purchase is initiated by an invoice approval, not an invoice. An invoice approval verifies that the amount is consistent with that requested, ordered, and received. This controls and verifies purchases and related liabilities.

As each step in the checklist is approved, the person initials the invoice approval and records the current date. Final approval implies the following steps have occurred:

1. **Requisition check:** Items on invoice are requested per purchase requisition.
2. **Purchase order check:** Items on invoice are ordered per purchase order.
3. **Receiving report check:** Items on invoice are received per receiving report.
4. **Invoice check: Price:** Invoice prices are as agreed with the vendor.
   Calculations: Invoice has no mathematical errors.
   Terms: Terms are as agreed with the vendor.

Voucher Once an invoice has been checked and approved, the voucher is complete. A complete voucher is a record summarizing a transaction. Once the voucher certifies a transaction, it authorizes recording an obligation. A voucher also contains approval for paying the obligation on an appropriate date. The physical form of a voucher varies across companies. Many are designed so that the invoice and other related source documents are placed inside the voucher, which can be a folder.

Completion of a voucher usually requires a person to enter certain information on both the inside and outside of the voucher. Typical information required on the inside of a voucher is shown in Exhibit 6A.4, and that for the outside is shown in Exhibit 6A.5. This information is taken from the invoice and the supporting documents filed in the voucher. A complete voucher is sent to an authorized individual (often called an *auditor*). This person performs a final review, approves the accounts and amounts for debiting (called the *accounting distribution*), and authorizes recording of the voucher.

EXHIBIT 6A.4

Inside of a Voucher

After a voucher is approved and recorded (in a journal called a **voucher register**), it is filed by its due date. A check is then sent on the payment date from the cashier, the voucher is marked "paid," and the voucher is sent to the accounting department and recorded (in a journal called the **check register**). The person issuing checks relies on the approved voucher and its signed supporting documents as proof that an obligation has been incurred and must be paid. The purchase requisition and purchase order confirm the purchase was authorized. The receiving report shows that items have been received, and the invoice approval form verifies that the invoice has been checked for errors. There is little chance for error and even less chance for fraud without collusion unless all the documents and signatures are forged.

EXHIBIT 6A.5

Outside of a Voucher

APPENDIX 6B

Control of Purchase Discounts

This appendix explains how a company can better control its cash *disbursements* to take advantage of favorable purchases discounts. Chapter 4 described the entries to record the receipt and payment of an invoice for a merchandise purchase with and without discount terms. Those entries were prepared under what is called the **gross method** of recording purchases, which initially records the invoice at its *gross* amount ignoring any cash discount.

The **net method** is another means of recording purchases, which initially records the invoice at its *net* amount of any cash discount. The net method gives management an advantage in controlling and monitoring cash payments involving purchase discounts.

To explain, when invoices are recorded at *gross* amounts, the amount of any discounts taken is deducted from the balance of the Merchandise Inventory account when cash payment is made. This means that the amount of any discounts lost is not reported in any account or on the income statement. Lost discounts recorded in this way are unlikely to come to the attention of management. When purchases are recorded at *net* amounts, a **Discounts Lost** expense account is recorded and brought to management's attention. Management can then seek to identify the reason for discounts lost such as oversight, carelessness, or unfavorable terms. (Chapter 4 explains how managers assess whether a discount is favorable or not.)

P5 Apply the net method to control purchase discounts.

Perpetual Inventory System To illustrate, assume that a company purchases merchandise on November 2 at a $1,200 invoice price with terms of 2/10, n/30. Its November 2 entries under the gross and net methods are

Gross Method—Perpetual			Net Method—Perpetual		
Merchandise Inventory	1,200		Merchandise Inventory	1,176	
Accounts Payable		1,200	Accounts Payable		1,176

If the invoice is paid on November 12 within the discount period, it records the following:

Gross Method—Perpetual			Net Method—Perpetual		
Accounts Payable	1,200		Accounts Payable	1,176	
Merchandise Inventory		24	Cash		1,176
Cash		1,176			

If the invoice is *not* paid within the discount period, it records the following November 12 entry (which is the date corresponding to the end of the discount period):

Gross Method—Perpetual	Net Method—Perpetual
No entry	Discounts Lost 24
	Accounts Payable 24

Then, when the invoice is later paid on December 2, outside the discount period, it records the following:

Gross Method—Perpetual	Net Method—Perpetual
Accounts Payable 1,200	Accounts Payable 1,200
Cash 1,200	Cash 1,200

(The discount lost can be recorded when the cash payment is made with a single entry. However, in this case, when financial statements are prepared after a discount is lost and before the cash payment is made, an adjusting entry is required to recognize any unrecorded discount lost in the period when incurred.)

Periodic Inventory System The preceding entries assume a perpetual inventory system. If a company is using a periodic system, its November 2 entries under the gross and net methods are

Gross Method—Periodic	Net Method—Periodic
Purchases 1,200	Purchases 1,176
Accounts Payable 1,200	Accounts Payable 1,176

If the invoice is paid on November 12 within the discount period, it records the following:

Gross Method—Periodic	Net Method—Periodic
Accounts Payable 1,200	Accounts Payable 1,176
Purchases Discounts 24	Cash 1,176
Cash 1,176	

If the invoice is *not* paid within the discount period, it records the following November 12 entry:

Gross Method—Periodic	Net Method—Periodic
No entry	Discounts Lost 24
	Accounts Payable 24

Then, when the invoice is later paid on December 2, outside the discount period, it records the following:

Gross Method—Periodic	Net Method—Periodic
Accounts Payable 1,200	Accounts Payable 1,200
Cash 1,200	Cash 1,200

Summary

C1 **Define internal control and identify its purpose and principles.** An internal control system consists of the policies and procedures managers use to protect assets, ensure reliable accounting, promote efficient operations, and urge adherence to company policies. It can prevent avoidable losses and help managers both plan operations and monitor company and human performance. Principles of good internal control include establishing responsibilities, maintaining adequate records, insuring assets and bonding employees, separating recordkeeping from custody of assets, dividing responsibilities for related transactions, applying technological controls, and performing regular independent reviews.

C2 **Define cash and cash equivalents and explain how to report them.** Cash includes currency, coins, and amounts on (or acceptable for) deposit in checking and savings accounts. Cash equivalents are short-term, highly liquid investment assets readily convertible to a known cash amount and sufficiently close to their maturity date so that market value is not sensitive to interest rate changes. Cash and cash equivalents are liquid assets because they are readily converted into other assets or can be used to pay for goods, services, or liabilities.

A1 **Compute the days' sales uncollected ratio and use it to assess liquidity.** Many companies attract customers by selling to them on credit. This means that cash receipts from customers are delayed until accounts receivable are collected. Users want to know how quickly a company can convert its accounts receivable into cash. The days' sales uncollected ratio, one measure reflecting company liquidity, is computed by dividing the ending balance of receivables by annual net sales, and then multiplying by 365.

P1 **Apply internal control to cash receipts and disbursements.** Internal control of cash receipts ensures that all cash received is properly recorded and deposited. Attention focuses on two important types of cash receipts: over-the-counter and by mail. Good internal control for over-the-counter cash receipts includes use of a cash register, customer review, use of receipts, a permanent transaction record, and separation of the custody of cash from its recordkeeping. Good internal control for cash receipts by mail includes at least two people assigned to open mail and a listing of each sender's name, amount, and explanation. (Banks offer several services that promote the control and safeguarding of cash.)

P2 **Explain and record petty cash fund transactions.** Petty cash disbursements are payments of small amounts for items such as postage, courier fees, minor repairs, and supplies. A company usually sets up one or more petty cash funds. A petty cash fund cashier is responsible for safekeeping the cash, making payments from this fund, and keeping receipts and records. A Petty Cash account is debited only when the fund is established or increased in amount. When the fund is replenished, petty cash disbursements are recorded with debits to expense (or asset) accounts and a credit to cash.

P3 **Prepare a bank reconciliation.** A bank reconciliation proves the accuracy of the depositor's and the bank's records. The bank statement balance is adjusted for items such as outstanding checks and unrecorded deposits made on or before the bank statement date but not reflected on the statement. The book balance is adjusted for items such as service charges, bank collections for the depositor, and interest earned on the account.

P4^A **Describe the use of documentation and verification to control cash disbursements.** A voucher system is a set of procedures and approvals designed to control cash disbursements and acceptance of obligations. The voucher system of control relies on several important documents, including the voucher and its supporting files. A key factor in this system is that only approved departments and individuals are authorized to incur certain obligations.

P5^B **Apply the net method to control purchase discounts.** The net method aids management in monitoring and controlling purchase discounts. When invoices are recorded at gross amounts, the amount of discounts taken is deducted from the balance of the Inventory account. This means that the amount of any discounts lost is not reported in any account and is unlikely to come to the attention of management. When purchases are recorded at net amounts, a Discounts Lost account is brought to management's attention as an operating expense. Management can then seek to identify the reason for discounts lost, such as oversight, carelessness, or unfavorable terms.

Guidance Answers to Decision Maker and Decision Ethics

Entrepreneur A forced vacation policy is part of a good system of internal controls. When employees are forced to take vacations, their ability to hide any fraudulent behavior decreases because others must perform the vacationers' duties. A replacement employee potentially can uncover fraudulent behavior or falsified records. A forced vacation policy is especially important for employees in sensitive positions of handling money or in control of easily transferable assets.

Sales Representative A salesperson can take several steps to reduce days' sales uncollected. These include (1) decreasing the ratio of sales on account to total sales by encouraging more cash sales, (2) identifying customers most delayed in their payments and encouraging earlier payments or cash sales, and (3) applying stricter credit policies to eliminate credit sales to customers that never pay.

Guidance Answers to Quick Checks

1. (*c*)
2. Technology reduces processing errors. It also allows more extensive testing of records, limits the amount of hard evidence, and highlights the importance of separation of duties.
3. A company holds liquid assets so that it can purchase other assets, buy services, and pay obligations.
4. It owns cash equivalents because they yield a return greater than what cash earns (and are readily exchanged for cash).
5. Examples of cash equivalents are 90-day (or less) U.S. Treasury bills, money market funds, and commercial paper (notes).
6. (*a*)
7. A voucher system is used when an owner/manager can no longer control purchasing procedures through personal supervision and direct participation.
8. If all cash payments are made by check, numerous checks for small amounts must be written. Since this practice is expensive and time-consuming, a petty cash fund is often established for making small (immaterial) cash payments.
9. If the petty cash fund is not reimbursed at the end of an accounting period, the transactions involving petty cash are not yet recorded and the petty cash asset is overstated.
10. First, petty cash transactions are recorded when the petty cash fund is reimbursed. Second, reimbursement provides cash to allow the fund to continue being used. Third, reimbursement identifies any cash shortage or overage in the fund.
11. A bank statement is a report prepared by the bank describing the activities in a depositor's account.

12. To reconcile a bank balance means to explain the difference between the cash balance in the depositor's accounting records and the cash balance on the bank statement.

13. The purpose of the bank reconciliation is to determine whether the bank or the depositor has made any errors and whether the bank has entered any transactions affecting the account that the depositor has not recorded.

14. Unrecorded deposits—added
Outstanding checks—subtracted

15. Interest earned—added Debit memos—subtracted
Credit memos—added NSF checks—subtracted
Bank service charges—subtracted

Key Terms

Bank reconciliation (p. 265)
Bank statement (p. 264)
Canceled checks (p. 265)
Cash (p. 255)
Cash equivalents (p. 255)
Cash Over and Short (p. 257)
Check (p. 262)
Check register (p. 274)
Committee of Sponsoring Organizations (COSO) (p. 251)
Days' sales uncollected (p. 269)
Deposit ticket (p. 262)

Deposits in transit (p. 265)
Discounts lost (p. 275)
Electronic funds transfer (EFT) (p. 263)
Gross method (p. 275)
Internal control system (p. 250)
Invoice (p. 273)
Invoice approval (p. 273)
Liquid assets (p. 255)
Liquidity (p. 255)
Net method (p. 275)
Outstanding checks (p. 265)
Petty cash (p. 260)

Principles of internal control (p. 251)
Purchase order (p. 272)
Purchase requisition (p. 272)
Receiving report (p. 273)
Sarbanes-Oxley Act (p. 250)
Section 404 (of SOX) (p. 251)
Signature card (p. 262)
Vendee (p. 273)
Vendor (p. 272)
Voucher (p. 259)
Voucher register (p. 274)
Voucher system (p. 258)

Multiple Choice Quiz Answers on p. 291 mhhe.com/wildFA6e

Additional quiz questions are available at the book's Website.

1. A company needs to replenish its $500 petty cash fund. Its petty cash box has $75 cash and petty cash receipts of $420. The journal entry to replenish the fund includes
  a. A debit to Cash for $75.
  b. A credit to Cash for $75.
  c. A credit to Petty Cash for $420.
  d. A credit to Cash Over and Short for $5.
  e. A debit to Cash Over and Short for $5.

2. The following information is available for Hapley Company:
  - The November 30 bank statement shows a $1,895 balance.
  - The general ledger shows a $1,742 balance at November 30.
  - A $795 deposit placed in the bank's night depository on November 30 does not appear on the November 30 bank statement.
  - Outstanding checks amount to $638 at November 30.
  - A customer's $335 note was collected by the bank in November. A collection fee of $15 was deducted by the bank and the difference deposited in Hapley's account.
  - A bank service charge of $10 is deducted by the bank and appears on the November 30 bank statement.

How will the customer's note appear on Hapley's November 30 bank reconciliation?
  a. $320 appears as an addition to the book balance of cash.
  b. $320 appears as a deduction from the book balance of cash.
  c. $320 appears as an addition to the bank balance of cash.
  d. $320 appears as a deduction from the bank balance of cash.
  e. $335 appears as an addition to the bank balance of cash.

3. Using the information from question 2, what is the reconciled balance on Hapley's November 30 bank reconciliation?
  a. $2,052
  b. $1,895
  c. $1,742
  d. $2,201
  e. $1,184

4. A company had net sales of $84,000 and accounts receivable of $6,720. Its days' sales uncollected is
  a. 3.2 days
  b. 18.4 days
  c. 230.0 days
  d. 29.2 days
  e. 12.5 days

5.[B] A company records its purchases using the net method. On August 1, it purchases merchandise on account for $6,000 with terms of 2/10, n/30. The August 1 journal entry to record this transaction includes a
  a. Debit to Merchandise Inventory for $6,000.
  b. Debit to Merchandise Inventory for $5,880.
  c. Debit to Merchandise Inventory for $120.
  d. Debit to Accounts Payable for $5,880.
  e. Credit to Accounts Payable for $6,000.

Discussion Questions

1. List the seven broad principles of internal control.
2. Internal control procedures are important in every business, but at what stage in the development of a business do they become especially critical?
3. Why should responsibility for related transactions be divided among different departments or individuals?
4. Why should the person who keeps the records of an asset not be the person responsible for its custody?
5. When a store purchases merchandise, why are individual departments not allowed to directly deal with suppliers?
6. What are the limitations of internal controls?
7. Which of the following assets is most liquid? Which is least liquid? Inventory, building, accounts receivable, or cash.
8. What is a petty cash receipt? Who should sign it?
9. Why should cash receipts be deposited on the day of receipt?
10. **Research In Motion**'s statement of cash flows in Appendix A describes changes in cash and cash equivalents for the year ended February 27, 2010. What total amount is provided (used) by investing activities? What amount is provided (used) by financing activities?
11. Refer to **Apple**'s financial statements in Appendix A. Identify Apple's net income for the year ended December 31, 2009. Is its net income equal to the increase in cash and cash equivalents for the year? Explain the difference between net income and the increase in cash and cash equivalents.
12. Refer to **Nokia**'s balance sheet in Appendix A. How does its cash (titled "bank and cash") compare with its other current assets (both in amount and percent) as of December 31, 2009? Compare and assess its cash at December 31, 2009, with its cash at December 31, 2008.
13. **Palm**'s balance sheet in Appendix A reports that cash and equivalents decreased during the fiscal year ended May, 31, 2009. Identify the cash generated (or used) by operating activities, by investing activities, and by financing activities.

QUICK STUDY

QS 6-1 Internal control objectives — C1

An internal control system consists of all policies and procedures used to protect assets, ensure reliable accounting, promote efficient operations, and urge adherence to company policies.
1. What is the main objective of internal control procedures? How is that objective achieved?
2. Why should recordkeeping for assets be separated from custody over those assets?
3. Why should the responsibility for a transaction be divided between two or more individuals or departments?

QS 6-2 Internal control for cash — P1

A good system of internal control for cash provides adequate procedures for protecting both cash receipts and cash disbursements.
1. What are three basic guidelines that help achieve this protection?
2. Identify two control systems or procedures for cash disbursements.

QS 6-3 Cash and equivalents — C2

Good accounting systems help in managing cash and controlling who has access to it.
1. What items are included in the category of cash?
2. What items are included in the category of cash equivalents?
3. What does the term *liquidity* refer to?

QS 6-4 Petty cash accounting — P2

1. The petty cash fund of the Rio Agency is established at $75. At the end of the current period, the fund contained $14 and had the following receipts: film rentals, $19, refreshments for meetings, $23 (both expenditures to be classified as Entertainment Expense); postage, $6; and printing, $13. Prepare journal entries to record (*a*) establishment of the fund and (*b*) reimbursement of the fund at the end of the current period.
2. Identify the two events that cause a Petty Cash account to be credited in a journal entry.

QS 6-5 Bank reconciliation — P3

1. For each of the following items, indicate whether its amount (i) affects the bank or book side of a bank reconciliation and (ii) represents an addition or a subtraction in a bank reconciliation.
   - a. Outstanding checks
   - b. Debit memos
   - c. NSF checks
   - d. Unrecorded deposits
   - e. Interest on cash balance
   - f. Credit memos
   - g. Bank service charges
2. Which of the items in part 1 require an adjusting journal entry?

QS 6-6
Bank reconciliation
P3

Cruz Company deposits all cash receipts on the day when they are received and it makes all cash payments by check. At the close of business on June 30, 2011, its Cash account shows an $11,352 debit balance. Cruz's June 30 bank statement shows $10,332 on deposit in the bank. Prepare a bank reconciliation for Cruz Company using the following information.

a. Outstanding checks as of June 30 total $1,713.

b. The June 30 bank statement included a $23 debit memorandum for bank services; Cruz has not yet recorded the cost of these services.

c. In reviewing the bank statement, a $90 check written by Cruz Company was mistakenly recorded in Cruz Company's books at $99.

d. June 30 cash receipts of $2,724 were placed in the bank's night depository after banking hours and were not recorded on the June 30 bank statement.

e. The bank statement included a $5 credit for interest earned on the cash in the bank.

QS 6-7
Days' sales uncollected
A1

The following annual account balances are taken from ProTeam Sports at December 31.

	2011	2010
Accounts receivable	$ 75,692	$ 70,484
Net sales	2,591,933	2,296,673

What is the change in the number of days' sales uncollected between years 2010 and 2011? According to this analysis, is the company's collection of receivables improving? Explain.

QS 6-8[A]
Documents in a voucher system
P4

Management uses a voucher system to help control and monitor cash disbursements. Identify and describe at least four key documents that are part of a voucher system of control.

QS 6-9[B]
Purchase discounts   P5

An important part of cash management is knowing when, and if, to take purchase discounts.

a. Which accounting method uses a Discounts Lost account?

b. What is the advantage of this method for management?

QS 6-10
International accounting and internal controls
C1   P1

Answer each of the following related to international accounting standards.

a. Explain how the purposes and principles of internal controls are different between accounting systems reporting under IFRS versus U.S. GAAP.

b. Cash presents special internal control challenges. How do internal controls for cash differ for accounting systems reporting under IFRS versus U.S. GAAP? How do the procedures applied differ across those two accounting systems?

QS 6-11
Reviewing bank statements
P3

An entrepreneur commented that a bank reconciliation may not be necessary as she regularly reviews her online bank statement for any unusual items and errors.

a. Describe how a bank reconciliation and an online review (or reading) of the bank statement are not equivalent.

b. Identify and explain at least two frauds or errors that would be uncovered through a bank reconciliation and that would *not* be uncovered through an online review of the bank statement.

EXERCISES

Exercise 6-1
Internal control recommendations
C1

What internal control procedures would you recommend in each of the following situations?

1. A concession company has one employee who sells towels, coolers, and sunglasses at the beach. Each day, the employee is given enough towels, coolers, and sunglasses to last through the day and enough cash to make change. The money is kept in a box at the stand.

2. An antique store has one employee who is given cash and sent to garage sales each weekend. The employee pays cash for any merchandise acquired that the antique store resells.

Exercise 6-2
Analyzing internal control
C1

Cantu Company is a rapidly growing start-up business. Its recordkeeper, who was hired nine months ago, left town after the company's manager discovered that a large sum of money had disappeared over the past three months. An audit disclosed that the recordkeeper had written and signed several checks made payable to her fiancé and then recorded the checks as salaries expense. The fiancé, who cashed the checks but never worked for the company, left town with the recordkeeper. As a result, the company incurred an uninsured loss of $84,000. Evaluate Cantu's internal control system and indicate which principles of internal control appear to have been ignored.

Exercise 6-3
Control of cash receipts by mail
P1

Some of Chester Company's cash receipts from customers are received by the company with the regular mail. Chester's recordkeeper opens these letters and deposits the cash received each day. (*a*) Identify any internal control problem(s) in this arrangement. (*b*) What changes to its internal control system do you recommend?

Exercise 6-4
Cash, liquidity, and return
C2

Good accounting systems help with the management and control of cash and cash equivalents.
1. Define and contrast the terms *liquid asset* and *cash equivalent*.
2. Why would companies invest their idle cash in cash equivalents?
3. Identify five principles of effective cash management.

Exercise 6-5
Petty cash fund with a shortage
P2

Hawk Company establishes a $400 petty cash fund on September 9. On September 30, the fund shows $166 in cash along with receipts for the following expenditures: transportation-in, $32; postage expenses, $113; and miscellaneous expenses, $87. The petty cashier could not account for a $2 shortage in the fund. Hawk uses the perpetual system in accounting for merchandise inventory. Prepare (1) the September 9 entry to establish the fund, (2) the September 30 entry to reimburse the fund, and (3) an October 1 entry to decrease the fund to $300.

Check (2) Cr. Cash $234 and (3) Dr. Cash $100

Exercise 6-6
Petty cash fund accounting
P2

NetPerks Co. establishes a $200 petty cash fund on January 1. On January 8, the fund shows $28 in cash along with receipts for the following expenditures: postage, $64; transportation-in, $19; delivery expenses, $36; and miscellaneous expenses, $53. NetPerks uses the perpetual system in accounting for merchandise inventory. Prepare journal entries to (1) establish the fund on January 1, (2) reimburse it on January 8, and (3) both reimburse the fund and increase it to $500 on January 8, assuming no entry in part 2. (*Hint*: Make two separate entries for part 3.)

Check (3) Cr. Cash $472 (total)

Exercise 6-7
Bank reconciliation and adjusting entries
P3

Prepare a table with the following headings for a monthly bank reconciliation dated September 30.

Bank Balance		Book Balance			Not Shown on the Reconciliation
Add	Deduct	Add	Deduct	Adjust	

For each item 1 through 12, place an *x* in the appropriate column to indicate whether the item should be added to or deducted from the book or bank balance, or whether it should not appear on the reconciliation. If the book balance is to be adjusted, place a *Dr.* or *Cr.* in the Adjust column to indicate whether the Cash balance should be debited or credited. At the left side of your table, number the items to correspond to the following list.

1. Bank service charge for September.
2. Checks written and mailed to payees on October 2.
3. Checks written by another depositor but charged against this company's account.
4. Principal and interest on a note receivable to this company is collected by the bank but not yet recorded by the company.
5. Special bank charge for collection of note in part 4 on this company's behalf.
6. Check written against the company's account and cleared by the bank; erroneously not recorded by the company's recordkeeper.
7. Interest earned on the September cash balance in the bank.
8. Night deposit made on September 30 after the bank closed.
9. Checks outstanding on August 31 that cleared the bank in September.
10. NSF check from customer is returned on September 25 but not yet recorded by this company.
11. Checks written by the company and mailed to payees on September 30.
12. Deposit made on September 5 and processed by the bank on September 6.

Exercise 6-8
Voucher system
P1

The voucher system of control is designed to control cash disbursements and the acceptance of obligations.
1. The voucher system of control establishes procedures for what two processes?
2. What types of expenditures should be overseen by a voucher system of control?
3. When is the voucher initially prepared? Explain.

Exercise 6-9
Bank reconciliation
P3

Frederick Clinic deposits all cash receipts on the day when they are received and it makes all cash payments by check. At the close of business on June 30, 2011, its Cash account shows a $15,141 debit balance. Frederick Clinic's June 30 bank statement shows $14,275 on deposit in the bank. Prepare a bank reconciliation for Frederick Clinic using the following information:

a. Outstanding checks as of June 30 total $2,500.
b. The June 30 bank statement included a $125 debit memorandum for bank services.
c. Check No. 919, listed with the canceled checks, was correctly drawn for $645 in payment of a utility bill on June 15. Frederick Clinic mistakenly recorded it with a debit to Utilities Expense and a credit to Cash in the amount of $654.
d. The June 30 cash receipts of $3,250 were placed in the bank's night depository after banking hours and were not recorded on the June 30 bank statement.

Check Reconciled bal., $15,025

Exercise 6-10
Adjusting entries from bank reconciliation P3

Prepare the adjusting journal entries that Frederick Clinic must record as a result of preparing the bank reconciliation in Exercise 6-9.

Exercise 6-11
Bank reconciliation
P3

Chung Company deposits all cash receipts on the day when they are received and it makes all cash payments by check. At the close of business on May 31, 2011, its Cash account shows a $15,500 debit balance. Chung's May 31 bank statement shows $13,800 on deposit in the bank. Prepare a bank reconciliation for Chung Company using the following information.

a. May 31 cash receipts of $2,200 were placed in the bank's night depository after banking hours and were not recorded on the May 31 bank statement.
b. Outstanding checks as of May 31 total $1,600.
c. The May 31 bank statement included a $100 debit memorandum for bank services; Chung has not yet recorded the cost of these services.
d. In reviewing the bank statement, a $400 check written by Wald Company was mistakenly drawn against Chung's account.
e. A debit memorandum for $600 refers to a $600 NSF check from a customer; Chung has not yet recorded this NSF check.

Check Reconciled bal., $14,800

Exercise 6-12
Liquid assets and accounts receivable
A1

Deacon Co. reported annual net sales for 2010 and 2011 of $565,000 and $647,000, respectively. Its year-end balances of accounts receivable follow: December 31, 2010, $51,000; and December 31, 2011, $83,000. (*a*) Calculate its days' sales uncollected at the end of each year. (*b*) Evaluate and comment on any changes in the amount of liquid assets tied up in receivables.

Exercise 6-13[A]
Documents in a voucher system
P4

Match each document in a voucher system in column one with its description in column two.

Document
1. Voucher
2. Invoice approval
3. Receiving report
4. Invoice
5. Purchase order
6. Purchase requisition

Description
A. A document used to notify the appropriate persons that ordered goods have arrived, including a description of the quantities and condition of goods.
B. An internal file used to store documents and information to control cash disbursements and to ensure that a transaction is properly authorized and recorded.
C. A document used to place an order with a vendor that authorizes the vendor to ship ordered merchandise at the stated price and terms.
D. A checklist of steps necessary for the approval of an invoice for recording and payment; also known as a check authorization.
E. A document used by department managers to inform the purchasing department to place an order with a vendor.
F. An itemized statement of goods prepared by the vendor listing the customer's name, items sold, sales prices, and terms of sale.

USA Imports uses the perpetual system in accounting for merchandise inventory and had the following transactions during the month of October. Prepare entries to record these transactions assuming that USA Imports records invoices (*a*) at gross amounts and (*b*) at net amounts.

Exercise 6-14^B
Record invoices at gross or net amounts
P5

Oct. 2 Purchased merchandise at a $4,000 price, invoice dated October 2, terms 2/10, n/30.
 10 Received a $400 credit memorandum (at full invoice price) for the return of merchandise that it purchased on October 2.
 17 Purchased merchandise at a $4,400 price, invoice dated October 16, terms 2/10, n/30.
 26 Paid for the merchandise purchased on October 17, less the discount.
 31 Paid for the merchandise purchased on October 2. Payment was delayed because the invoice was mistakenly filed for payment today. This error caused the discount to be lost.

For each of these five separate cases, identify the principle(s) of internal control that is violated. Recommend what the business should do to ensure adherence to principles of internal control.

PROBLEM SET A

Problem 6-1A
Analyzing internal control
C1

1. Heather Flat records all incoming customer cash receipts for her employer and posts the customer payments to their respective accounts.
2. At Netco Company, Jeff and Jose alternate lunch hours. Jeff is the petty cash custodian, but if someone needs petty cash when he is at lunch, Jose fills in as custodian.
3. Nadine Cox posts all patient charges and payments at the Dole Medical Clinic. Each night Nadine backs up the computerized accounting system to a tape and stores the tape in a locked file at her desk.
4. Barto Sayles prides himself on hiring quality workers who require little supervision. As office manager, Barto gives his employees full discretion over their tasks and for years has seen no reason to perform independent reviews of their work.
5. Desi West's manager has told her to reduce costs. Desi decides to raise the deductible on the plant's property insurance from $5,000 to $10,000. This cuts the property insurance premium in half. In a related move, she decides that bonding the plant's employees is a waste of money since the company has not experienced any losses due to employee theft. Desi saves the entire amount of the bonding insurance premium by dropping the bonding insurance.

Shawnee Co. set up a petty cash fund for payments of small amounts. The following transactions involving the petty cash fund occurred in May (the last month of the company's fiscal year).

Problem 6-2A
Establish, reimburse, and adjust petty cash
P2

May 1 Prepared a company check for $250 to establish the petty cash fund.
 15 Prepared a company check to replenish the fund for the following expenditures made since May 1.
  a. Paid $78 for janitorial services.
  b. Paid $63.68 for miscellaneous expenses.
  c. Paid postage expenses of $43.50.
  d. Paid $57.15 to *The County Gazette* (the local newspaper) for an advertisement.
  e. Counted $11.15 remaining in the petty cash box.
 16 Prepared a company check for $200 to increase the fund to $450.
 31 The petty cashier reports that $293.39 cash remains in the fund. A company check is drawn to replenish the fund for the following expenditures made since May 15.
  f. Paid postage expenses of $48.36.
  g. Reimbursed the office manager for business mileage, $38.50.
  h. Paid $39.75 to deliver merchandise to a customer, terms FOB destination.
 31 The company decides that the May 16 increase in the fund was too large. It reduces the fund by $50, leaving a total of $400.

Required

1. Prepare journal entries to establish the fund on May 1, to replenish it on May 15 and on May 31, and to reflect any increase or decrease in the fund balance on May 16 and May 31.

Check (1) Cr. to Cash: May 15, $238.85; May 16, $200.00

Analysis Component

2. Explain how the company's financial statements are affected if the petty cash fund is not replenished and no entry is made on May 31.

Problem 6-3A
Establish, reimburse, and increase petty cash

P2

Shelton Gallery had the following petty cash transactions in February of the current year.

Feb. 2 Wrote a $300 check, cashed it, and gave the proceeds and the petty cashbox to Bo Brown, the petty cashier.
5 Purchased bond paper for the copier for $10.13 that is immediately used.
9 Paid $22.50 COD shipping charges on merchandise purchased for resale, terms FOB shipping point. Shelton uses the perpetual system to account for merchandise inventory.
12 Paid $9.95 postage to express mail a contract to a client.
14 Reimbursed Alli Buck, the manager, $58 for business mileage on her car.
20 Purchased stationery for $77.76 that is immediately used.
23 Paid a courier $18 to deliver merchandise sold to a customer, terms FOB destination.
25 Paid $15.10 COD shipping charges on merchandise purchased for resale, terms FOB shipping point.
27 Paid $64 for postage expenses.
28 The fund had $21.23 remaining in the petty cash box. Sorted the petty cash receipts by accounts affected and exchanged them for a check to reimburse the fund for expenditures.
28 The petty cash fund amount is increased by $100 to a total of $400.

Required

1. Prepare the journal entry to establish the petty cash fund.
2. Prepare a petty cash payments report for February with these categories: delivery expense, mileage expense, postage expense, merchandise inventory (for transportation-in), and office supplies expense. Sort the payments into the appropriate categories and total the expenditures in each category.
3. Prepare the journal entries for part 2 to both (a) reimburse and (b) increase the fund amount.

Check (3a & 3b) Total Cr. to Cash $378.77

Problem 6-4A
Prepare a bank reconciliation and record adjustments

P3

mhhe.com/wildFA6e

The following information is available to reconcile Clark Company's book balance of cash with its bank statement cash balance as of July 31, 2011.

a. On July 31, the company's Cash account has a $26,193 debit balance, but its July bank statement shows a $28,020 cash balance.
b. Check No. 3031 for $1,380 and Check No. 3040 for $552 were outstanding on the June 30 bank reconciliation. Check No. 3040 is listed with the July canceled checks, but Check No. 3031 is not. Also, Check No. 3065 for $336 and Check No. 3069 for $2,148, both written in July, are not among the canceled checks on the July 31 statement.
c. In comparing the canceled checks on the bank statement with the entries in the accounting records, it is found that Check No. 3056 for July rent was correctly written and drawn for $1,250 but was erroneously entered in the accounting records as $1,230.
d. A credit memorandum enclosed with the July bank statement indicates the bank collected $9,000 cash on a non-interest-bearing note for Clark, deducted a $45 collection fee, and credited the remainder to its account. Clark had not recorded this event before receiving the statement.
e. A debit memorandum for $805 lists a $795 NSF check plus a $10 NSF charge. The check had been received from a customer, Jim Shaw. Clark has not yet recorded this check as NSF.
f. Enclosed with the July statement is a $15 debit memorandum for bank services. It has not yet been recorded because no previous notification had been received.
g. Clark's July 31 daily cash receipts of $10,152 were placed in the bank's night depository on that date, but do not appear on the July 31 bank statement.

Required

1. Prepare the bank reconciliation for this company as of July 31, 2011.
2. Prepare the journal entries necessary to bring the company's book balance of cash into conformity with the reconciled cash balance as of July 31, 2011.

Check (1) Reconciled balance, $34,308; (2) Cr. Note Receivable $9,000

Analysis Component

3. Assume that the July 31, 2011, bank reconciliation for this company is prepared and some items are treated incorrectly. For each of the following errors, explain the effect of the error on (i) the adjusted bank statement cash balance and (ii) the adjusted cash account book balance.
   a. The company's unadjusted cash account balance of $26,193 is listed on the reconciliation as $26,139.
   b. The bank's collection of the $9,000 note less the $45 collection fee is added to the bank statement cash balance on the reconciliation.

Els Company most recently reconciled its bank statement and book balances of cash on August 31 and it reported two checks outstanding, No. 5888 for $1,038.05 and No. 5893 for $484.25. The following information is available for its September 30, 2011, reconciliation.

Problem 6-5A
Prepare a bank reconciliation and record adjustments

P3

mhhe.com/wildFA6e

From the September 30 Bank Statement

PREVIOUS BALANCE	TOTAL CHECKS AND DEBITS	TOTAL DEPOSITS AND CREDITS	CURRENT BALANCE
16,800.45	9,620.05	11,182.85	18,363.25

CHECKS AND DEBITS			DEPOSITS AND CREDITS		DAILY BALANCE	
Date	No.	Amount	Date	Amount	Date	Amount
09/03	5888	1,038.05	09/05	1,103.75	08/31	16,800.45
09/04	5902	731.90	09/12	2,226.90	09/03	15,762.40
09/07	5901	1,824.25	09/21	4,093.00	09/04	15,030.50
09/17		588.25 NSF	09/25	2,351.70	09/05	16,134.25
09/20	5905	937.00	09/30	22.50 IN	09/07	14,310.00
09/22	5903	399.10	09/30	1,385.00 CM	09/12	16,536.90
09/22	5904	2,080.00			09/17	15,948.65
09/28	5907	213.85			09/20	15,011.65
09/29	5909	1,807.65			09/21	19,104.65
					09/22	16,625.55
					09/25	18,977.25
					09/28	18,763.40
					09/29	16,955.75
					09/30	18,363.25

From Els Company's Accounting Records

Cash Receipts Deposited

Date		Cash Debit
Sept.	5	1,103.75
	12	2,226.90
	21	4,093.00
	25	2,351.70
	30	1,582.75
		11,358.10

Cash Disbursements

Check No.		Cash Credit
5901		1,824.25
5902		731.90
5903		399.10
5904		2,050.00
5905		937.00
5906		859.30
5907		213.85
5908		276.00
5909		1,807.65
		9,099.05

Cash   Acct. No. 101

Date		Explanation	PR	Debit	Credit	Balance
Aug.	31	Balance				15,278.15
Sept.	30	Total receipts	R12	11,358.10		26,636.25
	30	Total disbursements	D23		9,099.05	17,537.20

Additional Information

Check No. 5904 is correctly drawn for $2,080 to pay for computer equipment; however, the recordkeeper misread the amount and entered it in the accounting records with a debit to Computer Equipment and a credit to Cash of $2,050. The NSF check shown in the statement was originally received from a customer, S. Nilson, in payment of her account. Its return has not yet been recorded by the company. The credit memorandum is from the collection of a $1,400 note for Els Company by the bank. The bank deducted a $15 collection fee. The collection and fee are not yet recorded.

Required

1. Prepare the September 30, 2011, bank reconciliation for this company.
2. Prepare the journal entries to adjust the book balance of cash to the reconciled balance.

Check (1) Reconciled balance, $18,326.45 (2) Cr. Note Receivable $1,400

Analysis Component

3. The bank statement reveals that some of the prenumbered checks in the sequence are missing. Describe three situations that could explain this.

PROBLEM SET B

Problem 6-1B
Analyzing internal control
C1

For each of these five separate cases, identify the principle(s) of internal control that is violated. Recommend what the business should do to ensure adherence to principles of internal control.

1. Latoya Tally is the company's computer specialist and oversees its computerized payroll system. Her boss recently asked her to put password protection on all office computers. Latoya has put a password in place that allows only the boss access to the file where pay rates are changed and personnel are added or deleted from the payroll.
2. Lake Theater has a computerized order-taking system for its tickets. The system is active all week and backed up every Friday night.
3. X2U Company has two employees handling acquisitions of inventory. One employee places purchase orders and pays vendors. The second employee receives the merchandise.
4. The owner of Super-Aid Pharmacy uses a check protector to perforate checks, making it difficult for anyone to alter the amount of the check. The check protector is on the owner's desk in an office that contains company checks and is normally unlocked.
5. LeAnn Company is a small business that has separated the duties of cash receipts and cash disbursements. The employee responsible for cash disbursements reconciles the bank account monthly.

Problem 6-2B
Establishing, reimbursing, and adjusting petty cash
P2

Pepco Co. establishes a petty cash fund for payments of small amounts. The following transactions involving the petty cash fund occurred in January (the last month of the company's fiscal year).

Jan. 3   A company check for $150 is written and made payable to the petty cashier to establish the petty cash fund.

    14   A company check is written to replenish the fund for the following expenditures made since January 3.
         a. Purchased office supplies for $16.29 that are immediately used up.
         b. Paid $17.60 COD shipping charges on merchandise purchased for resale, terms FOB shipping point. Pepco uses the perpetual system to account for inventory.
         c. Paid $36.57 to All-Tech for minor repairs to a computer.
         d. Paid $14.82 for items classified as miscellaneous expenses.
         e. Counted $62.28 remaining in the petty cash box.

    15   Prepared a company check for $25 to increase the fund to $175.

    31   The petty cashier reports that $17.35 remains in the fund. A company check is written to replenish the fund for the following expenditures made since January 14.
         f. Paid $40 to *The Smart Shopper* for an advertisement in January's newsletter.
         g. Paid $38.19 for postage expenses.
         h. Paid $58 to Take-You-There for delivery of merchandise, terms FOB destination.

    31   The company decides that the January 15 increase in the fund was too little. It increases the fund by another $75, leaving a total of $250.

Required

1. Prepare journal entries to establish the fund on January 3, to replenish it on January 14 and January 31, and to reflect any increase or decrease in the fund balance on January 15 and 31.

Check (1) Cr. to Cash: Jan. 14, $87.72; Jan. 31 (total), $232.65

Analysis Component

2. Explain how the company's financial statements are affected if the petty cash fund is not replenished and no entry is made on January 31.

RPM Music Center had the following petty cash transactions in March of the current year.

March 5   Wrote a $200 check, cashed it, and gave the proceeds and the petty cashbox to Liz Buck, the petty cashier.
       6   Paid $14.50 COD shipping charges on merchandise purchased for resale, terms FOB shipping point. RPM uses the perpetual system to account for merchandise inventory.
      11   Paid $8.75 delivery charges on merchandise sold to a customer, terms FOB destination.
      12   Purchased file folders for $12.13 that are immediately used.
      14   Reimbursed Will Nelson, the manager, $9.65 for office supplies purchased and used.
      18   Purchased printer paper for $22.54 that is immediately used.
      27   Paid $47.10 COD shipping charges on merchandise purchased for resale, terms FOB shipping point.
      28   Paid postage expenses of $16.
      30   Reimbursed Nelson $58.80 for business car mileage.
      31   Cash of $11.53 remained in the fund. Sorted the petty cash receipts by accounts affected and exchanged them for a check to reimburse the fund for expenditures.
      31   The petty cash fund amount is increased by $50 to a total of $250.

Problem 6-3B
Establish, reimburse, and increase petty cash
P2

Required

1. Prepare the journal entry to establish the petty cash fund.
2. Prepare a petty cash payments report for March with these categories: delivery expense, mileage expense, postage expense, merchandise inventory (for transportation-in), and office supplies expense. Sort the payments into the appropriate categories and total the expenses in each category.
3. Prepare the journal entries for part 2 to both (a) reimburse and (b) increase the fund amount.

Check (2) Total expenses $189.47

(3a & 3b) Total Cr. to Cash $238.47

The following information is available to reconcile Style Co.'s book balance of cash with its bank statement cash balance as of December 31, 2011.

a. The December 31 cash balance according to the accounting records is $31,743.70, and the bank statement cash balance for that date is $45,091.80.

b. Check No. 1273 for $1,084.20 and Check No. 1282 for $390, both written and entered in the accounting records in December, are not among the canceled checks. Two checks, No. 1231 for $2,289 and No. 1242 for $370.50, were outstanding on the most recent November 30 reconciliation. Check No. 1231 is listed with the December canceled checks, but Check No. 1242 is not.

c. When the December checks are compared with entries in the accounting records, it is found that Check No. 1267 had been correctly drawn for $2,435 to pay for office supplies but was erroneously entered in the accounting records as $2,453.

d. Two debit memoranda are enclosed with the statement and are unrecorded at the time of the reconciliation. One debit memorandum is for $749.50 and dealt with an NSF check for $732 received from a customer, Titus Industries, in payment of its account. The bank assessed a $17.50 fee for processing it. The second debit memorandum is a $79 charge for check printing. Style did not record these transactions before receiving the statement.

e. A credit memorandum indicates that the bank collected $20,000 cash on a note receivable for the company, deducted a $20 collection fee, and credited the balance to the company's Cash account. Style did not record this transaction before receiving the statement.

f. Style's December 31 daily cash receipts of $7,666.10 were placed in the bank's night depository on that date, but do not appear on the December 31 bank statement.

Problem 6-4B
Prepare a bank reconciliation and record adjustments
P3

Required

1. Prepare the bank reconciliation for this company as of December 31, 2011.
2. Prepare the journal entries necessary to bring the company's book balance of cash into conformity with the reconciled cash balance as of December 31, 2011.

Check (1) Reconciled balance, $50,913.20; (2) Cr. Note Receivable $20,000

Analysis Component

3. Explain the nature of the communications conveyed by a bank when the bank sends the depositor (a) a debit memorandum and (b) a credit memorandum.

Problem 6-5B
Prepare a bank reconciliation and record adjustments

P3

Safe Systems most recently reconciled its bank balance on April 30 and reported two checks outstanding at that time, No. 1771 for $781 and No. 1780 for $1,325.90. The following information is available for its May 31, 2011, reconciliation.

From the May 31 Bank Statement

PREVIOUS BALANCE	TOTAL CHECKS AND DEBITS	TOTAL DEPOSITS AND CREDITS	CURRENT BALANCE
18,290.70	12,898.90	16,416.80	21,808.60

CHECKS AND DEBITS			DEPOSITS AND CREDITS		DAILY BALANCE	
Date	No.	Amount	Date	Amount	Date	Amount
05/01	1771	781.00	05/04	2,438.00	04/30	18,290.70
05/02	1783	195.30	05/14	2,898.00	05/01	17,509.70
05/04	1782	1,285.50	05/22	1,801.80	05/02	17,314.40
05/11	1784	1,449.60	05/25	7,200.00 CM	05/04	18,466.90
05/18		431.80 NSF	05/26	2,079.00	05/11	17,017.30
05/25	1787	8,032.50			05/14	19,915.30
05/26	1785	157.20			05/18	19,483.50
05/29	1788	554.00			05/22	21,285.30
05/31		12.00 SC			05/25	20,452.80
					05/26	22,374.60
					05/29	21,820.60
					05/31	21,808.60

From Safe Systems' Accounting Records

Cash Receipts Deposited

Date		Cash Debit
May 4		2,438.00
14		2,898.00
22		1,801.80
26		2,079.00
31		2,526.30
		11,743.10

Cash Disbursements

Check No.		Cash Credit
1782		1,285.50
1783		195.30
1784		1,449.60
1785		157.20
1786		353.10
1787		8,032.50
1788		544.00
1789		639.50
		12,656.70

Cash   Acct. No. 101

Date	Explanation	PR	Debit	Credit	Balance
Apr. 30	Balance				16,183.80
May 31	Total receipts	R7	11,743.10		27,926.90
31	Total disbursements	D8		12,656.70	15,270.20

Additional Information

Check No. 1788 is correctly drawn for $554 to pay for May utilities; however, the recordkeeper misread the amount and entered it in the accounting records with a debit to Utilities Expense and a credit to Cash for $544. The bank paid and deducted the correct amount. The NSF check shown in the statement was originally received from a customer, S. Bax, in payment of her account. The company has not yet recorded its return. The credit memorandum is from a $7,300 note that the bank collected for the company. The bank deducted a $100 collection fee and deposited the remainder in the company's account. The collection and fee have not yet been recorded.

Required

1. Prepare the May 31, 2011, bank reconciliation for Safe Systems.
2. Prepare the journal entries to adjust the book balance of cash to the reconciled balance.

Check (1) Reconciled balance, $22,016.40; (2) Cr. Note Receivable $7,300

Analysis Component

3. The bank statement reveals that some of the prenumbered checks in the sequence are missing. Describe three possible situations to explain this.

SERIAL PROBLEM
Business Solutions
P3

(This serial problem began in Chapter 1 and continues through most of the book. If previous chapter segments were not completed, the serial problem can begin at this point. It is helpful, but not necessary, to use the Working Papers that accompany the book.)

SP 6 Santana Rey receives the March bank statement for Business Solutions on April 11, 2012. The March 31 bank statement shows an ending cash balance of $67,566. A comparison of the bank statement with the general ledger Cash account, No. 101, reveals the following.

a. S. Rey notices that the bank erroneously cleared a $500 check against her account in March that she did not issue. The check documentation included with the bank statement shows that this check was actually issued by a company named Business Systems.
b. On March 25, the bank issued a $50 debit memorandum for the safety deposit box that Business Solutions agreed to rent from the bank beginning March 25.
c. On March 26, the bank issued a $102 debit memorandum for printed checks that Business Solutions ordered from the bank.
d. On March 31, the bank issued a credit memorandum for $33 interest earned on Business Solutions' checking account for the month of March.
e. S. Rey notices that the check she issued for $128 on March 31, 2012, has not yet cleared the bank.
f. S. Rey verifies that all deposits made in March do appear on the March bank statement.
g. The general ledger Cash account, No. 101, shows an ending cash balance per books of $68,057 as of March 31 (prior to any reconciliation).

Required

1. Prepare a bank reconciliation for Business Solutions for the month ended March 31, 2012.
2. Prepare any necessary adjusting entries. Use Miscellaneous Expenses, No. 677, for any bank charges. Use Interest Revenue, No. 404, for any interest earned on the checking account for the month of March.

Check (1) Adj. bank bal. $67,938

Beyond the Numbers

BTN 6-1 Refer to **Research In Motion**'s financial statements in Appendix A to answer the following.

1. For both fiscal year-ends February 27, 2010, and February 28, 2009, identify the total amount of cash and cash equivalents. Determine the percent this amount represents of total current assets, total current liabilities, total shareholders' equity, and total assets for both years. Comment on any trends.
2. For fiscal years ended February 27, 2010, and February 28, 2009, use the information in the statement of cash flows to determine the percent change between the beginning and ending year amounts of cash and cash equivalents.
3. Compute the days' sales uncollected as of February 27, 2010, and February 28, 2009. Has the collection of receivables improved? Are accounts receivable an important asset for Research In Motion? Explain.

REPORTING IN ACTION
C2 A1

RIM

Fast Forward

4. Access Research In Motion's financial statements for fiscal years ending after February 27, 2010, from its Website (RIM.com) or the SEC's EDGAR database (www.sec.gov). Recompute its days' sales uncollected for fiscal years ending after February 27, 2010. Compare this to the days' sales uncollected for 2010 and 2009.

COMPARATIVE ANALYSIS

A1

RIM

Apple

BTN 6-2 Key comparative figures for **Research In Motion** and **Apple** follow.

($ millions)	Research In Motion Current Year	Research In Motion Prior Year	Apple Current Year	Apple Prior Year
Accounts receivable	$ 2,594	$ 2,112	$ 3,361	$ 2,422
Net sales	14,953	11,065	42,905	37,491

Required

Compute days' sales uncollected for these companies for each of the two years shown. Comment on any trends for the companies. Which company has the largest percent change in days' sales uncollected?

ETHICS CHALLENGE

C1

BTN 6-3 Carol Benton, Sue Knox, and Marcia Diamond work for a family physician, Dr. Gwen Conrad, who is in private practice. Dr. Conrad is knowledgeable about office management practices and has segregated the cash receipt duties as follows. Benton opens the mail and prepares a triplicate list of money received. She sends one copy of the list to Knox, the cashier, who deposits the receipts daily in the bank. Diamond, the recordkeeper, receives a copy of the list and posts payments to patients' accounts. About once a month the office clerks have an expensive lunch they pay for as follows. First, Knox endorses a patient's check in Dr. Conrad's name and cashes it at the bank. Benton then destroys the remittance advice accompanying the check. Finally, Diamond posts payment to the customer's account as a miscellaneous credit. The three justify their actions by their relatively low pay and knowledge that Dr. Conrad will likely never miss the money.

Required

1. Who is the best person in Dr. Conrad's office to reconcile the bank statement?
2. Would a bank reconciliation uncover this office fraud?
3. What are some procedures to detect this type of fraud?
4. Suggest additional internal controls that Dr. Conrad could implement.

COMMUNICATING IN PRACTICE

P5

BTN 6-4[B] Assume you are a business consultant. The owner of a company sends you an e-mail expressing concern that the company is not taking advantage of its discounts offered by vendors. The company currently uses the gross method of recording purchases. The owner is considering a review of all invoices and payments from the previous period. Due to the volume of purchases, however, the owner recognizes that this is time-consuming and costly. The owner seeks your advice about monitoring purchase discounts in the future. Provide a response in memorandum form.

TAKING IT TO THE NET

C1 P1

BTN 6-5 Visit the Association of Certified Fraud Examiners Website at cfenet.com. Find and open the file "2008 Report to the Nation." Read the two-page Executive Summary and fill in the following blanks. (The report is under its *Fraud Resources* tab or under its *About the ACFE* tab [under Press Room]; we can also use the *Search* tab.)

1. The median loss caused by occupational frauds was $_____.
2. More than _____ of fraud cases caused at least $1 million in losses.
3. Companies lose ___% of their annual revenues to fraud; this figure translates to $_____ billion in fraud losses.
4. The typical length of fraud schemes was ____ years from the time the fraud began until it was detected.
5. Companies that conducted surprise audits suffered a median loss of $_____, whereas those without surprise audits had a median loss of $_____.
6. The median loss suffered by companies with fewer than 100 employees was $_____ per scheme.
7. _____ and _____ were the most common small business fraud schemes.
8. ___% of respondents cited inadequate internal controls as the primary contributing factor in the frauds investigated.
9. Only ___% of the perpetrators had convictions prior to committing their frauds.

BTN 6-6 Organize the class into teams. Each team must prepare a list of 10 internal controls a consumer could observe in a typical retail department store. When called upon, the team's spokesperson must be prepared to share controls identified by the team that have not been shared by another team's spokesperson.

TEAMWORK IN ACTION
C1

BTN 6-7 Review the opening feature of this chapter that highlights Kim Jordan and her company **New Belgium Brewing Company**.

Required
1. List the seven principles of internal control and explain how Kim could implement each of them in one of her retail brewing pubs.
2. Do you believe that Kim will need to add controls as her business expands? Explain.

ENTREPRENEURIAL DECISION
C1 P1

BTN 6-8 Visit an area of your college that serves the student community with either products or services. Some examples are food services, libraries, and bookstores. Identify and describe between four and eight internal controls being implemented.

HITTING THE ROAD
C1

BTN 6-9 The following information is from **Nokia** (www.Nokia.com), which is a leading global manufacturer of mobile devices and services.

GLOBAL DECISION
C2 A1

NOKIA

EUR millions	Current Year	Prior Year
Cash	1,142	1,706
Accounts receivable	7,981	9,444
Current assets	23,613	24,470
Total assets	35,738	39,582
Current liabilities	15,188	20,355
Shareholders' equity	14,749	16,510
Net sales	40,984	50,710

Required
1. For each year, compute the percentage that cash represents of current assets, total assets, current liabilities, and shareholders' equity. Comment on any trends in these percentages.
2. Determine the percentage change between the current and prior year cash balances.
3. Compute the days' sales uncollected at the end of both the current year and the prior year. Has the collection of receivables improved? Explain.

ANSWERS TO MULTIPLE CHOICE QUIZ

1. e; The entry follows.

Debits to expenses (or assets)	420	
Cash Over and Short	5	
Cash		425

2. a; recognizes cash collection of note by bank.
3. a; the bank reconciliation follows.

4. d; ($6,720/$84,000) × 365 = 29.2 days
5. b; The entry follows.

Merchandise Inventory*	5,880	
Accounts Payable		5,880

*$6,000 × 98%

Bank Reconciliation
November 30

Balance per bank statement	$1,895	Balance per books	$1,742
Add: Deposit in transit	795	Add: Note collected less fee	320
Deduct: Outstanding checks	(638)	Deduct: Service charge	(10)
Reconciled balance	$2,052	Reconciled balance	$2,052

A Look Back	A Look at This Chapter	A Look Ahead
Chapter 6 focused on internal control and reporting for cash. We described internal control procedures and the accounting for and management of cash.	This chapter emphasizes receivables. We explain that they are liquid assets and describe how companies account for and report them. We also discuss the importance of estimating uncollectibles.	Chapter 8 focuses on plant assets, natural resources, and intangible assets. We explain how to account for, report, and analyze these long-term assets.

7 Reporting and Analyzing Receivables

Learning Objectives

CAP

CONCEPTUAL

- **C1** Describe accounts receivable and how they occur and are recorded. (p. 294)
- **C2** Describe a note receivable, the computation of its maturity date, and the recording of its existence. (p. 304)
- **C3** Explain how receivables can be converted to cash before maturity. (p. 307)

ANALYTICAL

- **A1** Compute accounts receivable turnover and use it to help assess financial condition. (p. 309)

LP7

PROCEDURAL

- **P1** Apply the direct write-off method to account for accounts receivable. (p. 297)
- **P2** Apply the allowance method and estimate uncollectibles based on sales and accounts receivable. (p. 300)
- **P3** Record the honoring and dishonoring of a note and adjustments for interest. (p. 306)

Decision Insight

Heeeere's Johnny!

"I'll sit down with my customers, take them out to eat, hang out. . . with them."
—JOHN EARLE

BOSTON, MS—Working at a music store, John Earle's co-workers coined new nicknames for him on an almost daily basis: Johnny Appleseed, Johnny Pancakes, Johnny Cupcakes. As a joke, John printed up a few t-shirts with the Johnny Cupcakes nickname for the heavy-metal band he played in. The shirts, based on a skull and crossbones design with a cupcake replacing the skull, drew attention, and John dropped his heavy-metal dreams to start his company, **Johnny Cupcakes, Inc. (JohnnyCupcakes.com).**

John was always a small-scale serial entrepreneur, operating lemonade stands, peddling glow sticks on the beach near his home, and selling packs of pranks and magic tricks. Like his itching powder prank that went awry at his school, "the Johnny Cupcakes brand started as a complete joke," admits John. One day John's mother Lorraine interrupted his band's tour to tell him he had a real business on his hands. Now, the company's designs—like a Statue of Liberty holding a cupcake, Marilyn Monroe with a tiny cupcake-shaped mole, and the cupcakes and crossbones motif—attract a cult following. By the time John opened his first store, over 500 people had lined up to get in (see photo above).

Sales quickly soared, and John had to contend with receivables and day-to-day recordkeeping. Special attention was focused on monitoring receivables, including decisions on credit sales and policies for extending credit. John explains that he understands his customers, including cash payment patterns that allow him to estimate uncollectibles and minimize bad debts. Both accounts and notes receivables receive John's attention, along with regular reviews of the allowance for doubtful accounts.

Though still a prankster, John knows that successful entrepreneurs must understand receivables to succeed. Identifying nonpaying customers and cultivating relationships with credit customers are as crucial as his new limited edition T-shirts. With an expanding product line, an understanding of receivables and how uncollectibles relate to income become even more important.

From a handful of gag T-shirts made as a joke, Johnny Cupcakes now boasts sales of nearly $4 million per year. "I never expected it to get this big," John says, encouraging potential entrepreneurs to get out and make it happen. "I work very hard," he says, "and I enjoy every minute of it."

[Sources: *Johnny Cupcakes Website,* January 2012; *Boston Globe,* October 2007; *Businessweek.com,* August 2008; *Inc magazine,* May 2010; *NPR.org,* August 2006; *Quick Sprout,* February 2011]

Chapter Preview

This chapter focuses on accounts receivable and short-term notes receivable. We describe each of these assets, their uses, and how they are accounted for and reported in financial statements. This knowledge helps us use accounting information to make better business decisions. It can also help in predicting future company performance and financial condition as well as in managing one's own business.

Reporting and Analyzing Receivables

Accounts Receivable
- Recognizing accounts receivable
- Valuing accounts receivable
- Estimating bad debts

Notes Receivable
- Computing maturity and interest
- Recognizing notes receivable
- Valuing and settling notes

Disposal of Receivables
- Selling receivables
- Pledging receivables

ACCOUNTS RECEIVABLE

A *receivable* is an amount due from another party. The two most common receivables are accounts receivable and notes receivable. Other receivables include interest receivable, rent receivable, tax refund receivable, and receivables from employees. **Accounts receivable** are amounts due from customers for credit sales. This section begins by describing how accounts receivable occur. It includes receivables that occur when customers use credit cards issued by third parties and when a company gives credit directly to customers. When a company does extend credit directly to customers, it (1) maintains a separate account receivable for each customer and (2) accounts for bad debts from credit sales.

Recognizing Accounts Receivable

C1 Describe accounts receivable and how they occur and are recorded.

Accounts receivable occur from credit sales to customers. The amount of credit sales has increased in recent years, reflecting several factors including an efficient financial system. Retailers such as **Costco** and **Best Buy** hold millions of dollars in accounts receivable. Similar amounts are held by wholesalers such as **SUPERVALU** and **SYSCO**. Exhibit 7.1 shows recent dollar amounts of receivables and their percent of total assets for four well-known companies.

EXHIBIT 7.1

Accounts Receivable for Selected Companies

Company	Amount	Percent of total assets
Abercrombie & Fitch	$53 Mil.	1.9%
Pfizer	$14,645 Mil.	6.9%
Callaway Golf	$140 Mil.	16%
John Deere	$21,883 Mil.	53%

Sales on Credit Credit sales are recorded by increasing (debiting) Accounts Receivable. A company must also maintain a separate account for each customer that tracks how much that customer purchases, has already paid, and still owes. This information provides the basis for sending bills to customers and for other business analyses. To maintain this information, companies that extend credit directly to their customers keep a separate account receivable for each one of them. The general ledger continues to have a single Accounts Receivable account along with the other financial statement accounts, but a supplementary record is created to maintain a separate account for each customer. This supplementary record is called the *accounts receivable ledger*.

Exhibit 7.2 shows the relation between the Accounts Receivable account in the general ledger and its individual customer accounts in the accounts receivable ledger for TechCom, a small electronics wholesaler. This exhibit reports a $3,000 ending balance of TechCom's accounts receivable for June 30. TechCom's transactions are mainly in cash, but it has two major credit customers: CompStore and RDA Electronics. Its *schedule of accounts receivable* shows that the $3,000 balance of the Accounts Receivable account in the general ledger equals the total of its two customers' balances in the accounts receivable ledger.

EXHIBIT 7.2

General Ledger and the Accounts Receivable Ledger (before July 1 transactions)

General Ledger — Accounts Receivable

Date	PR	Debit	Credit	Balance
June 30		3,000		3,000

Accounts Receivable Ledger

RDA Electronics

Date	PR	Debit	Credit	Balance
June 30		1,000		1,000

CompStore

Date	PR	Debit	Credit	Balance
June 30		2,000		2,000

TechCom — Schedule of Accounts Receivable

RDA Electronics	$1,000
CompStore	2,000
Total	$3,000

To see how accounts receivable from credit sales are recognized in the accounting records, we look at two transactions on July 1 between TechCom and its credit customers—see Exhibit 7.3. The first is a credit sale of $950 to CompStore. A credit sale is posted with both a debit to the Accounts Receivable account in the general ledger and a debit to the customer account in the accounts receivable ledger. The second transaction is a collection of $720 from RDA Electronics from a prior credit sale. Cash receipts from a credit customer are posted with a credit to the Accounts Receivable account in the general ledger and flow through to credit the customer account in the accounts receivable ledger. (Posting debits or credits to Accounts Receivable in two separate ledgers does not violate the requirement that debits equal credits. The equality of debits and credits is maintained in the general ledger. The accounts receivable ledger is a *supplementary* record providing information on each customer.)

EXHIBIT 7.3

Accounts Receivable Transactions

July 1	Accounts Receivable—CompStore	950	
	Sales		950
	To record credit sales*		
July 1	Cash	720	
	Accounts Receivable—RDA Electronics		720
	To record collection of credit sales.		

Assets = Liabilities + Equity
+ 950   +950

Assets = Liabilities + Equity
+720
−720

* We omit the entry to Dr. Cost of Sales and Cr. Merchandise Inventory to focus on sales and receivables.

Exhibit 7.4 shows the general ledger and the accounts receivable ledger after recording the two July 1 transactions. The general ledger shows the effects of the sale, the collection, and the resulting balance of $3,230. These events are also reflected in the individual customer accounts: RDA Electronics has an ending balance of $280, and CompStore's ending balance is $2,950.

EXHIBIT 7.4

General Ledger and the Accounts Receivable Ledger (after July 1 transactions)

General Ledger — Accounts Receivable

Date	PR	Debit	Credit	Balance
June 30		3,000		3,000
July 1		950		3,950
July 1			720	3,230

Accounts Receivable Ledger

RDA Electronics

Date	PR	Debit	Credit	Balance
June 30		1,000		1,000
July 1			720	280

CompStore

Date	PR	Debit	Credit	Balance
June 30		2,000		2,000
July 1		950		2,950

TechCom — Schedule of Accounts Receivable

RDA Electronics	$ 280
CompStore	2,950
Total	$3,230

The $3,230 sum of the individual accounts equals the debit balance of the Accounts Receivable account in the general ledger.

Like TechCom, many large retailers such as **Sears** and **JCPenney** sell on credit. Many also maintain their own credit cards to grant credit to approved customers and to earn interest on any balance not paid within a specified period of time. This allows them to avoid the fee charged by credit card companies. The entries in this case are the same as those for TechCom except for the possibility of added interest revenue. If a customer owes interest on a bill, we debit Interest Receivable and credit Interest Revenue for that amount.

Credit Card Sales Many companies allow their customers to pay for products and services using third-party credit cards such as **Visa**, **MasterCard**, or **American Express**, and debit cards (also called ATM or bank cards). This practice gives customers the ability to make purchases without cash or checks. Once credit is established with a credit card company or bank, the customer does not have to open an account with each store. Customers using these cards can make single monthly payments instead of several payments to different creditors and can defer their payments.

Many sellers allow customers to use third-party credit cards and debit cards instead of granting credit directly for several reasons. First, the seller does not have to evaluate each customer's credit standing or make decisions about who gets credit and how much. Second, the seller avoids the risk of extending credit to customers who cannot or do not pay. This risk is transferred to the card company. Third, the seller typically receives cash from the card company sooner than had it granted credit directly to customers. Fourth, a variety of credit options for customers offers a potential increase in sales volume. **Sears** historically offered credit only to customers using a Sears card but later changed its policy to permit customers to charge purchases to third-party credit card companies in a desire to increase sales. It reported: "SearsCharge increased its share of Sears retail sales even as the company expanded the payment options available to its customers with the acceptance ... of Visa, MasterCard, and American Express in addition to the [Sears] Card."

There are guidelines for how companies account for credit card and debit card sales. Some credit cards, but nearly all debit cards, credit a seller's Cash account immediately upon deposit. In this case the seller deposits a copy of each card sales receipt in its bank account just as it deposits a customer's check. The majority of credit cards, however, require the seller to remit a copy (often electronically) of each receipt to the card company. Until payment is received, the seller has an account receivable from the card company. In both cases, the seller pays a fee for services provided by the card company, often ranging from 1% to 5% of card sales. This charge is deducted from the credit to the seller's account or the cash payment to the seller.

Point: Visa USA now transacts more than $1 trillion from its credit, debit, and prepaid cards.

Decision Insight

Debit Card vs. Credit Card A buyer's debit card purchase reduces the buyer's cash account balance at the card company, which is often a bank. Since the buyer's cash account balance is a liability (with a credit balance) for the card company to the buyer, the card company would debit that account for a buyer's purchase—hence, the term *debit card*. A credit card reflects authorization by the card company of a line of credit for the buyer with preset interest rates and payment terms—hence, the term *credit card*. Most card companies waive interest charges if the buyer pays its balance each month. ■

Point: Web merchants pay twice as much in credit card association fees as other retailers because they suffer 10 times as much fraud.

The procedures used in accounting for credit card sales depend on whether cash is received immediately on deposit or cash receipt is delayed until the credit card company makes the payment.

Cash Received Immediately on Deposit To illustrate, if TechCom has $100 of credit card sales with a 4% fee, and its $96 cash is received immediately on deposit, the entry is

Assets = Liabilities + Equity
+96   +100
                         −4

July 15	Cash	96	
	Credit Card Expense	4	
	Sales		100
	To record credit card sales less a 4% credit card expense.*		

* We omit the entry to Dr. Cost of Sales and Cr. Merchandise Inventory to focus on credit card expense.

Cash Received Some Time after Deposit However, if instead TechCom must remit electronically the credit card sales receipts to the credit card company and wait for the $96 cash payment, the entry on the date of sale is

July 15	Accounts Receivable—Credit Card Co.	96	
	Credit Card Expense	4	
	Sales		100
	To record credit card sales less 4% credit card expense.*		

Assets = Liabilities + Equity
+96   +100
                                      −4

* We omit the entry to Dr. Cost of Sales and Cr. Merchandise Inventory to focus on credit card expense.

When cash is later received from the credit card company, usually through electronic funds transfer, the entry is

July 20	Cash	96	
	Accounts Receivable—Credit Card Co.		96
	To record cash receipt.		

Assets = Liabilities + Equity
+96
−96

Some firms report credit card expense in the income statement as a type of discount deducted from sales to get net sales. Other companies classify it as a selling expense or even as an administrative expense. Arguments can be made for each approach.

Point: Third-party credit card costs can be large. JCPenney reported third-party credit card costs exceeding $10 million.

Installment Sales and Receivables Many companies allow their credit customers to make periodic payments over several months. For example, **Ford Motor Company** reports more than $75 billion in installment receivables. The seller refers to such assets as *installment accounts* (or *finance*) *receivable,* which are amounts owed by customers from credit sales for which payment is required in periodic amounts over an extended time period. Source documents for installment accounts receivable include sales slips or invoices describing the sales transactions. The customer is usually charged interest. Although installment accounts receivable can have credit periods of more than one year, they are classified as current assets if the seller regularly offers customers such terms.

Decision Maker   Answer — p. 312

Entrepreneur As a small retailer, you are considering allowing customers to buy merchandise using credit cards. Until now, your store accepted only cash and checks. What analysis do you use to make this decision? ■

Quick Check   Answers — 313

1. In recording credit card sales, when do you debit Accounts Receivable and when do you debit Cash?
2. A company accumulates sales receipts and remits them to the credit card company for payment. When are the credit card expenses recorded? When are these expenses incurred?

Valuing Accounts Receivable—Direct Write-Off Method

When a company directly grants credit to its customers, it expects that some customers will not pay what they promised. The accounts of these customers are *uncollectible accounts,* commonly called **bad debts.** The total amount of uncollectible accounts is an expense of selling on credit. Why do companies sell on credit if they expect some accounts to be uncollectible? The answer is that companies believe that granting credit will increase total sales and net income enough to offset bad debts. Companies use two methods to account for uncollectible accounts: (1) direct write-off method and (2) allowance method. We describe both.

P1 Apply the direct write-off method to account for accounts receivable.

Recording and Writing Off Bad Debts The **direct write-off method** of accounting for bad debts records the loss from an uncollectible account receivable when it is determined to be uncollectible. No attempt is made to predict bad debts expense. To illustrate, if TechCom

Point: Managers realize that some portion of credit sales will be uncollectible, but which credit sales are uncollectible is unknown.

determines on January 23 that it cannot collect $520 owed to it by its customer J. Kent, it recognizes the loss using the direct write-off method as follows:

Jan. 23	Bad Debts Expense	520	
	Accounts Receivable—J. Kent		520
	To write off an uncollectible account.		

The debit in this entry charges the uncollectible amount directly to the current period's Bad Debts Expense account. The credit removes its balance from the Accounts Receivable account in the general ledger (and its subsidiary ledger).

Recovering a Bad Debt Although uncommon, sometimes an account written off is later collected. This can be due to factors such as continual collection efforts or a customer's good fortune. If the account of J. Kent that was written off directly to Bad Debts Expense is later collected in full, the following two entries record this recovery.

Mar. 11	Accounts Receivable—J. Kent.....................	520	
	Bad Debts Expense		520
	To reinstate account previously written off.		
Mar. 11	Cash	520	
	Accounts Receivable—J. Kent		520
	To record full payment of account.		

Assessing the Direct Write-Off Method Examples of companies that use the direct write-off method include **Rand Medical Billing**, **Gateway Distributors**, **Microwave Satellite Technologies**, **First Industrial Realty**, **New Frontier Energy**, and **Sub Surface Waste Management**. The following disclosure by **Pharma-Bio Serv** is typical of the justification for this method: Bad debts are accounted for using the direct write-off method whereby an expense is recognized only when a specific account is determined to be uncollectible. The effect of using this method approximates that of the allowance method. Companies must weigh at least two accounting concepts when considering the use of the direct write-off method: the (1) matching principle and (2) materiality constraint.

Matching principle applied to bad debts. The **matching (expense recognition) principle** requires expenses to be reported in the same accounting period as the sales they helped produce. This means that if extending credit to customers helped produce sales, the bad debts expense linked to those sales is matched and reported in the same period. The direct write-off method usually does *not* best match sales and expenses because bad debts expense is not recorded until an account becomes uncollectible, which often occurs in a period after that of the credit sale. To match bad debts expense with the sales it produces therefore requires a company to estimate future uncollectibles.

Materiality constraint applied to bad debts. The **materiality constraint** states that an amount can be ignored if its effect on the financial statements is unimportant to users' business decisions. The materiality constraint permits the use of the direct write-off method when bad debts expenses are very small in relation to a company's other financial statement items such as sales and net income.

Fraud

Receivables Protection. One accounts receivable fraud involves accepting cash payments from customers and not depositing that money in the company's bank account. Instead, a credit memo is issued to the customer's account, so that there are no collection calls to the customer. This fraud can be exposed by reviewing credit memos issued to customers and confirming the reason they were issued.

Valuing Accounts Receivable—Allowance Method

The **allowance method** of accounting for bad debts matches the *estimated* loss from uncollectible accounts receivable against the sales they helped produce. We must use estimated losses because when sales occur, management does not know which customers will not pay their bills. This means that at the end of each period, the allowance method requires an estimate of the total bad debts expected to result from that period's sales. This method has two advantages over the direct write-off method: (1) it records estimated bad debts expense in the period when the related sales are recorded and (2) it reports accounts receivable on the balance sheet at the estimated amount of cash to be collected.

Recording Bad Debts Expense The allowance method estimates bad debts expense at the end of each accounting period and records it with an adjusting entry. TechCom, for instance, had credit sales of $300,000 during its first year of operations. At the end of the first year, $20,000 of credit sales remained uncollected. Based on the experience of similar businesses, TechCom estimated that $1,500 of its accounts receivable would be uncollectible. This estimated expense is recorded with the following adjusting entry.

Dec. 31	Bad Debts Expense	1,500	
	Allowance for Doubtful Accounts		1,500
	To record estimated bad debts.		

Assets = Liabilities + Equity
−1,500   −1,500

The estimated Bad Debts Expense of $1,500 is reported on the income statement (as either a selling expense or an administrative expense) and offsets the $300,000 credit sales it helped produce. The **Allowance for Doubtful Accounts** is a contra asset account. A contra account is used instead of reducing accounts receivable directly because at the time of the adjusting entry, the company does not know which customers will not pay. After the bad debts adjusting entry is posted, TechCom's account balances (in T-account form) for Accounts Receivable and its Allowance for Doubtful Accounts are as shown in Exhibit 7.5.

Point: Credit approval is usually not assigned to the selling dept. because its goal is to increase sales, and it may approve customers at the cost of increased bad debts. Instead, approval is assigned to a separate credit-granting or administrative dept.

Accounts Receivable		Allowance for Doubtful Accounts	
Dec. 31 20,000			Dec. 31 1,500

EXHIBIT 7.5
General Ledger Entries after Bad Debts Adjusting Entry

The Allowance for Doubtful Accounts credit balance of $1,500 has the effect of reducing accounts receivable to its estimated realizable value. **Realizable value** refers to the expected proceeds from converting an asset into cash. Although credit customers owe $20,000 to TechCom, only $18,500 is expected to be realized in cash collections from these customers. In the balance sheet, the Allowance for Doubtful Accounts is subtracted from Accounts Receivable and is often reported as shown in Exhibit 7.6.

Point: Bad Debts Expense is also called *Uncollectible Accounts Expense*. The Allowance for Doubtful Accounts is also called *Allowance for Uncollectible Accounts*.

Current assets		
Accounts receivable	$20,000	
Less allowance for doubtful accounts	1,500	$18,500

EXHIBIT 7.6
Balance Sheet Presentation of the Allowance for Doubtful Accounts

Sometimes the Allowance for Doubtful Accounts is not reported separately. This alternative presentation is shown in Exhibit 7.7 (also see Appendix A).

Current assets	
Accounts receivable (net of $1,500 doubtful accounts)	$18,500

EXHIBIT 7.7
Alternative Presentation of the Allowance for Doubtful Accounts

Writing Off a Bad Debt When specific accounts are identified as uncollectible, they are written off against the Allowance for Doubtful Accounts. To illustrate, TechCom decides that J. Kent's $520 account is uncollectible and makes the following entry to write it off.

Jan. 23	Allowance for Doubtful Accounts	520	
	Accounts Receivable—J. Kent		520
	To write off an uncollectible account.		

Assets = Liabilities + Equity
+520
−520

Posting this write-off entry to the Accounts Receivable account removes the amount of the bad debt from the general ledger (it is also posted to the accounts receivable subsidiary ledger). The general ledger accounts now appear as in Exhibit 7.8 (assuming no other transactions affecting these accounts).

Point: The Bad Debts Expense account is not debited in the write-off entry because it was recorded in the period when sales occurred.

Accounts Receivable			Allowance for Doubtful Accounts		
Dec. 31 20,000					Dec. 31 1,500
	Jan. 23	520	Jan. 23 520		

EXHIBIT 7.8
General Ledger Entries after Write-Off

Point: In posting a write-off, the ledger's Explanation column indicates the reason for this credit so it is not misinterpreted as payment in full.

The write-off does *not* affect the realizable value of accounts receivable as shown in Exhibit 7.9. Neither total assets nor net income is affected by the write-off of a specific account. Instead, both assets and net income are affected in the period when bad debts expense is predicted and recorded with an adjusting entry.

EXHIBIT 7.9

Realizable Value before and after Write-Off of a Bad Debt

	Before Write-Off	After Write-Off
Accounts receivable	$ 20,000	$ 19,480
Less allowance for doubtful accounts	1,500	980
Estimated realizable accounts receivable	**$18,500**	**$18,500**

Recovering a Bad Debt When a customer fails to pay and the account is written off as uncollectible, his or her credit standing is jeopardized. To help restore credit standing, a customer sometimes volunteers to pay all or part of the amount owed. A company makes two entries when collecting an account previously written off by the allowance method. The first is to reverse the write-off and reinstate the customer's account. The second entry records the collection of the reinstated account. To illustrate, if on March 11 Kent pays in full his account previously written off, the entries are

Assets = Liabilities + Equity
+520
−520

Assets = Liabilities + Equity
+520
−520

Mar. 11	Accounts Receivable—J. Kent	520	
	Allowance for Doubtful Accounts		520
	To reinstate account previously written off.		
Mar. 11	Cash	520	
	Accounts Receivable—J. Kent		520
	To record full payment of account.		

Example: If TechCom used a collection agency and paid a 35% commission on $520 collected from Kent, how is this recorded? *Answer:*
Cash 338
Collection Expense 182
   Accts. Recble.—J. Kent 520

In this illustration, Kent paid the entire amount previously written off, but sometimes a customer pays only a portion of the amount owed. A question then arises as to whether the entire balance of the account or just the amount paid is returned to accounts receivable. This is a matter of judgment. If we believe this customer will later pay in full, we return the entire amount owed to accounts receivable, but if we expect no further collection, we return only the amount paid.

Decision Insight

PayPal PayPal is legally just a money transfer agent, but it is increasingly challenging big credit card brands—see chart. PayPal is successful because: (1) online credit card processing fees often exceed $0.15 per dollar, but PayPal's fees are under $0.10 per dollar. (2) PayPal's merchant fraud losses are under 0.2% of revenues, which compares to nearly 2% for online merchants using credit cards. ■

Global accounts (in mil.):
JP Morgan 30; Discover 53; MBNA 56; American Express 65; PayPal 72; Master Card 680; VISA 1,200

Estimating Bad Debts—Percent of Sales Method

P2 Apply the allowance method and estimate uncollectibles based on sales and accounts receivable.

The allowance method requires an estimate of bad debts expense to prepare an adjusting entry at the end of each accounting period. There are two common methods. One is based on the income statement relation between bad debts expense and sales. The second is based on the balance sheet relation between accounts receivable and the allowance for doubtful accounts.

The *percent of sales method,* also referred to as the *income statement method,* is based on the idea that a given percent of a company's credit sales for the period is uncollectible. To illustrate, assume that Musicland has credit sales of $400,000 in year 2011. Based on past experience,

Musicland estimates 0.6% of credit sales to be uncollectible. This implies that Musicland expects $2,400 of bad debts expense from its sales (computed as $400,000 × 0.006). The adjusting entry to record this estimated expense is

Dec. 31	Bad Debts Expense	2,400	
	Allowance for Doubtful Accounts		2,400
	To record estimated bad debts.		

Point: Focus is on *credit* sales because cash sales do not produce bad debts. If cash sales are a small or stable percent of credit sales, total sales can be used.

Assets = Liabilities + Equity
−2,400   −2,400

The allowance account ending balance on the balance sheet for this method would rarely equal the bad debts expense on the income statement. This is so because unless a company is in its first period of operations, its allowance account has a zero balance only if the prior amounts written off as uncollectible *exactly* equal the prior estimated bad debts expenses. (When computing bad debts expense as a percent of sales, managers monitor and adjust the percent so it is not too high or too low.)

Point: When using the *percent of sales method* for estimating uncollectibles, the estimate of bad debts is the number used in the adjusting entry.

Estimating Bad Debts—Percent of Receivables Method

The *accounts receivable methods,* also referred to as *balance sheet methods,* use balance sheet relations to estimate bad debts—mainly the relation between accounts receivable and the allowance amount. The goal of the bad debts adjusting entry for these methods is to make the Allowance for Doubtful Accounts balance equal to the portion of accounts receivable that is estimated to be uncollectible. The estimated balance for the allowance account is obtained in one of two ways: (1) computing the percent uncollectible from the total accounts receivable or (2) aging accounts receivable.

The *percent of accounts receivable method* assumes that a given percent of a company's receivables is uncollectible. This percent is based on past experience and is impacted by current conditions such as economic trends and customer difficulties. The total dollar amount of all receivables is multiplied by this percent to get the estimated dollar amount of uncollectible accounts—reported in the balance sheet as the Allowance for Doubtful Accounts.

To illustrate, assume that Musicland has $50,000 of accounts receivable on December 31, 2011. Experience suggests 5% of its receivables is uncollectible. This means that *after* the adjusting entry is posted, we want the Allowance for Doubtful Accounts to show a $2,500 credit balance (5% of $50,000). We are also told that its beginning balance is $2,200, which is 5% of the $44,000 accounts receivable on December 31, 2010—see Exhibit 7.10.

Point: When using an accounts receivable method for estimating uncollectibles, the allowance account balance is adjusted to equal the estimate of uncollectibles.

EXHIBIT 7.10

Allowance for Doubtful Accounts after Bad Debts Adjusting Entry

Allowance for Doubtful Accounts

			Dec. 31, 2010, bal.	2,200
Feb. 6	800			
July 10	700			
Nov. 20	500			
			Unadjusted bal.	200
			Dec. 31 adjustment	2,300
			Dec. 31, 2011, bal.	2,500

Current year write-offs → Feb. 6, July 10, Nov. 20
Prior year estimate of allowance for doubtful accounts → Dec. 31, 2010, bal.
Adjusting entry → Dec. 31 adjustment
Current year estimate of allowance for doubtful accounts → Dec. 31, 2011, bal.

During 2011, accounts of customers are written off on February 6, July 10, and November 20. Thus, the account has a $200 credit balance *before* the December 31, 2011, adjustment. The adjusting entry to give the allowance account the estimated $2,500 balance is

Dec. 31	Bad Debts Expense	2,300	
	Allowance for Doubtful Accounts		2,300
	To record estimated bad debts.		

Assets = Liabilities + Equity
−2,300   −2,300

> **Decision Insight**
>
> **Aging Pains** Experience shows that the longer a receivable is past due, the lower is the likelihood of its collection. An *aging schedule* uses this knowledge to estimate bad debts. The chart here is from a survey that reported estimates of bad debts for receivables grouped by how long they were past their due dates. Each company sets its own estimates based on its customers and its experiences with those customers' payment patterns.
>
> Bad debts percentage by months past due:
> - 1: 6%
> - 2: 15%
> - 3–5: 27%
> - 6–8: 43%
> - 9–11: 58%
> - 12–23: 76%
> - >24: 89%

Estimating Bad Debts—Aging of Receivables Method

The **aging of accounts receivable** method uses both past and current receivables information to estimate the allowance amount. Specifically, each receivable is classified by how long it is past its due date. Then estimates of uncollectible amounts are made assuming that the longer an amount is past due, the more likely it is to be uncollectible. Classifications are often based on 30-day periods. After the amounts are classified (or aged), experience is used to estimate the percent of each uncollectible class. These percents are applied to the amounts in each class and then totaled to get the estimated balance of the Allowance for Doubtful Accounts. This computation is performed by setting up a schedule such as Exhibit 7.11.

EXHIBIT 7.11

Aging of Accounts Receivable

MUSICLAND
Schedule of Accounts Receivable by Age
December 31, 2011

Customer	Totals	Not Yet Due	1 to 30 Days Past Due	31 to 60 Days Past Due	61 to 90 Days Past Due	Over 90 Days Past Due
Carlie Abbott	$ 450	$ 450				
Jamie Allen	710			$ 710		
Chavez Andres	500	300	$ 200			
Balicia Company	740				$ 100	$ 640
⋮						
Zamora Services	1,000	810	190			
Total receivables*	$50,000	$37,000	$6,500	$3,700	$1,900	$ 900
Percent uncollectible		× 2%	× 5%	× 10%	× 25%	× 40%
Estimated uncollectible	**$ 2,270**	$ 740	$ 325	$ 370	$ 475	$ 360

- Each receivable is grouped by how long it is past its due date
- Each age group is multiplied by its estimated bad debts percent
- Estimated bad debts for each group are totaled

*The "white line break" means that additional customer accounts are not shown in the table but are included in each column's total.

Exhibit 7.11 lists each customer's individual balances assigned to one of five classes based on its days past due. The amounts in each class are totaled and multiplied by the estimated percent of uncollectible accounts for each class. The percents used are regularly reviewed to reflect changes in the company and economy.

To explain, Musicland has $3,700 in accounts receivable that are 31 to 60 days past due. Its management estimates 10% of the amounts in this age class are uncollectible, or a total of $370 (computed as $3,700 × 10%). Similar analysis is done for each of the other four classes. The final total of $2,270 ($740 + $325 + 370 + $475 + $360) shown in the first column is the estimated balance for the Allowance for Doubtful Accounts. Exhibit 7.12 shows that since the allowance

EXHIBIT 7.12

Computation of the Required Adjustment for the Accounts Receivable Method

Unadjusted balance	$ 200 credit
Estimated balance	2,270 credit
Required adjustment	**$2,070 credit**

account has an unadjusted credit balance of $200, the required adjustment to the Allowance for Doubtful Accounts is $2,070. (We could also use a T-account for this analysis as shown in the margin.) This yields the following end-of-period adjusting entry.

Dec. 31	Bad Debts Expense	2,070	
	Allowance for Doubtful Accounts		2,070
	To record estimated bad debts.		

Allowance for Doubtful Accounts

	Unadj. bal.	200
	Req. adj.	2,070
	Estim. bal.	2,270

Assets = Liabilities + Equity
−2,070   −2,070

Alternatively, if the allowance account had an unadjusted *debit* balance of $500 (instead of the $200 credit balance), its required adjustment would be computed as follows. (Again, a T-account can be used for this analysis as shown in the margin.)

Point: A debit balance implies that write-offs for that period exceed the total allowance.

Unadjusted balance......... $ 500 debit
Estimated balance..........   2,270 credit   ← Current year estimate of allowance for doubtful accounts
Required adjustment...... $ 2,770 credit

Adjusting entry amount

Allowance for Doubtful Accounts

Unadj. bal.	500		
		Req. adj.	2,770
		Estim. bal.	2,270

The entry to record the end-of-period adjustment for this alternative case is

Dec. 31	Bad Debts Expense	2,770	
	Allowance for Doubtful Accounts		2,770
	To record estimated bad debts.		

Assets = Liabilities + Equity
−2,770   −2,770

The aging of accounts receivable method is an examination of specific accounts and is usually the most reliable of the estimation methods.

Estimating Bad Debts—Summary of Methods Exhibit 7.13 summarizes the principles guiding all three estimation methods and their focus of analysis. Percent of sales, with its income statement focus, does a good job at matching bad debts expense with sales. The accounts receivable methods, with their balance sheet focus, do a better job at reporting accounts receivable at realizable value.

EXHIBIT 7.13

Methods to Estimate Bad Debts

Bad Debts Estimation
or
Income Statement Focus / **Balance Sheet Focus**

- **Percent of Sales** [Emphasis on Matching]
  - Sales × Rate = Bad Debts Expense
- **Percent of Receivables** [Emphasis on Realizable Value]
  - Accounts Receivable × Rate = Allowance for Doubtful Accounts
- **Aging of Receivables** [Emphasis on Realizable Value]
  - Accounts Receivable (by Age) × Rates (by Age) = Allowance for Doubtful Accounts

Decision Maker   Answer — p. 312

Labor Union Chief One week prior to labor contract negotiations, financial statements are released showing no income growth. A 10% growth was predicted. Your analysis finds that the company increased its allowance for uncollectibles from 1.5% to 4.5% of receivables. Without this change, income would show a 9% growth. Does this analysis impact negotiations? ■

> **Quick Check** Answers — p. 313
>
> 3. Why must bad debts expense be estimated if such an estimate is possible?
> 4. What term describes the balance sheet valuation of Accounts Receivable less the Allowance for Doubtful Accounts?
> 5. Why is estimated bad debts expense credited to a contra account (Allowance for Doubtful Accounts) rather than to the Accounts Receivable account?
> 6. SnoBoard Company's year-end balance in its Allowance for Doubtful Accounts is a credit of $440. By aging accounts receivable, it estimates that $6,142 is uncollectible. Prepare SnoBoard's year-end adjusting entry for bad debts.
> 7. Record entries for these transactions assuming the allowance method is used:
>   Jan. 10 The $300 account of customer Cool Jam is determined uncollectible.
>   April 12 Cool Jam unexpectedly pays in full the account deemed uncollectible on Jan. 10.

NOTES RECEIVABLE

C2 Describe a note receivable, the computation of its maturity date, and the recording of its existence.

A **promissory note** is a written promise to pay a specified amount of money, usually with interest, either on demand or at a definite future date. Promissory notes are used in many transactions, including paying for products and services, and lending and borrowing money. Sellers sometimes ask for a note to replace an account receivable when a customer requests additional time to pay a past-due account. For legal reasons, sellers generally prefer to receive notes when the credit period is long and when the receivable is for a large amount. If a lawsuit is needed to collect from a customer, a note is the buyer's written acknowledgment of the debt, its amount, and its terms.

Exhibit 7.14 shows a simple promissory note dated July 10, 2011. For this note, Julia Browne promises to pay TechCom or to its order (according to TechCom's instructions) a specified amount of money ($1,000), called the **principal of a note,** at a definite future date (October 8, 2011). As the one who signed the note and promised to pay it at maturity, Browne is the **maker of the note.** As the person to whom the note is payable, TechCom is the **payee of the note.** To Browne, the note is a liability called a *note payable*. To TechCom, the same note is an asset called a *note receivable*. This note bears interest at 12%, as written on the note. **Interest** is the charge for using the money until its due date. To a borrower, interest is an expense. To a lender, it is revenue.

EXHIBIT 7.14

Promissory Note

```
                    Promissory Note
Amount: $1,000                    Date: July 10, 2011

  Ninety days  after date _____!_____ promise to pay to the order of
                    TechCom Company
                    Los Angeles, CA
  One thousand and no/100 -------------------------------- Dollars
  for value received with interest at the annual rate of ..12%..
  payable at  First National Bank of Los Angeles, CA
                                        Julia Browne
```

- Principal
- Date of note
- Due date
- Payee
- Interest rate
- Maker

Computing Maturity and Interest

This section describes key computations for notes including the determination of maturity date, period covered, and interest computation.

Maturity Date and Period The **maturity date of a note** is the day the note (principal and interest) must be repaid. The *period* of a note is the time from the note's (contract) date to its maturity date. Many notes mature in less than a full year, and the period they cover is often expressed in days. When the time of a note is expressed in days, its maturity date is the specified number of days after the note's date. As an example, a five-day note dated June 15 matures and is due on June 20. A 90-day note dated July 10 matures on October 8. This October 8 due date is computed as shown in Exhibit 7.15. The period of a note is sometimes expressed in months or years. When months are used, the note matures and is payable in the month of its maturity on the *same day of the month* as its original date. A nine-month note dated July 10, for instance, is payable on April 10. The same analysis applies when years are used.

Days in July	31
Minus the date of the note	10
Days remaining in July	21 ← July 11–31
Add days in August	31 ← Aug. 1–31
Add days in September	30 ← Sept. 1–30
Days to equal 90 days, or **maturity date of October 8**	8 ← Oct. 1–8
Period of the note in days	90

EXHIBIT 7.15

Maturity Date Computation

Interest Computation *Interest* is the cost of borrowing money for the borrower or, alternatively, the profit from lending money for the lender. Unless otherwise stated, the rate of interest on a note is the rate charged for the use of the principal for one year. The formula for computing interest on a note is shown in Exhibit 7.16.

$$\text{Principal of the note} \times \text{Annual interest rate} \times \text{Time expressed in fraction of year} = \text{Interest}$$

EXHIBIT 7.16

Computation of Interest Formula

To simplify interest computations, a year is commonly treated as having 360 days (called the *banker's rule* in the business world and widely used in commercial transactions). **We treat a year as having 360 days for interest computations in the examples and assignments**. Using the promissory note in Exhibit 7.14 where we have a 90-day, 12%, $1,000 note, the total interest is computed as follows.

$$\$1{,}000 \times 12\% \times \frac{90}{360} = \$1{,}000 \times 0.12 \times 0.25 = \$30$$

Recognizing Notes Receivable

Notes receivable are usually recorded in a single Notes Receivable account to simplify recordkeeping. The original notes are kept on file, including information on the maker, rate of interest, and due date. (When a company holds a large number of notes, it sometimes sets up a controlling account and a subsidiary ledger for notes. This is similar to the handling of accounts receivable.) To illustrate the recording for the receipt of a note, we use the $1,000, 90-day, 12% promissory note in Exhibit 7.14. TechCom received this note at the time of a product sale to Julia Browne. This transaction is recorded as follows.

July 10*	Notes Receivable	1,000	
	Sales		1,000
	Sold goods in exchange for a 90-day, 12% note.		

Assets = Liabilities + Equity
+1,000   +1,000

* We omit the entry to Dr. Cost of Sales and Cr. Merchandise Inventory to focus on sales and receivables.

When a seller accepts a note from an overdue customer as a way to grant a time extension on a past-due account receivable, it will often collect part of the past-due balance in cash. This partial payment forces a concession from the customer, reduces the customer's debt (and the seller's risk), and produces a note for a smaller amount. To illustrate, assume that TechCom agreed to accept $232 in cash along with a $600, 60-day, 15% note from Jo Cook to

Point: Notes receivable often are a major part of a company's assets. Likewise, notes payable often are a large part of a company's liabilities.

settle her $832 past-due account. TechCom made the following entry to record receipt of this cash and note.

Oct. 5	Cash...	232	
	Notes Receivable	600	
	Accounts Receivable—J. Cook		832
	Received cash and note to settle account.		

Assets = Liabilities + Equity
+232
+600
−832

Valuing and Settling Notes

Recording an Honored Note The principal and interest of a note are due on its maturity date. The maker of the note usually *honors* the note and pays it in full. To illustrate, when J. Cook pays the note above on its due date, TechCom records it as follows.

P3 Record the honoring and dishonoring of a note and adjustments for interest.

Dec. 4	Cash...	615	
	Notes Receivable		600
	Interest Revenue		15
	Collect note with interest of $600 × 15% × 60/360.		

Assets = Liabilities + Equity
+615   +15
−600

Interest Revenue, also called *Interest Earned,* is reported on the income statement.

Recording a Dishonored Note When a note's maker is unable or refuses to pay at maturity, the note is *dishonored*. The act of dishonoring a note does not relieve the maker of the obligation to pay. The payee should use every legitimate means to collect. How do companies report this event? The balance of the Notes Receivable account should include only those notes that have not matured. Thus, when a note is dishonored, we remove the amount of this note from the Notes Receivable account and charge it back to an account receivable from its maker. To illustrate, TechCom holds an $800, 12%, 60-day note of Greg Hart. At maturity, Hart dishonors the note. TechCom records this dishonoring of the note as follows.

Point: When posting a dishonored note to a customer's account, an explanation is included so as not to misinterpret the debit as a sale on account.

Oct. 14	Accounts Receivable—G. Hart.....................	816	
	Interest Revenue		16
	Notes Receivable		800
	To charge account of G. Hart for a dishonored note and interest of $800 × 12% × 60/360.		

Assets = Liabilities + Equity
+816   +16
−800

Point: Reporting the details of notes is consistent with the **full disclosure principle,** which requires financial statements (including footnotes) to report all relevant information.

Charging a dishonored note back to the account of its maker serves two purposes. First, it removes the amount of the note from the Notes Receivable account and records the dishonored note in the maker's account. Second, and more important, if the maker of the dishonored note applies for credit in the future, his or her account will reveal all past dealings, including the dishonored note. Restoring the account also reminds the company to continue collection efforts from Hart for both principal and interest. The entry records the full amount, including interest, to ensure that it is included in collection efforts.

Recording End-of-Period Interest Adjustment When notes receivable are outstanding at the end of a period, any accrued interest earned is computed and recorded. To illustrate, on December 16, TechCom accepts a $3,000, 60-day, 12% note from a customer in granting an extension on a past-due account. When TechCom's accounting period ends on December 31, $15 of interest has accrued on this note ($3,000 × 12% × 15/360). The following adjusting entry records this revenue.

Dec. 31	Interest Receivable	15	
	Interest Revenue		15
	To record accrued interest earned.		

Assets = Liabilities + Equity
+15   +15

Interest Revenue appears on the income statement, and Interest Receivable appears on the balance sheet as a current asset. When the December 16 note is collected on February 14, TechCom's entry to record the cash receipt is

Feb. 14	Cash	3,060	
	Interest Revenue		45
	Interest Receivable		15
	Notes Receivable		3,000
	Received payment of note and its interest.		

Assets = Liabilities + Equity
+3,060   +45
−15
−3,000

Total interest earned on the 60-day note is $60. The $15 credit to Interest Receivable on February 14 reflects the collection of the interest accrued from the December 31 adjusting entry. The $45 interest earned reflects TechCom's revenue from holding the note from January 1 to February 14 of the current period.

Fraud

Skimming. *Skimming* refers to stealing money from a cash register, a customer's payment, or refunds received. A point-of-sale employee who operates a cash register is especially at risk for skimming. For example, a cash register employee might receive $900 cash but only ring up $600 on the register (or nothing), which enables the employee to steal $300 cash (or the entire amount). A crucial control is to require that each sale is entered into the register. Skimming is then revealed when the record on the register differs from the cash in the register. To ensure that *all* sales are recorded on the register, we use customer help by hanging a sign: "Sales without a receipt are free!"

Quick Check   Answers — p. 313

8. Irwin purchases $7,000 of merchandise from Stamford on December 16, 2011. Stamford accepts Irwin's $7,000, 90-day, 12% note as payment. Stamford's accounting period ends on December 31, and it does not make reversing entries. Prepare entries for Stamford on December 16, 2011, and December 31, 2011.
9. Using the information in Quick Check 8, prepare Stamford's March 16, 2012, entry if Irwin dishonors the note.

DISPOSAL OF RECEIVABLES

Companies can convert receivables to cash before they are due. Reasons for this include the need for cash or the desire not to be involved in collection activities. Converting receivables is usually done either by (1) selling them or (2) using them as security for a loan. A recent survey shows that about 20% of companies obtain cash from either selling receivables or pledging them as security. In some industries such as textiles, apparel and furniture, this is common practice.

C3 Explain how receivables can be converted to cash before maturity.

Selling Receivables

A company can sell all or a portion of its receivables to a finance company or bank. The buyer, called a *factor,* charges the seller a *factoring fee* and then the buyer takes ownership of the receivables and receives cash when they come due. By incurring a factoring fee, the seller receives cash earlier and can pass the risk of bad debts to the factor. The seller can also choose to avoid costs of billing and accounting for the receivables. To illustrate, if TechCom sells $20,000 of its accounts receivable and is charged a 4% factoring fee, it records this sale as follows.

Global: Firms in export sales increasingly sell their receivables to factors.

Aug. 15	Cash	19,200	
	Factoring Fee Expense	800	
	Accounts Receivable		20,000
	Sold accounts receivable for cash, less 4% fee.		

Assets = Liabilities + Equity
+19,200   −800
−20,000

The accounting for sales of notes receivable is similar to that for accounts receivable. The detailed entries are covered in advanced courses.

Pledging Receivables

A company can raise cash by borrowing money and *pledging* its receivables as security for the loan. Pledging receivables does not transfer the risk of bad debts to the lender because the borrower retains ownership of the receivables. If the borrower defaults on the loan, the lender has a right to be paid from the cash receipts of the receivable when collected. To illustrate, when TechCom borrows $35,000 and pledges its receivables as security, it records this transaction as follows.

Assets = Liabilities + Equity
+35,000   +35,000

Aug. 20	Cash	35,000	
	Notes Payable		35,000
	Borrowed money with a note secured by pledging receivables.		

Since pledged receivables are committed as security for a specific loan, the borrower's financial statements disclose the pledging of them. TechCom, for instance, includes the following note with its statements: Accounts receivable of $40,000 are pledged as security for a $35,000 note payable.

Decision Insight

What's the Proper Allowance? How can we assess whether a company has properly estimated its allowance for uncollectibles? One way is to compute the ratio of the allowance account to the gross accounts receivable. When this ratio is analyzed over several consecutive periods, trends often emerge that reflect on the adequacy of the allowance amount. ■

GLOBAL VIEW

This section discusses similarities and differences between U.S. GAAP and IFRS regarding the recognition, measurement, and disposition of receivables.

Recognition of Receivables Both U.S. GAAP and IFRS have similar asset criteria that apply to recognition of receivables. Further, receivables that arise from revenue-generating activities are subject to broadly similar criteria for U.S. GAAP and IFRS. Specifically, both refer to the realization principle and an earnings process. The realization principle under U.S. GAAP implies an *arm's-length transaction* occurs, whereas under IFRS this notion is applied in terms of reliable measurement and likelihood of economic benefits. Regarding U.S. GAAP's reference to an earnings process, IFRS instead refers to risk transfer and ownership reward. While these criteria are broadly similar, differences do exist, and they arise mainly from industry-specific guidance under U.S. GAAP, which is very limited under IFRS.

Valuation of Receivables Both U.S. GAAP and IFRS require that receivables be reported net of estimated uncollectibles. Further, both systems require that the expense for estimated uncollectibles be recorded in the same period when any revenues from those receivables are recorded. This means that for accounts receivable, both U.S. GAAP and IFRS require the allowance method for uncollectibles (unless uncollectibles are immaterial). The allowance method using percent of sales, percent of receivables, and aging was explained in this chapter. **Nokia** reports the following for its allowance for uncollectibles:

NOKIA

> Management specifically analyzes accounts receivables and historical bad debt, customer concentrations, customer creditworthiness, current economic trends and changes in our customer payment terms when evaluating the adequacy of the allowance.

Disposition of Receivables Both U.S. GAAP and IFRS apply broadly similar rules in recording dispositions of receivables. Those rules are discussed in this chapter. We should be aware of an important difference in terminology. Companies reporting under U.S. GAAP disclose Bad Debts Expense, which is also referred to as Provision for Bad Debts or the Provision for Uncollectible Accounts. For U.S. GAAP, *provision* here refers to expense. Under IFRS, the term *provision* usually refers to a liability whose amount or timing (or both) is uncertain.

Accounts Receivable Turnover

Decision Analysis

For a company selling on credit, we want to assess both the quality and liquidity of its accounts receivable. *Quality* of receivables refers to the likelihood of collection without loss. Experience shows that the longer receivables are outstanding beyond their due date, the lower the likelihood of collection. *Liquidity* of receivables refers to the speed of collection. **Accounts receivable turnover** is a measure of both the quality and liquidity of accounts receivable. It indicates how often, on average, receivables are received and collected during the period. The formula for this ratio is shown in Exhibit 7.17.

A1 Compute accounts receivable turnover and use it to help assess financial condition.

$$\text{Accounts receivable turnover} = \frac{\text{Net sales}}{\text{Average accounts receivable, net}}$$

EXHIBIT 7.17
Accounts Receivable Turnover

We prefer to use net *credit* sales in the numerator because cash sales do not create receivables. However, since financial statements rarely report net credit sales, our analysis uses net sales. The denominator is the *average* accounts receivable balance, computed as (Beginning balance + Ending balance) ÷ 2. TechCom has an accounts receivable turnover of 5.1. This indicates its average accounts receivable balance is converted into cash 5.1 times during the period. Exhibit 7.18 shows graphically this turnover activity for TechCom.

EXHIBIT 7.18
Rate of Accounts Receivable Turnover for TechCom

Accounts receivable turnover also reflects how well management is doing in granting credit to customers in a desire to increase sales. A high turnover in comparison with competitors suggests that management should consider using more liberal credit terms to increase sales. A low turnover suggests management should consider stricter credit terms and more aggressive collection efforts to avoid having its resources tied up in accounts receivable.

To illustrate, we take fiscal year data from two competitors: **Dell** and **Apple**. Exhibit 7.19 shows accounts receivable turnover for both companies.

Point: Credit risk ratio is computed by dividing the Allowance for Doubtful Accounts by Accounts Receivable. The higher this ratio, the higher is credit risk.

Company	Figure ($ millions)	2008	2007	2006	2005
Dell	Net sales	$61,101	$61,133	$57,420	$55,788
	Average accounts receivable, net	$ 5,346	$ 5,292	$ 4,352	$ 3,826
	Accounts receivable turnover	11.4	11.6	13.2	14.6
Apple	Net sales	$32,479	$24,006	$19,315	$13,931
	Average accounts receivable, net	$ 2,030	$ 1,445	$ 1,074	$ 835
	Accounts receivable turnover	16.0	16.6	18.0	16.7

EXHIBIT 7.19
Analysis Using Accounts Receivable Turnover

Dell's 2008 turnover is 11.4, computed as $61,101/$5,346 ($ millions). This means that Dell's average accounts receivable balance was converted into cash 11.4 times in 2008. Its turnover declined in 2008, as it has for each of the past 3 years. Apple's turnover exceeds that for Dell in each of the past 4 years. Is either company's turnover too high? Since sales are stable or markedly growing

Decision Maker

Answer — p. 312

Family Physician Your medical practice is barely profitable, so you hire a health care analyst. The analyst highlights several points including the following: *"Accounts receivable turnover is too low. Tighter credit policies are recommended along with discontinuing service to those most delayed in payments."* How do you interpret these recommendations? What actions do you take?

DEMONSTRATION PROBLEM

Clayco Company completes the following selected transactions during year 2011.

July 14   Writes off a $750 account receivable arising from a sale to Briggs Company that dates to 10 months ago. (Clayco Company uses the allowance method.)

     30   Clayco Company receives a $1,000, 90-day, 10% note in exchange for merchandise sold to Sumrell Company (the merchandise cost $600).

Aug. 15   Receives $2,000 cash plus a $10,000 note from JT Co. in exchange for merchandise that sells for $12,000 (its cost is $8,000). The note is dated August 15, bears 12% interest, and matures in 120 days.

Nov. 1   Completed a $200 credit card sale with a 4% fee (the cost of sales is $150). The cash is received immediately from the credit card company.

     3   Sumrell Company refuses to pay the note that was due to Clayco Company on October 28. Prepare the journal entry to charge the dishonored note plus accrued interest to Sumrell Company's accounts receivable.

     5   Completed a $500 credit card sale with a 5% fee (the cost of sales is $300). The payment from the credit card company is received on Nov. 9.

    15   Received the full amount of $750 from Briggs Company that was previously written off on July 14. Record the bad debts recovery.

Dec. 13   Received payment of principal plus interest from JT for the August 15 note.

Required

1. Prepare journal entries to record these transactions on Clayco Company's books.
2. Prepare an adjusting journal entry as of December 31, 2011, assuming the following:
   a. Bad debts are estimated to be $20,400 by aging accounts receivable. The unadjusted balance of the Allowance for Doubtful Accounts is $1,000 debit.
   b. Alternatively, assume that bad debts are estimated using the percent of sales method. The Allowance for Doubtful Accounts had a $1,000 debit balance before adjustment, and the company estimates bad debts to be 1% of its credit sales of $2,000,000.

PLANNING THE SOLUTION

- Examine each transaction to determine the accounts affected, and then record the entries.
- For the year-end adjustment, record the bad debts expense for the two approaches.

---

[1] As an estimate of *average days' sales uncollected,* we compute how many days (*on average*) it takes to collect receivables as follows: 365 days ÷ accounts receivable turnover. An increase in this *average collection period* can signal a decline in customers' financial condition.

SOLUTION TO DEMONSTRATION PROBLEM

1.

Date	Account	Debit	Credit
July 14	Allowance for Doubtful Accounts	750	
	Accounts Receivable—Briggs Co.		750
	Wrote off an uncollectible account.		
July 30	Notes Receivable—Sumrell Co.	1,000	
	Sales		1,000
	Sold merchandise for a 90-day, 10% note.		
July 30	Cost of Goods Sold	600	
	Merchandise Inventory		600
	To record the cost of July 30 sale.		
Aug. 15	Cash	2,000	
	Notes Receivable—JT Co.	10,000	
	Sales		12,000
	Sold merchandise to customer for $2,000 cash and $10,000 note.		
Aug. 15	Cost of Goods Sold	8,000	
	Merchandise Inventory		8,000
	To record the cost of Aug. 15 sale.		
Nov. 1	Cash	192	
	Credit Card Expense	8	
	Sales		200
	To record credit card sale less a 4% credit card expense.		
Nov. 1	Cost of Goods Sold	150	
	Merchandise Inventory		150
	To record the cost of Nov. 1 sale.		
Nov. 3	Accounts Receivable—Sumrell Co.	1,025	
	Interest Revenue		25
	Notes Receivable—Sumrell Co.		1,000
	To charge account of Sumrell Company for a $1,000 dishonored note and interest of $1,000 × 10% × 90/360.		
Nov. 5	Accounts Receivable—Credit Card Co.	475	
	Credit Card Expense	25	
	Sales		500
	To record credit card sale less a 5% credit card expense.		
Nov. 5	Cost of Goods Sold	300	
	Merchandise Inventory		300
	To record the cost of Nov. 5 sale.		
Nov. 9	Cash	475	
	Accounts Receivable—Credit Card Co.		475
	To record cash receipt from Nov. 5 sale.		
Nov. 15	Accounts Receivable—Briggs Co.	750	
	Allowance for Doubtful Accounts		750
	To reinstate the account of Briggs Company previously written off.		
Nov. 15	Cash	750	
	Accounts Receivable—Briggs Co.		750
	Cash received in full payment of account.		
Dec. 13	Cash	10,400	
	Interest Revenue		400
	Note Receivable—JT Co.		10,000
	Collect note with interest of $10,000 × 12% × 120/360.		

2a. Aging of accounts receivable method.

Dec. 31	Bad Debts Expense	21,400	
	Allowance for Doubtful Accounts		21,400
	To adjust allowance account from a $1,000 debit balance to a $20,400 credit balance.		

2b. Percent of sales method.*

Dec. 31	Bad Debts Expense	20,000	
	Allowance for Doubtful Accounts		20,000
	To provide for bad debts as 1% × $2,000,000 in credit sales.		

---

* For the income statement approach, which requires estimating bad debts as a percent of sales or credit sales, the Allowance account balance is *not* considered when making the adjusting entry.

Summary

C1 **Describe accounts receivable and how they occur and are recorded.** Accounts receivable are amounts due from customers for credit sales. A subsidiary ledger lists amounts owed by each customer. Credit sales arise from at least two sources: (1) sales on credit and (2) credit card sales. *Sales on credit* refers to a company's granting credit directly to customers. Credit card sales involve customers' use of third-party credit cards.

C2 **Describe a note receivable, the computation of its maturity date, and the recording of its existence.** A note receivable is a written promise to pay a specified amount of money at a definite future date. The maturity date is the day the note (principal and interest) must be repaid. Interest rates are normally stated in annual terms. The amount of interest on the note is computed by expressing time as a fraction of one year and multiplying the note's principal by this fraction and the annual interest rate. A note received is recorded at its principal amount by debiting the Notes Receivable account. The credit amount is to the asset, product, or service provided in return for the note.

C3 **Explain how receivables can be converted to cash before maturity.** Receivables can be converted to cash before maturity in three ways. First, a company can sell accounts receivable to a factor, who charges a factoring fee. Second, a company can borrow money by signing a note payable that is secured by pledging the accounts receivable. Third, notes receivable can be discounted at (sold to) a financial institution.

A1 **Compute accounts receivable turnover and use it to help assess financial condition.** Accounts receivable turnover is a measure of both the quality and liquidity of accounts receivable. The accounts receivable turnover measure indicates how often, on average, receivables are received and collected during the period. Accounts receivable turnover is computed as net sales divided by average accounts receivable.

P1 **Apply the direct write-off method to account for accounts receivable.** The direct write-off method charges Bad Debts Expense when accounts are written off as uncollectible. This method is acceptable only when the amount of bad debts expense is immaterial.

P2 **Apply the allowance method and estimate uncollectibles based on sales and accounts receivable.** Under the allowance method, bad debts expense is recorded with an adjustment at the end of each accounting period that debits the Bad Debts Expense account and credits the Allowance for Doubtful Accounts. The uncollectible accounts are later written off with a debit to the Allowance for Doubtful Accounts. Uncollectibles are estimated by focusing on either (1) the income statement relation between bad debts expense and credit sales or (2) the balance sheet relation between accounts receivable and the allowance for doubtful accounts. The first approach emphasizes the matching principle using the income statement. The second approach emphasizes realizable value of accounts receivable using the balance sheet.

P3 **Record the honoring and dishonoring of a note and adjustments for interest.** When a note is honored, the payee debits the money received and credits both Notes Receivable and Interest Revenue. Dishonored notes are credited to Notes Receivable and debited to Accounts Receivable (to the account of the maker in an attempt to collect), and Interest Revenue is recorded for interest earned for the time the note is held.

Guidance Answers to Decision Maker and Decision Ethics

Entrepreneur Analysis of credit card sales should weigh the benefits against the costs. The primary benefit is the potential to increase sales by attracting customers who prefer the convenience of credit cards. The primary cost is the fee charged by the credit card company for providing this service. Analysis should therefore estimate the expected increase in dollar sales from allowing credit card sales and then subtract (1) the normal costs and expenses and (2) the credit card fees associated with this expected increase in dollar sales. If your analysis shows an increase in profit from allowing credit card sales, your store should probably accept them.

Labor Union Chief Yes, this information is likely to impact your negotiations. The obvious question is why the company markedly increased this allowance. The large increase in this allowance means a substantial increase in bad debts expense *and* a decrease in earnings. This change (coming immediately prior to labor contract discussions) also raises concerns since it reduces the union's bargaining power for increased compensation. You want to ask management for supporting documentation justifying this increase. You also want data for two or three prior years and similar data from competitors.

These data should give you some sense of whether the change in the allowance for uncollectibles is justified.

Family Physician The recommendations are twofold. First, the analyst suggests more stringent screening of patients' credit standing. Second, the analyst suggests dropping patients who are most overdue in payments. You are likely bothered by both suggestions. They are probably financially wise recommendations, but you are troubled by eliminating services to those less able to pay. One alternative is to follow the recommendations while implementing a care program directed at patients less able to pay for services. This allows you to continue services to patients less able to pay and lets you discontinue services to patients able but unwilling to pay.

Guidance Answers to Quick Checks

1. If cash is immediately received when credit card sales receipts are deposited, the company debits Cash at the time of sale. If the company does not receive payment until after it submits receipts to the credit card company, it debits Accounts Receivable at the time of sale. (Cash is later debited when payment is received from the credit card company.)
2. Credit card expenses are usually *recorded* and *incurred* at the time of their related sales, not when cash is received from the credit card company.
3. If possible, bad debts expense must be matched with the sales that gave rise to the accounts receivable. This requires that companies estimate future bad debts at the end of each period before they learn which accounts are uncollectible.
4. Realizable value (also called *net realizable value*).
5. The estimated amount of bad debts expense cannot be credited to the Accounts Receivable account because the specific customer accounts that will prove uncollectible cannot yet be identified and removed from the accounts receivable subsidiary ledger. Moreover, if only the Accounts Receivable account is credited, its balance would not equal the sum of its subsidiary account balances.
6.

Dec. 31	Bad Debts Expense	5,702	
	Allowance for Doubtful Accounts		5,702

7.

Jan. 10	Allowance for Doubtful Accounts	300	
	Accounts Receivable—Cool Jam		300
Apr. 12	Accounts Receivable—Cool Jam	300	
	Allowance for Doubtful Accounts		300
Apr. 12	Cash	300	
	Accounts Receivable—Cool Jam		300

8.

Dec. 16	Note Receivable—Irwin	7,000	
	Sales		7,000
Dec. 31	Interest Receivable	35	
	Interest Revenue		35
	($7,000 × 12% × 15/360)		

9.

Mar. 16	Accounts Receivable—Irwin	7,210	
	Interest Revenue		175
	Interest Receivable		35
	Notes Receivable—Irwin		7,000

Key Terms

Accounts receivable (p. 294)
Accounts receivable turnover (p. 309)
Aging of accounts receivable (p. 302)
Allowance for Doubtful Accounts (p. 299)
Allowance method (p. 298)
Bad debts (p. 297)
Credit risk ratio (p. 309)

Direct write-off method (p. 297)
Full disclosure principle (p. 306)
Interest (p. 304)
Maker of the note (p. 304)
Matching (expense recognition) principle (p. 298)
Materiality constraint (p. 298)

Maturity date of a note (p. 304)
Payee of the note (p. 304)
Principal of a note (p. 304)
Promissory note (or **note**) (p. 304)
Realizable value (p. 299)

Multiple Choice Quiz

Answers on p. 325

mhhe.com/wildFA6e

Additional quiz questions are available at the book's Website.

1. A company's Accounts Receivable balance at its December 31 year-end is $125,650, and its Allowance for Doubtful Accounts has a credit balance of $328 before year-end adjustment. Its net sales are $572,300. It estimates that 4% of outstanding accounts receivable are uncollectible. What amount of Bad Debts Expense is recorded at December 31?
   a. $5,354
   b. $328
   c. $5,026
   d. $4,698
   e. $34,338

2. A company's Accounts Receivable balance at its December 31 year-end is $489,300, and its Allowance for Doubtful Accounts has a debit balance of $554 before year-end adjustment. Its net sales are $1,300,000. It estimates that 6% of outstanding accounts receivable are uncollectible. What amount of Bad Debts Expense is recorded at December 31?
   a. $29,912
   b. $28,804
   c. $78,000
   d. $29,358
   e. $554

3. Total interest to be earned on a $7,500, 5%, 90-day note is
   a. $93.75
   b. $375.00
   c. $1,125.00
   d. $31.25
   e. $125.00

4. A company receives a $9,000, 8%, 60-day note. The maturity value of the note is
   a. $120
   b. $9,000
   c. $9,120
   d. $720
   e. $9,720

5. A company has net sales of $489,600 and average accounts receivable of $40,800. What is its accounts receivable turnover?
   a. 0.08
   b. 30.41
   c. 1,341.00
   d. 12.00
   e. 111.78

Icon denotes assignments that involve decision making.

Discussion Questions

1. How do sellers benefit from allowing their customers to use credit cards?
2. Why does the direct write-off method of accounting for bad debts usually fail to match revenues and expenses?
3. Explain the accounting constraint of materiality.
4. Explain why writing off a bad debt against the Allowance for Doubtful Accounts does not reduce the estimated realizable value of a company's accounts receivable.
5. Why does the Bad Debts Expense account usually not have the same adjusted balance as the Allowance for Doubtful Accounts?
6. Why might a business prefer a note receivable to an account receivable?
7. Refer to the financial statements and notes of **Research In Motion** in Appendix A. In its presentation of accounts receivable on the balance sheet, how does it title accounts receivable? What does it report for its allowance as of February 27, 2010?
8. Refer to the balance sheet of **Apple** in Appendix A. Does it use the direct write-off method or allowance method in accounting for its Accounts Receivable? What is the realizable value of its receivable's balance as of September 26, 2009?
9. Refer to the financial statements of **Palm** in Appendix A. What are Palm's gross accounts receivable at May 31, 2009? What percentage of its accounts receivable does it believe to be uncollectible at this date?
10. Refer to the December 31, 2009, financial statements of **Nokia** in Appendix A. What does it title its accounts receivable on its statement of financial position? What percent of its accounts receivable does it believe to be uncollectible?

QUICK STUDY

QS 7-1
Credit card sales
C1

Prepare journal entries for the following credit card sales transactions (the company uses the perpetual inventory system).

1. Sold $10,000 of merchandise, that cost $7,500, on MasterCard credit cards. The net cash receipts from sales are immediately deposited in the seller's bank account. MasterCard charges a 5% fee.
2. Sold $3,000 of merchandise, that cost $1,500, on an assortment of credit cards. Net cash receipts are received 7 days later, and a 4% fee is charged.

QS 7-2
Allowance method for bad debts
P2

Milner Corp. uses the allowance method to account for uncollectibles. On October 31, it wrote off a $1,000 account of a customer, C. Schaub. On December 9, it receives a $200 payment from Schaub.
1. Prepare the journal entry or entries for October 31.
2. Prepare the journal entry or entries for December 9; assume no additional money is expected from Schaub.

QS 7-3
Percent of accounts receivable method
P2

Wecker Company's year-end unadjusted trial balance shows accounts receivable of $89,000, allowance for doubtful accounts of $500 (credit), and sales of $270,000. Uncollectibles are estimated to be 1.5% of accounts receivable.
1. Prepare the December 31 year-end adjusting entry for uncollectibles.
2. What amount would have been used in the year-end adjusting entry if the allowance account had a year-end unadjusted debit balance of $200?

QS 7-4
Percent of sales method P2

Assume the same facts as in QS 7-3, except that Wecker estimates uncollectibles as 1.0% of sales. Prepare the December 31 year-end adjusting entry for uncollectibles.

QS 7-5
Note receivable C2

On August 2, 2011, JLK Co. receives a $5,500, 90-day, 12% note from customer Tom Menke as payment on his $9,000 account. (1) Compute the maturity date for this note. (2) Prepare JLK's journal entry for August 2.

QS 7-6
Note receivable P3

Refer to the information in QS 7-5 and prepare the journal entry assuming the note is honored by the customer on October 31, 2011.

QS 7-7
Note receivable P3

Dekon Company's December 31 year-end unadjusted trial balance shows a $8,000 balance in Notes Receivable. This balance is from one 6% note dated December 1, with a period of 45 days. Prepare any necessary journal entries for December 31 and for the note's maturity date assuming it is honored.

QS 7-8
Disposing receivables C3

Record the sale by Kroll Company of $1,000 in accounts receivable on May 1. Kroll is charged a 3% factoring fee.

QS 7-9
Direct write-off method P1

Krugg Company determines on May 1 that it cannot collect $1,000 of its accounts receivable from its customer P. Carroll. Apply the direct write-off method to record this loss as of May 1.

QS 7-10
Recovering a bad debt P1

Refer to the information in QS 7-9. On May 30, P. Carroll unexpectedly paid his account in full to Krugg Company. Record Krugg's entry(ies) to reflect this recovery of this bad debt.

QS 7-11
Accounts receivable turnover
A1

The following data are taken from the comparative balance sheets of Fulton Company. Compute and interpret its accounts receivable turnover for year 2011 (competitors average a turnover of 7.5).

	2011	2010
Accounts receivable, net	$152,900	$133,700
Net sales	754,200	810,600

QS 7-12
International accounting standards
C1

Answer each of the following related to international accounting standards.
a. Explain (in general terms) how the accounting for recognition of receivables is different between IFRS and U.S. GAAP.
b. Explain (in general terms) how the accounting for valuation of receivables is different between IFRS and U.S. GAAP.

EXERCISES

Exercise 7-1
Accounting for credit card sales
C1

Petri Company uses the perpetual inventory system and allows customers to use two credit cards in charging purchases. With the Omni Bank Card, Petri receives an immediate credit to its account when it deposits sales receipts. Omni assesses a 4% service charge for credit card sales. The second credit card that Petri accepts is the Continental Card. Petri sends its accumulated receipts to Continental on a weekly basis and is paid by Continental about a week later. Continental assesses a 2.5% charge on sales for using its card. Prepare journal entries to record the following selected credit card transactions of Petri Company.

Apr. 8 Sold merchandise for $9,200 (that had cost $6,800) and accepted the customer's Omni Bank Card. The Omni receipts are immediately deposited in Petri's bank account.
12 Sold merchandise for $5,400 (that had cost $3,500) and accepted the customer's Continental Card. Transferred $5,400 of credit card receipts to Continental, requesting payment.
20 Received Continental's check for the April 12 billing, less the service charge.

Exercise 7-2
Accounts receivable subsidiary ledger; schedule of accounts receivable
C1

Sami Company recorded the following selected transactions during November 2011.

Nov. 5	Accounts Receivable—Surf Shop	4,417	
	Sales		4,417
10	Accounts Receivable—Yum Enterprises	1,250	
	Sales		1,250
13	Accounts Receivable—Matt Albin	733	
	Sales		733
21	Sales Returns and Allowances	189	
	Accounts Receivable—Matt Albin		189
30	Accounts Receivable—Surf Shop	2,606	
	Sales		2,606

1. Open a general ledger having T-accounts for Accounts Receivable, Sales, and Sales Returns and Allowances. Also open an accounts receivable subsidiary ledger having a T-account for each customer. Post these entries to both the general ledger and the accounts receivable ledger.

Check Accounts Receivable ending balance, $8,817

2. Prepare a schedule of accounts receivable (see Exhibit 7.4) and compare its total with the balance of the Accounts Receivable controlling account as of November 30.

Exercise 7-3
Direct write-off method
P1

Diablo Company applies the direct write-off method in accounting for uncollectible accounts. Prepare journal entries to record the following selected transactions of Diablo.

June 11 Diablo determines that it cannot collect $9,000 of its accounts receivable from its customer Chaffey Company.
29 Chaffey Company unexpectedly pays its account in full to Diablo Company. Diablo records its recovery of this bad debt.

Exercise 7-4
Percent of sales method; write-off
P2

At year-end (December 31), Alvare Company estimates its bad debts as 0.5% of its annual credit sales of $875,000. Alvare records its Bad Debts Expense for that estimate. On the following February 1, Alvare decides that the $420 account of P. Coble is uncollectible and writes it off as a bad debt. On June 5, Coble unexpectedly pays the amount previously written off. Prepare the journal entries of Alvare to record these transactions and events of December 31, February 1, and June 5.

Exercise 7-5
Percent of accounts receivable method
P2

At each calendar year-end, Cabool Supply Co. uses the percent of accounts receivable method to estimate bad debts. On December 31, 2011, it has outstanding accounts receivable of $53,000, and it estimates that 4% will be uncollectible. Prepare the adjusting entry to record bad debts expense for year 2011 under the assumption that the Allowance for Doubtful Accounts has (*a*) a $915 credit balance before the adjustment and (*b*) a $1,332 debit balance before the adjustment.

Exercise 7-6
Aging of receivables method
P2

Hecter Company estimates uncollectible accounts using the allowance method at December 31. It prepared the following aging of receivables analysis.

			Days Past Due			
	Total	0	1 to 30	31 to 60	61 to 90	Over 90
Accounts receivable	$190,000	$132,000	$30,000	$12,000	$6,000	$10,000
Percent uncollectible		1%	2%	4%	7%	12%

a. Estimate the balance of the Allowance for Doubtful Accounts using the aging of accounts receivable method.
b. Prepare the adjusting entry to record Bad Debts Expense using the estimate from part a. Assume the unadjusted balance in the Allowance for Doubtful Accounts is a $600 credit.
c. Prepare the adjusting entry to record Bad Debts Expense using the estimate from part a. Assume the unadjusted balance in the Allowance for Doubtful Accounts is a $400 debit.

Refer to the information in Exercise 7-6 to complete the following requirements.
a. Estimate the balance of the Allowance for Doubtful Accounts assuming the company uses 3.5% of total accounts receivable to estimate uncollectibles, instead of the aging of receivables method.
b. Prepare the adjusting entry to record Bad Debts Expense using the estimate from part a. Assume the unadjusted balance in the Allowance for Doubtful Accounts is a $300 credit.
c. Prepare the adjusting entry to record Bad Debts Expense using the estimate from part a. Assume the unadjusted balance in the Allowance for Doubtful Accounts is a $200 debit.

Exercise 7-7
Percent of receivables method
P2

Refer to the information in Exercise 7-6 to complete the following requirements.
a. On February 1 of the next period, the company determined that $1,900 in customer accounts is uncollectible; specifically, $400 for Oxford Co. and $1,500 for Brookes Co. Prepare the journal entry to write off those accounts.
b. On June 5 of that next period, the company unexpectedly received a $400 payment on a customer account, Oxford Company, that had previously been written off in part a. Prepare the entries necessary to reinstate the account and to record the cash received.

Exercise 7-8
Writing off receivables
P2

At December 31, GreenTea Company reports the following results for its calendar-year.

Cash sales $1,200,000
Credit sales 900,000

Its year-end unadjusted trial balance includes the following items.

Accounts receivable .... $195,000 debit
Allowance for doubtful accounts .... 3,000 debit

a. Prepare the adjusting entry to record Bad Debts Expense assuming uncollectibles are estimated to be 1.5% of credit sales.
b. Prepare the adjusting entry to record Bad Debts Expense assuming uncollectibles are estimated to be 0.5% of total sales.
c. Prepare the adjusting entry to record Bad Debts Expense assuming uncollectibles are estimated to be 6% of year-end accounts receivable.

Exercise 7-9
Estimating bad debts
P2

Check Dr. Bad Debts Expense:
(a) $13,500

(c) $14,700

On June 30, Roman Co. has $125,900 of accounts receivable. Prepare journal entries to record the following selected July transactions. Also prepare any footnotes to the July 31 financial statements that result from these transactions. (The company uses the perpetual inventory system.)

July 4 Sold $6,295 of merchandise (that had cost $4,000) to customers on credit.
9 Sold $18,000 of accounts receivable to Center Bank. Center charges a 4% factoring fee.
17 Received $3,436 cash from customers in payment on their accounts.
27 Borrowed $10,000 cash from Center Bank, pledging $13,000 of accounts receivable as security for the loan.

Exercise 7-10
Selling and pledging accounts receivable
C3

Prepare journal entries to record these selected transactions for Eduardo Company.

Nov. 1 Accepted a $5,000, 180-day, 6% note dated November 1 from Melosa Allen in granting a time extension on her past-due account receivable.
Dec. 31 Adjusted the year-end accounts for the accrued interest earned on the Allen note.
Apr. 30 Allen honors her note when presented for payment; February has 28 days for the current year.

Exercise 7-11
Honoring a note
P3

Exercise 7-12
Dishonoring a note
P3

Prepare journal entries to record the following selected transactions of Paloma Company.

Mar. 21 Accepted a $3,100, 180-day, 10% note dated March 21 from Salma Hernandez in granting a time extension on her past-due account receivable.
Sept. 17 Hernandez dishonors her note when it is presented for payment.
Dec. 31 After exhausting all legal means of collection, Paloma Company writes off Hernandez's account against the Allowance for Doubtful Accounts.

Exercise 7-13
Notes receivable transactions
C2

Check Dec. 31, Cr. Interest Revenue $40

Prepare journal entries for the following selected transactions of Deshawn Company for 2010.

2010

Dec. 13 Accepted a $10,000, 45-day, 8% note dated December 13 in granting Latisha Clark a time extension on her past-due account receivable.
  31 Prepared an adjusting entry to record the accrued interest on the Clark note.

Exercise 7-14
Notes receivable transactions
P3

Check Jan. 27, Dr. Cash $10,100

June 1, Dr. Cash $4,100

Refer to the information in Exercise 7-13 and prepare the journal entries for the following selected transactions of Deshawn Company for 2011.

2011

Jan. 27 Received Clark's payment for principal and interest on the note dated December 13.
Mar. 3 Accepted a $4,000, 10%, 90-day note dated March 3 in granting a time extension on the past-due account receivable of Shandi Company.
  17 Accepted a $2,000, 30-day, 9% note dated March 17 in granting Juan Torres a time extension on his past-due account receivable.
Apr. 16 Torres dishonors his note when presented for payment.
May 1 Wrote off the Torres account against the Allowance for Doubtful Accounts.
June 1 Received the Shandi payment for principal and interest on the note dated March 3.

Exercise 7-15
Accounts receivable turnover
A1

The following information is from the annual financial statements of Waseem Company. Compute its accounts receivable turnover for 2010 and 2011. Compare the two years results and give a possible explanation for any change (competitors average a turnover of 11).

	2011	2010	2009
Net sales	$305,000	$236,000	$288,000
Accounts receivable, net (year-end)	22,900	20,700	17,400

Exercise 7-16
Accounting for bad debts following IFRS
P2

Hitachi, Ltd., reports total revenues of ¥10,000,369 million for its fiscal year ending March 31, 2009, and its March 31, 2009, unadjusted trial balance reports a debit balance for trade receivables (gross) of ¥2,179,764 million.

a. Prepare the adjusting entry to record its Bad Debts Expense assuming uncollectibles are estimated to be 0.4% of total revenues and its unadjusted trial balance reports a credit balance of ¥10,000 million.

b. Prepare the adjusting entry to record Bad Debts Expense assuming uncollectibles are estimated to be 2.1% of year-end trade receivables (gross) and its unadjusted trial balance reports a credit balance of ¥10,000 million.

PROBLEM SET A

Problem 7-1A
Sales on account and credit card sales
C1

Atlas Co. allows select customers to make purchases on credit. Its other customers can use either of two credit cards: Zisa or Access. Zisa deducts a 3% service charge for sales on its credit card and credits the bank account of Atlas immediately when credit card receipts are deposited. Atlas deposits the Zisa credit card receipts each business day. When customers use Access credit cards, Atlas accumulates the receipts for several days before submitting them to Access for payment. Access deducts a 2% service charge and usually pays within one week of being billed. Atlas completes the following transactions in June. (The terms of all credit sales are 2/15, n/30, and all sales are recorded at the gross price.)

June 4 Sold $750 of merchandise (that had cost $500) on credit to Anne Cianci.
  5 Sold $5,900 of merchandise (that had cost $3,200) to customers who used their Zisa cards.

6   Sold $4,800 of merchandise (that had cost $2,800) to customers who used their Access cards.
8   Sold $3,200 of merchandise (that had cost $1,900) to customers who used their Access cards.
10 Submitted Access card receipts accumulated since June 6 to the credit card company for payment.
13 Wrote off the account of Nakia Wells against the Allowance for Doubtful Accounts. The $329 balance in Wells's account stemmed from a credit sale in October of last year.
17 Received the amount due from Access.
18 Received Cianci's check in full payment for the purchase of June 4.

Check June 17, Dr. Cash $7,840

Required

Prepare journal entries to record the preceding transactions and events. (The company uses the perpetual inventory system. Round amounts to the nearest dollar.)

Lopez Company began operations on January 1, 2010, and it estimates uncollectible accounts using the allowance method. During its first two years, the company completed a number of transactions involving sales on credit, accounts receivable collections, and bad debts. These transactions are summarized as follows.

Problem 7-2A
Accounts receivable transactions and bad debts adjustments
C1 P2

2010

a. Sold $1,803,750 of merchandise (that had cost $1,475,000) on credit, terms n/30.
b. Wrote off $20,300 of uncollectible accounts receivable.
c. Received $789,200 cash in payment of accounts receivable.
d. In adjusting the accounts on December 31, the company estimated that 1.5% of accounts receivable will be uncollectible.

Check (d) Dr. Bad Debts Expense $35,214

2011

e. Sold $1,825,700 of merchandise (that had cost $1,450,000) on credit, terms n/30.
f. Wrote off $28,800 of uncollectible accounts receivable.
g. Received $1,304,800 cash in payment of accounts receivable.
h. In adjusting the accounts on December 31, the company estimated that 1.5% of accounts receivable will be uncollectible.

(h) Dr. Bad Debts Expense $36,181

Required

Prepare journal entries to record Lopez's 2010 and 2011 summarized transactions and its year-end adjustments to record bad debts expense. (The company uses the perpetual inventory system. Round amounts to the nearest dollar.)

At December 31, 2011, Ethan Company reports the following results for its calendar-year.

Cash sales	$1,803,750
Credit sales	3,534,000

Problem 7-3A
Estimating and reporting bad debts
P2

In addition, its unadjusted trial balance includes the following items.

Accounts receivable	$1,070,100 debit
Allowance for doubtful accounts	15,750 debit

Required

1. Prepare the adjusting entry for this company to recognize bad debts under each of the following independent assumptions.
   a. Bad debts are estimated to be 2% of credit sales.
   b. Bad debts are estimated to be 1% of total sales.
   c. An aging analysis estimates that 5% of year-end accounts receivable are uncollectible.
2. Show how Accounts Receivable and the Allowance for Doubtful Accounts appear on its December 31, 2011, balance sheet given the facts in part 1a.
3. Show how Accounts Receivable and the Allowance for Doubtful Accounts appear on its December 31, 2011, balance sheet given the facts in part 1c.

Check Bad Debts Expense: (1a) $70,680, (1c) $69,255

Problem 7-4A
Aging accounts receivable and accounting for bad debts

P2

Carmack Company has credit sales of $2.6 million for year 2011. On December 31, 2011, the company's Allowance for Doubtful Accounts has an unadjusted credit balance of $13,400. Carmack prepares a schedule of its December 31, 2011, accounts receivable by age. On the basis of past experience, it estimates the percent of receivables in each age category that will become uncollectible. This information is summarized here.

December 31, 2011 Accounts Receivable	Age of Accounts Receivable	Expected Percent Uncollectible
$730,000	Not yet due	1.25%
354,000	1 to 30 days past due	2.00
76,000	31 to 60 days past due	6.50
48,000	61 to 90 days past due	32.75
12,000	Over 90 days past due	68.00

Required
1. Estimate the required balance of the Allowance for Doubtful Accounts at December 31, 2011, using the aging of accounts receivable method.
2. Prepare the adjusting entry to record bad debts expense at December 31, 2011.

Check (2) Dr. Bad Debts Expense $31,625

Analysis Component
3. On June 30, 2012, Carmack Company concludes that a customer's $3,750 receivable (created in 2011) is uncollectible and that the account should be written off. What effect will this action have on Carmack's 2012 net income? Explain.

Problem 7-5A
Analyzing and journalizing notes receivable transactions

C2 C3 P3

The following selected transactions are from Ohlde Company.

2010

Dec. 16 Accepted a $9,600, 60-day, 9% note dated this day in granting Todd Duke a time extension on his past-due account receivable.
    31 Made an adjusting entry to record the accrued interest on the Duke note.

2011

Feb. 14 Received Duke's payment of principal and interest on the note dated December 16.
Mar. 2 Accepted an $4,120, 8%, 90-day note dated this day in granting a time extension on the past-due account receivable from Mare Co.
    17 Accepted a $2,400, 30-day, 7% note dated this day in granting Jolene Halaam a time extension on her past-due account receivable.
Apr. 16 Halaam dishonored her note when presented for payment.
June 2 Mare Co. refuses to pay the note that was due to Ohlde Co. on May 31. Prepare the journal entry to charge the dishonored note plus accrued interest to Mare Co.'s accounts receivable.
July 17 Received payment from Mare Co. for the maturity value of its dishonored note plus interest for 46 days beyond maturity at 8%.
Aug. 7 Accepted an $5,440, 90-day, 10% note dated this day in granting a time extension on the past-due account receivable of Birch and Byer Co.
Sept. 3 Accepted a $2,080, 60-day, 10% note dated this day in granting Kevin York a time extension on his past-due account receivable.
Nov. 2 Received payment of principal plus interest from York for the September 3 note.
Nov. 5 Received payment of principal plus interest from Birch and Byer for the August 7 note.
Dec. 1 Wrote off the Jolene Halaam account against Allowance for Doubtful Accounts.

Check Feb. 14, Cr. Interest Revenue $108

June 2, Cr. Interest Revenue $82

Nov. 2, Cr. Interest Revenue $35

Required
1. Prepare journal entries to record these transactions and events. (Round amounts to the nearest dollar.)

Analysis Component
2. What reporting is necessary when a business pledges receivables as security for a loan and the loan is still outstanding at the end of the period? Explain the reason for this requirement and the accounting principle being satisfied.

Able Co. allows select customers to make purchases on credit. Its other customers can use either of two credit cards: Commerce Bank or Aztec. Commerce Bank deducts a 3% service charge for sales on its credit card and immediately credits the bank account of Able when credit card receipts are deposited. Able deposits the Commerce Bank credit card receipts each business day. When customers use the Aztec card, Able accumulates the receipts for several days and then submits them to Aztec for payment. Aztec deducts a 2% service charge and usually pays within one week of being billed. Able completed the following transactions in August (terms of all credit sales are 2/10, n/30; and all sales are recorded at the gross price).

Aug. 4 Sold $2,780 of merchandise (that had cost $1,750) on credit to Stacy Dalton.
10 Sold $3,248 of merchandise (that had cost $2,456) to customers who used their Commerce Bank credit cards.
11 Sold $1,575 of merchandise (that had cost $1,150) to customers who used their Aztec cards.
14 Received Dalton's check in full payment for the purchase of August 4.
15 Sold $2,960 of merchandise (that had cost $1,758) to customers who used their Aztec cards.
18 Submitted Aztec card receipts accumulated since August 11 to the credit card company for payment.
22 Wrote off the account of Ness City against the Allowance for Doubtful Accounts. The $398 balance in Ness City's account stemmed from a credit sale in November of last year.
25 Received the amount due from Aztec.

PROBLEM SET B

Problem 7-1B
Sales on account and credit card sales

C1

Check Aug. 25, Dr. Cash $4,444

Required

Prepare journal entries to record the preceding transactions and events. (The company uses the perpetual inventory system. Round amounts to the nearest dollar.)

Crist Co. began operations on January 1, 2010, and it estimates uncollectible accounts using the allowance method. It completed several transactions during 2010 and 2011 that involved sales on credit, accounts receivable collections, and bad debts. These transactions are summarized as follows.

2010

a. Sold $673,490 of merchandise (that had cost $500,000) on credit, terms n/30.
b. Received $437,250 cash in payment of accounts receivable.
c. Wrote off $8,330 of uncollectible accounts receivable.
d. In adjusting the accounts on December 31, the company estimated that 1% of accounts receivable will be uncollectible.

2011

e. Sold $930,100 of merchandise (that had cost $650,000) on credit, terms n/30.
f. Received $890,220 cash in payment of accounts receivable.
g. Wrote off $10,090 of uncollectible accounts receivable.
h. In adjusting the accounts on December 31, the company estimated that 1% of accounts receivable will be uncollectible.

Problem 7-2B
Accounts receivable transactions and bad debts adjustments

C1 P2

Check (d) Dr. Bad Debts Expense $10,609

(h) Dr. Bad Debts Expense $10,388

Required

Prepare journal entries to record Crist's 2010 and 2011 summarized transactions and its year-end adjusting entry to record bad debts expense. (The company uses the perpetual inventory system. Round amounts to the nearest dollar.)

At December 31, 2011, Klimek Company reports the following results for the year.

Cash sales	$1,015,000
Credit sales	1,241,000

In addition, its unadjusted trial balance includes the following items.

Accounts receivable	$475,000 debit
Allowance for doubtful accounts	5,200 credit

Problem 7-3B
Estimating and reporting bad debts

P2

Required

1. Prepare the adjusting entry for Klimek Co. to recognize bad debts under each of the following independent assumptions.
   a. Bad debts are estimated to be 2.5% of credit sales.
   b. Bad debts are estimated to be 1.5% of total sales.
   c. An aging analysis estimates that 6% of year-end accounts receivable are uncollectible.
2. Show how Accounts Receivable and the Allowance for Doubtful Accounts appear on its December 31, 2011, balance sheet given the facts in part 1a.
3. Show how Accounts Receivable and the Allowance for Doubtful Accounts appear on its December 31, 2011, balance sheet given the facts in part 1c.

Check Bad debts expense:
(1b) $33,840, (1c) $23,300

Problem 7-4B
Aging accounts receivable and accounting for bad debts
P2

Quisp Company has credit sales of $3.5 million for year 2011. At December 31, 2011, the company's Allowance for Doubtful Accounts has an unadjusted debit balance of $4,100. Quisp prepares a schedule of its December 31, 2011, accounts receivable by age. On the basis of past experience, it estimates the percent of receivables in each age category that will become uncollectible. This information is summarized here.

December 31, 2011 Accounts Receivable	Age of Accounts Receivable	Expected Percent Uncollectible
$296,400	Not yet due	2.0%
177,800	1 to 30 days past due	4.0
58,000	31 to 60 days past due	8.5
7,600	61 to 90 days past due	39.0
3,700	Over 90 days past due	82.0

Required

1. Compute the required balance of the Allowance for Doubtful Accounts at December 31, 2011, using the aging of accounts receivable method.
2. Prepare the adjusting entry to record bad debts expense at December 31, 2011.

Check (2) Dr. Bad Debts Expense $28,068

Analysis Component

3. On July 31, 2012, Quisp concludes that a customer's $2,345 receivable (created in 2011) is uncollectible and that the account should be written off. What effect will this action have on Quisp's 2012 net income? Explain.

Problem 7-5B
Analyzing and journalizing notes receivable transactions
C2 C3 P3

The following selected transactions are from Seeker Company.

2010
Nov. 1 Accepted a $4,800, 90-day, 8% note dated this day in granting Julie Stephens a time extension on her past-due account receivable.
Dec. 31 Made an adjusting entry to record the accrued interest on the Stephens note.

2011
Jan. 30 Received Stephens's payment for principal and interest on the note dated November 1.
Feb. 28 Accepted a $12,600, 6%, 30-day note dated this day in granting a time extension on the past-due account receivable from Kramer Co.
Mar. 1 Accepted a $6,200, 60-day, 8% note dated this day in granting Shelly Myers a time extension on her past-due account receivable.
     30 The Kramer Co. dishonored its note when presented for payment.
April 30 Received payment of principal plus interest from Myers for the March 1 note.
June 15 Accepted a $2,000, 60-day, 10% note dated this day in granting a time extension on the past-due account receivable of Rhonda Rye.
     21 Accepted a $9,500, 90-day, 12% note dated this day in granting J. Striker a time extension on his past-due account receivable.
Aug. 14 Received payment of principal plus interest from R. Rye for the note of June 15.
Sep. 19 Received payment of principal plus interest from J. Striker for the June 21 note.
Nov. 30 Wrote off Kramer's account against Allowance for Doubtful Accounts.

Check Jan. 30, Cr. Interest Revenue $32

April 30, Cr. Interest Revenue $83

Sep. 19, Cr. Interest Revenue $285

Required

1. Prepare journal entries to record these transactions and events. (Round amounts to the nearest dollar.)

Analysis Component

2. What reporting is necessary when a business pledges receivables as security for a loan and the loan is still outstanding at the end of the period? Explain the reason for this requirement and the accounting principle being satisfied.

SERIAL PROBLEM
Business Solutions
P1 P2

(This serial problem began in Chapter 1 and continues through most of the book. If previous chapter segments were not completed, the serial problem can begin at this point. It is helpful, but not necessary, to use the Working Papers that accompany the book.)

SP 7 Santana Rey, owner of Business Solutions, realizes that she needs to begin accounting for bad debts expense. Assume that Business Solutions has total revenues of $44,000 during the first three months of 2012, and that the Accounts Receivable balance on March 31, 2012, is $22,867.

Required

1. Prepare the adjusting entry needed for Business Solutions to recognize bad debts expense on March 31, 2012, under each of the following independent assumptions (assume a zero unadjusted balance in the Allowance for Doubtful Accounts at March 31).
   a. Bad debts are estimated to be 1% of total revenues. (Round amounts to the dollar.)
   b. Bad debts are estimated to be 2% of accounts receivable. (Round amounts to the dollar.)

2. Assume that Business Solutions' Accounts Receivable balance at June 30, 2012, is $20,250 and that one account of $100 has been written off against the Allowance for Doubtful Accounts since March 31, 2012. If S. Rey uses the method prescribed in Part 1*b*, what adjusting journal entry must be made to recognize bad debts expense on June 30, 2012?

Check (2) Bad Debts Expense, $48

3. Should S. Rey consider adopting the direct write-off method of accounting for bad debts expense rather than one of the allowance methods considered in part 1? Explain.

Beyond the Numbers

BTN 7-1 Refer to **Research In Motion**'s financial statements in Appendix A to answer the following.

REPORTING IN ACTION
A1
RIM

1. What is the amount of Research In Motion's accounts receivable as of February 27, 2010?
2. Compute Research In Motion's accounts receivable turnover as of February 27, 2010.
3. How long does it take, *on average*, for the company to collect receivables? Do you believe that customers actually pay the amounts due within this short period? Explain.
4. Research In Motion's most liquid assets include (*a*) cash and cash equivalents, (*b*) short-term investments, and (*c*) receivables. Compute the percentage that these liquid assets make up of current liabilities as of February 27, 2010. Do the same computations for February 28, 2009. Comment on the company's ability to satisfy its current liabilities as of its 2010 fiscal year-end compared to its 2009 fiscal year-end.
5. What criteria did Research In Motion use to classify items as cash equivalents?

Fast Forward

6. Access Research In Motion's financial statements for fiscal years after February 27, 2010, at its Website (www.RIM.com) or the SEC's EDGAR database (www.sec.gov). Recompute parts 2 and 4 and comment on any changes since February 27, 2010.

BTN 7-2 Comparative figures for **Research In Motion** and **Apple** follow.

COMPARATIVE ANALYSIS
A1 P2
RIM
Apple

($ millions)	Research In Motion Current Year	Research In Motion One Year Prior	Research In Motion Two Years Prior	Apple Current Year	Apple One Year Prior	Apple Two Years Prior
Accounts receivable, net	$ 2,594	$ 2,112	$1,175	$ 3,361	$ 2,422	$ 1,637
Net sales	14,953	11,065	6,009	42,905	37,491	24,578

Required

1. Compute the accounts receivable turnover for Research In Motion and Apple for each of the two most recent years using the data shown.
2. Using results from part 1, compute how many days it takes each company, *on average,* to collect receivables. Compare the collection periods for RIM and Apple, and suggest at least one explanation for the difference.
3. Which company is more efficient in collecting its accounts receivable? Explain.

Hint: Average collection period equals 365 divided by the accounts receivable turnover.

ETHICS CHALLENGE
P2

BTN 7-3 Kelly Steinman is the manager of a medium-size company. A few years ago, Steinman persuaded the owner to base a part of her compensation on the net income the company earns each year. Each December she estimates year-end financial figures in anticipation of the bonus she will receive. If the bonus is not as high as she would like, she offers several recommendations to the accountant for year-end adjustments. One of her favorite recommendations is for the controller to reduce the estimate of doubtful accounts.

Required

1. What effect does lowering the estimate for doubtful accounts have on the income statement and balance sheet?
2. Do you believe Steinman's recommendation to adjust the allowance for doubtful accounts is within her right as manager, or do you believe this action is an ethics violation? Justify your response.
3. What type of internal control(s) might be useful for this company in overseeing the manager's recommendations for accounting changes?

COMMUNICATING IN PRACTICE
P2

BTN 7-4 As the accountant for Pure-Air Distributing, you attend a sales managers' meeting devoted to a discussion of credit policies. At the meeting, you report that bad debts expense is estimated to be $59,000 and accounts receivable at year-end amount to $1,750,000 less a $43,000 allowance for doubtful accounts. Sid Omar, a sales manager, expresses confusion over why bad debts expense and the allowance for doubtful accounts are different amounts. Write a one-page memorandum to him explaining why a difference in bad debts expense and the allowance for doubtful accounts is not unusual. The company estimates bad debts expense as 2% of sales.

TAKING IT TO THE NET
C1

BTN 7-5 Access **eBay**'s February 17, 2010, filing of its 10-K report for the year ended December 31, 2009, at **www.sec.gov**.

Required

1. What is the amount of eBay's net accounts receivable at December 31, 2009, and at December 31, 2008?
2. "Financial Statement Schedule II" to its financial statements lists eBay's allowance for doubtful accounts (including authorized credits). For the two years ended December 31, 2009 and 2008, compute its allowance for doubtful accounts (including authorized credits) as a percent of gross accounts receivable.
3. Do you believe that these percentages are reasonable based on what you know about eBay? Explain.

TEAMWORK IN ACTION
P2

BTN 7-6 Each member of a team is to participate in estimating uncollectibles using the aging schedule and percents shown in Problem 7-4A. The division of labor is up to the team. Your goal is to accurately complete this task as soon as possible. After estimating uncollectibles, check your estimate with the instructor. If the estimate is correct, the team then should prepare the adjusting entry and the presentation of accounts receivable (net) for the December 31, 2011, balance sheet.

ENTREPRENEURIAL DECISION
C1

BTN 7-7 John Earle of **Johnny Cupcakes** is introduced in the chapter's opening feature. John currently sells his products through multiple outlets. Assume that he is considering two new selling options.

Plan A. Johnny Cupcakes would begin selling additional products online directly to customers, which are only currently sold directly to outlet stores. These new online customers would use their credit cards. It currently has the capability of selling through its Website with no additional investment in hardware or software. Credit sales are expected to increase by $250,000 per year. Costs associated with this plan are: cost of these sales will be $135,500, credit card fees will be 4.75% of sales, and additional recordkeeping and shipping costs will be 6% of sales. These online sales will reduce the sales to stores by $35,000 because some customers will now purchase items online. Sales to stores have a 25% gross margin percentage.

Plan B. Johnny Cupcakes would expand its market to more outlet stores. It would make additional credit sales of $500,000 to those stores. Costs associated with those sales are: cost of sales will be $375,000, additional recordkeeping and shipping will be 4% of sales, and uncollectible accounts will be 6.2% of sales.

Required

1. Compute the additional annual net income or loss expected under (a) Plan A and (b) Plan B.
2. Should Johnny Cupcakes pursue either plan? Discuss both the financial and nonfinancial factors relevant to this decision.

Check (1b) Net income, $74,000

BTN 7-8 Many commercials include comments similar to the following: "We accept **VISA**" or "We do not accept **American Express**." Conduct your own research by contacting at least five companies via interviews, phone calls, or the Internet to determine the reason(s) companies discriminate in their use of credit cards. Collect information on the fees charged by the different cards for the companies contacted. (The instructor can assign this as a team activity.)

HITTING THE ROAD

C1

BTN 7-9 Key information from Nokia (www.Nokia.com), which is a leading global manufacturer of mobile devices and services, follows.

GLOBAL DECISION

C1 P2

NOKIA
RIM
Apple

EUR millions	Current Year	Prior Year
Accounts receivable, net*	7,981	9,444
Sales	40,984	50,710

*Nokia refers to it as "Accounts receivable, net of allowance for doubtful accounts."

1. Compute the accounts receivable turnover for the current year.
2. How long does it take on average for Nokia to collect receivables?
3. Refer to BTN 7-2. How does Nokia compare to Research In Motion and Apple in terms of its accounts receivable turnover and its collection period?
4. Nokia reports an aging analysis of its receivables, based on due dates, as follows (in EUR millions) as of December 31, 2009. Compute the percent of receivables in each category.

EUR millions	Total Receivables
Current	7,302
Past due 1–30 days	393
Past due 31–180 days	170
More than 180 days	116

ANSWERS TO MULTIPLE CHOICE QUIZ

1. d; Desired balance in Allowance for Doubtful Accounts = $ 5,026 cr.
   ($125,650 × 0.04)
   Current balance in Allowance for Doubtful Accounts = (328) cr.
   Bad Debts Expense to be recorded = $ 4,698
2. a; Desired balance in Allowance for Doubtful Accounts = $29,358 cr.
   ($489,300 × 0.06)
   Current balance in Allowance for Doubtful Accounts = 554 dr.
   Bad Debts Expense to be recorded = $29,912
3. a; $7,500 × 0.05 × 90/360 = $93.75

4. c; Principal amount $9,000
   Interest accrued . . . . 120 ($9,000 × 0.08 × 60/360)
   Maturity value $9,120
5. d; $489,600/$40,800 = 12

A Look Back	A Look at This Chapter	A Look Ahead
Chapters 6 and 7 focused on short-term assets: cash, cash equivalents, and receivables. We explained why they are known as liquid assets and described how companies account and report for them.	This chapter introduces us to long-term assets. We explain how to account for a long-term asset's cost, the allocation of an asset's cost to periods benefiting from it, the recording of additional costs after an asset is purchased, and the disposal of an asset.	Chapter 9 focuses on current liabilities. We explain how they are computed, recorded, and reported in financial statements. We also explain the accounting for company payroll and contingencies.

8 Reporting and Analyzing Long-Term Assets

Learning Objectives

CAP

CONCEPTUAL

C1 Explain the cost principle for computing the cost of plant assets. (p. 329)

C2 Explain depreciation for partial years and changes in estimates. (p. 336)

C3 Distinguish between revenue and capital expenditures, and account for them. (p. 338)

ANALYTICAL

A1 Compute total asset turnover and apply it to analyze a company's use of assets. (p. 347)

LP8

PROCEDURAL

P1 Compute and record depreciation using the straight-line, units-of-production, and declining-balance methods. (p. 332)

P2 Account for asset disposal through discarding or selling an asset. (p. 340)

P3 Account for natural resource assets and their depletion. (p. 342)

P4 Account for intangible assets. (p. 343)

P5 *Appendix 8A*—Account for asset exchanges. (p. 350)

Decision Insight

Gaming Assets

"We want the average kid to have a party like a rock star."
—DAVID PIKOFF

AUSTIN, TX—Fun and games are the common bond for brothers Stuart and David Pikoff. That bond was also the driving force for an excursion into business. "We're both fun guys, we love kids, and we love games," explains David. "So we thought, 'Why not create our own game franchise?'" What they did was create **Games2U (Games2U.com),** a business focused on bringing fun and games to children and adults, using vans and trailers outfitted with state-of-the-art games and activities.

The brothers started operations by scraping up just enough money. However, long-term assets such as mobile vehicles outfitted with video games, large flat-screen displays, high-quality sound systems, and laser-light and fog machines for effects, are very expensive. David explains that financing such equipment, machinery, and similar assets is a struggle. "We would be much bigger, much quicker, if we didn't have that challenge." The owners had to work out depreciation schedules and estimate payback for different games and accessories.

Games2U is now rocking—employing nearly 20 workers, offering franchise agreements to others interested in mimicking their fun and games business, and generating several million in annual sales. Still, a constant challenge for the brothers is maintaining the right kind and amount of assets to meet people's demands and be profitable. "That made us hone in on product development," explains David. "How do we provide unique entertainment at your doorstep?" Games2U's success depends on monitoring and controlling those asset costs, which range from a mobile 4-D movie theater to decked-out trailers to a patented seven-foot tall kid-controlled robot.

Each of these tangible and intangible assets commands Stuart and David's attention. The brothers account for, manage, and focus on recovering all costs of these long-term assets. "We're never done," says David. "We're always challenging ourselves." Their success in asset management permits them to pursue further expansion and new ideas for gaming experiences. They have expanded into outdoor laser tag, human gyros, air cannons, and a version of capture-the-flag called "Booger Wars." "We have a unique concept, a solid infrastructure," explains David. "We provide unique entertainment."

[Sources: *Games2U Website,* January 2012; *Entrepreneur,* June 2009; *The Wall Street Journal,* March 2010; *Inc.com* October 2009; *The Monitor,* September 2009; *Franchise Update,* August 2009; *AOL,* January 2011]

Chapter Preview

This chapter focuses on long-term assets, which can be grouped into plant assets, natural resource assets, and intangible assets. Plant assets make up a large part of assets on most balance sheets, and they yield depreciation, often one of the largest expenses on income statements. The acquisition or building of a plant asset is often referred to as a *capital expenditure*. Capital expenditures are important events because they impact both the short- and long-term success of a company. Natural resource assets and intangible assets have similar impacts. This chapter describes the purchase and use of these assets. We also explain what distinguishes these assets from other types of assets, how to determine their cost, how to allocate their costs to periods benefiting from their use, and how to dispose of them.

Reporting and Analyzing Long-Term Assets

Plant Assets
- Cost determination
- Depreciation
- Additional expenditures
- Disposals

Natural Resources
- Cost determination
- Depletion
- Plant assets used in extracting resources

Intangible Assets
- Cost determination
- Amortization
- Types of intangibles

Section 1—Plant Assets

Plant assets are tangible assets used in a company's operations that have a useful life of more than one accounting period. Plant assets are also called *plant and equipment; property, plant, and equipment;* or *fixed assets.* For many companies, plant assets make up the single largest class of assets they own. Exhibit 8.1 shows plant assets as a percent of total assets for several companies. Not only do they make up a large percent of many companies' assets, but their dollar values are large. **McDonald's** plant assets, for instance, are reported at more than $20 billion, and **Walmart** reports plant assets of more than $92 billion.

EXHIBIT 8.1

Plant Assets of Selected Companies

- eBay: $1,120 mil. — 7%
- Walmart: $92,856 mil. — 57%
- Boston Beer: $148 mil. — 67%
- McDonald's: $20,255 mil. — 71%

As a Percent of Total Assets

Plant assets are set apart from other assets by two important features. First, *plant assets are used in operations.* This makes them different from, for instance, inventory that is held for sale and not used in operations. The distinctive feature here is use, not type of asset. A company that purchases a computer to resell it reports it on the balance sheet as inventory. If the same company purchases this computer to use in operations, however, it is a plant asset. Another example is land held for future expansion, which is reported as a long-term investment. However, if this land holds a factory used in operations, the land is part of plant assets. Another example is equipment held for use in the event of a breakdown or for peak periods of production, which is reported in plant assets. If this same equipment is removed from use and held for sale, however, it is not reported in plant assets.

The second important feature is that *plant assets have useful lives extending over more than one accounting period.* This makes plant assets different from current assets such as supplies that are normally consumed in a short time period after they are placed in use.

The accounting for plant assets reflects these two features. Since plant assets are used in operations, we try to match their costs against the revenues they generate. Also, since their useful lives extend over more than one period, our matching of costs and revenues must extend over several periods. Specifically, we value plant assets (balance sheet effect) and then, for many of them, we allocate their costs to periods benefiting from their use (income statement effect). An important exception is land; land cost is not allocated to expense when we expect it to have an indefinite life.

Exhibit 8.2 shows four main issues in accounting for plant assets: (1) computing the costs of plant assets, (2) allocating the costs of most plant assets (less any salvage amounts) against revenues for the periods they benefit, (3) accounting for expenditures such as repairs and improvements to plant assets, and (4) recording the disposal of plant assets. The following sections discuss these issues.

Point: It can help to view plant assets as prepaid expenses that benefit several future accounting periods.

EXHIBIT 8.2

Issues in Accounting for Plant Assets

COST DETERMINATION

Plant assets are recorded at cost when acquired. This is consistent with the *cost principle*. **Cost** includes all normal and reasonable expenditures necessary to get the asset in place and ready for its intended use. The cost of a factory machine, for instance, includes its invoice cost less any cash discount for early payment, plus any necessary freight, unpacking, assembling, installing, and testing costs. Examples are the costs of building a base or foundation for a machine, providing electrical hookups, and testing the asset before using it in operations.

To be recorded as part of the cost of a plant asset, an expenditure must be normal, reasonable, and necessary in preparing it for its intended use. If an asset is damaged during unpacking, the repairs are not added to its cost. Instead, they are charged to an expense account. Nor is a paid traffic fine for moving heavy machinery on city streets without a proper permit part of the machinery's cost, but payment for a proper permit is included in the cost of machinery. Charges are sometimes incurred to modify or customize a new plant asset. These charges are added to the asset's cost. We explain in this section how to determine the cost of plant assets for each of its four major classes.

C1 Explain the cost principle for computing the cost of plant assets.

Land

When land is purchased for a building site, its cost includes the total amount paid for the land, including any real estate commissions, title insurance fees, legal fees, and any accrued property taxes paid by the purchaser. Payments for surveying, clearing, grading, and draining also are included in the cost of land. Other costs include government assessments, whether incurred at the time of purchase or later, for items such as public roadways, sewers, and sidewalks. These assessments are included because they permanently add to the land's value. Land purchased as a building site sometimes includes structures that must be removed. In such cases, the total purchase price is charged to the Land account as is the cost of removing the structures, less any amounts recovered through sale of salvaged materials. To illustrate, assume that **Starbucks** paid $167,000 cash to acquire land for a retail store. This land had an old service garage that was removed at a net cost of

EXHIBIT 8.3

Computing Cost of Land

Cash price of land	$167,000
Net cost of garage removal	13,000
Closing costs	10,000
Cost of land	**$190,000**

$13,000 ($15,000 in costs less $2,000 proceeds from salvaged materials). Additional closing costs total $10,000, consisting of brokerage fees ($8,000), legal fees ($1,500), and title costs ($500). The cost of this land to Starbucks is $190,000 and is computed as shown in Exhibit 8.3.

Land Improvements

Land has an indefinite (unlimited) life and is not usually used up over time. **Land improvements** such as parking lot surfaces, driveways, fences, shrubs, and lighting systems, however, have limited useful lives and are used up. While the costs of these improvements increase the usefulness of the land, they are charged to a separate Land Improvement account so that their costs can be allocated to the periods they benefit.

Buildings

A Building account is charged for the costs of purchasing or constructing a building that is used in operations. When purchased, a building's costs usually include its purchase price, brokerage fees, taxes, title fees, and attorney fees. Its costs also include all expenditures to ready it for its intended use, including any necessary repairs or renovations such as wiring, lighting, flooring, and wall coverings. When a company constructs a building or any plant asset for its own use, its costs include materials and labor plus a reasonable amount of indirect overhead cost. Overhead includes the costs of items such as heat, lighting, power, and depreciation on machinery used to construct the asset. Costs of construction also include design fees, building permits, and insurance during construction. However, costs such as insurance to cover the asset *after* it is placed in use are operating expenses.

Machinery and Equipment

The costs of machinery and equipment consist of all costs normal and necessary to purchase them and prepare them for their intended use. These include the purchase price, taxes, transportation charges, insurance while in transit, and the installing, assembling, and testing of the machinery and equipment.

Lump-Sum Purchase

Plant assets sometimes are purchased as a group in a single transaction for a lump-sum price. This transaction is called a *lump-sum purchase,* or *group, bulk,* or *basket purchase.* When this occurs, we allocate the cost of the purchase among the different types of assets acquired based on their *relative market values,* which can be estimated by appraisal or by using the tax-assessed valuations of the assets. To illustrate, assume **CarMax** paid $90,000 cash to acquire a group of items consisting of land appraised at $30,000, land improvements appraised at $10,000, and a building appraised at $60,000. The $90,000 cost is allocated on the basis of these appraised values as shown in Exhibit 8.4.

Example: If appraised values in Exhibit 8.4 are land, $24,000; land improvements, $12,000; and building, $84,000, what cost is assigned to the building? *Answer:*
(1) $24,000 + $12,000 + $84,000 = $120,000 (total appraisal)
(2) $84,000/$120,000 = 70% (building's percent of total)
(3) 70% × $90,000 = $63,000 (building's apportioned cost)

EXHIBIT 8.4

Computing Costs in a Lump-Sum Purchase

	Appraised Value	Percent of Total	Apportioned Cost
Land	$ 30,000	30% ($30,000/$100,000)	**$27,000** ($90,000 × 30%)
Land improvements	10,000	10 ($10,000/$100,000)	9,000 ($90,000 × 10%)
Building	60,000	60 ($60,000/$100,000)	54,000 ($90,000 × 60%)
Totals	$100,000	100%	$ 90,000

Quick Check
Answers — p. 353

1. Identify the asset class for each of the following: (*a*) supplies, (*b*) office equipment, (*c*) inventory, (*d*) land for future expansion, and (*e*) trucks used in operations.
2. Identify the account charged for each of the following: (*a*) the purchase price of a vacant lot to be used in operations and (*b*) the cost of paving that same vacant lot.
3. Compute the amount recorded as the cost of a new machine given the following payments related to its purchase: gross purchase price, $700,000; sales tax, $49,000; purchase discount taken, $21,000; freight cost—terms FOB shipping point, $3,500; normal assembly costs, $3,000; cost of necessary machine platform, $2,500; cost of parts used in maintaining machine, $4,200.

DEPRECIATION

Depreciation is the process of allocating the cost of a plant asset to expense in the accounting periods benefiting from its use. Depreciation does not measure the decline in the asset's market value each period, nor does it measure the asset's physical deterioration. Since depreciation reflects the cost of using a plant asset, depreciation charges are only recorded when the asset is actually in service. This section describes the factors we must consider in computing depreciation, the depreciation methods used, revisions in depreciation, and depreciation for partial periods.

Factors in Computing Depreciation

Factors that determine depreciation are (1) cost, (2) salvage value, and (3) useful life.

Cost The **cost** of a plant asset consists of all necessary and reasonable expenditures to acquire it and to prepare it for its intended use.

Salvage Value The total amount of depreciation to be charged off over an asset's benefit period equals the asset's cost minus its salvage value. **Salvage value,** also called *residual value* or *scrap value,* is an estimate of the asset's value at the end of its benefit period. This is the amount the owner expects to receive from disposing of the asset at the end of its benefit period. If the asset is expected to be traded in on a new asset, its salvage value is the expected trade-in value.

Point: If we expect additional costs in preparing a plant asset for disposal, the salvage value equals the expected amount from disposal less any disposal costs.

Useful Life The **useful life** of a plant asset is the length of time it is productively used in a company's operations. Useful life, also called *service life,* might not be as long as the asset's total productive life. For example, the productive life of a computer can be eight years or more. Some companies, however, trade in old computers for new ones every two years. In this case, these computers have a two-year useful life, meaning the cost of these computers (less their expected trade-in values) is charged to depreciation expense over a two-year period.

Point: Useful life and salvage value are estimates. Estimates require judgment based on all available information.

Several variables often make the useful life of a plant asset difficult to predict. A major variable is the wear and tear from use in operations. Two other variables, inadequacy and obsolescence, also require consideration. **Inadequacy** refers to the insufficient capacity of a company's plant assets to meet its growing productive demands. **Obsolescence** refers to the condition of a plant asset that is no longer useful in producing goods or services with a competitive advantage because of new inventions and improvements. Both inadequacy and obsolescence are difficult to predict because of demand changes, new inventions, and improvements. A company usually disposes of an inadequate or obsolete asset before it wears out.

A company is often able to better predict a new asset's useful life when it has past experience with a similar asset. When it has no such experience, a company relies on the experience of others or on engineering studies and judgment. In note 1 of its annual report, **Tootsie Roll**, a snack food manufacturer, reports the following useful lives:

Buildings	20–35 years
Machinery and Equipment	5–20 years

Decision Insight

Life Line Life expectancy of plant assets is often in the eye of the beholder. For instance, **Hershey Foods** and **Tootsie Roll** are competitors and apply similar manufacturing processes, yet their equipment's life expectancies are different. Hershey depreciates equipment over 3 to 15 years, but Tootsie Roll depreciates them over 5 to 20 years. Such differences markedly impact financial statements. ■

Depreciation Methods

P1 Compute and record depreciation using the straight-line, units-of-production, and declining-balance methods.

Depreciation methods are used to allocate a plant asset's cost over the accounting periods in its useful life. The most frequently used method of depreciation is the straight-line method. Another common depreciation method is the units-of-production method. We explain both of these methods in this section. This section also describes accelerated depreciation methods, with a focus on the declining-balance method.

The computations in this section use information about a machine that inspects athletic shoes before packaging. Manufacturers such as **Converse**, **Reebok**, **adidas**, and **Fila** use this machine. Data for this machine are in Exhibit 8.5.

EXHIBIT 8.5

Data for Athletic Shoe-Inspecting Machine

Cost	$10,000
Salvage value	1,000
Depreciable cost	$ 9,000
Useful life	
Accounting periods	5 years
Units inspected	36,000 shoes

Straight-Line Method *Straight-line depreciation* charges the same amount of expense to each period of the asset's useful life. A two-step process is used. We first compute the *depreciable cost* of the asset, also called the *cost to be depreciated*. It is computed by subtracting the asset's salvage value from its total cost. Second, depreciable cost is divided by the number of accounting periods in the asset's useful life. The formula for straight-line depreciation, along with its computation for the inspection machine just described, is shown in Exhibit 8.6.

EXHIBIT 8.6

Straight-Line Depreciation Formula and Example

$$\frac{\text{Cost} - \text{Salvage value}}{\text{Useful life in periods}} = \frac{\$10,000 - \$1,000}{5 \text{ years}} = \$1,800 \text{ per year}$$

If this machine is purchased on December 31, 2010, and used throughout its predicted useful life of five years, the straight-line method allocates an equal amount of depreciation to each of the years 2011 through 2015. We make the following adjusting entry at the end of each of the five years to record straight-line depreciation of this machine.

Assets = Liabilities + Equity
−1,800   −1,800

Dec. 31	Depreciation Expense	1,800	
	Accumulated Depreciation—Machinery		1,800
	To record annual depreciation.		

Example: If the salvage value of the machine is $2,500, what is the annual depreciation? *Answer:* ($10,000 − $2,500)/5 years = $1,500

The $1,800 Depreciation Expense is reported on the income statement among operating expenses. The $1,800 Accumulated Depreciation is a contra asset account to the Machinery account in the balance sheet. The graph on the left in Exhibit 8.7 shows the $1,800 per year expenses reported in each of the five years. The graph on the right shows the amounts reported on each of the six December 31 balance sheets.

EXHIBIT 8.7

Financial Statement Effects of Straight-Line Depreciation

The net balance sheet amount is the **asset book value,** or simply *book value,* and is computed as the asset's total cost less its accumulated depreciation. For example, at the end of year 2 (December 31, 2012), its book value is $6,400 and is reported in the balance sheet as follows:

Machinery	$10,000	
Less accumulated depreciation	3,600	$6,400

The book value of this machine declines by $1,800 each year due to depreciation. From the graphs in Exhibit 8.7 we can see why this method is called straight-line.

We also can compute the *straight-line depreciation rate,* defined as 100% divided by the number of periods in the asset's useful life. For the inspection machine, this rate is 20% (100% ÷ 5 years, or 1/5 per period). We use this rate, along with other information, to compute the machine's *straight-line depreciation schedule* shown in Exhibit 8.8. Note three points in this exhibit. First, depreciation expense is the same each period. Second, accumulated depreciation is the sum of current and prior periods' depreciation expense. Third, book value declines each period until it equals salvage value at the end of the machine's useful life.

Point: Depreciation requires estimates for salvage value and useful life. Ethics are relevant when managers might be tempted to choose estimates to achieve desired results on financial statements.

EXHIBIT 8.8

Straight-Line Depreciation Schedule

Annual Period	Depreciation for the Period			End of Period	
	Depreciable Cost*	Depreciation Rate	Depreciation Expense	Accumulated Depreciation	Book Value†
2010	—	—	—	—	$10,000
2011	$9,000	20%	$1,800	$1,800	8,200
2012	9,000	20	1,800	3,600	6,400
2013	9,000	20	1,800	5,400	4,600
2014	9,000	20	1,800	7,200	2,800
2015	9,000	20	1,800	9,000	1,000

* $10,000 − $1,000. † Book value is total cost minus accumulated depreciation.

Units-of-Production Method The straight-line method charges an equal share of an asset's cost to each period. If plant assets are used up in about equal amounts each accounting period, this method produces a reasonable matching of expenses with revenues. However, the use of some plant assets varies greatly from one period to the next. A builder, for instance, might use a piece of construction equipment for a month and then not use it again for several months. When equipment use varies from period to period, the units-of-production depreciation method can better match expenses with revenues. **Units-of-production depreciation** charges a varying amount to expense for each period of an asset's useful life depending on its usage.

334 Chapter 8 Reporting and Analyzing Long-Term Assets

A two-step process is used to compute units-of-production depreciation. We first compute *depreciation per unit* by subtracting the asset's salvage value from its total cost and then dividing by the total number of units expected to be produced during its useful life. Units of production can be expressed in product or other units such as hours used or miles driven. The second step is to compute depreciation expense for the period by multiplying the units produced in the period by the depreciation per unit. The formula for units-of-production depreciation, along with its computation for the machine described in Exhibit 8.5, is shown in Exhibit 8.9. (7,000 shoes are inspected and sold in its first year.)

EXHIBIT 8.9
Units-of-Production Depreciation Formula and Example

Step 1

$$\text{Depreciation per unit} = \frac{\text{Cost} - \text{Salvage value}}{\text{Total units of production}} = \frac{\$10{,}000 - \$1{,}000}{36{,}000 \text{ shoes}} = \$0.25 \text{ per shoe}$$

Step 2

$$\text{Depreciation expense} = \text{Depreciation per unit} \times \text{Units produced in period}$$
$$\$0.25 \text{ per shoe} \times 7{,}000 \text{ shoes} = \$1{,}750$$

Using data on the number of shoes inspected by the machine, we can compute the *units-of-production depreciation schedule* shown in Exhibit 8.10. For example, depreciation for the first year is $1,750 (7,000 shoes at $0.25 per shoe). Depreciation for the second year is $2,000 (8,000 shoes at $0.25 per shoe). Other years are similarly computed. Exhibit 8.10 shows that (1) depreciation expense depends on unit output, (2) accumulated depreciation is the sum of current and prior periods' depreciation expense, and (3) book value declines each period until it equals salvage value at the end of the asset's useful life. **Deltic Timber** is one of many companies using the units-of-production depreciation method. It reports that depreciation "is calculated over the estimated useful lives of the assets by using the units of production method for machinery and equipment."

Example: Refer to Exhibit 8.10. If the number of shoes inspected in 2015 is 5,500, what is depreciation for 2015? *Answer:* $1,250 (never depreciate below salvage value).

EXHIBIT 8.10
Units-of-Production Depreciation Schedule

Annual Period	Number of Units	Depreciation per Unit	Depreciation Expense	Accumulated Depreciation	Book Value
2010	—	—	—	—	$10,000
2011	7,000	$0.25	$1,750	$1,750	8,250
2012	8,000	0.25	2,000	3,750	6,250
2013	9,000	0.25	2,250	6,000	4,000
2014	7,000	0.25	1,750	7,750	2,250
2015	5,000	0.25	1,250	9,000	1,000

Declining-Balance Method An **accelerated depreciation method** yields larger depreciation expenses in the early years of an asset's life and less depreciation in later years. The most common accelerated method is the **declining-balance method** of depreciation, which uses a depreciation rate that is a multiple of the straight-line rate and applies it to the asset's beginning-of-period book value. The amount of depreciation declines each period because book value declines each period.

A common depreciation rate for the declining-balance method is double the straight-line rate. This is called the *double-declining-balance* (*DDB*) method. This method is applied in three steps: (1) compute the asset's straight-line depreciation rate, (2) double the straight-line rate, and (3) compute depreciation expense by multiplying this rate by the asset's beginning-of-period book value. To illustrate, let's return to the machine in Exhibit 8.5 and apply the double-declining-balance method to compute depreciation expense. Exhibit 8.11 shows the first-year depreciation computation for the machine. The three-step process is to (1) divide 100% by five years to determine the straight-line rate of 20%, or 1/5, per year, (2) double this 20% rate to get the

Point: In the DDB method, *double* refers to the rate and *declining balance* refers to book value. The rate is applied to beginning book value each period.

declining-balance rate of 40%, or 2/5, per year, and (3) compute depreciation expense as 40%, or 2/5, multiplied by the beginning-of-period book value.

EXHIBIT 8.11
Double-Declining-Balance Depreciation Formula*

Step 1
Straight-line rate = 100% ÷ Useful life = 100% ÷ 5 years = 20%

Step 2
Double-declining-balance rate = 2 × Straight-line rate = 2 × 20% = 40%

Step 3
Depreciation expense = Double-declining-balance rate × Beginning-period book value
40% × $10,000 = $4,000 (for 2011)

* To simplify: DDB depreciation = (2 × Beginning-period book value)/Useful life.

The *double-declining-balance depreciation schedule* is shown in Exhibit 8.12. The schedule follows the formula except for year 2015, when depreciation expense is $296. This $296 is not equal to 40% × $1,296, or $518.40. If we had used the $518.40 for depreciation expense in 2015, the ending book value would equal $777.60, which is less than the $1,000 salvage value. Instead, the $296 is computed by subtracting the $1,000 salvage value from the $1,296 book value at the beginning of the fifth year (the year when DDB depreciation cuts into salvage value).

Example: What is the DDB depreciation expense in year 2014 if the salvage value is $2,000?
Answer: $2,160 − $2,000 = $160

EXHIBIT 8.12
Double-Declining-Balance Depreciation Schedule

Annual Period	Beginning of Period Book Value	Depreciation Rate	Depreciation Expense	Accumulated Depreciation	Book Value
2010	—	—	—	—	$10,000
2011	$10,000	40%	$4,000	$4,000	6,000
2012	6,000	40	2,400	6,400	3,600
2013	3,600	40	1,440	7,840	2,160
2014	2,160	40	864	8,704	1,296
2015	1,296	40	296*	9,000	1,000

* Year 2015 depreciation is $1,296 − $1,000 = $296 (never depreciate book value below salvage value).

Comparing Depreciation Methods Exhibit 8.13 shows depreciation expense for each year of the machine's useful life under each of the three depreciation methods. While depreciation expense per period differs for different methods, total depreciation expense of $9,000 is the same over the machine's useful life.

EXHIBIT 8.13
Depreciation Expense for the Different Methods

Period	Straight-Line	Units-of-Production	Double-Declining-Balance
2011	$1,800	$1,750	$4,000
2012	1,800	2,000	2,400
2013	1,800	2,250	1,440
2014	1,800	1,750	864
2015	1,800	1,250	296
Totals	$9,000	$9,000	$9,000

Each method starts with a total cost of $10,000 and ends with a salvage value of $1,000. The difference is the pattern in depreciation expense over the useful life. The book value of the asset when using straight-line is always greater than the book value from using double-declining-balance, except at the beginning and end of the asset's useful life, when it is the same. Also,

Point: Depreciation is higher and income lower in the short run when using accelerated versus straight-line methods.

the straight-line method yields a steady pattern of depreciation expense while the units-of-production depreciation depends on the number of units produced. Each of these methods is acceptable because it allocates cost in a systematic and rational manner.

Decision Insight

In Vogue About 87% of companies use straight-line depreciation for plant assets, 4% use units-of-production, and 4% use declining-balance. Another 5% use an unspecified accelerated method—most likely declining-balance. ■

- Straight-line, 87%
- Accelerated and other, 5%
- Declining-balance, 4%
- Units-of-production, 4%

Depreciation for Tax Reporting The records a company keeps for financial accounting purposes are usually separate from the records it keeps for tax accounting purposes. This is so because financial accounting aims to report useful information on financial performance and position, whereas tax accounting reflects government objectives in raising revenues. Differences between these two accounting systems are normal and expected. Depreciation is a common example of how the records differ. For example, many companies use accelerated depreciation in computing taxable income. Reporting higher depreciation expense in the early years of an asset's life reduces the company's taxable income in those years and increases it in later years, when the depreciation expense is lower. The company's goal here is to *postpone* its tax payments.

The U.S. federal income tax law has rules for depreciating assets. These rules include the **Modified Accelerated Cost Recovery System (MACRS),** which allows straight-line depreciation for some assets but requires accelerated depreciation for most kinds of assets. MACRS separates depreciable assets into different classes and defines the depreciable life and rate for each class. MACRS is *not* acceptable for financial reporting because it often allocates costs over an arbitrary period that is less than the asset's useful life and it fails to estimate salvage value. Details of MACRS are covered in tax accounting courses.

Point: Understanding depreciation for financial accounting will help in learning MACRS for tax accounting. Rules for MACRS are available from www.IRS.gov.

Partial-Year Depreciation

C2 Explain depreciation for partial years and changes in estimates.

Plant assets are purchased and disposed of at various times. When an asset is purchased (or disposed of) at a time other than the beginning or end of an accounting period, depreciation is recorded for part of a year. This is done so that the year of purchase or the year of disposal is charged with its share of the asset's depreciation.

To illustrate, assume that the machine in Exhibit 8.5 is purchased and placed in service on October 8, 2010, and the annual accounting period ends on December 31. Since this machine is purchased and used for nearly three months in 2010, the calendar-year income statement should report depreciation expense on the machine for that part of the year. Normally, depreciation assumes that the asset is purchased on the first day of the month nearest the actual date of purchase. In this case, since the purchase occurred on October 8, we assume an October 1 purchase date. This means that three months' depreciation is recorded in 2010. Using straight-line depreciation, we compute three months' depreciation of $450 as follows.

$$\frac{\$10{,}000 - \$1{,}000}{5 \text{ years}} \times \frac{3}{12} = \$450$$

A similar computation is necessary when an asset disposal occurs during a period. To illustrate, assume that the machine is sold on June 24, 2015. Depreciation is recorded for the period January 1 through June 24 when it is disposed of. This partial year's depreciation, computed to the nearest whole month, is

$$\frac{\$10{,}000 - \$1{,}000}{5 \text{ years}} \times \frac{6}{12} = \$900$$

Example: If the machine's salvage value is zero and purchase occurs on Oct. 8, 2010, how much depreciation is recorded at Dec. 31, 2010?
Answer: $10,000/5 × 3/12 = $500

Change in Estimates for Depreciation

Depreciation is based on estimates of salvage value and useful life. During the useful life of an asset, new information may indicate that these estimates are inaccurate. If our estimate of an asset's useful life and/or salvage value changes, what should we do? The answer is to use the new estimate to compute depreciation for current and future periods. This means that we revise the depreciation expense computation by spreading the cost yet to be depreciated over the remaining useful life. This approach is used for all depreciation methods.

Let's return to the machine described in Exhibit 8.8 using straight-line depreciation. At the beginning of this asset's third year, its book value is $6,400, computed as $10,000 minus $3,600. Assume that at the beginning of its third year, the estimated number of years remaining in its useful life changes from three to four years *and* its estimate of salvage value changes from $1,000 to $400. Straight-line depreciation for each of the four remaining years is computed as shown in Exhibit 8.14.

Point: Remaining depreciable cost equals book value less revised salvage value at the point of revision.

Point: Income is overstated (and depreciation understated) when useful life is too high; when useful life is too low, the opposite results.

$$\frac{\text{Book value} - \text{Revised salvage value}}{\text{Revised remaining useful life}} = \frac{\$6,400 - \$400}{4 \text{ years}} = \$1,500 \text{ per year}$$

EXHIBIT 8.14
Computing Revised Straight-Line Depreciation

Thus, $1,500 of depreciation expense is recorded for the machine at the end of the third through sixth years—each year of its remaining useful life. Since this asset was depreciated at $1,800 per year for the first two years, it is tempting to conclude that depreciation expense was overstated in the first two years. However, these expenses reflected the best information available at that time. We do not go back and restate prior years' financial statements for this type of new information. Instead, we adjust the current and future periods' statements to reflect this new information. Revising an estimate of the useful life or salvage value of a plant asset is referred to as a **change in an accounting estimate** and is reflected in current and future financial statements, not in prior statements.

Example: If at the beginning of its second year the machine's remaining useful life changes from four to three years and salvage value from $1,000 to $400, how much straight-line depreciation is recorded in remaining years?
Answer: Revised depreciation = ($8,200 − $400)/3 = $2,600.

Reporting Depreciation

Both the cost and accumulated depreciation of plant assets are reported on the balance sheet or in its notes. **Dale Jarrett Racing Adventure**, for instance, reports the following.

Office furniture and equipment	$ 54,593
Shop and track equipment	202,973
Race vehicles and other	975,084
Property and equipment, gross	1,232,650
Less accumulated depreciation	628,355
Property and equipment, net	$ 604,295

Many companies also show plant assets on one line with the net amount of cost less accumulated depreciation. When this is done, the amount of accumulated depreciation is disclosed in a note. **Apple** reports only the net amount of its property, plant and equipment in its balance sheet in Appendix A. To satisfy the full-disclosure principle, Apple describes its depreciation methods in its Note 1 and the amounts comprising plant assets in its Note 5—see its 10-K at **www.SEC.gov**.

Reporting both the cost and accumulated depreciation of plant assets helps users compare the assets of different companies. For example, a company holding assets costing $50,000 and accumulated depreciation of $40,000 is likely in a situation different from a company with new assets costing $10,000. While the net undepreciated cost of $10,000 is the same in both cases, the first company may have more productive capacity available but likely is facing the need to replace older assets. These insights are not provided if the two balance sheets report only the $10,000 book values.

Users must remember that plant assets are reported on a balance sheet at their undepreciated costs (book value), not at fair (market) values. This emphasis on costs rather than fair values is based on the *going-concern assumption* described in Chapter 1. This assumption states that, unless there is evidence to the contrary, we assume that a company continues in business. This implies

Point: A company usually keeps records for each asset showing its cost and depreciation to date. The combined records for individual assets are a type of *plant asset subsidiary ledger*.

338   Chapter 8   Reporting and Analyzing Long-Term Assets

that plant assets are held and used long enough to recover their cost through the sale of products and services. Because plant assets are not for sale, their fair values are not reported. An exception is when there is a *permanent decline* in the fair value of an asset relative to its book value, called an asset **impairment.** In this case the company writes the asset down to this fair value (details for the two-step process for assessing and computing the impairment loss are in advanced courses).

Accumulated Depreciation is a contra asset account with a normal credit balance. It does *not* reflect funds accumulated to buy new assets when the assets currently owned are replaced. If a company has funds available to buy assets, the funds are shown on the balance sheet among liquid assets such as Cash or Investments.

> **Example:** Assume equipment carries a book value of $800 ($900 cost less $100 accumulated depreciation) and a fair (market) value of $750, *and* this $50 decline in value meets the 2-step impairment test. The entry to record this impairment is:
> Impairment Loss $50
>   Accum Depr-Equip. $50

Decision Ethics   Answer — p. 352

Controller You are the controller for a struggling company. Its operations require regular investments in equipment, and depreciation is its largest expense. Its competitors frequently replace equipment—often depreciated over three years. The company president instructs you to revise useful lives of equipment from three to six years and to use a six-year life on all new equipment. What actions do you take? ■

Quick Check   Answers — p. 353

4. On January 1, 2011, a company pays $77,000 to purchase office furniture with a zero salvage value. The furniture's useful life is somewhere between 7 and 10 years. What is the year 2011 straight-line depreciation on the furniture using (*a*) a 7-year useful life and (*b*) a 10-year useful life?
5. What does the term *depreciation* mean in accounting?
6. A company purchases a machine for $96,000 on January 1, 2011. Its useful life is five years or 100,000 units of product, and its salvage value is $8,000. During 2011, 10,000 units of product are produced. Compute the book value of this machine on December 31, 2011, assuming (*a*) straight-line depreciation and (*b*) units-of-production depreciation.
7. In early January 2011, a company acquires equipment for $3,800. The company estimates this equipment to have a useful life of three years and a salvage value of $200. Early in 2013, the company changes its estimates to a total four-year useful life and zero salvage value. Using the straight-line method, what is depreciation for the year ended 2013?

ADDITIONAL EXPENDITURES

C3 Distinguish between revenue and capital expenditures, and account for them.

After a company acquires a plant asset and puts it into service, it often makes additional expenditures for that asset's operation, maintenance, repair, and improvement. In recording these expenditures, it must decide whether to capitalize or expense them (to capitalize an expenditure is to debit the asset account). The issue is whether these expenditures are reported as current period expenses or added to the plant asset's cost and depreciated over its remaining useful life.

Revenue expenditures, also called *income statement expenditures,* are additional costs of plant assets that do not materially increase the asset's life or productive capabilities. They are recorded as expenses and deducted from revenues in the current period's income statement. Examples of revenue expenditures are cleaning, repainting, adjustments, and lubricants. **Capital expenditures,** also called *balance sheet expenditures,* are additional costs of plant assets that provide benefits extending beyond the current period. They are debited to asset accounts and reported on the balance sheet. Capital expenditures increase or improve the type or amount of service an asset provides. Examples are roofing replacement, plant expansion, and major overhauls of machinery and equipment.

Financial statements are affected for several years by the accounting choice of recording costs as either revenue expenditures or capital expenditures. This decision is based on whether the expenditures are identified as ordinary repairs or as betterments and extraordinary repairs.

	Financial Statement Effect	
	Accounting	Expense Timing
Revenue expenditure	Income stmt. account debited	Expensed currently
Capital expenditure	Balance sheet account debited	Expensed in future

Ordinary Repairs

Ordinary repairs are expenditures to keep an asset in normal, good operating condition. They are necessary if an asset is to perform to expectations over its useful life. Ordinary repairs do not extend an asset's useful life beyond its original estimate or increase its productivity beyond original expectations. Examples are normal costs of cleaning, lubricating, adjusting, and replacing small parts of a machine. Ordinary repairs are treated as *revenue expenditures*. This means their costs are reported as expenses on the current period income statement. Following this rule, **Brunswick** reports that "maintenance and repair costs are expensed as incurred." If Brunswick's current year repair costs are $9,500, it makes the following entry.

Dec. 31	Repairs Expense	9,500	
	Cash		9,500
	To record ordinary repairs of equipment.		

Point: Many companies apply the *materiality constraint* to treat *low-cost plant assets* (say, less than $500) as revenue expenditures. This practice is referred to as a "capitalization policy."

Assets = Liabilities + Equity
−9,500   −9,500

Betterments and Extraordinary Repairs

Accounting for betterments and extraordinary repairs is similar—both are treated as *capital expenditures*.

Betterments (Improvements) Betterments, also called *improvements,* are expenditures that make a plant asset more efficient or productive. A betterment often involves adding a component to an asset or replacing one of its old components with a better one, and does not always increase an asset's useful life. An example is replacing manual controls on a machine with automatic controls. One special type of betterment is an *addition,* such as adding a new wing or dock to a warehouse. Since a betterment benefits future periods, it is debited to the asset account as a capital expenditure. The new book value (less salvage value) is then depreciated over the asset's remaining useful life. To illustrate, suppose a company pays $8,000 for a machine with an eight-year useful life and no salvage value. After three years and $3,000 of depreciation, it adds an automated control system to the machine at a cost of $1,800. This results in reduced labor costs in future periods. The cost of the betterment is added to the Machinery account with this entry.

Example: Assume a firm owns a Web server. Identify each cost as a revenue or capital expenditure: (1) purchase price, (2) necessary wiring, (3) platform for operation, (4) circuits to increase capacity, (5) cleaning after each month of use, (6) repair of a faulty switch, and (7) replaced a worn fan. *Answer:* Capital expenditures: 1, 2, 3, 4; revenue expenditures: 5, 6, 7.

Jan. 2	Machinery	1,800	
	Cash		1,800
	To record installation of automated system.		

Assets = Liabilities + Equity
+1,800
−1,800

After the betterment is recorded, the remaining cost to be depreciated is $6,800, computed as $8,000 − $3,000 + $1,800. Depreciation expense for the remaining five years is $1,360 per year, computed as $6,800/5 years.

Point: Both extraordinary repairs and betterments require revising future depreciation.

Extraordinary Repairs (Replacements) Extraordinary repairs are expenditures extending the asset's useful life beyond its original estimate. Extraordinary repairs are *capital expenditures* because they benefit future periods. Their costs are debited to the asset account (or to accumulated depreciation). For example, **Delta Air Lines** reports, "modifications that . . . extend the useful lives of airframes or engines are capitalized and amortized [depreciated] over the remaining estimated useful life of the asset."

■ **Decision Maker**   Answer — p. 352

Entrepreneur Your start-up Internet services company needs cash, and you are preparing financial statements to apply for a short-term loan. A friend suggests that you treat as many expenses as possible as capital expenditures. What are the impacts on financial statements of this suggestion? What do you think is the aim of this suggestion? ■

DISPOSALS OF PLANT ASSETS

Plant assets are disposed of for several reasons. Some are discarded because they wear out or become obsolete. Others are sold because of changing business plans. Regardless of the reason, disposals of plant assets occur in one of three basic ways: discarding, sale, or exchange. The general steps in accounting for a disposal of plant assets are described in Exhibit 8.15.

EXHIBIT 8.15

Accounting for Disposals of Plant Assets

1. Record depreciation up to the date of disposal—this also updates Accumulated Depreciation.
2. Record the removal of the disposed asset's account balances—including its Accumulated Depreciation.
3. Record any cash (and/or other assets) received or paid in the disposal.
4. Record any gain or loss—computed by comparing the disposed asset's book value with the market value of any assets received.*

* An exception to step 4 is the case of an exchange that lacks *commercial substance*—see Appendix 8A.

Discarding Plant Assets

P2 Account for asset disposal through discarding or selling an asset.

A plant asset is *discarded* when it is no longer useful to the company and it has no market value. To illustrate, assume that a machine costing $9,000 with accumulated depreciation of $9,000 is discarded. When accumulated depreciation equals the asset's cost, it is said to be *fully depreciated* (zero book value). The entry to record the discarding of this asset is

Assets = Liabilities + Equity
+9,000
−9,000

June 5	Accumulated Depreciation—Machinery	9,000	
	Machinery		9,000
	To discard fully depreciated machinery.		

This entry reflects all four steps of Exhibit 8.15. Step 1 is unnecessary since the machine is fully depreciated. Step 2 is reflected in the debit to Accumulated Depreciation and credit to Machinery. Since no other asset is involved, step 3 is irrelevant. Finally, since book value is zero and no other asset is involved, no gain or loss is recorded in step 4.

How do we account for discarding an asset that is not fully depreciated or one whose depreciation is not up-to-date? To answer this, consider equipment costing $8,000 with accumulated depreciation of $6,000 on December 31 of the prior fiscal year-end. This equipment is being depreciated using the straight-line method over eight years with zero salvage. On July 1 of the current year it is discarded. Step 1 is to bring depreciation up-to-date.

Point: Recording depreciation expense up-to-date gives an up-to-date book value for determining gain or loss.

Assets = Liabilities + Equity
−500   −500

July 1	Depreciation Expense	500	
	Accumulated Depreciation—Equipment		500
	To record 6 months' depreciation ($1,000 × 6/12).		

Steps 2 through 4 of Exhibit 8.15 are reflected in the second (and final) entry.

Assets = Liabilities + Equity
+6,500   −1,500
−8,000

July 1	Accumulated Depreciation—Equipment	6,500	
	Loss on Disposal of Equipment	1,500	
	Equipment		8,000
	To discard equipment with a $1,500 book value.		

Point: Gain or loss is determined by comparing "value given" (book value) to "value received."

This loss is computed by comparing the equipment's $1,500 book value ($8,000 − $6,000 − $500) with the zero net cash proceeds. The loss is reported in the Other Expenses and Losses section of the income statement. Discarding an asset can sometimes require a cash payment that would increase the loss.

Selling Plant Assets

Companies often sell plant assets when they restructure or downsize operations. To illustrate the accounting for selling plant assets, we consider BTO's March 31 sale of equipment that cost $16,000 and has accumulated depreciation of $12,000 at December 31 of the prior calendar year-end. Annual depreciation on this equipment is $4,000 computed using straight-line depreciation. Step 1 of this sale is to record depreciation expense and update accumulated depreciation to March 31 of the current year.

March 31	Depreciation Expense	1,000	
	Accumulated Depreciation—Equipment		1,000
	To record 3 months' depreciation ($4,000 × 3/12).		

Assets = Liabilities + Equity
−1,000   −1,000

Steps 2 through 4 of Exhibit 8.15 can be reflected in one final entry that depends on the amount received from the asset's sale. We consider three different possibilities.

Sale at Book Value If BTO receives $3,000 cash, an amount equal to the equipment's book value as of March 31 (book value = $16,000 − $12,000 − $1,000), no gain or loss occurs on disposal. The entry is

Sale price = Book value → No gain or loss

March 31	Cash	3,000	
	Accumulated Depreciation—Equipment	13,000	
	Equipment		16,000
	To record sale of equipment for no gain or loss.		

Assets = Liabilities + Equity
+3,000
+13,000
−16,000

Sale above Book Value If BTO receives $7,000, an amount that is $4,000 above the equipment's $3,000 book value as of March 31, a gain on disposal occurs. The entry is

Sale price > Book value → Gain

March 31	Cash	7,000	
	Accumulated Depreciation—Equipment	13,000	
	Gain on Disposal of Equipment		4,000
	Equipment		16,000
	To record sale of equipment for a $4,000 gain.		

Assets = Liabilities + Equity
+7,000   +4,000
+13,000
−16,000

Sale below Book Value If BTO receives $2,500, an amount that is $500 below the equipment's $3,000 book value as of March 31, a loss on disposal occurs. The entry is

Sale price < Book value → Loss

March 31	Cash	2,500	
	Loss on Disposal of Equipment	500	
	Accumulated Depreciation—Equipment	13,000	
	Equipment		16,000
	To record sale of equipment for a $500 loss.		

Assets = Liabilities + Equity
+2,500   −500
+13,000
−16,000

IFRS

Unlike U.S. GAAP, IFRS requires an annual review of useful life and salvage value estimates. IFRS also permits revaluation of plant assets to market value if market value is reliably determined. ●

Quick Check
Answers — p. 353

8. Early in the fifth year of a machine's six-year useful life, it is overhauled, and its useful life is extended to nine years. This machine originally cost $108,000 and the overhaul cost is $12,000. Prepare the entry to record the overhaul cost.
9. Explain the difference between revenue expenditures and capital expenditures and how both are recorded.
10. What is a betterment? How is a betterment recorded?
11. A company acquires equipment on January 10, 2011, at a cost of $42,000. Straight-line depreciation is used with a five-year life and $7,000 salvage value. On June 27, 2012, the company sells this equipment for $32,000. Prepare the entry(ies) for June 27, 2012.

Section 2—Natural Resources

P3 Account for natural resource assets and their depletion.

Natural resources are assets that are physically consumed when used. Examples are standing timber, mineral deposits, and oil and gas fields. Since they are consumed when used, they are often called *wasting assets*. These assets represent soon-to-be inventories of raw materials that will be converted into one or more products by cutting, mining, or pumping. Until that conversion takes place, they are noncurrent assets and are shown in a balance sheet using titles such as timberlands, mineral deposits, or oil reserves. Natural resources are reported under either plant assets or their own separate category. **Alcoa**, for instance, reports its natural resources under the balance sheet title *Properties, plants and equipment.* In a note to its financial statements, Alcoa reports a separate amount for *Land and land rights, including mines.* **Weyerhaeuser**, on the other hand, reports its timber holdings in a separate balance sheet category titled *Timber and timberlands.*

Cost Determination and Depletion

Natural resources are recorded at cost, which includes all expenditures necessary to acquire the resource and prepare it for its intended use. **Depletion** is the process of allocating the cost of a natural resource to the period when it is consumed. Natural resources are reported on the balance sheet at cost less *accumulated depletion.* The depletion expense per period is usually based on units extracted from cutting, mining, or pumping. This is similar to units-of-production depreciation. **Exxon Mobil** uses this approach to amortize the costs of discovering and operating its oil wells.

To illustrate depletion of natural resources, let's consider a mineral deposit with an estimated 250,000 tons of available ore. It is purchased for $500,000, and we expect zero salvage value. The depletion charge per ton of ore mined is $2, computed as $500,000 ÷ 250,000 tons. If 85,000 tons are mined and sold in the first year, the depletion charge for that year is $170,000. These computations are detailed in Exhibit 8.16.

EXHIBIT 8.16
Depletion Formula and Example

Step 1

$$\text{Depletion per unit} = \frac{\text{Cost} - \text{Salvage value}}{\text{Total units of capacity}} = \frac{\$500,000 - \$0}{250,000 \text{ tons}} = \$2 \text{ per ton}$$

Step 2

$$\text{Depletion expense} = \text{Depletion per unit} \times \text{Units extracted and sold in period}$$
$$= \$2 \times 85,000 = \$170,000$$

Depletion expense for the first year is recorded as follows.

Assets	= Liabilities +	Equity
−170,000		−170,000

Dec. 31	Depletion Expense—Mineral Deposit	170,000	
	Accumulated Depletion—Mineral Deposit		170,000
	To record depletion of the mineral deposit.		

The period-end balance sheet reports the mineral deposit as shown in Exhibit 8.17.

EXHIBIT 8.17
Balance Sheet Presentation of Natural Resources

Mineral deposit	$500,000	
Less accumulated depletion	170,000	$330,000

Since all 85,000 tons of the mined ore are sold during the year, the entire $170,000 of depletion is reported on the income statement. If some of the ore remains unsold at year-end, however, the depletion related to the unsold ore is carried forward on the balance sheet and reported as

Ore Inventory, a current asset. To illustrate, and continuing with our example, assume that 40,000 tons are mined in the second year, but only 34,000 tons are sold. We record depletion of $68,000 (34,000 tons × $2 depletion per unit) and the remaining Ore Inventory of $12,000 (6,000 tons × $2 depletion per unit) as follows.

Dec. 31	Depletion Expense—Mineral Deposit	68,000	
	Ore Inventory	12,000	
	Accumulated Depletion—Mineral Deposit		80,000
	To record depletion and inventory of mineral deposit.		

Assets = Liabilities + Equity
−80,000   −68,000
+12,000

Plant Assets Used in Extracting

The conversion of natural resources by mining, cutting, or pumping usually requires machinery, equipment, and buildings. When the usefulness of these plant assets is directly related to the depletion of a natural resource, their costs are depreciated using the units-of-production method in proportion to the depletion of the natural resource. For example, if a machine is permanently installed in a mine and 10% of the ore is mined and sold in the period, then 10% of the machine's cost (less any salvage value) is allocated to depreciation expense. The same procedure is used when a machine is abandoned once resources have been extracted. If, however, a machine will be moved to and used at another site when extraction is complete, the machine is depreciated over its own useful life.

Fraud

Asset Control. Long-term assets must be safeguarded against theft, misuse, and other damages. Controls take many forms depending on the asset, including use of security tags, the legal monitoring of rights infringements, and approvals of all asset disposals. A study reports that 44% of employees in operations and service areas witnessed the wasting, mismanaging, or abusing of assets in the past year (KPMG 2009). Another 21% in general management and administration observed stealing or misappropriation of assets.

Section 3—Intangible Assets

Intangible assets are nonphysical assets (used in operations) that confer on their owners long-term rights, privileges, or competitive advantages. Examples are patents, copyrights, licenses, leaseholds, franchises, goodwill, and trademarks. Lack of physical substance does not necessarily imply an intangible asset. Notes and accounts receivable, for instance, lack physical substance, but they are not intangibles. This section identifies the more common types of intangible assets and explains the accounting for them.

P4 Account for intangible assets.

Cost Determination and Amortization

An intangible asset is recorded at cost when purchased. Intangibles are then separated into those with limited lives or indefinite lives. If an intangible has a **limited life,** its cost is systematically allocated to expense over its estimated useful life through the process of **amortization.** If an intangible asset has an **indefinite life**—meaning that no legal, regulatory, contractual, competitive, economic, or other factors limit its useful life—it should not be amortized. (If an intangible with an indefinite life is later judged to have a limited life, it is amortized over that limited life.) Amortization of intangible assets is similar to depreciation of plant assets and the depletion of natural resources in that it is a process of cost allocation. However, only the straight-line method is used for amortizing intangibles *unless* the company can show that another method is preferred. The effects of amortization are recorded in a contra account (Accumulated Amortization). The gross acquisition cost of intangible assets is disclosed in the balance sheet along with their accumulated amortization (these disclosures are new). The eventual disposal of an intangible asset involves removing its book value, recording any other asset(s) received or given up, and recognizing any gain or loss for the difference.

Point: The cost to acquire a Website address is an intangible asset.

Point: Goodwill is not amortized; instead, it is annually tested for impairment.

Many intangibles have limited lives due to laws, contracts, or other asset characteristics. Examples are patents, copyrights, and leaseholds. Other intangibles such as goodwill, trademarks, and trade names have lives that cannot be easily determined. The cost of intangible assets is amortized over the periods expected to benefit by their use, but in no case can this period be longer than the asset's legal existence. The values of some intangible assets such as goodwill continue indefinitely into the future and are not amortized. (An intangible asset that is not amortized is tested annually for **impairment**—if necessary, an impairment loss is recorded. Details for this test are in advanced courses.)

Intangible assets are often shown in a separate section of the balance sheet immediately after plant assets. **Callaway Golf**, for instance, follows this approach in reporting nearly $150 million of intangible assets in its balance sheet. Companies usually disclose their amortization periods for intangibles. The remainder of our discussion focuses on accounting for specific types of intangible assets.

Types of Intangibles

Patents The federal government grants patents to encourage the invention of new technology, mechanical devices, and production processes. A **patent** is an exclusive right granted to its owner to manufacture and sell a patented item or to use a process for 20 years. When patent rights are purchased, the cost to acquire the rights is debited to an account called Patents. If the owner engages in lawsuits to successfully defend a patent, the cost of lawsuits is debited to the Patents account. However, the costs of research and development leading to a new patent are expensed when incurred.

A patent's cost is amortized over its estimated useful life (not to exceed 20 years). If we purchase a patent costing $25,000 with a useful life of 10 years, we make the following adjusting entry at the end of each of the 10 years to amortize one-tenth of its cost.

Assets = Liabilities + Equity
−2,500   −2,500

Dec. 31	Amortization Expense—Patents	2,500	
	Accumulated Amortization—Patents		2,500
	To amortize patent costs over its useful life.		

The $2,500 debit to Amortization Expense appears on the income statement as a cost of the product or service provided under protection of the patent. The Accumulated Amortization—Patents account is a contra asset account to Patents.

Decision Insight

Mention "drug war" and most people think of illegal drug trade. But another drug war is under way: Brand-name drugmakers are fighting to stop generic copies of their products from hitting the market once patents expire. Delaying a generic rival can yield millions in extra sales. ■

Percent of Prescriptions That Specify Generics

Copyrights A **copyright** gives its owner the exclusive right to publish and sell a musical, literary, or artistic work during the life of the creator plus 70 years, although the useful life of most copyrights is much shorter. The costs of a copyright are amortized over its useful life. The only identifiable cost of many copyrights is the fee paid to the Copyright Office of the federal government or international agency granting the copyright. If this fee is immaterial, it is charged directly to an expense account; but if the identifiable costs of a copyright are material, they are capitalized (recorded in an asset account) and periodically amortized by debiting an account called Amortization Expense—Copyrights.

Franchises and Licenses **Franchises** and **licenses** are rights that a company or government grants an entity to deliver a product or service under specified conditions. Many organizations grant franchise and license rights—**McDonald's**, **Pizza Hut**, and **Major**

League Baseball are just a few examples. The costs of franchises and licenses are debited to a Franchises and Licenses asset account and are amortized over the lives of the agreements. If an agreement is for an indefinite or perpetual period, those costs are not amortized.

Trademarks and Trade Names Companies often adopt unique symbols or select unique names and brands in marketing their products. A **trademark** or **trade (brand) name** is a symbol, name, phrase, or jingle identified with a company, product, or service. Examples are Nike swoosh, Marlboro Man, Big Mac, Coca-Cola, and Corvette. Ownership and exclusive right to use a trademark or trade name are often established by showing that one company used it before another. Ownership is best established by registering a trademark or trade name with the government's Patent Office. The cost of developing, maintaining, or enhancing the value of a trademark or trade name (such as advertising) is charged to expense when incurred. If a trademark or trade name is purchased, however, its cost is debited to an asset account and then amortized over its expected life. If the company plans to renew indefinitely its right to the trademark or trade name, the cost is not amortized.

Point: McDonald's "golden arches" are one of the world's most valuable trademarks, yet this asset is not shown on McDonald's balance sheet.

Goodwill Goodwill has a specific meaning in accounting. Goodwill is the amount by which a company's value exceeds the value of its individual assets and liabilities. This usually implies that the company as a whole has certain valuable attributes not measured among its individual assets and liabilities. These can include superior management, skilled workforce, good supplier or customer relations, quality products or services, good location, or other competitive advantages.

To keep accounting information from being too subjective, goodwill is not recorded unless an entire company or business segment is purchased. Purchased goodwill is measured by taking the purchase price of the company and subtracting the market value of its individual net assets (excluding goodwill). For instance, Yahoo! paid nearly $3.0 billion to acquire GeoCities; about $2.8 of the $3.0 billion was for goodwill and other intangibles.

Goodwill is measured as the excess of the cost of an acquired entity over the value of the acquired net assets. Goodwill is recorded as an asset, and it is *not* amortized. Instead, goodwill is annually tested for impairment. If the book value of goodwill does not exceed its fair (market) value, goodwill is not impaired. However, if the book value of goodwill does exceed its fair value, an impairment loss is recorded equal to that excess. (Details of this test are in advanced courses.)

Point: Amortization of goodwill is different for financial accounting and tax accounting. The IRS requires the amortization of goodwill over 15 years.

Example: Assume goodwill carries a book value of $500 and has an implied fair value of $475, *and* this $25 decline in value meets the 2-step impairment test. The entry to record this impairment is:
Impairment Loss $25
   Goodwill $25

Leaseholds Property is rented under a contract called a **lease**. The property's owner, called the **lessor**, grants the lease. The one who secures the right to possess and use the property is called the **lessee**. A **leasehold** refers to the rights the lessor grants to the lessee under the terms of the lease. A leasehold is an intangible asset for the lessee.

Certain leases require no advance payment from the lessee but require monthly rent payments. In this case, we do not set up a Leasehold account. Instead, the monthly payments are debited to a Rent Expense account. If a long-term lease requires the lessee to pay the final period's rent in advance when the lease is signed, the lessee records this advance payment with a debit to the Leasehold account. Since the advance payment is not used until the final period, the Leasehold account balance remains intact until that final period when its balance is transferred to Rent Expense. (Some long-term leases give the lessee essentially the same rights as a purchaser. This results in a tangible asset and a liability reported by the lessee. Chapter 10 describes these so-called *capital leases*.)

A long-term lease can increase in value when current rental rates for similar property rise while the required payments under the lease remain constant. This increase in value of a lease is not reported on the lessee's balance sheet. However, if the property is subleased and the new tenant makes a cash payment to the original lessee for the rights under the old lease, the new tenant debits this payment to a Leasehold account, which is amortized to Rent Expense over the remaining life of the lease.

Point: A leasehold account implies existence of future benefits that the lessee controls because of a prepayment. It also meets the definition of an asset.

Leasehold Improvements A lessee sometimes pays for alterations or improvements to the leased property such as partitions, painting, and storefronts. These alterations and improvements are called **leasehold improvements,** and the lessee debits these costs to a Leasehold Improvements account. Since leasehold improvements become part of the property and revert to the lessor at the end of the lease, the lessee amortizes these costs over the life of the lease or the life of the improvements, whichever is shorter. The amortization entry debits

Amortization Expense—Leasehold Improvements and credits Accumulated Amortization—Leasehold Improvements.

Other Intangibles There are other types of intangible assets such as *software, noncompete covenants, customer lists,* and so forth. Our accounting for them is the same. First, we record the intangible asset's costs. Second, we determine whether the asset has a limited or indefinite life. If limited, we allocate its costs over that period. If indefinite, its costs are not amortized.

Fraud

Hidden Assets. Most view fraud involving long-term assets as low risk. Yet, the opportunity for fraud in a one-time transaction is reasonably high and requires scrutiny. Concealment of an asset theft can include recording it as scrap, obsolescence, donated, or destroyed. More generally, the following business activities can be used to conceal asset theft:

- Recording an asset disposal as customer adjustment, no charge, or promotional.
- Recording false receiving reports as to asset quantity.
- False counts or record alteration after a physical count.
- Nonbilling of an asset sale.
- Write-off of an asset.

Quick Check
Answers — p. 353

12. Give an example of a natural resource and of an intangible asset.
13. A company pays $650,000 for an ore deposit. The deposit is estimated to have 325,000 tons of ore that will be mined over the next 10 years. During the first year, it mined, processed, and sold 91,000 tons. What is that year's depletion expense?
14. On January 6, 2011, a company pays $120,000 for a patent with a remaining 17-year legal life to produce a toy expected to be marketable for three years. Prepare entries to record its acquisition and the December 31, 2011, amortization entry.

GLOBAL VIEW

This section discusses similarities and differences between U.S. GAAP and IFRS in accounting and reporting for plant assets and intangible assets.

Accounting for Plant Assets Issues involving cost determination, depreciation, additional expenditures, and disposals of plant assets are subject to broadly similar guidance for both U.S. GAAP and IFRS. Although differences exist, the similarities vastly outweigh the differences. **Nokia** describes its accounting for plant assets as follows:

NOKIA

> Property, plant and equipment are stated at cost less accumulated depreciation. Depreciation is recorded on a straight-line basis over the expected useful lives of the assets. Maintenance, repairs and renewals are generally charged to expense during the financial period in which they are incurred. However, major renovations are capitalized and included in the carrying amount of the asset ... Major renovations are depreciated over the remaining useful life of the related asset.

One area where notable differences exist is in accounting for changes in the value of plant assets (between the time they are acquired and when disposed of). Namely, how do IFRS and U.S. GAAP treat decreases and increases in the value of plant assets subsequent to acquisition?

Decreases in the Value of Plant Assets When the value of plant assets declines after acquisition, but before disposition, both U.S. GAAP and IFRS require companies to record those decreases as *impairment losses*. While the *test for impairment* uses a different base between U.S. GAAP and IFRS, a more fundamental difference is that U.S. GAAP revalues impaired plant assets to *fair value* whereas IFRS revalues them to a *recoverable amount* (defined as fair value less costs to sell).

Increases in the Value of Plant Assets U.S. GAAP prohibits companies from recording increases in the value of plant assets. However, IFRS permits upward *asset revaluations*. Namely, under IFRS, if an impairment was previously recorded, a company would reverse that impairment to the extent necessary and record that increase in income. If the increase is beyond the original cost, that increase is recorded in comprehensive income.

Accounting for Intangible Assets For intangible assets, the accounting for cost determination, amortization, additional expenditures, and disposals is subject to broadly similar guidance for U.S. GAAP and IFRS. Although differences exist, the similarities vastly outweigh differences. Again, and consistent with the accounting for plant assets, U.S. GAAP and IFRS handle decreases and increases in the value of intangible assets differently. However, IFRS requirements for recording increases in the value of intangible assets are so restrictive that such increases are rare. **Nokia** describes its accounting for intangible assets as follows:

> [Intangible assets] are capitalized and amortized using the straight-line method over their useful lives. Where an indication of impairment exists, the carrying amount of any intangible asset is assessed and written down to its recoverable amount.

NOKIA

Total Asset Turnover — Decision Analysis

A company's assets are important in determining its ability to generate sales and earn income. Managers devote much attention to deciding what assets a company acquires, how much it invests in assets, and how to use assets most efficiently and effectively. One important measure of a company's ability to use its assets is **total asset turnover**, defined in Exhibit 8.18.

A1 Compute total asset turnover and apply it to analyze a company's use of assets.

EXHIBIT 8.18
Total Asset Turnover

$$\text{Total asset turnover} = \frac{\text{Net sales}}{\text{Average total assets}}$$

The numerator reflects the net amounts earned from the sale of products and services. The denominator reflects the average total resources devoted to operating the company and generating sales.

To illustrate, let's look at total asset turnover in Exhibit 8.19 for two competing companies: **Molson Coors** and **Boston Beer**.

EXHIBIT 8.19
Analysis Using Total Asset Turnover

Company	Figure ($ millions)	2009	2008	2007	2006	2005
Molson Coors	Net sales	$ 3,032.4	$ 4,774.3	$ 6,190.6	$ 5,845.0	$ 5,506.9
	Average total assets	$11,203.9	$11,934.1	$12,527.5	$11,701.4	$ 8,228.4
	Total asset turnover	0.27	0.40	0.49	0.50	0.67
Boston Beer	Net sales	$ 415.053	$ 398.400	$ 341.647	$ 285.431	$238.304
	Average total assets	$ 241.347	$ 208.856	$ 176.215	$ 136.765	$113.258
	Total asset turnover	1.72	1.91	1.94	2.09	2.10

To show how we use total asset turnover, let's look at Molson Coors. We express Molson Coors's use of assets in generating net sales by saying "it turned its assets over 0.27 times during 2009." This means that each $1.00 of assets produced $0.27 of net sales. Is a total asset turnover of 0.27 good or bad? It is safe to say that all companies desire a high total asset turnover. Like many ratio analyses, however, a company's total asset turnover must be interpreted in comparison with those of prior years and of its competitors. Interpreting the total asset turnover also requires an understanding of the company's operations. Some operations are capital intensive, meaning that a relatively large amount is invested in assets to generate sales. This suggests a relatively lower total asset turnover. Other companies' operations are labor intensive, meaning that they generate sales more by the efforts of people than the use of assets. In that case, we expect a higher total asset turnover. Companies with low total asset turnover require higher profit margins (examples are hotels and real estate); companies with high total asset turnover can succeed with lower profit margins (examples are food stores and toy merchandisers). Molson Coors's turnover recently declined and is now much lower than that for Boston Beer and many other competitors. Total asset turnover for Molson Coors's competitors, available in industry publications such as Dun & Bradstreet, is generally in the range of 0.5 to 1.0 over this same period. Overall, Molson Coors must improve relative to its competitors on total asset turnover.

Point: An estimate of **plant asset useful life** equals the plant asset cost divided by depreciation expense.

Point: The **plant asset age** is estimated by dividing accumulated depreciation by depreciation expense. Older plant assets can signal needed asset replacements; they may also signal less efficient assets.

> **Decision Maker** — Answer — p. 352
>
> **Environmentalist** A paper manufacturer claims it cannot afford more environmental controls. It points to its low total asset turnover of 1.9 and argues that it cannot compete with companies whose total asset turnover is much higher. Examples cited are food stores (5.5) and auto dealers (3.8). How do you respond?

DEMONSTRATION PROBLEM

On July 14, 2011, Tulsa Company pays $600,000 to acquire a fully equipped factory. The purchase involves the following assets and information.

Asset	Appraised Value	Salvage Value	Useful Life	Depreciation Method
Land	$160,000			Not depreciated
Land improvements	80,000	$ 0	10 years	Straight-line
Building	320,000	100,000	10 years	Double-declining-balance
Machinery	240,000	20,000	10,000 units	Units-of-production*
Total	$800,000			

* The machinery is used to produce 700 units in 2011 and 1,800 units in 2012.

Required

1. Allocate the total $600,000 purchase cost among the separate assets.
2. Compute the 2011 (six months) and 2012 depreciation expense for each asset, and compute the company's total depreciation expense for both years.
3. On the last day of calendar year 2013, Tulsa discarded machinery that had been on its books for five years. The machinery's original cost was $12,000 (estimated life of five years) and its salvage value was $2,000. No depreciation had been recorded for the fifth year when the disposal occurred. Journalize the fifth year of depreciation (straight-line method) and the asset's disposal.
4. At the beginning of year 2013, Tulsa purchased a patent for $100,000 cash. The company estimated the patent's useful life to be 10 years. Journalize the patent acquisition and its amortization for the year 2013.
5. Late in the year 2013, Tulsa acquired an ore deposit for $600,000 cash. It added roads and built mine shafts for an additional cost of $80,000. Salvage value of the mine is estimated to be $20,000. The company estimated 330,000 tons of available ore. In year 2013, Tulsa mined and sold 10,000 tons of ore. Journalize the mine's acquisition and its first year's depletion.
6.[A] On the first day of 2013, Tulsa exchanged the machinery that was acquired on July 14, 2011, along with $5,000 cash for machinery with a $210,000 market value. Journalize the exchange of these assets assuming the exchange lacked commercial substance. (Refer to background information in parts 1 and 2.)

PLANNING THE SOLUTION

- Complete a three-column table showing the following amounts for each asset: appraised value, percent of total value, and apportioned cost.
- Using allocated costs, compute depreciation for 2011 (only one-half year) and 2012 (full year) for each asset. Summarize those computations in a table showing total depreciation for each year.
- Remember that depreciation must be recorded up-to-date before discarding an asset. Calculate and record depreciation expense for the fifth year using the straight-line method. Since salvage value is not received at the end of a discarded asset's life, the amount of any salvage value becomes a loss on disposal. Record the loss on the disposal as well as the removal of the discarded asset and its related accumulated depreciation.
- Record the patent (an intangible asset) at its purchase price. Use straight-line amortization over its useful life to calculate amortization expense.
- Record the ore deposit (a natural resource asset) at its cost, including any added costs to ready the mine for use. Calculate depletion per ton using the depletion formula. Multiply the depletion per ton by the amount of tons mined and sold to calculate depletion expense for the year.
- Remember that gains and losses on asset exchanges that lack commercial substance are not recognized. Make a journal entry to add the acquired machinery to the books and to remove the old machinery, along with its accumulated depreciation, and to record the cash given in the exchange.

SOLUTION TO DEMONSTRATION PROBLEM

1. Allocation of the total cost of $600,000 among the separate assets.

Asset	Appraised Value	Percent of Total Value	Apportioned Cost
Land	$160,000	20%	$120,000 ($600,000 × 20%)
Land improvements	80,000	10	60,000 ($600,000 × 10%)
Building	320,000	40	240,000 ($600,000 × 40%)
Machinery	240,000	30	180,000 ($600,000 × 30%)
Total	$800,000	100%	$600,000

2. Depreciation for each asset. (Land is not depreciated.)

Land Improvements

Cost	$60,000
Salvage value	0
Depreciable cost	$60,000
Useful life	10 years
Annual depreciation expense ($60,000/10 years)	$6,000
2011 depreciation ($6,000 × 6/12)	**$3,000**
2012 depreciation	**$6,000**

Building
Straight-line rate = 100%/10 years = 10%
Double-declining-balance rate = 10% × 2 = 20%
2011 depreciation ($240,000 × 20% × 6/12) **$24,000**
2012 depreciation [($240,000 − $24,000) × 20%] **$43,200**

Machinery

Cost	$180,000
Salvage value	20,000
Depreciable cost	$160,000
Total expected units of production	10,000 units
Depreciation per unit ($160,000/10,000 units)	$16
2011 depreciation ($16 × 700 units)	**$11,200**
2012 depreciation ($16 × 1,800 units)	**$28,800**

Total depreciation expense for each year:

	2011	2012
Land improvements	$3,000	$6,000
Building	24,000	43,200
Machinery	11,200	28,800
Total	$38,200	$78,000

3. Record the depreciation up-to-date on the discarded asset.

Depreciation Expense—Machinery	2,000	
Accumulated Depreciation—Machinery		2,000
To record depreciation on date of disposal: ($12,000 − $2,000)/5		

Record the removal of the discarded asset and its loss on disposal.

Accumulated Depreciation—Machinery	10,000	
Loss on Disposal of Machinery	2,000	
Machinery		12,000
To record the discarding of machinery with a $2,000 book value.		

4.

Patent	100,000	
Cash		100,000
To record patent acquisition.		

Amortization Expense—Patent	10,000	
Accumulated Amortization—Patent		10,000
To record amortization expense: $100,000/10 years = $10,000.		

5.

Ore Deposit	680,000	
Cash		680,000
To record ore deposit acquisition and its related costs.		

Depletion Expense—Ore Deposit	20,000	
Accumulated Depletion—Ore Deposit		20,000
To record depletion expense: ($680,000 − $20,000)/330,000 tons = $2 per ton. 10,000 tons mined and sold × $2 = $20,000 depletion.		

6. Record the asset exchange: The book value on the exchange date is $180,000 (cost) − $40,000 (accumulated depreciation). The book value of the machinery given up in the exchange ($140,000) plus the $5,000 cash paid is less than the $210,000 value of the machine acquired. The entry to record this exchange of assets that lacks commercial substance does not recognize the $65,000 "gain."

Machinery (new)	145,000*	
Accumulated Depreciation—Machinery (old)	40,000	
Machinery (old)		180,000
Cash		5,000
To record asset exchange that lacks commercial substance.		

* Market value of the acquired asset of $210,000 minus $65,000 "gain."

APPENDIX 8A — Exchanging Plant Assets

P5A Account for asset exchanges.

Many plant assets such as machinery, automobiles, and office equipment are disposed of by exchanging them for newer assets. In a typical exchange of plant assets, a *trade-in allowance* is received on the old asset and the balance is paid in cash. Accounting for the exchange of assets depends on whether the transaction has *commercial substance* (per *SFAS 153,* commercial substance implies that it alters the company's future cash flows). If an asset exchange has commercial substance, a gain or loss is recorded based on the difference between the book value of the asset(s) given up and the market value of the asset(s) received. If an asset exchange lacks commercial substance, no gain or loss is recorded, and the asset(s) received is recorded based on the book value of the asset(s) given up. An exchange has commercial substance if the company's future cash flows change as a result of the transaction. This section describes the accounting for the exchange of assets.

Exchange with Commercial Substance: A Loss A company acquires $42,000 in new equipment. In exchange, the company pays $33,000 cash and trades in old equipment. The old equipment originally cost $36,000 and has accumulated depreciation of $20,000, which implies a $16,000 book value at the time of exchange. We are told this exchange has commercial substance and that the old equipment has a trade-in allowance of $9,000. This exchange yields a loss as computed in the middle (Loss) columns of Exhibit 8A.1; the loss is computed as Asset received − Assets given = $42,000 − $49,000 = $(7,000). We can also compute the loss as Trade-in allowance − Book value of asset given = $9,000 − $16,000 = $(7,000).

EXHIBIT 8A.1
Computing Gain or Loss on Asset Exchange with Commercial Substance

Asset Exchange Has Commercial Substance	Loss		Gain	
Market value of asset received		$42,000		$52,000
Book value of assets given:				
Equipment ($36,000 − $20,000)	$16,000		$16,000	
Cash	33,000	49,000	33,000	49,000
Gain (loss) on exchange		**$(7,000)**		**$ 3,000**

The entry to record this asset exchange is

Jan. 3	Equipment (new)	42,000	
	Loss on Exchange of Assets	7,000	
	Accumulated Depreciation—Equipment (old)	20,000	
	Equipment (old)		36,000
	Cash		33,000
	To record exchange (with commercial substance) of old equipment and cash for new equipment.		

Assets = Liabilities + Equity
+42,000   −7,000
+20,000
−36,000
−33,000

Point: Parenthetical notes to "new" and "old" equipment are for illustration only. Both the debit and credit are to the same Equipment account.

Exchange with Commercial Substance: A Gain Let's assume the same facts as in the preceding asset exchange *except* that the new equipment received has a market value of $52,000 instead of $42,000. We are told that this exchange has commercial substance and that the old equipment has a trade-in allowance of $19,000. This exchange yields a gain as computed in the right-most (Gain) columns of Exhibit 8A.1; the gain is computed as Asset received − Assets given = $52,000 − $49,000 = $3,000. We can also compute the gain as Trade-in allowance − Book value of asset given = $19,000 − $16,000 = $3,000. The entry to record this asset exchange is

Jan. 3	Equipment (new)	52,000	
	Accumulated Depreciation—Equipment (old)	20,000	
	Equipment (old)		36,000
	Cash		33,000
	Gain on Exchange of Assets		3,000
	To record exchange (with commercial substance) of old equipment and cash for new equipment.		

Assets = Liabilities + Equity
+52,000   +3,000
+20,000
−36,000
−33,000

Exchanges without Commercial Substance Let's assume the same facts as in the preceding asset exchange involving new equipment received with a market value of $52,000, but let's instead assume the transaction *lacks commercial substance*. The entry to record this asset exchange is

Jan. 3	Equipment (new)	49,000	
	Accumulated Depreciation—Equipment (old)	20,000	
	Equipment (old)		36,000
	Cash		33,000
	To record exchange (without commercial substance) of old equipment and cash for new equipment.		

Assets = Liabilities + Equity
+49,000
+20,000
−36,000
−33,000

The $3,000 gain recorded when the transaction has commercial substance is *not* recognized in this entry because of the rule prohibiting recording a gain or loss on asset exchanges without commercial substance. The $49,000 recorded for the new equipment equals its cash price ($52,000) less the unrecognized gain ($3,000) on the exchange. The $49,000 cost recorded is called the *cost basis* of the new machine. This cost basis is the amount we use to compute depreciation and its book value. The cost basis of the new asset also can be computed by summing the book values of the assets given up as shown in Exhibit 8A.2. The same analysis and approach are taken for a loss on an asset exchange without commercial substance.

Point: No gain or loss is recorded for exchanges *without* commercial substance.

EXHIBIT 8A.2
Cost Basis of New Asset When Gain Not Recorded on Asset Exchange without Commercial Substance

Cost of old equipment	$ 36,000
Less accumulated depreciation	20,000
Book value of old equipment	16,000
Cash paid in the exchange	33,000
Cost recorded for new equipment	**$49,000**

Quick Check
Answer — p. 353

15. A company trades an old Web server for a new one. The cost of the old server is $30,000, and its accumulated depreciation at the time of the trade is $23,400. The new server has a cash price of $45,000. Prepare entries to record the trade under two different assumptions where the company receives a trade-in allowance of (*a*) $3,000 and the exchange has commercial substance, and (*b*) $7,000 and the exchange lacks commercial substance.

Summary

C1 Explain the cost principle for computing the cost of plant assets. Plant assets are set apart from other tangible assets by two important features: use in operations and useful lives longer than one period. Plant assets are recorded at cost when purchased. Cost includes all normal and reasonable expenditures necessary to get the asset in place and ready for its intended use. The cost of a lump-sum purchase is allocated among its individual assets.

C2 Explain depreciation for partial years and changes in estimates. Partial-year depreciation is often required because assets are bought and sold throughout the year. Depreciation is revised when changes in estimates such as salvage value and useful life occur. If the useful life of a plant asset changes, for instance, the remaining cost to be depreciated is spread over the remaining (revised) useful life of the asset.

C3 Distinguish between revenue and capital expenditures, and account for them. Revenue expenditures expire in the current period and are debited to expense accounts and matched with current revenues. Ordinary repairs are an example of revenue expenditures. Capital expenditures benefit future periods and are debited to asset accounts. Examples of capital expenditures are extraordinary repairs and betterments.

A1 Compute total asset turnover and apply it to analyze a company's use of assets. Total asset turnover measures a company's ability to use its assets to generate sales. It is defined as net sales divided by average total assets. While all companies desire a high total asset turnover, it must be interpreted in comparison with those for prior years and its competitors.

P1 Compute and record depreciation using the straight-line, units-of-production, and declining-balance methods. *Depreciation* is the process of allocating to expense the cost of a plant asset over the accounting periods that benefit from its use. Depreciation does not measure the decline in a plant asset's market value or its physical deterioration. Three factors determine depreciation: cost, salvage value, and useful life. Salvage value is an estimate of the asset's value at the end of its benefit period. Useful (service) life is the length of time an asset is productively used. The straight-line method divides cost less salvage value by the asset's useful life to determine depreciation expense per period. The units-of-production method divides cost less salvage value by the estimated number of units the asset will produce over its life to determine depreciation per unit. The declining-balance method multiplies the asset's beginning-of-period book value by a factor that is often double the straight-line rate.

P2 Account for asset disposal through discarding or selling an asset. When a plant asset is discarded or sold, its cost and accumulated depreciation are removed from the accounts. Any cash proceeds from discarding or selling an asset are recorded and compared to the asset's book value to determine gain or loss.

P3 Account for natural resource assets and their depletion. The cost of a natural resource is recorded in a noncurrent asset account. Depletion of a natural resource is recorded by allocating its cost to depletion expense using the units-of-production method. Depletion is credited to an Accumulated Depletion account.

P4 Account for intangible assets. An intangible asset is recorded at the cost incurred to purchase it. The cost of an intangible asset with a definite useful life is allocated to expense using the straight-line method, and is called *amortization*. Goodwill and intangible assets with an indefinite useful life are not amortized—they are annually tested for impairment. Intangible assets include patents, copyrights, leaseholds, goodwill, and trademarks.

P5A Account for asset exchanges. For an asset exchange with commercial substance, a gain or loss is recorded based on the difference between the book value of the asset given up and the market value of the asset received. For an asset exchange without commercial substance, no gain or loss is recorded, and the asset received is recorded based on the book value of the asset given up.

Guidance Answers to Decision Maker and Decision Ethics

Controller The president's instructions may reflect an honest and reasonable prediction of the future. Since the company is struggling financially, the president may have concluded that the normal pattern of replacing assets every three years cannot continue. Perhaps the strategy is to avoid costs of frequent replacements and stretch use of equipment a few years longer until financial conditions improve. However, if you believe the president's decision is unprincipled, you might confront the president with your opinion that it is unethical to change the estimate to increase income. Another possibility is to wait and see whether the auditor will prohibit this change in estimate. In either case, you should insist that the statements be based on reasonable estimates.

Entrepreneur Treating an expense as a capital expenditure means that reported expenses will be lower and income higher in the short run. This is so because a capital expenditure is not expensed immediately but is spread over the asset's useful life. Treating an expense as a capital expenditure also means that asset and equity totals are reported at larger amounts in the short run. This continues until the asset is fully depreciated. Your friend is probably trying to help, but the suggestion is misguided. Only an expenditure benefiting future periods is a capital expenditure.

Environmentalist The paper manufacturer's comparison of its total asset turnover with food stores and auto dealers is misdirected. These other industries' turnovers are higher because their profit margins are lower (about 2%). Profit margins for the paper industry are usually 3% to 3.5%. You need to collect data from competitors in the paper industry to show that a 1.9 total asset turnover is about the norm for this industry. You might also want to collect data on this company's revenues and expenses, along with compensation data for its high-ranking officers and employees.

Guidance Answers to Quick Checks

1. a. Supplies—current assets
   b. Office equipment—plant assets
   c. Inventory—current assets
   d. Land for future expansion—long-term investments
   e. Trucks used in operations—plant assets
2. a. Land   b. Land Improvements
3. $700,000 + $49,000 − $21,000 + $3,500 + $3,000 + $2,500 = $737,000
4. a. Straight-line with 7-year life: ($77,000/7) = $11,000
   b. Straight-line with 10-year life: ($77,000/10) = $7,700
5. Depreciation is a process of allocating the cost of plant assets to the accounting periods that benefit from the assets' use.
6. a. Book value using straight-line depreciation:
      $96,000 − [($96,000 − $8,000)/5] = $78,400
   b. Book value using units of production:
      $96,000 − [($96,000 − $8,000) × (10,000/100,000)]
      = $87,200
7. ($3,800 − $200)/3 = $1,200 (original depreciation per year)
   $1,200 × 2 = $2,400 (accumulated depreciation)
   ($3,800 − $2,400)/2 = $700 (revised depreciation)
8.

Machinery	12,000	
Cash		12,000

9. A revenue expenditure benefits only the current period and should be charged to expense in the current period. A capital expenditure yields benefits that extend beyond the end of the current period and should be charged to an asset.
10. A betterment involves modifying an existing plant asset to make it more efficient, usually by replacing part of the asset with an improved or superior part. The cost of a betterment is debited to the asset account.

11.

Depreciation Expense	3,500	
Accumulated Depreciation		3,500
Cash	32,000	
Accumulated Depreciation	10,500	
Gain on Sale of Equipment		500
Equipment		42,000

12. Examples of natural resources are timberlands, mineral deposits, and oil reserves. Examples of intangible assets are patents, copyrights, leaseholds, leasehold improvements, goodwill, trademarks, and licenses.
13. ($650,000/325,000 tons) × 91,000 tons = $182,000
14.

Jan. 6	Patents		120,000	
		Cash		120,000
Dec. 31	Amortization Expense		40,000*	
		Accumulated Amortization—Patents		40,000

* $120,000/3 years = $40,000.

15. (a)

Equipment (new)	45,000	
Loss on Exchange of Assets	3,600	
Accumulated Depreciation—Equipment (old)	23,400	
Equipment (old)		30,000
Cash ($45,000 − $3,000)		42,000

(b)

Equipment (new)*	44,600	
Accumulated Depreciation—Equipment (old)	23,400	
Equipment (old)		30,000
Cash ($45,000 − $7,000)		38,000

* Includes $400 unrecognized gain.

Key Terms

Accelerated depreciation method (p. 334)	**Copyright** (p. 344)	**Franchises** (p. 344)
Amortization (p. 343)	**Cost** (p. 329)	**Goodwill** (p. 345)
Asset book value (p. 333)	**Declining-balance method** (p. 334)	**Impairment** (p. 338)
Betterments (p. 339)	**Depletion** (p. 342)	**Inadequacy** (p. 331)
Capital expenditures (p. 338)	**Depreciation** (p. 331)	**Indefinite life** (p. 343)
Change in an accounting estimate (p. 337)	**Extraordinary repairs** (p. 339)	**Intangible assets** (p. 343)

Land improvements (p. 330)
Lease (p. 345)
Leasehold (p. 345)
Leasehold improvements (p. 345)
Lessee (p. 345)
Lessor (p. 345)
Licenses (p. 344)
Limited life (p. 343)

Modified Accelerated Cost Recovery System (MACRS) (p. 336)
Natural resources (p. 342)
Obsolescence (p. 331)
Ordinary repairs (p. 338)
Patent (p. 344)
Plant asset age (p. 347)
Plant asset useful life (p. 347)

Plant assets (p. 328)
Revenue expenditures (p. 338)
Salvage value (p. 331)
Straight-line depreciation (p. 332)
Total asset turnover (p. 347)
Trademark or trade (brand) name (p. 345)
Units-of-production depreciation (p. 333)
Useful life (p. 331)

Multiple Choice Quiz

Answers on p. 367   mhhe.com/wildFA6e

Additional quiz questions are available at the book's Website.

1. A company paid $326,000 for property that included land, land improvements, and a building. The land was appraised at $175,000, the land improvements were appraised at $70,000, and the building was appraised at $105,000. What is the allocation of property costs to the three assets purchased?
   a. Land, $150,000; Land Improvements, $60,000; Building, $90,000
   b. Land, $163,000; Land Improvements, $65,200; Building, $97,800
   c. Land, $150,000; Land Improvements, $61,600; Building, $92,400
   d. Land, $159,000; Land Improvements, $65,200; Building, $95,400
   e. Land, $175,000; Land Improvements, $70,000; Building, $105,000

2. A company purchased a truck for $35,000 on January 1, 2011. The truck is estimated to have a useful life of four years and an estimated salvage value of $1,000. Assuming that the company uses straight-line depreciation, what is the depreciation expense on the truck for the year ended December 31, 2012?
   a. $8,750
   b. $17,500
   c. $8,500
   d. $17,000
   e. $25,500

3. A company purchased machinery for $10,800,000 on January 1, 2011. The machinery has a useful life of 10 years and an estimated salvage value of $800,000. What is the depreciation expense on the machinery for the year ended December 31, 2012, assuming that the double-declining-balance method is used?
   a. $2,160,000
   b. $3,888,000
   c. $1,728,000
   d. $2,000,000
   e. $1,600,000

4. A company sold a machine that originally cost $250,000 for $120,000 when accumulated depreciation on the machine was $100,000. The gain or loss recorded on the sale of this machine is
   a. $0 gain or loss.
   b. $120,000 gain.
   c. $30,000 loss.
   d. $30,000 gain.
   e. $150,000 loss.

5. A company had average total assets of $500,000, gross sales of $575,000, and net sales of $550,000. The company's total asset turnover is
   a. 1.15
   b. 1.10
   c. 0.91
   d. 0.87
   e. 1.05

A Superscript letter A denotes assignments based on Appendix 8A.
Icon denotes assignments that involve decision making.

Discussion Questions

1. What characteristics of a plant asset make it different from other assets?
2. What is the general rule for cost inclusion for plant assets?
3. What is different between land and land improvements?
4. Why is the cost of a lump-sum purchase allocated to the individual assets acquired?
5. Does the balance in the Accumulated Depreciation—Machinery account represent funds to replace the machinery when it wears out? If not, what does it represent?
6. Why is the Modified Accelerated Cost Recovery System not generally accepted for financial accounting purposes?

7. What accounting concept justifies charging low-cost plant asset purchases immediately to an expense account?
8. What is the difference between ordinary repairs and extraordinary repairs? How should each be recorded?
9. Identify events that might lead to disposal of a plant asset.
10. What is the process of allocating the cost of natural resources to expense as they are used?
11. Is the declining-balance method an acceptable way to compute depletion of natural resources? Explain.
12. What are the characteristics of an intangible asset?
13. What general procedures are applied in accounting for the acquisition and potential cost allocation of intangible assets?
14. When do we know that a company has goodwill? When can goodwill appear in a company's balance sheet?
15. Assume that a company buys another business and pays for its goodwill. If the company plans to incur costs each year to maintain the value of the goodwill, must it also amortize this goodwill?
16. How is total asset turnover computed? Why would a financial statement user be interested in total asset turnover?
17. Refer to **Research In Motion**'s balance sheet in Appendix A. What property, plant and equipment assets does RIM list on its balance sheet? What is the book value of its total net property, plant and equipment assets at February 27, 2010?
18. **Apple** lists its plant assets as "Property, plant and equipment, net." What does "net" mean in this title?
19. Refer to **Nokia**'s balance sheet in Appendix A. What does it title its plant assets? What is the book value of its plant assets at December 31, 2009?
20. Refer to the May 31, 2009, balance sheet of **Palm** in Appendix A. What long-term assets discussed in this chapter are reported by the company?

connect

QUICK STUDY

QS 8-1 Cost of plant assets C1

Strike Bowling installs automatic scorekeeping equipment with an invoice cost of $180,000. The electrical work required for the installation costs $8,000. Additional costs are $3,000 for delivery and $12,600 for sales tax. During the installation, a component of the equipment is carelessly left on a lane and hit by the automatic lane-cleaning machine. The cost of repairing the component is $2,250. What is the total recorded cost of the automatic scorekeeping equipment?

QS 8-2 Defining assets C1

Identify the main difference between (1) plant assets and inventory, (2) plant assets and current assets, and (3) plant assets and long-term investments.

QS 8-3 Straight-line depreciation P1

On January 2, 2011, the Crossover Band acquires sound equipment for concert performances at a cost of $55,900. The band estimates it will use this equipment for four years, during which time it anticipates performing about 120 concerts. It estimates that after four years it can sell the equipment for $1,900. During year 2011, the band performs 40 concerts. Compute the year 2011 depreciation using the straight-line method.

QS 8-4 Units-of-production depreciation P1

Refer to the information in QS 8-3. Compute the year 2011 depreciation using the units-of-production method.

QS 8-5 Computing revised depreciation C2

Refer to the facts in QS 8-3. Assume that the Crossover Band uses straight-line depreciation but realizes at the start of the second year that due to concert bookings beyond expectations, this equipment will last only a total of three years. The salvage value remains unchanged. Compute the revised depreciation for both the second and third years.

QS 8-6 Double-declining-balance method P1

A fleet of refrigerated delivery trucks is acquired on January 5, 2011, at a cost of $930,000 with an estimated useful life of eight years and an estimated salvage value of $150,000. Compute the depreciation expense for the first three years using the double-declining-balance method.

QS 8-7 Recording plant asset impairment C2

Assume a company's equipment carries a book value of $4,000 ($4,500 cost less $500 accumulated depreciation) and a fair value of $3,750, *and* that the $250 decline in fair value in comparison to the book value meets the 2-step impairment test. Prepare the entry to record this $250 impairment.

QS 8-8
Revenue and capital expenditures
C3

1. Classify the following as either revenue or capital expenditures.
   a. Completed an addition to an office building for $250,000 cash.
   b. Paid $160 for the monthly cost of replacement filters on an air-conditioning system.
   c. Paid $300 cash per truck for the cost of their annual tune-ups.
   d. Paid $50,000 cash to replace a compressor on a refrigeration system that extends its useful life by four years.
2. Prepare the journal entries to record transactions *a* and *d* of part 1.

QS 8-9
Disposal of assets P2

Horizon Co. owns equipment that cost $138,750, with accumulated depreciation of $81,000. Horizon sells the equipment for cash. Record the sale of the equipment assuming Horizon sells the equipment for (1) $63,000 cash, (2) $57,750 cash, and (3) $46,500 cash.

QS 8-10
Natural resources and depletion
P3

Diamond Company acquires an ore mine at a cost of $1,300,000. It incurs additional costs of $200,000 to access the mine, which is estimated to hold 500,000 tons of ore. The estimated value of the land after the ore is removed is $150,000.
1. Prepare the entry(ies) to record the cost of the ore mine.
2. Prepare the year-end adjusting entry if 90,000 tons of ore are mined and sold the first year.

QS 8-11
Classify assets
P3 P4

Which of the following assets are reported on the balance sheet as intangible assets? Which are reported as natural resources? (*a*) timberland, (*b*) patent, (*c*) leasehold, (*d*) Oil well, (*e*) equipment, (*f*) copyright, (*g*) franchise, (*h*) gold mine.

QS 8-12
Intangible assets and amortization P4

On January 4 of this year, Larsen Boutique incurs a $95,000 cost to modernize its store. Improvements include new floors, ceilings, wiring, and wall coverings. These improvements are estimated to yield benefits for 10 years. Larsen leases its store and has eight years remaining on the lease. Prepare the entry to record (1) the cost of modernization and (2) amortization at the end of this current year.

QS 8-13
Computing total asset turnover
A1

Eastman Company reports the following (dollar amounts are in thousands): net sales of $13,557 for 2011 and $12,670 for 2010; end-of-year total assets of $14,968 for 2011 and $18,810 for 2010. Compute its total asset turnover for 2011, and assess its level if competitors average a total asset turnover of 2.0 times.

QS 8-14^A
Asset exchange
P5

Esteban Co. owns a machine that costs $38,400 with accumulated depreciation of $20,400. Esteban exchanges the machine for a newer model that has a market value of $48,000. (1) Record the exchange assuming Esteban paid $32,000 cash and the exchange has commercial substance. (2) Record the exchange assuming Esteban pays $24,000 cash and the exchange lacks commercial substance.

QS 8-15
International accounting standards
C1 C3

Answer each of the following related to international accounting standards.
a. Accounting for plant assets involves cost determination, depreciation, additional expenditures, and disposals. Is plant asset accounting broadly similar or dissimilar between IFRS and U.S. GAAP? Identify one notable difference between IFRS and U.S. GAAP in accounting for plant assets.
b. Describe how IFRS and U.S. GAAP treat increases in the value of plant assets subsequent to their acquisition (but before their disposition).

EXERCISES

Exercise 8-1
Cost of plant assets
C1

Farha Co. purchases a machine for $11,500, terms 2/10, n/60, FOB shipping point. The seller prepaid the $260 freight charges, adding the amount to the invoice and bringing its total to $11,760. The machine requires special steel mounting and power connections costing $795. Another $375 is paid to assemble the machine and get it into operation. In moving the machine to its steel mounting, $190 in damages occurred. Materials costing $30 are used in adjusting the machine to produce a satisfactory product. The adjustments are normal for this machine and are not the result of the damages. Compute the cost recorded for this machine. (Farha pays for this machine within the cash discount period.)

Cerner Manufacturing purchases a large lot on which an old building is located as part of its plans to build a new plant. The negotiated purchase price is $225,000 for the lot plus $120,000 for the old building. The company pays $34,500 to tear down the old building and $51,000 to fill and level the lot. It also pays a total of $1,440,000 in construction costs—this amount consists of $1,354,500 for the new building and $85,500 for lighting and paving a parking area next to the building. Prepare a single journal entry to record these costs incurred by Cerner, all of which are paid in cash.

Exercise 8-2
Recording costs of assets
C1

Ming Yue Company pays $368,250 for real estate plus $19,600 in closing costs. The real estate consists of land appraised at $166,320; land improvements appraised at $55,440; and a building appraised at $174,240. Allocate the total cost among the three purchased assets and prepare the journal entry to record the purchase.

Exercise 8-3
Lump-sum purchase of plant assets C1

In early January 2011, LabTech purchases computer equipment for $147,000 to use in operating activities for the next four years. It estimates the equipment's salvage value at $30,000. Prepare a table showing depreciation and book value for each of the four years assuming straight-line depreciation.

Exercise 8-4
Straight-line depreciation P1

Refer to the information in Exercise 8-4. Prepare a table showing depreciation and book value for each of the four years assuming double-declining-balance depreciation.

Exercise 8-5
Double-declining-balance depreciation P1

Feng Company installs a computerized manufacturing machine in its factory at the beginning of the year at a cost of $42,300. The machine's useful life is estimated at 10 years, or 363,000 units of product, with a $6,000 salvage value. During its second year, the machine produces 35,000 units of product. Determine the machine's second-year depreciation under the straight-line method.

Exercise 8-6
Straight-line depreciation
P1

Refer to the information in Exercise 8-6. Determine the machine's second-year depreciation using the units-of-production method.

Exercise 8-7
Units-of-production depreciation
P1

Refer to the information in Exercise 8-6. Determine the machine's second-year depreciation using the double-declining-balance method.

Exercise 8-8
Double-declining-balance depreciation P1

On April 1, 2010, Stone's Backhoe Co. purchases a trencher for $250,000. The machine is expected to last five years and have a salvage value of $25,000. Compute depreciation expense for both 2010 and 2011 assuming the company uses the straight-line method.

Exercise 8-9
Straight-line, partial-year depreciation C2

Refer to the information in Exercise 8-9. Compute depreciation expense for both 2010 and 2011 assuming the company uses the double-declining-balance method.

Exercise 8-10
Double-declining-balance, partial-year depreciation C2

Supreme Fitness Club uses straight-line depreciation for a machine costing $21,750, with an estimated four-year life and a $2,250 salvage value. At the beginning of the third year, Supreme determines that the machine has three more years of remaining useful life, after which it will have an estimated $1,800 salvage value. Compute (1) the machine's book value at the end of its second year and (2) the amount of depreciation for each of the final three years given the revised estimates.

Exercise 8-11
Revising depreciation
C2

Check (2) $3,400

Mulan Enterprises pays $235,200 for equipment that will last five years and have a $52,500 salvage value. By using the equipment in its operations for five years, the company expects to earn $85,500 annually, after deducting all expenses except depreciation. Prepare a table showing income before depreciation, depreciation expense, and net (pretax) income for each year and for the total five-year period, assuming straight-line depreciation.

Exercise 8-12
Straight-line depreciation and income effects P1

Refer to the information in Exercise 8-12. Prepare a table showing income before depreciation, depreciation expense, and net (pretax) income for each year and for the total five-year period, assuming double-declining-balance depreciation is used.

Exercise 8-13
Double-declining-balance depreciation P1

Check Year 3 NI, $53,328

Exercise 8-14
Extraordinary repairs; plant asset age

C3

Check (3) $207,450

Passat Company owns a building that appears on its prior year-end balance sheet at its original $561,000 cost less $420,750 accumulated depreciation. The building is depreciated on a straight-line basis assuming a 20-year life and no salvage value. During the first week in January of the current calendar year, major structural repairs are completed on the building at a $67,200 cost. The repairs extend its useful life for 7 years beyond the 20 years originally estimated.

1. Determine the building's age (plant asset age) as of the prior year-end balance sheet date.
2. Prepare the entry to record the cost of the structural repairs that are paid in cash.
3. Determine the book value of the building immediately after the repairs are recorded.
4. Prepare the entry to record the current calendar year's depreciation.

Exercise 8-15
Ordinary repairs, extraordinary repairs and betterments

C3

Patterson Company pays $262,500 for equipment expected to last four years and have a $30,000 salvage value. Prepare journal entries to record the following costs related to the equipment.

1. During the second year of the equipment's life, $21,000 cash is paid for a new component expected to increase the equipment's productivity by 10% a year.
2. During the third year, $5,250 cash is paid for normal repairs necessary to keep the equipment in good working order.
3. During the fourth year, $13,950 is paid for repairs expected to increase the useful life of the equipment from four to five years.

Exercise 8-16
Disposal of assets

P2

Millworks Company owns a milling machine that cost $125,000 and has accumulated depreciation of $91,000. Prepare the entry to record the disposal of the milling machine on January 5 under each of the following independent situations.

1. The machine needed extensive repairs, and it was not worth repairing. Millworks disposed of the machine, receiving nothing in return.
2. Millworks sold the machine for $17,500 cash.
3. Millworks sold the machine for $34,000 cash.
4. Millworks sold the machine for $40,000 cash.

Exercise 8-17
Partial-year depreciation; disposal of plant asset

P2

Finesse Co. purchases and installs a machine on January 1, 2011, at a total cost of $92,750. Straight-line depreciation is taken each year for four years assuming a seven-year life and no salvage value. The machine is disposed of on July 1, 2015, during its fifth year of service. Prepare entries to record the partial year's depreciation on July 1, 2015, and to record the disposal under the following separate assumptions: (1) the machine is sold for $35,000 cash and (2) Finesse receives an insurance settlement of $30,000 resulting from the total destruction of the machine in a fire.

Exercise 8-18
Depletion of natural resources

P1 P3

On April 2, 2011, Idaho Mining Co. pays $3,633,750 for an ore deposit containing 1,425,000 tons. The company installs machinery in the mine costing $171,000, with an estimated seven-year life and no salvage value. The machinery will be abandoned when the ore is completely mined. Idaho begins mining on May 1, 2011, and mines and sells 156,200 tons of ore during the remaining eight months of 2011. Prepare the December 31, 2011, entries to record both the ore deposit depletion and the mining machinery depreciation. Mining machinery depreciation should be in proportion to the mine's depletion.

Exercise 8-19
Amortization of intangible assets

P4

Busch Gallery purchases the copyright on an oil painting for $236,700 on January 1, 2011. The copyright legally protects its owner for 12 more years. The company plans to market and sell prints of the original for 15 years. Prepare entries to record the purchase of the copyright on January 1, 2011, and its annual amortization on December 31, 2011.

Exercise 8-20
Goodwill

P4

On January 1, 2011, Timothy Company purchased Macys Company at a price of $3,750,000. The fair market value of the net assets purchased equals $2,700,000.

1. What is the amount of goodwill that Timothy records at the purchase date?
2. Explain how Timothy would determine the amount of goodwill amortization for the year ended December 31, 2011.
3. Timothy Company believes that its employees provide superior customer service, and through their efforts, Timothy Company believes it has created $1,350,000 of goodwill. How would Timothy Company record this goodwill?

Exercise 8-21
Cash flows related to assets
C1
Apple

Refer to the statement of cash flows for **Apple** in Appendix A for the fiscal year ended September 26, 2009, to answer the following.
1. What amount of cash is used to purchase property, plant, and equipment?
2. How much depreciation, amortization, and accretion are recorded?
3. What total amount of net cash is used in investing activities?

Exercise 8-22
Evaluating efficient use of assets
A1

Joy Co. reports net sales of $4,862,000 for 2010 and $7,542,000 for 2011. End-of-year balances for total assets are 2009, $1,586,000; 2010, $1,700,000; and 2011, $1,882,000. (*a*) Compute Joy's total asset turnover for 2010 and 2011. (*b*) Comment on Joy's efficiency in using its assets if its competitors average a total asset turnover of 3.0.

Exercise 8-23A
Exchanging assets
P5

Ramond Construction trades in an old tractor for a new tractor, receiving a $31,850 trade-in allowance and paying the remaining $93,275 in cash. The old tractor had cost $107,900, and straight-line accumulated depreciation of $58,500 had been recorded to date under the assumption that it would last eight years and have a $14,300 salvage value. Answer the following questions assuming the exchange has commercial substance.
1. What is the book value of the old tractor at the time of exchange?
2. What is the loss on this asset exchange?
3. What amount should be recorded (debited) in the asset account for the new tractor?

Check (2) $17,550

Exercise 8-24A
Recording plant asset disposals
P2 P5

On January 5, 2011, Holstrom Co. disposes of a machine costing $65,500 with accumulated depreciation of $35,284. Prepare the entries to record the disposal under each of the following separate assumptions.
1. The machine is sold for $25,343 cash.
2. The machine is traded in for a newer machine having an $86,125 cash price. A $31,912 trade-in allowance is received, and the balance is paid in cash. Assume the asset exchange lacks commercial substance.
3. The machine is traded in for a newer machine having an $86,125 cash price. A $23,393 trade-in allowance is received, and the balance is paid in cash. Assume the asset exchange has commercial substance.

Check (2) Dr. Machinery (new), $84,429

Exercise 8-25
Accounting for plant assets under IFRS
C2 P1 P2

Volkswagen Group reports the following information for property, plant and equipment as of December 31, 2008, along with additions, disposals, depreciation, and impairments for the year ended December 31, 2008 (euros in millions):

Property, plant and equipment, net	€23,121
Additions to property, plant and equipment	6,651
Disposals of property, plant and equipment	2,322
Depreciation on property, plant and equipment	4,625
Impairments to property, plant and equipment	184

1. Prepare Volkswagen's journal entry to record its depreciation for 2008.
2. Prepare Volkswagen's journal entry to record its additions for 2008 assuming they are paid in cash and are treated as "betterments (improvements)" to the assets.
3. Prepare Volkswagen's journal entry to record its €2,322 in disposals for 2008 assuming it receives €700 cash in return and the accumulated depreciation on the disposed assets totals €1,322.
4. Volkswagen reports €184 of impairments. Do these impairments increase or decrease the property, plant and equipment account? And, by what amount?

connect

PROBLEM SET A

Xavier Construction negotiates a lump-sum purchase of several assets from a company that is going out of business. The purchase is completed on January 1, 2011, at a total cash price of $787,500 for a building, land, land improvements, and four vehicles. The estimated market values of the assets are building, $408,000; land, $289,000; land improvements, $42,500; and four vehicles, $110,500. The company's fiscal year ends on December 31.

Problem 8-1A
Plant asset costs; depreciation methods C1 P1

mhhe.com/wildFA6e

Required
1. Prepare a table to allocate the lump-sum purchase price to the separate assets purchased (round percents to the nearest 1%). Prepare the journal entry to record the purchase.

Check (2) $23,490

(3) $15,750

2. Compute the depreciation expense for year 2011 on the building using the straight-line method, assuming a 15-year life and a $25,650 salvage value.

3. Compute the depreciation expense for year 2011 on the land improvements assuming a five-year life and double-declining-balance depreciation.

Analysis Component

4. Defend or refute this statement: Accelerated depreciation results in payment of less taxes over the asset's life.

Problem 8-2A
Asset cost allocation; straight-line depreciation

C1   P1

mhhe.com/wildFA6e

In January 2011, Keona Co. pays $2,800,000 for a tract of land with two buildings on it. It plans to demolish Building 1 and build a new store in its place. Building 2 will be a company office; it is appraised at $641,300, with a useful life of 20 years and an $80,000 salvage value. A lighted parking lot near Building 1 has improvements (Land Improvements 1) valued at $408,100 that are expected to last another 14 years with no salvage value. Without the buildings and improvements, the tract of land is valued at $1,865,600. The company also incurs the following additional costs:

Cost to demolish Building 1	$ 422,600
Cost of additional land grading	167,200
Cost to construct new building (Building 3), having a useful life of 25 years and a $390,100 salvage value	2,019,000
Cost of new land improvements (Land Improvements 2) near Building 2 having a 20-year useful life and no salvage value	158,000

Required

Check (1) Land costs, $2,381,800; Building 2 costs, $616,000

1. Prepare a table with the following column headings: Land, Building 2, Building 3, Land Improvements 1, and Land Improvements 2. Allocate the costs incurred by Keona to the appropriate columns and total each column (round percents to the nearest 1%).

2. Prepare a single journal entry to record all the incurred costs assuming they are paid in cash on January 1, 2011.

(3) Depr.—Land Improv. 1 and 2, $28,000 and $7,900

3. Using the straight-line method, prepare the December 31 adjusting entries to record depreciation for the 12 months of 2011 when these assets were in use.

Problem 8-3A
Computing and revising depreciation; revenue and capital expenditures

C1   C2   C3

Clarion Contractors completed the following transactions and events involving the purchase and operation of equipment in its business.

2010

Jan. 1   Paid $255,440 cash plus $15,200 in sales tax and $2,500 in transportation (FOB shipping point) for a new loader. The loader is estimated to have a four-year life and a $34,740 salvage value. Loader costs are recorded in the Equipment account.

Jan. 3   Paid $3,660 to enclose the cab and install air conditioning in the loader to enable operations under harsher conditions. This increased the estimated salvage value of the loader by another $1,110.

Check Dec. 31, 2010, Dr. Depr. Expense—Equip., $60,238

Dec. 31   Recorded annual straight-line depreciation on the loader.

2011

Jan. 1   Paid $4,500 to overhaul the loader's engine, which increased the loader's estimated useful life by two years.

Feb. 17   Paid $920 to repair the loader after the operator backed it into a tree.

Check Dec. 31, 2011, Dr. Depr. Expense—Equip., $37,042

Dec. 31   Recorded annual straight-line depreciation on the loader.

Required

Prepare journal entries to record these transactions and events.

Problem 8-4A
Computing and revising depreciation; selling plant assets

C2   P1   P2

Chen Company completed the following transactions and events involving its delivery trucks.

2010

Jan. 1   Paid $19,415 cash plus $1,165 in sales tax for a new delivery truck estimated to have a five-year life and a $3,000 salvage value. Delivery truck costs are recorded in the Trucks account.

Dec. 31   Recorded annual straight-line depreciation on the truck.

2011

Dec. 31 Due to new information obtained earlier in the year, the truck's estimated useful life was changed from five to four years, and the estimated salvage value was increased to $3,500. Recorded annual straight-line depreciation on the truck.

Check Dec. 31, 2011, Dr. Depr. Expense—Trucks, $4,521

2012

Dec. 31 Recorded annual straight-line depreciation on the truck.
Dec. 31 Sold the truck for $6,200 cash.

Dec. 31, 2012, Dr. Loss on Disposal of Trucks, $1,822

Required
Prepare journal entries to record these transactions and events.

A machine costing $210,000 with a four-year life and an estimated $20,000 salvage value is installed in Calhoon Company's factory on January 1. The factory manager estimates the machine will produce 475,000 units of product during its life. It actually produces the following units: year 1, 121,400; year 2, 122,400; year 3, 119,600; and year 4, 118,200. The total number of units produced by the end of year 4 exceeds the original estimate—this difference was not predicted. (The machine must not be depreciated below its estimated salvage value.)

Problem 8-5A
Depreciation methods
P1

Required
Prepare a table with the following column headings and compute depreciation for each year (and total depreciation of all years combined) for the machine under each depreciation method.

Year	Straight-Line	Units-of-Production	Double-Declining-Balance

Check Year 4: units-of-production depreciation, $44,640; DDB depreciation, $6,250

Saturn Co. purchases a used machine for $167,000 cash on January 2 and readies it for use the next day at an $3,420 cost. On January 3, it is installed on a required operating platform costing $1,080, and it is further readied for operations. The company predicts the machine will be used for six years and have a $14,600 salvage value. Depreciation is to be charged on a straight-line basis. On December 31, at the end of its fifth year in operations, it is disposed of.

Problem 8-6A
Disposal of plant assets
C1 P1 P2

Required

1. Prepare journal entries to record the machine's purchase and the costs to ready and install it. Cash is paid for all costs incurred.
2. Prepare journal entries to record depreciation of the machine at December 31 of (*a*) its first year in operations and (*b*) the year of its disposal.
3. Prepare journal entries to record the machine's disposal under each of the following separate assumptions: (*a*) it is sold for $13,500 cash; (*b*) it is sold for $45,000 cash; and (*c*) it is destroyed in a fire and the insurance company pays $24,000 cash to settle the loss claim.

Check (2*b*) Depr. Exp., $26,150

(3*c*) Dr. Loss from Fire, $16,750

On July 23 of the current year, Dakota Mining Co. pays $4,836,000 for land estimated to contain 7,800,000 tons of recoverable ore. It installs machinery costing $390,000 that has a 10-year life and no salvage value and is capable of mining the ore deposit in eight years. The machinery is paid for on July 25, seven days before mining operations begin. The company removes and sells 400,000 tons of ore during its first five months of operations ending on December 31. Depreciation of the machinery is in proportion to the mine's depletion as the machinery will be abandoned after the ore is mined.

Problem 8-7A
Natural resources
P3

Required
Prepare entries to record (*a*) the purchase of the land, (*b*) the cost and installation of machinery, (*c*) the first five months' depletion assuming the land has a net salvage value of zero after the ore is mined, and (*d*) the first five months' depreciation on the machinery.

Check (*c*) Depletion, $248,000
(*d*) Depreciation, $20,000

Analysis Component
Describe both the similarities and differences in amortization, depletion, and depreciation.

Problem 8-8A
Intangible assets

P4

On July 1, 2006, Sweetman Company signed a contract to lease space in a building for 15 years. The lease contract calls for annual (prepaid) rental payments of $70,000 on each July 1 throughout the life of the lease and for the lessee to pay for all additions and improvements to the leased property. On June 25, 2011, Sweetman decides to sublease the space to Kirk & Associates for the remaining 10 years of the lease—Kirk pays $185,000 to Sweetman for the right to sublease and it agrees to assume the obligation to pay the $70,000 annual rent to the building owner beginning July 1, 2011. After taking possession of the leased space, Kirk pays for improving the office portion of the leased space at a $129,840 cost. The improvements are paid for by Kirk on July 5, 2011, and are estimated to have a useful life equal to the 16 years remaining in the life of the building.

Required

1. Prepare entries for Kirk to record (*a*) its payment to Sweetman for the right to sublease the building space, (*b*) its payment of the 2011 annual rent to the building owner, and (*c*) its payment for the office improvements.

Check Dr. Rent Expense for (2*a*) $9,250, (2*c*) $35,000

2. Prepare Kirk's year-end adjusting entries required at December 31, 2011, to (*a*) amortize the $185,000 cost of the sublease, (*b*) amortize the office improvements, and (*c*) record rent expense.

PROBLEM SET B

Problem 8-1B
Plant asset costs; depreciation methods

C1 P1

Racerback Company negotiates a lump-sum purchase of several assets from a contractor who is relocating. The purchase is completed on January 1, 2011, at a total cash price of $1,610,000 for a building, land, land improvements, and six trucks. The estimated market values of the assets are building, $784,800; land, $540,640; land improvements, $226,720; and six trucks, $191,840. The company's fiscal year ends on December 31.

Required

1. Prepare a table to allocate the lump-sum purchase price to the separate assets purchased (round percents to the nearest 1%). Prepare the journal entry to record the purchase.

Check (2) $52,000

2. Compute the depreciation expense for year 2011 on the building using the straight-line method, assuming a 12-year life and a $100,500 salvage value.

(3) $41,860

3. Compute the depreciation expense for year 2011 on the land improvements assuming a 10-year life and double-declining-balance depreciation.

Analysis Component

4. Defend or refute this statement: Accelerated depreciation results in payment of more taxes over the asset's life.

Problem 8-2B
Asset cost allocation; straight-line depreciation

C1 P1

In January 2011, InTech Co. pays $1,350,000 for a tract of land with two buildings. It plans to demolish Building A and build a new shop in its place. Building B will be a company office; it is appraised at $472,770, with a useful life of 15 years and a $90,000 salvage value. A lighted parking lot near Building B has improvements (Land Improvements B) valued at $125,145 that are expected to last another six years with no salvage value. Without the buildings and improvements, the tract of land is valued at $792,585. The company also incurs the following additional costs.

Cost to demolish Building A	$ 117,000
Cost of additional land grading	172,500
Cost to construct new building (Building C), having a useful life of 20 years and a $295,500 salvage value	1,356,000
Cost of new land improvements (Land Improvements C) near Building C, having a 10-year useful life and no salvage value	101,250

Required

Check (1) Land costs, $1,059,000; Building B costs, $459,000

1. Prepare a table with the following column headings: Land, Building B, Building C, Land Improvements B, and Land Improvements C. Allocate the costs incurred by InTech to the appropriate columns and total each column (round percents to the nearest 1%).

2. Prepare a single journal entry to record all incurred costs assuming they are paid in cash on January 1, 2011.

(3) Depr.—Land Improv. B and C, $20,250 and $10,125

3. Using the straight-line method, prepare the December 31 adjusting entries to record depreciation for the 12 months of 2011 when these assets were in use.

Problem 8-3B
Computing and revising depreciation; revenue and capital expenditures
C1 C2 C3

Xpress Delivery Service completed the following transactions and events involving the purchase and operation of equipment for its business.

2010

Jan. 1 Paid $24,950 cash plus $1,950 in sales tax for a new delivery van that was estimated to have a five-year life and a $3,400 salvage value. Van costs are recorded in the Equipment account.
Jan. 3 Paid $1,550 to install sorting racks in the van for more accurate and quicker delivery of packages. This increases the estimated salvage value of the van by another $200.
Dec. 31 Recorded annual straight-line depreciation on the van.

Check Dec. 31, 2010, Dr. Depr. Expense—Equip., $4,970

2011

Jan. 1 Paid $1,970 to overhaul the van's engine, which increased the van's estimated useful life by two years.
May 10 Paid $600 to repair the van after the driver backed it into a loading dock.
Dec. 31 Record annual straight-line depreciation on the van. (Round to the nearest dollar.)

Check Dec. 31, 2011, Dr. Depr. Expense—Equip., $3,642

Required

Prepare journal entries to record these transactions and events.

Field Instruments completed the following transactions and events involving its machinery.

Problem 8-4B
Computing and revising depreciation; selling plant assets
C2 P1 P2

2010

Jan. 1 Paid $106,600 cash plus $6,400 in sales tax for a new machine. The machine is estimated to have a six-year life and a $9,800 salvage value.
Dec. 31 Recorded annual straight-line depreciation on the machinery.

2011

Dec. 31 Due to new information obtained earlier in the year, the machine's estimated useful life was changed from six to four years, and the estimated salvage value was increased to $13,050. Recorded annual straight-line depreciation on the machinery.

Check Dec. 31, 2011, Dr. Depr. Expense—Machinery, $27,583

2012

Dec. 31 Recorded annual straight-line depreciation on the machinery.
Dec. 31 Sold the machine for $25,240 cash.

Dec. 31, 2012, Dr. Loss on Disposal of Machinery, $15,394

Required

Prepare journal entries to record these transactions and events.

On January 2, Gannon Co. purchases and installs a new machine costing $312,000 with a five-year life and an estimated $28,000 salvage value. Management estimates the machine will produce 1,136,000 units of product during its life. Actual production of units is as follows: year 1, 245,600; year 2, 230,400; year 3, 227,000; year 4, 232,600; and year 5, 211,200. The total number of units produced by the end of year 5 exceeds the original estimate—this difference was not predicted. (The machine must not be depreciated below its estimated salvage value.)

Problem 8-5B
Depreciation methods
P1

Required

Prepare a table with the following column headings and compute depreciation for each year (and total depreciation of all years combined) for the machine under each depreciation method.

Year	Straight-Line	Units-of-Production	Double-Declining-Balance

Check DDB Depreciation, Year 3, $44,928; U-of-P Depreciation, Year 4, $58,150

On January 1, Jefferson purchases a used machine for $130,000 and readies it for use the next day at a cost of $3,390. On January 4, it is mounted on a required operating platform costing $4,800, and it is further readied for operations. Management estimates the machine will be used for seven years and have an $18,000 salvage value. Depreciation is to be charged on a straight-line basis. On December 31, at the end of its sixth year of use, the machine is disposed of.

Problem 8-6B
Disposal of plant assets
C1 P1 P2

Required

1. Prepare journal entries to record the machine's purchase and the costs to ready and install it. Cash is paid for all costs incurred.
2. Prepare journal entries to record depreciation of the machine at December 31 of (*a*) its first year in operations and (*b*) the year of its disposal.
3. Prepare journal entries to record the machine's disposal under each of the following separate assumptions: (*a*) it is sold for $30,000 cash; (*b*) it is sold for $50,000 cash; and (*c*) it is destroyed in a fire and the insurance company pays $20,000 cash to settle the loss claim.

Check (2*b*) Depr. Exp., $17,170

(3*c*) Dr. Loss from Fire, $15,170

Problem 8-7B
Natural resources
P3

On February 19 of the current year, Rock Chalk Co. pays $4,450,000 for land estimated to contain 5 million tons of recoverable ore. It installs machinery costing $200,000 that has a 16-year life and no salvage value and is capable of mining the ore deposit in 12 years. The machinery is paid for on March 21, eleven days before mining operations begin. The company removes and sells 352,000 tons of ore during its first nine months of operations ending on December 31. Depreciation of the machinery is in proportion to the mine's depletion as the machinery will be abandoned after the ore is mined.

Required

Prepare entries to record (*a*) the purchase of the land, (*b*) the cost and installation of the machinery, (*c*) the first nine months' depletion assuming the land has a net salvage value of zero after the ore is mined, and (*d*) the first nine months' depreciation on the machinery.

Check (*c*) Depletion, $313,280; (*d*) Depreciation, $14,080

Analysis Component

Describe both the similarities and differences in amortization, depletion, and depreciation.

Problem 8-8B
Intangible assets
P4

On January 1, 2004, Liberty Co. entered into a 12-year lease on a building. The lease contract requires (1) annual (prepaid) rental payments of $26,400 each January 1 throughout the life of the lease and (2) for the lessee to pay for all additions and improvements to the leased property. On January 1, 2011, Liberty decides to sublease the space to Moberly Co. for the remaining five years of the lease—Moberly pays $30,000 to Liberty for the right to sublease and agrees to assume the obligation to pay the $26,400 annual rent to the building owner beginning January 1, 2011. After taking possession of the leased space, Moberly pays for improving the office portion of the leased space at an $18,000 cost. The improvements are paid for by Moberly on January 3, 2011, and are estimated to have a useful life equal to the 13 years remaining in the life of the building.

Required

1. Prepare entries for Moberly to record (*a*) its payment to Liberty for the right to sublease the building space, (*b*) its payment of the 2011 annual rent to the building owner, and (*c*) its payment for the office improvements.
2. Prepare Moberly's year-end adjusting entries required on December 31, 2011, to (*a*) amortize the $30,000 cost of the sublease, (*b*) amortize the office improvements, and (*c*) record rent expense.

Check Dr. Rent Expense: (2*a*) $6,000, (2*c*) $26,400

SERIAL PROBLEM
Business Solutions
P1 A1

(This serial problem began in Chapter 1 and continues through most of the book. If previous chapter segments were not completed, the serial problem can begin at this point. It is helpful, but not necessary, to use the Working Papers that accompany the book.)

SP 8 Selected ledger account balances for Business Solutions follow.

	For Three Months Ended December 31, 2011	For Three Months Ended March 31, 2012
Office equipment	$ 8,000	$ 8,000
Accumulated depreciation—Office equipment	400	800
Computer equipment	20,000	20,000
Accumulated depreciation—Computer equipment	1,250	2,500
Total revenue	31,284	44,000
Total assets	83,460	120,268

Required

1. Assume that Business Solutions does not acquire additional office equipment or computer equipment in 2012. Compute amounts for *the year ended* December 31, 2012, for Depreciation Expense—Office Equipment and for Depreciation Expense—Computer Equipment (assume use of the straight-line method).
2. Given the assumptions in part 1, what is the book value of both the office equipment and the computer equipment as of December 31, 2012?
3. Compute the three-month total asset turnover for Business Solutions as of March 31, 2012. Use total revenue for the numerator and average the December 31, 2011, total assets and the March 31, 2012, total assets for the denominator. Interpret its total asset turnover if competitors average 2.5 for annual periods. (Round turnover to two decimals.)

Check (3) Three-month (annual) turnover = 0.43 (1.73 annual)

Beyond the Numbers

BTN 8-1 Refer to the financial statements of **Research In Motion** in Appendix A to answer the following.
1. What percent of the original cost of RIM's property, plant and equipment remains to be depreciated as of February 27, 2010, and at February 28, 2009? Assume these assets have no salvage value.
2. Over what length(s) of time is RIM depreciating its major categories of property, plant and equipment?
3. What is the change in total property, plant and equipment (before accumulated depreciation) for the year ended February 27, 2010? What is the amount of cash provided (used) by investing activities for property, plant and equipment for the year ended February 27, 2010? What is one possible explanation for the difference between these two amounts?
4. Compute its total asset turnover for the year ended February 27, 2010, and the year ended February 28, 2009. Assume total assets at March 1, 2008, are $5,511 ($ millions).

REPORTING IN ACTION
A1
RIM

Fast Forward

5. Access RIM's financial statements for fiscal years ending after February 27, 2010, at its Website (**RIM.com**) or the SEC's EDGAR database (**www.sec.gov**). Recompute RIM's total asset turnover for the additional years' data you collect. Comment on any differences relative to the turnover computed in part 4.

BTN 8-2 Comparative figures for **Research In Motion** and **Apple** follow.

COMPARATIVE ANALYSIS
A1
RIM
Apple

	Research In Motion			Apple		
($ millions)	Current Year	One Year Prior	Two Years Prior	Current Year	One Year Prior	Two Years Prior
Total assets	$10,204	$ 8,101	$5,511	$47,501	$36,171	$25,347
Net sales	14,953	11,065	6,009	42,905	37,491	24,578

Required

1. Compute total asset turnover for the most recent two years for Research In Motion and Apple using the data shown.
2. Which company is more efficient in generating net sales given the total assets it employs? Assume an industry average of 1.0 for asset turnover.

BTN 8-3 Flo Choi owns a small business and manages its accounting. Her company just finished a year in which a large amount of borrowed funds was invested in a new building addition as well as in equipment and fixture additions. Choi's banker requires her to submit semiannual financial statements so he can monitor the financial health of her business. He has warned her that if profit margins erode, he might raise the interest rate on the borrowed funds to reflect the increased loan risk from the bank's point of view. Choi knows profit margin is likely to decline this year. As she prepares year-end adjusting entries, she decides to apply the following depreciation rule: All asset additions are considered to be in use on the first day of the following month. (The previous rule assumed assets are in use on the first day of the month nearest to the purchase date.)

ETHICS CHALLENGE
C1

Chapter 8 Reporting and Analyzing Long-Term Assets

Required

1. Identify decisions that managers like Choi must make in applying depreciation methods.
2. Is Choi's rule an ethical violation, or is it a legitimate decision in computing depreciation?
3. How will Choi's new depreciation rule affect the profit margin of her business?

COMMUNICATING IN PRACTICE
A1

BTN 8-4 Teams are to select an industry, and each team member is to select a different company in that industry. Each team member is to acquire the financial statements (Form 10-K) of the company selected—see the company's Website or the SEC's EDGAR database (www.sec.gov). Use the financial statements to compute total asset turnover. Communicate with teammates via a meeting, e-mail, or telephone to discuss the meaning of this ratio, how different companies compare to each other, and the industry norm. The team must prepare a one-page report that describes the ratios for each company and identifies the conclusions reached during the team's discussion.

TAKING IT TO THE NET
P4

BTN 8-5 Access the **Yahoo!** (ticker: YHOO) 10-K report for the year ended December 31, 2009, filed on February 26, 2010, at www.sec.gov.

Required

1. What amount of goodwill is reported on Yahoo!'s balance sheet? What percentage of total assets does its goodwill represent? Is goodwill a major asset for Yahoo!? Explain.
2. Locate Note 5 to its financial statements. Identify the change in goodwill from December 31, 2008, to December 31, 2009. Comment on the change in goodwill over this period.
3. Locate Note 6 to its financial statements. What are the three categories of intangible assets that Yahoo! reports at December 31, 2009? What proportion of total assets do the intangibles represent?
4. What does Yahoo! indicate is the life of "Trade names, trademarks, and domain names" according to its Note 6? Comment on the difference between the estimated useful life and the legal life of Yahoo!'s trademark.

TEAMWORK IN ACTION
P1

BTN 8-6 Each team member is to become an expert on one depreciation method to facilitate teammates' understanding of that method. Follow these procedures:

a. Each team member is to select an area for expertise from one of the following depreciation methods: straight-line, units-of-production, or double-declining-balance.
b. Expert teams are to be formed from those who have selected the same area of expertise. The instructor will identify the location where each expert team meets.
c. Using the following data, expert teams are to collaborate and develop a presentation answering the requirements. Expert team members must write the presentation in a format they can show to their learning teams.

Data and Requirements On January 8, 2009, Waverly Riders purchases a van to transport rafters back to the point of departure at the conclusion of the rafting adventures they operate. The cost of the van is $44,000. It has an estimated salvage value of $2,000 and is expected to be used for four years and driven 60,000 miles. The van is driven 12,000 miles in 2009, 18,000 miles in 2010, 21,000 in 2011, and 10,000 in 2012.

1. Compute the annual depreciation expense for each year of the van's estimated useful life.
2. Explain when and how annual depreciation is recorded.
3. Explain the impact on income of this depreciation method versus others over the van's life.
4. Identify the van's book value for each year of its life and illustrate the reporting of this amount for any one year.

d. Re-form original learning teams. In rotation, experts are to present to their teams the results from part c. Experts are to encourage and respond to questions.

Point: This activity can follow an overview of each method. Step 1 allows for three areas of expertise. Larger teams will have some duplication of areas, but the straight-line choice should not be duplicated. Expert teams can use the book and consult with the instructor.

ENTREPRENEURIAL DECISION
A1

BTN 8-7 Review the chapter's opening feature involving **Games2U**. Assume that the company currently has net sales of $8,000,000, and that it is planning an expansion that will increase net sales by $4,000,000. To accomplish this expansion, Games2U must increase its average total assets from $2,500,000 to $3,000,000.

Required

1. Compute the company's total asset turnover under (a) current conditions and (b) proposed conditions.
2. Evaluate and comment on the merits of the proposal given your analysis in part 1. Identify any concerns you would express about the proposal.

Chapter 8 Reporting and Analyzing Long-Term Assets

BTN 8-8 Team up with one or more classmates for this activity. Identify companies in your community or area that must account for at least one of the following assets: natural resource; patent; lease; leasehold improvement; copyright; trademark; or goodwill. You might find a company having more than one type of asset. Once you identify a company with a specific asset, describe the accounting this company uses to allocate the cost of that asset to the periods benefited from its use.

HITTING THE ROAD
P3 P4

BTN 8-9 Nokia (www.Nokia.com), Research In Motion, and Apple are all competitors in the global marketplace. Comparative figures for these companies' recent annual accounting periods follow.

GLOBAL DECISION
A1

NOKIA
RIM
Apple

(in millions, except turnover)	Nokia (EUR millions) Current Year	Prior Year	Two Years Prior	Research In Motion Current Year	Prior Year	Apple Current Year	Prior Year
Total assets	35,738	39,582	37,599	$10,204	$ 8,101	$47,501	$36,171
Net sales	40,984	50,710	51,058	14,953	11,065	42,905	37,491
Total asset turnover	?	?	—	1.63	1.63	1.03	1.22

Required
1. Compute total asset turnover for the most recent two years for Nokia using the data shown.
2. Which company is most efficient in generating net sales given the total assets it employs?

ANSWERS TO MULTIPLE CHOICE QUIZ

1. b;

	Appraisal Value	%	Total Cost	Allocated
Land	$175,000	50%	$326,000	$163,000
Land improvements	70,000	20	326,000	65,200
Building	105,000	30	326,000	97,800
Totals	$350,000			$326,000

2. c; ($35,000 − $1,000)/4 years = $8,500 per year.
3. c; 2011: $10,800,000 × (2 × 10%) = $2,160,000
   2012: ($10,800,000 − $2,160,000) × (2 × 10%) = $1,728,000
4. c;

Cost of machine	$250,000
Accumulated depreciation	100,000
Book value	150,000
Cash received	120,000
Loss on sale	$ 30,000

5. b; $550,000/$500,000 = 1.10

A Look Back	A Look at This Chapter	A Look Ahead
Chapter 8 focused on long-term assets including plant assets, natural resources, and intangibles. We showed how to account for and analyze those assets.	This chapter explains how to identify, compute, record, and report current liabilities in financial statements. We also analyze and interpret these liabilities, including those related to employee costs.	Chapter 10 focuses on long-term liabilities. We explain how to value, record, amortize, and report these liabilities in financial statements.

9 Reporting and Analyzing Current Liabilities

Learning Objectives

CAP

CONCEPTUAL

- **C1** Describe current and long-term liabilities and their characteristics. (p. 370)
- **C2** Identify and describe known current liabilities. (p. 372)
- **C3** Explain how to account for contingent liabilities. (p. 382)

ANALYTICAL

- **A1** Compute the times interest earned ratio and use it to analyze liabilities. (p. 384)

PROCEDURAL

- **P1** Prepare entries to account for short-term notes payable. (p. 373)
- **P2** Compute and record *employee* payroll deductions and liabilities. (p. 376)
- **P3** Compute and record *employer* payroll expenses and liabilities. (p. 377)
- **P4** Account for estimated liabilities, including warranties and bonuses. (p. 379)
- **P5** *Appendix 9A*—Identify and describe the details of payroll reports, records, and procedures. (p. 387)

LP9

Decision Insight

No Stuffed Shirts

"Part of the fun is the journey . . . working til 2 am every day."
—MATT WALLS

ATLANTA, GA—Brothers Matt and Bryan Walls never planned to be entrepreneurs in the T-shirt business. "[It was] an idea we had while hanging out in our parents' basement," explains Matt. "We were naive and, like many first-time entrepreneurs, just dove right in." Matt and Bryan's plans involved making T-shirts with visual humor and pop culture themes. Their company, **SnorgTees (SnorgTees.com),** had a shaky start but soon found its groove with best-selling T-shirts such as "With a shirt like this, who needs pants?" "Don't act like you're not impressed," and "I'm kind of a big deal."

"We dreamed it would be successful overnight," recalls Matt. "But when things first started we had a huge reality check, and at that point I don't know if I believed." Today their business is thriving. Their commitment to success carries over to the financial side. They especially focus on the important task of managing liabilities for payroll, supplies, employee benefits, training, and taxes. Both insist that effective management of liabilities, especially payroll and employee benefits, is crucial. They stress that monitoring and controlling liabilities are a must.

To help control liabilities, Matt and Bryan describe how they began by working out of their parents' home to reduce liabilities. "Most people think all we do is sit around and think up funny ideas," explains Matt. "In reality most of the time is spent on executing projects and managing the business . . . [including] order fulfillment, supply chain management, marketing, and accounting." In short, creative reduction of liabilities can mean success or failure.

The two continue to monitor liabilities and their payment patterns. "I'm pretty conservative about spending money," admits Matt. "If you want to run a successful company, you can't forget all the details." The two insist that accounting for and monitoring liabilities are one key to a successful start-up. Their company now generates sufficient income to pay for liabilities and produces revenue growth for expansion. "We plan to keep having fun," insists Matt. "We do business with people all over the world."

[Sources: *SnorgTees Website,* January 2012; *Entrepreneur,* September 2009; *RetireAt21.com,* October 2008; *Business to Business,* January 2008; *WannaBeMogul.com,* November 2007; *SweetStrangers.com,* February 2011]

Chapter Preview

Previous chapters introduced liabilities such as accounts payable, notes payable, wages payable, and unearned revenues. This chapter further explains these liabilities and additional ones such as warranties, taxes, payroll, vacation pay, and bonuses. It also describes contingent liabilities and introduces long-term liabilities. The focus is on how to define, classify, measure, report, and analyze these liabilities so that this information is useful to business decision makers.

Reporting and Analyzing Current Liabilities

Liability Characteristics	Known Liabilities	Estimated Liabilities	Contingent Liabilities
• Definition • Classification • Uncertainty	• Accounts payable • Sales taxes payable • Unearned revenues • Short-term notes • Payroll liabilities	• Health and pension benefits • Vacation benefits • Bonus plans • Warranty liabilities	• Accounting for contingencies • Reasonably possible contingencies

CHARACTERISTICS OF LIABILITIES

This section discusses important characteristics of liabilities and how liabilities are classified and reported.

Defining Liabilities

C1 Describe current and long-term liabilities and their characteristics.

A *liability* is a probable future payment of assets or services that a company is presently obligated to make as a result of past transactions or events. This definition includes three crucial factors:

1. A past transaction or event.
2. A present obligation.
3. A future payment of assets or services.

These three important elements are portrayed visually in Exhibit 9.1. Liabilities reported in financial statements exhibit those characteristics. No liability is reported when one or more of those characteristics is absent. For example, most companies expect to pay wages to their employees in upcoming months and years, but these future payments are *not* liabilities because no past event such as employee work resulted in a present obligation. Instead, such liabilities arise when employees perform their work and earn the wages.

EXHIBIT 9.1

Characteristics of a Liability

Due to a past event ... → Company has a present obligation → ... For future sacrifices

Past — Present — Future

Classifying Liabilities

Information about liabilities is more useful when the balance sheet identifies them as either current or long term. Decision makers need to know when obligations are due so they can plan for them and take appropriate action.

Current Liabilities Current liabilities, also called *short-term liabilities,* are obligations due within one year or the company's operating cycle, whichever is longer. They are expected to be paid using current assets or by creating other current liabilities. Common examples of current liabilities are accounts payable, short-term notes payable, wages payable, warranty liabilities, lease liabilities, taxes payable, and unearned revenues.

Current liabilities differ across companies because they depend on the type of company operations. **MGM Mirage**, for instance, included the following current liabilities related to its gaming, hospitality, and entertainment operations ($000s):

Advance deposits and ticket sales	$104,911
Casino outstanding chip liability	83,957
Casino front money deposits	80,944

Harley-Davidson reports a much different set of current liabilities. It discloses current liabilities made up of items such as warranty, recall, and dealer incentive liabilities.

Point: Improper classification of liabilities can distort ratios used in financial statement analysis and business decisions.

Long-Term Liabilities A company's obligations not expected to be paid within the longer of one year or the company's operating cycle are reported as **long-term liabilities.** They can include long-term notes payable, warranty liabilities, lease liabilities, and bonds payable. They are sometimes reported on the balance sheet in a single long-term liabilities total or in multiple categories. **Domino's Pizza**, for instance, reports long-term liabilities of $1,555 million. They are reported after current liabilities. A single liability also can be divided between the current and noncurrent sections if a company expects to make payments toward it in both the short and long term. Domino's reports ($ millions) long-term debt, $1,522; and current portion of long-term debt, $50. The second item is reported in current liabilities. We sometimes see liabilities that do not have a fixed due date but instead are payable on the creditor's demand. These are reported as current liabilities because of the possibility of payment in the near term. Exhibit 9.2 shows amounts of current liabilities and as a percent of total liabilities for selected companies.

Point: The current ratio is overstated if a company fails to classify any portion of long-term debt due next period as a current liability.

Company	Amount	As a percent of total liabilities
Six Flags	$443 mil.	16%
Bowl America	$3.2 mil.	54%
Columbia Sportswear	$179 mil.	83%
Apple	$19,282 mil.	74%

EXHIBIT 9.2

Current Liabilities of Selected Companies

Uncertainty in Liabilities

Accounting for liabilities involves addressing three important questions: Whom to pay? When to pay? How much to pay? Answers to these questions are often decided when a liability is incurred. For example, if a company has a $100 account payable to a specific individual, payable on March 15, the answers are clear. The company knows whom to pay, when to pay, and how much to pay. However, the answers to one or more of these questions are uncertain for some liabilities.

Uncertainty in Whom to Pay Liabilities can involve uncertainty in whom to pay. For instance, a company can create a liability with a known amount when issuing a note that is payable to its holder. In this case, a specific amount is payable to the note's holder at a specified date, but the company does not know who the holder is until that date. Despite this uncertainty, the company reports this liability on its balance sheet.

Point: An *accrued expense* is an unpaid expense, and is also called an *accrued liability.*

Uncertainty in When to Pay A company can have an obligation of a known amount to a known creditor but not know when it must be paid. For example, a legal services firm can accept fees in advance from a client who plans to use the firm's services in the future. This means that the firm has a liability that it settles by providing services at an unknown future date. Although this uncertainty exists, the legal firm's balance sheet must report this liability. These types of obligations are reported as current liabilities because they are likely to be settled in the short term.

Uncertainty in How Much to Pay A company can be aware of an obligation but not know how much will be required to settle it. For example, a company using electrical power is billed only after the meter has been read. This cost is incurred and the liability created before a bill is received. A liability to the power company is reported as an estimated amount if the balance sheet is prepared before a bill arrives.

IFRS

IFRS records a contingent liability when an obligation exists from a past event if there is a 'probable' outflow of resources and the amount can be estimated reliably. However, IFRS defines probable as 'more likely than not' while U.S. GAAP defines it as 'likely to occur.'

Quick Check
Answers — p. 395

1. What is a liability? Identify its crucial characteristics.
2. Is every expected future payment a liability?
3. If a liability is payable in 15 months, is it classified as current or long term?

KNOWN LIABILITIES

C2 Identify and describe known current liabilities.

Most liabilities arise from situations with little uncertainty. They are set by agreements, contracts, or laws and are measurable. These liabilities are **known liabilities,** also called *definitely determinable liabilities.* Known liabilities include accounts payable, notes payable, payroll, sales taxes, unearned revenues, and leases. We describe how to account for these known liabilities in this section.

Accounts Payable

Accounts payable, or trade accounts payable, are amounts owed to suppliers for products or services purchased on credit. Accounting for accounts payable is primarily explained and illustrated in our discussion of merchandising activities in Chapters 4 and 5.

Sales Taxes Payable

Nearly all states and many cities levy taxes on retail sales. Sales taxes are stated as a percent of selling prices. The seller collects sales taxes from customers when sales occur and remits these collections (often monthly) to the proper government agency. Since sellers currently owe these collections to the government, this amount is a current liability. **Home Depot**, for instance, reports sales taxes payable of $362 million in its recent annual report. To illustrate, if Home Depot sells materials on August 31 for $6,000 cash that are subject to a 5% sales tax, the revenue portion of this transaction is recorded as follows:

Assets = Liabilities + Equity
+6,300   +300   +6,000

Aug. 31	Cash	6,300	
	Sales		6,000
	Sales Taxes Payable ($6,000 × 0.05)		300
	To record cash sales and 5% sales tax.		

Sales Taxes Payable is debited and Cash credited when it remits these collections to the government. Sales Taxes Payable is not an expense. It arises because laws require sellers to collect this cash from customers for the government.[1]

Unearned Revenues

Unearned revenues (also called *deferred revenues, collections in advance,* and *prepayments*) are amounts received in advance from customers for future products or services. Advance ticket sales for sporting events or music concerts are examples. **Beyoncé**, for instance, has "deferred revenues" from advance ticket sales. To illustrate, assume that Beyoncé sells $5 million in tickets for eight concerts; the entry is

June 30	Cash	5,000,000	
	Unearned Ticket Revenue		5,000,000
	To record sale of concert tickets.		

Point: To *defer* a revenue means to postpone recognition of a revenue collected in advance until it is earned. Sport teams must defer recognition of ticket sales until games are played.

Assets = Liabilities + Equity
+5,000,000   +5,000,000

When a concert is played, Beyoncé would record revenue for the portion earned.

Oct. 31	Unearned Ticket Revenue	625,000	
	Ticket Revenue		625,000
	To record concert ticket revenues earned.		

Assets = Liabilities + Equity
           −625,000   +625,000

Unearned Ticket Revenue is an unearned revenue account and is reported as a current liability. Unearned revenues also arise with airline ticket sales, magazine subscriptions, construction projects, hotel reservations, and custom orders.

Decision Insight

Reward Programs Gift card sales now exceed $100 billion annually, and reward (also called loyalty) programs are growing. There are no exact rules for how retailers account for rewards. When **Best Buy** launched its "Reward Zone," shoppers earned $5 on each $125 spent and had 90 days to spend it. Retailers make assumptions about how many reward program dollars will be spent and how to report it. Best Buy sets up a liability and reduces revenue by the same amount. **Talbots** does not reduce revenue but instead increases selling expense. **Men's Wearhouse** records rewards in cost of goods sold, whereas **Neiman Marcus** subtracts them from revenue. The FASB continues to review reward programs. ■

Short-Term Notes Payable

A **short-term note payable** is a written promise to pay a specified amount on a definite future date within one year or the company's operating cycle, whichever is longer. These promissory notes are negotiable (as are checks), meaning they can be transferred from party to party by endorsement. The written documentation provided by notes is helpful in resolving disputes and for pursuing legal actions involving these liabilities. Most notes payable bear interest to compensate for use of the money until payment is made. Short-term notes payable can arise from many transactions. A company that purchases merchandise on credit can sometimes extend the credit period by signing a note to replace an account payable. Such notes also can arise when money is borrowed from a bank. We describe both of these cases.

P1 Prepare entries to account for short-term notes payable.

Point: Required characteristics for negotiability of a note: (1) unconditional promise, (2) in writing, (3) specific amount, and (4) definite due date.

---

[1] Sales taxes can be computed from total sales receipts when sales taxes are not separately identified on the register. To illustrate, assume a 5% sales tax and $420 in total sales receipts (which includes sales taxes). Sales are computed as follows:

Sales = Total sales receipts/(1 + Sales tax percentage) = $420/1.05 = $400

Thus, the sales tax amount equals total sales receipts minus sales, or $420 − $400 = $20.

Note Given to Extend Credit Period A company can replace an account payable with a note payable. A common example is a creditor that requires the substitution of an interest-bearing note for an overdue account payable that does not bear interest. A less common situation occurs when a debtor's weak financial condition motivates the creditor to accept a note, sometimes for a lesser amount, and to close the account to ensure that this customer makes no additional credit purchases.

To illustrate, let's assume that on August 23, Brady Company asks to extend its past-due $600 account payable to McGraw. After some negotiations, McGraw agrees to accept $100 cash and a 60-day, 12%, $500 note payable to replace the account payable. Brady records the transaction with this entry:

Assets = Liabilities + Equity
−100   −600
          +500

Aug. 23	Accounts Payable—McGraw	600	
	Cash		100
	Notes Payable—McGraw		500
	Gave $100 cash and a 60-day, 12% note for payment on account.		

Point: Accounts payable are detailed in a subsidiary ledger, but notes payable are sometimes not. A file with copies of notes can serve as a subsidiary ledger.

Signing the note does not resolve Brady's debt. Instead, the form of debt is changed from an account payable to a note payable. McGraw prefers the note payable over the account payable because it earns interest and it is written documentation of the debt's existence, term, and amount. When the note comes due, Brady pays the note and interest by giving McGraw a check for $510. Brady records that payment with this entry:

Assets = Liabilities + Equity
−510   −500   −10

Oct. 22	Notes Payable—McGraw	500	
	Interest Expense	10	
	Cash		510
	Paid note with interest ($500 × 12% × 60/360).		

Point: Commercial companies commonly compute interest using a 360-day year. This is known as the *banker's rule*.

Interest expense is computed by multiplying the principal of the note ($500) by the annual interest rate (12%) for the fraction of the year the note is outstanding (60 days/360 days).

Note Given to Borrow from Bank A bank nearly always requires a borrower to sign a promissory note when making a loan. When the note matures, the borrower repays the note with an amount larger than the amount borrowed. The difference between the amount borrowed and the amount repaid is *interest*. This section considers a type of note whose signer promises to pay *principal* (the amount borrowed) plus interest. In this case, the *face value* of the note equals principal. Face value is the value shown on the face (front) of the note. To illustrate, assume that a company needs $2,000 for a project and borrows this money from a bank at 12% annual interest. The loan is made on September 30, 2011, and is due in 60 days. Specifically, the borrowing company signs a note with a face value equal to the amount borrowed. The note includes a statement similar to this: "*I promise to pay $2,000 plus interest at 12% within 60 days after September 30.*" This simple note is shown in Exhibit 9.3.

Point: When money is borrowed from a bank, the loan is reported as an asset (receivable) on the bank's balance sheet.

EXHIBIT 9.3

Note with Face Value Equal to Amount Borrowed

Promissory Note

$2,000 — Face Value   Sept. 30, 2011 — Date

Sixty days after date, I promise to pay to the order of

National Bank
Boston, MA

Two thousand and no/100 ---------------- Dollars

plus interest at the annual rate of 12%.

Janet Lee

The borrower records its receipt of cash and the new liability with this entry:

Sept. 30	Cash	2,000	
	Notes Payable		2,000
	Borrowed $2,000 cash with a 60-day, 12%, $2,000 note.		

Assets = Liabilities + Equity
+2,000   +2,000

When principal and interest are paid, the borrower records payment with this entry:

Nov. 29	Notes Payable	2,000	
	Interest Expense	40	
	Cash		2,040
	Paid note with interest ($2,000 × 12% × 60/360).		

Assets = Liabilities + Equity
−2,040   −2,000   −40

End-of-period interest adjustment. When the end of an accounting period occurs between the signing of a note payable and its maturity date, the *matching principle* requires us to record the accrued but unpaid interest on the note. To illustrate, let's return to the note in Exhibit 9.3, but assume that the company borrows $2,000 cash on December 16, 2011, instead of September 30. This 60-day note matures on February 14, 2012, and the company's fiscal year ends on December 31. Thus, we need to record interest expense for the final 15 days in December. This means that one-fourth (15 days/60 days) of the $40 total interest is an expense of year 2011. The borrower records this expense with the following adjusting entry:

2011			
Dec. 31	Interest Expense	10	
	Interest Payable		10
	To record accrued interest on note ($2,000 × 12% × 15/360).		

Assets = Liabilities + Equity
             +10   −10

Example: If this note is dated Dec. 1 instead of Dec. 16, how much expense is recorded on Dec. 31? *Answer:* $2,000 × 12% × 30/360 = $20

When this note matures on February 14, the borrower must recognize 45 days of interest expense for year 2012 and remove the balances of the two liability accounts:

2012			
Feb. 14	Interest Expense*	30	
	Interest Payable	10	
	Notes Payable	2,000	
	Cash		2,040
	Paid note with interest. *($2,000 × 12% × 45/360)		

Assets = Liabilities + Equity
−2,040   −10   −30
            −2,000

Decision Insight

Many franchisors such as **Baskin-Robbins**, **Dunkin' Donuts**, and **Cold Stone Creamery**, use notes to help entrepreneurs acquire their own franchises, including using notes to pay for the franchise fee and any equipment. Payments on these notes are usually collected monthly and often are secured by the franchisees' assets. ■

Payroll Liabilities

An employer incurs several expenses and liabilities from having employees. These expenses and liabilities are often large and arise from salaries and wages earned, from employee benefits, and from payroll taxes levied on the employer. **Boston Beer**, for instance, reports payroll-related current liabilities of more than $6.6 million from accrued "employee wages, benefits and reimbursements." We discuss payroll liabilities and related accounts in this section. Appendix 9A describes details about payroll reports, records, and procedures.

P2 Compute and record *employee* payroll deductions and liabilities.

Point: Deductions at some companies, such as those for insurance coverage, are "required" under its own labor contracts.

EXHIBIT 9.4

Payroll Deductions

Employee Payroll Deductions **Gross pay** is the total compensation an employee earns including wages, salaries, commissions, bonuses, and any compensation earned before deductions such as taxes. (*Wages* usually refer to payments to employees at an hourly rate. *Salaries* usually refer to payments to employees at a monthly or yearly rate.) **Net pay,** also called *take-home pay,* is gross pay less all deductions. **Payroll deductions,** commonly called *withholdings,* are amounts withheld from an employee's gross pay, either required or voluntary. Required deductions result from laws and include income taxes and Social Security taxes. Voluntary deductions, at an employee's option, include pension and health contributions, health and life insurance premiums, union dues, and charitable giving. Exhibit 9.4 shows the typical payroll deductions of an employee. The employer withholds payroll deductions from employees' pay and is obligated to transmit this money to the designated organization. The employer records payroll deductions as current liabilities until these amounts are transmitted. This section discusses the major payroll deductions.

Gross Pay

Federal Income Tax | State and Local Income Taxes | Net Pay | Voluntary Deductions | FICA Taxes (Medicare) | FICA Taxes (Social Security)

Employee FICA taxes. The federal Social Security system provides retirement, disability, survivorship, and medical benefits to qualified workers. Laws *require* employers to withhold **Federal Insurance Contributions Act (FICA) taxes** from employees' pay to cover costs of the system. Employers usually separate FICA taxes into two groups: (1) retirement, disability, and survivorship and (2) medical. For the first group, the Social Security system provides monthly cash payments to qualified retired workers for the rest of their lives. These payments are often called *Social Security benefits.* Taxes related to this group are often called *Social Security taxes.* For the second group, the system provides monthly payments to deceased workers' surviving families and to disabled workers who qualify for assistance. These payments are commonly called *Medicare benefits;* like those in the first group, they are paid with *Medicare taxes* (part of FICA taxes).

Law requires employers to withhold FICA taxes from each employee's salary or wages on each payday. The taxes for Social Security and Medicare are computed separately. For example, for 2012, the amount scheduled to be withheld from each employee's pay for Social Security tax is 6.2% of the first $110,100 the employee earns in the calendar year, or a maximum of $6,826.20. The Medicare tax is 1.45% of *all* amounts the employee earns; there is no maximum limit to Medicare tax. (Politicians could pass a 2012 adjustment; for example, politicians reduced the 2011 *employee* share from 6.2% to 4.2%.)

Employers must pay withheld taxes to the Internal Revenue Service (IRS) on specific filing dates during the year. Employers who fail to send the withheld taxes to the IRS on time can be assessed substantial penalties. Until all the taxes are sent to the IRS, they are included in employers' current liabilities. For any changes in rates or with the maximum earnings level, check the IRS Website at www.IRS.gov or the SSA Website at www.SSA.gov.

Point: The sources of U.S. tax receipts are roughly as follows:
50% Personal income tax
35   FICA and FUTA taxes
10   Corporate income tax
5   Other taxes

Point: Part-time employees may claim "exempt from withholding" if they did not have any income tax liability in the prior year and do not expect any in the current year.

Employee income tax. Most employers are required to withhold federal income tax from each employee's paycheck. The amount withheld is computed using tables published by the IRS. The amount depends on the employee's annual earnings rate and the number of *withholding allowances* the employee claims. Allowances reduce the amount of taxes one owes the government. The more allowances one claims, the less tax the employer will withhold. Employees can claim allowances for themselves and their dependents. They also can claim additional allowances if they expect major declines in their taxable income for medical expenses. (An employee who claims more allowances than appropriate is subject to a fine.) Most states and many local governments require employers to withhold income taxes from employees' pay and to remit them promptly to the proper government agency. Until they are paid, withholdings are reported as a current liability on the employer's balance sheet.

Point: IRS withholding tables are based on projecting weekly (or other period) pay into an annual figure.

Employee voluntary deductions. Beyond Social Security, Medicare, and income taxes, employers often withhold other amounts from employees' earnings. These withholdings arise from employee requests, contracts, unions, or other agreements. They can include amounts for charitable giving, medical and life insurance premiums, pension contributions, and union dues. Until they are paid, such withholdings are reported as part of employers' current liabilities.

Recording employee payroll deductions. Employers must accrue payroll expenses and liabilities at the end of each pay period. To illustrate, assume that an employee earns a salary of $2,000 per month. At the end of January, the employer's entry to accrue payroll expenses and liabilities for this employee is

Jan. 31	Salaries Expense	2,000	
	FICA—Social Security Taxes Payable (6.2%)		124
	FICA—Medicare Taxes Payable (1.45%)		29
	Employee Federal Income Taxes Payable*		213
	Employee Medical Insurance Payable*		85
	Employee Union Dues Payable*		25
	Salaries Payable		1,524
	To record accrued payroll for January.		

Assets = Liabilities + Equity
+124   −2,000
+29
+213
+85
+25
+1,524

* Amounts taken from employer's accounting records.

Salaries Expense (debit) shows that the employee earns a gross salary of $2,000. The first five payables (credits) show the liabilities the employer owes on behalf of this employee to cover FICA taxes, income taxes, medical insurance, and union dues. The Salaries Payable account (credit) records the $1,524 net pay the employee receives from the $2,000 gross pay earned. When the employee is paid, another entry (or a series of entries) is required to record the check written and distributed (or funds transferred). The entry to record cash payment to this employee is to debit Salaries Payable and credit Cash for $1,524.

Salaries Payable 1,524
  Cash 1,524

Decision Insight

A company's delay or failure to pay withholding taxes to the government has severe consequences. For example, a 100% penalty can be levied, with interest, on the unpaid balance. The government can even close a company, take its assets, and pursue legal actions against those involved. ■

Employer Payroll Taxes Employers must pay payroll taxes in addition to those required of employees. Employer taxes include FICA and unemployment taxes.

P3 Compute and record *employer* payroll expenses and liabilities.

Employer FICA tax. Employers must pay FICA taxes on their payroll to employees. For 2012, the employer must pay Social Security tax of 6.2% on the first $110,100 earned by each employee and a Medicare tax of 1.45% on all earnings of each employee. An employer's tax is credited to the same FICA Taxes Payable accounts used to record the Social Security and Medicare taxes withheld from employees. (A self-employed person must pay both the employee and employer FICA taxes.)

Federal and state unemployment taxes. The federal government participates with states in a joint federal and state unemployment insurance program. Each state administers its program. These programs provide unemployment benefits to qualified workers. The federal government approves state programs and pays a portion of their administrative expenses.

Federal Unemployment Taxes (FUTA). Employers are subject to a federal unemployment tax on wages and salaries paid to their employees. For the year 2012, employers were required to pay FUTA taxes of as much as 6.2% of the first $7,000 earned by each employee. This federal tax can be reduced by a credit of up to 5.4% for taxes paid to a state program. As a result, the net federal unemployment tax is often only 0.8%.

State Unemployment Taxes (SUTA). All states support their unemployment insurance programs by placing a payroll tax on employers. (A few states require employees to make a contribution. In the book's assignments, we assume that this tax is only on the employer.) In most states, the base rate for SUTA taxes is 5.4% of the first $7,000 paid each employee. This base rate is adjusted according to an employer's merit rating. The state assigns a **merit rating** that reflects a company's stability or instability in employing workers. A good rating reflects stability in employment and means an employer can pay less than the 5.4% base rate. A low rating reflects high turnover or seasonal hirings and layoffs. To illustrate, an employer with 50 employees each of whom earns $7,000 or more per year saves $15,400 annually if it has a merit rating of 1.0% versus 5.4%. This is computed by comparing taxes of $18,900 at the 5.4% rate to only $3,500 at the 1.0% rate.

Recording employer payroll taxes. Employer payroll taxes are an added expense beyond the wages and salaries earned by employees. These taxes are often recorded in an entry separate from the one recording payroll expenses and deductions. To illustrate, assume that the $2,000 recorded salaries expense from the previous example is earned by an employee whose earnings have not yet reached $5,000 for the year. This means the entire salaries expense for this period is subject to tax because year-to-date pay is under $7,000. Also assume that the federal unemployment tax rate is 0.8% and the state unemployment tax rate is 5.4%. Consequently, the FICA portion of the employer's tax is $153, computed by multiplying both the 6.2% and 1.45% by the $2,000 gross pay. Moreover, state unemployment (SUTA) taxes are $108 (5.4% of the $2,000 gross pay), and federal unemployment (FUTA) taxes are $16 (0.8% of $2,000). The entry to record the employer's payroll tax expense and related liabilities is

Example: If the employer's merit rating in this example reduces its SUTA rate to 2.9%, what is its SUTA liability?
Answer: SUTA payable = $2,000 × 2.9% = $58

Assets = Liabilities + Equity
 +124 −277
 +29
 +108
 +16

Jan. 31	Payroll Taxes Expense	277	
	FICA—Social Security Taxes Payable (6.2%)		124
	FICA—Medicare Taxes Payable (1.45%)		29
	State Unemployment Taxes Payable		108
	Federal Unemployment Taxes Payable		16
	To record employer payroll taxes.		

Point: Internal control is important for payroll accounting. Managers must monitor (1) employee hiring, (2) timekeeping, (3) payroll listings, and (4) payroll payments. Poor controls led the U.S. Army to pay nearly $10 million to deserters, fictitious soldiers, and other unauthorized entities.

■ **Decision** Ethics   Answer — p. 394

Web Designer You take a summer job working for a family friend who runs a small IT service. On your first payday, the owner slaps you on the back, gives you full payment in cash, winks, and adds: "No need to pay those high taxes, eh." What action, if any, do you take? ■

Multi-Period Known Liabilities

Many known liabilities extend over multiple periods. These often include unearned revenues and notes payable. For example, if **Sports Illustrated** sells a four-year magazine subscription, it records amounts received for this subscription in an Unearned Subscription Revenues account. Amounts in this account are liabilities, but are they current or long term? They are *both*. The portion of the Unearned Subscription Revenues account that will be fulfilled in the next year is reported as a current liability. The remaining portion is reported as a long-term liability.

The same analysis applies to notes payable. For example, a borrower reports a three-year note payable as a long-term liability in the first two years it is outstanding. In the third year, the borrower reclassifies this note as a current liability since it is due within one year or the operating cycle, whichever is longer. The **current portion of long-term debt** refers to that part of long-term debt due within one year or the operating cycle, whichever is longer. Long-term debt is reported under long-term liabilities, but the *current portion due* is reported under current liabilities. To illustrate, assume that a $7,500 debt is paid in installments of $1,500 per year for five years. The $1,500 due within the year is reported as a current liability. No journal entry is necessary for this reclassification. Instead, we simply classify the amounts for debt as either current or long term when the balance sheet is prepared.

Some known liabilities are rarely reported in long-term liabilities. These include accounts payable, sales taxes, and wages and salaries.

Point: Some accounting systems do make an entry to transfer the current amount due out of Long-Term Debt and into the Current Portion of Long-Term Debt as follows:

Long-Term Debt 1,500
   Current Portion of L-T Debt . . . 1,500

Fraud

Liability Limits. Probably the greatest number of frauds involve payroll. Companies must safeguard payroll activities. Controls include proper approvals and processes for employee additions, deletions, and pay rate changes. A common fraud is a manager adding a fictitious employee to the payroll and then cashing the fictitious employee's check. A study reports that 28% of employees in operations and service areas witnessed violations of employee wage, overtime, or benefit rules in the past year (KPMG 2009). Another 21% observed falsifying of time and expense reports.

Quick Check

Answers — p. 395

4. Why does a creditor prefer a note payable to a past-due account payable?
5. A company pays its one employee $3,000 per month. This company's FUTA rate is 0.8% on the first $7,000 earned; its SUTA rate is 4.0% on the first $7,000; its Social Security tax rate is 6.2% of the first $110,100; and its Medicare tax rate is 1.45% of all amounts earned. The entry to record this company's March payroll includes what amount for total payroll taxes expense?
6. Identify whether the employer or employee or both incurs each of the following: (*a*) FICA taxes, (*b*) FUTA taxes, (*c*) SUTA taxes, and (*d*) withheld income taxes.

ESTIMATED LIABILITIES

An **estimated liability** is a known obligation that is of an uncertain amount but that can be reasonably estimated. Common examples are employee benefits such as pensions, health care and vacation pay, and warranties offered by a seller. We discuss each of these in this section. Other examples of estimated liabilities include property taxes and certain contracts to provide future services.

P4 Account for estimated liabilities, including warranties and bonuses.

Health and Pension Benefits

Many companies provide **employee benefits** beyond salaries and wages. An employer often pays all or part of medical, dental, life, and disability insurance. Many employers also contribute to *pension plans,* which are agreements by employers to provide benefits (payments) to employees after retirement. Many companies also provide medical care and insurance benefits to their retirees. When payroll taxes and charges for employee benefits are totaled, payroll cost often exceeds employees' gross earnings by 25% or more.

To illustrate, assume that an employer agrees to (1) pay an amount for medical insurance equal to $8,000 and (2) contribute an additional 10% of the employees' $120,000 gross salary to a retirement program. The entry to record these accrued benefits is

Dec. 31	Employee Benefits Expense	20,000	
	Employee Medical Insurance Payable		8,000
	Employee Retirement Program Payable		12,000
	To record costs of employee benefits.		

Assets = Liabilities + Equity
+8,000   −20,000
+12,000

Decision Insight

Postgame Spoils Baseball was the first pro sport to set up a pension, originally up to $100 per month depending on years played. Many former players now take home six-figure pensions. Cal Ripken Jr.'s pension when he reaches 62 is estimated at $160,000 per year (he played 21 seasons). The requirement is only 43 games for a full pension and just one game for full medical benefits.

Vacation Benefits

Many employers offer paid vacation benefits, also called *paid absences*. To illustrate, assume that salaried employees earn two weeks' vacation per year. This benefit increases employers' payroll expenses because employees are paid for 52 weeks but work for only 50 weeks. Total annual salary is the same, but the cost per week worked is greater than the amount paid per week. For example, if an employee is paid $20,800 for 52 weeks but works only 50 weeks, the total weekly expense to the employer is $416 ($20,800/50 weeks) instead of the $400 cash paid weekly to the employee ($20,800/52 weeks). The $16 difference between these two amounts is recorded weekly as follows:

Assets = Liabilities + Equity
         +16   −16

Vacation Benefits Expense....................	16	
Vacation Benefits Payable................		16
To record vacation benefits accrued.		

Vacation Benefits Payable .... #
   Cash .... #

Vacation Benefits Expense is an operating expense, and Vacation Benefits Payable is a current liability. When the employee takes a vacation, the employer reduces (debits) the Vacation Benefits Payable and credits Cash (no additional expense is recorded).

Bonus Plans

Many companies offer bonuses to employees, and many of the bonuses depend on net income. To illustrate, assume that an employer offers a bonus to its employees equal to 5% of the company's annual net income (to be equally shared by all). The company's expected annual net income is $210,000. The year-end adjusting entry to record this benefit is

Assets = Liabilities + Equity
         +10,000   −10,000

Dec. 31	Employee Bonus Expense*................	10,000	
	Bonus Payable		10,000
	To record expected bonus costs.		

* Bonus Expense (B) equals 5% of net income, which equals $210,000 minus the bonus; this is computed as:

$$B = 0.05 (\$210,000 - B)$$
$$B = \$10,500 - 0.05B$$
$$1.05B = \$10,500$$
$$B = \$10,500/1.05 = \$10,000$$

When the bonus is paid, Bonus Payable is debited and Cash is credited for $10,000.

Warranty Liabilities

Point: Kodak recently reported $60 million in warranty obligations.

A **warranty** is a seller's obligation to replace or correct a product (or service) that fails to perform as expected within a specified period. Most new cars, for instance, are sold with a warranty covering parts for a specified period of time. **Ford Motor Company** reported more than $15 billion in "dealer and customer allowances and claims" in its annual report. To comply with the *full disclosure* and *matching principles,* the seller reports the expected warranty expense in the period when revenue from the sale of the product or service is reported. The seller reports this warranty obligation as a liability, although the existence, amount, payee, and date of future sacrifices are uncertain. This is because such warranty costs are probable and the amount can be estimated using, for instance, past experience with warranties.

To illustrate, a dealer sells a used car for $16,000 on December 1, 2011, with a maximum one-year or 12,000-mile warranty covering parts. This dealer's experience shows that warranty expense averages about 4% of a car's selling price, or $640 in this case ($16,000 × 4%). The dealer records the estimated expense and liability related to this sale with this entry:

2011			
Dec. 1	Warranty Expense	640	
	Estimated Warranty Liability		640
	To record estimated warranty expense.		

Assets = Liabilities + Equity
          +640   −640

This entry alternatively could be made as part of end-of-period adjustments. Either way, the estimated warranty expense is reported on the 2011 income statement and the warranty liability on the 2011 balance sheet. To further extend this example, suppose the customer returns the car for warranty repairs on January 9, 2012. The dealer performs this work by replacing parts costing $200. The entry to record partial settlement of the estimated warranty liability is

Point: Recognition of warranty liabilities is necessary to comply with the matching and full disclosure principles.

2012			
Jan. 9	Estimated Warranty Liability	200	
	Auto Parts Inventory		200
	To record costs of warranty repairs.		

Assets = Liabilities + Equity
 −200   −200

This entry reduces the balance of the estimated warranty liability. Warranty expense was previously recorded in 2011, the year the car was sold with the warranty. Finally, what happens if total warranty expenses are more or less than the estimated 4%, or $640? The answer is that management should monitor actual warranty expenses to see whether the 4% rate is accurate. If experience reveals a large difference from the estimate, the rate for current and future sales should be changed. Differences are expected, but they should be small.

Point: Both U.S. GAAP and IFRS account for restructuring costs in a manner similar to accounting for warranties.

Decision Insight

Guaranteed Profits Best Buy earns a 60% profit margin on its warranty contracts, and those contracts are a large part of its profit—see table to the side [*BusinessWeek*]. ■

Warranty contracts as a percentage of sales	4%
Warranty contracts as a percentage of operating profit	45%
Profit margin on warranty contracts	60%

Multi-Period Estimated Liabilities

Estimated liabilities can be both current and long term. For example, pension liabilities to employees are long term to workers who will not retire within the next period. For employees who are retired or will retire within the next period, a portion of pension liabilities is current. Other examples include employee health benefits and warranties. Specifically, many warranties are for 30 or 60 days in length. Estimated costs under these warranties are properly reported in current liabilities. Many other automobile warranties are for three years or 36,000 miles. A portion of these warranties is reported as long term.

Quick Check
Answers — p. 395

7. Estimated liabilities involve an obligation to pay which of these? (*a*) An uncertain but reasonably estimated amount owed on a known obligation or (*b*) A known amount to a specific entity on an uncertain due date.
8. A car is sold for $15,000 on June 1, 2011, with a one-year warranty on parts. Warranty expense is estimated at 1.5% of selling price at each calendar year-end. On March 1, 2012, the car is returned for warranty repairs costing $135. The amount recorded as warranty expense on March 1 is (*a*) $0; (*b*) $60; (*c*) $75; (*d*) $135; (*e*) $225.

CONTINGENT LIABILITIES

C3 Explain how to account for contingent liabilities.

A **contingent liability** is a potential obligation that depends on a future event arising from a past transaction or event. An example is a pending lawsuit. Here, a past transaction or event leads to a lawsuit whose result depends on the outcome of the suit. Future payment of a contingent liability depends on whether an uncertain future event occurs.

Accounting for Contingent Liabilities

Accounting for contingent liabilities depends on the likelihood that a future event will occur and the ability to estimate the future amount owed if this event occurs. Three different possibilities are identified in the following chart: record liability, disclose in notes, or no disclosure.

```
                 Future event is    Amount owed is
                                    Estimable ────────→ Record liability
                    Probable ──────┤
Contingent ────────┤                Nonestimable ─────→ Disclose in notes
liability          │   Possible ───────────────────────→ Disclose in notes
                   └── Remote ─────────────────────────→ No disclosure
```

The conditions that determine each of these three possibilities follow:

1. The future event is *probable* (likely) and the amount owed can be *reasonably estimated*. We then record this amount as a liability. Examples are the estimated liabilities described earlier such as warranties, vacation pay, and income taxes.
2. The future event is *reasonably possible* (could occur). We disclose information about this type of contingent liability in notes to the financial statements.
3. The future event is *remote* (unlikely). We do not record or disclose information on remote contingent liabilities.

Point: A contingency is an *if*. Namely, if a future event occurs, then financial consequences are likely for the entity.

Reasonably Possible Contingent Liabilities

This section identifies and discusses contingent liabilities that commonly fall in the second category—when the future event is reasonably possible. Disclosing information about contingencies in this category is motivated by the *full-disclosure principle,* which requires information relevant to decision makers be reported and not ignored.

Potential Legal Claims Many companies are sued or at risk of being sued. The accounting issue is whether the defendant should recognize a liability on its balance sheet or disclose a contingent liability in its notes while a lawsuit is outstanding and not yet settled. The answer is that a potential claim is recorded in the accounts *only* if payment for damages is probable and the amount can be reasonably estimated. If the potential claim cannot be reasonably estimated or is less than probable but reasonably possible, it is disclosed. **Ford Motor Company**, for example, includes the following note in its annual report: "Various legal actions, governmental investigations and proceedings and claims are pending . . . arising out of alleged defects in our products."

Point: A sale of a note receivable is often a contingent liability. It becomes a liability if the original signer of the note fails to pay it at maturity.

Debt Guarantees Sometimes a company guarantees the payment of debt owed by a supplier, customer, or another company. The guarantor usually discloses the guarantee in its financial statement notes as a contingent liability. If it is probable that the debtor will default, the guarantor needs to record and report the guarantee in its financial statements as a liability. The **Boston Celtics** report a unique guarantee when it comes to coaches and players: "Certain of the contracts provide for guaranteed payments which must be paid even if the employee [player] is injured or terminated."

Other Contingencies Other examples of contingencies include environmental damages, possible tax assessments, insurance losses, and government investigations. **Sunoco**, for instance, reports that "federal, state and local laws . . . result in liabilities and loss contingencies. Sunoco accrues . . . cleanup costs [that] are probable and reasonably estimable. Management believes it is reasonably possible (i.e., less than probable but greater than remote) that additional . . . losses will be incurred." Many of Sunoco's contingencies are revealed only in notes.

Point: Auditors and managers often have different views about whether a contingency is recorded, disclosed, or omitted.

Decision Insight

Pricing Priceless What's it worth to see from one side of the Grand Canyon to the other? What's the cost when gulf coast beaches are closed due to an oil well disaster? A method to measure environmental liabilities is *contingent valuation,* by which people answer such questions. Regulators use their answers to levy fines and assess punitive damages.

Uncertainties That Are Not Contingencies

All organizations face uncertainties from future events such as natural disasters and the development of new competing products or services. These uncertainties are not contingent liabilities because they are future events *not* arising from past transactions. Accordingly, they are not disclosed.

Fraud

Risky Payables. Following are some warning signs of potential fraud involving payables:

- **Duplicate** payments in the same or similar amount to the same vendor (or invoices to the same vendor with the same or similar date).
- **Invoices** at amounts just below the limit requiring managerial approval.
- **Irregular vendor information** such as the absence of a business/home phone number or phone numbers that always go to an answering system; multiple vendors with the same phone number; vendors with PO box billing addresses; vendors with similar-sounding or similar-spelled names.
- **Unusual invoice activity** such as increases or decreases in invoice activity, or above-average invoice amounts, or activity at abnormal dates.

Quick Check
Answers — p. 395

9. A future payment is reported as a liability on the balance sheet if payment is contingent on a future event that (*a*) is reasonably possible but the payment cannot be reasonably estimated; (*b*) is probable and the payment can be reasonably estimated; or (*c*) is not probable but the payment is known.
10. Under what circumstances is a future payment reported in the notes to the financial statements as a contingent liability?

GLOBAL VIEW

This section discusses similarities and differences between U.S. GAAP and IFRS in accounting and reporting for current liabilities.

Characteristics of Liabilities The definitions and characteristics of current liabilities are broadly similar for both U.S. GAAP and IFRS. Although differences exist, the similarities vastly outweigh any differences. Remembering that "provision" is typically used under IFRS to refer to what is titled "liability" under U.S. GAAP, **Nokia** describes its recognition of liabilities as follows:

> Provisions are recognized when the Group has a present legal or constructive obligation as a result of past events, it is probable that an outflow of resources will be required to settle the obligation and a reliable estimate of the amount can be made.

NOKIA

Known (Determinable) Liabilities When there is little uncertainty surrounding current liabilities, both U.S. GAAP and IFRS require companies to record them in a similar manner. This correspondence in accounting applies to accounts payable, sales taxes payable, unearned revenues, short-term notes, and payroll liabilities. Of course, tax regulatory systems of countries are different, which implies use of different rates and levels. Still, the basic approach is the same.

Estimated Liabilities When there is a known current obligation that involves an uncertain amount, but one that can be reasonably estimated, both U.S. GAAP and IFRS require similar treatment. This treatment extends to many obligations such as those arising from vacations, warranties, restructurings, pensions, and health care. Both accounting systems require that companies record estimated expenses related to these obligations when they can reasonably estimate the amounts. **Nokia** reports wages, salaries and bonuses of €5,658 million. It also reports pension expenses of €427 million.

Decision Analysis — Times Interest Earned Ratio

A1 Compute the times interest earned ratio and use it to analyze liabilities.

A company incurs interest expense on many of its current and long-term liabilities. Examples extend from its short-term notes and the current portion of long-term liabilities to its long-term notes and bonds. Interest expense is often viewed as a *fixed expense* because the amount of these liabilities is likely to remain in one form or another for a substantial period of time. This means that the amount of interest is unlikely to vary due to changes in sales or other operating activities. While fixed expenses can be advantageous when a company is growing, they create risk. This risk stems from the possibility that a company might be unable to pay fixed expenses if sales decline. To illustrate, consider Diego Co.'s results for 2011 and two possible outcomes for year 2012 in Exhibit 9.5.

EXHIBIT 9.5
Actual and Projected Results

		2012 Projections	
($ thousands)	2011	Sales Increase	Sales Decrease
Sales	$600	$900	$300
Expenses (75% of sales)	450	675	225
Income before interest	150	225	75
Interest expense (fixed)	60	60	60
Net income	$ 90	$165	$ 15

Expenses excluding interest are at, and expected to remain at, 75% of sales. Expenses such as these that change with sales volume are called *variable expenses*. However, interest expense is at, and expected to remain at, $60,000 per year due to its fixed nature.

The middle numerical column of Exhibit 9.5 shows that Diego's income increases by 83% to $165,000 if sales increase by 50% to $900,000. In contrast, the far right column shows that income decreases by 83% if sales decline by 50%. These results reveal that the amount of fixed interest expense affects a company's risk of its ability to pay interest, which is numerically reflected in the **times interest earned** ratio in Exhibit 9.6.

EXHIBIT 9.6
Times Interest Earned

$$\text{Times interest earned} = \frac{\text{Income before interest expense and income taxes}}{\text{Interest expense}}$$

For 2011, Diego's times interest earned is computed as $150,000/$60,000, or 2.5 times. This ratio suggests that Diego faces low to moderate risk because its sales must decline sharply before it would be unable to cover its interest expenses. (Diego is an LLC and does not pay income taxes.)

Experience shows that when times interest earned falls below 1.5 to 2.0 and remains at that level or lower for several periods, the default rate on liabilities increases sharply. This reflects increased risk for companies and their creditors. We also must interpret the times interest earned ratio in light of information about the variability of a company's income before interest. If income is stable from year to year or if it is growing, the company can afford to take on added risk by borrowing. If its income greatly varies from year to year, fixed interest expense can increase the risk that it will not earn enough income to pay interest.

Decision Maker

Answer — p. 394

Entrepreneur You wish to invest in a franchise for either one of two national chains. Each franchise has an expected annual net income *after* interest and taxes of $100,000. Net income for the first franchise includes a regular fixed interest charge of $200,000. The fixed interest charge for the second franchise is $40,000. Which franchise is riskier to you if sales forecasts are not met? Does your decision change if the first franchise has more variability in its income stream? ∎

DEMONSTRATION PROBLEM

The following transactions and events took place at Kern Company during its recent calendar-year reporting period (Kern does not use reversing entries).

a. In September 2011, Kern sold $140,000 of merchandise covered by a 180-day warranty. Prior experience shows that costs of the warranty equal 5% of sales. Compute September's warranty expense and prepare the adjusting journal entry for the warranty liability as recorded at September 30. Also prepare the journal entry on October 8 to record a $300 cash expenditure to provide warranty service on an item sold in September.

b. On October 12, 2011, Kern arranged with a supplier to replace Kern's overdue $10,000 account payable by paying $2,500 cash and signing a note for the remainder. The note matures in 90 days and has a 12% interest rate. Prepare the entries recorded on October 12, December 31, and January 10, 2012, related to this transaction.

c. In late December, Kern learns it is facing a product liability suit filed by an unhappy customer. Kern's lawyer advises that although it will probably suffer a loss from the lawsuit, it is not possible to estimate the amount of damages at this time.

d. Sally Bline works for Kern. For the pay period ended November 30, her gross earnings are $3,000. Bline has $800 deducted for federal income taxes and $200 for state income taxes from each paycheck. Additionally, a $35 premium for her health care insurance and a $10 donation for the United Way are deducted. Bline pays FICA Social Security taxes at a rate of 6.2% and FICA Medicare taxes at a rate of 1.45%. She has not earned enough this year to be exempt from any FICA taxes. Journalize the accrual of salaries expense of Bline's wages by Kern.

e. On November 1, Kern borrows $5,000 cash from a bank in return for a 60-day, 12%, $5,000 note. Record the note's issuance on November 1 and its repayment with interest on December 31.

f.[B] Kern has estimated and recorded its quarterly income tax payments. In reviewing its year-end tax adjustments, it identifies an additional $5,000 of income tax expense that should be recorded. A portion of this additional expense, $1,000, is deferrable to future years. Record this year-end income taxes expense adjusting entry.

g. For this calendar-year, Kern's net income is $1,000,000, its interest expense is $275,000, and its income taxes expense is $225,000. Calculate Kern's times interest earned ratio.

PLANNING THE SOLUTION

- For *a*, compute the warranty expense for September and record it with an estimated liability. Record the October expenditure as a decrease in the liability.
- For *b*, eliminate the liability for the account payable and create the liability for the note payable. Compute interest expense for the 80 days that the note is outstanding in 2011 and record it as an additional liability. Record the payment of the note, being sure to include the interest for the 10 days in 2012.
- For *c*, decide whether the company's contingent liability needs to be disclosed or accrued (recorded) according to the two necessary criteria: probable loss and reasonably estimable.
- For *d*, set up payable accounts for all items in Bline's paycheck that require deductions. After deducting all necessary items, credit the remaining amount to Salaries Payable.
- For *e*, record the issuance of the note. Calculate 60 days' interest due using the 360-day convention in the interest formula.
- For *f*, determine how much of the income taxes expense is payable in the current year and how much needs to be deferred.
- For *g*, apply and compute times interest earned.

SOLUTION TO DEMONSTRATION PROBLEM

a. Warranty expense = 5% × $140,000 = $7,000

Sept. 30	Warranty Expense	7,000	
	Estimated Warranty Liability		7,000
	To record warranty expense for the month.		
Oct. 8	Estimated Warranty Liability	300	
	Cash		300
	To record the cost of the warranty service.		

b. Interest expense for 2011 = 12% × $7,500 × 80/360 = $200
Interest expense for 2012 = 12% × $7,500 × 10/360 = $25

Oct. 12	Accounts Payable	10,000	
	Notes Payable		7,500
	Cash		2,500
	Paid $2,500 cash and gave a 90-day, 12% note to extend the due date on the account.		
Dec. 31	Interest Expense	200	
	Interest Payable		200
	To accrue interest on note payable.		
Jan. 10	Interest Expense	25	
	Interest Payable	200	
	Notes Payable	7,500	
	Cash		7,725
	Paid note with interest, including the accrued interest payable.		

c. Disclose the pending lawsuit in the financial statement notes. Although the loss is probable, no liability can be accrued since the loss cannot be reasonably estimated.

d.

Nov. 30	Salaries Expense	3,000.00	
	FICA—Social Security Taxes Payable (6.2%)		186.00
	FICA—Medicare Taxes Payable (1.45%)		43.50
	Employee Federal Income Taxes Payable		800.00
	Employee State Income Taxes Payable		200.00
	Employee Medical Insurance Payable		35.00
	Employee United Way Payable		10.00
	Salaries Payable		1,725.50
	To record Bline's accrued payroll.		

e.

Nov. 1	Cash	5,000	
	Notes Payable		5,000
	Borrowed cash with a 60-day, 12% note.		

When the note and interest are paid 60 days later, Kern Company records this entry:

Dec. 31	Notes Payable	5,000	
	Interest Expense	100	
	Cash		5,100
	Paid note with interest ($5,000 × 12% × 60/360).		

f.

Dec. 31	Income Taxes Expense	5,000	
	Income Taxes Payable		4,000
	Deferred Income Tax Liability		1,000
	To record added income taxes expense and the deferred tax liability.		

g. Times interest earned $= \dfrac{\$1,000,000 + \$275,000 + \$225,000}{\$275,000} = \underline{\underline{5.45 \text{ times}}}$

APPENDIX 9A

Payroll Reports, Records, and Procedures

Understanding payroll procedures and keeping adequate payroll reports and records are essential to a company's success. This appendix focuses on payroll accounting and its reports, records, and procedures.

P5 Identify and describe the details of payroll reports, records, and procedures.

Payroll Reports Most employees and employers are required to pay local, state, and federal payroll taxes. Payroll expenses involve liabilities to individual employees, to federal and state governments, and to other organizations such as insurance companies. Beyond paying these liabilities, employers are required to prepare and submit reports explaining how they computed these payments.

Reporting FICA Taxes and Income Taxes The Federal Insurance Contributions Act (FICA) requires each employer to file an Internal Revenue Service (IRS) **Form 941,** the *Employer's Quarterly Federal Tax Return,* within one month after the end of each calendar quarter. A sample Form 941 is shown in Exhibit 9A.1 for Phoenix Sales & Service, a landscape design company. Accounting information and software are helpful in tracking payroll transactions and reporting the accumulated information on Form 941. Specifically, the employer reports total wages subject to income tax withholding on line 2 of Form 941. (For simplicity, this appendix uses *wages* to refer to both wages and salaries.) The income tax withheld is reported on line 3. The combined amount of employee and employer FICA (Social Security) taxes for Phoenix Sales & Service is reported on line 5a (taxable Social Security wages, $36,599 × 12.4% = $4,538.28). The 12.4% is the sum of the Social Security tax withheld, computed as 6.2% tax withheld from the employee wages for the quarter plus the 6.2% tax levied on the employer. The combined amount of employee Medicare wages is reported on line 5c. The 2.9% is the sum of 1.45% withheld from employee wages for the quarter plus 1.45% tax levied on the employer. Total FICA taxes are reported on line 5d and are added to the total income taxes withheld of $3,056.47 to yield a total of $8,656.12. For this year, assume that income up to $110,100 is subject to Social Security tax. There is no income limit on amounts subject to Medicare tax. Congress sets annual limits on the amount owed for Social Security tax.

Federal depository banks are authorized to accept deposits of amounts payable to the federal government. Deposit requirements depend on the amount of tax owed. For example, when the sum of FICA taxes plus the employee income taxes is less than $2,500 for a quarter, the taxes can be paid when Form 941 is filed. Companies with large payrolls are often required to pay monthly or even semiweekly.

Reporting FUTA Taxes and SUTA Taxes An employer's federal unemployment taxes (FUTA) are reported on an annual basis by filing an *Annual Federal Unemployment Tax Return,* IRS **Form 940.** It must be mailed on or before January 31 following the end of each tax year. Ten more days are allowed if all required tax deposits are filed on a timely basis and the full amount of tax is paid on or before January 31. FUTA payments are made quarterly to a federal depository bank if the total amount due exceeds $500. If $500 or less is due, the taxes are remitted annually. Requirements for paying and reporting state unemployment taxes (SUTA) vary depending on the laws of each state. Most states require quarterly payments and reports.

EXHIBIT 9A.1
Form 941

Form 941 — Employer's QUARTERLY Federal Tax Return
Department of the Treasury — Internal Revenue Service

(EIN) Employer identification number: 86-3214587

Name (not your trade name): Phoenix Sales & Service

Trade name (if any):

Address: 1214 Mill Road
City: Phoenix   State: AZ   ZIP code: 85621

Report for this Quarter ... (Check one.)
- [ ] 1: January, February, March
- [ ] 2: April, May, June
- [ ] 3: July, August, September
- [X] 4: October, November, December

Part 1: Answer these questions for this quarter.

1. Number of employees who received wages, tips, or other compensation for the pay period including: Mar. 12 (Quarter 1), June 12 (Quarter 2), Sept. 12 (Quarter 3), Dec. 12 (Quarter 4) — **1**: 1
2. Wages, tips, and other compensation — **2**: 36,599.00
3. Total income tax withheld from wages, tips, and other compensation — **3**: 3,056.47
4. If no wages, tips, and other compensation are subject to social security or Medicare tax. ☐ Check and go to line 6.
5. Taxable social security and Medicare wages and tips:

	Column 1		Column 2
5a Taxable social security wages	36,599.00	× .124 =	4,538.28
5b Taxable social security tips	.	× .124 =	.
5c Taxable Medicare wages & tips	36,599.00	× .029 =	1,061.37

5d. Total social security and Medicare taxes (Column 2, lines 5a + 5b + 5c = line 5d) — **5d**: 5,599.65

6. Total taxes before adjustments (lines 3 + 5d = line 6) — **6**: 8,656.12

7. TAX ADJUSTMENTS (Read the instructions for line 7 before completing lines 7a through 7h.):
   - 7a Current quarter's fractions of cents: .
   - 7b Current quarter's sick pay: .
   - 7c Current quarter's adjustments for tips and group-term life insurance: .
   - 7d Current year's income tax withholding (attach Form 941c): .
   - 7e Prior quarters' social security and Medicare taxes (attach Form 941c): .
   - 7f Special additions to federal income tax (attach Form 941c): .
   - 7g Special additions to social security and Medicare (attach Form 941c): .
   - 7h TOTAL ADJUSTMENTS (Combine all amounts: lines 7a through 7g.) — **7h**: 0.00

8. Total taxes after adjustments (Combine lines 6 and 7h.) — **8**: 8,656.12
9. Advance earned income credit (EIC) payments made to employees — **9**: .
10. Total taxes after adjustment for advance EIC (lines 8 − line 9 = line 10) — **10**: 8,656.12
11. Total deposits for this quarter, including overpayment applied from a prior quarter — **11**: 8,656.12
12. Balance due (If line 10 is more than line 11, write the difference here.) Make checks payable to *United States Treasury*. — **12**: 0.00
13. Overpayment (If line 11 is more than line 10, write the difference here.) 0.00 — Check one ☐ Apply to next return. ☐ Send a refund.

Part 2: Tell us about your deposit schedule and tax liability for this quarter.

If you are unsure about whether you are a monthly schedule depositor or a semiweekly schedule depositor, see Pub. 15 (Circular E), section 11.

14. Write the state abbreviation for the state where you made your deposits OR write "MU" if you made your deposits in *multiple* states: **AZ**

15. Check one:
    - ☐ Line 10 is less than $2,500. Go to Part 3.
    - [X] You were a monthly schedule depositor for the entire quarter. Fill out your tax liability for each month. Then go to Part 3.

Tax liability:	Amount
Month 1	3,079.11
Month 2	2,049.77
Month 3	3,527.24
Total liability for quarter	8,656.12

    Total must equal line 10.

    - ☐ You were a semiweekly schedule depositor for any part of this quarter. Fill out *Schedule B (Form 941): Report of Tax Liability for Semiweekly Schedule Depositors*, and attach it to this form.

Part 3: Tell us about your business. If a question does NOT apply to your business, leave it blank.

16. If your business has closed or you stopped paying wages . . . ☐ Check here, and enter the final date you paid wages __/__/__
17. If you are a seasonal employer and you do not have to file a return for every quarter of the year. ☐ Check here.

Part 4: May we speak with your third-party designee?

Do you want to allow an employee, a paid tax preparer, or another person to discuss this return with the IRS? See the instructions for details.

- ☐ Yes. Designee's name: _____ Phone (___) ___-____ Personal Identification Number (PIN) ☐☐☐☐☐
- [X] No.

Part 5: Sign here. You MUST fill out both sides of this form and SIGN it.

Under penalties of perjury, I declare that I have examined this return, including accompanying schedules and statements, and to the best of my knowledge and belief, it is true, correct, and complete.

X Sign your name here: _____
Print name and title: _____
Date: __/__/__   Phone: (___) ___-____

388

Reporting Wages and Salaries Employers are required to give each employee an annual report of his or her wages subject to FICA and federal income taxes along with the amounts of these taxes withheld. This report is called a *Wage and Tax Statement,* or **Form W-2**. It must be given to employees before January 31 following the year covered by the report. Exhibit 9A.2 shows Form W-2 for one of the employees at Phoenix Sales & Service. Copies of the W-2 Form must be sent to the Social Security Administration, where the amount of the employee's wages subject to FICA taxes and FICA taxes withheld are posted to each employee's Social Security account. These posted amounts become the basis for determining an employee's retirement and survivors' benefits. The Social Security Administration also transmits to the IRS the amount of each employee's wages subject to federal income taxes and the amount of taxes withheld.

EXHIBIT 9A.2

Form W-2

Field	Value
a Control number	AR101
	22222
	OMB No. 1545-0006
b Employer identification number (EIN)	86-3214587
1 Wages, tips, other compensation	4,910.00
2 Federal income tax withheld	333.37
c Employer's name, address and ZIP code	Phoenix Sales & Service / 1214 Mill Road / Phoenix, AZ 85621
3 Social security wages	4,910.00
4 Social security tax withheld	304.42
5 Medicare wages and tips	4,910.00
6 Medicare tax withheld	71.20
7 Social security tips	
8 Allocated tips	
d Employee's social security number	333-22-9999
9 Advance EIC payment	
10 Dependent care benefits	
e Employee's first name and initial	Robert J.
Last name	Austin
11 Nonqualified plans	
12a Code	
f Employee's address and ZIP code	18 Roosevelt Blvd., Apt. C / Tempe, AZ 86322
13 Statutory employee / Retirement plan / Third-party sick pay	
12b Code	
14 Other	
12c Code	
12d Code	
15 State	AZ
Employer's state ID number	13-902319
16 State wages, tips, etc.	4,910.00
17 State income tax	26.68
18 Local wages, tips, etc.	
19 Local income tax	
20 Locality name	

Form W-2 Wage and Tax Statement — Copy 1–For State, City, or Local Tax Department — Department of Treasury—Internal Revenue Service

Payroll Records Employers must keep payroll records in addition to reporting and paying taxes. These records usually include a payroll register and an individual earnings report for each employee.

Payroll Register A **payroll register** usually shows the pay period dates, hours worked, gross pay, deductions, and net pay of each employee for each pay period. Exhibit 9A.3 shows a payroll register for Phoenix Sales & Service. It is organized into nine columns:

Col. 1 Employee identification (ID); Employee name; Social Security number (SS No.); Reference (check number); and Date (date check issued)
Col. 2 Pay Type (regular and overtime)
Col. 3 Pay Hours (number of hours worked as regular and overtime)
Col. 4 Gross Pay (amount of gross pay)[2]
Col. 5 FIT (federal income taxes withheld); FUTA (federal unemployment taxes)
Col. 6 SIT (state income taxes withheld); SUTA (state unemployment taxes)
Col. 7 FICA-SS_EE (social security taxes withheld, employee); FICA-SS_ER (social security taxes, employer)
Col. 8 FICA-Med_EE (medicare tax withheld, employee); FICA-Med_ER (medicare tax, employer)
Col. 9 Net pay (Gross pay less amounts withheld from employees)

---

[2] The Gross Pay column shows regular hours worked on the first line multiplied by the regular pay rate—this equals regular pay. Overtime hours multiplied by the overtime premium rate equals overtime premium pay reported on the second line. If employers are engaged in interstate commerce, federal law sets a minimum overtime rate of pay to employees. For this company, workers earn 150% of their regular rate for hours in excess of 40 per week.

EXHIBIT 9A.3

Payroll Register

Phoenix Sales & Service
Payroll Register
For Week Ended Oct. 8, 2012

Employee ID / Employee / SS No. / Refer., Date	Pay Type	Pay Hours	Gross Pay	FIT / FUTA	SIT / SUTA	FICA-SS_EE / FICA-SS_ER	FICA-Med_EE / FICA-Med_ER	Net Pay
AR101 Robert Austin 333-22-9999 9001, 10/8/12	Regular Overtime	40.00 0.00	400.00 0.00 400.00	−28.99 −3.20	−2.32 −10.80	−24.80 −24.80	−5.80 −5.80	338.09
CJ102 Judy Cross 299-11-9201 9002, 10/8/12	Regular Overtime	40.00 1.00	560.00 21.00 581.00	−52.97 −4.65	−4.24 −15.69	−36.02 −36.02	−8.42 −8.42	479.35
DJ103 John Diaz 444-11-9090 9003, 10/8/12	Regular Overtime	40.00 2.00	560.00 42.00 602.00	−48.33 −4.82	−3.87 −16.25	−37.32 −37.32	−8.73 −8.73	503.75
KK104 Kay Keife 909-11-3344 9004, 10/8/12	Regular Overtime	40.00 0.00	560.00 0.00 560.00	−68.57 −4.48	−5.49 −15.12	−34.72 −34.72	−8.12 −8.12	443.10
ML105 Lee Miller 444-56-3211 9005, 10/8/12	Regular Overtime	40.00 0.00	560.00 0.00 560.00	−34.24 −4.48	−2.74 −15.12	−34.72 −34.72	−8.12 −8.12	480.18
SD106 Dale Sears 909-33-1234 9006, 10/8/12	Regular Overtime	40.00 0.00	560.00 0.00 560.00	−68.57 −4.48	−5.49 −15.12	−34.72 −34.72	−8.12 −8.12	443.10
Totals	Regular Overtime	240.00 3.00	3,200.00 63.00 3,263.00	−301.67 −26.11	−24.15 −88.10	−202.30 −202.30	−47.31 −47.31	2,687.57

Net pay for each employee is computed as gross pay minus the items on the first line of columns 5–8. The employer's payroll tax for each employee is computed as the sum of items on the third line of columns 5–8. A payroll register includes all data necessary to record payroll. In some software programs the entries to record payroll are made in a special *payroll journal*.

Payroll Check Payment of payroll is usually done by check or electronic funds transfer. Exhibit 9A.4 shows a *payroll check* for a Phoenix employee. This check is accompanied with a detachable *statement of earnings* (at top) showing gross pay, deductions, and net pay.

Employee Earnings Report An **employee earnings report** is a cumulative record of an employee's hours worked, gross earnings, deductions, and net pay. Payroll information on this report is taken from the payroll register. The employee earnings report for R. Austin at Phoenix Sales & Service is shown in Exhibit 9A.5. An employee earnings report accumulates information that can show when an employee's earnings reach the tax-exempt points for FICA, FUTA, and SUTA taxes. It also gives data an employer needs to prepare Form W-2.

Payroll Procedures Employers must be able to compute federal income tax for payroll purposes. This section explains how we compute this tax and how to use a payroll bank account.

Computing Federal Income Taxes To compute the amount of taxes withheld from each employee's wages, we need to determine both the employee's wages earned and the employee's number of *withholding*

Chapter 9 Reporting and Analyzing Current Liabilities

EXHIBIT 9A.4

Check and Statement of Earnings

EMPLOYEE NO.	EMPLOYEE NAME	SOCIAL SECURITY NO.	PAY PERIOD END	CHECK DATE
AR101	Robert Austin	333-22-9999	10/8/12	10/8/12

ITEM	RATE	HOURS	TOTAL	ITEM	THIS CHECK	YEAR TO DATE
Regular	10.00	40.00	400.00	Gross	400.00	400.00
Overtime	15.00			Fed. Income tax	−28.99	−28.99
				FICA-Soc. Sec.	−24.80	−24.80
				FICA-Medicare	−5.80	−5.80
				State Income tax	−2.32	−2.32

HOURS WORKED	GROSS THIS PERIOD	GROSS YEAR TO DATE	NET CHECK	CHECK No.
40.00	400.00	400.00	$338.09	9001

(Detach and retain for your records)

PHOENIX SALES & SERVICE
1214 Mill Road
Phoenix, AZ 85621
602-555-8900

Phoenix Bank and Trust
Phoenix, AZ 85621
3312-87044

No. 9001

DATE October 8, 20 12

Check No. 9001

Amount Three Hundred Thirty-Eight and 9/100 Dollars $ **************$338.09*

Pay to the order of
Robert Austin
18 Roosevelt Blvd., Apt C
Tempe, AZ 86322

Mary Wills
AUTHORIZED SIGNATURE

EXHIBIT 9A.5

Employee Earnings Report

Phoenix Sales & Service
Employee Earnings Report
For Month Ended Dec. 31, 2012

Employee ID / Employee / SS No.	Date Reference	Gross Pay	FIT / [blank] / FUTA	SIT / [blank] / SUTA	FICA-SS_EE / [blank] / FICA-SS_ER	FICA-Med_EE / [blank] / FICA-Med_ER	Net Pay
Beginning Balance for Robert Austin		2,910.00	−188.42	−15.08	−180.42	−42.20	2,483.88
			−23.28	−78.57	−180.42	−42.20	
AR101 Robert Austin 333-22-9999	12/03/12 9049	400.00	−28.99	−2.32	−24.80	−5.80	338.09
			−3.20	−10.80	−24.80	−5.80	
AR101 Robert Austin 333-22-9999	12/10/12 9055	400.00	−28.99	−2.32	−24.80	−5.80	338.09
			−3.20	−10.80	−24.80	−5.80	
AR101 Robert Austin 333-22-9999	12/17/12 9061	400.00	−28.99	−2.32	−24.80	−5.80	338.09
			−3.20	−10.80	−24.80	−5.80	
AR101 Robert Austin 333-22-9999	12/24/12 9067	400.00	−28.99	−2.32	−24.80	−5.80	338.09
			−3.20	−10.80	−24.80	−5.80	
AR101 Robert Austin 333-22-9999	12/31/12 9073	400.00	−28.99	−2.32	−24.80	−5.80	338.09
			−3.20	−10.80	−24.80	−5.80	
Total 12/01/12 thru 12/31/12		2,000.00	−144.95	−11.60	−124.00	−29.00	1,690.45
			−16.00	−54.00	−124.00	−29.00	
Year-to-date Total for Robert Austin		4,910.00	−333.37	−26.68	−304.42	−71.20	4,174.33
			−39.28	−132.57	−304.42	−71.20	

allowances. Each employee records the number of withholding allowances claimed on a withholding allowance certificate, **Form W-4,** filed with the employer. When the number of withholding allowances increases, the amount of income taxes withheld decreases.

Employers often use a **wage bracket withholding table** similar to the one shown in Exhibit 9A.6 to compute the federal income taxes withheld from each employee's gross pay. The table in Exhibit 9A.6 is for a single employee paid weekly. Tables are also provided for married employees and for biweekly, semimonthly, and monthly pay periods (most payroll software includes these tables). When using a wage bracket withholding table to compute federal income tax withheld from an employee's gross wages, we need to locate an employee's wage bracket within the first two columns. We then find the amount withheld by looking in the withholding allowance column for that employee.

EXHIBIT 9A.6

Wage Bracket Withholding Table

SINGLE Persons—WEEKLY Payroll Period

If the wages are—		And the number of withholding allowances claimed is—										
At least	But less than	0	1	2	3	4	5	6	7	8	9	10
		The amount of income tax to be withheld is—										
$600	$610	$76	$67	$58	$49	$39	$30	$21	$12	$6	$0	$0
610	620	79	69	59	50	41	32	22	13	7	1	0
620	630	81	70	61	52	42	33	24	15	8	2	0
630	640	84	72	62	53	44	35	25	16	9	3	0
640	650	86	73	64	55	45	36	27	18	10	4	0
650	660	89	75	65	56	47	38	28	19	11	5	0
660	670	91	76	67	58	48	39	30	21	12	6	0
670	680	94	78	68	59	50	41	31	22	13	7	1
680	690	96	81	70	61	51	42	33	24	14	8	2
690	700	99	83	71	62	53	44	34	25	16	9	3
700	710	101	86	73	64	54	45	35	27	17	10	4
710	720	104	88	74	65	56	47	37	28	19	11	5
720	730	106	91	76	67	57	48	39	30	20	12	6
730	740	109	93	78	68	59	50	40	31	22	13	7
740	750	111	96	80	70	60	51	42	33	23	14	8

Payroll Bank Account Companies with few employees often pay them with checks drawn on the company's regular bank account. Companies with many employees often use a special **payroll bank account** to pay employees. When this account is used, a company either (1) draws one check for total payroll on the regular bank account and deposits it in the payroll bank account or (2) executes an *electronic funds transfer* to the payroll bank account. Individual payroll checks are then drawn on this payroll bank account. Since only one check for the total payroll is drawn on the regular bank account each payday, use of a special payroll bank account helps with internal control. It also helps in reconciling the regular bank account. When companies use a payroll bank account, they usually include check numbers in the payroll register. The payroll register in Exhibit 9A.3 shows check numbers in column 1. For instance, Check No. 9001 is issued to Robert Austin. With this information, the payroll register serves as a supplementary record of wages earned by and paid to employees.

Who Pays What Payroll Taxes and Benefits

We conclude this appendix with the following table identifying who pays which payroll taxes and which common employee benefits such as medical, disability, pension, charitable, and union costs. Who pays which employee benefits, and what portion, is subject to agreements between companies and their workers. Also, self-employed workers must pay both the employer and employee FICA taxes for Social Security and Medicare.

Employer Payroll Taxes and Costs	Employee Payroll Deductions
• FICA—Social Security Taxes	• FICA—Social Security taxes
• FICA—Medicare Taxes	• FICA—Medicare taxes
• FUTA (Federal Unemployment Taxes)	• Federal Income taxes
• SUTA (State Unemployment Taxes)	• State and local income taxes
• Share of medical coverage, if any	• Share of medical coverage, if any
• Share of pension coverage, if any	• Share of pension coverage, if any
• Share of other benefits, if any	• Share of other benefits, if any

Quick Check

Answers — p. 395

11. What three items determine the amount deducted from an employee's wages for federal income taxes?
12. What amount of income tax is withheld from the salary of an employee who is single with three withholding allowances and earnings of $675 in a week? (*Hint:* Use the wage bracket withholding table in Exhibit 9A.6.)
13. Which of the following steps are executed when a company draws one check for total payroll and deposits it in a special payroll bank account? (*a*) Write a check to the payroll bank account for the total payroll and record it with a debit to Salaries Payable and a credit to Cash. (*b*) Deposit a check (or transfer funds) for the total payroll in the payroll bank account. (*c*) Issue individual payroll checks drawn on the payroll bank account. (*d*) All of the above.

APPENDIX 9B

Corporate Income Taxes

This appendix explains current liabilities involving income taxes for corporations.

Income Tax Liabilities Corporations are subject to income taxes and must estimate their income tax liability when preparing financial statements. Since income tax expense is created by earning income, a liability is incurred when income is earned. This tax must be paid quarterly under federal regulations. To illustrate, consider a corporation that prepares monthly financial statements. Based on its income in January 2011, this corporation estimates that it owes income taxes of $12,100. The following adjusting entry records this estimate:

Jan. 31	Income Taxes Expense	12,100	
	Income Taxes Payable		12,100
	To accrue January income taxes.		

Assets = Liabilities + Equity
         +12,100   −12,100

The tax liability is recorded each month until the first quarterly payment is made. If the company's estimated taxes for this first quarter total $30,000, the entry to record its payment is

Apr. 10	Income Taxes Payable	30,000	
	Cash		30,000
	Paid estimated quarterly income taxes based on first quarter income.		

Assets = Liabilities + Equity
−30,000   −30,000

This process of accruing and then paying estimated income taxes continues through the year. When annual financial statements are prepared at year-end, the corporation knows its actual total income and the actual amount of income taxes it must pay. This information allows it to properly record income taxes expense for the fourth quarter so that the total of the four quarters' expense amounts equals the actual taxes paid to the government.

Deferred Income Tax Liabilities An income tax liability for corporations can arise when the amount of income before taxes that the corporation reports on its income statement is not the same as the amount of income reported on its income tax return. This difference occurs because income tax laws and GAAP measure income differently. (Differences between tax laws and GAAP arise because Congress uses tax laws to generate receipts, stimulate the economy, and influence behavior, whereas GAAP are intended to provide financial information useful for business decisions. Also, tax accounting often follows the cash basis, whereas GAAP follows the accrual basis.)

Some differences between tax laws and GAAP are temporary. *Temporary differences* arise when the tax return and the income statement report a revenue or expense in different years. As an example, companies are often able to deduct higher amounts of depreciation in the early years of an asset's life and smaller amounts in later years for tax reporting in comparison to GAAP. This means that in the early years, depreciation for tax reporting is often more than depreciation on the income statement. In later years, depreciation for tax reporting is often less than depreciation on the income statement. When temporary differences exist between taxable income on the tax return and the income before taxes on the income statement, corporations compute income taxes expense based on the income reported on the income statement. The result is that income taxes expense reported in the income statement is often different from the amount of income taxes payable to the government. This difference is the **deferred income tax liability.**

To illustrate, assume that in recording its usual quarterly income tax payments, a corporation computes $25,000 of income taxes expense. It also determines that only $21,000 is currently due and $4,000 is deferred to future years (a timing difference). The entry to record this end-of-period adjustment is

Assets = Liabilities + Equity
         +21,000   −25,000
         +4,000

Dec. 31	Income Taxes Expense	25,000	
	Income Taxes Payable		21,000
	Deferred Income Tax Liability		4,000
	To record tax expense and deferred tax liability.		

The credit to Income Taxes Payable reflects the amount currently due to be paid. The credit to Deferred Income Tax Liability reflects tax payments deferred until future years when the temporary difference reverses.

Temporary differences also can cause a company to pay income taxes *before* they are reported on the income statement as expense. If so, the company reports a *Deferred Income Tax Asset* on its balance sheet.

Summary

C1 **Describe current and long-term liabilities and their characteristics.** Liabilities are probable future payments of assets or services that past transactions or events obligate an entity to make. Current liabilities are due within one year or the operating cycle, whichever is longer. All other liabilities are long term.

C2 **Identify and describe known current liabilities.** Known (determinable) current liabilities are set by agreements or laws and are measurable with little uncertainty. They include accounts payable, sales taxes payable, unearned revenues, notes payable, payroll liabilities, and the current portion of long-term debt.

C3 **Explain how to account for contingent liabilities.** If an uncertain future payment depends on a probable future event and the amount can be reasonably estimated, the payment is recorded as a liability. The uncertain future payment is reported as a contingent liability (in the notes) if (*a*) the future event is reasonably possible but not probable or (*b*) the event is probable but the payment amount cannot be reasonably estimated.

A1 **Compute the times interest earned ratio and use it to analyze liabilities.** Times interest earned is computed by dividing a company's net income before interest expense and income taxes by the amount of interest expense. The times interest earned ratio reflects a company's ability to pay interest obligations.

P1 **Prepare entries to account for short-term notes payable.** Short-term notes payable are current liabilities; most bear interest. When a short-term note's face value equals the amount borrowed, it identifies a rate of interest to be paid at maturity.

P2 **Compute and record *employee* payroll deductions and liabilities.** Employee payroll deductions include FICA taxes, income taxes, and voluntary deductions such as for pensions and charities. They make up the difference between gross and net pay.

P3 **Compute and record *employer* payroll expenses and liabilities.** An employer's payroll expenses include employees' gross earnings, any employee benefits, and the payroll taxes levied on the employer. Payroll liabilities include employees' net pay amounts, withholdings from employee wages, any employer-promised benefits, and the employer's payroll taxes.

P4 **Account for estimated liabilities, including warranties and bonuses.** Liabilities for health and pension benefits, warranties, and bonuses are recorded with estimated amounts. These items are recognized as expenses when incurred and matched with revenues generated.

P5A **Identify and describe the details of payroll reports, records, and procedures.** Employers report FICA taxes and federal income tax withholdings using Form 941. FUTA taxes are reported on Form 940. Earnings and deductions are reported to each employee and the federal government on Form W-2. An employer's payroll records often include a payroll register for each pay period, payroll checks and statements of earnings, and individual employee earnings reports.

Guidance Answers to Decision Maker and Decision Ethics

Web Designer You need to be concerned about being an accomplice to unlawful payroll activities. Not paying federal and state taxes on wages earned is illegal and unethical. Such payments also will not provide the employee with Social Security and some Medicare credits. The best course of action is to request payment by check. If this fails to change the owner's payment practices, you must consider quitting this job.

Entrepreneur Risk is partly reflected by the times interest earned ratio. This ratio for the first franchise is 1.5 [($100,000 + $200,000)/$200,000], whereas the ratio for the second franchise is 3.5 [($100,000 + $40,000)/$40,000]. This analysis shows that the first franchise is more at risk of incurring a loss if its sales decline. The second question asks about variability of income. If income greatly varies, this increases the risk an owner will not earn sufficient income to cover interest. Since the first franchise has the greater variability, it is a riskier investment.

Guidance Answers to Quick Checks

1. A liability involves a probable future payment of assets or services that an entity is presently obligated to make as a result of past transactions or events.
2. No, an expected future payment is not a liability unless an existing obligation was created by a past event or transaction.
3. In most cases, a liability due in 15 months is classified as long term. It is classified as a current liability if the company's operating cycle is 15 months or longer.
4. A creditor prefers a note payable instead of a past-due account payable so as to (a) charge interest and/or (b) have evidence of the debt and its terms for potential litigation or disputes.
5. $1,000* × (.008) + $1,000* × (.04) + $3,000 × (.062) + $3,000 × (.0145) = $277.50

---

* $1,000 of the $3,000 March pay is subject to FUTA and SUTA—the entire $6,000 pay from January and February was subject to them.

6. (a) FICA taxes are incurred by both employee and employer.
   (b) FUTA taxes are incurred by the employer.
   (c) SUTA taxes are incurred by the employer.
   (d) Withheld income taxes are incurred by the employee.
7. (a)
8. (a) Warranty expense was previously estimated and recorded.
9. (b)
10. A future payment is reported in the notes as a contingent liability if (a) the uncertain future event is probable but the amount of payment cannot be reasonably estimated or (b) the uncertain future event is not probable but has a reasonable possibility of occurring.
11. An employee's marital status, gross earnings and number of withholding allowances determine the deduction for federal income taxes.
12. $59
13. (d)

Key Terms

Contingent liability (p. 382)
Current liabilities (p. 371)
Current portion of long-term debt (p. 379)
Deferred income tax liability (p. 394)
Employee benefits (p. 379)
Employee earnings report (p. 390)
Estimated liability (p. 379)
Federal depository bank (p. 387)
Federal Insurance Contributions Act (FICA) taxes (p. 376)

Federal Unemployment Taxes (FUTA) (p. 378)
Form 940 (p. 387)
Form 941 (p. 387)
Form W-2 (p. 389)
Form W-4 (p. 392)
Gross pay (p. 376)
Known liabilities (p. 372)
Long-term liabilities (p. 371)
Merit rating (p. 378)

Net pay (p. 376)
Payroll bank account (p. 392)
Payroll deductions (p. 376)
Payroll register (p. 389)
Short-term note payable (p. 373)
State Unemployment Taxes (SUTA) (p. 378)
Times interest earned (p. 384)
Wage bracket withholding table (p. 392)
Warranty (p. 380)

Multiple Choice Quiz

Answers on p. 411   mhhe.com/wildFA6e

Additional quiz questions are available at the book's Website.

1. On December 1, a company signed a $6,000, 90-day, 5% note payable, with principal plus interest due on March 1 of the following year. What amount of interest expense should be accrued at December 31 on the note?
   a. $300
   b. $25
   c. $100
   d. $75
   e. $0

2. An employee earned $50,000 during the year. FICA tax for social security is 6.2% and FICA tax for Medicare is 1.45%. The employer's share of FICA taxes is
   a. Zero, since the employee's pay exceeds the FICA limit.
   b. Zero, since FICA is not an employer tax.
   c. $3,100
   d. $725
   e. $3,825

3. Assume the FUTA tax rate is 0.8% and the SUTA tax rate is 5.4%. Both taxes are applied to the first $7,000 of an employee's pay. What is the total unemployment tax an employer must pay on an employee's annual wages of $40,000?
   a. $2,480
   b. $434
   c. $56
   d. $378
   e. Zero; the employee's wages exceed the $7,000 maximum.

4. A company sells big screen televisions for $3,000 each. Each television has a two-year warranty that covers the replacement of defective parts. It is estimated that 1% of all televisions sold will be returned under warranty at an average cost of $250 each. During July, the company sold 10,000 big screen televisions, and 80 were serviced under the warranty during July at a total cost of $18,000. The credit balance in the Estimated

Warranty Liability account at July 1 was $26,000. What is the company's warranty expense for the month of July?
a. $51,000
b. $1,000
c. $25,000
d. $33,000
e. $18,000

5. Employees earn vacation pay at the rate of 1 day per month. During October, 150 employees qualify for one vacation day each. Their average daily wage is $175 per day. What is the amount of vacation benefit expense for October?
a. $26,250
b. $175
c. $2,100
d. $63,875
e. $150

A(B) *Superscript letter A (B) denotes assignments based on Appendix 9A (9B).*

Icon denotes assignments that involve decision making.

Discussion Questions

1. What are the three important questions concerning the uncertainty of liabilities?
2. What is the difference between a current and a long-term liability?
3. What is an estimated liability?
4. If $988 is the total of a sale that includes its sales tax of 4%, what is the selling price of the item only?
5. What is the combined amount (in percent) of the employee and employer Social Security tax rate?
6. What is the current Medicare tax rate? This rate is applied to what maximum level of salary and wages?
7. What determines the amount deducted from an employee's wages for federal income taxes?
8. Which payroll taxes are the employee's responsibility and which are the employer's responsibility?
9. What is an employer's unemployment merit rating? How are these ratings assigned to employers?
10. Why are warranty liabilities usually recognized on the balance sheet as liabilities even when they are uncertain?
11. Suppose that a company has a facility located where disastrous weather conditions often occur. Should it report a probable loss from a future disaster as a liability on its balance sheet? Explain.
12.A What is a wage bracket withholding table?
13.A What amount of income tax is withheld from the salary of an employee who is single with two withholding allowances and earning $725 per week? What if the employee earned $625 and has no withholding allowances? (Use Exhibit 9A.6.)
14. Refer to **Research In Motion**'s balance sheet in Appendix A. What revenue-related liability does Research In Motion report at February 27, 2010? **RIM**
15. Refer to **Apple**'s balance sheet in Appendix A. What is the amount of Apple's accounts payable as of September 26, 2009? **Apple**
16. Refer to **Nokia**'s balance sheet in Appendix A. List Nokia's current liabilities as of December 31, 2009. **NOKIA**
17. Refer to **Palm**'s balance sheet in Appendix A. What current liabilities related to income taxes are on its balance sheet? Explain the meaning of each income tax account identified. **Palm**

QUICK STUDY

QS 9-1
Classifying liabilities C1

Which of the following items are normally classified as a current liability for a company that has a 15-month operating cycle?
1. Salaries payable.
2. Note payable due in 19 months.
3. FICA taxes payable.
4. Note payable maturing in 3 years.
5. Note payable due in 10 months.
6. Portion of long-term note due in 15 months.

QS 9-2
Accounting for sales taxes
C2

Wrecker Computing sells merchandise for $5,000 cash on September 30 (cost of merchandise is $2,900). The sales tax law requires Wrecker to collect 4% sales tax on every dollar of merchandise sold. Record the entry for the $5,000 sale and its applicable sales tax. Also record the entry that shows the remittance of the 4% tax on this sale to the state government on October 15.

QS 9-3
Unearned revenue C2

Tickets, Inc., receives $5,500,000 cash in advance ticket sales for a four-date tour of Bruce Springsteen. Record the advance ticket sales on October 31. Record the revenue earned for the first concert date of November 8, assuming it represents one-fourth of the advance ticket sales.

The following legal claims exist for Kalamazoo Co. Identify the accounting treatment for each claim as either (a) a liability that is recorded or (b) an item described in notes to its financial statements.

1. Kalamazoo (defendant) estimates that a pending lawsuit could result in damages of $1,000,000; it is reasonably possible that the plaintiff will win the case.
2. Kalamazoo faces a probable loss on a pending lawsuit; the amount is not reasonably estimable.
3. Kalamazoo estimates damages in a case at $2,500,000 with a high probability of losing the case.

QS 9-4
Accounting for contingent liabilities
C3

On November 7, 2011, Ortez Company borrows $150,000 cash by signing a 90-day, 8% note payable with a face value of $150,000. (1) Compute the accrued interest payable on December 31, 2011, (2) prepare the journal entry to record the accrued interest expense at December 31, 2011, and (3) prepare the journal entry to record payment of the note at maturity.

QS 9-5
Interest-bearing note transactions P1

On January 14, the end of the first bi-weekly pay period of the year, Rockin Company's payroll register showed that its employees earned $14,000 of sales salaries. Withholdings from the employees' salaries include FICA Social Security taxes at the rate of 6.2%, FICA Medicare taxes at the rate of 1.45%, $2,600 of federal income taxes, $309 of medical insurance deductions, and $120 of union dues. No employee earned more than $7,000 in this first period. Prepare the journal entry to record Rockin Company's January 14 (employee) payroll expenses and liabilities.

QS 9-6
Record employee payroll taxes
P2

Merger Co. has ten employees, each of whom earns $2,000 per month and has been employed since January 1. FICA Social Security taxes are 6.2% of the first $110,100 paid to each employee, and FICA Medicare taxes are 1.45% of gross pay. FUTA taxes are 0.8% and SUTA taxes are 5.4% of the first $7,000 paid to each employee. Prepare the March 31 journal entry to record the March payroll taxes expense.

QS 9-7
Record employer payroll taxes
P3

On September 11, 2010, Home Store sells a mower for $400 with a one-year warranty that covers parts. Warranty expense is estimated at 5% of sales. On July 24, 2011, the mower is brought in for repairs covered under the warranty requiring $35 in materials taken from the Repair Parts Inventory. Prepare the July 24, 2011, entry to record the warranty repairs.

QS 9-8
Recording warranty repairs
P4

Paris Company offers an annual bonus to employees if the company meets certain net income goals. Prepare the journal entry to record a $10,000 bonus owed to its workers (to be shared equally) at calendar year-end.

QS 9-9
Accounting for bonuses P4

Chester Co.'s salaried employees earn four weeks vacation per year. It pays $192,000.12 in total employee salaries for 52 weeks but its employees work only 48 weeks. This means Chester's total weekly expense is $4,000 ($192,000/48 weeks) instead of the $3,692.31 cash paid weekly to the employees ($192,000/52 weeks). Record Chester's weekly vacation benefits expense.

QS 9-10
Accounting for vacations
P4

Compute the times interest earned for Weltin Company, which reports income before interest expense and income taxes of $2,044,000, and interest expense of $350,000. Interpret its times interest earned (assume that its competitors average a times interest earned of 4.0).

QS 9-11
Times interest earned A1

The payroll records of Clix Software show the following information about Trish Farqua, an employee, for the weekly pay period ending September 30, 2012. Farqua is single and claims one allowance. Compute her Social Security tax (6.2%), Medicare tax (1.45%), federal income tax withholding, state income tax (1.0%), and net pay for the current pay period. (Use the withholding table in Exhibit 9A.6 and round tax amounts to the nearest cent.)

Total (gross) earnings for current pay period..........	$ 735
Cumulative earnings of previous pay periods..........	9,700

QS 9-12^A
Net pay and tax computations
P5

Check Net pay, $578.42

Cather Corporation has made and recorded its quarterly income tax payments. After a final review of taxes for the year, the company identifies an additional $30,000 of income tax expense that should be recorded. A portion of this additional expense, $8,000, is deferred for payment in future years. Record Cather's year-end adjusting entry for income tax expense.

QS 9-13^B
Record deferred income tax liability P4

Answer each of the following related to international accounting standards.
a. In general, how similar or different are the definitions and characteristics of current liabilities between IFRS and U.S. GAAP?
b. Companies reporting under IFRS often reference a set of current liabilities with the title *financial liabilities*. Identify two current liabilities that would be classified under financial liabilities per IFRS. (*Hint:* **Nokia** provides examples in this chapter and in Appendix A.)

QS 9-14
International accounting standards
C1 C2

EXERCISES

Exercise 9-1
Classifying liabilities
C1

The following items appear on the balance sheet of a company with a two-month operating cycle. Identify the proper classification of each item as follows: *C* if it is a current liability, *L* if it is a long-term liability, or *N* if it is not a liability.

_____ 1. Sales taxes payable.
_____ 2. FUTA taxes payable.
_____ 3. Accounts receivable.
_____ 4. Wages payable.
_____ 5. Salaries payable.
_____ 6. Notes payable (due in 6 to 12 months).
_____ 7. Notes payable (due in 120 days).
_____ 8. Current portion of long-term debt.
_____ 9. Notes payable (mature in five years).
_____10. Notes payable (due in 13 to 24 months).

Exercise 9-2
Recording known current liabilities
C2

Prepare any necessary adjusting entries at December 31, 2011, for Yacht Company's year-end financial statements for each of the following separate transactions and events.

1. Yacht Company records an adjusting entry for $2,000,000 of previously unrecorded cash sales (costing $1,000,000) and its sales taxes at a rate of 5%.
2. The company earned $40,000 of $100,000 previously received in advance for services.

Exercise 9-3
Accounting for contingent liabilities
C3

Prepare any necessary adjusting entries at December 31, 2011, for Moor Company's year-end financial statements for each of the following separate transactions and events.

1. A disgruntled employee is suing Moor Company. Legal advisers believe that the company will probably need to pay damages, but the amount cannot be reasonably estimated.
2. Moor Company guarantees the $5,000 debt of a supplier. The supplier will probably not default on the debt.

Exercise 9-4
Accounting for note payable
P1

Check (2b) Interest expense, $1,880

Perfect Systems borrows $94,000 cash on May 15, 2011, by signing a 60-day, 12% note.
1. On what date does this note mature?
2. Suppose the face value of the note equals $94,000, the principal of the loan. Prepare the journal entries to record (*a*) issuance of the note and (*b*) payment of the note at maturity.

Exercise 9-5
Interest-bearing notes payable with year-end adjustments
P1

Check (2) $2,250
(3) $1,125

Kwon Co. borrows $150,000 cash on November 1, 2011, by signing a 90-day, 9% note with a face value of $150,000.
1. On what date does this note mature? (Assume that February of 2011 has 28 days.)
2. How much interest expense results from this note in 2011? (Assume a 360-day year.)
3. How much interest expense results from this note in 2012? (Assume a 360-day year.)
4. Prepare journal entries to record (*a*) issuance of the note, (*b*) accrual of interest at the end of 2011, and (*c*) payment of the note at maturity.

Exercise 9-6
Computing payroll taxes
P2 P3

Check (a) FUTA, $4.80; SUTA, $17.40

MRI Company has one employee. FICA Social Security taxes are 6.2% of the first $110,100 paid to its employee, and FICA Medicare taxes are 1.45% of gross pay. For MRI, its FUTA taxes are 0.8% and SUTA taxes are 2.9% of the first $7,000 paid to its employee. Compute MRI's amounts for each of these four taxes as applied to the employee's gross earnings for September under each of three separate situations (*a*), (*b*), and (*c*).

	Gross Pay through August	Gross Pay for September
a.	$ 6,400	$ 800
b.	18,200	2,100
c.	103,800	8,000

Exercise 9-7
Payroll-related journal entries P2

Using the data in situation *a* of Exercise 9-6, prepare the employer's September 30 journal entries to record salary expense and its related payroll liabilities for this employee. The employee's federal income taxes withheld by the employer are $135 for this pay period.

Exercise 9-8
Payroll-related journal entries P3

Using the data in situation *a* of Exercise 9-6, prepare the employer's September 30 journal entries to record the *employer's* payroll taxes expense and its related liabilities.

Exercise 9-9
Computing and recording bonuses P4

For the year ended December 31, 2011, Winter Company has implemented an employee bonus program equal to 3% of Winter's net income, which employees will share equally. Winter's net income (prebonus) is expected to be $1,000,000, and bonus expense is deducted in computing net income.

1. Compute the amount of the bonus payable to the employees at year-end (use the method described in the chapter and round to the nearest dollar).
2. Prepare the journal entry at December 31, 2011, to record the bonus due the employees.
3. Prepare the journal entry at January 19, 2012, to record payment of the bonus to employees.

Check (1) $29,126

Exercise 9-10
Accounting for estimated liabilities P4

Prepare any necessary adjusting entries at December 31, 2011, for Jester Company's year-end financial statements for each of the following separate transactions and events.

1. During December, Jester Company sold 3,000 units of a product that carries a 60-day warranty. December sales for this product total $120,000. The company expects 8% of the units to need warranty repairs, and it estimates the average repair cost per unit will be $15.
2. Employees earn vacation pay at a rate of one day per month. During December, 20 employees qualify for one vacation day each. Their average daily wage is $120 per employee.

Exercise 9-11
Warranty expense and liability computations and entries P4

Chang Co. sold a copier costing $3,800 with a two-year parts warranty to a customer on August 16, 2011, for $5,500 cash. Chang uses the perpetual inventory system. On November 22, 2012, the copier requires on-site repairs that are completed the same day. The repairs cost $199 for materials taken from the Repair Parts Inventory. These are the only repairs required in 2012 for this copier. Based on experience, Chang expects to incur warranty costs equal to 4% of dollar sales. It records warranty expense with an adjusting entry at the end of each year.

1. How much warranty expense does the company report in 2011 for this copier?
2. How much is the estimated warranty liability for this copier as of December 31, 2011?
3. How much warranty expense does the company report in 2012 for this copier?
4. How much is the estimated warranty liability for this copier as of December 31, 2012?
5. Prepare journal entries to record (a) the copier's sale; (b) the adjustment on December 31, 2011, to recognize the warranty expense; and (c) the repairs that occur in November 2012.

Check (1) $220

(4) $21

Exercise 9-12
Computing and interpreting times interest earned A1

Use the following information from separate companies a through f to compute times interest earned. Which company indicates the strongest ability to pay interest expense as it comes due?

	Net Income (Loss)	Interest Expense	Income Taxes
a.	$140,000	$48,000	$ 35,000
b.	140,000	15,000	50,000
c.	140,000	8,000	70,000
d.	265,000	12,000	130,000
e.	79,000	12,000	30,000
f.	(4,000)	12,000	0

Check (b) 13.67

Exercise 9-13A
Gross and net pay computation P5

Tony Newbern, an unmarried employee, works 48 hours in the week ended January 12. His pay rate is $12 per hour, and his wages are subject to no deductions other than FICA—Social Security, FICA—Medicare, and federal income taxes. He claims two withholding allowances. Compute his regular pay, overtime pay (for this company, workers earn 150% of their regular rate for hours in excess of 40 per week), and gross pay. Then compute his FICA tax deduction (use 6.2% for the Social Security portion and 1.45% for the Medicare portion), income tax deduction (use the wage bracket withholding table of Exhibit 9A.6), total deductions, and net pay. (Round tax amounts to the nearest cent.)

Check Net pay, $515.26

Exercise 9-14B
Accounting for income taxes P4

Ming Corporation prepares financial statements for each month-end. As part of its accounting process, estimated income taxes are accrued each month for 30% of the current month's net income. The income taxes are paid in the first month of each quarter for the amount accrued for the prior quarter. The following information is available for the fourth quarter of year 2011. When tax computations are completed on January 20, 2012, Ming determines that the quarter's Income Taxes Payable account balance should be $29,100 on December 31, 2011 (its unadjusted balance is $23,640).

October 2011 net income	$27,900
November 2011 net income	18,200
December 2011 net income	32,700

Check (1) $5,460

1. Determine the amount of the accounting adjustment (dated as of December 31, 2011) to produce the proper ending balance in the Income Taxes Payable account.
2. Prepare journal entries to record (a) the December 31, 2011, adjustment to the Income Taxes Payable account and (b) the January 20, 2012, payment of the fourth-quarter taxes.

Exercise 9-15
Accounting for current liabilities under IFRS
P4

Volvo Group reports the following information for its product warranty costs as of December 31, 2008, along with provisions and utilizations of warranty liabilities for the year ended December 31, 2008 (SEK in millions).

Product warranty costs

Estimated costs for product warranties are charged to cost of sales when the products are sold. Estimated warranty costs include contractual warranty and goodwill warranty. Warranty provisions are estimated with consideration of historical claims statistics, the warranty period, the average time-lag between faults occurring and claims to the company, and anticipated changes in quality indexes. Differences between actual warranty claims and the estimated claims generally affect the recognized expense and provisions in future periods. At December 31, 2008, warranty cost provisions amounted to 10,354.

Product warranty liabilities, December 31, 2007	SEK 9,373
Additional provisions to product warranty liabilities	6,201
Utilizations and reductions of product warranty liabilities	(5,220)
Product warranty liabilities, December 31, 2008	10,354

1. Prepare Volvo's journal entry to record its estimated warranty liabilities (provisions) for 2008.
2. Prepare Volvo's journal entry to record its costs (utilizations) related to its warranty program for 2008. Assume those costs involve replacements taken out of Inventory, with no cash involved.
3. How much warranty expense does Volvo report for 2008?

Exercise 9-16
Recording payroll
P2 P3

The following monthly data are taken from Nunez Company at July 31: Sales salaries, $120,000; Office salaries, $60,000; Federal income taxes withheld, $45,000; State income taxes withheld, $10,000; Social security taxes withheld, $11,160; Medicare taxes withheld, $2,610; Medical insurance premiums, $7,000; Life insurance premiums, $4,000; Union dues deducted, $1,000; and Salaries subject to unemployment taxes, $50,000. The employee pays forty percent of medical and life insurance premiums.

Prepare journal entries to record: (1) accrued payroll, including employee deductions, for July; (2) cash payment of the net payroll (salaries payable) for July; (3) accrued employer payroll taxes, and other related employment expenses, for July—assume that FICA taxes are identical to those on employees and that SUTA taxes are 5.4% and FUTA taxes are 0.8%; and (4) cash payment of all liabilities related to the July payroll.

Exercise 9-17
Computing payroll taxes
P2 P3

Madison Company has nine employees. FICA Social Security taxes are 6.2% of the first $110,100 paid to each employee, and FICA Medicare taxes are 1.45% of gross pay. FUTA taxes are 0.8% and SUTA taxes are 5.4% of the first $7,000 paid to each employee. Cumulative pay for the current year for each of its employees follows.

Employee	Cumulative Pay	Employee	Cumulative Pay	Employee	Cumulative Pay
Steve S.	$ 6,000	Christina S.	$156,600	Dana W.	$116,600
Tim V.	60,000	Michelle H.	106,900	Stewart M.	36,800
Brent G.	87,000	Kathleen K.	110,100	Sankha B.	4,000

a. Prepare a table with the following column headings: Employee; Cumulative Pay; Pay Subject to FICA Social Security Taxes; Pay Subject to FICA Medicare Taxes; Pay Subject to FUTA Taxes; Pay Subject to SUTA Taxes. Compute the amounts in this table for each employee and total the columns.
b. For the company, compute each total for: FICA Social Security taxes, FICA Medicare taxes, FUTA taxes, and SUTA taxes. (*Hint:* Remember to include in those totals any employee share of taxes that the company must collect.)

Exercise 9-18
Preparing payroll register and related entries **P5**

SP Company has five employees. Employees paid by the hour receive a $10 per hour pay rate for the regular 40-hour work week plus one and one-half times the hourly rate for each overtime hour beyond the 40-hours per week. Hourly employees are paid every two weeks, but salaried employees are paid monthly on the last biweekly payday of each month. FICA Social Security taxes are 6.2% of the first $110,100 paid to each employee, and FICA Medicare taxes are 1.45% of gross pay. FUTA taxes are 0.8% and SUTA taxes are 5.4% of the first $7,000 paid to each employee. The company has a benefits plan that includes medical insurance, life insurance, and retirement funding for employees. Under this plan, employees must contribute 5 percent of their gross income as a payroll withholding, which the company matches with double the amount. Following is the partially completed payroll register for the biweekly period ending August 31, which is the last payday of August.

Employee	Cumulative Pay (Excludes Current Period)	Current Period Gross Pay - Pay Type	Pay Hours	Gross Pay	FIT / SIT	FUTA / SUTA	FICA-SS_EE / FICA-SS_ER	FICA-Med_EE / FICA-Med_ER	EE-Ben_Plan Withholding / ER-Ben_Plan Withholding	Employee Net Pay
Kathleen	$108,300.00	Salary	---	$7,000.00	$2,000.00 / 300.00					
Nichole	6,800.00	Salary	---	500.00	80.00 / 20.00					
Anthony	15,000.00	Regular / Overtime	80 / 8		110.00 / 25.00					
Zoey	6,500.00	Regular / Overtime	80 / 4		100.00 / 22.00					
Gracie	5,000.00	Regular / Overtime	74 / 0	740.00 / 0.00	90.00 / 21.00					
Totals	141,600.00				2,380.00 / 388.00					

Note: Table abbreviations follow those in Exhibit 9A.3 (see pages 389–390); and, "Ben_Plan" refers to employee (EE) or employer (ER) withholding for the benefits plan.

a. Complete this payroll register by filling in all cells for the pay period ended August 31. *Hint:* See Exhibit 9A.3 for guidance. (Round amounts to cents.)
b. Prepare the August 31 journal entry to record the accrued biweekly payroll and related liabilities for deductions.
c. Prepare the August 31 journal entry to record the employer's cash payment of the net payroll of part *b*.
d. Prepare the August 31 journal entry to record the employer's payroll taxes including the contribution to the benefits plan.
e. Prepare the August 31 journal entry to pay all liabilities (expect net payroll in part *c*) for this biweekly period.

connect

Tytus Co. entered into the following transactions involving short-term liabilities in 2010 and 2011.

2010

Apr. 20 Purchased $38,500 of merchandise on credit from Frier, terms are 1/10, n/30. Tytus uses the perpetual inventory system.
May 19 Replaced the April 20 account payable to Frier with a 90-day, $30,000 note bearing 9% annual interest along with paying $8,500 in cash.
July 8 Borrowed $60,000 cash from Community Bank by signing a 120-day, 10% interest-bearing note with a face value of $60,000.
___?___ Paid the amount due on the note to Frier at the maturity date.
___?___ Paid the amount due on the note to Community Bank at the maturity date.
Nov. 28 Borrowed $21,000 cash from UMB Bank by signing a 60-day, 8% interest-bearing note with a face value of $21,000.
Dec. 31 Recorded an adjusting entry for accrued interest on the note to UMB Bank.

2011

___?___ Paid the amount due on the note to UMB Bank at the maturity date.

Required

1. Determine the maturity date for each of the three notes described.
2. Determine the interest due at maturity for each of the three notes. (Assume a 360-day year.)
3. Determine the interest expense to be recorded in the adjusting entry at the end of 2010.
4. Determine the interest expense to be recorded in 2011.
5. Prepare journal entries for all the preceding transactions and events for years 2010 and 2011.

PROBLEM SET A

Problem 9-1A
Short-term notes payable transactions and entries

P1

mhhe.com/wildFA6e

Check (2) Frier, $675
(3) $154
(4) $126

Problem 9-2A
Warranty expense and liability estimation
P4

On October 29, 2010, Lue Co. began operations by purchasing razors for resale. Lue uses the perpetual inventory method. The razors have a 90-day warranty that requires the company to replace any nonworking razor. When a razor is returned, the company discards it and mails a new one from Merchandise Inventory to the customer. The company's cost per new razor is $18 and its retail selling price is $80 in both 2010 and 2011. The manufacturer has advised the company to expect warranty costs to equal 7% of dollar sales. The following transactions and events occurred.

2010

Nov. 11 Sold 75 razors for $6,000 cash.
     30 Recognized warranty expense related to November sales with an adjusting entry.
Dec. 9 Replaced 15 razors that were returned under the warranty.
    16 Sold 210 razors for $16,800 cash.
    29 Replaced 30 razors that were returned under the warranty.
    31 Recognized warranty expense related to December sales with an adjusting entry.

2011

Jan. 5 Sold 130 razors for $10,400 cash.
   17 Replaced 50 razors that were returned under the warranty.
   31 Recognized warranty expense related to January sales with an adjusting entry.

Required

1. Prepare journal entries to record these transactions and adjustments for 2010 and 2011.
2. How much warranty expense is reported for November 2010 and for December 2010?
3. How much warranty expense is reported for January 2011?
4. What is the balance of the Estimated Warranty Liability account as of December 31, 2010?
5. What is the balance of the Estimated Warranty Liability account as of January 31, 2011?

Check (3) $728
(4) $786 Cr.
(5) $614 Cr.

Problem 9-3A
Computing and analyzing times interest earned
A1

Shown here are condensed income statements for two different companies (both are organized as LLCs and pay no income taxes).

Ace Company	
Sales	$500,000
Variable expenses (80%)	400,000
Income before interest	100,000
Interest expense (fixed)	30,000
Net income	$ 70,000

Deuce Company	
Sales	$500,000
Variable expenses (60%)	300,000
Income before interest	200,000
Interest expense (fixed)	130,000
Net income	$ 70,000

Required

1. Compute times interest earned for Ace Company.
2. Compute times interest earned for Deuce Company.
3. What happens to each company's net income if sales increase by 30%?
4. What happens to each company's net income if sales increase by 50%?
5. What happens to each company's net income if sales increase by 80%?
6. What happens to each company's net income if sales decrease by 10%?
7. What happens to each company's net income if sales decrease by 20%?
8. What happens to each company's net income if sales decrease by 40%?

Analysis Component

9. Comment on the results from parts 3 through 8 in relation to the fixed-cost strategies of the two companies and the ratio values you computed in parts 1 and 2.

Check (3) Ace net income, $100,000 (43% increase)

(6) Deuce net income, $50,000 (29% decrease)

Problem 9-4A
Payroll expenses, withholdings, and taxes
P2 P3

Legal Stars has four employees. FICA Social Security taxes are 6.2% of the first $110,100 paid to each employee, and FICA Medicare taxes are 1.45% of gross pay. Also, for the first $7,000 paid to each employee, the company's FUTA taxes are 0.8% and SUTA taxes are 2.15%. The company is preparing its payroll calculations for the week ended August 25. Payroll records show the following information for the company's four employees.

	Name	Gross Pay through 8/18	Current Week Gross Pay	Current Week Income Tax Withholding
3	Dale	$108,600	$2,000	$252
4	Ted	36,650	900	99
5	Kate	6,750	450	54
6	Chas	1,050	400	36

In addition to gross pay, the company must pay one-half of the $32 per employee weekly health insurance; each employee pays the remaining one-half. The company also contributes an extra 8% of each employee's gross pay (at no cost to employees) to a pension fund.

Required

Compute the following for the week ended August 25 (round amounts to the nearest cent):

1. Each employee's FICA withholdings for Social Security.
2. Each employee's FICA withholdings for Medicare.
3. Employer's FICA taxes for Social Security.
4. Employer's FICA taxes for Medicare.
5. Employer's FUTA taxes.
6. Employer's SUTA taxes.
7. Each employee's net (take-home) pay.
8. Employer's total payroll-related expense for each employee.

Check (3) $201.50
(4) $54.38
(5) $5.20

(7) Total net pay, $2,989.12

Problem 9-5A
Entries for payroll transactions
P2 P3

On January 8, the end of the first weekly pay period of the year, Royal Company's payroll register showed that its employees earned $11,380 of office salaries and $32,920 of sales salaries. Withholdings from the employees' salaries include FICA Social Security taxes at the rate of 6.2%, FICA Medicare taxes at the rate of 1.45%, $6,340 of federal income taxes, $670 of medical insurance deductions, and $420 of union dues. No employee earned more than $7,000 in this first period.

Required

1. Calculate FICA Social Security taxes payable and FICA Medicare taxes payable. Prepare the journal entry to record Royal Company's January 8 (employee) payroll expenses and liabilities.
2. Prepare the journal entry to record Royal's (employer) payroll taxes resulting from the January 8 payroll. Royal's merit rating reduces its state unemployment tax rate to 4% of the first $7,000 paid each employee. The federal unemployment tax rate is 0.8%.

Check (1) Cr. Salaries Payable, $33,481.05

(2) Dr. Payroll Taxes Expense, $5,515.35

Problem 9-6A[A]
Entries for payroll transactions
P2 P3 P5

Polo Company has 10 employees, each of whom earns $2,600 per month and is paid on the last day of each month. All 10 have been employed continuously at this amount since January 1. Polo uses a payroll bank account and special payroll checks to pay its employees. On March 1, the following accounts and balances exist in its general ledger:

a. FICA—Social Security Taxes Payable, $3,224; FICA—Medicare Taxes Payable, $754. (The balances of these accounts represent total liabilities for *both* the employer's and employees' FICA taxes for the February payroll only.)
b. Employees' Federal Income Taxes Payable, $3,900 (liability for February only).
c. Federal Unemployment Taxes Payable, $416 (liability for January and February together).
d. State Unemployment Taxes Payable, $2,080 (liability for January and February together).

During March and April, the company had the following payroll transactions.

Mar. 15 Issued check payable to Fleet Bank, a federal depository bank authorized to accept employers' payments of FICA taxes and employee income tax withholdings. The $7,878 check is in payment of the February FICA and employee income taxes.
    31 Recorded the March payroll and transferred funds from the regular bank account to the payroll bank account. Issued checks payable to each employee in payment of the March payroll. The payroll register shows the following summary totals for the March pay period.

Check March 31: Cr. Salaries Payable, $20,111

	Salaries and Wages					
	Office Salaries	Shop Wages	Gross Pay	FICA Taxes*	Federal Income Taxes	Net Pay
	$10,400	$15,600	$26,000	$1,612 $ 377	$3,900	$20,111

* FICA taxes are Social Security and Medicare, respectively.

March 31: Dr. Payroll Taxes Expenses, $2,853

31 Recorded the employer's payroll taxes resulting from the March payroll. The company has a merit rating that reduces its state unemployment tax rate to 4.0% of the first $7,000 paid each employee. The federal rate is 0.8%.

April 15: Cr. Cash, $7,878 (Fleet Bank)

Apr. 15 Issued check to Fleet Bank in payment of the March FICA and employee income taxes.
15 Issued check to the State Tax Commission for the January, February, and March state unemployment taxes. Mailed the check and the first quarter tax return to the Commission.
30 Issued check payable to Fleet Bank in payment of the employer's FUTA taxes for the first quarter of the year.
30 Mailed Form 941 to the IRS, reporting the FICA taxes and the employees' federal income tax withholdings for the first quarter.

Required

Prepare journal entries to record the transactions and events for both March and April.

PROBLEM SET B

Bargen Co. entered into the following transactions involving short-term liabilities in 2010 and 2011.

Problem 9-1B
Short-term notes payable transactions and entries
P1

2010

Apr. 22 Purchased $4,000 of merchandise on credit from Quinn Products, terms are 1/10, n/30. Bargen uses the perpetual inventory system.
May 23 Replaced the April 22 account payable to Quinn Products with a 60-day, $3,600 note bearing 15% annual interest along with paying $400 in cash.
July 15 Borrowed $9,000 cash from Blackhawk Bank by signing a 120-day, 10% interest-bearing note with a face value of $9,000.
___?___ Paid the amount due on the note to Quinn Products at maturity.
___?___ Paid the amount due on the note to Blackhawk Bank at maturity.
Dec. 6 Borrowed $16,000 cash from City Bank by signing a 45-day, 9% interest-bearing note with a face value of $16,000.
31 Recorded an adjusting entry for accrued interest on the note to City Bank.

2011

___?___ Paid the amount due on the note to City Bank at maturity.

Required

Check (2) Quinn, $90
(3) $100
(4) $80

1. Determine the maturity date for each of the three notes described.
2. Determine the interest due at maturity for each of the three notes. (Assume a 360-day year.)
3. Determine the interest expense to be recorded in the adjusting entry at the end of 2010.
4. Determine the interest expense to be recorded in 2011.
5. Prepare journal entries for all the preceding transactions and events for years 2010 and 2011.

Problem 9-2B
Warranty expense and liability estimation
P4

On November 10, 2011, Byung Co. began operations by purchasing coffee grinders for resale. Byung uses the perpetual inventory method. The grinders have a 60-day warranty that requires the company to replace any nonworking grinder. When a grinder is returned, the company discards it and mails a new one from Merchandise Inventory to the customer. The company's cost per new grinder is $14 and its retail selling price is $35 in both 2011 and 2012. The manufacturer has advised the company to expect warranty costs to equal 10% of dollar sales. The following transactions and events occurred.

2011

Nov. 16 Sold 50 grinders for $1,750 cash.
30 Recognized warranty expense related to November sales with an adjusting entry.
Dec. 12 Replaced six grinders that were returned under the warranty.
18 Sold 150 grinders for $5,250 cash.
28 Replaced 17 grinders that were returned under the warranty.
31 Recognized warranty expense related to December sales with an adjusting entry.

2012

Jan. 7 Sold 60 grinders for $2,100 cash.
21 Replaced 38 grinders that were returned under the warranty.
31 Recognized warranty expense related to January sales with an adjusting entry.

Required

1. Prepare journal entries to record these transactions and adjustments for 2011 and 2012.
2. How much warranty expense is reported for November 2011 and for December 2011?
3. How much warranty expense is reported for January 2012?
4. What is the balance of the Estimated Warranty Liability account as of December 31, 2011?
5. What is the balance of the Estimated Warranty Liability account as of January 31, 2012?

Check (3) $210
(4) $378 Cr.
(5) $56 Cr.

Shown here are condensed income statements for two different companies (both are organized as LLCs and pay no income taxes).

Problem 9-3B
Computing and analyzing times interest earned
A1

Virgo Company	
Sales	$120,000
Variable expenses (50%)	60,000
Income before interest	60,000
Interest expense (fixed)	45,000
Net income	$ 15,000

Zodiac Company	
Sales	$120,000
Variable expenses (75%)	90,000
Income before interest	30,000
Interest expense (fixed)	15,000
Net income	$ 15,000

Required

1. Compute times interest earned for Virgo Company.
2. Compute times interest earned for Zodiac Company.
3. What happens to each company's net income if sales increase by 10%?
4. What happens to each company's net income if sales increase by 40%?
5. What happens to each company's net income if sales increase by 90%?
6. What happens to each company's net income if sales decrease by 20%?
7. What happens to each company's net income if sales decrease by 50%?
8. What happens to each company's net income if sales decrease by 80%?

Check (4) Virgo net income, $39,000 (160% increase)

(6) Zodiac net income, $9,000 (40% decrease)

Analysis Component

9. Comment on the results from parts 3 through 8 in relation to the fixed-cost strategies of the two companies and the ratio values you computed in parts 1 and 2.

Sea Biz Co. has four employees. FICA Social Security taxes are 6.2% of the first $110,100 paid to each employee, and FICA Medicare taxes are 1.45% of gross pay. Also, for the first $7,000 paid to each employee, the company's FUTA taxes are 0.8% and SUTA taxes are 1.75%. The company is preparing its payroll calculations for the week ended September 30. Payroll records show the following information for the company's four employees.

Problem 9-4B
Payroll expenses, withholdings, and taxes
P2 P3

Name	Gross Pay through 9/23	Current Week Gross Pay	Income Tax Withholding
Alli	$107,600	$2,500	$198
Eve	36,650	1,515	182
Hong	6,650	475	52
Juan	22,200	600	48

In addition to gross pay, the company must pay one-half of the $44 per employee weekly health insurance; each employee pays the remaining one-half. The company also contributes an extra 5% of each employee's gross pay (at no cost to employees) to a pension fund.

Required

Compute the following for the week ended September 30 (round amounts to the nearest cent):

1. Each employee's FICA withholdings for Social Security.
2. Each employee's FICA withholdings for Medicare.
3. Employer's FICA taxes for Social Security.
4. Employer's FICA taxes for Medicare.
5. Employer's FUTA taxes.
6. Employer's SUTA taxes.
7. Each employee's net (take-home) pay.
8. Employer's total payroll-related expense for each employee.

Check (3) $315.58
(4) $73.81
(5) $2.80
(7) Total net pay, $4,132.61

Problem 9-5B
Entries for payroll transactions
P2 P3

Palmer Company's first weekly pay period of the year ends on January 8. On that date, the column totals in Palmer's payroll register indicate its sales employees earned $69,490, its office employees earned $42,450, and its delivery employees earned $2,060. The employees are to have withheld from their wages FICA Social Security taxes at the rate of 6.2%, FICA Medicare taxes at the rate of 1.45%, $17,250 of federal income taxes, $2,320 of medical insurance deductions, and $275 of union dues. No employee earned more than $7,000 in the first pay period.

Required

1. Calculate FICA Social Security taxes payable and FICA Medicare taxes payable. Prepare the journal entry to record Palmer Company's January 8 (employee) payroll expenses and liabilities.
2. Prepare the journal entry to record Palmer's (employer) payroll taxes resulting from the January 8 payroll. Palmer's merit rating reduces its state unemployment tax rate to 3.4% of the first $7,000 paid each employee. The federal unemployment tax rate is 0.8%.

Check (1) Cr. Salaries Payable, $85,434
(2) Dr. Payroll Taxes Expense, $13,509

Problem 9-6B[A]
Entries for payroll transactions
P2 P3 P5

JLK Company has five employees, each of whom earns $1,200 per month and is paid on the last day of each month. All five have been employed continuously at this amount since January 1. JLK uses a payroll bank account and special payroll checks to pay its employees. On June 1, the following accounts and balances exist in its general ledger:

a. FICA—Social Security Taxes Payable, $744; FICA—Medicare Taxes Payable, $174. (The balances of these accounts represent total liabilities for *both* the employer's and employees' FICA taxes for the May payroll only.)
b. Employees' Federal Income Taxes Payable, $900 (liability for May only).
c. Federal Unemployment Taxes Payable, $96 (liability for April and May together).
d. State Unemployment Taxes Payable, $480 (liability for April and May together).

During June and July, the company had the following payroll transactions.

June 15 Issued check payable to Security Bank, a federal depository bank authorized to accept employers' payments of FICA taxes and employee income tax withholdings. The $1,818 check is in payment of the May FICA and employee income taxes.

30 Recorded the June payroll and transferred funds from the regular bank account to the payroll bank account. Issued checks payable to each employee in payment of the June payroll. The payroll register shows the following summary totals for the June pay period.

Check June 30: Cr. Salaries Payable, $4,641

Salaries and Wages			FICA Taxes*	Federal Income Taxes	Net Pay
Office Salaries	Shop Wages	Gross Pay			
$2,000	$4,000	$6,000	$372	$900	$4,641
			$ 87		

* FICA taxes are Social Security and Medicare, respectively.

Check June 30: Dr. Payroll Taxes Expenses, $699

July 15: Cr. Cash $1,818 (Security Bank)

30 Recorded the employer's payroll taxes resulting from the June payroll. The company has a merit rating that reduces its state unemployment tax rate to 4.0% of the first $7,000 paid each employee. The federal rate is 0.8%.

July 15 Issued check payable to Security Bank in payment of the June FICA and employee income taxes.
15 Issued check to the State Tax Commission for the April, May and June state unemployment taxes. Mailed the check and the second quarter tax return to the State Tax Commission.
31 Issued check payable to Security Bank in payment of the employer's FUTA taxes for the first quarter of the year.
31 Mailed Form 941 to the IRS, reporting the FICA taxes and the employees' federal income tax withholdings for the second quarter.

Required

Prepare journal entries to record the transactions and events for both June and July.

(This serial problem began in Chapter 1 and continues through most of the book. If previous chapter segments were not completed, the serial problem can begin at this point. It is helpful, but not necessary, to use the Working Papers that accompany the book.)

SERIAL PROBLEM
Business Solutions

P2 P3 C2

SP 9 Review the February 26 and March 25 transactions for Business Solutions (SP 4) from Chapter 4.

Required

1. Assume that Lyn Addie is an unmarried employee. Her $1,000 of wages are subject to no deductions other than FICA Social Security taxes, FICA Medicare taxes, and federal income taxes. Her federal income taxes for this pay period total $159. Compute her net pay for the eight days' work paid on February 26. (Round amounts to the nearest cent.)
2. Record the journal entry to reflect the payroll payment to Lyn Addie as computed in part 1.
3. Record the journal entry to reflect the (employer) payroll tax expenses for the February 26 payroll payment. Assume Lyn Addie has not met earnings limits for FUTA and SUTA—the FUTA rate is 0.8% and the SUTA rate is 4% for Business Solutions. (Round amounts to the nearest cent.)
4. Record the entry(ies) for the merchandise sold on March 25 if a 4% sales tax rate applies.

CP 9 Bug-Off Exterminators provides pest control services and sells extermination products manufactured by other companies. The following six-column table contains the company's unadjusted trial balance as of December 31, 2011.

COMPREHENSIVE PROBLEM
Bug-Off Exterminators
(Review of Chapters 1–9)

BUG-OFF EXTERMINATORS
December 31, 2011

	Unadjusted Trial Balance		Adjustments	Adjusted Trial Balance
Cash..................	$ 17,000			
Accounts receivable	4,000			
Allowance for doubtful accounts		$ 828		
Merchandise inventory	11,700			
Trucks	32,000			
Accum. depreciation—Trucks		0		
Equipment	45,000			
Accum. depreciation—Equipment		12,200		
Accounts payable.............		5,000		
Estimated warranty liability		1,400		
Unearned services revenue		0		
Interest payable		0		
Long-term notes payable		15,000		
Common stock		10,000		
Retained earnings		49,700		
Dividends................	10,000			
Extermination services revenue		60,000		
Interest revenue		872		
Sales (of merchandise)		71,026		
Cost of goods sold	46,300			
Depreciation expense—Trucks	0			
Depreciation expense—Equipment	0			
Wages expense	35,000			
Interest expense	0			
Rent expense	9,000			
Bad debts expense	0			
Miscellaneous expense	1,226			
Repairs expense	8,000			
Utilities expense	6,800			
Warranty expense	0			
Totals	$226,026	$226,026		

Chapter 9 Reporting and Analyzing Current Liabilities

The following information in *a* through *h* applies to the company at the end of the current year.

a. The bank reconciliation as of December 31, 2011, includes the following facts.

Cash balance per bank	$15,100
Cash balance per books	17,000
Outstanding checks	1,800
Deposit in transit	2,450
Interest earned (on bank account)	52
Bank service charges (miscellaneous expense)	15

Reported on the bank statement is a canceled check that the company failed to record. (Information from the bank reconciliation allows you to determine the amount of this check, which is a payment on an account payable.)

b. An examination of customers' accounts shows that accounts totaling $679 should be written off as uncollectible. Using an aging of receivables, the company determines that the ending balance of the Allowance for Doubtful Accounts should be $700.

c. A truck is purchased and placed in service on January 1, 2011. Its cost is being depreciated with the straight-line method using the following facts and estimates.

Original cost	$32,000
Expected salvage value	8,000
Useful life (years)	4

d. Two items of equipment (a sprayer and an injector) were purchased and put into service in early January 2009. They are being depreciated with the straight-line method using these facts and estimates.

	Sprayer	Injector
Original cost	$27,000	$18,000
Expected salvage value	3,000	2,500
Useful life (years)	8	5

e. On August 1, 2011, the company is paid $3,840 cash in advance to provide monthly service for an apartment complex for one year. The company began providing the services in August. When the cash was received, the full amount was credited to the Extermination Services Revenue account.

f. The company offers a warranty for the services it sells. The expected cost of providing warranty service is 2.5% of the extermination services revenue of $57,760 for 2011. No warranty expense has been recorded for 2011. All costs of servicing warranties in 2011 were properly debited to the Estimated Warranty Liability account.

g. The $15,000 long-term note is an 8%, five-year, interest-bearing note with interest payable annually on December 31. The note was signed with First National Bank on December 31, 2011.

h. The ending inventory of merchandise is counted and determined to have a cost of $11,700. Bug-Off uses a perpetual inventory system.

Required

1. Use the preceding information to determine amounts for the following items.
   a. Correct (reconciled) ending balance of Cash, and the amount of the omitted check.
   b. Adjustment needed to obtain the correct ending balance of the Allowance for Doubtful Accounts.
   c. Depreciation expense for the truck used during year 2011.
   d. Depreciation expense for the two items of equipment used during year 2011.
   e. The adjusted 2011 ending balances of the Extermination Services Revenue and Unearned Services Revenue accounts.
   f. The adjusted 2011 ending balances of the accounts for Warranty Expense and Estimated Warranty Liability.
   g. The adjusted 2011 ending balances of the accounts for Interest Expense and Interest Payable. (Round amounts to nearest whole dollar.)

Check (1*a*) Cash bal. $15,750
(1*b*) $551 credit

(1*f*) Estim. warranty liability, $2,844 Cr.

2. Use the results of part 1 to complete the six-column table by first entering the appropriate adjustments for items *a* through *g* and then completing the adjusted trial balance columns. (*Hint:* Item *b* requires two adjustments.)

3. Prepare journal entries to record the adjustments entered on the six-column table. Assume Bug-Off's adjusted balance for Merchandise Inventory matches the year-end physical count.

4. Prepare a single-step income statement, a statement of retained earnings (cash dividends declared during 2011 were $10,000), and a classified balance sheet.

(2) Adjusted trial balance totals, $238,207

(4) Net income, $9,274; Total assets, $82,771

Beyond the Numbers

BTN 9-1 Refer to the financial statements of **Research In Motion** in Appendix A to answer the following.

1. Compute times interest earned for the fiscal years ended 2010, 2009, and 2008. Comment on RIM's ability to cover its interest expense for this period. Assume interest expense of $1, $502, and $31 for fiscal years ended 2010, 2009, and 2008 ($ thousands); and, assume an industry average of 18.1 for times interest earned.

2. RIM's current liabilities include "deferred revenue"; assume that this account reflects "Unredeemed gift card liabilities." Explain how this liability is created and how RIM satisfies this liability.

3. Does RIM have any commitments or contingencies? Briefly explain them.

Fast Forward

4. Access RIM's financial statements for fiscal years ending after February 27, 2010, at its Website (**RIM.com**) or the SEC's EDGAR database (**www.sec.gov**). Compute its times interest earned for years ending after February 27, 2010, and compare your results to those in part 1.

REPORTING IN ACTION
A1 P4

RIM

BTN 9-2 Key figures for **Research In Motion** and **Apple** follow. (Interest expense figures for Apple are assumed as it has no interest expense for these years.)

($ millions)	Research In Motion Current Year	Research In Motion One Year Prior	Research In Motion Two Years Prior	Apple Current Year	Apple One Year Prior	Apple Two Years Prior
Net income	$2,457.144	$1,892.616	$1,293.867	$8,235	$6,119	$3,495
Income taxes	809.366	907.747	516.653	3,831	2,828	1,511
Interest expense	.001	.502	.031	3	2	1

COMPARATIVE ANALYSIS
A1

RIM
Apple

Required

1. Compute times interest earned for the three years' data shown for each company.
2. Comment on which company appears stronger in its ability to pay interest obligations if income should decline. Assume an industry average of 18.1.

BTN 9-3 Connor Bly is a sales manager for an automobile dealership. He earns a bonus each year based on revenue from the number of autos sold in the year less related warranty expenses. Actual warranty expenses have varied over the prior 10 years from a low of 3% of an automobile's selling price to a high of 10%. In the past, Bly has tended to estimate warranty expenses on the high end to be conservative. He must work with the dealership's accountant at year-end to arrive at the warranty expense accrual for cars sold each year.

1. Does the warranty accrual decision create any ethical dilemma for Bly?
2. Since warranty expenses vary, what percent do you think Bly should choose for the current year? Justify your response.

ETHICS CHALLENGE
P4

BTN 9-4 Dustin Clemens is the accounting and finance manager for a manufacturer. At year-end, he must determine how to account for the company's contingencies. His manager, Madeline Pretti, objects to Clemens's proposal to recognize an expense and a liability for warranty service on units of a new product introduced in the fourth quarter. Pretti comments, "There's no way we can estimate this warranty cost. We don't owe anyone anything until a product fails and it is returned. Let's report an expense if and when we do any warranty work."

COMMUNICATING IN PRACTICE
C3

Required

Prepare a one-page memorandum for Clemens to send to Pretti defending his proposal.

TAKING IT TO THE NET
C1 A1

BTN 9-5 Access the February 26, 2010, filing of the December 31, 2009, annual 10-K report of **McDonald's Corporation** (Ticker: MCD), which is available from **www.sec.gov**.

Required

1. Identify the current liabilities on McDonald's balance sheet as of December 31, 2009.
2. What portion (in percent) of McDonald's long-term debt matures within the next 12 months?
3. Use the consolidated statement of income for the year ended December 31, 2009, to compute McDonald's times interest earned ratio. Comment on the result. Assume an industry average of 12.0.

TEAMWORK IN ACTION
C2 P1

BTN 9-6 Assume that your team is in business and you must borrow $6,000 cash for short-term needs. You have been shopping banks for a loan, and you have the following two options.

A. Sign a $6,000, 90-day, 10% interest-bearing note dated June 1.
B. Sign a $6,000, 120-day, 8% interest-bearing note dated June 1.

Required

1. Discuss these two options and determine the best choice. Ensure that all teammates concur with the decision and understand the rationale.
2. Each member of the team is to prepare *one* of the following journal entries.
   a. Option A—at date of issuance.
   b. Option B—at date of issuance.
   c. Option A—at maturity date.
   d. Option B—at maturity date.
3. In rotation, each member is to explain the entry he or she prepared in part 2 to the team. Ensure that all team members concur with and understand the entries.
4. Assume that the funds are borrowed on December 1 (instead of June 1) and your business operates on a calendar-year reporting period. Each member of the team is to prepare *one* of the following entries.
   a. Option A—the year-end adjustment.
   b. Option B—the year-end adjustment.
   c. Option A—at maturity date.
   d. Option B—at maturity date.
5. In rotation, each member is to explain the entry he or she prepared in part 4 to the team. Ensure that all team members concur with and understand the entries.

ENTREPRENEURIAL DECISION
A1

BTN 9-7 Review the chapter's opening feature about Matt and Bryan Walls, and their start-up company, **SnorgTees**. Assume that these young entrepreneurs are considering expanding their business to open an outlet in Europe. Assume their current income statement is as follows.

SNORGTEES Income Statement For Year Ended December 31, 2011	
Sales	$1,000,000
Cost of goods sold (30%)	300,000
Gross profit	700,000
Operating expenses (25%)	250,000
Net income	$ 450,000

SnorgTees currently has no interest-bearing debt. If it expands to open a European location, it will require a $300,000 loan. SnorgTees has found a bank that will loan it the money on a 7% note payable. The company believes that, at least for the first few years, sales at its European location will be $250,000, and that all expenses (including cost of goods sold) will follow the same patterns as its current locations.

Required

1. Prepare an income statement (showing three separate columns for current operations, European, and total) for SnorgTees assuming that it borrows the funds and expands to Europe. Annual revenues for current operations are expected to remain at $1,000,000.
2. Compute SnorgTees' times interest earned under the expansion assumptions in part 1.
3. Assume sales at its European location are $400,000. Prepare an income statement (with columns for current operations, European, and total) for the company and compute times interest earned.
4. Assume sales at its European location are $100,000. Prepare an income statement (with columns for current operations, European, and total) for the company and compute times interest earned.
5. Comment on your results from parts 1 through 4.

HITTING THE ROAD
P2

BTN 9-8 Check your phone book or the Social Security Administration Website (www.ssa.gov) to locate the Social Security office near you. Visit the office to request a personal earnings and estimate form. Fill out the form and mail according to the instructions. You will receive a statement from the Social Security Administration regarding your earnings history and future Social Security benefits you can receive. (Formerly the request could be made online. The online service has been discontinued and is now under review by the Social Security Administration due to security concerns.) It is good to request an earnings and benefit statement every 5 to 10 years to make sure you have received credit for all wages earned and for which you and your employer have paid taxes into the system.

GLOBAL DECISION
A1

NOKIA
RIM
Apple

BTN 9-9 **Nokia**, **Research In Motion**, and **Apple** are all competitors in the global marketplace. Comparative figures for Nokia (www.Nokia.com), along with selected figures from Research In Motion and Apple, follow.

Key Figures	Nokia (EUR millions) Current Year	Nokia Prior Year	Research In Motion Current Year	Research In Motion Prior Year	Apple Current Year	Apple Prior Year
Net income	260	3,889	—	—	—	—
Income taxes	702	1,081	—	—	—	—
Interest expense	243	185	—	—	—	—
Times interest earned	?	?	3,267	5,579	4,023	4,475

Required

1. Compute the times interest earned ratio for the most recent two years for Nokia using the data shown.
2. Which company of the three presented provides the best coverage of interest expense? Explain.

ANSWERS TO MULTIPLE CHOICE QUIZ

1. b; $6,000 × 0.05 × 30/360 = $25
2. e; $50,000 × (.062 + .0145) = $3,825
3. b; $7,000 × (.008 + .054) = $434
4. c; 10,000 television sets × .01 × $250 = $25,000
5. a; 150 employees × $175 per day × 1 vacation day earned = $26,250

A Look Back
Chapter 9 focused on how current liabilities are identified, computed, recorded, and reported. Attention was directed at notes, payroll, sales taxes, warranties, employee benefits, and contingencies.

A Look at This Chapter
This chapter describes the accounting for and analysis of bonds and notes. We explain their characteristics, payment patterns, interest computations, retirement, and reporting requirements. An appendix to this chapter introduces leases and pensions.

A Look Ahead
Chapter 11 focuses on corporate equity transactions, including stock issuances and dividends. We also explain how to report and analyze income, earnings per share, and retained earnings.

10 Reporting and Analyzing Long-Term Liabilities

Learning Objectives

CAP

CONCEPTUAL

- **C1** Explain the types and payment patterns of notes. (p. 424)
- **C2** *Appendix 10A*—Explain and compute the present value of an amount(s) to be paid at a future date(s). (p. 432)
- **C3** *Appendix 10C*—Describe interest accrual when bond payment periods differ from accounting periods. (p. 436)
- **C4** *Appendix 10D*—Describe accounting for leases and pensions. (p. 438)

ANALYTICAL

- **A1** Compare bond financing with stock financing. (p. 414)
- **A2** Assess debt features and their implications. (p. 428)
- **A3** Compute the debt-to-equity ratio and explain its use. (p. 428)

LP10

PROCEDURAL

- **P1** Prepare entries to record bond issuance and interest expense. (p. 416)
- **P2** Compute and record amortization of bond discount. (p. 417)
- **P3** Compute and record amortization of bond premium. (p. 420)
- **P4** Record the retirement of bonds. (p. 423)
- **P5** Prepare entries to account for notes. (p. 426)

Decision Insight

Love at First Bite

"Each individual problem you face is totally surmountable."
—WARREN BROWN

WASHINGTON, DC—Warren Brown started baking cakes in his apartment after work each evening. He sold his sweet concoctions mostly to coworkers and friends, and even held a cake open house at the local art gallery. But Warren was determined to grow his business. He took a course in entrepreneurship at his local community college, and there he discovered the importance of financial reporting and accounting.

Launching his fledgling cake business presented Warren with many challenges. He needed to especially focus on the important task of managing liabilities for payroll, baking supplies, employee benefits, training, and taxes. Warren insists that effective management of liabilities, especially long-term financing from sources such as bonds and notes, is crucial to business success. "Everything feels like a disaster when it's right in your face," says Warren. "You just have to be calm, look at what you're doing, and fix the problem."

Warren fixed the problems and unveiled his business called **CakeLove (CakeLove.com),** funded with short- and long-term notes. "I opened up this tiny retail, walk-up bakery . . . [to sell] goodies that are baked from scratch," Warren explains. Today CakeLove entices the neighborhood with a gentle scent of fresh bakery and a sidewalk view into the kitchen. Warmly painted walls, comfy window seats, and free wireless Internet encourage customers to lounge for hours. "I want it to be relaxed and comfortable," says Warren. "People can bring their work, their kids, their friends, and just relax."

Warren continues to monitor liabilities and their payment patterns, and he is not shy about striving to better learn the accounting side. "I'm always getting better, improving my skills," he explains. Warren insists that accounting for and monitoring liabilities of long-term financing are important ingredients to a successful start-up. His company now generates sufficient income to pay for liabilities of interest and principal on long-term debt and still produces revenue growth for expansion. He shows a keen appetite for using accounting information to make good business decisions. "But," says Warren, "I love eating what I make more."

"The bigger message of CakeLove is finding your passion and working to reach your goals," explains Warren. That's a slice of advice worth more than any amount of dough.

[Sources: *CakeLove Website,* January 2012; *Black Enterprise,* September 2004; *Georgetown Voice,* March 2005; *National Public Radio (NPR) Website,* May 2005; *Inc.com,* April 2005; *Plain Dealer,* May 2011]

Chapter Preview

Individuals, companies, and governments issue bonds to finance their activities. In return for financing, bonds promise to repay the lender with interest. This chapter explains the basics of bonds and the accounting for their issuance and retirement. The chapter also describes long-term notes as another financing source. We explain how present value concepts impact both the accounting for and reporting of bonds and notes. Appendixes to this chapter discuss present value concepts applicable to liabilities, effective interest amortization, and the accounting for leases and pensions.

Reporting and Analyzing Long-Term Liabilities

Bond Basics	Bond Issuances	Bond Retirement	Long-Term Notes
• Bond financing • Bond trading • Issuance procedures	• Issuance at par • Issuance at a discount • Issuance at a premium • Bond pricing	• At maturity • Before maturity • By conversion	• Installment notes • Mortgage terms

BASICS OF BONDS

This section explains the basics of bonds and a company's motivation for issuing them.

Bond Financing

A1 Compare bond financing with stock financing.

Projects that demand large amounts of money often are funded from bond issuances. (Both for-profit and nonprofit companies, as well as governmental units, such as nations, states, cities, and school districts, issue bonds.) A **bond** is its issuer's written promise to pay an amount identified as the par value of the bond with interest. The **par value of a bond,** also called the *face amount* or *face value,* is paid at a specified future date known as the bond's *maturity date.* Most bonds also require the issuer to make semiannual interest payments. The amount of interest paid each period is determined by multiplying the par value of the bond by the bond's contract rate of interest for that same period. This section explains both advantages and disadvantages of bond financing.

Advantages of Bonds There are three main advantages of bond financing:

1. *Bonds do not affect owner control.* Equity financing reflects ownership in a company, whereas bond financing does not. A person who contributes $1,000 of a company's $10,000 equity financing typically controls one-tenth of all owner decisions. A person who owns a $1,000, 11%, 20-year bond has no ownership right. This person, or bondholder, is to receive from the bond issuer 11% interest, or $110, each year the bond is outstanding and $1,000 when it matures in 20 years.
2. *Interest on bonds is tax deductible.* Bond interest payments are tax deductible for the issuer, but equity payments (distributions) to owners are not. To illustrate, assume that a corporation with no bond financing earns $15,000 in income *before* paying taxes at a 40% tax rate, which amounts to $6,000 ($15,000 × 40%) in taxes. If a portion of its financing is in bonds, however, the resulting bond interest is deducted in computing taxable income. That is, if bond interest expense is $10,000, the taxes owed would be $2,000 ([$15,000 − $10,000] × 40%), which is less than the $6,000 owed with no bond financing.
3. *Bonds can increase return on equity.* A company that earns a higher return with borrowed funds than it pays in interest on those funds increases its return on equity. This process is called *financial leverage* or *trading on the equity.*

Point: Financial leverage reflects issuance of bonds, notes, or preferred stock.

To illustrate the third point, consider Magnum Co., which has $1 million in equity and is planning a $500,000 expansion to meet increasing demand for its product. Magnum predicts the

$500,000 expansion will yield $125,000 in additional income before paying any interest. It currently earns $100,000 per year and has no interest expense. Magnum is considering three plans. Plan A is to not expand. Plan B is to expand and raise $500,000 from equity financing. Plan C is to expand and issue $500,000 of bonds that pay 10% annual interest ($50,000). Exhibit 10.1 shows how these three plans affect Magnum's net income, equity, and return on equity (net income/equity). The owner(s) will earn a higher return on equity if expansion occurs. Moreover, the preferred expansion plan is to issue bonds. Projected net income under Plan C ($175,000) is smaller than under Plan B ($225,000), but the return on equity is larger because of less equity investment. Plan C has another advantage if income is taxable. This illustration reflects a general rule: *Return on equity increases when the expected rate of return from the new assets is higher than the rate of interest expense on the debt financing.*

Example: Compute return on equity for all three plans if Magnum currently earns $150,000 instead of $100,000.
Answer ($ 000s):
Plan A = 15%   ($150/$1,000)
Plan B = 18.3%   ($275/$1,500)
Plan C = 22.5%   ($225/$1,000)

	Plan A: Do Not Expand	Plan B: Equity Financing	Plan C: Bond Financing
Income before interest expense	$ 100,000	$ 225,000	$ 225,000
Interest expense	—	—	(50,000)
Net income	$ 100,000	$ 225,000	$ 175,000
Equity	$1,000,000	$1,500,000	$1,000,000
Return on equity	10.0%	15.0%	17.5%

EXHIBIT 10.1
Financing with Bonds versus Equity

Disadvantages of Bonds The two main disadvantages of bond financing are these:

1. *Bonds can decrease return on equity.* When a company earns a lower return with the borrowed funds than it pays in interest, it decreases its return on equity. This downside risk of financial leverage is more likely to arise when a company has periods of low income or net losses.
2. *Bonds require payment of both periodic interest and the par value at maturity.* Bond payments can be especially burdensome when income and cash flow are low. Equity financing, in contrast, does not require any payments because cash withdrawals (dividends) are paid at the discretion of the owner (or board).

A company must weigh the risks and returns of the disadvantages and advantages of bond financing when deciding whether to issue bonds to finance operations.

Point: Debt financing is desirable when interest is tax deductible, when owner control is preferred, and when return on equity exceeds the debt's interest rate.

Bond Trading

Bonds are securities that can be readily bought and sold. A large number of bonds trade on both the New York Exchange and the American Exchange. A bond *issue* consists of a number of bonds, usually in denominations of $1,000 or $5,000, and is sold to many different lenders. After bonds are issued, they often are bought and sold by investors, meaning that any particular bond probably has a number of owners before it matures. Since bonds are exchanged (bought and sold) in the market, they have a market value (price). For convenience, bond market values are expressed as a percent of their par (face) value. For example, a company's bonds might be trading at 103½, meaning they can be bought or sold for 103.5% of their par value. Bonds can also trade below par value. For instance, if a company's bonds are trading at 95, they can be bought or sold at 95% of their par value.

Decision Insight

Quotes The **IBM** bond quote here is interpreted (left to right) as **Bonds,** issuer name; **Rate,** contract interest rate (7%); **Mat,** matures in year 2025 when principal is paid; **Yld,** yield rate (5.9%) of bond at current price; **Vol,** daily dollar worth ($130,000) of trades (in 1,000s); **Close,** closing price (119.25) for the day as percentage of par value; **Chg,** change (+1.25) in closing price from prior day's close. ∎

Bonds	Rate	Mat	Yld	Vol	Close	Chg
IBM	7	25	5.9	130	119¼	+1¼

EXHIBIT 10.2

Bond Certificate

Bond-Issuing Procedures

State and federal laws govern bond issuances. Bond issuers also want to ensure that they do not violate any of their existing contractual agreements when issuing bonds. Authorization of bond issuances includes the number of bonds authorized, their par value, and the contract interest rate. The legal document identifying the rights and obligations of both the bondholders and the issuer is called the **bond indenture,** which is the legal contract between the issuer and the bondholders. A bondholder may also receive a bond certificate as evidence of the company's debt. A **bond certificate,** such as that shown in Exhibit 10.2, includes specifics such as the issuer's name, the par value, the contract interest rate, and the maturity date. Many companies reduce costs by not issuing paper certificates to bondholders.[1]

Point: *Indenture* refers to a bond's legal contract; *debenture* refers to an unsecured bond.

BOND ISSUANCES

This section explains accounting for bond issuances at par, below par (discount), and above par (premium). It also describes how to amortize a discount or premium and record bonds issued between interest payment dates.

Issuing Bonds at Par

P1 Prepare entries to record bond issuance and interest expense.

To illustrate an issuance of bonds at par value, suppose a company receives authorization to issue $800,000 of 9%, 20-year bonds dated January 1, 2011, that mature on December 31, 2030, and pay interest semiannually on each June 30 and December 31. After accepting the bond indenture on behalf of the bondholders, the trustee can sell all or a portion of the bonds to an underwriter. If all bonds are sold at par value, the issuer records the sale as follows.

Assets = Liabilities + Equity
+800,000   +800,000

2011			
Jan. 1	Cash	800,000	
	Bonds Payable		800,000
	Sold bonds at par.		

This entry reflects increases in the issuer's cash *and* long-term liabilities.
The issuer records the first semiannual interest payment as follows.

Assets = Liabilities + Equity
−36,000   −36,000

2011			
June 30	Bond Interest Expense	36,000	
	Cash		36,000
	Paid semiannual interest (9% × $800,000 × ½ year).		

Point: The *spread* between the dealer's cost and what buyers pay can be huge. Dealers earn more than $25 billion in annual spread revenue.

Global: In the United Kingdom, government bonds are called *gilts*— short for gilt-edged investments.

---

[1] The issuing company normally sells its bonds to an investment firm called an *underwriter,* which resells them to the public. An issuing company can also sell bonds directly to investors. When an underwriter sells bonds to a large number of investors, a *trustee* represents and protects the bondholders' interests. The trustee monitors the issuer to ensure that it complies with the obligations in the bond indenture. Most trustees are large banks or trust companies. The trustee writes and accepts the terms of a bond indenture before it is issued. When bonds are offered to the public, called *floating an issue,* they must be registered with the Securities and Exchange Commission (SEC). SEC registration requires the issuer to file certain financial information. Most company bonds are issued in par value units of $1,000 or $5,000. A *baby bond* has a par value of less than $1,000, such as $100.

The issuer pays and records its semiannual interest obligation every six months until the bonds mature. When they mature, the issuer records its payment of principal as follows.

2030 Dec. 31	Bonds Payable	800,000	
	Cash		800,000
	Paid bond principal at maturity.		

Assets = Liabilities + Equity
−800,000   −800,000

Bond Discount or Premium

The bond issuer pays the interest rate specified in the indenture, the **contract rate**, also referred to as the *coupon rate, stated rate,* or *nominal rate*. The annual interest paid is determined by multiplying the bond par value by the contract rate. The contract rate is usually stated on an annual basis, even if interest is paid semiannually. For example, if a company issues a $1,000, 8% bond paying interest semiannually, it pays annual interest of $80 (8% × $1,000) in two semiannual payments of $40 each.

The contract rate sets the amount of interest the issuer pays in *cash,* which is not necessarily the *bond interest expense* actually incurred by the issuer. Bond interest expense depends on the bond's market value at issuance, which is determined by market expectations of the risk of lending to the issuer. The bond's **market rate** of interest is the rate that borrowers are willing to pay and lenders are willing to accept for a particular bond and its risk level. As the risk level increases, the rate increases to compensate purchasers for the bonds' increased risk. Also, the market rate is generally higher when the time period until the bond matures is longer due to the risk of adverse events occurring over a longer time period.

Many bond issuers try to set a contract rate of interest equal to the market rate they expect as of the bond issuance date. When the contract rate and market rate are equal, a bond sells at par value, but when they are not equal, a bond does not sell at par value. Instead, it is sold at a *premium* above par value or at a *discount* below par value. Exhibit 10.3 shows the relation between the contract rate, market rate, and a bond's issue price.

Bond Sets — Contract rate
Market Sets — Market rate

Bond Price Determined

Contract rate > Market rate	➡	Bond sells at premium
Contract rate = Market rate	➡	Bond sells at par
Contract rate < Market rate	➡	Bond sells at discount

EXHIBIT 10.3

Relation between Bond Issue Price, Contract Rate, and Market Rate

Quick Check
Answers — p. 441

1. A company issues $10,000 of 9%, 5-year bonds dated January 1, 2011, that mature on December 31, 2015, and pay interest semiannually on each June 30 and December 31. Prepare the entry to record this bond issuance and the first semiannual interest payment.
2. How do you compute the amount of interest a bond issuer pays in cash each year?
3. When the contract rate is above the market rate, do bonds sell at a premium or a discount? Do purchasers pay more or less than the par value of the bonds?

Issuing Bonds at a Discount

A **discount on bonds payable** occurs when a company issues bonds with a contract rate less than the market rate. This means that the issue price is less than par value. To illustrate, assume that **Fila** announces an offer to issue bonds with a $100,000 par value, an 8% annual contract rate (paid semiannually), and a two-year life. Also assume that the market rate for Fila bonds is

P2 Compute and record amortization of bond discount.

Point: The difference between the contract rate and the market rate of interest on a new bond issue is usually a fraction of a percent. We use a difference of 2% to emphasize the effects.

10%. These bonds then will sell at a discount since the contract rate is less than the market rate. The exact issue price for these bonds is stated as 96.454 (implying 96.454% of par value, or $96,454); we show how to compute this issue price later in the chapter. These bonds obligate the issuer to pay two separate types of future cash flows:

1. Par value of $100,000 cash at the end of the bonds' two-year life.
2. Cash interest payments of $4,000 (4% × $100,000) at the end of each semiannual period during the bonds' two-year life.

The exact pattern of cash flows for the Fila bonds is shown in Exhibit 10.4.

EXHIBIT 10.4

Cash Flows for Fila Bonds

When Fila accepts $96,454 cash for its bonds on the issue date of December 31, 2011, it records the sale as follows.

Assets = Liabilities + Equity
+96,454   +100,000
          −3,546

Dec. 31	Cash	96,454	
	Discount on Bonds Payable	3,546	
	Bonds Payable		100,000
	Sold bonds at a discount on their issue date.		

Point: Book value at issuance always equals the issuer's cash borrowed.

These bonds are reported in the long-term liability section of the issuer's December 31, 2011, balance sheet as shown in Exhibit 10.5. A discount is deducted from the par value of bonds to yield the **carrying (book) value of bonds**. Discount on Bonds Payable is a contra liability account.

EXHIBIT 10.5

Balance Sheet Presentation of Bond Discount

Long-term liabilities
Bonds payable, 8%, due December 31, 2013 .... $100,000
Less discount on bonds payable 3,546 $96,454

Point: *Zero-coupon bonds* do not pay periodic interest (contract rate is zero). These bonds always sell at a discount because their 0% contract rate is always below the market rate.

Amortizing a Bond Discount Fila receives $96,454 for its bonds; in return it must pay bondholders $100,000 after two years (plus semiannual interest payments). The $3,546 discount is paid to bondholders at maturity and is part of the cost of using the $96,454 for two years. The upper portion of panel A in Exhibit 10.6 shows that total bond interest expense of $19,546 is the difference between the total amount repaid to bondholders ($116,000) and the amount borrowed from bondholders ($96,454). Alternatively, we can compute total bond interest expense as the sum of the four interest payments and the bond discount. This alternative computation is shown in the lower portion of panel A.

The total $19,546 bond interest expense must be allocated across the four semiannual periods in the bonds' life, and the bonds' carrying value must be updated at each balance sheet date. This is accomplished using the straight-line method (or the effective interest method in Appendix 10B). Both methods systematically reduce the bond discount to zero over the two-year life. This process is called *amortizing a bond discount.*

Straight-Line Method The **straight-line bond amortization** method allocates an equal portion of the total bond interest expense to each interest period. To apply the straight-line method to Fila's bonds, we divide the total bond interest expense of $19,546 by 4 (the number of semiannual periods in the bonds' life). This gives a bond interest expense of $4,887 per period, which is $4,886.5 rounded to the nearest dollar per period (all computations, including those for assignments, are rounded to the nearest whole dollar). Alternatively, we can find this number by first dividing the $3,546 discount by 4, which yields the $887 amount of discount to be amortized each interest period. When the $887 is added to the $4,000 cash payment, the bond

EXHIBIT 10.6
Interest Computation and Entry for Bonds Issued at a Discount

Panel A: Interest Computations

Amount repaid to bondholders
- Four interest payments of $4,000 .... $ 16,000
- Par value at maturity 100,000
- Total repaid to bondholders 116,000
- Less amount borrowed from bondholders .... (96,454)
- **Total bond interest expense** **$19,546**

Alternative Computation
- Four payments of $4,000 .... $ 16,000
- Plus discount 3,546
- **Total bond interest expense** **$19,546**

$$\frac{\text{Bond interest expense}}{\text{(per interest period)}} = \frac{\text{Total bond interest expense}}{\text{Number of interest periods}} = \frac{\$19,546}{4} = \$4,887$$

Panel B: Entry to Record Interest Payment and Amortization

2012–2013			
June 30 and Dec. 31	Bond Interest Expense	4,887	
	Discount on Bonds Payable		887
	Cash		4,000
	To record semiannual interest and discount amortization (straight-line method).		

(Discount ÷ periods)
(Par value × contract rate)

interest expense for each period is $4,887. Panel B of Exhibit 10.6 shows how the issuer records bond interest expense and updates the balance of the bond liability account at the end of *each* of the four semiannual interest periods (June 30, 2012, through December 31, 2013).

Exhibit 10.7 shows the pattern of decreases in the Discount on Bonds Payable account and the pattern of increases in the bonds' carrying value. The following points summarize the discount bonds' straight-line amortization:

1. At issuance, the $100,000 par value consists of the $96,454 cash received by the issuer plus the $3,546 discount.

2. During the bonds' life, the (unamortized) discount decreases each period by the $887 amortization ($3,546/4), and the carrying value (par value less unamortized discount) increases each period by $887.

3. At maturity, the unamortized discount equals zero, and the carrying value equals the $100,000 par value that the issuer pays the holder.

Semiannual Period-End	Unamortized Discount*	Carrying Value†
(0) 12/31/2011	$3,546	$ 96,454
(1) 6/30/2012	2,659	97,341
(2) 12/31/2012	1,772	98,228
(3) 6/30/2013	885	99,115
(4) 12/31/2013	0‡	100,000

* Total bond discount (of $3,546) less accumulated periodic amortization ($887 per semiannual interest period).
† Bond par value (of $100,000) less unamortized discount.
‡ Adjusted for rounding.

EXHIBIT 10.7
Straight-Line Amortization of Bond Discount

The two columns always sum to par value for a discount bond.

We see that the issuer incurs a $4,887 bond interest expense each period but pays only $4,000 cash. The $887 unpaid portion of this expense is added to the bonds' carrying value. (The total $3,546 unamortized discount is "paid" when the bonds mature; $100,000 is paid at maturity but only $96,454 was received at issuance.)

Decision Insight

Ratings Game Many bond buyers rely on rating services to assess bond risk. The best known are **Standard & Poor's**, **Moody's**, and **Fitch**. These services focus on the issuer's financial statements and other factors in setting ratings. Standard & Poor's ratings, from best quality to default, are AAA, AA, A, BBB, BB, B, CCC, CC, C, and D. Ratings can include a plus (+) or minus (−) to show relative standing within a category. ■

Quick Check
Answers — p. 441

Five-year, 6% bonds with a $100,000 par value are issued at a price of $91,893. Interest is paid semiannually, and the bonds' market rate is 8% on the issue date. Use this information to answer the following questions:

4. Are these bonds issued at a discount or a premium? Explain your answer.
5. What is the issuer's journal entry to record the issuance of these bonds?
6. What is the amount of bond interest expense recorded at the first semiannual period using the straight-line method?

Issuing Bonds at a Premium

P3 Compute and record amortization of bond premium.

When the contract rate of bonds is higher than the market rate, the bonds sell at a price higher than par value. The amount by which the bond price exceeds par value is the **premium on bonds**. To illustrate, assume that Adidas issues bonds with a $100,000 par value, a 12% annual contract rate, semiannual interest payments, and a two-year life. Also assume that the market rate for Adidas bonds is 10% on the issue date. The Adidas bonds will sell at a premium because the contract rate is higher than the market rate. The issue price for these bonds is stated as 103.546 (implying 103.546% of par value, or $103,546); we show how to compute this issue price later in the chapter. These bonds obligate the issuer to pay out two separate future cash flows:

1. Par value of $100,000 cash at the end of the bonds' two-year life.
2. Cash interest payments of $6,000 (6% × $100,000) at the end of each semiannual period during the bonds' two-year life.

The exact pattern of cash flows for the Adidas bonds is shown in Exhibit 10.8.

EXHIBIT 10.8
Cash Flows for Adidas Bonds

0	6 mo.	12 mo.	18 mo.	24 mo.
	$6,000	$6,000	$6,000	$6,000 + $100,000

When Adidas accepts $103,546 cash for its bonds on the issue date of December 31, 2011, it records this transaction as follows.

Assets = Liabilities + Equity
+103,546   +100,000
           +3,546

Dec. 31	Cash	103,546	
	Premium on Bonds Payable		3,546
	Bonds Payable		100,000
	Sold bonds at a premium on their issue date.		

These bonds are reported in the long-term liability section of the issuer's December 31, 2011, balance sheet as shown in Exhibit 10.9. A premium is added to par value to yield the carrying (book) value of bonds. Premium on Bonds Payable is an adjunct (also called *accretion*) liability account.

EXHIBIT 10.9
Balance Sheet Presentation of Bond Premium

Long-term liabilities		
Bonds payable, 12%, due December 31, 2013	$100,000	
Plus premium on bonds payable	3,546	$103,546

Amortizing a Bond Premium Adidas receives $103,546 for its bonds; in return, it pays bondholders $100,000 after two years (plus semiannual interest payments). The $3,546 premium not repaid to issuer's bondholders at maturity goes to reduce the issuer's expense of using the $103,546 for two years. The upper portion of panel A of Exhibit 10.10 shows that total bond interest expense of $20,454 is the difference between the total amount repaid to bondholders ($124,000) and the amount borrowed from bondholders ($103,546). Alternatively, we can compute total bond interest expense as the sum of the four interest payments less the bond premium. The premium is

EXHIBIT 10.10
Interest Computation and Entry for Bonds Issued at a Premium

Panel A: Interest Computations

Amount repaid to bondholders
- Four interest payments of $6,000 .... $ 24,000
- Par value at maturity 100,000
- Total repaid to bondholders 124,000
- Less amount borrowed from bondholders .... (103,546)
- **Total bond interest expense** .... **$ 20,454**

Alternative Computation
- Four payments of $6,000 .... $ 24,000
- Less premium .... (3,546)
- **Total bond interest expense** .... **$ 20,454**

$$\frac{\text{Bond interest expense}}{\text{(per interest period)}} = \frac{\text{Total bond interest expense}}{\text{Number of interest periods}} = \frac{\$20{,}454}{4} = \$5{,}113$$

Panel B: Entry to Record Interest Payment and Amortization

2012–2013			
June 30 and Dec. 31	Bond Interest Expense....................	5,113	
	Premium on Bonds Payable................	887	
	Cash...................................		6,000
	To record semiannual interest and premium amortization (straight-line method).		

- 5,113 ← Total bond interest expense / periods
- 887 ← Premium ÷ periods
- 6,000 ← Par value × contract rate

---

subtracted because it will not be paid to bondholders when the bonds mature; see the lower portion of panel A. Total bond interest expense must be allocated over the four semiannual periods using the straight-line method (or the effective interest method in Appendix 10B).

Straight-Line Method The straight-line method allocates an equal portion of total bond interest expense to each of the bonds' semiannual interest periods. To apply this method to Adidas bonds, we divide the two years' total bond interest expense of $20,454 by 4 (the number of semiannual periods in the bonds' life). This gives a total bond interest expense of $5,113 per period, which is $5,113.5 rounded down so that the journal entry balances and for simplicity in presentation (alternatively, one could carry cents). Panel B of Exhibit 10.10 shows how the issuer records bond interest expense and updates the balance of the bond liability account for *each* semiannual period (June 30, 2012, through December 31, 2013).

Exhibit 10.11 shows the pattern of decreases in the unamortized Premium on Bonds Payable account and in the bonds' carrying value. The following points summarize straight-line amortization of the premium bonds:

Point: A premium decreases Bond Interest Expense; a discount increases it.

EXHIBIT 10.11
Straight-Line Amortization of Bond Premium

Semiannual Period-End	Unamortized Premium*	Carrying Value†
(0) 12/31/2011	$3,546	$103,546
(1) 6/30/2012	2,659	102,659
(2) 12/31/2012	1,772	101,772
(3) 6/30/2013	885	100,885
(4) 12/31/2013	0‡	100,000

* Total bond premium (of $3,546) less accumulated periodic amortization ($887 per semiannual interest period).

† Bond par value (of $100,000) plus unamortized premium.

‡ Adjusted for rounding.

During the bond life, carrying value is adjusted to par and the amortized premium to zero.

1. At issuance, the $100,000 par value plus the $3,546 premium equals the $103,546 cash received by the issuer.
2. During the bonds' life, the (unamortized) premium decreases each period by the $887 amortization ($3,546/4), and the carrying value decreases each period by the same $887.
3. At maturity, the unamortized premium equals zero, and the carrying value equals the $100,000 par value that the issuer pays the holder.

The next section describes bond pricing. An instructor can choose to cover bond pricing or not. Assignments requiring the next section are Quick Study 10-5, and Exercises 10-9 & 10-10.

Bond Pricing

Prices for bonds traded on an organized exchange are often published in newspapers and through online services. This information normally includes the bond price (called *quote*), its contract rate, and its current market (called *yield*) rate. However, only a fraction of bonds are traded on organized exchanges. To compute the price of a bond, we apply present value concepts. This section explains how to use *present value concepts* to price the Fila discount bond and the Adidas premium bond described earlier.

Point: InvestingInBonds.com is a bond research and learning source.

Present Value of a Discount Bond

The issue price of bonds is found by computing the present value of the bonds' cash payments, discounted at the bonds' market rate. When computing the present value of the Fila bonds, we work with *semiannual* compounding periods because this is the time between interest payments; the annual market rate of 10% is considered a semiannual rate of 5%. Also, the two-year bond life is viewed as four semiannual periods. The price computation is twofold: (1) Find the present value of the $100,000 par value paid at maturity and (2) find the present value of the series of four semiannual payments of $4,000 each; see Exhibit 10.4. These present values can be found by using *present value tables*. Appendix B at the end of this book shows present value tables and describes their use. Table B.1 at the end of Appendix B is used for the single $100,000 maturity payment, and Table B.3 in Appendix B is used for the $4,000 series of interest payments. Specifically, we go to Table B.1, row 4, and across to the 5% column to identify the present value factor of 0.8227 for the maturity payment. Next, we go to Table B.3, row 4, and across to the 5% column, where the present value factor is 3.5460 for the series of interest payments. We compute bond price by multiplying the cash flow payments by their corresponding present value factors and adding them together; see Exhibit 10.12.

Point: A bond's market value (price) at issuance equals the present value of its future cash payments, where the interest (discount) rate used is the bond's market rate.

Point: Many calculators have present value functions for computing bond prices.

EXHIBIT 10.12

Computing Issue Price for the Fila Discount Bonds

Cash Flow	Table	Present Value Factor	Amount	Present Value
$100,000 par (maturity) value	B.1	0.8227	× $100,000 =	$ 82,270
$4,000 interest payments	B.3	3.5460	× 4,000 =	14,184
Price of bond				$96,454

Present Value of a Premium Bond

We find the issue price of the Adidas bonds by using the market rate to compute the present value of the bonds' future cash flows. When computing the present value of these bonds, we again work with *semiannual* compounding periods because this is the time between interest payments. The annual 10% market rate is applied as a semiannual rate of 5%, and the two-year bond life is viewed as four semiannual periods. The computation is twofold: (1) Find the present value of the $100,000 par value paid at maturity and (2) find the present value of the series of four payments of $6,000 each; see Exhibit 10.8. These present values can be found by using present value tables. First, go to Table B.1, row 4, and across to the 5% column where the present value factor is 0.8227 for the maturity payment. Second, go to Table B.3, row 4, and across to the 5% column, where the present value factor is 3.5460 for the series of interest payments. The bonds' price is computed by multiplying the cash flow payments by their corresponding present value factors and adding them together; see Exhibit 10.13.

Point: There are nearly 5 million individual U.S. bond issues, ranging from huge treasuries to tiny municipalities. This compares to about 12,000 individual U.S. stocks that are traded.

EXHIBIT 10.13

Computing Issue Price for the Adidas Premium Bonds

Cash Flow	Table	Present Value Factor	Amount	Present Value
$100,000 par (maturity) value	B.1	0.8227	× $100,000 =	$ 82,270
$6,000 interest payments	B.3	3.5460	× 6,000 =	21,276
Price of bond				$103,546

Fraud

Unreported Liabilities Drove U.S. Financial Crisis? Many argue that unreported liabilities were a major cause of the financial crisis. They assert that "off-balance-sheet accounting" encouraged bad loans, securitizations, and derivatives that drove much of the crisis. It is argued that balance sheets failed to report many of these liabilities. For example, because bank liabilities used to finance assets were not transparent, the markets failed to penalize banks that used derivatives and variable interest entities (VIEs) to take excessive risks. Arguably, such accounting is fraudulent.

Quick Check
Answers — p. 441

On December 31, 2010, a company issues 16%, 10-year bonds with a par value of $100,000. Interest is paid on June 30 and December 31. The bonds are sold to yield a 14% annual market rate at an issue price of $110,592. Use this information to answer questions 7 through 9:

7. Are these bonds issued at a discount or a premium? Explain your answer.
8. Using the straight-line method to allocate bond interest expense, the issuer records the second interest payment (on December 31, 2011) with a debit to Premium on Bonds Payable in the amount of (a) $7,470, (b) $530, (c) $8,000, or (d) $400.
9. How are these bonds reported in the long-term liability section of the issuer's balance sheet as of December 31, 2011?

BOND RETIREMENT

This section describes the retirement of bonds (1) at maturity, (2) before maturity, and (3) by conversion to stock.

P4 Record the retirement of bonds.

Bond Retirement at Maturity

The carrying value of bonds at maturity always equals par value. For example, both Exhibits 10.7 (a discount) and 10.11 (a premium) show that the carrying value of bonds at the end of their lives equals par value ($100,000). The retirement of these bonds at maturity, assuming interest is already paid and entered, is recorded as follows:

2013 Dec. 31	Bonds Payable	100,000	
	Cash		100,000
	To record retirement of bonds at maturity.		

Assets = Liabilities + Equity
−100,000   −100,000

Bond Retirement before Maturity

Issuers sometimes wish to retire some or all of their bonds prior to maturity. For instance, if interest rates decline greatly, an issuer may wish to replace high-interest-paying bonds with new low-interest bonds. Two common ways to retire bonds before maturity are to (1) exercise a call option or (2) purchase them on the open market. In the first instance, an issuer can reserve the right to retire bonds early by issuing callable bonds. The bond indenture can give the issuer an option to *call* the bonds before they mature by paying the par value plus a *call premium* to bondholders. In the second case, the issuer retires bonds by repurchasing them on the open market at their current price. Whether bonds are called or repurchased, the issuer is unlikely to pay a price that exactly equals their carrying value. When a difference exists between the bonds' carrying value and the amount paid, the issuer records a gain or loss equal to the difference.

To illustrate the accounting for retiring callable bonds, assume that a company issued callable bonds with a par value of $100,000. The call option requires the issuer to pay a call premium of $3,000 to bondholders in addition to the par value. Next, assume that after the June 30, 2011, interest payment, the bonds have a carrying value of $104,500. Then on July 1, 2011, the issuer

Point: Bond retirement is also referred to as *bond redemption*.

Point: Gains and losses from retiring bonds were previously reported as extraordinary items. New standards require that they now be judged by the "unusual and infrequent" criteria for reporting purposes.

calls these bonds and pays $103,000 to bondholders. The issuer recognizes a $1,500 gain from the difference between the bonds' carrying value of $104,500 and the retirement price of $103,000. The issuer records this bond retirement as follows.

July 1	Bonds Payable	100,000	
	Premium on Bonds Payable	4,500	
	Gain on Bond Retirement		1,500
	Cash		103,000
	To record retirement of bonds before maturity.		

Assets = Liabilities + Equity
−103,000 −100,000   +1,500
          −4,500

An issuer usually must call all bonds when it exercises a call option. However, to retire as many or as few bonds as it desires, an issuer can purchase them on the open market. If it retires less than the entire class of bonds, it recognizes a gain or loss for the difference between the carrying value of those bonds retired and the amount paid to acquire them.

Bond Retirement by Conversion

Holders of convertible bonds have the right to convert their bonds to stock. When conversion occurs, the bonds' carrying value is transferred to equity accounts and no gain or loss is recorded. (We further describe convertible bonds in the Decision Analysis section of this chapter.)

To illustrate, assume that on January 1 the $100,000 par value bonds of **Converse**, with a carrying value of $100,000, are converted to 15,000 shares of $2 par value common stock. The entry to record this conversion follows (the market prices of the bonds and stock are *not* relevant to this entry; the material in Chapter 11 is helpful in understanding this transaction):

Jan. 1	Bonds Payable	100,000	
	Common Stock		30,000
	Paid-In Capital in Excess of Par Value		70,000
	To record retirement of bonds by conversion.		

Assets = Liabilities + Equity
          −100,000   +30,000
                     +70,000

Decision Insight

Junk Bonds Junk bonds are company bonds with low credit ratings due to a higher than average likelihood of default. On the upside, the high risk of junk bonds can yield high returns if the issuer survives and repays its debt. ■

Quick Check   Answer — p. 441

10. Six years ago, a company issued $500,000 of 6%, eight-year bonds at a price of 95. The current carrying value is $493,750. The company decides to retire 50% of these bonds by buying them on the open market at a price of 102½. What is the amount of gain or loss on the retirement of these bonds?

LONG-TERM NOTES PAYABLE

C1 Explain the types and payment patterns of notes.

Like bonds, notes are issued to obtain assets such as cash. Unlike bonds, notes are typically transacted with a *single* lender such as a bank. An issuer initially records a note at its selling price—that is, the note's face value minus any discount or plus any premium. Over the note's life, the amount of interest expense allocated to each period is computed by multiplying the market rate (at issuance of the note) by the beginning-of-period note balance. The note's carrying (book) value at any time equals its face value minus any unamortized discount or plus any unamortized premium; carrying value is also computed as the present value of all remaining payments, discounted using the market rate at issuance.

Installment Notes

An **installment note** is an obligation requiring a series of payments to the lender. Installment notes are common for franchises and other businesses when lenders and borrowers agree to spread payments over several periods. To illustrate, assume that Foghog borrows $60,000 from a bank to purchase equipment. It signs an 8% installment note requiring six annual payments of principal plus interest and it records the note's issuance at January 1, 2011, as follows.

Jan. 1	Cash	60,000	
	Notes Payable		60,000
	Borrowed $60,000 by signing an 8%, six-year installment note.		

Assets = Liabilities + Equity
+60,000   +60,000

Payments on an installment note normally include the accrued interest expense plus a portion of the amount borrowed (the *principal*). This section describes an installment note with equal payments.

The equal total payments pattern consists of changing amounts of both interest and principal. To illustrate, assume that Foghog borrows $60,000 by signing a $60,000 note that requires six *equal payments* of $12,979 at the end of each year. (The present value of an annuity of six annual payments of $12,979, discounted at 8%, equals $60,000; we show this computation in footnote 2 on the next page.) The $12,979 includes both interest and principal, the amounts of which change with each payment. Exhibit 10.14 shows the pattern of equal total payments and its two parts, interest and principal. Column A shows the note's beginning balance. Column B shows accrued interest for each year at 8% of the beginning note balance. Column C shows the impact on the

Point: Most consumer notes are installment notes that require equal total payments.

EXHIBIT 10.14
Installment Note: Equal Total Payments

Period Ending Date	(A) Beginning Balance	(B) Debit Interest Expense 8% × (A)	(C) Debit Notes Payable (D) − (B)	(D) Credit Cash (computed)	(E) Ending Balance (A) − (C)
(1) 12/31/2011	$60,000	$ 4,800	$ 8,179	$12,979	$51,821
(2) 12/31/2012	51,821	4,146	8,833	12,979	42,988
(3) 12/31/2013	42,988	3,439	9,540	12,979	33,448
(4) 12/31/2014	33,448	2,676	10,303	12,979	23,145
(5) 12/31/2015	23,145	1,852	11,127	12,979	12,018
(6) 12/31/2016	12,018	961	12,018	12,979	0
		$17,874	$60,000	$77,874	

note's principal, which equals the difference between the total payment in column D and the interest expense in column B. Column E shows the note's year-end balance.

> **Fraud**
>
> **Where's the Debt?** A study reports that 13% of employees in finance and accounting witnessed the falsifying or manipulating of accounting information in the past year (KPMG 2009). This is of special concern with long-term liabilities. For example, Enron violated GAAP to keep debt off its balance sheet. This concern extends to hidden environmental liabilities. That same study reports 27% of employees in quality, safety, and environmental areas observed violations of environmental standards, which can yield massive liabilities.

P5 Prepare entries to account for notes.

Although the six cash payments are equal, accrued interest decreases each year because the principal balance of the note declines. As the amount of interest decreases each year, the portion of each payment applied to principal increases. This pattern is graphed in the lower part of Exhibit 10.14. Foghog uses the amounts in Exhibit 10.14 to record its first two payments (for years 2011 and 2012) as follows:

Assets = Liabilities + Equity
−12,979   −8,179   −4,800

2011			
Dec. 31	Interest Expense	4,800	
	Notes Payable	8,179	
	Cash		12,979
	To record first installment payment.		

Assets = Liabilities + Equity
−12,979   −8,833   −4,146

2012			
Dec. 31	Interest Expense	4,146	
	Notes Payable	8,833	
	Cash		12,979
	To record second installment payment.		

Foghog records similar entries but with different amounts for each of the remaining four payments. After six years, the Notes Payable account balance is zero.[2]

> **Decision Maker** — Answer — p. 441
>
> **Entrepreneur** You are an electronics retailer planning a holiday sale on a custom stereo system that requires no payments for two years. At the end of two years, buyers must pay the full amount. The system's suggested retail price is $4,100, but you are willing to sell it today for $3,000 cash. What is your holiday sale price if payment will not occur for two years and the market interest rate is 10%?

Mortgage Notes and Bonds

Point: The Truth-in-Lending Act requires lenders to provide information about loan costs including finance charges and interest rate.

A **mortgage** is a legal agreement that helps protect a lender if a borrower fails to make required payments on notes or bonds. A mortgage gives the lender a right to be paid from the cash proceeds of the sale of a borrower's assets identified in the mortgage. A legal document, called a *mortgage contract,* describes the mortgage terms.

Mortgage notes carry a mortgage contract pledging title to specific assets as security for the note. Mortgage notes are especially popular in the purchase of homes and the acquisition of plant assets. Less common *mortgage bonds* are backed by the issuer's assets. Accounting for mortgage

---

Example: Suppose the $60,000 installment loan has an 8% interest rate with eight equal annual payments. What is the annual payment? *Answer* (using Table B.3): $60,000/5.7466 = $10,441

[2] Table B.3 in Appendix B is used to compute the dollar amount of the six payments that equal the initial note balance of $60,000 at 8% interest. We go to Table B.3, row 6, and across to the 8% column, where the present value factor is 4.6229. The dollar amount is then computed by solving this relation:

Table	Present Value Factor		Dollar Amount		Present Value
B.3	4.6229	×	?	=	$60,000

The dollar amount is computed by dividing $60,000 by 4.6229, yielding $12,979.

notes and bonds is similar to that for unsecured notes and bonds, except that the mortgage agreement must be disclosed. For example, **TIBCO Software** reports that its "mortgage note payable...is collateralized by the commercial real property acquired [corporate headquarters]."

> **Global:** Countries vary in the preference given to debtholders vs. stockholders when a company is in financial distress. Some countries such as Germany, France, and Japan give preference to stockholders over debtholders.

Fraud

Hidden Liabilities. Some companies arguably "hide" debt from their balance sheets by pursuing joint ventures, R&D partnerships, operating leases, and the like. While there are many sound economic reasons to pursue these activities, they also present the "less-principled" company with an opportunity to deceive readers of its balance sheet. Specifically, under certain conditions, companies can hide liabilities from such transactions when the economics suggest they should not. Notes to financial statements can often reveal this risk, but not always.

Quick Check
Answers — p. 441

11. Which of the following is true for an installment note requiring a series of equal total cash payments? (*a*) Payments consist of increasing interest and decreasing principal; (*b*) payments consist of changing amounts of principal but constant interest; or (*c*) payments consist of decreasing interest and increasing principal.
12. How is the interest portion of an installment note payment computed?
13. When a borrower records an interest payment on an installment note, how are the balance sheet and income statement affected?

GLOBAL VIEW

This section discusses similarities and differences between U.S. GAAP and IFRS in accounting and reporting for long-term liabilities such as bonds and notes.

Accounting for Bonds and Notes The definitions and characteristics of bonds and notes are broadly similar for both U.S. GAAP and IFRS. Although slight differences exist, accounting for bonds and notes under U.S. GAAP and IFRS is similar. Specifically, the accounting for issuances (including recording discounts and premiums), market pricing, and retirement of both bonds and notes follows the procedures in this chapter. **Nokia** describes its accounting for bonds, which follows the amortized cost approach explained in this chapter (and in Appendix 10B), as follows: Loans payable [bonds] are recognized initially at fair value, net of transaction costs incurred. In the subsequent periods, they are stated at amortized cost.

NOKIA

Both U.S. GAAP and IFRS allow companies to account for bonds and notes using fair value (different from the amortized value described in this chapter). This method is referred to as the **fair value option.** This method is similar to that applied in measuring and accounting for debt and equity securities. *Fair value* is the amount a company would receive if it settled a liability (or sold an asset) in an orderly transaction as of the balance sheet date. Companies can use several sources of inputs to determine fair value, and those inputs fall into three classes (ranked in order of preference):

Level 1: Observable quoted market prices in active markets for identical items.
Level 2: Observable inputs other than those in Level 1 such as prices from inactive markets or from similar, but not identical, items.
Level 3: Unobservable inputs reflecting a company's assumptions about value.

The exact procedures for marking liabilities to fair value at each balance sheet date are in advanced courses.

Accounting for Leases and Pensions Both U.S. GAAP and IFRS require companies to distinguish between operating leases and capital leases; the latter is referred to as *finance leases* under IFRS. The accounting and reporting for leases are broadly similar for both U.S. GAAP and IFRS. The main difference is the criteria for identifying a lease as a capital lease are more general under IFRS. However, the basic approach applies. **Nokia** describes its accounting for operating leases as follows: the payments... are treated as rentals and recognized in the profit and loss account.

For pensions, both U.S. GAAP and IFRS require companies to record costs of retirement benefits as employees work and earn them. The basic methods are similar in accounting and reporting for pensions.

428   Chapter 10   Reporting and Analyzing Long-Term Liabilities

Decision Analysis

Debt Features and the Debt-to-Equity Ratio

Collateral agreements can reduce the risk of loss for both bonds and notes. Unsecured bonds and notes are riskier because the issuer's obligation to pay interest and principal has the same priority as all other unsecured liabilities in the event of bankruptcy. If a company is unable to pay its debts in full, the unsecured creditors (including the holders of debentures) lose all or a portion of their balances. These types of legal agreements and other characteristics of long-term liabilities are crucial for effective business decisions. The first part of this section describes the different types of features sometimes included with bonds and notes. The second part explains and applies the debt-to-equity ratio.

A2 Assess debt features and their implications.

Features of Bonds and Notes

This section describes common features of debt securities.

Secured or Unsecured **Secured bonds** (and notes) have specific assets of the issuer pledged (or *mortgaged*) as collateral. This arrangement gives holders added protection against the issuer's default. If the issuer fails to pay interest or par value, the secured holders can demand that the collateral be sold and the proceeds used to pay the obligation. **Unsecured bonds** (and notes), also called *debentures,* are backed by the issuer's general credit standing. Unsecured debt is riskier than secured debt. *Subordinated debentures* are liabilities that are not repaid until the claims of the more senior, unsecured (and secured) liabilities are settled.

Secured Debt

Unsecured Debt

Term or Serial **Term bonds** (and notes) are scheduled for maturity on one specified date. **Serial bonds** (and notes) mature at more than one date (often in series) and thus are usually repaid over a number of periods. For instance, $100,000 of serial bonds might mature at the rate of $10,000 each year from 6 to 15 years after they are issued. Many bonds are **sinking fund bonds,** which to reduce the holder's risk require the issuer to create a *sinking fund* of assets set aside at specified amounts and dates to repay the bonds.

Registered or Bearer Bonds issued in the names and addresses of their holders are **registered bonds.** The issuer makes bond payments by sending checks (or cash transfers) to registered holders. A registered holder must notify the issuer of any ownership change. Registered bonds offer the issuer the practical advantage of not having to actually issue bond certificates. Bonds payable to whoever holds them (the *bearer*) are called **bearer bonds** or *unregistered bonds*. Sales or exchanges might not be recorded, so the holder of a bearer bond is presumed to be its rightful owner. As a result, lost bearer bonds are difficult to replace. Many bearer bonds are also **coupon bonds.** This term reflects interest coupons that are attached to the bonds. When each coupon matures, the holder presents it to a bank or broker for collection. At maturity, the holder follows the same process and presents the bond certificate for collection. Issuers of coupon bonds cannot deduct the related interest expense for taxable income. This is to prevent abuse by taxpayers who own coupon bonds but fail to report interest income on their tax returns.

Convertible and/or Callable **Convertible bonds** (and notes) can be exchanged for a fixed number of shares of the issuing corporation's common stock. Convertible debt offers holders the potential to participate in future increases in stock price. Holders still receive periodic interest while the debt is held and the par value if they hold the debt to maturity. In most cases, the holders decide whether and when to convert debt to stock. **Callable bonds** (and notes) have an option exercisable by the issuer to retire them at a stated dollar amount before maturity.

Convertible Debt   **Callable Debt**

Decision Insight

Munis More than a million municipal bonds, or "munis," exist, and many are tax exempt. Munis are issued by state, city, town, and county governments to pay for public projects including schools, libraries, roads, bridges, and stadiums. ■

A3 Compute the debt-to-equity ratio and explain its use.

Debt-to-Equity Ratio

Beyond assessing different characteristics of debt as just described, we want to know the level of debt, especially in relation to total equity. Such knowledge helps us assess the risk of a company's financing structure. A company financed mainly with debt is more risky because liabilities must be repaid—usually with periodic interest—whereas equity financing does not. A measure to assess the risk of a company's financing structure is the **debt-to-equity ratio** (see Exhibit 10.15).

$$\text{Debt-to-equity} = \frac{\text{Total liabilities}}{\text{Total equity}}$$

EXHIBIT 10.15

Debt-to-Equity Ratio

The debt-to-equity ratio varies across companies and industries. Industries that are more variable and less stable tend to have lower ratios, while more stable industries tend to have higher ratios. To apply the debt-to-equity ratio, let's look at this measure for **Cedar Fair** in Exhibit 10.16.

($ millions)	2009	2008	2007	2006	2005
Total liabilities	$2,017.577	$2,079.297	$2,133.576	$2,100.306	$590.560
Total equity	$ 127.862	$ 106.786	$ 285.092	$ 410.615	$434.234
Debt-to-equity	15.8	19.5	7.5	5.1	1.4
Industry debt-to-equity	11.4	10.3	5.7	3.2	1.2

EXHIBIT 10.16

Cedar Fair's Debt-to-Equity Ratio

Cedar Fair's 2009 debt-to-equity ratio is 15.8, meaning that debtholders contributed $15.8 for each $1 contributed by equityholders. This implies a fairly risky financing structure for Cedar Fair. A similar concern is drawn from a comparison of Cedar Fair with its competitors, where the 2009 industry ratio is 11.4. Analysis across the years shows that Cedar Fair's financing structure has grown increasingly risky in recent years. Given its sluggish revenues and increasing operating expenses in recent years (see its annual report), Cedar Fair is increasingly at risk of financial distress.

Decision Maker Answer — p. 441

Bond Investor You plan to purchase debenture bonds from one of two companies in the same industry that are similar in size and performance. The first company has $350,000 in total liabilities, and $1,750,000 in equity. The second company has $1,200,000 in total liabilities, and $1,000,000 in equity. Which company's debenture bonds are less risky based on the debt-to-equity ratio? ■

DEMONSTRATION PROBLEM

Water Sports Company (WSC) patented and successfully test-marketed a new product. To expand its ability to produce and market the new product, WSC needs to raise $800,000 of financing. On January 1, 2011, the company obtained the money in two ways:

a. WSC signed a $400,000, 10% installment note to be repaid with five equal annual installments to be made on December 31 of 2011 through 2015.

b. WSC issued five-year bonds with a par value of $400,000. The bonds have a 12% annual contract rate and pay interest on June 30 and December 31. The bonds' annual market rate is 10% as of January 1, 2011.

Required

1. For the installment note, (a) compute the size of each annual payment, (b) prepare an amortization table such as Exhibit 10.14, and (c) prepare the journal entry for the first payment.
2. For the bonds, (a) compute their issue price; (b) prepare the January 1, 2011, journal entry to record their issuance; (c) prepare an amortization table using the straight-line method; (d) prepare the June 30, 2011, journal entry to record the first interest payment; and (e) prepare a journal entry to record retiring the bonds at a $416,000 call price on January 1, 2013.
3.[B] Redo parts 2(c), 2(d), and 2(e) assuming the bonds are amortized using the effective interest method.

PLANNING THE SOLUTION

- For the installment note, divide the borrowed amount by the annuity factor (from Table B.3) using the 10% rate and five payments to compute the amount of each payment. Prepare a table similar to Exhibit 10.14 and use the numbers in the table's first line for the journal entry.
- Compute the bonds' issue price by using the market rate to find the present value of their cash flows (use tables found in Appendix B). Then use this result to record the bonds' issuance. Next, prepare an amortization table like Exhibit 10.11 (and Exhibit 10B.2) and use it to get the numbers needed for the journal entry. Also use the table to find the carrying value as of the date of the bonds' retirement that you need for the journal entry.

SOLUTION TO DEMONSTRATION PROBLEM

Part 1: Installment Note

a. Annual payment = Note balance/Annuity factor = $400,000/3.7908 = $105,519 (The annuity factor is for five payments and a rate of 10%.)

b. An amortization table follows.

Annual Period Ending	(a) Beginning Balance	(b) Debit Interest Expense	(c) Debit Notes Payable	(d) Credit Cash	(e) Ending Balance
(1) 12/31/2011	$400,000	$ 40,000	$ 65,519	$105,519	$334,481
(2) 12/31/2012	334,481	33,448	72,071	105,519	262,410
(3) 12/31/2013	262,410	26,241	79,278	105,519	183,132
(4) 12/31/2014	183,132	18,313	87,206	105,519	95,926
(5) 12/31/2015	95,926	9,593	95,926	105,519	0
		$127,595	$400,000	$527,595	

c. Journal entry for December 31, 2011, payment.

Dec. 31	Interest Expense	40,000	
	Notes Payable	65,519	
	Cash		105,519
	To record first installment payment.		

Part 2: Bonds (Straight-Line Amortization)

a. Compute the bonds' issue price.

Cash Flow	Table	Present Value Factor*	Amount	Present Value
Par (maturity) value	B.1 in App. B (PV of 1)	0.6139	× 400,000	= $245,560
Interest payments	B.3 in App. B (PV of annuity)	7.7217	× 24,000	= 185,321
Price of bond				$430,881

* Present value factors are for 10 payments using a semiannual market rate of 5%.

b. Journal entry for January 1, 2011, issuance.

Jan. 1	Cash	430,881	
	Premium on Bonds Payable		30,881
	Bonds Payable		400,000
	Sold bonds at a premium.		

c. Straight-line amortization table for premium bonds.

Semiannual Period-End	Unamortized Premium	Carrying Value
(0) 1/1/2011	$30,881	$430,881
(1) 6/30/2011	27,793	427,793
(2) 12/31/2011	24,705	424,705
(3) 6/30/2012	21,617	421,617
(4) 12/31/2012	18,529	418,529
(5) 6/30/2013	15,441	415,441
(6) 12/31/2013	12,353	412,353
(7) 6/30/2014	9,265	409,265
(8) 12/31/2014	6,177	406,177
(9) 6/30/2015	3,089	403,089
(10) 12/31/2015	0*	400,000

* Adjusted for rounding.

d. Journal entry for June 30, 2011, bond payment.

June 30	Bond Interest Expense	20,912	
	Premium on Bonds Payable	3,088	
	Cash		24,000
	Paid semiannual interest on bonds.		

e. Journal entry for January 1, 2013, bond retirement.

Jan. 1	Bonds Payable	400,000	
	Premium on Bonds Payable	18,529	
	Cash		416,000
	Gain on Retirement of Bonds		2,529
	To record bond retirement (carrying value as of Dec. 31, 2012).		

Part 3: Bonds (Effective Interest Amortization)[B]

c. The effective interest amortization table for premium bonds.

	(A)	(B)	(C)	(D)	(E)
Semiannual Interest Period	Cash Interest Paid 6% × $400,000	Interest Expense 5% × Prior (E)	Premium Amortization (A) − (B)	Unamortized Premium Prior (D) − (C)	Carrying Value $400,000 + (D)
(0) 1/1/2011				$30,881	$430,881
(1) 6/30/2011	$ 24,000	$ 21,544	$ 2,456	28,425	428,425
(2) 12/31/2011	24,000	21,421	2,579	25,846	425,846
(3) 6/30/2012	24,000	21,292	2,708	23,138	423,138
(4) 12/31/2012	24,000	21,157	2,843	20,295	420,295
(5) 6/30/2013	24,000	21,015	2,985	17,310	417,310
(6) 12/31/2013	24,000	20,866	3,134	14,176	414,176
(7) 6/30/2014	24,000	20,709	3,291	10,885	410,885
(8) 12/31/2014	24,000	20,544	3,456	7,429	407,429
(9) 6/30/2015	24,000	20,371	3,629	3,800	403,800
(10) 12/31/2015	24,000	20,200*	3,800	0	400,000
	$240,000	$209,119	$30,881		

* Adjusted for rounding

d. Journal entry for June 30, 2011, bond payment.

June 30	Bond Interest Expense	21,544	
	Premium on Bonds Payable	2,456	
	Cash		24,000
	Paid semiannual interest on bonds.		

e. Journal entry for January 1, 2013, bond retirement.

Jan. 1	Bonds Payable	400,000	
	Premium on Bonds Payable	20,295	
	Cash		416,000
	Gain on Retirement of Bonds		4,295
	To record bond retirement (carrying value as of December 31, 2012).		

APPENDIX 10A — Present Values of Bonds and Notes

This appendix explains how to apply present value techniques to measure a long-term liability when it is created and to assign interest expense to the periods until it is settled. Appendix B at the end of the book provides additional discussion of present value concepts.

C2 Explain and compute the present value of an amount(s) to be paid at a future date(s).

Present Value Concepts The basic present value concept is that cash paid (or received) in the future has less value now than the same amount of cash paid (or received) today. To illustrate, if we must pay $1 one year from now, its present value is less than $1. To see this, assume that we borrow $0.9259 today that must be paid back in one year with 8% interest. Our interest expense for this loan is computed as $0.9259 × 8%, or $0.0741. When the $0.0741 interest is added to the $0.9259 borrowed, we get the $1 payment necessary to repay our loan with interest. This is formally computed in Exhibit 10A.1. The $0.9259 borrowed is the present value of the $1 future payment. More generally, an amount borrowed equals the present value of the future payment. (This same interpretation applies to an investment. If $0.9259 is invested at 8%, it yields $0.0741 in revenue after one year. This amounts to $1, made up of principal and interest.)

EXHIBIT 10A.1 Components of a One-Year Loan

Amount borrowed	$0.9259
Interest for one year at 8%	0.0741
Amount owed after 1 year	$1.0000

Point: Benjamin Franklin is said to have described compounding as "the money, money makes, makes more money."

To extend this example, assume that we owe $1 two years from now instead of one year, and the 8% interest is compounded annually. *Compounded* means that interest during the second period is based on the total of the amount borrowed plus the interest accrued from the first period. The second period's interest is then computed as 8% multiplied by the sum of the amount borrowed plus interest earned in the first period. Exhibit 10A.2 shows how we compute the present value of $1 to be paid in two years. This amount is $0.8573. The first year's interest of $0.0686 is added to the principal so that the second year's interest is based on $0.9259. Total interest for this two-year period is $0.1427, computed as $0.0686 plus $0.0741.

EXHIBIT 10A.2 Components of a Two-Year Loan

Amount borrowed	$0.8573
Interest for first year ($0.8573 × 8%)	0.0686
Amount owed after 1 year	0.9259
Interest for second year ($0.9259 × 8%)	0.0741
Amount owed after 2 years	$1.0000

Present Value Tables The present value of $1 that we must repay at some future date can be computed by using this formula: $1/(1 + i)^n$. The symbol i is the interest rate per period and n is the number of periods until the future payment must be made. Applying this formula to our two-year loan, we get $1/(1.08)^2$, or $0.8573. This is the same value shown in Exhibit 10A.2. We can use this formula to find any present value. However, a simpler method is to use a *present value table,* which lists present values computed with this formula for various interest rates and time periods. Many people find it helpful in learning present value concepts to first work with the table and then move to using a calculator.

Exhibit 10A.3 shows a present value table for a future payment of 1 for up to 10 periods at three different interest rates. Present values in this table are rounded to four decimal places. This table is drawn from the larger and more complete Table B.1 in Appendix B at the end of the book. Notice that the first value in the 8% column is 0.9259, the value we computed earlier for the present value of a $1 loan for one year at 8% (see Exhibit 10A.1). Go to the second row in the same 8% column and find the present value of 1 discounted at 8% for two years, or 0.8573. This $0.8573 is the present value of our obligation to repay $1 after two periods at 8% interest (see Exhibit 10A.2).

EXHIBIT 10A.3
Present Value of 1

	Rate		
Periods	6%	8%	10%
1	0.9434	**0.9259**	0.9091
2	0.8900	**0.8573**	0.8264
3	0.8396	0.7938	0.7513
4	0.7921	0.7350	0.6830
5	0.7473	0.6806	0.6209
6	0.7050	0.6302	0.5645
7	0.6651	0.5835	0.5132
8	0.6274	0.5403	0.4665
9	0.5919	0.5002	0.4241
10	0.5584	0.4632	0.3855

Example: Use Exhibit 10A.3 to find the present value of $1 discounted for 2 years at 6%. *Answer:* $0.8900

Applying a Present Value Table To illustrate how to measure a liability using a present value table, assume that a company plans to borrow cash and repay it as follows: $2,000 after one year, $3,000 after two years, and $5,000 after three years. How much does this company receive today if the interest rate on this loan is 10%? To answer, we need to compute the present value of the three future payments, discounted at 10%. This computation is shown in Exhibit 10A.4 using present values from Exhibit 10A.3. The company can borrow $8,054 today at 10% interest in exchange for its promise to make these three payments at the scheduled dates.

EXHIBIT 10A.4
Present Value of a Series of Unequal Payments

Periods	Payments	Present Value of 1 at 10%	Present Value of Payments
1	$2,000	0.9091	$ 1,818
2	3,000	0.8264	2,479
3	5,000	0.7513	3,757
Present value of all payments			$8,054

Present Value of an Annuity The $8,054 present value for the loan in Exhibit 10A.4 equals the sum of the present values of the three payments. When payments are not equal, their combined present value is best computed by adding the individual present values as shown in Exhibit 10A.4. Sometimes payments follow an **annuity,** which is a series of *equal* payments at equal time intervals. The present value of an annuity is readily computed.

To illustrate, assume that a company must repay a 6% loan with a $5,000 payment at each year-end for the next four years. This loan amount equals the present value of the four payments discounted at 6%. Exhibit 10A.5 shows how to compute this loan's present value of $17,326 by multiplying each payment by its matching present value factor taken from Exhibit 10A.3.

However, the series of $5,000 payments is an annuity, so we can compute its present value with either of two shortcuts. First, the third column of Exhibit 10A.5 shows that the sum of the present values of 1 at 6% for periods 1 through 4 equals 3.4651. One shortcut is to multiply this total of 3.4651 by the $5,000 annual payment to get the combined present value of $17,326. It requires one multiplication instead of four.

EXHIBIT 10A.5
Present Value of a Series of Equal Payments (Annuity) by Discounting Each Payment

Periods	Payments	Present Value of 1 at 6%	Present Value of Payments
1	$5,000	0.9434	$ 4,717
2	5,000	0.8900	4,450
3	5,000	0.8396	4,198
4	5,000	0.7921	3,961
Present value of all payments		3.4651	$17,326

EXHIBIT 10A.6

Present Value of an Annuity of 1

Periods	6%	8%	10%
1	0.9434	0.9259	0.9091
2	1.8334	1.7833	1.7355
3	2.6730	2.5771	2.4869
4	**3.4651**	3.3121	3.1699
5	4.2124	3.9927	3.7908
6	4.9173	4.6229	4.3553
7	5.5824	5.2064	4.8684
8	6.2098	5.7466	5.3349
9	6.8017	6.2469	5.7590
10	7.3601	6.7101	6.1446

Example: Use Exhibit 10A.6 to find the present value of an annuity of eight $15,000 payments with an 8% interest rate. Answer: $15,000 × 5.7466 = $86,199

Example: If this borrower makes five semiannual payments of $8,000, what is the present value of this annuity at a 12% rate? Answer: 4.2124 × $8,000 = $33,699

The second shortcut uses an *annuity table* such as the one shown in Exhibit 10A.6, which is drawn from the more complete Table B.3 in Appendix B. We go directly to the annuity table to get the present value factor for a specific number of payments and interest rate. We then multiply this factor by the amount of the payment to find the present value of the annuity. Specifically, find the row for four periods and go across to the 6% column, where the factor is 3.4651. This factor equals the present value of an annuity with four payments of 1, discounted at 6%. We then multiply 3.4651 by $5,000 to get the $17,326 present value of the annuity.

Compounding Periods Shorter Than a Year

The present value examples all involved periods of one year. In many situations, however, interest is compounded over shorter periods. For example, the interest rate on bonds is usually stated as an annual rate but interest is often paid every six months (semiannually). This means that the present value of interest payments from such bonds must be computed using interest periods of six months.

Assume that a borrower wants to know the present value of a series of 10 *semiannual payments* of $4,000 made over five years at an *annual interest rate* of 12%. The interest rate is stated as an annual rate of 12%, but it is actually a rate of 6% per semiannual interest period. To compute the present value of this series of $4,000 payments, go to row 10 of Exhibit 10A.6 and across to the 6% column to find the factor 7.3601. The present value of this annuity is $29,440 (7.3601 × $4,000).

Appendix B further describes present value concepts and includes more complete present value tables and assignments.

Quick Check

Answers — p. 441

14. A company enters into an agreement to make four annual year-end payments of $1,000 each, starting one year from now. The annual interest rate is 8%. The present value of these four payments is (a) $2,923, (b) $2,940, or (c) $3,312.

15. Suppose a company has an option to pay either (a) $10,000 after one year or (b) $5,000 after six months and another $5,000 after one year. Which choice has the lower present value?

APPENDIX 10B

Effective Interest Amortization

Effective Interest Amortization of a Discount Bond The straight-line method yields changes in the bonds' carrying value while the amount for bond interest expense remains constant. This gives the impression of a changing interest rate when users divide a constant bond interest expense over a changing carrying value. As a result, accounting standards allow use of the straight-line method only when its results do not differ materially from those obtained using the effective interest method. The **effective interest method,** or simply *interest method,* allocates total bond interest expense over the bonds' life in a way that yields a constant rate of interest. This constant rate of interest is the market rate at the issue date. Thus, bond interest expense for a period equals the carrying value of the bond at the beginning of that period multiplied by the market rate when issued.

Point: The effective interest method computes bond interest expense using the market rate at issuance. This rate is applied to a changing carrying value.

Exhibit 10B.1 shows an effective interest amortization table for the Fila bonds (as described in Exhibit 10.4). The key difference between the effective interest and straight-line methods lies in computing bond interest expense. Instead of assigning an equal amount of bond interest expense to each period, the effective interest method assigns a bond interest expense amount that increases over the life of a discount bond. **Both methods allocate the *same* $19,546 of total bond interest expense to the bonds' life, but in different patterns.** Specifically, the amortization table in Exhibit 10B.1 shows that the balance of the discount (column D) is amortized until it reaches zero. Also, the bonds' carrying value (column E) changes each period until it equals par value at maturity. Compare columns D and E to the corresponding columns in Exhibit 10.7 to see the amortization patterns. Total bond interest expense is $19,546, consisting of $16,000 of semiannual cash payments and $3,546 of the original bond discount, the same for both methods.

EXHIBIT 10B.1

Effective Interest Amortization of Bond Discount

Bonds: $100,000 Par Value, Semiannual Interest Payments, Two-Year Life, 4% Semiannual Contract Rate, 5% Semiannual Market Rate

Semiannual Interest Period-End	(A) Cash Interest Paid	(B) Bond Interest Expense	(C) Discount Amortization	(D) Unamortized Discount	(E) Carrying Value
(0) 12/31/2011				$3,546	$ 96,454
(1) 6/30/2012	$4,000	$4,823	$ 823	2,723	97,277
(2) 12/31/2012	4,000	4,864	864	1,859	98,141
(3) 6/30/2013	4,000	4,907	907	952	99,048
(4) 12/31/2013	4,000	4,952	952	0	100,000
	$16,000	$19,546	$3,546		

Column (A) is the par value ($100,000) multiplied by the semiannual contract rate (4%).
Column (B) is the prior period's carrying value multiplied by the semiannual market rate (5%).
Column (C) is the difference between interest paid and bond interest expense, or [(B) − (A)].
Column (D) is the prior period's unamortized discount less the current period's discount amortization.
Column (E) is the par value less unamortized discount, or [$100,000 − (D)].

Except for differences in amounts, journal entries recording the expense and updating the liability balance are the same under the effective interest method and the straight-line method. We can use the numbers in Exhibit 10B.1 to record each semiannual entry during the bonds' two-year life (June 30, 2012, through December 31, 2013). For instance, we record the interest payment at the end of the first semiannual period as follows:

2012			
June 30	Bond Interest Expense	4,823	
	Discount on Bonds Payable		823
	Cash		4,000
	To record semiannual interest and discount amortization (effective interest method).		

Assets	=	Liabilities	+	Equity
−4,000		+823		−4,823

Effective Interest Amortization of a Premium Bond Exhibit 10B.2 shows the amortization table using the effective interest method for the Adidas bonds (as described in Exhibit 10.8). Column A lists the semiannual cash payments. Column B shows the amount of bond interest expense, computed as the 5% semiannual market rate at issuance multiplied by the beginning-of-period carrying value. The amount of cash paid in column A is larger than the bond interest expense because the cash payment is based on the higher 6% semiannual contract rate. The excess cash payment over the interest expense reduces the principal. These amounts are shown in column C. Column E shows the carrying value after

EXHIBIT 10B.2

Effective Interest Amortization of Bond Premium

Bonds: $100,000 Par Value, Semiannual Interest Payments, Two-Year Life, 6% Semiannual Contract Rate, 5% Semiannual Market Rate

Semiannual Interest Period-End	(A) Cash Interest Paid	(B) Bond Interest Expense	(C) Premium Amortization	(D) Unamortized Premium	(E) Carrying Value
(0) 12/31/2011				$3,546	$103,546
(1) 6/30/2012	$6,000	$5,177	$823	2,723	102,723
(2) 12/31/2012	6,000	5,136	864	1,859	101,859
(3) 6/30/2013	6,000	5,093	907	952	100,952
(4) 12/31/2013	6,000	5,048	952	0	100,000
	$24,000	$20,454	$3,546		

Column (A) is the par value ($100,000) multiplied by the semiannual contract rate (6%).
Column (B) is the prior period's carrying value multiplied by the semiannual market rate (5%).
Column (C) is the difference between interest paid and bond interest expense, or [(A) − (B)].
Column (D) is the prior period's unamortized premium less the current period's premium amortization.
Column (E) is the par value plus unamortized premium, or [$100,000 + (D)].

deducting the amortized premium in column C from the prior period's carrying value. Column D shows the premium's reduction by periodic amortization. When the issuer makes the first semiannual interest payment, the effect of premium amortization on bond interest expense and bond liability is recorded as follows:

Assets = Liabilities + Equity
−6,000   −823   −5,177

2012			
June 30	Bond Interest Expense	5,177	
	Premium on Bonds Payable	823	
	Cash		6,000
	To record semiannual interest and premium amortization (effective interest method).		

Similar entries with different amounts are recorded at each payment date until the bond matures at the end of 2013. The effective interest method yields decreasing amounts of bond interest expense and increasing amounts of premium amortization over the bonds' life.

IFRS

Unlike U.S. GAAP, IFRS requires that interest expense be computed using the effective interest method with *no exemptions.*

APPENDIX 10C

Issuing Bonds between Interest Dates

C3 Describe interest accrual when bond payment periods differ from accounting periods.

An issuer can sell bonds at a date other than an interest payment date. When this occurs, the buyers normally pay the issuer the purchase price plus any interest accrued since the prior interest payment date. This accrued interest is then repaid to these buyers on the next interest payment date. To illustrate, suppose **Avia** sells $100,000 of its 9% bonds at par on March 1, 2011, 60 days after the stated issue date. The interest on Avia bonds is payable semiannually on each June 30 and December 31. Since 60 days have passed, the issuer collects accrued interest from the buyers at the time of issuance. This amount is $1,500 ($100,000 × 9% × 60/360 year). This case is reflected in Exhibit 10C.1.

EXHIBIT 10C.1

Accruing Interest between Interest Payment Dates

```
Stated issue         Date of sale                        First interest
date January 1       March 1                             date June 30
      │                 │                                     │
      ▼                 ▼                                     ▼
      ├─── $1,500 accrued ───┼────────── $3,000 earned ──────┤
                         ▲                                     ▲
                         │                                     │
                    Bondholder pays                        Issuer pays
                    $1,500 to issuer                       $4,500 to bondholder
```

Avia records the issuance of these bonds on March 1, 2011, as follows:

Mar. 1	Cash	101,500	
	Interest Payable		1,500
	Bonds Payable................................		100,000
	Sold bonds at par with accrued interest.		

Assets = Liabilities + Equity
+101,500   +100,000
           +1,500

Liabilities for interest payable and bonds payable are recorded in separate accounts. When the June 30, 2011, semiannual interest date arrives, Avia pays the full semiannual interest of $4,500 ($100,000 × 9% × ½ year) to the bondholders. This payment includes the four months' interest of $3,000 earned by the bondholders from March 1 to June 30 *plus* the repayment of the 60 days' accrued interest collected by Avia when the bonds were sold. Avia records this first semiannual interest payment as follows:

Example: How much interest is collected from a buyer of $50,000 of Avia bonds sold at par 150 days after the contract issue date? *Answer:* $1,875 (computed as $50,000 × 9% × 150/360 year)

June 30	Interest Payable	1,500	
	Bond Interest Expense........................	3,000	
	Cash		4,500
	Paid semiannual interest on the bonds.		

Assets = Liabilities + Equity
−4,500   −1,500   −3,000

The practice of collecting and then repaying accrued interest with the next interest payment is to simplify the issuer's administrative efforts. To explain, suppose an issuer sells bonds on 15 or 20 different dates between the stated issue date and the first interest payment date. If the issuer does not collect accrued interest from buyers, it needs to pay different amounts of cash to each of them according to the time that passed after purchasing the bonds. The issuer needs to keep detailed records of buyers and the dates they bought bonds. Issuers avoid this recordkeeping by having each buyer pay accrued interest at purchase. Issuers then pay the full semiannual interest to all buyers, regardless of when they bought bonds.

Accruing Bond Interest Expense If a bond's interest period does not coincide with the issuer's accounting period, an adjusting entry is needed to recognize bond interest expense accrued since the most recent interest payment. To illustrate, assume that the stated issue date for Adidas bonds described in Exhibit 10.10 is September 1, 2011, instead of December 31, 2011, and that the bonds are sold on September 1, 2011. As a result, four months' interest (and premium amortization) accrue before the end of the 2011 calendar year. Interest for this period equals $3,409, or 4/6 of the first six months' interest of $5,113. Also, the premium amortization is $591, or 4/6 of the first six months' amortization of $887. The sum of the bond interest expense and the amortization is $4,000 ($3,409 + $591), which equals 4/6 of the $6,000 cash payment due on February 28, 2012. Adidas records these effects with an adjusting entry at December 31, 2011.

Point: Computation of accrued bond interest may use months instead of days for simplicity purposes. For example, the accrued interest computation for the Adidas bonds is based on months.

Dec. 31	Bond Interest Expense	3,409	
	Premium on Bonds Payable	591	
	Interest Payable		4,000
	To record four months' accrued interest and premium amortization.		

Assets = Liabilities + Equity
           −591   −3,409
           +4,000

Similar entries are made on each December 31 throughout the bonds' two-year life. When the $6,000 cash payment occurs on each February 28 interest payment date, Adidas must recognize bond interest expense and amortization for January and February. It must also eliminate the interest payable liability created by the December 31 adjusting entry. For example, Adidas records its payment on February 28, 2012, as follows:

Assets = Liabilities + Equity
−6,000   −4,000   −1,704
             −296

Feb. 28	Interest Payable	4,000	
	Bond Interest Expense ($5,113 × 2/6)	1,704	
	Premium on Bonds Payable ($887 × 2/6)	296	
	Cash		6,000
	To record 2 months' interest and amortization, and eliminate accrued interest liability.		

The interest payments made each August 31 are recorded as usual because the entire six-month interest period is included within this company's calendar-year reporting period.

Decision Maker
Answer — p. 441

Bond Rater You must assign a rating to a bond that reflects its risk to bondholders. Identify factors you consider in assessing bond risk. Indicate the likely levels (relative to the norm) for the factors you identify for a bond that sells at a discount. ■

Quick Check
Answer — p. 441

16. On May 1, a company sells 9% bonds with a $500,000 par value that pay semiannual interest on each January 1 and July 1. The bonds are sold at par plus interest accrued since January 1. The issuer records the first semiannual interest payment on July 1 with (a) a debit to Interest Payable for $15,000, (b) a debit to Bond Interest Expense for $22,500, or (c) a credit to Interest Payable for $7,500.

APPENDIX 10D

Leases and Pensions

This appendix briefly explains the accounting and analysis for both leases and pensions.

C4 Describe accounting for leases and pensions.

Lease Liabilities A **lease** is a contractual agreement between a *lessor* (asset owner) and a *lessee* (asset renter or tenant) that grants the lessee the right to use the asset for a period of time in return for cash (rent) payments. Nearly one-fourth of all equipment purchases are financed with leases. The advantages of lease financing include the lack of an immediate large cash payment and the potential to deduct rental payments in computing taxable income. From an accounting perspective, leases can be classified as either operating or capital leases.

Point: Home Depot reports that its rental expenses from operating leases total more than $900 million.

Operating Leases **Operating leases** are short-term (or cancelable) leases in which the lessor retains the risks and rewards of ownership. Examples include most car and apartment rental agreements. The lessee records such lease payments as expenses; the lessor records them as revenue. The lessee does not report the leased item as an asset or a liability (it is the lessor's asset). To illustrate, if an employee of Amazon leases a car for $300 at an airport while on company business, Amazon (lessee) records this cost as follows:

Assets = Liabilities + Equity
−300   −300

July 4	Rental Expense	300	
	Cash		300
	To record lease rental payment.		

Capital Leases **Capital leases** are long-term (or noncancelable) leases by which the lessor transfers substantially all risks and rewards of ownership to the lessee.[3] Examples include most leases of airplanes and department store buildings. The lessee records the leased item as its own asset along with a lease liability at the start of the lease term; the amount recorded equals the present value of all lease payments. To illustrate, assume that K2 Co. enters into a six-year lease of a building in which it will sell sporting equipment. The lease transfers all building ownership risks and rewards to K2 (the present value of its $12,979 annual lease payments is $60,000). K2 records this transaction as follows:

2011			
Jan. 1	Leased Asset—Building	60,000	
	Lease Liability		60,000
	To record leased asset and lease liability.		

Assets = Liabilities + Equity
+60,000   +60,000

K2 reports the leased asset as a plant asset and the lease liability as a long-term liability. The portion of the lease liability expected to be paid in the next year is reported as a current liability.[4] At each year-end, K2 records depreciation on the leased asset (assume straight-line depreciation, six-year lease term, and no salvage value) as follows:

Point: Home Depot reports "*certain locations ... are leased under capital leases.*" The net present value of this Lease Liability is about $400 million.

Dec. 31	Depreciation Expense—Building	10,000	
	Accumulated Depreciation—Building		10,000
	To record depreciation on leased asset.		

Assets = Liabilities + Equity
−10,000   −10,000

K2 also accrues interest on the lease liability at each year-end. Interest expense is computed by multiplying the remaining lease liability by the interest rate on the lease. Specifically, K2 records its annual interest expense as part of its annual lease payment ($12,979) as follows (for its first year):

2011			
Dec. 31	Interest Expense	4,800	
	Lease Liability	8,179	
	Cash		12,979
	To record first annual lease payment.*		

Assets = Liabilities + Equity
−12,979   −8,179   −4,800

*These numbers are computed from a *lease payment schedule*. For simplicity, we use the same numbers from Exhibit 10.14 for this lease payment schedule—with different headings as follows:

	(A)	(B) Debit	(C) Debit	(D) Credit	(E)
Period Ending Date	Beginning Balance of Lease Liability	Interest on Lease Liability 8% × (A)	+ Lease Liability (D) − (B)	= Cash Lease Payment	Ending Balance of Lease Liability (A) − (C)
12/31/2011	$60,000	$ 4,800	$ 8,179	$12,979	$51,821
12/31/2012	51,821	4,146	8,833	12,979	42,988
12/31/2013	42,988	3,439	9,540	12,979	33,448
12/31/2014	33,448	2,676	10,303	12,979	23,145
12/31/2015	23,145	1,852	11,127	12,979	12,018
12/31/2016	12,018	961	12,018	12,979	0
		$17,874	$60,000	$77,874	

---

[3] A *capital lease* meets any one or more of four criteria: (1) transfers title of leased asset to lessee, (2) contains a bargain purchase option, (3) has a lease term that is 75% or more of the leased asset's useful life, or (4) has a present value of lease payments that is 90% or more of the leased asset's market value.

[4] Most lessees try to keep leased assets and lease liabilities off their balance sheets by failing to meet any one of the four criteria of a capital lease. This is because a lease liability increases a company's total liabilities, making it more difficult to obtain additional financing. The acquisition of assets without reporting any related liabilities (or other asset outflows) on the balance sheet is called **off-balance-sheet financing.**

Point: Fringe benefits are often 40% or more of salaries and wages, and pension benefits make up nearly 15% of fringe benefits.

Pension Liabilities A **pension plan** is a contractual agreement between an employer and its employees for the employer to provide benefits (payments) to employees after they retire. Most employers pay the full cost of the pension, but sometimes employees pay part of the cost. An employer records its payment into a pension plan with a debit to Pension Expense and a credit to Cash. A *plan administrator* receives payments from the employer, invests them in pension assets, and makes benefit payments to *pension recipients* (retired employees). Insurance and trust companies often serve as pension plan administrators.

Many pensions are known as *defined benefit plans* that define future benefits; the employer's contributions vary, depending on assumptions about future pension assets and liabilities. Several disclosures are necessary in this case. Specifically, a pension liability is reported when the accumulated benefit obligation is *more than* the plan assets, a so-called *underfunded plan*. The accumulated benefit obligation is the present value of promised future pension payments to retirees. *Plan assets* refer to the market value of assets the plan administrator holds. A pension asset is reported when the accumulated benefit obligation is *less than* the plan assets, a so-called *overfunded plan*. An employer reports pension expense when it receives the benefits from the employees' services, which is sometimes decades before it pays pension benefits to employees. (*Other Postretirement Benefits* refer to nonpension benefits such as health care and life insurance benefits. Similar to a pension, costs of these benefits are estimated and liabilities accrued when the employees earn them.)

Point: Two types of pension plans are (1) *defined benefit plan*—the retirement benefit is defined and the employer estimates the contribution necessary to pay these benefits—and (2) *defined contribution plan*—the pension contribution is defined and the employer and/or employee contributes amounts specified in the pension agreement.

Summary

C1 **Explain the types and payment patterns of notes.** Notes repaid over a period of time are called *installment notes* and usually follow one of two payment patterns: (1) decreasing payments of interest plus equal amounts of principal or (2) equal total payments. Mortgage notes also are common.

C2A **Explain and compute the present value of an amount(s) to be paid at a future date(s).** The basic concept of present value is that an amount of cash to be paid or received in the future is worth less than the same amount of cash to be paid or received today. Another important present value concept is that interest is compounded, meaning interest is added to the balance and used to determine interest for succeeding periods. An annuity is a series of equal payments occurring at equal time intervals. An annuity's present value can be computed using the present value table for an annuity (or a calculator).

C3C **Describe interest accrual when bond payment periods differ from accounting periods.** Issuers and buyers of debt record the interest accrued when issue dates or accounting periods do not coincide with debt payment dates.

C4D **Describe accounting for leases and pensions.** A lease is a rental agreement between the lessor and the lessee. When the lessor retains the risks and rewards of asset ownership (an *operating lease*), the lessee debits Rent Expense and credits Cash for its lease payments. When the lessor substantially transfers the risks and rewards of asset ownership to the lessee (a *capital lease*), the lessee capitalizes the leased asset and records a lease liability. Pension agreements can result in either pension assets or pension liabilities.

A1 **Compare bond financing with stock financing.** Bond financing is used to fund business activities. Advantages of bond financing versus stock include (1) no effect on owner control, (2) tax savings, and (3) increased earnings due to financial leverage. Disadvantages include (1) interest and principal payments and (2) amplification of poor performance.

A2 **Assess debt features and their implications.** Certain bonds are secured by the issuer's assets; other bonds, called *debentures,* are unsecured. Serial bonds mature at different points in time; term bonds mature at one time. Registered bonds have each bondholder's name recorded by the issuer; bearer bonds are payable to the holder. Convertible bonds are exchangeable for shares of the issuer's stock. Callable bonds can be retired by the issuer at a set price. Debt features alter the risk of loss for creditors.

A3 **Compute the debt-to-equity ratio and explain its use.** Both creditors and equity holders are concerned about the relation between the amount of liabilities and the amount of equity. A company's financing structure is at less risk when the debt-to-equity ratio is lower, as liabilities must be paid and usually with periodic interest.

P1 **Prepare entries to record bond issuance and interest expense.** When bonds are issued at par, Cash is debited and Bonds Payable is credited for the bonds' par value. At bond interest payment dates (usually semiannual), Bond Interest Expense is debited and Cash credited—the latter for an amount equal to the bond par value multiplied by the bond contract rate.

P2 **Compute and record amortization of bond discount.** Bonds are issued at a discount when the contract rate is less than the market rate, making the issue (selling) price less than par. When this occurs, the issuer records a credit to Bonds Payable (at par) and debits both Discount on Bonds Payable and Cash. The amount of bond interest expense assigned to each period is computed using either the straight-line or effective interest method.

P3 **Compute and record amortization of bond premium.** Bonds are issued at a premium when the contract rate is higher than the market rate, making the issue (selling) price greater than par. When this occurs, the issuer records a debit to Cash and credits both Premium on Bonds Payable and Bonds Payable (at par). The amount of bond interest expense assigned to each period is computed using either the straight-line or effective interest method. The Premium on Bonds Payable is allocated to reduce bond interest expense over the life of the bonds.

P4 **Record the retirement of bonds.** Bonds are retired at maturity with a debit to Bonds Payable and a credit to Cash at par value. The issuer can retire the bonds early by exercising a call option or purchasing them in the market. Bondholders can also retire bonds early by exercising a conversion feature on convertible bonds. The issuer recognizes a gain or loss for the difference between the amount paid and the bond carrying value.

P5 **Prepare entries to account for notes.** Interest is allocated to each period in a note's life by multiplying its beginning-period carrying value by its market rate at issuance. If a note is repaid with equal payments, the payment amount is computed by dividing the borrowed amount by the present value of an annuity factor (taken from a present value table) using the market rate and the number of payments.

Guidance Answers to Decision Maker

Entrepreneur This is a "present value" question. The market interest rate (10%) and present value ($3,000) are known, but the payment required two years later is unknown. This amount ($3,630) can be computed as $3,000 × 1.10 × 1.10. Thus, the sale price is $3,630 when no payments are received for two years. The $3,630 received two years from today is equivalent to $3,000 cash today.

Bond Investor The debt-to-equity ratio for the first company is 0.2 ($350,000/$1,750,000) and for the second company is 1.2 ($1,200,000/$1,000,000), suggesting that the financing structure of the second company is more risky than that of the first company. Consequently, as a buyer of unsecured debenture bonds, you prefer the first company (all else equal).

Bond Rater Bonds with longer repayment periods (life) have higher risk. Also, bonds issued by companies in financial difficulties or facing higher than normal uncertainties have higher risk. Moreover, companies with higher than normal debt and large fluctuations in earnings are considered of higher risk. Discount bonds are more risky on one or more of these factors.

Guidance Answers to Quick Checks

1.
2011			
Jan. 1	Cash	10,000	
	Bonds Payable		10,000
June 30	Bond Interest Expense	450	
	Cash		450

2. Multiply the bond's par value by its contract rate of interest.
3. Bonds sell at a premium when the contract rate exceeds the market rate and the purchasers pay more than their par value.
4. The bonds are issued at a discount, meaning that issue price is less than par value. A discount occurs because the bond contract rate (6%) is less than the market rate (8%).
5.
Cash	91,893	
Discount on Bonds Payable	8,107	
Bonds Payable		100,000

6. $3,811 (total bond interest expense of $38,107 divided by 10 periods; or the $3,000 semiannual cash payment plus the $8,107 discount divided by 10 periods).
7. The bonds are issued at a premium, meaning issue price is higher than par value. A premium occurs because the bonds' contract rate (16%) is higher than the market rate (14%).
8. (b) For each semiannual period: $10,592/20 periods = $530 premium amortization.

9.
Bonds payable, 16%, due 12/31/2020		$100,000
Plus premium on bonds payable		9,532* $109,532

*Original premium balance of $10,592 less $530 and $530 amortized on 6/30/2011 and 12/31/2011, respectively.

10. $9,375 loss, computed as the difference between the repurchase price of $256,250 [50% of ($500,000 × 102.5%)] and the carrying value of $246,875 (50% of $493,750).
11. (c)
12. The interest portion of an installment payment equals the period's beginning loan balance multiplied by the market interest rate at the time of the note's issuance.
13. On the balance sheet, the account balances of the related liability (note payable) and asset (cash) accounts are decreased. On the income statement, interest expense is recorded.
14. (c), computed as 3.3121 × $1,000 = $3,312.
15. The option of paying $10,000 after one year has a lower present value. It postpones paying the first $5,000 by six months. More generally, the present value of a further delayed payment is always lower than a less delayed payment.
16. (a) Reflects payment of accrued interest recorded back on May 1; $500,000 × 9% × 2/12 = $15,000.

Key Terms

Annuity (p. 433)
Bearer bonds (p. 428)
Bond (p. 414)

Bond certificate (p. 416)
Bond indenture (p. 416)
Callable bonds (p. 428)

Capital leases (p. 439)
Carrying (book) value of bonds (p. 418)
Contract rate (p. 417)

Convertible bonds (p. 428)
Coupon bonds (p. 428)
Debt-to-equity ratio (p. 429)
Discount on bonds payable (p. 417)
Effective interest method (p. 434)
Fair value option (p. 427)
Installment note (p. 425)
Lease (p. 438)

Market rate (p. 417)
Mortgage (p. 426)
Off-balance-sheet financing (p. 439)
Operating leases (p. 438)
Par value of a bond (p. 414)
Pension plan (p. 440)
Premium on bonds (p. 420)
Registered bonds (p. 428)

Secured bonds (p. 428)
Serial bonds (p. 428)
Sinking fund bonds (p. 428)
Straight-line bond amortization (p. 418)
Term bonds (p. 428)
Unsecured bonds (p. 428)

Multiple Choice Quiz

Answers on p. 455

mhhe.com/wildFA6e

Additional quiz questions are available at the book's Website.

1. A bond traded at 97½ means that
   a. The bond pays 97½% interest.
   b. The bond trades at $975 per $1,000 bond.
   c. The market rate of interest is below the contract rate of interest for the bond.
   d. The bonds can be retired at $975 each.
   e. The bond's interest rate is 2½%.

2. A bondholder that owns a $1,000, 6%, 15-year bond has
   a. The right to receive $1,000 at maturity.
   b. Ownership rights in the bond issuing entity.
   c. The right to receive $60 per month until maturity.
   d. The right to receive $1,900 at maturity.
   e. The right to receive $600 per year until maturity.

3. A company issues 8%, 20-year bonds with a par value of $500,000. The current market rate for the bonds is 8%. The amount of interest owed to the bondholders for each semiannual interest payment is
   a. $40,000.
   b. $0.
   c. $20,000.
   d. $800,000.
   e. $400,000.

4. A company issued 5-year, 5% bonds with a par value of $100,000. The company received $95,735 for the bonds. Using the straight-line method, the company's interest expense for the first semiannual interest period is
   a. $2,926.50.
   b. $5,853.00.
   c. $2,500.00.
   d. $5,000.00.
   e. $9,573.50.

5. A company issued 8-year, 5% bonds with a par value of $350,000. The company received proceeds of $373,745. Interest is payable semiannually. The amount of premium amortized for the first semiannual interest period, assuming straight-line bond amortization, is
   a. $2,698.
   b. $23,745.
   c. $8,750.
   d. $9,344.
   e. $1,484.

B(C,D) *Superscript letter B(C, D) denotes assignments based on Appendix 10B (10C, 10D).*
Icon denotes assignments that involve decision making.

Discussion Questions

1. What is the main difference between a bond and a share of stock?
2. What is the main difference between notes payable and bonds payable?
3. What is the advantage of issuing bonds instead of obtaining financing from the company's owners?
4. What are the duties of a trustee for bondholders?
5. What is a bond indenture? What provisions are usually included in it?
6. What are the *contract* rate and the *market* rate for bonds?
7. What factors affect the market rates for bonds?
8.[B] Does the straight-line or effective interest method produce an interest expense allocation that yields a constant rate of interest over a bond's life? Explain.
9.[C] Why does a company that issues bonds between interest dates collect accrued interest from the bonds' purchasers?
10. If you know the par value of bonds, the contract rate, and the market rate, how do you compute the bonds' price?
11. What is the issue price of a $2,000 bond sold at 98¼? What is the issue price of a $6,000 bond sold at 101½?
12. Describe the debt-to-equity ratio and explain how creditors and owners would use this ratio to evaluate a company's risk.

13. What obligation does an entrepreneur (owner) have to investors that purchase bonds to finance the business?
14. Refer to **Research In Motion**'s annual report in Appendix A. Is there any indication that RIM has issued bonds?
15. By what amount did **Palm**'s long-term debt increase or decrease in 2009?
16. Refer to the statement of cash flows for **Nokia** in Appendix A. For the year ended December 31, 2009, what was the amount for repayment of bank loans?
17. Refer to the annual report for **Apple** in Appendix A. For the year ended September 26, 2009, what is its debt-to-equity ratio? What does this ratio tell us?
18.^D When can a lease create both an asset and a liability for the lessee?
19.^D Compare and contrast an operating lease with a capital lease.
20.^D Describe the two basic types of pension plans.

connect

Round dollar amounts to the nearest whole dollar.

Enter the letter of the description A through H that best fits each term or phrase 1 through 8.
- **A.** Records and tracks the bondholders' names.
- **B.** Is unsecured; backed only by the issuer's credit standing.
- **C.** Has varying maturity dates for amounts owed.
- **D.** Identifies rights and responsibilities of the issuer and the bondholders.
- **E.** Can be exchanged for shares of the issuer's stock.
- **F.** Is unregistered; interest is paid to whoever possesses them.
- **G.** Maintains a separate asset account from which bondholders are paid at maturity.
- **H.** Pledges specific assets of the issuer as collateral.

1. _____ Debenture
2. _____ Bond indenture
3. _____ Bearer bond
4. _____ Registered bond
5. _____ Sinking fund bond
6. _____ Convertible bond
7. _____ Secured bond
8. _____ Serial bond

QUICK STUDY

QS 10-1
Bond features and terminology
A2

Alberto Company issues 8%, 10-year bonds with a par value of $350,000 and semiannual interest payments. On the issue date, the annual market rate for these bonds is 10%, which implies a selling price of 87½. The straight-line method is used to allocate interest expense.
1. What are the issuer's cash proceeds from issuance of these bonds?
2. What total amount of bond interest expense will be recognized over the life of these bonds?
3. What is the amount of bond interest expense recorded on the first interest payment date?

QS 10-2
Bond computations—straight-line
P1 P2

Sanchez Company issues 10%, 15-year bonds with a par value of $120,000 and semiannual interest payments. On the issue date, the annual market rate for these bonds is 8%, which implies a selling price of 117¼. The effective interest method is used to allocate interest expense.
1. What are the issuer's cash proceeds from issuance of these bonds?
2. What total amount of bond interest expense will be recognized over the life of these bonds?
3. What amount of bond interest expense is recorded on the first interest payment date?

QS 10-3^B
Bond computations—effective interest
P1 P3

Prepare the journal entries for the issuance of the bonds in both QS 10-2 and QS 10-3. Assume that both bonds are issued for cash on January 1, 2011.

QS 10-4
Journalize bond issuance P1

Using the bond details in both QS 10-2 and QS 10-3, confirm that the bonds' selling prices given in each problem are approximately correct. Use the present value tables B.1 and B.3 in Appendix B.

QS 10-5
Computing bond price P2 P3

QS 10-6
Recording bond issuance and discount amortization P1 P2

Bellvue Company issues 10%, five-year bonds, on December 31, 2010, with a par value of $100,000 and semiannual interest payments. Use the following straight-line bond amortization table and prepare journal entries to record (*a*) the issuance of bonds on December 31, 2010; (*b*) the first interest payment on June 30, 2011; and (*c*) the second interest payment on December 31, 2011.

Semiannual Period-End	Unamortized Discount	Carrying Value
(0) 12/31/2010	$7,360	$92,640
(1) 6/30/2011	6,624	93,376
(2) 12/31/2011	5,888	94,112

QS 10-7
Bond retirement by call option P4

On July 1, 2011, Jackson Company exercises a $5,000 call option (plus par value) on its outstanding bonds that have a carrying value of $208,000 and par value of $200,000. The company exercises the call option after the semiannual interest is paid on June 30, 2011. Record the entry to retire the bonds.

QS 10-8
Bond retirement by stock conversion P4

On January 1, 2011, the $1,000,000 par value bonds of Gruden Company with a carrying value of $1,000,000 are converted to 500,000 shares of $0.50 par value common stock. Record the entry for the conversion of the bonds.

QS 10-9
Computing payments for an installment note C1

Valdez Company borrows $170,000 cash from a bank and in return signs an installment note for five annual payments of equal amount, with the first payment due one year after the note is signed. Use Table B.3 in Appendix B to compute the amount of the annual payment for each of the following annual market rates: (*a*) 4%, (*b*) 8%, and (*c*) 12%.

QS 10-10
Debt-to-equity ratio A2

Compute the debt-to-equity ratio for each of the following companies. Which company appears to have a riskier financing structure? Explain.

	Canal Company	Sears Company
Total liabilities	$492,000	$ 384,000
Total equity	656,000	1,200,000

QS 10-11^C
Issuing bonds between interest dates P1

Kemper Company plans to issue 6% bonds on January 1, 2011, with a par value of $1,000,000. The company sells $900,000 of the bonds on January 1, 2011. The remaining $100,000 sells at par on March 1, 2011. The bonds pay interest semiannually as of June 30 and December 31. Record the entry for the March 1 cash sale of bonds.

QS 10-12^D
Recording operating leases C4

Lauren Wright, an employee of ETrain.com, leases a car at O'Hare airport for a three-day business trip. The rental cost is $350. Prepare the entry by ETrain.com to record Lauren's short-term car lease cost.

QS 10-13^D
Recording capital leases C4

Juicyfruit, Inc., signs a five-year lease for office equipment with Office Solutions. The present value of the lease payments is $20,859. Prepare the journal entry that Juicyfruit records at the inception of this capital lease.

QS 10-14
International liabilities disclosures P1 P2

Vodafone Group Plc reports the following information among its bonds payable as of March 31, 2009 (pounds in millions).

Financial Long-Term Liabilities Measured at Amortised Cost			
(£ millions)	Nominal (par) Value	Carrying Value	Fair Value
4.625% (US dollar 500 million) bond due July 2018	£350	£392	£315

a. What is the par value of the 4.625% bond issuance? What is its book (carrying) value?
b. Was the 4.625% bond sold at a discount or a premium? Explain.

Refer to the information in QS 10-14 for **Vodafone Group Plc**. The following price quotes (from Yahoo! Finance Bond Center) relate to its bonds payable as of late 2009. For example, the price quote indicates that the 4.625% bonds have a market price of 98.0 (98.0% of par value), resulting in a yield to maturity of 4.899%.

QS 10-15
International liabilities disclosures and interpretations
P1 P2

Price	Contract Rate (coupon)	Maturity Date	Market Rate (YTM)
98.0	4.625%	15-Jul-2018	4.899%

a. Assuming that the 4.625% bonds were originally issued at par value, what does the market price reveal about interest rate changes since bond issuance? (Assume that Vodafone's credit rating has remained the same.)
b. Does the change in market rates since the issuance of these bonds affect the amount of interest expense reported on Vodafone's income statement? Explain.
c. How much cash would Vodafone need to pay to repurchase the 4.625% bonds at the quoted market price of 98.0? (Assume no interest is owed when the bonds are repurchased.)
d. Assuming that the 4.625% bonds remain outstanding until maturity, at what market price will the bonds sell on the due date in 2018?

connect

Round dollar amounts to the nearest whole dollar. Assume no reversing entries are used.

EXERCISES

On January 1, 2011, Kidman Enterprises issues bonds that have a $1,700,000 par value, mature in 20 years, and pay 9% interest semiannually on June 30 and December 31. The bonds are sold at par.
1. How much interest will Kidman pay (in cash) to the bondholders every six months?
2. Prepare journal entries to record (*a*) the issuance of bonds on January 1, 2011; (*b*) the first interest payment on June 30, 2011; and (*c*) the second interest payment on December 31, 2011.
3. Prepare the journal entry for issuance assuming the bonds are issued at (*a*) 98 and (*b*) 102.

Exercise 10-1
Recording bond issuance and interest
P1

Moss issues bonds with a par value of $90,000 on January 1, 2011. The bonds' annual contract rate is 8%, and interest is paid semiannually on June 30 and December 31. The bonds mature in three years. The annual market rate at the date of issuance is 10%, and the bonds are sold for $85,431.
1. What is the amount of the discount on these bonds at issuance?
2. How much total bond interest expense will be recognized over the life of these bonds?
3. Prepare an amortization table like the one in Exhibit 10.7 for these bonds; use the straight-line method to amortize the discount.

Exercise 10-2
Straight-line amortization of bond discount
P2

Welch issues bonds dated January 1, 2011, with a par value of $250,000. The bonds' annual contract rate is 9%, and interest is paid semiannually on June 30 and December 31. The bonds mature in three years. The annual market rate at the date of issuance is 12%, and the bonds are sold for $231,570.
1. What is the amount of the discount on these bonds at issuance?
2. How much total bond interest expense will be recognized over the life of these bonds?
3. Prepare an amortization table like the one in Exhibit 10B.1 for these bonds; use the effective interest method to amortize the discount.

Exercise 10-3[B]
Effective interest amortization of bond discount
P2

Prairie Dunes Co. issues bonds dated January 1, 2011, with a par value of $800,000. The bonds' annual contract rate is 13%, and interest is paid semiannually on June 30 and December 31. The bonds mature in three years. The annual market rate at the date of issuance is 12%, and the bonds are sold for $819,700.
1. What is the amount of the premium on these bonds at issuance?
2. How much total bond interest expense will be recognized over the life of these bonds?
3. Prepare an amortization table like the one in Exhibit 10.11 for these bonds; use the straight-line method to amortize the premium.

Exercise 10-4
Straight-line amortization of bond premium
P3

Exercise 10-5^B
Effective interest amortization of bond premium P3

Refer to the bond details in Exercise 10-4 and prepare an amortization table like the one in Exhibit 10B.2 for these bonds using the effective interest method to amortize the premium.

Exercise 10-6
Recording bond issuance and premium amortization P1 P3

Jobbs Company issues 10%, five-year bonds, on December 31, 2010, with a par value of $100,000 and semiannual interest payments. Use the following straight-line bond amortization table and prepare journal entries to record (a) the issuance of bonds on December 31, 2010; (b) the first interest payment on June 30, 2011; and (c) the second interest payment on December 31, 2011.

Semiannual Period-End		Unamortized Premium	Carrying Value
(0)	12/31/2010	$8,111	$108,111
(1)	6/30/2011	7,300	107,300
(2)	12/31/2011	6,489	106,489

Exercise 10-7
Recording bond issuance and discount amortization P1 P2

Matchbox Company issues 6%, four-year bonds, on December 31, 2011, with a par value of $100,000 and semiannual interest payments. Use the following straight-line bond amortization table and prepare journal entries to record (a) the issuance of bonds on December 31, 2011; (b) the first interest payment on June 30, 2012; and (c) the second interest payment on December 31, 2012.

Semiannual Period-End		Unamortized Discount	Carrying Value
(0)	12/31/2011	$6,733	$93,267
(1)	6/30/2012	5,891	94,109
(2)	12/31/2012	5,049	94,951

Exercise 10-8
Recording bond issuance and discount amortization P1 P2

Oneil Company issues 5%, two-year bonds, on December 31, 2011, with a par value of $100,000 and semiannual interest payments. Use the following straight-line bond amortization table and prepare journal entries to record (a) the issuance of bonds on December 31, 2011; (b) the first through fourth interest payments on each June 30 and December 31; and (c) the maturity of the bond on December 31, 2013.

Semiannual Period-End		Unamortized Discount	Carrying Value
(0)	12/31/2011	$6,000	$ 94,000
(1)	6/30/2012	4,500	95,500
(2)	12/31/2012	3,000	97,000
(3)	6/30/2013	1,500	98,500
(4)	12/31/2013	0	100,000

Exercise 10-9
Computing bond interest and price; recording bond issuance P2

Jester Company issues bonds with a par value of $600,000 on their stated issue date. The bonds mature in 10 years and pay 6% annual interest in semiannual payments. On the issue date, the annual market rate for the bonds is 8%.

1. What is the amount of each semiannual interest payment for these bonds?
2. How many semiannual interest payments will be made on these bonds over their life?
3. Use the interest rates given to determine whether the bonds are issued at par, at a discount, or at a premium.
4. Compute the price of the bonds as of their issue date.
5. Prepare the journal entry to record the bonds' issuance.

Check (4) $518,465

Exercise 10-10
Computing bond interest and price; recording bond issuance P3

Metro Company issues bonds with a par value of $75,000 on their stated issue date. The bonds mature in five years and pay 10% annual interest in semiannual payments. On the issue date, the annual market rate for the bonds is 8%.

1. What is the amount of each semiannual interest payment for these bonds?
2. How many semiannual interest payments will be made on these bonds over their life?
3. Use the interest rates given to determine whether the bonds are issued at par, at a discount, or at a premium.

4. Compute the price of the bonds as of their issue date.
5. Prepare the journal entry to record the bonds' issuance.

Check (4) $81,086

On January 1, 2011, Steadman issues $350,000 of 10%, 15-year bonds at a price of 97¾. Six years later, on January 1, 2017, Steadman retires 20% of these bonds by buying them on the open market at 104½. All interest is accounted for and paid through December 31, 2016, the day before the purchase. The straight-line method is used to amortize any bond discount.

1. How much does the company receive when it issues the bonds on January 1, 2011?
2. What is the amount of the discount on the bonds at January 1, 2011?
3. How much amortization of the discount is recorded on the bonds for the entire period from January 1, 2011, through December 31, 2016?
4. What is the carrying (book) value of the bonds as of the close of business on December 31, 2016? What is the carrying value of the 20% soon-to-be-retired bonds on this same date?
5. How much did the company pay on January 1, 2017, to purchase the bonds that it retired?
6. What is the amount of the recorded gain or loss from retiring the bonds?
7. Prepare the journal entry to record the bond retirement at January 1, 2017.

Exercise 10-11
Bond computations, straight-line amortization, and bond retirement
P2 P4

Check (6) $4,095 loss

On May 1, 2011, Fellenger Enterprises issues bonds dated January 1, 2011, that have a $1,700,000 par value, mature in 20 years, and pay 9% interest semiannually on June 30 and December 31. The bonds are sold at par plus four months' accrued interest.

1. How much accrued interest do the bond purchasers pay Fellenger on May 1, 2011?
2. Prepare Fellenger's journal entries to record (a) the issuance of bonds on May 1, 2011; (b) the first interest payment on June 30, 2011; and (c) the second interest payment on December 31, 2011.

Exercise 10-12^C
Recording bond issuance with accrued interest
C4 P1

Check (1) $51,000

Simon issues four-year bonds with a $50,000 par value on June 1, 2011, at a price of $47,974. The annual contract rate is 7%, and interest is paid semiannually on November 30 and May 31.

1. Prepare an amortization table like the one in Exhibit 10.7 for these bonds. Use the straight-line method of interest amortization.
2. Prepare journal entries to record the first two interest payments and to accrue interest as of December 31, 2011.

Exercise 10-13
Straight-line amortization and accrued bond interest expense
P1 P2

On January 1, 2011, Randa borrows $25,000 cash by signing a four-year, 7% installment note. The note requires four equal total payments of accrued interest and principal on December 31 of each year from 2011 through 2014.

1. Compute the amount of each of the four equal total payments.
2. Prepare an amortization table for this installment note like the one in Exhibit 10.14.

Exercise 10-14
Installment note with equal total payments C1 P5

Check (1) $7,381

Use the information in Exercise 10-14 to prepare the journal entries for Randa to record the loan on January 1, 2011, and the four payments from December 31, 2011, through December 31, 2014.

Exercise 10-15
Installment note entries P5

Ramirez Company is considering a project that will require a $500,000 loan. It presently has total liabilities of $220,000, and total assets of $620,000.

1. Compute Ramirez's (a) present debt-to-equity ratio and (b) the debt-to-equity ratio assuming it borrows $500,000 to fund the project.
2. Evaluate and discuss the level of risk involved if Ramirez borrows the funds to pursue the project.

Exercise 10-16
Applying debt-to-equity ratio
A3

Indicate whether the company in each separate case 1 through 3 has entered into an operating lease or a capital lease.

1. The present value of the lease payments is 95% of the leased asset's market value, and the lease term is 70% of the leased asset's useful life.
2. The title is transferred to the lessee, the lessee can purchase the asset for $1 at the end of the lease, and the lease term is five years. The leased asset has an expected useful life of six years.
3. The lessor retains title to the asset, and the lease term is three years on an asset that has a five-year useful life.

Exercise 10-17^D
Identifying capital and operating leases
C4

448   Chapter 10   Reporting and Analyzing Long-Term Liabilities

Exercise 10-18^D
Accounting for capital lease
C4

Flyer (lessee) signs a five-year capital lease for office equipment with a $20,000 annual lease payment. The present value of the five annual lease payments is $82,000, based on a 7% interest rate.

1. Prepare the journal entry Flyer will record at inception of the lease.
2. If the leased asset has a five-year useful life with no salvage value, prepare the journal entry Flyer will record each year to recognize depreciation expense related to the leased asset.

Exercise 10-19^D
Analyzing lease options
C2 C3 C4

General Motors advertised three alternatives for a 25-month lease on a new Chevrolet Volt: (1) zero dollars down and a lease payment of $1,750 per month for 25 months, (2) $5,000 down and $1,500 per month for 25 months, or (3) $38,500 down and no payments for 25 months. Use the present value Table B.3 in Appendix B to determine which is the best alternative (assume you have enough cash to accept any alternative and the annual interest rate is 12% compounded monthly).

Exercise 10-20
Accounting for long-term liabilities under IFRS
P1 P2 P3

Heineken N.V. reports the following information for its Loans and Borrowings as of December 31, 2008, including proceeds and repayments for the year ended December 31, 2008 (euros in millions).

Loans and borrowings (noncurrent liabilities)	
Loans and borrowings, December 31, 2008	€ 9,084
Proceeds (cash) from issuances of loans and borrowings	6,361
Repayments (in cash) of loans and borrowings	(2,532)

1. Prepare Heineken's journal entry to record its cash proceeds from issuances of its loans and borrowings for 2008. Assume that the par value of these issuances is €6,000.
2. Prepare Heineken's journal entry to record its cash repayments of its loans and borrowings for 2008. Assume that the par value of these issuances is €2,400, and the premium on them is €32.
3. Compute the discount or premium on its loans and borrowings as of December 31, 2008, assuming that the par value of these liabilities is €9,000.
4. Given the facts in part 3 and viewing the entirety of loans and borrowings as one issuance, was the contract rate on these loans and borrowings higher or lower than the market rate at the time of issuance? Explain. (Assume that Heineken's credit rating has remained the same.)

PROBLEM SET A

Round dollar amounts to the nearest whole dollar. Assume no reversing entries are used.

Problem 10-1A
Computing bond price and recording issuance
P1 P2 P3

Check (1) Premium, $2,718

(3) Discount, $2,294

Stowers Research issues bonds dated January 1, 2011, that pay interest semiannually on June 30 and December 31. The bonds have a $20,000 par value and an annual contract rate of 10%, and they mature in 10 years.

Required

For each of the following three separate situations, (*a*) determine the bonds' issue price on January 1, 2011, and (*b*) prepare the journal entry to record their issuance.

1. The market rate at the date of issuance is 8%.
2. The market rate at the date of issuance is 10%.
3. The market rate at the date of issuance is 12%.

Problem 10-2A
Straight-line amortization of bond discount
P1 P2

mhhe.com/wildFA6e

Check (3) $2,071,776

(4) 12/31/2012 carrying value, $1,764,460

Heathrow issues $2,000,000 of 6%, 15-year bonds dated January 1, 2011, that pay interest semiannually on June 30 and December 31. The bonds are issued at a price of $1,728,224.

Required

1. Prepare the January 1, 2011, journal entry to record the bonds' issuance.
2. For each semiannual period, compute (*a*) the cash payment, (*b*) the straight-line discount amortization, and (*c*) the bond interest expense.
3. Determine the total bond interest expense to be recognized over the bonds' life.
4. Prepare the first two years of an amortization table like Exhibit 10.7 using the straight-line method.
5. Prepare the journal entries to record the first two interest payments.

Problem 10-3A
Straight-line amortization of bond premium
P1 P3

Refer to the bond details in Problem 10-2A, *except* assume that the bonds are issued at a price of $2,447,990.

Required

1. Prepare the January 1, 2011, journal entry to record the bonds' issuance.
2. For each semiannual period, compute (*a*) the cash payment, (*b*) the straight-line premium amortization, and (*c*) the bond interest expense.
3. Determine the total bond interest expense to be recognized over the bonds' life.
4. Prepare the first two years of an amortization table like Exhibit 10.7 using the straight-line method.
5. Prepare the journal entries to record the first two interest payments.

Check (3) $1,352,010
(4) 12/31/2012 carrying value, $2,388,258

Problem 10-4A
Straight-line amortization of bond premium
P1 P3

Saturn issues 6.5%, five-year bonds dated January 1, 2011, with a $500,000 par value. The bonds pay interest on June 30 and December 31 and are issued at a price of $510,666. The annual market rate is 6% on the issue date.

Required

1. Calculate the total bond interest expense over the bonds' life.
2. Prepare a straight-line amortization table like Exhibit 10.11 for the bonds' life.
3. Prepare the journal entries to record the first two interest payments.

mhhe.com/wildFA6e

Check (2) 6/30/2013 carrying value, $505,331

Problem 10-5A[B]
Effective interest amortization of bond premium; computing bond price **P1 P3**

Refer to the bond details in Problem 10-4A.

Required

1. Compute the total bond interest expense over the bonds' life.
2. Prepare an effective interest amortization table like the one in Exhibit 10B.2 for the bonds' life.
3. Prepare the journal entries to record the first two interest payments.
4. Use the market rate at issuance to compute the present value of the remaining cash flows for these bonds as of December 31, 2013. Compare your answer with the amount shown on the amortization table as the balance for that date (from part 2) and explain your findings.

Check (2) 6/30/2013 carrying value, $505,728
(4) $504,653

Problem 10-6A
Straight-line amortization of bond discount
P1 P2

Patton issues $650,000 of 5%, four-year bonds dated January 1, 2011, that pay interest semiannually on June 30 and December 31. They are issued at $584,361 and their market rate is 8% at the issue date.

Required

1. Prepare the January 1, 2011, journal entry to record the bonds' issuance.
2. Determine the total bond interest expense to be recognized over the bonds' life.
3. Prepare a straight-line amortization table like the one in Exhibit 10.7 for the bonds' first two years.
4. Prepare the journal entries to record the first two interest payments.

Check (2) $195,639
(3) 12/31/2012 carrying value, $617,181

Analysis Component

5. Assume the market rate on January 1, 2011, is 4% instead of 8%. Without providing numbers, describe how this change affects the amounts reported on Patton's financial statements.

Problem 10-7A[B]
Effective interest amortization of bond discount **P1 P2**

Refer to the bond details in Problem 10-6A.

Required

1. Prepare the January 1, 2011, journal entry to record the bonds' issuance.
2. Determine the total bond interest expense to be recognized over the bonds' life.
3. Prepare an effective interest amortization table like the one in Exhibit 10B.1 for the bonds' first two years.
4. Prepare the journal entries to record the first two interest payments.

Check (2) $195,639
(3) 12/31/2012 carrying value, $614,614

mhhe.com/wildFA6e

Problem 10-8A[B]
Effective interest amortization of bond premium; retiring bonds

P1 P3 P4

Check (3) 6/30/2012 carrying value, $91,224

(5) $2,635 gain

mhhe.com/wildFA6e

McFad issues $90,000 of 11%, three-year bonds dated January 1, 2011, that pay interest semiannually on June 30 and December 31. They are issued at $92,283. Their market rate is 10% at the issue date.

Required

1. Prepare the January 1, 2011, journal entry to record the bonds' issuance.
2. Determine the total bond interest expense to be recognized over the bonds' life.
3. Prepare an effective interest amortization table like Exhibit 10B.2 for the bonds' first two years.
4. Prepare the journal entries to record the first two interest payments.
5. Prepare the journal entry to record the bonds' retirement on January 1, 2013, at 98.

Analysis Component

6. Assume that the market rate on January 1, 2011, is 12% instead of 10%. Without presenting numbers, describe how this change affects the amounts reported on McFad's financial statements.

Problem 10-9A
Installment notes

C1 P5

Check (2) 10/31/2015 ending balance, $92,759

On November 1, 2011, Leetch Ltd. borrows $400,000 cash from a bank by signing a five-year installment note bearing 8% interest. The note requires equal total payments each year on October 31.

Required

1. Compute the total amount of each installment payment.
2. Complete an amortization table for this installment note similar to the one in Exhibit 10.14.
3. Prepare the journal entries in which Leetch records (*a*) accrued interest as of December 31, 2011 (the end of its annual reporting period), and (*b*) the first annual payment on the note.

Problem 10-10A
Applying the debt-to-equity ratio

A3

At the end of the current year, the following information is available for both Kumar Company and Asher Company.

	Kumar Company	Asher Company
Total assets	$2,254,500	$1,123,500
Total liabilities	904,500	598,500
Total equity	1,350,000	525,000

Required

1. Compute the debt-to-equity ratios for both companies.
2. Comment on your results and discuss the riskiness of each company's financing structure.

Problem 10-11A[D]
Capital lease accounting

C4

Check (1) $79,854

(3) Year 3 ending balance, $35,664

Montana Company signs a five-year capital lease with Elway Company for office equipment. The annual lease payment is $20,000, and the interest rate is 8%.

Required

1. Compute the present value of Montana's five-year lease payments.
2. Prepare the journal entry to record Montana's capital lease at its inception.
3. Complete a lease payment schedule for the five years of the lease with the following headings. Assume that the beginning balance of the lease liability (present value of lease payments) is $79,854. (*Hint:* To find the amount allocated to interest in year 1, multiply the interest rate by the beginning-of-year lease liability. The amount of the annual lease payment not allocated to interest is allocated to principal. Reduce the lease liability by the amount allocated to principal to update the lease liability at each year-end.)

Period Ending Date	Beginning Balance of Lease Liability	Interest on Lease Liability	Reduction of Lease Liability	Cash Lease Payment	Ending Balance of Lease Liability

4. Use straight-line depreciation and prepare the journal entry to depreciate the leased asset at the end of year 1. Assume zero salvage value and a five-year life for the office equipment.

Round dollar amounts to the nearest whole dollar. Assume no reversing entries are used.

Sedona Systems issues bonds dated January 1, 2011, that pay interest semiannually on June 30 and December 31. The bonds have a $45,000 par value and an annual contract rate of 12%, and they mature in five years.

Required

For each of the following three separate situations, (*a*) determine the bonds' issue price on January 1, 2011, and (*b*) prepare the journal entry to record their issuance.
1. The market rate at the date of issuance is 10%.
2. The market rate at the date of issuance is 12%.
3. The market rate at the date of issuance is 14%.

ParFour issues $1,700,000 of 10%, 10-year bonds dated January 1, 2011, that pay interest semiannually on June 30 and December 31. The bonds are issued at a price of $1,505,001.

Required

1. Prepare the January 1, 2011, journal entry to record the bonds' issuance.
2. For each semiannual period, compute (*a*) the cash payment, (*b*) the straight-line discount amortization, and (*c*) the bond interest expense.
3. Determine the total bond interest expense to be recognized over the bonds' life.
4. Prepare the first two years of an amortization table like Exhibit 10.7 using the straight-line method.
5. Prepare the journal entries to record the first two interest payments.

Refer to the bond details in Problem 10-2B, *except* assume that the bonds are issued at a price of $2,096,466.

Required

1. Prepare the January 1, 2011, journal entry to record the bonds' issuance.
2. For each semiannual period, compute (*a*) the cash payment, (*b*) the straight-line premium amortization, and (*c*) the bond interest expense.
3. Determine the total bond interest expense to be recognized over the bonds' life.
4. Prepare the first two years of an amortization table like Exhibit 10.7 using the straight-line method.
5. Prepare the journal entries to record the first two interest payments.

Zooba Company issues 9%, five-year bonds dated January 1, 2011, with a $160,000 par value. The bonds pay interest on June 30 and December 31 and are issued at a price of $166,494. Their annual market rate is 8% on the issue date.

Required

1. Calculate the total bond interest expense over the bonds' life.
2. Prepare a straight-line amortization table like Exhibit 10.11 for the bonds' life.
3. Prepare the journal entries to record the first two interest payments.

Refer to the bond details in Problem 10-4B.

Required

1. Compute the total bond interest expense over the bonds' life.
2. Prepare an effective interest amortization table like the one in Exhibit 10B.2 for the bonds' life.
3. Prepare the journal entries to record the first two interest payments.
4. Use the market rate at issuance to compute the present value of the remaining cash flows for these bonds as of December 31, 2013. Compare your answer with the amount shown on the amortization table as the balance for that date (from part 2) and explain your findings.

PROBLEM SET B

Problem 10-1B
Computing bond price and recording issuance
P1 P2 P3

Check (1) Premium, $3,475

(3) Discount, $3,162

Problem 10-2B
Straight-line amortization of bond discount
P1 P2

Check (3) $1,894,999

(4) 6/30/2012 carrying value, $1,534,251

Problem 10-3B
Straight-line amortization of bond premium
P1 P3

Check (3) $1,303,534

(4) 6/30/2012 carrying value, $2,036,997

Problem 10-4B
Straight-line amortization of bond premium
P1 P3

Check (2) 6/30/2013 carrying value, $163,249

Problem 10-5B[B]
Effective interest amortization of bond premium; computing bond price P1 P3

Check (2) 6/30/2013 carrying value, $163,568

(4) $162,903

452 Chapter 10 Reporting and Analyzing Long-Term Liabilities

Problem 10-6B
Straight-line amortization of bond discount
P1 P2

Check (2) $128,753
(3) 6/30/2012 carrying value, $101,323

Roney issues $120,000 of 6%, 15-year bonds dated January 1, 2011, that pay interest semiannually on June 30 and December 31. They are issued at $99,247, and their market rate is 8% at the issue date.

Required

1. Prepare the January 1, 2011, journal entry to record the bonds' issuance.
2. Determine the total bond interest expense to be recognized over the life of the bonds.
3. Prepare a straight-line amortization table like the one in Exhibit 10.7 for the bonds' first two years.
4. Prepare the journal entries to record the first two interest payments.

Problem 10-7B[B]
Effective interest amortization of bond discount
P1 P2

Check (2) $128,753;
(3) 6/30/2012 carrying value, $100,402

Refer to the bond details in Problem 10-6B.

Required

1. Prepare the January 1, 2011, journal entry to record the bonds' issuance.
2. Determine the total bond interest expense to be recognized over the bonds' life.
3. Prepare an effective interest amortization table like the one in Exhibit 10B.1 for the bonds' first two years.
4. Prepare the journal entries to record the first two interest payments.

Problem 10-8B[B]
Effective interest amortization of bond premium; retiring bonds
P1 P3 P4

Check (3) 6/30/2012 carrying value, $958,406

(5) $6,174 loss

Hutton issues $900,000 of 13%, four-year bonds dated January 1, 2011, that pay interest semiannually on June 30 and December 31. They are issued at $987,217, and their market rate is 10% at the issue date.

Required

1. Prepare the January 1, 2011, journal entry to record the bonds' issuance.
2. Determine the total bond interest expense to be recognized over the bonds' life.
3. Prepare an effective interest amortization table like the one in Exhibit 10B.2 for the bonds' first two years.
4. Prepare the journal entries to record the first two interest payments.
5. Prepare the journal entry to record the bonds' retirement on January 1, 2013, at 106.

Analysis Component

6. Assume that the market rate on January 1, 2011, is 14% instead of 10%. Without presenting numbers, describe how this change affects the amounts reported on Hutton's financial statements.

Problem 10-9B
Installment notes
C1 P5

Check (2) 9/30/2013 ending balance, $109,673

On October 1, 2011, Milan Enterprises borrows $300,000 cash from a bank by signing a three-year installment note bearing 10% interest. The note requires equal total payments each year on September 30.

Required

1. Compute the total amount of each installment payment.
2. Complete an amortization table for this installment note similar to the one in Exhibit 10.14.
3. Prepare the journal entries to record (*a*) accrued interest as of December 31, 2011 (the end of its annual reporting period) and (*b*) the first annual payment on the note.

Problem 10-10B
Applying the debt-to-equity ratio
A3

At the end of the current year, the following information is available for both West Elm Company and East Park Company.

	West Elm Company	East Park Company
Total assets	$396,396	$1,650,000
Total liabilities	178,596	1,237,500
Total equity	217,800	412,500

Required

1. Compute the debt-to-equity ratios for both companies.
2. Comment on your results and discuss what they imply about the relative riskiness of these companies.

Preston Company signs a five-year capital lease with Starbuck Company for office equipment. The annual lease payment is $10,000, and the interest rate is 10%.

Problem 10-11B^D
Capital lease accounting
C4

Required

1. Compute the present value of Preston's lease payments.
2. Prepare the journal entry to record Preston's capital lease at its inception.
3. Complete a lease payment schedule for the five years of the lease with the following headings. Assume that the beginning balance of the lease liability (present value of lease payments) is $37,908. (*Hint:* To find the amount allocated to interest in year 1, multiply the interest rate by the beginning-of-year lease liability. The amount of the annual lease payment not allocated to interest is allocated to principal. Reduce the lease liability by the amount allocated to principal to update the lease liability at each year-end.)

Check (1) $37,908

(3) Year 3 ending balance, $17,356

Period Ending Date	Beginning Balance of Lease Liability	Interest on Lease Liability	Reduction of Lease Liability	Cash Lease Payment	Ending Balance of Lease Liability

4. Use straight-line depreciation and prepare the journal entry to depreciate the leased asset at the end of year 1. Assume zero salvage value and a five-year life for the office equipment.

(*This serial problem began in Chapter 1 and continues through most of the book. If previous chapter segments were not completed, the serial problem can begin at this point. It is helpful, but not necessary, to use the Working Papers that accompany the book.*)

SERIAL PROBLEM
Business Solutions
A1 A3

SP 10 Santana Rey has consulted with her local banker and is considering financing an expansion of her business by obtaining a long-term bank loan. Selected account balances at March 31, 2012, for Business Solutions follow.

Total assets	$120,268	Total liabilities	$875	Total equity	$119,393

Required

1. The bank has offered a long-term secured note to Business Solutions. The bank's loan procedures require that a client's debt-to-equity ratio not exceed 0.8. As of March 31, 2012, what is the maximum amount that Business Solutions could borrow from this bank (rounded to nearest dollar)?
2. If Business Solutions borrows the maximum amount allowed from the bank, what percentage of assets would be financed (*a*) by debt and (*b*) by equity?
3. What are some factors Santana Rey should consider before borrowing the funds?

Check (1) $94,639

Beyond the Numbers

BTN 10-1 Refer to **Research In Motion**'s financial statements in Appendix A to answer the following.

1. Identify the items, if any, that make up RIM's long-term debt as reported on its balance sheet at February 27, 2010.
2. Assume that RIM has $402,000 thousand in convertible debentures that carry a 2.25% contract rate of interest. How much annual cash interest must be paid on those convertible debentures?
3. How much cash did it generate from issuance of debt for the year-ended February 27, 2010? How much cash did it use for repayments of debt for that same year?

REPORTING IN ACTION
A1 A2

RIM

Fast Forward

4. Access Research In Motion's financial statements for the years ending after February 27, 2010, from its Website (**RIM.com**) or the SEC's EDGAR database (**www.sec.gov**). Has it issued additional long-term debt since the year-end February 27, 2010? If yes, identify the amount(s).

COMPARATIVE ANALYSIS

A3

RIM

Apple

BTN 10-2 Key figures for **Research In Motion** and **Apple** follow.

($ millions)	Research In Motion Current Year	Research In Motion Prior Year	Apple Current Year	Apple Prior Year
Total assets	$10,204	$8,101	$47,501	$36,171
Total liabilities	2,602	2,227	15,861	13,874
Total equity	7,603	5,874	31,640	22,297

Required

1. Compute the debt-to-equity ratios for Research In Motion and Apple for both the current year and the prior year.
2. Use the ratios you computed in part 1 to determine which company's financing structure is least risky. Assume an industry average of 0.64 for debt-to-equity.

ETHICS CHALLENGE

C4 A1

BTN 10-3 Holly County needs a new county government building that would cost $24 million. The politicians feel that voters will not approve a municipal bond issue to fund the building since it would increase taxes. They opt to have a state bank issue $24 million of tax-exempt securities to pay for the building construction. The county then will make yearly lease payments (of principal and interest) to repay the obligation. Unlike conventional municipal bonds, the lease payments are not binding obligations on the county and, therefore, require no voter approval.

Required

1. Do you think the actions of the politicians and the bankers in this situation are ethical?
2. How do the tax-exempt securities used to pay for the building compare in risk to a conventional municipal bond issued by Holly County?

COMMUNICATING IN PRACTICE

P3

BTN 10-4 Your business associate mentions that she is considering investing in corporate bonds currently selling at a premium. She says that since the bonds are selling at a premium, they are highly valued and her investment will yield more than the going rate of return for the risk involved. Reply with a memorandum to confirm or correct your associate's interpretation of premium bonds.

TAKING IT TO THE NET

A2

BTN 10-5 Access the March 25, 2010, filing of the 10-K report of **Home Depot** for the year ended January 31, 2010, from www.sec.gov (Ticker: HD). Refer to Home Depot's balance sheet, including its note 4 (on debt).

Required

1. Identify Home Depot's long-term liabilities and the amounts for those liabilities from Home Depot's balance sheet at January 31, 2010.
2. Review Home Depot's note 5. The note reports that as of January 31, 2010, it had $2.96 billion of "5.875% Senior Notes; due December 16, 2036; interest payable semiannually on June 16 and December 16." These notes have a face value of $3.0 billion and were originally issued at $2.958 billion.
   a. Why would Home Depot issue $3.0 billion of its notes for only $2.958 billion?
   b. How much cash interest must Home Depot pay each June 16 and December 16 on these notes?

TEAMWORK IN ACTION

P2 P3

BTN 10-6[B] Break into teams and complete the following requirements related to effective interest amortization for a premium bond.

1. Each team member is to independently prepare a blank table with proper headings for amortization of a bond premium. When all have finished, compare tables and ensure that all are in agreement.

Parts 2 and 3 require use of these facts: On January 1, 2010, Caleb issues $100,000, 9%, five-year bonds at 104.1. The market rate at issuance is 8%. Caleb pays interest semiannually on June 30 and December 31.

2. In rotation, *each* team member must explain how to complete *one* line of the bond amortization table, including all computations for his or her line. (Round amounts to the nearest dollar.) All members are to fill in their tables during this process. You need not finish the table; stop after all members have explained a line.

3. In rotation, *each* team member is to identify a separate column of the table and indicate what the final number in that column will be and explain the reasoning.
4. Reach a team consensus as to what the total bond interest expense on this bond issue will be if the bond is not retired before maturity.
5. As a team, prepare a list of similarities and differences between the amortization table just prepared and the amortization table if the bond had been issued at a discount.

Hint: Rotate teams to report on parts 4 and 5. Consider requiring entries for issuance and interest payments.

BTN 10-7 Warren Brown is the founder of **CakeLove**. Assume that his company currently has $250,000 in equity, and he is considering a $100,000 expansion to meet increased demand. The $100,000 expansion would yield $16,000 in additional annual income before interest expense. Assume that the business currently earns $40,000 annual income before interest expense of $10,000, yielding a return on equity of 12% ($30,000/$250,000). To fund the expansion, he is considering the issuance of a 10-year, $100,000 note with annual interest payments (the principal due at the end of 10 years).

ENTREPRENEURIAL DECISION
A1

Required
1. Using return on equity as the decision criterion, show computations to support or reject the expansion if interest on the $100,000 note is (*a*) 10%, (*b*) 15%, (*c*) 16%, (*d*) 17%, and (*e*) 20%.
2. What general rule do the results in part 1 illustrate?

BTN 10-8 Visit your city or county library. Ask the librarian to help you locate the recent financial records of your city or county government. Examine those records.

HITTING THE ROAD
A1

Required
1. Determine the amount of long-term bonds and notes currently outstanding.
2. Read the supporting information to your municipality's financial statements and record
   a. The market interest rate(s) when the bonds and/or notes were issued.
   b. The date(s) when the bonds and/or notes will mature.
   c. Any rating(s) on the bonds and/or notes received from **Moody's**, **Standard & Poor's**, or another rating agency.

BTN 10-9 **Nokia** (www.Nokia.com), **Research In Motion**, and **Apple** are competitors in the global marketplace. Selected results from these companies follow.

GLOBAL DECISION
A3

NOKIA
RIM
Apple

Key Figures	Nokia (EURm) Current Year	Nokia (EURm) Prior Year	Research In Motion ($ millions) Current Year	Research In Motion ($ millions) Prior Year	Apple ($ millions) Current Year	Apple ($ millions) Prior Year
Total assets	€35,738	€39,582	$10,204	$8,101	$47,501	$36,171
Total liabilities	20,989	23,072	2,602	2,227	15,861	13,874
Total equity	14,749	16,510	7,603	5,874	31,640	22,297
Debt-to-equity ratio	?	?	0.34	0.38	0.50	0.62

Required
1. Compute Nokia's debt-to-equity ratios for the current year and the prior year.
2. Use the data provided and the ratios computed in part 1 to determine which company's financing structure is least risky.

ANSWERS TO MULTIPLE CHOICE QUIZ

1. b
2. a
3. c; $500,000 × 0.08 × ½ year = $20,000
4. a; Cash interest paid = $100,000 × 5% × ½ year = $2,500
   Discount amortization = ($100,000 − $95,735)/10 periods = $426.50
   Interest expense = $2,500.00 + $426.50 = $2,926.50
5. e; ($373,745 − $350,000)/16 periods = $1,484

11 Reporting and Analyzing Equity

A Look Back

Chapter 10 focused on long-term liabilities, which are a main part of most companies' financing. We explained how to value, record, amortize, and report these liabilities in financial statements.

A Look at This Chapter

This chapter emphasizes details of the corporate form of organization. The accounting concepts and procedures for equity transactions are explained. We also describe how to report and analyze income, earnings per share, and retained earnings.

A Look Ahead

Chapter 12 focuses on reporting and analyzing a company's cash flows. Special emphasis is directed at the statement of cash flows and the methods for reporting that statement.

Learning Objectives

CAP

CONCEPTUAL

- **C1** Identify characteristics of corporations and their organization. (p. 458)
- **C2** Explain characteristics of, and distribute dividends between, common and preferred stock. (p. 468)
- **C3** Explain the items reported in retained earnings. (p. 474)

ANALYTICAL

- **A1** Compute earnings per share and describe its use. (p. 477)
- **A2** Compute price-earnings ratio and describe its use in analysis. (p. 477)
- **A3** Compute dividend yield and explain its use in analysis. (p. 478)
- **A4** Compute book value and explain its use in analysis. (p. 478)

PROCEDURAL

- **P1** Record the issuance of corporate stock. (p. 462)
- **P2** Record transactions involving cash dividends, stock dividends, and stock splits. (p. 465)
- **P3** Record purchases and sales of treasury stock and the retirement of stock. (p. 472)

LP11

Decision Insight

Well...Mow Me Down!

"Every part of our business is... profitable."
—KELLY GIARD

FORT COLLINS, CO—According to the U.S. Environmental Protection Agency, a gas-powered lawn mower produces as much air pollution as 43 new cars each driven 12,000 miles. "At least 5 percent of pollution is caused by gas-powered maintenance equipment," explains Kelly Giard, owner of **Clean Air Lawn Care (CleanAirLawnCare.com)**. "This is one of the last dirty frontiers in America that can be easily solved."

Kelly launched his business four years ago, which is a full-service sustainable lawn care company dedicated to using clean electrical and biodiesel powered equipment. His equipment is charged by solar panels during the day and by wind power overnight. "I started [it] out of my garage mostly for fun," says Kelly. "And business took off."

Kelly explains that his success would not have been possible without equity financing and knowledge of business operations. To make it happen, says Kelly, he studied corporate formation, equity issuance, stock types, retaining earnings, and dividend policies. After that analysis, Kelly set up Clean Air Lawn Care as a corporation, which had several benefits given his business goals and strategies. With his corporate structure in place, Kelly was ready to attack the market. "Only about 1% of the country uses an electrical mower," says Kelly. "That's awful, and that's something we're committed to changing."

The success of Kelly's corporate structure and his equity financing brings both opportunities and challenges. The positive is being part of the green movement, yielding "a ripple effect where there's profit, happy customers and an environmental benefit." The challenge is effectively using accounting for equity as a tool to achieve those objectives. That includes his knowledge of corporate formation, stock types, and equity transactions. "This is critical to us doing well in the long term," explains Kelly. Still, the focus remains on the environment. "We want [consumers] to have a choice when they hire a service: sustainable vs. dirty."

[Sources: *Clean Air Lawn Care Website,* January 2012; *Entrepreneur,* January 2010; *Lawn & Landscape,* April 2010; *Charles & Hudson Website,* 2010; *PacificSun,* June 2011]

Chapter Preview

This chapter focuses on equity transactions. The first part of the chapter describes the basics of the corporate form of organization and explains the accounting for common and preferred stock. We then focus on several special financing transactions, including cash and stock dividends, stock splits, and treasury stock. The final section considers accounting for retained earnings, including prior period adjustments, retained earnings restrictions, and reporting guidelines.

Reporting and Analyzing Equity

Corporations	Common Stock	Dividends	Preferred Stock	Treasury Stock	Reporting on Equity
• Characteristics • Organization and management • Stockholders • Stock basics	• Par value • No-par value • Stated value • Stock for non-cash assets	• Cash dividends • Stock dividends • Stock splits	• Issuance • Dividend preferences • Convertible preferred • Callable preferred	• Purchasing treasury stock • Reissuing treasury stock • Retiring stock	• Statement of retained earnings • Statement of stockholders' equity • Stock options

CORPORATE FORM OF ORGANIZATION

C1 Identify characteristics of corporations and their organization.

A **corporation** is an entity created by law that is separate from its owners. It has most of the rights and privileges granted to individuals. Owners of corporations are called *stockholders* or *shareholders*. Corporations can be separated into two types. A *privately held* (or *closely held*) corporation does not offer its stock for public sale and usually has few stockholders. A *publicly held* corporation offers its stock for public sale and can have thousands of stockholders. *Public sale* usually refers to issuance and trading on an organized stock market.

Characteristics of Corporations

Corporations represent an important type of organization. Their unique characteristics offer advantages and disadvantages.

Advantages of Corporate Characteristics

- **Separate legal entity:** A corporation conducts its affairs with the same rights, duties, and responsibilities of a person. It takes actions through its agents, who are its officers and managers.
- **Limited liability of stockholders:** Stockholders are liable for neither corporate acts nor corporate debt.

Point: The *business entity assumption* requires a corporation to be accounted for separately from its owners (shareholders).

Global: U.S., U.K., and Canadian corporations finance much of their operations with stock issuances, but companies in countries such as France, Germany, and Japan finance mainly with note and bond issuances.

- **Transferable ownership rights:** The transfer of shares from one stockholder to another usually has no effect on the corporation or its operations except when this causes a change in the directors who control or manage the corporation.
- **Continuous life:** A corporation's life continues indefinitely because it is not tied to the physical lives of its owners.
- **Lack of mutual agency for stockholders:** A corporation acts through its agents, who are its officers and managers. Stockholders, who are not its officers and managers, do not have the power to bind the corporation to contracts—referred to as *lack of mutual agency*.
- **Ease of capital accumulation:** Buying stock is attractive to investors because (1) stockholders are not liable for the corporation's acts and debts, (2) stocks usually are transferred easily, (3) the life of the corporation is unlimited, and (4) stockholders are not corporate agents. These advantages enable corporations to accumulate large amounts of capital from the combined investments of many stockholders.

Disadvantages of Corporate Characteristics

- **Government regulation:** A corporation must meet requirements of a state's incorporation laws, which subject the corporation to state regulation and control. Proprietorships and partnerships avoid many of these regulations and governmental reports.
- **Corporate taxation:** Corporations are subject to the same property and payroll taxes as proprietorships and partnerships plus *additional* taxes. The most burdensome of these are federal and state income taxes that together can take 40% or more of corporate pretax income. Moreover, corporate income is usually taxed a second time as part of stockholders' personal income when they receive cash distributed as dividends. This is called *double taxation*. (The usual dividend tax is 15%; however, it is less than 15% for lower income taxpayers, and in some cases zero.)

Point: Proprietorships and partnerships are not subject to income taxes. Their income is taxed as the personal income of their owners.

Point: Double taxation is less severe when a corporation's owner-manager collects a salary that is taxed only once as part of his or her personal income.

Decision Insight

Stock Financing Marc Andreessen cofounded **Netscape** at age 22, only four months after earning his degree. One year later, he and friends issued Netscape shares to the public. The stock soared, making Andreessen a multimillionaire.

Corporate Organization and Management

This section describes the incorporation, costs, and management of corporate organizations.

Incorporation A corporation is created by obtaining a charter from a state government. A charter application usually must be signed by the prospective stockholders called *incorporators* or *promoters* and then filed with the proper state official. When the application process is complete and fees paid, the charter is issued and the corporation is formed. Investors then purchase the corporation's stock, meet as stockholders, and elect a board of directors. Directors oversee a corporation's affairs.

Point: A corporation is not required to have an office in its state of incorporation.

Organization Expenses Organization expenses (also called *organization costs*) are the costs to organize a corporation; they include legal fees, promoters' fees, and amounts paid to obtain a charter. The corporation records (debits) these costs to an expense account called *Organization Expenses*. Organization costs are expensed as incurred because it is difficult to determine the amount and timing of their future benefits.

Management of a Corporation The ultimate control of a corporation rests with stockholders who control a corporation by electing its *board of directors,* or simply, *directors.* Each stockholder usually has one vote for each share of stock owned. This control relation is shown in Exhibit 11.1. Directors are responsible for and have final authority for managing corporate activities. A board can act only as a collective body and usually limits its actions to setting general policy.

A corporation usually holds a stockholder meeting at least once a year to elect directors and transact business as its bylaws require. A group of stockholders owning or controlling votes of more than a 50% share of a corporation's stock can elect the board and control the corporation. Stockholders who do not attend stockholders' meetings must have an opportunity to delegate their voting rights to an agent by signing a **proxy,** a document that gives a designated agent the right to vote the stock.

EXHIBIT 11.1

Corporate Structure

Stockholders → Board of Directors → President, Vice President, and Other Officers → Employees of the Corporation

Day-to-day direction of corporate business is delegated to executive officers appointed by the board. A corporation's chief executive officer (CEO) is often its president. Several vice presidents, who report to the president, are commonly assigned specific areas of management responsibility such as finance, production, and marketing. One person often has the dual role

Point: *Bylaws* are guidelines that govern the behavior of individuals employed by and managing the corporation.

Global: Some corporate labels are:

Country	Label
United States	Inc.
France	SA
United Kingdom	
Public	PLC
Private	Ltd
Germany & Austria	
Public	AG
Private	GmbH
Sweden & Finland	AB
Italy	SpA
Netherlands	NV
Australia	AG
Mexico	SA
Bahamas	IBC

of chairperson of the board of directors and CEO. In this case, the president is usually designated the chief operating officer (COO).

Decision Insight

Seed Money Sources for start-up money include (1) "angel" investors such as family, friends, or anyone who believes in a company, (2) employees, investors, and even suppliers who can be paid with stock, and (3) venture capitalists (investors) who have a record of entrepreneurial success. See the National Venture Capital Association (**NVCA.org**) for information.

Stockholders of Corporations

This section explains stockholder rights, stock purchases and sales, and the role of registrar and transfer agents.

Rights of Stockholders When investors buy stock, they acquire all *specific* rights the corporation's charter grants to stockholders. They also acquire *general* rights granted stockholders by the laws of the state in which the company is incorporated. When a corporation has only one class of stock, it is identified as **common stock.** State laws vary, but common stockholders usually have the general right to

1. Vote at stockholders' meetings.
2. Sell or otherwise dispose of their stock.
3. Purchase their proportional share of any common stock later issued by the corporation. This **preemptive right** protects stockholders' proportionate interest in the corporation. For example, a stockholder who owns 25% of a corporation's common stock has the first opportunity to buy 25% of any new common stock issued.
4. Receive the same dividend, if any, on each common share of the corporation.
5. Share in any assets remaining after creditors and preferred stockholders are paid when, and if, the corporation is liquidated. Each common share receives the same amount.

Stockholders also have the right to receive timely financial reports.

Stock Certificates and Transfer Investors who buy a corporation's stock, sometimes receive a *stock certificate* as proof of share ownership. Many corporations issue only one certificate for each block of stock purchased. A certificate can be for any number of shares. Exhibit 11.2 shows a stock certificate of the **Green Bay Packers**. A certificate shows the company name, stockholder name, number of shares, and other crucial information. Issuance of certificates is becoming less common. Instead, many stockholders maintain accounts with the corporation or their stockbrokers and never receive actual certificates.

EXHIBIT 11.2
Stock Certificate

Registrar and Transfer Agents If a corporation's stock is traded on a major stock exchange, the corporation must have a registrar and a transfer agent. A *registrar* keeps stockholder records and prepares official lists of stockholders for stockholder meetings and dividend payments. A *transfer agent* assists with purchases and sales of shares by receiving and issuing certificates as necessary. Registrars and transfer agents are usually large banks or trust companies with computer facilities and staff to do this work.

> **Decision Insight**
>
> **Pricing Stock** A prospectus accompanies a stock's initial public offering (IPO), giving financial information about the company issuing the stock. A prospectus should help answer these questions to price an IPO: (1) Is the underwriter reliable? (2) Is there growth in revenues, profits, and cash flows? (3) What is management's view of operations? (4) Are current owners selling? (5) What are the risks? ∎

Basics of Capital Stock

Capital stock is a general term that refers to any shares issued to obtain capital (owner financing). This section introduces terminology and accounting for capital stock.

Authorized Stock   **Authorized stock** is the number of shares that a corporation's charter allows it to sell. The number of authorized shares usually exceeds the number of shares issued (and outstanding), often by a large amount. (*Outstanding stock* refers to issued stock held by stockholders.) No formal journal entry is required for stock authorization. A corporation must apply to the state for a change in its charter if it wishes to issue more shares than previously authorized. A corporation discloses the number of shares authorized in the equity section of its balance sheet or notes. **Apple**'s balance sheet in Appendix A reports 1.8 billion common shares authorized as of the start of its 2010 fiscal year.

Subcategories of Authorized Stock

Authorized
Authorized & Issued
Authorized, Issued and Outstanding

Selling (Issuing) Stock   A corporation can sell stock directly or indirectly. To *sell directly*, it advertises its stock issuance to potential buyers. This type of issuance is most common with privately held corporations. To *sell indirectly*, a corporation pays a brokerage house (investment banker) to issue its stock. Some brokerage houses *underwrite* an indirect issuance of stock; that is, they buy the stock from the corporation and take all gains or losses from its resale.

Market Value of Stock   **Market value per share** is the price at which a stock is bought and sold. Expected future earnings, dividends, growth, and other company and economic factors influence market value. Traded stocks' market values are available daily in newspapers such as *The Wall Street Journal* and online. The current market value of previously issued shares (for example, the price of stock in trades between investors) does not impact the issuing corporation's stockholders' equity.

Classes of Stock   When all authorized shares have the same rights and characteristics, the stock is called *common stock*. A corporation is sometimes authorized to issue more than one class of stock, including preferred stock and different classes of common stock. **American Greetings**, for instance, has two types of common stock: Class A stock has 1 vote per share and Class B stock has 10 votes per share.

Par Value Stock   **Par value stock** is stock that is assigned a **par value,** which is an amount assigned per share by the corporation in its charter. For example, **Palm**'s common stock has a par value of $0.001. Other commonly assigned par values are $10, $5, $1 and $0.01. There is no restriction on the assigned par value. In many states, the par value of a stock establishes **minimum legal capital,** which refers to the least amount that the buyers of stock must contribute to the corporation or be subject to paying at a future date. For example, if a corporation issues 1,000 shares of $10 par value stock, the corporation's minimum legal capital in these states would be $10,000. Minimum legal capital is intended to protect a corporation's creditors. Since creditors cannot demand payment from stockholders' personal assets, their claims are limited to the corporation's assets and any minimum legal capital. At liquidation, creditor claims are paid before any amounts are distributed to stockholders.

Point: Managers are motivated to set a low par value when minimum legal capital or state issuance taxes are based on par value.

Point: Minimum legal capital was intended to protect creditors by requiring a minimum level of net assets.

No-Par Value Stock   **No-par value stock,** or simply *no-par stock,* is stock *not* assigned a value per share by the corporate charter. Its advantage is that it can be issued at any price without the possibility of a minimum legal capital deficiency.

Point: Par, no-par, and stated value do *not* set the stock's market value.

EXHIBIT 11.3
Equity Composition

Corporation

Common Stock
Normal bal.

Paid-In Capital in Excess of Par
Normal bal.

(Total Paid-In Capital)

Retained Earnings
Normal bal.

Point: Paid-in capital comes from stock-related transactions, whereas retained earnings comes from operations.

Stated Value Stock Stated value stock is no-par stock to which the directors assign a "stated" value per share. Stated value per share becomes the minimum legal capital per share in this case.

Stockholders' Equity A corporation's equity is known as **stockholders' equity**, also called *shareholders' equity* or *corporate capital*. Stockholders' equity consists of (1) paid-in (or contributed) capital and (2) retained earnings; see Exhibit 11.3. **Paid-in capital** is the total amount of cash and other assets the corporation receives from its stockholders in exchange for its stock. **Retained earnings** is the cumulative net income (and loss) not distributed as dividends to its stockholders.

Decision Insight

Stock Quote The **Best Buy** stock quote is interpreted as (left to right): **Hi,** highest price in past 52 weeks; **Lo,** lowest price in past 52 weeks;

52 Weeks				Yld		Vol				Net
Hi	Lo	Sym	Div	%	PE	mil.	Hi	Lo	Close	Chg
54.15	41.85	BBY	0.13	0.98	19	7.2	53.14	52.36	52.91	+0.20

Sym, company exchange symbol; **Div,** dividends paid per share in past year; **Yld %,** dividend divided by closing price; **PE,** stock price per share divided by earnings per share; **Vol mil.,** number (in millions) of shares traded; **Hi,** highest price for the day; **Lo,** lowest price for the day; **Close,** closing price for the day; **Net Chg,** change in closing price from prior day.

Quick Check   Answers — p. 483

1. Which of the following is *not* a characteristic of the corporate form of business? (*a*) Ease of capital accumulation, (*b*) Stockholder responsibility for corporate debts, (*c*) Ease in transferability of ownership rights, or (*d*) Double taxation.
2. Why is a corporation's income said to be taxed twice?
3. What is a proxy?

COMMON STOCK

P1 Record the issuance of corporate stock.

Accounting for the issuance of common stock affects only paid-in (contributed) capital accounts; no retained earnings accounts are affected.

Issuing Par Value Stock

Par value stock can be issued at par, at a premium (above par), or at a discount (below par). In each case, stock can be exchanged for either cash or noncash assets.

Issuing Par Value Stock at Par When common stock is issued at par value, we record amounts for both the asset(s) received and the par value stock issued. To illustrate, the entry to record Dillon Snowboards' issuance of 30,000 shares of $10 par value stock for $300,000 cash on June 5, 2011, follows.

Assets = Liabilities + Equity
+300,000   +300,000

$10 par value × 30,000 shares

June 5	Cash	300,000	
	Common Stock, $10 Par Value		300,000
	Issued 30,000 shares of $10 par value common stock at par.		

Exhibit 11.4 shows the stockholders' equity of Dillon Snowboards at year-end 2011 (its first year of operations) after income of $65,000 and no dividend payments.

EXHIBIT 11.4
Stockholders' Equity for Stock Issued at Par

Stockholders' Equity	
Common Stock—$10 par value; 50,000 shares authorized; 30,000 shares issued and outstanding	$300,000
Retained earnings	65,000
Total stockholders' equity	$365,000

Issuing Par Value Stock at a Premium A **premium on stock** occurs when a corporation sells its stock for more than par (or stated) value. To illustrate, if Dillon Snowboards issues its $10 par value common stock at $12 per share, its stock is sold at a $2 per share premium. The premium, known as **paid-in capital in excess of par value,** is reported as part of equity; it is not revenue and is not listed on the income statement. The entry to record Dillon Snowboards' issuance of 30,000 shares of $10 par value stock for $12 per share on June 5, 2011, follows

Point: A *premium* is the amount by which issue price exceeds par (or stated) value. It is recorded in the "Paid-In Capital in Excess of Par Value, Common Stock" account; also called "Additional Paid-In Capital, Common Stock."

June 5	Cash	360,000	
	Common Stock, $10 Par Value		300,000
	Paid-In Capital in Excess of Par Value, Common Stock		60,000
	Sold and issued 30,000 shares of $10 par value common stock at $12 per share.		

Assets = Liabilities + Equity
+360,000   +300,000
                           +60,000

$10 par value × 30,000 shares

[$12 issue price − $10 par value] × 30,000 shares

The Paid-In Capital in Excess of Par Value account is added to the par value of the stock in the equity section of the balance sheet as shown in Exhibit 11.5.

Point: The *Paid-In Capital* terminology is interchangeable with *Contributed Capital.*

EXHIBIT 11.5
Stockholders' Equity for Stock Issued at a Premium

Stockholders' Equity	
Common Stock—$10 par value; 50,000 shares authorized; 30,000 shares issued and outstanding	$300,000
Paid-in capital in excess of par value, common stock	60,000
Retained earnings	65,000
Total stockholders' equity	$425,000

Issuing Par Value Stock at a Discount A **discount on stock** occurs when a corporation sells its stock for less than par (or stated) value. Most states prohibit the issuance of stock at a discount. In states that allow stock to be issued at a discount, its buyers usually become contingently liable to creditors for the discount. If stock is issued at a discount, the amount by which issue price is less than par is debited to a *Discount on Common Stock* account, a contra to the common stock account, and its balance is subtracted from the par value of stock in the equity section of the balance sheet. This discount is not an expense and does not appear on the income statement.

Point: Retained earnings can be negative, reflecting accumulated losses. Amazon.com had an accumulated deficit of $730 million at the start of 2009.

Issuing No-Par Value Stock

When no-par stock is issued and is not assigned a stated value, the amount the corporation receives becomes legal capital and is recorded as Common Stock. This means that the entire proceeds are credited to a no-par stock account. To illustrate, a corporation records its October 20 issuance of 1,000 shares of no-par stock for $40 cash per share as follows.

Oct. 20	Cash	40,000	
	Common Stock, No-Par Value		40,000
	Issued 1,000 shares of no-par value common stock at $40 per share.		

Assets = Liabilities + Equity
+40,000   +40,000

$40 issue price × 1,000 no-par shares

Issuing Stated Value Stock

When no-par stock is issued and assigned a stated value, its stated value becomes legal capital and is credited to a stated value stock account. Assuming that stated value stock is issued at an amount in excess of stated value (the usual case), the excess is credited to Paid-In Capital in Excess of Stated Value, Common Stock, which is reported in the stockholders' equity section. To illustrate, a corporation that issues 1,000 shares of no-par common stock having a stated value of $40 per share in return for $50 cash per share records this as follows.

Frequency of Stock Types
- Par 88%
- Stated 3%
- No-Par 9%

Assets = Liabilities + Equity
+50,000   +40,000
                   +10,000

$40 stated value × 1,000 shares

[$50 issue price − $40 stated value] × 1,000 shares

Oct. 20	Cash	50,000	
	Common Stock, $40 Stated Value		40,000
	Paid-In Capital in Excess of Stated Value, Common Stock		10,000
	Issued 1,000 shares of $40 per share stated value stock at $50 per share.		

Issuing Stock for Noncash Assets

A corporation can receive assets other than cash in exchange for its stock. (It can also assume liabilities on the assets received such as a mortgage on property received.) The corporation records the assets received at their market values as of the date of the transaction. The stock given in exchange is recorded at its par (or stated) value with any excess recorded in the Paid-In Capital in Excess of Par (or Stated) Value account. (If no-par stock is issued, the stock is recorded at the assets' market value.) To illustrate, the entry to record receipt of land valued at $105,000 in return for issuance of 4,000 shares of $20 par value common stock on June 10 is

Point: Stock issued for noncash assets should be recorded at the market value of either the stock or the noncash asset, whichever is more clearly determinable.

Assets = Liabilities + Equity
+105,000   +80,000
                    +25,000

$20 par value × 4,000 shares

$105,000 asset value − $80,000 stock value

June 10	Land	105,000	
	Common Stock, $20 Par Value		80,000
	Paid-In Capital in Excess of Par Value, Common Stock		25,000
	Exchanged 4,000 shares of $20 par value common stock for land.		

A corporation sometimes gives shares of its stock to promoters in exchange for their services in organizing the corporation, which the corporation records as **Organization Expenses.** The entry to record receipt of services valued at $12,000 in organizing the corporation in return for 600 shares of $15 par value common stock on June 5 is

Point: Any type of stock can be issued for noncash assets.

Assets = Liabilities + Equity
                    −12,000
                    +9,000
                    +3,000

$15 par value × 600 shares

$12,000 services value − $9,000 stock value

June 5	Organization Expenses	12,000	
	Common Stock, $15 Par Value		9,000
	Paid-In Capital in Excess of Par Value, Common Stock		3,000
	Gave promoters 600 shares of $15 par value common stock in exchange for their services.		

Quick Check
Answers — p. 483

4. A company issues 7,000 shares of its $10 par value common stock in exchange for equipment valued at $105,000. The entry to record this transaction includes a credit to (a) Paid-In Capital in Excess of Par Value, Common Stock, for $35,000. (b) Retained Earnings for $35,000. (c) Common Stock, $10 Par Value, for $105,000.
5. What is a premium on stock issuance?
6. Who is intended to be protected by minimum legal capital?

DIVIDENDS

This section describes both cash and stock dividend transactions.

Cash Dividends

The decision to pay cash dividends rests with the board of directors and involves more than evaluating the amounts of retained earnings and cash. The directors, for instance, may decide to keep the cash to invest in the corporation's growth, to meet emergencies, to take advantage of unexpected opportunities, or to pay off debt. Alternatively, many corporations pay cash dividends to their stockholders at regular dates. These cash flows provide a return to investors and almost always affect the stock's market value.

P2 Record transactions involving cash dividends, stock dividends, and stock splits.

Accounting for Cash Dividends Dividend payment involves three important dates: declaration, record, and payment. **Date of declaration** is the date the directors vote to declare and pay a dividend. This creates a legal liability of the corporation to its stockholders. **Date of record** is the future date specified by the directors for identifying those stockholders listed in the corporation's records to receive dividends. The date of record usually follows the date of declaration by at least two weeks. Persons who own stock on the date of record receive dividends. **Date of payment** is the date when the corporation makes payment; it follows the date of record by enough time to allow the corporation to arrange checks, money transfers, or other means to pay dividends.

Percent of Corporations Paying Dividends

Cash Dividend to Common: 75%
Cash Dividend to Preferred: 22%

To illustrate, the entry to record a January 9 declaration of a $1 per share cash dividend by the directors of Z-Tech, Inc., with 5,000 outstanding shares is

Date of Declaration

Jan. 9	Retained Earnings	5,000	
	Common Dividend Payable		5,000
	Declared $1 per common share cash dividend.[1]		

Assets = Liabilities + Equity
+5,000 −5,000

$1 per share declared dividend × 5,000 shares

Common Dividend Payable is a current liability. The date of record for the Z-Tech dividend is January 22. *No formal journal entry is needed on the date of record.* The February 1 date of payment requires an entry to record both the settlement of the liability and the reduction of the cash balance, as follows:

Date of Payment

Feb. 1	Common Dividend Payable	5,000	
	Cash		5,000
	Paid $1 per common share cash dividend.		

Assets = Liabilities + Equity
−5,000 −5,000

Deficits and Cash Dividends A corporation with a debit (abnormal) balance for retained earnings is said to have a **retained earnings deficit,** which arises when a company incurs cumulative losses and/or pays more dividends than total earnings from current and prior years. A deficit is reported as a deduction on the balance sheet, as shown in Exhibit 11.6. Most states prohibit a corporation with a deficit from paying a cash dividend to its stockholders. This legal restriction is designed to protect creditors by preventing distribution of assets to stockholders when the company may be in financial difficulty.

Point: It is often said a dividend is a distribution of retained earnings, but it is more precise to describe a dividend as a distribution of assets to satisfy stockholder claims.

Point: The Retained Earnings Deficit account is also called *Accumulated Deficit.*

---

[1] An alternative entry is to debit Dividends instead of Retained Earnings. The balance in Dividends is then closed to Retained Earnings at the end of the reporting period. The effect is the same: Retained Earnings is decreased and a Dividend Payable is increased. For simplicity, all assignments in this chapter use the Retained Earnings account to record dividend declarations.

EXHIBIT 11.6

Stockholders' Equity with a Deficit

Common stock—$10 par value, 5,000 shares authorized, issued, and outstanding	$50,000
Retained earnings deficit	(6,000)
Total stockholders' equity	$44,000

Some state laws allow cash dividends to be paid by returning a portion of the capital contributed by stockholders. This type of dividend is called a **liquidating cash dividend,** or simply *liquidating dividend,* because it returns a part of the original investment back to the stockholders. This requires a debit entry to one of the contributed capital accounts instead of Retained Earnings at the declaration date.

Point: Amazon.com has never declared a cash dividend.

Quick Check

Answers — p. 483

7. What type of an account is the Common Dividend Payable account?
8. What three crucial dates are involved in the process of paying a cash dividend?
9. When does a dividend become a company's legal obligation?

Stock Dividends

A **stock dividend,** declared by a corporation's directors, is a distribution of additional shares of the corporation's own stock to its stockholders without the receipt of any payment in return. Stock dividends and cash dividends are different. A stock dividend does not reduce assets and equity but instead transfers a portion of equity from retained earnings to contributed capital.

Reasons for Stock Dividends Stock dividends exist for at least two reasons. First, directors are said to use stock dividends to keep the market price of the stock affordable. For example, if a corporation continues to earn income but does not issue cash dividends, the price of its common stock likely increases. The price of such a stock may become so high that it discourages some investors from buying the stock (especially in lots of 100 and 1,000). When a corporation has a stock dividend, it increases the number of outstanding shares and lowers the per share stock price. Another reason for a stock dividend is to provide evidence of management's confidence that the company is doing well and will continue to do well.

Accounting for Stock Dividends A stock dividend affects the components of equity by transferring part of retained earnings to contributed capital accounts, sometimes described as *capitalizing* retained earnings. Accounting for a stock dividend depends on whether it is a small or large stock dividend. A **small stock dividend** is a distribution of 25% or less of previously outstanding shares. It is recorded by capitalizing retained earnings for an amount equal to the market value of the shares to be distributed. A **large stock dividend** is a distribution of more than 25% of previously outstanding shares. A large stock dividend is recorded by capitalizing retained earnings for the minimum amount required by state law governing the corporation. Most states require capitalizing retained earnings equal to the par or stated value of the stock.

To illustrate stock dividends, we use the equity section of Quest's balance sheet shown in Exhibit 11.7 just *before* its declaration of a stock dividend on December 31.

EXHIBIT 11.7

Stockholders' Equity *before* Declaring a Stock Dividend

Stockholders' Equity (before dividend)	
Common stock—$10 par value, 15,000 shares authorized, 10,000 shares issued and outstanding	$100,000
Paid-in capital in excess of par value, common stock	8,000
Retained earnings	35,000
Total stockholders' equity	$143,000

Recording a small stock dividend. Assume that Quest's directors declare a 10% stock dividend on December 31. This stock dividend of 1,000 shares, computed as 10% of its 10,000 issued and outstanding shares, is to be distributed on January 20 to the stockholders of record on January 15. Since the market price of Quest's stock on December 31 is $15 per share, this small stock dividend declaration is recorded as follows:

Point: Small stock dividends are recorded at market value.

Date of Declaration—Small Stock Dividend

Dec. 31	Retained Earnings	15,000	
	Common Stock Dividend Distributable		10,000
	Paid-In Capital in Excess of Par Value, Common Stock		5,000
	Declared a 1,000-share (10%) stock dividend.		

Assets = Liabilities + Equity
−15,000
+10,000
+5,000

10% dividend × 10,000 issued shares × $10 par value

10% dividend × 10,000 issued shares × [$15 market price − $10 par value]

The $10,000 credit in the declaration entry equals the par value of the shares and is recorded in *Common Stock Dividend Distributable,* an equity account. Its balance exists only until the shares are issued. The $5,000 credit equals the amount by which market value exceeds par value. This amount increases the Paid-In Capital in Excess of Par Value account in anticipation of the issuance of shares. In general, the balance sheet changes in three ways when a stock dividend is declared. First, the amount of equity attributed to common stock increases; for Quest, from $100,000 to $110,000 for 1,000 additional declared shares. Second, paid-in capital in excess of par increases by the excess of market value over par value for the declared shares. Third, retained earnings decreases, reflecting the transfer of amounts to both common stock and paid-in capital in excess of par. The stockholders' equity of Quest is shown in Exhibit 11.8 *after* its 10% stock dividend is declared on December 31—the items impacted are in bold.

Point: The term *Distributable* (not *Payable*) is used for stock dividends. A stock dividend is never a liability because it never reduces assets.

Point: The credit to Paid-In Capital in Excess of Par Value is recorded when the stock dividend is declared. This account is not affected when stock is later distributed.

EXHIBIT 11.8
Stockholders' Equity *after* Declaring a Stock Dividend

Stockholders' Equity (after dividend)	
Common stock—$10 par value, 15,000 shares authorized, 10,000 shares issued and outstanding	$100,000
Common stock dividend distributable—1,000 shares	**10,000**
Paid-in capital in excess of par value, common stock	**13,000**
Retained earnings	**20,000**
Total stockholders' equity	$143,000

No entry is made on the date of record for a stock dividend. On January 20, the date of payment, Quest distributes the new shares to stockholders and records this entry:

Date of Payment—Small Stock Dividend

Jan. 20	Common Stock Dividend Distributable	10,000	
	Common Stock, $10 Par Value		10,000
	To record issuance of common stock dividend.		

Assets = Liabilities + Equity
−10,000
+10,000

The combined effect of these stock dividend entries is to transfer (or capitalize) $15,000 of retained earnings to paid-in capital accounts. The amount of capitalized retained earnings equals the market value of the 1,000 issued shares ($15 × 1,000 shares). A stock dividend has no effect on the ownership percent of individual stockholders.

Point: A stock dividend does not affect assets.

Recording a large stock dividend. A corporation capitalizes retained earnings equal to the minimum amount required by state law for a large stock dividend. For most states, this amount is the par or stated value of the newly issued shares. To illustrate, suppose Quest's board declares a stock dividend of 30% instead of 10% on December 31. Since this dividend is more

Point: Large stock dividends are recorded at par or stated value.

than 25%, it is treated as a large stock dividend. Thus, the par value of the 3,000 dividend shares is capitalized at the date of declaration with this entry:

Date of Declaration—Large Stock Dividend

Dec. 31	Retained Earnings	30,000	
	Common Stock Dividend Distributable		30,000
	Declared a 3,000-share (30%) stock dividend.		

Assets = Liabilities + Equity
−30,000
+30,000

30% dividend × 10,000 issued shares × $10 par value

This transaction decreases retained earnings and increases contributed capital by $30,000. On the date of payment the company debits Common Stock Dividend Distributable and credits Common Stock for $30,000. The effects from a large stock dividend on balance sheet accounts are similar to those for a small stock dividend except for the absence of any effect on paid-in capital in excess of par.

Stock Splits

A **stock split** is the distribution of additional shares to stockholders according to their percent ownership. When a stock split occurs, the corporation "calls in" its outstanding shares and issues more than one new share in exchange for each old share. Splits can be done in any ratio, including 2-for-1, 3-for-1, or higher. Stock splits reduce the par or stated value per share. The reasons for stock splits are similar to those for stock dividends.

To illustrate, CompTec has 100,000 outstanding shares of $20 par value common stock with a current market value of $88 per share. A 2-for-1 stock split cuts par value in half as it replaces 100,000 shares of $20 par value stock with 200,000 shares of $10 par value stock. Market value is reduced from $88 per share to about $44 per share. The split does not affect any equity amounts reported on the balance sheet or any individual stockholder's percent ownership. Both the Paid-In Capital and Retained Earnings accounts are unchanged by a split, and *no journal entry is made*. The only effect on the accounts is a change in the stock account description. CompTec's 2-for-1 split on its $20 par value stock means that after the split, it changes its stock account title to Common Stock, $10 Par Value. This stock's description on the balance sheet also changes to reflect the additional authorized, issued, and outstanding shares and the new par value.

The difference between stock splits and large stock dividends is often blurred. Many companies report stock splits in their financial statements without calling in the original shares by simply changing their par value. This type of "split" is really a large stock dividend and results in additional shares issued to stockholders by capitalizing retained earnings or transferring other paid-in capital to Common Stock. This approach avoids administrative costs of splitting the stock. **Harley-Davidson** recently declared a 2-for-1 stock split executed in the form of a 100% stock dividend.

Before 5:1 Split: 1 share, $50 par

After 5:1 Split: 5 shares, $10 par

Point: Berkshire Hathaway has resisted a stock split. Its recent stock price was $150,000 per share.

Point: A **reverse stock split** is the opposite of a stock split. It increases both the market value per share and the par or stated value per share with a split ratio less than 1-for-1, such as 1-for-2. A reverse split results in fewer shares.

Decision Maker   Answer — p. 483

Entrepreneur A company you cofounded and own stock in announces a 50% stock dividend. Has the value of your stock investment increased, decreased, or remained the same? Would it make a difference if it was a 3-for-2 stock split executed in the form of a dividend? ■

Quick Check   Answers — p. 483

10. How does a stock dividend impact assets and retained earnings?
11. What distinguishes a large stock dividend from a small stock dividend?
12. What amount of retained earnings is capitalized for a small stock dividend?

PREFERRED STOCK

C2 Explain characteristics of, and distribute dividends between, common and preferred stock.

A corporation can issue two basic kinds of stock, common and preferred. **Preferred stock** has special rights that give it priority (or senior status) over common stock in one or more areas. Special rights typically include a preference for receiving dividends and for the distribution of assets if the corporation is liquidated. Preferred stock carries all rights of common stock unless the corporate charter nullifies them. Most preferred stock, for instance, does not confer the right to vote. Exhibit 11.9 shows that preferred stock is issued by about one-fourth of corporations. All corporations issue common stock.

EXHIBIT 11.9
Corporations and Preferred Stock

No Preferred Stock 73%
Issued Preferred Stock 27%

Issuance of Preferred Stock

Preferred stock usually has a par value. Like common stock, it can be sold at a price different from par. Preferred stock is recorded in its own separate capital accounts. To illustrate, if Dillon Snowboards issues 50 shares of $100 par value preferred stock for $6,000 cash on July 1, 2011, the entry is

July 1	Cash..	6,000	
	Preferred Stock, $100 Par Value................		5,000
	Paid-In Capital in Excess of Par Value, Preferred Stock............................		1,000
	Issued preferred stock for cash.		

Assets = Liabilities + Equity
+6,000   +5,000
               +1,000

$100 par value × 50 shares

$6,000 cash − [$100 par value × 50 shares]

The equity section of the year-end balance sheet for Dillon Snowboards, including preferred stock, is shown in Exhibit 11.10. (This exhibit assumes that common stock was issued at par.) Issuing no-par preferred stock is similar to issuing no-par common stock. Also, the entries for issuing preferred stock for noncash assets are similar to those for common stock.

EXHIBIT 11.10
Stockholders' Equity with Common and Preferred Stock

Stockholders' Equity
Common stock—$10 par value; 50,000 shares authorized;
   30,000 shares issued and outstanding $300,000
Preferred stock—$100 par value; 1,000 shares authorized;
   50 shares issued and outstanding 5,000
Paid-in capital in excess of par value, preferred stock 1,000
Retained earnings 65,000
Total stockholders' equity $371,000

Dividend Preference of Preferred Stock

Preferred stock usually carries a preference for dividends, meaning that preferred stockholders are allocated their dividends before any dividends are allocated to common stockholders. The dividends allocated to preferred stockholders are usually expressed as a dollar amount per share or a percent applied to par value. A preference for dividends does *not* ensure dividends. If the directors do not declare a dividend, neither the preferred nor the common stockholders receive one.

Cumulative or Noncumulative Dividend Most preferred stocks carry a cumulative dividend right. **Cumulative preferred stock** has a right to be paid both the current and all prior periods' unpaid dividends before any dividend is paid to common stockholders. When preferred stock is cumulative and the directors either do not declare a dividend to preferred stockholders or declare one that does not cover the total amount of cumulative dividend, the unpaid dividend amount is called **dividend in arrears.** Accumulation of dividends in arrears on cumulative preferred stock does not guarantee they will be paid. **Noncumulative preferred stock** confers no right to prior periods' unpaid dividends if they were not declared in those prior periods.

To illustrate the difference between cumulative and noncumulative preferred stock, assume that a corporation's outstanding stock includes (1) 1,000 shares of $100 par, 9% preferred

Point: Dividend preference does not imply that preferred stockholders receive more dividends than common stockholders, nor does it guarantee a dividend.

stock—yielding $9,000 per year in potential dividends, and (2) 4,000 shares of $50 par value common stock. During 2010, the first year of operations, the directors declare cash dividends of $5,000. In year 2011, they declare cash dividends of $42,000. See Exhibit 11.11 for the allocation of dividends for these two years. Allocation of year 2011 dividends depends on whether the preferred stock is noncumulative or cumulative. With noncumulative preferred, the preferred stockholders never receive the $4,000 skipped in 2010. If the preferred stock is cumulative, the $4,000 in arrears is paid in 2011 before any other dividends are paid.

EXHIBIT 11.11

Allocation of Dividends (noncumulative vs. cumulative preferred stock)

	Preferred	Common
Preferred Stock Is Noncumulative		
Year 2010	$ 5,000	$ 0
Year 2011		
Step 1: Current year's preferred dividend	$ 9,000	
Step 2: Remainder to common		$33,000
Preferred Stock Is Cumulative		
Year 2010	$ 5,000	$ 0
Year 2011		
Step 1: Dividend in arrears	$ 4,000	
Step 2: Current year's preferred dividend	9,000	
Step 3: Remainder to common		$29,000
Totals for year 2011	$13,000	$29,000

Example: What dividends do cumulative preferred stockholders receive in 2011 if the corporation paid only $2,000 of dividends in 2010? How does this affect dividends to common stockholders in 2011? *Answers:* $16,000 ($7,000 dividends in arrears, plus $9,000 current preferred dividends). Dividends to common stockholders decrease to $26,000.

A liability for a dividend does not exist until the directors declare a dividend. If a preferred dividend date passes and the corporation's board fails to declare the dividend on its cumulative preferred stock, the dividend in arrears is not a liability. The *full-disclosure principle* requires a corporation to report (usually in a note) the amount of preferred dividends in arrears as of the balance sheet date.

Participating or Nonparticipating Dividend Nonparticipating preferred stock has a feature that limits dividends to a maximum amount each year. This maximum is often stated as a percent of the stock's par value or as a specific dollar amount per share. Once preferred stockholders receive this amount, the common stockholders receive any and all additional dividends. **Participating preferred stock** has a feature allowing preferred stockholders to share with common stockholders in any dividends paid in excess of the percent or dollar amount stated on the preferred stock. This participation feature does not apply until common stockholders receive dividends equal to the preferred stock's dividend percent. Many corporations are authorized to issue participating preferred stock but rarely do, and most managers never expect to issue it.[2]

Convertible Preferred Stock

Preferred stock is more attractive to investors if it carries a right to exchange preferred shares for a fixed number of common shares. **Convertible preferred stock** gives holders the option to

---

[2] Participating preferred stock is usually authorized as a defense against a possible corporate *takeover* by an "unfriendly" investor (or a group of investors) who intends to buy enough voting common stock to gain control. Taking a term from spy novels, the financial world refers to this type of plan as a *poison pill* that a company swallows if enemy investors threaten its capture. A poison pill usually works as follows: A corporation's common stockholders on a given date are granted the right to purchase a large amount of participating preferred stock at a very low price. This right to purchase preferred shares is *not* transferable. If an unfriendly investor buys a large block of common shares (whose right to purchase participating preferred shares does *not* transfer to this buyer), the board can issue preferred shares at a low price to the remaining common shareholders who retained the right to purchase. Future dividends are then divided between the newly issued participating preferred shares and the common shares. This usually transfers value from common shares to preferred shares, causing the unfriendly investor's common stock to lose much of its value and reduces the potential benefit of a hostile takeover.

exchange their preferred shares for common shares at a specified rate. When a company prospers and its common stock increases in value, convertible preferred stockholders can share in this success by converting their preferred stock into more valuable common stock.

Callable Preferred Stock

Callable preferred stock gives the issuing corporation the right to purchase (retire) this stock from its holders at specified future prices and dates. The amount paid to call and retire a preferred share is its **call price,** or *redemption value,* and is set when the stock is issued. The call price normally includes the stock's par value plus a premium giving holders additional return on their investment. When the issuing corporation calls and retires a preferred stock, the terms of the agreement often require it to pay the call price *and* any dividends in arrears.

Point: The issuing corporation has the right, or option, to retire its callable preferred stock.

IFRS

Like U.S. GAAP, IFRS requires that preferred stocks be classified as debt or equity based on analysis of the stock's contractual terms. However, IFRS uses different criteria for such classification.

Reasons for Issuing Preferred Stock

Corporations issue preferred stock for several reasons. One is to raise capital without sacrificing control. For example, suppose a company's organizers have $100,000 cash to invest and organize a corporation that needs $200,000 of capital to start. If they sell $200,000 worth of common stock (with $100,000 to the organizers), they would have only 50% control and would need to negotiate extensively with other stockholders in making policy. However, if they issue $100,000 worth of common stock to themselves and sell outsiders $100,000 of 8%, cumulative preferred stock with no voting rights, they retain control.

A second reason to issue preferred stock is to boost the return earned by common stockholders. To illustrate, suppose a corporation's organizers expect to earn an annual after-tax income of $24,000 on an investment of $200,000. If they sell and issue $200,000 worth of common stock, the $24,000 income produces a 12% return on the $200,000 of common stockholders' equity. However, if they issue $100,000 of 8% preferred stock to outsiders and $100,000 of common stock to themselves, their own return increases to 16% per year, as shown in Exhibit 11.12.

Net (after-tax) income	$24,000
Less preferred dividends at 8%	(8,000)
Balance to common stockholders	$16,000
Return to common stockholders ($16,000/$100,000)	16%

EXHIBIT 11.12

Return to Common Stockholders When Preferred Stock Is Issued

Common stockholders earn 16% instead of 12% because assets contributed by preferred stockholders are invested to earn $12,000 while the preferred dividend is only $8,000. Use of preferred stock to increase return to common stockholders is an example of **financial leverage** (also called *trading on the equity*). As a general rule, when the dividend rate on preferred stock is less than the rate the corporation earns on its assets, the effect of issuing preferred stock is to increase (or *lever*) the rate earned by common stockholders.

Point: Financial leverage also occurs when debt is issued and the interest rate paid on it is less than the rate earned from using the assets the creditors lend the company.

Other reasons for issuing preferred stock include its appeal to some investors who believe that the corporation's common stock is too risky or that the expected return on common stock is too low.

Decision Maker

Answer — p. 483

Concert Organizer Assume that you alter your business strategy from organizing concerts targeted at under 1,000 people to those targeted at between 5,000 to 20,000 people. You also incorporate because of increased risk of lawsuits and a desire to issue stock for financing. It is important that you control the company for decisions on whom to schedule. What types of stock do you offer?

Quick Check

Answers — p. 483

13. In what ways does preferred stock often have priority over common stock?
14. Increasing the return to common stockholders by issuing preferred stock is an example of (*a*) Financial leverage. (*b*) Cumulative earnings. (*c*) Dividend in arrears.
15. A corporation has issued and outstanding (i) 9,000 shares of $50 par value, 10% cumulative, nonparticipating preferred stock and (ii) 27,000 shares of $10 par value common stock. No dividends have been declared for the two prior years. During the current year, the corporation declares $288,000 in dividends. The amount paid to common shareholders is (*a*) $243,000. (*b*) $153,000. (*c*) $135,000.

TREASURY STOCK

P3 Record purchases and sales of treasury stock and the retirement of stock.

Corporations and Treasury Stock

With Treasury Stock 62%
No Treasury Stock 38%

Corporations acquire shares of their own stock for several reasons: (1) to use their shares to acquire another corporation, (2) to purchase shares to avoid a hostile takeover of the company, (3) to reissue them to employees as compensation, and (4) to maintain a strong market for their stock or to show management confidence in the current price.

A corporation's reacquired shares are called **treasury stock,** which is similar to unissued stock in several ways: (1) neither treasury stock nor unissued stock is an asset, (2) neither receives cash dividends or stock dividends, and (3) neither allows the exercise of voting rights. However, treasury stock does differ from unissued stock in one major way: The corporation can resell treasury stock at less than par without having the buyers incur a liability, provided it was originally issued at par value or higher. Treasury stock purchases also require management to exercise ethical sensitivity because funds are being paid to specific stockholders instead of all stockholders. Managers must be sure the purchase is in the best interest of all stockholders. These concerns cause companies to fully disclose treasury stock transactions.

Purchasing Treasury Stock

Purchasing treasury stock reduces the corporation's assets and equity by equal amounts. (We describe the *cost method* of accounting for treasury stock, which is the most widely used method. The *par value* method is another method explained in advanced courses.) To illustrate, Exhibit 11.13 shows Cyber Corporation's account balances *before* any treasury stock purchase (Cyber has no liabilities).

EXHIBIT 11.13

Account Balances *before* Purchasing Treasury Stock

Assets		Stockholders' Equity	
Cash	$ 30,000	Common stock—$10 par; 10,000 shares authorized, issued, and outstanding	$100,000
Other assets	95,000	Retained earnings	25,000
Total assets	$125,000	Total stockholders' equity	$125,000

Cyber then purchases 1,000 of its own shares for $11,500 on May 1, which is recorded as follows.

Assets = Liabilities + Equity
−11,500   −11,500

$11.50 cost per share × 1,000 shares

May 1	Treasury Stock, Common	11,500	
	Cash		11,500
	Purchased 1,000 treasury shares at $11.50 per share.		

This entry reduces equity through the debit to the Treasury Stock account, which is a contra equity account. Exhibit 11.14 shows account balances *after* this transaction.

Assets			Stockholders' Equity	
Cash	$ 18,500	Common stock—$10 par; 10,000 shares authorized and issued; 1,000 shares in treasury		$100,000
Other assets	95,000	Retained earnings, $11,500 restricted by treasury stock purchase		25,000
		Less cost of treasury stock		**(11,500)**
Total assets	$113,500	Total stockholders' equity		$113,500

EXHIBIT 11.14

Account Balances *after* Purchasing Treasury Stock

The treasury stock purchase reduces Cyber's cash, total assets, and total equity by $11,500 but does not reduce the balance of either the Common Stock or the Retained Earnings account. The equity reduction is reported by deducting the cost of treasury stock in the equity section. Also, two disclosures are evident. First, the stock description reveals that 1,000 issued shares are in treasury, leaving only 9,000 shares still outstanding. Second, the description for retained earnings reveals that it is partly restricted.

Point: The Treasury Stock account is *not* an asset. Treasury stock does not carry voting or dividend rights.

Point: A treasury stock purchase is also called a *stock buyback*.

Reissuing Treasury Stock

Treasury stock can be reissued by selling it at cost, above cost, or below cost.

Selling Treasury Stock at Cost If treasury stock is reissued at cost, the entry is the reverse of the one made to record the purchase. For instance, if on May 21 Cyber reissues 100 of the treasury shares purchased on May 1 at the same $11.50 per share cost, the entry is

May 21	Cash	1,150	
	Treasury Stock, Common		1,150
	Received $11.50 per share for 100 treasury shares costing $11.50 per share.		

Assets = Liabilities + Equity
+1,150   +1,150

$11.50 cost per share × 100 shares

Selling Treasury Stock *above* Cost If treasury stock is sold for more than cost, the amount received in excess of cost is credited to the Paid-In Capital, Treasury Stock account. This account is reported as a separate item in the stockholders' equity section. No gain is ever reported from the sale of treasury stock. To illustrate, if Cyber receives $12 cash per share for 400 treasury shares costing $11.50 per share on June 3, the entry is

Point: Treasury stock does not represent ownership. A company cannot own a part of itself.

June 3	Cash	4,800	
	Treasury Stock, Common		4,600
	Paid-In Capital, Treasury Stock		**200**
	Received $12 per share for 400 treasury shares costing $11.50 per share.		

Assets = Liabilities + Equity
+4,800   +4,600
                +200

$11.50 cost per share × 400 shares

[$12 issue price − $11.50 cost per share] × 400 shares

Selling Treasury Stock *below* Cost When treasury stock is sold below cost, the entry to record the sale depends on whether the Paid-In Capital, Treasury Stock account has a credit balance. If it has a zero balance, the excess of cost over the sales price is debited to Retained Earnings. If the Paid-In Capital, Treasury Stock account has a credit balance, it is debited for the excess of the cost over the selling price but not to exceed the balance in this account. When the credit balance in this paid-in capital account is eliminated, any remaining difference between the cost and selling price is debited to Retained Earnings. To illustrate, if Cyber sells its remaining 500 shares of treasury stock at $10 per share on July 10, equity is

Point: The phrase *treasury stock* is believed to arise from the fact that reacquired stock is held in a corporation's treasury.

Point: The Paid-In Capital, Treasury Stock account can have a zero or credit balance but never a debit balance.

reduced by $750 (500 shares × $1.50 per share excess of cost over selling price), as shown in this entry:

July 10	Cash	5,000	
	Paid-In Capital, Treasury Stock	200	
	Retained Earnings	550	
	Treasury Stock, Common		5,750
	Received $10 per share for 500 treasury shares costing $11.50 per share.		

Assets = Liabilities + Equity
+5,000
                  −200
                  −550
                  +5,750

[$10 issue price − $11.50 cost per share] × 500 shares; not to exceed $200

For any amount exceeding $200

$11.50 cost per share × 500 shares

This entry eliminates the $200 credit balance in the paid-in capital account created on June 3 and then reduces the Retained Earnings balance by the remaining $550 excess of cost over selling price. A company never reports a loss (or gain) from the sale of treasury stock.

Retiring Stock

A corporation can purchase its own stock and retire it. Retiring stock reduces the number of issued shares. Retired stock is the same as authorized and unissued shares. Purchases and retirements of stock are permissible under state law only if they do not jeopardize the interests of creditors and stockholders. When stock is purchased for retirement, we remove all capital amounts related to the retired shares. If the purchase price exceeds the net amount removed, this excess is debited to Retained Earnings. If the net amount removed from all capital accounts exceeds the purchase price, this excess is credited to the Paid-In Capital from Retirement of Stock account. A company's assets and equity are always reduced by the amount paid for the retiring stock.

Point: Recording stock retirement results in canceling the equity from the original issuance of the shares.

Quick Check   Answers — p. 483

16. Purchase of treasury stock (*a*) has no effect on assets; (*b*) reduces total assets and total equity by equal amounts; or (*c*) is recorded with a debit to Retained Earnings.
17. Southern Co. purchases shares of Northern Corp. Should either company classify these shares as treasury stock?
18. How does treasury stock affect the authorized, issued, and outstanding shares?
19. When a company purchases treasury stock, (*a*) retained earnings are restricted by the amount paid; (*b*) Retained Earnings is credited; or (*c*) it is retired.

REPORTING OF EQUITY

C3 Explain the items reported in retained earnings.

Statement of Retained Earnings

Retained earnings generally consist of a company's cumulative net income less any net losses and dividends declared since its inception. Retained earnings are part of stockholders' claims on the company's net assets, but this does *not* imply that a certain amount of cash or other assets is available to pay stockholders. For example, **Research In Motion** has $5,274,365 thousand in retained earnings, but only $1,550,861 thousand in cash. This section describes events and transactions affecting retained earnings and how retained earnings are reported.

Restrictions and Appropriations The term **restricted retained earnings** refers to both statutory and contractual restrictions. A common *statutory* (or *legal*) *restriction* is to limit treasury stock purchases to the amount of retained earnings. The balance sheet in Exhibit 11.14 provides an example. A common *contractual restriction* involves loan agreements that restrict paying dividends beyond a specified amount or percent of retained earnings. Restrictions are usually described in the notes. The term **appropriated retained earnings** refers to a voluntary transfer of amounts from the Retained Earnings account to the Appropriated Retained Earnings account to inform users of special activities that require funds.

Prior Period Adjustments **Prior period adjustments** are corrections of material errors in prior period financial statements. These errors include arithmetic mistakes, unacceptable accounting, and missed facts. Prior period adjustments are reported in the *statement of retained earnings* (or the statement of stockholders' equity), net of any income tax effects. Prior period adjustments result in changing the beginning balance of retained earnings for events occurring prior to the earliest period reported in the current set of financial statements. To illustrate, assume that ComUS makes an error in a 2009 journal entry for the purchase of land by incorrectly debiting an expense account. When this is discovered in 2011, the statement of retained earnings includes a prior period adjustment, as shown in Exhibit 11.15. This exhibit also shows the usual format of the statement of retained earnings.

Point: If a year 2009 error is discovered in 2010, the company records the adjustment in 2010. But if the financial statements include 2009 and 2010 figures, the statements report the correct amounts for 2009, and a note describes the correction.

EXHIBIT 11.15
Statement of Retained Earnings with a Prior Period Adjustment

ComUS Statement of Retained Earnings For Year Ended December 31, 2011	
Retained earnings, Dec. 31, 2010, as previously reported	$4,745,000
Prior period adjustment	
Cost of land incorrectly expensed (net of $63,000 income taxes)	147,000
Retained earnings, Dec. 31, 2010, as adjusted	4,892,000
Plus net income	1,224,300
Less cash dividends declared	(301,800)
Retained earnings, Dec. 31, 2011	$5,814,500

Many items reported in financial statements are based on estimates. Future events are certain to reveal that some of these estimates were inaccurate even when based on the best data available at the time. These inaccuracies are *not* considered errors and are *not* reported as prior period adjustments. Instead, they are identified as **changes in accounting estimates** and are accounted for in current and future periods. To illustrate, we know that depreciation is based on estimated useful lives and salvage values. As time passes and new information becomes available, managers may need to change these estimates and the resulting depreciation expense for current and future periods.

Point: Accounting for changes in estimates is sometimes criticized as two wrongs to make a right. Consider a change in an asset's life. Depreciation neither before nor after the change is the amount computed if the revised estimate were originally selected. Regulators chose this approach to avoid restating prior period numbers.

Closing Process The closing process was explained earlier in the book as: (1) Close credit balances in revenue accounts to Income Summary, (2) Close debit balances in expense accounts to Income Summary, and (3) Close Income Summary to Retained Earnings. If dividends are recorded in a Dividends account, and not as an immediate reduction to Retained Earnings (as shown in this chapter), a fourth step is necessary to close the Dividends account to Retained Earnings.

Statement of Stockholders' Equity

Instead of a separate statement of retained earnings, companies commonly report a statement of stockholders' equity that includes changes in retained earnings. A **statement of stockholders' equity** lists the beginning and ending balances of key equity accounts and describes the changes that occur during the period. The companies in Appendix A report such a statement. The usual format is to provide a column for each component of equity and use the rows to describe events occurring in the period. Exhibit 11.16 shows a condensed statement for **Apple**.

EXHIBIT 11.16
Statement of Stockholders' Equity

Apple

APPLE Statement of Stockholders' Equity					
($ millions, shares in thousands)	Common Stock Shares	Common Stock Amount	Retained Earnings	Other	Total Equity
Balance, Sept. 27, 2008	888,326	$7,177	$15,129	$(9)	$22,297
Net income	—	—	8,235	—	8,235
Issuance of Common Stock	11,480	404	(11)	—	393
Other	—	629	—	86	715
Cash Dividends ($0.00 per share)	—	—	—	—	—
Balance, Sept. 26, 2009	899,806	$8,210	$23,353	$77	$31,640

Reporting Stock Options

The majority of corporations whose shares are publicly traded issue **stock options,** which are rights to purchase common stock at a fixed price over a specified period. As the stock's price rises, the option's value increases. Starbucks and Home Depot offer stock options to both full- and part-time employees. Stock options are said to motivate managers and employees to (1) focus on company performance, (2) take a long-run perspective, and (3) remain with the company. A stock option is like having an investment with no risk ("a carrot with no stick").

To illustrate, Quantum grants each of its employees the option to purchase 100 shares of its $1 par value common stock at its current market price of $50 per share anytime within the next 10 years. If the stock price rises to $70 per share, an employee can exercise the option at a gain of $20 per share (acquire a $70 stock at the $50 option price). With 100 shares, a single employee would have a total gain of $2,000, computed as 20×100 shares. Companies report the cost of stock options in the income statement. Measurement of this cost is explained in advanced courses.

Fraud

Pump 'n Dump. Fraudulent information can be used by the owners of a company's stock to pump it up and claim it is undervalued, which causes naïve investors to seek to acquire the stock and drive up its price. After that, those behind the release of fraudulent information dump the stock at an inflated price. When later information reveals that the stock is overvalued, its price declines and investors still holding the stock lose value. This scheme is called *pump 'n dump.* Jonathan Lebed, at 15 years old, is one of the most infamous cases of pump 'n dump, in which he allegedly made about $1 million.

GLOBAL VIEW

This section discusses similarities and differences between U.S. GAAP and IFRS in accounting and reporting for equity.

Accounting for Common Stock The accounting for and reporting of common stock under U.S. GAAP and IFRS are similar. Specifically, procedures for issuing common stock at par, at a premium, at a discount, and for noncash assets are similar across the two systems. However, we must be aware of legal and cultural differences across the world that can impact the rights and responsibilities of common shareholders. Nokia's terminology is a bit different as it uses the phrase "share capital" in reference to what U.S. GAAP would title "common shares" (see Appendix A). It also discloses that it has issued (and outstanding) shares of 3,744,956,052.

Accounting for Dividends Accounting for and reporting of dividends under U.S. GAAP and IFRS are consistent. This applies to cash dividends, stock dividends, and stock splits. For Nokia, a "dividend of EUR 0.40 per share is to be paid out on the shares of the Company." Nokia, like many other companies, follows a dividend policy set by management and its board.

Accounting for Preferred Stock Accounting and reporting for preferred stock are similar for U.S. GAAP and IFRS, but there are some important differences. First, preferred stock that is redeemable at the option of the preferred stockholders is reported *between* liabilities and equity in U.S. GAAP balance sheets. However, that same stock is reported as a liability in IFRS balance sheets. Second, the issue price of convertible preferred stock (and bonds) is recorded entirely under preferred stock (or bonds) *and none is assigned to the conversion feature* under U.S. GAAP. However, IFRS requires that a portion of the issue price be allocated to the conversion feature when it exists. Nokia has no preferred stock.

Accounting for Treasury Stock Both U.S. GAAP and IFRS apply the principle that companies do not record gains or losses on transactions involving their own stock. This applies to purchases, reissuances, and retirements of treasury stock. Consequently, the accounting for treasury stock explained in this chapter is consistent with that under IFRS. However, IFRS in this area is less detailed than that of U.S. GAAP. Nokia's policy regarding treasury stock follows: "[It] recognizes acquired treasury shares as a deduction from equity at their acquisition cost."

Chapter 11 Reporting and Analyzing Equity

Earnings per Share, Price-Earnings Ratio, Dividend Yield, and Book Value per Share

Decision Analysis

Earnings per Share

The income statement reports **earnings per share,** also called *EPS* or *net income per share,* which is the amount of income earned per each share of a company's outstanding common stock. The **basic earnings per share** formula is shown in Exhibit 11.17. When a company has no preferred stock, then preferred dividends are zero. The weighted-average common shares outstanding is measured over the income reporting period; its computation is explained in advanced courses.

A1 Compute earnings per share and describe its use.

$$\text{Basic earnings per share} = \frac{\text{Net income} - \text{Preferred dividends}}{\text{Weighted-average common shares outstanding}}$$

EXHIBIT 11.17
Basic Earnings per Share

To illustrate, assume that Quantum Co. earns $40,000 net income in 2011 and declares dividends of $7,500 on its noncumulative preferred stock. (If preferred stock is *non*cumulative, the income available [numerator] is the current period net income less any preferred dividends *declared* in that same period. If preferred stock is cumulative, the income available [numerator] is the current period net income less the preferred dividends whether declared or not.) Quantum has 5,000 weighted-average common shares outstanding during 2011. Its basic EPS[3] is

$$\text{Basic earnings per share} = \frac{\$40,000 - \$7,500}{5,000 \text{ shares}} = \$6.50$$

Price-Earnings Ratio

A stock's market value is determined by its *expected* future cash flows. A comparison of a company's EPS and its market value per share reveals information about market expectations. This comparison is traditionally made using a **price-earnings (or PE) ratio,** expressed also as *price earnings, price to earnings,* or *PE*. Some analysts interpret this ratio as what price the market is willing to pay for a company's current earnings stream. Price-earnings ratios can differ across companies that have similar earnings because of either higher or lower expectations of future earnings. The price-earnings ratio is defined in Exhibit 11.18.

A2 Compute price-earnings ratio and describe its use in analysis.

Point: The average PE ratio of stocks in the 1950–2010 period is about 14.

$$\text{Price-earnings ratio} = \frac{\text{Market value (price) per share}}{\text{Earnings per share}}$$

EXHIBIT 11.18
Price-Earnings Ratio

This ratio is often computed using EPS from the most recent period (for Amazon, its PE is 52; for Altria, its PE is 13). However, many users compute this ratio using *expected* EPS for the next period.

Some analysts view stocks with high PE ratios (higher than 20 to 25) as more likely to be overpriced and stocks with low PE ratios (less than 5 to 8) as more likely to be underpriced. These investors prefer to sell or avoid buying stocks with high PE ratios and to buy or hold stocks with low PE ratios. However, investment decision making is rarely so simple as to rely on a single ratio. For instance, a stock with a high PE ratio can prove to be a good investment if its earnings continue to increase beyond current expectations. Similarly, a stock with a low PE ratio can prove to be a poor investment if its earnings decline below expectations.

Point: Average PE ratios for U.S. stocks increased over the past two decades. Some analysts interpret this as a signal the market is overpriced. But higher ratios can at least partly reflect accounting changes that have reduced reported earnings.

---

[3] A corporation can be classified as having either a simple or complex capital structure. The term **simple capital structure** refers to a company with only common stock and nonconvertible preferred stock outstanding. The term **complex capital structure** refers to companies with dilutive securities. **Dilutive securities** include options, rights to purchase common stock, and any bonds or preferred stock that are convertible into common stock. A company with a complex capital structure must often report two EPS figures: basic and diluted. **Diluted earnings per share** is computed by adding all dilutive securities to the denominator of the basic EPS computation. It reflects the decrease in basic EPS *assuming* that all dilutive securities are converted into common shares.

Chapter 11 Reporting and Analyzing Equity

> **Decision Maker** — Answer — p. 483
>
> **Money Manager** You plan to invest in one of two companies identified as having identical future prospects. One has a PE of 19 and the other a PE of 25. Which do you invest in? Does it matter if your *estimate* of PE for these two companies is 29 as opposed to 22? ■

Dividend Yield

A3 Compute dividend yield and explain its use in analysis.

Investors buy shares of a company's stock in anticipation of receiving a return from either or both cash dividends and stock price increases. Stocks that pay large dividends on a regular basis, called *income stocks,* are attractive to investors who want recurring cash flows from their investments. In contrast, some stocks pay little or no dividends but are still attractive to investors because of their expected stock price increases. The stocks of companies that distribute little or no cash but use their cash to finance expansion are called *growth stocks*. One way to help identify whether a stock is an income stock or a growth stock is to analyze its dividend yield. **Dividend yield,** defined in Exhibit 11.19, shows the annual amount of cash dividends distributed to common shares relative to their market value.

EXHIBIT 11.19
Dividend Yield

$$\text{Dividend yield} = \frac{\text{Annual cash dividends per share}}{\text{Market value per share}}$$

Dividend yield can be computed for current and prior periods using actual dividends and stock prices and for future periods using expected values. Exhibit 11.20 shows recent dividend and stock price data for **Amazon** and **Altria Group** to compute dividend yield.

EXHIBIT 11.20
Dividend and Stock Price Information

Company	Cash Dividends per Share	Market Value per Share	Dividend Yield
Amazon	$0.00	$80	0.0%
Altria Group	1.68	20	8.4

Point: The *payout ratio* equals cash dividends declared on common stock divided by net income. A low payout ratio suggests that a company is retaining earnings for future growth.

Dividend yield is zero for Amazon, implying it is a growth stock. An investor in Amazon would look for increases in stock prices (and eventual cash from the sale of stock). Altria has a dividend yield of 8.4%, implying it is an income stock for which dividends are important in assessing its value.

Book Value per Share

A4 Compute book value and explain its use in analysis.

Case 1: Common Stock (Only) Outstanding. **Book value per common share,** defined in Exhibit 11.21, reflects the amount of equity applicable to *common* shares on a per share basis. To illustrate, we use Dillon Snowboards' data from Exhibit 11.4. Dillon has 30,000 outstanding common shares, and the stockholders' equity applicable to common shares is $365,000. Dillon's book value per common share is $12.17, computed as $365,000 divided by 30,000 shares.

EXHIBIT 11.21
Book Value per Common Share

$$\text{Book value per common share} = \frac{\text{Stockholders' equity applicable to common shares}}{\text{Number of common shares outstanding}}$$

Point: Book value per share is also referred to as *stockholders' claim to assets on a per share basis*.

Case 2: Common and Preferred Stock Outstanding. To compute book value when both common and preferred shares are outstanding, we allocate total equity between the two types of shares. The **book value per preferred share** is computed first; its computation is shown in Exhibit 11.22.

EXHIBIT 11.22
Book Value per Preferred Share

$$\text{Book value per preferred share} = \frac{\text{Stockholders' equity applicable to preferred shares}}{\text{Number of preferred shares outstanding}}$$

The equity applicable to preferred shares equals the preferred share's call price (or par value if the preferred is not callable) plus any cumulative dividends in arrears. The remaining equity is the portion applicable to common shares. To illustrate, consider LTD's equity in Exhibit 11.23. Its preferred stock is callable at $108 per share, and two years of cumulative preferred dividends are in arrears.

EXHIBIT 11.23
Stockholders' Equity with Preferred and Common Stock

Stockholders' Equity	
Preferred stock—$100 par value, 7% cumulative, 2,000 shares authorized, 1,000 shares issued and outstanding	$100,000
Common stock—$25 par value, 12,000 shares authorized, 10,000 shares issued and outstanding	250,000
Paid-in capital in excess of par value, common stock	15,000
Retained earnings	82,000
Total stockholders' equity	$447,000

The book value computations are in Exhibit 11.24. Equity is first allocated to preferred shares before the book value of common shares is computed.

EXHIBIT 11.24
Computing Book Value per Preferred and Common Share

Total stockholders' equity			$447,000
Less equity applicable to preferred shares			
Call price (1,000 shares × $108)		$108,000	
Dividends in arrears ($100,000 × 7% × 2 years)		14,000	(122,000)
Equity applicable to common shares			$325,000
Book value per preferred share ($122,000/1,000 shares)			$122.00
Book value per common share ($325,000/10,000 shares)			$32.50

Book value per share reflects the value per share if a company is liquidated at balance sheet amounts. Book value is also the starting point in many stock valuation models, merger negotiations, price setting for public utilities, and loan contracts. The main limitation in using book value is the potential difference between recorded value and market value for assets and liabilities. Investors often adjust their analysis for estimates of these differences.

Decision Maker
Answer — p. 483

Investor You are considering investing in **BMX**, whose book value per common share is $4 and price per common share on the stock exchange is $7. From this information, are BMX's net assets priced higher or lower than its recorded values? ■

DEMONSTRATION PROBLEM 1

Barton Corporation began operations on January 1, 2010. The following transactions relating to stockholders' equity occurred in the first two years of the company's operations.

2010

Jan. 1 Authorized the issuance of 2 million shares of $5 par value common stock and 100,000 shares of $100 par value, 10% cumulative, preferred stock.
Jan. 2 Issued 200,000 shares of common stock for $12 cash per share.
Jan. 3 Issued 100,000 shares of common stock in exchange for a building valued at $820,000 and merchandise inventory valued at $380,000.
Jan. 4 Paid $10,000 cash to the company's founders for organization activities.
Jan. 5 Issued 12,000 shares of preferred stock for $110 cash per share.

2011

June 4 Issued 100,000 shares of common stock for $15 cash per share.

Required

1. Prepare journal entries to record these transactions.
2. Prepare the stockholders' equity section of the balance sheet as of December 31, 2010, and December 31, 2011, based on these transactions.
3. Prepare a table showing dividend allocations and dividends per share for 2010 and 2011 assuming Barton declares the following cash dividends: 2010, $50,000, and 2011, $300,000.

4. Prepare the January 2, 2010, journal entry for Barton's issuance of 200,000 shares of common stock for $12 cash per share assuming
   a. Common stock is no-par stock without a stated value.
   b. Common stock is no-par stock with a stated value of $10 per share.

PLANNING THE SOLUTION

- Record journal entries for the transactions for 2010 and 2011.
- Determine the balances for the 2010 and 2011 equity accounts for the balance sheet.
- Prepare the contributed capital portion of the 2010 and 2011 balance sheets.
- Prepare a table similar to Exhibit 11.11 showing dividend allocations for 2010 and 2011.
- Record the issuance of common stock under both specifications of no-par stock.

SOLUTION TO DEMONSTRATION PROBLEM 1

1. Journal entries.

2010			
Jan. 2	Cash	2,400,000	
	Common Stock, $5 Par Value		1,000,000
	Paid-In Capital in Excess of Par Value, Common Stock		1,400,000
	Issued 200,000 shares of common stock.		
Jan. 3	Building	820,000	
	Merchandise Inventory	380,000	
	Common Stock, $5 Par Value		500,000
	Paid-In Capital in Excess of Par Value, Common Stock		700,000
	Issued 100,000 shares of common stock.		
Jan. 4	Organization Expenses	10,000	
	Cash		10,000
	Paid founders for organization costs.		
Jan. 5	Cash	1,320,000	
	Preferred Stock, $100 Par Value		1,200,000
	Paid-In Capital in Excess of Par Value, Preferred Stock		120,000
	Issued 12,000 shares of preferred stock.		
2011			
June 4	Cash	1,500,000	
	Common Stock, $5 Par Value		500,000
	Paid-In Capital in Excess of Par Value, Common Stock		1,000,000
	Issued 100,000 shares of common stock.		

2. Balance sheet presentations (at December 31 year-end).

	2011	2010
Stockholders' Equity		
Preferred stock—$100 par value, 10% cumulative, 100,000 shares authorized, 12,000 shares issued and outstanding	$1,200,000	$1,200,000
Paid-in capital in excess of par value, preferred stock	120,000	120,000
Total paid-in capital by preferred stockholders	1,320,000	1,320,000
Common stock—$5 par value, 2,000,000 shares authorized, 300,000 shares issued and outstanding in 2010, and 400,000 shares issued and outstanding in 2011	2,000,000	1,500,000
Paid-in capital in excess of par value, common stock	3,100,000	2,100,000
Total paid-in capital by common stockholders	5,100,000	3,600,000
Total paid-in capital	$6,420,000	$4,920,000

3. Dividend allocation table.

	Common	Preferred
2010 ($50,000)		
Preferred—current year (12,000 shares × $10 = $120,000)	$ 0	$ 50,000
Common—remainder (300,000 shares outstanding)	0	0
Total for the year	$ 0	$ 50,000
2011 ($300,000)		
Preferred—dividend in arrears from 2010 ($120,000 − $50,000)	$ 0	$ 70,000
Preferred—current year	0	120,000
Common—remainder (400,000 shares outstanding)	110,000	0
Total for the year	$110,000	$190,000
Dividends per share		
2010	$ 0.00	$ 4.17
2011	$ 0.28	$ 15.83

4. Journal entries.

   a. For 2010 (no-par stock without a stated value):

Jan. 2	Cash	2,400,000	
	Common Stock, No-Par Value		2,400,000
	Issued 200,000 shares of no-par common stock at $12 per share.		

   b. For 2010 (no-par stock with a stated value):

Jan. 2	Cash	2,400,000	
	Common Stock, $10 Stated Value		2,000,000
	Paid-In Capital in Excess of Stated Value, Common Stock		400,000
	Issued 200,000 shares of $10 stated value common stock at $12 per share.		

DEMONSTRATION PROBLEM 2

Precision Company began year 2011 with the following balances in its stockholders' equity accounts.

Common stock—$10 par, 500,000 shares authorized, 200,000 shares issued and outstanding	$2,000,000
Paid-in capital in excess of par, common stock	1,000,000
Retained earnings	5,000,000
Total	$8,000,000

All outstanding common stock was issued for $15 per share when the company was created. Prepare journal entries to account for the following transactions during year 2011.

Jan. 10 The board declared a $0.10 cash dividend per share to shareholders of record Jan. 28.
Feb. 15 Paid the cash dividend declared on January 10.
Mar. 31 Declared a 20% stock dividend. The market value of the stock is $18 per share.
May 1   Distributed the stock dividend declared on March 31.
July 1   Purchased 30,000 shares of treasury stock at $20 per share.
Sept. 1 Sold 20,000 treasury shares at $26 cash per share.
Dec. 1   Sold the remaining 10,000 shares of treasury stock at $7 cash per share.

PLANNING THE SOLUTION

- Calculate the total cash dividend to record by multiplying the cash dividend declared by the number of shares as of the date of record.
- Decide whether the stock dividend is a small or large dividend. Then analyze each event to determine the accounts affected and the appropriate amounts to be recorded.

SOLUTION TO DEMONSTRATION PROBLEM 2

Date	Account	Debit	Credit
Jan. 10	Retained Earnings	20,000	
	Common Dividend Payable		20,000
	Declared a $0.10 per share cash dividend.		
Feb. 15	Common Dividend Payable	20,000	
	Cash		20,000
	Paid $0.10 per share cash dividend.		
Mar. 31	Retained Earnings	720,000	
	Common Stock Dividend Distributable		400,000
	Paid-In Capital in Excess of Par Value, Common Stock		320,000
	Declared a small stock dividend of 20% or 40,000 shares; market value is $18 per share.		
May 1	Common Stock Dividend Distributable	400,000	
	Common Stock		400,000
	Distributed 40,000 shares of common stock.		
July 1	Treasury Stock, Common	600,000	
	Cash		600,000
	Purchased 30,000 common shares at $20 per share.		
Sept. 1	Cash	520,000	
	Treasury Stock, Common		400,000
	Paid-In Capital, Treasury Stock		120,000
	Sold 20,000 treasury shares at $26 per share.		
Dec. 1	Cash	70,000	
	Paid-In Capital, Treasury Stock	120,000	
	Retained Earnings	10,000	
	Treasury Stock, Common		200,000
	Sold 10,000 treasury shares at $7 per share.		

Summary

C1 **Identify characteristics of corporations and their organization.** Corporations are legal entities whose stockholders are not liable for its debts. Stock is easily transferred, and the life of a corporation does not end with the incapacity of a stockholder. A corporation acts through its agents, who are its officers and managers. Corporations are regulated and subject to income taxes. Authorized stock is the stock that a corporation's charter authorizes it to sell. Issued stock is the portion of authorized shares sold. Par value stock is a value per share assigned by the charter. No-par value stock is stock *not* assigned a value per share by the charter. Stated value stock is no-par stock to which the directors assign a value per share.

C2 **Explain characteristics of, and distribute dividends between, common and preferred stock.** Preferred stock has a priority (or senior status) relative to common stock in one or more areas, usually (1) dividends and (2) assets in case of liquidation. Preferred stock usually does not carry voting rights and can be convertible or callable. Convertibility permits the holder to convert preferred to common. Callability permits the issuer to buy back preferred stock under specified conditions. Preferred stockholders usually hold the right to dividend distributions before common stockholders. When preferred stock is cumulative and in arrears, the amount in arrears must be distributed to preferred before any dividends are distributed to common.

C3 **Explain the items reported in retained earnings.** Stockholders' equity is made up of (1) paid-in capital and (2) retained earnings. Paid-in capital consists of funds raised by stock issuances. Retained earnings consists of cumulative net income (losses) not distributed. Many companies face statutory and contractual restrictions on retained earnings. Corporations can voluntarily appropriate retained earnings to inform others about their disposition. Prior period adjustments are corrections of errors in prior financial statements.

A1 **Compute earnings per share and describe its use.** A company with a simple capital structure computes basic EPS by dividing net income less any preferred dividends by the weighted-average number of outstanding common shares. A company with a complex capital structure must usually report both basic and diluted EPS.

A2 **Compute price-earnings ratio and describe its use in analysis.** A common stock's price-earnings (PE) ratio is computed by dividing the stock's market value (price) per share by its EPS. A stock's PE is based on expectations that can prove to be better or worse than eventual performance.

A3 **Compute dividend yield and explain its use in analysis.** Dividend yield is the ratio of a stock's annual cash dividends per share to its market value (price) per share. Dividend yield can be compared with the yield of other companies to determine whether the stock is expected to be an income or growth stock.

A4 **Compute book value and explain its use in analysis.** Book value per common share is equity applicable to common shares divided by the number of outstanding common shares. Book value per preferred share is equity applicable to preferred shares divided by the number of outstanding preferred shares.

P1 **Record the issuance of corporate stock.** When stock is issued, its par or stated value is credited to the stock account and any excess is credited to a separate contributed capital account. If a stock has neither par nor stated value, the entire proceeds are credited to the stock account. Stockholders must contribute assets equal to minimum legal capital or be potentially liable for the deficiency.

P2 **Record transactions involving cash dividends, stock dividends, and stock splits.** Cash dividends involve three events. On the date of declaration, the directors bind the company to pay the dividend. A dividend declaration reduces retained earnings and creates a current liability. On the date of record, recipients of the dividend are identified. On the date of payment, cash is paid to stockholders and the current liability is removed. Neither a stock dividend nor a stock split alters the value of the company. However, the value of each share is less due to the distribution of additional shares. The distribution of additional shares is according to individual stockholders' ownership percent. Small stock dividends (≤25%) are recorded by capitalizing retained earnings equal to the market value of distributed shares. Large stock dividends (>25%) are recorded by capitalizing retained earnings equal to the par or stated value of distributed shares. Stock splits do not necessitate journal entries but do necessitate changes in the description of stock.

P3 **Record purchases and sales of treasury stock and the retirement of stock.** When a corporation purchases its own previously issued stock, it debits the cost of these shares to Treasury Stock. Treasury stock is subtracted from equity in the balance sheet. If treasury stock is reissued, any proceeds in excess of cost are credited to Paid-In Capital, Treasury Stock. If the proceeds are less than cost, they are debited to Paid-In Capital, Treasury Stock to the extent a credit balance exists. Any remaining amount is debited to Retained Earnings. When stock is retired, all accounts related to the stock are removed.

Guidance Answers to Decision Maker and Decision Ethics

Entrepreneur The 50% stock dividend provides you no direct income. A stock dividend often reveals management's optimistic expectations about the future and can improve a stock's marketability by making it affordable to more investors. Accordingly, a stock dividend usually reveals "good news" and because of this, it likely increases (slightly) the market value for your stock. The same conclusions apply to the 3-for-2 stock split.

Concert Organizer You have two basic options: (1) different classes of common stock or (2) common and preferred stock. Your objective is to issue to yourself stock that has all or a majority of the voting power. The other class of stock would carry limited or no voting rights. In this way, you maintain control and are able to raise the necessary funds.

Money Manager Since one company requires a payment of $19 for each $1 of earnings, and the other requires $25, you would prefer the stock with the PE of 19; it is a better deal given identical prospects. You should make sure these companies' earnings computations are roughly the same, for example, no extraordinary items, unusual events, and so forth. Also, your PE estimates for these companies do matter. If you are willing to pay $29 for each $1 of earnings for these companies, you obviously expect both to exceed current market expectations.

Investor Book value reflects recorded values. BMX's book value is $4 per common share. Stock price reflects the market's expectation of net asset value (both tangible and intangible items). BMX's market value is $7 per common share. Comparing these figures suggests BMX's market value of net assets is higher than its recorded values (by an amount of $7 versus $4 per share).

Guidance Answers to Quick Checks

1. (b)
2. A corporation pays taxes on its income, and its stockholders normally pay personal income taxes (at the 15% rate or lower) on any cash dividends received from the corporation.
3. A proxy is a legal document used to transfer a stockholder's right to vote to another person.
4. (a)
5. A stock premium is an amount in excess of par (or stated) value paid by purchasers of newly issued stock.
6. Minimum legal capital intends to protect creditors of a corporation by obligating stockholders to some minimum level of

equity financing and by constraining a corporation from excessive payments to stockholders.

7. Common Dividend Payable is a current liability account.
8. The date of declaration, date of record, and date of payment.
9. A dividend is a legal liability at the date of declaration, on which date it is recorded as a liability.
10. A stock dividend does not transfer assets to stockholders, but it does require an amount of retained earnings to be transferred to a contributed capital account(s).
11. A small stock dividend is 25% or less of the previous outstanding shares. A large stock dividend is more than 25%.
12. Retained earnings equal to the distributable shares' market value should be capitalized for a small stock dividend.
13. Typically, preferred stock has a preference in receipt of dividends and in distribution of assets.

14. (a)
15. (b)

Total cash dividend	$288,000
To preferred shareholders	135,000*
Remainder to common shareholders	$153,000

* 9,000 × $50 × 10% × 3 years = $135,000.

16. (b)
17. No. The shares are an investment for Southern Co. and are issued and outstanding shares for Northern Corp.
18. Treasury stock does not affect the number of authorized or issued shares, but it reduces the outstanding shares.
19. (a)

Key Terms

Appropriated retained earnings (p. 474)
Authorized stock (p. 461)
Basic earnings per share (p. 477)
Book value per common share (p. 478)
Book value per preferred share (p. 478)
Call price (p. 471)
Callable preferred stock (p. 471)
Capital stock (p. 461)
Changes in accounting estimates (p. 475)
Common stock (p. 460)
Complex capital structure (p. 477)
Convertible preferred stock (p. 470)
Corporation (p. 458)
Cumulative preferred stock (p. 469)
Date of declaration (p. 465)
Date of payment (p. 465)
Date of record (p. 465)
Diluted earnings per share (p. 477)
Dilutive securities (p. 477)

Discount on stock (p. 463)
Dividend in arrears (p. 469)
Dividend yield (p. 478)
Earnings per share (EPS) (p. 477)
Financial leverage (p. 471)
Large stock dividend (p. 466)
Liquidating cash dividend (p. 466)
Market value per share (p. 461)
Minimum legal capital (p. 461)
Noncumulative preferred stock (p. 469)
Nonparticipating preferred stock (p. 470)
No-par value stock (p. 461)
Organization expenses (p. 459)
Paid-in capital (p. 462)
Paid-in capital in excess of par value (p. 463)
Participating preferred stock (p. 470)
Par value (p. 461)
Par value stock (p. 461)

Preemptive right (p. 460)
Preferred stock (p. 468)
Premium on stock (p. 463)
Price-earnings (PE) ratio (p. 477)
Prior period adjustments (p. 475)
Proxy (p. 459)
Restricted retained earnings (p. 474)
Retained earnings (p. 462)
Retained earnings deficit (p. 465)
Reverse stock split (p. 468)
Simple capital structure (p. 477)
Small stock dividend (p. 466)
Stated value stock (p. 462)
Statement of stockholders' equity (p. 475)
Stock dividend (p. 466)
Stock options (p. 476)
Stock split (p. 468)
Stockholders' equity (p. 462)
Treasury stock (p. 472)

Multiple Choice Quiz

Answers on p. 499   mhhe.com/wildFA6e

Additional quiz questions are available at the book's Website.

1. A corporation issues 6,000 shares of $5 par value common stock for $8 cash per share. The entry to record this transaction includes:
   a. A debit to Paid-In Capital in Excess of Par Value for $18,000.
   b. A credit to Common Stock for $48,000.
   c. A credit to Paid-In Capital in Excess of Par Value for $30,000.
   d. A credit to Cash for $48,000.
   e. A credit to Common Stock for $30,000.

2. A company reports net income of $75,000. Its weighted-average common shares outstanding is 19,000. It has no other stock outstanding. Its earnings per share is:
   a. $4.69
   b. $3.95
   c. $3.75
   d. $2.08
   e. $4.41

3. A company has 5,000 shares of $100 par preferred stock and 50,000 shares of $10 par common stock outstanding. Its total stockholders' equity is $2,000,000. Its book value per common share is:
   a. $100.00
   b. $ 10.00
   c. $ 40.00
   d. $ 30.00
   e. $ 36.36
4. A company paid cash dividends of $0.81 per share. Its earnings per share is $6.95 and its market price per share is $45.00. Its dividend yield is:
   a. 1.8%
   b. 11.7%
   c. 15.4%
   d. 55.6%
   e. 8.6%
5. A company's shares have a market value of $85 per share. Its net income is $3,500,000, and its weighted-average common shares outstanding is 700,000. Its price-earnings ratio is:
   a. 5.9
   b. 425.0
   c. 17.0
   d. 10.4
   e. 41.2

Icon denotes assignments that involve decision making.

Discussion Questions

1. What are organization expenses? Provide examples.
2. How are organization expenses reported?
3. Who is responsible for directing a corporation's affairs?
4. What is the preemptive right of common stockholders?
5. List the general rights of common stockholders.
6. What is the difference between authorized shares and outstanding shares?
7. Why would an investor find convertible preferred stock attractive?
8. What is the difference between the market value per share and the par value per share?
9. What is the difference between the par value and the call price of a share of preferred stock?
10. Identify and explain the importance of the three dates relevant to corporate dividends.
11. Why is the term *liquidating dividend* used to describe cash dividends debited against paid-in capital accounts?
12. How does declaring a stock dividend affect the corporation's assets, liabilities, and total equity? What are the effects of the eventual distribution of that stock?
13. What is the difference between a stock dividend and a stock split?
14. Courts have ruled that a stock dividend is not taxable income to stockholders. What justifies this decision?
15. How does the purchase of treasury stock affect the purchaser's assets and total equity?
16. Why do laws place limits on treasury stock purchases?
17. How are EPS results computed for a corporation with a simple capital structure?
18. What is a stock option?
19. How is book value per share computed for a corporation with no preferred stock? What is the main limitation of using book value per share to value a corporation?
20. Review the 2009 balance sheet for **Nokia** in Appendix A and list the amounts for treasury shares and retained earnings.
21. Refer to **Research In Motion**'s 2010 balance sheet in Appendix A. How many shares of common stock are authorized? How many shares of voting common stock are issued?
22. Refer to the 2009 balance sheet for **Palm** in Appendix A. What is the par value per share of its common stock? Suggest a rationale for the amount of par value it assigned.
23. Refer to the financial statements for **Apple** in Appendix A. What are its cash proceeds from issuance of common stock *and* its cash repurchases of common stock for the year ended September 26, 2009? Explain.

connect

Of the following statements, which are true for the corporate form of organization?
1. Owners are not agents of the corporation.
2. It is a separate legal entity.
3. It has a limited life.
4. Capital is more easily accumulated than with most other forms of organization.
5. Corporate income that is distributed to shareholders is usually taxed twice.
6. Owners have unlimited liability for corporate debts.
7. Ownership rights cannot be easily transferred.

QUICK STUDY

QS 11-1
Characteristics of corporations
C1

QS 11-2
Issuance of common stock
P1

Prepare the journal entry to record Channel One Company's issuance of 100,000 shares of $0.50 par value common stock assuming the shares sell for:
a. $0.50 cash per share.
b. $2 cash per share.

QS 11-3
Issuance of no-par common stock
P1

Prepare the journal entry to record Selectist Company's issuance of 104,000 shares of no-par value common stock assuming the shares:
a. Sell for $15 cash per share.
b. Are exchanged for land valued at $1,560,000.

QS 11-4
Issuance of par and stated value common stock
P1

Prepare the journal entry to record Typist Company's issuance of 250,000 shares of its common stock assuming the shares have a:
a. $1 par value and sell for $10 cash per share.
b. $1 stated value and sell for $10 cash per share.

QS 11-5
Issuance of common stock
P1

Prepare the issuer's journal entry for each separate transaction. (*a*) On March 1, Edgar Co. issues 44,500 shares of $4 par value common stock for $255,000 cash. (*b*) On April 1, GT Co. issues no-par value common stock for $50,000 cash. (*c*) On April 6, MTV issues 2,000 shares of $20 par value common stock for $35,000 of inventory, $135,000 of machinery, and acceptance of an $84,000 note payable.

QS 11-6
Issuance of preferred stock
P1 P2

a. Prepare the journal entry to record Stefan Company's issuance of 12,000 shares of $50 par value 6% cumulative preferred stock for $75 cash per share.
b. Assuming the facts in part 1, if Stefan declares a year-end cash dividend, what is the amount of dividend paid to preferred shareholders? (Assume no dividends in arrears.)

QS 11-7
Accounting for cash dividends
P2

Prepare journal entries to record the following transactions for Emerson Corporation.

April 15   Declared a cash dividend payable to common stockholders of $40,000.
May 15   Date of record is May 15 for the cash dividend declared on April 15.
May 31   Paid the dividend declared on April 15.

QS 11-8
Dividend allocation between classes of shareholders
C2

Stockholders' equity of STIX Company consists of 75,000 shares of $5 par value, 8% cumulative preferred stock and 200,000 shares of $1 par value common stock. Both classes of stock have been outstanding since the company's inception. STIX did not declare any dividends in the prior year, but it now declares and pays a $108,000 cash dividend at the current year-end. Determine the amount distributed to each class of stockholders for this two-year-old company.

QS 11-9
Accounting for small stock dividend
P2

The stockholders' equity section of Zacman Company's balance sheet as of April 1 follows. On April 2, Zacman declares and distributes a 10% stock dividend. The stock's per share market value on April 2 is $25 (prior to the dividend). Prepare the stockholders' equity section immediately after the stock dividend.

Common stock—$5 par value, 375,000 shares authorized, 150,000 shares issued and outstanding	$ 750,000
Paid-in capital in excess of par value, common stock	352,500
Retained earnings	633,000
Total stockholders' equity	$1,735,500

QS 11-10
Accounting for changes in estimates; error adjustments
C3

Answer the following questions related to a company's activities for the current year:

1. After using an expected useful life of 20 years and no salvage value to depreciate its office equipment over the preceding 15 years, the company decided early this year that the equipment will last only two more years. How should the effects of this decision be reported in the current year financial statements?
2. A review of the notes payable files discovers that two years ago the company reported the entire amount of a payment (principal and interest) on an installment note payable as interest expense. This mistake had a material effect on the amount of income in that year. How should the correction be reported in the current year financial statements?

On May 3, Lassman Corporation purchased 3,000 shares of its own stock for $27,000 cash. On November 4, Lassman reissued 750 shares of this treasury stock for $7,080. Prepare the May 3 and November 4 journal entries to record Lassman's purchase and reissuance of treasury stock.	**QS 11-11** Purchase and sale of treasury stock **P3**
Barnes Company earned net income of $450,000 this year. The number of common shares outstanding during the entire year was 200,000, and preferred shareholders received a $10,000 cash dividend. Compute Barnes Company's basic earnings per share.	**QS 11-12** Basic earnings per share **A1**
Campbell Company reports net income of $1,200,000 for the year. It has no preferred stock, and its weighted-average common shares outstanding is 300,000 shares. Compute its basic earnings per share.	**QS 11-13** Basic earnings per share **A1**
Compute Fox Company's price-earnings ratio if its common stock has a market value of $30.75 per share and its EPS is $4.10. Would an analyst likely consider this stock potentially over- or underpriced? Explain.	**QS 11-14** Price-earnings ratio **A2**
Fiona Company expects to pay a $2.10 per share cash dividend this year on its common stock. The current market value of Fiona stock is $28.50 per share. Compute the expected dividend yield on the Fiona stock. Would you classify the Fiona stock as a growth or an income stock? Explain.	**QS 11-15** Dividend yield **A3**
The stockholders' equity section of Axel Company's balance sheet follows. The preferred stock's call price is $30. Determine the book value per share of the common stock.	**QS 11-16** Book value per common share **A4**

Preferred stock—5% cumulative, $10 par value, 10,000 shares authorized, issued and outstanding	$100,000
Common stock—$5 par value, 100,000 shares authorized, 75,000 shares issued and outstanding	375,000
Retained earnings	445,000
Total stockholders' equity	$920,000

Air France-KLM reports the following equity information for its fiscal year ended March 31, 2009 (euros in millions). Prepare its journal entry, using its account titles, to record the issuance of capital stock assuming that its entire par value stock was issued on March 31, 2009, for cash.	**QS 11-17** International equity disclosures **P1**

March 31	2009
Issued capital	€2,552
Additional paid-in capital	765

Describe how each of the following characteristics of organizations applies to corporations.

1. Duration of life
2. Owner liability
3. Legal status
4. Tax status of income
5. Owner authority and control
6. Ease of formation
7. Transferability of ownership
8. Ability to raise large capital amounts

EXERCISES

Exercise 11-1
Characteristics of corporations
C1

Aloha Corporation issues 6,000 shares of its common stock for $144,000 cash on February 20. Prepare journal entries to record this event under each of the following separate situations.
1. The stock has neither par nor stated value.
2. The stock has a $20 par value.
3. The stock has an $8 stated value.

Exercise 11-2
Accounting for par, stated, and no-par stock issuances
P1

Exercise 11-3
Recording stock issuances
P1

Prepare journal entries to record the following four separate issuances of stock.

1. A corporation issued 2,000 shares of no-par common stock to its promoters in exchange for their efforts, estimated to be worth $30,000. The stock has no stated value.
2. A corporation issued 2,000 shares of no-par common stock to its promoters in exchange for their efforts, estimated to be worth $30,000. The stock has a $1 per share stated value.
3. A corporation issued 4,000 shares of $10 par value common stock for $70,000 cash.
4. A corporation issued 1,000 shares of $100 par value preferred stock for $120,000 cash.

Exercise 11-4
Stock issuance for noncash assets
P1

Soku Company issues 36,000 shares of $9 par value common stock in exchange for land and a building. The land is valued at $225,000 and the building at $360,000. Prepare the journal entry to record issuance of the stock in exchange for the land and building.

Exercise 11-5
Identifying characteristics of preferred stock
C2

Match each description 1 through 6 with the characteristic of preferred stock that it best describes by writing the letter of that characteristic in the blank next to each description.

- **A.** Cumulative
- **B.** Noncumulative
- **C.** Convertible
- **D.** Callable
- **E.** Nonparticipating
- **F.** Participating

____ 1. Holders of the stock lose any dividends that are not declared in the current year.
____ 2. The issuing corporation can retire the stock by paying a prespecified price.
____ 3. Holders of the stock can receive dividends exceeding the stated rate under certain conditions.
____ 4. Holders of the stock are not entitled to receive dividends in excess of the stated rate.
____ 5. Holders of this stock can exchange it for shares of common stock.
____ 6. Holders of the stock are entitled to receive current and all past dividends before common stockholders receive any dividends.

Exercise 11-6
Stock dividends and splits
P2

On June 30, 2011, Quinn Corporation's common stock is priced at $31 per share before any stock dividend or split, and the stockholders' equity section of its balance sheet appears as follows.

Common stock—$10 par value, 60,000 shares authorized, 25,000 shares issued and outstanding	$250,000
Paid-in capital in excess of par value, common stock	100,000
Retained earnings	330,000
Total stockholders' equity	$680,000

1. Assume that the company declares and immediately distributes a 100% stock dividend. This event is recorded by capitalizing retained earnings equal to the stock's par value. Answer these questions about stockholders' equity as it exists *after* issuing the new shares.
    - **a.** What is the retained earnings balance?
    - **b.** What is the amount of total stockholders' equity?
    - **c.** How many shares are outstanding?

Check (1*b*) $680,000

2. Assume that the company implements a 2-for-1 stock split instead of the stock dividend in part 1. Answer these questions about stockholders' equity as it exists *after* issuing the new shares.
    - **a.** What is the retained earnings balance?
    - **b.** What is the amount of total stockholders' equity?
    - **c.** How many shares are outstanding?

(2*a*) $330,000

3. Explain the difference, if any, to a stockholder from receiving new shares distributed under a large stock dividend versus a stock split.

Exercise 11-7
Stock dividends and per share book values
P2

The stockholders' equity of Whiz.com Company at the beginning of the day on February 5 follows.

Common stock—$25 par value, 150,000 shares authorized, 60,000 shares issued and outstanding	$1,500,000
Paid-in capital in excess of par value, common stock	525,000
Retained earnings	675,000
Total stockholders' equity	$2,700,000

On February 5, the directors declare a 20% stock dividend distributable on February 28 to the February 15 stockholders of record. The stock's market value is $40 per share on February 5 before the stock dividend. The stock's market value is $34 per share on February 28.

1. Prepare entries to record both the dividend declaration and its distribution.
2. One stockholder owned 750 shares on February 5 before the dividend. Compute the book value per share and total book value of this stockholder's shares immediately before *and* after the stock dividend of February 5.
3. Compute the total market value of the investor's shares in part 2 as of February 5 and February 28.

Check (2) Book value per share: before, $45; after, $37.50

Wade's outstanding stock consists of 40,000 shares of *noncumulative* 7.5% preferred stock with a $10 par value and also 100,000 shares of common stock with a $1 par value. During its first four years of operation, the corporation declared and paid the following total cash dividends.

2011	$ 10,000
2012	24,000
2013	100,000
2014	196,000

Determine the amount of dividends paid each year to each of the two classes of stockholders: preferred and common. Also compute the total dividends paid to each class for the four years combined.

Exercise 11-8
Dividends on common and noncumulative preferred stock
C2

Check 4-year total paid to preferred, $94,000

Use the data in Exercise 11-8 to determine the amount of dividends paid each year to each of the two classes of stockholders assuming that the preferred stock is *cumulative*. Also determine the total dividends paid to each class for the four years combined.

Exercise 11-9
Dividends on common and cumulative preferred stock C2

On October 10, the stockholders' equity of Noble Systems appears as follows.

Common stock—$10 par value, 36,000 shares authorized, issued, and outstanding	$360,000
Paid-in capital in excess of par value, common stock	108,000
Retained earnings	432,000
Total stockholders' equity	$900,000

1. Prepare journal entries to record the following transactions for Noble Systems.
   a. Purchased 4,500 shares of its own common stock at $30 per share on October 11.
   b. Sold 1,200 treasury shares on November 1 for $36 cash per share.
   c. Sold all remaining treasury shares on November 25 for $25 cash per share.
2. Explain how the company's equity section changes after the October 11 treasury stock purchase, and prepare the revised equity section of its balance sheet at that date.

Exercise 11-10
Recording and reporting treasury stock transactions
P3

Check (1c) Dr. Retained Earnings, $9,300

The following information is available for Ballard Company for the year ended December 31, 2011.
a. Balance of retained earnings, December 31, 2010, prior to discovery of error, $850,000.
b. Cash dividends declared and paid during 2011, $15,000.
c. It neglected to record 2009 depreciation expense of $55,600, which is net of $5,500 in income taxes.
d. The company earned $205,000 in 2011 net income.

Prepare a 2011 statement of retained earnings for Ballard Company.

Exercise 11-11
Preparing a statement of retained earnings
C3

Guess Company reports $648,500 of net income for 2011 and declares $102,500 of cash dividends on its preferred stock for 2011. At the end of 2011, the company had 260,000 weighted-average shares of common stock.

1. What amount of net income is available to common stockholders for 2011?
2. What is the company's basic EPS for 2011?

Exercise 11-12
Earnings per share
A1

Check (2) $2.10

Exercise 11-13
Earnings per share
A1

Check (2) $3.56

Franklin Company reports $698,000 of net income for 2011 and declares $75,500 of cash dividends on its preferred stock for 2011. At the end of 2011, the company had 175,000 weighted-average shares of common stock.

1. What amount of net income is available to common stockholders for 2011?
2. What is the company's basic EPS for 2011? Round your answer to the nearest whole cent.

Exercise 11-14
Dividend yield computation and interpretation
A3

Compute the dividend yield for each of these four separate companies. Which company's stock would probably *not* be classified as an income stock? Explain.

Company	Annual Cash Dividend per Share	Market Value per Share
1	$15.00	$216.00
2	12.00	128.00
3	6.00	61.00
4	1.20	86.00

Exercise 11-15
Price-earnings ratio computation and interpretation
A2

Compute the price-earnings ratio for each of these four separate companies. Which stock might an analyst likely investigate as being potentially undervalued by the market? Explain.

Company	Earnings per Share	Market Value per Share
1	$10.00	$166.00
2	9.00	90.00
3	6.50	84.50
4	40.00	240.00

Exercise 11-16
Book value per share
A4

The equity section of Webster Corporation's balance sheet shows the following.

Preferred stock—5% cumulative, $10 par value, $15 call price, 10,000 shares issued and outstanding	$100,000
Common stock—$10 par value, 55,000 shares issued and outstanding	550,000
Retained earnings	267,500
Total stockholders' equity	$917,500

Determine the book value per share of the preferred and common stock under two separate situations.

Check (1) Book value of common, $13.95

1. No preferred dividends are in arrears.
2. Three years of preferred dividends are in arrears.

Exercise 11-17
Accounting for equity under IFRS
C3 P1

Unilever Group reports the following equity information for the years ended December 31, 2007 and 2008 (euros in millions).

December 31	2008	2007
Share capital	€ 484	€ 484
Share premium	121	153
Other reserves	(6,469)	(3,412)
Retained profit	15,812	15,162
Shareholders' equity	€ 9,948	€12,387

1. For each of the three account titles *share capital, share premium,* and *retained profit,* match it with the usual account title applied under U.S. GAAP from the following options:
   a. Paid-in capital in excess of par value, common stock
   b. Retained earnings
   c. Common stock, par value
2. Prepare Unilever's journal entry, using its account titles, to record the issuance of capital stock assuming that its entire par value stock was issued on December 31, 2007, for cash.
3. What were Unilever's 2008 dividends assuming that only dividends and income impacted retained profit for 2008 and that its 2008 income totaled €2,692?

Kroll Corporation reports the following components of stockholders' equity on December 31, 2011.

Common stock—$25 par value, 40,000 shares authorized, 30,000 shares issued and outstanding	$ 750,000
Paid-in capital in excess of par value, common stock	50,000
Retained earnings	260,000
Total stockholders' equity	$1,060,000

Exercise 11-18
Cash dividends, treasury stock, and statement of retained earnings

C3 P2 P3

In year 2012, the following transactions affected its stockholders' equity accounts.

Jan. 2 Purchased 2,000 shares of its own stock at $25 cash per share.
Jan. 7 Directors declared a $2 per share cash dividend payable on Feb. 28 to the Feb. 9 stockholders of record.
Feb. 28 Paid the dividend declared on January 7.
July 9 Sold 500 of its treasury shares at $30 cash per share.
Aug. 27 Sold 1,500 of its treasury shares at $23 cash per share.
Sept. 9 Directors declared a $2 per share cash dividend payable on October 22 to the September 23 stockholders of record.
Oct. 22 Paid the dividend declared on September 9.
Dec. 31 Closed the $8,000 credit balance (from net income) in the Income Summary account to Retained Earnings.

Required
1. Prepare journal entries to record each of these transactions for 2012.
2. Prepare a statement of retained earnings for the year ended December 31, 2012.
3. Prepare the stockholders' equity section of the company's balance sheet as of December 31, 2012.

---

connect

Oxygen Co. is incorporated at the beginning of this year and engages in a number of transactions. The following journal entries impacted its stockholders' equity during its first year of operations.

PROBLEM SET A

Problem 11-1A
Stockholders' equity transactions and analysis

C2 P1

a.		Cash	150,000	
		Common Stock, $25 Par Value		125,000
		Paid-In Capital in Excess of Par Value, Common Stock		25,000
b.		Organization Expenses	75,000	
		Common Stock, $25 Par Value		62,500
		Paid-In Capital in Excess of Par Value, Common Stock		12,500
c.		Cash	21,500	
		Accounts Receivable	7,500	
		Building	30,000	
		Notes Payable		19,000
		Common Stock, $25 Par Value		25,000
		Paid-In Capital in Excess of Par Value, Common Stock		15,000

[continued on next page]

d.	Cash	60,000	
	Common Stock, $25 Par Value		37,500
	Paid-In Capital in Excess of Par Value, Common Stock		22,500

Required

1. Explain the transaction(s) underlying each journal entry (*a*) through (*d*).
2. How many shares of common stock are outstanding at year-end?
3. What is the amount of minimum legal capital (based on par value) at year-end?
4. What is the total paid-in capital at year-end?
5. What is the book value per share of the common stock at year-end if total paid-in capital plus retained earnings equals $347,500?

Check (2) 10,000 shares
(3) $250,000
(4) $325,000

Problem 11-2A
Cash dividends, treasury stock, and statement of retained earnings

C3 P2 P3

Context Corporation reports the following components of stockholders' equity on December 31, 2011.

Common stock—$10 par value, 50,000 shares authorized, 20,000 shares issued and outstanding	$200,000
Paid-in capital in excess of par value, common stock	30,000
Retained earnings	135,000
Total stockholders' equity	$365,000

In year 2012, the following transactions affected its stockholders' equity accounts.

Jan. 1 Purchased 2,000 shares of its own stock at $20 cash per share.
Jan. 5 Directors declared a $2 per share cash dividend payable on Feb. 28 to the Feb. 5 stockholders of record.
Feb. 28 Paid the dividend declared on January 5.
July 6 Sold 750 of its treasury shares at $24 cash per share.
Aug. 22 Sold 1,250 of its treasury shares at $17 cash per share.
Sept. 5 Directors declared a $2 per share cash dividend payable on October 28 to the September 25 stockholders of record.
Oct. 28 Paid the dividend declared on September 5.
Dec. 31 Closed the $194,000 credit balance (from net income) in the Income Summary account to Retained Earnings.

Required

1. Prepare journal entries to record each of these transactions for 2012.
2. Prepare a statement of retained earnings for the year ended December 31, 2012.
3. Prepare the stockholders' equity section of the company's balance sheet as of December 31, 2012.

Check (2) Retained earnings, Dec. 31, 2012, $252,250

Problem 11-3A
Equity analysis—journal entries and account balances

P2

At September 30, the end of Excel Company's third quarter, the following stockholders' equity accounts are reported.

Common stock, $12 par value	$720,000
Paid-in capital in excess of par value, common stock	180,000
Retained earnings	640,000

In the fourth quarter, the following entries related to its equity are recorded.

Oct. 2	Retained Earnings	120,000	
	Common Dividend Payable		120,000
Oct. 25	Common Dividend Payable	120,000	
	Cash		120,000
Oct. 31	Retained Earnings	150,000	
	Common Stock Dividend Distributable		72,000
	Paid-In Capital in Excess of Par Value, Common Stock		78,000

[continued on next page]

Nov. 5	Common Stock Dividend Distributable	72,000	
	Common Stock, $12 Par Value		72,000
Dec. 1	Memo—Change the title of the common stock account to reflect the new par value of $4.		
Dec. 31	Income Summary	420,000	
	Retained Earnings		420,000

Required

1. Explain the transaction(s) underlying each journal entry.
2. Complete the following table showing the equity account balances at each indicated date (include the balances from September 30).

	Oct. 2	Oct. 25	Oct. 31	Nov. 5	Dec. 1	Dec. 31
Common stock	$____	$____	$____	$____	$____	$____
Common stock dividend distributable	____	____	____	____	____	____
Paid-in capital in excess of par, common stock	____	____	____	____	____	____
Retained earnings	____	____	____	____	____	____
Total equity	$____	$____	$____	$____	$____	$____

Check Total equity: Oct. 2, $1,420,000; Dec. 31, $1,840,000

The equity sections from Salazar Group's 2011 and 2012 year-end balance sheets follow.

Problem 11-4A
Analysis of changes in stockholders' equity accounts

C3 P2 P3

Stockholders' Equity (December 31, 2011)

Common stock—$4 par value, 50,000 shares authorized, 20,000 shares issued and outstanding	$ 80,000
Paid-in capital in excess of par value, common stock	60,000
Retained earnings	160,000
Total stockholders' equity	$300,000

Stockholders' Equity (December 31, 2012)

Common stock—$4 par value, 50,000 shares authorized, 23,700 shares issued, 1,500 shares in treasury	$ 94,800
Paid-in capital in excess of par value, common stock	89,600
Retained earnings ($15,000 restricted by treasury stock)	200,000
	384,400
Less cost of treasury stock	(15,000)
Total stockholders' equity	$369,400

The following transactions and events affected its equity during year 2012.

Jan. 5 Declared a $0.50 per share cash dividend, date of record January 10.
Mar. 20 Purchased treasury stock for cash.
Apr. 5 Declared a $0.50 per share cash dividend, date of record April 10.
July 5 Declared a $0.50 per share cash dividend, date of record July 10.
July 31 Declared a 20% stock dividend when the stock's market value is $12 per share.
Aug. 14 Issued the stock dividend that was declared on July 31.
Oct. 5 Declared a $0.50 per share cash dividend, date of record October 10.

Required

1. How many common shares are outstanding on each cash dividend date?
2. What is the total dollar amount for each of the four cash dividends?
3. What is the amount of the capitalization of retained earnings for the stock dividend?
4. What is the per share cost of the treasury stock purchased?
5. How much net income did the company earn during year 2012?

Check (3) $44,400
(4) $10
(5) $124,000

Problem 11-5A
Computation of book values and dividend allocations

C2 A4

Razz Corporation's common stock is currently selling on a stock exchange at $170 per share, and its current balance sheet shows the following stockholders' equity section.

Preferred stock—5% cumulative, $___ par value, 1,000 shares authorized, issued, and outstanding	$100,000
Common stock—$___ par value, 4,000 shares authorized, issued, and outstanding	160,000
Retained earnings	300,000
Total stockholders' equity	$560,000

Required (Round per share amounts to cents.)

1. What is the current market value (price) of this corporation's common stock?
2. What are the par values of the corporation's preferred stock and its common stock?
3. If no dividends are in arrears, what are the book values per share of the preferred stock and the common stock?
4. If two years' preferred dividends are in arrears, what are the book values per share of the preferred stock and the common stock?
5. If two years' preferred dividends are in arrears and the preferred stock is callable at $110 per share, what are the book values per share of the preferred stock and the common stock?
6. If two years' preferred dividends are in arrears and the board of directors declares cash dividends of $20,000, what total amount will be paid to the preferred and to the common shareholders? What is the amount of dividends per share for the common stock?

Analysis Component

7. What are some factors that can contribute to a difference between the book value of common stock and its market value (price)?

Check (4) Book value of common, $112.50
(5) Book value of common, $110
(6) Dividends per common share, $1.25

PROBLEM SET B

Problem 11-1B
Stockholders' equity transactions and analysis

C2 P1

Nilson Company is incorporated at the beginning of this year and engages in a number of transactions. The following journal entries impacted its stockholders' equity during its first year of operations.

a.	Cash	60,000	
	Common Stock, $1 Par Value		1,500
	Paid-In Capital in Excess of Par Value, Common Stock		58,500
b.	Organization Expenses	20,000	
	Common Stock, $1 Par Value		500
	Paid-In Capital in Excess of Par Value, Common Stock		19,500
c.	Cash	6,650	
	Accounts Receivable	4,000	
	Building	12,500	
	Notes Payable		3,150
	Common Stock, $1 Par Value		400
	Paid-In Capital in Excess of Par Value, Common Stock		19,600
d.	Cash	30,000	
	Common Stock, $1 Par Value		600
	Paid-In Capital in Excess of Par Value, Common Stock		29,400

Required

1. Explain the transaction(s) underlying each journal entry (*a*) through (*d*).
2. How many shares of common stock are outstanding at year-end?
3. What is the amount of minimum legal capital (based on par value) at year-end?

Check (2) 3,000 shares
(3) $3,000

4. What is the total paid-in capital at year-end? (4) $130,000
5. What is the book value per share of the common stock at year-end if total paid-in capital plus retained earnings equals $141,500?

Baycore Corp. reports the following components of stockholders' equity on December 31, 2011.

Common stock—$1 par value, 160,000 shares authorized, 100,000 shares issued and outstanding	$ 100,000
Paid-in capital in excess of par value, common stock	700,000
Retained earnings	1,080,000
Total stockholders' equity	$1,880,000

Problem 11-2B
Cash dividends, treasury stock, and statement of retained earnings
C3 P2 P3

It completed the following transactions related to stockholders' equity in year 2012.

Jan. 10 Purchased 20,000 shares of its own stock at $12 cash per share.
Mar. 2 Directors declared a $1.50 per share cash dividend payable on March 31 to the March 15 stockholders of record.
Mar. 31 Paid the dividend declared on March 2.
Nov. 11 Sold 12,000 of its treasury shares at $13 cash per share.
Nov. 25 Sold 8,000 of its treasury shares at $9.50 cash per share.
Dec. 1 Directors declared a $2.50 per share cash dividend payable on January 2 to the December 10 stockholders of record.
Dec. 31 Closed the $536,000 credit balance (from net income) in the Income Summary account to Retained Earnings.

Required

1. Prepare journal entries to record each of these transactions for 2012.
2. Prepare a statement of retained earnings for the year ended December 31, 2012.
3. Prepare the stockholders' equity section of the company's balance sheet as of December 31, 2012.

Check (2) Retained earnings, Dec. 31, 2012, $1,238,000

At December 31, the end of Intertec Communication's third quarter, the following stockholders' equity accounts are reported.

Common stock, $10 par value	$480,000
Paid-in capital in excess of par value, common stock	192,000
Retained earnings	800,000

Problem 11-3B
Equity analysis—journal entries and account balances
P2

In the fourth quarter, the following entries related to its equity are recorded.

Date	Account	Debit	Credit
Jan. 17	Retained Earnings	48,000	
	Common Dividend Payable		48,000
Feb. 5	Common Dividend Payable	48,000	
	Cash		48,000
Feb. 28	Retained Earnings	126,000	
	Common Stock Dividend Distributable		60,000
	Paid-In Capital in Excess of Par Value, Common Stock		66,000
Mar. 14	Common Stock Dividend Distributable	60,000	
	Common Stock, $10 Par Value		60,000
Mar. 25	Memo—Change the title of the common stock account to reflect the new par value of $5.		
Mar. 31	Income Summary	360,000	
	Retained Earnings		360,000

Required

1. Explain the transaction(s) underlying each journal entry.
2. Complete the following table showing the equity account balances at each indicated date (include the balances from December 31).

	Jan. 17	Feb. 5	Feb. 28	Mar. 14	Mar. 25	Mar. 31
Common stock	$____	$____	$____	$____	$____	$____
Common stock dividend distributable	____	____	____	____	____	____
Paid-in capital in excess of par, common stock	____	____	____	____	____	____
Retained earnings	____	____	____	____	____	____
Total equity	$____	$____	$____	$____	$____	$____

Check Total equity: Jan. 17, $1,424,000; Mar. 31, $1,784,000

Problem 11-4B
Analysis of changes in stockholders' equity accounts

C3 P2 P3

The equity sections from Jetta Corporation's 2011 and 2012 balance sheets follow.

Stockholders' Equity (December 31, 2011)

Common stock—$20 par value, 15,000 shares authorized, 8,500 shares issued and outstanding	$170,000
Paid-in capital in excess of par value, common stock	30,000
Retained earnings	135,000
Total stockholders' equity	$335,000

Stockholders' Equity (December 31, 2012)

Common stock—$20 par value, 15,000 shares authorized, 9,500 shares issued, 500 shares in treasury	$190,000
Paid-in capital in excess of par value, common stock	52,000
Retained earnings ($20,000 restricted by treasury stock)	147,600
	389,600
Less cost of treasury stock	(20,000)
Total stockholders' equity	$369,600

The following transactions and events affected its equity during year 2012.

Feb. 15 Declared a $0.40 per share cash dividend, date of record five days later.
Mar. 2 Purchased treasury stock for cash.
May 15 Declared a $0.40 per share cash dividend, date of record five days later.
Aug. 15 Declared a $0.40 per share cash dividend, date of record five days later.
Oct. 4 Declared a 12.5% stock dividend when the stock's market value is $42 per share.
Oct. 20 Issued the stock dividend that was declared on October 4.
Nov. 15 Declared a $0.40 per share cash dividend, date of record five days later.

Required

1. How many common shares are outstanding on each cash dividend date?
2. What is the total dollar amount for each of the four cash dividends?
3. What is the amount of the capitalization of retained earnings for the stock dividend?
4. What is the per share cost of the treasury stock purchased?
5. How much net income did the company earn during year 2012?

Check (3) $42,000
(4) $40
(5) $68,000

Problem 11-5B
Computation of book values and dividend allocations

C2 A4

Scotch Company's common stock is currently selling on a stock exchange at $45 per share, and its current balance sheet shows the following stockholders' equity section.

Preferred stock—8% cumulative, $____ par value, 1,500 shares authorized, issued, and outstanding	$ 187,500
Common stock—$____ par value, 18,000 shares authorized, issued, and outstanding	450,000
Retained earnings	562,500
Total stockholders' equity	$1,200,000

Required (Round per share amounts to cents.)

1. What is the current market value (price) of this corporation's common stock?
2. What are the par values of the corporation's preferred stock and its common stock?
3. If no dividends are in arrears, what are the book values per share of the preferred stock and the common stock? (Round per share values to the nearest cent.)
4. If two years' preferred dividends are in arrears, what are the book values per share of the preferred stock and the common stock? (Round per share values to the nearest cent.)
5. If two years' preferred dividends are in arrears and the preferred stock is callable at $140 per share, what are the book values per share of the preferred stock and the common stock? (Round per share values to the nearest cent.)
6. If two years' preferred dividends are in arrears and the board of directors declares cash dividends of $50,000, what total amount will be paid to the preferred and to the common shareholders? What is the amount of dividends per share for the common stock? (Round per share values to the nearest cent.)

Check (4) Book value of common, $54.58

(5) Book value of common, $53.33

(6) Dividends per common share, $0.28

Analysis Component

7. Discuss why the book value of common stock is not always a good estimate of its market value.

(This serial problem began in Chapter 1 and continues through most of the book. If previous chapter segments were not completed, the serial problem can begin at this point. It is helpful, but not necessary, to use the Working Papers that accompany the book.)

SERIAL PROBLEM
Business Solutions
P1 C1 C2

SP 11 Santana Rey created Business Solutions on October 1, 2011. The company has been successful, and Santana plans to expand her business. She believes that an additional $86,000 is needed and is investigating three funding sources.

a. Santana's sister Cicely is willing to invest $86,000 in the business as a common shareholder. Since Santana currently has about $129,000 invested in the business, Cicely's investment will mean that Santana will maintain about 60% ownership, and Cicely will have 40% ownership of Business Solutions.
b. Santana's uncle Marcello is willing to invest $86,000 in the business as a preferred shareholder. Marcello would purchase 860 shares of $100 par value, 7% preferred stock.
c. Santana's banker is willing to lend her $86,000 on a 7%, 10-year note payable. She would make monthly payments of $1,000 per month for 10 years.

Required

1. Prepare the journal entry to reflect the initial $86,000 investment under each of the options (a), (b), and (c).
2. Evaluate the three proposals for expansion, providing the pros and cons of each option.
3. Which option do you recommend Santana adopt? Explain.

Beyond the Numbers

BTN 11-1 Refer to **Research In Motion**'s financial statements in Appendix A to answer the following.

1. How many shares of common stock are issued and outstanding at February 27, 2010, and February 28, 2009? How do these numbers compare with the basic weighted-average common shares outstanding at February 27, 2010, and February 28, 2009?
2. What is the book value of its entire common stock at February 27, 2010?
3. What is the total amount of cash dividends paid to common stockholders for the years ended February 27, 2010, and February 28, 2009?
4. Identify and compare basic EPS amounts across fiscal years 2010, 2009, and 2008. Identify and comment on any notable changes.
5. How many shares does Research In Motion hold in treasury stock, if any, as of February 27, 2010? As of February 28, 2009?

REPORTING IN ACTION
C2 A1 A4

RIM

Fast Forward

6. Access Research In Motion's financial statements for fiscal years ending after February 27, 2010, from its Website (**RIM.com**) or the SEC's EDGAR database (**www.sec.gov**). Has the number of common shares outstanding increased since that date? Has the company increased the total amount of cash dividends paid compared to the total amount for fiscal year 2010?

COMPARATIVE ANALYSIS

A1 A2 A3 A4

RIM
Palm
Apple

BTN 11-2 Key comparative figures for **Research In Motion**, **Palm**, and **Apple** follow.

Key Figures	Research In Motion	Palm	Apple
Net income (in millions)	$2,457	$ (753)	$8,235
Cash dividends declared per common share	$ —	$ —	$ —
Common shares outstanding (in millions)	557	140	900
Weighted-average common shares outstanding (in mil.)	564	116	893
Market value (price) per share	$69.76	$12.19	$184.40
Equity applicable to common shares (in millions)	$7,603	$ (414)	$31,640

Required

1. Compute the book value per common share for each company using these data.
2. Compute the basic EPS for each company using these data.
3. Compute the dividend yield for each company using these data. Does the dividend yield of any of the companies characterize it as an income or growth stock? Explain.
4. Compute, compare, and interpret the price-earnings ratio for each company using these data.

ETHICS CHALLENGE

C3

BTN 11-3 Gianna Tuck is an accountant for Post Pharmaceuticals. Her duties include tracking research and development spending in the new product development division. Over the course of the past six months, Gianna notices that a great deal of funds have been spent on a particular project for a new drug. She hears "through the grapevine" that the company is about to patent the drug and expects it to be a major advance in antibiotics. Gianna believes that this new drug will greatly improve company performance and will cause the company's stock to increase in value. Gianna decides to purchase shares of Post in order to benefit from this expected increase.

Required

What are Gianna's ethical responsibilities, if any, with respect to the information she has learned through her duties as an accountant for Post Pharmaceuticals? What are the implications to her planned purchase of Post shares?

COMMUNICATING IN PRACTICE

A1 A2

Hint: Make a transparency of each team's memo for a class discussion.

BTN 11-4 Teams are to select an industry, and each team member is to select a different company in that industry. Each team member then is to acquire the selected company's financial statements (or Form 10-K) from the SEC site (www.SEC.gov). Use these data to identify basic EPS. Use the financial press (or finance.yahoo.com) to determine the market price of this stock, and then compute the price-earnings ratio. Communicate with teammates via a meeting, e-mail, or telephone to discuss the meaning of this ratio, how companies compare, and the industry norm. The team must prepare a single memorandum reporting the ratio for each company and identifying the team conclusions or consensus of opinion. The memorandum is to be duplicated and distributed to the instructor and teammates.

TAKING IT TO THE NET

C1 C3

BTN 11-5 Access the February 26, 2010, filing of the 2009 calendar-year 10-K report of **McDonald's**, (ticker MCD) from www.SEC.gov.

Required

1. Review McDonald's balance sheet and identify how many classes of stock it has issued.
2. What are the par values, number of authorized shares, and issued shares of the classes of stock you identified in part 1?
3. Review its statement of cash flows and identify what total amount of cash it paid in 2009 to purchase treasury stock.
4. What amount did McDonald's pay out in common stock cash dividends for 2009?

TEAMWORK IN ACTION

P3

Hint: Instructor should be sure each team accurately completes part 1 before proceeding.

BTN 11-6 This activity requires teamwork to reinforce understanding of accounting for treasury stock.

1. Write a brief team statement (*a*) generalizing what happens to a corporation's financial position when it engages in a stock "buyback" and (*b*) identifying reasons why a corporation would engage in this activity.
2. Assume that an entity acquires 100 shares of its $100 par value common stock at a cost of $134 cash per share. Discuss the entry to record this acquisition. Next, assign *each* team member to prepare *one* of the following entries (assume each entry applies to all shares):
   a. Reissue treasury shares at cost.
   b. Reissue treasury shares at $150 per share.

c. Reissue treasury shares at $120 per share; assume the paid-in capital account from treasury shares has a $1,500 balance.

d. Reissue treasury shares at $120 per share; assume the paid-in capital account from treasury shares has a $1,000 balance.

e. Reissue treasury shares at $120 per share; assume the paid-in capital account from treasury shares has a zero balance.

3. In sequence, each member is to present his/her entry to the team and explain the *similarities* and *differences* between that entry and the previous entry.

BTN 11-7 Assume that Kelly Giard of Clean Air Lawn Care decides to launch a new retail chain to market electrical mowers. This chain, named Mow Green, requires $500,000 of start-up capital. Kelly contributes $375,000 of personal assets in return for 15,000 shares of common stock, but he must raise another $125,000 in cash. There are two alternative plans for raising the additional cash. *Plan A* is to sell 3,750 shares of common stock to one or more investors for $125,000 cash. *Plan B* is to sell 1,250 shares of cumulative preferred stock to one or more investors for $125,000 cash (this preferred stock would have a $100 par value, an annual 8% dividend rate, and be issued at par).

ENTREPRENEURIAL DECISION
C2 P2

1. If the new business is expected to earn $72,000 of after-tax net income in the first year, what rate of return on beginning equity will Kelly earn under each alternative plan? Which plan will provide the higher expected return?
2. If the new business is expected to earn $16,800 of after-tax net income in the first year, what rate of return on beginning equity will Kelly earn under each alternative plan? Which plan will provide the higher expected return?
3. Analyze and interpret the differences between the results for parts 1 and 2.

BTN 11-8 Review 30 to 60 minutes of financial news programming on television. Take notes on companies that are catching analysts' attention. You might hear reference to over- and undervaluation of firms and to reports about PE ratios, dividend yields, and earnings per share. Be prepared to give a brief description to the class of your observations.

HITTING THE ROAD
A1 A2 A3

BTN 11-9 Financial information for Nokia Corporation (www.nokia.com) follows.

Net income (in millions)	€ 260
Cash dividends declared (in millions)	€ 1,481
Cash dividends declared per share	€ 0.40
Number of shares outstanding (in millions)*	3,708
Equity applicable to shares (in millions)	€14,749

*Assume that for Nokia the year-end number of shares outstanding approximates the weighted-average shares outstanding.

GLOBAL DECISION
A1 C3

NOKIA

Required

1. Compute book value per share for Nokia.
2. Compute earnings per share (EPS) for Nokia.
3. Compare Nokia's dividends per share with its EPS. Is Nokia paying out a large or small amount of its income as dividends? Explain.

ANSWERS TO MULTIPLE CHOICE QUIZ

1. e; Entry to record this stock issuance is:

Cash (6,000 × $8)	48,000	
Common Stock (6,000 × $5)		30,000
Paid-In Capital in Excess of Par Value, Common Stock		18,000

2. b; $75,000/19,000 shares = $3.95 per share

3. d; Preferred stock = 5,000 × $100 = $500,000
   Book value per share = ($2,000,000 − $500,000)/50,000 shares = $30 per common share
4. a; $0.81/$45.00 = 1.8%
5. c; Earnings per share = $3,500,000/700,000 shares = $5 per share
   PE ratio = $85/$5 = 17.0

Appendix A

Financial Statement Information

This appendix includes financial information for (1) **Research In Motion**, (2) **Apple**, (3) **Palm**, and (4) **Nokia**. This information is taken from their annual reports (Form 10-K for Apple and Palm, 40-F for RIM, and 20-F for Nokia) filed with the SEC. An **annual report** is a summary of a company's financial results for the year along with its current financial condition and future plans. This report is directed to external users of financial information, but it also affects the actions and decisions of internal users.

A company often uses an annual report to showcase itself and its products. Many annual reports include photos, diagrams, and illustrations related to the company. The primary objective of annual reports, however, is the *financial section,* which communicates much information about a company, with most data drawn from the accounting information system. The layout of an annual report's financial section is fairly established and typically includes the following:

- Letter to Shareholders
- Financial History and Highlights
- Management Discussion and Analysis
- Management's Report on Financial Statements and on Internal Controls
- Report of Independent Accountants (Auditor's Report) and on Internal Controls
- Financial Statements
- Notes to Financial Statements
- List of Directors and Officers

This appendix provides the financial statements for Research In Motion (plus selected notes), Apple, Palm, and Nokia. The appendix is organized as follows:

- **Research In Motion** A-2 through A-18
- **Apple** A-19 through A-23
- **Palm** A-24 through A-28
- **Nokia** A-29 through A-33

RIM
Apple
Palm
NOKIA

Many assignments at the end of each chapter refer to information in this appendix. We encourage readers to spend time with these assignments; they are especially useful in showing the relevance and diversity of financial accounting and reporting.

Special note: The SEC maintains the EDGAR (**E**lectronic **D**ata **G**athering, **A**nalysis, and **R**etrieval) database at www.sec.gov. The **Form 10-K** is the annual report form for most companies; **Form 10-K/A** refers to an amendment of the original Form 10-K. It provides electronically accessible information. The **Form 10-KSB** is the annual report form filed by small businesses. It requires slightly less information than the Form 10-K. One of these forms must be filed within 90 days after the company's fiscal year-end. (Forms 10-K405, 10-KT, 10-KT405, and 10-KSB405 are slight variations of the usual form due to certain regulations or rules; Forms 40-F and 20-F are common for international companies.)

A-1

Research In Motion Financial Report

Research In Motion Limited
Summary Data—Management's Discussion and Analysis of Financial Condition and Results of Operations

As at and for the Fiscal Year Ended	February 27, 2010	February 28, 2009	March 1, 2008	March 3, 2007	March 4, 2006
	(in thousands, except for per share amounts)				
Revenue	$ 14,953,224	$ 11,065,186	$ 6,009,395	$ 3,037,103	$ 2,065,845
Cost of sales	8,368,958	5,967,888	2,928,814	1,379,301	925,598
Gross margin	6,584,266	5,097,298	3,080,581	1,657,802	1,140,247
Operating expenses					
Research and development	964,841	684,702	359,828	236,173	158,887
Selling, marketing, and administration	1,907,398	1,495,697	881,482	537,922	314,317
Amortization	310,357	194,803	108,112	76,879	49,951
Litigation	163,800	—	—	—	201,791
Total operating expenses	3,346,396	2,375,202	1,349,422	850,974	724,946
Income from operations	3,237,870	2,722,096	1,731,159	806,828	415,301
Investment income	28,640	78,267	79,361	52,117	66,218
Income before income taxes	3,266,510	2,800,363	1,810,520	858,945	481,519
Provision for income taxes	809,366	907,747	516,653	227,373	106,863
Net income	$ 2,457,144	$ 1,892,616	$ 1,293,867	$ 631,572	$ 374,656
Earnings per share					
Basic	$ 4.35	$ 3.35	$ 2.31	$ 1.14	$ 0.66
Diluted	$ 4.31	$ 3.30	$ 2.26	$ 1.10	$ 0.64
Weighted-average number of shares outstanding (000's)					
Basic	564,492	565,059	559,778	556,059	566,742
Diluted	569,759	574,156	572,830	571,809	588,468
Total asset	$ 10,204,409	$ 8,101,372	$ 5,511,187	$ 3,088,949	$ 2,314,349
Total liabilities	$ 2,601,746	$ 2,227,244	$ 1,577,621	$ 605,449	$ 318,934
Total long-term liabilities	$ 169,969	$ 111,893	$ 103,190	$ 58,874	$ 34,709
Shareholders' equity	$ 7,602,663	$ 5,874,128	$ 3,933,566	$ 2,483,500	$ 1,995,415

REPORT OF
INDEPENDENT REGISTERED PUBLIC ACCOUNTING FIRM

To the Shareholders of **Research In Motion Limited**

We have audited the accompanying consolidated balance sheets of **Research In Motion Limited** [the "Company"] as at February 27, 2010 and February 28, 2009, and the related consolidated statements of operations, shareholders' equity and cash flows for the years ended February 27, 2010, February 28, 2009 and March 1, 2008. These financial statements are the responsibility of the Company's management. Our responsibility is to express an opinion on these financial statements based on our audits.

We conducted our audits in accordance with Canadian generally accepted auditing standards and the standards of the Public Company Accounting Oversight Board (United States). Those standards require that we plan and perform the audit to obtain reasonable assurance about whether the financial statements are free of material misstatement. An audit includes examining, on a test basis, evidence supporting the amounts and disclosures in the financial statements. An audit also includes assessing the accounting principles used and significant estimates made by management, as well as evaluating the overall financial statement presentation. We believe that our audits provide a reasonable basis for our opinion.

In our opinion, the consolidated financial statements referred to above present fairly, in all material respects, the financial position of the Company as at February 27, 2010 and February 28, 2009, and the results of its operations and its cash flows for the years ended February 27, 2010, February 28, 2009 and March 1, 2008, in conformity with United States generally accepted accounting principles.

We also have audited, in accordance with the standards of the Public Company Accounting Oversight Board (United States), the Company's internal control over financial reporting as of February 27, 2010, based on criteria established in Internal Control-Integrated Framework issued by the Committee of Sponsoring Organizations of the Treadway Commission and our report dated April 1, 2010 expressed an unqualified opinion thereon.

Ernst & Young LLP

Kitchener, Canada,
April 1, 2010.

Chartered Accountants
Licensed Public Accountants

REPORT OF
INDEPENDENT REGISTERED PUBLIC ACCOUNTING FIRM
ON INTERNAL CONTROL OVER FINANCIAL REPORTING

To the Shareholders of **Research In Motion Limited**

We have audited **Research In Motion Limited's** [the "Company"] internal control over financial reporting as of February 27, 2010, based on criteria established in Internal Control — Integrated Framework issued by the Committee of Sponsoring Organizations of the Treadway Commission ["the COSO criteria"]. The Company's management is responsible for maintaining effective internal control over financial reporting, and for its assessment of the effectiveness of internal control over financial reporting. Our responsibility is to express an opinion on the Company's internal control over financial reporting based on our audit.

We conducted our audit in accordance with the standards of the Public Company Accounting Oversight Board (United States). Those standards require that we plan and perform the audit to obtain reasonable assurance about whether effective internal control over financial reporting was maintained in all material respects. Our audit included obtaining an understanding of internal control over financial reporting, assessing the risk that a material weakness exists, testing and evaluating the design and operating effectiveness of internal control based on the assessed risk, and performing such other procedures as we considered necessary in the circumstances. We believe that our audit provides a reasonable basis for our opinion.

A company's internal control over financial reporting is a process designed to provide reasonable assurance regarding the reliability of financial reporting and the preparation of financial statements for external purposes in accordance with generally accepted accounting principles. A company's internal control over financial reporting includes those policies and procedures that [1] pertain to the maintenance of records that, in reasonable detail, accurately and fairly reflect the transactions and dispositions of the assets of the company; [2] provide reasonable assurance that transactions are recorded as necessary to permit preparation of financial statements in accordance with generally accepted accounting principles, and that receipts and expenditures of the company are being made only in accordance with authorizations of management and directors of the company; and [3] provide reasonable assurance regarding prevention or timely detection of unauthorized acquisition, use or disposition of the company's assets that could have a material effect on the financial statements.

Because of its inherent limitations, internal control over financial reporting may not prevent or detect misstatements. Also, projections of any evaluation of effectiveness to future periods are subject to the risk that controls may become inadequate because of changes in conditions, or that the degree of compliance with the policies or procedures may deteriorate.

In our opinion, the Company maintained, in all material respects, effective internal control over financial reporting as of February 27, 2010, based on the COSO criteria.

We also have audited, in accordance with the standards of the Public Company Accounting Oversight Board (United States), the consolidated balance sheets of the Company as at February 27, 2010 and February 28, 2009, and the consolidated statements of operations, shareholders' equity and cash flows for the years ended February 27, 2010, February 28, 2009 and March 1, 2008 of the Company and our report dated April 1, 2010 expressed an unqualified opinion thereon.

Ernst & Young LLP

Kitchener, Canada,
April 1, 2010.

Chartered Accountants
Licensed Public Accountants

Research In Motion Limited
Consolidated Balance Sheets

($US, in thousands)	February 27, 2010	February 28, 2009
Assets		
Current		
Cash and cash equivalents	$ 1,550,861	$ 835,546
Short-term investments	360,614	682,666
Accounts receivable, net	2,593,742	2,112,117
Other receivables	206,373	157,728
Inventories	621,611	682,400
Other current assets	285,539	187,257
Deferred income tax asset	193,916	183,872
Total current assets	5,812,656	4,841,586
Long-term investments	958,248	720,635
Property, plant and equipment, net	1,956,581	1,334,648
Intangible assets, net	1,326,363	1,066,527
Goodwill	150,561	137,572
Deferred income tax asset	—	404
Total assets	$10,204,409	$8,101,372
Liabilities		
Current		
Accounts payable	$ 615,620	$ 448,339
Accrued liabilities	1,638,260	1,238,602
Income taxes payable	95,650	361,460
Deferred revenue	67,573	53,834
Deferred income tax liability	14,674	13,116
Total current liabilities	2,431,777	2,115,351
Deferred income tax liability	141,382	87,917
Income taxes payable	28,587	23,976
Total liabilities	2,601,746	2,227,244
Shareholders' Equity		
Capital stock		
Preferred shares, authorized unlimited number of non-voting, cumulative, redeemable and retractable	—	—
Common shares, authorized unlimited number of non-voting, redeemable, retractable Class A common shares and unlimited number of voting common shares. Issued — 557,328,394 voting common shares (February 28, 2009 — 566,218,819)	2,207,609	2,208,235
Treasury stock		
February 27, 2010 — 1,458,950 (February 28, 2009 — nil)	(94,463)	—
Retained earnings	5,274,365	3,545,710
Additional paid-in capital	164,060	119,726
Accumulated other comprehensive income	51,092	457
Total shareholders equity	7,602,663	5,874,128
Total liabilities and shareholders' equity	$10,204,409	$8,101,372

Research In Motion Limited
Consolidated Statements of Operations

($US, in thousands, except per share data)

For the Year Ended	February 27, 2010	February 28, 2009	March 1, 2008
Revenue			
Devices and other	$12,535,998	$9,410,755	$4,914,366
Service and software	2,417,226	1,654,431	1,095,029
Total revenue	$14,953,224	11,065,186	6,009,395
Cost of sales			
Devices and other	7,979,163	5,718,041	2,758,250
Service and software	389,795	249,847	170,564
Total cost of sales	8,368,958	5,967,888	2,928,814
Gross margin	6,584,266	5,097,298	3,080,581
Operating expenses			
Research and development	964,841	684,702	359,828
Selling, marketing, and administration	1,907,398	1,495,697	881,482
Amortization	310,357	194,803	108,112
Litigation	163,800	—	—
Total operating expenses	3,346,396	2,375,202	1,349,422
Income from operations	3,237,870	2,722,096	1,731,159
Investment income	28,640	78,267	79,361
Income before income taxes	3,266,510	2,800,363	1,810,520
Provision for income taxes	809,366	907,747	516,653
Net income	$2,457,144	$1,892,616	$1,293,867
Earnings per share			
Basic	$ 4.35	$ 3.35	$ 2.31
Diluted	$ 4.31	$ 3.30	$ 2.26

Research In Motion Limited
Consolidated Statements of Shareholders' Equity

($US, in thousands)	Capital Stock	Additional Paid-In Capital	Treasury Stock	Retained Earnings	Accumulated Other Comprehensive Income (Loss)	Total
Balance as at March 3, 2007	$2,099,696	$36,093	$ —	$359,227	$(11,516)	$2,483,500
Comprehensive income (loss):						
Net income	—	—	—	1,293,867	—	1,293,867
Net change in unrealized gains on available-for-sale investments	—	—	—	—	13,467	13,467
Net change in fair value of derivatives designated as cash flow hedges during the year	—	—	—	—	37,564	37,564
Amounts reclassified to earnings during the year	—	—	—	—	(9,232)	(9,232)
Other paid-in capital	—	9,626	—	—	—	9,626
Shares issued:						
Exercise of stock options	62,889	—	—	—	—	62,889
Transfers to capital stock from stock option exercises	7,271	(7,271)	—	—	—	—
Stock-based compensation	—	33,700	—	—	—	33,700
Excess tax benefits from stock-based compensation	—	8,185	—	—	—	8,185
Balance as at March 1, 2008	$2,169,856	$80,333	$ —	$1,653,094	$30,283	$3,933,566
Comprehensive income (loss):						
Net income	—	—	—	1,892,616	—	1,892,616
Net change in unrealized gains on available-for-sale investments	—	—	—	—	(7,161)	(7,161)
Net change in fair value of derivatives designated as cash flow hedges during the year	—	—	—	—	(6,168)	(6,168)
Amounts reclassified to earnings during the year	—	—	—	—	(16,497)	(16,497)
Shares issued:						
Exercise of stock options	27,024	—	—	—	—	27,024
Transfers to capital stock from stock option exercises	11,355	(11,355)	—	—	—	—
Stock-based compensation	—	38,100	—	—	—	38,100
Excess tax benefits from stock-based compensation	—	12,648	—	—	—	12,648
Balance as at February 28, 2009	$2,208,235	$119,726	$ —	$3,545,710	$457	$5,874,128
Comprehensive income:						
Net income	—	—	—	2,457,144	—	2,457,144
Net change in unrealized gains on available-for-sale investments	—	—	—	—	6,803	6,803
Net change in fair value of derivatives designated as cash flow hedges during the year	—	—	—	—	28,324	28,324
Amounts reclassified to earnings during the year	—	—	—	—	15,508	15,508
Shares issued:						
Exercise of stock options	30,246	—	—	—	—	30,246
Transfers to capital stock from stock option exercises	15,647	(15,647)	—	—	—	—
Stock-based compensation	—	58,038	—	—	—	58,038
Excess tax benefits from stock-based compensation	—	1,943	—	—	—	1,943
Purchase of treasury stock	—	—	(94,463)	—	—	(94,463)
Common shares repurchased	(46,519)	—	—	(728,489)	—	(775,008)
Balance as at February 27, 2010	$2,207,609	$164,060	$(94,463)	$5,274,365	$51,092	$7,602,663

Research In Motion Limited
Consolidated Statements of Cash Flows

For the Year Ended ($US, in thousands)	February 27, 2010	February 28, 2009	March 1, 2008
Cash flows from operating activities			
Net income	$ 2,457,144	$ 1,892,616	$ 1,293,867
Adjustments to reconcile net income to net cash provided by operating activities:			
Amortization	615,621	327,896	177,366
Deferred income taxes	51,363	(36,623)	(67,244)
Income taxes payable	4,611	(6,897)	4,973
Stock-based compensation	58,038	38,100	33,700
Other	8,806	5,867	3,303
Net changes in working capital items	(160,709)	(769,114)	130,794
Net cash provided by operating activities	3,034,874	1,451,845	1,576,759
Cash flows from investing activities			
Acquisition of long-term investments	(862,977)	(507,082)	(757,656)
Proceeds on sale or maturity of long-term investments	473,476	431,713	260,393
Acquisition of property, plant and equipment	(1,009,416)	(833,521)	(351,914)
Acquisition of intangible assets	(421,400)	(687,913)	(374,128)
Business acquisitions, net of cash acquired	(143,375)	(48,425)	(6,200)
Acquisition of short-term investments	(476,956)	(917,316)	(1,249,919)
Proceeds on sale or maturity of short-term investments	970,521	739,021	1,325,487
Net cash used in investing activities	(1,470,127)	(1,823,523)	(1,153,937)
Cash flows from financing activities			
Issuance of common shares	30,246	27,024	62,889
Additional paid-in capital	—	—	9,626
Excess tax benefits from stock-based compensation	1,943	12,648	8,185
Purchase of treasury stock	(94,463)	—	—
Common shares repurchased	(775,008)	—	—
Repayment of debt	(6,099)	(14,305)	(302)
Net cash provided by (used in) financing activities	(843,381)	25,367	80,398
Effect of foreign exchange gain (loss) on cash and cash equivalents	(6,051)	(2,541)	4,034
Net increase (decrease) in cash and cash equivalents for the year	715,315	(348,852)	507,254
Cash and cash equivalents, beginning of year	835,546	1,184,398	677,144
Cash and cash equivalents, end of year	$ 1,550,861	$ 835,546	$ 1,184,398

RIM—SELECTED Notes to the Consolidated Financial Statements

$US in thousands, except share and per share data, and where otherwise indicated

1. RESEARCH IN MOTION LIMITED AND SUMMARY OF SIGNIFICANT ACCOUNTING POLICIES

Research In Motion Limited ("RIM" or the "Company") is a leading designer, manufacturer and marketer of innovative wireless solutions for the worldwide mobile communications market. Through the development of integrated hardware, software and services that support multiple wireless network standards, RIM provides platforms and solutions for seamless access to time-sensitive information including email, phone, short messaging service (SMS), Internet and intranet-based applications. RIM technology also enables a broad array of third party developers and manufacturers to enhance their products and services with wireless connectivity to data. RIM's portfolio of award-winning products, services and embedded technologies are used by thousands of organizations and millions of consumers around the world and include the BlackBerry wireless solution, and other software and hardware. The Company's sales and marketing efforts include collaboration with strategic partners and distribution channels, as well as its own supporting sales and marketing teams, to promote the sale of its products and services.

Basis of presentation and preparation

The consolidated financial statements include the accounts of all subsidiaries of the Company with intercompany transactions and balances eliminated on consolidation. All of the Company's subsidiaries are wholly-owned. These consolidated financial statements have been prepared by management in accordance with United States generally accepted accounting principles ("U.S. GAAP") on a basis consistent for all periods presented except as described in note 2. Certain of the comparative figures have been reclassified to conform to the current year presentation. The Company's fiscal year end date is the 52 or 53 weeks ending on the last Saturday of February, or the first Saturday of March. The fiscal years ended February 27, 2010, February 28, 2009, and March 1, 2008 comprise 52 weeks.

The significant accounting policies used in these U.S. GAAP consolidated financial statements are as follows:

Use of estimates

The preparation of the consolidated financial statements requires management to make estimates and assumptions with respect to the reported amounts of assets, liabilities, revenues and expenses and the disclosure of contingent assets and liabilities. Significant areas requiring the use of management estimates relate to the determination of reserves for various litigation claims, provisions for excess and obsolete inventories and liabilities for purchase commitments with contract manufacturers and suppliers, fair values of assets acquired and liabilities assumed in business combinations, royalties, amortization expense, implied fair value of goodwill, provision for income taxes, realization of deferred income tax assets and the related components of the valuation allowance, provisions for warranty and the fair values of financial instruments. Actual results could differ from these estimates.

Foreign currency translation

The U.S. dollar is the functional and reporting currency of the Company. Foreign currency denominated assets and liabilities of the Company and all of its subsidiaries are translated into U.S. dollars. Accordingly, monetary assets and liabilities are translated using the exchange rates in effect at the consolidated balance sheet date and revenues and expenses at the rates of exchange prevailing when the transactions occurred. Remeasurement adjustments are included in income. Non-monetary assets and liabilities are translated at historical exchange rates.

Cash and cash equivalents

Cash and cash equivalents consist of balances with banks and liquid investments with maturities of three months or less at the date of acquisition.

Accounts receivable, net

The accounts receivable balance which reflects invoiced and accrued revenue is presented net of an allowance for doubtful accounts. The allowance for doubtful accounts reflects estimates of probable losses in accounts receivables. The Company is dependent on a number of significant customers and on large complex contracts with respect to sales of the majority of its products, software and services. The Company expects the majority of its accounts receivable balances to continue to come from large customers as it sells the majority of its devices and software products and service relay access through network carriers and resellers rather than directly.

The Company evaluates the collectability of its accounts receivables based upon a combination of factors on a periodic basis such as specific credit risk of its customers, historical trends and economic circumstances. The Company, in the normal course of business, monitors the financial condition of its customers and reviews the credit history of each new

$US in thousands, except share and per share data, and where otherwise indicated

customer. When the Company becomes aware of a specific customer's inability to meet its financial obligations to the Company (such as in the case of bankruptcy filings or material deterioration in the customer's operating results or financial position, and payment experiences), RIM records a specific bad debt provision to reduce the customer's related accounts receivable to its estimated net realizable value. If circumstances related to specific customers change, the Company's estimates of the recoverability of accounts receivables balances could be further adjusted. The allowance for doubtful accounts as at February 27, 2010 is $2.0 million (February 28, 2009- $2.1 million).

Investments

The Company's investments, other than cost method investments of $2.5 million and equity method investments of $4.1 million, consist of money market and other debt securities, and are classified as available-for-sale for accounting purposes. The Company does not exercise significant influence with respect to any of these investments.

Investments with maturities one year or less, as well as any investments that management intends to hold for less than one year, are classified as short-term investments. Investments with maturities in excess of one year are classified as long-term investments.

The Company determines the appropriate classification of investments at the time of purchase and subsequently reassesses the classification of such investments at each balance sheet date. Investments classified as available-for-sale are carried at fair value with unrealized gains and losses recorded in accumulated other comprehensive income (loss) until such investments mature or are sold. The Company uses the specific identification method of determining the cost basis in computing realized gains or losses on available-for-sale investments which are recorded in investment income.

The Company assesses individual investments in an unrealized loss position to determine whether the unrealized loss is other-than-temporary. The Company makes this assessment by considering available evidence, including changes in general market conditions, specific industry and individual company data, the length of time and the extent to which the fair value has been less than cost, the financial condition, the near-term prospects of the individual investment and the Company's intent and ability to hold the investments. In the event that a decline in the fair value of an investment occurs and the decline in value is considered to be other-than-temporary, an impairment charge is recorded in investment income equal to the difference between the cost basis and the fair value of the individual investment at the balance sheet date of the reporting period for which the assessment was made. The fair value of the investment then becomes the new cost basis of the investment.

Effective in the second quarter of fiscal 2010, if a debt security's market value is below its amortized cost and the Company either intends to sell the security or it is more likely than not that the Company will be required to sell the security before its anticipated recovery, the Company records an other-than-temporary impairment charge to investment income for the entire amount of the impairment. For other-than-temporary impairments on debt securities that the Company does not intend to sell and it is not more likely than not that the entity will be required to sell the security before its anticipated recovery, the Company would separate the other-than-temporary impairment into the amount representing the credit loss and the amount related to all other factors. The Company would record the other-than-temporary impairment related to the credit loss as a charge to investment income and the remaining other-than-temporary impairment would be recorded as a component of accumulated other comprehensive income.

Derivative financial instruments

The Company uses derivative financial instruments, including forward contracts and options, to hedge certain foreign currency exposures. The Company does not use derivative financial instruments for speculative purposes.

Inventories

Raw materials are stated at the lower of cost and replacement cost. Work in process and finished goods inventories are stated at the lower of cost and net realizable value. Cost includes the cost of materials plus direct labour applied to the product and the applicable share of manufacturing overhead. Cost is determined on a first-in-first-out basis.

Property, plant and equipment, net

Property, plant and equipment is stated at cost less accumulated amortization. No amortization is provided for construction in progress until the assets are ready for use. Amortization is provided using the following rates and methods:

Buildings, leaseholds and other	Straight-line over terms between 5 and 40 years
BlackBerry operations and other information technology	Straight-line over terms between 3 and 5 years
Manufacturing equipment, R&D equipment and tooling	Straight-line over terms between 2 and 8 years
Furniture and fixtures	Declining balance at 20% per annum

$US in thousands, except share and per share data, and where otherwise indicated

Intangible assets, net

Intangible assets are stated at cost less accumulated amortization and are comprised of acquired technology, licenses, and patents. Acquired technology consists of purchased developed technology arising from the Company's business acquisitions. Licenses include licenses or agreements that the Company has negotiated with third parties upon use of third parties' technology. Patents comprise trademarks, internally developed patents, as well as individual patents or portfolios of patents acquired from third parties. Costs capitalized and subsequently amortized include all costs necessary to acquire intellectual property, such as patents and trademarks, as well as legal defense costs arising out of the assertion of any Company-owned patents.

Intangible assets are amortized as follows:

Acquired technology	Straight-line over 2 to 5 years
Licenses	Straight-line over terms of the license agreements or on a per unit basis based upon the anticipated number of units sold during the terms, subject to a maximum of 5 years
Patents	Straight-line over 17 years or over estimated useful life

Goodwill

Goodwill represents the excess of the purchase price of business acquisitions over the fair value of identifiable net assets acquired. Goodwill is allocated as at the date of the business combination. Goodwill is not amortized, but is tested for impairment annually, or more frequently if events or changes in circumstances indicate the asset may be impaired.

Impairment of long-lived assets

The Company reviews long-lived assets such as property, plant and equipment and intangible assets with finite useful lives for impairment whenever events or changes in circumstances indicate that the carrying amount may not be recoverable. If the total of the expected undiscounted future cash flows is less than the carrying amount of the asset, a loss is recognized for the excess of the carrying amount over the fair value of the asset.

Income taxes

The Company uses the liability method of tax allocation to account for income taxes. Deferred income tax assets and liabilities are recognized based upon temporary differences between the financial reporting and tax bases of assets and liabilities, and measured using enacted tax rates and laws that will be in effect when the differences are expected to reverse. The Company records a valuation allowance to reduce deferred income tax assets to the amount that is more likely than not to be realized. The Company considers both positive evidence and negative evidence, to determine whether, based upon the weight of that evidence, a valuation allowance is required. Judgment is required in considering the relative impact of negative and positive evidence.

Revenue recognition

The Company recognizes revenue when it is realized or realizable and earned. The Company considers revenue realized or realizable and earned when it has persuasive evidence of an arrangement, the product has been delivered or the services have been provided to the customer, the sales price is fixed or determinable and collectability is reasonably assured. In addition to this general policy, the following paragraphs describe the specific revenue recognition policies for each major category of revenue.

Devices

Revenue from the sales of BlackBerry devices is recognized when title is transferred to the customer and all significant contractual obligations that affect the customer's final acceptance have been fulfilled. For hardware products for which software is deemed not to be incidental, the Company recognizes revenue in accordance with industry specific software revenue recognition guidance. The Company records reductions to revenue for estimated commitments related to price protection and for customer incentive programs, including reseller and end-user rebates. The estimated cost of the incentive programs are accrued based on historical experience, as a reduction to revenue in the period the Company has sold the product and committed to a plan. Price protection is accrued as a reduction to revenue based on estimates of future price reductions and certain agreed customer inventories at the date of the price adjustment. In addition, provisions are made at the time of sale for warranties and royalties.

Service

Revenue from service is recognized rateably on a monthly basis when the service is provided. In instances where the Company bills the customer prior to performing the service, the prebilling is recorded as deferred revenue.

Software

Revenue from licensed software is recognized at the inception of the license term and in accordance with industry

$US in thousands, except share and per share data, and where otherwise indicated

specific software revenue recognition guidance. When the fair value of a delivered element has not been established, the Company uses the residual method to recognize revenue if the fair value of undelivered elements is determinable. Revenue from software maintenance, unspecified upgrades and technical support contracts is recognized over the period that such items are delivered or that services are provided.

Other

Revenue from the sale of accessories is recognized when title is transferred to the customer and all significant contractual obligations that affect the customer's final acceptance have been fulfilled. Technical support ("T-Support") contracts extending beyond the current period are recorded as deferred revenue. Revenue from repair and maintenance programs is recognized when the service is delivered which is when the title is transferred to the customer and all significant contractual obligations that affect the customer's final acceptance have been fulfilled. Revenue for non-recurring engineering contracts is recognized as specific contract milestones are met. The attainment of milestones approximates actual performance.

Shipping and handling costs

Shipping and handling costs charged to income are included in cost of sales where they can be reasonably attributed to certain revenue; otherwise they are included in selling, marketing and administration.

Multiple-element arrangements

The Company enters into transactions that represent multiple-element arrangements which may include any combination of hardware and/or service or software and T-Support. These multiple-element arrangements are assessed to determine whether they can be separated into more than one unit of accounting or element for the purpose of revenue recognition. When the appropriate criteria for separating revenue into more than one unit of accounting is met and there is vendor specific objective evidence of fair value for all units of accounting or elements in an arrangement, the arrangement consideration is allocated to the separate units of accounting or elements based on each unit's relative fair value. When the fair value of a delivered element has not been established, the Company uses the residual method to recognize revenue if the fair value of undelivered elements is determinable. This vendor specific objective evidence of fair value is established through prices charged for each revenue element when that element is sold separately. The revenue recognition policies described above are then applied to each unit of accounting.

Research and development

Research costs are expensed as incurred. Development costs for BlackBerry devices and licensed software to be sold, leased or otherwise marketed are subject to capitalization beginning when a product's technological feasibility has been established and ending when a product is available for general release to customers. The Company's products are generally released soon after technological feasibility has been established and therefore costs incurred subsequent to achievement of technological feasibility are not significant and have been expensed as incurred.

Comprehensive income (loss)

Comprehensive income (loss) is defined as the change in net assets of a business enterprise during a period from transactions and other events and circumstances from non-owner sources and includes all changes in equity during a period except those resulting from investments by owners and distributions to owners. The Company's reportable items of comprehensive income are cash flow hedges and changes in the fair value of available-for-sale investments. Realized gains or losses on available-for-sale investments are reclassified into investment income using the specific identification basis.

Earnings per share

Earnings per share is calculated based on the weighted-average number of shares outstanding during the year. The treasury stock method is used for the calculation of the dilutive effect of stock options.

Stock-based compensation plans

The Company has stock-based compensation plans.

Warranty

The Company provides for the estimated costs of product warranties at the time revenue is recognized. BlackBerry devices are generally covered by a time-limited warranty for varying periods of time. The Company's warranty obligation is affected by product failure rates, differences in warranty periods, regulatory developments with respect to warranty obligations in the countries in which the Company carries on business, freight expense, and material usage and other related repair costs. The Company's estimates of costs are based upon historical experience and expectations of future return rates and unit warranty repair cost. If the Company experiences increased or decreased warranty activity, or increased or decreased costs associated with servicing those obligations, revisions to the estimated warranty liability would be recognized in the reporting period when such revisions are made.

Advertising costs

The Company expenses all advertising costs as incurred. These costs are included in selling, marketing, and administration.

$US in thousands, except share and per share data, and where otherwise indicated

4. CASH, CASH EQUIVALENTS AND INVESTMENTS

The components of cash, cash equivalents and investments were as follows:

	Cost Basis	Unrealized Gains	Unrealized Losses	Recorded Basis	Cash and Cash Equivalents	Short-term Investments	Long-term Investments
As at February 27, 2010							
Bank balances	$ 535,445	$ —	$ —	$ 535,445	$ 535,445	$ —	$ —
Money market fund	3,278	—	—	3,278	3,278	—	—
Bankers acceptances and term deposits/certificates	377,596	—	—	377,596	377,596	—	—
Commercial paper and corporate notes/bonds	855,145	6,528	(49)	861,624	472,312	187,369	201,943
Treasury bills/notes	203,514	129	(12)	203,631	92,272	50,786	60,573
Government sponsored enterprise notes	447,131	2,590	(13)	449,708	69,958	111,977	267,773
Asset-backed securities	393,751	5,280	(50)	398,981	—	10,482	388,499
Auction-rate securities	40,527	—	(7,688)	32,839	—	—	32,839
Other investments	6,621	—	—	6,621	—	—	6,621
	$2,863,008	$14,527	$ (7,812)	$2,869,723	$1,550,861	$360,614	$958,248

Realized gains and losses on available-for-sale securities comprise the following:

For the year ended	February 27, 2010	February 28, 2009	March 1, 2008
Realized gains	$439	$ 158	$ 10
Realized losses	(17)	(1,801)	(410)
Net realized gains (losses)	$422	$(1,643)	$(400)

The contractual maturities of available-for-sale investments at February 27, 2010 were as follows:

	Cost Basis	Fair Value
Due in one year or less	$1,371,047	$1,372,752
Due in one to five years	773,471	783,451
Due after five years	173,146	168,176
No fixed maturity date	3,278	3,278
	$2,320,942	$2,327,657

5. FAIR VALUE MEASUREMENTS

The Company defines fair value as the price that would be received to sell an asset or paid to transfer a liability in an orderly transaction between market participants at the measurement date. When determining the fair value measurements for assets and liabilities required to be recorded at fair value, the Company considers the principal or most advantageous market in which it would transact and considers assumptions that market participants would use in pricing the asset or liability such as inherent risk, non-performance risk, and credit risk. The Company applies the following fair value hierarchy, which prioritizes the inputs used in the valuation methodologies in measuring fair value into three levels:

- Level 1 — Unadjusted quoted prices at the measurement date for identical assets or liabilities in active markets.

- Level 2 — Observable inputs other than quoted prices included in Level 1, such as quoted prices for similar assets and liabilities in active markets; quoted prices for identical or similar assets and liabilities in markets that are not active; or other inputs that are observable or can be corroborated by observable market data.

- Level 3 — Significant unobservable inputs which are supported by little or no market activity.

The fair value hierarchy also requires the Company to maximize the use of observable inputs and minimize the use of unobservable inputs when measuring fair value. The carrying amounts of the Company's cash and cash equivalents, accounts receivable, other receivables, accounts payable and accrued liabilities, approximate fair value due to their short maturities. When determining the fair value of its investments held, the Company primarily relies on an independent third party valuator for the fair valuation of securities.

$US in thousands, except share and per share data, and where otherwise indicated

6. INVENTORIES

Inventories were comprised as follows:

	February 27, 2010	February 28, 2009
Raw materials	$ 490,063	$464,497
Work in process	231,939	250,728
Finished goods	17,068	35,264
Provision for excess and obsolete inventories	(117,459)	(68,089)
	$ 621,611	$682,400

7. PROPERTY, PLANT AND EQUIPMENT, NET

Property, plant and equipment were comprised of the following:

February 27, 2010	Cost	Accumulated amortization	Net book value
Land	$ 104,254	$ —	$ 104,254
Buildings, leaseholds and other	926,747	115,216	811,531
BlackBerry operations and other information technology	1,152,637	484,180	668,457
Manufacturing equipment, research and development equipment, and tooling	347,692	182,228	165,464
Furniture and fixtures	346,641	139,766	206,875
	$2,877,971	$921,390	$1,956,581

As at February 27, 2010, the carrying amount of assets under construction was $254.3 million (February 28, 2009 — $88.9 million). Of this amount, $110.9 million (February 28, 2009 — $50.0 million) was included in buildings, leaseholds and other; $102.5 million (February 28, 2009 - $35.8 million) was included in BlackBerry operations and other information technology; and $40.9 million (February 28, 2009 — $3.2 million) was included in manufacturing equipment, research and development equipment, and tooling. As at February 27, 2010, $31.7 million has been classified as an asset held for sale and accordingly has been reclassified from property, plant and equipment to other current assets. For the year ended February 27, 2010, amortization expense related to property, plant and equipment was $344.5 million (February 28, 2009 — $203.4 million; March 1, 2008 — $133.1 million).

8. INTANGIBLE ASSETS, NET

Intangible assets were comprised of the following:

February 27, 2010	Cost	Accumulated amortization	Net book value
Acquired technology	$ 165,791	$ 70,777	$ 95,014
Licenses	711,969	196,618	515,351
Patents	889,467	173,469	715,998
	$1,767,227	$440,864	$1,326,363

For the year ended February 27, 2010, amortization expense related to intangible assets was $271.1 million (February 28, 2009 — $124.5 million; March 1, 2008 — $44.3 million). Total additions to intangible assets in fiscal 2010 were $531.0 million (2009 — $721.1 million). Based on the carrying value of the identified intangible assets as at February 27, 2010 and assuming no subsequent impairment of the underlying assets, the annual amortization expense for the next five fiscal years is expected to be as follows: 2011 — $324 million; 2012 — $275 million; 2013 — $227 million; 2014 — $139 million; and 2015 — $61 million. The weighted-average remaining useful life of the acquired technology is 3.4 years (2009 – 3.7 years).

$US in thousands, except share and per share data, and where otherwise indicated

10. INCOME TAXES

The difference between the amount of the provision for income taxes and the amount computed by multiplying income before income taxes by the statutory Canadian tax rate is reconciled as follows:

For the year ended	February 27, 2010	February 28, 2009
Statutory Canadian tax rate	32.8%	33.4%
Expected income tax provision	$1,072,395	$935,881
Differences in income taxes resulting from:		
Impact of Canadian U.S. dollar functional currency election	(145,000)	—
Investment tax credits	(101,214)	(81,173)
Manufacturing and processing activities	(52,053)	(49,808)
Foreign exchange	2,837	99,575
Foreign tax rate differences	5,291	(16,273)
Non-deductible stock compensation	9,600	10,500
Adjustments to deferred tax balances for enacted changes in tax laws and rates	7,927	1,260
Other differences	9,583	7,785
	$809,366	$907,747

11. CAPITAL STOCK

(a) Capital stock

The Company is authorized to issue an unlimited number of non-voting, redeemable, retractable Class A common shares, an unlimited number of voting common shares and an unlimited number of non-voting, cumulative, redeemable, retractable preferred shares. At February 27, 2010 and February 28, 2009, there were no Class A common shares or preferred shares outstanding. The Company declared a 3-for-1 stock split of the Company's outstanding common shares on June 28, 2007. The stock split was implemented by way of a stock dividend. Shareholders received an additional two common shares of the Company for each common share held. The stock dividend was paid on August 20, 2007 to common shareholders of record at the close of business on August 17, 2007. All share, earnings per share and stock option data have been adjusted to reflect this stock dividend.

The following details the changes in issued and outstanding common shares for the year ended February 27, 2010:

	Capital Stock Outstanding (000's)	Capital Stock Amount	Treasury Stock Outstanding (000's)	Treasury Stock Amount
Common shares outstanding as at February 28, 2009	566,219	2,208,235	—	—
Exercise of stock options	3,408	30,246	—	—
Conversion of restricted share units	2	—	—	—
Transfers to capital stock resulting from stock option exercises	—	15,647	—	—
Restricted share unit plan purchase of shares	—	—	1,459	(94,463)
Common shares repurchased	(12,300)	(46,519)	—	—
Common shares outstanding as at February 27, 2010	557,329	$2,207,609	1,459	$(94,463)

On November 4, 2009, the Company's Board of Directors authorized a Common Share Repurchase Program for the repurchase and cancellation, through the facilities of the NASDAQ Stock Market, common shares having an aggregate purchase price of up to $1.2 billion, or approximately 21 million common shares based on trading prices at the time of the authorization. This represents approximately 3.6% of the outstanding common shares of the Company at the time of the authorization. All common shares repurchased by the Company pursuant to the Common Share Repurchase Program have been cancelled. The Common Share Repurchase Program will remain in place for up to 12 months from November 4, 2009 or until the purchases are completed or the program is terminated by the Company.

(b) Stock-based compensation

Stock Option Plan

The Company recorded a charge to income and a credit to paid-in-capital of $37.0 million in fiscal 2010 (fiscal 2009 — $38.1 million; fiscal 2008 — $33.7 million) in relation to stock-based compensation expense.

The Company has not paid a dividend in the previous twelve fiscal years and has no current expectation of paying cash dividends on its common shares.

Restricted Share Unit Plan

During fiscal 2010, the trustee purchased 1,458,950 common shares for total consideration of approximately $94.5 million

$US in thousands, except share and per share data, and where otherwise indicated

to comply with its obligations to deliver shares upon vesting. These purchased shares are classified as treasury stock for accounting purposes and included in the shareholders' equity section of the Company's consolidated balance sheet. The Company recorded compensation expense with respect to RSUs of $21.0 million in the year ended February 27, 2010 (February 28, 2009 — $196; March 1, 2008 — $33).

Deferred Share Unit Plan

The Company issued 14,593 DSUs in the year ended February 27, 2010. There are 34,801 DSUs outstanding as at February 27, 2010 (February 28, 2009 — 20,208). The Company had a liability of $2.5 million in relation to the DSU plan as at February 27, 2010 (February 28, 2009 — $834).

12. COMMITMENTS AND CONTINGENCIES

(a) Credit Facility

The Company has $150.0 million in unsecured demand credit facilities (the "Facilities") to support and secure operating and financing requirements. As at February 27, 2010, the Company has utilized $6.9 million of the Facilities for outstanding letters of credit, and $143.1 million of the Facilities are unused.

(b) Lease commitments

The Company is committed to future minimum annual lease payments under operating leases as follows:

For the years ending	Real Estate	Equipment and other	Total
2011	$ 35,088	$1,917	$ 37,005
2012	30,611	1,202	31,813
2013	27,841	163	28,004
2014	26,178	—	26,178
2015	21,755	—	21,755
Thereafter	63,631	—	63,631
	$205,104	$3,282	$208,386

For the year ended February 27, 2010, the Company incurred rental expense of $39.6 million (February 28, 2009 — $22.7 million; March 1, 2008 — $15.5 million).

(c) Litigation

The Company is involved in litigation in the normal course of its business, both as a defendant and as a plaintiff. The Company may be subject to claims (including claims related to patent infringement, purported class actions and derivative actions) either directly or through indemnities against these claims that it provides to certain of its partners.

13. PRODUCT WARRANTY

The Company estimates its warranty costs at the time of revenue recognition based on historical warranty claims experience and records the expense in cost of sales. The warranty accrual balance is reviewed quarterly to establish that it materially reflects the remaining obligation based on the anticipated future expenditures over the balance of the obligation period. Adjustments are made when the actual warranty claim experience differs from estimates. The change in the Company's warranty expense and actual warranty experience from March 3, 2007 to February 27, 2010 as well as the accrued warranty obligations as at February 27, 2010 are set forth in the following table:

Accrued warranty obligations as at March 3, 2007	$ 36,669
Actual warranty experience during fiscal 2008	(68,166)
Fiscal 2008 warranty provision	116,045
Accrued warranty obligations as at March 1, 2008	84,548
Actual warranty experience during fiscal 2009	(146,434)
Fiscal 2009 warranty provision	258,757
Adjustments for changes in estimate	(12,536)
Accrued warranty obligations as at February 28, 2009	184,335
Actual warranty experience during fiscal 2010	(416,393)
Fiscal 2010 warranty provision	462,834
Adjustments for changes in estimate	21,541
Accrued warranty obligations as at February 27, 2010	$ 252,317

$US in thousands, except share and per share data, and where otherwise indicated

14. EARNINGS PER SHARE

The following table sets forth the computation of basic and diluted earnings per share:

For the year ended	February 27, 2010	February 28, 2009	March 1, 2008
Net income for basic and diluted earnings per share available to common shareholders	$2,457,144	$1,892,616	$1,293,867
Weighted-average number of shares outstanding (000's) — basic	564,492	565,059	559,778
Effect of dilutive securities (000's) — stock-based compensation	5,267	9,097	13,052
Weighted-average number of shares and assumed conversions (000's) — diluted	569,759	574,156	572,830
Earnings per share — reported			
Basic	$ 4.35	$ 3.35	$ 2.31
Diluted	$ 4.31	$ 3.30	$ 2.26

15. COMPREHENSIVE INCOME (LOSS)

The components of comprehensive income (loss) are shown in the following table:

For the year ended	February 27, 2010	February 28, 2009	March 1, 2008
Net income	$2,457,144	$1,892,616	$1,293,867
Net change in unrealized gains (losses) on available-for-sale investments	6,803	(7,161)	13,467
Net change in fair value of derivatives designated as cash flow hedges during the year, net of income taxes of $13,190 (February 28, 2009 - tax recovery of $8,641; March 1, 2008 - income taxes of $19,238)	28,324	(6,168)	37,564
Amounts reclassified to earnings during the year, net of income tax recovery of $6,079 (February 28, 2009 - income taxes of $4,644; March 1, 2008 - income taxes of $5,142)	15,508	(16,497)	(9,232)
Comprehensive income	$2,507,779	$1,862,790	$1,335,666

The components of accumulated other comprehensive income (loss) are as follows:

	February 27, 2010	February 28, 2009	March 1, 2008
Accumulated net unrealized gains (losses) on available-for-sale investments	$ 6,715	$ (88)	$ 7,073
Accumulated net unrealized gains on derivative instruments designated as cash flow hedges	44,377	545	23,210
Total accumulated other comprehensive income	$51,092	$457	$30,283

16. SUPPLEMENTAL INFORMATION

(a) Cash flows resulting from net changes in working capital items are as follows:

For the year ended	February 27, 2010	February 28, 2009	March 1, 2008
Accounts receivable	$(480,610)	$(936,514)	$(602,055)
Other receivables	(44,719)	(83,039)	(34,515)
Inventories	60,789	(286,133)	(140,360)
Other current assets	(52,737)	(50,280)	(26,161)
Accounts payable	167,281	177,263	140,806
Accrued liabilities	442,065	506,859	383,020
Income taxes payable	(266,517)	(113,868)	401,270
Deferred revenue	13,739	16,598	8,789
	$(160,709)	$(769,114)	$ 130,794

(b) Certain statement of cash flow information related to interest and income taxes paid is summarized as follows:

For the year ended	February 27, 2010	February 28, 2009	March 1, 2008
Interest paid during the year	$ —	$ 502	$ 518
Income taxes paid during the year	$1,081,720	$946,237	$216,095

$US in thousands, except share and per share data, and where otherwise indicated

(c) The following items are included in the accrued liabilities balance:

	February 27, 2010	February 28, 2009
Marketing costs	$ 91,554	$ 91,160
Vendor inventory liabilities	125,761	18,000
Warranty	252,316	184,335
Royalties	383,939	279,476
Rebates	146,304	134,788
Other	638,386	530,843
	$1,638,260	$1,238,602

Other accrued liabilities as noted in the above chart, include, among other things, salaries, payroll withholding taxes and incentive accruals, none of which are greater than 5% of the current liability balance.

(d) Additional information

Advertising expense, which includes media, agency, and promotional expenses totalling $790.8 million (February 28, 2009 — $718.9 million; March 1, 2008 — $336.0 million) is included in selling, marketing, and administration expense.

Selling, marketing, and administration expense for the fiscal year includes $58.4 million with respect to foreign exchange losses (February 28, 2009 – loss of $6.1 million; March 1, 2008 – loss of $5.3 million). For the year ended February 27, 2010, the Company recorded a $54.3 million charge primarily relating to the reversal of foreign exchange gains previously recorded in fiscal 2009 on the revaluation of Canadian dollar denominated tax liability balances.

17. DERIVATIVE FINANCIAL INSTRUMENTS

The Company uses derivative instruments to manage exposures to foreign exchange risk resulting from transactions in currencies other than its functional currency, the U.S. dollar. The Company's risk management objective in holding derivative instruments is to reduce the volatility of current and future income as a result of changes in foreign currency. To limit its exposure to adverse movements in foreign currency exchange rates, the Company enters into foreign currency forward and option contracts.

18. SEGMENT DISCLOSURES

The Company is organized and managed as a single reportable business segment. The Company's operations are substantially all related to the research, design, manufacture, and sales of wireless communications products, services, and software. Selected financial information is as follows:

Revenue, classified by major geographic segments in which our customers are located, was as follows:

For the year ended	February 27, 2010	February 28, 2009	March 1, 2008
Revenue			
Canada	$ 843,762	$ 887,005	$ 438,302
United States	8,619,762	6,967,598	3,528,858
United Kingdom	1,447,417	711,536	461,592
Other	4,042,283	2,499,047	1,580,643
	$14,953,224	$11,065,186	$6,009,395

	February 27, 2010	February 28, 2009
Total assets		
Canada	$ 4,502,522	$3,218,640
United States	4,059,174	2,646,783
United Kingdom	1,195,534	1,931,387
Other	447,179	304,562
	$10,204,409	$8,101,372

Apple Financial Report

APPLE

APPLE INC.
CONSOLIDATED BALANCE SHEETS
(in millions, except share amounts)

	September 26, 2009	September 27, 2008
ASSETS		
Current assets		
Cash and cash equivalents	$ 5,263	$11,875
Short-term marketable securities	18,201	10,236
Accounts receivable, less allowances of $52 and $47, respectively	3,361	2,422
Inventories	455	509
Deferred tax assets	1,135	1,044
Other current assets	3,140	3,920
Total current assets	31,555	30,006
Long-term marketable securities	10,528	2,379
Property, plant and equipment, net	2,954	2,455
Goodwill	206	207
Acquired intangible assets, net	247	285
Other assets	2,011	839
Total assets	$47,501	$36,171
LIABILITIES AND SHAREHOLDERS' EQUITY		
Current liabilities		
Accounts payable	$ 5,601	$ 5,520
Accrued expenses	3,852	4,224
Deferred revenue	2,053	1,617
Total current liabilities	11,506	11,361
Deferred revenue – non-current	853	768
Other non-current liabilities	3,502	1,745
Total liabilities	15,861	13,874
Shareholders' equity		
Common stock, no par value; 1,800,000,000 shares authorized; 899,805,500 and 888,325,973 shares issued and outstanding, respectively	8,210	7,177
Retained earnings	23,353	15,129
Accumulated other comprehensive income/(loss)	77	(9)
Total shareholders' equity	31,640	22,297
Total liabilities and shareholders' equity	$47,501	$36,171

APPLE INC.
CONSOLIDATED STATEMENTS OF OPERATIONS
(in millions, except share amounts which are reflected in thousands and per share amounts)

For fiscal year ended	September 26, 2009	September 27, 2008	September 29, 2007
Net sales	$ 42,905	$ 37,491	$ 24,578
Cost of sales	25,683	24,294	16,426
Gross margin	17,222	13,197	8,152
Operating expenses			
Research and development	1,333	1,109	782
Selling, general and administrative	4,149	3,761	2,963
Total operating expenses	5,482	4,870	3,745
Operating income	11,740	8,327	4,407
Other income and expense	326	620	599
Income before provision for income taxes	12,066	8,947	5,006
Provision for income taxes	3,831	2,828	1,511
Net income	$ 8,235	$ 6,119	$ 3,495
Earnings per common share:			
Basic	$ 9.22	$ 6.94	$ 4.04
Diluted	$ 9.08	$ 6.78	$ 3.93
Shares used in computing earnings per share:			
Basic	893,016	881,592	864,595
Diluted	907,005	902,139	889,292

APPLE INC.
CONSOLIDATED STATEMENTS OF SHAREHOLDERS' EQUITY
(in millions, except share amounts which are reflected in thousands)

	Common Stock Shares	Common Stock Amount	Retained Earnings	Accumulated Other Comprehensive Income	Total Shareholders' Equity
Balances as of September 30, 2006	855,263	$ 4,355	$ 5,607	$ 22	$ 9,984
Components of comprehensive income:					
Net income	—	—	3,495	—	3,495
Change in foreign currency translation	—	—	—	51	51
Change in unrealized loss on available-for-sale securities, net of tax	—	—	—	(7)	(7)
Change in unrealized gain on derivative instruments, net of tax	—	—	—	(3)	(3)
Total comprehensive income					3,536
Stock-based compensation	—	251	—	—	251
Common stock issued under stock plans, net of shares withheld for employee taxes	17,066	364	(2)	—	362
Tax benefit from employee stock plan awards	—	398	—	—	398
Balances as of September 29, 2007	872,329	5,368	9,100	63	14,531
Cumulative effect of change in accounting principle	—	45	11	—	56
Components of comprehensive income:					
Net income	—	—	6,119	—	6,119
Change in foreign currency translation	—	—	—	(28)	(28)
Change in unrealized loss on available-for-sale securities, net of tax	—	—	—	(63)	(63)
Change in unrealized gain on derivative instruments, net of tax	—	—	—	19	19
Total comprehensive income					6,047
Stock-based compensation	—	513	—	—	513
Common stock issued under stock plans, net of shares withheld for employee taxes	15,888	460	(101)	—	359
Issuance of common stock in connection with an asset acquisition	109	21	—	—	21
Tax benefit from employee stock plan awards	—	770	—	—	770
Balances as of September 27, 2008	888,326	7,177	15,129	(9)	22,297
Components of comprehensive income:					
Net income	—	—	8,235	—	8,235
Change in foreign currency translation	—	—	—	(14)	(14)
Change in unrealized loss on available-for-sale securities, net of tax	—	—	—	118	118
Change in unrealized gain on derivative instruments, net of tax	—	—	—	(18)	(18)
Total comprehensive income					8,321
Stock-based compensation	—	707	—	—	707
Common stock issued under stock plans, net of shares withheld for employee taxes	11,480	404	(11)	—	393
Tax benefit from employee stock plan awards, including transfer pricing adjustments	—	(78)	—	—	(78)
Balances as of September 26, 2009	899,806	$ 8,210	$23,353	$ 77	$31,640

APPLE INC.
CONSOLIDATED STATEMENTS OF CASH FLOWS
(in millions)

For fiscal year ended	September 26, 2009	September 27, 2008	September 29, 2007
Cash and cash equivalents, beginning of the year	$ 11,875	$ 9,352	$ 6,392
Operating Activities			
Net income	8,235	6,119	3,495
Adjustments to reconcile net income to cash generated by operating activities			
Depreciation, amortization and accretion	734	496	327
Stock-based compensation expense	710	516	242
Deferred income tax expense	1,040	398	73
Loss on disposition of property, plant and equipment	26	22	12
Changes in operating assets and liabilities			
Accounts receivable, net	(939)	(785)	(385)
Inventories	54	(163)	(76)
Other current assets	749	(274)	(1,279)
Other assets	(902)	289	285
Accounts payable	92	596	1,494
Deferred revenue	521	718	566
Other liabilities	(161)	1,664	716
Cash generated by operating activities	10,159	9,596	5,470
Investing Activities			
Purchases of marketable securities	(46,724)	(22,965)	(11,719)
Proceeds from maturities of marketable securities	19,790	11,804	6,483
Proceeds from sales of marketable securities	10,888	4,439	2,941
Purchases of other long-term investments	(101)	(38)	(17)
Payments made in connection with business acquisitions, net of cash acquired	—	(220)	—
Payment for acquisition of property, plant and equipment	(1,144)	(1,091)	(735)
Payment for acquisition of intangible assets	(69)	(108)	(251)
Other	(74)	(10)	49
Cash used in investing activities	(17,434)	(8,189)	(3,249)
Financing Activities			
Proceeds from issuance of common stock	475	483	365
Excess tax benefits from stock-based compensation	270	757	377
Cash used to net share settle equity awards	(82)	(124)	(3)
Cash generated by financing activities	663	1,116	739
(Decrease)/increase in cash and cash equivalents	(6,612)	2,523	2,960
Cash and cash equivalents, end of the year	$ 5,263	$11,875	$ 9,352
Supplemental cash flow disclosures:			
Cash paid for income taxes, net	$ 2,997	$ 1,267	$ 863

Palm Financial Report

PALM

Palm, Inc.
Consolidated Balance Sheets
(In thousands, except par value amounts)

	May 31, 2009	May 31, 2008
ASSETS		
Current assets		
Cash and cash equivalents	$ 152,400	$ 176,918
Short-term investments	102,733	81,830
Accounts receivable, net of allowance for doubtful accounts of $350 and $1,169, respectively	66,452	116,430
Inventories	19,716	67,461
Deferred income taxes	174	82,011
Prepaids and other	12,104	15,436
Total current assets	353,579	540,086
Restricted investments	9,496	8,620
Non-current auction rate securities	6,105	29,944
Deferred costs	14,896	—
Property and equipment, net	31,167	39,636
Goodwill	166,320	166,332
Intangible assets, net	48,914	61,048
Deferred income taxes	331	318,850
Other assets	12,428	15,746
Total assets	$ 643,236	$1,180,262
LIABILITIES AND STOCKHOLDERS' EQUITY (DEFICIT)		
Current liabilities		
Accounts payable	$ 105,628	$ 161,642
Income taxes payable	475	1,088
Deferred revenues	18,429	4,080
Accrued restructuring	6,090	8,058
Current portion of long-term debt	4,000	4,000
Other accrued liabilities	207,820	232,478
Total current liabilities	342,442	411,346
Non-current liabilities		
Long-term debt	390,000	394,000
Non-current deferred revenues	13,077	—
Non-current tax liabilities	5,783	6,127
Other non-current liabilities	—	2,098
Series B redeemable convertible preferred stock, $0.001 par value, 325 shares authorized and outstanding; aggregate liquidation value: $325,000	265,412	255,671
Series C redeemable convertible preferred stock, $0.001 par value, 100 shares authorized; outstanding: 51 shares and 0 shares, respectively; aggregate liquidation value: $51,000 and $0, respectively	40,387	—
Stockholders' equity (deficit)		
Preferred stock, $0.001 par value, 125,000 shares authorized:		
Series A: 2,000 shares authorized, none outstanding	—	—
Common stock, $0.001 par value, 2,000,000 shares authorized; outstanding: 139,687 shares and 108,369 shares, respectively	140	108
Additional paid-in capital	854,649	659,141
Accumulated deficit	(1,269,672)	(537,484)
Accumulated other comprehensive income (loss)	1,018	(10,745)
Total stockholders' equity (deficit)	(413,865)	111,020
Total liabilities and stockholders' equity (deficit)	$ 643,236	$1,180,262

Palm, Inc.
Consolidated Statements of Operations
(In thousands, except per share amounts)

Years Ended May 31	2009	2008	2007
Revenues	$ 735,872	$1,318,691	$1,560,507
Cost of revenues	576,113	916,810	985,369
Gross profit	159,759	401,881	575,138
Operating expenses			
Sales and marketing	174,052	229,702	248,685
Research and development	177,210	202,764	190,952
General and administrative	55,923	60,778	59,762
Amortization of intangible assets	3,054	3,775	1,981
Restructuring charges	16,134	30,353	—
Casualty recovery	(268)	—	—
Patent acquisition cost (refund)	(1,537)	5,000	—
Gain on sale of land	—	(4,446)	—
In-process research and development	—	—	3,700
Total operating expenses	424,568	527,926	505,080
Operating income (loss)	(264,809)	(126,045)	70,058
Impairment of non-current auction rate securities	(35,885)	(32,175)	—
Interest (expense)	(25,299)	(20,397)	(1,970)
Interest income	5,840	21,860	25,958
Loss on series C derivative	(2,515)	—	—
Other income (expense), net	(5,255)	(1,471)	(1,619)
Income (loss) before income taxes	(327,923)	(158,228)	92,427
Income tax provision (benefit)	404,265	(52,809)	36,044
Net income (loss)	(732,188)	(105,419)	56,383
Accretion of series B and series C redeemable convertible preferred stock	21,285	5,516	—
Net income (loss) applicable to common shareholders	$(753,473)	$ (110,935)	$ 56,383
Net income (loss) per common share:			
Basic	$ (6.51)	$ (1.05)	$ 0.55
Diluted	$ (6.51)	$ (1.05)	$ 0.54
Shares used to compute net income (loss) per common share:			
Basic	115,725	105,891	102,757
Diluted	115,725	105,891	104,442

Palm, Inc.
Consolidated Statements of Stockholders' Equity (Deficit) and Comprehensive Income (Loss)
(In thousands)

	Common Stock	Additional Paid-In Capital	Unamortized Deferred Stock-Based Compensation	Accumulated Deficit	Accumulated Other Comprehensive Income (Loss)	Total
Balances, May 31, 2006	$ 103	$1,475,319	$ (2,752)	$ (488,081)	$ (684)	$ 983,905
Components of comprehensive income:						
Net income	—	—	—	56,383	—	56,383
Net unrealized gains on available-for-sale investments	—	—	—	—	1,522	1,522
Recognized gains included in results of operations	—	—	—	—	(110)	(110)
Accumulated translation adjustments	—	—	—	—	915	915
Total comprehensive income	—	—	—	—	—	58,710
Common stock issued under stock plans, net	3	21,923	—	—	—	21,926
Stock-based compensation expense	—	21,503	2,752	—	—	24,255
Tax benefit from employee stock options	—	4,578	—	—	—	4,578
Shares repurchased and retired	(2)	(30,961)				(30,963)
Balances, May 31, 2007	104	1,492,362	—	(431,698)	1,643	1,062,411
Components of comprehensive loss:						
Net loss	—	—	—	(105,419)	—	(105,419)
Net unrealized losses on available-for-sale investments	—	—	—	—	(1,261)	(1,261)
Net unrealized losses in value of non-current auction rate securities	—	—	—	—	(44,706)	(44,706)
Net recognized losses on non-current auction rate securities included in results of operations	—	—	—	—	32,175	32,175
Net recognized gains on available-for-sale investments included in results of operations	—	—	—	—	(68)	(68)
Accumulated translation adjustments	—	—	—	—	1,472	1,472
Total comprehensive loss	—	—	—	—	—	(117,807)
Common stock issued under stock plans, net	4	28,433	—	—	—	28,437
Stock-based compensation expense	—	32,181	—	—	—	32,181
Tax deficiency from employee stock options	—	(3,663)	—	—	—	(3,663)
Cash distribution to stockholders	—	(949,691)	—	—	—	(949,691)
Discount recognized on issuance of series B redeemable convertible preferred stock	—	65,035	—	—	—	65,035
Accretion of series B redeemable convertible preferred stock	—	(5,516)	—	—	—	(5,516)
Adjustment to accumulated deficit due to adoption of FIN No. 48 (see Note 16)	—	—	—	(367)	—	(367)
Balances, May 31, 2008	108	659,141	—	(537,484)	(10,745)	111,020
Components of comprehensive loss:						
Net loss	—	—	—	(732,188)	—	(732,188)
Net unrealized losses on available-for-sale investments	—	—	—	—	(1,649)	(1,649)
Net unrealized losses in value of non-current auction rate securities	—	—	—	—	(23,354)	(23,354)
Net recognized losses on non-current auction rate securities included in results of operations	—	—	—	—	35,885	35,885
Net recognized losses on available-for-sale investments included in results of operations	—	—	—	—	3,594	3,594
Accumulated translation adjustments	—	—	—	—	(2,713)	(2,713)
Total comprehensive loss	—	—	—	—	—	(720,425)
Common stock issued under stock plans, net	5	15,531	—	—	—	15,536
Stock-based compensation expense	—	23,853	—	—	—	23,853
Tax benefit from employee stock options	—	1,924	—	—	—	1,924
Distribution liability related to canceled shares of restricted stock	—	34	—	—	—	34
Accretion of series B and series C redeemable convertible preferred stock	—	(21,285)	—	—	—	(21,285)
Warrants recorded in connection with issuance of series C units	—	21,966	—	—	—	21,966
Conversion of series C units and issuance of additional common stock, net	27	101,544	—	—	—	101,571
Discount recognized on issuance of series C redeemable convertible preferred stock	—	51,941	—	—	—	51,941
Balances, May 31, 2009	$ 140	$ 854,649	$ —	$ (1,269,672)	$ 1,018	$ (413,865)

Palm, Inc.
Consolidated Statements of Cash Flows
(In thousands)

Years Ended May 31	2009	2008	2007
Cash flows from operating activities			
Net income (loss)	$(732,188)	$(105,419)	$ 56,383
Adjustments to reconcile net income (loss) to net cash flows from operating activities			
Depreciation	19,677	19,699	13,316
Stock-based compensation	23,853	32,181	24,255
Amortization of intangible assets	12,134	16,510	8,315
Amortization of debt issuance costs	3,139	1,834	—
In-process research and development	—	—	3,700
Deferred income taxes	401,670	(58,227)	11,313
Realized (gain) loss on short-term investments	3,594	(68)	(110)
Excess tax benefit related to stock-based compensation	(142)	(40)	(5,241)
Realized loss (gain) on disposition of property and equipment and sale of land	619	(4,446)	—
Impairment of non-current auction rate securities	35,885	32,175	—
Loss on series C derivative	2,515	—	—
Changes in assets and liabilities			
Accounts receivable	48,425	89,312	2
Inventories	47,571	(28,147)	18,842
Prepaids and other	4,542	736	1,790
Accounts payable	(54,883)	(35,840)	11,654
Income taxes payable	(346)	3,033	16,421
Accrued restructuring	(361)	6,303	(1,803)
Deferred revenues/costs, net	12,530	—	—
Other accrued liabilities	(16,746)	12,866	9,354
Net cash provided by (used in) operating activities	(188,512)	(17,538)	168,191
Cash flows from investing activities			
Purchase of brand name intangible asset	—	(1,500)	(44,000)
Purchase of property and equipment	(13,452)	(22,999)	(24,651)
Proceeds from sale of land	—	64,446	—
Cash paid for business acquisitions	—	(495)	(19,000)
Purchase of short-term investments	(112,385)	(517,104)	(682,882)
Sales/maturities of short-term investments	88,109	777,917	671,623
Purchase of restricted investments	(2,000)	(8,951)	—
Sale of restricted investments	1,124	331	—
Proceeds related to investments in non-current auction rate securities	485	250	—
Net cash provided by (used in) investing activities	(38,119)	291,895	(98,910)
Cash flows from financing activities			
Proceeds from issuance of common stock, net	104,049	—	—
Proceeds from issuance of common stock, employee stock plans	15,536	28,437	21,926
Purchase and subsequent retirement of common stock	—	—	(30,963)
Excess tax benefit related to stock-based compensation	142	40	5,241
Proceeds from issuance of redeemable convertible preferred stock and series C units, net	99,173	315,190	—
Proceeds from issuance of debt, net	—	381,107	—
Repayment of debt	(14,446)	(3,089)	(50,816)
Cash distribution to stockholders	(439)	(948,949)	—
Net cash provided by (used in) financing activities	204,015	(227,264)	(54,612)
Effects of exchange rate changes on cash and cash equivalents	(1,902)	1,695	—
Change in cash and cash equivalents	(24,518)	48,788	14,669
Cash and cash equivalents, beginning of period	176,918	128,130	113,461
Cash and cash equivalents, end of period	$ 152,400	$ 176,918	$ 128,130
Supplemental cash flow information:			
Cash paid for income taxes	$ 3,402	$ 3,391	$ 8,900
Cash paid for interest	$ 21,828	$ 18,042	$ 1,741
Non-cash investing and financing activities:			
Liability for property and equipment acquired	$ —	$ 3,334	$ 2,309

Nokia Financial Report

Nokia Corporation and Subsidiaries
Consolidated Statements of Financial Position

December 31	2009 EURm	2008 EURm
ASSETS		
Non-current assets		
Capitalized development costs	143	244
Goodwill	5 171	6 257
Other intangible assets	2 762	3 913
Property, plant and equipment	1 867	2 090
Investments in associated companies	69	96
Available-for-sale investments	554	512
Deferred tax assets	1 507	1 963
Long-term loans receivable	46	27
Other non-current assets	6	10
	12 125	15 112
Current assets		
Inventories	1 865	2 533
Accounts receivable, net of allowances for doubtful accounts (2009: EUR 391 million, 2008: EUR 415 million)	7 981	9 444
Prepaid expenses and accrued income	4 551	4 538
Current portion of long-term loans receivable	14	101
Other financial assets	329	1 034
Investments at fair value through profit and loss, liquid assets	580	—
Available-for-sale investments, liquid assets	2 367	1 272
Available-for-sale investments, cash equivalents	4 784	3 842
Bank and cash	1 142	1 706
	23 613	24 470
Total assets	35 738	39 582
SHAREHOLDERS' EQUITY AND LIABILITIES		
Capital and reserves attributable to equity holders of the parent		
Share capital	246	246
Share issue premium	279	442
Treasury shares, at cost	(681)	(1 881)
Translation differences	(127)	341
Fair value and other reserves	69	62
Reserve for invested non-restricted equity	3 170	3 306
Retained earnings	10 132	11 692
	13 088	14 208
Minority interests	1 661	2 302
Total equity	14 749	16 510
Non-current liabilities		
Long-term interest-bearing liabilities	4 432	861
Deferred tax liabilities	1 303	1 787
Other long-term liabilities	66	69
	5 801	2 717
Current liabilities		
Current portion of long-term loans	44	13
Short-term borrowings	727	3 578
Other financial liabilities	245	924
Accounts payable	4 950	5 225
Accrued expenses	6 504	7 023
Provisions	2 718	3 592
	15 188	20 355
Total shareholders' equity and liabilities	35 738	39 582

Nokia Corporation and Subsidiaries
Consolidated Income Statements

Financial Year Ended December 31	2009 EURm	2008 EURm	2007 EURm
Net sales	**40 984**	50 710	51 058
Cost of sales	(27 720)	(33 337)	(33 781)
Gross profit	**13 264**	17 373	17 277
Research and development expenses	(5 909)	(5 968)	(5 636)
Selling and marketing expenses	(3 933)	(4 380)	(4 379)
Administrative and general expenses	(1 145)	(1 284)	(1 165)
Impairment of goodwill	(908)	—	—
Other income	338	420	2 312
Other expenses	(510)	(1 195)	(424)
Operating profit	**1 197**	4 966	7 985
Share of results of associated companies	30	6	44
Financial income and expenses	(265)	(2)	239
Profit before tax	**962**	4 970	8 268
Tax	(702)	(1 081)	(1 522)
Profit	**260**	3 889	6 746
Profit attributable to equity holders of the parent	**891**	3 988	7 205
Loss attributable to minority interests	**(631)**	(99)	(459)
	260	3 889	6 746

Earnings per share (for profit attributable to the equity holders of the parent)	2009 EUR	2008 EUR	2007 EUR
Basic	0.24	1.07	1.85
Diluted	0.24	1.05	1.83

Average number of shares (000's shares)	2009	2008	2007
Basic	3 705 116	3 743 622	3 885 408
Diluted	3 721 072	3 780 363	3 932 008

Nokia Corporation and Subsidiaries
Consolidated Statements of Comprehensive Income

Financial Year Ended December 31	2009 EURm	2008 EURm	2007 EURm
Profit	**260**	3 889	6 746
Other comprehensive income			
Translation differences	(563)	595	(151)
Net investment hedge gains (losses)	114	(123)	51
Cash flow hedges	25	(40)	(7)
Available-for-sale investments	48	(15)	49
Other increase (decrease), net	(7)	28	(46)
Income tax related to components of other comprehensive income	(44)	58	(12)
Other comprehensive income (expense), net of tax	**(427)**	503	(116)
Total comprehensive income (expense)	**(167)**	4 392	6 630
Total comprehensive income (expense) attributable to:			
Equity holders of the parent	429	4 577	7 073
Minority interests	(596)	(185)	(443)
	(167)	4 392	6 630

Nokia Corporation and Subsidiaries
Consolidated Statements of Changes in Shareholders' Equity

	Number of shares (000's)	Share capital	Share issue premium	Treasury shares	Translation differences	Fair value and other reserves	Reserve for invested non-restrict. equity	Retained earnings	Before minority interests	Minority interests	Total
Balance at December 31, 2007	3 845 950	246	644	(3 146)	(163)	23	3 299	13 870	14 773	2 565	17 338
Translation differences					595				595		595
Net investment hedge gains, net of tax					(91)				(91)		(91)
Cash flow hedges, net of tax						42			42	(67)	(25)
Available-for-sale investments, net of tax						(3)			(3)	(2)	(5)
Other increase, net								46	46	(17)	29
Profit								3 988	3 988	(99)	3 889
Total comprehensive income		—	—	—	504	39	—	4 034	4 577	(185)	4 392
Stock options exercised	3 547							51	51		51
Stock options exercised related to acquisitions			1						1		1
Share-based compensation			74						74		74
Excess tax benefit on share-based compensation			(117)						(117)	(6)	(124)
Settlement of performance and restricted shares	5 622		(179)	154				(44)	(69)		(69)
Acquisition of treasury shares	(157 390)			(3 123)					(3 123)		(3 123)
Reissuance of treasury shares	143			2					2		2
Cancellation of treasury shares			0	4 232				(4 232)	—		—
Dividend								(1 992)	(1 992)	(35)	(2 027)
Acquisitions and other change in minority interests										(37)	(37)
Vested portion of share-based payment awards related to acquisitions			19						19		19
Acquisition of Symbian								12	12		12
Total of other equity movements		—	(202)	1 265	—	—	7	(6 212)	(5 142)	(78)	(5 220)
Balance at December 31, 2008	3 697 872	246	442	(1 881)	341	62	3 306	11 692	14 208	2 302	16 510
Translation differences					(552)				(552)	(9)	(561)
Net investment hedge gains, net of tax					84				84		84
Cash flow hedges, net of tax						(35)			(35)	49	14
Available-for-sale investments, net of tax						42			42	2	44
Other decrease, net								(1)	(1)	(7)	(8)
Profit								891	891	(631)	260
Total comprehensive income		—	—	—	(468)	7	—	890	429	(596)	(167)
Stock options exercised	7										
Stock options exercised related to acquisitions			(1)						(1)		(1)
Share-based compensation			16						16		16
Excess tax benefit on share-based compensation			(12)						(12)	(1)	(13)
Settlement of performance and restricted shares	10 352		(166)	230				(136)	(72)		(72)
Acquisition of treasury shares									—		—
Reissuance of treasury shares	31			1					1		1
Cancellation of treasury shares				969				(969)	—		—
Dividend								(1 481)	(1 481)	(44)	(1 525)
Total of other equity movements		—	(163)	1 200	—	—	(136)	(2 450)	(1 549)	(45)	(1 594)
Balance at December 31, 2009	3 708 262	246	279	(681)	(127)	69	3 170	10 132	13 088	1 661	14 749

Dividends declared per share were EUR 0.40 for 2009 (EUR 0.40 for 2008 and EUR 0.53 for 2007), subject to shareholders' approval.

Nokia Corporation and Subsidiaries
Consolidated Statements of Cash Flows

Financial Year Ended December 31	2009 EURm	2008 EURm	2007 EURm
Cash flow from operating activities			
Profit attributable to equity holders of the parent	891	3 988	7 205
Adjustments, total	3 390	3 024	1 159
Change in net working capital	140	(2 546)	605
Cash generated from operations	4 421	4 466	8 969
Interest received	125	416	362
Interest paid	(256)	(155)	(59)
Other financial income and expenses, net received	(128)	250	67
Income taxes paid, net received	(915)	(1 780)	(1 457)
Net cash from operating activities	**3 247**	**3 197**	**7 882**
Cash flow from investing activities			
Acquisition of Group companies, net of acquired cash	(29)	(5 962)	253
Purchase of current available-for-sale investments, liquid assets	(2 800)	(669)	(4 798)
Purchase of investments at fair value through profit and loss, liquid assets	(695)	—	—
Purchase of non-current available-for-sale investments	(95)	(121)	(126)
Purchase of shares in associated companies	(30)	(24)	(25)
Additions to capitalized development costs	(27)	(131)	(157)
Long-term loans made to customers	—	—	(261)
Proceeds from repayment and sale of long-term loans receivable	—	129	163
Proceeds from (+) / payment of (-) other long-term receivables	2	(1)	5
Proceeds from (+) / payment of (-) short-term loans receivable	2	(15)	(119)
Capital expenditures	(531)	(889)	(715)
Proceeds from disposal of shares in associated companies	40	3	6
Proceeds from disposal of businesses	61	41	—
Proceeds from maturities and sale of current available-for-sale investments, liquid assets	1 730	4 664	4 930
Proceeds from maturities and sale of investments at fair value through profit and loss, liquid assets	108	—	—
Proceeds from sale of non-current available-for-sale investments	14	10	50
Proceeds from sale of fixed assets	100	54	72
Dividends received	2	6	12
Net cash used in investing activities	**(2 148)**	**(2 905)**	**(710)**
Cash flow from financing activities			
Proceeds from stock option exercises	—	53	987
Purchase of treasury shares	—	(3 121)	(3 819)
Proceeds from long-term borrowings	3 901	714	115
Repayment of long-term borrowings	(209)	(34)	(16)
Proceeds from (+) / repayment of (-) short-term borrowings	(2 842)	2 891	661
Dividends paid	(1 546)	(2 048)	(1 760)
Net cash used in financing activities	**(696)**	**(1 545)**	**(3 832)**
Foreign exchange adjustment	**(25)**	**(49)**	**(15)**
Net increase (+) / decrease (-) in cash and cash equivalents	378	(1 302)	3 325
Cash and cash equivalents at beginning of period	5 548	6 850	3 525
Cash and cash equivalents at end of period	5 926	5 548	6 850
Cash and cash equivalents comprise of:			
Bank and cash	1 142	1 706	2 125
Current available-for-sale investments, cash equivalents	4 784	3 842	4 725
	5 926	5 548	6 850

Glossary

Accelerated depreciation method Method that produces larger depreciation charges in the early years of an asset's life and smaller charges in its later years. *(p. 334)*

Account Record within an accounting system of increases and decreases in a specific asset, liability, equity, revenue, or expense. *(p. 53)*

Account balance Difference between total debits and total credits (including the beginning balance) for an account. *(p. 57)*

Account form balance sheet Balance sheet that lists assets on the left side and liabilities and equity on the right. *(p. 22)*

Account payable Liability created by buying goods or services on credit; backed by the buyer's general credit standing.

Accounting Information and measurement system that identifies, records, and communicates relevant information about a company's business activities. *(p. 4)*

Accounting cycle Recurring steps performed each accounting period, starting with analyzing transactions and continuing through the post-closing trial balance (or reversing entries). *(p. 114)*

Accounting equation Equality involving a company's assets, liabilities, and equity; Assets = Liabilities + Equity; also called *balance sheet equation*. *(p. 15)*

Accounting information system People, records, and methods that collect and process data from transactions and events, organize them in useful forms, and communicate results to decision makers. *(p. E-2)*

Accounting period Length of time covered by financial statements; also called *reporting period*. *(p. 96)*

Accounts payable ledger Subsidiary ledger listing individual creditor (supplier) accounts. *(p. E-7)*

Accounts receivable Amounts due from customers for credit sales; backed by the customer's general credit standing. *(p. 294)*

Accounts receivable ledger Subsidiary ledger listing individual customer accounts. *(p. E-7)*

Accounts receivable turnover Measure of both the quality and liquidity of accounts receivable; indicates how often receivables are received and collected during the period; computed by dividing net sales by average accounts receivable. *(p. 309)*

Accrual basis accounting Accounting system that recognizes revenues when earned and expenses when incurred; the basis for GAAP. *(p. 97)*

Accrued expenses Costs incurred in a period that are both unpaid and unrecorded; adjusting entries for recording accrued expenses involve increasing expenses and increasing liabilities. *(p. 103)*

Accrued revenues Revenues earned in a period that are both unrecorded and not yet received in cash (or other assets); adjusting entries for recording accrued revenues involve increasing assets and increasing revenues. *(p. 105)*

Accumulated depreciation Cumulative sum of all depreciation expense recorded for an asset. *(p. 101)*

Acid-test ratio Ratio used to assess a company's ability to settle its current debts with its most liquid assets; defined as quick assets (cash, short-term investments, and current receivables) divided by current liabilities. *(p. 174)*

Adjusted trial balance List of accounts and balances prepared after period-end adjustments are recorded and posted. *(p. 108)*

Adjusting entry Journal entry at the end of an accounting period to bring an asset or liability account to its proper amount and update the related expense or revenue account. *(p. 98)*

Aging of accounts receivable Process of classifying accounts receivable by how long they are past due for purposes of estimating uncollectible accounts. *(p. 302)*

Allowance for Doubtful Accounts Contra asset account with a balance approximating uncollectible accounts receivable; also called *Allowance for Uncollectible Accounts*. *(p. 299)*

Allowance method Procedure that (a) estimates and matches bad debts expense with its sales for the period and/or (b) reports accounts receivable at estimated realizable value. *(p. 298)*

Amortization Process of allocating the cost of an intangible asset to expense over its estimated useful life. *(p. 343)*

Annual financial statements Financial statements covering a one-year period; often based on a calendar year, but any consecutive 12-month (or 52-week) period is acceptable. *(p. 96)*

Annual report Summary of a company's financial results for the year with its current financial condition and future plans; directed to external users of financial information. *(p. A-1)*

Annuity Series of equal payments at equal intervals. *(p. 433)*

Appropriated retained earnings Retained earnings separately reported to inform stockholders of funding needs. *(p. 474)*

Asset book value (See *book value*.) *(p. 333)*

Assets Resources a business owns or controls that are expected to provide current and future benefits to the business. *(p. 15)*

Audit Analysis and report of an organization's accounting system, its records, and its reports using various tests. *(p. 13)*

Auditors Individuals hired to review financial reports and information systems. *Internal auditors* of a company are employed to assess and evaluate its system of internal controls, including the resulting reports. *External auditors* are independent of a company and are hired to assess and evaluate the "fairness" of financial statements (or to perform other contracted financial services) *(p. 13)*.

Authorized stock Total amount of stock that a corporation's charter authorizes it to issue. *(p. 461)*

Available-for-sale (AFS) securities Investments in debt and equity securities that are not classified as trading securities or held-to-maturity securities. *(p. C-5)*

Average cost See *weighted average*. *(pp. 212 & 227)*

Bad debts Accounts of customers who do not pay what they have promised to pay; an expense of selling on credit; also called *uncollectible accounts*. *(p. 297)*

Balance column account Account with debit and credit columns for recording entries and another column for showing the balance of the account after each entry. *(p. 60)*

Balance sheet Financial statement that lists types and dollar amounts of assets, liabilities, and equity at a specific date. *(p. 20)*

Balance sheet equation See *accounting equation*.

Bank reconciliation Report that explains the difference between the book (company) balance of cash and the cash balance reported on the bank statement. *(p. 265)*

Bank statement Bank report on the depositor's beginning and ending cash balances, and a listing of its changes, for a period. *(p. 264)*

Basic earnings per share Net income less any preferred dividends and then divided by weighted-average common shares outstanding. *(p. 477)*

Batch processing Accumulating source documents for a period of time and then processing them all at once such as once a day, week, or month. *(p. E-16)*

Bearer bonds Bonds made payable to whoever holds them (the *bearer*); also called *unregistered bonds*. *(p. 428)*

Benchmarking Practice of comparing and analyzing company financial performance or position with other companies or standards. *(p. 558)*

Betterments Expenditures to make a plant asset more efficient or productive; also called *improvements*. *(p. 339)*

Bond Written promise to pay the bond's par (or face) value and interest at a stated contract rate; often issued in denominations of $1,000. *(p. 414)*

Bond certificate Document containing bond specifics such as issuer's name, bond par value, contract interest rate, and maturity date. *(p. 416)*

Bond indenture Contract between the bond issuer and the bondholders; identifies the parties' rights and obligations. *(p. 416)*

Book value Asset's acquisition costs less its accumulated depreciation (or depletion, or amortization); also sometimes used synonymously as the *carrying value* of an account. *(p. 102)*

Book value per common share Recorded amount of equity applicable to common shares divided by the number of common shares outstanding. *(p. 478)*

Book value per preferred share Equity applicable to preferred shares (equals its call price [or par value if it is not callable] plus any cumulative dividends in arrears) divided by the number of preferred shares outstanding. *(p. 478)*

Bookkeeping See *recordkeeping*. *(p. 4)*

Business An organization of one or more individuals selling products and/or services for profit. *(p. 11)*

Business entity assumption Principle that requires a business to be accounted for separately from its owner(s) and from any other entity. *(p. 11)*

Business segment Part of a company that can be separately identified by the products or services that it provides or by the geographic markets that it serves; also called *segment*. *(p. 580)*

C corporation Corporation that does not qualify for nor elect to be treated as a proprietorship or partnership for income tax purposes and therefore is subject to income taxes; also called *C corp*. *(p. D-4)*

Call price Amount that must be paid to call and retire a callable preferred stock or a callable bond. *(p. 471)*

Callable bonds Bonds that give the issuer the option to retire them at a stated amount prior to maturity. *(p. 428)*

Callable preferred stock Preferred stock that the issuing corporation, at its option, may retire by paying the call price plus any dividends in arrears. *(p. 471)*

Canceled checks Checks that the bank has paid and deducted from the depositor's account. *(p. 265)*

Capital expenditures Additional costs of plant assets that provide material benefits extending beyond the current period; also called *balance sheet expenditures*. *(p. 338)*

Capital leases Long-term leases in which the lessor transfers substantially all risk and rewards of ownership to the lessee. *(p. 439)*

Capital stock General term referring to a corporation's stock used in obtaining capital (owner financing). *(p. 461)*

Capitalize Record the cost as part of a permanent account and allocate it over later periods. *(p. 338)*

Carrying (book) value of bonds Net amount at which bonds are reported on the balance sheet; equals the par value of the bonds less any unamortized discount or plus any unamortized premium; also called *carrying amount* or *book value*. *(p. 418)*

Cash Includes currency, coins, and amounts on deposit in bank checking or savings accounts. *(p. 255)*

Cash basis accounting Accounting system that recognizes revenues when cash is received and records expenses when cash is paid. *(p. 97)*

Cash disbursements journal Special journal normally used to record all payments of cash; also called *cash payments journal*. *(p. E-14)*

Cash discount Reduction in the price of merchandise granted by a seller to a buyer when payment is made within the discount period. *(p. 161)*

Cash equivalents Short-term, investment assets that are readily convertible to a known cash amount or sufficiently close to their maturity date (usually within 90 days) so that market value is not sensitive to interest rate changes. *(p. 255)*

Cash flow on total assets Ratio of operating cash flows to average total assets; not sensitive to income recognition and measurement; partly reflects earnings quality. *(p. 520)*

Cash Over and Short Income statement account used to record cash overages and cash shortages arising from errors in cash receipts or payments. *(p. 257)*

Cash receipts journal Special journal normally used to record all receipts of cash. *(p. E-11)*

Change in an accounting estimate Change in an accounting estimate that results from new information, subsequent developments, or improved judgment that impacts current and future periods. *(pp. 337 & 475)*

Chart of accounts List of accounts used by a company; includes an identification number for each account. *(p. 56)*

Check Document signed by a depositor instructing the bank to pay a specified amount to a designated recipient. *(p. 262)*

Check register Another name for a cash disbursements journal when the journal has a column for check numbers. *(pp. 274 & E-14)*

Classified balance sheet Balance sheet that presents assets and liabilities in relevant subgroups, including current and noncurrent classifications. *(p. 115)*

Closing entries Entries recorded at the end of each accounting period to transfer end-of-period balances in revenue, gain, expense, loss, and withdrawal (dividend for a corporation) accounts to the capital account (to retained earnings for a corporation). *(p. 110)*

Closing process Necessary end-of-period steps to prepare the accounts for recording the transactions of the next period. *(p. 110)*

Columnar journal Journal with more than one column. *(p. E-8)*

Committee on Sponsoring Organizations (COSO) Committee devoted to improving the quality of financial reporting through effective internal controls, consisting of five interrelated components, along with other mechanisms (www.COSO.org). *(p. 251)*

Common stock Corporation's basic ownership share; also generically called *capital stock*. *(pp. 12, 55, & 460)*

Common-size financial statement Statement that expresses each amount as a percent of a base amount. In the balance sheet, total assets is usually the base and is expressed as 100%. In the income statement, net sales is usually the base. *(p. 563)*

Comparative financial statement Statement with data for two or more successive periods placed in side-by-side columns, often with changes shown in dollar amounts and percents. *(p. 559)*

Compatibility principle Information system principle that prescribes an accounting system to conform with a company's activities, personnel, and structure. *(p. E-3)*

Complex capital structure Capital structure that includes outstanding rights or options to purchase common stock, or securities that are convertible into common stock. *(p. 477)*

Components of accounting systems Five basic components of accounting systems are source documents, input devices, information processors, information storage, and output devices. *(p. E-3)*

Compound journal entry Journal entry that affects at least three accounts. *(p. 63)*

Comprehensive income Net change in equity for a period, excluding owner investments and distributions. *(p. C-9)*

Computer hardware Physical equipment in a computerized accounting information system.

Computer network Linkage giving different users and different computers access to common databases and programs. *(p. E-16)*

Computer software Programs that direct operations of computer hardware.

Conceptual framework A written framework to guide the development, preparation, and interpretation of financial accounting information. *(p. 10)*

Conservatism constraint Principle that prescribes the less optimistic estimate when two estimates are about equally likely. *(p. 216)*

Consignee Receiver of goods owned by another who holds them for purposes of selling them for the owner. *(p. 206)*

Consignor Owner of goods who ships them to another party who will sell them for the owner. *(p. 206)*

Consistency concept Principle that prescribes use of the same accounting method(s) over time so that financial statements are comparable across periods. *(p. 215)*

Consolidated financial statements Financial statements that show all (combined) activities under the parent's control, including those of any subsidiaries. *(p. C-8)*

Contingent liability Obligation to make a future payment if, and only if, an uncertain future event occurs. *(p. 382)*

Contra account Account linked with another account and having an opposite normal balance; reported as a subtraction from the other account's balance. *(p. 101)*

Contract rate Interest rate specified in a bond indenture (or note); multiplied by the par value to determine the interest paid each period; also called *coupon rate, stated rate,* or *nominal rate*. *(p. 417)*

Contributed capital Total amount of cash and other assets received from stockholders in exchange for stock; also called *paid-in capital*. *(p. 15)*

Contributed capital in excess of par value Difference between the par value of stock and its issue price when issued at a price above par.

Contribution margin Sales revenue less total variable costs.

Control principle Information system principle that prescribes an accounting system to aid managers in controlling and monitoring business activities. *(p. E-2)*

Controlling account General ledger account, the balance of which (after posting) equals the sum of the balances in its related subsidiary ledger. *(p. E-7)*

Convertible bonds Bonds that bondholders can exchange for a set number of the issuer's shares. *(p. 428)*

Convertible preferred stock Preferred stock with an option to exchange it for common stock at a specified rate. *(p. 470)*

Copyright Right giving the owner the exclusive privilege to publish and sell musical, literary, or artistic work during the creator's life plus 70 years. *(p. 334)*

Corporation Business that is a separate legal entity under state or federal laws with owners called *shareholders* or *stockholders*. *(pp. 12 & 458)*

Cost All normal and reasonable expenditures necessary to get an asset in place and ready for its intended use. *(p. 329)*

Cost-benefit constraint Notion that only information with benefits of disclosure greater than the costs of disclosure need be disclosed. *(p. 13)*

Cost-benefit principle Information system principle that prescribes the benefits from an activity in an accounting system to outweigh the costs of that activity. *(p. E-3)*

Cost of goods available for sale Consists of beginning inventory plus net purchases of a period. *(p. 181)*

Cost of goods sold Cost of inventory sold to customers during a period; also called *cost of sales*. *(p. 158)*

Cost principle Accounting principle that prescribes financial statement information to be based on actual costs incurred in business transactions. *(p. 11)*

Coupon bonds Bonds with interest coupons attached to their certificates; bondholders detach coupons when they mature and present them to a bank or broker for collection. *(p. 428)*

Credit Recorded on the right side; an entry that decreases asset and expense accounts, and increases liability, revenue, and most equity accounts; abbreviated Cr. *(p. 57)*

Credit memorandum Notification that the sender has credited the recipient's account in the sender's records. *(p. 167)*

Credit period Time period that can pass before a customer's payment is due. *(p. 161)*

Credit terms Description of the amounts and timing of payments that a buyer (debtor) agrees to make in the future. *(p. 161)*

Creditors Individuals or organizations entitled to receive payments. *(p. 54)*

Cumulative preferred stock Preferred stock on which undeclared dividends accumulate until paid; common stockholders cannot receive dividends until cumulative dividends are paid. *(p. 469)*

Current assets Cash and other assets expected to be sold, collected, or used within one year or the company's operating cycle, whichever is longer. *(p. 116)*

Current liabilities Obligations due to be paid or settled within one year or the company's operating cycle, whichever is longer. *(pp. 117 & 371)*

Current portion of long-term debt Portion of long-term debt due within one year or the operating cycle, whichever is longer; reported under current liabilities. *(p. 379)*

Current ratio Ratio used to evaluate a company's ability to pay its short-term obligations, calculated by dividing current assets by current liabilities. *(p. 119)*

Date of declaration Date the directors vote to pay a dividend. *(p. 465)*

Date of payment Date the corporation makes the dividend payment. *(p. 465)*

Date of record Date directors specify for identifying stockholders to receive dividends. *(p. 465)*

Days' sales in inventory Estimate of number of days needed to convert inventory into receivables or cash; equals ending inventory divided by cost of goods sold and then multiplied by 365; also called *days' stock on hand*. *(p. 219)*

Days' sales uncollected Measure of the liquidity of receivables computed by dividing the current balance of receivables by the annual credit (or net) sales and then multiplying by 365; also called *days' sales in receivables*. *(p. 269)*

Debit Recorded on the left side; an entry that increases asset and expense accounts, and decreases liability, revenue, and most equity accounts; abbreviated Dr. *(p. 57)*

Debit memorandum Notification that the sender has debited the recipient's account in the sender's records. *(p. 162)*

Debtors Individuals or organizations that owe money. *(p. 53)*

Debt ratio Ratio of total liabilities to total assets; used to reflect risk associated with a company's debts. *(p. 72)*

Debt-to-equity ratio Defined as total liabilities divided by total equity; shows the proportion of a company financed by non-owners (creditors) in comparison with that financed by owners. *(p. 429)*

Declining-balance method Method that determines depreciation charge for the period by multiplying a depreciation rate (often twice the straight-line rate) by the asset's beginning-period book value. *(p. 334)*

Deferred income tax liability Corporation income taxes that are deferred until future years because of temporary differences between GAAP and tax rules. *(p. 394)*

Depletion Process of allocating the cost of natural resources to periods when they are consumed and sold. *(p. 242)*

Deposit ticket Lists items such as currency, coins, and checks deposited and their corresponding dollar amounts. *(p. 262)*

Deposits in transit Deposits recorded by the company but not yet recorded by its bank. *(p. 265)*

Depreciable cost Cost of a plant asset less its salvage value. *(p. 332)*

Depreciation Expense created by allocating the cost of plant and equipment to periods in which they are used; represents the expense of using the asset. *(pp. 101 & 331)*

Diluted earnings per share Earnings per share calculation that requires dilutive securities be added to the denominator of the basic EPS calculation. *(p. 477)*

Dilutive securities Securities having the potential to increase common shares outstanding; examples are options, rights, convertible bonds, and convertible preferred stock. *(p. 477)*

Direct method Presentation of net cash from operating activities for the statement of cash flows that lists major operating cash receipts less major operating cash payments. *(p. 508)*

Direct write-off method Method that records the loss from an uncollectible account receivable at the time it is determined to be uncollectible; no attempt is made to estimate bad debts. *(p. 297)*

Discount on bonds payable Difference between a bond's par value and its lower issue price or carrying value; occurs when the contract rate is less than the market rate. *(p. 417)*

Discount on note payable Difference between the face value of a note payable and the (lesser) amount borrowed; reflects the added interest to be paid on the note over its life.

Discount on stock Difference between the par value of stock and its issue price when issued at a price below par value. *(p. 463)*

Discount period Time period in which a cash discount is available and the buyer can make a reduced payment. *(p. 161)*

Discount rate Expected rate of return on investments; also called *cost of capital, hurdle rate,* or *required rate of return*. *(p. B-2)*

Discounts lost Expenses resulting from not taking advantage of cash discounts on purchases. *(p. 275)*

Dividend in arrears Unpaid dividend on cumulative preferred stock; must be paid before any regular dividends on preferred stock and before any dividends on common stock. *(p. 469)*

Dividends Corporation's distributions of assets to its owners. *(pp. 15 & 55)*

Dividend yield Ratio of the annual amount of cash dividends distributed to common shareholders relative to the common stock's market value (price). *(p. 478)*

Double-declining-balance (DDB) depreciation Depreciation equals beginning book value multiplied by 2 times the straight-line rate. *(p. 334)*

Double taxation Corporate income is taxed and then its later distribution through dividends is normally taxed again for shareholders. *(p. 12)*

Double-entry accounting Accounting system in which each transaction affects at least two accounts and has at least one debit and one credit. *(p. 57)*

Earnings See *net income*.

Earnings per share (EPS) Amount of income earned by each share of a company's outstanding common stock; also called *net income per share*. *(p. 477)*

Effective interest method Allocates interest expense over the bond life to yield a constant rate of interest; interest expense for a period is found by multiplying the balance of the liability at the beginning of the period by the bond market rate at issuance; also called *interest method*. *(p. 434)*

Efficiency Company's productivity in using its assets; usually measured relative to how much revenue a certain level of assets generates. *(p. 557)*

Electronic funds transfer (EFT) Use of electronic communication to transfer cash from one party to another. *(p. 263)*

Employee benefits Additional compensation paid to or on behalf of employees, such as premiums for medical, dental, life, and disability insurance, and contributions to pension plans. *(p. 379)*

Employee earnings report Record of an employee's net pay, gross pay, deductions, and year-to-date payroll information. *(p. 390)*

Enterprise resource planning (ERP) software Programs that manage a company's vital operations, which range from order taking to production to accounting. *(p. E-17)*

Entity Organization that, for accounting purposes, is separate from other organizations and individuals. *(p. 11)*

EOM Abbreviation for *end of month;* used to describe credit terms for credit transactions. *(p. 161)*

Equity Owner's claim on the assets of a business; equals the residual interest in an entity's assets after deducting liabilities; also called *net assets*. *(p. 15)*

Equity method Accounting method used for long-term investments when the investor has "significant influence" over the investee. *(p. C-7)*

Equity ratio Portion of total assets provided by equity, computed as total equity divided by total assets. *(p. 571)*

Equity securities with controlling influence Long-term investment when the investor is able to exert controlling influence over the investee; investors owning 50% or more of voting stock are presumed to exert controlling influence. *(p. C-8)*

Equity securities with significant influence Long-term investment when the investor is able to exert significant influence over the investee; investors owning 20 percent or more (but less than 50 percent) of voting stock are presumed to exert significant influence. *(p. C-7)*

Estimated liability Obligation of an uncertain amount that can be reasonably estimated. *(p. 379)*

Ethics Beliefs that distinguish right from wrong; the accepted standards of good and bad behavior. *(p. 8)*

Events Happenings that both affect an organization's financial position and can be reliably measured. *(p. 16)*

Expanded accounting equation Assets = Liabilities + Equity; Equity equals [Owner capital − Owner withdrawals + Revenues − Expenses] for a noncorporation; Equity equals [Contributed Capital + Retained Earnings + Revenues − Expenses] for a corporation where dividends are subtracted from retained earnings. *(p. 15)*

Expense recognition (or **matching**) **principle** See *matching principle*. *(pp. 11 & 98)*

Expenses Outflows or using up of assets as part of operations of a business to generate sales. *(p. 15)*

External transactions Exchanges of economic value between one entity and another entity. *(p. 16)*

External users Persons using accounting information who are not directly involved in running the organization. *(p. 5)*

Extraordinary gains and losses Gains or losses reported separately from continuing operations because they are both unusual and infrequent. *(p. 580)*

Extraordinary repairs Major repairs that extend the useful life of a plant asset beyond prior expectations; treated as a capital expenditure. *(p. 339)*

Fair value option Reporting option that permits a company to use fair value in reporting certain assets and liabilities, which is presently based on a 3-level system to determine fair value. *(p. 427)*

Federal depository bank Bank authorized to accept deposits of amounts payable to the federal government. *(p. 387)*

Federal Insurance Contributions Act (FICA) taxes Taxes assessed on both employers and employees; for Social Security and Medicare programs. *(p. 376)*

Federal Unemployment Taxes (FUTA) Payroll taxes on employers assessed by the federal government to support its unemployment insurance program. *(p. 378)*

FIFO method See *first-in, first-out*. *(p. 211)*

Financial accounting Area of accounting aimed mainly at serving external users. *(p. 5)*

Financial Accounting Standards Board (FASB) Independent group of full-time members responsible for setting accounting rules. *(p. 9)*

Financial leverage Earning a higher return on equity by paying dividends on preferred stock or interest on debt at a rate lower than the return earned with the assets from issuing preferred stock or debt; also called *trading on the equity*. *(p. 471)*

Financial reporting Process of communicating information relevant to investors, creditors, and others in making investment, credit, and business decisions. *(p. 557)*

Financial statement analysis Application of analytical tools to general-purpose financial statements and related data for making business decisions. *(p. 556)*

Financial statements Includes the balance sheet, income statement, statement of owner's (or stockholders') equity, and statement of cash flows. *(p. 20)*

Financing activities Transactions with owners and creditors that include obtaining cash from issuing debt, repaying amounts borrowed, and obtaining cash from or distributing cash to owners. *(p. 504)*

First-in, first-out (FIFO) Method to assign cost to inventory that assumes items are sold in the order acquired; earliest items purchased are the first sold. *(p. 211)*

Fiscal year Consecutive 12-month (or 52-week) period chosen as the organization's annual accounting period. *(p. 97)*

Flexibility principle Information system principle that prescribes an accounting system be able to adapt to changes in the company, its operations, and needs of decision makers. *(p. E-3)*

FOB Abbreviation for *free on board;* the point when ownership of goods passes to the buyer; *FOB shipping point* (or *factory*) means the buyer pays shipping costs and accepts ownership of goods when the seller transfers goods to carrier; *FOB destination* means the seller pays shipping costs and buyer accepts ownership of goods at the buyer's place of business. *(p. 163)*

Foreign exchange rate Price of one currency stated in terms of another currency. *(p. C-15)*

Form 940 IRS form used to report an employer's federal unemployment taxes (FUTA) on an annual filing basis. *(p. 387)*

Form 941 IRS form filed to report FICA taxes owed and remitted. *(p. 387)*

Form 10-K (or 10-KSB) Annual report form filed with SEC by businesses (small businesses) with publicly traded securities. *(p. A-1)*

Form W-2 Annual report by an employer to each employee showing the employee's wages subject to FICA and federal income taxes along with amounts withheld. *(p. 389)*

Form W-4 Withholding allowance certificate, filed with the employer, identifying the number of withholding allowances claimed. *(p. 392)*

Franchises Privileges granted by a company or government to sell a product or service under specified conditions. *(p. 344)*

Full disclosure principle Principle that prescribes financial statements (including notes) to report all relevant information about an entity's operations and financial condition. *(pp. 11 & 306)*

GAAP See *generally accepted accounting principles. (p. 9)*

General and administrative expenses Expenses that support the operating activities of a business. *(p. 171)*

General journal All-purpose journal for recording the debits and credits of transactions and events. *(pp. 58 & E-6)*

General ledger See *ledger. (p. 53)*

General partner Partner who assumes unlimited liability for the debts of the partnership; responsible for partnership management. *(p. D-3)*

General partnership Partnership in which all partners have mutual agency and unlimited liability for partnership debts. *(p. D-3)*

Generally accepted accounting principles (GAAP) Rules that specify acceptable accounting practices. *(p. 9)*

Generally accepted auditing standards (GAAS) Rules that specify auditing practices.

General-purpose financial statements Statements published periodically for use by a variety of interested parties; includes the income statement, balance sheet, statement of owner's equity (or statement of retained earnings for a corporation), statement of cash flows, and notes to these statements. *(p. 557)*

Going-concern assumption Principle that prescribes financial statements to reflect the assumption that the business will continue operating. *(p. 11)*

Goodwill Amount by which a company's (or a segment's) value exceeds the value of its individual assets less its liabilities. *(p. 345)*

Gross margin See *gross profit. (p. 159)*

Gross margin ratio Gross margin (net sales minus cost of goods sold) divided by net sales; also called *gross profit ratio. (p. 174)*

Gross method Method of recording purchases at the full invoice price without deducting any cash discounts. *(p. 275)*

Gross pay Total compensation earned by an employee. *(p. 376)*

Gross profit Net sales minus cost of goods sold; also called *gross margin. (p. 158)*

Gross profit method Procedure to estimate inventory when the past gross profit rate is used to estimate cost of goods sold, which is then subtracted from the cost of goods available for sale. *(p. 230)*

Held-to-maturity (HTM) securities Debt securities that a company has the intent and ability to hold until they mature. *(p. C-5)*

Horizontal analysis Comparison of a company's financial condition and performance across time. *(p. 558)*

Impairment Diminishment of an asset value. *(pp. 338 & 344)*

Imprest system Method to account for petty cash; maintains a constant balance in the fund, which equals cash plus petty cash receipts. *(p. 260)*

Inadequacy Condition in which the capacity of plant assets is too small to meet the company's production demands. *(p. 331)*

Income See *net income. (p. 15)*

Income statement Financial statement that subtracts expenses from revenues to yield a net income or loss over a specified period of time; also includes any gains or losses. *(p. 20)*

Income Summary Temporary account used only in the closing process to which the balances of revenue and expense accounts (including any gains or losses) are transferred; its balance is transferred to the capital account (or retained earnings for a corporation). *(p. 111)*

Indefinite life Asset life that is not limited by legal, regulatory, contractual, competitive, economic, or other factors. *(p. 343)*

Indirect method Presentation that reports net income and then adjusts it by adding and subtracting items to yield net cash from operating activities on the statement of cash flows. *(p. 508)*

Information processor Component of an accounting system that interprets, transforms, and summarizes information for use in analysis and reporting. *(p. E-4)*

Information storage Component of an accounting system that keeps data in a form accessible to information processors. *(p. E-4)*

Infrequent gain or loss Gain or loss not expected to recur given the operating environment of the business. *(p. 580)*

Input device Means of capturing information from source documents that enables its transfer to information processors. *(p. E-4)*

Installment note Liability requiring a series of periodic payments to the lender. *(p. 425)*

Intangible assets Long-term assets (resources) used to produce or sell products or services; usually lack physical form and have uncertain benefits. *(pp. 117 & 343)*

Interest Charge for using money (or other assets) loaned from one entity to another. *(p. 304)*

Interim financial statements Financial statements covering periods of less than one year; usually based on one-, three-, or six-month periods. *(pp. 96 & 229)*

Internal control system Policies and procedures managers use to monitor and control business activities. *(p. 250)*

Internal controls or **Internal control system** All policies and procedures used to protect assets, ensure reliable accounting, promote efficient operations, and urge adherence to company policies. *(pp. 6 & E-2)*

Internal transactions Activities within an organization that can affect the accounting equation. *(p. 16)*

Internal users Persons using accounting information who are directly involved in managing the organization. *(p. 6)*

International Accounting Standards Board (IASB) Group that identifies preferred accounting practices and encourages global acceptance; issues International Financial Reporting Standards (IFRS). *(p. 9)*

International Financial Reporting Standards (IFRS) International Financial Reporting Standards (IFRS) are required or allowed by over 100 countries; IFRS is set by the International Accounting Standards Board (IASB), which aims to develop a single set of global standards, to promote those standards, and to converge national and international standards globally. *(p. 9)*

Inventory Goods a company owns and expects to sell in its normal operations. *(p. 159)*

Inventory turnover Number of times a company's average inventory is sold during a period; computed by dividing cost of goods sold by average inventory; also called *merchandise turnover*. *(p. 219)*

Investing activities Transactions that involve purchasing and selling of long-term assets, includes making and collecting notes receivable and investments in other than cash equivalents. *(p. 504)*

Invoice Itemized record of goods prepared by the vendor that lists the customer's name, items sold, sales prices, and terms of sale. *(p. 273)*

Invoice approval Document containing a checklist of steps necessary for approving the recording and payment of an invoice; also called *check authorization*. *(p. 273)*

Journal Record in which transactions are entered before they are posted to ledger accounts; also called *book of original entry*. *(p. 58)*

Journalizing Process of recording transactions in a journal. *(p. 58)*

Known liabilities Obligations of a company with little uncertainty; set by agreements, contracts, or laws; also called *definitely determinable liabilities*. *(p. 372)*

Land improvements Assets that increase the benefits of land, have a limited useful life, and are depreciated. *(p. 330)*

Large stock dividend Stock dividend that is more than 25% of the previously outstanding shares. *(p. 466)*

Last-in, first-out (LIFO) Method to assign cost to inventory that assumes costs for the most recent items purchased are sold first and charged to cost of goods sold. *(p. 211)*

Lease Contract specifying the rental of property. *(pp. 345 & 438)*

Leasehold Rights the lessor grants to the lessee under the terms of a lease. *(p. 345)*

Leasehold improvements Alterations or improvements to leased property such as partitions and storefronts. *(p. 345)*

Ledger Record containing all accounts (with amounts) for a business; also called *general ledger*. *(p. 53)*

Lessee Party to a lease who secures the right to possess and use the property from another party (the lessor). *(p. 345)*

Lessor Party to a lease who grants another party (the lessee) the right to possess and use its property. *(p. 345)*

Liabilities Creditors' claims on an organization's assets; involves a probable future payment of assets, products, or services that a company is obligated to make due to past transactions or events. *(p. 15)*

Licenses See *franchises*. *(p. 344)*

Limited liability Owner can lose no more than the amount invested. *(p. 12)*

Limited liability company Organization form that combines select features of a corporation and a limited partnership; provides limited liability to its members (owners), is free of business tax, and allows members to actively participate in management. *(p. D-4)*

Limited liability partnership Partnership in which a partner is not personally liable for malpractice or negligence unless that partner is responsible for providing the service that resulted in the claim. *(p. D-3)*

Limited life See *useful life*. *(p. 343)*

Limited partners Partners who have no personal liability for partnership debts beyond the amounts they invested in the partnership. *(p. D-3)*

Limited partnership Partnership that has two classes of partners, limited partners and general partners. *(p. D-3)*

Liquid assets Resources such as cash that are easily converted into other assets or used to pay for goods, services, or liabilities. *(p. 255)*

Liquidating cash dividend Distribution of assets that returns part of the original investment to stockholders; deducted from contributed capital accounts. *(p. 466)*

Liquidation Process of going out of business; involves selling assets, paying liabilities, and distributing remainder to owners.

Liquidity Availability of resources to meet short-term cash requirements. *(pp. 255 & 557)*

List price Catalog (full) price of an item before any trade discount is deducted. *(p. 160)*

Long-term investments Long-term assets not used in operating activities such as notes receivable and investments in stocks and bonds. *(pp. 117 & C-1)*

Long-term liabilities Obligations not due to be paid within one year or the operating cycle, whichever is longer. *(pp. 117 & 371)*

Lower of cost or market (LCM) Required method to report inventory at market replacement cost when that market cost is lower than recorded cost. *(p. 215)*

Maker of the note Entity who signs a note and promises to pay it at maturity. *(p. 304)*

Managerial accounting the area of accounting that serves the decision-making needs of internal users. *(p. 6)*

Manufacturer Company that uses labor and operating assets to convert raw materials to finished goods. *(p. 16)*

Market prospects Expectations (both good and bad) about a company's future performance as assessed by users and other interested parties. *(p. 557)*

Market rate Interest rate that borrowers are willing to pay and lenders are willing to accept for a specific lending agreement given the borrowers' risk level. *(p. 417)*

Market value per share Price at which stock is bought or sold. *(p. 461)*

Matching (or expense recognition) principle Prescribes expenses to be reported in the same period as the revenues that were earned as a result of the expenses. *(pp. 11 & 298)*

Materiality constraint Prescribes that accounting for items that significantly impact financial statements and any inferences from them adhere strictly to GAAP. *(pp. 13 & 298)*

Maturity date of a note Date when a note's principal and interest are due. *(p. 304)*

Measurement principle Accounting information is based on cost with potential subsequent adjustments to fair value; see also *cost principle*. *(p. 11)*

Merchandise See *merchandise inventory*. *(p. 158)*

Merchandise inventory Goods that a company owns and expects to sell to customers; also called *merchandise* or *inventory*. *(p. 159)*

Merchandiser Entity that earns net income by buying and selling merchandise. *(p. 158)*

Merit rating Rating assigned to an employer by a state based on the employer's record of employment. *(p. 378)*

Minimum legal capital Amount of assets defined by law that stockholders must (potentially) invest in a corporation; usually defined as par value of the stock; intended to protect creditors. *(p. 461)*

Modified Accelerated Cost Recovery System (MACRS) Depreciation system required by federal income tax law. *(p. 336)*

Monetary unit assumption Principle that assumes transactions and events can be expressed in money units. *(p. 11)*

Mortgage Legal loan agreement that protects a lender by giving the lender the right to be paid from the cash proceeds from the sale of a borrower's assets identified in the mortgage. *(p. 426)*

Multinational Company that operates in several countries. *(p. C-15)*

Multiple-step income statement Income statement format that shows subtotals between sales and net income, categorizes expenses, and often reports the details of net sales and expenses. *(p. 171)*

Mutual agency Legal relationship among partners whereby each partner is an agent of the partnership and is able to bind the partnership to contracts within the scope of the partnership's business. *(p. D-2)*

Natural business year Twelve-month period that ends when a company's sales activities are at their lowest point. *(p. 97)*

Natural resources Assets physically consumed when used; examples are timber, mineral deposits, and oil and gas fields; also called *wasting assets*. *(p. 342)*

Net assets See *equity*.

Net income Amount earned after subtracting all expenses necessary for and matched with sales for a period; also called *income, profit,* or *earnings*. *(p. 15)*

Net loss Excess of expenses over revenues for a period. *(p. 15)*

Net method Method of recording purchases at the full invoice price less any cash discounts. *(p. 275)*

Net pay Gross pay less all deductions; also called *take-home pay*. *(p. 376)*

Net realizable value Expected selling price (value) of an item minus the cost of making the sale. *(p. 206)*

Noncumulative preferred stock Preferred stock on which the right to receive dividends is lost for any period when dividends are not declared. *(p. 469)*

Noninterest-bearing note Note with no stated (contract) rate of interest; interest is implicitly included in the note's face value.

Nonparticipating preferred stock Preferred stock on which dividends are limited to a maximum amount each year. *(p. 470)*

Non-sufficient funds (NSF) check Maker's bank account has insufficient money to pay the check; also called *hot check*. *(p. 265)*

No-par value stock Stock class that has not been assigned a par (or stated) value by the corporate charter. *(p. 461)*

Note See *promissory note*.

Note payable Liability expressed by a written promise to pay a definite sum of money on demand or on a specific future date(s). *(p. 54)*

Note receivable Asset consisting of a written promise to receive a definite sum of money on demand or on a specific future date(s). *(p. 53)*

Objectivity principle Principle that prescribes independent, unbiased evidence to support financial statement information. *(p. 11)*

Obsolescence Condition in which, because of new inventions and improvements, a plant asset can no longer be used to produce goods or services with a competitive advantage. *(p. 331)*

Off-balance-sheet financing Acquisition of assets by agreeing to liabilities not reported on the balance sheet. *(p. 439)*

Online processing Approach to inputting data from source documents as soon as the information is available. *(p. E-16)*

Operating activities Activities that involve the production or purchase of merchandise and the sale of goods or services to customers, including expenditures related to administering the business. *(p. 503)*

Operating cycle Normal time between paying cash for merchandise or employee services and receiving cash from customers. *(p. 115)*

Operating leases Short-term (or cancelable) leases in which the lessor retains risks and rewards of ownership. *(p. 438)*

Ordinary repairs Repairs to keep a plant asset in normal, good operating condition; treated as a revenue expenditure and immediately expensed. *(p. 338)*

Organization expenses (costs) Costs such as legal fees and promoter fees to bring an entity into existence. *(pp. 459 & 464)*

Other comprehensive income Equals net income less comprehensive income; includes unrealized gains and losses on available-for-sale securities, foreign currency adjustments, and pension adjustments. *(p. C-9)*

Output devices Means by which information is taken out of the accounting system and made available for use. *(p. E-5)*

Outsourcing Manager decision to buy a product or service from another part of a *make-or-buy* decision; also called *make or buy*.

Outstanding checks Checks written and recorded by the depositor but not yet paid by the bank at the bank statement date. *(p. 265)*

Outstanding stock Corporation's stock held by its shareholders. *(p. 461)*

Owner, Capital Account showing the owner's claim on company assets; equals owner investments plus net income (or less net losses) minus owner withdrawals since the company's inception; also referred to as *equity*. *(p. 15)*

Owner investment Assets put into the business by the owner.

Owner's equity See *equity*.

Owner, withdrawals Account used to record asset distributions to the owner. (See also *withdrawals*.)

Paid-in capital See *contributed capital*. *(p. 462)*

Paid-in capital in excess of par value Amount received from issuance of stock that is in excess of the stock's par value. *(p. 463)*

Par value Value assigned a share of stock by the corporate charter when the stock is authorized. *(p. 461)*

Par value of a bond Amount the bond issuer agrees to pay at maturity and the amount on which cash interest payments are based; also called *face amount* or *face value* of a bond. *(p. 414)*

Par value stock Class of stock assigned a par value by the corporate charter. *(p. 461)*

Parent Company that owns a controlling interest in a corporation (requires more than 50% of voting stock). *(p. C-8)*

Participating preferred stock Preferred stock that shares with common stockholders any dividends paid in excess of the percent stated on preferred stock. *(p. 470)*

Partner return on equity Partner net income divided by average partner equity for the period. *(p. D-14)*

Partnership Unincorporated association of two or more persons to pursue a business for profit as co-owners. *(pp. 12 & D-2)*

Partnership contract Agreement among partners that sets terms under which the affairs of the partnership are conducted; also called *articles of partnership*. *(p. D-2)*

Partnership liquidation Dissolution of a partnership by (1) selling noncash assets and allocating any gain or loss according to partners' income-and-loss ratio, (2) paying liabilities, and (3) distributing any remaining cash according to partners' capital balances. *(p. D-11)*

Patent Exclusive right granted to its owner to produce and sell an item or to use a process for 20 years. *(p. 344)*

Payee of the note Entity to whom a note is made payable. *(p. 304)*

Payroll bank account Bank account used solely for paying employees; each pay period an amount equal to the total employees' net pay is deposited in it and the payroll checks are drawn on it. *(p. 392)*

Payroll deductions Amounts withheld from an employee's gross pay; also called *withholdings*. *(p. 376)*

Payroll register Record for a pay period that shows the pay period dates, regular and overtime hours worked, gross pay, net pay, and deductions. *(p. 389)*

Pension plan Contractual agreement between an employer and its employees for the employer to provide benefits to employees after they retire; expensed when incurred. *(p. 440)*

Periodic inventory system Method that records the cost of inventory purchased but does not continuously track the quantity available or sold to customers; records are updated at the end of each period to reflect the physical count and costs of goods available. *(p. 160)*

Permanent accounts Accounts that reflect activities related to one or more future periods; balance sheet accounts whose balances are not closed; also called *real accounts*. *(p. 110)*

Perpetual inventory system Method that maintains continuous records of the cost of inventory available and the cost of goods sold. *(p. 160)*

Petty cash Small amount of cash in a fund to pay minor expenses; accounted for using an imprest system. *(p. 260)*

Plant asset age Estimate of the age of a company's plant assets, computed by dividing accumulated depreciation by depreciation expense. *(p. 347)*

Plant assets Tangible long-lived assets used to produce or sell products and services; also called *property, plant and equipment (PP&E)* or *fixed assets*. *(pp. 101 & 328)*

Pledged assets to secured liabilities Ratio of the book value of a company's pledged assets to the book value of its secured liabilities. *(p. 571)*

Post-closing trial balance List of permanent accounts and their balances from the ledger after all closing entries are journalized and posted. *(p. 112)*

Posting Process of transferring journal entry information to the ledger; computerized systems automate this process. *(p. 58)*

Posting reference (PR) column A column in journals in which individual ledger account numbers are entered when entries are posted to those ledger accounts. *(p. 60)*

Preemptive right Stockholders' right to maintain their proportionate interest in a corporation with any additional shares issued. *(p. 460)*

Preferred stock Stock with a priority status over common stockholders in one or more ways, such as paying dividends or distributing assets. *(p. 468)*

Premium on bonds Difference between a bond's par value and its higher carrying value; occurs when the contract rate is higher than the market rate; also called *bond premium*. *(p. 420)*

Premium on stock See *contributed capital in excess of par value.* (p. 463)

Prepaid expenses Items paid for in advance of receiving their benefits; classified as assets. (p. 99)

Price-earnings (PE) ratio Ratio of a company's current market value per share to its earnings per share; also called *price-to-earnings.* (p. 477)

Principal of a note Amount that the signer of a note agrees to pay back when it matures, not including interest. (p. 304)

Principles of internal control Principles prescribing management to establish responsibility, maintain records, insure assets, separate record-keeping from custody of assets, divide responsibility for related transactions, apply technological controls, and perform reviews. (p. 251)

Prior period adjustment Correction of an error in a prior year that is reported in the statement of retained earnings (or statement of stockholders' equity) net of any income tax effects. (p. 475)

Pro forma financial statements Statements that show the effects of proposed transactions and events as if they had occurred. (p. 126)

Profit See *net income.*

Profit margin Ratio of a company's net income to its net sales; the percent of income in each dollar of revenue; also called *net profit margin.* (p. 119)

Profitability Company's ability to generate an adequate return on invested capital. (p. 557)

Promissory note (or **note**) Written promise to pay a specified amount either on demand or at a definite future date; is a *note receivable* for the lender but a *note payable* for the lendee. (p. 304)

Proprietorship See *sole proprietorship.* (p. 11)

Proxy Legal document giving a stockholder's agent the power to exercise the stockholder's voting rights. (p. 459)

Purchase discount Term used by a purchaser to describe a cash discount granted to the purchaser for paying within the discount period. (p. 161)

Purchase order Document used by the purchasing department to place an order with a seller (vendor). (p. 272)

Purchase requisition Document listing merchandise needed by a department and requesting it be purchased. (p. 272)

Purchases journal Journal normally used to record all purchases on credit. (p. E-13)

Ratio analysis Determination of key relations between financial statement items as reflected in numerical measures. (p. 558)

Realizable value Expected proceeds from converting an asset into cash. (p. 299)

Receiving report Form used to report that ordered goods are received and to describe their quantity and condition. (p. 273)

Recordkeeping Part of accounting that involves recording transactions and events, either manually or electronically; also called *bookkeeping.* (p. 4)

Registered bonds Bonds owned by investors whose names and addresses are recorded by the issuer; interest payments are made to the registered owners. (p. 428)

Relevance principle Information system principle prescribing that its reports be useful, understandable, timely, and pertinent for decision making. (p. E-2)

Report form balance sheet Balance sheet that lists accounts vertically in the order of assets, liabilities, and equity. (p. 70)

Restricted retained earnings Retained earnings not available for dividends because of legal or contractual limitations. (p. 474)

Retail inventory method Method to estimate ending inventory based on the ratio of the amount of goods for sale at cost to the amount of goods for sale at retail. (p. 229)

Retailer Intermediary that buys products from manufacturers or wholesalers and sells them to consumers. (p. 158)

Retained earnings Cumulative income less cumulative losses and dividends. (pp. 15 & 462)

Retained earnings deficit Debit (abnormal) balance in Retained Earnings; occurs when cumulative losses and dividends exceed cumulative income; also called *accumulated deficit.* (p. 465)

Return Monies received from an investment; often in percent form. (p. 28)

Return on assets See *return on total assets* (p. 24)

Return on equity Ratio of net income to average equity for the period.

Return on total assets Ratio reflecting operating efficiency; defined as net income divided by average total assets for the period; also called *return on assets* or *return on investment.* (p. C-10)

Revenue expenditures Expenditures reported on the current income statement as an expense because they do not provide benefits in future periods. (p. 338)

Revenue recognition principle The principle prescribing that revenue is recognized when earned. (p. 11)

Revenues Gross increase in equity from a company's business activities that earn income; also called *sales.* (p. 15)

Reverse stock split Occurs when a corporation calls in its stock and replaces each share with less than one new share; increases both market value per share and any par or stated value per share. (p. 468)

Reversing entries Optional entries recorded at the beginning of a period that prepare the accounts for the usual journal entries as if adjusting entries had not occurred in the prior period. (p. 127)

Risk Uncertainty about an expected return. (p. 28)

S corporation Corporation that meets special tax qualifications so as to be treated like a partnership for income tax purposes. (p. D-4)

Sales See *revenues.*

Sales discount Term used by a seller to describe a cash discount granted to buyers who pay within the discount period. (p. 161)

Sales journal Journal normally used to record sales of goods on credit. (p. E-8)

Salvage value Estimate of amount to be recovered at the end of an asset's useful life; also called *residual value* or *scrap value.* (p. 331)

Sarbanes-Oxley Act (SOX) Created the *Public Company Accounting Oversight Board,* regulates analyst conflicts, imposes corporate governance requirements, enhances accounting and control disclosures, impacts insider transactions and executive loans, establishes new types of criminal conduct, and expands penalties for violations of federal securities laws. *(pp. 13 & 250)*

Schedule of accounts payable List of the balances of all accounts in the accounts payable ledger and their totals. *(p. E-14)*

Schedule of accounts receivable List of the balances of all accounts in the accounts receivable ledger and their totals. *(p. E-9)*

Section 404 (of SOX) Section 404 of SOX requires that company management document and assess the effectiveness of all internal control processes that can affect financial reporting; company auditors express an opinion on whether management's assessment of the effectiveness of internal controls is fairly stated. *(p. 251)*

Secured bonds Bonds that have specific assets of the issuer pledged as collateral. *(p. 428)*

Securities and Exchange Commission (SEC) Federal agency Congress has charged to set reporting rules for organizations that sell ownership shares to the public. *(p. 9)*

Segment return on assets Segment operating income divided by segment average (identifiable) assets for the period. *(p. E-18)*

Selling expenses Expenses of promoting sales, such as displaying and advertising merchandise, making sales, and delivering goods to customers. *(p. 171)*

Serial bonds Bonds consisting of separate amounts that mature at different dates. *(p. 428)*

Service company Organization that provides services instead of tangible products.

Shareholders Owners of a corporation; also called *stockholders. (p. 12)*

Shares Equity of a corporation divided into ownership units; also called *stock. (p. 12)*

Short-term investments Debt and equity securities that management expects to convert to cash within the next 3 to 12 months (or the operating cycle if longer); also called *temporary investments* or *marketable securities. (p. C-1)*

Short-term note payable Current obligation in the form of a written promissory note. *(p. 373)*

Shrinkage Inventory losses that occur as a result of theft or deterioration. *(p. 168)*

Signature card Includes the signatures of each person authorized to sign checks on the bank account. *(p. 262)*

Simple capital structure Capital structure that consists of only common stock and nonconvertible preferred stock; consists of no dilutive securities. *(p. 477)*

Single-step income statement Income statement format that includes cost of goods sold as an expense and shows only one subtotal for total expenses. *(p. 172)*

Sinking fund bonds Bonds that require the issuer to make deposits to a separate account; bondholders are repaid at maturity from that account. *(p. 428)*

Small stock dividend Stock dividend that is 25% or less of a corporation's previously outstanding shares. *(p. 466)*

Social responsibility Being accountable for the impact that one's actions might have on society. *(p. 8)*

Sole proprietorship Business owned by one person that is not organized as a corporation; also called *proprietorship. (p. 11)*

Solvency Company's long-run financial viability and its ability to cover long-term obligations. *(p. 557)*

Source documents Source of information for accounting entries that can be in either paper or electronic form; also called *business papers. (p. 52)*

Special journal Any journal used for recording and posting transactions of a similar type. *(p. E-6)*

Specific identification Method to assign cost to inventory when the purchase cost of each item in inventory is identified and used to compute cost of inventory. *(p. 209)*

Spreadsheet Computer program that organizes data by means of formulas and format; also called *electronic work sheet. (p. 524)*

State Unemployment Taxes (SUTA) State payroll taxes on employers to support its unemployment programs. *(p. 378)*

Stated value stock No-par stock assigned a stated value per share; this amount is recorded in the stock account when the stock is issued. *(p. 462)*

Statement of cash flows A financial statement that lists cash inflows (receipts) and cash outflows (payments) during a period; arranged by operating, investing, and financing. *(pp. 20 & 502)*

Statement of owner's equity Report of changes in equity over a period; adjusted for increases (owner investment and net income) and for decreases (withdrawals and net loss).

Statement of partners' equity Financial statement that shows total capital balances at the beginning of the period, any additional investment by partners, the income or loss of the period, the partners' withdrawals, and the partners' ending capital balances; also called *statement of partners' capital. (p. D-7)*

Statement of retained earnings Report of changes in retained earnings over a period; adjusted for increases (net income), for decreases (dividends and net loss), and for any prior period adjustment. *(p. 20)*

Statement of stockholders' equity Financial statement that lists the beginning and ending balances of each major equity account and describes all changes in those accounts. *(p. 475)*

Statements of Financial Accounting Standards (SFAS) FASB publications that establish U.S. GAAP.

Stock See *shares. (p. 12)*

Stock dividend Corporation's distribution of its own stock to its stockholders without the receipt of any payment. *(p. 466)*

Stock options Rights to purchase common stock at a fixed price over a specified period of time. *(p. 476)*

Stock split Occurs when a corporation calls in its stock and replaces each share with more than one new share; decreases both the market value per share and any par or stated value per share. *(p. 468)*

Stock subscription Investor's contractual commitment to purchase unissued shares at future dates and prices.

Stockholders See *shareholders. (p. 12)*

Stockholders' equity A corporation's equity; also called *shareholders' equity* or *corporate capital. (p. 462)*

Straight-line depreciation Method that allocates an equal portion of the depreciable cost of plant asset (cost minus salvage) to each accounting period in its useful life. *(pp. 101 & 332)*

Straight-line bond amortization Method allocating an equal amount of bond interest expense to each period of the bond life. *(p. 418)*

Subsidiary Entity controlled by another entity (parent) in which the parent owns more than 50% of the subsidiary's voting stock. *(p. C-8)*

Subsidiary ledger List of individual subaccounts and amounts with a common characteristic; linked to a controlling account in the general ledger. *(p. E-6)*

Supplementary records Information outside the usual accounting records; also called *supplemental records*. *(p. 164)*

Supply chain Linkages of services or goods extending from suppliers, to the company itself, and on to customers.

T-account Tool used to show the effects of transactions and events on individual accounts. *(p. 57)*

Temporary accounts Accounts used to record revenues, expenses, and withdrawals (dividends for a corporation); they are closed at the end of each period; also called *nominal accounts*. *(p. 110)*

Term bonds Bonds scheduled for payment (maturity) at a single specified date. *(p. 428)*

Time period assumption Assumption that an organization's activities can be divided into specific time periods such as months, quarters, or years. *(pp. 11 & 96)*

Times interest earned Ratio of income before interest expense (and any income taxes) divided by interest expense; reflects risk of covering interest commitments when income varies. *(p. 384)*

Total asset turnover Measure of a company's ability to use its assets to generate sales; computed by dividing net sales by average total assets. *(p. 347)*

Trade discount Reduction from a list or catalog price that can vary for wholesalers, retailers, and consumers. *(p. 160)*

Trademark or **trade (brand) name** Symbol, name, phrase, or jingle identified with a company, product, or service. *(p. 345)*

Trading on the equity See *financial leverage*.

Trading securities Investments in debt and equity securities that the company intends to actively trade for profit. *(p. C-4)*

Transaction Exchange of economic consideration affecting an entity's financial position that can be reliably measured.

Treasury stock Corporation's own stock that it reacquired and still holds. *(p. 472)*

Trial balance List of accounts and their balances at a point in time; total debit balances equal total credit balances. *(p. 67)*

Unadjusted trial balance List of accounts and balances prepared before accounting adjustments are recorded and posted. *(p. 108)*

Unclassified balance sheet Balance sheet that broadly groups assets, liabilities, and equity accounts. *(p. 115)*

Unearned revenue Liability created when customers pay in advance for products or services; earned when the products or services are later delivered. *(pp. 54 & 102)*

Unit contribution margin Amount a product's unit selling price exceeds its total unit variable cost.

Units-of-production depreciation Method that charges a varying amount to depreciation expense for each period of an asset's useful life depending on its usage. *(p. 333)*

Unlimited liability Legal relationship among general partners that makes each of them responsible for partnership debts if the other partners are unable to pay their shares. *(p. D-3)*

Unrealized gain (loss) Gain (loss) not yet realized by an actual transaction or event such as a sale. *(p. C-4)*

Unsecured bonds Bonds backed only by the issuer's credit standing; almost always riskier than secured bonds; also called *debentures*. *(p. 428)*

Unusual gain or loss Gain or loss that is abnormal or unrelated to the company's ordinary activities and environment. *(p. 580)*

Useful life Length of time an asset will be productively used in the operations of a business; also called *service life* or *limited life*. *(p. 331)*

Vendee Buyer of goods or services. *(p. 273)*

Vendor Seller of goods or services. *(p. 272)*

Vertical analysis Evaluation of each financial statement item or group of items in terms of a specific base amount. *(p. 558)*

Voucher Internal file used to store documents and information to control cash disbursements and to ensure that a transaction is properly authorized and recorded. *(p. 259)*

Voucher register Journal (referred to as *book of original entry*) in which all vouchers are recorded after they have been approved. *(p. 274)*

Voucher system Procedures and approvals designed to control cash disbursements and acceptance of obligations. *(p. 258)*

Wage bracket withholding table Table of the amounts of income tax withheld from employees' wages. *(p. 392)*

Warranty Agreement that obligates the seller to correct or replace a product or service when it fails to perform properly within a specified period. *(p. 380)*

Weighted average Method to assign inventory cost to sales; the cost of available-for-sale units is divided by the number of units available to determine per unit cost prior to each sale that is then multiplied by the units sold to yield the cost of that sale. *(pp. 212 & 227)*

Weighted-average method See *weighted average*.

Wholesaler Intermediary that buys products from manufacturers or other wholesalers and sells them to retailers or other wholesalers. *(p. 158)*

Withdrawals Payment of cash or other assets from a proprietorship or partnership to its owner or owners. *(p. 55)*

Work sheet Spreadsheet used to draft an unadjusted trial balance, adjusting entries, adjusted trial balance, and financial statements. *(p. 125)*

Working capital Current assets minus current liabilities at a point in time. *(p. 567)*

Working papers Analyses and other informal reports prepared by accountants and managers when organizing information for formal reports and financial statements. *(p. 125)*

Credits

Chapter 1
Page 3 © Gabriela Hasbun Photography
Page 9 © Hiroko Masuike/Getty Images
Page 10 © Martin Shields/Getty Images/Photographer's Choice
Page 11 © Scott Boehm/Getty Images
Page 16 © PAUL J. RICHARDS/AFP/Getty Images
Page 23 Map adapted from E. Maimon, J. H. Peritz, and K. B. Yancey, *A Writer's Resource*, 4/e. New York: McGraw-Hill, 2012.

Chapter 2
Page 51 Laura Boyd/Courtesy of CitySlips
Page 54 Laura Boyd/Courtesy of CitySlips
Page 55 © Sports Illustrated/Getty Images
Page 56 © Jed Jacobsohn/Getty Images

Chapter 3
Page 95 © John Keatley/Redux
Page 97 Ezio Petersen/UPI/Landov
Page 116 © Cameron Spencer/Getty Images

Chapter 4
Page 157 © Asia Kepka Photography
Page 158 Courtesy of Lim Ching, Singapore
Page 163 © Christie & Cole/photolibrary

Chapter 5
Page 205 © 2010 Fitness Anywhere, Inc. Used under license
Page 207 © Blend Images/Alamy

Chapter 6
Page 249 Courtesy of New Belgium Brewing Company
Page 252 © Lawrence Lawry/Getty Images/Photodisc

Chapter 7
Page 293 Courtesy of Dave Green/Johnny Cupcakes, Inc.
Page 296 © Ken Reid/Getty Images/Photographer's Choice
Page 297 © Stan Honda/AFP/Getty Images

Chapter 8
Page 327 Courtesy Emily O'Brien/Games2U
Page 330 Getty Images
Page 332 © Bradley C. Bower/Bloomberg via Getty Images

Page 337 ©Streeter Lecka/Getty Images
Page 342 ©Digital Vision/Getty Images
Page 344 ©Hunter Martin/Getty Images

Chapter 9
Page 369 Courtesy of Snorg Tees
Page 373 Dove Shore/Getty Images
Page 375 Adam Gault/Getty Images/OJO Images
Page 380 © Jeff Zelevansky/Getty Images
Page 383 ©John Burcham/National Geographic/Getty Images

Chapter 10
Page 413 © Josh Cogan
Page 416 Courtesy of Dow Chemicals

Chapter 11
Page 457 Courtesy of Clean Air Lawn Care
Page 460 Courtesy of Green Bay Packers, Inc.

Chapter 12
Page 501 © David Johnson
Page 502 AP Images/Brian Kersey

Chapter 13
Page 555 Carrie Devorah/WENN.com/newscom
Page 569 Stelios Varias/Reuters/Landov
Page 574 © Comstock Images/Jupiter Images

Appendix C
Page C-1 Courtesy of Scripophily.com

Appendix D
Page D-1 © Martin Harvey/Getty Images/Photodisc
Page D-2 AP Images/Frank Franklin II
Page D-3 © Royalty Free/Corbis

Appendix E
Page E-1 AP Images/Eric Risberg
Page E-2 ©Royalty-Free/Corbis
Page E-3 ©Jody Dole/Getty Images/The Image Bank
Page E-4 ©Nick Koudis/Getty Images/PhotoDisc

Index

Note: Entries and page numbers in **boldface type** indicate defined terms. Page numbers followed by *n* indicate material in footnotes.

Abbott-Langer.com, 7
Abercrombie & Fitch, 294
Ability to pay debts, 119–120, 130
Abnormal balance, 61, 129
Accelerated depreciation methods, 334–335
Account(s), 53–56, 76
   adjusting (*See* Adjusting accounts)
   asset accounts, 53–54, 113, 511–512
   balance column accounts, 60–61
   cash accounts, 53, 265, 268, 506–507
   chart of, 22, 55–56, 76, CA–CA-1
   cleared (*See* **Closing process**)
   contra accounts, 55, 101, 299, 338, 343
   equity accounts, 55–56, 113
   expense accounts (*See* Expense accounts)
   liability accounts, 54–55, 55*n*, 113
   noncash accounts, 507–508
   permanent accounts, 110, C-4
   prepaid, 53–54
   Retained Earnings account, 112
   revenue accounts (*See* Revenue accounts)
   T-accounts (*See* **T-account(s)**)
   temporary, 110, 111, C-4, C-7
   zero balances of, 57, 111, 473
Account balance, 57
Account form of balance sheet, 22, 70
Accounting, 2–30
   accounting equation (*See* **Accounting equation**)
   defined, 4
   financial accounting, 6
   financial statements (*See* Financial statement(s); *specific statements*)
   fundamentals of, 8–14, 254
   global view of (*See* Global view of accounting)
   importance of, 4–7, 29, 502, 556
   managerial accounting, 6
   off-balance sheet, 423
   principles-based, 10, 23, 118
   private vs. public, 6–7
   rules-based, 23, 118
   transaction analysis (*See* Transaction analysis)
Accounting assumptions, 11–12
Accounting constraints, 13
Accounting cycle, 114–115, 114*n*, 129
Accounting distribution, 275
Accounting equation, 15–16, 29, 53
   analysis of, 65–66
   business activities and, 28–29
   double-entry accounting and, 57
   elements of, 15
   expanded, 15, 57–58
   in preparing statement of cash flows, 507–508
   in transaction analysis, 16–20

Accounting errors, 68, 68*n*, 261–262, 265–266
Accounting period(s), 96, 96–97, 111, 160, 179
Accounting policies, A-9–A-12
Accounting principles, 10–11
   changes in, 581–582
   GAAP vs. IFRS on, 22
   generally accepted (GAAP), 9, 29, 504, C-6
   principles-based accounting, 10, 23, 118
Accounting year, 69
Accounts payable, 18–19, 54, 63
   adjustments for changes, 512
   as known liability, 372
   replacing with notes payable, 374
Accounts receivable, 53, 294–303, 298, 312
   adjusting entries for, 301, 311–312
   adjustments for changes in, 510–511
   aging of, 302–303, 312
   demonstration problem, 310–312
   note regarding, A-9–A-10
   ratio analysis, 309–310, 310*n*
   recognizing, 294–297, 308
   reconstruction analysis of, 527–528
   schedule of, 295
   transaction analysis, 18
   valuation of, 297–300, 308, 312
Accounts receivable ledger, 295
Accounts receivable methods of estimating bad debts, 301
Accounts receivable turnover ratio, 309–310, 310*n*, 312, 313, 569, 575, 580
Account titles, 55, 55*n*, 59
Accrual basis accounting, 97, 129, 527
Accrued expenses, 55, **103**–105, 129, 371
   ethical issues with recording, 107, 130
   financial statement links, 107
   interest expense, 104–105, 437–438, 440
   reversing entries for, 128
Accrued revenues, 105–106, 129, 130
Accumulated deficit, 465
Accumulated Depreciation account, 101
Accumulated other comprehensive income, C-9
ACFE (Association of Certified Fraud Examiners), 251, 254
Acid-test (quick) ratio, 174, 177–178, 184, 568–569, 575, 580
"Acts of God," 580
Additions, 339
Adelphia Communications, 13
adidas, 332, 420–421, 422, 435
Adjusted bank balance, 266
Adjusted trial balance, 108, 109, 129
   closing entries prepared from, 112, 175, 177
   financial statements prepared from, 122–123, 175–177
   preparing from work sheet, 126–127

Adjusting accounts, 98–108, 118
   accrued expenses, 103–105
   accrued revenues, 105–106, 130
   adjusted trial balance and, 108
   closing process and (*See* **Closing process**)
   ethical issues, 107, 130
   financial statement preparation and, 108–110
   framework for, 98–99
   links to financial statements, 107, 129
   prepaid (deferred) expenses, 99–102, 130
   unearned (deferred) revenues, 102–103
Adjusting entries, 98–99, 108, 120–121, 129
   accounts receivable, 301, 311–312
   for income tax liabilities, 393
   for investments (demonstration), C-12
   keying adjustments, 126–127
   for merchandisers, 168, 184
   periodic inventory system, 180–182, 181*n*
   prepaid expenses, 99–102, 130
   prepared from bank reconciliation, 267–268, 271
   for prepayments, 123–125
   reporting AFS securities, C-5
   reversing entries, 127–129
   for straight-line depreciation, 332
   for unearned revenues, 102–103
Adjusting entry method, 181*n*
Adjustments, 126–127, 475
   in cash flow reporting, 510–514
   end-of-period, 306–307, 375, 381
Advertising costs, A-12
AFS (available-for-sale) securities, C-2, C-5–C-6, C-9, C-10, C-18
Aging of accounts receivable, 302–303, 312
Aging schedule, 302
AICPA (American Institute of Certified Public Accountants), 9
Alcoa, 342
Allowance for Doubtful Accounts, 299
Allowance method, 298–300, 312
Altered checks, 265
Altria Group, 478
Amazon.com, 253, 438, 463, 466, 478, 501
American Express, 296, 300, 503
American Greetings, 461
American Institute of Certified Public Accountants (AICPA), 9
Amortization, 343
   bonds
      effective interest method, 429, 431–432, 434–436
      straight-line method, 418–421
   intangible assets, 343–344, 345, 350
Amortization tables, 430–431
Analysis period, 559

Andreesen, Marc, 459
"Angel" investors, 460
Animoto, 501
Animoto.com, 501
Annual Federal Unemployment Tax Return **(Form 940), 387**
Annual financial statements, 96
Annual interest rate, 162*n*, 434
Annual report(s), 70, A-1
   Apple, Inc., A-1, A-19–A-23
   Nokia, A-1, A-29–A-33
   Palm, A-1, A-24–A-28
   Research in Motion (RIM), A-1–A-18
Annual Statement Studies (The Risk Management Association), 24
Annual Statement Studies (Robert Morris Associates), 567
Annuity(ies), 433, B-1
   future value *(f)* of, B-6–B-7, B-11
   present value *(p)* of, 425, 426*n*, 433–434, B-5, B-7, B-11
Annuity table, 434, B-11
AOL Time Warner, 13
Apple, Inc., 4, 55*n*, 70, 309–310, 337, 371, 461, C-9
   consolidated financial statements of, A-1, A-19–A-23
   balance sheets, A-20
   statements of cash flows, A-23
   statements of operations, A-21
   statements of shareholders' equity, 475, A-22
   financial statement analysis, 556, 562, 566–574
Appropriated retained earnings, 474
Arm's-length transactions, 308
Asset(s), 15, 53–54, 174, 255, 440
   accrued (*See* **Accrued revenues**)
   book value of (*See* **Book value** of assets)
   classification of, 338
   current (*See* **Current assets**)
   custody of, 252, 256
   fixed (*See* **Plant asset(s)**)
   impairment of value, 336, 338, 344, 346, A-11
   intangible (*See* **Intangible assets**)
   keeping only necessary levels of, 256
   misappropriation of, 102, 307, 343, 346, 516
   noncash assets, 464, 510–512
   noncurrent, 515–516
Asset accounts, 53–54, 113, 511–512
Asset-backed securitization, 14
Asset book value. *See* **Book value** of assets
Asset disposals
   intangible assets, 343
   plant assets (*See* Plant asset disposals)
   receivables, 307–308, 309, 312

IND

Index

Asset management, 28
Association of Certified Fraud Examiners (ACFE), 251, 254
ATM cards (debit cards), 296
ATMs (automated teller machines), 264, 265
Audit, 13
Auditors, 8, **13,** 250, 275
   independent (external), 5, 556, A-3–A-4
   internal, 7, 252–253, 556
   reports of, A-3–A-4
Authorized stock, 461
Automated teller machines (ATMs), 264–265
Automatic payments, 265
Available-for-sale (AFS) securities, C-2, **C-5,** C-18
   fair value changes, C-9
   global view of, C-10
   selling, C-6
   valuing and reporting, C-5–C-6
Average collection period, 310n, 570
Average cost method. *See* **Weighted average (WA)**
Average days' sales uncollected, 310n
Average values, comparison to, 559
Avia, 436–437

Baby bond, 416n
Bad debts, 297
   allowance method, 298–300, 312
   direct write-off method, 297–298, 312
   estimating bad debts expense, 300–303, 312
      aging of receivables method, 302–303, 312
      percent of receivables method, 301
      percent of sales method, 300–301, 312
      summary of methods, 303
   notes regarding, 298, 308
Balance column accounts, 60–61
Balance per bank, 266
Balance per book, 266
Balance sheet, 20–22, 27, 423, 439n
   account form of, 22, 70
   cash and cash equivalents combined, 255
   classification of liabilities, 370–371
   classified, 115–117, 172–173
   common-size, 563–564
   comparative, 510, 518, 521, 560–561, 578–579
   consolidated, examples of, A-5, A-20, A-25, A-30
   effects of inventory errors, 218
   GAAP vs. IFRS regulations, 118
   long-term investments, C-14–C-15
   preparation of
      from adjusted trial balance, 123
      global issues, 173
      from trial balance, 69–70, 75, 109–110
   presentations, 342, 420, 480
   uses of, 22, 30
Balance sheet expenditures, 338
Balance sheet methods of estimating bad debts, 301
Banana Republic, C-8
Bank account, 262
Bank errors, 265–266
Banker's rule, 105, 305, 374
Banking activities, 262–268
   bank examiners, 571
   bank reconciliation (*See* **Bank reconciliation**)

   bank statement, 264–265
   basic services, 262–264, 265
   federal depository banks, 387
   global view of, 269
   notes given by borrowers, 374–375, 424–427
   online banking, 262
   payroll bank account, 392
Bank of America, 503
Bank reconciliation, 265–268, 270–271, 277
   adjusting entries prepared from, 267–268, 271
   error testing and correction, 266, 271
   illustration of, 266–267
   purpose of, 265–266
Bank service charges (fees), 265
Bank statement, 264–265
Bar code scanners, 207
Bare Escentuals, 164
Barnes & Noble, 184
Base amount, 563
Base period, 561
Basic earnings per share, 477, 477n
Basket purchases, 330
Baskin-Robbins, 375
Bearer bond(s), 428
Bear market, 572
Benchmarks (standards), 558, 582
Berkshire Hathaway, 468
Best Buy, 24, 294, 373, 381, 462
Betterments, 339
Beyoncé, 372
BMX, 479
Boanson, Jacqueline, 254
Board of directors, 5, 12, 459, 465, 556
Bond(s), 414–415, 428
   baby bonds, 416n
   bond financing, 414–415, 440
   bond quote, 415, 422
   book (carrying) value of, 418–419, 424
   callable, 423–424, 428
   corporate, high-risk, 28
   debenture bonds, 428–429, 441
   debt features, 428, 440
   demonstration problems, 429–432
   effective interest amortization, 434–436
      demonstration problem, 429, 431–432
      discount bonds, 434–435
      premium bonds, 435–436
   global view of, 427
   issuances, 416–423, 440
      accrued interest expense, 437–438, 440
      at discount, 417–419
      between interest dates, 436–438
      at par, 416–417
      at premium, 420–421
      pricing, 422
   issuing procedures, 416, 416n
   junk bonds, 424
   kinds of, 428
   present values of, 432–434
      annuities, 433–434, B-11
      applying present value tables, 433
      compounding periods, 434
      present value concepts, 422, 432, 440
      present value tables, 433, B-10
   retirement of, 440–441
      by conversion, 424
      journal entries for, 431–432
      at maturity, 423
      before maturity, 423–424
   return and risk analysis, 28
   straight-line amortization, 418–419, 421, 429–431

Bond certificate, 416, 416n
Bond indenture, 416
Bonding of employees, 251
Bond interest expense, 417, 421, 437–438
Bond issue, 415
Bond rating, 419, 438, 441
Bond redemption, 423–424
Bonds payable, 417–419
   amortizing bond discount, 418–419, 440
   effective interest amortization, 434–435
   mortgage bonds and notes, 426–427
   present value of, 422, B-10–B-11
   straight-line bond amortization, 418–419
Bonus plans, 380
Bookkeeping, 4
Book of original entry. *See* **Journal(s)**
Book value of assets, 101–**102,** 333–334
   impairment of asset value, 338
   recording up-to-date, 340
   sale of asset and, 341
Book (carrying) value of bonds, 418–419, 424
Book value of investment, C-7
Book (carrying) value of notes, 424
Book value per common share, 478–479, 483
Book value per preferred share, 478–479, 483
Book value per share, 477
Boston Beer, 328, 347, 375
Boston Celtics, 102, 382
Bot-networking, 254
Bottom line items, 173, 506
Bowl America, 371
Brand names, 345
Bristol-Myers Squibb, 13
Brokers, 557
Brown, Warren, 413
Brunswick, 339, C-8
Building blocks of financial statement analysis, 557, 567, 582
Buildings, 54, 329, 330
Bulk purchases, 330
Bull market, 572
Business activities, 4, 28–29
   financing (*See* **Financing activities**)
   investing (*See* **Investing activities**)
   operating (*See* **Operating activities**)
Business entity assumption, 11–12, 458
Business segments, 580, A-18
BusinessWeek magazine, 13
Bylaws, corporate, 459

Cake Love, 413
CakeLove.com, 413
Calculators, 422
Calendar-year companies, 69
Callable bond(s), 423–424, **428**
Callable preferred stock, 471
Callaway Golf, 294, 344
Call option, 423
Call premium, 423
Call price, 471
Cameron, Andrew, 254
Canceled checks, 265
Capital, 15, 458, 460, 471
   minimum legal capital, 461
   paid-in capital, 462
   paid-in capital in excess of par value, 463, 464, 467
   working capital, 567–568
Capital expenditures, 338, 339, 352
"Capitalization policy," 339
Capital leases, 345, 427, **439,** 439n

Capital stock, 461–462, A-15–A-16. *See also* **Common stock**
Capital structure, 477n
Career opportunities in accounting, 6–7, 29
Carrying (book) value of bonds, 418, 419, 424
Carrying (book) value of notes, 424
Cash, 255, 257, 276–277, 417, 508
   excess, investing, 256, C-1
   misappropriation of, 307, 516
   notes regarding, A-9, A-13
   sources and uses of, 520
Cash accounts, 53, 265, 268, 506–507
Cash basis accounting, 97, 527
Cash budget, 258
Cash controls, 255–262
   banking activities as (*See* Banking activities)
   cash, cash equivalents, and liquidity, 255
   cash disbursements, 258–262, 277, 516
   cash management, 255–256
   cash receipts, 256–258, 277
   days' sales uncollected ratio, 269, 277, 310n, 569–570, 575, 580
   global view of, 268
   misappropriation of cash, 307, 516
Cash coverage of debt ratio, 521, 575
Cash coverage of growth ratio, 521, 575
Cash disbursements, 258–262, 277, 516
Cash discount, 161
Cash dividends, 465, 465n, 483, C-7
   deficits and, 465–466
   liquidating dividend, 466
   transaction analysis, 19, 63
Cash equivalents, 255, 276–277, 503, A-9
Cash flow(s), 502–503
   for bonds, 418, 420
   classification of, 503–504, 506–507
   free cash flows, 520, 575
   net cash inflow, 503, 506, 532
   net cash outflow, 503
Cash flow analysis, 520–521, 532, 575
Cash flow on total assets ratio, 520–521, 532, 575
Cash flow reporting, 500–532, 515–516. *See also* **Statement of cash flows**
   adjustments in (*See* **Indirect method** of reporting operating cash flows)
   basics of, 502–508
   classification, 503–504
   importance of, 502–503
   measurement, 503
   noncash investing and financing, 505, 532
   purpose of, 502
   demonstration problem, 521–524
   financing cash flows, 517–519
      equity analysis, 518
      noncurrent liabilities, 517
      proving cash balances, 519
      three-stage analysis, 517
   global view of, 519
   IFRS on, 531
   investing cash flows, 21, 22, 515–516, 532
      global view of, 519
      noncurrent assets, 515–516
      other assets, 515–516
      three-stage analysis, 515
   operating cash flows
      direct method (*See* **Direct method** of reporting operating cash flows)
      indirect method (*See* **Indirect method** of reporting operating cash flows)

IND-2 Index

Cash management, 255–256
Cash over and short, 257, 261–262
Cash payments, 105, 528–531
Cash purchases, 16–17, 61–62, 64
Cash receipts
  control of, 256–258, 277
  in future period, 106
  operating cash receipts, 527–528
  petty cash, 260
  transaction analysis, 63–64
Cash registers, 53, 251, 256–258
Catalina Marketing, 10
Catalog price, 160
CB (certified bookkeeper), 7
C corporation, 12
CDC (Centers for Disease Control and Prevention), 102
Center for Women's Business Research, 54
Centers for Disease Control and Prevention (CDC), 102
CEO (chief executive officer), 459
Certificate in management accounting (CMA), 7
Certified bookkeeper (CB), 7
Certified forensic accountant (CrFA), 7
Certified fraud examiner (CFE), 7
Certified internal auditor (CIA), 7, 556
Certified payroll professional (CPP), 7
Certified public accountants (CPAs), 7, 556
CFE (certified fraud examiner), 7
cfenet.com, 251, 254
CFO (chief financial officer), 7
Change counters, 252
Change fund, 257
Changes in accounting estimates, 337, 475
  depreciation, 337, 352
  prospective application, 582
  useful life and salvage value of assets, 331, 333, 337
Changes in accounting principles, 581–582
Chart of Accounts, 22, 55–**56,** 76, CA–CA-1
Check(s), 262–263
  canceled, 265
  NSF checks, 265–268
  outstanding checks, 265
  payments by, 255, 264
  payroll check, 390–391
  printing, 266–267
  reimbursement of petty cash, 260–261
  remittance advice, 263
  restrictive endorsement of, 255
  in voucher system, 258
Check authorization, 273–274
Check fraud, 265
Checking accounts, 255, 267
Check kiting, 265
Check protector, 252
Check register, 275
Cheezburger.com/sites, 95
Cheezburger Network, 95
Chief executive officer (CEO), 459
Chief financial officer (CFO), 7
Chief operating officer (COO), 459–460
CIA (certified internal auditor), 7, 556
Citizens Against Government Waste, 102
CitySlips, 51
Classified balance sheet, 115–117, 172, 173
"Clawback," 14
Clean Air Lawn Care, 457
CleanAirLawnCare.com, 457
Cleared accounts. See **Closing process**
Clifton, Stevie, 501

Clifton, Tom, 501
Closely held corporations, 70, 458
Closing entries, 110–112, 129
  adjusted trial balance prepared from, 112, 175, 177
  for merchandisers, 169, 177, 184
  periodic inventory system, 180–182, 181n
Closing entry method, 180–181, 181n
Closing process, 110–115, 118
  accounting cycle and, 114–115, 114n
  post-closing trial balance, 112–114
  recording closing entries (See **Closing entries**)
  statement of retained earnings, 475
  temporary and permanent accounts, 110, 111
CMA (certificate in management accounting), 7
Coca-Cola Company, 54, 218, 558, C-1, C-15
Cold Stone Creamery, 375
Collateral agreements, 428
Collections, 265–266
Collusion, 252, 257–258
Columbia Sportswear, 371
Commercial substance, 350–351
Commitments, A-16
Committee of Sponsoring Organizations (COSO), 251, 253
Common-size analysis. See **Vertical analysis**
Common-size financial statements, 563–565
Common-size graphics, 565–566
Common-size percents, 563–564
Common stock, 12, 15, 55, 460, 461, 482
  dividends on (See **Dividend(s)**)
  global view of, 476
  issuing, 462–464
  participation feature, 470
  reconstruction analysis of transactions, 518
Common stock dividend distributable, 467
Common stock transactions, 518
Communicating business activities, 4
Comparability of financial statements, 97
Comparative financial statements, 559–561
  balance sheets, 510, 518, 521, 560–561, 578–579
  computation of dollar and percent changes, 559–560, 559n
  income statements, 561, 578–579
Comparative format, 559
Competitor standards, 558
Complex capital structure, 477n
Compounding, 422, 432, B-2
Compounding periods, 422, 434
Compound journal entry, 63, 65
Comprehensive income (loss), A-12, A-17, C-5, C-9
Computerized accounting systems, 111, 259, 390
  manual system compared, 59, 60, 61
  point-of-sale systems, 251, 258
Computer viruses, 253
Conceptual framework, 9, **10**
Condemnation of property, 580
Conn's, 24
Conservatism constraint, 216
Consignee, 206
Consignor, 206
Consistency concept, 215, 581

Consolidated financial statements, C-8
  balance sheets, A-5, A-20, A-25, A-30
  income statements, A-27, A-31
  with international subsidiaries, C-17
  statements of cash flows, A-8, A-23, A-28
  statements of operations, A-6, A-21, A-26
  statements of shareholders' equity, A-7, A-22, A-27, A-31
Consolidation method, C-10
Construction costs, 330
Contingencies, 382, A-16
Contingent liabilities, 382, 394
  disclosure of, 382–383, 386
  IFRS on, 372
  uncertainties, 383
Contingent valuation, 383
Continuous life of corporations, 458
Contra account(s), 55, **101,** 299, 338, 343
Contract rate on bonds, **417,** 418
Contractual restrictions, 474
Contributed capital, 15
Contributors to nonprofits, 5
Controlling influence, C-2, C-8, C-17
"Convenience" financial statements, 564
Convergence process, 9, 10, 23
Converse, 72, 332, 424
Conversion, retirement by, 424
Convertible bond(s), 428
Convertible preferred stock, 470–471
COO (chief operating officer), 459–460
Copyrights, 344
Corporate bonds, high-risk, 28
Corporate capital. See **Stockholders' equity**
Corporate income taxes. See Income taxes
Corporation(s), 12, 458–462
  capital stock in, 461–462, A-15–A-16
  capital structure of, 477n
  characteristics of, 458–459, 482
  common stock in (See **Common stock**)
  equity reporting for (See Equity reporting)
  financing of, globally, 458
  incorporation, 459
  management of, 459–460
  organization expenses, 459
  preferred stock in (See **Preferred stock**)
  shareholders in (See **Stockholders**)
  start-up money for, 460
  treasury stock, 472–474, 476, 483
Corrected bank balance, 266
Correcting entries, 68
COSO (Committee of Sponsoring Organizations), 251, 253
Cost(s), 329, 331
  of intangible assets, 343–344
  of inventory (See Merchandise inventory costing)
  of plant assets, 329–330, 349
Cost basis of new assets, 351
Cost-benefit constraint. See **Materiality constraint**
Cost-benefit principle, 265
Costco, 160, 294
Cost flow(s), 159–160, 168, 184
Cost flow assumptions, 208–209, 218
Cost method of accounting for treasury stock, 472–473
Cost of goods available for sale, 221
Cost of goods sold, 158, 169, 177, 182
Cost of sales. See **Cost of goods sold**
Cost per share, C-3

Cost principle, 11, 101, 328–329, 352
Cost to be depreciated, 332
Cost-to-retail ratio, 229
Counterfeit checks, 265
Coupon bond(s), 428
Coupon rate on bonds, 417
CPAs (certified public accountants), 7, 556
CPP (certified payroll professional), 7
Credit, decision to extend, 22, 30
Credit balances, 57, 111–112
Credit card(s), 253, 296, 297, 312–313
Credit card association fees, 296
Credit card sales, 296–297
Credit memoranda, 167, 265, 266–267
Creditor (nonowner) financing, 28, 72
Creditors (lenders), 5, **54,** 556, 572
Credit period, 161
Credit purchases
  purchase discounts (See **Purchase discounts**)
  transaction analysis, 17
Credit risk ratio, 309, 575
Credits, 57, 57n, 76
Credit sales, 11, 53, 294–296
  accounts receivable turnover and, 569
  in foreign currency, C-16
  transaction analysis, 18
Credit terms, 161
CrFA (certified forensic accountant), 7
Cuffe, Khary, 157
Cuffe, Selena, 157
Cumulative preferred stock, 469–470
Currency counters, 252
Current assets, 116–117
  composition of, 568
  inventory as, 169, 174, 182, 511–512
  noncash, adjustments for changes in, 510–512
Current liabilities, 256, **368**–394
  adjustments for changes in, 512–513
  contingent liabilities (See **Contingent liabilities**)
  defined, **117,** 371
  demonstration problem, 385–387
  estimated liabilities (See **Estimated liabilities**)
  global view of, 383–384
  known liabilities (See **Known liabilities**)
Current portion of long-term debt, 379
Current ratio, 119, 129, 567–568, 575, 580
  in approving loans, 568, 583
  classification of liabilities and, 371
  use of, 120, 130, 174, 184
Custody of assets, 252, 256
Customer(s), 6, 527–528, 556
Customer lists, 346
Cybercrime.gov, 254

Dale Jarrett Racing Adventure, 337
Dallas Cowboys, 11, 206
Date of declaration, 465
Date of payment, 465
Date of record, 465
Days' cash expense coverage, 256, 575
Days' sales in inventory ratio, **219,** 231, 570, 575
Days' sales uncollected, 269, 277, 310n, 569–570, 575, 580
Days' stock on hand, 219
DDB (double-declining-balance) depreciation, 334–335
Debenture, 416
Debenture bonds, 428, 429, 441
Debit(s), 57, 57n, 76

Debit balances, 57, 111, 112
Debit cards, 296
Debit memoranda, 162, 267
Debt, 374, 379, 426, 521
   bonds (*See* **Bond(s)**)
   retirement of
     bonds (*See* **Bond(s)**)
     gain on, 514, 530–531
     notes, 517
     taxes and interest on, 530
Debt financing, 415
Debt guarantees, 382
Debtors, 53
Debt ratio, 72, 76, 571, 575, 580
Debt securities, C-1–C-2, C-3, C-17
   available-for-sale securities, C-2, C-5–C-6, C-9, C-10, C-18
   held-to-maturity securities, C-2, C-5, C-10, C-18
   interest earned on, C-2–C-3
   trading securities, C-2, C-4–C-5, C-10, C-12, C-18
Debt-to-equity ratio, 428–429, 440, 571, 575, 580
Declining-balance depreciation, 334–335, 352
Default rate on liabilities, 384
Defective merchandise, 163, 167
Deferrals
   expenses (*See* **Prepaid expenses**)
   revenues (*See* **Unearned revenue(s)**)
Deferred income tax asset, 394
Deferred income tax liability, 393–394
Defined benefit plans, 440
Defined contribution plans, 440
Definitely determinable liabilities.
     See **Known liabilities**
Dell Computer, 24, 309
Deloitte, 7
Delta Air Lines, 339
Deltic Timber, 334
Demand deposits, 255
Demonstration problems
   accounts receivable, 310–312
   adjusting entries, 120–121
   bank reconciliation, 270–271
   bond interest amortization, 429–432
   cash flow reporting, 521–524
   current liabilities, 385–387
   dividends, 482
   equity reporting, 479–481
   financial statements, 25–27
     analysis, 577–580
     preparation, 122–123, 175–177
   investments, C-11–C-15
   merchandise inventory costing, 220–224
   merchandising transactions, 178
   petty cash fund, 271–272
   plant assets, 348–350
   ratios, 27, 76, 177, 178, 580
   transaction analysis, 72–76
Depletion of natural resources, **342–343,** 350, 352
Deposits in transit, 265
Deposit ticket, 262, 263
Depreciable basis, 102
Depreciable cost, 332
Depreciation, 101, 331–338, 340, 349
   adjusting entries for, 101–102
   changes in estimates for, 337, 352
   factors in computing, 331
   methods used, 332–336, 352
     comparison of methods, 335–336
     declining-balance depreciation, 334–335

     straight-line depreciation, 101, 332–333, 335
     for tax reporting, 336, 393–394
     units-of-production depreciation, 332, 333–334, 335, 343
   partial-year, 336, 352
   reporting, 337–338
   for tax reporting, 336, 393–394
   temporary differences in, 393–394
Depreciation expense, 515–516, 530
Depreciation per unit, 334
Derivatives, 14, 423, A-10, A-18
Diluted earnings per share, 477*n*
Dilutive securities, 477*n*
Direct method of reporting operating cash flows, **508,** 519, 524, 527–531, 532
   format of operating activities section, 507, 531
   operating cash payments, 528–531
     depreciation expense, 530
     gain on retirement of debt, 530–531
     for interest and income tax, 530
     loss on sale of assets, 530
     for merchandise, 528–529
     summary of adjustments, 531
     wages and operating expenses, 529, 529*n*, 530
   operating cash receipts, 527–528
Directors of corporation, 459
Direct sale of stock, 461
Direct write-off method, 297–298, 312
Disclosures, 22. *See also* Notes to financial statements
   of contingent liabilities, 382–383, 386
   of restricted cash accounts, 265
Discount(s), 160, 161, 417, B-2
   purchase discounts (*See* **Purchase discounts**)
   sales discounts, 161, 165, 166, 180
Discount on bonds payable, 417–419
   amortizing bond discount, 418–419, 440
   effective interest amortization, 434–435
   straight-line bond amortization, 418–419
   present value of, 422, B-10, B-11
Discount on stock, 463
Discount period, 161
Discount rate, B-2
Discounts Lost account, **275**
Discover, 300
Dishonored note, 306, 312
Distributed earnings, C-7
Distribution managers, 6
Dividend(s), 15, 55, 465–468, 476, 482
   in cash, 19, 63, 465–466, 465*n*, 483, C-7
   dividend preference of preferred stock, 469–470, 470*n*
   earned on equity securities, C-3
   stock dividends (*See* **Stock dividends**)
   stock splits, 468
Dividend allocation table, 481
Dividend in arrears, 469, 470
Dividend rights of stockholders, 460
Dividends account, closing, 112
Dividend yield ratio, **478,** 483, 574, 575
Documentation, 253, 258–259, 272–275, 277
Dodd-Frank Wall Street Reform and Consumer Protection Act, 14
Dollar changes, 559–560, 559*n*
Domini Social Index (DSI), 6
Domino's Pizza, 371
Dorsey, Jack, 3

Double-declining-balance (DDB) depreciation, 334–335
Double-declining-balance depreciation schedule, 335
Double-entry accounting, 57–58, 76, 507
Double taxation, 12, 459
DSI (Domini Social Index), 6
Dukes, Kenny, B-1
Dun & Bradstreet, 24, 347, 556, 558, 567
Dunkin' Donuts, 375

Earle, John, 293
Earle, Lorraine, 293
Earnings. *See* **Net income**
Earnings per share (EPS), 477, 477*n*, 483, 581, A-12, A-17
Earnings quality, 520–521
Earnings statement. *See* **Income statement**
eBay, 253, 328
Ebbers, Bernard, 9, 258
E-cash, 508
ECGs (electrocardiograms), 252
Echostar, 10
E-commerce, 253–254
EDGAR (Electronic Data Gathering, Analysis, and Retrieval) database (SEC), 16, A-1
Effective interest amortization, 434–436
   demonstration of, 429, 431–432
   discount bonds, 434–435
   premium bonds, 435–436
Efficiency, 557, 567
EFT (electronic funds transfer), 263–264, 392
Electrocardiograms (ECGs), 252
Electronic Data Gathering, Analysis, and Retrieval (EDGAR) database (SEC), 16, A-1
Electronic Data Systems, 10
Electronic funds transfer (EFT), 263–264, 392
Employee(s), 5, 251, 376, 556
   illegal acts by (*See* Illegal acts)
   payroll deductions for (*See* **Payroll deductions**)
Employee benefits, 379
Employee earnings report, 390, 391
Employer payroll taxes, 377–378, 394, 459
   FICA tax, 377, 387, 388
   FUTA and SUTA, 378, 387
Employer's Quarterly Federal Tax Return (**Form 941), 387,** 388
Encryption, 253–254
End of month (**EOM), 161**
End-of-period adjustments, 306–307, 375, 381
Enron, 9, 11, 13, 426
Entrepreneurship
   cash and internal controls, 249
   controlling cash flows, 501
   equity financing, 457
   financial statements, 95, 555
   inventory issues, 205
   long-term assets, 327
   merchandising activities, 157
   monetizing of business, 3
   monitoring liabilities, 369, 413
   transaction analysis, 51
   understanding receivables, 293
   women-owned businesses, 51, 54, 157, 249

Environmental issues, 348, 353, 383
EOM (end of month), 161
EPS. *See* **Earnings per share**
Equipment, 54, 62, 330
Equity, 15, 28, 55–56, 456–483
   common stock (*See* **Common stock**)
   corporations (*See* **Corporation(s)**)
   dividends (*See* **Dividend(s)**)
   preferred stock (*See* **Preferred stock**)
   reporting (*See* Equity reporting)
   return on, bonds and, 414, 415
   "trading on the equity," 414, 471
   treasury stock, 472–474, 476, 483
Equity accounts, 55–56, 113
Equity analysis, 518
Equity financing, 414, 440
Equity method, C-7, C-8, C-10
Equity method with consolidation, C-8
Equity ratio, 571, 575
Equity relations, 57–58
Equity reporting, 474–476
   in classified balance sheet, 117
   demonstration of, 479–481
   statement of retained earnings (*See* **Statement of retained earnings**)
   statement of stockholders' equity, 475, A-7, A-22, A-27, A-31
   stock options, 476
Equity securities, C-2, C-3, C-17
   available-for-sale securities, C-2, C-5–C-6, C-9, C-10, C-18
   Russian, C-15
   trading securities, C-2, C-4–C-5, C-10, C-12, C-18
Equity securities with controlling influence, C-2, **C-8,** C-17
Equity securities with significant influence, C-2, **C-7**–C-8, C-18
Ernst & Young, 7, 10
Error correction, 68, 68*n*, 217, 271
Error testing, 266
Estimate(s)
   allowance for uncollectibles, 308
   of bad debts expense (*See* **Bad debts**)
   changes in (*See* **Changes in accounting estimates**)
   of inventory costs, 218–219
   inventory estimation methods, 229–230, 231
   note regarding, A-9
   plant asset age, 347
   prior period adjustments, 475
   useful life and salvage value of assets, 331, 333, 337
Estimated liabilities, 379–381, 394
   global view of, 384
   health and pension benefits, 379
   multi-period, 380–381
Ethics, 8, 29
   adjusting accounts, 107, 130
   form of business organization, 12, 29
   inventory costing methods, 215, 231
   inventory manipulation, 218
   payment policies, 163, 184
   recording transactions, 53, 76
   state ethics codes, 9
   useful life of asset, 338, 352
   wages paid in cash, 378, 394
Events, 16
Exchange rate, 265
Executive compensation, 14
Exemption from withholding, 376
Expanded accounting equation, 15, 57–58
Expenditures, planning, 256

Expense(s), 15, 55, 98, 118, 257
   cash over and short, 257
   fixed or variable, 384
   general and administrative, 171
   joint relation with sales, 563, 582–583
   noncash charges, 509
   organization expenses, 459, 464
   other expenses, reporting, 172
   payment in cash, 62, 65, 529, 529n, 530
   selling expenses, 171
   treatment as capital expenditures, 339, 353
   wages and operating expenses, 529, 529n, 530
Expense accounts, 56
   adjusting (See Adjusting accounts)
   after closing process, 113
   alternative accounting for prepayments, 123–124
   closing to Income Summary, 111, 112
Expense recognition principle. *See* **Matching principle**
Explanation of transactions, 59, 60
Expropriation of property, 580
External (independent) auditors, 5, 556, A-3, A-4
External transactions, 16
External users of accounting information, **5**–**6**, 29, 556
Extraordinary gains and losses, 580
Extraordinary repairs, 339
ExxonMobil, 342

Face amount of bond, 414
Facebook, 3
Face-recognition software, 252
Face value of notes, 374
Factor, 307
Factoring fee, 307
Fair value, 11, 337–338, 346, 427
   adjustment computations, C-13, C-14
   changes in, C-9
   measurements, A-13
   noninfluential investments, C-2, C-4, C-5
Fair value option, 427, C-6, C-10
Fannie Mae, 13, 118
FASB. *See* **Financial Accounting Standards Board**
FASB.org, 9, 10
Fastow, Andrew, 9
Federal depository banks, 387
Federal income taxes. *See* Income taxes
Federal Insurance Contributions Act (FICA) taxes, 376, 377, 387, 388
Federal Trade Commission (FTC), 259
Federal Unemployment Taxes (FUTA), 378, 387
Federated Department Stores, 502
FICA (Federal Insurance Contributions Act) taxes, 376, 377, 387, 388
FIFO. *See* **First-in, first-out**
Fila, 332, 417–418, 422, 434
Finance leases, 427
Finance.Yahoo.com, 16
Financial accounting, 6
Financial Accounting Standards Board (FASB), 9
   convergence of GAAP and IFRS, 9, 10, 23
   on direct method of preparing statement of cash flows, 509, 531
   FASB.org, 9, 10
   reporting requirements of, 504

Statements of Financial Accounting Standards (SFAS), No. 153, "Exchanges of Nonmonetary Assets," 350
Financial assets at fair value through profit and loss. *See* **Trading securities**
Financial leverage, 72, 414, **471,** 571
Financial management, 28
Financial reporting, 336, **557**
Financial section of annual reports, A-1
Financial statement(s), 20–22, 29, 68, 71, 97
   adjusting entries linked to, 107, 129
   balance sheet (*See* **Balance sheet**)
   common-size, 563–564, 565
   comparative (*See* **Comparative financial statements**)
   confidence in, internal controls and, 253
   "convenience" statements, 564
   demonstration problem, 25–27
   examples of, A-1–A-33
      Apple, Inc., A-1, A-19–A-23
      Nokia, A-1, A-29–A-33
      Palm, A-1, A-24–A-28
      Research in Motion (RIM), A-1, A-2–A-18
   formatting, 21, 22, 70
   general-purpose, 5, 557
   IFRS requirements for, 59
   income statement (*See* **Income statement**)
   links among, 21, 69
   pro forma, 126
   reporting comprehensive income, C-9
   statement of cash flows (*See* **Statement of cash flows**)
   statement of retained earnings (*See* **Statement of retained earnings**)
Financial statement analysis, 554–582
   basics of, 556–558
      building blocks of, 557, 567, 582
      information for, 557
      purpose, 556
      standards for comparison, 558
      tools of analysis, 558
   defined, **556**
   demonstration problem, 577–580
   in fraud prevention, 558
   horizontal analysis (*See* **Horizontal analysis**)
   ratio analysis (*See* **Ratio analysis**)
   vertical analysis (*See* **Vertical analysis**)
Financial statement analysis report, 576–577, 582
Financial statement effects
   of adjusting entries, 121
   of asset classification, 338
   of inventory costing methods, 121, 214–215, 228
   of inventory errors, 216–218, 224, 231
Financial statement formats, 170–172
   classified balance sheet, 172
   multiple-step income statement, 171–172, 176–177, 184
   single-step income statement, 172, 177, 184
Financial statement preparation, 76
   from adjusted trial balance, 122–123, 175–177
   adjusting accounts and, 108–110
   global view of, 118
   for merchandisers, 169
   note regarding, A-9
   from trial balance, 68–70, 75, 109
   work sheet used in, 125–126, 127

Financing activities, 28, 29, **504,** 532
   accounting equation and, 28
   cash flows from, 21, 22, 517–519, 532
Firewalls, 253–254
First-in, first-out (FIFO), 211
   current ratio and, 568
   frequency of use, 208
   periodic inventory system, 225–226, 228
   perpetual inventory system, 211, 221–222
      changes in inventory value, 214, 231
      cost flow assumption, 208, 209
      financial statement effects, 214
First Industrial Realty, 298
Fiscal year, 69, **97**
Fitch, 419
FitnessAnywhere.com, 205
Fitness Anywhere Inc., 205
Fixed assets. *See* **Plant asset(s)**
Fixed expenses, 384
Fleming, 158
Floating an issue, 416n
FOB (free on board) point, **163**–164, 206
Fool.com, 555
Footing, 69
Ford Motor Company, 297, 380, 382
Foreign currency exchange, 265, A-9
   exchange rates, C-15, C-16, C-17, C-18
   sales and purchases in, C-16–C-17, C-18
Foreign exchange rate, C-15, C-16
Forged endorsements, 265
Forged signature, 265
Form 940 (Annual Federal Unemployment Tax Return), **387**
Form 941 (Employer's Quarterly Federal Tax Return), **387,** 388
Form 10–K, A-1
Form 10–KSB, A-1
Form W-2 (Wage and Tax Statement), **389**
Form W-4, 392
Franchises, 344–345, 375, 385, 394
Franklin, Benjamin, 432
Fraud, 7
   accounting controls, 71
   accounts receivable fraud, 298
   ACFE and, 251, 254
   cash disbursements, 516
   check fraud, forms of, 265
   collusion in, 252, 257, 258
   employee knowledge of, 268
   false or misleading invoices, 173
   financial regulation and, 576
   hiding debt, 426
   human fraud, 254
   involving assets, 102, 343, 346
   involving payables, 383
   in long-term liabilities, 426
   management override, 254
   merchant fraud losses, 300
   misappropriation of cash, 307, 516
   payroll fraud, 378, 379
   physical count of inventory and, 207
   prevention of, 8–9, 13, 259
      cash monitoring and, 504
      clues to internal control violations, 262
      embedded tags, 252
      with financial statement analysis, 558
      inventory controls, 213
      safeguarding assets, 343
   "pump 'n dump," 476
   religious organizations vulnerable to, 67
   in revenue and expense recognition, 118

   reversing sales returns, 167
   risk of, 426
   role of economic downturn in, 13
   sec.gov/investor/pubs/cyberfraud.htm, 253
   skimming, 307, 516
   unreliable accounting, 9
   unreported liabilities, 423
   www.fraud.org, 253
Fraud triangle, 8–9, 254
Free cash flows, 520, 575
Free on board **(FOB)** point, **163**–164, 206
Freight-in, 164, 179–180
Freight-out, 164
Fremont General, 10
FTC (Federal Trade Commission), 259
ftc.gov/bcp/consumer.shtm, 253
Full-disclosure principle, 11, 215, 306, 505
   contingent liabilities, 382–383
   dividends in arrears, 470
   warranties, 380, 381
FUTA (Federal Unemployment Taxes), 378, 387
Future value (f)
   of ordinary annuity, B-6–B-7, B-11
   of single amount, B-3–B-5, B-7, B-10
Future value tables, B-7, B-10, B-11
   of annuity of 1, B-11
   of single amount, B-10

GAAP. *See* **Generally accepted accounting principles**
Gains, 171–172, 580–581
   on foreign exchange, C-16
   nonoperating, adjustments for, 513–514
   plant asset exchanges, 351
   on retirement of debt, 514, 530–531
   unrealized, C-4, C-12
Games2U, 327
Games2U.com, 327
Gap, Inc., 97, 158, 514, C-1, C-8, C-11
Gardner, David, 555
Gardner, Tom, 555
Garza, Mary E., 503
Gateway Distributors, 298
General and administrative expenses, 171
General journal, 58–60, 73–74
General ledger, 53, 56, 295
Generally accepted accounting principles (GAAP), 9, 29
   fair value option, C-6
   IFRS compared (*See* Global view of accounting)
   on operating activities, 504
   rules-based accounting, 23, 118
   tax reporting and, 393–394
General principles, 10
General-purpose financial statements, 5, **557**
General rights of stockholders, 460
GeoCities, 345
Giard, Kelly, 457
Gift card sales, 373
Global Crossing, 13
Global view of accounting, 23, 71, 118, 173
   adjusting accounts, 118
   balance sheet, 173
   basic principles, 22
   closing process, 118
   for corporations, 460, 476
   income statement, 173
   intangible assets, 347

internal controls, 71, 268, 269
for investments, C-10
liabilities, 383–384
long-term liabilities, 427
merchandise inventory, 218–219
merchandise purchases and sales, 173
plant assets, 346–347
receivables, 308–309
Going-concern assumption, 11, 337–338
Goods damaged or obsolete, 206
Goods for sale, 117
Goods in transit, 206
Goods on consignment, 206
Goodwill, 345, A-11
Google, 255, 501
Governance systems, 13
Government officials, 5
Grant Thornton, 10
Graphical analysis, 562, 565
Green Bay Packers, Inc., 11, 460
Green Mountain Coffee Roasters, 167
Gross margin, 158–159
Gross margin ratio, 174–175, 177, 178, 184, 185
Gross method of recording purchases, 162, **275–**276
Gross pay, 376, 389, 389n
Gross profit, 158–159, 165
  inventory cost flow assumptions and, 208, 209
  reporting for merchandiser, 169, 171, 182
Gross profit method, 230, 231
Gross profit ratio. See **Gross margin ratio**
Group purchases, 330
Growth stocks, 478
Guidelines (rules of thumb), 558

Hackers, 253–254
Halliburton, 13
Harley-Davidson, 298, 371, 468, 514
Health benefits, 379
Held-to-maturity (HTM) securities, C-2, **C-5,** C-10, C-18
Heritage Link Brands, 157
HeritageLinkBrands.com, 157
Hershey Foods, 332
Hetrick, Randy, 205
The Home Depot, 184, 229, 372, 438, 439, 476
Honored note, 306, 312
Horizontal analysis, 558, 559–563, 576, 582
  comparative financial statements, 559–561
  balance sheets, 560–561
  dollar and percent changes, 559–560, 559n
  income statements, 561
  trend analysis, 561–563
Hostile takeovers, 470n
HTM (held-to-maturity) securities, C-2, **C-5,** C-10, C-18
Huh, Ben, 95
Human error, 254
Human fraud, 254
Human resource managers, 6
Hybrid inventory systems, 160, 164

IASB. See **International Accounting Standards Board**
IASB.org.uk, 9, 10
IBM, 415
IDEA. See EDGAR

Identifying business activities, 4
Identity theft, 253, 254
IFRS (International Financial Reporting Standards), 9
IFRS.com, 9
Illegal acts
  collusion, 252, 257, 258
  credit card number theft, 253
  fraud (See Fraud)
  identity theft, 253, 254
  misappropriation of assets, 102, 307, 343, 346, 516
  shrinkage, 168, 180–181, 229
ImClone, 13
Impairment of asset value, **338, 344**
  note regarding, A-11
  plant assets, 346
  recoverable amount of loss, 336
Impersonation online, 253
Implied annual interest rate, 162n
Imprest system, 260
Improvements (betterments), 339
Inadequacy of asset, **331**
Incentive-based compensation, 14
Income, 15, 158, 171, 173
  comprehensive income (loss), A-12, A-17, C-5, C-9
  net income, 15, 27, 171, 173, 477
  adjusting for statement of cash flows, 526
  computing from worksheet, 126, 127
  difference from operating cash flows, 514
  from long-term investments, C-10
  sustainable, 580–582
Income statement, 20, 21
  common-size, 563–564, 565
  comparative, 561, 578–579
  complete, 580, 582
  consolidated, examples of, A-6, A-21, A-26, A-27, A-31
  demonstration, 26
  long-term investments, C-14, C-15
  multiple-step, 171–172, 176–177, 184
  preparation of, 173
    from adjusted trial balance, 122
    from trial balance, 69, 75, 109, 110
  single-step, 172, 177, 184
  for specific accounting period, 111
Income statement effects of inventory errors, 216–218, 224
Income statement expenditures, 338
Income statement method of estimating bad debts, 300–301
Income stocks, 478
Income Summary account, **111–**112
Income taxes, 390–392, 513, 530. See also specific tax forms
  deferred liabilities, 393–394
  deferred tax asset, 394
  employee payroll deductions, 376–377
  notes regarding, A-11, A-15
  partnerships and proprietorships not subject to, 459
Incorporation, 459
Incorporators, 459, 464
Indefinite life of asset, **343,** 344
Independent (external) auditors, 5
Index number, 561
Index number trend analysis, 561–563
Indirect method of reporting operating cash flows, **508–**509, 510, 511
  adjustments, 510–514
    changes in current liabilities, 512–513

changes in noncash current assets, 510–512
  nonoperating items, 513–514
  operating items not providing or using cash, 513
  summary of, 514
application of, 509–514
demonstration of, 522–523
global view of, 519
spreadsheet preparation, 524–526
Indirect sale of stock, 461
Industry Norms & Key Business Ratios (Dun & Bradstreet), 24, 567
Industry standards, 558
Influential investments, C-7–C-9, C-10
  accounting summary, C-8–C-9
  comprehensive income, C-9
  controlling influence, C-2, C-8, C-17
  significant influence, C-2, C-7–C-8, C-18
Infrequent gain or loss, 580–581
Initial public offering (IPO), 461
Installment accounts receivable, 297
Installment notes, 425–426, 426n, 429, 430
Installment sales, 297
Insurance, 54, 64, 99–100, 251
Intangible assets, 54, **117, 343–**346, 352
  cost determination and amortization, 343–344
  disposal of, 343
  global view of, 347
  notes regarding, 347, A-11, A-14
  types of, 344–346
Interactive Data Electronic Applications (IDEA) database (SEC), A-1
Interest, 304
  on bonds (See **Bond(s)**)
  on checking accounts, 267
  on notes
    end-of-period adjustment, 375
    notes receivable, 304, 305, 306–307
    short-term notes payable, 374
  on retirement of debt, 530
  semiannual payment of, 434
  time value of money and (See Time value of money)
Interest expense, 573
  accrued, 104–105, 437–438, 440
  bond interest expense, 417, 421, 437–438, 440
  on short-term notes payable, 374, 386
Interest payable, 512–513
Interest rate, 162n
Interest revenue, 106, C-2–C-3
Interim financial statements, 96, 229
Intermediaries, 158
Internal auditors, 7, 252, 253, 556
Internal control(s), 6, 249, 250–254, 271, 276
  cash controls (See Cash controls)
  clues to violations of, 262
  global view of, 71, 268, 269
  inventory controls, 207, 213
  limitations on, 254, 265
  mandatory vacation policy, 251, 253, 277
  note regarding, 268
  in payroll accounting, 378
  principles of (See **Principles of internal control**)
  purpose of, 250–251
  technological, 5, 252, 253–254

bar code scanners, 207
e-commerce, increased, 253–254
electrocardiograms, 252
embedded tags, 252
face-recognition software, 252
limited evidence and, 253
processing errors, 253
records testing and, 253
separation of duties crucial to, 253
Internal control environment, 254
Internal control report, 251, A-4
Internal control systems, 250
Internal Revenue Service (IRS), 5, 68, 215, 345, 376
Internal transactions, 16
Internal users of accounting information, **6,** 29, 502, 556
International Accounting Standards Board (IASB), 9
  convergence of GAAP and IFRS, 9, 10, 23
  IASB.org.uk, 9, 10
International Financial Reporting Standards (IFRS), 9
  on cash flow reporting, 531
  on consolidated subsidiaries, C-8
  contingent liabilities, 372
  on effective interest method, 436
  fair value option, C-6
  financial statement requirements, 59
  GAAP compared (See Global view of accounting)
  on internal controls, 269
  on preferred stocks, 471
  principles-based, 23, 118
  revenue and expense recognition, 118
  useful life and salvage value estimates, 341
International operations, C-15–C-17
  consolidated financial statements, C-17
  exchange rates and, C-15, C-16
  sales and purchases, C-16–C-17, C-18
Intracompany standards, 558
Inventory(ies), 159, 160, 179, 205, 207
  cost determination (See Merchandise inventory costing)
  as current asset, 169, 174, 182
  ethical issues, 215, 218, 231
  inventory systems, 159–160, 164, 174, 256
  managerial decisions regarding, 208
  for merchandisers (See **Merchandise inventory**)
  notes regarding, 219, A-10, A-14
  physical count of, 179, 180
  write-downs of, 580
Inventory errors, 216–218, 224, 231
Inventory relation, 216
Inventory systems
  hybrid systems, 160, 164
  periodic (See **Periodic inventory system**)
  perpetual (See **Perpetual inventory system**)
Inventory turnover ratio, **219,** 231, 569, 575, 580
Investing activities, 28, 29, **504,** 532
  accounting equation and, 28
  cash flows from, 21, 22, 515–516, 519, 532
InvestingInBonds.com, 422

Index

Investment(s), C–C-18
  basics of, C1–C-3
  demonstration problems, C-11–C-15
  in franchises, 385, 394
  global view of, C-10
  influential (*See* **Influential investments**)
  in international operations (*See* **International operations**)
  long-term, 117, C-1, C-9, C-10, C-14, C-15
  noninfluential (*See* **Noninfluential investments**)
  notes regarding, A-10, A-13
  short-term, C-1, C-9
  strategies for holding, C-5, C-18
  using debt ratio in evaluating, 72, 76
Investment by owner, 16
Investors (shareholders), 5, 460
Investor's Business Daily, 574
Invoice(s), 53, 272, 273, 274
  false or misleading, 173
  fraud involving, 383
  as source documents, 160, 161
Invoice approval, 273–274
IPO (initial public offering), 461
IRS. *See* Internal Revenue Service

JCPenney, 174, 175, 296, 297
J.D. Power and Associates, C-8
Jefferson, Brad, 501
John Deere, 294
Johnny Cupcakes, Inc., 293
JohnnyCupcakes.com, 293
Joint relation between sales and expenses, 563, 582–583
Jordan, Kim, 249
Journal(s), 58–60, 73–74, 390
Journal entries, 63, 65, 76, 121
  for cash dividends, 465, 465*n*, 483
  demonstrations of, 73–74, 178, C-11–C-12, C-13, C-14
  explanation of transactions, 59, 60
  posting, 60, 61, 74
  receivables, 311, 312
  retirement of bonds, 431, 432
  for stockholders' equity, 480, 481, 482
Journalizing transactions, **58–**60
JP Morgan, 300
Junk bonds, 424
Just-in-time inventory, 174, 256

The Kellogg Company, 97
Keying adjustments, 126, 127
Kforce.com, 7
K2 Inc., 116, 117, 439
Kiting of cash, 516
Known liabilities, 372–379, 384, 394
  accounts payable, 372
  multi-period, 378–379
  payroll liabilities, 375–378, 388, 394, 459
  sales taxes payable, 372–373, 373*n*
  short-term notes payable, 373–375
  unearned revenues, 373
Kodak, 380
KPMG, 7, 118
Kyocera, 164

Labor unions, 5, 303, 313, 519, 532, 556
Land, 54, 101, 329–330
Land improvements, 330
Lapping, 516

Large stock dividend, 466, 467–468
Last-in, first-out (LIFO), 211
  current ratio and, 568
  frequency of use, 208
  periodic inventory system, 226–227, 228
  perpetual inventory system, 211–212
    cost flow assumption, 208, 209
    demonstration of, 208, 209, 222
    financial statement effects, 214
    tax effects, 214–215
LCM (lower of cost or market), 215–218
Lease(s), 345, 438–439, 440
  capital leases, 345, 427, 439, 439*n*
  operating leases, 427, 438
Leasehold(s), 345
Leasehold improvements, 345–346
Lease payment schedule, 439*n*
Lebed, Jonathan, 476
Ledger(s), 53, 56, 76
  explanation of transactions, 60
  general ledger, 53, 56, 295
  subsidiary ledgers, 207, 295, 337, 374
  in T-account form, 66
Legal claims, 382
Legal restriction, 474
Legislators, 5
Lenders (creditors), 5, 54, 556, 572
Lessee, 345, 438
Lessor, 345, 438
Levitt, Susie, 51
Liabilities, 15, 28, 54–55, 55*n*, 370–372, 394
  accrued (*See* **Accrued expenses**)
  classification of, 370–371
  current (*See* **Current liabilities**)
  long-term (*See* **Long-term liabilities**)
  defining, 370
  IFRS vs. GAAP on, 383–384
  income tax liabilities, 393–394
  known (*See* **Known liabilities**)
  note regarding, 383
  payroll liabilities, 375–378
    employee deductions, 376–377
    employer taxes, 377–378, 387, 388, 394, 459
  uncertainty in, 371–372
  unreported, 423
Liability accounts, 54–55, 55*n*, 113
Licenses, 344–345
LIFO. *See* **Last-in, first-out**
LIFO conformity rule, 215
Limited Brands, Inc., 119, 184
Limited liability company (LLC), 12
Limited liability of stockholders, 458
Limited liability partnership (LLP), 12
Limited life of asset, **343,** 344
Limited partnership (LP), 12
Line of credit, 296
Liquid assets, 255
Liquidating cash dividend, 466
Liquidating dividend, 466
Liquidity, 174, **255,** 557, 567
Liquidity and efficiency ratios, 24, 567–570, 575
  accounts receivable turnover, 309–310, 310*n*, 312, 313, 569, 575, 580
  acid-test (quick) ratio, 174, 177, 178, 184, 568–569, 580, 686
  current ratio, 119, 120, 129, 130, 174, 184, 371, 567–568, 575, 580, 583
  days' sales in inventory, 219, 231, 570, 575
  days' sales uncollected, 269, 277, 310*n*, 569–570, 575, 580

  inventory turnover ratio, 219, 231, 569, 575, 580
  total asset turnover, 347, 348, 352, 353, 569, 570, 572, 575, 580, C-10, C-11
List price, 160
LLC (limited liability company), 12
LLP (limited liability partnership), 12
Long-term assets, 326–352
  intangible (*See* **Intangible assets**)
  natural resources (*See* **Natural resources**)
  plant assets (*See* **Plant asset(s)**)
Long-term debt, 379
Long-term investments, 117, C-1, C-9
  in income statement, C-14, C-15
  net income from, C-10
Long-term liabilities, 117, 371, 394, 412–441, 426, 427
  bonds (*See* **Bond(s)**)
  in classified balance sheet, 117
  debt features, 428, 440
  lease liabilities
    capital leases, 345, 427, 439, 439*n*
    operating leases, 427, 438
  notes (*See* Long-term notes payable)
  pension liabilities, 440
Long-term notes payable, 424–427, 429, 430, 440, 441
  debt features, 428, 440
  installment notes, 425–426, 426*n*, B-11
  mortgage bonds and notes, 426–427
Los Angeles Lakers, 56
Losses, 172, 251, 580–581
  on foreign exchange, C-16
  merchant fraud losses, 300
  net loss, 15, 126, 127
  on plant assets, 336, 346, 350–351, 514, 530
  unrealized loss on trading securities, C-4, C-12
Lottery winners, B-1, B-6
Lower of cost or market (LCM), 215–218, 231
LP (limited partnership), 12
Lump-sum purchases, 330

Machinery, 330
MACRS (Modified Accelerated Cost Recovery System), 336
Macy's, 97, 502
Madoff, Bernard, 9
Madoff Investment Securities, 9
Major League Baseball, 344–345
Maker of check, 262
Maker of debit memorandum, 162
Maker of note, 304
Management override, 254
Management's Discussion and Analysis (MD&A), 28, 253, 557
Managerial accounting, 6
Managerial decisions, 208
Mandatory vacation policy, 251, 253, 277
Manual accounting system, 59, 60, 61
Manufacturers, 16
Marketable securities. *See* **Short-term investments**
Marketing managers, 6
Market prospects, 557
Market prospects ratios, 24, 573–574, 575
  dividend yield ratio, 478, 483, 574, 575
  price-earnings ratio, 477, 478, 483, 573–574, 575
Market rate on bonds, **417,** 418, 422

Market value(s), 215, 330
Market value per share, 461
MasterCard, 296, 300
Matching principle, 11, 98, 298, 375
  determining inventory costs, 207, 208
  warranties, 380, 381
Materiality constraint, 13, 207, **298,** 339
Maturity date of bond, 414, 423–424
Maturity date of note, 304–305
MBNA, 300
McDonald's, 328, 344–345, C-15
McGraw-Hill, C-8
MCI, 258
MD&A (Management's Discussion and Analysis), 28, 253, 557
Measurement principle. *See* **Cost principle**
Median values, 559, 559*n*
Medicare benefits, 376
Medicare taxes, 376, 377, 387
Memo line on check, 263
Men's Wearhouse, 373
Merchandise, 158, 163, 167, 528–529
Merchandise inventory, 117, 159, 204–231
  adjustments for changes, 511–512
  costing methods (*See* Merchandise inventory costing)
  as current asset, 169, 174, 182
  global view of, 218–219
  inventory estimation methods, 229–230, 231
  overview, 206–207, 230
  safe storage of data on, 230
  valuation of, 215–218, 219
    effects of inventory errors, 216–218
    GAAP vs. IFRS on, 218–219
    at lower of cost or market, 215–216
    net realizable value, 206, 216
    at replacement cost, 215, 216, 218
Merchandise inventory costing, 207, 208–215, 219
  change in inventory method, 224
  cost estimates, 218–219
  cost flow assumptions, 208, 209, 218
  ethical issues, 215, 231
  financial statement effects, 121, 214–215, 228
  periodic inventory system (*See* **Periodic inventory system**)
  perpetual inventory system (*See* **Perpetual inventory system**)
Merchandise inventory turnover, 219, 231, 569, 575, 580
Merchandise purchases, 160–167, 170, 173, 176, 184
  ethical issues, 163, 184
  journal entries for (demonstration), 178
  ownership and transportation costs, 163–164
  periodic inventory system, 179, 184, 276
  purchase discounts (*See* **Purchase discounts**)
  returns and allowances, 162–163, 179
Merchandisers, 16, 158–160, 163, 184
  accounting for purchases (*See* Merchandise purchases)
  accounting for sales (*See* Merchandise sales)
  completing accounting cycle for, 168–170, 177, 184
  cost of goods sold, 169, 182
  current ratios for, 568
  demands made to suppliers, 166
  financial statement formats (*See* Financial statement formats)

income reporting for, 158–159, 171
inventory systems for, 159–160
reporting gross profit, 169, 171, 182
Merchandise sales, 165–167, 170, 173, 178, 184
allowances, 167, 180
discounts, 165, 166, 180
parts of sales, 165
periodic inventory system, 180
returns, 166–167, 180
selling price, 160
Mercury Marine, C-8
Merit rating, 378
MGM Mirage, 371
Microwave Satellite Technologies, 298
Minimum legal capital, 461
Miscellaneous revenues, 257
Modified Accelerated Cost Recovery System (MACRS), 336
Molson Coors, 347
Monetary unit assumption, 11
Monetizing of business, 3
Moody's, 419, 556, 558
Mortgage, 426
Mortgage bonds, 426–427, 428
Mortgage contract, 426
Mortgage notes, 426–427
The Motley Fool, 555
Multinationals, C-15
Multi-period estimated liabilities, 380–381
Multiple-step income statement, 171–172, 176–177, 184
Municipal bonds ("munis"), 428
Mutual agency, 458

National Basketball Association (NBA), 56, 102
National Football League (NFL), 11
National Retail Federation, 103
National Venture Capital Association, 460
Natural business year, 97
Natural resources, 342, 350, 352
cost determination and depletion, 342–343, 350, 352
plant assets used in extracting, 343
Navistar, 10
NBA (National Basketball Association), 56, 102
Neiman Marcus, 373
Net amount. *See* **Book value** of assets
Net assets. *See* **Equity**
Net cash inflow, 503, 506, 532
Net cash outflow, 503
Net income, 15, 27, 171, 173
adjusting for statement of cash flows, 526
computing from worksheet, 126, 127
difference from operating cash flows, 514
from long-term investments, C-10
Net income per share, 477
Net loss, 15, 126, 127
Net method of recording purchases, **275**–276, 277
Net pay, 376
Net realizable value, 206, 216
Netscape, 459
Net working capital, 567–568
New Belgium Brewing Company, 249
NewBelgium.com, 249
New Frontier Energy, 298
New Orleans Saints, 55
New York Stock Exchange, 573
The New York Times Company, 102
NFL (National Football League), 11
Nike, 520–521, 577

Nokia, 4, 24, 70, 71, 118, 173, 346, 347, 383, 384, 427, 476, 519, C-10
financial statement analysis, 556, 566, 576
financial statements of (consolidated), A-1, A-29–A-33
income statements, A-31
statements of changes in shareholders' equity, A-31
statements of comprehensive income, A-31
statements of financial position, A-30
Nominal accounts. *See* **Temporary accounts**
Nominal rate on bonds, 417
Noncalendar-year companies, 69
Noncash accounts, 507–508
Noncash assets, 464, 510–512
Noncash charges, 509
Noncash credits, 509
Noncash investing and financing, 505, 532
Noncash proceeds, 11
Noncompete covenants, 346
Noncumulative preferred stock, 469–470, 477
Noncurrent assets, 515–516
Noncurrent investments. *See* **Long-term investments**
Noncurrent liabilities, 517
Noninfluential investments, C-4–C-6, C-10
available-for-sale securities, C-2, C-5–C-6, C-9, C-10, C-18
held-to-maturity securities, C-2, C-5, C-10, C-18
reporting at fair value, C-2, C-4, C-5
trading securities, C-2, C-4–C-5, C-10, C-12, C-18
Nonoperating activities, 171
Nonoperating gains (losses), 513–514
Nonowner (creditor) financing, 28, 72
Nonparticipating preferred stock, 470
Non-sufficient funds (NSF) checks, 265–268
No-par value stock, 461, 463
Normal balance, 57, 60
Nortel Networks, 10, 13
Notes payable, 54, 304, 517
long-term notes (*See* Long-term notes payable)
short-term notes (*See* **Short-term notes payable**)
Notes receivable, 53, 304–307, 312
adjusting entry for, 267
interest computation, 305
maturity date and period, 304–305
recognizing, 305–306
valuing and settling, 306–307, 312
Notes to financial statements, A-9–A-18
accounts receivable, A-9–A-10
advertising costs, A-12
bad debts, 298, 308
business segments, A-18
capital stock, A-15–A-16
cash and cash equivalents, A-9, A-13
commitments and contingencies, A-16
comprehensive income (loss), A-12, A-17
derivatives, A-10, A-18
earnings per share, A-12, A-17
estimates, A-9
fair value measurements, A-13
financial statement preparation, A-9
foreign currency translation, A-9
goodwill, A-11
impairment of asset value, A-11
income taxes, A-11, A-15

intangible assets, 347, A-11, A-14
internal controls, 268
inventories, 219, A-10, A-14
investments, A-10, A-13
liabilities, 383
plant assets, 346, A-10, A-14
product warranties, A-16
research and development, A-12
revealing risk of fraud, 426
revenue recognition, A-11–A-12
stock-based compensation, A-12
summary of accounting policies, A-9–A-12
supplemental information, A-17–A-18
warranties, A-12
NSF (non-sufficient funds) checks, 265–268
NVCA.org, 460

Oakley, 158
Objectivity, 11
Obsolescence of asset, **331**
Off-balance sheet accounting, 423
Off-balance-sheet agreements, 576
Off-balance sheet financing, 439n
Office equipment, 54
Office supplies, 54
Old Navy, C-8
1-800-FLOWERS.COM, 163–164
Online banking, 262
Operating activities, 29, 173, **503,** 532
accounting equation and, 28–29
cash flows from, 21, 22, 503–504, 508–514, 519, 532
difference from net income, 514
major classes of, 527
reporting directly (*See* **Direct method** of reporting operating cash flows)
reporting indirectly (*See* **Indirect method** of reporting operating cash flows)
plant assets used in, 328
Operating cash flow to sales ratio, 521
Operating cash payments (direct method), 528–531
depreciation expense, 530
gain on retirement of debt, 530–531
for interest and income tax, 530
loss on sale of assets, 530
for merchandise, 528–529
summary of adjustments, 531
wages and operating expenses, 529, 529n, 530
Operating cash receipts (direct method), 527–528
Operating cycle, 115, 159
Operating expenses, 529, 529n, 530
Operating leases, 427, **438**
Opportunity, 8–9, 254
Ordinary annuity
future value (f) of, B-6–B-7, B-11
present value (p) of, 425, 426n, B-5, B-11
Ordinary repairs, 338–339
Organization expenses, 459, 464
Organization Expenses account, 459
Other comprehensive income, C-9
Other expenses and losses, 172
Other postretirement benefits, 440
Other revenues and gains, 171–172
Outstanding checks, 265
Outstanding deposits, 265
Outstanding stock, 461

Overfunded pension plan, 440
Over-the-counter cash receipts, 256, 257
Overtime pay, 389, 389n
Owner control, 414
Owner financing, 28, 72
Owner investment, 61
Ownership of goods, 163–164, 206
Ownership rights, 458

Pacioli, Luca, 64
Paid-in capital, 462
Paid-in capital in excess of par value, 463, 464, 467
Palm, 4, 70, 172, 461
consolidated financial statements of, A-1, A-24–A-28
balance sheets, A-25
statements of cash flows, A-28
statements of comprehensive income (loss), A-27
statements of operations, A-26
statements of stockholders' equity, A-27
financial statement analysis, 556, 562, 567–570
Parent company, C-8
Parking fees, 53
Partial payments, 63, 300
Partial-year depreciation, 336, 352
Participating preferred stock, 470, 470n
Partnership, 12, 459
Part-time employees, 376
Par value, 461
Par value method, 472
Par value of bond, 414, 415
Par value stock, 461, 462–463, 469
Passwords, 253
Patents, 344, 350
Payables, 15
Payee of check, 262
Payee of note, 304
Payer of check, 262
Payment of rent, 17–18, 100, 345
Payout ratio, 478, 575
PayPal, 300, 501
Payroll bank account, 392
Payroll check, 390, 391
Payroll deductions, 376–377, 394
Payroll fraud, 378, 379
Payroll journal, 390
Payroll liabilities, 375–378
employee deductions, 376–377
employer payroll taxes, 377–378, 387, 388, 394, 459
Payroll procedures, 392, 394
computing federal income taxes, 390, 392
fraud in, 378, 379
Payroll records, 394
employee earnings report, 390, 391
payroll check, 390, 391
payroll register, 389–390, 389n
Payroll register, 389–390, 389n
Payroll reports, 387–389, 394
Form 940, 387
Form 941, 387, 388
Form W-2, 389
PCAOB (Public Company Accounting Oversight Board), 250
Pension(s), 427
Pension benefits, 379, 381
Pension plan(s), 379, 380, **440**
Pension recipients, 440
PepsiCo, 558

PE (price-earnings) ratio, **477**, 478, 483, 573–574, 575
P-E (price-earnings) ratio, **477**, 478, 483, 573–574, 575
Percent changes, 559–560, 559*n*
Percent of receivables method (bad debts), 301
Percent of sales method (bad debts), 300–301, 312
Periodic inventory system, 160, 179–182, 224–228, 231
  adjusting and closing entries in, 180–182, 181*n*
  financial statement preparation, 182
  gross method of recording purchases, 276
  merchandise inventory costing
    financial statement effects of, 228
    first-in, first-out (FIFO), 225–226, 228
    last-in, first-out (LIFO), 226–227, 228
    specific identification 224–225, 228
    weighted average (WA), 227, 228
  merchandise sales, 180
  purchase discounts, 179, 276
  recording transactions, 179–180, 184, 276
  transportation-in, 179–180
Period of note, 304–305
Period of time, 21, 68, B-2, B-4
Permanent accounts, 110, C-4
Perpetual inventory system, 160, 164, 183, 184
  completing accounting cycle, 168–170
  financial statement formats, 170–172
  merchandise inventory costing, 209, 220–224, 231
    consistency concept, 215
    financial statement effects, 214–215
    first-in, first-out (FIFO) (*See* **First-in, first-out (FIFO)**)
    last-in, first-out (LIFO) (*See* **Last-in, first-out (LIFO)**)
    specific identification, 208, 209–210, 223
    tax effects of, 214–215, 230–231
    weighted average, 212–213
  merchandise purchases under, 160–167, 275–276
  merchandise sales under, 165–167
Personal financial specialist (PFS), 7
Personal scanners, 252
Petty cashbox, 260
Petty cash fund, 260–262, 277
  cash over and short, 261–262
  demonstration problem, 271–272
  illustrated, 260–261
  increasing or decreasing, 261
  surprise counts, 260
Petty cashier, 260
Petty cash receipts, 260
Pfizer, 294, C-1
PFS (personal financial specialist), 7
Pharma-Bio Serv, 298
Pharmaceutical industry, 344
Pharming, 254
Phishing, 254
Physical count of inventory, 179, 180, 207, 229
Physical flow of goods, 208
Pikoff, David, 327
Pikoff, Stuart, 327
Pizza Hut, 344–345
Plan administrator, 440

Plan assets, 440
Planning, 28
Plant asset(s), 101, 328–341
  additional expenditures for, 338–339
  analysis of transactions, 515–516
  in classified balance sheet, 117
  cost determination, 329–330, 349
  demonstration problem, 348–350
  depreciation of, 331–338, 349
    adjusting entries, 101–102
    changes in estimates for, 337, 352
    factors in computing, 331
    methods used, 332–336
    partial-year, 336
    reporting, 337–338
  disposals of (*See* Plant asset disposals)
  global view of, 346–347
  low-cost, materiality and, 339
  notes regarding, 346, A-10, A-14
  purchasing, 330, 336
  safeguarding against fraud, 343
  used in extracting natural resources, 343
Plant asset age, 347, 575
Plant asset disposals, 339–341
  by discarding, 340, 349, 352
  by exchange, 352
  partial-year depreciation, 336
  by selling, 340–341, 352
Plant asset subsidiary ledger, 337
Plant & equipment. *See* **Plant asset(s)**
Platt's, C-8
P&L (profit and loss) statement. *See* **Income statement**
Point in time, 21, 68
Point-of-sale systems, 251, 258, 307, 516
Poison pill, 470*n*
Post-closing trial balance, 112–114, 129
Posting, 58, 60, 61, 74, 76
Posting reference (PR) column, 60
PR (posting reference) column, 60
Preemptive right, 460
Preferred stock, 468–471, 476, 482
  callable, 471
  control of corporation and, 471, 483
  convertible, 470–471
  dividend preference of, 469–470, 470*n*, 477
  issuance of, 469
  reasons for issuing, 471
Premium, 417, 463
Premium on bonds, 420–421, 423
  amortizing, 420–421, 435–436, 440
  present value of, 422, B-10, B-11
Premium on stock, 463
Prenumbered inventory tickets, 207
Prepaid accounts, 53–54
Prepaid expenses (deferrals), 53–54, **99,** 129
  adjusting entries for, 99–102
    author signing fees, 100, 130
    depreciation, 101–102
    other prepaids, 100
    prepaid insurance, 99–100
    supplies, 100
  adjustments for changes, 512
  alternative accounting for, 123–124, 129
  financial statement links, 107
  transaction analysis, 64
Prepayments, 123–125, 129
Present value (*p*)
  of annuity of one, 434, B-5, B-7, B-11
  of bonds (*See* **Bond(s)**)
  of single amount, B-1–B-3, B-7, B-10
Present value concepts
  bonds and notes, 422, 432, 440
  time value of money, B-1, B-7

Present value factor, 426*n*, B-11
Present value tables, 433, B-7, B-10, B-11
  of annuity of 1, 434, B-11
  of single amount, B-10
Pressure, in fraud triangle, 8, 254
Price-earnings (P-E) ratio, 477, 478, 483, 573–574, 575
PricewaterhouseCoopers, 7
Principal of a note, 304, 374, 425
Principles and assumptions of accounting, 10–13
Principles-based accounting, 10, 23, 118
Principles of internal control, 251–252
  custody of assets, 252, 256
  establishing responsibilities, 251
  insurance and bonding, 251
  recordkeeping, 251, 256
  regular reviews, 252
  separation of duties, 252
  technological controls, 252
Prior period adjustments, 475
Private accounting, 6, 7
Privately held corporations, 70, 458
Processing errors, 253
Product businesses, 55*n*, 115
Production managers, 6
Product warranties, A-16
Profit. *See* Net income
Profitability, 557, 572
Profitability ratios, 24, 572–573, 575
  basic earnings per share, 477, 477*n*
  book value per common share, 478, 479, 483
  book value per preferred share, 478–479, 483
  book value per share, 477
  earnings per share, 477, 483, 581, A-12, A-17
  gross margin ratio, 174–175, 177, 178, 184, 185
  profit margin, 119, 129, 381, 572, 575, 580, C-10, C-11
  return on assets (ROA), 24, 25, 27, 28, 29, 30
  return on common stockholders' equity, 573, 575, 580
  return on total assets, 572–573, 575, 580, C-10–C-11, C-18
Profit and loss (P&L) statement. *See* **Income statement**
Profit margin ratio, **119,** 129, 381, 572, 575, 580, C-10, C-11
Pro forma financial statements, 126
Promissory notes, 304, 374–375
Promoters, 459, 464
Property, plant & equipment. *See* **Plant asset(s)**
Property taxes, 459
Proprietorship, 11–12, 459
Prospective application, 582
Prospectus, 461
Proving balances, 67, 519
Proxy, 459
Public accounting, 6, 7
Public Company Accounting Oversight Board (PCAOB), 250
Publicly held corporations, 70, 250–251, 458
Public sale of stock, 458
"Pump 'n dump," 476
Purchase allowances, 163
Purchase discounts, 161–162, 162*n*, 184
  gross and net methods, 275–276, 277
  periodic inventory system, 179, 276
  perpetual inventory system, 275–276

Purchase invoice, 273
Purchase order, 272, 274
Purchase requisition, 258, 272, 274
Purchase returns, 163
Purchases
  basket purchases, 330
  in cash, 16, 17, 61, 62, 64
  on credit, 17, 62, 174, 184
  discounts (*See* **Purchase discounts**)
  in foreign currency, C-16–C-17, C-18
  of merchandise (*See* Merchandise purchases)
Purchasing managers, 6

Quick assets, 174
Quick ratio. *See* **Acid-test (quick) ratio**
Quote (price), 415, 422, 462
Qwest Communications, 13

RadioShack, 24
Raju, Ramalinga, 9
Rand Medical Billing, 298
Ratio(s), 567
Ratio analysis, 558, 566–575, 582
  accounts receivable turnover, 309–310, 310*n*, 312, 313, 569, 575, 580
  acid-test (quick) ratio, 174, 177, 178, 184, 568–569, 580, 686
  in analysis of inventory management, 219–220, 231
  basic earnings per share, 477, 477*n*
  book value per common share, 478, 479, 483
  book value per preferred share, 478–479, 483
  cash coverage of debt, 521, 575
  cash coverage of debt ratio, 521, 575
  cash coverage of growth, 521
  cash flow on total assets, 520–521, 532
  classification of liabilities and, 371
  current ratio, 119, 120, 129, 130, 174, 184, 371, 567–568, 575, 580, 583
  days' sales in inventory, 219, 231, 570, 575
  days' sales uncollected, 269, 277, 310*n*, 569–570, 575, 580
  debt ratio, 72, 76, 571, 575, 580
  debt-to-equity ratio, 428–429, 440, 571, 575, 580
  demonstration of, 580
  dividend yield ratio, 478, 483, 574, 575
  earnings per share, 477, 483, 581, A-12, A-17
  equity ratio, 571, 575
  global view of, 576
  gross margin ratio, 174–175, 177, 178, 184, 185
  inventory turnover ratio, 219, 231, 569, 575, 580
  liquidity and efficiency ratios, 24, 567–570, 575
  accounts receivable turnover, 309–310, 310*n*, 312, 313, 569, 575, 580
  acid-test (quick) ratio, 174, 177, 178, 184, 568–569, 580, 686
  current ratio, 119, 120, 129, 130, 174, 184, 371, 567–568, 575, 580, 583
  days' sales in inventory, 219, 231, 570, 575
  days' sales uncollected, 269, 277, 310*n*, 569–570, 575, 580

Index

inventory turnover ratio, 219, 231, 569, 575, 580
total asset turnover, 347, 348, 352, 353, 569, 570, 572, 575, 580, C-10, C-11
market prospects ratios, 24, 573–574, 575
dividend yield ratio, 478, 483, 574, 575
price-earnings ratio, 477, 478, 483, 573–574, 575
operating cash flow to sales, 521
price-earnings ratio, 477, 478, 483, 573–574, 575
profitability ratios, 24, 572–573, 575
basic earnings per share, 477, 477n
book value per common share, 478, 479, 483
book value per preferred share, 478–479, 483
book value per share, 477
earnings per share, 477, 483, 581, A-12, A-17
gross margin ratio, 174–175, 177, 178, 184, 185
profit margin, 119, 129, 381, 572, 575, 580, C-10, C-11
return on assets (ROA), 24, 25, 27, 28, 29, 30
return on common stockholders' equity, 573, 575, 580
return on total assets, 572–573, 575, 580, C-10–C-11, C-18
profit margin, 119, 129, 381, 572, 575, 580, C-10, C-11
return on assets (ROA) ratio, 24, 25, 27, 28, 29, 30
return on common stockholders' equity, 573, 575, 580
return on total assets, 572–573, 575, 580, C-10–C-11, C-18
solvency ratios, 24, 571–572, 575
debt ratio, 72, 76, 571, 575, 580
debt-to-equity ratio, 428–429, 440, 571, 575, 580
equity ratio, 571, 575
times interest earned, 384, 387, 394, 571–572, 575, 580
summary of ratios, 574, 575
times interest earned, 384, 387, 394, 571–572, 575, 580
total asset turnover, 347, 348, 352, 353, 569, 570, 572, 575, 580, C-10, C-11
Rationalization, 8, 254
Real (permanent) accounts, 110, C-4
Realizable value, 299
"Reasonableness" criterion, 563
Receivables, 15, 256, 292–312
accounts receivable (See **Accounts receivable**)
disposal of, 307–308, 309, 312
estimating bad debts expense, 301, 302–303, 312
global view of, 308–309
journal entries for, 311, 312
notes receivable (See Notes receivable)
write-offs of, 580
Receiving report, 272, 273
Reconciled bank balance, 266
Reconstruction analysis, 523
of accounts receivable, 527–528
equity analysis, 518
operating cash payments, 528–529
plant asset transactions, 515–516

Recording business activities, 4
Recording transactions, 4, 52–56
acquisition of natural resources, 350
closing entries, 110–112
ethical issues, 53, 76, 107, 130
merchandise purchases, 162, 179–180, 184, 216, 275–276, 277
notes payable (See **Notes payable**)
notes receivable (See Notes receivable)
Recordkeeping, 4, 251, 256
Records testing, 253
Recoverable amount, 336
Reebok, 332
Registered bond(s), 428
Registrar, 460
Regular reviews, 252
Regulation of corporations, 14, 459, 576
Regulators, 5, 571
Related-party transactions, 576
Relative market values, 330
Religious organizations, 67
Remittance advice, 263
Replacement cost, 215, 216, 218
Report form of balance sheet, 22, 70
Reporting accounting information, 96–98, 129
accounting period and, 96–97
accrual basis vs. cash basis, 97
financial statements (See Financial statement(s); specific statements and reports)
methods (See specific reporting methods)
revenue and expense recognition, 98
Reporting period(s), 69
Research and development, A-12
Research and development managers, 6
Research In Motion (RIM), 4, 15, 16, 55n, 69, 70, 216, 218, 474
comparative financial statements of, 560–561, 564, 565
consolidated financial statements of, A-1, A-2–A-18
balance sheets, A-5
internal controls report, A-4
management discussion and analysis, A-3
reports of independent auditors, A-3, A-4
selected notes to, A-9–A-18
statements of cash flows, A-8
statements of operations, A-6
statements of shareholders' equity, A-7
financial statement analysis, 556, 557, 558, 559
common-size graphics, 565–566
horizontal analysis, 560–561
ratio analysis, 567–574
trend analysis, 562
vertical analysis, 563–566
Residual. See **Equity**
Residual equity. See **Equity**
Residual interest, 55
Residual value. See **Salvage value** of asset
Responsibility, 251
Restatements, 10
Restricted retained earnings, 474
Retail amount of inventory, 229
Retailers, 158
Retail inventory method, 229, 231
Retained earnings, 15, 462, 466, 474, 482, 518
Retained Earnings account, 112
Retained earnings deficit, 465

Retirement of debt. See Debt
Retiring stock, 474, 483
Retrospective application, 581–582
Return, 27
Return and risk analysis, 27–28, 29
Return on assets (ROA) ratio, **24,** 25, 27, 28, 29, 30
Return on common stockholders' equity, 573, 575, 580
Return on equity, 414, 415
Return on investment (ROI) ratio, 24, 25, 27, 28, 29, 30
Return on sales. See **Profit margin** ratio
Return on total assets ratio, 572–573, 575, 580, **C-10**–C-11, C-18
Reuters.com/finance, 567
Revenue(s), 11, 15, 257
equity increased by, 55
interest revenue, C-2–C-3
noncash credits, 509
other, reporting, 171–172
recognizing, 98
unearned (See **Unearned revenue(s)**)
Revenue accounts, 56
adjusting (See Adjusting accounts)
alternative accounting for prepayments, 124–125
closing process, 111, 112, 113
contra-revenue accounts, 299
Revenue expenditures, 338–339, 352
Revenue recognition, 11, 98, 118, A-11–A-12
Revenue recognition principle, 11, 63, 98, 103, 106
Reverse stock split, 468
Reversing entries, 114, 115, **127–**129, 130
Rex Stores, 24
RIM. See Research In Motion
RIM.com, 16, 557
Ripken, Cal, Jr., 380
Risk, 28
The Risk Management Association, 24
ROA (return on assets) ratio, **24,** 25, 27, 28, 29, 30
Robert Morris Associates, 567
ROI (return on investment) ratio, 24, 25, 27, 28, 29, 30
Romo, Tony, 206
Rounding, 70
Rules-based accounting, 23, 118
Rules of thumb (guidelines), 558

Salaries expense, accrued, 104
Sales, 97, 180, 297, 373
cost of (See **Cost of goods sold**)
in foreign currency, C-16
joint relation with expenses, 563, 582–583
of merchandise (See Merchandise sales)
point-of-sale systems, 251, 258, 307, 516
ticket sales and subscriptions, 55, 102
Sales allowances, 166, 167
Sales discounts, 161, 165, 166, 180
Sales invoice, 53, 273
Sales on account. See Credit sales
Sales on credit. See Credit sales
Sales receipts, 296–297, 373n
Sales returns, 166–167, 180
Sales taxes payable, 372–373, 373n
Salvage value of asset, **331,** 333, 336, 337
Sam's Club, 160

Sarbanes-Oxley Act (SOX) of 2002, **8, 13,** 14, **250**–251
control procedures under, 71
financial statement requirements, 109
Satyam Computers, 9
Schedule of accounts receivable, 295
S corporation, 12
Scrap value. See **Salvage value** of asset
Sea Ray, C-8
Sears, 296
SEC. See Securities and Exchange Commission
sec.gov/investor/pubs/cyberfraud.htm, 253
Section 404 (Sarbanes-Oxley Act), **251**
Secured bond(s), 428
Securities and Exchange Commission (SEC), 9, 14, 16, A-1
fines for WorldCom accounting fraud, 258
income statement presentation requirements, 173
private companies not subject to oversight of, 70
registration of bond issue, 416n
Self-correcting errors, 217
Self-employed workers, 392
Selling expenses, 171
Selling price of merchandise, 160
Semiannual compounding, 422
Separate legal entity, 458
Separation of duties
bank reconciliation, 266
cash registers, 251, 256, 257
as internal control, 252, 253
Serial bond(s), 428
Service charges (fees), 265
Service companies, 16, 55n, 158, 568
Service life. See **Useful life** of asset
Service managers, 6
Services, 62, 63. See also Banking activities
Services revenue, accrued, 105–106
Shareholders. See **Stockholders**
Shareholders' equity. See **Stockholders' equity**
Shares. See **Stock**
Shea, Katie, 51
Shoplifting, 168
Short selling, 574, 577
Short-term investments, C-1, C-9
Short-term liabilities. See **Current liabilities**
Short-term notes payable, 373–375, 378, 394
Shrinkage, 168, 180–181, 229
Signature card, 262
Significant influence, C-2, C-7–C-8, C-18
Simple capital structure, 477n
Single-step income statement, 172, 177, 184
Sinking fund, 428
Sinking fund bond(s), 428
Six Flags, 371
Skechers, 72
Skimming, 307, 516
Small stock dividend, 466, 467
Snorg Tees, 369
SnorgTees.com, 369
Social responsibility, 6, 8
Social Security benefits, 376
Social Security taxes, 376, 377, 387
SocialTwist, 3
Software, 252, 346, 507
Sole proprietorship, 11–12, 459
Solvency, 557

Solvency ratios, 24, 571–572, 575
   debt ratio, 72, 76, 571, 575, 580
   debt-to-equity ratio, 428–429, 440, 571, 575, 580
   equity ratio, 571, 575
   times interest earned, 384, 387, 394, 571–572, 575, 580
Source documents, 52–53, 76, 508
   adjusting entries and, 98
   invoices, 160, 161
SOX. *See* **Sarbanes-Oxley Act (SOX)** of 2002
Specific identification, 208, **209,** 214
   periodic inventory system, 224–225, 228
   perpetual inventory system, 208, 209–210, 223
Specific principles, 10
Specific rights of stockholders, 460
S&P 500 index, 6
Sports Illustrated, 378
Spreadsheet. *See* **Work sheet**
Standard & Poor's, 419, 556, 557, 558, C-8
Standard & Poor's Industry Surveys, 567
Standards (benchmarks), 558, 582
Standard setting, 10
Staples, 169
Starbucks, 329–330, 476, 514, C-1
Start-up businesses, 506, 532
Start-up money, 460
Stated rate on bonds, 417
Stated value stock, 462, 464
State ethics codes, 9
Statement of cash flows, 20, 21, 22, **502,** 532
   classification of activities, 503–504
   consolidated, examples of, A-8, A-23, A-28
   demonstration, 27
   format of, 505–506
   preparation of, 506–508
      direct method (*See* **Direct method** of reporting operating cash flows)
      FASB on, 509, 531
      indirect method (*See* **Indirect method** of reporting operating cash flows)
      from spreadsheet, 524–526, 532
   purpose of, 502
Statement of Financial Accounting Standards (SFAS) No. 153, "Exchanges of Nonmonetary Assets," 350
Statement of financial position. *See* **Balance sheet**
Statement of operations. *See* **Income statement**
Statement of retained earnings, 20, 21, 474–475
   demonstration, 26
   preparation of
      from adjusted trial balance, 122
      from trial balance, 69, 70, 75, 109, 110
Statement of stockholders' equity, 475, A-7, A-22, A-27, A-31
State Unemployment Taxes (SUTA), 378, 387
Statutory restriction, 474
Stock, 12, 458, 461–464, 471, 483
   blue chips, 557
   common (*See* **Common stock**)
   discount on, 463
   growth or income stocks, 478
   preferred (*See* **Preferred stock**)

   pricing, 461, 462
   retiring, 474, 483
   short selling, 574, 577
   stock certificates, 460
   stock quote, 462
   treasury stock, 472–474, 476, 483
Stock-based compensation, A-12
Stock buyback, 472–473
Stock certificate, 460
Stock dividends, 466–468, 483, 505
   dividend distributable, 467
   large stock dividend, 466, 467–468
   small stock dividend, 466, 467
Stockholders, 5, **12,** 458, 460, 556
   as external users of accounting information, 5
   lack of mutual agency for, 458
   meetings of, 459
   registrar and transfer agents, 460–461
   rights of, 460, 476
   stock certificates, 460
Stockholders' equity, 55–56, **462,** 480
   journal entries for, 480, 481, 482
   return on, 573, 575, 580
Stock options, 476
Stock splits, 468, 483
Stone, Biz, 3
Store promotions, 106, 130, 427, 441
Store supplies, 54
Straight-line bond amortization, 418
   demonstration of, 429, 430–431
   discount on bonds payable, 418–419
   premium on bonds, 421
Straight-line depreciation, 101, 332–333, 335, 352
Straight-line depreciation rate, 333
Straight-line depreciation schedule, 333
Strategic management, 28
Subordinated debentures, 428
Subscriptions, 55
Subsidiary companies, C-8, C-17
Subsidiary ledgers, 207, 295, 337, 374
Sub Surface Waste Management, 298
Summary of entries for merchandisers, 169, 170
Summary of transactions, 19–20, 26
Sunoco, 382–383
SuperValu, 158, 294
Supplementary records, 164, 176, 295, A-17–A-18
Suppliers, 5–6, 166
Supplies, 54, 100
   purchased for cash, 61, 64
   purchased on credit, 62, 174, 184
Sustainable income, 580–582
   changes in accounting principles, 581–582
   continuing operations, 580
   discontinued segments, 580
   earnings per share, 581
   extraordinary items, 580–581
SUTA (State Unemployment Taxes), 378, 387
SYSCO, 158, 294

T-account(s), 57, 58
   accounts receivable, 527–528
   for adjusting journal entries, 121
   cash account, 268
   current assets, 511, 512
   current liabilities, 512, 513
   ledger in T-account form, 66
Talbots, 373
Target, 97, 158

Taxation, 12, 459
   effects of inventory costing, 214–215, 230–231
   employer payroll taxes, 377–378, 387, 388, 394, 459
   income taxes (*See* Income taxes)
   Medicare and Social Security, 376, 377, 387
   sales taxes payable, 372–373, 373*n*
   temporary differences, 393–394
Tax reporting, 336, 393–394
Technology, as internal control. *See* Internal control(s)
Temporary accounts, 110, 111, C-4, C-7
Temporary differences, 393–394
Temporary investments. *See* **Short-term investments**
Term bond(s), 428
360-Day year, 105, 305, 374
Three-stage analysis, 515, 517
TIBCO Software, 427
Ticker prices, 574
TicketMaster, 4
Time clocks, 252
Time deposits, 255
Time period assumption, 11, 96, 129
Times interest earned ratio, **384,** 387, 394, 571–572, 575, 580
Time value of money, B–B-7
   future value
      of annuities, B-6–B-7, B-11
      of single amount, B-3–B-5
   lottery winnings, B-1, B-6
   present and future value concepts, B-1, B-7
   present value
      of annuities, 425, 426*n*, 433–434, B-5, B-7, B-11
      of single amount, B-1–B-3, B-10
Tootsie Roll, 331, 332
Top line items, 173
Total asset turnover, 347, 348, 352, 353, 568, 570, 572, 575, 580, C-10, C-11
Toys "R" Us, 219–220
Trade discount, 160
Trade-in allowance on assets, 350
Trademarks, 345
Trade names, 345
Trade payables, 54
Trading on the equity, 414, 471
Trading securities, C-2, **C-4**–C-5, C-18
   global view of, C-10
   unrealized loss on, C-4, C-12
   valuing and reporting, C-4
Transaction(s), 16, 58–60
   arm's-length, 308
   ethics in recording, 53, 76
   involving plant assets, 515–516
   merchandising (demonstration), 178
   recording (*See* Recording transactions)
   summary of, 19–20, 26
Transaction analysis, 29, 50–76
   accounting equation in, 16–20
   accounts payable, 18–19, 63
   accounts receivable, 18
   analyzing and recording process, 52–56
   account analysis, 53–56
   source documents, 52–53, 76, 160, 161
   cash dividends, 19, 63
   cash purchases, 16, 17, 61, 62, 64
   cash receipts, 63, 64
   credit purchases, 17
   credit sales, 18

   demonstration problem, 72–76
   entrepreneurship, 51
   GAAP vs. IFRS on, 23
   global view of, 23, 71
   investment by owner, 16
   notes payable, 517
   payments, 17–18, 62–65
   for plant assets, 515–516
   processing transactions (*See* Transaction processing)
   summary of transactions, 19–20
   trial balance, 67–70, 75, 109
Transaction processing, 56–66, 76
   accounting equation analysis, 65, 66
   debits and credits, 57, 57*n*
   double-entry accounting, 57–58
   illustration of, 61–65
   journalizing and posting, 58–61, 74
   ledger and chart of accounts, 56
Transfer agents, 460–461
Transportation costs, 163–164
Transportation-in, 164, 179–180
Transportation-out, 164
Transposition errors, 68*n*
Treasurer of company, 256
Treasury stock, 472–474, 476, 483
   purchasing, 472–473
   reissuing, 473–474
   retiring, 474, 483
Trend analysis, 561–563
Trial balance, 67–70, 76
   adjusted (*See* **Adjusted trial balance**)
   in financial statement preparation, 68–70, 75, 109, 110
   post-closing trial balance, 112–114, 129
   preparation of, 67–68, 75
   unadjusted, 67, 108, 126, 127
Triple-threat of fraud, 8–9, 254
Trustee, 416, 416*n*
Truth-in-Lending Act, 426
Twitter, 3, 16
Twitter.com, 3
Tyco International, 13
Typo-squatting, 254

Unadjusted financial statements, 68
Unadjusted trial balance, 67, **108,** 126, 127
Uncertainty in liabilities, 371–372, 383
Unclassified balance sheet, 115
Uncollectible accounts. *See* **Bad debts**
Uncollectible items, 265
Underfunded pension plan, 440
Underwriters, 416, 416*n*, 461
Undistributed earnings, C-7
Unearned revenue(s), 54–55, 64, **102,** 107, 129
   adjusting entries for, 102–103
   alternative accounting for, 124–125, 129
   as known liability, 378
   ticket sales and subscriptions, 55, 102
U.S. Army, 378
U.S. Marine, C-8
U.S. Navy Seals, 205
U.S. Treasury bonds, 28
Units-of-production depreciation, 332, **333**–334, 335, 343, 352
Units-of-production depreciation schedule, 334
Unlimited liability, 12
Unlimited life of land, 330
Unrealized gain (loss), C-4, C-12
Unregistered bonds, 428
Unsecured bonds, 428

Index

"Unusual and infrequent" criterion, 423
Unusual gain or loss, 580–581
Upper Deck, 206
Useful life of asset, 101, 328, **331, 347,** 575
  changes in estimates, 337
  in computing depreciation, 331, 332, 333
  IFRS on, 341
  total asset turnover and, 347
Users of accounting information
  external, 5–6, 29, 556
  internal, 6, 29, 502, 556

Vacation(s)
  benefits as estimated liabilities, 380
  mandatory vacation policy, 251, 253, 277
  pay as accrued expense, 104
Valuation
  of accounts receivable, 308
    allowance method, 298–300
    direct write-off method, 297–298
  of assets
    book value, 101–102, 333, 334
    salvage value, 101, 331, 333, 336, 337
  fair value (*See* Fair value)
  of merchandise inventory, 215–218, 219
    effects of inventory errors, 216–218
    GAAP vs. IFRS on, 218–219

  at lower of cost or market, 215–216
  net realizable value, 206, 216
  at replacement cost, 215, 216, 218
Variable expenses, 384
Variable interest entities (VIEs), 423
Vendee, 273
Vendor, 272, 383
Venture capitalists, 460
Verification, 253, 277
Vertical analysis, 558, 563–566, 576, 582
  common-size graphics, 565–566
  common-size statements, 563–564, 565
    balance sheets, 563, 564
    income statements, 563–564, 565
Vice presidents, 459
VIEs (variable interest entities), 423
VISA, 296, 300
Volcker Rule, 14
Voluntary deductions, 377
Voters, 5
Voting rights of stockholders, 460
Voucher, 259, 274, 275
Voucher register, 275
Voucher system, 258, 272–275
  as cash control, 258–259
  invoice, 273, 274
  invoice approval, 273–274
  purchase order, 272, 274
  purchase requisition, 272, 274
  receiving report, 273, 274
  voucher, 259, 274, 275

W. T. Grant Co., 503
WA. *See* **Weighted average (WA)**
Wage and Tax Statement
  (Form W-2), 389
Wage bracket withholding table, 392
Wages, 529, 529*n*, 530
Walls, Bryan, 369
Walls, Matt, 369
Wall Street, 573
The Wall Street Journal, 461, 574
Walmart, 97, 158, 184, 258, 328
Walt Disney, 98
Warranty(ies), 380–381, 386, A-12
Websites, 16
Weighted average (WA), 208, **212,** 214, 223
  cost flow assumption, 208, 209
  periodic inventory system, 227, 228
  perpetual inventory system, 212–213
WeMarket4U.net/FatFoe, 259
WeMarket4U.net/SundaeStation, 259
Weyerhaeuser, 342
Whittaker, Andrew "Jack," B-6
Wholesalers, 158
Williams, Evan, 3
Wi-phishing, 254
Withholding allowances, 376–377, 390, 392
Withholdings. *See* **Payroll deductions**
Women-owned businesses, 51, 54, 157

Working capital, 567–568
Working papers, 125
Work sheet, 125–127, 130
  applications and analysis, 109, 126
  perpetual inventory system, 183
  in preparing statement of cash flows, 524–526, 532
WorldCom, 9, 13, 118, 258
Write-downs of inventory, 580
Write-offs of receivables, 580
www.AICPA.org, 7, 8
www.cityslips.com, 51
www.COSO.org, 251
www.fraud.org, 253
www.IRS.gov, 336, 376
www.SEC.gov, 337, A-1
www.SEC.gov/edgar.shtml, 16
www.SSA.gov, 376
www.standardandpoors.com, 557

XE.com, 11, C-15
Xerox, 13, 118

Yahoo!, 345
Yield rate on bonds, 417, 418, 422

Zero balance(s), 57, 111, 473
Zero-coupon bonds, 418

Chart of Accounts

Following is a typical chart of accounts, which is used in several assignments. Every company has its own unique accounts and numbering system.

Assets

Current Assets

101 Cash
102 Petty cash
103 Cash equivalents
104 Short-term investments
105 Fair value adjustment, _____ securities (S-T)
106 Accounts receivable
107 Allowance for doubtful accounts
108 Legal fees receivable
109 Interest receivable
110 Rent receivable
111 Notes receivable
119 Merchandise inventory
120 _____ inventory
121 _____ inventory
124 Office supplies
125 Store supplies
126 _____ supplies
128 Prepaid insurance
129 Prepaid interest
131 Prepaid rent
132 Raw materials inventory
133 Goods in process inventory, _____
134 Goods in process inventory, _____
135 Finished goods inventory

Long-Term Investments

141 Long-term investments
142 Fair value adjustment, _____ securities (L-T)
144 Investment in _____
145 Bond sinking fund

Plant Assets

151 Automobiles
152 Accumulated depreciation—Automobiles
153 Trucks
154 Accumulated depreciation—Trucks
155 Boats
156 Accumulated depreciation—Boats
157 Professional library
158 Accumulated depreciation—Professional library
159 Law library
160 Accumulated depreciation—Law library
161 Furniture
162 Accumulated depreciation—Furniture
163 Office equipment
164 Accumulated depreciation—Office equipment
165 Store equipment
166 Accumulated depreciation—Store equipment
167 _____ equipment
168 Accumulated depreciation—_____ equipment
169 Machinery
170 Accumulated depreciation—Machinery
173 Building _____
174 Accumulated depreciation—Building _____
175 Building _____
176 Accumulated depreciation—Building _____
179 Land improvements _____
180 Accumulated depreciation—Land improvements _____
181 Land improvements _____
182 Accumulated depreciation—Land improvements _____
183 Land

Natural Resources

185 Mineral deposit
186 Accumulated depletion—Mineral deposit

Intangible Assets

191 Patents
192 Leasehold
193 Franchise
194 Copyrights
195 Leasehold improvements
196 Licenses
197 Accumulated amortization—_____

Liabilities

Current Liabilities

201 Accounts payable
202 Insurance payable
203 Interest payable
204 Legal fees payable
207 Office salaries payable
208 Rent payable
209 Salaries payable
210 Wages payable
211 Accrued payroll payable
214 Estimated warranty liability
215 Income taxes payable
216 Common dividend payable
217 Preferred dividend payable
218 State unemployment taxes payable
219 Employee federal income taxes payable
221 Employee medical insurance payable
222 Employee retirement program payable
223 Employee union dues payable
224 Federal unemployment taxes payable
225 FICA taxes payable
226 Estimated vacation pay liability

Unearned Revenues

230 Unearned consulting fees
231 Unearned legal fees
232 Unearned property management fees
233 Unearned _____ fees
234 Unearned _____ fees
235 Unearned janitorial revenue
236 Unearned _____ revenue
238 Unearned rent

Notes Payable

240 Short-term notes payable
241 Discount on short-term notes payable
245 Notes payable
251 Long-term notes payable
252 Discount on long-term notes payable

Long-Term Liabilities

253 Long-term lease liability
255 Bonds payable
256 Discount on bonds payable
257 Premium on bonds payable
258 Deferred income tax liability

Equity

Owner's Equity

301 _____, Capital
302 _____, Withdrawals
303 _____, Capital
304 _____, Withdrawals
305 _____, Capital
306 _____, Withdrawals

Paid-In Capital

307 Common stock, $_____ par value
308 Common stock, no-par value
309 Common stock, $_____ stated value
310 Common stock dividend distributable
311 Paid-in capital in excess of par value, Common stock

CA

Chart of Accounts

312 Paid-in capital in excess of stated value, No-par common stock
313 Paid-in capital from retirement of common stock
314 Paid-in capital, Treasury stock
315 Preferred stock
316 Paid-in capital in excess of par value, Preferred stock

Retained Earnings

318 Retained earnings
319 Cash dividends (or Dividends)
320 Stock dividends

Other Equity Accounts

321 Treasury stock, Common
322 Unrealized gain—Equity
323 Unrealized loss—Equity

Revenues

401 _____ fees earned
402 _____ fees earned
403 _____ services revenue
404 _____ services revenue
405 Commissions earned
406 Rent revenue (or Rent earned)
407 Dividends revenue (or Dividend earned)
408 Earnings from investment in _____
409 Interest revenue (or Interest earned)
410 Sinking fund earnings
413 Sales
414 Sales returns and allowances
415 Sales discounts

Cost of Sales

Cost of Goods Sold

502 Cost of goods sold
505 Purchases
506 Purchases returns and allowances
507 Purchases discounts
508 Transportation-in

Manufacturing

520 Raw materials purchases
521 Freight-in on raw materials
530 Factory payroll
531 Direct labor
540 Factory overhead
541 Indirect materials
542 Indirect labor
543 Factory insurance expired
544 Factory supervision
545 Factory supplies used
546 Factory utilities
547 Miscellaneous production costs
548 Property taxes on factory building
549 Property taxes on factory equipment
550 Rent on factory building
551 Repairs, factory equipment
552 Small tools written off
560 Depreciation of factory equipment
561 Depreciation of factory building

Standard Cost Variance

580 Direct material quantity variance
581 Direct material price variance
582 Direct labor quantity variance
583 Direct labor price variance
584 Factory overhead volume variance
585 Factory overhead controllable variance

Expenses

Amortization, Depletion, and Depreciation

601 Amortization expense—_____
602 Amortization expense—_____
603 Depletion expense—_____
604 Depreciation expense—Boats
605 Depreciation expense—Automobiles
606 Depreciation expense—Building _____
607 Depreciation expense—Building _____
608 Depreciation expense—Land improvements _____
609 Depreciation expense—Land improvements _____
610 Depreciation expense—Law library
611 Depreciation expense—Trucks
612 Depreciation expense—_____ equipment
613 Depreciation expense—_____ equipment
614 Depreciation expense—_____
615 Depreciation expense—_____

Employee-Related Expenses

620 Office salaries expense
621 Sales salaries expense
622 Salaries expense
623 _____ wages expense
624 Employees' benefits expense
625 Payroll taxes expense

Financial Expenses

630 Cash over and short
631 Discounts lost
632 Factoring fee expense
633 Interest expense

Insurance Expenses

635 Insurance expense—Delivery equipment
636 Insurance expense—Office equipment
637 Insurance expense—_____

Rental Expenses

640 Rent expense
641 Rent expense—Office space
642 Rent expense—Selling space
643 Press rental expense
644 Truck rental expense
645 _____ rental expense

Supplies Expenses

650 Office supplies expense
651 Store supplies expense
652 _____ supplies expense
653 _____ supplies expense

Miscellaneous Expenses

655 Advertising expense
656 Bad debts expense
657 Blueprinting expense
658 Boat expense
659 Collection expense
661 Concessions expense
662 Credit card expense
663 Delivery expense
664 Dumping expense
667 Equipment expense
668 Food and drinks expense
671 Gas and oil expense
672 General and administrative expense
673 Janitorial expense
674 Legal fees expense
676 Mileage expense
677 Miscellaneous expenses
678 Mower and tools expense
679 Operating expense
680 Organization expense
681 Permits expense
682 Postage expense
683 Property taxes expense
684 Repairs expense—_____
685 Repairs expense—_____
687 Selling expense
688 Telephone expense
689 Travel and entertainment expense
690 Utilities expense
691 Warranty expense
695 Income taxes expense

Gains and Losses

701 Gain on retirement of bonds
702 Gain on sale of machinery
703 Gain on sale of investments
704 Gain on sale of trucks
705 Gain on _____
706 Foreign exchange gain or loss
801 Loss on disposal of machinery
802 Loss on exchange of equipment
803 Loss on exchange of _____
804 Loss on sale of notes
805 Loss on retirement of bonds
806 Loss on sale of investments
807 Loss on sale of machinery
808 Loss on _____
809 Unrealized gain—Income
810 Unrealized loss—Income
811 Impairment gain
812 Impairment loss

Clearing Accounts

901 Income summary
902 Manufacturing summary

A Rose by Any Other Name

The same financial statement sometimes receives different titles. Following are some of the more common aliases.*

Balance Sheet	Statement of Financial Position Statement of Financial Condition
Income Statement	Statement of Income Operating Statement Statement of Operations Statement of Operating Activity Earnings Statement Statement of Earnings Profit and Loss (P&L) Statement
Statement of Cash Flows	Statement of Cash Flow Cash Flows Statement Statement of Changes in Cash Position Statement of Changes in Financial Position
Statement of Stockholders' Equity	Statement of Shareholders' Equity Statement of Changes in Shareholders' Equity Statement of Stockholders' Equity and Comprehensive Income Statement of Changes in Owner's Equity Statement of Changes in Owner's Capital Statement of Changes in Capital Accounts

*The term **Consolidated** often precedes or follows these statement titles to reflect the combination of different entities, such as a parent company and its subsidiaries.

We thank Dr. Louella Moore from Arkansas State University for suggesting this listing.

SELECTED TRANSACTIONS AND RELATIONS

① Merchandising Transactions Summary

	Merchandising Transactions	Merchandising Entries	Dr.	Cr.
Purchases	Purchasing merchandise for resale.	• Merchandise Inventory .... Cash or Accounts Payable	#	#
	Paying freight costs on purchases; FOB shipping point.	• Merchandise Inventory .... Cash	#	#

	Paying within discount period.	• Accounts Payable ....
		    Merchandise Inventory ....
		    Cash ....
			#	#
				#

	Recording purchase returns or allowances.	• Cash or Accounts Payable .... Merchandise Inventory	#	#

Sales	Selling merchandise.	• Cash or Accounts Receivable ....
		    Sales ....
		• Cost of Goods Sold ....
		    Merchandise Inventory ....
			#
			#
				#
				#

	Receiving payment within discount period.	• Cash ....
		    Sales Discounts ....
		    Accounts Receivable ....
			#
			#
				#

	Granting sales returns or allowances.	• Sales Returns and Allowances...........
		    Cash or Accounts Receivable ....
		• Merchandise Inventory ....
		    Cost of Goods Sold ....
			#
			#
				#
				#

	Paying freight costs on sales; FOB destination.	• Delivery Expense .... Cash	#	#

	Merchandising Events	Adjusting and Closing Entries	Dr.	Cr.
Adjusting	Adjusting due to shrinkage (occurs when recorded amount larger than physical inventory).	Cost of Goods Sold .... Merchandise Inventory	#	#
Closing	Closing temporary accounts with credit balances.	Sales .... Income Summary	#	#

	Closing temporary accounts with debit balances.	Income Summary ....
		    Sales Returns and Allowances ....
		    Sales Discounts ....
		    Cost of Goods Sold ....
		    Delivery Expense ....
		    "Other Expenses" ....
			#	#
				#
				#
				#
				#

④ Bad Debts Estimation

Bad Debts Estimation
- Income Statement Focus
  - Percent of Sales [Emphasis on Matching]
    - Sales × Rate = Bad Debts Expense
- Balance Sheet Focus
  - Percent of Receivables [Emphasis on Realizable Value]
    - Accounts Receivable × Rate = Allowance for Doubtful Accounts
  - Aging of Receivables [Emphasis on Realizable Value]
    - Accounts Receivable (by Age) × Rates (by Age) = Allowance for Doubtful Accounts

⑥ Stock Transactions Summary

	Stock Transactions	Stock Entries	Dr.	Cr.
Issue Common Stock	Issue par value common stock at par (par stock recorded at par).	Cash .... Common Stock	#	#

	Issue par value common stock at premium (par stock recorded at par).	Cash ....
		    Common Stock ....
		    Paid-In Capital in Excess of Par Value, Common Stock .....
			#	#
				#

	Issue no-par value common stock (no-par stock recorded at amount received).	Cash .... Common Stock	#	#
	Issue stated value common stock at stated value (stated stock recorded at stated value).	Cash .... Common stock	#	#

	Issue stated value common stock at premium (stated stock recorded at stated value).	Cash ....
		    Common stock ....
		    Paid-In Capital in Excess of Stated Value, Common Stock ....
			#	#
				#

Issue Preferred Stock	Issue par value preferred stock at par (par stock recorded at par).	Cash .... Preferred Stock	#	#

	Issue par value preferred stock at premium (par stock recorded at par).	Cash ....
		    Preferred Stock ....
		    Paid-In Capital in Excess of Par Value, Preferred Stock .....
			#	#
				#

Reacquire Common Stock	Reacquire its own common stock (treasury stock recorded at cost).	Treasury Stock, Common .... Cash	#	#
Reissue Common Stock	Reissue its treasury stock at cost (treasury stock removed at cost).	Cash .... Treasury Stock, Common	#	#

	Reissue its treasury stock above cost (treasury stock removed at cost).	Cash ....
		    Treasury Stock, Common........
		    Paid-In Capital, Treasury ....
			#	#
				#

	Reissue its treasury stock below cost (treasury stock removed at cost; if paid-in capital is insufficient to cover amount below cost, retained earnings is debited for remainder).	Cash ....
		    Paid-In Capital, Treasury ....
		    Retained Earnings (if necessary) ....
		    Treasury Stock, Common ....
			#
			#
			#
				#

② Merchandising Cost Flows

Period 1
Beginning inventory + Net cost of purchases (From supplier) → Merchandise available for sale → Ending inventory / Cost of goods sold → To Income Statement; Ending inventory → To Balance Sheet

Period 2
Beginning inventory + Net cost of purchases (From supplier) → Merchandise available for sale → Ending inventory / Cost of goods sold → To Income Statement; Ending inventory → To Balance Sheet

③ Credit Terms and Amounts

Credit Terms: Credit period; Discount* period
Time: Date of invoice
Amount Due: Due: Invoice price minus discount* ; Due: Invoice price

*Discount refers to a purchase discount for a buyer and a sales discount for a seller.

⑤ Bond Valuation

Bond Sets	Market Sets	Bond Price Determined
Contract rate	Market rate	Contract rate > Market rate → Bond sells at Premium
		Contract rate = Market rate → Bond sells at Par
		Contract rate < Market rate → Bond sells at Discount

⑦ Dividend Transactions

Account Affected	Cash Dividend	Stock Dividend	Stock Split
Cash.............	Decrease	—	—
Common Stock....	—	Increase	—
Retained Earnings..	Decrease	Decrease	—

⑧ A Rose by Any Other Name

The same financial statement sometimes receives different titles. Following are some of the more common aliases.*

Balance Sheet	Statement of Financial Position Statement of Financial Condition
Income Statement	Statement of Income Operating Statement Statement of Operations Statement of Operating Activity Earnings Statement Statement of Earnings Profit and Loss (P&L) Statement
Statement of Cash Flows	Statement of Cash Flow Cash Flows Statement Statement of Changes in Cash Position Statement of Changes in Financial Position
Statement of Stockholders' Equity	Statement of Shareholders' Equity Statement of Changes in Shareholders' Equity Statement of Stockholders' Equity and Comprehensive Income Statement of Changes in Owner's Equity Statement of Changes in Owner's Capital Statement of Changes in Capital Accounts

*The term **Consolidated** often precedes or follows these statement titles to reflect the combination of different entities, such as a parent company and its subsidiaries.

FUNDAMENTALS

① Accounting Equation

$$\text{Assets} = \text{Liabilities} + \text{Equity}$$

Assets	=	Liabilities	+	Equity
↑ Debit for increases	↓ Credit for decreases	↓ Debit for decreases	↑ Credit for increases	↓ Debit for decreases	↑ Credit for increases

Equity = Contributed Capital* + Retained Earnings

Retained Earnings = Common Stock − Dividends + Revenues − Expenses

Common Stock	Dividends	Revenues	Expenses
Dr. for decreases / Cr. for increases	Dr. for increases / Cr. for decreases	Dr. for decreases / Cr. for increases	Dr. for increases / Cr. for decreases

■ Indicates normal balance.
*Includes common stock and any preferred stock.

② Accounting Cycle

1. Analyze transactions
2. Journalize
3. Post
4. Prepare unadjusted trial balance
5. Adjust
6. Prepare adjusted trial balance
7. Prepare statements
8. Close
9. Prepare post-closing trial balance
10. Reverse (Optional)

③ Adjustments and Entries

Type	Adjusting Entry
Prepaid Expenses	Dr. Expense / Cr. Asset*
Unearned Revenues	Dr. Liability / Cr. Revenue
Accrued Expenses	Dr. Expense / Cr. Liability
Accrued Revenues	Dr. Asset / Cr. Revenue

*For depreciation, credit Accumulated Depreciation (contra asset).

④ 4-Step Closing Process

1. Transfer revenue and gain account balances to Income Summary.
2. Transfer expense and loss account balances to Income Summary.
3. Transfer Income Summary balance to Retained Earnings.
4. Transfer Dividends balance to Retained Earnings.

⑤ Accounting Concepts

Characteristics	Assumptions	Principles	Constraints
Relevance	Business entity	Measurement (historical cost)	Cost-benefit
Reliability	Going concern	Revenue recognition	Materiality
Comparability	Monetary unit	Expense recognition	Industry practice
Consistency	Periodicity	Full disclosure	Conservatism

⑥ Ownership of Inventory

	Ownership Transfers When Goods Passed To	Transportation Costs Paid By
FOB Shipping Point	Carrier	Buyer
FOB Destination	Buyer	Seller

⑦ Inventory Costing Methods

- Specific identification
- First-in, first-out (FIFO)
- Weighted-average
- Last-in, first-out (LIFO)

⑧ Depreciation and Depletion

Straight-line: $\dfrac{\text{Cost} - \text{Salvage value}}{\text{Useful life in periods}} \times \text{Periods expired}$

Units-of-production: $\dfrac{\text{Cost} - \text{Salvage value}}{\text{Useful life in units}} \times \text{Units produced}$

Declining-balance: Rate* × Beginning-of-period book value
*Rate is often double the straight-line rate, or 2 × (1/Useful life)

Depletion: $\dfrac{\text{Cost} - \text{Salvage value}}{\text{Total capacity in units}} \times \text{Units extracted}$

⑨ Interest Computation

Interest = Principal (face) × Rate × Time

⑩ Accounting for Investment Securities

Classification*	Accounting
Short-Term Investment in Securities	
Held-to-maturity (debt) securities	**Cost** (without any discount or premium amortization)
Trading (debt and equity) securities	**Fair value** (with fair value adjustment to income)
Available-for-sale (debt and equity) securities	**Fair value** (with fair value adjustment to equity)
Long-Term Investment in Securities	
Held-to-maturity (debt) securities	**Cost** (with any discount or premium amortization)
Available-for-sale (debt and equity) securities	**Fair value** (with fair value adjustment to equity)
Equity securities with significant influence	Equity method
Equity securities with controlling influence	Equity method (with consolidation)

*A *fair value option* allows companies to report HTM and AFS securities much like trading securities.

ANALYSES

① Liquidity and Efficiency

Current ratio = $\dfrac{\text{Current assets}}{\text{Current liabilities}}$ — pp. 119 & 567

Working capital = Current assets − Current liabilities — p. 567

Acid-test ratio = $\dfrac{\text{Cash} + \text{Short-term investments} + \text{Current receivables}}{\text{Current liabilities}}$ — p. 174

Accounts receivable turnover = $\dfrac{\text{Net sales}}{\text{Average accounts receivable, net}}$ — pp. 309 & 569

Credit risk ratio = $\dfrac{\text{Allowance for doubtful accounts}}{\text{Accounts receivable, net}}$ — p. 309

Inventory turnover = $\dfrac{\text{Cost of goods sold}}{\text{Average inventory}}$ — pp. 219 & 569

Days' sales uncollected = $\dfrac{\text{Accounts receivable, net}}{\text{Net sales}} \times 365^*$ — p. 569

Days' sales in inventory = $\dfrac{\text{Ending inventory}}{\text{Cost of goods sold}} \times 365^*$ — pp. 219 & 570

Total asset turnover = $\dfrac{\text{Net sales}}{\text{Average total assets}}$ — pp. 347 & 570

Plant asset useful life = $\dfrac{\text{Plant asset cost}}{\text{Depreciation expense}}$ — p. 347

Plant asset age = $\dfrac{\text{Accumulated depreciation}}{\text{Depreciation expense}}$ — p. 347

Days' cash expense coverage = $\dfrac{\text{Cash and cash equivalents}}{\text{Average daily cash expenses}}$ — p. 256

*360 days is also commonly used.

② Solvency

Debt ratio = $\dfrac{\text{Total liabilities}}{\text{Total assets}}$ Equity ratio = $\dfrac{\text{Total equity}}{\text{Total assets}}$ — pp. 72 & 571

Debt-to-equity = $\dfrac{\text{Total liabilities}}{\text{Total equity}}$ — pp. 429 & 571

Times interest earned = $\dfrac{\text{Income before interest expense and income taxes}}{\text{Interest expense}}$ — pp. 384 & 572

Cash coverage of growth = $\dfrac{\text{Cash flow from operations}}{\text{Cash outflow for plant assets}}$ — p. 521

Cash coverage of debt = $\dfrac{\text{Cash flow from operations}}{\text{Total noncurrent liabilities}}$ — p. 521

③ Profitability

Profit margin ratio = $\dfrac{\text{Net income}}{\text{Net sales}}$ — p. 119

Gross margin ratio = $\dfrac{\text{Net sales} - \text{Cost of goods sold}}{\text{Net sales}}$ — p. 174

Return on total assets = $\dfrac{\text{Net income}}{\text{Average total assets}}$ — pp. 24 & 572

= Profit margin ratio × Total asset turnover — p. 573

Return on common stockholders' equity = $\dfrac{\text{Net income} - \text{Preferred dividends}}{\text{Average common stockholders' equity}}$ — p. 573

Book value per common share = $\dfrac{\text{Stockholders' equity applicable to common shares}}{\text{Number of common shares outstanding}}$ — p. 478

Basic earnings per share = $\dfrac{\text{Net income} - \text{Preferred dividends}}{\text{Weighted-average common shares outstanding}}$ — p. 477

Cash flow on total assets = $\dfrac{\text{Cash flow from operations}}{\text{Average total assets}}$ — p. 520

Payout ratio = $\dfrac{\text{Cash dividends declared on common stock}}{\text{Net income}}$ — p. 478

④ Market

Price-earnings ratio = $\dfrac{\text{Market value (price) per share}}{\text{Earnings per share}}$ — pp. 477 & 573

Dividend yield = $\dfrac{\text{Annual cash dividends per share}}{\text{Market price per share}}$ — pp. 478 & 574

Residual income = Net income − Target net income

FINANCIAL REPORTS

Income Statement*
For _period_ Ended _date_

Net sales (revenues)	$	#
Cost of goods sold (cost of sales)		#
Gross margin (gross profit)		#
Operating expenses		
Examples: Depreciation, salaries, ...	$	#
wages, rent, utilities, interest, ...		#
amortization, advertising, taxes		#
Total operating expenses		#
Nonoperating gains and losses		#
Net income (net profit or earnings)	$	#

*A typical chart of accounts is at the end of the book and classifies all accounts by financial statement categories.

Balance Sheet
Date

ASSETS
Current assets
Examples: Cash, Cash equivalents, Short-term investments,
  Accounts receivable, Current portion of notes .... $ #
  receivable, Inventory, Prepaid expenses .... #
Total current assets .... $ #
Long-term investments
Examples: Investment in stock, Investment in bonds, ... #
  Land for expansion .... #
Total long-term investments .... #
Plant assets
Examples: Equipment, Machinery, Buildings, Land .... #
Total plant assets, net of depreciation .... #
Intangible assets
Examples: Patent, Trademark, Copyright, License, Goodwill .. #
Total intangible assets, net of amortization .... #
Total assets .... $ #

LIABILITIES AND EQUITY
Current liabilities
Examples: Accounts payable, Wages payable, Salaries .... $ #
  payable, Current notes payable, Taxes payable, ... #
  Interest payable, Unearned revenues .... #
Total current liabilities .... $ #
Long-term liabilities
Examples: Notes payable, Bonds payable, Lease liability ...... #
Total long-term liabilities .... #
Total liabilities .... #
Equity
Common stock .... #
Paid-in capital in excess of par or stated value .... #
Retained earnings .... #
Less treasury stock .... (#)
Total liabilities and equity .... $ #

Statement of Cash Flows
For _period_ Ended _date_

Cash flows from operating activities
  [Prepared using the indirect (see below)† or direct method]
  Net cash provided (used) by operating activities .... $ #
Cash flows from investing activities
  [List of individual investing inflows and outflows]
  Net cash provided (used) by investing activities .... #
Cash flows from financing activities
  [List of individual financing inflows and outflows]
  Net cash provided (used) by financing activities .... #
Net increase (decrease) in cash .... $ #
Cash (and equivalents) balance at beginning of period .... #
Cash (and equivalents) balance at end of period .... $ #

Attach separate schedule or note disclosure of "Noncash investing and financing transactions."

†Indirect Method: Cash Flows from Operating Activities

Cash flows from operating activities
  Net income .... $ #
  Add: Decreases in noncash current assets .... $ #
    Increases in current liabilities .... #
    Expenses with no cash outflows (examples: depreciation,
      and amortization of both intangibles and bond discounts) ..... #
    Nonoperating losses (examples: losses from asset sales
      and from debt retirements) .... # #
  Less: Increases in noncash current assets .... #
    Decreases in current liabilities .... #
    Revenues with no cash inflows (examples:
      amortization of bond premiums) .... #
    Nonoperating gains (examples: gains from asset sales
      and from debt retirements) .... # #
  Net cash provided (used) by operating activities .... $ #

Statement of Retained Earnings
For _period_ Ended _date_

Retained earnings, beginning	$	#
Add: Net income		#
		#
Less: Dividends declared		#
Retained earnings, ending	$	#

Statement of Stockholders' Equity†
For _period_ Ended _date_

	Common Stock	Capital in Excess of Par	Retained Earnings	Treasury Stock	Total
Balances, beginning	$ #	$ #	$ #	$ #	$ #
Net income					
Cash dividends					
Stock issuance					
Treasury stock purchase					
Treasury stock reissuance					
Other					
Balances, ending	$ #	$ #	$ #	$ #	$ #

† Additional columns and account titles commonly include number of shares, preferred stock, unrealized gains and losses on available-for-sale securities, foreign currency translation, and comprehensive income.

Premium Bond Amortization (Straight-Line) Table†

Semiannual Period-End	Unamortized Bond Premium*	Bond Carrying Value**
Bond life-start	$ #	$ #
...	:	:
Bond life-end	0	par

† Bond carrying value is adjusted to par and its amortized premium to zero over the bond life (note: carrying value less unamortized bond premium equals par).
* Equals total bond premium less its accumulated amortization.
** Equals bond par value plus its unamortized bond premium.

Discount Bond Amortization (Straight-Line) Table†

Semiannual Period-End	Unamortized Bond Discount*	Bond Carrying Value**
Bond life-start	$ #	$ #
...	:	:
Bond life-end	0	par

† Bond carrying value is adjusted to par and its amortized discount to zero over the bond life (note: unamortized bond discount plus carrying value equals par).
* Equals total bond discount less its accumulated amortization.
** Equals bond par value less its unamortized bond discount.

Effective Interest Amortization Table for Bonds with Semiannual Interest Payment

Semiannual Interest Period-End	Cash Interest Paid[A]	Bond Interest Expense[B]	Discount or Premium Amortization[C]	Unamortized Discount or Premium[D]	Carrying Value[E]
#	#	#	#	#	#
:	:	:	:	:	:

[A] Par value multiplied by the semiannual contract rate.
[B] Prior period's carrying value multiplied by the semiannual market rate.
[C] The difference between interest paid and bond interest expense.
[D] Prior period's unamortized discount or premium less the current period's discount or premium amortization.
[E] Par value less unamortized discount or plus unamortized premium.

Installment Notes Payment Table

Period Ending Date	Beginning Balance	Debit Interest Expense	+	Debit Notes Payable	=	Credit Cash	Ending Balance
#	#	#		#		#	#
:	:	:		:		:	:

Bank Reconciliation
Date

Bank statement balance	$#	Book balance		$#
Add: Unrecorded deposits	#	Add: Unrecorded bank credit memoranda		#
Bank errors understating the balance	#	Book errors understating the balance		#
Less: Outstanding checks	#	Less: Unrecorded bank debit memoranda		#
Bank errors overstating the balance	#	Book errors overstating the balance		#
Adjusted bank balance	$#	**Adjusted book balance**		$#

Balances are equal (reconciled)